3

guide to the ANTIQUE SHOPS of BRITAIN

2006-2007

compiled by

Carol Adams

British Library CIP Data.
A catalogue record for this book is available from the British Library.

Origination by Antique Collectors' Club Ltd., England. Printed and bound in China

U.K. Office	U.S. Office
Sandy Lane, Old Martlesham, Woodbridge,	Eastworks, 116 Pleasant Street - Suite ≠ 60B,
Suffolk, IP12 4SD.	Easthampton, MA 01027.
Tel: 01394 389950 Fax: 01394 389999	Tel: (413) 529 0861 Fax: (413) 529 0862
Email: editorial@antique-acc.com	Email: info@antiquecc.com
Website: www.antiquecollectorsclub.com	Website: www.antiquecollectorsclub.com

COTSWOLD ART & ANTIQUE DEALERS' ASSOCIATION

A wealth of Antiques and Fine Art in the heart of England

from a Brass in Northleach Church

Please write to the Secretary
for a free brochure.

FOR ASSISTANCE WITH BUYING, SHIPPING, ACCOMMODATION DURING YOUR VISIT, WRITE TO:

Secretary, CADA, Broadwell House, Sheep Street,
Stow-on-the-Wold, Gloucestershire GL54 1JS
Tel/Fax: 01451 810407
www.cotswolds-antiques-art.com

8

International Fine Art Packers & Shippers

Founded in London in 1933, Gander & White has established a reputation as one of the world's leading packers and shippers of antiques and works of art. A family owned business with staff of over 100, we pride ourselves on our skills at combining the traditional standards of service with the modern skills and expertise needed to meet the requirements of museums, dealers and individuals for the packing, shipping and storage of antiques and fine art.

London   –   Unit 1, St Martin's Way
Wimbledon, London SW17 0JH
Tel: (020) 8971 7171   Fax: (020) 8946 8062

Sussex   –   Newpound, Wisborough Green, Nr. Billingshurst
West Sussex, RH14 0AZ
Tel: (01403) 700044   Fax: (01403) 700814

Paris   –   2 Boulevard de la Liberation
93200 Saint Denis, Paris
Tel: 00 33 1 55 87 67 10   Fax: 00 33 1 42 43 20 18

New York   –   21-44 44th Road, Long Island City, New York 11101
Tel: (718) 784 8444   Fax: (718) 784 9337

Palm Beach –   2206 Mercer Avenue
West Palm Beach, Florida 33401
Tel: (561) 655 4204   Fax: (561) 655 4224

10

W. R. Harvey & Co (Antiques) Ltd.

FINE ANTIQUE FURNITURE & WORKS OF ART, CONSERVATION & CONSULTANCY

*A very pretty and small William and Mary period walnut and
feather-banded Bureau Bookcase, Ca. 1690.*

86 Corn Street, Witney, Oxfordshire OX28 6BU.
Tel: 01993 706501 Fax: 01993 706601
Web Site: www.wrharvey.co.uk e-mail: antiques@wrharvey.co.uk

ANTIQUES
FOR LIVING

When visiting Antiquarius you will have the opportunity to browse and discover a variety of antiques sure to enrich your mind and complement your lifestyle. With over 120 dealers catering to everyone from the casual browser to the dedicated collector, you can immerse yourself in an inspiring range of authentic antiques encompassing jewellery, silver, glass, porcelain, clocks, watches, lighting, furniture, antiquarian books, prints, paintings and collector's items. From objets d'art to Art Deco, from Oriental art to contemporary collectables, these truly are antiques for living.

15

CONTENTS

INTRODUCTION

This is the 34th edition of the **Guide to the Antique Shops of Britain** which is now universally accepted as *the* guide for anybody who wishes to buy antiques in Britain.

All the entries listed have been confirmed before reprinting. We appreciate, however, that quantity without quality is meaningless and therefore the range of information we provide is more detailed and up-to-date than in any other publication. We state the obvious facts - name of proprietor, address, telephone number, opening hours and stock and also size of showroom and price range (where supplied). Additional information gives details of major trade association members, the date the business was established, the location and also the parking situation. Whilst none of these points are decisive in themselves, we feel they build up to a useful picture of the sort of establishment likely to be found and may well influence a prospective buyer's decision whether or not to visit a particular shop.

We start preparing the next edition in early 2006. Please let us know of any changes in your area - openings and closures. We do not print information about other dealers without first contacting them, but obviously the more shops in a particular town or village, the more attractive it is to prospective buyers on trips around the country. We would also be grateful for your comments on the Guide and, if you find any information given in the Guide to be incorrect, please let us know. We have occasionally had prospective customers telephoning to say that the stock listed is not what they found when visiting a particular establishment but then refuse to tell us the name of the shop - which means we can do nothing about the complaint. Constructive criticism is welcomed and we look forward to your comments.

ACKNOWLEDGEMENTS

Our main sources of information are still the trade magazines but we would like to thank those dealers who provide information about new shops and closures in their area. Without their assistance our job would be far more difficult.

We would also like to thank those dealers who have supported us with advertising. It is because of their valued patronage that we can continue to produce such a high-quality, informative volume at such a low retail price. Each year we include a form at the end of the Guide which dealers can use to up-date details about their own business, or you could email your corrections to editorial@antique-acc.com

Editorial **Carol Adams**
Advertising Sales **Jean Johnson and Alison Hart**

HOW TO USE THIS GUIDE

The Guide is set out under six main headings; London, Counties, Channel Islands, Northern Ireland, Scotland and Wales. Counties are listed alphabetically, within counties the towns are listed alphabetically and within towns the shops are listed, again alphabetically. London is divided into postal districts.

To make route planning easier there is a map at the beginning of each county, and a list showing the number of shops in any one town or village. The roads indicated on the map are only a broad intimation of the routes available and it is advisable to use an up-to-date map showing the latest improvements in the road system.

Apart from the six main headings above, there are further helpful lists - an alphabetical list of towns, showing the counties in which they will be found for those not familiar with the location of towns within counties, e.g. Woodbridge is shown in the county of Suffolk. One therefore turns to the Suffolk section to look up Woodbridge. This listing is a valuable aid to the overseas visitor. The second is particularly important to British dealers and collectors - giving an alphabetical list of the name of every shop, proprietor and company director known to be connected with a shop or gallery. Thus, if A. Bloggs and B. Brown own an antique shop called Castle Antiques, there will be entries under Bloggs, A., Brown, B., and Castle Antiques. Listings of specialist dealers, auctioneers, shippers and packers and services are also included.

We strongly suggest making a prior telephone call to confirm opening hours before setting off on a long journey. In the main, dealers are factual and accurate in describing their stock to us but there are probably a few who list what they would like to stock rather than as it is! We would appreciate you letting us know of any such anomalies. Please telephone (01394) 389968 or drop us a postcard and help us to ensure that the Guide remains Britain's premier listing of antique shops and galleries.

ABBREVIATIONS IN ENTRIES

BADA:	British Antique Dealers Association
LAPADA:	The Association of Art and Antique Dealers
BABAADA:	Bath and Bradford on Avon Antique Dealers Association
EADA:	Essex Antique Dealers Association
KCSADA:	Kensington Church Street Antique Dealers Association
PAADA:	Petworth Art & Antique Dealers Association
TADA:	Tetbury Antique Dealers Association
TVADA:	Thames Valley Antique Dealers Association
CADA:	Cotswold Antique Dealers Association
BAFRA:	British Antique Furniture Restorers' Association
CL:	When the business is normally closed in addition to Sunday
SIZE:	Showroom size. Small - under 60 sq. metres; medium - between 60 and 150 sq. metres; large over 150 sq. metres
LOC:	Location of shop
SER:	Additional services which the dealer offers

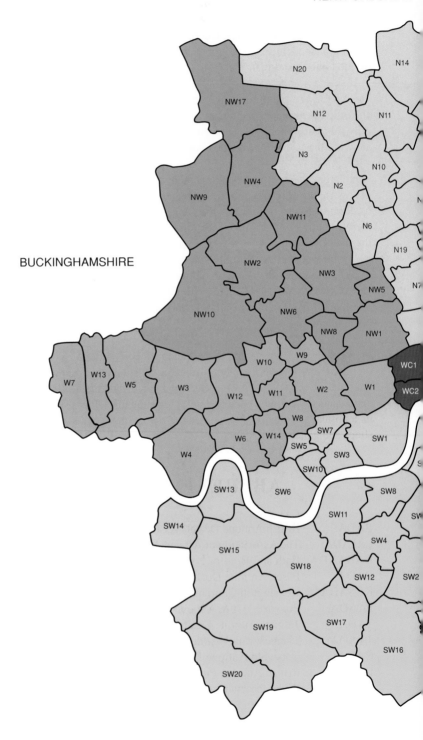

HERTFORDSHIRE

BUCKINGHAMSHIRE

N20

N14

NW17

N12

N11

N3

N10

NW4

N2

NW9

N6

NW11

N19

NW2

NW3

N7

NW5

NW10

NW6

NW8

NW1

W10

W9

WC1

W2

W1

WC2

W7

W13

W5

W3

W12

W11

W8

SW7

SW1

W6

W14

SW5

SW3

W4

SW10

SW13

SW6

SW8

SW14

SW11

SW4

SW15

SW18

SW12

SW2

SW19

SW17

SW16

SW20

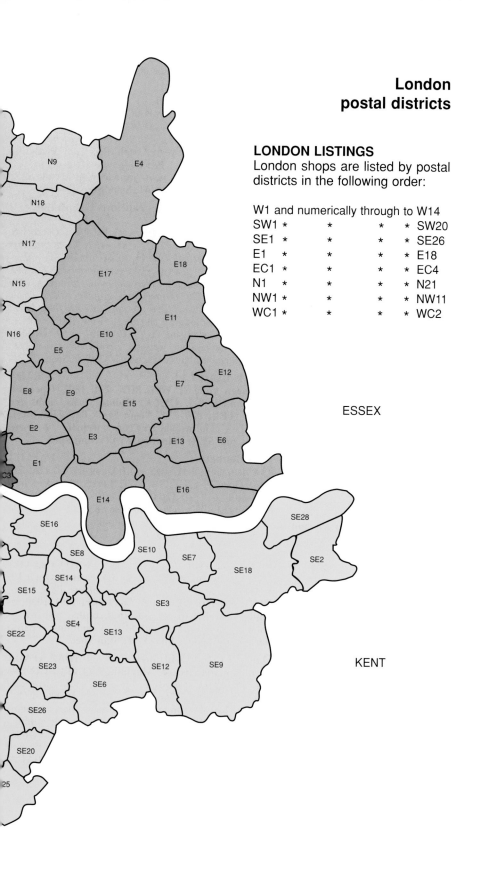

London
postal districts

LONDON LISTINGS
London shops are listed by postal districts in the following order:

W1 and numerically through to W14

SW1 *	*	*	* SW20
SE1 *	*	*	* SE26
E1 *	*	*	* E18
EC1 *	*	*	* EC4
N1 *	*	*	* N21
NW1 *	*	*	* NW11
WC1 *	*	*	* WC2

ESSEX

KENT

W1

A.D.C. Heritage Ltd BADA
W1K 2ST. (F. Raeymaekers and E.Bellord). Open by appointment. *STOCK: Silver, old Sheffield plate.* LOC: Mayfair. PARK: Meters. TEL: 020 7355 1444; fax - 020 7355 2444. SER: Valuations; restorations; buys at auction. VAT: Spec.

David Aaron Ancient Arts & Rare Carpets
LAPADA
22 Berkeley Sq., Mayfair. W1J 6EH. Est. 1910. Open 9-6, Sat. by appointment. SIZE: Large. *STOCK: Islamic and ancient art; antique carpets.* PARK: Easy. TEL: 020 7491 9588; fax - 020 7491 9522; e-mail - david_aaron @hotmail.com SER: Valuations; restorations. VAT: Stan/Spec.

Aaron Gallery
125 Mount St. W1K 3NS. (Manouchehr and Simon Aaron). Est. 1910. Open 10-6, Sat. by appointment. *STOCK: Ancient art; Greek, Roman, Egyptian, Near Eastern and Islamic antiquities.* TEL: 020 7499 9434; fax - 020 7499 0072; e-mail - simon@aarongallery.com website - www.aarongallery.com

Agnew's
BADA
43 Old Bond St. W1S 4BA. SLAD. Est. 1817. Open 9.30-5.30, Sat.11-4. SIZE: Large. *STOCK: Paintings, drawings, watercolours, engravings of all schools; contemporary art.* TEL: 020 7290 9250; fax - 020 7629 4359; e-mail - agnews@agnewsgallery.co.uk website - www.agnewsgallery.co.uk VAT: Spec.

Adrian Alan Ltd
BADA LAPADA
66/67 South Audley St. W1K 2QX. Est. 1963. Open 10-6. CL: Sat. SIZE: Large. *STOCK: English and Continental furniture, especially fine 19th C; sculpture and works of art.* TEL: 020 7495 2324; fax - 020 7495 0204; e-mail - enquiries@adrianalan.com website - www.adrianalan.com SER: Transport, storage and shipping; insurance and finance. VAT: Stan/Spec.

Altea Gallery
35 St. George St. W1S 2FN. (Massimo De Martini). PBFA. ABA. ILAB. IMCOS. Est. 1993. Open Mon.-Fri. 10-6 or by appointment. SIZE: Medium. *STOCK: Antiquarian maps, 15th-19th C, £50-£5,000; travel books, atlases, 16th-19th C, £200-£20,000; globes, 17th-20th C, £200-£20,000.* LOC: 200 yards from Oxford Circus. PARK: NCP nearby. TEL: 020 7491 0010; fax - 020 7491 0015; e-mail - info@alteamaps.com website - www.alteamaps.com SER: Valuations; restorations (paper, cleaning, colouring and book binding); buys at auction (maps, books and globes). FAIRS: London Map, Olympia (June); ABA Olympia (June). VAT: Stan.

Argyll Etkin Gallery
Ramillies Buildings, 1-9 Hills Place, Oxford Circus. W1F 7SA. (Argyll Etkin Ltd). PTS. MS. UACC. Est. 1954. Open 9-5.30. CL: Sat. SIZE: Medium. *STOCK: Classic postage stamps, postal history and covers, Royal autographs, signed photographs, historical documents and antique letters, 1400-1950, £50-£25,000; stamp boxes and associated writing equipment, 1700-1930, £50-£500.* TEL: 020 7437 7800 (6 lines); fax - 020 7434 1060; e-mail - philatelists@argyll-etkin.com website - www.argyll-etkin.com SER: Valuations; collections purchased. FAIRS: Major stamp exhibitions worldwide. VAT: Stan.

Armour-Winston Ltd
43 Burlington Arcade. W1J 0QQ. Est. 1952. Open 9-5. Sat. 10-4. SIZE: Small. *STOCK: Jewellery, especially Victorian; gentlemen's cufflinks, classic watches.* LOC: Off Piccadilly. Between Green Park and Piccadilly underground stations. PARK: Savile Row. TEL: 020 7493 8937; website - www.armourwinston.co.uk SER: Valuations; restorations. VAT: Stan/Spec.

Victor Arwas Gallery - Editions Graphiques Gallery Ltd
3 Clifford St. W1S 2LF. (V. Arwas). Est. 1966. Open 11-6, Sat. 10-2. SIZE: Large. *STOCK: Art Nouveau and Art Deco glass, ceramics, bronzes, sculpture, furniture, jewellery, silver, pewter, books and posters 1880-1940, £25-£50,000; paintings, watercolours and drawings, 1880 to date, £100-£20,000; original graphics, lithographs, etchings, woodcuts, 1890 to date, £5-£10,000.* LOC: Between New Bond St. and Savile Row. PARK: 50yds. TEL: 020 7734 3944; fax - 020 7437 1859; e-mail - art@victorarwas.com website - www.victorarwas.com SER: Valuations; buys at auction. VAT: Stan/Spec.

J. & A. Beare Ltd
BADA
30 Queen Anne St. W1G 8HX. Est. 1892. Open 10-12.30 and 1.30-5. *STOCK: Violins, violas, cellos and bows.* TEL: 020 7307 9666; fax - 020 7307 9651; e-mail - violins@beares.com website - www.beares.com SER: Valuations. VAT: Stan/Spec.

Paul Bennett
LAPADA
48A George St. W1U 7DY. (M.J. Dubiner). CINOA. Est. 1970. Open 10-6. CL: Sat. SIZE: Large. *STOCK: Silver, 17th-20th C, £10-£10,000; Sheffield plate.* PARK: Meters. TEL: 020 7935 1555/7486 8836; fax - 020 7224 4858; e-mail - info@paulbennettonline.co.uk website - www.paulbennettonline.co.uk FAIRS: Olympia; Claridges. VAT: Stan/Spec.

Bentley & Skinner
BADA LAPADA
8 New Bond St. W1S 3SL. (Mark Evans). Open 10-5.30. *STOCK: Jewellery, Fabergé, objets d'art, silver.* PARK: Meters. TEL: 020 7629 0651/7491 1030; e-mail - info@bentley-skinner.co.uk website - www.bentley-skinner.co.uk SER: Valuations; repairs; tiara and jewellery hire. VAT: Stan/Spec.

Daniel Bexfield Antiques
BADA LAPADA
26 Burlington Arcade, Mayfair. W1J 0PU. CINOA. Est. 1980. Open 9-6. SIZE: Large. *STOCK: Silver and objects of vertu, 17th-20th C, £200-£25,000.* LOC: Next to Royal Academy, Piccadilly. PARK: Nearby. TEL: 020 7491 1720; fax - 020 7491 1730; e-mail - antiques@bexfield.co.uk website - www.bexfield.co.uk SER: Valuations; restorations (repairs and polishing silver, blue glass liners). FAIRS: BADA. VAT: Spec.

Peter Biddulph
34 St George St., Hanover Sq. W1S 2ND. Open 10-6. CL: Sat. *STOCK: Violins, violas, cellos and bows.* TEL: 020 7491 8621; fax - 020 7495 1428; website - www.peterbiddulph.com SER: Valuations; restorations.

BOND STREET
ANTIQUES CENTRE
124 New Bond Street, London W1

"The most prestigious antiques centre
in London"

Antique Monthly

Enquiries: Mike Spooner
Tel: 020-7351 5353 Fax: 020-7969 1639

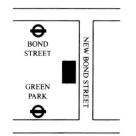

H. Blairman and Sons Ltd.   **BADA**
**119 Mount St. W1K 3NL. (M.P., P.A. and W.Y. Levy
and P.A. Hannen). Est. 1884. Open daily. CL: Sat.
SIZE: Medium.** *STOCK: English and Continental
furniture and works of art, 1800-1900.* **TEL: 020 7493
0444; fax - 020 7495 0766; e-mail - blairman@atlas.
co.uk website - www.blairman.co.uk FAIRS:
Grosvenor House; IFAAD, New York. VAT: Spec.**

Blunderbuss Antiques
29 Thayer St. W1U 2QW. (C. and P. Greenaway). Open
9.30-4.30. CL: Mon. *STOCK: Arms and armour,
militaria.* TEL: 020 7486 2444; fax - 020 7935 1645;
e-mail - mail@blunderbuss-antiques.co.uk website -
www.blunderbuss-antiques.co.uk

Bond Street Antiques Centre
124 New Bond St. W1Y 9AE. (Atlantic Antique Centres
Ltd). Est. 1970. Open 10-5.30, Sat. 11-5.30. SIZE: Large
- 27 dealers. *STOCK: Wide range of general antiques
especially jewellery - see dealers listed below.* LOC:
Bond St., Oxford St. or Green Park underground stations.
TEL: Enquiries - 020 7351 5353; fax - 020 7969 1639;
e-mail - antique@dial.pipex.com

Philip Cyrlin & Co
Stand 17. *Watches.* TEL: 020 7629 0133; mobile -
07905 105471; e-mail - watches@cyrlin.co.uk
website - www.cyrlin.co.uk

Adele de Havilland
Stands 18. *Oriental porcelain, netsuke, jade.* TEL:
020 7499 7127.

David Duggan Watches   LAPADA
Stands 1A, 1B, 22. *Vintage watches.* TEL: 020 7491
1362; fax - 020 7408 1727; mobile - 07836 726260;
e-mail - enquiries@daviddugganwatches.co.uk
website - www.daviddugganwatches.co.uk

Elisabeth's Antiques   LAPADA
Stand 7. (Mrs E. Hage). *Jewellery.* TEL: 020 7491
1723.

Matthew Foster Ltd
Stand 5. *Jewellery.* TEL: 020 7629 4977; fax - same;
mobile - 07850 964103; e-mail - info@matthew-
foster.com website - www. matthew-foster.com

Saul Greenstein
Stand 9. *Jewellery.* TEL: 020 7629 9282; mobile -
07900 067548; e-mail - saul@hotmail.com

Jan Havlik Fine Jewels
Stand 21. *Jewellery.* TEL: 020 7629 9007; fax -
same; mobile - 07775 708198.

Janis Collection
Stand 1D. *Jewellery.* TEL: 020 7629 0277.

Massada Antiques Ltd   LAPADA
Stand 2. (Mr. and Mrs Yacobi). Est. 1970. *Jewellery
and silver.* TEL: 020 7493 4792.

Nonsuch Antiques   LAPADA
Stand 3. (E. Michelson). *Jewellery and objects.* TEL:
020 7629 6783.

John Silverman
Stand 4. *Jewellery.* TEL: 020 7499 3256.

Sergio Tencati
Stand 16. *Jewellery and silver.* TEL: 020 7493 6272.

Trianon Antiques Ltd   LAPADA
Stand 1C, 10, 11. (Mrs L. Horton). *Jewellery.* TEL:
020 7629 6678; fax - 020 7355 2055; e-mail -
trianonantiques@hotmail.com

Yamamoto Antiques
Stands 14/15. *Jewellery and porcelain.* TEL: 020
7491 0983; fax - same.

Brandt Oriental Art
First Floor, 29 New Bond St. W1Y 9HD. (R. Brandt).
Est. 1981. Open by appointment. *STOCK: Oriental
works of art, £500-£10,000.* TEL: 020 7499 8835;
mobile - 07774 989661. VAT: Spec.

Browse and Darby Ltd
19 Cork St. W1S 3LP. SLAD. Est. 1977. Open Mon.-Fri.
10-5.30. *STOCK: French and British paintings,
drawings and sculpture, contemporary British artists,
19th-20th C.* TEL: 020 7734 7984; e-mail - art@
browseanddarby.co.uk website - www.browseanddarby.
co.uk VAT: Spec.

Bruford & Heming Ltd   LAPADA
Rear Ground Floor, Renoir House, 136 New Bond St.
W1S 2TH. (Alan Kinsey). Est. 1858. SIZE: Small.
STOCK: Jewellery, domestic silverware and cutlery.
TEL: 020 7499 7644; 020 7629 4289; fax - 020 7493
5879; e-mail - sales@bruford-heming.co.uk SER:
Valuations; restorations (jewellery and silver).

John Bull (Antiques) Ltd JB Silverware LAPADA
139A New Bond St. W1S 2TN. (John and Kenneth D. Bull). Est. 1953. Open 9-5. CL: Sat. *STOCK: Antique silver and reproduction giftware, photo frames, cutlery.* TEL: 020 7629 1251; fax - 020 7495 3001; e-mail - sales@jbsilverware.co.uk website - www.jbsilverware. co.uk and www.antique-silver.co.uk SER: Valuations; repairs. FAIRS: Antiques For Everyone, NEC. VAT: Global/Margin.

Burlington Paintings Ltd BADA
10 and 12 Burlington Gardens. W1S 3EY. (A. Lloyd, M. Day and A. Hardy). Est. 1981. Open 9.30-5.30, Sat. 10-5. SIZE: Medium. *STOCK: British and European oil paintings, 19th-20th C, from £1,000.* LOC: Between Old Bond St. and Regent St., facing Savile Row. PARK: APCOA, Old Burlington St. TEL: 020 7734 9984; fax - 020 7494 3770; e-mail - pictures@ burlington.co.uk website - www.burlington.co.uk SER: Valuations; restorations (lining, cleaning, reframing oils and watercolours); buys at auction (pictures). VAT: Stan/Spec.

C. & L. Burman BADA
5 Vigo St. W1S 3HF. (Charles Truman). Open by appointment. *STOCK: 18th-19th works of art including silver, glass, furniture, ceramics and sculpture.* TEL: 020 7439 6604; fax - 020 7439 6605; e-mail - charles-truman@lineone.net SER: Valuations; restorations; buys at auction. FAIRS: Grosvenor House (June). VAT: Spec.

The Button Queen Ltd.
19 Marylebone Lane. W1U 2NF. (I. and M. Frith). GMC. Est. 1953. Open 10-5, Thurs. and Fri. 10-6, Sat. 10-4. SIZE: Large. *STOCK: Antique, old and modern buttons.* LOC: Off Wigmore St. TEL: 020 7935 1505. VAT: Stan.

Carrington and Co. Ltd
170 Regent St. W1R 6BQ. Open 10-6. *STOCK: Regimental jewellery and silver.* TEL: 020 7734 3727.

Paul Champkins BADA
41 Dover St. W1S 4NS. Est. 1995. Open by appointment. SIZE: Small. *STOCK: Chinese, Korean and Japanese art, £1,000-£100,000.* LOC: Off Piccadilly. TEL: 020 7495 4600; fax - 01235 751658; mobile - 07785 765508; e-mail - pc@paulchampkins. demon.co.uk SER: Valuations; restorations. FAIRS: Grosvenor House; BADA (March). VAT: Spec.

Antoine Cheneviere Fine Arts BADA
27 Bruton St. W1J 6QN. Open 9.30-6. CL: Sat. *STOCK: 18th-19th C furniture and paintings, objets d'art from Russia, Italy, Austria, Sweden and Germany.* TEL: 020 7491 1007.

Andrew Clayton-Payne Ltd
2nd Floor, 14 Old Bond St. W1S 4PP. Open by appointment. SIZE: Small. *STOCK: British paintings and watercolours, 1700-1850, £2,000-£500,000.* PARK: Easy. TEL: 020 7493 6980; fax - 020 7629 9151; mobile - 07771 563850; e-mail - andrew@clayton-payne.com SER: Valuations; buys at auction (pictures). VAT: Spec.

Sibyl Colefax & John Fowler LAPADA
39 Brook St. W1K 4JE. Est. 1933. Open 9.30-5.30. CL: Sat. SIZE: Large. *STOCK: Decorative furniture, pictures, lamps and carpets, 18th-19th C.* PARK: Meters. TEL: 020 7493 2231/7355 4037; e-mail - antiques@ sibylcolefax.com website - www.colefaxantiques.com FAIRS: Olympia (June). VAT: Spec.

P. and D. Colnaghi & Co Ltd BADA
15 Old Bond St. W1S 4AX. SLAD. Est. 1760. Open Mon.-Fri. 10-6. SIZE: Large. *STOCK: Old Master paintings and drawings, 14th-19th C.* TEL: 020 7491 7408; fax - 020 7491 8851; e-mail - contact@colnaghi. co.uk SER: Experts and appraisers. FAIRS: TEFAF, Maastricht; IFAAD, New York; Grosvenor House, London; Biennale des Antiquaires, Paris; Palm Beach Classic; Salon du Dessin, Paris; Les Antiquaires, Brussels. VAT: Spec.

Connaught Brown plc
2 Albemarle St. W1X 3HF. (A. Brown). SLAD. Est. 1985. Open 10-6, Sat. 10-12.30. SIZE: Medium. *STOCK: Post Impressionist, Scandinavian and modern works, from £5,000+; contemporary, from £500+.* LOC: Off Piccadilly and parallel to Bond St. PARK: Berkeley Sq. TEL: 020 7408 0362. SER: Valuations; restorations (paintings, drawings, watercolours and sculpture). FAIRS: Olympia. VAT: Stan/Spec.

Sandra Cronan Ltd BADA
18 Burlington Arcade. W1J 0PN. Est. 1975. Open 10-5. *STOCK: Fine and unusual jewels, 18th to early 20th C, £500-£150,000.* TEL: 020 7491 4851; fax - 020 7493 2758. SER: Valuations; design commissions. FAIRS: Fine Art & Antiques; BADA (March); Grosvenor House (June). VAT: Stan/Spec.

A. B. Davis Ltd
18 Brook St., (Corner of New Bond St). W1S 1BF. NAG. Est. 1920. Open 10-5. CL: Sat. *STOCK: Antique and secondhand jewellery, small silver items, objets d'art and gold coins.* TEL: 020 7629 1053/7483 1666/7629 3611; fax and ansaphone - 020 7499 6454. SER: Valuations; repairs (jewellery and silver). VAT: Stan/Spec.

Day & Faber
173 New Bond St. W1S 4RF. (Richard Day and James Faber). SLAD. Est. 1970. Open 10-5 by appointment. CL: Sat. *STOCK: Old Master drawings.* TEL: 020 7629 2991; fax - 020 7493 7569; e-mail - jf@dayfaber.com website - www.dayfaber.com VAT: Stan.

David Duggan Watches LAPADA
63 Burlington Arcade. W1J 0QS. (David and Denise Duggan). MBHI. Est. 1976. Open 10-5.30. SIZE: Small. *STOCK: Old and current wristwatches - Patek Phillipe, Rolex, Cartier, Panerai, Roger Dubuis, Lange & Sohne, Franck Muller, Audemars Piguet, Vacheron Constantin, Breguet.* LOC: West End. PARK: Meters nearby. TEL: 020 7491 1362/1675; fax - 020 7408 1727; website - www.daviddugganwatches.co.uk SER: Valuations; restorations (comprehensive repairs on site, Swiss trained technician)

Charles Ede Ltd BADA
20 Brook St. W1K 5DE. Est. 1970. Open 12.30-4.30 or by appointment. CL: Mon and Sat. *STOCK: Greek, Roman and Egyptian antiquities, £50-£50,000.* PARK:

Meters. TEL: 020 7493 4944; fax - 020 7491 2548; e-mail - charlesede@attglobal.net website - www.charlesede.com SER: Valuations; buys at auction. VAT: Spec.

Andrew Edmunds
44 Lexington St. W1F 0LW. Open Mon.-Fri. 10-6, appointment advisable. SIZE: Small. *STOCK: 18th to early 19th C caricature and decorative prints and drawings.* TEL: 020 7437 8594; fax - 020 7439 2551; e-mail - prints@andrewedmunds.com FAIRS: London Original Print; Grosvenor House. VAT: Stan/Spec.

Emanouel Corporation (UK) Ltd   LAPADA
64 & 64a South Audley St. W1K 2QT. (E. Naghi). Est. 1974. Open 10-6, Sat. by appointment. *STOCK: Important antiques and fine works of art, 18th-19th C; Islamic works of art.* TEL: 020 7493 4350/7499 0996; fax - 020 7629 3125; mobile - 07831 241899; e-mail - emanouelnaghi@aol.com website - www.emanouel.net VAT: Stan/Spec.

Eskenazi Ltd   BADA
10 Clifford St. W1S 2LJ. (J.E. Eskenazi, P.S. Constantinidi and D.M. Eskenazi). Est. 1960. Open 9.30-5.30, Sat. by appointment. SIZE: Large. *STOCK: Early Chinese ceramics; bronzes, sculpture, works of art; Japanese porcelain and screens.* TEL: 020 7493 5464; fax - 020 7499 3136; e-mail - gallery@eskenazi.co.uk website - www.eskenazi.co.uk VAT: Spec.

John Eskenazi Ltd   BADA
15 Old Bond St. W1S 4AX. Open 9.30-6, Sat. by appointment. SIZE: Medium. *STOCK: Oriental art, rugs and textiles; Indian, Himalayan and South East Asian art, sculpture and works of art.* PARK: Meters. TEL: 020 7409 3001; fax - 020 7629 2146; e-mail - john.eskenazi@john-eskenazi.com FAIRS: International Asian Art, New York (March); Asian Art, London (Nov). VAT: Spec.

Essie Carpets
62 Piccadilly. W1J 0DZ. (E. Sakhai). Est. 1766. Open 9.30-6.30, Sun. 10.30-6. CL: Sat. SIZE: Large. *STOCK: Persian and Oriental carpets and rugs.* LOC: Opposite St. James St. and Ritz Hotel. PARK: Easy. TEL: 020 7493 7766. SER: Valuations; restorations; commissions undertaken; exchange. VAT: Stan/Spec.

The Fine Art Society plc
148 New Bond St. W1S 2JT. SLAD. IFPDA. Est. 1876. Open 9.30-5.30, Sat. 10-1. SIZE: Large. *STOCK: British fine and decorative arts, 19th-20th C.* LOC: Bond St. or Green Park underground stations. PARK: 300yds. TEL: 020 7629 5116/7491 9454; e-mail - art@faslondon.com website - www.faslondon.com SER: Buys at auction. FAIRS: London Original Print; Winter Show and IFPDA Print, New York. VAT: Stan/Spec.

Sam Fogg   BADA
15d Clifford St. W1S 4JZ. ABA. Est. 1971. Open Mon.-Fri. 9.30-5.30 or by appointment. *STOCK: Manuscripts - Western medieval, Islamic and Oriental and works of art; Indian paintings.* LOC: Off New Bond St. PARK: NCP Burlington Gardens. TEL: 020 7534 2100; fax - 020 7534 2122; e-mail - info@samfogg.com website - www.samfogg.com SER:

Valuations; buys at auction. FAIRS: Asian Art, New York; Biennale, Paris. VAT: Margin.

Deborah Gage (Works of Art) Ltd
38 Old Bond St. W1S 4QW. Est. 1982. Open 9.30-5.30. CL: Sat. *STOCK: European decorative arts, British and European paintings, Renaissance to 1940, from £5,000.* TEL: 020 7493 3249; fax - 020 7495 1352; e-mail - art@deborahgage.com SER: Valuations; cataloguing; buys at auction. VAT: Stan/Spec.

Thomas Goode and Co (London) Ltd
19 South Audley St., Mayfair. W1K 2BN. Est. 1827. Open 10-6. SIZE: Large. *STOCK: China, glass, silver, tableware, ornamental, lamps, mirrors and furniture.* TEL: 020 7499 2823; fax - 020 7629 4230; e-mail - info@thomasgoode.co.uk website - www.thomasgoode.com SER: Restorations. VAT: Spec.

Grays Antique Markets
58 Davies St. and 1-7 Davies Mews. W1K 5LP. Est. 1970. Open 10-6. CL: Sat. TEL: 020 7629 7034; fax - 020 7629 3279; e-mail - grays@clara.net website - www.graysantiques.com SER: Engraving and jewellery repair. Below are listed the dealers at this market.

A & T Jewellers
Stand G104. *Jewellery.* TEL: 020 7495 7068; e-mail - touro@grays.clara.net

Emmy Abe
Stand G324. *Jewellery.* TEL: 020 7629 1826; e-mail - emmy@grays.clara.net

Accurate Trading Co. Ltd
Stand G325-6. *Jewellery.* TEL: 020 7629 0277; e-mail - ellisfahimian@aol.com

Maria Alcazar
Stand G323. *Jewellery.* TEL: 020 7629 6219; e-mail - alcazar@grays.clara.net

Anthea A.G. Antiques   LAPADA
Stand G154-5. (Anthea Geshua). *Jewellery.* TEL: 020 7493 7564; e-mail - anthea@grays.clara.net

Antik Dekor
Stand MC20. (Nabi Ozbek). *Islamic items and antiquities.* TEL: 020 7629 1353; e-mail - nabiozbek@hotmail.com

Arca
Stand G351-353. (R. & E. Innocenti). *Objets d'art and miniatures.* TEL: 020 7629 2729; e-mail - arca@grays.clara.net

Armoury of St. James
Stand MB16. (Richard Kirch). *Militaria.* TEL: 020 7493 5082; e-mail - welcome@armoury.co.uk

Artenotria
Stand MK32. *Small antiques.* TEL: 020 7493 0900; e-mail - enotria@crescenzi.freeserve.co.uk

Elias Assad
Stand MJ28-K13. *Islamic and antiquities.* TEL: 020 7499 4778; e-mail - assad@grays.clara.net

Atighi
Stand ME14-15. *Islamic items and antiquities.* TEL: 020 7629 7272; e-mail - atighi@grays.clara.net

Aurum Antiques
Stand G310-11. *Jewellery.* TEL: 020 7409 0215; e-mail - aurum@tinyworld.com

Aytac Antiques
Stand G331-2. *Watches and clocks.* TEL: 020 7629 7380; e-mail - aytac@grays.clara.net

B & T Engraving
Stand G109. TEL: 020 7408 1880; e-mail - engraving@grays.clara.net

Colin Baddiel
Stand MB24-25. *Toys.* TEL: 020 7408 1239; e-mail - toychemcol@hotmail.com

David Baker
Stand M10/11. *Asian art.* TEL: Mobile - 07973 625229; e-mail - david@asianartlondon.com

Vivien Barnett
Stand MC10-11. *Vintage fashion.* TEL: 020 7409 0400; e-mail - vivien@grays.clara.net

Don Bayney
Stand MA20-21. *Militaria.* TEL: 020 7491 7200; e-mail - donbayney@aol.com

Karen Beagle
Stand MFS010. *Asian.* TEL: 020 7629 7034; e-mail - karenbeagle@aol.com

Linda Bee
Stand ML18-21. *Jewellery, vintage fashion.* TEL: 020 7629 5921; e-mail - lindabee@grays.clara.net

Barbara Berg
Stand G333/4. *Jewellery.* TEL: 020 7499 0560; e-mail - berg@grays.clara.net

Beverley R
Stand G342/4. *Jewellery.* TEL: 020 7408 1129; e-mail - beverley@grays.clara.net

Biblion
(Leo Harrison). *Books.* TEL: 020 7629 1374; e-mail - info@biblion.com

Bjs.Online.com/Bijoux Signes
Stand G384. (Mrs Relcha). *Glass and perfume bottles, watches, clocks and timepieces.* TEL: 020 7495 6814; e-mail - mail@bjsonline.com

David Bowden   LAPADA
Stand G304-6. CINOA. *Asian.* TEL: 020 7495 1773; e-mail - bowden@grays.clara.net

Patrick Boyd-Carpenter
Stand G127. *Prints and paintings.* TEL: 020 7491 7623; e-mail - patrickboyd_carpenter@hotmail.com

Britannia
Stand G159-160. (Rita Smythe). *Ceramics.* TEL: 020 7629 6772; e-mail - britannia@grays.clara.net

Sue Brown
Stand MM12. *Jewellery.* TEL: 020 7491 4287; e-mail - sue@antique-rings.co.uk

C20 Fashion
Stand MM13. (Mark and Cleo Butterfield). *Vintage fashion.* TEL: 01626 366437; e-mail - enquiries@c20vintagefashion.co.uk

Cat Antiques
Stand M Exhibit SC. (Caterina Krumrey). *Ceramics.* TEL: 020 7629 7034; e-mail - catantiques@grays.clara.net

Chris Cavey & Associates
Stand G178. *Gems and precious stones.* TEL: 020 7495 1743; e-mail - chriscavey@grays-uk.com

Cekay
Stand G172. (Diane Matlock). *Small antiques.* TEL: 020 7629 7034; e-mail - cekay@grays.clara.net

D. & J. Church
Stand G163. *Jewellery.* TEL: 020 7499 7935; e-mail - d&j@grays.clara.net

Collection Antiques
Stand G329/30. (John Shockett). *Jewellery.* TEL: 020 7493 2654; e-mail - collection@grays.clara.net

Olivia Howard Collins   LAPADA
Stand G103. *Jewellery.* TEL: 01428 645435; e-mail - howardcollins@grays.clara.net

Ethel Corduff
Stand MV14. *Ceramics.* TEL: 020 7629 7034; e-mail - corduff@grays.clara.net

Caroline Cox
Stand MV009. *Jewellery.* TEL: 020 7629 7034; e-mail - cox@grays.clara.net

Stuart Craig
Stand D12. *Vintage fashion.* TEL: 020 7409 0400; e-mail - stuartcraig@grays.clara.net

The Cushion Corner
Stand MV8/V15. (Ela Sosnowska). *Textiles.* TEL: 020 7629 7034; e-mail - cushioncorner@grays.clara.net

Anthony Douch Antiques
Stand G10/11. (Anthony Douch and Nicolov Valarie). *Jewellery.* TEL: 020 7493 9413; e-mail - vivianedouch@fsmail.net

Sallie Ead
Stand MD13/14. *Vintage and fashion.* TEL: 020 7409 0400; e-mail - sallie_ead@ lycos.com

Ealing Import & Export
Stand MK36-38. *Antiquities and Islamic items.* TEL: 020 7409 1900; e-mail - al7473@aol.com

Eastern Satrapy
Stand MM20/21. (Amin Rezai). *Coins and medals.* TEL: Mobile - 07956 597075; e-mail - satrapy@grays.clara.net

Evonne Antiques
Stand G301. (Evonne Muszkowska). *Silver.* TEL: 020 7491 0143; e-mail - evonne@grays.clara.net

Sandra Fellner
Stand MA18-19. *Dolls and teddy bears.* TEL: 020 7948 5613; e-mail - sandrafellner@blueyonder.co.uk

Finishing Touch
Stand G176. (Pauline Boxsey). *Jewellery.* TEL: 020 7495 0592; e-mail - ftouch@netcomuk.co.uk

Forever Young
Stand G371. *Jewellery.* TEL: Mobile - 07970 832026.

Gallery Diem
Stand G171. (Boris Boscovic and Andrew Day). *Jewellery.* TEL: 020 7493 0224; e-mail - gallerydiem@supernet.com

C. Garreta
Stand MV007. *Jewellery.* TEL: 020 7629 7034; e-mail - garreta@grays.clara.net

Peter Gaunt
Stand G120. *Silver.* TEL: 020 7629 1072; e-mail - ptg@peter-gaunt.freeserve.co.uk

Ghazi Ghafoori
Stand MC27. *Islamic items, antiquities and jewellery.* TEL:

020 7629 7212; e-mail - ghazighafoori2003@yahoo.co.uk

Gilded Lily **LAPADA**
Stand G145/6. (Korin Harvey and Brian Murray-Smith). *Jewellery.* TEL: 020 7499 6260; e-mail - jewellery@gilded-lily.co.uk

Gordon's Medals
Stand MG14/15. (Malcolm Gordon). *Coins, medals and militaria.* TEL: 020 7495 0900; e-mail - malcolm@cocollector.co.uk

R.G. Grahame
Stand G129/30. *Prints and paintings.* TEL: Mobile - 07969 444239; e-mail - grahame@grays.clara.net

Solveig & Anita Gray **LAPADA**
Stand G307-309. *Asian.* TEL: 020 7408 1638; e-mail - info@chinese-porcelain.co.uk

Sarah Groombridge **LAPADA**
Stand G335-7. *Jewellery.* TEL: 020 7629 0225.

Guest & Gray
Stand MH25-28. (Anthony Gray and Louise Guest). *Asian.* TEL: 020 7408 1252; e-mail - info@chinese-porcelain-art.com

Abdul Hadi
Stand MA12/13. *Islamic and antiquities.* TEL: 020 7491 3335; e-mail - hadi@grays.clara.net

Hallmark Antiques
Stand G319. *Jewellery.* TEL: 020 7629 8757; e-mail - hallmark@grays.clara.net

H.M. Hannaby
Stand MV010. *Small items.* TEL: 020 7629 7034; e-mail - hannaby@grays.clara.net

Diane Harby
Stand G148. *Textiles.* TEL: 020 7629 5130; e-mail - harby@grays.clara.net

Satoe Hatrell
Stand G156/166. *Jewellery and jet.* TEL: 020 7629 4296; e-mail - satoe@grays.clara.net

E. Hopkins
Stand MB027. *Dolls and teddy bears.* TEL: 020 7629 7034.

P. Hubble
Stand MV006. *Watches and clocks.* TEL: 020 7629 7034.

J.L.A.
Stand G364-76. (Alan Jacobs and Stephen Lack). *Jewellery.* TEL: 020 7499 1681.

Linda Jackson
Stand MFS004. *Jewellery.* TEL: 020 7629 7034; e-mail - lindajackson@grays.clara.net

Baba Jethwa
Stand G136. *Clocks and watches.* TEL: 020 7495 7327; e-mail - baba@grays.clara.net

John Joseph **LAPADA**
Stand G345-7. *Jewellery.* TEL: 020 7629 1140; e-mail - jewellery@john-joseph.co.uk

JUS Watches
Stand G108. *Clocks and watches.* TEL: 020 7495 7404; e-mail - swisswatch@webcom.com

K & M Antiques
Stand G369/70. (Martin Harris). *Ceramics.* TEL: 020 7491 4310; e-mail - kandmantiques@aol.com

K. & Y. Oriental Art
Stand MK24-7. *Asian.* TEL: 020 7491 0264; e-mail - yusui@freeuk.com

Minoo & Andre Kaae **LAPADA**
Stand MG22/23. *Jewellery.* TEL: 020 7629 1200; e-mail - andrekaae@aol.com

Kikuchi Trading Co Ltd **LAPADA**
Stand G357-359. *Jewellery and watches.* TEL: 020 7629 6808; e-mail - kikuchi@grays.clara.net

Lazarel
Stand G302-3. *Objets d'art.* TEL: 020 7408 0154; e-mail - pgszuhay@aol.com

Monty Lo
Stand G369/70. *Ceramics.* TEL: 020 7493 7457.

Michael Longmore **LAPADA**
Stand G378/379. *Jewellery.* TEL: 020 7491 2764; e-mail - michaellongmore@aol.com

C. Malbon
Stand MV005. *Toys.* TEL: 020 7629 7034.

Marco Polo Antiques Ltd
Stand MA16-17. *Islamic.* TEL: 020 7629 3788; e-mail - marcopolo@grays.clara.net

Michael Marks
Stand G385. *Jewellery.* TEL: 020 7491 0332; e-mail - marks@grays.clara.net

Allison Massey
Stand MB32-33. *Jewellery.* TEL: 020 7629 7034; e-mail - massey@grays.clara.net

Mazar Antiques
Stand MA28/29. *Islamic.* TEL: 020 7491 3001; e-mail - adadajan@aol.com

Michael's Boxes
Stand ML14/15. *Objets d'art and miniatures.* TEL: 020 7629 5716; e-mail - info@michaelsboxes.com

A. Mirecko
Stand MV011. *Jewellery.* TEL: 020 7629 7034; e-mail - annamirecko@grays.clara.net

Brian Moore
Stand MFS003. *Ceramics.* TEL: 020 7629 7034; e-mail - brianmoore@grays.clara.net

Howard Neville
Stand G127. *Objets d'art and miniatures.* TEL: 020 7491 7623.

James Norbury
Stand ML26-27. *Asian.* TEL: Mobile - 07887 836291; e-mail - norbury@grays.clara.net

Glenda O'Connor
Stand MA18/19. *Dolls and teddy bears.* TEL: 020 8367 2441; e-mail - glenda@glenda-antiquedoll.com

Pavlos Pavlou
Stand ML17. *Coins and medals.* TEL: 020 7629 9449; e-mail - pspavlou@hotmail.com

The Pearl Gallery
Stand G328. *Jewellery.* TEL: 020 7409 2743; e-mail - pearlgallery@freenetname.co.uk

Persepolis Gallery
Stand MK10-12. *Islamic.* TEL: 020 7629 7388; e-mail - persepolisgall@aol.com

Pieces of Time   BADA
Stand MM17-19. (Johnny Wachsman). *Watches and clocks.* **TEL: 020 7629 3272; e-mail - info@antique-watch.com**

Jack Podlewski
Stand G320. *Silver.* TEL: 020 7409 1468; e-mail - podlewski@grays.clara.net

Lance Poynter
Stand GB093/4. *Glass and perfume bottles.* TEL: 020 7491 7623; e-mail - poynter@grays.clara.net

Lucinda Prince
Stand MMB023-24. *Dolls and teddy bears.* TEL: 020 7629 7034; e-mail - lucindaprince@aol.com

Hilary Proctor
Stand ME18-20. *Vintage fashion.* TEL: 020 7499 7001; e-mail - secondhandfurs@aol.com

Pushkin Antiques
Stand G371. *Jewellery.* TEL: Mobile - 07900 000562.

Rasoul Gallery
Stand MK34/35. *Islamic and antiquities.* TEL: 020 7495 7422; e-mail - rasoul@grays.clara.net

RBR Grp
Stand G158. (Olivia Gerrish). *Jewellery.* TEL: 020 7629 4769; e-mail - rbr@grays.clara.net

Regal Watches
Stand G128-140. *Clocks and watches.* TEL: 020 7491 7722.

Ian Roper
Stand ML10-13. *Coins and medals.* TEL: 020 7491 4009; e-mail - ropewine@aol.com

Charlotte Sayers
Stand G313-315. *Jewellery.* TEL: 020 7499 5478.

Walter Schaetzka
Stand MV013. *Ceramics.* TEL: 020 7629 7034; e-mail - schaetzke@grays.clara.net

Second Time Around
Stand G316-318. *Clocks and watches.* TEL: 020 7499 7442; e-mail - k.waite@secondtimearound.com

Chris Seidler
Stand MG12/13. *Militaria.* TEL: 020 7629 2851; e-mail - chris@antique-militaria.co.uk

Sarah Sellers
Stand MA25/B14. *Dolls and teddy bears.* TEL: 020 7629 7034; e-mail - sarah@allyoucanbear.com

Shapiro & Co   LAPADA
Stand G380. *Jewellery.* TEL: 020 7491 2720; e-mail - shapiro@grays.clara.net

Mousa Shavolian
Stand MB19-21. *Glass and perfume bottles.* TEL: 020 7499 8273; e-mail - mousaantiques@yahoo.com

Shiraz Antiques
Stand MH10/11. (Reza Kiadeh). *Islamic and antiquities.* TEL: 020 7495 0635; e-mail - rezkia7@hotmail.com

Peter Sloane
Stand ME12/13. *Asian.* TEL: 020 7408 1043; e-mail - petersloane@grays.clara.net

Solaimani Gallery
Stand ME16/17. *Islamic and antiquities.* TEL: 020 7491 2562; e-mail - solaimanigallery@aol.com

Boris Sosna
Stand G374/5. *Jewellery.* TEL: 020 7629 2371; e-mail - bomax@freenetname.co.uk

Spectrum
Stand G372/3. *Jewellery.* TEL: 020 7629 3501; e-mail - spectrum@grays.clara.net

Jane Stewart
Stand ML25. *Pewter and medieval items.* TEL: 020 7355 3333; e-mail - janestewart@grays.clara.net

Sultani Antiques
Stand MK28-31. *Islamic and antiquities.* TEL: 020 7629 7034; e-mail - sultani@grays.clara.net

Timespec
Stand G366. *Watches and clocks.* TEL: 020 7499 9814; e-mail - timespec@grays.clara.net

Trio
Stand ML24. (Teresa Clayton). *Glass and perfume bottles.* TEL: 020 7493 2736; e-mail - trio@grays.clara.net

Michael Ventura-Pauly
Stand G354-355. *Jewellery.* TEL: 020 7495 6868; e-mail - venturapauly@grays.clara.net

June Victor
Stand MC10/11. *Vintage fashion.* TEL: 020 7409 0400; e-mail - junevictor@grays.clara.net

Mary Wellard
Stand G165. *Small antiques.* TEL: 020 7629 7034; e-mail - wellard@grays.clara.net

Westleigh Antiques
Stand G341. (Pat Sneath). *Jewellery.* TEL: 020 7493 0123; e-mail - westleigh@grays.clara.net

Westminster Group   LAPADA
Stand G322. (Paulette Bates and Richard Harrison). *Jewellery, watches and clocks.* TEL: 020 7493 8672; e-mail - westminster@grays.clara.net

David Wheatley   LAPADA
Stand G106. *Asian.* TEL: 020 7629 1352; e-mail - wheatley.antiques@btinternet.com

Wheels of Steel
Stand MB10-11. (Jeff Williams). *Toys.* TEL: 020 7629 2813; e-mail - wheelsofsteel@grays.clara.net

Margaret Williamson
Stand MD10-11. *Vintage fashion.* TEL: 020 7702 8180; e-mail - margaretwilliamson@grays.clara.net

Alan Wilson
Stand MFS008. *Asian.* TEL: 020 7629 7034; e-mail - alanwilson@grays.clara.net

Wimpole Antiques   LAPADA
Stand G338-349. *Jewellery.* TEL: 020 7499 2889; e-mail - wimpoleantiques@compuserve.com

ZMS Antiques
Stand G125. *Silver.* TEL: 020 7491 1144; e-mail - mara@zmsantiques.com

Richard Green   BADA
147 New Bond St., 33 New Bond St. and 39 Dover St. W1S 2TS. SLAD. Open 9.30-6, Sat. by appointment. *STOCK: Paintings - British, sporting and marine, French Impressionist and Modern British, Victorian and European, fine Old Masters.* **PARK: Meters. TEL: 020 7493 3939; fax - 020 7629 2609; e-mail - paintings**

@richard-green.com website - www.richard-green. com. FAIRS: Grosvenor House; 20th-21st British Art; London Art. VAT: Stan/Spec.

Simon Griffin Antiques Ltd
3 Royal Arcade, 28 Old Bond St. W1S 4SB. (S.J. Griffin). Est. 1979. Open 10-5, Sat. 10-5.30. *STOCK: Silver, old Sheffield plate.* TEL: 020 7491 7367; fax - same. VAT: Stan/Spec.

Hadji Baba Ancient Art Ltd
34a Davies St. W1K 4NE. (Hadji Soleimani). Est. 1939. Open 9.30-6, Sat. and Sun. by appointment. SIZE: Medium. *STOCK: Antiquities and Islamic art.* LOC: Mayfair, near Claridges. PARK: Meters. TEL: 020 7499 9363/9384; mobile - 07899 974974; fax - 020 7493 5504. SER: Valuations.

Halcyon Days   BADA
14 Brook St. W1S 1BD. Est. 1950. Open 9.30-6. *STOCK: 18th to early 19th C enamels, fans, treen, objects of vertu, Georgian and Victorian scent bottles.* **LOC: Hanover Sq. end of Brook St. PARK: Meters and Hanover Sq. TEL: 020 7629 8811; fax - 020 7409 0280; e-mail - info@halcyondays.co.uk website - www.halcyondays.co.uk** VAT: Stan/Spec.

Robert Hall
15c Clifford St. W1X 1RF. Est. 1976. SIZE: Large. *STOCK: Chinese snuff bottles, Ching dynasty; Oriental works of art, 17th-19th C; all £300-£20,000; contemporary Chinese paintings.* LOC: Mayfair. PARK: Meters. TEL: 020 7734 4008; fax - 020 7734 4408; e-mail - roberthall@snuffbottle.com website - www. snuffbottle.com SER: Buys at auction. FAIRS: Maastricht (TEFAF); Asian Art, New York. VAT: Stan/Spec.

Hancocks and Co   BADA
52 & 53 Burlington Arcade. W1J 0HH. Est. 1849. Open 9.30-5.30. CL: Sat. SIZE: Medium. *STOCK: Fine estate jewellery and silver.* **PARK: Old Burlington St.** TEL: 020 7493 8904; fax - 020 7493 8905; e-mail - info@hancocks-london.com website - www.hancocks-london.com. SER: Valuations; re-modelling. FAIRS: Grosvenor House; Miami Beach; Palm Beach; Maastricht (TEFAF); IFAAD, New York. VAT: Stan/Spec.

William Hanham Ltd
14 Old Bond St. W1S 4PP. Est. 1993. SIZE: Medium. *STOCK: Old Master and British paintings, 1500-1830; 20th C British art.* LOC: 150 yards from Piccadilly. TEL: 020 7491 4966; fax - 020 7491 4976; e-mail - wh@ williamhanham.com website - www.williamhanham. com SER: Valuations. FAIRS: Olympia; IFAAD, New York. VAT: Stan/Spec.

Harcourt Antiques
5 Harcourt St. W1 1DS. (J. Christophe). Est. 1961. Open by appointment. SIZE: Medium. *STOCK: English, Continental and Oriental porcelain, pre-1830.* PARK: Easy. TEL: 020 7727 6936. VAT: Stan. *Trade Only.*

Brian Haughton Antiques
3B Burlington Gardens, Old Bond St. W1S 3EP. Est. 1965. Open 10-5.30. SIZE: Large. *STOCK: British and European ceramics, porcelain and pottery, 18th-19th C,*

£100-£100,000. PARK: Nearby, Savile Row NCP. TEL: 020 7734 5491; fax - 020 7494 4604; e-mail - info@ haughton.com website - www.haughton.com SER: Buys at auction (porcelain and pottery). FAIRS: Organiser - International Ceramics Fair & Seminar, Park Lane Hotel; IFAAD; International Fine Art; International Asian Art; International Art & Design; New York. VAT: Spec.

Gerard Hawthorn Ltd   BADA
104 Mount St., Mayfair. W1K 2TL. Open 10-6, Sat. by appointment. *STOCK: Chinese, Japanese and Korean works of art.* **LOC: Opposite Connaught Hotel. PARK: Easy. TEL: 020 7409 2888; fax - 020 7409 2777. SER: Valuations; restorations; buys at auction; exhibitions twice yearly (illustrated catalogues). FAIRS: New York; Olympia (June).**

G. Heywood Hill Ltd
10 Curzon St. W1J 5HH. Open 9-5.30, Sat. 9-12.30. *STOCK: Books, new and old, architecture, history, literature, children's, natural history and illustrated.* TEL: 020 7629 0647; fax - 020 7408 0286; e-mail - books@ gheywoodhill.com website - www.gheywoodhill.com

Hirsh London
56/57 Burlington Arcade. W1J 0QN. Open 10-5.30. *STOCK: Fine jewellery and objets d'art.* LOC: West end. TEL: 020 7499 6814; fax - 020 7430 0107; e-mail - enquiries@hirsh.co.uk SER: Valuations; jewellery designed and re-modelled.

Holland & Holland
31 and 33 Bruton St. W1X 8JS. Est. 1835. Open 9.30-

5.30, Sat. 10-4. SIZE: Medium. *STOCK: Modern and antique guns, rifles, associated items; sporting prints, pictures and antiquarian books; antique sporting objects.* PARK: Meters. TEL: 020 7499 4411; fax - 020 7499 4544.

Holmes Ltd
24 Burlington Arcade. W1V 9AD. (A.N., B.J. and I.J. Neale). Open 9.30-5. *STOCK: Jewels and silver.* TEL: 020 7629 8380. SER: Valuations; restorations. VAT: Stan.

C. John (Rare Rugs) Ltd   BADA
70 South Audley St., Mayfair. W1K 2RA. Est. 1947. Open 9-5. CL: Sat. *STOCK: Rugs, carpets, tapestries, textiles and embroideries, 16th - 19th C.* TEL: 020 7493 5288; fax - 020 7409 7030; e-mail - cjohn@dircon. co.uk website - www.cjohn.com SER: Restorations, cleaning. FAIRS: Grosvenor House. VAT: Stan/Spec.

Johnson Walker & Tolhurst Ltd   BADA
64 Burlington Arcade. W1J 0QT. (Miss R. Gill). Est. 1849. Open 9.30-5.30. *STOCK: Antique and secondhand jewellery, objets d'art, silver.* TEL: 020 7629 2615. SER: Restorations (jewellery, pearl-stringing). VAT: Stan/Spec.

Daniel Katz Ltd
13 Old Bond St. W1S 4SX. (Daniel Katz and Stuart Lochhead). SLAD. Est. 1970. Open 9-6. CL: Sat. SIZE: Large. *STOCK: European sculpture, early medieval to 19th C, from £5,000.* LOC: Near Green Park underground station. TEL: 020 7493 0688; fax - 020 7499 7493; e-mail - info@katz.co.uk website - www. katz.co.uk VAT: Spec.

Roger Keverne   BADA
2nd Floor, 16 Clifford St. W1S 3RG. Est. 1996. Open Mon.-Fri. 9.30-5.30. SIZE: Large. *STOCK: Chinese ceramics and works of art including jade, lacquer, bronzes, ivories and enamels, from 2500 BC to 1916.* PARK: Meters. TEL: 020 7434 9100; fax - 020 7434 9101; e-mail - enquiries@keverne.co.uk website - www.keverne.co.uk SER: Valuations; restorations; buys at auction; two exhibitions a year; catalogues available. FAIRS: New York (Winter and March Oriental). VAT: Stan/Spec.

D.S. Lavender (Antiques) Ltd   BADA
26 Conduit St. W1S 2XX. Est. 1945. Open 9.30-5. CL: Sat. *STOCK: Jewels, miniatures, works of art.* PARK: Meters. TEL: 020 7629 1782; fax - 020 7629 3106; e-mail - dslavender@clara.net SER: Valuations. VAT: Stan/Spec.

Liberty
Regent St. W1R 6AH. Est. 1875. Open 10-6.30, Thurs. 10-8, Fri. and Sat. 10-7. SIZE: Large. *STOCK: British furniture, ceramics, glass and metalware, 1860-1930, Gothic Revival, Aesthetic Movement and Arts & Crafts.* LOC: Regent St. joins Piccadilly and Oxford Circus. PARK: Meters and underground station in Cavendish Sq. TEL: 020 7734 1234. VAT: Stan.

Maas Gallery
15a Clifford St. W1S 4JZ. (R.N. Maas). SLAD. Est. 1960. Open Mon.-Fri. 10-5.30. SIZE: Medium. *STOCK: Victorian and Pre-Raphaelite paintings, drawings, watercolours and illustrations.* LOC: Between New Bond St. and Cork St. PARK: Easy. TEL: 020 7734 2302; fax - 020 7287 4836; e-mail - mail@ maasgallery.co.uk website - www.maasgallery.com SER: Valuations; buys at auction. VAT: Spec.

Maggs Bros Ltd   BADA
50 Berkeley Sq. W1J 5BA. (J.F., B.D. and E.F. Maggs, P. Harcourt, R. Harding, H. Bett and J. Collins). ABA. Est. 1853. Open 9.30-5. CL: Sat. SIZE: Large. *STOCK: Rare books, manuscripts, autograph letters and medieval miniatures.* PARK: Meters. TEL: 020 7493 7160 (6 lines); fax - 020 7499 2007; e-mail - ed@maggs.com website - www.maggs.com VAT: Stan/Spec.

Mahboubian Gallery
65 Grosvenor St. W1K 3JJ. (H. Mahboubian). Open 10-6. CL: Sat. TEL: 020 7493 9112; e-mail - kmahboubian@aol.com

Mallett and Son (Antiques) Ltd   BADA
141 New Bond St. W1S 2BS. Est. 1865. Open 9.15-6, Sat. 10-4. SIZE: Large. *STOCK: English furniture, 1690-1835; clocks, 17th-18th C; china, needlework, paintings and watercolours, objects and glass.* PARK: Meters in Berkeley Sq. TEL: 020 7499 7411; fax - 020 7495 3179; e-mail - info@mallettantiques.com website - www.mallettantiques.com FAIRS: Grosvenor House; Maastricht; IFAAD New York; Winter Show, New York; Palm Beach; San Francisco (Fall).

Mallett at Bourdon House
2 Davies St., Berkeley Sq. W1K 3DJ. Est. 1962. Open 9.30-6. SIZE: Large. *STOCK: 18th-19th C Continental furniture, clocks, objets d'art; garden statuary, ornaments, pictures.* PARK: Meters. TEL: 020 7629 2444; fax - 020 7499 2670; e-mail - info@mallett antiques.com website - www.mallettantiques.com FAIRS: Winter Antiques; Palm Beach; Maastricht; Grosvenor House; IFAAD. VAT: Stan.

Mallett Gallery   BADA
141 New Bond St. W1S 2BS. SLAD. Open 9.15-6, Sat. 10-4. *STOCK: 18th to early 20th C paintings, watercolours and drawings.* PARK: Meters nearby. TEL: 020 7499 7411; fax - 020 7495 3179; e-mail - info@mallettantiques.com website - www.mallett antiques.com FAIRS: Olympia; Grosvenor House; IFAAD, New York; Maastricht; Palm Beach. VAT: Spec.

Mansour Gallery   BADA
46-48 Davies St. W1K 5JB. (M.Mokhtarzadeh). Open 9.30-5.30, Sat. by appointment. *STOCK: Islamic works of art, miniatures; ancient glass and glazed wares; Greek, Roman and Egyptian antiquities.* TEL: 020 7491 7444/7499 0510; e-mail - masil@ mansourgallery.com VAT: Stan.

Map World   LAPADA
25 Burlington Arcade, Piccadilly. W1J 0PT. (J. T. Sharpe). IMCOS. Est. 1982. Open 10-5.30. SIZE: Small. *STOCK: Maps, worldwide, 1480-1850, £50-£150,000.* TEL: 020 7495 5377; fax - same; e-mail - info@map-world.com website - www.map-world.com SER: Valuations; buys at auction.

Marks Antiques BADA LAPADA
49 Curzon St. W1J 7UN. (Anthony Marks). Est. 1935.
Open 9.30-6, Sat. 9.30-5. SIZE: Large. *STOCK: Fine
17th-19th C silver and Fabergé.* LOC: Green Park
underground station, opposite Washington Hotel.
PARK: Meters. TEL: 020 7499 1788; fax - 020 7409
3183; e-mail - marks@marksantiques.com website -
www.marksantiques.com SER: Valuations; buys at
auction. FAIRS: Grosvenor House; BADA; Olympia;
Hong Kong; Palm Beach; Dallas. VAT: Stan/Spec.

Marlborough Fine Art (London) Ltd
6 Albemarle St. W1S 4BY. SLAD. Est. 1946. Open 10-
5.30, Sat. 10-12.30. *STOCK: Graphic works and
exhibitions by leading contemporary artists and
sculptors.* PARK: Meters or near Cork St. TEL: 020 7629
5161; fax - 020 7629 6338; e-mail - mfa@marlborough
fineart.com website - www.marlboroughfineart.com
FAIRS: Madrid; Maastricht; Miami; Moscow; Basel;
Paris.

Marlborough Rare Books Ltd
144-146 New Bond St. W1S 2TR. (Jonathan Gestetner).
ABA. Est. 1946. Open 9.30-5.30. CL: Sat. SIZE:
Medium. *STOCK: Illustrated books of all periods; rare
books on fine and applied arts and architecture; English
literature.* PARK: Meters. TEL: 020 7493 6993; e-mail -
sales@mrb-books.co.uk SER: Buys at auction;
valuations; catalogues available. FAIRS: Olympia;
Chelsea; California; New York.

Mayfair Gallery Ltd
39 South Audley St. W1K 2PP. (M. Sinai). Open 9.30-6,
Sat. by appointment. *STOCK: 19th C antiques and
decorative Continental furniture, clocks, chandeliers,
Meissen, ivories and objets d'art.* LOC: Mayfair. TEL:
020 7491 3435/3436; fax - 020 7491 3437; e-mail -
mayfairgallery@mayfairgallery.com SER: Valuations;
restorations; shipping. FAIRS: Miami Beach; Olympia
(June).

Melton's
27 Bruton Place. W1J 6NQ. (Cecilia Neal). IIDA. BIDA.
Est. 1990. Open Mon.-Fri. 9.30-5.30. *STOCK: Small
antiques and decorative accessories: lamps, prints,
porcelain, textiles, English and Continental.* LOC:
Mayfair, near Bond St. PARK: Meters Berkeley Sq.
TEL: 020 7629 3612; fax - 020 7495 3196; e-mail -
sales@meltons.co.uk website - www.meltons.co.uk
SER: Interior design and decoration.

Messum's BADA LAPADA
8 Cork St. W1S 3LJ. SLAD. SOFAA. Open 10-6, Sat.
11-5, other times by appointment. *STOCK: British
Impressionist and contemporary paintings and
sculpture.* TEL: 020 7437 5545; fax - 020 7734 7018; e-
mail - support@messums.com website - www.
messums.com SER: Valuations; restorations;
framing. VAT: Stan/Spec.

John Mitchell and Son
44 Old Bond St. W1S 4GB. SLAD. Est. 1931. Open
9.30-5, Sat. by appointment. SIZE: Medium. *STOCK:
Old Master paintings, drawings and watercolours,
especially flower paintings, 17th C Dutch, 18th C
English and 19th C French; Alpine paintings;*

*contemporary, representing Julian Barrow and James
Hart-Dyke.* PARK: Meters. TEL: 020 7493 7567; fax -
020 7493 5537; e-mail - enquiries@johnmitchell.net
website - www.johnmitchell.net SER: Valuations;
restorations (pictures); buys at auction. FAIRS: TEFAF;
Palm Beach; IFAAD New York; Milan.

Paul Mitchell Ltd BADA
17 Avery Row, Brook St. W1K 4BF. Open 9.30-5.30.
CL: Sat. SIZE: Large. *STOCK: Picture frames.*
PARK: Meters. TEL: 020 7493 8732/0860. VAT: Stan.

Moira
11 New Bond St. W1S 3SR. Open 9-6. *STOCK: Fine
antique and Art Deco jewellery.* TEL: 020 7629 0160.
SER: Valuations; repairs.

Sydney L. Moss Ltd BADA
51 Brook St. W1K 4HP. (P.G. Moss). Est. 1910. Open
Mon.-Fri. 10-5.30. SIZE: Large. *STOCK: Chinese and
Japanese paintings and works of art; Japanese netsuke
and lacquer, 17th-20th C; reference books (as stock).*
LOC: From Grosvenor Sq., up Brook St. to
Claridges. PARK: Meters. TEL: 020 7629 4670/7493
7374; fax - 020 7491 9278; e-mail - pasi@slmoss.com
website - www.slmoss.com SER: Valuations and
advice; buys at auction. FAIRS: Asian Art, New York
(March). VAT: Spec.

Richard Ogden Ltd BADA
28 and 29 Burlington Arcade, Piccadilly. W1J 0NX.
Est. 1948. Open 9.30-5.30, Sat. 9.30-5. SIZE:
Medium. *STOCK: Antique jewellery.* PARK: Meters
and NCP. TEL: 020 7493 9136; e-mail - admin
@richardogden.com SER: Valuations; repairs. VAT:
Spec.

Partridge Fine Arts plc BADA
144-146 New Bond St. W1S 2PF. (John Partridge,
Michael Pick, Lucy Morton and Anthony Smith).
SLAD. CINOA. Est. 1905. Open 9-5.30, Sat. 11-4
(Oct-July - check beforehand), other times by
appointment. SIZE: Very large - 4 floors. *STOCK:
18th-19th C English, French and Continental
furniture; works of art; paintings, silver, clocks,
chandeliers, tapestries, lamps, needlework, carpets,
sculpture.* LOC: North of Bruton St.-Conduit St.
crossing. PARK: Meters and NCP nearby. TEL: 020
7629 0834; fax - 020 7495 6266; e-mail - enquiries
@partridgeplc.com website - www.partridgeplc.com
SER: Valuations; buys at auction; upholstery;
restorations; carving and gilding; annual exhibitions.
FAIRS: Grosvenor House; October International,
New York. VAT: Spec.

A. Pash & Sons
37 South Audley St. W1K 2PN. (Arnold and Robert
Pash). Est. 1940. Open 9-6. SIZE: Large. *STOCK: Silver.*
PARK: NCP nearby. TEL: 020 7493 5176; fax - 020
7355 3676; e-mail - david.pash@idnet.co.uk website -
www.pashantiques.com

W.H. Patterson Ltd BADA
19 Albemarle St. W1S 4BB. (Cory, Anthony and
Glenn Fuller and Wayne Thornton). SLAD. Open
9.30-6. SIZE: Large. *STOCK: 19th C and regular
exhibitions for contemporary artists, the New English*

Art Club, Paul Brown, Peter Brown, Willem and Walter Dolphyn, Clive McCartney, Lionel Aggett. LOC: Near Green Park underground station. PARK: Meters. TEL: 020 7629 4119; fax - 020 7499 0119; e-mail - info@whpatterson.com website - www.whpatterson. com SER: Valuations; restorations. FAIRS: New York Armoury; Affordable Art, Battersea; Watercolours and Drawings, Royal Academy. VAT: Spec.

Pelham Galleries Ltd   BADA
24/25 Mount St., Mayfair. W1K 2RR. (Alan and L.J. Rubin). Est. 1928. Open Mon.-Fri. 9-5.30. STOCK: Furniture, English and Continental; tapestries, decorative works of art and musical instruments. TEL: 020 7629 0905; fax - 020 7495 4511; e-mail - alan@ pelhamgalleries.com SER: Valuations. FAIRS: Palm Beach; Maastricht; Grosvenor House; Biennale Paris; New York. VAT: Spec.

Pendulum of Mayfair Ltd
King House, 51 Maddox St. W1S 2PJ. (K.R. Clements and Dr H. Specht). Open 10-6, Sat. 10-5, other times by appointment. STOCK: Clocks, mainly longcase, also bracket, mantel and wall; Georgian mahogany furniture. TEL: 020 7629 6606; fax - 020 7629 6616; e-mail - pendulumclocks@aol.com website - www.pendulum ofmayfair.co.uk SER: Valuations; repairs. VAT: Spec.

Ronald Phillips Ltd   BADA
26 Bruton St. W1J 6QL. (Simon Phillips). Est. 1952. Open Mon.-Fri. 9-5.30. STOCK: English 18th C furniture, objets d'art, glass, clocks and barometers. LOC: Mayfair. TEL: 020 7493 2341; fax - 020 7495 0843; e-mail - advice@ronaldphillips.co.uk website - www.ronaldphillips.co.uk FAIRS: Grosvenor House (June); IFAAD, New York (Oct). VAT: Mainly Spec.

S.J. Phillips Ltd   BADA
139 New Bond St. W1A 3DL. (M.S., N.E.L., J.P. and F.E. Norton). Est. 1869. Open 10-5. CL: Sat. SIZE: Large. STOCK: Silver, jewellery, gold boxes, miniatures. LOC: Near Bond St. underground station. PARK: Meters. TEL: 020 7629 6261; fax - 020 7495 6180; website - www.sjphillips.com SER: Restorations; buys at auction. FAIRS: Grosvenor House; Maastricht. VAT: Stan/Spec.

Piccadilly Gallery
43 Dover St. W1S 4NU. (R.G. and E.E. Pilkington). SLAD. Est. 1953. Open 10-5.30. STOCK: Symbolist and Art Nouveau works, 20th C; drawings and watercolours. PARK: Meters. TEL: 020 7629 2875; fax - 020 7499 0431; e-mail - art@piccadillygall.demon.co. uk website - www.piccadillygall.demon.co.uk VAT: Spec.

Pickering and Chatto
1st Floor, 36 St George St. W1S 2FN. Est. 1820. Open Mon.-Fri. 9.30-5.30 or by appointment. SIZE: Medium. STOCK: Literature, economics, politics, philosophy, science, medicine, general antiquarian. PARK: Meters. TEL: 020 7491 2656; fax - 020 7491 9161; e-mail - rarebooks@pickering-chatto.com

Portal Gallery
43 Dover St. W1S 4NU. (Lionel Levy and Jess Wilder). Est. 1959. Open 10-5.30, Sat. 10-4. SIZE: Medium. STOCK: Curios, bygones, artefacts, country pieces and objects of virtue, 19th C, £50-£500; contemporary British idiosyncratic paintings, including Beryl Cook. TEL: 020 7493 0706; fax - 020 7629 3506; e-mail - portalgallery@btinternet.com website - www.portal-gallery.com

Jonathan Potter Ltd   BADA LAPADA
125 New Bond St. W1S 1DY. ABA. Est. 1975. Open 10-6, Sat. by appointment. STOCK: Maps - worldwide including Britain, atlases and travel books, 16th-19th C, £50-£10,000. PARK: Meters nearby. TEL: 020 7491 3520; fax - 020 7491 9754; e-mail - jpmaps@ attglobal.net website - www.jpmaps.co.uk SER: Valuations; restorations; colouring; framing; buys at auction (maps and prints); catalogue available. VAT: Stan.

Pullman Gallery
116 Mount St., Mayfair. W1K 3NH. (Simon Khachadourian). Est. 1980. Open 10-6, Sat. by appointment. SIZE: Medium. STOCK: Objets de luxe, 19th-20th C, £200-£20,000; automobile art, pre-1950, £1,000-£20,000; cocktail shakers, bar accessories, cigar memorabilia, 1880-1950, £250-£25,000; René Lalique glass, 1900-1940, from £3,000. TEL: 020 7499 8080; fax - 020 7499 9090; mobile - 07973 141606; email - sk@pullmangallery.com website - www. pullmangallery.com VAT: Stan.

Bernard Quaritch Ltd (Booksellers)   BADA
8 Lower John St., Golden Sq. W1F 9AU. (Lord

Parmoor). ABA. Est. 1847. Open 9-6. CL: Sat. SIZE: Large. *STOCK: Rare books and manuscripts.* LOC: Piccadilly Circus. PARK: Meters, 50yds. TEL: 020 7734 2983; fax - 020 7437 0967; e-mail - rarebooks@quaritch.com website - www.quaritch. com SER: Buys at auction; valuations. FAIRS: Various International. VAT: Stan.

Rabi Gallery Ltd
82P Portland Place. W1B 1NS. (V.R. Soleymani). Est. 1878. Open by appointment. *STOCK: Ancient art and works of art.* TEL: 020 7580 9064; fax - 020 7436 0772.

Gordon Reece Gallery
16 Clifford St., Mayfair. W1S 3RG. Est. 1981. Open Tues.-Sat. 11-5.30. SIZE: Large. *STOCK: Chinese and Japanese antique furniture, south-east Asian sculpture, tribal art including jewellery, textiles and sculpture.* TEL: 020 7439 0007; fax - 020 7437 5715; e-mail - london@gordonreecegalleries.com website - www. gordonreecegalleries.com

David Richards and Sons
10 New Cavendish St. W1G 8UL. (M. and E. Richards). Est. 1970. Open 9.30-6. SIZE: Large. *STOCK: Antique and reproduction silver and plate.* LOC: Off Harley St., at corner of Marylebone High St. PARK: Nearby. TEL: 020 7935 3206/0322; fax - 020 7224 4423; e-mail - richards@thesilvershop.net website - www.the-silver shop.co.uk SER: Valuations; restorations. VAT: Stan/Spec.

Michael Rose - Source of the Unusual
3, 15, 44 Burlington Arcade, Piccadilly. W1J 0QY. NAG. Est. 1980. Open 9.30-5.30. *STOCK: Victorian, antique and period diamonds, jewellery and watches.* TEL: 020 7493 0714; 020 7491 1051; e-mail - michael@rose jewels.com website - www.rosejewels.co.uk FAIRS: Miami; Las Vegas.

Rossi & Rossi Ltd
13 Old Bond St. W1S 4SX. (Anna Maria Rossi and Fabio Rossi). Est. 1984. Open 10-5, Sat. and Sun. by appointment. SIZE: Medium. *STOCK: Himalayan art, 12th-18th C, to £150,000; early Chinese textiles.* LOC: Off Piccadilly. PARK: Meters. TEL: 020 7355 1804; fax - 020 7355 1806; e-mail - info@rossirossi.com website - www.asianart.com/rossi SER: Valuations; buys at auction. VAT: Spec.

The Royal Arcade Watch Shop
4 Royal Arcade at 28 Old Bond St. W1S 4SD. (Frank H. Lord and Daniel Pizzigoni). Est. 1995. Open 10.30-5.30. SIZE: Small. *STOCK: Modern and vintage Rolex, Cartier, Patek Philippe.* PARK: Easy. TEL: 020 7495 4882; website - www.royalarcadewatches.com

Frank T. Sabin Ltd   BADA
46 Albemarle St. W1S 4JN. (John and Mark Sabin). Open 9.30-6, Sat. by appointment. *STOCK: 19th-20th C paintings, contemporary sculpture.* TEL: 020 7493 3288; fax - 020 7499 3593; e-mail - ft.sabin@ btinternet.com website - www.ftsabin.com

Alistair Sampson Antiques Ltd   BADA
120 Mount St., Mayfair. (Formerly of 156 Brompton Rd). W1K 3NN. Est. 1968. Open 9.30-5.30. SIZE: Large. *STOCK: English pottery, oak and country furniture, metalwork, needlework, primitive pictures, decorative and interesting items, 17th-18th C.* PARK: Meters. TEL: 020 7409 1799; fax - 020 7409 7717; e-mail - info@alistairsampson.com website - www. alistairsampson.com FAIRS: Olympia; Grosvenor House; IFAAD; International Ceramics. VAT: Spec.

Robert G. Sawers
PO Box 4QA. W1A 4QA. ABA. Est. 1970. Open by appointment. *STOCK: Books on the Orient, Japanese prints, screens, paintings.* LOC: West Hampstead. TEL: 020 7794 9618; fax - 020 7794 9571; e-mail - bobsawers@clara.net

Seaby Antiquities
14 Old Bond St. W1S 4PP. (Dr. J.M. Eisenberg). ADA. Est. 1980. Open 10-5. CL: Sat. SIZE: Medium. *STOCK: Antiquities.* LOC: Just off Piccadilly, nearest underground station Green Park. PARK: Meters. TEL: 020 7495 2590; fax - 020 7491 1595.

Jeremy Seale Antiques/Interiors
15 St. Andrews Mansions, Dorset St. W1U 4EQ. Est. 1988. Open by appointment. SIZE: Small. *STOCK: Furniture, 18th-19th C, £300-£6,000; decorative items, 19th C; pictures and prints, 18th-19th C; both £50-£500.* TEL: 020 7935 5131; mobile - 07956 457795. SER: Finder; valuations; interior design consultant; homefinder. VAT: Stan/Spec.

Shapero Gallery   BADA
32 St George St. W1S 2EA. ABA, ILAB, IMCoS. Est. 1979. Open 9.30-6.30, Sat. 11-5. SIZE: Large. *STOCK: Rare maps and atlases, fine prints and travel photography, 16th-20th C; 19th C photographs; all £50-£50,000; antiquarian books - travel, natural history, modern first edition, colour plate.* LOC: Near Hanover Sq. and Bond St. TEL: 020 7493 0876; fax - 020 7229 7860; e-mail - rarebooks@shapero.com website - www.shapero.com SER: Valuations; restorations; framing. FAIRS: Palm Beach International; Maastricht TEFAF; Grosvenor House; ABA Olympia; Paris, New York, San Francisco, Los Angeles, Boston.

W. Sitch and Co. Ltd.
48 Berwick St. W1V 4JD. (R. Sitch). Est. 1776. Open 8-5. SIZE: Large. *STOCK: Edwardian and Victorian lighting fixtures and floor standards.* LOC: Off Oxford St. TEL: 020 7437 3776; fax - 020 7437 5707; e-mail - wsitch_co@hotmail.com website - www.wsitch.co.uk SER: Valuations; restorations; repairs. VAT: Stan.

The Sladmore Gallery of Sculpture   BADA
32 Bruton Place, Berkeley Sq. W1J 6NW. (E.F. and N. Horswell and G. Farrell). SLAD. Est. 1962. Open 10-6. CL: Sat. SIZE: Large. *STOCK: Bronze sculptures, 19th C - Mene, Barye, Fremiet, Bonheur; Impressionist, Bugatti, Troubetzkoy, Pompon, Degas, Rodin, Maillol; contemporary, Geoffrey Dashwood, Mark Coreth, Nic Fiddian-Green.* TEL: 020 7499 0365; fax - 020 7409 1381; e-mail - sculpture@ sladmore.com website - www.sladmore.com SER: Valuations; restorations. FAIRS: Grosvenor House. VAT: Stan/Spec.

Henry Sotheran Ltd
2/5 Sackville St., Piccadilly. W1S 3DP. ABA. PBFA. ILAB. Est. 1761. Open 9.30-6, Sat. 10-4. *STOCK: Antiquarian books and prints.* TEL: 020 7439 6151; fax - 020 7434 2019; e-mail - sotherans@sotherans.co.uk website - www.sotherans.co.uk SER: Restorations and binding (books, prints); buys at auction. VAT: Stan.

A. & J. Speelman Ltd   BADA
129 Mount St. W1K 3NX. Est. 1931. Open 9.30-6. SIZE: Large. *STOCK: Rare Chinese, Japanese and Himalayan works of art including Tang pottery and Chinese export ceramics, Buddhist images and ritual objects.* LOC: Mayfair. TEL: 020 7499 5126; fax - 020 7355 3391; e-mail - enquiries@ajspeelman.com website - www.ajspeelman.com SER: Valuations. FAIRS: Asian, New York. VAT: Spec.

Jacob Stodel   BADA
Flat 53 Macready House, 75 Crawford St. W1H 5LP. Est. 1949. Open by appointment. *STOCK: Continental furniture, objets d'art, ceramics.* TEL: 020 7723 3732; fax - 020 7723 9938; e-mail - jacobstodel@aol.com SER: Consultancy; valuations. FAIRS: Maastricht (TEFAF). VAT: Margin/Spec.

Stoppenbach & Delestre Ltd
25 Cork St. W1S 3NB. SLAD. Open 10-5.30, Sat. 10-1. *STOCK: French paintings, drawings and sculpture, 19th-20th C.* TEL: 020 7734 3534; e-mail - contact@ artfrancais.com website - www.artfrancais.com

Tessiers Ltd   BADA
1st Floor Gallery, 12 St. George St. W1S 2FB. Est. 1851. Open Mon.-Fri. 10-5, other times by appointment. *STOCK: Jewellery, silver, objets d'art.* LOC: Mayfair. TEL: 020 7629 0458; fax - 020 7629 1857. SER: Valuations; restorations. VAT: Spec.

William Thuillier
14 Old Bond St. W1S 4PP. Est. 1982. Open by appointment. *STOCK: European and British paintings, 1600-1850.* TEL: 020 7499 0106; e-mail - thuillart@ aol.com website - www.thuillart.com SER: Valuations; research. FAIRS: Olympia (Feb., June and Nov).

M. Turpin Ltd   LAPADA
27 Bruton St. W1J 6QN. CINOA. Est. 1948. Open Mon.-Fri. 10-6 or by appointment. SIZE: Large. *STOCK: English and Continental furniture, mirrors, chandeliers, objets d'art, 17th to early 19th C.* LOC: Between Berkeley Sq. and Bond St. PARK: Meters. TEL: 020 7493 3275; fax - 020 7408 1869; mobile - 07799 664322; e-mail - mturpin@mturpin.co.uk website - www. mturpin.co.uk SER: Restorations; upholstery; buys at auction. VAT: Spec.

Jan van Beers Oriental Art   BADA
34 Davies St. W1Y 1LG. Est. 1978. Open 10-6. CL: Sat. SIZE: Medium. *STOCK: Chinese and Japanese ceramics and works of art, 200BC to 1800AD.* LOC: Between Berkeley Sq. and Oxford St. PARK: Easy. TEL: 020 7408 0434; website - www.janvanbeers.com SER: Valuations. VAT: Spec.

Vigo Carpet Gallery   LAPADA
6a Vigo St. W1S 3HF. Open 10-6, Sat. 11-5. *STOCK: Oriental antique carpets and rugs; re-creations of hand-made carpets and rugs in vegetable dyes and hand-spun wool.* TEL: 020 7439 6971; fax - 020 7439 2353; e-mail - vigo@btinternet.com SER: Valuations; restorations.

Rupert Wace Ancient Art Ltd   BADA
14 Old Bond St. W1S 4PP. IADAA. ADA. Est. 1984. Open Mon.-Fri. 10-5 or by appointment. *STOCK: Ancient Egyptian, Classical, Near Eastern and Celtic antiquities.* LOC: West End. TEL: 020 7495 1623; fax - 020 7495 8495; e-mail - info@rupertwace.co.uk website - www.rupertwace.co.uk SER: Valuations. FAIRS: Ancient Art, Basel; Winter Antiques Show, New York.

Wartski Ltd   BADA
14 Grafton St. W1S 4DE. Est. 1865. Open 9.30-5. CL: Sat. SIZE: Medium. *STOCK: Jewellery, 18th C gold boxes, Fabergé, Russian works of art, silver.* PARK: Meters. TEL: 020 7493 1141. SER: Restorations. FAIRS: IFAAD, New York; European Fine Art; Maastricht (TEFAF); Grosvenor House. VAT: Stan/Spec.

Waterhouse and Dodd   BADA
26 Cork St. W1S 3MQ. (R. Waterhouse and J. Dodd). Est. 1987. Open 9.30-6, Sat. by appointment. SIZE: Medium. *STOCK: British and European oil paintings, watercolours and drawings, 1850-1950, £2,000-£50,000.* TEL: 020 7734 7800; e-mail - info@ european-paintings.com website - www.european-paintings.com SER: Valuations; restorations; buys at auction (paintings). FAIRS: Antiques & Fine Art; Olympia. VAT: Spec.

William Weston Gallery
7 Royal Arcade, Albemarle St. W1S 4SG. SLAD. IFPDA. Est. 1964. Open 9.30-5.30, Sat. 11-4. SIZE: Small. *STOCK: Lithographs and etchings, 1890-2000.* LOC: Off Piccadilly. TEL: 020 7493 0722; fax - 020 7491 9240; e-mail - www@williamweston.co.uk website - www.williamweston.co.uk FAIRS: Grosvenor House; 20th/21st C British Art; Royal Academy Print: New York. VAT: Spec.

Wilkins and Wilkins
1 Barrett St., St Christophers Pl. W1M 6DN. (M. Wilkins). Est. 1981. Open 10-5. CL: Sat. SIZE: Small. *STOCK: English 17th-18th C portraits and decorative paintings, £700-£20,000.* LOC: Near Selfridges. TEL: 020 7935 9613; fax - 020 7935 4696; e-mail - info@wilkinsandwilkins.com FAIRS: Olympia (June). VAT: Stan/Spec.

Wilkinson plc
1 Grafton St. W1S 4EA. Est. 1947. Open 9.30-5. CL: Sat. *STOCK: Glass, especially chandeliers, 18th C and reproduction; art metal work.* LOC: Nearest underground station - Green Park. TEL: 020 7495 2477; fax - 020 7491 1737; e-mail - enquiries@wilkinson-plc.com website - www.wilkinson-plc.com SER: Restorations and repairs (glass and metalwork).

Williams and Son
2 Grafton St. W1X 3LB. (J.R. Williams). Est. 1931. Open 9.30-6. CL: Sat. SIZE: Large. *STOCK: British and European paintings, 19th-20th C.* LOC: Between Bond

St. and Berkeley Sq. TEL: 020 7493 4985/5751; fax - 020 7409 7363; e-mail - art@williamsandson.com website - www.williamsandson.com VAT: Stan/Spec.

Thomas Williams (Fine Art) Ltd
22 Old Bond St. W1S 4PY. Open 9-6. CL: Sat. STOCK: Old Master drawings, £300-£1,000,000. TEL: 020 7491 1485; fax - 020 7408 0197; e-mail - thomas. williams@thomaswilliamsfineart.com website - www. thomaswilliamsfineart.com SER: Valuations; buys at auction (paintings and drawings).

Windsor House Antiques Ltd LAPADA
28-29 Dover St., Mayfair. W1S 4NA. (D.K. Smith). CINOA. Est. 1957. Open Mon.-Fri. 10-6. SIZE: Large plus Georgian town house. STOCK: English and Continental furniture, 18th-19th C; paintings and objects. TEL: 020 7659 0340; fax - 020 7499 6728; e-mail - sales@windsorhouseantiques.co.uk website - www.windsorhouseantiques.co.uk SER: Interior design; shipping arranged. VAT: Stan/Spec.

Linda Wrigglesworth Ltd LAPADA
34 Brook St. W1K 5DN. Est. 1978. Open Mon.-Fri. 11-6 by appointment. STOCK: Chinese, Korean and Tibetan costume and textiles, 14th-19th C. LOC: Corner of South Molton Lane, Brook St. end. PARK: Grosvenor Square. TEL: 020 7486 8990; fax - 020 7935 1511; e-mail - info @lindawrigglesworth.com website - www.linda wrigglesworth.com SER: Valuations; restorations; mounting, framing; buys on commission (Oriental). FAIRS: Maastricht; Asian Art, London and New York; San Francisco.

A. Zadah
2nd Floor, 2/3 Woodstock St. W1C 2AB. Est. 1976. Open 9.30-6. STOCK: Oriental and European carpets, rugs, tapestries and textiles. TEL: 020 7493 2622; fax - 020 7491 2236; e-mail - zadah@btconnect.com website - www.zadah.com

W2

Sean Arnold Sporting Antiques
21-22 Chepstow Corner, off Westbourne Grove. W2 4XE. Est. 1980. Open 10-6. SIZE: Large. STOCK: Sporting antiques and decorative items; golf clubs, 1840-1915, £30-£6,000; tennis racquets, £10-£3,000; football memorablia, globes and pond yachts; vintage luggage. LOC: Notting Hill Gate. PARK: Meters. TEL: 020 7221 2267; fax - 020 7221 5464. SER: Mail order. VAT: Stan.

David Black Carpets
27 Chepstow Corner, Chepstow Place. W2 4XE. (David Black and Richard Morant). Est. 1966. Open 11-6. SIZE: Large. STOCK: Custom made and outsize carpets, rugs, kilims, dhurries and silk embroideries, some antique, £500-£25,000. LOC: Notting Hill/Portobello. PARK: Meters. TEL: 020 7727 2566; fax - 020 7229 4599; e-mail - richardmorant@david-black.com website - www. david-black.com SER: Valuations; restorations; cleaning underfelt; design. VAT: Spec.

Craven Gallery
16 Craven Terrace. W2 3QD. (A. Quaradeghini). Est. 1974. By appointment only. SIZE: Large and warehouse.

STOCK: Silver and plate, 19th-20th C; Victorian furniture, china and glass. LOC: Off Bayswater Rd. PARK: Easy. TEL: 020 7402 2802; e-mail - cravengallery@btconnect.com VAT: Stan. Trade Only.

Hosains Books and Antiques
25 Connaught St. W2 2AY. (K.S. and Mrs. Y. Hosain). Est. 1979. Open by appointment. STOCK: Secondhand and antiquarian books on India, Middle East, Central Asia; miniatures; prints of India and Middle East; Islamic manuscripts. TEL: 020 7262 7900; fax - 020 7433 3126; website - www.indoislamica.com

Manya Igel Fine Arts Ltd LAPADA
21/22 Peters Court, Porchester Rd. W2 5DR. (M. Igel and B.S. Prydal). Est. 1977. Open Mon.-Fri. 10-5 by appointment only. SIZE: Large. STOCK: Traditional Modern British Art, £250-£25,000. LOC: Off Queensway. PARK: Nearby. TEL: 020 7229 1669/8429; fax - 020 7229 6770; e-mail - paintings@manyaigelfine arts.com website - www.manyaigelfinearts.com FAIRS: 20th/21st C British Art; Olympia (Spring); Chelsea (Spring); Claridges; VAT: Spec.

The Mark Gallery BADA
9 Porchester Place, Marble Arch. W2 2BS. (H. Mark). CINOA. Est. 1969. Open 10-1 and 2-6, Sat. 11-1. SIZE: Medium. STOCK: Russian icons, 16th-19th C; modern graphics - French school. LOC: Near Marble Arch. TEL: 020 7262 4906; fax - 020 7224 9416. SER: Valuations; restorations; buys at auction. FAIRS: Olympia (June and Nov); BADA. VAT: Spec.

Richard Nagy Fine Art Ltd
17 Hyde Park Gardens. W2 2LU. SLAD. Est. 1978. Open Mon.-Fri. 10-6 by appointment. SIZE: Large. STOCK: Classic Modernism, German Expressionists including Gustav Klimt and Egon Schiele; Modern British from Sickert to Auerbach. TEL: 020 7262 6400; fax - 020 7262 6464; e-mail - info@RichardNagy.com website - www.RichardNagy.com SER: Valuations; buys at auction. FAIRS: Maastricht (TEFAF); Art Basel. VAT: Spec.

W4

The Chiswick Fireplace Co.
68 Southfield Rd., Chiswick. W4 1BD. Open 9.30-5. SIZE: Medium. STOCK: Original cast iron fireplaces, late Victorian to early 1900's, £200-£1,000; marble, wood and limestone surrounds. LOC: 8 mins. walk from Turnham Green underground station. PARK: Easy. TEL: 020 8995 4011; fax - 020 8995 4012. SER: Restorations; installation. VAT: Stan.

David Edmonds
1-4 Prince of Wales Terrace, Chiswick. W4 2EY. Est. 1985. Open 10-5, Sun. by appointment. SIZE: Large. STOCK: Antiques and architecture from India and subcontinent, £10-£10,000. LOC: Off Devonshire Rd. PARK: Easy. TEL: 020 8742 1920; fax - 020 8742 3030; mobile - 07831 666436; e-mail - dareindia@aol.com SER: Valuations; restorations; buys at auction (as stock). VAT: Stan.

Marshall Phillips
38 Chiswick Lane, Chiswick. W4 2JQ. (John Phillips).

Est. 1985. Open 10-6, Sat. 10-5. SIZE: Medium. *STOCK: Decorative and unusual objects, furniture, bronzes and chandeliers, £100-£50,000; garden statuary and furniture, to £30,000.* LOC: Off A4/M4 at the Hogarth roundabout or Chiswick High Rd. PARK: Easy. TEL: 020 8742 8089; fax - same; e-mail - john@ marshallphillips.com website - www.marshallphillips. com SER: Valuations; restorations (oil and water gilding; metal patination and non-ferrous casting). VAT: Spec.

The Old Cinema Antique Department Store
160 Chiswick High Rd. W4 1PR. Est. 1977. Open 10-6, Sun. 12-5. SIZE: Large. *STOCK: General antiques including furniture, 20th C design, gardenalia, decorative and architectural items, 1660-1960, £100-£6,000.* PARK: Easy. TEL: 020 8995 4166; fax - 020 8995 4167; e-mail - theoldcinema@antiques-uk.co.uk website - www.theoldcinema.co.uk SER: Restorations; delivery. VAT: Stan/Spec.

Strand Antiques
46 Devonshire Rd., Chiswick. W4 2HD. Est. 1977. Open Tues.-Sat. 10.30-5.30. SIZE: Medium. *STOCK: English and French brocante, furniture, glass, lighting, ceramics, jewellery and silver, garden and kitchenware, books and prints, textiles and collectables, £1-£500.* LOC: Off Chiswick High Rd. 5 mins. Turnham Green underground station. PARK: Meters. TEL: 020 8994 1912.

W6

Architectural Antiques
351 King St. W6 9NH. (G.P.A. Duc). Est. 1985. Open Mon.-Fri. 8.30-4.30. SIZE: Medium. *STOCK: Marble/stone chimney pieces, 18th-19th C, £500-£15,000; gilt/painted overmantels, 19th C, £300-£1,500; antique French doors, £200-£1,000; bathroom fixtures, basins, £200-£800.* PARK: Easy and Black Lion Lane. TEL: 020 8741 7883; fax - 020 8741 1109; mobile - 07831 127541; website - www.aa-fireplaces.co.uk SER: Valuations; restorations and installations of marble. VAT: Stan. *Trade Only.*

Paravent
Flat 10, Ranelagh Gardens, Stamford Brook Ave. W6 0YE. (M. Aldbrook). Est. 1989. Open by appointment. *STOCK: Screens, 17th-20th C, £500-£10,000 - on view at Lelievre Showroom, Chelsea Harbour Design Centre.* TEL: 020 8748 6323; fax - 020 8563 2912; e-mail - aldbrook@paravent.freeserve.co.uk website - www. paravent.co.uk SER: Restorations; finder (screens); lectures worldwide. VAT: Stan/Spec.

Richard Philp   BADA
7 Ravenscourt Sq. W6 0TW. Est. 1961. Open by appointment. STOCK: Old Master drawings, 16th-17th C English portraiture and Old Master paintings, medieval sculpture, early furniture and 20th C drawings, £50-£40,000. PARK: Easy. TEL: 020 8748 5678; website - www.richardphilp.com FAIRS: Grosvenor House. VAT: Spec.

W7

Campbell's of London
1/5 Exhibition Rd. W7 28E. Open 9.30-5.30. *STOCK:*

20th C Impressionist and Modern British oils and watercolours. TEL: 020 7584 9268; fax - 020 7581 3499. SER: Master framing, carving, gilding; restorations.

W8

AntikWest AB
150-152 Kensington Church St. W8 4BN. (Bjorn Gremner and Jonathan Robinson). CINOA. KCSADA. Est. 1979. Open 10-6, Sat. 10-4. SIZE: Small. *STOCK: Chinese pottery and porcelain, Tang to late 19th C, £200-£35,000; Chinese furniture, £200-£2,000.* LOC: 100 yards south of Notting Hill Gate. PARK: Meters. TEL: 020 7229 4115; e-mail - china@antikwest.com website - www.antikwest.com FAIRS: Olympia (June); Stockholm, Alvsjo; Helsingborg, Sweden. VAT: Spec.

Valerie Arieta
97b Kensington Church St. W8 7LN. Est. 1972. Open 10.30-5, appointment advisable. *STOCK: American Indian, Eskimo and Folk art; English and Continental antiques.* TEL: 020 7243 1074/7794 7613. FAIRS: Santa Fe Ethnographic Art.

Gregg Baker Asian Art   BADA LAPADA
142 Kensington Church St. W8 4BN. KCSADA. Est. 1985. Open Tues.-Fri. 10-6, Sat. 11-4 or by appointment. SIZE: Medium. STOCK: Japanese and Chinese works of art and screens, mainly 18th-19th C, £500-£250,000. PARK: Meters. TEL: 020 7221 3533; fax - 020 7221 4410; e-mail - info@japanesescreens. com website - www.japanesescreens.com SER: Valuations. FAIRS: Olympia (June); NY Asian Art (March). VAT: Stan/Spec.

Eddy Bardawil   BADA
106 Kensington Church St. W8 4BH. (E.S. Bardawil). KCSADA. Est. 1979. Open 10-1 and 2-5.30, Sat. 10-1.30. SIZE: Medium. STOCK: English furniture - mahogany, satinwood, walnut; mirrors, brassware, tea-caddies, all pre-1830, £500-£50,000; prints, 18th C. LOC: Corner premises, Berkeley Gardens/Church St. PARK: Easy. TEL: 020 7221 3967; fax - 020 7221 5124. SER: Valuations; restorations (furniture); polishing. VAT: Stan/Spec.

Baumkotter Gallery   LAPADA
63a Kensington Church St. W8 4BA. (N. and Mrs L. Baumkotter). KCSADA. BAPCR. Est. 1968. Open 10.30-6, Sat. and Sun. by appointment. SIZE: Large. *STOCK: 17th-20th C fine oil paintings.* PARK: Own. TEL: 020 7937 5171 and 020 8395 5394; e-mail - n.baumkotter@btclick.com website - www.baumkottergallery.com SER: Restorations (pictures); framing. VAT: Spec.

David Brower Antiques   LAPADA
113 Kensington Church St. W8 7LN. KCSADA. Est. 1970. Open 11-6, Sat. by appointment. SIZE: Large. *STOCK: Specialist in Meissen, KPM, European and Oriental porcelain, French bronzes and Japanese works of art.* PARK: Meters nearby. TEL: 020 7221 4155; fax - 020 7221 6211; e-mail - David@davidbrower-antiques.com website - www.davidbrower-antiques.com SER: Buys at auction. FAIRS: Olympia (June). VAT: Stan/Spec.

Butchoff Antiques   LAPADA
154 Kensington Church St. W8 4BN. (Ian Butchoff).

KCSADA. Est. 1964. Open 9.30-6, Sat. 9.30-4. SIZE: Large. *STOCK: Fine 18th-19th C English and Continental furniture, mirrors, lighting, objets d'art and paintings.* PARK: Easy. TEL: 020 7221 8174; fax - 020 7792 8923; e-mail - enquiries@butchoff.com website - www.butchoff.com SER: Restorations (furniture). FAIRS: Olympia (Spring, Summer and Winter).

The Lucy B. Campbell Gallery
123 Kensington Church St. W8 7LP. Est. 1983. Open 10-6, Sat. 10-4. SIZE: Medium. *STOCK: Figurative, contemporary, naive and botanical paintings.* PARK: Meters. TEL: 020 7727 2205; fax - 020 7229 4252; e-mail - lucy@lucybcampbell.co.uk website - www. lucybcampbell.com SER: Framing. FAIRS: Olympia (Spring). VAT: Stan.

Cohen & Cohen   BADA
101B Kensington Church St. W8 7LN. (Ewa and Michael Cohen). KCSADA. TEFAF. Est. 1973. Open 10-6, Sat. 11-3. SIZE: Large. *STOCK: Chinese export porcelain and works of art.* TEL: 020 7727 7677; fax - 020 7229 9653; e-mail - info@cohenandcohen.co.uk website - www.cohenandcohen.co.uk SER: Valuations; buys at auction. FAIRS: Grosvenor House; Maastricht; Palm Beach Classic; New York Ceramics. VAT: Stan/Spec.

Garrick D. Coleman
5 Kensington Court. W8 5DL. Est. 1944. Open by appointment. SIZE: Medium. *STOCK: Chess sets, 1750-1880, £400-£10,000; decorative items, £50-£5,000; glass paperweights, £200-£3,000; conjuring and magic items.* PARK: Easy. TEL: 020 7937 5524; fax - 020 7937 5530; e-mail - coleman-antiques-london@compuserve. com website - www.antiquechess.co.uk VAT: Stan/Spec.

Mrs. M.E. Crick Chandeliers
166 Kensington Church St. W8 4BN. (M.T. and E.R. Denton). Est. 1897. Open Mon.-Fri. 9.30-5.30. SIZE: Large. *STOCK: English and Continental crystal, glass and ormulu chandeliers, 18th-19th C.* PARK: Meters. TEL: 020 7229 1338; fax - 020 7792 1073; e-mail - info@crick-chandeliers.co.uk website - www.crick-chandeliers.co.uk

Barry Davies Oriental Art   BADA
Est. 1983. Open Mon.-Fri. 10.30-5.30. STOCK: Japanese works of art, netsuke, lacquer and bronzes. TEL: 020 7408 0207; fax - 020 7603 0348; e-mail - bdoa@btopenworld.com website - www.barrydavies. com

Denton Antiques
156 Kensington Church St. W8 4BN. (M.T., E.R., and A.C. Denton). Est. 1897. Open Mon.-Fri. 9.30-5.30. SIZE: Large. *STOCK: Glass and metal chandeliers, wall lights and candelabra, 18th-19th C.* PARK: Meters. TEL: 020 7229 5866; fax - 020 7792 1073; e-mail - info@denton-antiques.co.uk website - www.denton-antiques.co.uk

H. and W. Deutsch Antiques   LAPADA
111 Kensington Church St. W8 7LN. Est. 1897. Open 10-5. CL: Wed. and Sat. SIZE: Large. *STOCK: 18th-19th C Continental and English porcelain and glassware; silver, plate and enamel ware, miniature portraits;*

Oriental porcelain, cloisonné, bronzes, £300-£5,000. TEL: 020 7727 5984. VAT: Stan/Spec.

C. Fredericks and Son   BADA
(R.F. Fredericks). Est. 1947. By appointment only. SIZE: Medium. *STOCK: Furniture, 18th C, £500-£15,000.* LOC: Near Notting Hill Gate underground station. TEL: 020 7727 2240; fax - same; mobile - 07831 336937; e-mail - richard.fredericks@ cfredericksandson.com website - www.cfrederick sandson.com SER: Restorations. FAIRS: BADA; Olympia (Winter). VAT: Stan/Spec.

Michael German Antiques Ltd   BADA LAPADA
38B Kensington Church St. W8 4BX. KCSADA. Est. 1954. Open 10-5, Sat. 10-12.30. *STOCK: European and Oriental arms and armour; walking stick specialist.* TEL: 020 7937 2771; fax - 020 7937 8566; website - www.antiquecanes.com and www.antique weapons.com

Green's Antique Galleries
117 Kensington Church St. W8 7LN. (S. Green). Open 9-5. SIZE: Medium. *STOCK: Jewellery, 18th C to date; pre-1930 clothes and lace; dolls, china, silver, furniture, paintings, masonic, crocodile and leather items.* PARK: Easy. TEL: 020 7229 9618. VAT: Stan/Spec.

Adrian Harrington
64A Kensington Church St. W8 4DB. ABA. ILAB. PBFA. KCSADA. Est. 1970. Open 10-6. SIZE: Large. *STOCK: Fine and rare antiquarian books, first editions, literature, children's, fore-edge paintings, library sets, Winston Churchill.* LOC: 5 mins. from Kensington High St. and Notting Hill Gate underground stations. PARK: Meters. TEL: 020 7937 1465; fax - 020 7368 0912; e-mail - rare@harringtonbooks.co.uk website - www. harringtonbooks.co.uk SER: Bookbinding; restoration. FAIRS: Olympia Book (June); Chelsea Book (Nov). VAT: Stan.

Haslam and Whiteway
105 Kensington Church St. W8 7LN. (T.M. Whiteway). KCSADA. Est. 1972. Open 10-6, Sat. 10-2. SIZE: Small. *STOCK: British furniture, £300-£50,000; British decorative arts, £200-£50,000; Continental and American decorative arts, £200-£10,000; all 1850-1930.* LOC: From Notting Hill Gate underground station, in Kensington Church St., premises approx. 300yds. on right. PARK: Meters. TEL: 020 7229 1145; fax - 020 7221 7065. SER: Valuations; buys at auction. VAT: Stan.

Jeanette Hayhurst Fine Glass   BADA
32A Kensington Church St. W8 4BX. KCSADA. Open 10-5, Sat. 12-5. STOCK: Glass - 18th C English drinking, fine 19th C engraved, table decanters, contemporary art, scent bottles, Roman and Continental. TEL: 020 7938 1539; website - www. antiqueglasslondon.com FAIRS: BADA; Antiques For Everyone (Birmingham); Harrogate Fine Art & Antiques Fair. VAT: Spec.

D. Holmes
47c Earls Court Rd. (in Abingdon Villas), Kensington. W8 6EE. (Don and Sarah Holmes). Est. 1965. Open Fri. 9-7, Sat. 9-12 or by appointment. *STOCK: Decorative items and furniture, 18th-19th C.* PARK: Meters. TEL:

020 7937 6961 or 01208 880254; mobile - 07790 431895. SER: Restorations (furniture). VAT: Stan/Spec.

Hope and Glory
(Commemorative Ceramics Specialists) 131a Kensington Church St. W8 7LP. (R.R. Lower). KCSADA. Est. 1982. Open 10-5. *STOCK: Commemorative china.* LOC: Entrance in Peel St. TEL: 020 7727 8424. SER: Mail order (no catalogue).

Jonathan Horne   BADA
66c Kensington Church St. W8 4BY. KCSADA. CINOA. Est. 1968. Open 9.30-5.30, Sat. and Sun. by appointment. SIZE: Medium. *STOCK: Early English pottery, needlework and works of art.* TEL: 020 7221 5658; fax - 020 7792 3090; e-mail - JH@ jonathanhorne.co.uk website - www.jonathan horne.co.uk SER: Valuations. FAIRS: BADA; Olympia (June and Nov); Grosvenor House; International Ceramics; New York Ceramics; Buxton; IFAAD. VAT: Stan/Spec.

Howard-Jones - The Silver Shop
43 Kensington Church St. W8 4BA. (H. Howard-Jones). Est. 1971. Open 10-5.30. SIZE: Small. *STOCK: Silver, antique and modern, £10-£3,000.* PARK: Nearby. TEL: 020 7937 4359; fax - same. VAT: Stan.

Iona Antiques   BADA
PO Box 285. W8 6HZ. Est. 1974. Open by appointment. SIZE: Large. *STOCK: 19th C animal paintings, £2,000-£30,000.* LOC: 3 mins. walk from Odeon Cinema, Kensington High St. PARK: Nearby. TEL: 020 7602 1193; fax - 020 7371 2843; e-mail - iona@ionaantiques.com website - www.ionaantiques. com FAIRS: Grosvenor House, Olympia.

J.A.N. Fine Art
132-134 Kensington Church St. W8 4BH. (Mrs F.K. Shimizu). KCSADA. Est. 1976. Open 10-6, Sat. by appointment. SIZE: Large. *STOCK: Japanese and Chinese porcelain, 1st to 20th C, from £150; Japanese bronzes and works of art, 15th-20th C, from £150; Japanese paintings and screens, 16th-20th C, from £250; Tibetan thankas and ritual objects, 12th-18th C, from £250.* PARK: Meters. TEL: 020 7792 0736; fax - 020 7221 1380; e-mail - fusashimizu@aol.com website - www.jan-fineart-london.com FAIRS: Olympia (June). VAT: Spec.

Japanese Gallery
66d Kensington Church St. W8 4BY. (Mr and Mrs C.D. Wertheim). Est. 1977. Open 10-6. *STOCK: Japanese wood-cut prints; books, porcelain, netsuke.* TEL: 020 7229 2934; fax - same; e-mail - sales@japanesegallery.co.uk website - www.japanesegallery.co.uk SER: Free authentification; on-the-spot framing for Japanese prints; sales exhibitions.

John Jesse
160 Kensington Church St. W8 4BN. Est. 1963. Open 10-6, Sat. 11-4. *STOCK: Decorative arts, 1880-1980, especially Art Nouveau and Art Deco silver, glass, bronzes and jewellery.* LOC: Near Notting Hill Gate underground. TEL: 020 7229 0312; fax - 020 7229 4732; e-mail - jj@johnjesse.com website - www.johnjesse.com

Peter Kemp
170 Kensington Church St. W8 4BN. KCSADA. Est. 1975. Open 10-5. CL: Sat. SIZE: Medium. *STOCK: Porcelain - 10th-19th C Chinese, 17th-19th C Japanese, 18th C Continental; Oriental works of art and porcelain, 18th-19th C.* LOC: 200yds. from Notting Hill underground station. PARK: Meters nearby. TEL: 020 7229 2988. SER: Valuations; restorations (porcelain). VAT: Spec.

Kensington Church Street Antiques Centre
58-60 Kensington Church St. W8 4DB. KCSADA. Open 10-6. TEL: 020 7937 4600; fax - 020 7937 3400. Below are listed some of the dealers at this Centre.

Abstract   LAPADA
20th C decorative arts and design. TEL: 020 7376 2652; fax - same; website - www.abstract-antiques.com

Nicolaus Boston
Majolica, Palissy, Dresser and Aesthetic movement porcelain. TEL: 020 7937 2237; fax - 01386 584004; e-mail - sales@majolica.co.uk website - www.majolica.co.uk

Didier Antiques   LAPADA
Jewellery and silver, objets d'art, 1860-1960. TEL: 020 7938 2537; fax - same; e-mail - didier.antiques@virgin.net

FCR Gallery
20th C metalware, glass, ceramics; Arts and Crafts, Art Nouveau, Art Deco, Modernism. TEL: 020 7938 5385; fax - same; website - www.fcrgallery.com

David Glick   LAPADA
Antique glass. TEL: Mobile - 07850 615867; website - www.georgianglass.com

James Miles
20th C ceramics and metalware. TEL: Mobile - 07815 301990; website - www.james-miles.com

Colin D. Monk
Oriental porcelain. TEL: 020 7229 3727; fax - 020 7376 1501; e-mail - colindmonk@yahoo.co.uk

Christopher Sheppard
Ancient and antique glass. TEL: 020 7937 3450.

Sandy Stanley
20th C jewellery and metalware. TEL: Mobile - 07973 147072; website - www.net-jewels.co.uk

The Lacquer Chest
71 and 75 Kensington Church St. W8 4BG. (G. and V. Andersen). Est. 1959. Open 9.30-5.30, Sat. 10.30-4.30. SIZE: Large. *STOCK: Furniture - painted, oak, mahogany; blue and white, Staffordshire, lamps, candlesticks, samplers, prints, paintings, brass, mirrors, garden furniture, unusual items.* LOC: Half-way up left-hand side from High St. PARK: Meters. TEL: 020 7937 1306; fax - 020 7376 0223. VAT: Stan/Spec.

Lev (Antiques) Ltd
97A & B Kensington Church St. W8 7LN. (Mrs Lev). Est. 1882. Open 10.30-5.30. SIZE: Medium. *STOCK: Jewellery, silver, plate, curios and pictures.* PARK: Meters. TEL: 020 7727 9248. SER: Restorations (pictures).

Libra Antiques
131d Kensington Church St. W8 7LP. KCSADA. Open 10-5, Sat. 10-4. *STOCK: Blue and white pottery, lustre ware.* TEL: 020 7727 2990.

London Antique Gallery
66E Kensington Church St. W8 4BY. (Mr and Mrs C.D. Wertheim). Open 10-6. *STOCK: Porcelain including English, Worcester, Meissen, Dresden and Sèvres; French and German bisque dolls.* TEL: 020 7229 2934; fax - same. SER: Restorations (prints, porcelain and dolls).

E. and H. Manners   BADA
66a Kensington Church St. W8 4BY. (Errol and Henriette Manners). KCSADA. Est. 1986. Open Mon.-Fri. 10-5.30 appointment advisable. *STOCK: European ceramics, pre-19th C.* TEL: 020 7229 5516; fax - same; home - 020 8741 7084; e-mail - manners@ europeanporcelain.com website - www.european porcelain.com FAIRS: International Ceramic. VAT: Spec.

S. Marchant & Son   BADA
120 Kensington Church St. W8 4BH. (R.P. and S.J. Marchant). KCSADA. Est. 1925. Open 9.30-5.30. CL: Sat. *STOCK: Chinese and Japanese pottery and porcelain, jades, cloisonné, Chinese furniture and paintings.* PARK: Easy. TEL: 020 7229 5319/3770; fax - 020 7792 8979; e-mail - gallery@marchant asianart.com website - www.marchantasianart.com SER: Valuations; restorations (porcelain); buys at auction. FAIRS: Grosvenor House; Asian Art New York. VAT: Stan/Spec.

R. and G. McPherson Antiques   BADA
40 Kensington Church St. W8 4BX. (Robert and Georgina McPherson). KCSADA. Est. 1985. Open 10-5.30. SIZE: Large. *STOCK: Chinese, Japanese and

other south-east Asian ceramics, including song monochromes, Chinese export ware, shipwreck ceramics, blue and white and blanc de Chine. **LOC: Kensington High St. underground station. PARK: Meters. TEL: 020 7937 0812; fax - 020 7938 2032; mobile - 07768 432630; e-mail - rmcpherson@ orientalceramics.com website - www.oriental ceramics.com SER: Valuations (verbal); identification. FAIRS: Olympia (June). Asian Art, London (Nov). VAT: Spec.**

Michael Coins
6 Hillgate St., (off Notting Hill Gate). W8 7SR. (M. Gouby). Est. 1966. Open 10-5. CL: Mon. and Sat. SIZE: Small. *STOCK: Coins, English and foreign, 1066 A.D. to date; stamps, banknotes and general items.* LOC: From Marble Arch to Notting Hill Gate, turn left at corner of Coronet Cinema. PARK: Easy. TEL: 020 7727 1518; fax - 020 7727 1518; website - www.michael-coins.co.uk SER: Valuations; buys at auction. VAT: Stan/Spec.

Millner Manolatos
2 Campden St. W8 7EP. (Arthur Millner and Alex Manolatos). KCSADA. Est. 1996. Open Tues.-Fri. 12-6, Sat. 12-4.30. SIZE: Small. *STOCK: Indian objects, 10th-19th C, up to £8,000; Indian paintings, 17th-19th C, £200-£4,000; Islamic art, 15th-19th C, £500-£8,000.* LOC: Off Kensington Church St., Notting Hill Gate underground station. PARK: Meters. TEL: 020 7229 3268; e-mail - info@millnermanolatos.com website - www.millnermanolatos.com SER: Valuations. FAIRS: Olympia. VAT: Spec.

Amir Mohtashemi Ltd

131 Kensington Church St. W8 7LP. (Amir Mohtashemi and Farah Hakemi). KCSADA. Est. 1989. Open 10.30-6.30, Sat. 10.30-4.30. SIZE: Small. *STOCK: Indian and Islamic works of art especially colonial items (boxes, ivory and furniture); Islamic tiles, ceramics and Ottoman furniture; arms and armour.* PARK: Nearby. TEL: 020 7727 2628; fax - 020 7727 5734; e-mail - info@ amirmohtashemi.com website - www.amirmohtashemi. com SER: Valuations. FAIRS: Olympia (Summer).

Pawsey and Payne   BADA

PO Box 11830 W8. (The Hon. NicholasWallop). Est. 1910. Open by appointment. *STOCK: English oils and watercolours, 18th-19th C.* TEL: 020 7930 4221; fax - 020 7937 3440; e-mail - nicholas.wallop@btconnect. com SER: Valuations; restorations. VAT: Stan/Spec.

Pruskin Gallery

73 Kensington Church St. W8 4BG. KCSADA.Open 10-6, Sat. 11-5. *STOCK: Fine Art Nouveau and Art Deco glass, bronzes, silver, furniture, ceramics, paintings, posters and prints.* TEL: 020 7937 1994.

Puritan Values

69 Kensington Church St. W8 4BG. (A.F. Geering). Est. 1987. Open 10.30-5. CL: Tues. *STOCK: Arts & Crafts movement, Gothic Revival, Aesthetic, Art Nouveau, £50-£20,000; decorative and important works of art.* TEL: 020 7937 2410; e-mail - sales@puritanvalues.com website - www.puritanvalues.com SER: Valuations; restorations. VAT: Stan/Spec.

Raffety & Walwyn Ltd   BADA LAPADA

79 Kensington Church St. W8 4BG. CINOA. KCSADA. Open 10-5.30, Sat. 11-2.30. *STOCK: Fine English longcase and bracket clocks, 17th-18th C; barometers and period furniture.* TEL: 020 7938 1100; fax - 020 7938 2519; e-mail - raffety@globalnet.co.uk website - www.raffetyantiqueclocks.com SER: Valuations; buys at auction. FAIRS: BADA, Olympia (June); Grosvenor House. VAT: Stan/Spec.

Paul Reeves

32B Kensington Church St. W8 4HA. Est. 1976. Open 10-5.30, Sat. 11-4. *STOCK: Architect designed furniture and artefacts, 1860-1960.* TEL: 020 7937 1594; fax - 020 7938 2163; e-mail - paul@paulreeveslondon.com website - www.paulreeveslondon.com VAT: Spec.

Reindeer Antiques Ltd   BADA LAPADA

81 Kensington Church St. W8 4BG. (Peter Alexander). KCSADA. Open 9.30-6, Sat. 10.30-5.30. *STOCK: Period English and Continental furniture and works of art.* PARK: Meters. TEL: 020 7937 3754; fax - 020 7937 7199; e-mail - london@reindeer antiques.co.uk website - www.reindeerantiques.co.uk FAIRS: BADA: Olympia (Nov). VAT: Stan/Spec.

Roderick Antique Clocks   LAPADA

23 Vicarage Gate, Kensington. W8 4AA. (Roderick Mee). Est. 1975. Open 10-5.15, Sat. 10-4. *STOCK: Clocks - French decorative and carriage, 19th C, £250-£3,500; English longcase and bracket, 18th-19th C, £2,000-£12,000.* LOC: At junction of Kensington Church St. PARK: Easy. TEL: 020 7937 8517; e-mail -

rick@roderickantiqueclocks.com website - www.roderickantiqueclocks.com SER: Valuations; restorations (English and French movements and cases). VAT: Spec.

Brian Rolleston Antiques Ltd   BADA
104A Kensington Church St. W8 4BU. KCSADA. Est. 1950. Open 10-1 and 2-5.30, Sat. by appointment. SIZE: Large. *STOCK: English furniture, 18th C.* TEL: 020 7229 5892; fax - same; e-mail - antiques@ brianrolleston.freeserve.co.uk FAIRS: BADA; Grosvenor House.

Patrick Sandberg Antiques Ltd   BADA
150-152 Kensington Church St. W8 4BN. (P.C.F. Sandberg). KCSADA. Est. 1983. Open 10-6, Sat. 10-4. SIZE: Large. *STOCK: 18th to early 19th C English furniture and accessories - candlesticks, tea caddies, clocks and prints.* TEL: 020 7229 0373; fax - 020 7792 3467; e-mail - psand@antiquefurniture.net website - www.antiquefurniture.net FAIRS: Olympia (June and Nov); BADA. VAT: Spec.

Santos   BADA
21 Old Court House. W8 4PD. CINOA. Open by appointment. *STOCK: Chinese export porcelain, 17th-18th C.* TEL: 020 7937 6000; fax - 020 7937 3351; e-mail - companhiaindias@aol.com website - www.santoslondon.com FAIRS: Olympia (June); New York Ceramics; Lisbon Biennal. VAT: Spec.

B. Silverman   BADA
4 Campden St., Off Kensington Church St. W8 7EP. (Robin Silverman and Bill Brackenbury). Open 10-6, Sat. 10-4. SIZE: Large. *STOCK: Fine antique silver including flatware.* TEL: 020 7985 0555/6; e-mail - silver@silverman-london.com website - www.silverman-london.com SER: Valuations. FAIRS: Olympia; BADA. VAT: Stan/Spec.

Sinai Antiques Ltd
219-221 Kensington Church St. W8 7LX. (E. Sinai Ltd). KCSADA. Est. 1973. Open 10-6, Sat. and Sun. by appointment. *STOCK: Fine 19th C Continental furniture, clocks, porcelain, chandeliers and objet d'art; Oriental and Islamic decorative arts and antiques.* TEL: 020 7229 6190; fax - 020 7221 0543; e-mail - sinaiantiquesltd@aol.com

Simon Spero
3A Campden St., Off Kensington Church St. W8 4EP. KCSADA. Author of 'The Price Guide to 18th C English Porcelain' and three other standard reference books. Est. 1964. Open 10-5, Sat. by appointment. SIZE: Medium. *STOCK: 18th C English ceramics and enamels.* PARK: Meters. TEL: 020 7727 7413; fax - 020 7727 7414. SER: Valuations; buys at auction; lecturer. VAT: Spec.

Stockspring Antiques   BADA
114 Kensington Church St. W8 4BH. (Antonia Agnew and Felicity Marno). KCSADA. Est. 1979. Open 10-5.30, Sat. 10-1. SIZE: 2 floors. *STOCK: English, European and Oriental pottery and porcelain.* TEL: 020 7727 7995; fax - same; e-mail - stockspring@ antique-porcelain.co.uk SER: Packing and shipping; valuations. FAIRS: Olympia (June and Nov). VAT: Spec.

Through the Looking Glass Ltd
137 Kensington Church St. W8 7LP. (J.J.A. and D.A. Pulton). KCSADA.Est. 1958. Open 10-5.30. SIZE: Medium. *STOCK: English, French and Continental mirrors, 19th C, £500-£10,000.* LOC: 200yds. from Notting Hill Gate. PARK: Side roads. TEL: 020 7221 4026; fax - same; website - www.throughthelookingglass.co.uk VAT: Spec.

Geoffrey Waters Ltd   BADA
133 Kensington Church St. W8 7LP. Open 10.15-5.30, Sat. 10.30-4.30. SIZE: Medium. *STOCK: 16th-18th C Chinese porcelain, mainly export.* TEL: 020 7243 6081; fax - 020 7243 6081; e-mail - info@antique-chinese-porcelain.com website - www.antique-chinese-porcelain.com

Jorge Welsh Oriental Porcelain & Works of Art   BADA
116 Kensington Church St. W8 4BH. KCSADA. Est. 1987. Open 10-5.30, Sat. 10-2. SIZE: Medium. *STOCK: Chinese export porcelain and Oriental works of art.* LOC: Off Kensington High St. PARK: NCP Bayswater Rd. TEL: 020 7229 2140; fax - 020 7792 3535; e-mail - uk@jorgewelsh.com website - www.jorgewelsh.com SER: Valuations; restorations; buys at auction. FAIRS: International Ceramic. VAT: Spec.

Neil Wibroe and Natasha MacIlwaine
77 Kensington Church St. W8 4BG. Est. 1984. Open 10-6. *STOCK: 18th C English furniture and works of art.* TEL: 020 7937 2461; fax - 020 7938 3286; mobile - 07831 748433. SER: Restorations.

Mary Wise & Grosvenor Antiques   BADA
27 Holland St., Kensington. W8 4NA. (Elisabeth Lorie). Est. 1959. Open Mon.-Fri. 10-5 or by appointment. *STOCK: English porcelain, works of art, bronzes, Chinese paintings.* **Not Stocked: English pottery, jewellery. PARK: Meters and nearby. TEL: 020 7937 8649; fax - 020 7937 7179; e-mail - info@ wiseantiques.com website - www.wiseantiques.com SER: Buys at auction (Chinese and English porcelain). FAIRS: BADA; Grosvenor House; Olympia (Nov); San Francisco. VAT: Spec.**

W9

Cox Interiors Ltd
5 Formosa St., Little Venice. W9 1EE. (Kaley Cox). Est. 1994. Open 10-6. SIZE: Medium. *STOCK: French and Italian furniture, 18th-20th C; lighting including chandeliers and lanterns, mirrors; painted, decorative, fruitwood and walnut furniture.* PARK: Easy. TEL: 020 7266 2620; fax - 020 7266 2622; e-mail - info@coxinteriors.com website - www.coxinteriors.com SER: Restorations; upholstery.

Fluss and Charlesworth Ltd   BADA LAPADA
1 Lauderdale Rd. W9 1LT. (J. Charlesworth). Est. 1970. Open by appointment. *STOCK: 18th to early 19th C furniture and works of art.* **TEL: 020 7286 8339; mobile - 07831 830323. SER: Interior decor. FAIRS: Olympia (June and Nov); LAPADA; Palm Beach.**

Vale Antiques
245 Elgin Ave., Maida Vale. W9 1NJ. (P. Gooley). *STOCK: General antiques.* TEL: 020 7328 4796.

W10

Crawley and Asquith Ltd   BADA
133 Oxford Gardens. W10 6NE. Open by appointment. *STOCK: 18th-19th C paintings, watercolours, prints, books.* **TEL: 020 8969 6161; fax - 020 8960 6494; e-mail - az@crawleyandasquith.com**

W11

Admiral Vernon Antiques Market
141-149 Portobello Rd. W11 2DY. (Portobello Group). PADA. Est. 1995. Open Sat. 5-5. SIZE: 200+ dealers. *STOCK: Wide range of general antiques and collectables.* TEL: 020 7727 5240; mobile - 07956 851283; e-mail - leeclifford@portobellogroup.com website - www.portobellogroup.com SER: Valuations; repairs (pens, jewellery, watches, and lighters).

Alice's
86 Portobello Rd. W11 2QD. (D. Carter). Est. 1960. Open Tues.-Fri. 9-5, Sat. 7-4. SIZE: Large. *STOCK: General antiques and decorative items.* TEL: 020 7229 8187; fax - 020 7792 2456.

Arbras Gallery
292 Westbourne Grove. W11 2PS. Est. 1972. Open Fri. 10-4, Sat. 7-5. SIZE: 2 floors. *STOCK: General antiques - silver, cutlery, jewellery, glass, porcelain, decorative arts and antiquities.* LOC: 50 yards from Portobello Road. TEL: 020 7229 6772; fax - same. VAT: Stan/Spec.

Axia Art Consultants Ltd
121 Ledbury Rd. W11 2AQ. (Yanni Petsopoulos). Est. 1974. Open Mon.-Fri. 10-6. *STOCK: Works of art, icons, textiles, metalwork, woodwork and ceramics, Islamic and Byzantine.* TEL: 020 7727 9724; fax - 020 7229 1272; e-mail - axia@axia-art.com

B. and T. Antiques   LAPADA
79/81 Ledbury Rd. W11 2AG. (Mrs B. Lewis). Est. 1984. Open 10-6. SIZE: 2 floors. *STOCK: Furniture especially mirrored, silver, objets d'art, Art Deco.* LOC: Notting Hill. PARK: Easy. TEL: 020 7229 7001; fax - 020 7229 2033; e-mail - bernadette@btantiques. freeserve.co.uk website - www.bntantiques.co.uk SER: Restorations. VAT: Stan/Spec.

Sebastiano Barbagallo
15-17 Pembridge Rd., Notting Hill Gate. W11 3HL. Est. 1975. Open 10.30-6 including Sun., Sat. 9-7. SIZE: Medium. *STOCK: Chinese furniture; antiques and handicrafts from India, Tibet, SE Asia and China.* LOC: Just before Portobello Road. TEL: 020 7792 3320; fax - same. VAT: Stan.

Barham Antiques
83 Portobello Rd. W11 2QB. Est. 1954. Open 10.30-5, Sat. 7.30-5. SIZE: Large. *STOCK: Victorian and Georgian writing boxes, tea caddies, inkwells and inkstands, glass epergnes, silver plate, clocks, paintings, Victorian furniture, tantalus and jewellery boxes.* TEL: 020 7727 3845; fax - same; e-mail - mchlbarham@ aol.com website - www.barhamantiques.co.uk SER: Valuations; buys at auction.

Elizabeth Bradwin
73 Portobello Rd., Notting Hill. W11 2QB. PADA. Est. 1989. Open Sat. 7-4. SIZE: Small. *STOCK: Animal subjects including animalier bronzes, 19th-20th C, £100-£4,000; Vienna bronzes, Staffordshire, carved wood, inkwells, tobacco jars.* TEL: Home and fax - 020 8947 2629; mobile - 07940 952450; e-mail - eliz@ elizabethbradwin.com website - www.elizabethbradwin. com VAT: Spec.

Caelt Gallery
182 Westbourne Grove. W11 2RH. (Edward T. Crawshaw). PADA. Est. 1967. Open 9.30-8, Sun. 10.30-6. SIZE: Large. *STOCK: Oil paintings, 17th-20th C, £200-£10,000 but mainly £300-£900: Soviet and Russian oils.* PARK: Easy. TEL: 020 7229 9309; fax - 020 7727 8746; mobile - 07973 412601; e-mail - art@ caeltgallery.com website - www.caeltgallery.com SER: Re-lining; cleaning and restoration; framing. VAT: Spec.

Jack Casimir Ltd   BADA LAPADA
23 Pembridge Rd. W11 3HG. Est. 1933. Open 10-5 and by appointment. SIZE: Large. *STOCK: 16th-19th C British and European brass, copper, pewter, paktong.* **Not Stocked: Silver, china, jewellery. LOC: 2 mins. walk from Notting Hill Gate underground station. PARK: 100yds. TEL: 020 7727 8643. SER: Exports. VAT: Stan/Spec.**

Central Gallery (Portobello)
125 Portobello Rd. W11 2DY. (C. Hickey). Est. 1996. Open Sat. 6-3. SIZE: 25+ dealers. *STOCK: Jewellery - 18th C to 1960s, including cameos, hardstone, shell,*

lava, coral, amber, ivory, jet, tortoiseshell, piqué, micro-mosaics, pietra-dura, Art Nouveau, plique é jour, horn pendants, Art Deco, enamels, Austro-Hungarian, cut-steel, Berlin iron, Scottish, Victorian silver and gold, Alberts, Albertines, longuards, curbs, gates, fobs, seals, intaglios, pocket watches, vintage wristwatches, cufflinks, fine diamonds, rare gemstones, signed pieces, pearls, platinum jewellery; from £50-£5,000+. LOC: Notting Hill. PARK: Pay and Display. TEL: 020 7243 8027; fax - same; e-mail - jewellery@centralgallery.com website - www.centralgallery.com FAIRS: Olympia; Park Lane Hotel; NEC. VAT: Stan/Spec/Global.

Chelsea Clocks & Antiques
73 Portobello Rd., Notting Hill. W11 2QB. (Peter Dixon). Est. 1978. Open 10-5. SIZE: Small. *STOCK: English, French and German clocks, especially dial, 1800-1930, £150-£10,000; brass, fireplace tools, stationery items, globes, boxes, scales, barometers.* PARK: Easy. TEL: 020 7229 7762; fax - 020 7274 5198; e-mail - info@chelseaclocks.co.uk website - www. chelseaclocks.co.uk

Garrick D. Coleman
75 Portobello Rd. W11 2QB. Est. 1944. Open 10.30-4.30, Sat. 8.30-3.30. *STOCK: Chess sets, 1750-1880, £300-£15,000; works of art £50-£3,000; glass paperweights, £200-£3,000; also conjuring and magic items.* TEL: 020 7937 5524; fax - 020 7937 5530; e-mail - coleman-antiques-london@compuserve.com website - www.antiquechess.co.uk/ VAT: Stan/Spec.

Sheila Cook Textiles
184 Westbourne Grove. W11 2RH. Est. 1970. Open by appointment only. SIZE: Small. *STOCK: Textiles, costume and accessories, 1750-1980, £15-£3,000.* PARK: Meters. TEL: 020 7792 8001; ; fax - 020 7243 1744; e-mail - sheilacook@sheilacook.co.uk website - www.sheilacook.co.uk SER: Valuations. VAT: Global.

The Corner Portobello Antiques Supermarket
282-290 Westbourne Grove. W11 2PS. (B. Lipka & Son Ltd). Open Fri. 12-4, Sat. 7-5. SIZE: 150 dealers. *STOCK: General miniature antiques, silver and jewellery.* TEL: 020 7727 2027. SER: Valuations; restorations.

Crown Arcade
119 Portobello Rd. W11 2DY. (Angelo Soteriades). PADA. Est. 1986. Open Sat. 5.30-5. SIZE: Medium, 25 stalls. *STOCK: 18th-19th C glass, bronzes, sculpture, silver, jewellery, Arts & Crafts, Art Nouveau, Art Deco, treen, boxes, humidors, tortoiseshell, ivory, Austrian glass, pewter, decorative prints, Italian glass, decanters, decorative objects.* LOC: Near Westbourne Grove Corner. TEL: 020 7436 9416/7792 3619 (Sat. only); mobile - 07956 277077; e-mail - info@portobello-antiques.co.uk website - www.portobello-antiques.co.uk SER: Valuations.

Curá Antiques
34 Ledbury Rd. W11 2AB. (G. and M. Antichi). Open 11-6, Sat. 10.30-1. *STOCK: Continental furniture, sculptures, majolica and paintings.* TEL: 020 7229 6880; e-mail - mail@cura-antiques.com website - www.cura-antiques.com

Daggett Gallery   LAPADA
1st and 2nd Floors, 153 Portobello Rd. W11 2DY. (Caroline Daggett). Est. 1992. Open 10-5 (prior telephone call advisable), Sat. 9-3.30. SIZE: Medium. *STOCK: Frames, 18th-20th C, from £1.* LOC: 200 yards from Westbourne Grove towards Elgin Crescent. PARK: Meters. TEL: 020 7229 2248. SER: Restorations (frames); gilding; framing. VAT: Stan/Spec.

Charles Daggett Gallery   LAPADA
1st and 2nd Floors, 153 Portobello Rd. W11 2DY. (Charles and Caroline Daggett). Est. 1977. Open 10-4 (prior telephone call advisable), Sat. 9-3.30. SIZE: Medium. *STOCK: British pictures, 1740-1840.* LOC: 200 yards from Westbourne Grove, towards Elgin Crescent. PARK: Meters. TEL: 020 7229 2248; fax - 020 7229 0193. SER: Restorations (pictures and frames); framing. VAT: Stan/Spec.

John Dale
87 Portobello Rd. W11 2QB. Est. 1950. Open Sun., Mon. and Fri. 10-5, Sat. 7-5, other times by appointment. SIZE: Medium. *STOCK: General antiques.* TEL: 020 7727 1304. VAT: Stan.

Delehar
146 Portobello Rd. W11 2DZ. Est. 1919. Open Sat. 9-4. SIZE: Medium. *STOCK: General antiques, works of art.* Not Stocked: Furniture. TEL: 020 7727 9860. VAT: Spec.

Peter Delehar
146 Portobello Rd. W11 2DZ. Est. 1919. Open Sat. 10-4. SIZE: Medium. *STOCK: Fine and interesting antique works of art, scientific and medical instruments.* TEL: 020 7727 9860 (Sat.) or 020 8423 8600; fax - same; e-mail - peter@peterdelehar.co.uk FAIRS: International Scientific and Medical Instrument. VAT: Spec.

Demetzy Books
113 Portobello Rd. W11 2QB. (P. and M. Hutchinson). ABA. PBFA. Est. 1972. Open Sat. 7.30-3.30. SIZE: Medium. *STOCK: Antiquarian leather bound books, 18th-19th C, £5-£1,000; Dickens' first editions and children's and illustrated books, 18th-20th C, £5-£200.* LOC: 20yds. from junction with Westbourne Grove, opposite Earl of Lonsdale public house. PARK: Meters. TEL: 01993 702209; e-mail - demetzybooks@ tiscali.co.uk SER: Valuations; buys at auction (books). FAIRS: ABA Chelsea; PBFA Russell Hotel, London (monthly); Randolph Hotel, Oxford; York.

Gavin Douglas Fine Antiques Ltd   LAPADA
75 Portobello Rd. W11 2QB. (G.A. Douglas). PADA. CINOA. Est. 1993. Open 10.30-4.30, Sat. 7.30-5. SIZE: Medium. *STOCK: Neo-classical clocks, 18th-19th C, to £100,000; bronzes, sculpture, porcelain and objects, to £50,000.* PARK: Easy. TEL: 020 7221 1121; 01825 723441; fax - 01825 724418; e-mail - gavin@antique-clocks.co.uk website - www.antique-clocks.co.uk SER: Valuations; restorations; buys at auction. FAIRS: Olympia (Summer, Winter and Spring); LAPADA; Harrogate; New York. VAT: Stan/Spec.

Eureka Antiques
105 Portobello Rd. W11 2QB. (Noel Gibson and Alex O'Donnell). Est. 1965. Open Sat. 7-3 or by appointment.

STOCK: Mauchlineware, tartanware, papier mâché, glass. TEL: 0161 941 5453; mobile - 07798 573332. FAIRS: Olympia; NEC.

Fleur de Lys Gallery
227a Westbourne Grove. W11 2SE. (H.S. and B.S. Coronel). PADA. Est. 1967. Open 1-5. SIZE: Medium. *STOCK: Oil paintings, 19th C, £2,000-£8,000.* PARK: Easy, but limited. TEL: 020 7727 8595; fax - same; home - 01372 467934; e-mail - fleurdelysgallery@yahoo.com website - www.fleur-de-lys.com VAT: Spec.

Judy Fox   LAPADA
81 Portobello Rd. W11 2QB. Est. 1970. Open 10-5. SIZE: Large. *STOCK: Furniture and decorative items, 18th-20th C; inlaid furniture, mainly 19th C; pottery and porcelain.* TEL: 020 7229 8130; fax - 020 7229 6998; e-mail - judy@judy-fox.com website - www.judy-fox.com VAT: Stan.

Graham and Green
4 Elgin Crescent. W11 2JA. (A. and J. Graham and R. Harrison). Est. 1974. Open 10-6, Sun. 11-5. SIZE: Medium. *STOCK: Indian, Vietnamese and Chinese furniture; decorative objects and textiles; Chinese hairpins and embroidered skirts.* LOC: Near Portobello Rd. PARK: Nearby. TEL: 020 7727 4594; fax - 020 7229 9717; e-mail - info@grahamandgreen.co.uk website - www.grahamandgreen.co.uk VAT: Stan.

Henry Gregory
82 Portobello Rd. W11 2QD. (H. and C. Gregory). Est. 1969. Open 10-4, Sat. 8-5. SIZE: Medium. *STOCK: Antique silver and decorative objects, vintage sports items and luggage.* LOC: Between Westbourne Grove and Chepstow Villas. PARK: Easy. TEL: 020 7792 9221; fax - same; e-mail - hgregoryantiques@aol.com SER: Export packing and shipping. VAT: Stan/Spec.

The Harris's Arcade
161-163 Portobello Rd. W11 2DY. (Angelo Soteriades). PADA. Est. 1951. Open Fri. and Sat. or by appointment. SIZE: 40 dealers. *STOCK: General antiques including ethnic antiquities, bronzes, ivory statues, jade, precious metals, silver and plate, drinking vessels, costumes, Oriental and Western porcelain, furniture, collectables, prints, lace, linen, books, manuscripts, paintings, etchings, sporting memorabilia, Tibetan, East and South East Asian antiquities, decorative arts and designer objects, jewellery - gold, silver, pearls, semi-precious stones.* TEL: 020 7727 5242; fax- same; mobile - 07956 277077; e-mail - info@portobello-antiques.co.uk website - www.portobello-antiques.co.uk SER: Valuations; shipping.

Hickmet Fine Arts   LAPADA
75 Portobello Rd. W11 2QB. (David Hickmet). CINOA. PADA. Open 10-4, Sat. 8-5. SIZE: Medium. *STOCK: Art Deco sculpture, £500-£5,000; Art glass, £200-£2,000.* PARK: Easy. TEL: 020 7221 1121; mobile - 07050 123450; fax - 01342 841879; e-mail - david@ hickmet.com website - www.hickmet.com SER: Valuations; commission purchases. FAIRS: Olympia; LAPADA; NEC; Harrogate; GMEX; SECC; New York; Palm Beach. VAT: Spec.

Hirst Antiques
59 Pembridge Rd. W11 3HG. Est. 1963. Open 10-6.

SIZE: Medium. *STOCK: Four poster and half-tester beds; decorative furniture and articles; bronze and marble sculpture; vintage costume jewellery.* LOC: Start of Portobello Rd., near Notting Hill Gate underground station. TEL: 020 7727 9364. SER: Valuations; repairs (jewellery).

Humbleyard Fine Art
141-149 Portobello Rd. W11 2DY. (James Layte). PADA. Est. 1973. Open Sat. 6-2. SIZE: Small. *STOCK: Scientific, medical and marine items, sailors' woolworks, shell valentines, primitive pictures, needleworks, boxes, pottery and curiosities, 18th-19th C, £50-£5,000.* PARK: Easy. TEL: 01362 637793; fax - same; mobile - 07836 349416. SER: Valuations. FAIRS: Olympia (June, Nov); Decorative (Jan., Sept); Little Chelsea (April, Oct); Scientific Instrument (April, Oct). VAT: Spec.

Jones Antique Lighting
194 Westbourne Grove. W11 2RH. (Judy Jones). Est. 1978. Open 9.30-6 or by appointment. SIZE: Large. *STOCK: Original decorative lighting, 1860-1960.* PARK: Meters. TEL: 020 7229 6866; fax - 020 7243 3547; e-mail - judy@jonesantiquelighting.com website - www.jonesantiquelighting.com SER: Valuations; repairs; prop hire. VAT: Stan.

Peter Kennedy
87 Portobello Rd. W11 2QB. ABA. Est. 1974. Sat. only 8.30-4, other times by appointment. SIZE: Small. *STOCK: Antiquarian prints and books, 1650-1880, £5-£5,000.* TEL: 020 7243 1416; home - 01483 797293; fax - 01483 488006; e-mail - peter@peterkennedy.com SER: Valuations; restorations including print cleaning and colouring; books re-bound.

Lacy Gallery
203 Westbourne Grove. W11 2SB. Est. 1960. Open Tues.-Fri.10-5, Sat. 10-4. SIZE: Large. *STOCK: Period frames, 1700 to secondhand modern; decorative paintings and art, posters; 20th C paintings from St. Petersburg.* LOC: Two roads east of Portobello Rd. PARK: Meters. TEL: 020 7229 6340; fax - 020 7229 9105. VAT: Stan/Spec.

M. and D. Lewis
1 Lonsdale Rd. W11 2BY. Est. 1960. Open 9.30-5.30, Sat. 9.30-4. *STOCK: Continental and Victorian furniture, porcelain, bronzes.* TEL: 020 7727 3908; email - mdlewisantiques@hotmail.com VAT: Stan.

M.C.N. Antiques
183 Westbourne Grove. W11 2SB. Est. 1971. Open 10-6, Sat. 11-3 or by appointment. *STOCK: Japanese porcelain, cloisonné, Satsuma, bronze, lacquer, ivory.* LOC: Near Portobello Rd. market. PARK: Easy. TEL: 020 7727 3796; fax - 020 7229 8839. VAT: Stan.

Robin Martin Antiques
44 Ledbury Rd. W11 2AB. (Paul Martin). Est. 1972. Open 10-6. SIZE: Medium. *STOCK: English and Continental furniture and works of art, 17th-19th C.* LOC: Westbourne Grove area. TEL: 020 7727 1301; fax - same; mobile - 07831 544055; e-mail - paul.martin11 @virgin.net FAIRS: Olympia (June and Nov). VAT: Spec.

Mercury Antiques   BADA
1 Ladbroke Rd. W11 3PA. (L. Richards). Est. 1963.
Open 10-5.30, Sat. 10-1. SIZE: Medium. *STOCK:
English porcelain, 1745-1840; English pottery and
Delft, 1700-1850; glass, 1780-1850.* Not Stocked:
Jewellery, silver, plate, Art Nouveau. LOC: From
Notting Hill Gate underground station, turn into
Pembridge Rd., bear left. TEL: 020 7727 5106; fax -
020 7229 3738. VAT: Spec.

Milne and Moller   LAPADA
W11 2BU. (Mr and Mrs C. Moller). Est. 1976. Open by
appointment. SIZE: Small. *STOCK: Watercolours, oils,
ceramics and sculpture, 20th C to contemporary.* LOC:
Near junction of Westbourne Grove and Ledbury Rd.
PARK: Easy. TEL: 020 7727 1679; home - same; e-mail
-   juliet@milneandmoller.co.uk   SER: Portrait
commissioning. FAIRS: Olympia. VAT: Spec.

Mimi Fifi
27 Pembridge Rd., Notting Hill Gate. W11 3HG. (Mrs
Rita Delaforge). Est. 1990. Open 11-6.30, Sat. 10-7, Sun.
11-4. SIZE: Medium. *STOCK: Vintage and collectable
toys, especially Snoopy, Smurfs, Betty Boop, Simpsons,
and memorabilia, 20th C, £5-£500; perfume miniatures
and related collectables, 19th-20th C, £5-£1,000;
perfume bottles by appointment.* LOC: 200 yards from
Notting Hill underground station. PARK: Nearby. TEL:
020 7243 3154; fax - 020 7938 4222; website -
www.mimififi.com

Myriad Antiques
131 Portland Rd., Holland Park Ave. W11 4LW. (S.
Nickerson). Est. 1970. Open Tues.-Sat. 11-6. CL: Aug.
SIZE: Medium. *STOCK: Decorative and unusual
furniture (including garden) and objects, mainly French,
19th C, £20-£2,500.* LOC: Between Notting Hill Gate
and Shepherds Bush roundabout. PARK: Meters. TEL:
020 7229 1709; fax - 020 7221 3882. VAT: Stan.

The Nanking Porcelain Co. Ltd
Admiral Vernon Arcade, 141-149 Portobello Rd. W11
2DY. (Maurice Hyams and Elizabeth Porter). Open Sat.
8.30-3.30. SIZE: Large. *STOCK: Chinese export
porcelain, Oriental ivories.* TEL: 020 7924 2349; fax -
020 7924 2352; mobile - 07836 594885; e-mail -
nankingporcelain@aol.com SER: Valuations. FAIRS:
Olympia (June).

Piano Nobile Fine Paintings
129 Portland Rd., Holland Park. W11 4LW. (Dr Robert
A. Travers). SLAD. Est. 1986. Open Tues.-Sat. 10.30-
5.30. SIZE: Medium. *STOCK: Fine 19th C Impressionist
and 20th C Post-Impressionist and Modern British and
Continental oil paintings and sculpture, Les Petit
Maitres of the Paris Schools; representing leading
contemporary figurative painters & sculptors including
Adam Birtwistle, Peter Coker RA, Dora Holzhandler and
Eduardo Paolozzi, £100-£250,000.* PARK: Easy. TEL:
020 7229 1099; fax - same; e-mail - art@piano-
nobile.com website - www.piano-nobile.com SER:
Valuations; restorations (paintings and sculptures);
framing; buys at auction (19th-20th C oil paintings).
FAIRS: Grosvenor; 20th C British Art; Olympia; BADA;
Art London.

Portobello Antique Store
79 Portobello Rd. W11 2QB. (T.J. Evans). Est. 1971.
Open Tues.-Fri. 10-4, Sat. 8.15-4. SIZE: Large. *STOCK:
Silver and plate, £2-£3,000.* LOC: Notting Hill end of
Portobello Rd. PARK: Easy weekdays. TEL: 020 7221
1994. SER: Export. VAT: Stan.

Quadrille
146 Portobello Rd. W11 2DZ. (Valerie Jackson-Harris).
Open Sat. 9-4. *STOCK: Ephemera especially Royal and
rare commemoratives, performing arts, valentines,
children's toys, games and unusual items, appertaining
to the history of London.* TEL: 01923 829079; fax -
01923 825079. FAIRS: Ephemera Society; NEC; ABA.

The Red Lion Antiques Arcade
165/169 Portobello Rd. W11 2DY. (Angelo Soteriades).
PADA. Est. 1951. Open Sat. 5.30-5.30. SIZE: 80 dealers.
*STOCK: General antiques including ethnic antiquities,
bronzes, ivory statues, jade, precious metals, dolls, silver
and plate, drinking vessels, costumes, Oriental and Western
porcelain, furniture, collectables, prints, lace, linen, books,
manuscripts, stamps, coins, banknotes, paintings, etchings,
sporting memorabilia, Tibetan, East and South East Asian
antiquities, decorative arts and designer objects, jewellery -
gold, silver, pearls, semi-precious stones.* TEL: 020 7727
5242; fax- same; mobile - 07956 277077; e-mail -
info@portobello-antiques.com website - www.portobello-
antiques.co.uk SER: Valuations; shipping.

Rezai Persian Carpets
123 Portobello Rd. W11 2DY. (A. Rezai). Est. 1966.
Open 10-5. *STOCK: Oriental carpets, kilims, tribal rugs,
tapestries, runners, Aubussons and silk embroideries.*
TEL: 020 7221 5012; fax - 020 7229 6690; website -
www.rezaipersiancarpets.co.uk   SER: Valuations;
cleaning and restorations.

Roger's Antiques Gallery
65 Portobello Rd. W11 3DB. (Bath Antiques Market
Ltd). Open Sat. 7-4.30. SIZE: 65 dealers. *STOCK: Wide
range of general antiques and collectables with
specialist dealers in most fields, especially jewellery.*
TEL: Enquiries - 020 7351 5353; fax - 020 7351 5350.
SER: Valuations.

Schredds of Portobello   LAPADA
107 Portobello Rd. W11 2QB. (H.J. and G.R. Schrager).
Est. 1969. Open Sat. 7.30-3. SIZE: Small. *STOCK:
Silver, 17th-19th C, £10-£5,000; Wedgwood, 18th-19th
C.* LOC: Portobello Market. PARK: Free after 1.30 pm.
TEL: 020 8348 3314; home - same; fax - 020 8341 5971;
e-mail - silver@schredds.com website - www.schredds.
com/ SER: Valuations; buys at auction; worldwide
shipping. FAIRS: Kensington (Jan); Chelsea Town Hall
(Mar). VAT: Stan/Spec.

The Silver Fox Gallery (Portobello)
121 Portobello Rd. W11 2DY. (C. Hickey). Est. 1993.
Open Sat. 6-3. SIZE: 25+ dealers. *STOCK: Jewellery -
18th C to 1960s including Victorian, Art Nouveau, Arts
& Crafts, Art Deco, rings (diamond and gemset),
earrings, brooches, pendants, gold and silver, Alberts,
Albertines, chains longuards, bracelets, curbs, gates,
fobs, seals, intaglios, pocket watches, vintage
wristwatches, cufflinks, fine diamonds, rare gemstones,*

Justin F. Skrebowski Ground Floor, 177 Portobello Road, London, W11 2DY, UK
Tel/Fax/Answerphone: 020 7792 9742 Mobile: 07774 612474
e-mail: justin@skreb.co.uk website: www.skreb.co.uk

■ Folio Stands/Browsers

■ Display Easels

■ Desk Top Stands

■ Solid Mahogany

■ Beautiful Antique Finish

■ Exported Worldwide

■ Used by Galleries & Museums

■ Ideal for Studies & Homes

---

cameos, coral, amber, ivory, jet tortoiseshell, piqué, micro-mosaics, pietra-dura, lava, horn pendants, enamels, pearls, Austro-Hungarian cut steel, Berlin iron, Scottish, niello, £50-£5,000+. LOC: Notting Hill. PARK: Pay and Display. TEL: 020 7243 8027; fax - same; e-mail - jewellery@silverfoxgallery.com website - www. silverfoxgallery.com FAIRS: Olympia; Park Lane Hotel; NEC. VAT: Stan/Spec/Global.

Justin F. Skrebowski Prints
Ground Floor, 177 Portobello Rd. W11 2DY. Est. 1985. Open Sat. 9-4, other times by appointment. SIZE: Small. *STOCK: Prints, engravings and lithographs, 1700-1850, £50-£500; oil paintings, 1700-1900, £200-£1,500; watercolours, drawings including Old Masters, 1600-1900, £50-£1,000; modern mahogany folio stands and easels; frames - gilt, rosewood, maple, carved, 18th-19th C.* PARK: Meters. TEL: 020 7792 9742; mobile - 07774 612474; e-mail - justin@skreb.co.uk website - www.skreb.co.uk SER: Valuations. FAIRS: PBFA; Hotel Russell (Monthly). VAT: Stan/Spec.

Colin Smith and Gerald Robinson Antiques
105 Portobello Rd. W11 2QB. Est. 1979. Open Sat., Fri. by appointment. SIZE: Large. *STOCK: Tortoiseshell, £100-£2,000; silver, ivory and crocodile items.* TEL: 020 8994 3783/020 7225 1163. FAIRS: Olympia. VAT: Stan.

Stern Pissarro Gallery   LAPADA
46 Ledbury Rd. W11 2AB. (David Stern). SLAD. Est. 1963. Open 10-6. SIZE: Medium. *STOCK: English and European oil paintings, 19th-20th C, especially the Pissarro family.* LOC: Off Westbourne Grove near Portobello. PARK: Easy. TEL: 020 7229 6187; fax - 020 7229 7016; e-mail - stern@pissarro.com website - www. stern-art.com SER: Valuations; restorations. VAT: Stan.

Temple Gallery
6 Clarendon Cross. W11 4AP. (R.C.C. Temple). Est. 1959. Open 10-6, weekends and evenings by appointment. SIZE: Large. *STOCK: Icons, Russian and Greek, 12th-16th C, £1,000-£50,000.* PARK: Easy. TEL: 020 7727 3809; fax - 020 7727 1546; e-mail - info@ templegallery.com website - www.templegallery.com SER: Valuations; restorations; buys at auction (icons); illustrated catalogues published. VAT: Spec.

Themes and Variations
231 Westbourne Grove. W11 2SE. (L. Fawcett). Open 10-1 and 2-6, Sat 10-6. *STOCK: Post war and contemporary decorative arts, furniture, glass, ceramics, carpets, lamps, jewellery.* TEL: 020 7727 5531; fax - 020 7221 6378; e-mail - go@themesandvariations.com website - www.themesandvariations.com

Christina Truscott
Geoffrey Van Arcade, 105-107 Portobello Rd. W11 2QB. PADA. Est. 1967. Open Sat. 6.45-3.30. *STOCK: Chinese export lacquer, papier-mâché, tortoiseshell, fans.* TEL: 01403 730554; Sat. only - 020 7229 5577; e-mail - christina.truscott@btopenworld.com

Victoriana Dolls
101 Portobello Rd. W11 2BQ. (Mrs H. Bond). Open Sat. 8-3 or by appointment. *STOCK: Dolls, toys and accessories.* TEL: Home - 01737 249525.

Virginia
98 Portland Rd., Holland Park. W11 4LQ. (V. Bates). Est. 1971. Open 11-6, Sat. by appointment. SIZE: Medium. *STOCK: Clothes and lace, 1880-1940, from £100.* LOC: Holland Park Ave. PARK: Easy. TEL: 020 7727 9908; fax - 020 7229 2198. VAT: Stan.

Johnny Von Pflugh Antiques
286 Westbourne Grove. W11 2PS. Est. 1985. Open Sat. 8-5 at Portobello Market or by appointment. SIZE: Small. *STOCK: European works of art, Italian oil paintings, gouaches, 17th-19th C, £300-£1,500; fine ironware, 17th-18th C, £300-£800; medical and scientific instruments, 18th-19th C, £200-£1,000.* PARK: Easy. TEL: 020 8740 5306; fax - 020 8749 2868; mobile - 07949 086243. SER: Valuations; buys at auction (keys, caskets, medical instruments, Italian oil paintings and gouaches). FAIRS: Olympia (June); Scientific and Medical (April and Oct). VAT: Spec.

Walpoles   BADA
Geoffrey Van Arcade, 107 Portobello Rd. W11 2QB. (Graham Walpole). PADA. Open Sat. 7-4. STOCK: British Army and Navy, campaign and colonial furniture, Chinese export trade and English country house, mid-18th to mid-20th C; fine and folk art. TEL: Mobile - 07831 561042; e-mail - info@walpoleantiques.com website - www.walpoleantiques.com

Trude Weaver   LAPADA
71 Portobello Rd. W11 2QB. Est. 1968. Open Wed.-Sat. 9-5. SIZE: Medium. *STOCK: 18th-19th C furniture, associated accessories.* PARK: Easy. TEL: 020 7229 8738; fax - same; mobile - 07768 551269. SER: Valuations.

Wolseley Fine Arts Ltd
12 Needham Rd. W11 2RP. (Rupert Otten and Hanneke van der Werf). SLAD. TEFAF. Open during exhibitions Wed., Thurs. and Fri. 11-6, Sat. 11-5 or by appointment. *STOCK: British and European 20th C works on paper and sculpture, works by David Jones, Eric Gill, John Buckland Wright, Pierre Bonnard, Edouard Vuillard, Ker Xavier Roussel and Eugeen van Mieghem; contemporary still life paintings, art, sculpture and carved lettering.* TEL: 020 7792 2788; fax - 020 7792 2988; e-mail - info@wolseleyfinearts.com website - www.wolseleyfinearts.com SER: Regular catalogues by subscription. FAIRS: Works on Paper; New York; TEFAF; Art London; 20th/21st C British Art.

World Famous Portobello Market
177 Portobello Rd. W11 2DY. (Angelo Soteriades). PADA. Est. 1951. Open Sat. 5.30-5.30. SIZE: 60 dealers. *STOCK: Stamps, coins, Art Deco, amber, jewellery, oils, watercolours, engravings, prints, maps, books, photographs, objects, teddy bears, toys, dolls, wood, soapstone, Africana, picture frames, ephemera, auction catalogues.* TEL: 020 7727 5242; mobile - 07956 277077; e-mail - info@portobello-antiques.co.uk website - www.portobello-collections.co.uk SER: Valuations; framing.

W13

W.13 Antiques
10 The Avenue, Ealing. W13 8PH. Est. 1977. Open Tues., Thurs. and Sat. 10-5 or by appointment. SIZE: Medium. *STOCK: Furniture, china and general antiques, 18th-20th C.* LOC: Off Uxbridge Rd., West Ealing. PARK: Easy. TEL: 020 8998 0390; mobile - 07778 177102. SER: Valuations. VAT: Stan.

W14

Marshall Gallery
67 Masbro Rd. W14 0LS. (D.A. and J. Marshall). Resident. Est. 1978. Open 10-6, Sat. 10-5. CL: Mon. SIZE: Medium. *STOCK: French and decorative furniture, £500-£20,000; objects and lighting, £200-£12,000; pictures, from £100; all 18th-20th C.* LOC: Just behind Olympia, off Hammersmith Rd. PARK: Easy. TEL: 020 7602 3317. SER: Restorations (furniture, re-gilding, re-wiring). VAT: Spec.

D. Parikian
3 Caithness Rd. W14 0JB. ABA. Est. 1960. Open by appointment. *STOCK: Antiquarian books, mythology, iconography, emblemata, Continental books, pre-1800.* TEL: 020 7603 8375; fax - 020 7602 1178; e-mail - dparikian@aol.com

J. Roger (Antiques) Ltd   BADA
(C. Bayley). Open by appointment. *STOCK: Late 18th to early 19th C small elegant pieces furniture, mirrors, prints, porcelain and boxes.* TEL: 020 7603 7627.

SW1

Didier Aaron (London)Ltd   BADA
21 Ryder St., St. James's. SW1Y 6PX. (Didier Leblanc and Marc Fecker). Open 10-1 and 2-5.30 and by appointment. SIZE: Large. *STOCK: Mainly French 18th-19th C furniture and objets d'art; 17th-19th C paintings and drawings.* LOC: 20 yds. from Christie's. PARK: Meters nearby. TEL: 020 7839 4716; fax - 020 7930 6699; e-mail - contact@ didieraaronltd.com FAIRS: Paris Biennale, Maastricht (TEFAF); Salon du Dessin, Paris; International Fine Art, New York; Master Drawings, London.

Ackermann & Johnson   BADA
27 Lowndes St. SW1X 9HY. (Peter Johnson). Est. 1783. Open 9-5.30, Sat. by appointment. SIZE: Medium. *STOCK: British paintings and watercolours, especially sporting, marine and landscapes including the Norwich School, 18th-20th C.* LOC: Opposite Carlton Tower Hotel. PARK: Meters. TEL: 020 7235 6464; fax - 020 7823 1057; e-mail - ackermann johnson@btconnect.com website - www.artnet. com/ackermann.johnson SER: Valuations; restorations; framing. VAT: Spec.

Adam Gallery Ltd
35 Ponsonby Terrace. SW1P 4PZ. (Paul and Philip Dye). *STOCK: 20th C British and international paintings and prints especially St. Ives, Bacon, Nicholson, Francis, Piper, Debuffet, Kandinsky, Lanyon, Moore, Picasso, Delaunay, Hitchens, Hilton, Heron and Scott; British contemporary, £500-£50,000.* TEL: 020 7630 0599; fax - same; e-mail - enquiries@adamgallery.com website - www.adamgallery.com

John Adams Fine Art Ltd
Ebury Galleries, 200 Ebury St. SW1W 8UN. Est. 1980. Open 10-6, Sat. 10-4. SIZE: Medium. *STOCK: Antique and modern paintings, drawings and watercolours, £1,000-£25,000.* PARK: Easy. TEL: 020 7730 8999; fax - 020 7259 9015; e-mail - johnadamsfineart@onetel.com website - www.johnadamsfineart.com SER: Valuations; restorations.

ADEC
227 Ebury St. SW1W 8UT. (A. De Cacqueray). Est. 1985. Open 10-6, Sat. 11-4. *STOCK: French and Continental furniture, objets d'art.* TEL: 020 7730 5000; fax - 020 7730 0005. SER: Interior design.

Verner Åmell Ltd
4 Ryder St., St. James's. SW1Y 6QB. SLAD. Est. 1988. Open 10-5.30. CL: Sat. *STOCK: Dutch and Flemish Old Masters, 16th-17th C; 18th C French and 19th C Scandinavian paintings.* TEL: 020 7925 2759; website - www.amells.com FAIRS: TEFAF; Grosvenor House. VAT: Spec.

Albert Amor Ltd
37 Bury St., St. James's. SW1Y 6AU. Est. 1903. Open Tues.-Thurs. 9.30-5. SIZE: Small. *STOCK: 18th to early 19th C English ceramics, especially first period Worcester.* PARK: Meters. TEL: 020 7930 2444; fax - 020 7930 9067; website - www.albertamor.co.uk SER: Valuations. VAT: Spec.

Anno Domini Antiques   BADA
66 Pimlico Rd. SW1W 8LS. (F. Bartman and D. Cohen). Est. 1960. Open 10-1 and 2.15-5.30, Sat. 10-3. SIZE: Large. *STOCK: Furniture, 17th to early 19th C, £500-£20,000; mirrors, 17th-19th C, £300-£3,000; glass, screens, decorative items and tapestries, £15-£10,000. Not Stocked: Silver, jewellery, arms, coins.* LOC: From Sloane Sq. go down Lower Sloane St., turn left at traffic lights. PARK: Easy. TEL: 020 7730 5496; home - 020 7352 3084. SER: Buys at auction. VAT: Stan/Spec.

Antiquus
90-92 Pimlico Rd. SW1W 8PL. (E. Amati). Open 9.30-5.30. SIZE: Large. *STOCK: Classical, medieval and Renaissance works of art, paintings, textiles and glass.* LOC: Near Sloane Sq. underground station. PARK: Meters in Holbein Place and Lower Sloane St. TEL: 020 7730 8681; fax - 020 7823 6409; e-mail - antiquus@antiquus-london.co.uk website - www.antiquus-london.co.uk

Appley Hoare Antiques
30 Pimlico Rd. SW1W 8LJ. Est. 1980. Open 10.30-6, Sat. 11-5. SIZE: Medium. *STOCK: House and garden furniture, French 18th-19th C, with original paint and patination; decorative items; English 18th-19th C stone ornaments and statuary.* LOC: Corner Pimlico Green. PARK: Easy. TEL: 020 7730 7070; fax - 020 7730 8188; e-mail - appley@appleyhoare.com website - www.appleyhoare.com SER: Shipping. VAT: Spec.

The Armoury of St. James's Military Antiquarians
17 Piccadilly Arcade, Piccadilly. SW1Y 6NH. GMC. Est. 1965. Open 9.30-6. SIZE: Small. *STOCK: British and foreign Orders of Chivalry, 18th C to date, £50-£50,000; militaria, including regimental brooches and drums; toy and hand-painted model soldiers, £4-£4,000.* LOC: Between Piccadilly and Jermyn St. TEL: 020 7493 5082; e-mail - welcome@armoury.co.uk website - www.armoury.co.uk SER: Valuations. special commissions. VAT: Stan/Spec.

Artemis Fine Arts Limited   LAPADA
15 Duke St., St. James's. SW1Y 6DB. (Timothy Bathurst, Adrian Eeles, Armin Kunz and Francois Borne). SLAD. Open 9.30-5.30. CL: Sat. *STOCK: Old Master, 19th C and modern paintings, drawings and prints; Scandinavian paintings.* TEL: 020 7930 8733; fax - 020 7839 5009; e-mail - info@artemisfinearts.co.uk website - www.artemisfinearts.com FAIRS: Maastricht; London Original Print. VAT: Margin.

Nigel A. Bartlett
22 Pimlico Rd. SW1W 8LJ. Open 9.30-5.30. CL: Sat. *STOCK: Marble, pine and stone chimney pieces.* TEL: 020 7730 3223; fax - 020 7730 2332.

Hilary Batstone Antiques inc. Rose Uniacke Design   LAPADA
8 Holbein Place. SW1W 8NL. Est. 1983. Open 10.30-5.30, Sat. by appointment. SIZE: Medium. *STOCK: 19th-20th C decorative furniture, mirrors and lighting.* TEL: 020 7730 5335; e-mail - hilary@batstone.com SER: Interior design. VAT: Spec.

Chris Beetles Ltd
10 Ryder St., St. James's. SW1Y 6QB. Est. 1976. Open 10-5.30. SIZE: Large. *STOCK: English watercolours, paintings and illustrations, 18th-20th C, £500-£50,000.* LOC: 100yds. from Royal Academy. PARK: Meters. TEL: 020 7839 7551; e-mail - gallery@chrisbeetles.com website - www.chrisbeetles.com SER: Valuations; framing. VAT: Spec.

Belgrave Carpet Gallery Ltd
91 Knightsbridge. SW1X 7RB. (A.H. Khawaja). Open 9.30-6.30. *STOCK: Hand knotted Oriental carpets and rugs.* TEL: 020 7235 2541/7245 9749.

Blanchard Ltd   LAPADA
86/88 Pimlico Rd. SW1W 8PL. Est. 1990. Open 10-6, Sat. 10-3. SIZE: Medium. *STOCK: English and Continental furniture, lighting and objets d'art, 1700-1950.* LOC: Near Sloane Sq. underground station. TEL: 020 7823 6310; fax - 020 7823 6303. SER: Valuations; restorations; buys at auction. VAT: Stan/Spec.

John Bly   BADA
27 Bury St., St. James's. SW1Y 6AL. (J. and V. Bly). CINOA. Est. 1891. Open by appointment. *STOCK: Fine English furniture, silver, glass, porcelain and fine paintings, 18th-19th C.* TEL: 020 7930 1292; fax - 020 7839 4775; e-mail - john@johnbly.com website - www.johnbly.com SER: Restorations; valuations; consultancy. FAIRS: BADA; Grosvenor House; W. Palm Beach.

J.H. Bourdon-Smith Ltd   BADA
24 Mason's Yard, Duke St., St. James's. SW1Y 6BU. CINOA. Est. 1954. Open 9.30-6. CL: Sat. SIZE: Medium. *STOCK: Silver, 1680-1830, £50-£15,000; Victorian and modern silver, 1830 to date, £25-£10,000.* PARK: Meters. TEL: 020 7839 4714/3951; e-mail - enquiries@bourdonsmith.co.uk SER: Valuations; restorations (silver); buys at auction. FAIRS: Olympia (Nov); Harrogate; Grosvenor House; BADA; New York; NEC (Jan). VAT: Stan/Spec.

Robert Bowman
8 Duke St., St. James's. SW1Y 6BN. SLAD. Est. 1992. Open Mon.-Fri. 10-6. SIZE: Medium. *STOCK: Sculpture in bronze, marble and terracotta, 19th C to date, £3,000-£200,000.* PARK: Meters. TEL: 020 7839 3100; fax - 020 7839 3223; e-mail - info@robertbowman.com website - www.robertbowman.com SER: Valuations; restorations (bronze, marble and terracotta). FAIRS: Olympia; Maastricht; Palm Beach; New York; Chicago. VAT: Spec.

Brisigotti Antiques Ltd
44 Duke St., St. James's. SW1Y 6DD. Open 9.30-1 and 2-6. *STOCK: European works of art, Old Master paintings.* TEL: 020 7839 4441; fax - 020 7976 1663.

John Carlton-Smith   BADA
19 Ryder St., St. James's. SW1Y 6PY. (John and Michelle Carlton-Smith). Open 9.30-5.30. CL: Sat. *STOCK: Clocks, barometers, chronometers, 17th-19th C.* TEL: 020 7930 6622; fax - 020 7930 1370; mobile - 07967 180682; e-mail - info@fineantiqueclocks.com website - www.fineantiqueclocks.com SER: Valuations. FAIRS: Grosvenor House; BADA (Chelsea); Olympia (Nov). VAT: Spec.

Anno Domini

Antiques

66 Pimlico Road, London S.W.1
020-7730 5496

Fine small Regency rosewood brass inlaid sofa table,
c.1820. 30in. x 12in. x 28½in. (high)

Miles Wynn Cato
60 Lower Sloane St. SW1W 8BP. Est. 1995. Open Mon.-Fri. 9.30-5.30 and by appointment. SIZE: Medium. *STOCK: English and Welsh pictures and works of art, 1550-1950.* LOC: 100 yds. south of Sloane Sq. PARK: Easy - meters. TEL: 020 7259 0306; fax - 020 7259 0305; e-mail - wynncato@welshart.co.uk website - www.welshart.co.uk SER: Valuations; restorations; framing; appraisals.

Chelsea Antique Mirrors
72 Pimlico Rd. SW1W 8LS. (A. Koll). Est. 1976. Open 10-6, Sat. 10-2. SIZE: Medium. *STOCK: Antique mirrors, £1,000-£25,000.* PARK: Easy. TEL: 020 7824 8024; fax - 020 7824 8233. SER: Valuations; restorations (gilding).

Ciancimino Ltd
99 Pimlico Rd. SW1W 8PH. Open 10-6, Sat. 11-5. *STOCK: Art Deco furniture, Oriental art and ethnography.* TEL: 020 7730 9950/9959; fax - 020 7730 5365.

Classic Bindings Ltd
61 Cambridge St. SW1V 4PS. (Sasha Poklewski-Koziell). Est. 1989. Open Mon.-Fri. 9.30-5.30 and by appointment. *STOCK: English and French literature, history and politics, first editions, travel, illustrated, fine bindings, architecture and furniture, biographies, natural history and sciences, art and sport.* LOC: Off Warwick Way, Pimlico. PARK: Easy. TEL: 020 7834 5554; fax - 020 7630 6632; e-mail - info@classicbindings.net website - www.classicbindings.net FAIRS: ABA Olympia and Chelsea; PBFA London.

Cobra and Bellamy
149 Sloane St. SW1X 9BZ. (V. Manussis and T. Hunter). Est. 1976. Open 10.30-5.30. SIZE: Medium. *STOCK: 20th C and modern jewellery, £50-£5,000.* TEL: 020 7730 9993; e-mail - cobrabellamy@hotmail.com VAT: Stan/Margin.

Cornucopia
12 Upper Tachbrook St. SW1V 1SH. (G. Richards and V. Rosato). Est. 1967. Open 11-6. SIZE: Large. *STOCK: Jewellery, 20th C clothing and accessories.* LOC: Victoria. PARK: Meters. TEL: 020 7828 5752.

Cox and Company
37 Duke St., St. James's. SW1Y 6DF. (Mr and Mrs R. Cox). Est. 1972. Open 10-5.30, Sat. by appointment. SIZE: Small. *STOCK: European paintings, 19th-20th C, £1,000-£20,000; sporting (racing) and wildlife paintings.* LOC: Off Piccadilly. TEL: 020 7930 1987/7839 4539; e-mail - coxco@bellatlantic.net website - www.coxco.uk.com SER: Valuations; restorations; buys at auction. VAT: Spec.

Peter Dale Ltd   LAPADA
12 Royal Opera Arcade, Pall Mall. SW1Y 4UY. Est. 1955. Open 9.30-5. CL: Sat. SIZE: Medium. *STOCK: Firearms, 16th-19th C; edged weapons, armour, 14th-19th C; militaria.* LOC: Arcade behind Her Majesty's Theatre and New Zealand House. PARK: 350yds. Whitcomb St. public garage. TEL: 020 7930 3695; e-mail - robin@peterdaleltd.com website - www.peterdaleltd.com SER: Valuations; buys at auction. VAT: Spec.

Kenneth Davis (Works of Art) Ltd
15 King St., St. James's. SW1Y 6QU. Open 9-5. CL: Sat. *STOCK: Antique silver and works of art.* TEL: 020 7930 0313; fax - 020 7976 1306.

Alastair Dickenson Ltd   BADA
90 Jermyn St. SW1Y 6JD. (Alastair Dickenson and Melanie Cuchet). CINOA. Est. 2002. Open 9.30-5.30. CL: Sat. SIZE: Small. *STOCK: Fine English, Irish and Scottish silver, 16th to early 19th C; unusual silver - vinaigrettes, wine labels, card cases, caddy spoons, snuff boxes; Arts and Crafts silver including Omar Ramsden.* LOC: Off Duke St. PARK: Meters. TEL: 020 7839 2808; fax - 020 7839 2809; mobile - 07976 283530; e-mail - adickensonsilver@btconnect.com SER: Valuations; restorations (repairs, gilding, re-plating), replacement cruet and ink bottles; buys at auction. VAT: Spec.

Simon C. Dickinson Ltd
58 Jermyn St. SW1Y 6LX. (Simon Dickinson, David Ker and James Roundell). SLAD. Est. 1993. Open 10-5.30, Fri. 10-4.30. CL: Sat. SIZE: Large. *STOCK: Important Old, Modern and contemporary Master paintings.* LOC: 2 mins. from Piccadilly. TEL: 020 7493 0340; fax - 020 7493 0796; e-mail - info.uk@simondickinson.com website - www.simondickinson.com SER: Valuations; restorations; buys at auction. FAIRS: Maastricht. VAT: Spec.

Douwes Fine Art Ltd
Apartment 1B, 37 Duke St., St. James's. SW1Y 6DF. SLAD. Est. 1805. By appointment only. SIZE: Medium. *STOCK: 16th-20th C paintings, drawings and watercolours, Dutch, Flemish, French and Russian schools.* PARK: Meters. TEL: 020 7839 5795. e-mail - info@douwesfineart.com website - www.douwesfineart.com SER: Valuations; restorations. FAIRS: TEFAF (Maastricht); PAN (Amsterdam). VAT: Spec.

Eaton Gallery   LAPADA
34 Duke St., St. James's and 9 and 12a Princes Arcade, Jermyn St. SW1Y 6DF. (Dr J.D. George). Est. 1976. Open 10-5.30. *STOCK: English and European paintings, 19th-20th C and contemporary.* TEL: 020 7930 5950; fax - 020 7839 8076.

N. and I. Franklin   BADA
11 Bury St., St. James's. SW1Y 6AB. Est. 1984. Open 9.30-5.30. CL: Sat. *STOCK: Fine silver and works of art.* TEL: 020 7839 3131; fax - 020 7839 3132; e-mail - neil@franklinsilver.com website - www.franklinsilver.com FAIRS: Grosvenor House; New York.

Victor Franses Gallery   BADA
57 Jermyn St., St. James's. SW1Y 6LX. (Graham Franses). Est. 1972. Open 10-5, Sat. by appointment. *STOCK: 19th C animalier bronzes, paintings, watercolours and drawings.* TEL: 020 7493 6284/7629 1144; fax - 020 7495 3668. e-mail - bronzes@vfranses.com website - www.vfranses.com SER: Valuations; restorations. FAIRS: Grosvenor House.

S. Franses Ltd
80 Jermyn St. at Duke St., St. James's. SW1Y 6JD. Est. 1909. Open 9-5. CL: Sat. SIZE: Large. *STOCK: Historic and decorative tapestries, important carpets, needlework*

and textiles. TEL: 020 7976 1234; fax - 020 7930 8451; e-mail - gallery@franses.com website - www.franses. com SER: Valuations; restorations; cleaning. FAIRS: Biennale des Antiquaires, Paris. VAT: Spec.

Charles Frodsham & Co Ltd

32 Bury St., St. James's. SW1Y 6AU. (Richard Stenning and Philip Whyte). Est. 1834. Open by appointment. SIZE: Medium. *STOCK: Clocks, watches, marine chronometers and other horological items.* LOC: Between Jermyn St. and St. James's St. PARK: Meters. TEL: 020 7839 1234; fax - 020 7839 2000. VAT: Stan/Spec.

Frost and Reed Ltd (Est. 1808)   BADA

2-4 King St., St James's. SW1Y 6QP. Open 9-5.30. CL: Sat. *STOCK: Fine 19th C British and Continental paintings, marine and sporting pictures, Post-Impressionist drawings and watercolours; works by Sir Alfred Munnings, Montague Dawson, Marcel Dyf, Peter Smith, and Heather St Clair Davis.* **PARK: Meters. TEL: 020 7839 4645; fax - 020 7839 1166; e-mail - info@frostandreed.co.uk website - www. frostandreed.co.uk VAT: Spec.**

Gallery '25

26 Pimlico Rd. SW1W 8LJ. (D. Iglesis). Est. 1969. Open 10.30-5.30, Sat. 10.30-5. SIZE: Medium. *STOCK: Art glass, £100-£5,000; signed furniture, £1,000-£10,000; decorative fine art, £500-£5,000; all 1900-1960's.* TEL: 020 7730 7516; fax - same; e-mail - david@iglesis. ssnet.co.uk SER: Valuations; buys at auction (as stock). FAIRS: Park Lane; Olympia. VAT: Stan/Spec.

Christopher Gibbs Ltd

3 Dove Walk, Pimlico Rd. SW1W 8PS. Est. 1960. Open Mon.-Fri. 9.30-5.30. SIZE: Large. *STOCK: Unusual and decorative paintings, furniture, works of art and sculpture.* TEL: 020 7730 8200; fax - 020 7730 8420; website - www.christopher-gibbs.co.uk FAIRS: Consultancy. VAT: Spec.

Nicholas Gifford-Mead   BADA LAPADA

68 Pimlico Rd. SW1W 8LS. Est. 1972. Open 9.30-5.30. CL: Sat. SIZE: Medium. *STOCK: Chimney pieces and sculpture, 18th-19th C, from £1,000.* **LOC: 3 mins. from Sloane Sq. TEL: 020 7730 6233; fax - 020 7730 6239. SER: Valuations. VAT: Stan/Spec.**

Andi Gisel

69 Pimlico Rd. SW1W 8NE. Open 10-6, Sat. 11-5. *STOCK: French 18th-19th C furniture, mirrors, lighting, tapestries, stoneware and unusual items.* TEL: 020 7730 4187; fax - 020 7730 4025; e-mail - andigiselantique @aol.com VAT: Stan/Spec/Export.

Joss Graham Oriental Textiles

10 Eccleston St. SW1W 9LT. Est. 1980. Open 10-6, other times by appointment. SIZE: 2 floors. *STOCK: World textiles including rugs, kilims, embroideries, tribal costume and shawls; jewellery, metalwork, furniture, masks and primitive art - Indian, Middle Eastern, Central Asian and African.* LOC: 5 mins. walk from Victoria station. PARK: Meters. TEL: 020 7730 4370; fax - same; e-mail - joss.graham@btinternet.com SER: Valuations, conservation and repairs. FAIRS: Asian Art in London.

Martyn Gregory   BADA

34 Bury St., St. James's. SW1Y 6AU. SLAD. Open 10-6. CL: Sat. SIZE: Medium. *STOCK: China Trade paintings, pictures relating to China and the Far East; early English watercolours, 18th-20th C; British paintings, £500-£200,000.* PARK: Meters. TEL: 020 7839 3731; fax - 020 7930 0812; e-mail - mgregory@dircon.co.uk website - www.martyngregory.com SER: Valuations. FAIRS: Grosvenor House; Maastricht (TEFAF); New York Winter; Boston (Ellis Memorial); Philadelphia; London (Watercolours & Drawings). VAT: Spec.

Ross Hamilton Ltd   LAPADA

95 Pimlico Rd. SW1W 8PH. (Mark Boyce and John Underwood). Est. 1971. Open 9-6, Sat. 11-1 and 2.30-5. SIZE: Large. *STOCK: English and Continental furniture, 17th-19th C, £1,000-£100,000; porcelain and objects, 18th-19th C, £1,000-£8,000; paintings, 17th-19th C, £1,000-£10,000+.* LOC: 2 mins. walk from Sloane Square. PARK: Side streets. TEL: 020 7730 3015; website - www.lapada.co.uk/rosshamilton/ SER: Worldwide delivery. VAT: Stan/Spec.

Brian Harkins Oriental Art

3 Bury St., St. James's. SW1Y 6AB. Est. 1978. Open Mon.-Fri. 10-6. SIZE: Small. *STOCK: Japanese art, 19th-20th C, £2,000-£60,000; Japanese Art Deco, £500-£12,000; Chinese scholar's art and rocks from Ming (1368-1643) and Qing dynasties (1643-1912), £500-£20,000.* LOC: Near Green Park underground station. TEL: 020 7839 3338; fax - 0207 839 9339; e-mail - info @brianharkins.co.uk website - www.brianharkins.co.uk FAIRS: Asian Art, New York.

Harris Lindsay   BADA

67 Jermyn St. SW1Y 6NY. (Jonathan Harris and Bruce Lindsay). CINOA. Open 9.30-6. CL: Sat. *STOCK: English, Continental and Oriental furniture and works of art.* **TEL: 020 7839 5767; fax - 020 7839 5768; e-mail - info@harrislindsay.com website - www.harrislindsay.com FAIRS: Grosvenor House; IFAAD New York; TEFAF Maastricht. VAT: Spec.**

Harrods Ltd

Brompton Rd., Knightsbridge. SW1X 7XL. Open 10-7. SIZE: Large. *STOCK: Fine Victorian, Edwardian and period furniture and clocks.* PARK: Own. TEL: 020 7225 5940.

Harvey and Gore   BADA

41 Duke St., St. James's. SW1Y 6DF. (N.B. and A.J. Norman). CINOA. Est. 1723. Open 9.30-5. CL: Sat. SIZE: Medium. *STOCK: Jewellery, £150-£50,000; silver, £50-£15,000; old Sheffield plate, £125-£15,000; antique paste.* **TEL: 020 7839 4033; fax - 020 7839 3313; e-mail - norman@harveyandgore.co.uk website - www.harveyandgore.co.uk SER: Valuations; restorations (jewellery and silver); buys at auction. FAIRS: BADA. VAT: Stan/Spec.**

Hazlitt, Gooden and Fox Ltd

38 Bury St., St. James's. SW1Y 6BB. SLAD. Open 9.30-5.30. CL: Sat. SIZE: Large. *STOCK: Paintings, drawings and sculpture.* PARK: Meters. TEL: 020 7930 6422; fax - 020 7839 5984. SER: Valuations; restorations. VAT: Spec.

Thomas Heneage Art Books   LAPADA
42 Duke St., St. James's. SW1Y 6DJ. Est. 1975. Open 9.30-6 or by appointment. CL: Sat. *STOCK: Art reference books.* TEL: 020 7930 9223; fax - 020 7839 9223; e-mail - artbooks@heneage.com website - www. heneage.com FAIRS: Maastricht.

Hermitage Antiques Ltd
97 Pimlico Rd. SW1W 8PH. (B. Vieux-Pernon). Est. 1967. Open 10-6, Sat. 10-5, Sun. by appointment. SIZE: Large. *STOCK: Biedermeier, Empire and Russian furniture; oil paintings, decorative arts, chandeliers and bronzes.* Not Stocked: Silver and jewellery. LOC: Off Sloane Square. PARK: Easy. TEL: 020 7730 1973; fax - 020 7730 6586; e-mail - info@hermitage-antiques.co.uk website - www.hermitage-antiques.co.uk SER: Consultancy. VAT: Stan/Spec.

Carlton Hobbs   BADA
Est. 1975. Open by appointment. *STOCK: English and Continental furniture, paintings, chandeliers, works of art, £4,000-£850,000.* LOC: Westminster. TEL: 020 7340 1000; fax - 020 7340 1001; e-mail - carlton@carltonhobbs.com website - www.carlton hobbs.com

Christopher Hodsoll Ltd inc. Bennison   BADA
89-91 Pimlico Rd. SW1W 8PH. Est. 1991. Open 10-6 or by appointment. SIZE: 2 shops, 6 showrooms. *STOCK: Furniture, sculpture, pictures and objects.* PARK: Meters. TEL: 020 7730 3370; fax - 020 7730 1516; e-mail - info@hodsoll.com website - www. hodsoll.com SER: Search; interior design. VAT: Stan/Spec.

Hotspur Ltd   BADA
14 Lowndes St. SW1X 9EX. (R.A.B. Kern). Est. 1924. Open 8.30-6. SIZE: Large. *STOCK: Fine English furniture, 1680-1800.* LOC: Between Belgrave Sq. and Lowndes Sq. PARK: Underground within 100yds. TEL: 020 7235 1918; fax - 020 7235 4371; e-mail - enquiries@hotspurantiques.com FAIRS: Grosvenor House. VAT: Spec.

Christopher Howe
93 Pimlico Rd. SW1W 8PH. Est. 1982. Open 9-6, Sat. 10.30-4.30. SIZE: Large. *STOCK: British and European furniture, 16th-20th C, £100-£250,000; works of art, decorative objects and lighting.* LOC: Near Sloane Square. PARK: Meters nearby. TEL: 020 7730 7987; fax - 020 7730 0157; e-mail - antiques@howelondon.com website - www.howelondon.com SER: Sourcing. VAT: Stan/Spec.

Humphrey-Carrasco Ltd
43 Pimlico Rd. SW1W 8NE. (David Humphrey and Marylise Carrasco). Est. 1987. Open 10-6, Sat. by appointment. *STOCK: English furniture and lighting, architectural objects, 18th-19th C.* LOC: 10 mins. walk from Sloane Sq. PARK: Easy. TEL: 020 7730 9911; fax - 020 7730 9944; e-mail - hc@humphreycarrasco. demon.co.uk FAIRS: Olympia. VAT: Stan/Spec

Iconastas
5 Piccadilly Arcade. SW1Y 6NH. (John Gaze and Christopher Martin-Zakheim). Est. 1968. Open 10-6, Sat. 2-5. SIZE: Small. *STOCK: Russian art, 10th C to

1974. PARK: Meters. TEL: 020 7629 1433; fax - 020 7408 2015; e-mail - info@iconastas.com website - www.iconastas.com SER: Valuations.

Isaac and Ede   BADA
1 Duke of York St. St. James's. SW1Y 6JP. (David Isaac). Est. 2004. Open Mon.-Fri. 10-5.30. SIZE: Small. *STOCK: 18th-19th C decorative prints, £100-£5,000.* TEL: 020 7925 1177; fax - 020 7925 0606; e-mail - info@isaacandede.com website - www.isaac andede.com SER: Valuations; framing; restorations. FAIRS: Olympia (June); BADA (March); San Francisco (Fall). VAT: Stan/Spec.

Jeremy Ltd   BADA
29 Lowndes St. SW1X 9HX. (M. and J. Hill). Est. 1946. Open 8.30-6, Sat. by appointment. SIZE: Large. *STOCK: English, French and Russian furniture, objets d'art, glass chandeliers, 18th to early 19th C.* PARK: Nearby. TEL: 020 7823 2923; fax - 020 7245 6197; e-mail - jeremy@jeremique.co.uk website - www.jeremy.ltd.uk FAIRS: Grosvenor House; New York Armory Show. VAT: Spec.

Derek Johns Ltd
12 Duke St., St. James's. SW1Y 6BN. SLAD. Est. 1980. Open 9-6. *STOCK: Old Master paintings.* TEL: 020 7839 7671; fax - 020 7930 0986; e-mail - fineart@ derekjohns.co.uk FAIRS: Maastricht (TEFAF); IFAAD New York; Paris Biennale.

Peter Jones   LAPADA
Sloane Sqare. SW1W 8EL. (John Lewis Partnership). CINOA. Est. 1915. Open 9.30-7, Sun. 11-5. SIZE: Large. *STOCK: 18th-19th C furniture, mirrors, pictures, some glass.* LOC: Chelsea. TEL: 020 7730 3434, ext. 6382. VAT: Spec.

Keshishian   BADA
73 Pimlico Rd. SW1W 8NE. Est. 1978. Open 9.30-6, Sat. 10-5. SIZE: Large. *STOCK: European and Oriental carpets, to late 19th C; Aubussons, mid 19th C; European tapestries, 16th-18th C; Arts and Crafts and Art Deco carpet specialists.* LOC: Off Lower Sloane St. PARK: Easy. TEL: 020 7730 8810; fax - 020 7730 8803; e-mail - info@keshishiancarpets.com SER: Valuations; restorations. FAIRS: Grosvenor House; Winter Show, New York; Fall Show, San Francisco. VAT: Stan/Spec.

John King   BADA
74 Pimlico Rd. SW1W 8LS. Est. 1970. Open 10-6, Sat. by appointment. SIZE: Medium. *STOCK: Fine and unusual antiques, £500-£150,000.* PARK: Easy. TEL: 020 7730 0427; fax - 020 7730 2515; e-mail - kingj896@aol.com VAT: Spec.

Knightsbridge Coins
43 Duke St., St. James's. SW1Y 6DD. Open 10-6. CL: Sat. *STOCK: Coins - British, American and South African; medals.* TEL: 020 7930 7597/8215/7888.

Lamberty Ltd
46 Pimlico Rd. SW1W 8LP. (Andrew Lamberty). Est. 1992. Open 10-6, Sat. 10-5. SIZE: Large. *STOCK: Furniture and decorative items, to £500,000.* LOC: 5 mins. from Sloane Square. PARK: Private or pay &

display nearby. TEL: 020 7823 5115; fax - 020 7823 4433; e-mail - mail@lamberty.co.uk website - www. lamberty.co.uk

Bob Lawrence Gallery
93 Lower Sloane St. SW1W 8DA. Est. 1972. Open 10-6. SIZE: Medium. *STOCK: Decorative arts to Art Deco - furniture, paintings, objects and furnishings, £50-£10,000.* LOC: 2 mins. Sloane Sq., adjacent to Pimlico Rd. PARK: Easy. TEL: 020 7730 5900; fax - 020 7730 5902. SER: Valuations; restorations; buys at auction. VAT: Stan/Spec.

Longmire Ltd (Three Royal Warrants)
12 Bury St., St. James's. SW1Y 6AB. Open 9.30-5.30, Sat. in Nov. and Dec. only. *STOCK: Individual cufflink and dress sets: antique and contemporary, signed, platinum, gold, gem set, hardstone, pearl, carved crystal or enamel - four vices, fishing, polo, golfing, shooting, big game, ladybird and pigs.* LOC: Coming from Piccadilly, down Duke St., right into King St. past Christie's, first right into Bury St. PARK: Easy. TEL: 020 7930 8720; fax - 020 7930 1898. SER: Custom hand engraving or enamelling in colour - any corporate logo, initials, crest, coats of arms or tartan, any animal (cat, dog etc.), racing silks, sailing burgees, favourite hobbies or own automobiles.

MacConnal-Mason Gallery BADA
14 and 17 Duke St., St. James's. SW1Y 6DB. TEFAF. Est. 1893. Open 9-6, Sat. by appointment. SIZE: Large. *STOCK: Pictures and sculpture, 19th-20th C.* PARK: Meters. TEL: 020 7839 7693; fax - 020 7839 6797; e-mail - macconnal-mason@msn.com website - www.macconnal-mason-gallery.co.uk. SER: Valuations; restorations. FAIRS: TEFAF, Maastricht; International, New York; Palm Beach; Grosvenor House, Olympia, London; Harrogate. VAT: Spec.

The Mall Galleries
The Mall. SW1 5BD. Est. 1971. Open 10-5 seven days during exhibitions. *STOCK: Paintings, sculpture, prints and drawings.* LOC: Near Trafalgar Sq. PARK: Nearby. TEL: 020 7930 6844; fax - 020 7839 7830; e-mail - info @mallgalleries.com website - www.mallgalleries.org.uk SER: Contemporary art exhibitions; commissioning; gallery hire; workshops; education.

Paul Mason Gallery BADA
149 Sloane St. SW1X 9BZ. CINOA. IOD. Est. 1969. Open 9-6, Wed. 9-7, Sat. 10-5. *STOCK: Marine, yachting and naval paintings, prints, jewellery, barometers, chronometers and furniture; nautical artifacts; ship models; sporting and decorative paintings and prints; portfolio stands and old frames, 18th-20th C.* LOC: Sloane Sq. end of Sloane St. PARK: Easy. TEL: 020 7730 3683; fax - 020 7730 7359; e-mail - Paulmasonart@aol.com SER: Valuations; restorations (prints and paintings); buys at auction. FAIRS: England and Europe. VAT: Stan/Spec.

Jeremy Mason (Sainsbury & Mason)
145 Ebury St. SW1W 9QN. Est. 1968. Open 10-12.30 and 4-5.30 by appointment. *STOCK: Period Oriental and European works of art, especially Chinese and Japanese, bronzes, lacquer, porcelain, glass and pictures.* TEL: 020 7730 8331; fax - 020 7730 8334; mobile - 07939 240884. FAIRS: Olympia (June). VAT: Spec.

Mathaf Gallery Ltd LAPADA
24 Motcomb St. SW1X 8JU. (Brian and Gina MacDermot). SLAD. Est. 1975. Open 9.30-5.30, Sat. by appointment. *STOCK: Paintings, Middle East subjects, 19th C.* LOC: Knightsbridge. TEL: 020 7235 0010; e-mail - art@mathafgallery.demon.co.uk website - www.mathafgallery.com SER: Valuations. VAT: Spec.

Matthiesen Fine Art Ltd.
7-8 Mason's Yard, Duke St., St. James's. SW1Y 6BU. Est. 1978. Open by appointment. *STOCK: Fine Italian Old Master paintings, 1300-1800; French and Spanish Old Master paintings.* TEL: 020 7930 2437; fax - 020 7930 1387. SER: Valuations; buys at auction.

Duncan R. Miller Fine Arts BADA LAPADA
6 Bury St., St. James's. SW1Y 6AB. Est. 1975. Open 10-6. SIZE: Small. *STOCK: Modern British and European paintings, drawings and sculpture, especially Scottish Colourist paintings.* LOC: Green Park underground station. TEL: 020 7839 8806; e-mail - DMFineArts@aol.com website - www.duncanmiller. com SER: Valuations; conservation and restoration (oils, works on paper and Oriental rugs); buys at auction. FAIRS: Grosvenor House; BADA; Olympia. VAT: Spec.

Nigel Milne Ltd
38 Jermyn St. SW1Y 6DN. (Nigel and Cherry Milne). Est. 1979. Open 9.30-5.30. SIZE: Small. *STOCK: Jewellery, silver frames and objects.* TEL: 020 7434 9343; e-mail - jewels@nigelmilne.co.uk website - www. nigelmilne.co.uk SER: Valuations. VAT: Stan/Spec.

Mrs Monro Ltd
Jubilee House, 70 Cadogan Place. SW1X 9AH. (John Lusk). BIDA. Est. 1926. Open 9.30-5.30, Fri. 9.30-5. CL: Sat. SIZE: Medium. *STOCK: Small decorative furniture, £500-£1,000+; china, £50-£500+; rugs, prints, lamps, pictures and general decorative items, from £50; all 18th-19th C.* LOC: Between Sloane Sq. and Cadogan Place. PARK: Garage nearby. TEL: 020 7235 0326; fax - 020 7259 6305; e-mail - design@mrsmonro. co.uk website - www.mrsmonro.co.uk SER: Restorations (furniture and china). VAT: Stan/Spec.

Moreton Contemporary Art Ltd
40 Moreton St. SW1V 2PB. (C.K. Pearson). Est. 1972. Open 9-1 and 2-6. CL: Sat. SIZE: Medium. *STOCK: Contemporary oils, watercolours, limited editions, posters.* LOC: Off Belgrave Rd. PARK: Easy. TEL: 020 7834 7773/5; fax - 020 7834 7834. SER: Valuations; restorations; buys at auction (originals and engravings). VAT: Stan.

Peter Nahum At The Leicester Galleries BADA
5 Ryder St. SW1Y 6PY. SLAD. CINOA. Est. 1983. Open 9.30-6, Sat. and Sun. by appointment. SIZE: Large. *STOCK: British and European paintings, works on paper and bronzes, including Victorian, the Pre-Raphaelites, Symbolists and Modern British, 19th-20th C, £1,000-£100,000+.* LOC: 100yds. from Royal

Academy. PARK: Meters. TEL: 020 7930 6059; fax - 020 7930 4678; e-mail - peternahum@leicester galleries.com website - www.leicestergalleries.com SER: Valuations; restorations; framing. FAIRS: Grosvenor House; 20th/21st C British Art; IFAAD, New York; London Art. VAT: Spec.

Oakham Gallery BADA LAPADA
27 Bury St., St. James's. SW1 6AL. (Dr A.J. Smith). Open 10-5, Sat. and other times by appointment. *STOCK: Continental oils and watercolours, Victorian and 19th C.* TEL: 020 7839 8800; fax - 020 7976 2266; mobile - 07885 281041; e-mail - asmith@oakham gallery.fsnet.co.uk

Odyssey Fine Arts Ltd LAPADA
24 Holbein Place. SW1W 8NL. (Andrew Korom-Vokis). Est. 1992. Open 10-6. SIZE: Small. *STOCK: 18th to early 19th C Italian and French provincial furniture; 18th C engravings.* TEL: 020 7730 9942; fax - 020 7259 9941; e-mail - odysseyfinearts@aol.com website - www.odysseyart.co.uk FAIRS: Olympia. *Trade Only.*

Old Maps and Prints
3rd Floor, Harrods, Knightsbridge. SW1X 7XL. Est. 1976. Open 10-7. SIZE: Large. *STOCK: Maps, 16th C to 1900; engravings (all subjects); watercolours.* TEL: 020 7730 1234, ext. 2124; fax - 020 7893 8346; e-mail - oldmapsandprints@btconnect.com

Ossowski BADA
83 Pimlico Rd. SW1W 8PH. Est. 1960. Open 10-6. CL: Sat. pm. SIZE: Medium. *STOCK: Carved gilt, 18th C; mirrors, consoles, wood carvings.* TEL: 020 7730 3256. SER: Restorations (gilt furniture). FAIRS: New York International (Oct). VAT: Stan/Spec.

Paisnel Gallery
22 Mason's Yard, Duke St., St James's. SW1Y 6BU. (Stephen and Sylvia Paisnel). SLAD. Est. 1977. Open 10-6. CL: Sat. SIZE: Small. *STOCK: Modern British paintings, £5,000-£50,000.* LOC: Duke St. runs between Piccadilly and King St. 1 min. from Christies. PARK: St. James Sq. TEL: 020 7930 9293; fax - 020 7930 7282; e-mail - info@paisnelgallery.co.uk VAT: Spec.

The Parker Gallery BADA
28 Pimlico Rd. SW1W 8LJ. (Thomas H. Parker Ltd). SLAD. Est. 1750. Open 9.30-5.30, Sat. by appointment. SIZE: Medium. *STOCK: Historical prints, £45-£1,200; English paintings, £1,000-£30,000; ship models, £95-£30,000.* LOC: 5 mins. from Sloane Sq. TEL: 020 7730 6768; fax - 020 7259 9180; website - www.theparkergallery.com SER: Restorations (as stock); mounting; framing. VAT: Stan/Spec.

Michael Parkin Fine Art Ltd
Studio 4, Sedding St., 1/6 Sloane Sq. SW1W 8EE. SLAD. Open by appointment. *STOCK: British paintings, watercolours, drawings and prints, 1860-1960, £250-£100,000.* PARK: Easy. TEL: 020 7730 9784; fax - 01263 768964. FAIRS: 20th-21st C British Art. VAT: Spec.

Trevor Philip and Sons Ltd BADA
75a Jermyn St., St. James's. SW1Y 6NP. (T. and S. Waterman). Est. 1972. Open 9.30-6, Sat. by appointment. SIZE: Medium. *STOCK: Early scientific instruments, globes, barometers and ships models; silver and vertu.* PARK: At rear. TEL: 020 7930 2954; fax - 020 7321 0212; e-mail - globe@trevorphilip.com website - www.trevorphilip.com SER: Valuations; restorations (clocks and scientific instruments); buys at auction. FAIRS: Grosvenor House; Maastricht. VAT: Stan/Spec.

Portland Gallery
9 Bury St., St. James's. SW1Y 6AB. SLAD. Est. 1985. Open 10-6. CL: Sat. SIZE: Medium. *STOCK: Scottish pictures, 20th C, £500-£250,000.* TEL: 020 7321 0422. SER: Valuations; buys at auction. VAT: Spec.

Pullman Gallery
14 King St., St. James's. SW1Y 6QU. (Simon Khachadourian). Est. 1980. Open 10-6, Sat. by appointment. SIZE: Medium. *STOCK: Objets de luxe, 19th-20th C, £200-£20,000; automobile art, pre-1950, £1,000-£20,000; cocktail shakers, bar accessories, cigar memorabilia, 1880-1950, £250-£25,000; René Lalique glass, 1900-1940, from £3,000.* LOC: Corner of Bury St., adjacent Christie's. PARK: Easy. TEL: 020 7930 9595; fax - 020 7930 9494; mobile - 07973 141606; e-mail - sk@pullmangallery.com website - www.pullmangallery.com VAT: Stan.

Mark Ransom Ltd
62, 64 and 105 Pimlico Rd. SW1W 8LS. Est. 1989. Open 10-6. SIZE: Large. *STOCK: Furniture - French Empire and Russian, early 19th C; Continental, decorative, from late 18th C, all to £1,000+; sculpture and prints, contemporary art and furniture.* LOC: Close to Sloane Sq. underground station - turn left left, 5 mins. walk. PARK: Side streets. TEL: 020 7259 0220; fax - 020 7259 0323. e-mail - contact@markransom.co.uk website - www.markransom.co.uk VAT: Stan/Spec.

Steven Rich & Michael Rich
39 Duke St., St. James's. SW1Y 6DF. SLAD. Open daily, Sat. by appointment. SIZE: Medium. *STOCK: Master paintings, 16th-19th C; natural history; works of art.* LOC: Just off Piccadilly. PARK: St. James's Sq. TEL: 020 7930 9308; fax - 020 7930 2088; e-mail - art@richonline.com SER: Valuations. VAT: Spec.

Rogier et Rogier
20A Pimlico Rd. SW1W 8LJ. (Miss Lauriance Rogier). Est. 1980. Open 10-6, Sat. 11-4. SIZE: Small. *STOCK: French and Continental painted and country furniture, 18th-19th C, £1,000-£5,000; lamps and wall sconces, 19th C, from £500; decorative antique and reproduction items, from £300.* LOC: 5 mins. walk from Sloane Sq. PARK: Meters. TEL: 020 7823 4780; e-mail - rogier@easynet.co.uk SER: Restorations (decoration, painted effects, murals, trompe l'oeil). VAT: Spec.

Royal Exchange Art Gallery
7 Bury St., St James's. SW1Y 6AL. Est. 1974. Open 10-6, Fri. 10-5. *STOCK: Fine marine oils, watercolours and etchings.* TEL: 020 7839 4477; fax - 020 7839 8085; e-mail - enquiries@marinepictures.com website - www.marinepictures.com

Julian Simon Fine Art Ltd BADA
70 Pimlico Rd. SW1W 8LS. (M. and J. Brookstone). Open 10-6, Sat. 10-4 or by appointment. *STOCK: Fine English and Continental pictures, 18th-20th C.* LOC: Near Sloane Sq. TEL: 020 7730 8673; fax - 020 7823 6116; e-mail - juliansimon@compuserve.com website - www.19thcenturypaintings.com FAIRS: Olympia.

Sims Reed Gallery
The Economist Building, 23A St James's. SW1A 1HA. Est. 1977. Open 10-6 or by appointment. *STOCK: Modern and contemporary prints by artists including Picasso, Miro, Warhol, Chagall, Hockney.* TEL: 020 7930 5111; fax - 020 7930 1555; e-mail - gallery@simsreed.com website - www.simsreed.com

Sims Reed Ltd
43a Duke St., St James's. SW1Y 6DD. ABA. Est. 1977. Open 10-6 or by appointment. *STOCK: Illustrated, rare and in-print books on the fine and applied arts; leather-bound literary sets; contemporary books.* TEL: 020 7493 5660; fax - 020 7493 8468; e-mail - info@simsreed.com website - www.simsreed.com FAIRS: London ABA.

Peta Smyth - Antique Textiles LAPADA
42 Moreton St., Pimlico. SW1V 2PB. Est. 1977. Open 9.30-5.30. CL: Sat. *STOCK: European textiles, 16th-19th C - needlework, silks and velvets, hangings and curtains, tapestries and cushions, £50-£20,000.* PARK: Easy. TEL: 020 7630 9898; fax - 020 7630 5398; e-mail - petasmyth@ukonline.co.uk FAIRS: Olympia; Palm Beach Jewellery and Antique. VAT: Spec.

Somlo Antiques BADA
7 Piccadilly Arcade. SW1Y 6NH. Est. 1972. Open 10-5.30, Sat. 10.30-5.30. SIZE: Medium. *STOCK: Vintage wrist and antique pocket watches, from £1,000.* LOC: Between Piccadilly and Jermyn St. PARK: Meters. TEL: 020 7499 6526. SER: Restorations.

thesilverfund.com LAPADA
1 Duke of York St. SW1Y 6JP. (Alastair Crawford and Michael James). Open daily, Sat. and Sun. by appointment. SIZE: Large. *STOCK: Old Georg Jensen silver, £500-£100,000.* LOC: Opposite Christies (King St/Bury St). PARK: NCP Mayfair. TEL: 020 7839 7664; fax - 020 7839 8935; e-mail - dealers@thesilverfund.com SER: Valuations; restorations. VAT: Stan/Spec.

THE PARKER GALLERY
(ESTABLISHED 1750)

28, PIMLICO ROAD, LONDON SW1W 8LJ
TEL: 0207-730 6768   FAX: 0207-259 9180

Calshot Castle, The Solent Beyond
Oil painting by J. Tobias Young 1824
Panel size 13½ x 20 inches (34.3 x 50.8 cms)

The Liner Achille Lauro 23,629 tons
Oil painting by W. Eric Thorp. 1966.
Canvas size 16½ x 20 inches (41.9 x 50.8 cms)

DEALERS IN PRINTS, PAINTINGS AND WATERCOLOURS OF
THE 18th, 19th & 20th CENTURY, COVERING MARINE,
MILITARY, TOPOGRAPHICAL AND SPORTING
SUBJECTS, MAPS & SHIP MODELS

Bill Thomson - Albany Gallery
1 Bury St., St. James's. SW1Y 6AB. (W.B. Thomson). Est. 1964. Open Tues.-Fri. 10-5 by appointment only. *STOCK: British drawings, watercolours and paintings, 1700-1850 and some 20th C.* TEL: 020 7839 6119; fax - 020 7839 6614.

Kate Thurlow   LAPADA
41 Moreton St. SW1V 2NY. CINOA. Est. 1970. Open Tues.-Sat. 10-6, other times by appointment. SIZE: Medium. *STOCK: European furniture, including English, and accessories, 16th-18th C, £500-£20,000.* LOC: Lupus St. end of Moreton St. Pimlico underground station. PARK: Meters. TEL: 020 7932 0033; fax - 020 7738 0792; mobile - 07836 588776; e-mail - katethurlow@onetel.com SER: Valuations; restorations (furniture); buys at auction. FAIRS: Olympia. VAT: Spec.

Trafalgar Galleries   BADA
35 Bury St., St. James's. SW1Y 6AY. Open 9.30-6. CL: Sat. STOCK: Old Master paintings. LOC: Just south of Piccadilly. TEL: 020 7839 6466.

Tryon Gallery (incorporating Malcolm Innes)
7 Bury St., St James's. SW1Y 6AL. (Oliver Swann). SLAD. Est. 1955. Open 10-6. CL: Sat. (except during some exhibitions). SIZE: Large. *STOCK: Sporting, wildlife and natural history subjects; Scottish landscape and military pictures; paintings, bronzes, books, £150-£50,000.* TEL: 020 7839 8083; fax - 020 7839 8085; e-mail - tryon@tryon.co.uk website - www.tryon.co.uk SER: Valuations; framing; restoration; advising; commission buying. FAIRS: Game. VAT: Spec.

Rafael Valls Ltd   BADA
11 Duke St., St. James's. SW1Y 6BN. SLAD. Est. 1976. Open Mon.-Fri. 9.30-5.30. STOCK: Old Master paintings. TEL: 020 7930 1144; fax - 020 7976 1596. FAIRS: Maastricht: Grosvenor House: BADA. VAT: Spec.

Rafael Valls Ltd   BADA
6 Ryder St., St. James's. SW1Y 6QB. SLAD. Est. 1976. Open Mon.-Fri. 9.30-6. STOCK: Fine European paintings. Contemporary exhibitions. TEL: 020 7930 0029; fax - 020 7976 1596; e-mail - info@rafaelvalls.demon.co.uk VAT: Spec.

Johnny Van Haeften Ltd   BADA
13 Duke St., St. James's. SW1Y 6DB. (J. and S. Van Haeften). SLAD. TEFAF. Est. 1978. Open 10-6, Sat. and Sun. by appointment. SIZE: Medium. STOCK: Dutch and Flemish Old Master paintings, 16th-17th C, £5,000-£5m. LOC: Middle of Duke St. TEL: 020 7930 3062/3; fax - 020 7839 6303; e-mail - paintings@ johnnyvanhaeften.com website - www.johnnyvan haeften.com SER: Valuations; restorations (Old Masters); buys at auction (paintings including Old Masters). FAIRS: Grosvenor House; Maastricht. VAT: Spec.

Waterman Fine Art Ltd
75A Jermyn St., St. James's. SW1Y 6NP. (Mrs. R. Waterman). Open 9-6, Sat. 10-4. SIZE: Medium. *STOCK: 20th C paintings and watercolours.* PARK: At rear. TEL: 020 7839 5203; fax - 020 7321 0212.

The Weiss Gallery
59 Jermyn St. SW1Y 6LX. Open 10-6. *STOCK: Early English, Dutch, Flemish and French portraits.* TEL: 020 7409 0035; fax - 020 7491 9604; e-mail - mark@weissgallery.com website - www.weissgallery. com SER: Valuations; restorations.

Westenholz Antiques Ltd
76-78 Pimlico Rd. SW1W 8PL. Open 10-6, Sat. by appointment. *STOCK: 18th-19th C furniture, pictures, objects, lamps, mirrors.* TEL: 020 7824 8090.

Rollo Whately Ltd
41 St. James's Place, St. James's. SW1A 1NS. Est. 1995. Open 9-6. CL: Sat. SIZE: Small. *STOCK: Picture frames, 16th-19th C, £500-£2,000.* TEL: 020 7629 7861; e-mail - frames@rollowhately.demon.co.uk SER: Valuations; restorations (frames); search; buys at auction. VAT: Stan.

Whitford Fine Art
6 Duke St., St. James's. SW1Y 6BN. (Adrian Mibus). Est. 1973. Open 10-6. CL: Sat. *STOCK: Oil paintings and sculpture, late 19th to 20th C; Modernism, post war abstract and pop art.* TEL: 020 7930 9332; fax - 020 7930 5577; e-mail - info@whitfordfineart.com website - www.whitfordfineart.com VAT: Spec.

Arnold Wiggins and Sons Ltd   BADA
4 Bury St., St. James's. SW1Y 6AB. (Michael Gregory). Open Mon.-Fri 9-5.30. STOCK: Picture frames, 16th-19th C. PARK: Meters. TEL: 020 7925 0195; e-mail - info@arnoldwiggins.com website - www.artsolutionnet/wiggins SER: Restorations; adaptations. FAIRS: Grosvenor House.

Wildenstein and Co Ltd
46 St. James's Place. SW1A 1NS. SLAD. Est. 1934. Open by appointment. *STOCK: Impressionist and Old Master paintings and drawings.* TEL: 020 7629 0602; fax - 020 7493 3924.

SW2

Chris Baron Interiors
87 Streatham Hill. SW2 4UB. Est. 1976. Open 9.30-5.30, Thurs. until 6.30, Sat. 9.30-5. SIZE: Small. *STOCK: Desks, from Victorian, £250-£1,250; bureaux, from Georgian, £200-£2,000; chests of drawers, from Georgian, £300-£1,000; all mainly mahogany, oak and walnut. Lighting and interesting items.* PARK: Easy. TEL: 020 8671 8732; fax - 020 8671 1984; e-mail - baronsx3@aol.com website - www.chrisbaroninteriors. co.uk SER: Valuations; restorations and repairs.

SW3

Norman Adams Ltd   BADA
8/10 Hans Rd., Knightsbridge. SW3 1RX. Est. 1923. Open 9-5.30, Sat. and Sun. by appointment. SIZE: Large. STOCK: English furniture, 18th C, £650-£250,000; objets d'art (English and French) £500-£50,000; mirrors, glass pictures, 18th C; clocks and barometers. LOC: 30yds. off the Brompton Rd., opposite west side entrance to Harrods. TEL: 020 7589 5266; fax - 020 7589 1968; e-mail - antiques@

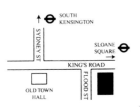

ANTIQUARIUS
131-141 King's Road, London SW3

"A fine example of what the best antiques centre can offer"
Antique Dealer and Collectors Guide
Enquiries: Neil Jackson
Tel: 020-7351 5353
Antiquarius Ltd., 15 Flood Street, London SW3 5ST
www.antiquarius.co.uk

normanadams.com website - www.normanadams.com FAIRS: Grosvenor House; BADA. VAT: Spec.

After Noah
261 King's Rd. Chelsea. SW3 5EL. (M. Crawford and Z. Candlin). Est. 1990. Open 10-6, Sun. 12-5. SIZE: Large. *STOCK: Arts and Craft oak and similar furniture, leather sofas and chairs, 1880s to 1950s, £1-£5,000; iron, iron and brass beds; decorative items, bric-a-brac including candlesticks, mirrors, lighting, kitchenalia and jewellery.* TEL: 020 7351 2610; fax - same; e-mail - enquiries@afternoah.com website - www.afternoah.com SER: Restorations. VAT: Stan/Margin.

The Andipa Gallery   LAPADA
162 Walton St. SW3 2JL. Est. 1969. Open 11-6. *STOCK: Icons from Byzantium, Greece, Russia, Eastern Europe, Asia Minor and North Africa; Italian Masters and Old Masters, all from 14th-19th C; Asian art and antiquities, from 500 BC; modern and contemporary prints, drawings, paintings and sculpture.* LOC: Knightsbridge. TEL: 020 7589 2371; fax - 020 7225 0305; e-mail - art@andipa.com website - www.andipa.com SER: Valuations; restorations; research; collections.

Antiquarius
131/141 King's Rd. SW3 4PW. (Atlantic Antiques Centres Ltd). Est. 1970. Open 10-6. *STOCK: Below are listed some of the many specialist dealers at this market.* LOC: On the corner of King's Rd. and Flood St., next to Chelsea Town Hall. TEL: Enquiries - 020 7351 5353; fax - 020 7969 1639; e-mail - antique@dial.pipex.com

Jaki Abbott
Stand M12. *Jewellery.* TEL: 020 7352 7989.

Aesthetics   LAPADA
Stand V1. (Peter and Philip Jeffs). *Silver, ceramics and decorative arts, 1860-1960.*

AM-PM
Stand V11. (Jane Yeganeh). *Vintage watches.* TEL: 020 7351 5654; fax - same.

Alexia Amato
Stand V8. *Decorative antiques, Bohemian glass.* TEL: 020 7352 3666; fax - same; mobile - 07770 826254; e-mail - alexia@amato.freeserve.co.uk website - www.amato.freeserve.co.uk

Antiques Rug Gallery
Stand V19 *Oriental carpets and Persian rugs.*

Baker Fine Arts
Stands L1/10. *20th C Russian paintings.* TEL: Mobile - 07879 055347.

Beauty & The Beast
Stand Q9. (J. Rothman). *Costume jewellery, handbags.* TEL: 020 7351 5149.

Bellum Antiques
Stand V12. *Fine jewellery and bronzes.* TEL: 020 7352 1444; mobile - 07710 945942.

Alexandra Bolla
Stand J1. *Jewellery.* TEL: 020 7352 7989.

Brown
Stand J4. *Jewellery.*

Brown & Kingston
Stand V5. (Dennis Kingston). *Furniture, Imari, blue and white, Staffordshire porcelain.* TEL: 020 7376 8881.

Teresa Buchinger
Stand Q2. *Jewellery and match strikers.* TEL: 020 7352 8734; mobile - 07752 407479.

Jasmine Cameron
Stand M1. *Glass.* TEL: 020 7351 4154; fax - same; mobile - 07774 871257; e-mail - jasmine.cameron@mail.com

Chelsea Military Antiques
Stand F1. *Militaria.* TEL: 020 7352 0308.

Claxton
Stand H3. *Furniture.*

The Cufflink Shop
Stand G2. (John Szwarc). *Jewellery and cuff-links.* TEL: 020 7352 8201; mobile - 07715 381175; e-mail - john.szwarc@btopenworld.com

Jesse Davis Antiques
Stand D5. *General antiques.* TEL: 020 7352 4314; fax - 020 7384 1435; mobile - 07887 998798; e-mail - monicadavis @btinternet.com website - www.jessedavis-antiques.co.uk

Glen Dewart
Stands P7/8. *Prints and paintings.* TEL: 020 7352 4777; mobile - 07751 153916.

Ferguson Fine Art
Stand V13. (Serena Ferguson). *Sporting collectables.* TEL: 020 7352 5272; fax - 020 8892 4039.

Gallison
Stand L9. *Jewellery and decorative accessories.*

Angelo Gibson
Stand M10. *Silver plate, general antiques.* TEL: 020 7352

4690; mobile - 079951 929015; e-mail - quicksilverangelo@zoom.co.uk

Brian Gordon LAPADA
Stand G1. *Silver and plate.* TEL: 020 7351 5808.

Robin Haydock - Rare Antiques & Textiles
LAPADA
Stand V15. *Antique textiles.* TEL: 020 7349 9110; fax - same; e-mail - robinhaydock@talk21.com

Hayman & Hayman
Stands K2-K5. *Photo frames, scent bottles.* TEL: 020 7351 6568; mobile - 07803 015779; e-mail - georgina@haymanframes.com

Islamic Art
Stand V14. *Islamic art.*

Martin Kaye Watches
Stands V3/4. *Rolex watches.*

Michael Kelleher
Stand V7. *Decorative prints and paintings.* TEL: Mobile - 07944 212311.

Sophie Ketley
Stands J9/11. *Giltwood furniture, decorative items including glass.* TEL: 020 7351 0005.

Claude & Martine Latreville
Stand V16. *Fine silver and jewellery.*

Little River
Stand D5. (David Dykes). *Asian prints, Oriental china and porcelain.* TEL: 020 7349 9080; fax - same; e-mail - littleriveroa@aol.com SER: *Restorations (Oriental furniture).*

Mariad Antique Jewellery
Stand V38. (Mrs M. McLean). *Vienna bronzes and jewellery.* TEL: 020 7351 9526.

Martinez-Negrillo
Stands P1/2/3. *Jewellery, porcelain, glass, paintings, objets de vertu.* TEL: 020 7349 0038; mobile - 07778 336781; e-mail - negrilloc@aol.com

Gerald Mathias
Stands R3-6. *Boxes.* TEL: 020 7351 0484; e-mail - gm@geraldmathias.com website - www.geraldmathias.com

Mrs N. McDonald-Hobley
Stand L7. *Jewellery.* TEL: 020 7351 0154; mobile - 07774 920251.

William McLeod-Brown
Stands L5/6. *Prints.* TEL: 020 7352 4690, ext. 6.

Molloy
Stand E2. *Oil paintings.*

Mrs. D. Mousavi
Stand D4. *Jewellery.*

Nina Antiquarius
Stand P9. *Jewellery.* TEL: 020 7351 2317; mobile - 07710 263742; e-mail - dsantamarinella@aol.com

Sue Norman
Stand L3. *19th C blue and white transferware.* TEL: 020 7352 7217; fax - 020 8870 4677; e-mail - sue@sue-norman.demon.co.uk website - www.sue-norman.demon.co.uk

Maria Perez
Stands V23/24. *Jewellery.* TEL: 020 7351 1986.

The Poster Shop
Stand N1. *Vintage and original movie posters.* TEL: 020 7351 5166; mobile - 07944 428544.

Abdul Rabi
Stand P4. SER: Jewellery and watch repairs and engraving.

Keiron Reilly
Stand K1. *Art Nouveau and Art Deco.*

Simar Antiques
Stand A18. (A. Cohen). *Silver.* TEL: 020 7352 7155; mobile - 07973 222520; e-mail - silver@adrian-cohen.co.uk website - www.adrian-cohen.co.uk

D. M. Simpson
Stand E1. *Ivory.*

Ouji Sormeh
Stand D1. *Jewellery.* TEL: 020 7352 5592.

Miwa Thorpe
Stands M8/9. *Silver and jewellery.* TEL: 020 7351 2911; fax - 0207351 6690; e-mail - miwathorpe@waitrose.com

William Wain
Stand J6. *Vintage costume jewellery.* TEL: 020 7351 4905; fax - 020 8693 1814; e-mail - williamwain@hotmail.com

Weast
Stand V20. *Pearls and semi-precious stone jewellery.* TEL: 020 7751 5588; website - www.weast.co.uk

West Country Jewellery
Stands M5/6/7. (David Billing). *Jewellery, objects, silver.*

XS Baggage
Stand A1-4, B1-5, C1/2. (Mr and Mrs Lehane). *Antique luggage and travel requisites.* TEL: 020 7376 8781; e-mail - xsbaggage@postmaster.co.uk website - www.xsbaggage.co.uk

Apter Fredericks Ltd BADA
265-267 Fulham Rd. SW3 6HY. Est. 1946. Open 9.30-5.30, Sat. and evenings by appointment. SIZE: 6 showrooms. STOCK: English furniture, 17th to early 19th C. TEL: 020 7352 2188; fax - 020 7376 5619; e-mail - antiques@apter-fredericks.com website - www.apter-fredericks.com FAIRS: Grosvenor House; IFAAD, New York.

Joanna Booth BADA
247 King's Rd., Chelsea. SW3 5EL. Est. 1963. Open 10-6. SIZE: Medium. STOCK: Sculpture, 12th-17th C; tapestries, textiles, 16th-18th C; Old Master drawings, £50-£50,000; early furniture, works of art. PARK: Meters. TEL: 020 7352 8998; fax - 020 7376 7350; e-mail - joanna@joannabooth.co.uk website - www.joannabooth.co.uk SER: Buys at auction. FAIRS: Olympia. VAT: Spec.

Bourbon-Hanby Antiques Centre
151 Sydney St. Chelsea. SW3 6NT. Est. 1976. Open 10-6, Sun. 11-5. *STOCK: Jewellery, silver, furniture, paintings, ivory and general antiques.* LOC: Just off Kings Road, opposite town hall. PARK: NCP next door. TEL: 020 7352 2106; website - www.bourbonhanby.co.uk SER: Jewellery repairs, design and manufacturing. VAT: Margin.

Butler and Wilson
189 Fulham Rd. SW3 6JN. Open 10-6, Wed. 10-7, Sun. 12-6. CL: Sat. *STOCK: Jewellery, Art Deco, vintage*

bags and clothes, 1950s jewellery, objects and accessories. TEL: 020 7352 3045; fax - 020 7376 5981; e-mail - info@butlerandwilson.co.uk

Richard Courtney Ltd BADA
112-114 Fulham Rd. SW3 6HU. Est. 1959. Open 9.30-1 and 2-6. CL: Sat. SIZE: Large. *STOCK: English furniture, 18th C, £5,000-£50,000.* PARK: Easy. TEL: 020 7370 4020. FAIRS: Grosvenor House; BADA; Olympia. VAT: Spec.

Robert Dickson and Lesley Rendall Antiques BADA
263 Fulham Rd. SW3 6HY. Est. 1969. Open 9.30-5.30, Sat. 10-5 or by appointment. SIZE: Medium. *STOCK: Late 18th to early 19th C furniture, mirrors, lighting and works of art, £500-£100,000.* PARK: Easy. TEL: 020 7351 0330; e-mail - info@dicksonrendall-antiques.co.uk website - www.dicksonrendall-antiques.co.uk SER: Restorations; valuations. VAT: Spec.

Drummonds Architectural Antiques Ltd
78 Royal Hospital Rd., Chelsea. SW3 4HN. SALVO. Est. 1988. Open 10-6, Sat. by appointment. SIZE: Large. *STOCK: Original architectural materials including wood and stone flooring, restored period bathrooms, fireplaces, radiators and garden ornaments.* PARK: Easy. TEL: 020 7376 4499; fax - 020 7376 4488; e-mail - London@drummonds-arch.co.uk website - www.drummonds-arch.co.uk SER: Manufacturer of cast-iron baths, iron conservatories and brassware; restorations (stonework and gates); vitreous re-enamelling of baths.

Michael Foster BADA
118 Fulham Rd., Chelsea. SW3 6HU. (Margaret and Michael Susands). Est. 1963. Open 9.30-5.30, Sat. by appointment. *STOCK: 18th C English furniture and works of art.* TEL: 020 7373 3636/3040; fax - 020 7373 4042.

Gallery Yacou LAPADA
127 Fulham Rd. SW3 6RT. (Y. and R. Yacoubian). Est. 1920. Open 10.30-6, Sat. 11.30-5. *STOCK: Decorative and antique Oriental and European carpets (room-size and over-size).* TEL: 020 7584 2929; fax - 020 7584 3535; e-mail - galleryyacou@aol.com SER: Consultation, repairs and cleaning. FAIRS: Olympia: LAPADA.

General Trading Co Ltd LAPADA
2 Symons St. SW3 2TJ. Est. 1920. Open 10-6.30. SIZE: Medium. *STOCK: English and Continental furniture, £100-£10,000; objects, both 18th-20th C.* LOC: Near Sloane Sq. TEL: 020 7730 0411, 020 7823 5426; e-mail - enquiries@general-trading.co.uk website - www.general-trading.co.uk VAT: Stan/Spec.

David Gill LAPADA
60 Fulham Rd. SW3 6HH. Est. 1986. Open 10-6. SIZE: Medium. *STOCK: Decorative and fine arts, Picasso, Cocteau ceramics and drawings, 1900 to present day.* PARK: Onslow Sq. TEL: 020 7589 5946; fax - 020 7584 9184. VAT: Stan.

Godson and Coles BADA
92 Fulham Rd. SW3 6HR. (Richard Godson and Richard Coles). Est. 1978. Open 9.30-5.30, Sat. by appointment. *STOCK: Fine 17th to early 19th C English furniture and works of art.* TEL: 020 7584 2200; fax - 020 7584 2223; e-mail - godsonandcoles@aol.com website - www.godsonandcoles.co.uk FAIRS: Grosvenor House.

Green and Stone
259 Kings Rd. SW3 5EL. (R.J.S. Baldwin). FATG. Est. 1927. Open 9-6, Sat. 9.30-6, Sun. 12-5. *STOCK: 18th-19th C writing and artists' materials, glass and china.* LOC: At junction with Old Church St. PARK: Meters. TEL: 020 7352 0837; fax - 020 7351 1098; e-mail - antiques@greenandstone.com SER: Restorations (pictures and frames). VAT: Stan.

James Hardy and Co
235 Brompton Rd. SW3 2EP. Est. 1853. Open 10-5.30. *STOCK: Silver including tableware, and jewellery.* PARK: Meters. TEL: 020 7589 5050; fax - 020 7589 9009. SER: Valuations; repairs.

Peter Harrington Antiquarian Bookseller
100 Fulham Rd., Chelsea. SW3 6HS. (Peter and Mati Harrington). ABA. ILAB. PBFA. Est. 1969. Open 10-6. SIZE: Large. *STOCK: Antiquarian and collectable books, 1500-2000, £20-£50,000+.* TEL: 020 7591 0220; fax - 020 7225 7054; e-mail - books@peter-harrington-books.com website - www.peter-harrington-books.com SER: Valuations; restorations (full bookbinding); buys at auction. FAIRS: Olympia Books & Antiques, Chelsea, New York, Boston, California. *Trade Only.*

Michael Hughes BADA
88 Fulham Rd., Chelsea. SW3 6HR. Est. 1970. Open 9.30-5.30, Sat. by appointment. SIZE: Large. *STOCK: Fine 18th-19th C English furniture and works of art.* TEL: 020 7589 0660; fax - 020 7823 7618; mobile - 07880 505123; e-mail - antiques@michaelhughes.freeserve.co.uk and info@michaelhughesantiques.co.uk website - www.michaelhughesantiques.co.uk FAIRS: Olympia (June and Nov). VAT: Spec.

Anthony James and Son Ltd BADA
88 Fulham Rd. SW3 6HR. CINOA. Est. 1949. Open 9.30-5.30, Sat. by appointment. SIZE: Large. *STOCK: Furniture, 1700-1880, £200-£50,000; mirrors, bronzes, ormolu and decorative items, £200-£20,000.* PARK: Easy. TEL: 020 7584 1120; fax - 020 7823 7618; e-mail - info@anthony-james.com website - www.anthony-james.com SER: Valuations; buys at auction. FAIRS: Olympia (June). VAT: Spec.

John Keil Ltd BADA
1st Floor, 154 Brompton Rd. SW3 1HX. Est. 1959. Open 9.30-5.30, Sat. by appointment. *STOCK: Fine English furniture, 18th to early 19th C.* LOC: Near Knightsbridge underground station. PARK: 200 yds. TEL: 020 7589 6454; fax - 020 7823 8235; e-mail - antiques@johnkeil.com website - www.johnkeil.com VAT: Spec.

Peter Lipitch Ltd BADA
120/124 Fulham Rd. SW3 6HU. Est. 1954. Open 9.30-5.30. SIZE: Large. *STOCK: Fine English furniture and mirrors.* TEL: 020 7373 3328; fax - 020 7373 8888; website - www.peterlipitch.com FAIRS: BADA; Grosvenor House. VAT: Spec.

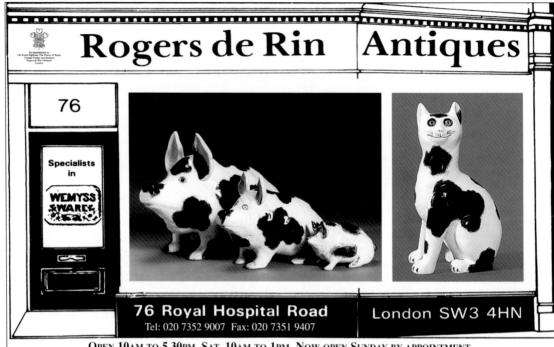

Rogers de Rin Antiques

76

Specialists in WEMYSS WARE

76 Royal Hospital Road
Tel: 020 7352 9007 Fax: 020 7351 9407

London SW3 4HN

OPEN 10AM TO 5.30PM, SAT. 10AM TO 1PM. NOW OPEN SUNDAY BY APPOINTMENT.
We would like to buy collections of Wemyss Ware or individual pieces - Free colour catalogue on request
Email: rogersderin@rogersderin.co.uk   Website: www.rogersderin.co.uk

The Map House   BADA
54 Beauchamp Place. SW3 1NY. (P. Curtis and P. Stuchlik). ABA. IMCOS. Est. 1907. Open 9.45-5.45, Sat. 10.30-5 or by appointment. SIZE: Large. *STOCK: Antique and rare maps, atlases, engravings and globes.* LOC: Knightsbridge, near Harrods. TEL: 020 7589 4325/7584 8559; fax - 020 7589 1041; e-mail - maps@themaphouse.com website - www.themap house.com FAIRS: Grosvenor House. VAT: Stan.

McKenna and Co   LAPADA
28 Beauchamp Place. SW3 1NJ. (C. and M. McKenna). CINOA. NAG. Est. 1982. Open 10-6. SIZE: Medium. *STOCK: Fine jewellery, Georgian to post war, £250-£200,000; some silver and objects.* LOC: Off Brompton Rd., near Harrods. PARK: Meters. TEL: 020 7584 1966; fax - 020 7225 2893; e-mail - info@mckennajewels.com website - www.mckennajewels.com SER: Valuations; restorations. VAT: Stan/Margin.

Old Church Galleries
98 Fulham Rd., Chelsea. SW3 6HS. (Nicky Ranson and Mrs M. Harrington). FATG. ABA. Open 10-6. SIZE: Large. *STOCK: Maps and engravings, sporting and decorative prints.* TEL: 020 7591 8790; fax - 020 7591 8791; e-mail - sales@old-church-galleries.com website - www.old-church-galleries.com SER: Framing. FAIRS: Olympia; Boston International.

Orientalist   LAPADA
152-154 Walton St. SW3 2JJ. (E., H. and M. Sakhai). Est. 1985. Open 10.30-5.15, appointment advisable.

SIZE: Large. *STOCK: Oriental, European, antique and reproduction rugs - classic and tribal Persian, Caucasian, Indian and Turkish, especially over-sized; Aubusson, tapestries, cushions and contemporary rugs.* PARK: Easy. TEL: 020 7581 2332; e-mail - rugs@orientalist.demon.co.uk website - www.orientalist. demon.co.uk/orientalist SER: Valuations; restorations (cleaning and repairing rugs, carpets and tapestries).

Prides of London
15 Paultons House. Paultons Sq. SW3 5DU. Open by appointment. *STOCK: Fine 18th-19th C English and Continental furniture; objets d'art.* TEL: 020 7586 1227. SER: Interior design.

Rogers de Rin   BADA
76 Royal Hospital Rd., Chelsea. SW3 4HN. (V. de Rin). Est. 1950. Open 10-5.30, Sat. 10-1, Sun. by appointment, SIZE: Small. *STOCK: Wemyss pottery, objets d'art, decorative furnishings (Regency taste), collectors' specialities, Vienna bronzes, treen, sewing items and needleworks, 18th-19th C, £50-£10,000.* LOC: Just beyond Royal Hospital, corner of Paradise Walk. PARK: Easy. TEL: 020 7352 9007; fax - 020 7351 9407; e-mail - rogersderin@rogersderin.co.uk website - www.rogersderin.co.uk FAIRS: Olympia (June and Nov); BADA (March). VAT: Spec.

Russell Rare Books
239A Fulham Rd., Chelsea. SW3 6HY. (C. Russell). ABA. PBFA. Est. 1978. Open Mon.-Fri. 2-6. SIZE: Small. *STOCK: Antiquarian books.* LOC: At junction

O.F. WILSON LTD.

QUEEN'S ELM PARADE

**OLD CHURCH STREET
LONDON, SW3 6EJ
Tel: 020 7352 9554
Fax: 020 7351 0765**

*English and
Continental period
decorative
furniture, mirrors,
objets d'art; period
English & French
mantelpieces*

Mon.–Fri. 9.30–5.30

Sat. 10.30–1

Valuations given

Old Church St. TEL: 020 7351 5119; fax - 020 7376 7227; e-mail - c.russell@russellrarebooks.com website - www.russellrarebooks.com FAIRS: Russell Hotel (monthly); Olympia (June).

Charles Saunders Antiques
255 Fulham Rd. SW3 6HY. Est. 1987. Open Mon.-Fri. 9.30-5.30. *STOCK: Continental and English decorative furniture, objects and lighting, 18th to early 20th C.* TEL: 020 7351 5242; e-mail - info@charlessaundersantiques.com website - www.charlessaundersantiques. com VAT: Spec.

Christine Schell
15 Cale St. SW3 3QS. Est. 1973. Open 10-5.30. SIZE: Small. *STOCK: Unusual tortoiseshell, silver and enamel objects, late 19th-20th C, £150-£2,500.* LOC: North of King's Rd., between Sloane Ave. and Sydney St. PARK: Easy. TEL: 020 7352 5563; e-mail - c.schell@eidosnet. co.uk website - www.christineschell.co.uk SER: Valuations; restorations (tortoiseshell, ivory, shagreen, crocodile, leather, enamels, silver, hairbrush re-bristling). VAT: Stan/Spec.

Robert Stephenson
1 Elystan St. Chelsea Green. SW3 3NT. Est. 1984. Open 9.30-5.30, Sat. 10.30-2. *STOCK: Antique and decorative room-sized carpets and kilims; antique Oriental rugs, European tapestries and Aubussons, textiles, needlepoints and cushions; modern Bessarabian kilims, traditional and own contemporary designs.* TEL: 020 7225 2343; fax - same; e-mail - stephensoncarpets@ tiscali.co.uk SER: Cleaning; restorations; valuations.

Gordon Watson Ltd   LAPADA
50 Fulham Rd. SW3 6HH. Est. 1977. Open 11-6. *STOCK: Art Deco and 1940s glass, jewellery and furniture, £1,000-£50,000; silver by Jensen and Jean E. Puiforcat, 1920s, £500-£30,000.* LOC: At junction with Sydney St. PARK: Sydney St. TEL: 020 7589 3108/7584 6328; e-mail - gordonwatson@btinternet.com FAIRS: Olympia. VAT: Stan/Spec.

O.F. Wilson Ltd   BADA LAPADA
Queen's Elm Parade, Old Church St. (corner Fulham Rd.), Chelsea. SW3 6EJ. (P. and V.E. Jackson and K.E. Simmonds). Est. 1935. Open 9.30-5.30, Sat. 10.30-1. SIZE: 6 showrooms. *STOCK: English and French furniture, mirrors, mantelpieces, objets d'art.* TEL: 020 7352 9554; fax - 020 7351 0765. SER: Valuations. VAT: Spec.

SW4

Antiques and Things
SW4 (Mrs V. Crowther). Est. 1986. Open by appointment. SIZE: Small. *STOCK: 18th-19th C French furniture, lighting and decorative items including curtain furniture and textiles, £5-£10,000.* LOC: Clapham. TEL: 020 7498 1303; fax - same; mobile - 07767 262096; website - www.antiquesandthings.co.uk FAIRS: Decorative Antiques and Textiles.

Places and Spaces
30 Old Town, Clapham. SW4 0LB. (Laura Slack). Est. 1996. Open 10.30-6, Sun. 12-4. CL: Mon. SIZE: Small.

STOCK: Furniture and lighting, 20th C, £45-£3,000. LOC: Near Clapham Common underground station. PARK: Meters. TEL: 020 7498 0998; fax - 020 7627 2625; e-mail - contact@placesandspaces.com website - www.placesandspaces.com SER: Valuations; sourcing.

SW5

Beaver Coin Room
Beaver Hotel, 57 Philbeach Gdns. SW5 9ED. (J. Lis). Est. 1971. Open by appointment. SIZE: Small. *STOCK: European coins, 10th-18th C; commemorative medals, 15th-20th C; all £5-£5,000.* LOC: 2 mins. walk from Earls Court Rd. PARK: Easy. TEL: 020 7373 4553; fax - 020 7373 4555; e-mail - hotelbeaver@hotmail.com SER: Valuations; buys at auction (coins and medals). FAIRS: London Coin and Coinex. VAT: Stan.

SW6

20th Century Gallery
821 Fulham Rd. SW6 5HG. (E. Brandl and H. Chapman). Open 10-6, Sat. 10-1. SIZE: Small. *STOCK: Post impressionist and modern British oils and watercolours; original prints.* LOC: Near Munster Rd. junction. PARK: Easy. TEL: 020 7731 5888. SER: Restorations (paintings); framing. VAT: Spec.

275 Antiques
275 Lillie Rd., Fulham. SW6 7LL. (David Fisher). Open 10-5.30. SIZE: Medium. *STOCK: English and Continental decorative furniture, £200-£1,200; decorative objects and mirrors, £50-£500; unique American Lucite 1960s table lamps and furniture, £250-£800.* PARK: Easy. TEL: 020 7386 7382.

291 Antiques
291 Lillie Rd., Fulham. SW6 7LL. Open 11-5.30. SIZE: Large. *STOCK: Highly decorative antiques, Gothic style and 18th C splendour; mirrors, garden statuary and textiles; oil paintings and watercolours.* TEL: 020 7381 5008. SER: Lavish interior design.

313 Antiques
313 Lillie Rd., Fulham. SW6 7LL. (Marc Costantini Art & Antiques). Open 10.30-5.30. *STOCK: 17th-19th C furniture, £200-£3,000; decorative and interesting objects, £20-£500; pictures especially portrait oils; decorative wood frames, mirrors, carpets.* LOC: From Old Brompton Rd., west for half a mile after crossing Northend Rd. PARK: Easy and nearby. TEL: 020 7610 2380; fax - same. SER: Shipping arranged.

(55) For Decorative Living
55 New King's Rd., Chelsea. SW6 4SE. (Mrs J. Rhodes). BFS. Est. 1987. Open 10.30-5.30. SIZE: Large. *STOCK: Furniture, lighting and decorative items, European, Colonial and garden.* PARK: Pay & Display. TEL: 020 7736 5623. e-mail - info@decorativeliving.co.uk website - www.decorativeliving.co.uk SER: Design.

And So To Bed Limited
638/640 King's Rd. SW6 2DU. Est. 1973. Open 10-6. SIZE: Large. *STOCK: Brass, lacquered and wooden beds.* LOC: End of King's Rd., towards Fulham. PARK: Easy. TEL: 020 7731 3593/4/5; freephone - 0808

1444343; fax - 020 7371 5272; e-mail - enquiries @andsotobed.co.uk website - www.andsotobed.co.uk SER: Restorations; spares; interior design. VAT: Stan.

The Antique Lamp Shop
at Christopher Wray Lighting, 591-593 King's Rd. SW6 2YW. Est. 1964. Open 10-6. SIZE: Large. *STOCK: Victorian and Edwardian oil lamps, spare parts, wicks, chimneys, glass shades; 19th C French and English decorative light fittings, Art Deco wall brackets and pendants, piano candle sconces; also door furniture, old signage and some furniture.* LOC: From Sloane Sq. over Stanley Bridge. PARK: Own at rear. TEL: 020 7751 8701; fax - 020 7751 8699. SER: Repairs and renovations. VAT: Stan.

Christopher Bangs Ltd   BADA LAPADA
P O Box 6077. SW6 7XS. (Christopher Bangs and Judy Wentworth). CINOA. Est. 1971. Open by appointment. *STOCK: Domestic metalwork and metalware, works of art, decorative objects, 18th-19th C textiles.* TEL: 020 7381 3532 (24 hrs); fax - 020 7381 2192 (24 hrs). SER: Research; commission buys at auction; finder. VAT: Stan/Spec.

Sebastiano Barbagallo
661 Fulham Rd. SW6 5PZ. Est. 1975. Open 10-6 including Sun. *STOCK: Chinese furniture; antiques and handicrafts from India, Tibet, SE Asia and China.* LOC: Near Fulham Broadway. TEL: 020 7751 0691.

Barclay Samson Ltd
65 Finlay St. SW6 6HF. (Richard Barclay). IVPDA. Open by appointment. *STOCK: Pre 1950 original lithographic posters: French, German, Swiss, American, British and Russian Constructivist schools.* TEL: 020 7731 8012 or 00 33 2975 88104 (France); e-mail - richard@barclaysamson.com website - www.barclay samson.com FAIRS: Olympia (June); USA. VAT: Spec.

Robert Barley Antiques
(R.A. Barley). Est. 1965. Open by appointment. SIZE: Medium. *STOCK: Rare and bizarre objects, sculpture and pictures, 2000BC to date.* TEL: 020 7736 4429; fax - same. FAIRS: Olympia (Spring, Summer and Winter); Decorative Antiques and Textiles (Jan., April and Sept). VAT: Stan/Spec.

Julia Boston   LAPADA
588 King's Rd. SW6 2DX. CINOA. Est. 1976. Open 10-6 or by appointment. SIZE: Large. *STOCK: 18th-19th C furniture, lighting, tapestry cartoons, antiquarian prints and decoration.* TEL: 020 7610 6783; fax - 020 7610 6784; e-mail - julia@juliaboston.com website - www. juliaboston.com VAT: Spec.

I. and J.L. Brown Ltd
634-636 King's Rd. SW6 2DU. Open 9-6. SIZE: Large. *STOCK: English and French provincial furniture including tables, country chairs, dressers, armoires, side tables and servers; decorative items.* TEL: 020 7736 4141; fax - 020 7736 9164; e-mail - sales@brownantiqueslondon.com SER: Restorations; chair re-rushing.

Rupert Cavendish Antiques
610 King's Rd. SW6 2DX. (Rupert Cavendish and Hakan Groth). Est. 1980. Open 10-6. SIZE: Large.

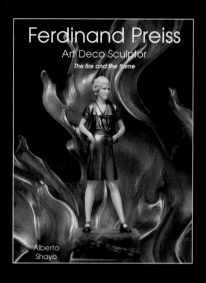
STOCK: Biedermeier, Art Deco and Empire furniture, 20th C French and Scandinavian paintings and alabaster lamps. LOC: Just before New King's Rd. PARK: Easy. TEL: 020 7731 7041; fax - 020 7731 8302; e-mail - RCavendish@aol.com website - www.rupertcavendish.co.uk SER: Valuations; restorations (furniture). VAT: Spec.

Hilary Chapman Fine Prints
20th Century Gallery, 821 Fulham Rd. SW6 5HG. Est. 1984. Open 10-6, Sat. 10-1. SIZE: Small. STOCK: Early 20th C British prints, etchings, engravings including wood, lithographs especially colour woodcuts and linocuts of 1920s and 1930s, £50-£2,000. LOC: Central Fulham. PARK: Side roads. TEL: 020 7384 1334; fax - 020 7384 1334; mobile - 07808 415048; e-mail - chapmanprints@aol.com website - www.hilarychapmanfineprints.co.uk SER: Valuations. FAIRS: Royal College of Art - Art on Paper; Chelsea Art.

Chelminski Gallery
616 King's Rd., Chelsea. SW6 2DU. (Hilary Chelminski). SALVO. Est. 1970. Open by appointment only. SIZE: Medium. STOCK: Antique sculpture and fine garden ornaments, mainly British and European, £500-£150,000. LOC: Near corner with Maxwell Rd. PARK: Easy. TEL: 020 7384 2227; fax - 020 7384 2229; mobile - 07989 033831; e-mail - enquiries@chelminski.com website - www.chelminski.com SER: Restoration; exhibitions.

John Clay
263 New King's Rd., Fulham. SW6 4RB. Est. 1974. Open 10-6. SIZE: Medium. STOCK: Furniture, £50-£10,000; objets d'art and animal objects, silver and clocks, £10-£5,000; all 18th-19th C. Not Stocked: Pine. LOC: Close to Parsons Green, A3. PARK: Easy. TEL: 020 7731 5677; e-mail - johnclayantiques@btconnect.com SER: Restorations (furniture, objets d'art). VAT: Stan/Spec.

Decorative Antiques   LAPADA
284 Lillie Rd., Fulham. SW6 7PX. (Anthony Harley). Est. 1991. Open 10-5.30. SIZE: Medium. STOCK: French country furniture, 18th C; decorative items. PARK: Easy. TEL: 020 7610 2694; fax - 020 7386 0103. SER: Valuations; restorations. VAT: Spec.

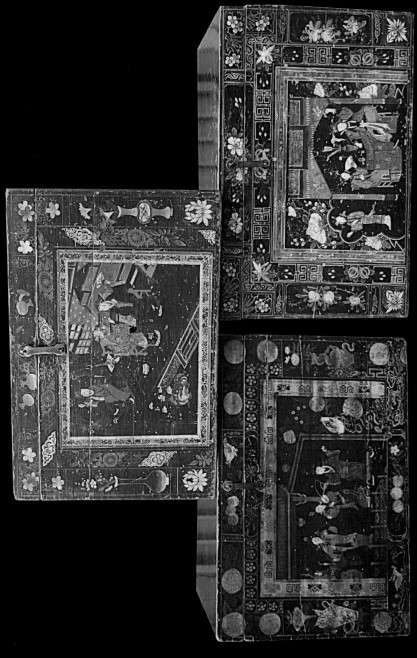

Charles Edwards
BADA
19A Rumbold Rd. SW6 2HX. Est. 1972. Open 9.30-6, Sat. 10-5. SIZE: Medium. *STOCK: Antique light fixtures; furniture, 18th-19th C; decorative items.* LOC: Just off King's Rd. PARK: Meters. TEL: 020 7736 7172; fax - 020 7731 7388; e-mail - charles@charlesedwards. com website - www.charlesedwards.com VAT: Stan/ Spec.

Hector Finch Lighting
90 Wandsworth Bridge Rd. SW6 2TF. (Mr and Mrs H. Finch). Est. 1988. Open 10-5.30. SIZE: Medium. *STOCK: Antiques and period lighting, early 20th C contemporary and reproduction.* PARK: Side streets or Pay and Display. TEL: 020 7731 8886; fax - 020 7731 7408; e-mail - hector@hectorfinch.com website - www.hectorfinch.com SER: Restorations (period lighting). VAT: Global.

Birdie Fortescue Antiques
LAPADA
Studio GJ, Cooper House, 2 Michael Rd. SW6 2AD. Open by appointment. SIZE: Large. *STOCK: Continental furniture, 18th-20th C, £500-£15,000.* LOC: Off King's Rd. TEL: 01206 337557; fax - same; mobile - 07778 263467; e-mail - bfortescueantiques@ btopenworld.com website - www.birdiefortescue.com FAIRS: Olympia (Feb., June and Nov): Decorative (Sept). VAT: Spec.

The French House (Antiques) Ltd
Unit A, Parsons Green Depot, Parsons Green Lane. SW6 4HH. (S.B. and M.J. Hazell). Est. 1995. Open 10-6. SIZE: Medium. *STOCK: Wooden beds, 18th-19th, £900-£2,500; gilt mirrors, 19th C, £300-£2,000; lighting, 19th-20th C, £200-£1,000; all French.* TEL: 020 7371 7573; website - www.thefrenchhouse.co.uk SER: Restorations; cabinet making; upholstery; French polishing; painting. VAT: Stan/Spec.

Judy Greenwood
657-659 Fulham Rd. SW6 5PY. Est. 1978. Open 10-5.30, Sat. 10-5. *STOCK: French decorative furniture including armoires, tables and chairs, commodes, lighting, mirrors, beds, quilts, all 1870-1970.* LOC: Fulham Broadway or Parsons Green underground stations. TEL: 020 7736 6037; fax - 020 7736 1941; e-mail - judygantiques@aol.com website - www.judy greenwoodantiques.co.uk

Robin Greer
434 Fulham Palace Rd. SW6 6HX. ABA. PBFA. Est. 1965. Open by appointment. *STOCK: Children's and illustrated books, original illustrations.* TEL: 020 7381 9113; fax - 020 7381 6499; e-mail - rarities@rarerobin. com SER: Catalogues issued.

Gregory, Bottley and Lloyd
13 Seagrave Rd. SW6 1RP. Est. 1858. Open 9.30-5. CL: Sat. SIZE: Medium. *STOCK: Mineral specimens, £1-£5,000; fossils, £5-£500.* LOC: Nearest underground station - West Brompton. PARK: Easy. TEL: 020 7381 5522; fax - 020 7381 5512. website - www.bottley.co.uk VAT: Stan.

Guinevere Antiques
574/580 King's Rd. SW6 2DY. Open 9.30-6, Sat. 10-5.30 (warehouse by appointment only). SIZE: Large + trade warehouse. *STOCK: Period decorative antiques and accessories.* TEL: 020 7736 2917; fax - 020 7736 8267; e-mail - sales@guinevere.co.uk website - www. guinevere.co.uk

Gutlin Clocks and Antiques
606 King's Rd. SW6 2DX. Est. 1990. Open 10-6. SIZE: Large - two floors. *STOCK: Longcase clocks, £2,000-£8,000; mantel clocks, £300-£6,000; furniture and lighting, £500-£3,000; all 18th-19th C.* LOC: 200 yards from beginning of New King's Rd. PARK: Maxwell Rd. TEL: 020 7384 2439; fax - same; home - 020 8740 6830; e-mail - mark@gutlin.com website - www.gutlin.com SER: Valuations; restorations (clocks and clock cases); buys at auction (clocks).

House of Mirrors
597 King's Rd. SW6 2EL. (G. Witek). Est. 1960. Open 10-6. *STOCK: Mirrors.* TEL: 020 7736 5885; fax - 020 7610 9188; e-mail - info@houseofmirrors.co.uk website - www.houseofmirrors.co.uk SER: Restorations.

HRW Antiques (London) Ltd   **LAPADA**
26 Sulivan Rd. SW6 3DT. Open 9-5. CL: Sat. SIZE: Large. *STOCK: 18th-19th C English and Continental furniture and decorative items.* LOC: Within easy reach of the King's Rd. and Chelsea Harbour. TEL: 020 7371 7995; fax - 020 7371 9522; e-mail - iain@hrw-antiques.com website - www.hrw-antiques.com

Indigo
275 New King's Rd., Parsons Green. SW6 4RD. (Richard Lightbown and Marion Bender). Est. 1983. Open 10-6. SIZE: Medium. *STOCK: Chinese, Indian, Japanese and Tibetan furniture and accessories, Chinese porcelain, from early 19th C, £10-£5,000.* LOC: Near Parsons Green underground. PARK: Nearby. TEL: 020 7384 3101; e-mail - antiques@indigo-uk.com website - www.indigo-uk.com

Christopher Jones Antiques
618-620 King's Rd. SW6 2DU. Open 10-5.30. *STOCK: Continental and British decorative objects and furniture, screens and mirrors, 18th-19th C, £500-£10,000.* TEL: 020 7731 4655; fax - 020 7371 8682; e-mail - florehouse @msn.com website - www.christopherjonesantiques. co.uk VAT: Spec.

King's Court Galleries
949/953 Fulham Rd. SW6 5HY. (Mrs J. Joel). ABA. Est. 1983. Open 10-5.30. *STOCK: Antique maps, engravings, decorative and sporting prints.* PARK: Easy. TEL: 020 7610 6939; e-mail - sales@kingscourtgalleries.co.uk website - www.kingscourtgalleries.co.uk SER: Framing (on site).

Graham Kirkland
271 Lillie Rd. Fulham. SW6 7LL. and Est. 2003. Open 10-5.30, Sat. 11-4. SIZE: Small + warehouse at Heathrow. *STOCK: Religious antiques including candlesticks, statuary, Gothic and carved church woodwork.* TEL: 020 7381 3195; fax - same; e-mail - graham@grahamkirkland.co.uk website - www. grahamkirkland.co.uk SER: Buys at auction (religious items). VAT: Stan.

L. and E. Kreckovic
559 King's Rd. SW6 2EB. Open 10-6. *STOCK: 18th-19th C furniture.* TEL: 020 7736 0753; fax - 020 7731 5904. SER: Restorations.

Lunn Antiques Ltd
86 New Kings Rd., Parsons Green. SW6 4LU. (Stephen and Juliet Lunn). Est. 1976. Open 10-6. *STOCK: Antique lace, antique and modern bed linen, nightdresses, christening robes, period clothing, antique textiles.* TEL: 020 7736 4638; fax - 020 7371 7113; e-mail - lunnantiques@aol.com website - www.lunnantiques.com SER: Laundry and restoration (antique linen and lace). VAT: Margin.

Mark Maynard Antiques
651 Fulham Rd. SW6 5PU. Est. 1977. Open 10-5, Sun. by appointment. SIZE: Medium. *STOCK: Decorative items, £25-£300.* LOC: Near Fulham Broadway

underground station. PARK: Easy. TEL: 020 7731 3533; home - 020 7373 4681. VAT: Stan/Spec.

Mora & Upham Antiques
584 King's Rd. SW6 2DX. (Matthew Upham). Est. 1996. Open 10-6. SIZE: Medium. *STOCK: Chandeliers, English and Continental furniture, decorative items, garden statuary.* LOC: Corner premises. PARK: Meters. TEL: 020 7731 4444; fax - 020 7736 0440; e-mail - mora.upham@talk21.com website - www.moraand upham.com SER: Valuations; restorations (lighting); design advice; chandelier hanging. VAT: Spec.

Nimmo & Spooner
277 Lillie Rd., Fulham. SW6 7LL. (Catherine Nimmo and Myra Spooner). Est. 1996. Open 10.30-5.30. SIZE: Medium. *STOCK: Objects and furniture including painted dressers and chests of drawers, tables, mirrors, 18th-20th C, to £3,500.* LOC: Between Fulham Broadway and Hammersmith. PARK: Nearby. TEL: 020 7385 2724; fax - same.

Old World Trading Co
565 King's Rd. SW6 2EB. (R.J. Campion). Est. 1970. Open 9.30-6. *STOCK: Fireplaces, chimney pieces and accessories, chandeliers, mirrors, furniture including decorative, works of art.* TEL: 020 7731 4708; fax - 020 7731 1291; e-mail - oldworld@btinternet.com

Ossowski   BADA
595 King's Rd. SW6 2EL. Est. 1960. Open 9.30-5.30. SIZE: Large. *STOCK: Furniture, 18th C; mirrors and wood carvings.* TEL: 020 7731 0334. SER: Valuations; restorations. FAIRS: IFAAD, New York (Oct). VAT: Spec.

Anthony Outred   BADA
SW6 6HF. (Anthony and Anne Outred). Est. 1974. By appointment only. *STOCK: Exceptional English and Continental furniture and works of art especially the unusual and amusing, £1,000-£100,000.* TEL: 020 7371 9863; fax - 020 7371 9869; mobile - 07767 848132; e-mail - antiques@outred.co.uk website - www.outred.co.uk SER: Sourcing and advice. FAIRS: Olympia. VAT: Stan/Spec.

M. Pauw Antiques
Cooper House, 2 Michael Rd. SW6 2AD. Est. 1981. SIZE: Medium. *STOCK: English and Continental leather chairs, 18th-19th C; decorative items, lighting fixtures, metal planters.* PARK: Easy. TEL: 020 7731 4022; fax - 020 7731 7356; e-mail - info@mpauw.com website - www.mpauw.com VAT: Stan.

Perez Antique Carpets Gallery
150 Wandsworth Bridge Rd., Fulham. SW6 2UH. (K. Dinari). Est. 1984. Open 10-6, Wed. 10-7.30. SIZE: Large. *STOCK: Carpets, 19th C, £400-£40,000; rugs, 18th-20th C, £300-£3,000; textiles, 19th C, £70-£1,500.* PARK: Easy. TEL: 020 7371 9619. SER: Valuations; restorations; buys at auction (Oriental and European carpets, rugs and textiles, tapestries). VAT: Stan/Spec.

The Pine Mine (Crewe-Read Antiques)
100 Wandsworth Bridge Rd., Fulham. SW6 2TF. (D. and Caspian Crewe-Read). Est. 1971. Open 9.45-5.45, Sat. till 4.30. SIZE: Large. *STOCK: Georgian and Victorian pine, Welsh dressers, farmhouse tables, chests of drawers, boxes and some architectural items.* LOC: From Sloane Sq., down King's Rd., into New King's Rd., left into Wandsworth Bridge Rd. PARK: Outside. TEL: 020 7736 1092. SER: Furniture made from old wood; stripping; export.

Daphne Rankin and Ian Conn   LAPADA
608 King's Rd. SW6 2DX. Est. 1979. Open 10.30-6. SIZE: Medium. *STOCK: Oriental porcelain including Chinese, Japanese, Imari, Cantonese, Satsuma, Nanking, Famille Rose, £500-£25,000; Dutch Delft; tortoiseshell tea caddies.* PARK: Maxwell Rd. adjacent to shop. TEL: 020 7384 1847; fax - same; mobile - 07774 487713; e-mail - info@rankin-conn-chinatrade.com website - www.rankin-conn-chinatrade.com SER: Valuations; buys at auction (as stock). FAIRS: Olympia (June and Nov). VAT: Stan/Spec.

Richardson and Kailas Icons   BADA
65 Rivermead Court, Ranelagh Gardens. SW6 3RY. (C. Richardson). Open by appointment. *STOCK: Icons and frescoes.* TEL: 020 7371 0491; e-mail - chris.richardson1@virgin.net SER: Consultancy; valuations; restorations.

Rogers & Co   LAPADA
604 Fulham Rd. SW6 5RP. (M. and C. Rogers). Est. 1971. Open 10-6. SIZE: Large. *STOCK: Furniture, 18th-19th C, £100-£3,000; upholstery.* LOC: Near Fulham library, Parsons Green Lane. PARK: Side streets. TEL: 020 7731 8504; fax - 020 7610 6040. SER: Valuations. VAT: Stan/Spec.

Simon Horn Furniture Ltd
117-121 Wandsworth Bridge Rd. SW6 2TP. BIDDA. BCFA. Est. 1982. Open 9.30-5.30, Sun. by appointment. SIZE: Large. *STOCK: Wooden classically styled bedframes £1,500-£6,500; bedside tables £250-£1,100; all 1790-1910 or recent larger copies; superior bedding.* LOC: South from New King's Rd., towards river down Wandsworth Bridge Rd., premises on left at first zebra crossing. PARK: Easy. TEL: 020 7731 1279; fax - 020 7736 3522; e-mail - info@simonhorn.com website - www.simonhorn.com SER: Special orders undertaken. VAT: Stan.

Soo San
598A King's Rd. SW6 2DX. Est. 1996. Open 10-6. SIZE: Large. *STOCK: Chinese furniture and accessories - cabinets, coffee tables, chairs, consol tables, desks, stools, beds, leather trunks, wedding baskets, wooden food containers, birdcages, porcelain, 18th-19th C; lacquer ware and Burmese buddhas; all £50-£18,000.* TEL: 020 7731 2063; fax - 020 7731 1566; e-mail - enquiries@ soosan.co.uk website - www.soosan.co.uk SER: Valuations; restorations (re-lacquering, gilding and wood).

Trowbridge Gallery   LAPADA
555 King's Rd. SW6 2EB. (M. Trowbridge). Est. 1980. Open 9.30-6, Sat. 10-5.30. SIZE: Large. *STOCK: Decorative prints, 17th-19th C, £50-£10,000.* PARK: Easy. TEL: 020 7371 8733; e-mail - martin@trowbridge. co.uk website - www.trowbridgegallery.com SER: Buys at auction (antiquarian books and prints); hand-made frames; decorative mounting. VAT: Stan.

York Gallery Ltd — LAPADA
569 King's Rd. SW6 2EB. (Jane and Gerd Beyer). Est. 1984. Open 10.30-5.30. SIZE: Medium. STOCK: Antique prints. TEL: 020 7736 2260; fax - same; e-mail - prints@yorkgallery.co.uk website - www.yorkgallery.co.uk SER: Bespoke framing. VAT: Stan.

SW7

The Gloucester Road Bookshop
123 Gloucester Rd., South Kensington. SW7 4TE. (Nicholas Dennys). Est. 1983. Open 9.30-10.30 pm, Sat. and Sun. 10.30-6.30. SIZE: Medium. STOCK: Secondhand hardback and paperback books, all genres, mainly 19th-20th C, £1-£50; modern first editions, mainly 20th C, £5-£10,000; rare books, 17th-20th C, £70-£5,000. LOC: 150 yards Gloucester Road underground station. Come out of station, cross road and turn right. PARK: Loading; easy weekends. Meters nearby. TEL: 020 7370 3503; fax - 020 7373 0610. SER: Valuations; book search.

M.P. Levene Ltd — BADA
5 Thurloe Place. SW7 2RR. Est. 1889. Open 9.30-6. CL: Sat. pm. STOCK: English and Irish silver, old Sheffield plate, scale silver models and cufflinks, antique to 20th C. LOC: Few mins. past Harrods near South Kensington underground station. PARK: Easy. TEL: 020 7589 3755; fax - 020 7589 9908; e-mail - silver@mplevene.co.uk website - www.mplevene.co.uk SER: Valuations. VAT: Stan/Spec.

A. & H. Page (Est. 1840)
66 Gloucester Rd. SW7 4QT. NAG. Open 9-5.45, Sat. 10-2. STOCK: Silver, jewellery, watches. TEL: 020 7584 7349. SER: Valuations; repairs; silversmith; goldsmith.

Polonaise Gallery — BADA
35 Thurloe Place. SW7 2HJ. (W. Grodzinski). CINOA. Est. 1945. Open 9-4, Sat. by appointment. SIZE: Medium. STOCK: Antique Oriental and European carpets and textiles; Islamic and Indian art. TEL: 020 7689 8489; e-mail - polonaise@btconnect.com SER: Valuations; restorations; buys at auction (as stock). VAT: Spec.

The Taylor Gallery Ltd
1 Bolney Gate. SW7 1QW. (Jeremy Taylor). Est. 1986. Open by appointment. STOCK: Irish, British, China Trade and marine paintings, 19th-20th C. TEL: 020 7581 0253; fax - 020 7589 4495; e-mail - jeremy@taylor-gallery-london.com website - www.taylor-gallery-london.com FAIRS: Olympia (June); Palm Beach (Feb); Hong Kong (Oct).

The Wyllie Gallery
44 Elvaston Place. SW7 5NP. (J.G. Wyllie). Est. 1980. Open by appointment. STOCK: 19th-20th C marine paintings and etchings, especially works by the Wyllie family. LOC: Short walk from Gloucester Rd. underground. PARK: Easy. TEL: 020 7584 6024; e-mail - jgwyllie@hotmail.com

SW8

Davies Antiques — LAPADA
c/o Cadogan Tate, 6-12 Ponton Rd. SW8 5BA. (H.Q.V. Davies). Est. 1976. Open by appointment only. STOCK: Continental porcelain especially Meissen, 1710-1930. PARK: Own. TEL: 020 8947 1902; fax - same; mobile - 07753 739689; e-mail - hugh.davies@btconnect.com website - www.antique-meissen.com

The French House (Antiques) Ltd
125 Queenstown Rd. SW8 3PH. (S.B. and M.J. Hazell). Est. 1995. Open 10-6. SIZE: Medium. STOCK: Wooden beds, 18th-19th, £900-£2,500; gilt mirrors, 19th C, £300-£2,000; lighting, 19th-20th C, £200-£1,000; all French. LOC: Short drive from Victoria station. PARK: Sidestreets. TEL: 020 7978 2228; fax - 020 7978 2340; website - www.thefrenchhouse.co.uk SER: Restorations; cabinet making; upholstery; French polishing; painting. VAT: Stan/Spec.

Fay Lucas Artmetal — BADA
Christies Fine Art Security, 42 Ponton Rd. SW8 5BA. Est. 1977. Open by appointment. STOCK: Fine signed silver holloware, 20th C, £200-£50,000; signed furniture, 20th C, £5,000-£50,000; antique military and sporting jewellery, £100-£3,000. TEL: 020 7371 4404; fax - same; mobile - 07767 660550; e-mail - info@faylucas.com SER: Valuations; restorations; buys at auction. FAIRS: Olympia (Feb., June and Nov). VAT: Stan/Spec.

Paul Orssich
2 St. Stephen's Terrace, South Lambeth. SW8 1DH. Open by appointment. STOCK: Old, rare and out of print books on Spain and Hispanic studies; old maps of all parts of the world, from £20. LOC: Near Stockwell underground. PARK: Meters. TEL: 020 7787 0030; fax - 020 7735 9612; e-mail - paulo@orssich.com website - www.orssich.com. FAIRS: Madrid Book (Nov).

SW9

Rodney Franklin Antiques
Est. 1968. Open by appointment. STOCK: French and English mirrors and beds, furniture, lighting, architectural and garden items. TEL: 020 7274 0729. VAT: Stan/Spec.

SW10

Alasdair Brown
Unit 150, 405 King's Rd. SW10 0BB. Est. 1985. Open by appointment. STOCK: Furniture, to £15,000; decorative items, to £10,000; upholstery, lighting and the unusual. LOC: Chelsea. TEL: 020 7736 3664; fax - same; mobile - 07836 672857; e-mail - ab@ajcb.demon.co.uk SER: Valuations. FAIRS: Olympia (June).

Jonathan Clark & Co
18 Park Walk, Chelsea. SW10 0AQ. SLAD. Open 10-6.30, Sat. by appointment. STOCK: Modern British paintings and sculpture. TEL: 020 7351 3555; fax - 020 7823 3187; e-mail - galina@jonathanclarkfineart.com website - www.jc-art.com FAIRS: Islington; Art London; Commonwealth Institute; Grosvenor House. VAT: Margin

Carlton Davidson Antiques
507 King's Rd.,Chelsea. SW10 0TX. Est. 1981. Open

10-6. *STOCK: Lamps, chandeliers, mirrors and decorative items, £500-£5,000.* TEL: 020 7795 0905.

The Furniture Cave
533 King's Rd. SW10 0TZ. Est. 1967. Open 10-6, Sun. 11-5. SIZE: Large. *STOCK: See dealers listed below.* LOC: Corner of Lots Rd. PARK: Meters. TEL: 020 7352 4229/5478. SER: Shipping; forwarding. VAT: Stan/Spec.

Paul Andrews Antiques
Basement. *English and Continental decorative furniture; sculpture, Old Master paintings, prints and drawings.* TEL: 020 7352 4584; fax - 020 7351 7815.

Browns Antique Furniture
First Floor. *Library and dining furniture and decorative objects, from early 18th C.* TEL: 020 7352 2046.

Classic Furniture
First Floor. *Library furniture, paintings, prints and some maps, decorative objects; antique leather books, bindings, literature runs and individual volumes.* TEL: 020 7376 7653.

Stuart Duggan
First Floor. *Georgian and Victorian furniture especially 19th-20th C pianos.* TEL: 020 7352 2046; fax - 020 7352 3654.

Robert Grothier
TEL: 020 7352 2045; fax - 020 7352 6803.

Harpur Dearden
First Floor. TEL: 020 7352 3111; fax - 020 7351 5833.

Kenneth Harvey Antiques   LAPADA
Ground Floor. *Decorative furniture, mirrors, chandeliers, light fittings.* TEL: 020 7352 3775; fax - 020 7352 3759.

Simon Hatchwell Antiques
Ground Floor. Est. 1961. *English and Continental decorative furniture and objets d'art.* TEL: 020 7351 2344; fax - 020 7351 3520.

Heritage and Heritage Ltd
First Floor. *Furniture, from William IV to modern Danish.* TEL: 020 7352 6116; fax - 020 7352 3654; e-mail - info@ heritageandheritage.co.uk website - www.heritageand heritage.co.uk SER: Restorations.

Hill Farm Antiques
General antiques including large tables. TEL: 020 7352 2046; fax - 020 7352 3654.

David Loveday
First Floor. *English and Georgian large furniture.* TEL: 020 7352 1100; fax - 020 7351 5833.

John Nicholas Antiques
TEL: 020 7352 2046; fax - 020 7352 3654.

Phoenix Trading Company
Furniture including Indian, porcelain, bronzes. TEL: 020 7351 6543; fax - 020 7352 9803.

Christopher Preston Antiques   LAPADA
Ground Floor. *Early 19th C and Regency furniture.* TEL: 020 7352 8587; fax - 020 7376 3627.

Anthony Redmile
Basement. *Marble resin neo-classical Grand Tour objects.* TEL: 020 7351 3813; fax - 020 7352 8131.

Hollywood Road Gallery
12 Hollywood Rd. SW10 9HY. (P. and C. Kennaugh). Est. 1981. Open 10.30-7.00, Sat. 10-4. *STOCK: Oils, watercolours, 20th C and contemporary £300-£3,000.* LOC: Chelsea. TEL: 020 7351 1973. SER: Framing; restorations. FAIRS: Affordable Art; Decorative Art, Chelsea. VAT: Spec.

Hünersdorff Rare Books Ltd
P.O. Box 582. SW10 9RU. (J.R. von Hünersdorff). ABA. Est. 1969. Open by appointment. *STOCK: Continental books in rare editions, early printing, science and medicine, military, Latin America, natural history.* LOC: Chelsea. TEL: 020 7373 3899; fax - 020 7370 1244; e-mail - huner.rarebooks@dial.pipex.com website - www.abebooks.com/home/hunersdorff FAIRS: Olympia (June).

Lucy Johnson   BADA LAPADA
10 Billing Place. SW10 9UW. CINOA. Est. 1982. Open by appointment. STOCK: Early English and Continental furniture and works of art. PARK: Easy. TEL: 020 7352 0114; mobile - 07974 149912; e-mail - lucy-johnson@lucy-johnson.com SER: Restorations. FAIRS: Olympia. VAT: Margin.

Thomas Kerr Antiques Ltd
at L'Encoignure, 517 King's Rd. SW10 0TX. Est. 1977. Open 10-6. SIZE: Large. *STOCK: French and Italian country furniture, paintings, mirrors and decorative items.* TEL: 020 7351 6465; fax - 020 7351 4744. VAT: Stan/Spec.

Lane Fine Art Ltd
8 Drayton Gardens. SW10 9SA. (C. Foley). Est. 1958. Open by appointment. *STOCK: Oil paintings, 1500-1850, principally English, major works by the main artists of the period, £10,000-£1million+.* TEL: 020 7373 3130; fax - 020 7373 2277; e-mail - cf@ lanefineart.co.uk website - www.lanefineart.com SER: Valuations. VAT: Stan/Spec.

Langford's Marine Antiques   BADA LAPADA
The Plaza, 535 King's Rd. SW10 0SZ. (L.L. Langford). Est. 1941. STOCK: Ships models, marine instruments, globes, steam engine models. TEL: 020 7351 4881; fax - 020 7352 0763; e-mail - langford @dircon.co.uk website - www.langfords.co.uk VAT: Stan/Spec.

Stephen Long
348 Fulham Rd. SW10 9UH. Est. 1966. Open 9.30-1 and 2.15-5, Sat. pm. and Sun. by appointment. SIZE: Small. *STOCK: English pottery, 18th-19th C, to £400; English painted furniture, 18th to early 19th C; toys and games, household and kitchen items, chintz, materials and patchwork, to £1,000.* LOC: From South Kensington along road on right between Ifield Rd. and Billing Rd. PARK: Easy. TEL: 020 7352 8226. VAT: Spec.

McVeigh & Charpentier   LAPADA
498 King's Rd. SW10 0LE. (Maggie Charpentier). Est. 1979. Open 10.30-5, weekends by appointment only. SIZE: Medium. *STOCK: Continental furniture, mirrors, garden ironwork and stone, 17th-19th C.* LOC: Two blocks down from Earls Court. PARK: In cul de sac adjacent. TEL: 020 7351 1442; home - 020 7937 6459; mobile - 07801 480167. FAIRS: Olympia (June); Harvey (Sept., Jan. and March). VAT: Spec.

McWhirter
22 Park Walk, Chelsea. SW10 0AQ. (James McWhirter). Est. 1988. Open 9.30-5.30 or by appointment. SIZE: Medium. *STOCK: Works of art, objects, unusual furniture.* LOC: Near Fulham Road Cinema. PARK: Meters. TEL: 020 7351 5399; fax - 020 7352 9821. SER: Consultancy (art and design). VAT: Spec.

Offer Waterman and Co. Fine Art
11 Langton St. SW10 0JL. SLAD. CINOA. Est. 1996. Open 10-6.30, Sat. 11-4. SIZE: 2 floors. *STOCK: Modern British and contemporary art.* LOC: Off Kings Rd. PARK: Easy. TEL: 020 7351 0068; fax - 020 7351 2269; e-mail - info@waterman.co.uk website - www.waterman.co.uk SER: Valuations; restorations (as stock); framing; buys at auction (Modern British paintings). FAIRS: Art 2004; 20th/21st C Art, Olympia; Grosvenor House. VAT: Stan/Spec.

Opium
414 King's Rd., Chelsea. SW10 0LJ. (Tracy Kitching). Est. 1999. Open 10-6.30, Sun. 12-5. SIZE: Large. *STOCK: Indian - mainly from Rajasthan, Gujarat and Kerala - furniture including dowry chests and day beds, marble and stone jalis, stone and teak columns, mainly 18th to early 20th C, to 2,500.* PARK: Pay & Display nearby. TEL: 020 7795 0700; fax - 020 7795 0800; e-mail - shop@opium.force9.co.uk website - www.opiumshop.co.uk

Orientation   LAPADA
2 Park Walk. SW10 0AD. (Evelyne Soler). Est. 1990. Open 10-5.30, Sat. by appointment. SIZE: Medium. *STOCK: Continental furniture, 18th-19th C; Chinese porcelain, ceramics, works of art, China trade items, to £20,000.* LOC: Off Fulham Rd. TEL: 020 7351 0234; fax - 020 7351 7535. FAIRS: Olympia. VAT: Spec.

Park Walk Gallery   BADA
20 Park Walk, Chelsea. SW10 0AQ. (J. Cooper). SLAD. Est. 1988. Open 10-6.30, Sat. 11-4. SIZE: Medium. *STOCK: Paintings, £250-£40,000; watercolours, £250-£30,000; drawings, £200-£15,000; all contemporary.* LOC: Off Fulham Rd. PARK: Easy. TEL: 020 7351 0410; fax - same; website - www.jonathancooper.co.uk SER: Valuations; restorations. FAIRS: Olympia; Art London; Art 2004. VAT: Spec.

H.W. Poulter and Son
279 Fulham Rd. SW10 9PZ. Est. 1946. Open 9.30-5. CL: Sat. pm. SIZE: Large. *STOCK: English and French marble chimney pieces, grates, fenders, fire-irons, brass, chandeliers.* PARK: Meters. TEL: 020 7352 7268. SER: Restorations (marble work). VAT: Stan/Spec.

John Thornton
455 Fulham Rd. SW10 9UZ. Open 10-5.30. *STOCK: Antiquarian books especially theology.* TEL: 020 7352 8810.

Toynbee-Clarke Interiors Ltd
18 Cresswell Place. SW10 9RB. (D. Toynbee-Clarke). Est. 1953. Open by appointment. SIZE: Medium. *STOCK: Decorative English and Continental furniture and objects, 17th-18th C; Chinese hand painted wallpapers, 18th C; French scenic wallpapers, early 19th C; Chinese and Japanese paintings and screens,*

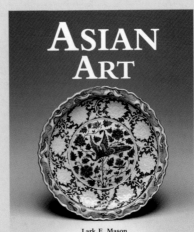

Lark E. Mason

Lark E. Mason offers a clear and concise guide to understanding the fine and decorative arts of Asia including the arts of the Islamic world. He addresses this complex subject in an easy to follow format beginning with an overview of the tumultuous history of the continent, leading into chapters on ceramics, metalwork, the arts of the craftsman, furniture and lacquer, textiles, prints and paintings. Each chapter includes a summary of the minor and major art forms with expert advice for judging quality and identifying fakes and over-restored objects. A valuable dictionary of terms and tables with reign dates and marks is included.

Specifications: 336pp., 336 col. illus., 11 x 9in./280 x 233mm. **£35.00 (hardback)**

17th-19th C. PARK: Meters. TEL: 020 7373 6889. SER: Buys at auction. VAT: Stan/Spec.

SW11

Braemar Antiques
113 Northcote Rd., Battersea. SW11 6PW. (Maria Elisabeth Ramos-de-Deus and Elizabeth Henderson). Est. 1995. SIZE: Small. *STOCK: Painted furniture including armoires, chests of drawers, mirrors and lamps; quilts, eiderdowns, china and glass.* LOC: Near Clapham junction. PARK: Easy. TEL: 020 7924 5628; e-mail - ramos-de-deus@msn.com FAIRS: Brocante, Chelsea.

Eccles Road Antiques
60 Eccles Rd., Battersea. SW11 1LX. (H. Rix). Open 10-5. *STOCK: General antiques, pine and painted furniture and smalls.* LOC: Off Clapham Common. TEL: 020 7228 1638.

Christopher Edwards
36 Roseneath Rd. SW11 6AH. Est. 1982. By appointment only. SIZE: Medium. *STOCK: Architecturally inspired furniture, unusual works of art, 19th C, £100-£10,000.* TEL: 020 7223 9962; fax - same; mobile - 07831 707043. SER: Valuations; buys at auction. VAT: Stan/Spec.

Garland Antiques

74 Chatham Rd., Battersea. SW11 6HG. (Garland Beech). Open 10-6, Sun. 12-5. CL: Mon. SIZE: Small. *STOCK: English and Continental furniture, 19th C; decorative objects, 18th-19th C.* PARK: Easy. TEL: 020 7924 4284.

Gideon Hatch Rugs

1 Port House, Plantation Wharf, Battersea. SW11 3TY. Est. 1985. Open by appointment. SIZE: Small. *STOCK: Oriental and European rugs, 19th to early 20th C, £500-£25,000.* LOC: Off York Rd., behind Homebase. PARK: Easy. TEL: 020 7223 3996; fax - 020 7223 3997; e-mail - info@gideonhatch.co.uk website - www.gideonhatch. co.uk SER: Valuations; restorations; cleaning; buys at auction (rare rugs). FAIRS: Olympia; Battersea. VAT: Stan/Spec.

Northcote Road Antiques Market

155A Northcote Rd., Battersea. SW11 6QB. Est. 1986. Open 10-6, Sun. 12-5. SIZE: 30 dealers. *STOCK: Victoriana and Art Deco collectables, silver, glass, studio pottery, furniture, lighting, jewellery, prints, mirrors, flatware.* TEL: 020 7228 6850; website - www.spectrumsoft.net/nam

Overmantels

66 Battersea Bridge Rd. SW11 3AG. (Seth Taylor). BCFA. Est. 1980. Open 9.30-5.30. SIZE: Medium. *STOCK: English giltwood mirrors, £400-£3,000; French giltwood mirrors, £700-£3,000; both 18th-19th C.* LOC: 200m south of Battersea Bridge. PARK: Outside shop. TEL: 020 7223 8151; fax - 020 7924 2283. SER: Valuations; restorations (gesso work and gilding). VAT: Stan/Spec.

Pairs Antiques Ltd

C14 The Imperial Laundry, 71-73 Warriner Gardens, Battersea. SW11 4XW. (Iain M. Brunt). Est. 1994. Open by appointment. SIZE: Large. *STOCK: Pairs only - 18th-19th C furniture, decorative objects and paintings, £500-£20,000.* TEL: 020 7622 6446; fax - 020 7622 3663; mobile - 07798 684694; e-mail - iain@ pairsantiques.co.uk; mail@iainb.com website - www. pairsantiques.co.uk; www.antiques.co.uk; www.polo antiques.com; www.metrodog.co.uk SER: Valuations; restorations; buys at auction. VAT: Stan/Spec.

Regent House Gallery

223 St John's Hill. SW11 1TH. (Nick & Jayne Underwood Thompson). Est. 1988. Open 10-6, Thurs. 10-7.30. CL: Mon. SIZE: Small. *STOCK: Watercolours and paintings, 19th-20th C, £50-£1,000; prints, drawings, cartoons, 18th-20th C, £10-£400; small antiques, books, 19th to early 20th C, £2-£200.* LOC: Top of St John's Hill, mid-way between Clapham Junction and Wandsworth Town. PARK: Pay and display (free Sat. and after 4.30 pm). TEL: 020 7228 9344; home and fax - 020 7228 9344; e-mail - nick@regenthouse gallery.com website - www.regenthousegallery.com SER: Framing.

Crispian Riley-Smith

P O Box 46890. SW11 1ZL. Est. 1997. By appointment only. SIZE: Medium. *STOCK: Old Master drawings, 1500-1900, £500-£100,000.* TEL: Mobile - 07771 552509; e-mail - crispian@riley-smith.com website - www.riley-smith.com SER: Valuations. FAIRS: Master Drawings in London.

The Woodpigeon

71 Webbs Rd. SW11 6SD. (Lucy Kallin). Est. 1995. Open Tues.-Sat. 10.30-5.30. SIZE: Small. *STOCK: Country furniture, mainly French - painted armoires, chests, wardrobes and beds; small decorative items and country antiques, mainly mid to late 19th C, £5-£1,500.* LOC: Parallel with Northcote Rd. PARK: Side roads. TEL: 020 7223 8668; website - www.woodpigeon.co.uk SER: Furniture painting and re-upholstery. VAT: Spec.

Robert Young Antiques   BADA

68 Battersea Bridge Rd. SW11 3AG. (Robert and Josyane Young). Est. 1974. Open 10-6, Sat. 10-5. SIZE: Medium. *STOCK: Fine country furniture, 17th-18th C, £500-£50,000; English and European treen and objects of folk art, £100-£25,000; English and European provincial pottery and metalwork, £100-£10,000.* LOC: Turn off King's Rd. or Chelsea Embankment into Beaufort St., cross over Battersea Bridge Rd., 9th shop on right. PARK: Opposite in side street, and in front of shop 10-4. TEL: 020 7228 7847; fax - 020 7585 0489; e-mail - office@ robertyoungantiques.com SER: Valuations; buys at auction (treen and country furniture). FAIRS: Olympia; Winter (New York); Fall (San Francisco). VAT: Stan/Spec.

SW12

Twentieth Century

(M. Taylor). Est. 1986. Open by appointment. *STOCK: Art Deco, Art Nouveau, Arts and Crafts, decorative arts items, £50-£500.* PARK: Easy. TEL: 020 8675 6351; fax - same; e-mail - martin@twentiethcentury.info FAIRS: Battersea Art Deco; Loughborough Art Deco; Manchester; Birmingham. VAT: Stan.

SW13

Christine Bridge   BADA LAPADA

78 Castelnau, Barnes. SW13 9EX. CINOA. Est. 1972. Open anytime by appointment. SIZE: Medium. *STOCK: Glass - 18th C collectors and 19th C coloured, engraved and decorative, £50-£15,000; small decorative items - papier mâché, bronzes, needlework, ceramics.* LOC: Main road from Hammersmith Bridge, 5 mins. from Olympia. PARK: Easy. TEL: 020 8741 5501; fax - 020 8255 0172; mobile - 07831 126668; e-mail - christine@bridge-antiques.com website - www. bridge-antiques.com and www.antiqueglass.co.uk SER: Valuations; restorations (glass - cutting, polishing, declouding); buys at auction; shipping. FAIRS: Olympia (June and Nov); BADA; Brussels; Tokyo; Melbourne; Sydney; Singapore; Santa Monica; Cleveland; Chicago. VAT: Stan/Spec.

Simon Coleman Antiques

40 White Hart Lane, Barnes. SW13 0PZ. Est. 1974. Open 9.30-6. SIZE: Large. *STOCK: 18th-19th C farm tables.* PARK: Easy. TEL: 020 8878 5037; e-mail - colemansimon@aol.com VAT: Stan/Spec.

Kate Dyson

THE DINING ROOM SHOP

62-64 White Hart Lane • London SW13 0PZ

Tel: 020-8878 1020   Fax: 020-8876 2367   Website: www.thediningroomshop.co.uk

Antique tables and sets of chairs, glass, china, cutlery, table linen, bespoke service – all for the dining room

---

The Dining Room Shop
62/64 White Hart Lane, Barnes. SW13 0PZ. (K. Dyson). Est. 1985. Open 10-5.30, Sun. by appointment. SIZE: Medium. *STOCK: Formal and country dining room furniture, 18th-19th C; glasses, china, pottery, cutlery, damask and lace table linen, 19th C; associated small and decorative items.* LOC: Near Barnes rail bridge, turning opposite White Hart public house. PARK: Easy. TEL: 020 8878 1020; fax - 020 8876 2367; e-mail - enquiries@thediningroomshop.co.uk website - www.thediningroomshop.co.uk SER: Valuations; restorations; bespoke furniture; finder; interior decorating. VAT: Stan/Spec.

Joy McDonald Antiques
50 Station Rd., Barnes. SW13 0LP. Resident. Est. 1966. Open 10.30-5.30, prior telephone call advisable. CL: Mon. SIZE: Small. *STOCK: 19th-21st C mirrors, chandeliers and lighting; decorative items and upholstered chairs.* TEL: 020 8876 6184.

New Grafton Gallery
49 Church Rd., Barnes. SW13 9HH. (Claudia Wolfers). Est. 1968. Open Tues.-Sat. 10-6. SIZE: Medium. *STOCK: Modern British and contemporary paintings, drawings and sculpture, from £150.* LOC: Off Castelnau which runs from Hammersmith Bridge. PARK: Easy. TEL: 020 8748 8850; fax - 020 8748 9818; e-mail - art@newgrafton.com website - www.newgrafton.com SER: Valuations; restorations. VAT: Stan/Spec.

John Spink   BADA
9 Richard Burbidge Mansions, 1 Brasenose Drive,

Barnes. SW13 8RB. Est. 1972. Open by appointment. *STOCK: Fine English watercolours and selected oils, 1720-1920.* TEL: **020 8741 6152; e-mail - john@ johnspink.com FAIRS: World of Watercolours; Olympia (Summer and Winter).**

Tobias and The Angel
68 White Hart Lane, Barnes. SW13 0PZ. (A. Hughes). Est. 1985. Open 10-6. SIZE: Large. *STOCK: Quilts, textiles, furniture, country and painted beds, decorative objects, from 1800.* LOC: Parallel to Barnes High St. PARK: Easy. TEL: 020 8878 8902; home - same; e-mail - enquiries@tobiasandtheangel.com website - www.tobiasandtheangel.com SER: Interior design; bespoke furniture. VAT: Stan/Spec.

SW14

Mary Cooke Antiques Ltd   BADA
12 The Old Power Station, 121 Mortlake High St. SW14 8SN. Open by appointment. *STOCK: Silver.* TEL: 020 8876 5777; fax - 020 8876 1652; mobile - 07836 521103; e-mail - silver@marycooke.co.uk SER: Valuations; restorations. FAIRS: Chelsea (Autumn); BADA; Olympia; Harrogate; NEC. VAT: Stan/Spec.

Paul Foster's Bookshop
119 Sheen Lane, East Sheen. SW14 8AE. ABA. PBFA. Est. 1983. Open Wed.-Sat. 10.30-6. SIZE: Medium. *STOCK: Books - antiquarian, 17th-19th C, £100-£1,000; out of print, 19th-20th C, £1-£500; general, 50p-£100.* LOC: 20 yards from South Circular. PARK: Easy. TEL: 020 8876 7424; fax - same.

SW15

The Clock Clinic Ltd   BADA LAPADA
85 Lower Richmond Rd., Putney. SW15 1EU. (R.S. Pedler). FBHI. Est. 1971. Open 9-6, Sat. 9-1. CL: Mon. *STOCK: Clocks and barometers.* PARK: Meters. TEL: 020 8788 1407; fax - 020 8780 2838; e-mail - clockclinic@btconnect.com website - www. clockclinic.co.uk SER: Valuations; restorations (as stock); buys at auction. FAIRS: Olympia (June and Nov). VAT: Stan/Spec.

Hanshan Tang Books
Unit 3 Ashburton Centre, 276 Cortis Rd. SW15 3AY. (John Constable, John Cayley and Myrna Chua). ABA. Open by appointment. *STOCK: Secondhand, antiquarian and new books and periodicals on Chinese, Japanese, Korean and Central Asian art and culture.* TEL: 020 8788 4464; fax - 020 8780 1565; e-mail - hst@hanshan.com website - www.hanshan.com/ SER: Regular and special catalogues; wants lists welcome.

SW16

H.C. Baxter and Sons   BADA LAPADA
40 Drewstead Rd. SW16 1AB. (T.J., J. and G.J. Baxter and T.J. Hunter). Est. 1928. Open Wed. and Thurs. 8.30-5.15 or by appointment. SIZE: Medium. *STOCK: English furniture, 1730-1830, £1,000-£35,000.* LOC: Near Streatham Hill station. PARK: Easy. TEL: 020 8769 5869/5969; fax - 020 8769 0898; e-mail - partnershcbaxter@tiscali.co.uk website - www.hcbaxter.co.uk FAIRS: Grosvenor House; BADA; Olympia (Nov). VAT: Spec.

A. and J. Fowle
542 Streatham High Rd. SW16 3QF. Est. 1962. Open 9.30-7. SIZE: Large. *STOCK: General antiques, Victorian and Edwardian furniture.* LOC: A23 towards Brighton from London. PARK: Easy. TEL: 020 8764 2896; mobile - 07968 058790. FAIRS: Ardingly; Newark.

SW17

Ash Rare Books
43 Huron Rd. SW17 8RE. (L. Worms). Est. 1946. Open by appointment only. SIZE: Small. *STOCK: Books, 1800-2000, £20-£2,500; prints, 1750-1900, £20-£500.* TEL: 020 8672 2263; e-mail - books@ashrare.com website - www.ashrare.com SER: Buys at auction (books and maps). VAT: Stan.

Ted Few
97 Drakefield Rd. SW17 8RS. Resident. Est. 1975. Open by appointment. SIZE: Medium. *STOCK: Paintings and sculpture, 1700-1940, £500-£5,000.* LOC: 5 mins. walk from Tooting Bec underground station. TEL: 020 8767 2314. SER: Valuations; buys at auction. FAIRS: Olympia. VAT: Spec.

Roger Lascelles
Wimbledon Stadium Business Centre, Riverside Rd. SW17 0BA. Est. 1978. Open Mon.-Fri. 10-5. SIZE: Medium. *STOCK: Longcase painted dial clocks, from £1,500; wall, retro and modern clocks, decorative antiques.* LOC: Warehouse on industrial estate off Garratt Lane.PARK: On premises. TEL: 020 8879 6011; fax - 020 8879 1818; e-mail - info@rogerlascelles.com website - www.rogerlascelles.com SER: Buys at auction.

SW18

Earlsfield Bookshop
513 Garratt Lane, Wandsworth. SW18 4SW. (Charles Dixon). Est. 1985. Open 4-6, Fri. 11-6, Sat. 10-5. SIZE: Small. *STOCK: Books, £1-£50.* LOC: Next to Earlsfield station. PARK: Limited. TEL: 020 8946 3744.

Just a Second
284 Merton Rd., Wandsworth. SW18 5JN. (James Ferguson). Est. 1980. Open 9.30-5.30. CL: Mon. SIZE: Medium. *STOCK: Victorian, Edwardian, pre-1920s and reproduction furniture and bric-a-brac.* LOC: 5 mins. from Southfields underground station. PARK: Easy. TEL: 020 8874 2520. SER: Valuations; restorations.

Thornhill Galleries
No. 319 Osiers Rd. SW18 1NL. (Graham and Anthony Wakefield). Est. 1880. Open 9-5.15, Sat. 10-12 by appointment. SIZE: Large. *STOCK: English and French period panelling, chimneypieces in wood, marble and stone; architectural items, wood carvings, 17th-19th C firegrates and fenders, fireplace accessories and iron interiors.* LOC: Off Putney Bridge Rd. PARK: Easy. TEL: 020 8874 2101/5669; fax - 020 8877 0313; e-mail - sales@thornhillgalleries.co.uk website - www.thornhillgalleries.co.uk SER: Valuations; restorations (architectural items); buys at auction (architectural items). VAT: Stan/Spec.

Mr Wandle's Workshop Ltd
202 Garratt Lane, Wandsworth. SW18 4ED. (S. Zoil). Open 9-5.30. *STOCK: Victorian and Edwardian fireplaces and surrounds especially cast iron.* TEL: 020 8870 5873. SER: Shot-blasting.

SW19

Corfield Potashnick   LAPADA
39 Church Rd., Wimbledon Village. SW19 5DQ. (Jonathan Corfield Fry and Simon Potashnick). Est. 1997. Open Thurs., Fri. and Sat. 10-6 or by appointment. *STOCK: Fine antique furniture.* TEL: 020 8944 9022. SER: Restorations; valuations. FAIRS: Harrogate (Spring).

The David Curzon Gallery
35 Church Rd., Wimbledon Village. SW19 5DQ. Est. 1985. Open 10-6. CL: Mon. and Tues. SIZE: Medium. *STOCK: Paintings and watercolours, from 1900, £350-£10,000.* LOC: 7 mins. walk from Wimbledon underground and BR stations. PARK: Reasonable. TEL: 020 8944 6098; fax - same; e-mail - curzgal@aol.com SER: Framing; restorations; valuations. VAT: Spec.

Shaikh and Son (Oriental Rugs) Ltd
139 Arthur Rd. SW19 8AB. (M. Shaikh). Open 10-6. CL: Sat. pm. *STOCK: Persian carpets, rugs, £100-£10,000.* TEL: 020 8947 9232. SER: Repairing and cleaning.

Mark J. West - Cobb Antiques Ltd   BADA
39B High St., Wimbledon Village. SW19 5BY. Open

10-5.30. SIZE: Large. *STOCK: Antique glass, £5-£20,000.* PARK: Easy. TEL: 020 8946 2811; e-mail - westglass@aol.com SER: Valuations; buys at auction. FAIRS: Olympia; Grosvenor House; New York Ceramics; BADA.

SW20

W.G.T. Burne (Antique Glass) Ltd   BADA
PO Box 9465. (Formerly of Chelsea) SW20 9ZD. (Mrs G. and A.T. Burne). Est. 1936. Open by appointment. *STOCK: English and Irish glassware, Georgian and Victorian decanters, chandeliers, candelabra and lustres.* TEL: 020 8543 6319; fax - same; mobile - 07774 72583; e-mail - antiqueglass@burne.plus.com SER: Valuations; restorations. VAT: Stan/Spec.

W. F. Turk Antique Clocks   BADA LAPADA
355 Kingston Rd., Wimbledon Chase. SW20 8JX. CINOA. Est. 1970. Open Tues.-Fri. 9-5.30, Sat. 9-4. SIZE: Large. *STOCK: Clocks, including longcase, 17th-19th C, £4,000-£150,000; bracket, 17th-19th C, £2,000-£100,000; mantel and carriage, 19th C, £450-£25,000.* LOC: Off A3. PARK: Easy. TEL: 020 8543 3231; fax - same; website - www.wfturk.com SER: Valuations; restorations. FAIRS: Olympia. VAT: Stan/Spec.

SE1

Antiques Exchange
170-172 Tower Bridge Rd. SE1 3LS. (Mr and Mrs R. Draysey). Est. 1966. Open 10-6, Sun. 11-5. SIZE: Large. *STOCK: Furniture, smalls, lighting, decorative items, from 1700.* PARK: Nearby. TEL: 020 7403 5568; fax - 020 7378 8828; e-mail - Ray@AntiquesExchange.com website - www.AntiquesExchange.com SER: Restorations (furniture).

Europa House Antiques
160-164 Tower Bridge Rd. SE1 3LS. (G. Viventi). Est. 1976. Open 9.30-5.15, Sat. 10-5.15. SIZE: Large. *STOCK: Furniture and general antiques.* TEL: 020 7403 0022; fax - 020 7277 5777; e-mail - viventi@btconnect.com

The Galleries
165 Tower Bridge Rd., Bermondsey. SE1 3LW. (Alan Bennett). Open 10-5, Fri. 10-4, Sat. and Sun. 11-5. SIZE: Large. *STOCK: Georgian and Victorian English and Continental furniture, some collectables.* TEL: 020 7407 5371; fax - 020 7403 0359. VAT: Stan/Spec.

Mayfair Carpet Gallery Ltd
301 Borough High St. SE1 1JH. *STOCK: Persian, Oriental rugs and carpets.* TEL: 020 7403 8228.

Tower Bridge Antiques
71 Tanner St. SE1 3PL. Open 9-5.30, Sat. 10.30-6, Sun. 11-5. SIZE: Large. *STOCK: Victorian, Georgian and Edwardian furniture, shipping goods.* TEL: 020 7403 3660; e-mail - towerbridgeant@aol.com VAT: Stan.

SE3

Michael Silverman
PO Box 350. SE3 0LZ. ABA. ILAB. Est. 1989. Open by appointment. *STOCK: Manuscripts, autograph letters, historical documents.* PARK: Free. TEL: 020 8319 4452; fax - 020 8856 6006; e-mail - ms@michael-silverman.com website - www.michael-silverman.com SER: Catalogue available. FAIRS: ABA - Olympia (June); ABAA, New York (April). *Postal Only.*

SE5

Robert E. Hirschhorn   BADA LAPADA
CINOA. Est. 1979. Visitors welcome by appointment. *STOCK: Distinctive English, Welsh and Continental country furniture, mainly oak, elm, walnut and fruitwood, and interesting objects, 18th C and earlier; ceramics, especially delftware; textiles, metalwork and treen.* PARK: Easy. TEL: 020 7703 7443; mobile - 07831 405937; e-mail - hirschhornantiques@macunlimited.net website - www.hirschhornantiques.com FAIRS: BADA (March); Olympia (March, June and Nov). VAT: Spec.

SE6

Ward Antique Fireplaces Ltd
1-5 Further Green Rd., Catford. SE6 1JU. (Michael and Terry Ward). Open 10-5, Sun. 11-2. *STOCK: Victorian and Edwardian fireplaces, some Victorian and Edwardian furniture.* TEL: 020 8697 6003; home - 020 8698 0771. SER: Restorations (fireplaces).

Wilkinson plc
5 Catford Hill. SE6 4NU. Est. 1947. Open 9-5. CL: Sat. SIZE: Medium. *STOCK: Glass especially chandeliers, 18th C and reproduction, art metal work.* LOC: Opposite Catford Bridge station. Entrance through Wickes DIY car park. PARK: Easy. TEL: 020 8314 1080; fax - 020 8690 1524; e-mail - enquiries@wilkinson-plc.com website - www.wilkinson-plc.com SER: Restorations and repairs (glass, metalwork).

SE7

Ward Antique Fireplaces Ltd
267 Woolwich Rd., Charlton. SE7 7RB. (T. and M. Ward). Est. 1981. Open 10-5, Sun. 11-2. SIZE: Medium. *STOCK: Victorian fireplaces, Victorian and Edwardian furniture, £50-£1,000.* LOC: From A102(M) take Woolwich/Woolwich ferry turn, 100yds. from roundabout immediately under rail bridge across the road. PARK: Easy. TEL: 020 8305 0963; home - 020 8698 0771.

SE9

The Fireplace
257 High St., Eltham. SE9 1TY. (A. Clark). Est. 1978. Open daily. SIZE: Medium. *STOCK: Fireplaces, 19th-20th C, £100-£1,000.* PARK: Adjacent side streets. TEL: 020 8850 4887. SER: Restorations (fireplaces). VAT: Stan.

R.E. Rose FBHI
731 Sidcup Rd., Eltham. SE9 3SA. Est. 1976. Open 9-5. SIZE: Small. *STOCK: Clocks and barometers, 1750-1930, £50-£5,000.* LOC: A20 from London, shop on left just past fiveways traffic lights at Green Lane. PARK: Easy. TEL: 020 8859 4754. SER: Restorations (clocks

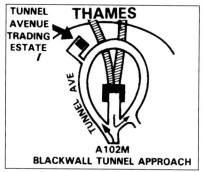
and barometers); spare parts for antique clocks and barometers. VAT: Stan/Spec.

SE10

Creek Antiques
23 Greenwich South St. SE10 8NW. Est. 1986. Open by appointment. SIZE: Small. *STOCK: General antiques, amusement machines, enamel signs, silver and plate.* LOC: 200 yards from British Rail station. PARK: Easy. TEL: 020 8293 5721; mobile - 07778 427521; e-mail - creekantiques@aol.com

Greenwich Antiques Market
Greenwich Church St. SE10. Open Thurs. and Fri. 7.30-5.30. SIZE: 40 stalls. *STOCK: General antiques and collectables.* PARK: Burney St. Cutty Sark Gdns. TEL: 020 8293 3110; website - www.greenwichmarket.net

The Greenwich Gallery
9 Nevada St. SE10 9JL. (R.F. Moy). Est. 1965. Open 10-5.30 including Sun. *STOCK: Mainly English oil paintings and watercolours, 18th C to 1950.* PARK: Opposite. TEL: 020 8305 1666. SER: Restorations; framing; exhibitions. VAT: Spec.

The Junk Shop
9 Greenwich South St. SE10 8NW. (T. and T.B.D. Moy). Est. 1985. Open 10-6 including Sun. SIZE: Large. *STOCK: Larger antique and decorative items, 18th C to 1950s; furniture, architectural items and bric-a-brac.* LOC: Opposite Greenwich B.R. TEL: 020 8305 1666. VAT: Stan/Spec.

Lamont Antiques Ltd   LAPADA
Tunnel Avenue Antique Warehouse, Tunnel Avenue Trading Estate, Greenwich. SE10 0QH. (N. Lamont and F. Llewellyn). Open 9-5.30. CL: Sat. SIZE: Large. *STOCK: Architectural fixtures and fittings, bars, stained glass, pub mirrors and signs, shipping furniture, £5-£25,000.* PARK: Own. TEL: 020 8305 2230; fax - 020 8305 1805; e-mail - lamontantiques@aol.com website - www.lamontantiques.com SER: Container packing.

The Warwick Leadlay Gallery
5 Nelson Rd., Greenwich. SE10 9JB. (Warwick Leadlay and Anthony Cross). Est. 1974. Open 9.30-5.30, Sun. and public holidays 11-5.30. SIZE: Large. *STOCK: Antique maps, prints, fine arts, Nelson specialists, 17th-20th C.* LOC: Head of Greenwich Market. PARK: Nearby. TEL: 020 8858 0317; fax - 020 8853 1773; e-mail - info@warwickleadlay.com website - www.warwickleadlay.com SER: Framing; restorations; valuations. VAT: Stan.

Marcet Books
4A Nelson Rd., Greenwich. SE10 9JB. (Martin Kemp). PBFA. Est. 1980. Open 10-5.30 including Sun. SIZE: Small. *STOCK: General secondhand and antiquarian books.* LOC: In alley off Nelson Rd., leading to Greenwich market. PARK: 200 yards. TEL: 020 8853 5408; e-mail - marcetbooks@btconnect.com website - www.marcetbooks.co.uk SER: Valuations. FAIRS: PBFA monthly Russell Hotel.

Minerva Antiques
90 Royal Hill, Greenwich. SE10 8RT. (Jonathan Atkins). Est. 1989. Open Tues.-Sun. 10-6. SIZE: Medium.

STOCK: Furniture, English and French mirrors, 19th C. PARK: Easy. TEL: 020 8691 2221; mobile - 07973 833441; e-mail - sales@minerva-antiques.co.uk website - www.minerva-antiques.co.uk SER: Restorations (repairs, caning, gilding and upholstery).

Rogers Turner Books
23a Nelson Rd., Greenwich. SE10 9JB. (P.J. Rogers and A.J. Turner). ABA. PBFA. Est. 1975. Open Thurs.-Fri. 10-6 or by appointment. *STOCK: Antiquarian books especially on clocks and scientific instruments.* TEL: 020 8853 5271; fax - same; Paris - 0033 13912 1191; e-mail - rogersturner@compuserve.com website - www.rogersturner@abebooks.com. SER: Buys at auction (British and European); catalogues available.

Spread Eagle Antiques
1 Stockwell St. SE10 9JL. (R.F. Moy). Est. 1954. Open 10-5.30 including Sun. SIZE: Large. *STOCK: Furniture, pictures and decorative items, 18th-19th C.* PARK: Opposite. TEL: 020 8305 1666; home - 020 8692 1618. SER: Valuations; restorations (pictures and furniture). VAT: Stan/Spec.

Spread Eagle Book & Curio Shop
8 Nevada St. SE10 9JL. (R.F. Moy). Est. 1954. Open 10-5.30 including Sun. SIZE: Large. *STOCK: Antiquarian and secondhand books, period costume, curios, china, bric-a-brac, prints, postcards.* LOC: A202. From London follow A2, then turn left at Deptford - or follow riverside road from Tower Bridge. TEL: 020 8305 1666. SER: Valuations; restorations (furniture, china and pictures). VAT: Stan/Spec/Global.

Walpoles   BADA
18 Nelson Rd., Greenwich. SE10 9JB. (Graham Walpole). PADA. Est. 1975. Open 10-5.30, Sat. and Sun. 12-5.30. SIZE: Medium. *STOCK: British Army and Navy, campaign and colonial furniture, Chinese export trade and English country house, mid-18th to mid-20th C; fine and folk art.* **LOC: Greenwich centre, near station and Greenwich Pier. PARK: Nearby. TEL: 020 8305 3080; mobile - 07831 561042; e-mail - info@walpoleantiques.com website - www.walpoleantiques.com SER: Stock hire for film and television. FAIRS: Olympia (June); BADA, London (Mar). VAT: Export/Stan/Spec.**

Robert Whitfield Antiques   LAPADA
Tunnel Avenue Antique Warehouse, Tunnel Avenue Trading Estate, Greenwich. SE10 0QH. Open 10-5. CL: Sat. *STOCK: Edwardian, Victorian and secondhand furniture, especially bentwood chairs.* PARK: Easy. TEL: 020 8305 2230; fax - 020 8305 1805; e-mail - robertwhitfield@btinternet.com SER: Container packing.

SE13

Robert Morley and Co Ltd   BADA
34 Engate St. SE13 7HA. Est. 1881. Open 9.30-5. *STOCK: Pianos, harpsichords, clavichords, spinets, virginals, harps; stools, music cabinets and stands.* **LOC: Lewisham. PARK: Own. TEL: 020 8318 5838; e-mail - jvm@morley-r.u-net.com website - www.morleypianos.com. SER: Restorations (musical instruments). FAIRS: Early Music Show, Greenwich. VAT: Stan.**

SE15

CASA
155 Bellenden Rd., Peckham. SE15 4DH. (M. Tree). Est. 1993. Open Tues.-Sat. 10-5. SIZE: Medium. *STOCK: Architectural salvage including doors, floorboards, radiators, baths, sinks and taps, 19th-20th C, £15-£600; furniture, 19th-20th C; fireplaces.* LOC: Bellenden village. PARK: Easy. TEL: 020 7732 3911; e-mail - info@casaonline.co.uk website - www.casaonline.co.uk SER: Fireplace fitting, shotblasting, floor sanding and plumbing.

SE19

Crystal Palace Antiques
Imperial House, Jasper Rd. SE19 1SJ. (L. Taylor and D. Roper). Est. 1994. Open 7 days 10-6. *STOCK: Furniture, £50-£3,000.* PARK: Easy. TEL: 020 8480 7042; mobile - 07818 237576. FAIRS: Ardingly, Newark, Kempton.

SE21

Acorn Antiques
111 Rosendale Rd., West Dulwich. SE21 8EZ. (Mrs G. Kingham). Est. 1976. Open 10-6, Sat. 10-5.30. *STOCK: Furniture, sterling silver, jewellery, ceramics, glassware and fireplace accessories.* TEL: 020 8761 3349. VAT: Stan.

Francis Jevons
80 Dulwich Village. SE21 7AJ. Est. 1983. Usually open 9.30-1 and 2.30-5.30, Sat. until 5, other times by appointment. CL: Wed. *STOCK: China and small furniture, late 18th to 19th C; interior design, lamps and decorative items.* LOC: Off South Circular leading down from either Gallery or College roads. PARK: Easy. TEL: 020 8693 1991. SER: Valuations; restorations. VAT: Stan/Spec.

SE25

Engine 'n' Tender
19 Spring Lane, Woodside Green. SE25 4SP. (Mrs Joyce M. Buttigieg). Est. 1957. Open Thurs. and Fri. 12-5.30, Sat. 10-5.30. SIZE: Small. *STOCK: Model railways, mainly pre 1939; Dinky toys, to 1968; old toys, mainly tinplate.* LOC: Near Croydon tramlink. PARK: Easy. TEL: 020 8654 0386. FAIRS: Local toy.

North London Clock Shop Ltd
Rear of 60 Saxon Rd. SE25 5EH. (D.S. Tomlin). Est. 1960. Open 9-6. CL: Sat. SIZE: Medium. *STOCK: Clocks, longcase, bracket, carriage, skeleton, 18th-19th C.* PARK: Easy. TEL: 020 8664 8089. SER: Restorations (clocks and barometers); wheel cutting; hand engraving; dial painting; clock reconversions. FAIRS: Olympia. VAT: Stan.

SE26

Behind the Boxes - Art Deco
98 Kirkdale, Sydenham. SE26 4BG. (Ray Owen). Est. 1987. Open 10.30-5, Sun. and Mon. by appointment. SIZE: Large. *STOCK: Furniture, lighting and costume jewellery, 1930s, from £25.* LOC: 1 mile from Crystal Palace. BR station Forest Hill. PARK: Loading, otherwise Fransfield Rd. TEL: 020 8291 6116. SER: Valuations; buys at auction. FAIRS: Decorama and Deco.

Oola Boola Antiques London
139-147 Kirkdale, Sydenham. SE26 4QJ. (R. Scales and S. Blackman). Est. 1968. Open 10-6, Sat.10-5, Sun. 11-5. SIZE: Large. *STOCK: Furniture, £5-£3,000; mahogany, oak, walnut, Victorian, Arts & Crafts, Art Nouveau, Edwardian, Art Deco, retro and shipping goods.* PARK: Forecourt. TEL: 020 8291 9999; fax - 020 8291 5759; e-mail - oola.boola@telco4u.net

Sydenham Antiques Centre
48 Sydenham Rd., Sydenham. SE26 5QF. (Mrs L. Cockton). Est. 1996. Open 10-5. SIZE: Medium. *STOCK: China, glass, silver, collectables, furniture and jewellery, 19th-20th C, £5-£500.* LOC: 2 doors down from Post Office in High St. PARK: Easy and nearby. TEL: 020 8778 1706. SER: Valuations; restorations (china).

E1

John Jackson at Town House   LAPADA
5 Fournier St., Spitalfields. E1 6QE. (Fiona Atkins). Est. 1984. Open Thurs. and Fri. 11.30-6, Sat. 11-5. SIZE: Small. *STOCK: 18th to early 19th C English furniture; portrait and still life paintings, prints, treen and curiosities.* LOC: Near Liverpool St. station. PARK: Commercial St. TEL: 020 7247 4745; mobile - 07711 319237; e-mail - fiona@townhousewindow.com website - www.townhousewindow.com FAIRS: Arundel.

La Maison
107/108 Shoreditch High St. E1 6JN. (Guillaume and Louise Bacou). Open 10-6, Sat. 11.30-6. SIZE: Large. *STOCK: Beds and French furniture.* TEL: 020 7729 9646; fax - 020 7729 6399. SER: Restorations. VAT: Margin.

E2

George Rankin Coin Co. Ltd
325 Bethnal Green Rd. E2 6AH. Est. 1965. *STOCK: Coins, medals, medallions and jewellery.* TEL: 020 7739 1840/7729 1280; fax - 020 7729 5023.

E3

Le Style 25
Unit 1A Riverbank Business Park, Dye House Lane, Bow. E3 2TB. (Philip Varma). Est. 1988. Open by appointment. SIZE: Medium. *STOCK: British and European Art Deco furniture, from coffee tables to dining, lounge and bedroom suites, lighting and decorative items.* PARK: Easy. TEL: 020 8983 4285; mobile - 07778 310293; e-mail - info@lestyle25.com website - www.lestyle25.com FAIRS: NEC; SECC; Earls Court.

E4

Record Detector
3 & 4 Station Approach, Station Rd., North Chingford. E4 6AL. (N. Salter). Est. 1992. Open 10-6. CL: Thurs. SIZE: Small (2 shops). *STOCK: Secondhand and collectable records, L.Ps, E.Ps, singles and CDs.* LOC: In forecourt of North Chingford station. PARK: Easy. TEL: 020 8529 6361/2938; e-mail - sales@salter.co.uk website - www.salter.co.uk

Nicholas Salter Antiques
8 Station Approach, Station Rd., North Chingford. E4 6AL. (Sherley Salter). Est. 1971. Open Tues. and Wed. 10-5, Fri. and Sat. 10-6. SIZE: Large. *STOCK: Furniture, 1850-1930, £150-£1,500; china and linen, 1870-1950, £30-£150; antiquarian and secondhand books; vintage clothes and accessories, 1860s-1970s, £5-£500.* LOC: Next to North Chingford station. PARK: Easy. TEL: 020 8529 2938; 020 8524 3101; e-mail - sherley@salter.co.uk website - www.salter.co.uk

E8

Boxes and Musical Instruments
2 Middleton Rd., Hackney. E8 4BL. (A. and J. O'Kelly). Est. 1974. Open any time by appointment. SIZE: Medium. *STOCK: Boxes - caddies, sewing, writing, snuff, vanity, jewellery and desk, £300-£5,000; musical instruments, plucked string, £1,000-£3,000; all 18th-19th C.* LOC: Off Kingsland Rd., continuation of Bishopsgate. PARK: Easy. TEL: 020 7254 7074; home - same; e-mail - boxes@hygra.com website - www.hygra.com SER: Valuations; restorations (exceptional instruments only). Registered with the Conservation Unit of the Museums and Galleries Commission.

E11

Old Cottage Antiques   LAPADA
8 High St., Wanstead. E11 2AJ. (P. Blake and B. Hawkins). Est. 1920. Open Fri. and Sat. 10-5 or by appointment. SIZE: Medium plus warehouse. *STOCK: Furniture, clocks, paintings, 19th-20th C.* LOC: Near Wanstead and Snaresbrook Central Line underground stations. PARK: Easy. TEL: 020 8989 2317; mobile - 07710 031079 and 07831 888736; e-mail - brianhawkinsantiques@hotmail.com SER: Buys at auction. VAT: Stan/Spec.

E14

Frontispiece Ltd
Promenade Level, Cabot Place East, Canary Wharf. E14 4QS. (Reginald and Jennifer Beer). EPSOC. Est. 1989. Open 9-7, Sat. 10-6, Sun. 12-6. SIZE: Medium. *STOCK: Over 5,000 antiquarian maps, prints and ephemera items.* LOC: Below Canary Wharf tower. PARK: Easy. TEL: 020 7363 6336; fax - 020 7515 1424; e-mail - sales@ frontispiece.co.uk website - www.frontispiece.co.uk

E17

Collectors Centre - Antique City
98 Wood St., Walthamstow. E17 3HX. (Woodstow Antiques Developments Ltd). Est. 1978. Open 9.30-5.30. CL: Thurs. SIZE: Large. *STOCK: Antiques, collectables, 40s, 50s, 60s, £1-£500.* PARK: Opposite. TEL: 020 8520 4032. *Trade Only.*

E18

Victoria Antiques
166A George Lane, South Woodford. E18 2HL. (M. A. Holman). Est. 1998. Open 11-5. CL: Tues. and Thurs. SIZE: Small. *STOCK: Clocks and carved chairs, 18th-*

19th C, £100-£1,000; pictures, 19th C, £50-£500; silver, £20-£500; bronze figures, £100-£1,000. LOC: 2 mins. walk from South Woodford station. PARK: George Lane. TEL: 020 8989 1002. SER: Valuations. VAT: Stan.

EC1

City Clocks
31 Amwell St. EC1R 1UN. (J. Rosson). FBHI. Est. 1960. Open Tues.- Sat. 9-5 or by appointment. SIZE: Medium. *STOCK: Clocks, some furniture, 18th-20th C, £100-£12,000.* PARK: Pay and Display. TEL: 020 7278 1154; freephone - 0800 7834587; e-mail - mail@cityclocks.co.uk website - www.cityclocks.co.uk SER: Valuations; restorations (clocks and watches, house calls to longcase); buys at auction. VAT: Spec.

Frosts of Clerkenwell Ltd
60-62 Clerkenwell Rd. EC1M 5PX. BCWMG. BHI. Est. 1932. Open 10-5. CL: Sat. SIZE: Large. *STOCK: Quality vintage clocks, watches and barometers.* TEL: 020 7253 0315; website - www.frostsofclerkenwell.co.uk SER: Restorations.

Jonathan Harris (Jewellery) Ltd
63-66 Hatton Garden (office). EC1N 8LE. (E.C., D. I. and J. Harris). Est. 1958. Open 9.30-4.30. CL: Sat. *STOCK: Antique and secondhand rings, brooches, pendants, bracelets and other jewellery, from £100.* PARK: Nearby. TEL: 020 7242 9115/7242 1558; fax - 020 7831 4417. SER: Valuations; export. VAT: Stan/Spec.

Hirsh Ltd
10 Hatton Garden. EC1N 8AH. (A. Hirsh). Open 10-5.30. *STOCK: Fine jewellery and objets d'art.* TEL: 020 7405 6080; fax - 020 7430 0107; e-mail - enquiries @hirsh.co.uk SER: Valuations; jewellery designed and re-modelled.

R. Holt and Co. Ltd
98 Hatton Garden. EC1N 8NX. (R. and J. Holt). GMC. BJA. London Diamond Bourse. Est. 1948. Open 9.30-5.30. CL: Sat. *STOCK: Gemstone specialists.* TEL: 020 7405 5286/0197; fax - 020 7430 1279; e-mail - info @rholt.co.uk website - www.rholt.co.uk SER: Valuations; restorations (gem stone cutting and testing, bead stringing and inlaid work).

Joseph and Pearce Ltd   LAPADA
63-66 Hatton Garden. EC1N 8LE. Est. 1896. Open by appointment. *STOCK: Jewellery, 1800-1960, £100-£5,000.* TEL: 020 7405 4604/7; fax - 020 7242 1902. FAIRS: Earls Court, NEC, Inhorgenta, New York. VAT: Stan/Spec. *Trade Only.*

A.R. Ullmann Ltd
10 Hatton Garden. EC1N 8AH. (J.S. Ullmann). Est. 1939. Open 9-5, Sat. 9.30-5. SIZE: Small. *STOCK: Jewellery, gold, silver and diamond; silver and objets d'art.* LOC: Close to Farringdon and Chancery Lane underground stations. PARK: Multi-storey in St. Cross St. TEL: 020 7405 1877; fax - 020 7404 7071; e-mail - enquiries@arullman.com website - www.arullman.com SER: Valuations; restorations. VAT: Stan/Spec.

EC2

LASSCO   LAPADA
St. Michael's, Mark St. (off Paul St.). EC2A 4ER. (Anthony Reeve). Est. 1979. Open 10-5. SIZE: Large plus walled garden. *STOCK: Architectural antiques including panelled rooms, chimney pieces, garden ornaments, lighting, door furniture, stained glass, columns and capitals, stonework, relics and curiosities.* PARK: Meters. TEL: 020 7749 9944; fax - 020 7749 9941; e-mail - st.michaels@lassco.co.uk website - www.lassco.co.uk/antiques

Westland London
St. Michael's Church, Leonard St. EC2A 4ER. (Geoffrey Westland). SALVO. Est. 1969. Open 9-6, Sat. 10-5, Sun. by appointment. SIZE: Large + warehouse. *STOCK: Period and prestigious chimneypieces, architectural elements, panelled rooms, light fittings, statuary, paintings and furniture, £100-£100,000.* LOC: Off Gt. Eastern St., near Old St. underground. PARK: Easy but in congestion zone. TEL: 020 7739 8094; fax - 020 7729 3620; e-mail - westland@westland.co.uk website - www.westland.co.uk SER: Restorations; installations; shipping. VAT: Stan/Spec.

EC3

Searle and Co Ltd
1 Royal Exchange, Cornhill. EC3V 3LL. NAG. Est. 1893. Open 9-5.30. SIZE: Medium. *STOCK: Georgian, Victorian, Art Nouveau, Art Deco and secondhand silver*

and jewellery; novelty pieces and collectibles. LOC: Near Bank underground station - exits 3 & 4. PARK: Meters. TEL: 020 7626 2456; fax - 020 7283 6384; e-mail - mail@searleandco.ltd.uk website - www. searleandco.ltd.uk SER: Commissions; valuations; restorations; repairs; engraving. VAT: Stan/Spec.

EC4

Gladwell and Company   LAPADA
68 Queen Victoria St. EC4N 4SJ. (Anthony Fuller). SLAD. Open 9-5.30, Sat. and Sun. by appointment. SIZE: Small. *STOCK: Oil paintings, watercolours, drawings, etchings and bronzes, £50-£50,000.* LOC: Near St Paul's cathedral and Bank of England. PARK: Easy. TEL: 020 7248 3824; fax - 020 7248 6899; e-mail - gladwells@btopenworld.com website - www. gladwells.co.uk SER: Valuations; restorations; consultant. FAIRS: LAPADA; NEC; Boston; Glasgow; New York; Chicago.

N1

After Noah
121 Upper St., Islington. N1 1QP. (M. Crawford and Z. Candlin). Est. 1990. Open 10-6, Sun. 12-5. SIZE: Medium. *STOCK: Arts and Craft oak and similar furniture, leather sofas and chairs, 1880s to 1950s, £1-£5,000; iron, iron and brass beds; decorative items, bric-a-brac including candlesticks, mirrors, lighting, kitchenalia and jewellery.* PARK: Side streets. TEL: 020 7359 4281; fax - same;

e-mail - enquiries@afternoah.com website - www. afternoah.com. SER: Restorations. VAT: Stan.

Meg Andrews
Islington. Est. 1982. Open by appointment. *STOCK: Worldwide collectable, hangable and wearable antique costume and textiles including Chinese embroideries and woven fabrics, robes, shoes, hats, large hangings; Morris and Arts and Crafts embroideries and woven cloths, Paisley shawls, samplers, silkwork pictures; European costumes and textiles.* TEL: 020 7359 7678; e-mail - meg@meg-andrews.com website - www.meg-andrews.com SER: Valuations; advice. FAIRS: Antique Textiles and Costumes, Manchester; Organisers - Textile Society (March); Antique Textiles, Costumes and Tribal Art, Hammersmith Town Hall. VAT: Spec.

The Angel Arcade
116 Islington High St., Camden Passage. N1 8EG. (Camden Passage Dealers Assn.). Open Wed. and Sat. 7.30-4.30. SIZE: Arcade with 14 shops. *STOCK: Decorative and interior design items and general antiques. Below are listed some of the dealers in this arcade.* PARK: Business Design Centre. Website - www.camdenpassageantiques.co.uk

Argosy Antiques
Shop 4. (Pat Buttigieg). *Silver and plate, bronzes, early lighting and early door knockers.* TEL: 020 7359 2517; home - 020 7402 4422.

Matthew Austin-Cooper
Shop C. *French and English decorative furniture, leather*

81

and antler items, Black Forest carvings, mirrors and lighting. TEL: 020 7226 4901; mobile - 07958 631690.

Kate Bannister
Shop C. Decorative antiques - tramp art, twig and bamboo furniture, lighting, inkwells, papier mâché and tôle trays, tôle scuttles, antler and horn accessories. TEL: 020 7704 6644.

Marilyn Bookal Antiques
Shop 10. French and painted decorative furniture, majolica, tôle, papier mâché and miniature bamboo furniture. TEL: Mobile - 07768 997687.

Burlington Designs
Shop 9. (Martin Lynn). Boule d'escaliers, lighting and fireside furniture. TEL: Mobile - 07730 037671. SER: Polishing and gilding.

Peter Collingridge Antiques Ltd
Shop 2. 18th-20th C metalware and lighting. TEL: 020 7354 9189; mobile - 07860 581858.

Val Cooper Antiques
Shop E. Bamboo furniture, majolica, papier mâché, brass frames, Black Forest carvings, decorative accessories. TEL: 020 7226 4901; 020 8505 2922; mobile - 07930 634015; e-mail - valcooperantique@aol.com SER: Restorations.

Feljoy Antiques
Shop 3. (J. Humphreys and F. Finburgh). Est. 1985. Chintzware, decorative items, beadwork cushions and textiles. TEL: 020 7354 5336; e-mail - joy@feljoy-antiques.demon.co.uk

Rosemary Hart
Shop 6. Est. 1980. Victorian silver plated tableware, decorative serving ware and small silver. TEL: 020 7359 6839; e-mail - contact@rosemaryhart.co.uk website - www.rosemaryhart.co.uk SER: Restorations; replating.

Lou, John & Chris
Shop 1. Decorative items.

Maureen Lyons
Shop 5. Chandeliers, decorative furniture and accessories. TEL: 020 7354 4245; fax - 020 7354 0508.

Lans Pickup
Shop G. Textiles and 18th C country furniture. TEL: 020 7359 8272.

Annie's Vintage Costume & Textiles
12 Camden Passage, Islington. N1 8ED. (A. Moss). Open 11-6 including Sun. STOCK: Vintage costume and textiles. PARK: Nearby and meters. TEL: 020 7359 0796.

The Antique Trader
The Millinery Works, 85/87 Southgate Rd. N1 3JS. (B. Thompson and D. Rothera). Est. 1968. Open 11-6 or by appointment. SIZE: Large. STOCK: Arts & Crafts, Art furniture and effects, £100-£15,000. LOC: Close to Camden Passage Antiques Centre. PARK: Meters. TEL: 020 7359 2019; fax - 020 7359 5792; e-mail - antiquetrader@milleryworks.co.uk website - www.milleryworks.co.uk VAT: Stan/Spec.

Banbury Fayre
6 Pierrepont Row Arcade, Camden Passage, Islington. N1 8EF. (N. Steel). Est. 1984. Open Wed. and Sat. SIZE: Small. STOCK: Collectables including commemoratives, shipping, Boer War, air line travel, and general small items. PARK: 200yds. TEL: Home - 020 8852 5675.

Camden Passage Antiques Market and Pierrepont Arcade Antiques Centre
Pierrepont Arcade, Islington. N1 8EF. Est. 1960. Open Wed. and Sat. 7.30-3.30 or by appointment. Thurs. - book market. SIZE: Over 400 dealers. STOCK: Wide range of general antiques and many specialists. PARK: Multi-storey and meters. TEL: 020 7359 0190; mobile - 07960 877035; e-mail - murdochkdr@aol.com website - www.camdenpassageantiques.com SER: Shipping.

Peter Chapman Antiques and Restoration
LAPADA
10 Theberton St., Islington. N1 0QX. (P.J. and Z.A. Chapman). CPTA. CINOA. Est. 1971. Open 9.30-6, Sun. and public holidays by appointment. SIZE: Medium. STOCK: Furniture and decorative objects, 1700-1900; paintings, drawings and prints, 17th to early 20th C; stained glass, hall lanterns; Grand Tour items. LOC: 5 mins. walk from Camden Passage down Upper St. PARK: Easy. TEL: 020 7226 5565; fax - 020 8348 4846; mobile - 07831 093662; e-mail - pchapman antiques@easynet.co.uk website - www.antiques-peterchapman.co.uk SER: Valuations; restorations (furniture and period objects); buys at auction. VAT: Stan/Spec.

Chapter One
2 Pierrepont Row Arcade, Camden Passage. N1 9EG. (Yvonne Gill). Est. 1993. Open Wed. 9-3, Sat. 9-5 or by appointment. SIZE: Small. STOCK: Handbags, costume jewellery, vintage accessories, fabrics, unusual collectors items, 1880-1960, £1-£300. TEL: 020 7359 1185; e-mail - yg@platinum.demon.co.uk SER: Jewellery repairs; search.

Charlton House Antiques
19 Camden Passage, Islington. N1 8EA. (Robin Sims and Stephen Burrows). Est. 1989. Open Wed. and Sat. 8-5, Tues. and Fri. 10-4. SIZE: Medium. STOCK: European and Art Deco furniture, 1840-1930, £100-£5,000; general antiques. LOC: Near Angel underground station. PARK: Easy. TEL: 020 7226 3141; fax - 020 7226 1123; e-mail - charlhse@aol.com VAT: Stan/Spec.

Chest of Drawers
281 Upper St., Islington. N1 2TZ. (J. Delf and K. Corbett). Open 10-6 including Sun. STOCK: Chinese and eastern European antiques in elm, oak, camphor and pine. TEL: 020 7359 5909; fax - 020 7704 6236; website - www.chestofdrawers.co.uk

Rosemary Conquest
27 Camden Passage. N1 8EA. Open 11-5.30, Wed. and Sat. 9-5.30. CL: Mon. SIZE: Medium - 2 floors. STOCK: Chandeliers and European decorative items. PARK: Easy. TEL: 020 7359 0616; mobile - 07710 486384. SER: Shipping. FAIRS: Battersea Decorative; Chelsea Village Brocante.

Carlton Davidson Antiques
33 Camden Passage, Islington. N1 8EA. Est. 1981. Open Wed.-Sat. 10-4. SIZE: Medium. STOCK: Lamps, chandeliers, mirrors and decorative items, £100-£3,000. LOC: Near Charlton Place. PARK: Meters. TEL: 020 7226 7491. VAT: Stan.

Donay Games & Pastimes
3 Pierrepont Row, Camden Passage, Islington. N1 8EF. (Carol E. Goddard). Est. 1980. Open Wed. and Sat. 9.30-3.30, office Mon.-Fri. SIZE: Medium. *STOCK: Board and mechanical games - horse racing, cricket, golf and football; treen, paper and metal puzzles including Journet and mechanical Hoffman; chess, backgammon, cribbage, dominoes; card games and scorers; tinplate including Schuco; dice, shakers, mah-jong, marbles, artists' colourboxes; animal bronzes, Punch & Judy puppets including ephemera, 1780-1950, £5-£5,000.* LOC: Near Angel underground station. PARK: Charlton Place, Colebrook Row. TEL: 020 7359 1880; office - 01444 416412; e-mail - donaygames@btconnect.com website - www.donaygames.co.uk

Eccentricities   LAPADA
The Merchants Hall, 46 Essex Rd. N1 8LN. (K. Skeel). SIZE: Very large. *STOCK: General small items especially curiosities and eccentricities.* TEL: 020 7359 5633; fax - 020 7226 3780; e-mail - info@keithskeel.com

Eclectica
2 Charlton Place. N1 8AJ. (Liz Wilson). Est. 1988. Open Mon., Tues., Thurs. and Fri. 11-6, Wed. and Sat. 10-6. *STOCK: Vintage costume jewellery.* TEL: 020 7226 5625; fax - same; website - www.eclectica.biz

The Fleamarket
7 Pierrepont Row Arcade, Camden Passage, Islington. N1 8EE. Open 9.30-6. CL: Mon. SIZE: Large. 26 standholders. *STOCK: Jewellery, furniture, objets d'art, militaria, guns, swords, pistols, porcelain, coins, medals, stamps, 18th-19th C, £1-£500; antiquarian books, prints, fine art, china, silver, glass and general antiques.* PARK: Easy. TEL: 020 7226 8211. SER: Valuations; buys at auction.

Vincent Freeman
1 Camden Passage, Islington. N1 8EA. Est. 1966. Open Wed. and Sat. 10-5. SIZE: Large. *STOCK: Music boxes, furniture and decorative items, from £100.* TEL: 020 7226 6178; fax - 020 7226 7231; e-mail - freemanvj @hotmail.com FAIRS: Olympia (June). VAT: Stan/Spec.

Furniture Vault
50 Camden Passage, Islington. N1 8AE. (David Loveday). Est. 1969. Open Tues.-Sat. 9.30-4.30. SIZE: Large. *STOCK: Furniture, 18th-20th C.* TEL: 020 7354 1047; e-mail - davidloveday1@aol.com

Get Stuffed
105 Essex Rd., Islington. N1 2SL. Est. 1975. Telephone mobile for appointment. *STOCK: Stuffed birds, fish, animals, trophy heads; rugs; butterflies, insects.* TEL: 020 7226 1364; fax - 020 7359 8253; mobile - 07831 260062; e-mail - taxidermy@thegetstuffed.co.uk website - www.thegetstuffed.co.uk SER: Restorations; taxidermy; glass domes and cases supplied.

David Griffiths Antiques
17 Camden Passage, Islington. N1 8EA. Open Tues., Wed., Fri. and Sat. 10-4 or by appointment. *STOCK: Decorative antiques including military and campaign furniture, leather chairs, pub accessories, club fenders and other fittings from hotels and gentlemen's clubs;*

Jubilee Photographica
Richard Meara
Fine Books and Photographs Ltd
Phone: 01932 863924 Fax: 01932 860318
Mobile:07860 793707 meara@btconnect.com
10 Pierrepont Row, Camden Passage Antiques Market, ISLINGTON, London N1 8EE (Nearest underground station - ANGEL)

quality vintage luggage. TEL: 020 7226 1991; tel/fax - 020 7226 1126; e-mail - dgantiques17@aol.com

Jonathan James   LAPADA
52/53 Camden Passage, Islington. N1 8EA. (Norman Petre). Est. 1970. Open 10-4.30, Wed. 9.30-4.30. CL: Mon. SIZE: Medium. *STOCK: Furniture, 18th-19th C, £1,000-£20,000.* PARK: 100 yds. TEL: 020 7704 8266; fax - same. SER: Valuations. VAT: Stan/Spec.

Japanese Gallery
23 Camden Passage, Islington. N1 8EA. Open 10-6. *STOCK: Japanese woodcut prints; books, porcelain, screens, kimonos, scrolls, furniture, netsuke, inro and Tsuba.* TEL: 020 7226 3347; fax - 020 7229 2934; e-mail - sales@japanesegallery.co.uk website - www. japanesegallery.co.uk SER: Framing; free authentification; interior design, ie. Tatami.

Jubilee Photographica
10 Pierrepont Row Arcade, Camden Passage, Islington. N1 8EE. (Richard Meara). Est. 1970. Open Wed. and Sat. 10-4 or by apppointment. SIZE: Small. *STOCK: Photographica - images, daguerreotypes, ambrotypes, tintypes, vintage paper prints, stereoscopic cards and viewers, magic lanterns and slides, topographical and family albums, cabinet cards and cartes de visite, £1-£1,000.* LOC: From Piccadilly Circus, take 19 bus to Angel, Islington. PARK: Meters. TEL: Home - 01932 863924; e-mail - meara@btconnect.com SER: Buys at auction. FAIRS: London Photograph; Photographica; Bievres, France; American Photo Historical Society, New York. VAT: Margin.

THE MALL
ANTIQUES ARCADE
Camden Passage, London N1

Over 35 Dealers in
London's premier centre for dealers,
decorators and collectors.

Enquiries: Mike Spooner
Tel: 020-7351 5353 Fax: 020-7969 1639

Carol Ketley Antiques   LAPADA
PO Box 16199. N1 7WD. Est. 1979. Open by appointment. SIZE: Medium. STOCK: *Mirrors, decanters, drinking glasses, decorative furniture and objects, 1780-1900, £10-£10,000.* LOC: Close to Camden Passage. PARK: Easy. TEL: 020 7359 5529; fax - 020 7226 4589; mobile - 07831 827284. FAIRS: Olympia (Feb., June and Nov); Decorative Antiques and Textiles (Jan., April and Sept). VAT: Global.

John Laurie (Antiques) Ltd   LAPADA
351/352 Upper St., Islington. N1 0PD. (R. Gewirtz). Est. 1962. Open 9.30-5. SIZE: Large. STOCK: *Silver, Sheffield plate.* TEL: 020 7226 0913/6969; fax - 020 7226 4599. SER: Restorations; packing and shipping. VAT: Stan.

London Militaria Market
Angel Arcade, Camden Passage, Islington. N1 8EG. (S. Bosley). Est. 1987. Open Sat. 8-1. SIZE: Large. 35 dealers. STOCK: *Militaria, 1800 to date.* LOC: Near Angel underground station. PARK: Meters and nearby. TEL: 01628 822503; website - www.londonmilitary market.com

The Mall Antiques Arcade
359 Upper St., Islington. N1 0PD. (Atlantic Antiques Centres Ltd). Est. 1979. Open 10-5, Wed. 7.30-5, Sat. 9-6. CL: Mon. STOCK: *See dealers listed below.* LOC: 5 mins. from Angel underground station. PARK: Meters. TEL: 020 7351 5353; enquiries - 020 7969 1634; e-mail - antique@dial.pipex.com

Alexandra Alfandary   LAPADA
Stand G9. *European porcelain especially Meissen.* TEL: 020 7354 9762; fax - 020 7727 4352; mobile - 07956 993233; e-mail - alex@alfandaryantiques.co.uk website - www.finemeissen.com

June and Heather Antiques
Stand G22. *Lighting.* TEL: Mobile - 07986 950049.

R. Arantes
Stand G27. *Lalique glass.* TEL: 020 7253 5303; mobile - 07712 189160; e-mail - rlaliqueglass@btinternet.com

Chancery Antiques
Stand G2. (R. Rote). *Oriental and Continental works of art.* TEL: 020 7359 9035; fax - same.

Li Min Chen
Stand G15. *Oriental items.*

Leolinda Costa
Stand G3. *Ethnic silver and gemstone jewellery.* TEL: 020 7226 3450.

Chris Dunn St. James
Stand G7. *Vintage jewellery.* TEL: 020 7704 0127.

GB Military Antiques
Stand G17. (Sean Edmunds). *Military antiques.*

Theo Ioannou
Stand G26. *Jewellery.*

Mosche Leibowitz   BADA
Stand G19/20. *Silver.* TEL: 020 7359 9588.

Leon's Militaria
Stand G21. (Leon Shrier). *Militaria.* TEL: 020 7288 1070; fax - 020 7288 1070; mobile - 07989 649972; e-mail - leonsmilitaria@yahoo.co.uk

Finbar Macdonnell
Stand G28. *Prints.* TEL: 020 7354 1706.

Paul Mayhew
Stand G11. *Clocks.* TEL: 020 7704 6510.

Rumours   LAPADA
Stand G4/5. (J. Donovan). *Art Nouveau, Art Deco china and objets d'art.* TEL: 020 7704 8416.

Count Alexander von Beregshasy
Stand G13. *Jewellery, French paste and tiaras (reproduction crown jewels).* TEL: 020 7354 0059.

Lower Mall

The Antique Barometer Co
Stand B5. *Barometers, scientific instruments and related accessories.* SM furniture, medical. TEL: 020 7226 4992; fax - same; e-mail - sales@antiquebarometer.com website - www.antiquebarometer.com

Patricia Baxter
Stand B2/3. *Furniture.* TEL: 020 7354 0886; home - 01992 574607; e-mail - baxantique@aol.com

Keith Birkett
Stand B9/10. *Furniture.* TEL: Mobile - 07813 613541.

Charles Woodage Antiques   LAPADA
Stand B4/7. *Furniture.* TEL: 020 7226 4173; fax - 01753 529047; mobile - 07950 561588; e-mail - woodage.antiques @btinternet.com website - www.woodageantiques.com

Graham Woodage Antiques
Stand B1. *Furniture and decorative accessories.* TEL: 020 8868 9514; fax - same; mobile - 07900 693650; e-mail - g.woodage@btopenworld.com

Kevin Page Oriental Art — LAPADA
2, 4 and 6 Camden Passage, Islington. N1 8ED. Est. 1968. Open 10.30-4. CL: Mon. and Thurs. SIZE: Large. *STOCK: Oriental porcelain and furniture, fine Japanese works of art from the Meiji period.* LOC: 1 min. from Angel underground station. PARK: Easy. TEL: 020 7226 8558. SER: Valuations. VAT: Stan.

Piers Rankin
14 Camden Passage, Islington. N1 8ED. Est. 1983. Open Tues.-Sat. 9.30-5.30, Mon. by appointment only. SIZE: Medium. *STOCK: Silver and plate, old Sheffield plate, 1700-1930.* PARK: NCP. TEL: 020 7354 3349; fax - 020 7359 8138; e-mail - piersrankin925@aol.com SER: Packing and shipping arranged.

Regent Antiques
North London Freight Depot, York Way. N1 0UZ. (T. Quaradeghini). Est. 1983. Open 9-5.30, other times by appointment. SIZE: Large. *STOCK: Furniture, 18th C to Edwardian.* LOC: 1/4 mile from Kings Cross station. PARK: Own. TEL: 020 7833 5545; fax - 020 7278 2236; e-mail - regentantiques@aol.com SER: Restorations (furniture). VAT: Stan/Spec. *Trade Only.*

Style Gallery
10 Camden Passage, Islington. N1 8ED. (M. Webb and P. Coakley-Webb). Est. 1980. Open Wed. and Sat. 9.30-4 or by appointment. *STOCK: Art Nouveau, WMF and Liberty pewter; Art Deco bronzes including Preiss and Chiparus; ceramics and glass.* TEL: 020 7359 7867; home - 020 8361 2357; fax - same; mobile - 07831 229640; e-mail - coakleywebb@btinternet.com website - www.styleantiques.co.uk

Sugar Antiques
8-9 Pierrepont Arcade, Camden Passage, Islington. N1 8EF. (Ted Kitagawa). Est. 1990. Open Wed. and Sat. 7.30-4. SIZE: Medium. *STOCK: Wrist and pocket watches, 19th-20th C, £25-£4,000; fountain pens and lighters, early 20th C to 1960s, £15-£1,000; costume jewellery and collectables, 19th-20th C, £5-£500.* LOC: 5 mins. walk from the Angel underground station (Northern Line). PARK: Meters. TEL: 020 7354 9896; fax - 01784 477460; mobile - 07779 636407; e-mail - info@sugarantiques.com website - www.sugarantiques.com SER: Repairs (as stock); buys at auction (as stock). VAT: Stan.

Swan Fine Art
12b Camden Passage, Islington. N1 8ED. (P. Child). Open 10-5, Wed. and Sat. 9-5 or by appointment. SIZE: Medium. *STOCK: Paintings, fine and decorative sporting and animal, portraits, 17th-19th C, £500-£25,000+.* PARK: Easy, except Wed. and Sat. TEL: 020 7226 5335; fax - 020 7359 2225; mobile - 07860 795336. VAT: Spec.

Tadema Gallery — BADA LAPADA
10 Charlton Place, Camden Passage, Islington. N1 8AJ. (S. and D. Newell-Smith). CINOA. Est. 1978. Open Wed. and Sat. 10-5 or by appointment. SIZE: Medium. STOCK: Jewellery - Art Nouveau, Art & Crafts, Art Deco to 1960s artist designed jewels; 20th C abstract art. PARK: Reasonable. TEL: 020 7359 1055; fax - same; e-mail - info@tademagallery.com website - www.tademagallery.com FAIRS: Grosvenor House; International Art & Design, New York. VAT: Spec.

C. Tapsell
16 Pierrepont Row, Camden Passage, Islington. N1 8EA. Est. 1970. Open Tues. and Fri. 10-5, Wed. 9-4.30, Sat. 9-5, other times by appointment. SIZE: Small. *STOCK: English mahogany and walnut furniture, 18th-19th C, £300-£15,000; Oriental china, 17th-19th C, £20-£5,000.* LOC: Near Angel underground station. TEL: 020 7354 3603. VAT: Stan/Spec.

Turn On Lighting
116/118 Islington High St., Camden Passage. N1 8EG. (J. Holdstock). Est. 1976. Open Tues.-Fri. 10.30-6, Sat. 9.30-4.30. *STOCK: Lighting, 1840-1940.* LOC: Angel underground station. PARK: Business Design Centre. TEL: 020 7359 7616; fax - same. SER: Interior design; museum commissions.

Vane House Antiques
15 Camden Passage, Islington. N1 8EA. (Michael J. Till). Est. 1950. Open 10-5. CL: Mon. and Thurs. *STOCK: 18th to early 19th C furniture.* TEL: 020 7359 1343; fax - same. VAT: Spec.

The Waterloo Trading Co.
The Granary, North London Freight Centre, York Way, King's Cross. N1 0AU. Est. 1989. Open 9-5. CL: Sat. SIZE: Large. *STOCK: Victorian, Edwardian and shipping furniture.* TEL: 020 7837 4806; fax - 020 7837 4815; e-mail - info@robertboysshipping.co.uk SER: Robert Boys shipping and packing worldwide. VAT: Stan.

Mike Weedon — LAPADA
7 Camden Passage, Islington. N1 8EA. (Mike and Hisako Weedon). Est. 1977. Open Wed. 9-5, Sat. 10-5. *STOCK: Large selection Art Nouveau glass - Gallé, Daum, Lötz; antique glass by artists and designers, from 1880 to 1939; Art Deco sculpture - bronze, bronze and ivory including Chiparus, Preiss, Lorenzl; lighting.* TEL: Wed and Sat. only - 020 7226 5319; fax - 020 7700 6387; home - 020 7609 6826; e-mail - info@mikeweedonantiques.com website - www.mikeweedonantiques.com and www.mikeweedonantiques.co.uk

York Gallery Ltd — LAPADA
51 Camden Passage. N1 8EA. (Jane and Gerd Beyer). Est. 1984. Open Wed. and Sat. 10-5. *STOCK: Antique prints.* TEL: 020 7354 8012; e-mail - prints@yorkgallery.co.uk website - www.yorkgallery.co.uk SER: Bespoke framing. VAT: Stan.

N2

Amazing Grates - Fireplaces Ltd
61-63 High Rd., East Finchley. N2 8AB. (T. Tew). Resident. Est. 1971. Open 10-6. SIZE: Large. *STOCK: Mantelpieces, grates and fireside items, £200-£5,000; Victorian tiling, £2-£20; early ironwork, all 19th C.* LOC: 100yds. north of East Finchley underground station. PARK: Own. TEL: 020 8883 9590/6017. SER: Valuations; reproduction mantelpieces in stone and marble; restorations (ironwork, welding of cast iron and brazing, polishing); installations. VAT: Stan.

Martin Henham (Antiques)
218 High Rd., East Finchley. N2 9AY. Est. 1967. Open 10-6. SIZE: Medium. *STOCK: Furniture and porcelain,*

1710-1920, £5-£3,500; paintings, 1650-1940, £10-£4,000. PARK: Easy. TEL: 020 8444 5274. SER: Valuations; restorations (furniture); buys at auction.

Barrie Marks Ltd
24 Church Vale, Fortis Green. N2 9PA. ABA. PBFA. Open by appointment. *STOCK: Antiquarian books - illustrated, private press, colourplate, colour printing; modern first editions.* TEL: 020 8883 1919.

Lauri Stewart - Fine Art
36 Church Lane. N2 8DT. Open Tues. and Wed. 10.30-4.30. *STOCK: Modern British oils and watercolours.* TEL: 020 8883 7719; e-mail - lste181072@aol.com

N3

Intercol London
43 Templars Crecent. N3 3QR. (Yasha Beresiner). Est. 1977. Open by appointment only. SIZE: Large. *STOCK: Playing cards, maps and banknotes and related literature, £5-£1,000+.* LOC: Finchley. PARK: Easy. TEL: 020 8349 2207; fax - 020 8346 9539; e-mail - yasha@intercol.co.uk website - www.intercol.co.uk SER: Valuations; restorations (maps including colouring); buys at auction (playing cards, maps, banknotes and books). FAIRS: Major specialist European, U.S.A. and Far Eastern. VAT: Stan.

N4

Chaucer Fine Arts Ltd
5 Victoria Terrace. N4 4DA. Est. 1978. Open by appointment. *STOCK: Old Master paintings, sculpture and works of art; 19th C European paintings, 20th C Russian paintings and drawings.* TEL: 020 7730 2972; fax - 020 7730 5861; e-mail - chaucer@atlas.co.uk FAIRS: Milan. VAT: Margin.

Alexander Juran and Co   BADA
at Nathan Azizollahoff, OCC, Top Floor & Lift, Building A, 105 Eade Rd. N4 1TJ. Est. 1951. Open 9.15-5.30. CL: Sat. *STOCK: Caucasian rugs, nomadic and tribal; carpets, rugs, tapestries.* TEL: 020 7435 0280; fax - same; 020 8809 5505. SER: Valuations; repairs. VAT: Stan/Spec.

Kennedy Carpets
OCC Building G, 105 Eade Rd. N4 1TJ. (M. Kennedy and V. Eder). Est. 1974. Open 9.30-6. SIZE: Large. *STOCK: Decorative carpets, collectable rugs and kelims, mid-19th C to new, £500-£50,000.* LOC: Off Seven Sisters Road. PARK: Free. TEL: 020 8800 4455; fax - 020 8800 4466; e-mail - kennedycarpets@ukonline.co.uk website - www.cloudband.com/occ/kennedycarpets SER: Valuations; restorations and cleaning; making to order. VAT: Stan.

Joseph Lavian
OCC, Building E, Ground Floor, 105 Eade Rd. N4 1TJ. Est. 1950. Open 9.30-5.30. SIZE: Large. *STOCK: Oriental carpets, rugs, kelims, tapestries and needlework, Aubusson, Savonnerie and textiles, 17th-19th C.* TEL: 020 8800 0707; fax - 020 8800 0404; mobile - 07767 797707; e-mail - Lavian@Lavian.com website - www.Lavian.com SER: Valuations; restorations.

Michael Slade Antiques
42 Quernmore Rd. N4 4QP. Est. 1987. Open 10-6. SIZE: Small. *STOCK: Period oak, Georgian, Victorian, Edwardian and Art Deco furniture, £300-£1,000.* PARK: Easy. TEL: 020 8341 3194; mobile - 07813 377029; website - www.antiquesnorthlondon.co.uk SER: Valuations; restorations (furniture including upholstery, French polishing and cabinet repairs). FAIRS: Alexandra Palace.

Teger Trading
318 Green Lanes. N4 1BX. Est. 1968. Open 9-6. CL: Sat. SIZE: Large. *STOCK: Reproduction bronzes, furniture, marble figures, paintings, mirrors, porcelain and unusual items.* PARK: Own. TEL: 020 8802 0156; fax - 020 8802 4110; e-mail - les@teger-trading.demon.co.uk SER: Restorations; film hire. *Trade Only.*

N5

Nicholas Goodyer
8 Framfield Rd., Highbury Fields. N5 1UU. ABA. ILAB. PBFA. Est. 1951. Open weekday business hours but prior telephone call advisable. *STOCK: Antiquarian books especially illustrated.* PARK: Nearby. TEL: 020 7226 5682; fax - 020 7354 4716; e-mail - email@nicholasgoodyer.com website - www.nicholasgoodyer.com FAIRS: International ILAB (London, Boston, San Francisco); monthly PBFA, London.

N6

Fisher and Sperr
46 Highgate High St. N6 5JB. (J.R. Sperr). Est. 1945. Open daily 10.30-5. SIZE: Large. *STOCK: Books, 15th C to date.* LOC: From centre of Highgate Village, nearest underground stations Archway (Highgate), Highgate. PARK: Easy. TEL: 020 8340 7244; fax - 020 8348 4293. SER: Valuations; restorations (books). VAT: Stan.

Betty Gould Antiques
408-410 Archway Rd., Highgate. N6 5AT. Est. 1964. Open 10-3. CL: Mon. and Thurs. SIZE: Medium. *STOCK: Furniture, 18th-20th C, £50-£5,000.* LOC: On A1, just below Highgate underground station (corner of Shepherds Hill). TEL: 020 8340 4987. SER: Restorations; French polishing; upholstery.

N7

Dome Antiques (Exports) Ltd   LAPADA
40 Queensland Rd., Islington. N7 7AJ. (Adam and Louise Woolf). Est. 1961. Open Mon.-Fri. SIZE: Large. *STOCK: 19th C furniture, £250-£10,000.* LOC: Near junction of Holloway and Hornsey roads. PARK: Easy. TEL: 020 7700 6266; fax - 020 7609 1692; mobile - 07831 805888; e-mail - info@domeantiques.co.uk SER: Valuations; restorations (furniture). FAIRS: LAPADA (NEC, April; Olympia, Feb. and June; Commonwealth Institute, Oct). VAT: Stan/Spec.

N8

Solomon
49 Park Rd., Crouch End. N8 8SY. (Solomon Salim). Est. 1982. Open 9.30-6. SIZE: Medium. *STOCK: Furniture including upholstered and Arts and Crafts,*

£200-£4,000; decorative items, £100-£500; all 1880-1970. LOC: 20 mins. off North Circular at Muswell Hill turn-off. PARK: Easy. TEL: 020 8341 1817; e-mail - solomon@solomonantiques.fsnet.co.uk website - www.solomonantiques.com SER: Valuations; restorations (furniture including upholstery). VAT: Spec.

N9

Anything Goes
83 Bounces Rd. N9 8LD. (C.J. Bednarz). Est. 1977. Open 10-5. CL: Mon. SIZE: Medium. *STOCK: General antiques including 18th-19th C furniture and bric-a-brac.* PARK: Easy. TEL: 020 8807 9399. SER: Valuations. FAIRS: Newark.

N10

Crafts Nouveau
112 Alexandra Park Rd., Muswell Hill. N10 2AE. (Laurie Strange). Est. 2003. Open Wed.-Sat. 10.30-6.30, Tues. and Sun. by appointment. CL: Mon. SIZE: Large. *STOCK: Arts and Crafts, Art Nouveau furniture and decorative art - desks and writing accessories, ceramics including Doulton, Moorcroft; glassware including Loetz; copper and pewter (Hugh Wallis, Archibald Knox, Liberty, Newlyn and Keswick schools); postcards, stamps, ephemera; Gallé and Daum reproduction lamps and glass.* LOC: Parade of shops, off Colney Hatch Lane. PARK: Easy and nearby. TEL: 020 8444 3300; fax - 020 8815 9945; mobile - 07958 448380; website - www.craftsnouveau.co.uk SER: Restorations (furniture including upholstery, metalware).

N12

Finchley Fine Art Galleries
983 High Rd., North Finchley. N12 8QR. (Sam Greenman). Est. 1972. Open 1-6, Sun. by appointment. SIZE: Large. *STOCK: 18th-20th C watercolours, paintings, etchings, prints, mostly English, £25-£10,000; Georgian, Victorian, Edwardian furniture, £50-£10,000;* china and porcelain - Moorcroft, Doulton, Worcester, Clarice Cliff, £5-£2,000; musical and scientific instruments, bronzes, early photographic apparatus, fire-arms, shotguns. LOC: Off M25, junction 23, take Barnet road. Gallery on right 3 miles south of Barnet church, opposite Britannia Road. PARK: Yellow line - call in and collect display card for 30 minutes free parking. TEL: 020 8446 4848; fax - 020 8445 2381; mobile - 07712 629282; e-mail - finchleyfineart@onetel.com SER: Valuations; restorations; picture relining, cleaning; framing.

Frames Stop
218 Woodhouse Rd., Friern Barnet. N12 0RS. (D. Georgiou and S. Kerr). Est. 1976. Open 10-5.30. SIZE: Small. *STOCK: General antiques, mirrors and frames.* LOC: Near Muswell Hill. PARK: Nearby. TEL: 020 8446 8409. SER: Restorations.

N13

Palmers Green Antiques Centre
472 Green Lanes, Palmers Green. N13 5PA. (Michael Webb). Est. 1976. Open 10-5.30, Sun. 11-5. CL: Tues. SIZE: Large. *STOCK: Furniture, general antiques and collectables.* PARK: Nearby. TEL: 020 8350 0878; mobile - 07986 730155. SER: Valuations. FAIRS: Alexandra Palace.

N14

C.J. Martin (Coins) Ltd   LAPADA
85 The Vale, Southgate. N14 6AT. Est. 1974. Open by appointment. *STOCK: Ancient and medieval coins and ancient artefacts.* TEL: 020 8882 1509/4359; e-mail - ancient.art@btinternet.com website - www.ancientart.co.uk/cjmartincoins

N16

The Cobbled Yard
1 Bouverie Rd., Stoke Newington. N16 0AB. (C. Lucas). Est. 2000. Open Wed.-Sun. 11-5.30. SIZE: Medium.

STOCK: Victorian pine furniture, £50-£750; iron and brass beds, 19th C, £200-£500; Edwardian and some period furniture, from £100; general antiques, collectors and decorative items, ceramics, bric-a-brac, £5-£500. LOC: Off Church St., behind Daniel Defoe public house. PARK: Easy. TEL: 020 8809 5286; e-mail - info@cobbled-yard.co.uk website - www.cobbled-yard.co.uk SER: Valuations; furniture restoration, polishing and upholstery; carpentry and bespoke furniture.

N19

Chesney's Antique Fireplace Warehouse
734-736 Holloway Rd. N19 3JF. Est. 1983. Open 9-5.30, Sat. 10-5. SIZE: Large. *STOCK: 18th-19th C marble, stone and timber chimney pieces, £1,000-£150,000; reproduction chimney pieces, £250-£7,500.* LOC: South of Archway roundabout on A1. PARK: Side streets adjacent. TEL: 020 7561 8280; fax - 020 7561 8288. SER: Valuations. VAT: Stan/Spec.

Squawk
130c Junction Rd., Tufnel Park. N19 5LB. Est. 1994. Open 11-7, Sun. 12-6. *STOCK: Decorative objects, original pine and reclaimed furniture, period garden furniture and some reproduction, general antiques.* TEL: 020 7272 5603.

N20

Julian Alexander Antiques
40 Totteridge Lane. N20 9QJ. (Julian A. Gonnermann). Est. 1991. Open 9.30-5. CL: Mon. and Thurs. SIZE: Medium. *STOCK: 18th-20th C furniture, £50-£5,000.* LOC: Close to Totteridge and Whetstone underground stations. PARK: Outside. TEL: 020 8446 6663; e-mail - julian@jag.uk.com website - www.jag.uk.com SER: French polishing; re-upholstery.

N21

Dolly Land
864 Green Lanes, Winchmore Hill. N21 2RS. Est. 1987. Open 9.30-4.30. CL: Mon. and Wed. *STOCK: Dolls, teddies, trains, die-cast limited editions.* PARK: Easy. TEL: 020 8360 1053; fax - 020 8364 1370; website - www.dolly-land.co.uk SER: Restorations; part exchange; dolls' hospital. FAIRS: Doll and Bear.

NW1

Art Furniture
158 Camden St. NW1 9PA. Est. 1989. Open 12-5 including Sun. SIZE: Warehouse. *STOCK: Decorative arts 1851-1951, Arts & Crafts furniture by Heal's, Liberty and others.* LOC: Under rail bridge on Camden St. going south. PARK: Easy. TEL: 020 7267 4324; e-mail - arts-and-crafts@artfurniture.co.uk website - www.artfurniture.co.uk SER: Export; hire. VAT: Stan/Spec.

Madeline Crispin Antiques
95 Lisson Grove. NW1 6UP. Est. 1971. Open 10-5.30. *STOCK: General antiques.* LOC: Near Church St. and Alfie's Market. TEL: 020 7402 6845; e-mail - madeline@crispinantiques.fsnet.uk

The Facade
99 Lisson Grove. NW1 6UP. (Mrs Gay Brown). Est. 1973. Open Tues.-Sat. 10.30-5. *STOCK: French and Italian decorative items and lighting, 1900-1940.* PARK: Easy. TEL: 020 7258 2017. VAT: Stan.

Angela Hone Watercolours BADA
CINOA. Open by appointment. *STOCK: English and French watercolours and pastels, 1850-1930.* TEL: 01628 484170; fax - same; e-mail - honewatercolours@aol.com FAIRS: Olympia; BADA; Harrogate.

Laurence Corner
62-64 Hampstead Rd. NW1 2NU. Est. 1955. Open 9.30-6. SIZE: Large. *STOCK: Military antiques - uniforms, helmets, militaria, theatrical costumes, props, fancy dress, flags.* LOC: From Tottenham Court Rd. - Warren St. end - continue into Hampstead Rd., then Drummond St. is first turning on right by traffic lights. PARK: Meters in nearby streets. TEL: 020 7813 1010; fax - 020 7813 1413; website - www.laurencecorner.com SER: Catalogue on request.

Relic Antiques Trade Warehouse
127 Pancras Rd. NW1 1UN. (Malcolm and Matthew Gliksten). Est. 1968. Open 10-5.30, Sun. by appointment. SIZE: Large. *STOCK: English and French decorative and country; architectural and garden; mirrors and French posters; fairground art, trade signs and marine antiques; shopfittings and showcases.* PARK: Meters. TEL: 020 7387 6039; fax - 020 7388 2691; mobile - 07831 785059; e-mail - malcolm.gliksten@blueyonder.co.uk website - www.rubylane.com/shops/relic SER: Antique tours - Languedoc, France. FAIRS: Chelsea Decorative; Montpellier, France. VAT: Stan.

David J. Wilkins
27 Princess Rd., Regents Park. NW1 8JR. Est. 1974. Open by appointment. SIZE: Large, warehouses. *STOCK: Oriental rugs.* LOC: Off Regent's Park Rd., near St Mark's church. PARK: Free. TEL: 020 7722 7608; home - 01371 831239; website - www.orientalrugexperts.com SER: Valuations; restorations; Oriental rug broker. VAT: Stan.

NW2

G. and F. Gillingham Ltd
62 Menelik Rd. NW2 3RH. (George and Fryda Gillingham). Est. 1960. Open by appointment. *STOCK: Furniture, 1750-1950.* TEL: 020 7435 5644; fax - same; mobile - 07958 484140. SER: Valuations; export.

Sabera Trading Co
2 Oxgate Parade, Crest Rd. NW2 7EU. (M. and Sabera Nawrozzadeh). Est. 1994. Open 10-6. SIZE: Large. *STOCK: Oriental carpets, 19th-20th C, £100-£12,000; porcelain, early 20th C, £100-£1,000; antiques and fine art, jewellery.* LOC: Cricklewood. PARK: Easy. TEL: 020 8450 0012; fax - same; home - 020 8450 4058. SER: Valuations.

Soviet Carpet & Art Galleries
303-305 Cricklewood Broadway. NW2 6PG. (R. Rabilizirov). Est. 1983. Open 10.30-5, Sun. 10.30-5.30. CL: Sat. SIZE: Large. *STOCK: Hand-made rugs, £100-*

£1,500; Russian art, £50-£5,000; all 19th-20th C. LOC: A5. PARK: Side road. TEL: 020 8452 2445. SER: Valuations; restorations (hand-made rugs). VAT: Stan.

NW3

Antiques 4 Ltd
116-118 Finchley Rd. NW3 5HT. (Andrew Harding and Simon Chaudhry). Est. 1994. Open 10-5.30 or by appointment. SIZE: Small. *STOCK: Clocks, including longcase and bracket, from 1650, £400-£60,000; furniture, from 1750; Victorian music boxes.* PARK: Own by arrangement. TEL: 020 7794 6043; fax - 020 7794 7368; mobile - 07712 009230; e-mail - antiques4 @btconnect.com website - www.antiques4.com SER: Valuations; restorations.

Patricia Beckman Antiques   LAPADA
(Patricia and Peter Beckman). Est. 1968. Open by appointment. *STOCK: Furniture, 18th-19th C.* LOC: Hampstead. TEL: 020 7435 5050/0500. VAT: Spec.

Tony Bingham   LAPADA
11 Pond St. NW3 2PN. Est. 1964. Open Mon.-Fri. 10-6.30. *STOCK: Musical instruments, books, music, oil paintings, engravings of musical interest.* TEL: 020 7794 1596; fax - 020 7433 3662; e-mail - tbingham @easynet.co.uk website - www.oldmusicalinstruments. co.uk VAT: Stan/Spec.

Keith Fawkes
1-3 Flask Walk, Hampstead. NW3 1HJ. Est. 1970. Open 10-5.30, Sun. 1-6. SIZE: 2 shops. *STOCK: Antiquarian and general books.* LOC: Near Hampstead underground station. PARK: Meters. TEL: 020 7435 0614.

Otto Haas
49 Belsize Park Gardens. NW3 4JL. (Maud and Julia Rosenthal). Est. 1866. Open by appointment. CL: Sat. *STOCK: Manuscripts, printed music, autographs, rare books on music.* PARK: Outside. TEL: 020 7722 1488; fax - 020 7722 2364; e-mail - contact@ottohaas-music. com SER: Auction representation; catalogues. FAIRS: Occasional international.

Hampstead Antique and Craft Emporium
12 Heath St., Hampstead. NW3 6TE. Est. 1967. Open 10.30-5, Sat. 10-6, Sun. 11.30-5.30. CL: Mon. SIZE: 24 units. *STOCK: General antiques, craft work and gifts.* LOC: 2 mins. walk from Hampstead underground station. TEL: 020 7794 3297.

Klaber and Klaber   BADA
PO Box 9445. NW3 1WD. (Mrs B. Klaber and Miss P. Klaber). Est. 1968. Open by appointment. STOCK: English and Continental porcelain and enamels, 18th-19th C. TEL: 020 7435 6537; fax - 020 7435 9459; e-mail - info@klaber.com website - www.klaber.com VAT: Spec.

Duncan R. Miller Fine Arts   BADA LAPADA
17 Flask Walk, Hampstead. NW3 1HJ. CINOA. Est. 1975. Open by appointment. SIZE: Small. STOCK: Modern British and European paintings, drawings and sculpture, especially Scottish Colourist paintings. LOC: Off Hampstead High St., near underground station. PARK: Nearby. TEL: 020 7435 5462; e-mail -

DMFineArts@aol.com website - www.duncanmiller. com SER: Valuations; conservation; restorations (oils, works on paper and Oriental rugs); buys at auction. FAIRS: Grosvenor House; BADA; Olympia. VAT: Spec.

Newhart (Pictures) Ltd
PO Box 1608. NW3 3LB. (Bernard Hart). Open by appointment. *STOCK: Oil paintings and watercolours, 1850-1930, from £500.* TEL: 020 7722 2537; fax - 020 7722 4335; e-mail - hart@newhartpictures.co.uk website - www.newhartpictures.co.uk SER: Valuations; restorations; framing. VAT: Spec.

Recollections Antiques Ltd
The Courtyard, Hampstead Antiques Emporium, 12 Heath St., Hampstead. NW3 6TE. (June Gilbert). Est. 1987. Open Tues.-Sat. 10.30-5. SIZE: Small. *STOCK: English blue and white transfer print pottery, 1820-1850; decorative furniture, 19th C; children's furniture and toys; unusual decorative items - glass and kitchenalia.* PARK: Nearby. TEL: 020 7431 9907; fax - 020 7794 9743; mobile - 07930 394014; e-mail - junal@recollectionsantiques.co.uk website - www. recollectionsantiques.co.uk

Malcolm Rushton - Early Oriental Art
13 Belsize Grove. NW3 4UX. (Dr Malcolm Rushton). Est. 1997. Open by appointment, mainly evenings and weekends. SIZE: Small. *STOCK: Fine 6th-8th C buddhist stone sculpture - China Northern Wei to Tang dynasties; fine bronze items - Shang to Han dynasties, with animal or human motif, to £50,000.* LOC: Near Belsize Park underground station, off Haverstock Hill. PARK: Easy. TEL: 020 7722 1989. e-mail - malcolm rushton@highstream.com SER: Valuations; restorations (ceramics, sculpture mounting). VAT: Stan.

M. and D. Seligmann
26 Belsize Park Gardens. NW3 4LH. (Maja and David Seligman). CINOA. Est. 1948. Open by appointment. *STOCK: Fine vernacular furniture, mainly English, 17th to early 19th C; antiquities and objets d'art.* PARK: Meters. TEL: 020 7722 4315; fax - same; mobile - 07946 634429. VAT: Stan/Spec.

NW4

Talking Machine
30 Watford Way, Hendon. NW4 3AL. Open 10-4, Sat. 9.30-1.30, prior telephone call advisable. *STOCK: Mechanical music, old gramophones, phonographs, vintage records and 78s, needles and spare parts, early radios and televisions, typewriters, sewing machines, juke boxes, early telephones.* LOC: 1 min. from Hendon Central underground station. TEL: 020 8202 3473; mobile - 07774 103139; e-mail - davepaul50@hotmail. com; davepauled1@yahoo.com and davepauled2@ yahoo.com website - www.gramophones.ndirect.co.uk SER: Buys at auction. VAT: Spec.

NW5

Acquisitions (Fireplaces) Ltd
24-26 Holmes Rd., Kentish Town. NW5 3AB. (K. Kennedy). NFA. GMC. Est. 1974. Open 9-5. SIZE:

Large. *STOCK: Fireplaces in marble, wood, cast-iron and stone, Georgian, Victorian, Edwardian reproduction, fire-side accessories, £195-£5,000.* LOC: 3 mins. walk from Kentish Town underground station. PARK: Forecourt. TEL: 020 7485 4955; fax - 020 7276 4361; e-mail - sales@acquisitions.co.uk website - www. acquisitions.co.uk SER: Bespoke manufacture of chimney pieces. VAT: Stan.

Lida Lavender   LAPADA
39-51 Highgate Rd. NW5 1RS. (Lida and Paul Lavender). Est. 1992. Open 10-6. SIZE: Large. *STOCK: Carpets including Aubusson, tapestries and textiles.* TEL: 020 7424 0600; fax - 020 7424 0404; e-mail - info@lavenders.co.uk website - www.lavenders.co.uk SER: Restorations. FAIRS: Olympia (Feb. and June).

Orientalist
74-78 Highgate Rd. NW5 1PB. (E. and H. Sakhai). Est. 1885. SIZE: Large. *STOCK: Rugs, carpets, needlepoints, tapestries and Aubussons, including reproduction.* PARK: Easy and nearby. TEL: 020 7482 0555; fax - 020 7267 9603. SER: Valuations; restorations (cleaning and repairing rugs, carpets and tapestries); buys at auction (Oriental carpets, rugs and textiles). VAT: Stan/Spec.

NW6

Gallery Kaleidoscope incorporating Scope Antiques
64-66 Willesden Lane. NW6 7SX. (K. Barrie). Est. 1965. Open Tues.-Sat. 10-6, Thurs. until 8. SIZE: Large. *STOCK: Oils, watercolours, prints, ceramics and sculpture, 19th-21st. C.* LOC: 10 mins. from Marble Arch. PARK: Easy. TEL: 020 7328 5833; fax - 020 7624 2913; e-mail - info@gallerykaleidoscope.com website - www.gallerykaleidoscope.com SER: Restorations; framing. FAIRS: Affordable Art (Spring). VAT: Stan/Spec.

NW8

Alfies Antique Market
13-25 Church St. NW8 8DT. Open Tues.-Sat. 10-6. SIZE: 300 stands with 180+ dealers on 4 floors. TEL: 020 7723 6066; fax - 020 7724 0999; e-mail - alfies@clara.net website - www.alfiesantiques.com

Beverley
30 Church St., Marylebone. NW8 8EP. Open 10-6 or by appointment. *STOCK: Art Nouveau, Art Deco, decorative objects.* TEL: 020 7262 1576. FAIRS: NEC.

Bizarre
24 Church St., Marylebone. NW8 8EP. (A. Taramasco and V. Conti). Open 10-5. *STOCK: Art Deco and Art Nouveau.* TEL: 020 7724 1305; fax - 020 7724 1316.

Church Street Antiques
8 Church St. NW8 8ED. (Stuart Shuster). Est. 1975. Open 10-5.30. CL: Mon. SIZE: Medium. *STOCK: English brown furniture, 18th to early 20th C, £500-£2,000.* LOC: Between Edgeware Rd. and Lisson Grove. PARK: Meters. TEL: 020 7723 7415; fax - 020 7723 7415; home - 020 8952 2249. SER: Valuations; restorations (polishing). FAIRS: NEC. VAT: Stan.

Davidson Antiques
5 Church St. NW8 8EE. (Edward Davidson). Est. 1982. Open 10-6. SIZE: Medium. *STOCK: Fine and decorative antiques; French, Continental and English furniture, 1780-1930; architectural antiques, objets d'art, paintings and eclectic items.* PARK: Easy. TEL: 020 7724 7781; fax - 020 7724 7783; e-mail - info@ canonbury-antiques.co.uk website - www.davidson antiques.com SER: Free sourcing; valuations. FAIRS: Decorative Antiques.

Nicholas Drummond/Wrawby Moor Art Gallery Ltd
6 St. John's Wood Rd. NW8 8RE. (J.N. Drummond). Est. 1972. Open by appointment. *STOCK: English and European oils, £250-£30,000; works on paper.* LOC: Pass Lords entrance and next lights, house last bow front on left, facing down Hamilton Terrace. TEL: 020 7286 6452; home - same; fax - 020 7266 9070; e-mail - drummonds@nixpix.fsnet.co.uk SER: Valuations; restorations (oils); buys at auction. VAT: Spec.

Gallery of Antique Costume and Textiles
2 Church St., Marylebone. NW8 8ED. Est. 1975. Open 10-5.30. *STOCK: Curtains, cushions, needleworks, paisley shawls, Aubussons, original clothing up to 1950s and English quilts, 19th-20th C; tassles, decorative borders, silk panels, velvets and brocades, £5-£20,000.* LOC: 500yds. from Marylebone underground station and 1/2 mile from Marble Arch. PARK: Easy. TEL: 020 7723 9981 (ansaphone); e-mail - info@gact.co.uk website - www.gact.co.uk FAIRS: Hali; Vintage Fashion and Textiles; New York.

Patricia Harvey Antiques and Decoration
42 Church St., Marylebone. NW8 8EP. Est. 1961. Open 10-5.30. SIZE: Medium. *STOCK: Decorative furniture, objets, accessories and paintings, £100-£20,000.* LOC: Between Lisson Grove and Edgware Rd., near Alfies Antique Market. PARK: Pay and Display. TEL: 020 7262 8989; fax - same; home - 020 7624 1787; e-mail - info@patriciaharveyantiques.co.uk website - www. patriciaharveyantiques.co.uk SER: Valuations; buys at auction; interior decoration. FAIRS: Decorative Antiques and Textiles. VAT: Spec.

Just Desks
20 Church St. NW8 8EP. (G. Gordon and N. Finch). Est. 1967. Open 9.30-6, Sat. 9.30-5 or by appointment. *STOCK: Victorian, Edwardian and reproduction desks, writing tables, bureaux, chairs, filing cabinets and roll tops.* PARK: Meters/Pay & Display. TEL: 020 7723 7976; fax - 020 7402 6416. VAT: Stan.

Leask Ward
NW8 9LP. Est. 1973. Open by appointment. *STOCK: Oriental and European antiques and paintings.* LOC: St John's Wood. TEL: 020 7289 2429; fax - same; e-mail - wardl5@aol.com SER: Consultancy. VAT: Spec.

Andrew Nebbett Antiques
35-37 Church St. NW8 8ES. Est. 1986. Open Tues.-Sat. 10-5.30. SIZE: Large. *STOCK: Refectory tables, leather sofas and chairs, light oak furniture, Heals, garden furniture, lamps, decorative items, military and ships furniture, 1760-1960.* LOC:

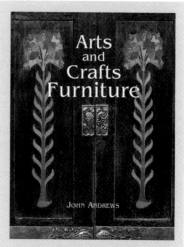
50m from Alfie's Antique Market. TEL: 020 7723 2303; e-mail - anebbett@aol.com website - www.andrewnebbett.com FAIRS: Olympia (Feb). VAT: Stan/Spec.

The Studio
(John Beer). Open by appointment. *STOCK: British Arts and Crafts, Gothic and Art Deco, especially furniture, 1830-1960's.* TEL: 01242 576080; mobile - 07976 704306. SER: Valuations; buys at auction.

Tara Antiques
6 Church St. NW8 8ED. (G. Robinson). Est. 1971. Open 10-6. CL: Mon. SIZE: Medium. *STOCK: Unusual marble and bronze statuary; Vienna bronzes, silver, furniture, paintings, ivory and tortoiseshell.* PARK: Easy. TEL: 020 7724 2405. SER: Buys at auction. VAT: Stan.

Townsends
81 Abbey Rd., St. John's Wood and 106 Boundary Rd. NW8 0AE. (M. Townsend). Est. 1972. Open 10-6. SIZE: Large + warehouse 96A Clifton Hill. *STOCK: Fireplaces, £250-£6,000; stained glass, £80-£1,000; architectural and garden antiques, £50-£2,000; all mainly 18th-19th C.* LOC: Corner of Abbey Rd. and Boundary Rd. PARK: Easy. TEL: 020 7624 4756; warehouse - 020 7372 4327; fax - 020 7372 3005. SER: Valuations; site surveys; free delivery. VAT: Stan.

Young & Son   LAPADA
12 Church St. NW8 8EP. (L. and S. Young). CINOA. Est. 1990. Open Tues.-Sat. 10-6. SIZE: Medium. *STOCK: Furniture, paintings, £100-£20,000; lighting and mirrors, £80-£5,000; decorative items, £100-£5,000; all 18th-20th C.* LOC: Off Lisson Grove and Edgeware Rd. PARK: Easy. TEL: 020 7723 5910; fax - same; mobile - 07958 437043; e-mail - youngfamily@fsmail.net

website - www.youngandson.com SER: Valuations; restorations (gilding, framing, French polishing, paintings lined, cleaned and restored). VAT: Stan/Spec.

NW9

B.C. Metalcrafts
69 Tewkesbury Gardens. NW9 0QU. (F. Burnell). Est. 1946. Open by appointment. *STOCK: Lighting, ormolu and marble lamps; Oriental and European vases; clocks, pre-1900, £5-£500.* TEL: 020 8204 2446; fax - 020 8206 2871. SER: Restorations; conversions; buys at auction. *Trade Only.*

NW10

David Malik and Son Ltd
5 Metro Centre, Britannia Way, Park Royal. NW10 7PA. Open 9-5. CL: Sat. *STOCK: Chandeliers, wall lights.* PARK: Easy. TEL: 020 8965 4232; fax - 020 8965 2401. VAT: Stan.

Willesden Green Architectural Salvage
189 High Rd., Willesden. NW10 2SD. (D. Harkin). Est. 1996. Open 9-6. *STOCK: Architectural items.* TEL: 020 8459 2947; fax - 020 8415 1515; mobile - 07971 176547.

NW11

Christopher Eimer
P.O. Box 352. NW11 7RF. BNTA. IAPN. Est. 1970. Open 9-5 by appointment. *STOCK: Commemorative and historical medals and related art.* TEL: 020 8458 9933; fax - 020 8455 3535; e-mail - art@christophereimer.co.uk website - www.christophereimer.co.uk VAT: Global/Margin.

WC1

Abbott and Holder Ltd   BADA
30 Museum St. WC1A 1LH. (Philip Athill). Est. 1936. Open 9.30-6, Thurs. till 7. SIZE: 3 floors. STOCK: English watercolours, drawings, oils and prints, 1760-2000. LOC: Opposite British Museum. PARK: Bloomsbury Sq. TEL: 020 7637 3981; fax - 020 7631 0575; e-mail - abbott.holder@virgin.net website - www.abbottandholder.co.uk SER: Conservation; framing and mounting; valuations. FAIRS: Watercolours and Drawings; BADA. VAT: Spec

Atlantis Bookshop
49a Museum St. WC1A 1LY. (Geraldine and Bali Beskin). Est. 1922. Open 10.30-6, Fri. 10.30-7.30. STOCK: Antiquarian books on the occult and esoteric sciences; occasional related artefacts and paintings, especially Austin Osman Spare and Aleister Crowley. LOC: Tottenham Court Rd. or Holborn underground stations. TEL: 020 7405 2120; e-mail - atlantis@the atlantisbookshop.com website - www.theatlantis bookshop.com

Austin/Desmond Fine Art
Pied Bull Yard, 68/69 Great Russell St. WC1B 3BN. (J. Austin). SLAD. Open 10.30-5.30, Sat. 11-2.30 during exhibitions. STOCK: Modern and contemporary British paintings and prints; ceramics. LOC: Near Bloomsbury. Holborn and Tottenham Court Rd. underground stations. PARK: Bloomsbury Sq. or Bury Place. TEL: 020 7242 4443; fax - 020 7404 4480; e-mail - gallery@ austindesmond.com website - www.austindesmond.com FAIRS: London Art; Olympia; London Original Print; 20th/21st British Art.

Cinema Bookshop
13-14 Great Russell St. WC1B 3NH. (F. Zentner). Est. 1969. Open 10.30-5.30. SIZE: Small. STOCK: Books, magazines, posters and stills. LOC: First right off Tottenham Court Rd. PARK: Easy. TEL: 020 7637 0206; fax - 020 7436 9979. SER: Mail order. VAT: Stan.

George and Peter Cohn
Unit 21, 21 Wren St. WC1X 0HF. Est. 1947. Open 9-5, Sat. and Fri. pm. by appointment. STOCK: Decorative lights. PARK: Forecourt. TEL: 020 7278 3749. SER: Restorations (chandeliers and wall-lights).

Fine Books Oriental
38 Museum St. WC1A 1LP. (Jeffrey Somers). PBFA. Est. 1970. Open 9.30-6, Sat. 11-6. SIZE: Medium. STOCK: Books. LOC: Near British Museum. PARK: Meters. TEL: 020 7242 5288; fax - 020 7242 5344; e-mail - oriental@finebooks.demon.co.uk website - www. finebooks.demon.co.uk

Michael Finney Antique Prints and Books
31 Museum St. WC1A 1LG. (Michael and Mirka Finney). ABA. PBFA. Est. 1979. Open 10-6. SIZE: Large. STOCK: Prints, 17th-19th C; decorative plate books and watercolours especially David Roberts, Piranesi and Spain; caricatures. PARK: Meters. TEL: 020 7631 3533; fax - 020 7637 1813; e-mail - prints@ michaelfinney.co.uk website - www.michaelfinney.co.uk FAIRS: ABA Olympia (June).

Robert Frew Ltd
106 Gt. Russell St. WC1B 3NB. ABA. PBFA. Est. 1978. Open 10-6, Sat. 10-2. STOCK: Books, 15th-20th C, £50-£50,000; maps and prints, 15th-19th C, £5-£5,000. LOC: Turn right off Tottenham Court Rd. to British Museum, shop on left past YMCA. PARK: Easy. TEL: 020 7580 2311; fax - 020 7580 2313; e-mail - shop@ robertfrew.com website - www.robertfrew.com FAIRS: ABA Olympia; Chelsea; PBFA; Hotel Russell; California; New York; Boston; Milan; Amsterdam. VAT: Stan.

Jessop Classic Photographica
67 Great Russell St. WC1B 3BN. Open 9-5.30. STOCK: Classic photographic equipment, cameras and lenses. TEL: 020 7831 3640; fax - 020 7831 3956; e-mail - classic@jessops.com website - www.jessops.com/classic

Spink and Son Ltd   BADA
69 Southampton Row. WC1B 4ET. BNTA. IAPN. Est. 1666. Open Mon.-Fri. 9.30-5.30. STOCK: Coins, medals, stamps, bank notes and related books. TEL: 020 7563 4000; fax - 020 7563 4066; e-mail - info@spink.com website - www.spink.com SER: Valuations. VAT: Stan/Spec.

WC2

Anchor Antiques Ltd
Suite 31, 26 Charing Cross Rd. WC2H 0DG. (K.B. Embden and H. Samne). Est. 1964. Open by appointment. STOCK: Continental and Oriental ceramics, European works of art and objets de vertu. TEL: 020 7836 5686. VAT: Spec. Trade Only.

Apple Market Stalls
Covent Garden Market. WC2E 8RF. Est. 1980. Open every Monday 10-6.30. SIZE: 48 stalls. STOCK: General antiques and quality collectables. LOC: North Hall. TEL: 020 7836 9136; e-mail - theapplemarket@ coventgardenmarket.co.uk website - www.covent gardenmarket.co.uk

A.H. Baldwin and Sons Ltd   BADA
11 Adelphi Terrace. WC2N 6BJ. IAPN. BNTA. Est. 1872. Open 9-5. CL: Sat. SIZE: Medium. STOCK: Coins, 600 BC to present; commemorative medals, 16th C to present, numismatic literature. LOC: Off Robert St., near Charing Cross. TEL: 020 7930 6879; fax - 020 7930 9450; e-mail - coins@baldwin.sh SER: Valuations; auctioneers and auction agents for selling and purchasing. VAT: Stan/Spec.

M. Bord (Gold Coin Exchange)
16 Charing Cross Rd. WC2H 0HR. Est. 1969. Open 10.30-5.30. SIZE: Small. STOCK: Gold, silver and copper coins, Roman to Elizabeth II, all prices; banknotes and medals, foreign coins. LOC: Near Leicester Sq. underground station. TEL: 020 7836 0631/7240 0479; fax - 020 7240 1920. SER: Valuations; buys at auction. FAIRS: All major coin. VAT: Stan/Spec.

Tim Bryars Ltd
8 Cecil Court. WC2N 4HE. ABA. ALAB. IAMA. IMCoS. Est. 2004. Open 11-6, Sat. 12-5. SIZE: Medium. STOCK: Early printed books, classical texts and

translations, atlases and maps of all regions, mainly pre 1800; topographical and natural history prints, all £10-£20,000. LOC: From Leicester Sq. underground, south down Charing Cross Rd.(towards Trafalgar Sq.), second left. PARK: Shelton St. or meters. TEL: 020 7836 1901; fax - 020 7836 1910; e-mail - tim@timbryars.co.uk website - www.timbryars.co.uk FAIRS: London Map (Rembrandt Hotel and Olympia). VAT: Stan.

Philip Cohen Numismatics
20 Cecil Court. WC2N 4HE. BNTA. Est. 1977. SIZE: Medium. *STOCK: English coins, 16th-20th C, £1-£1,000.* LOC: Off Charing Cross Road, near Leicester Sq. underground station. TEL: 020 7379 0615; fax - 020 7240 4300; e-mail - coinheritage@aol.com SER: Valuations.

Covent Garden Flea Market
Jubilee Market, Covent Garden. WC2E 8RB. (Sherman and Waterman Associates Ltd). Est. 1975. Open every Mon. from 6 am. SIZE: 150 stalls. *STOCK: General antiques.* LOC: South side of piazza, just off The Strand, via Southampton St. PARK: Easy and NCP Drury Lane. TEL: 020 7836 2139/7240 7405.

David Drummond at Pleasures of Past Times
11 Cecil Court, Charing Cross Rd. WC2N 4EZ. Est. 1962. Open 11-2.30 and 3.30-5.45 and usually 1st Sat. monthly, other times by appointment. SIZE: Medium. *STOCK: Scarce and out-of-print books of the performing arts; early juvenile and illustrated books; vintage postcards, valentines, entertainment ephemera and miscellaneous bygones.* Not Stocked: Coins, stamps, medals, jewellery, maps, cigarette cards. LOC: In pedestrian court between Charing Cross Rd. and St. Martin's Lane. TEL: 020 7836 1142; fax - same; e-mail - drummond@poptfsnet.co.uk VAT: Stan.

Elms-Lesters Tribal Art   LAPADA
1-5 Flitcroft St. WC2H 8DH. (Paul Jones and Fiona McKinnon). Est. 1972. Open 11-6 during exhibitions, other times by appointment. SIZE: Medium. *STOCK: Tribal art from Africa, Oceania and south-east Asia - sculptures, masks, ethnographic objects, furniture and textiles, 19th to mid-20th C.* LOC: Between Soho, Covent Garden and Bloomsbury. PARK: Meters and NCP nearby. TEL: 020 7836 6747; fax - 020 7379 0789; e-mail - gallery@elms-lesters.demon.co.uk website - www.elms-lesters.demon.co.uk SER: Valuations. FAIRS: LAPADA.

Stanley Gibbons
399 Strand. WC2R 0LX. PTS. Est. 1856. Open 9-5.30, Sat. 9.30-5.30. SIZE: Large. *STOCK: Popular and specialised stamps, postal history, catalogues, albums, accessories; autographs and memorabilia.* LOC: Opposite Savoy Hotel. TEL: 020 7836 8444; fax - 020 7836 7342; e-mail - shop@stanleygibbons.co.uk website - www.stanleygibbons.com SER: Valuations; auctions. VAT: Stan/Spec.

Gillian Gould at Ocean Leisure
Embankment Place, 11-14 Northumberland Avenue. WC2N 5AQ. Est. 1988. Open 9.30-6, Thurs. 9.30-7, Sat. 9.30-5.30 or by appointment. SIZE: Small. *STOCK: Marine antiques and collectables, scientific instruments,*

£30-£1,000. LOC: Embankment underground station. TEL: 020 7419 0500; fax - 020 7419 0400; mobile - 07831 150060; e-mail - gillgould@dealwith.com SER: Valuations; restorations; hire; sources gifts for personal and corporate presentation; buys at auction. VAT: Stan.

Grosvenor Prints
19 Shelton St., Covent Garden. WC2H 9JN. Est. 1975. Open 10-6, Sat. 11-4. SIZE: Large. *STOCK: 18th-19th C topographical and decorative prints, specialising in portraits, dogs and British field sports.* LOC: One street north of Covent Garden underground station. PARK: Easy. TEL: 020 7836 1979; fax - 020 7379 6695; e-mail - grosvenorprints@btinternet.com website - www.grosvenorprints.com SER: Valuations; restorations; buys at auction. FAIRS: ABA. VAT: Stan/Spec.

P. J. Hilton (Books)
12 Cecil Court. WC2N 4HE. (Paul Hilton). Est. 1980. Open 11-6, Sat. 11-5. SIZE: Medium. *STOCK: Antiquarian books, 16th-20th C, £75-£500; secondhand books; leather cloth bindings by the yard.* LOC: Off Charing Cross Rd. TEL: 020 7379 9825. SER: Valuations.

Raymond D Holdich International Medals & Militaria
7 Whitcomb St. WC2H 7HA. (D.C. Pratchett and R.D. Holdich). Est. 1979. Open 9.30-3.30. CL: Sat. *STOCK: Coins and military medals, bonds, banknotes, badges and militaria, 18th-20th C, £5-£10,000.* LOC: Next to National Gallery. PARK: NCP. TEL: 020 7930 1979; fax - 020 7930 1152; e-mail - rdhmedals@aol.com website - www.rdhmedals.com SER: Valuations; buys at auction (coins and military medals). VAT: Stan/Spec.

Koopman Ltd & Rare Art (London) Ltd BADA
Entrance to London Silver Vaults, Ground Floor, 53/64 Chancery Lane. WC2A 1QS. (Timo Koopman and Lewis Smith). Open 9-5.30, Sat. 10-1. *STOCK: Fine quality English Georgian and Continental silverware.* TEL: 020 7242 7624; fax - 020 7831 0221; e-mail - enquiries@rareartlondon.com website - www.rareartlondon.com FAIRS: Milan; Olympia; New York; Maastricht (TEFAF); Gotha, Parma; Palm Beach.

The London Silver Vaults
Chancery House, 53-64 Chancery Lane. WC2A 1QS. Est. 1892. Open 9-5.30, Sat. 9-1. SIZE: 34 shops. *STOCK: Antique and modern silver, plate, jewellery, objets d'art, clocks, watches, general items. See below details of some of the dealers at this address.* PARK: Meters. TEL: 020 7242 3844; website - www.thesilvervaults.com SER: Valuations; restorations. VAT: Stan/Global/Export.

A. M. W. Silverware
Vault 52-53. TEL: 020 7242 3620; fax - 020 7831 3923.

Argenteus Ltd   LAPADA
Vault 2. TEL: 020 7831 3637; fax - 020 7430 0126. VAT: Stan/Spec.

Belmonts

A. Bloom   LAPADA
Vault 27. *Victorian and Edwardian silver miniatures to*

monumental table centres. TEL: 020 7242 6189; fax - same; e-mail - bloomvault@aol.com website - www.bloomvault.com

Luigi Brian Antiques

Vault 17. *Fine English and European silver, objets d'art and icons.* TEL: 020 7405 2484; fax - same.

B.L. Collins

Vault 20. (Barry Collins). TEL: 020 7404 0628; fax - 020 7404 1451; e-mail - b.collins@silvervaults.idps.co.uk website - www.blcollins.co.uk

Crown Silver

Vault 30. TEL: 020 7242 4704. *Trade Only.*

P. Daniels

Vault 51. TEL: 020 7430 1327.

Bryan Douglas   LAPADA

Vault 12/14. (Ian Bryan). *Antique, old and modern silverware.* TEL: 020 7242 7073; fax - same; e-mail - sales@bryandouglas.co.uk website - www.bryandouglas.co.uk

R. Feldman Ltd   LAPADA

Vault 6. *Unusual and rare items, old Sheffield and Victorian plate, silver centrepieces, candelabra, epergnes combined with argenteus specialising in all patterns of flatware.* TEL: 020 7405 6111; fax - 020 7430 0126; e-mail - rfeldman@rfeldman.co.uk website - www.rfeldman.co.uk

I. Franks   LAPADA

Vault 9/11. Est. 1926. *Old and antique English silver and plate especially tableware, teasets, cutlery, epergnes, candlesticks and candelabra.* TEL: 020 7242 4035; fax - same; e-mail - info@ifranks.com website - www.ifranks.com

Anthony Green Antiques

Vault 54. *Vintage wrist watches.* TEL: 020 7430 0038

M. & J. Hamilton

Vault 25. *17th -20th C silver including cutlery.* TEL: 020 7831 7030; fax - 020 7831 5483; e-mail - hamiltonsilver@hotmail.com

Gary Hyams

Vault 48-50. *Silver and Sheffield Plate.* TEL: 020 7831 4330.

Stephen Kalms   LAPADA

Vault 15, 31, 32. TEL: 020 7430 1265; fax - 020 7405 6206; e-mail - stephen@skalms.freeserve.co.uk website - www.kalmsantiques.com

B. Lampert

Vault 19. TEL: 020 7242 4121.

Langfords   LAPADA

Vault 8/10. (Adam and Joel Langford). Est. 1940. *Silver and plate especially cutlery.* TEL: 020 7242 5506; fax - 020 7405 0431; e-mail - vault@langfords.com website - www.langfords.com SER: Valuations. VAT: Stan/Spec.

Leon Antiques

Vault 57.

Nat Leslie Ltd

Vault 21-23. (Mark Hyams). Est. 1940. *Victorian and 20th C silverware especially flatware and contemporary designers, especially Stuart Devlin.* TEL: 020 7242 4787; fax - 020 7242 4504; e-mail - nat.leslie@which.net website - www.natleslie.co.uk VAT: Stan/Spec.

Linden and Co. (Antiques) Ltd

Vault 7. (H.M. and S. C. Linden). *Silver and plate, specialising in gift items for weddings, christenings, silver weddings and retirements, £100-£750.* TEL: 020 7242 4863; fax - 020 7405 9946; e-mail - lindenandco@aol.com website - www.lindenantiquesilver.com VAT: Stan/Spec.

C. and T. Mammon

Vault 55-64. (Claude Mammon). *Victorian and old Sheffield plate, Continental and English silver and cutlery, mirror plateaux and centrepieces.* TEL: 020 7405 2397; fax - 020 7405 4900; e-mail - claudemammco@btinternet.com website - www.candtmammon.com

I. Nagioff (Jewellery)

Vault 63 and 69. (I. and R. Nagioff). Est. 1955. *Jewellery, 18th-20th C, £5-£2,000+; objets d'art, 19th C, to £200.* TEL: 020 7405 3766. SER: Valuations; restorations (jewellery). VAT: Stan.

Percy's (Silver Ltd).   LAPADA

Vault 16. (David and Paul Simons). *Fine decorative silver especially claret jugs, candelabra, candlesticks, flatware and collectables.* TEL: 020 7242 3618; fax - 020 7831 6541; e-mail - sales@percys-silver.com website - www.percys-silver.com

Terry Shaverin

Vault 143. TEL: 020 8368 5869; fax - 020 8361 7659; e-mail - terryshaverin@silverflatware.co.uk website - www.silverflatware.co.uk

David S. Shure and Co

Vault 1. (Lynn Bulka). Est. 1900. Author. *Antique and modern silverware, old Sheffield plate, cutlery and jewellery.* TEL: 020 7405 0011; fax - same. SER: Valuations. VAT: Stan.

Silstar (Antiques Ltd)

Vault 29. (B. Stern). Est. 1955. TEL: 020 7242 6740; fax - 020 7430 1745; e-mail - antique@silstar.fsnet.co.uk VAT: Stan/Spec.

S. and J. Stodel   BADA

Vault 24. (Jeremy Stodel). *Chinese export to English Art Deco silver including flatware.* TEL: 020 7405 7009; fax - 020 7242 6366; e-mail - stodel@msn.com website - www.chinesesilver.com

J. Surtees

Vault 65. *Silver.* TEL: 020 7242 0749.

William Walter Antiques Ltd   BADA LAPADA

Vault 3/5. (Elizabeth Simpson). Est. 1927. *Georgian silver, old Sheffield plate; also modern silver.* TEL: 020 7242 3284; fax - 020 7404 1280; e-mail - enq@wwantiques.prestel.co.uk website - www.williamwalter.co.uk SER: Valuations; restorations (silver, plate).

Peter K. Weiss

Vault 18. Est. 1955. *Watches, clocks.* TEL: 020 7242 8100; fax - 020 7242 7310. VAT: Stan.

Wolfe (Jewellery)

Vault 41. (John Petrook). TEL: 020 7405 2101; fax - same VAT: Stan/Spec.

Marchpane

16 Cecil Court, Charing Cross Rd. WC2N 4HE. (Kenneth Fuller). ABA. PBFA. ILAB. Est. 1989. Open 10.30-6. SIZE: Medium. *STOCK: Antiquarian children's and illustrated books, from 18th C to date.* TEL: 020 7836 8661; fax - 020 7497 0567; e-mail - k_fuller@btclick.com

Sir Charles Jackson's *English Goldsmiths and their Marks* is the classic reference work on British antique silver hallmarks. First written in 1905 and last revised in 1921, it is a mammoth endeavour which has remained in print ever since. It is still considered indispensable by silver collectors and dealers, despite shortcomings due to its age. This major new edition has been compiled by a team of distinguished experts to take account of the vast store of information which has been unearthed as a result of much detailed and wide ranging research over the last seventy years.

The text has been extensively updated with over 10,000 corrections and an enormous amount of entirely new material. For example, there are over 1,000 corrections to London eighteenth century makers' marks alone. Many ideas and attributions have changed since Jackson assembled his work and some of the makers he overlooked are now known to be of major significance.

There are not many standard reference works which survive for eighty years without being displaced. This revised edition reconfirms Jackson's status as the bible for all antique silver enthusiasts and a key reference for dealers, scholars and collectors.

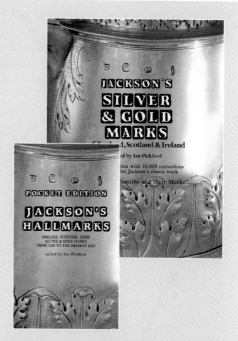

JACKSON'S
SILVER & GOLD MARKS
of England, Scotland & Ireland
edited by Ian Pickford

Specifications: 766pp., 400 b.&w. and approx. 15,000 marks, 11 x 8½in./279 x 216mm. **£49.50 (hardback)**
Pocket Edition: 172pp., over 1,000 marks, 8½ x 4½in./215 x 120mm. **£12.50 (hardback) £6.95 (paperback)**

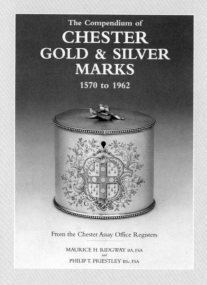

The Compendium of
CHESTER GOLD & SILVER MARKS
1570 to 1962
From the Chester Assay Office Registers
MAURICE RIDGWAY AND PHILIP PRIESTLEY

This is the first publication in a single work of all known Chester punch marks, and continues the tradition of the standard volumes of Jackson, Grimwade, Culme and Pickford. It is also the first time that the twentieth-century Chester marks have been published. It is produced in dictionary format, in alphabetical order from 1570, the date of the earliest known mark, to 1962 at which time the Chester assay office was closed. The authors, both members of the silver society, were given unlimited access to the Chester assay office records covering 1686 to 1962, and to the Chester Goldsmith's Company records dating from the 16th century.

The compendium has four sections. The preface provides an historical background and details of all extant records and copper plates. Part 1 is devoted to assay office marks, with a full set of date letter tables to assist the reader in dating wares. Part 2 covers nearly 10,000 entries for makers' marks, including pictograms and monograms. Finally, the appendices include items on assay volumes and charges, thimble makers, and Liverpool watchcase makers.

Since over 2,000 of the entries have Birmingham addresses, the new work will also enhance available information on jewellers and silversmiths working in this important trade center. The format of the marks' tables and the extensive index will also allow future research into the relationships between companies and agents.

Specifications:
520pp., approx. 10,000 marks recorded, 11 x 8½in./279 x 216mm.
£65.00 (hardback)

For full details of all ACC publications, log on to our website:
www.antiquecollectorsclub.com
or telephone 01394 389950 for a free catalogue

BEDFORDSHIRE

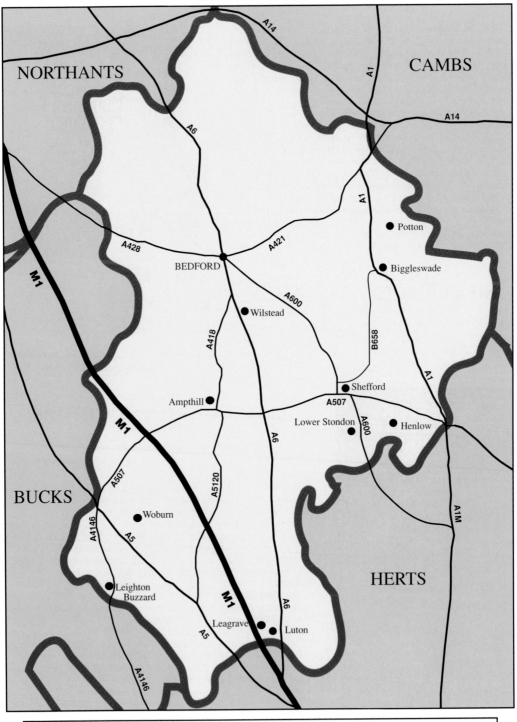

Dealers and Shops in Bedfordshire					
Ampthill	8	Leagrave	1	Potton	1
Bedford	2	Leighton Buzzard	1	Shefford	1
Biggleswade	2	Lower Stondon	1	Wilstead	1
Henlow	1	Luton	1	Woburn	4

AMPTHILL

Ampthill Antiques
Market Sq. MK45 2EH. (Lord J.E. Shayler). Est. 1980. Open 11-6 including Sun. SIZE: Large. *STOCK: Furniture, collectables, jewellery, clocks, china, glass, pictures.* LOC: Town centre. PARK: Easy and at rear. TEL: 01525 403344; e-mail - ampthillantiques@ btconnect.com

Ampthill Antiques Emporium
6 Bedford St. MK45 2NB. (Marc Legg). Est. 1979. Open 10-5 including Sun. CL: Tues. SIZE: Large - 50 dealers. *STOCK: Antique furniture, fireplaces, architectural items, smalls, ceramics, glass and jewellery.* LOC: 5 mins. from junction 13, M1. PARK: Easy. TEL: 01525 402131; fax - 01582 737527; e-mail - info@ampthill antiquesemporium.co.uk website - www.ampthill antiquesemporium.co.uk SER: Restorations (furniture); upholstery; caning and metal polishing.

Antiquarius of Ampthill
107 Dunstable St. MK45 2NG. (Peter Caldwell). Est. 1997. Open 10.30-5, Sun. 1-5. SIZE: Medium. *STOCK: Sitting and dining room furniture, 1800-1900, to £3,000.* LOC: Town centre. PARK: Nearby. TEL: 01525 841799; e-mail - peter.caldwell@tesco.net website - www. antiquariusofampthill.com SER: Restorations; re-upholstery.

House of Clocks
102-104 Dunstable St. MK45 2JP. (John and Helga Ginty). Resident. Est. 1957. Open 9-5, Sun. 11-4. SIZE: Medium. *STOCK: Clocks including longcase, bracket, carriage and wall, £150-£12,000.* PARK: Through narrow archway by shop, behind Market Sq. TEL: 01525 403136; e-mail - houseofclocks@tiscali.co.uk website - www.houseofclocks.co.uk SER: Valuations; restorations (clocks). FAIRS: Manchester; Birmingham: Uxbridge: Kettering: Luton. VAT: Stan/Spec.

David Litt Antiques
The Old Telephone Exchange, Claridges Lane. MK45 2NG. (David and Helen Litt). Est. 1967. Open 7.30-5, Sat. and Sun. by appointment. SIZE: Large. *STOCK: French country items especially armoires, farmhouse tables, sets of chairs, chandeliers and mirrors.* LOC: Off Woburn St. PARK: Easy. TEL: 01525 404825; fax - 01525 404563; mobile - 07802 449027; home - 01525 750359; e-mail - litt@ntlworld.com website - www. davidlittantiques.co.uk FAIRS: Decorative Antiques & Textile, Battersea; House & Garden; Olympia.

Paris Antiques
97B Dunstable St. MK45 2NG. (Paul and Elizabeth Northwood). Est. 1985. Open 9.30-5. CL: Mon. SIZE: Medium. *STOCK: Furniture, 18th to early 20th C, £250-£4,000; brass and copper, silver and plate, pictures and smalls.* LOC: Off junction 12, M1. PARK: Opposite. TEL: 01525 840488; home - 01525 861420; mobile - 07802 535059. SER: Valuations; restorations (mainly furniture, some metal); buys at auction.

Pilgrim Antiques
111 Dunstable St. MK45 1BY. (Gary Lester). Est. 1982. Open 10-5.30 including Sun. CL: Mon. SIZE: Large.

AMPTHILL ANTIQUES EMPORIUM

Experience shopping as it was nearly a century ago at this unique antique centre, housed in a purpose built Victorian department store, virtually unchanged since 1898. Three floors offering a variety of town, country & decorative Antiques to suit all tastes. Visit our rear yard for Architectural & Garden Antiques. Marvel at our magnificent mahogany pharmacy interior, which now incorporates our payment counter & reception area.

IN-HOUSE SERVICES
Traditional Upholsterer • Furniture Restorer • Picture Framer and the most comprehensive range of restoration materials in the area

Open every day **10.00am-5.00pm**
(except Tuesday closed all day)
6 Bedford Street, Ampthill
Telephone: 01525 402131
www.ampthillantiquesemporium.co.uk
email: info@ampthillantiquesemporium.co.uk

STOCK: Furniture including dining tables, bookcases, chairs, wardrobes, 18th-20th C, £500-£5,000. LOC: Town centre. PARK: Rear of premises. TEL: 01525 633023.

The Pine Parlour
82a Dunstable St. MK45 2LF. (Lynn Barker). Est. 1989. Open 10-5 including Sun. CL: Mon. SIZE: Small. *STOCK: Pine furniture, 19th C, £200-£800; kitchenalia, £5-£60.* PARK: Easy. TEL: 01525 403030; home - same. SER: Valuations.

BEDFORD

Architectural Antiques
70 Pembroke St. MK40 3RQ. (Paul and Linda Hoare). Est. 1989. Open 12-5, Sat. 10-5. SIZE: Medium. *STOCK: Early Georgian to early 20th C fireplaces, £500-£1,000; sanitary ware, from late Victorian, £100-£500; doors, panelling, pews, chimney pots and other architectural items, Georgian and Victorian, £50-£100.* LOC: Follow signs to town centre, turn on The Embankment or Castle Rd., shop is off Castle Rd., near Post Office. PARK: Easy. TEL: 01234 213131/308003; fax - 01234 309858. SER: Valuations; restorations; installations (period fireplaces).

Victoria House
70A Tavistock St. MK40 2RP. (Helen Felts). Est. 1989. Open 11.30-5. CL: Wed. SIZE: Medium. *STOCK: Victorian furniture, £100-£3,000.* LOC: A6 Kettering Rd. PARK: Easy. TEL: 01234 320000. SER: Valuations.

BIGGLESWADE

Shortmead Antiques
46 Shortmead St. SG18 0AP. (S.E. Sinfield). Open 10.30-4. CL: Mon. and Thurs. SIZE: Small. *STOCK: Furniture, £50-£1,000; boxes, porcelain, silver, bronzes, copper and brass, all pre-1930.* LOC: 1/2 mile from A1. TEL: 01767 601780 (ansaphone); e-mail - shortmead @lineone.net

Simply Oak
Oaktree Farm, Potton Rd. SG18 0EP. (R. Sturman and A. Kilgarriff). Est. 1996. Open 10-5, Sun. 11-4. SIZE: Large. *STOCK: Restored oak furniture, late Victorian to 1930s, £100-£2,000.* LOC: Off A1 towards Biggleswade, right turn onto B1040 - 3 miles towards Potton. PARK: Own. TEL: 01767 601559; e-mail - antiques@ simplyoak.freeserve.co.uk SER: Valuations; restorations (furniture especially oak).

HENLOW

Hanworth House Antiques & Interiors
Hanworth House, 92 High St. SG16 6AB. (Rosemarie Jarvis and Andrew Sell). Est. 2001. Open 11-5.30, Sun. 12-5.30. CL: Mon. SIZE: Small. *STOCK: English and Chinese furniture, mainly Victorian, £250-£5,500; glass and ceramics, 1880-1950, £50-£300; silver, 1890-1940, £50-£400; jewellery, 1900-1960, £40-£150; general small antiques including mirrors, lighting, watercolours, prints and etchings.* PARK: Own. TEL: 01462 814361; home/fax - same; e-mail - hanworthhouse@aol.com SER: Finder.

LEAGRAVE

Tomkinson Stained Glass
2 Neville Rd. LU3 2JQ. (S. Tomkinson). Open by appointment. *STOCK: Antique stained glass windows, from early Victorian to late Edwardian, Art Nouveau, Art Deco; religious church windows, French 1900; stained glass roundels.* LOC: 5 mins. from Luton station amd junction 11, M1. PARK: Easy. TEL: 01582 527866; mobile - 07831 861641; e-mail - sales@vitraux.co.uk website - www.vitraux.co.uk SER: Valuations; restorations. VAT: Stan.

LEIGHTON BUZZARD

Nick & Janet's Antiques
Buffalo House, Mill Rd., Slapton. LU7 9BT. (Janet and Nick Griffin). Est. 1992. Open by appointment. SIZE: Small. *STOCK: Pottery - South Devon including Torquay, £1-£2,000; North Devon including Brannam and Baron, £1-£1,000; Wesuma, £20-£400; Martin Brothers, £200-£5,000; modern Moorcroft, £30-£4,000; Cobridgeware, £20-£1,000.* PARK: Easy. TEL: 01525 220256; home - same; fax - 01525 229138; e-mail - nick@buffalogold.com website - www.buffalogold.com SER: Valuations.

LOWER STONDON

Memory Lane Antiques
14 Bedford Rd. SG16 6EA. (Elizabeth Henry). Est. 1985. Open 10.30-5, Sun. 11-4. CL: Wed. and Thurs. SIZE: Medium. *STOCK: General antiques including 19th oak, silver and plate, glass including coloured.* LOC: On A600 near RAF Henlow. PARK: Easy. TEL: 01462 811029/812716; fax - same. SER: Valuations.

LUTON

Bargain Box
4 & 6a Adelaide St. LU1 5BB. Open 9-6, Wed. 9-1. *STOCK: General antiques and collectables.* TEL: 01582 423809.

POTTON

W. J. West Antiques
58 High St. SG19 2QZ. (Alan, Richard and Wesley West). Est. 1930. Open 9-5.30, Sat. 9-12. SIZE: Small. *STOCK: Furniture, mainly Victorian, including upholstered, to £4,000.* LOC: Town centre. PARK: Easy. TEL: 01767 260589; fax - 01767 261513; mobile - 07989 257260; e-mail - emma_west32@yahoo.com SER: Valuations; restorations (furniture including upholstery).

SHEFFORD

S. and S. Timms Antiques Ltd   LAPADA
2/4 High St. SG17 5DG. Est. 1976. Open 9.30-5, Sat.11-5 or by appointment. SIZE: Large. *STOCK: 18th-19th C town and country furniture.* LOC: A507, centre of village. PARK: Easy. TEL: 01462 851051; mobile - 07885 458541; e-mail - info@timmsantiques.com website - www.timmsantiques.com FAIRS: Olympia x 3; Chelsea; Battersea. VAT: Stan/Spec.

WILSTEAD (WILSHAMSTEAD), Nr. Bedford

Manor Antiques

The Manor House, Cottonend Rd. MK45 3BT. (Mrs S. Bowen). Est. 1976. Open by appointment. SIZE: Large. STOCK: Furniture, 19th C to Edwardian, £100-£5,000; lighting, mirrors, decorative objects. LOC: Just off A6, 4 miles south of Bedford. PARK: Own. TEL: 01234 740262; home - same; e-mail - manorantiques@hotmail.com website - www.manorantiques.co.uk SER: Restorations (furniture); buys at auction. FAIRS: Olympia. VAT: Stan/Spec.

WOBURN

Christopher Sykes Antiques

The Old Parsonage, Bedford St. MK17 9QL. (Christopher and Margaret Sykes and Sally Lloyd). Est. 1949. Open by appointment but usually 9-5. SIZE: Large. STOCK: Collectors' items - attractive, early brass, copper and pewter; scientific and medical instruments; specialist in rare corkscrews, £10-£800; silver decanter labels, tastvins and funnels, pottery barrels and bin labels, glass decanters and tantalus. LOC: On A50, in main street next to Heritage Centre. PARK: Easy. TEL: 01525 290259/290467; fax - 01525 290061; e-mail - sykes.corkscrews@sykes-corkscrews.co.uk website - www.sykes-corkscrews.co.uk SER: 100 page illustrated mail order catalogue on corkscrews and wine related antiques available £7 each. Restoration and valuation of corkscrews. VAT: Stan/Spec.

Town Hall Antiques

Market Place. MK17 9PZ. (Elfyn and Elaine Groves). Est. 1993. Open 10-5.30, Sun. 11-5.30. SIZE: Medium. STOCK: Furniture, £50-£10,000; lighting, clocks, ceramics, glass, silver and plate, £10-£4,000; prints and pictures, £5-£4,000; all 18th to early 20th C; mirrors, domestic metalware; some antiquities; cigarette cards, tools, sporting memorabilia. LOC: Off A5 and off junction 12 or 13, M1. PARK: Easy. TEL: 01525 290950; fax - 01525 292501; e-mail - elfyn@townhallantiques.co.uk website - www.townhallantiques.co.uk SER: Valuations.

The Woburn Abbey Antiques Centre   BADA
                                              LAPADA

Woburn Abbey. MK17 9WA. (Woburn Enterprises Ltd). Est. 1967. Open every day (including Bank Holidays) 10-5.30. CL: Christmas holidays. SIZE: Over 75 shops and showcases on two floors. STOCK: English and Continental furniture, porcelain, glass, paintings, silver and decorative items. Not stocked: Reproduction. LOC: From M1 junction 13, signposted Woburn Abbey, centre is in South Courtyard. PARK: Easy. TEL: 01525 290350; fax - 01525 292102; e-mail - antiques@woburnabbey.co.uk website - www.woburnabbey.co.uk SER: Carriage for large items; worldwide shipping.

Woburn Fine Arts

12 Market Place. MK17 9PZ. (Z. Bieganski). Est. 1983. Open Tues.-Sun. 2.30-5.30. SIZE: Medium. STOCK: Post-impressionist paintings, 1880-1940; European paintings, 17th-18th C; British paintings, 20th C. PARK: Easy. TEL: 01525 290624; fax - 01525 290733; e-mail - info@abm.v.net.com SER: Restorations (oils and watercolours).

BERKSHIRE

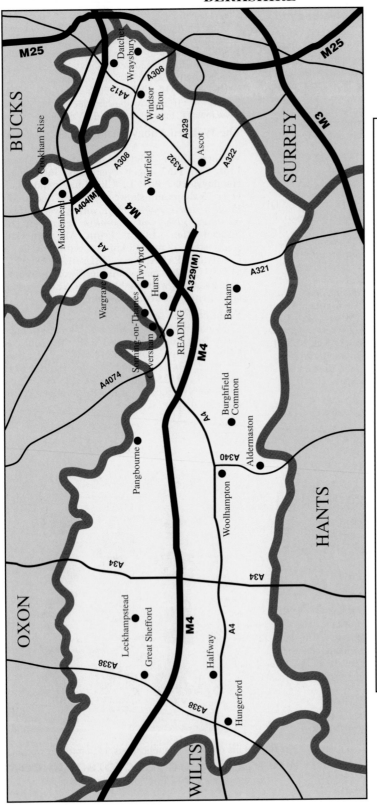

Dealers and Shops in Berkshire

Aldermaston	1	Cookham Rise	1	Hungerford	17	Twyford	1
Ascot	1	Datchet	1	Hurst	1	Warfield	1
Barkham	1	Great Shefford	1	Leckhampstead	1	Wargrave	1
Burghfield Comm	1	Halfway	1	Maidenhead	1	Windsor and Eton	14
Caversham	1	Horton	1	Pangbourne	1	Woolhampton	1
				Reading	2	Wraysbury	1
				Sonning-on-Thames	1		

ALDERMASTON, Nr. Reading

Aldermaston Antiques
The Old Dispensary. RG7 4LW. (Vivian and Roger Green). Est. 1994. Open 10-5.30. CL: Mon. SIZE: Medium + yard. *STOCK: Longcase clocks, furniture, lamps, silver, desks, mainly 19th C; architectural and garden stone and iron items.* LOC: A340, village centre. PARK: Easy and at rear. TEL: 01189 712370; home - same; website - www.aldermastonantiques.co.uk

ASCOT

Omell Galleries
The Corner House, Course Rd. SL5 7HL. (Omell Galleries (Windsor) Ltd). Est. 1947. Open 9.30-1 and 2-5 or by appointment. SIZE: Medium. *STOCK: Fine paintings, £400-£6,000.* LOC: Off High St. opposite garage. PARK: Easy. TEL: 01344 873443; fax - 01344 873467; e-mail - aomell@aol.com website - www.omellgalleries.co.uk SER: Valuations; restorations; cleaning; repairs (oils, watercolours and frames). VAT: Spec.

BARKHAM, Nr. Wokingham

Barkham Antique Centre
Barkham St. RG40 4PJ. (Len and Mary Collins). Open 10.30-5 including Sun. SIZE: Large - 50+ dealers. *STOCK: General antiques including furniture, china, kitchenalia, coins, Dinky toys, paintings, glassware, scientific instruments and brass; collectables including Beswick, Moorcroft, Royal Doulton, Wade.* LOC: Off M4, junction 10, A329M to Wokingham, over station crossing to Barkham (B3349), left at Bull public house, centre 300 yards on left. PARK: Easy. TEL: 01189 761355. SER: Valuations; restorations (china, French polishing, upholstery, cabinet making).

BURGHFIELD COMMON, Nr. Reading

Graham Gallery
Highwoods. RG7 3BG. (J. Steeds). Est. 1976. Open by appointment at any time. SIZE: Medium. *STOCK: English watercolours, £50-£1,500; English oil paintings, £200-£8,000; English prints, £25-£200; mainly 19th to early 20th C.* LOC: 4 miles west of Reading on Burghfield road. PARK: Easy. TEL: 01189 832320; fax - 01189 831070; e-mail - grahamgallery@freeuk.com website - www.grahamgallery.org.uk SER: Valuations; restorations; cleaning; framing.

CAVERSHAM, Nr. Reading

The Clock Workshop   LAPADA
17 Prospect St. RG4 8JB. (J.M. Yealland FBHI). TVADA. CINOA. Est. 1980. Open 9.30-5.30, Sat. 10-1. SIZE: Small. *STOCK: Clocks, late 17th to late 19th C, £350-£60,000; barometers, 18th-19th C, £500-£35,000.* LOC: Prospect St. is the beginning of main Reading to Henley road. PARK: Behind shop in North St. TEL: 01189 470741; mobile - 07788 410493; e-mail - theclockworkshop@hotmail.com SER: Valuations; restorations (clocks, barometers, chronometers, barographs); buys at auction. FAIRS: TVADA; LAPADA; Olympia. VAT: Stan/Spec.

COOKHAM RISE

Gary Wallis Antiques
35 Station Parade. SL6 9BR. TVADA. Est. 1990. Open 10-5, Sun. by appointment. SIZE: Warehouse. *STOCK: English, Continental and colonial furniture and decorative effects including desks, bookcases, farmhouse tables, cabinets, mirrors, architectural fittings, garden statuary, metalwork, stone and terracotta.* PARK: Easy and at rear. TEL: 01628 523224; mobile - 07778 020536; e-mail - garylloydwallis@aol.com SER: Valuations; restorations.

DATCHET

The Studio Gallery
The Old Bank, The Green, SL3 9JH. (Julian Bettney). Est. 1990. Open Mon.-Sat. 1.30-6.30, Sun. by prior appointment. SIZE: Medium. *STOCK: Fine paintings and prints, 1740-1940; architectural items and objets d'art.* LOC: Off junction 5, M4, opposite Manor Hotel. PARK: Horton Rd. or railway station. TEL: 01753 544100; fax - same; mobile - 07770 762468; e-mail - Julianbettney@talk21.com SER: Landscape paintings in oils painted to commission; bespoke framing (hand built, coloured, gilded and veneered).

GREAT SHEFFORD, Nr. Hungerford

Alan Hodgson
No 2 Ivy House, Wantage Rd. RG16 7DA. *STOCK: Boxes, country and general antiques, collectors' items.* LOC: A338, 10 mins. from Hungerford towards Wantage. TEL: 01488 648172. SER: Restorations (furniture).

HALFWAY, Nr. Newbury

Alan Walker   BADA
Halfway Manor. RG20 8NR. TVADA. Est. 1987. Open by appointment. SIZE: Large. *STOCK: Fine barometers and weather instruments.* LOC: 4 miles west of Newbury on A4. PARK: Easy. TEL: 01488 657670; mobile - 07770 728397; website - www.alan walker-barometers.com SER: Restorations. FAIRS: Major London; some regional.

HORTON, Nr. Slough

John A. Pearson Antiques   BADA
Horton Lodge, Horton Rd. SL3 9NU. (Mrs J.C. Sinclair Hill). Est. 1902. Open by appointment. SIZE: Large. *STOCK: English and Continental furniture, 1700-1850; oil paintings, 17th-19th C, all £50-£50,000; decorative objects.* Not Stocked: Items after 19th C. LOC: From London turn off M4, exit 5, past London Airport; from M25 take exit 14. 10 mins from Heathrow. PARK: Easy. TEL: 01753 682136; fax - 01753 687151. SER: Valuations.

HUNGERFORD

Beedham Antiques Ltd   BADA
Charnham Close. RG17 0EJ. Open 10-5 or by appointment. *STOCK: English oak furniture, 16th-18th C; objects and works of art.* TEL: 01488 684141; fax - 01488 684050. VAT: Spec.

GREAT GROOMS ANTIQUE CENTRES

GREAT GROOMS *of* DORKING
50/52 West Street,
Dorking
Surrey RH4 1BU

Tel: 01306 887076
Fax: 01306 881029
Email: dorking@greatgrooms.co.uk
Internet: www.greatgrooms.co.uk

GREAT GROOMS *of* HUNGERFORD
Riverside House, Charnham Street
Hungerford,
Berkshire RG17 0EP

Tel: 01488 682314
Fax: 01488 686677
Email: hungerford@greatgrooms.co.uk
Internet: www.greatgrooms.co.uk

www.greatgrooms.co.uk

Below Stairs of Hungerford
103 High St. RG17 0NB. (Stewart. L. Hofgartner). Est. 1974. Open 10-6, including Sun. and Bank Holidays. SIZE: Large. *STOCK: Kitchen and decorative garden items, lighting, collectables, sporting items, interior fittings, ironmongery, taxidermy, advertising items, mainly 19th C English, £20-£2,500.* Not Stocked: Reproductions. LOC: Main street. PARK: Easy. TEL: 01488 682317; fax - 01488 684294; e-mail - hofgartner @belowstairs.co.uk website - www.belowstairs.co.uk SER: Valuations; on-line catalogue. VAT: Stan.

Sir William Bentley Billiards (Antique Billiard Table Specialist Company)   **LAPADA**
Standen Manor Farm. RG17 0RB. GMC. Est. 1989. Open by appointment seven days a week. SIZE: Large. *STOCK: Billiard tables, billiard/dining tables; antique and modern accessories including panelling, brass lights, marker boards and seating.* PARK: Own; helicopter facilities. TEL: 01488 681711; 020 8940 1152; fax - 01488 685197; website - www.billiards.co.uk SER: Restorations; removals and storage. FAIRS: House & Garden; Ideal Home; Period Living; Decorex; Antiques & Fine Art; Palm Beach.

Bow House
4 Faulkner Sq., Charnham St. RG17 0EP. (Jo Preston). Open 9.30-5.30, Sun. 10-4. SIZE: 2 floors. *STOCK: 18th-19th C furniture and decoratives, contemporary accessories and gifts.* LOC: First shop in Hungerford from Newbury A4. PARK: Own. TEL: 01488 680826. VAT: Spec.

Bridge House Antiques & Interiors
7 Bridge St. RG17 0EH. (Kate Pols). Est. 1991. Open Tues.-Sat. 10-5.30. SIZE: Large. *STOCK: 19th C French, Georgian, Regency and Edwardian antiques and decorative items.* PARK: Easy. TEL: 01488 681999; fax - same; mobile - 07789 718048. SER: Restorations.

Franklin Antiques
25 Charnham St. RG17 0EJ. (Lynda Franklin). Est. 1973. Open 10-5.30. SIZE: Large. *STOCK: 18th-19th C French and English furniture and decorative items.* LOC: A4. PARK: Easy. TEL: 01488 682404; fax - 01488 686089; mobile - 07831 200834; home - 01488 684072; e-mail - antiques@lyndafranklin.com website - www.lyndafranklin.com SER: Valuations; restorations.

Garden Art
Barrs Yard, 1 Bath Rd. RG17 0HE. (Susan and Arnie Knowles). Est. 1980. Open 10-6, Sun. 11-4. SIZE: Large. *STOCK: Period garden items.* PARK: Easy. TEL: 01488 681881; home - 01488 681882; website - www. bigbronze.co.uk VAT: Stan/Spec.

Great Grooms of Hungerford
Riverside House, Charnham St. RG17 0EP. (J. Podger). Est. 1991. Open 9.30-5.30, Sun.and Bank Holidays 10-4. SIZE: 15 showrooms over 3 floors with over 60 dealers. *STOCK: Wide variety of fine Continental and English furniture, glass, ceramics, pictures including Old Masters, collectors' items, lighting.* LOC: From M4 junction 14 on to A338. PARK: Free at rear of premises. TEL: 01488 682314; fax - 01488 686677; e-mail - hungerford@greatgrooms.co.uk website - www.great grooms.co.uk SER: Valuations; restorations (furniture including upholstery, pictures, silver, jewellery, ceramics). VAT: Spec.

Griffin Fine Art & Antiques
20 Bridge St. RG17 0EL. (John and Margaret Riordan). TVADA. Est. 1992. Open 10-5, Sat. 10-5.30. SIZE: Medium. *STOCK: 19th C French bronzes, £800-£8,000; 18th-19th C furniture, some painted; lighting, to 1930; decorative objects, 19th to early 20th C.* PARK: Easy or at garage adjacent. TEL: 01488 684667; mobile - 07802 896427 and 07808 741823; e-mail - johnriordan@ griffinfineart.co.uk website - www.bronzegriffin.com SER: Valuations. FAIRS: Battersea Decorative; TVADA.

Hungerford Arcade
High St. RG17 0NF. (Wynsave Investments Ltd). Est. 1972. Open 9.30-5.30, Sun. 11-5. SIZE: Over 80 stallholders. *STOCK: General antiques and period furniture.* PARK: Easy. TEL: 01488 683701.

Roger King Antiques
111 High St. RG17 0NB. (Mr and Mrs R.F. King). Est. 1974. Open 9.30-5 and most Sun. 11-5. SIZE: Large. *STOCK: Furniture, 1750-1910, £100-£2,000; china, 19th C; oil paintings.* Not Stocked: Silver, jewellery. LOC: Opposite Hungerford Arcade. PARK: Easy. TEL: 01488 682256; website - www.kingantiques.co.uk VAT: Spec.

MJM Antiques
13 Bridge St. RG17 0EH. (Michael Mancey). Est. 1997. Open 10-4. SIZE: Small. *STOCK: Fine guns and swords,*

1700-1900, £300-£15,000. LOC: Town centre. PARK: Easy. TEL: 01488 684905; fax - 01488 684090; home - 01488 684999; e-mail - mike@oldguns.co.uk website - www.oldguns.co.uk SER: Valuations. FAIRS: London Arms; International Arms; Park Lane Arms; Bisley Arms.

The Old Malthouse   **BADA**
15 Bridge St. RG17 0EG. (P.F. Hunwick). CINOA. TVADA. Est. 1963. Open 10-5.30. SIZE: Large. *STOCK: 18th to early 19th C walnut and mahogany furniture - dining tables, sets of chairs, mirrors, chests of drawers; clocks, barometers, decorative items, boxes and tea caddies. Not Stocked: Orientalia.* LOC: A338, left at Bear Hotel, shop is approx. 120 yards on left, just before bridge. PARK: Front of premises. TEL: 01488 682209; fax - same. SER: Valuations. FAIRS: Chelsea (Sept); Olympia; Blue Coats - TVADA. VAT: Spec.

Principia Fine Art
111D High St. RG17 0NB. (Michael Forrer). Est. 1970. Open 9.30-5.30. SIZE: Large. *STOCK: Collectors items, scientific instruments, maritime, country furniture, treen, pictures, Oriental china, porcelain, books and clocks.* PARK: Easy. TEL: 01488 682873; fax - 01189 341989; e-mail - majingforrer@yahoo.com.cn SER: Valuations. FAIRS: Scientific Instrument; NEC. VAT: Spec.

Styles Silver   **LAPADA**
12 Bridge St. RG17 0EH. (P. and D. Styles). Est. 1974. Open 9.30-5.30, other times by appointment. SIZE: Medium. *STOCK: Antique, Victorian and secondhand silver including cutlery.* PARK: Easy. TEL: 01488 683922; home - same; fax - 01488 683488; mobile - 07778 769559; e-mail - george@styles-silver.co.uk website - www.styles-silver.co.uk SER: Repairs; finder.

Turpins Antiques   **BADA**
17 Bridge St. RG17 0EG. (Jane Sumner). CINOA. Open Wed. - Sat. or by appointment. SIZE: Small. *STOCK: 17th-18th C walnut, oak and mahogany furniture and metalware.* TEL: 01488 681886; home - 01672 870727. FAIRS: Olympia. VAT: Spec.

Youll's Antiques
28 Charnham St. RG17 0EJ. (B.Youll). Est. 1935. Open 10.30-5.30, Sun. 11-5. *STOCK: French and English furniture and decorative items.* TEL: 01488 682046; fax - 01488 684335; e-mail - bruce.youll@virgin.net FAIRS: Newark.

HURST, Nr. Reading

Peter Shepherd Antiques
Penfold, Lodge Rd. RG10 0EG. Est. 1962. Open by appointment. *STOCK: Glass, rarities and books.* TEL: 01189 34 0755.

LECKHAMPSTEAD, Nr. Newbury

Hill Farm Antiques
Hill Farm, Shop Lane. RG20 8QG. (Mike Beesley). Open 9-5, Sun. by appointment. *STOCK: 19th C dining tables, chairs and library furniture.* LOC: Off B4494 between Stag public house and church. PARK: Own at rear. TEL: 01488 638541/638361; website - www.hillfarmantiques.co.uk SER: Restorations; shipping arranged; buys at auction.

MAIDENHEAD

Widmerpool House Antiques
7 Lower Cookham Rd., Boulters Lock. SL6 8JN. (M.L. Coleman). Open by appointment. *STOCK: English furniture, oil paintings, watercolours, prints; porcelain and Swansea pottery, glass, silver, 18th-19th C.* PARK: Nearby. TEL: 01628 623752.

PANGBOURNE

Rita Butler
4 Station Rd. RG8 7AN. TVADA. Est. 1999. Open Tues.-Sat. 10-5. SIZE: 2 floors. *STOCK: General antiques including small furniture especially oak; early 19th C to early 20th C ceramics especially Art Deco; glass, early 1800s; silver, watercolours, 19th C prints.* LOC: Village centre. PARK: Opposite. TEL: 01189 845522; mobile - 07752 936327; e-mail - rita.butler @tesco.net website - www.ritabutlerantiques.co.uk FAIRS: TVADA; Thames; Silhouette: Jay; Cooper.

READING

Fanny's Antiques
1 Lynmouth Rd. RG1 8DE. (Julia Lyons). Est. 1988. Open 10.30-4, Sun. 12-4. SIZE: Large. *STOCK: Decorative, period and new furniture, smalls.* PARK: Easy. TEL: 01189 508261; home - 01491 671471. SER: Valuations; restorations. FAIRS: House & Gardens; Battersea Decorative.

Rupert Landen Antiques
Church Farm, Reading Rd., Woodcote. RG8 0QX. TVADA. Open 9-5, Sat. 10-3. CL: Mon. *STOCK: Late 18th to early 19th C furniture.* TEL: 01491 682396; mobile - 07974 732472; website - www.rupertsantiques.com

SONNING-ON-THAMES

Cavendish Fine Arts   BADA
The Dower House. RG4 6UL. (Janet Middlemiss and Guy Hazel). Est. 1972. Open by appointment. *STOCK: Fine Queen Anne and English Georgian furniture, glass and porcelain.* **LOC: 5 mins. from M4. TEL: 01189 691904; mobile - 07831 295575; e-mail - janet@cavendishfinearts.com website - www. cavendishfinearts.com SER: Valuations; shipping; interior decoration. FAIRS: Olympia; Chelsea; BADA; TVADA. VAT: Stan/Spec.**

TWYFORD, Nr. Reading

Bell Antiques
2B High St. RG10 9AE. (Nigel, Chris and Russell Timms). Est. 1989. Open 9.30-5.30, Sun. 10-5.30. SIZE: Small. *STOCK: General antiques including china and glass, silver and plate, small furniture, 18th-20th C, £10-£300.* LOC: Village centre on crossroads. PARK: Limited free nearby. TEL: 01189 342501. VAT: Spec.

WARFIELD

Moss End Antique Centre
Moss End Garden Centre. RG12 6EJ. (Maura Dorrington and Maureen Staite). TVADA. Est. 1988. Open 10.30-5 including Sun. SIZE: Large - 25 dealers. *STOCK: General antiques and collectables.* LOC: A3095. PARK: Own. TEL: 01344 861942; website - www. mossendantiques.co.uk SER: Restorations (furniture). FAIRS: TVADA (Spring and Autumn).

WARGRAVE

John Connell - Wargrave Antiques
66 High St. RG10 8BY. Est. 1979. Open Wed.-Sun. other times by appointment. SIZE: Large - several dealers. *STOCK: Furniture, Georgian-Edwardian; small items, china, glass, metal.* PARK: Nearby. TEL: 01189 402914. SER: Restorations (furniture); silver plating; metal polishing.

WINDSOR

Art & Antiques and Bridge Miniatures
69 High St., Eton. SL4 6AA. (Vivien and Eddie Rand). Est. 1982. Open 10.30-5.30, Sat. 10.30-6, Sun. 2.30-6. SIZE: Medium. *STOCK: Collectors' items, jewellery, furniture, dolls house miniatures, from Victorian, £1-£600.* LOC: 1st shop over Thames from Windsor at Eton. PARK: Nearby. TEL: 01753 855727; home - 01628 527127. SER: Restorations (furniture, dolls houses, jewellery).

Roger Barnett Antiques
91 High St., Eton. SL4 6AF. Est. 1975. Open by appointment. *STOCK: Mahogany furniture and clocks.* TEL: 01753 867785.

Berkshire Antiques Co Ltd
42 Thames St., SL4 1YY. Est. 1980. Open 10.30-5.30 including Sun. (Jan. to April - Sun. by appointment). SIZE: Large. *STOCK: Antique and modern designer jewellery; general antiques, china, porcelain and glass, silver and plate, Royal commemoratives, toys and dolls, £10-£25,000.* LOC: Opposite George V memorial fountain. PARK: Nearby. TEL: 01753 830100; fax - 01753 832278; e-mail - sales@jewels2go.co.uk website - www.jewels2go.co.uk SER: Valuations; repairs.

Dee's Antique Pine
89 Grove Rd. SL4 1HT. (Dee Waghorn). Est. 1975. Open Wed.-Sat. 10-6, Sun. 11-3, other times by appointment. SIZE: Medium. *STOCK: 19th to early 20th C pine wardrobes and chests of drawers.* LOC: 5 mins. from town centre. PARK: Easy. TEL: 01753 865627; mobile - 07711 902887; e-mail - dee@deesantiquepine.fsnet.co.uk website - www.deesantiquepine.co.uk SER: Free storage, local delivery and wardrobe assembly.

Eton Antique Bookshop
88 High St., Eton. SL4 6AF. (Maurice Bastians). Est. 1975. Open 11-6, Sun. 11-5. SIZE: Medium. *STOCK: Secondhand and antiquarian books; antiquarian prints.* PARK: Easy and at rear. TEL: 01753 855534. SER: Book search, book binding and repairs.

Eton Antiques Partnership
80 High St., Eton. SL4 6AF. (Mark Procter). Est. 1967. Open 10-5, Sun. 2-5.30. SIZE: Large. *STOCK: Mahogany and rosewood furniture, 18th-19th C.* LOC: Slough East exit from M4 westbound. PARK: Nearby. TEL: 01753 860752; home - same. SER: Exporting; interior design consultants. VAT: Stan/Spec.

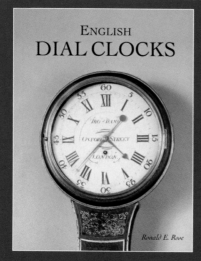
Marcelline Herald Antiques   LAPADA

41 High St., Eton. SL4 6BD. TVADA. Est. 1993. Open Tues.,Thurs., Fri. and Sat. 10-5, other days by appointment. SIZE: Medium. *STOCK: Furniture, £500-£15,000; mirrors, pelmets and screens, £200-£2,500; ceramics, lamps and prints, £50-£1,000; all 18th to early 19th C.* PARK: Loading and nearby. TEL: 01753 833924; fax - 01264 730376. FAIRS: TVADA; Decorative Antiques & Textile. VAT: Spec.

J. Manley

27 High St., Eton. SL4 6AX. (Malcolm Leach). BAPCR. Est. 1891. Open 10-5. *STOCK: Watercolours, old prints.* TEL: 01753 865647; e-mail - sales@manleygallery.com SER: Restorations; framing; mounting.

Peter J. Martin   LAPADA

40 High St., Eton. SL4 6BD. (Peter J. Martin & Son). TVADA. Est. 1963. Open 9-1 and 2-5. CL: Sun. SIZE: Large and warehouse. *STOCK: Period, Victorian and decorative furniture and furnishings, £50-£20,000; metalware, £10-£500, all from 1800.* PARK: 50yds. opposite. TEL: 01753 864901; home - 01753 863987; e-mail - pjmartin.antiques@btopenworld.com website - www.pjmartin-antiques.co.uk SER: Restorations; shipping arranged; buys at auction. VAT: Stan/Spec.

Mostly Boxes

93 High St., Eton. SL4 6AF. (G.S. Munday). Est. 1977. Open 10-6.30. *STOCK: Wooden, mother-of-pearl and tortoiseshell boxes; nautical instruments.* PARK: 100 yds. TEL: 01753 858470. SER: Restorations (boxes). VAT: Spec.

Rules Antiques

39 St Leonard's Rd. SL4 3BP. (Sue Rule and Kathryn Cale). Open 10.30-6. *STOCK: Lighting, door furniture, period fixtures and fittings; unusual small furniture.* PARK: Meters. TEL: 01753 833210; website - www.rulesantiques.co.uk

Studio 101

101 High St., Eton. SL4 6AF. (Anthony Cove). Est. 1959. SIZE: Medium. *STOCK: Mahogany furniture, some 18th C, mainly 19th C, £50-£1,000; brass, silver plate, 19th C, £10-£200.* LOC: Walk over Windsor Bridge from Windsor and Eton Riverside rail station. PARK: Public, at rear of premises. TEL: 01753 863333.

Times Past Antiques

59 High St., Eton. SL4 6BL. (P. Jackson). MBHI. Est. 1970. Open 10-6, Sun. 12-5. SIZE: Medium. *STOCK: Clocks, £100-£3,000.* PARK: Reasonable. TEL: 01753 857018; e-mail - philliptimespast@aol.com SER: Valuations; restorations (clocks). VAT: Stan/Spec.

Turks Head Antiques

98 High St., Eton. SL4 6AF. (Andrew Reeve and Anthea Baillie). Est. 1983. Open 10-5. *STOCK: Silver and plate, porcelain, glass and interesting collectables.* PARK: Nearby. TEL: 01753 863939.

WOOLHAMPTON, Nr. Reading

The Old Bakery Antiques

Bath Rd. RG7 5RE. (S. Everard). Resident. Est. 1969. Open 10.30-5.30 including Sun. SIZE: Medium. *STOCK: Furniture, objets d'art, collectors' items, general antiques.* PARK: Easy. TEL: 01189 712116. FAIRS: Newark; Ardingly.

WRAYSBURY

Wyrardisbury Antiques

23 High St. TW19 5DA. (C. Tuffs). Est. 1978. Open 10-5. CL: Mon. except by appointment. SIZE: Small. *STOCK: Clocks, £100-£6,000; barometers, small furniture, £100-£1,500.* LOC: A376 from Staines by-pass (A30) or from junction 5 M4/A4 via B470, then B376. PARK: Easy. TEL: 01784 483225. SER: Restorations (clocks).

BUCKINGHAMSHIRE

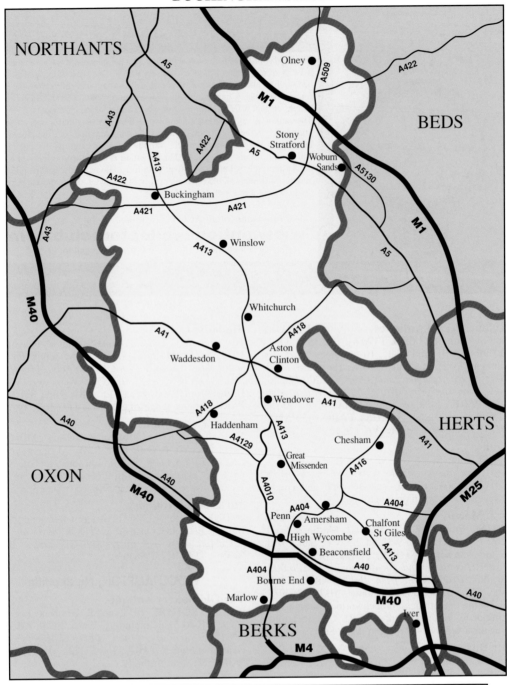

Dealers and Shops in Buckinghamshire

				Olney	3	
Amersham	4	Chesham	3	Penn	1	
Aston Clinton	1	Great Missenden	1	Stony Stratford	1	
Beaconsfield	4	Haddenham	1	Waddesdon	1	
Bourne End	2	High Wycombe	3	Wendover	2	
Buckingham	1	Iver	1	Whitchurch	1	
Chalfont St. Giles	2	Marlow	1	Winslow	1	

AMERSHAM

Carlton Clocks
Station Rd., Little Chalfont. HP7 9PP. (Ian Cherkas). BWCG. Est. 1981. Open 9-5.30, Sat. 9-4. *STOCK: Longcase, mantel, wall and carriage clocks, barometers and pocket watches, from 1700s to reproduction, £200-£15,000.* PARK: Easy. TEL: 01494 763793; fax - 01494 764989; e-mail - info@ukclocks.com website - www.ukclocks.com SER: Valuations; restorations (clocks, watches and barometers).

The Cupboard Antiques   LAPADA
80 High St., Old Amersham. HP7 0DS. (N. and C. Lucas). Est. 1965. Open 10-5. CL: Fri. SIZE: 3 showrooms. *STOCK: Georgian, Regency and early Victorian furniture and decorative items.* PARK: Easy. TEL: 01494 722882. FAIRS: Olympia (June).

Michael and Jackie Quilter
38 High St. HP7 0DJ. Est. 1970. Open 10-5. SIZE: 3 floors. *STOCK: General antiques, stripped pine, copper, brass, unusual objects.* PARK: Easy. TEL: 01494 433723; e-mail - jackie@quilters-antiques.fsnet.co.uk SER: Free local delivery. VAT: Stan.

Sundial Antiques
19 Whielden St. HP7 0HU. (A. and Mrs M. Macdonald). Est. 1970. Open 9.30-5.30. CL: Thurs. SIZE: Small. *STOCK: English and European brass, copper, metalware, fireplace equipment, 18th-19th C, £5-£500; small period furniture, 1670-1910, £25-£1,500; horse brasses, £10-£300; decorative items, 1750-1910, £5-£500; pottery, porcelain, curios, pre-1930, £10-£750.* Not Stocked: Jewellery, clocks, coins, oil paintings, stamps, books, silver, firegrates. LOC: On A404, in Old Town 200yds. from High St. on right; from High Wycombe, 500yds. from hospital on left. PARK: Easy. TEL: 01494 727955.

ASTON CLINTON

Dismantle and Deal Direct - Architectural Salvage Brokers
108 London Rd. HP22 5HS. (Tony Pattison). Est. 1992. Open 10-5. SIZE: Large *STOCK: Doors, glass, 18th C to 1930, £5-£1,000; fireplaces, marble and stone, 18th C to 1920, £500-£3,000; garden ornaments, 19th C to 1950, £1,000-£2,000.* LOC: Off M25 junction 20, take A41. PARK: Easy. TEL: 01296 632300; fax - 01296 631329; website - www.ddd-uk.com SER: Restorations (glass, marble, stone). VAT: Stan/Spec.

BEACONSFIELD

Buck House Antiques
47 Wycombe End, Old Town. HP9 1LZ. (C. and B. Whitby). Est. 1979. Open 10-5, Sun. 12-4. CL: Wed. SIZE: Medium. *STOCK: General antiques including English and Oriental porcelain, clocks, barometers, oak and mahogany furniture, boxes and beds, to 1930s, £5-£5,000.* LOC: A40. PARK: Easy. TEL: 01494 670714; e-mail - bachantiques@supanet.com SER: Valuations.

Ellison Fine Art   BADA
(Claudia Hill). Est. 2000. Open by appointment. *STOCK: 16th-19th C portrait miniatures, enamels and silhouettes, English and Continental, £250-£20,000+.* PARK: Easy. TEL: 01494 678880; home - 01494 670053; mobile - 07720 317899; e-mail - claudia.hill@ellisonfineart.co.uk website - www.ellisonfineart.com SER: Valuations; restorations (framing, glazing and conservation). FAIRS: BADA, Chelsea; Olympia; Harrogate. VAT: Margin.

Grosvenor House Interiors
51 Wycombe End, Old Town. HP9 1LX. (T.I. Marriott). Est. 1970. Open 10-1 and 2-5. CL: Wed. SIZE: Large. *STOCK: Furniture (especially walnut) and oils, 18th-19th C; fireplaces, traditional and modern, and accessories.* LOC: Centre of old town. PARK: Easy. TEL: 01494 677498. e-mail - terrymarriott@btconnect.com SER: Interior architectural design, fireplace specialists. VAT: Stan/Spec.

Period Furniture Showrooms
49 London End. HP9 2HW. (R.E.W. Hearne and N.J. Hearne). TVADA. Est. 1965. Open Mon.-Sat. 9-5.30. SIZE: Large. *STOCK: Furniture, 1700-1900, £50-£5,000.* LOC: A40 Beaconsfield Old Town. PARK: Own. TEL: 01494 674112; fax - 01494 681046; e-mail - sales @periodfurniture.net website - www.periodfurniture.net SER: Restorations (furniture). VAT: Stan/Spec.

BOURNE END

Bourne End Antiques Centre
67 The Parade. SL8 5SB. (S. Shepheard). Est. 1995. Open 10-5.30, Sun. 12-4. SIZE: Large. *STOCK: Furniture - pine, £100-£900, darkwood, £100-£800; both from 19th C; china and glass, £1-£250.* LOC: A4155, 2 miles from Marlow. PARK: Easy. TEL: 01628 533298; home - 01300 320125. VAT: Stan.

La Maison
The Crossings, Cores End Rd. SL8 5AL. (Jeremy D. Pratt). TVADA. Est. 1995. Open 10-5.30, Mon. 1-5.30, Sun. 11-4. SIZE: Medium. *STOCK: French antiques including armoires, mirrors, beds, clocks and chandeliers, 19th C, to £2,000; Victorian pine, £295-£795; antique and reproduction garden furniture, some mahogany furniture.* LOC: Take Marlow by-pass from junction 3, M40. PARK: Easy and opposite. TEL: 01628 525858; home - same; fax - 01494 670363; e-mail - jeremy@la-maison.co.uk website - www.la-maison.co.uk SER: Valuations; restorations including re-upholstery and repairs. VAT: Stan/Spec.

BUCKINGHAM

Buckingham Antiques Centre
5 West St. MK18 1HL. (Peter Walton). Est. 1975. Open 9.15-5.30, Sat. 9-5.30, Tues. and Sun. by appointment. SIZE: Medium. *STOCK: Furniture, 19th C, £50-£1,000; clocks, 18th-20th C, £50-£2,000; general antiques, £2-£500.* LOC: On A422 towards Brackley, near town centre. PARK: Nearby. TEL: 01280 824464; home - same; e-mail - peterwalton@whsmith.net.co.uk SER: Valuations; restorations (clocks).

CHALFONT ST. GILES

Gallery 23 Antiques
High St. HP9 4QH. (Mrs A. Vollaro). Est. 1991. Open 10-5. *STOCK: Furniture, clocks, silver, Continental and English porcelain, glass, paintings, prints and watercolours, tapestry cushions.* TEL: 01494 871512.

T. Smith
The Furniture Village, London Rd. HP8 4NN. Est. 1982. Open 10-5 including Sun. SIZE: Medium. *STOCK: Antique pine and architectural items.* LOC: Opposite Cape Fish. PARK: Easy. TEL: 01494 873031. SER: Valuations; restorations (including upholstery); buys at auction (furniture).

CHESHAM

Chess Antiques   LAPADA
85 Broad St. HP5 3EF. (M.P. Wilder). Est. 1966. Open 9-5, Sat. 10-5. SIZE: Small. *STOCK: Furniture and clocks.* PARK: Easy. TEL: 01494 783043. SER: Valuations; restorations. VAT: Stan/Spec.

Queen Anne House
57 Church St. HP5 1HY. (Miss A.E. Jackson). Est. 1918. Open Wed., Fri. and Sat. 9.30-5, other times by appointment. SIZE: Large. *STOCK: Furniture, decorative and furnishing pieces, china including porcelain figures, glass, silver plate, copper, brass, Victoriana, Persian rugs.* LOC: Near parish church. PARK: Easy. TEL: 01494 783811. SER: Buys at auction.

Stuff and Nonsense
68-70 Broad St. HP5 3DX. (Elaine and Helen Robb). Open 9.30-5.30, Sun. 11-5.30. CL: Wed. SIZE: Medium. *STOCK: General antiques and collectables - furniture including reproduction mahogany, books, commemoratives, records, haberdashery and clocks.* LOC: Just out of High St., on main road. PARK: Easy and at rear. TEL: 01494 775988; fax - same.

GREAT MISSENDEN

Peter Wright Antiques
(Incorporating Missenden Restorations and Abbey Clocks & Repairs), 32b High St. HP16 0AU. BHI. Est. 1992. Open by appointment. SIZE: Small. *STOCK: Clocks, curios and furniture.* LOC: A413. PARK: Opposite. TEL: 01494 891330. SER: Restorations; repairs (clocks).

HADDENHAM

H.S. Wellby Ltd
The Malt House, Church End. HP17 8AH. (C.S. Wellby). BAPCR. Est. 1820. Open by appointment 9-6. *STOCK: 18th-19th C paintings.* TEL: 01844 290036. SER: Restoration and conservation of oil paintings. VAT: Spec.

HIGH WYCOMBE

Browns' of West Wycombe
Church Lane, West Wycombe. HP14 3AH. BFM. Est. Pre 1900. Open 8-5.30. CL: Sat. *STOCK: Furniture.* LOC: On A40 approximately 3 miles west of High Wycombe on Oxford Road. PARK: Easy. TEL: 01494 524537; fax - 01494 439548; e-mail - enquiries@brownsofwestwycombe.com website - www.brownsofwestwycombe.com SER: Restorations; hand-made copies of period chairs.

Glade Antiques   BADA
P O Box 873. HP14 3ZQ. (Sonia Vaughan). CINOA. Open by appointment. *STOCK: Fine Oriental ceramics, bronzes and jades: Chinese items from Han, Tang, Song, Ming and Quing periods; Japanese items - mainly Kakiemon, Nabeshima, Kutani, Satsuma and Imari; also Korean Koryo, Yi and Choson periods.* TEL: 01494 882818; fax - 01494 882818; mobile - 07771 552328; e-mail - sonia@gladeantiques.com FAIRS: Olympia.

Windmill Fine Art
2 Windmill Drive, Widmer End. HP15 6BD. (Ray White). Open by appointment. *STOCK: Fine Victorian and early 20th C watercolours.* TEL: 01494 713757. SER: Valuations; commission search. FAIRS: Most major.

IVER

Yester-year
12 High St. SL0 9NG. (P.J. Frost). Resident. Est. 1969. Open 10-6. SIZE: Small. *STOCK: Furniture, porcelain, pottery, glass, metalwork, 18th to early 20th C.* PARK: Easy. TEL: 01753 652072. SER: Valuations; restorations (furniture and pictures); framing; buys at auction.

MARLOW

Marlow Antique Centre
35 Station Rd. SL7 1NW. Est. 1995. Open 10.30-5, Sun. 11-4. SIZE: Large - 30+ dealers. *STOCK: 18th-20th C furniture, collectors' china from Worcester to Clarice Cliff, Beswick, Staffordshire figures and dogs, chandeliers, silver, decorative glass, writing slopes, tea caddies, postcards, pens, cuff-links, equestrian items, jewellery, militaria, clocks and pocket watches.* LOC: Town centre. PARK: Nearby. TEL: 01628 473223; fax - 01628 478989. SER: International packing and shipping.

OLNEY

The Antiques Centre at Olney
13 Osborns Court, Off High St. South. MK46 4LA. (Robert Sklar). Open 10-5, Sun. 12-5. CL: Mon. SIZE:

Large, 80 dealers. *STOCK: General antiques, furniture, porcelain.* LOC: Town centre. PARK: Easy. TEL: 01234 710942; fax - 01234 710947; website - www.antiques-of-britain.co.uk

Leo Antiques & Collectables Ltd
19 Market Place. MK46 4BA. (Mrs G. Behari). Est. 2003. Open 10-5, Sun. and Bank Holidays 11-4. CL: Mon. SIZE: Large. *STOCK: Georgian to Edwardian furniture, to £5,000; silver, from 19th C; oils and watercolours, 19th-20th C, to £2,000; Doulton, Beswick, Royal Winton and Worcester; glass, clocks, books, country furniture and mirrors.* PARK: Easy. TEL: 01234 240003; fax - 01908 211112.

Pine Antiques
10 Market Place. MK46 4EA. (Linda Wilkinson). Est. 1976. Open 10-5, Sat. 9.30-5.30, Sun. 12-5. SIZE: 3 floors. *STOCK: Pine furniture, antique and reclaimed.* PARK: Easy. TEL: 01234 711065; 01908 510226; e-mail - pine-antiques@hotmail.com SER: Restorations; bespoke furniture.

Robin Unsworth Antiques
1 Weston Rd. MK46 5BD. (R. and Z. M. Unsworth). Est. 1971. Open 9-5, Sun. 9-4.30. SIZE: Small. *STOCK: Longcase and wall clocks, £1,000-£15,000; period and Victorian furniture, £1,000-£10,000; objects of art, £200-£5,000.* LOC: 6 miles from junction 14, M1. PARK: Easy. TEL: 01234 711210; home - 01908 617193. VAT: Spec.

PENN, Nr. High Wycombe

Penn Barn
By the Pond, Elm Rd. HP10 8LB. (P. J. M. Hunnings). Est. 1968. Open Tues.-Sat.10.30-4, (sometimes closed 1-2). SIZE: Large. *STOCK: Antiquarian books, maps and prints, 19th C, £5-£500; watercolours and oils, 19th-20th C, £50-£1,500.* LOC: B474. PARK: Easy. TEL: 01494 815691.

STONY STRATFORD, Nr. Milton Keynes

Circa
6 Church St. MK11 1BD. (Victoria Holton). Open Tues.-Sat. 10-5, other times by appointment. *STOCK: Victorian and Edwardian furniture, 1920s pieces; unusual objects, chandeliers, 1960s designer chrome, framed paintings and prints, vintage luggage, clocks, mirrors, upholstered items including wing chairs.* LOC: Opposite church. PARK: Easy and opposite. TEL: 01908 567100; e-mail - info@circa-antiques.co.uk website - www.circaantiques.co.uk SER: Valuations.

WADDESDON

Farrelly Antiques
68 High St. HP18 0JD. (P. Farrelly). Open 10-4. *STOCK: Furniture.* TEL: 01296 658210. SER: Restorations. VAT: Spec.

WENDOVER

Antiques at . . .Wendover Antiques Centre
The Old Post Office, 25 High St. HP22 6DU. (N. Gregory). Est. 1987. Open 10-5.30, Sun. and Bank

This is the first major book on English blue and white porcelain since the early 1970s. Not only is it the latest and most up-to-date work, but it includes types not previously studied and extends the range of wares into the early years of the nineteenth-century. It is a unique overall study.
Spec: 592pp., 153 col. illus., 711 b.&w. illus., 11 x 8½in./279 x 216mm. **£65.00 (hardback)**

Holidays 11-5. SIZE: Large - 30 dealers. *STOCK: General antiques dateline 1940/50 - town and country furniture, kitchenalia, gardenalia, pottery and porcelain, jewellery, Art Deco, watches, silver, lamps and lighting, clocks and barometers, telescopes, scientific and medical instruments, games, decorative items, glass, metalware, lace and linen, garden statuary, arms, pictures and prints.* LOC: A431. PARK: Own. TEL: 01296 625335; e-mail - antiques@antiquesatwendover.co.uk website - www.antiquesatwendover.co.uk SER: Restorations (china and furniture); metal polishing, gilding and re-upholstery.

Sally Turner Antiques   LAPADA
Hogarth House, High St. HP22 6DU. TVADA. Open 10-5. CL: Wed. and Sun. except Dec. SIZE: 7 showrooms + barn. *STOCK: Decorative and period furniture, paintings, jewellery and general antiques.* PARK: Own. TEL: 01296 624402; fax - same; mobile - 07860 201718; e-mail - majorsally@hotmail.com SER: Restorations.

WHITCHURCH

Deerstalker Antiques
28 High St. HP22 4JT. (R.J. and L.L. Eichler). Est. 1980. Open 10-5.30. CL: Mon. SIZE: Large. *STOCK: General antiques, including period oak furniture.* PARK: Easy. TEL: 01296 641505. SER: Restorations (furniture pre 1880); hand-made replicas. FAIRS: Milton Keynes; Brill.

WINSLOW

Winslow Antiques Centre
15 Market Sq. MK18 3AB. Est. 1992. Open 10-5, Sun. 1-5. CL: Wed. SIZE: 20 dealers. *STOCK: Furniture, English pottery, silver and jewellery, general antiques.* LOC: A413. TEL: 01296 714540; fax - 01296 714556.

CAMBRIDGESHIRE

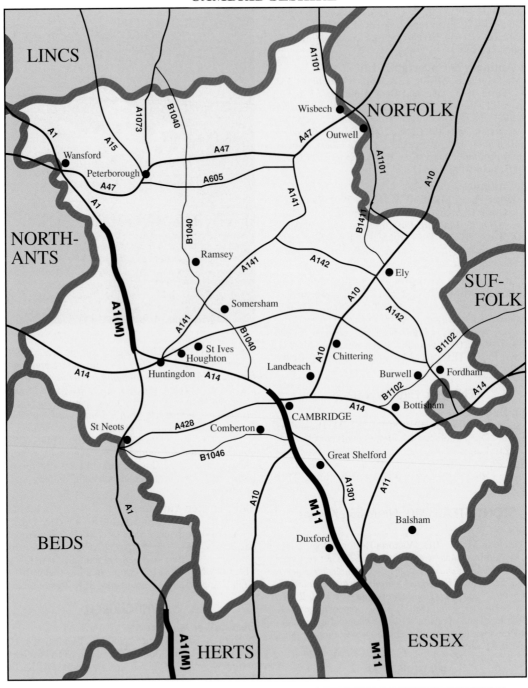

BALSHAM, Nr. Cambridge

Ward Thomas Antiques Ltd
7 High St. CB1 6DJ. (Christian Ward Thomas). Est. 1997. Open 9-5, Sat. 10-5, Sun. by appointment. *STOCK: Pine furniture, £210-£950.* LOC: Village centre, opposite primary school. TEL: 01223 892431; fax - 01223 892367; mobile - 07887 986566; e-mail - wtantiques@onetel.com SER: Valuations; restorations (Continental pine, oak flooring); bespoke kitchens.

BOTTISHAM, Nr. Cambridge

Cambridge Pine
Hall Farm, Lode Rd. CB5 9DN. (Mr and Mrs D. Weir). Est. 1980. Open seven days. SIZE: Large. *STOCK: Pine, 18th-19th C and reproduction, £25-£2,000.* LOC: Midway between Bottisham and Lode, near Anglesey Abbey. PARK: Easy. TEL: 01223 811208; home - same; e-mail - campinesales@btconnect.com website - www.cambridgepine.co.uk SER: Copies made in old timber with or without painted finish.

BURWELL

Peter Norman Antiques and Restorations
Sefton House, 55 North St. CB5 0BA. (P. Norman and A. Marpole). Est. 1977. Open 9-12.30 and 2-5.30. SIZE: Medium. *STOCK: Furniture, clocks, arms and Oriental rugs, 17th-19th C, £250-£10,000.* PARK: Easy. TEL: 01638 616914; mobile - 07714 279993; e-mail - amarpole@aol.com website - www.peternorman antiques.co.uk SER: Valuations; restorations (furniture, oil paintings, clocks and arms).

CAMBRIDGE

Jess Applin Antiques   BADA
8 Lensfield Rd. CB2 1EG. Est. 1968. Open 10-5. *STOCK: Furniture, 17th-19th C; works of art.* LOC: At junction with Hills Rd. opposite church. PARK: Pay and display nearby. TEL: 01223 315168. VAT: Spec.

John Beazor and Sons Ltd   BADA
78-80 Regent St. CB2 1DP. Est. 1875. Open 9.15-5, Sat. 10-4 and by appointment. *STOCK: English furniture, late 17th to early 19th C; clocks, barometers and period accessories.* PARK: Pay & Display and multi-storey. TEL: 01223 355178; fax - 01223 355183; e-mail - martin@johnbeazorantiques.co.uk website - www.johnbeazorantiques.co.uk SER: Valuations; sourcing.

The Bookshop
24 Magdalene St. CB3 0AF. (Hugh Hardinge and Peter Bright). Est. 1996. Open 10.30-5.30. SIZE: Medium. *STOCK: Secondhand and antiquarian books.* LOC: North of river. PARK: Meters. TEL: 01223 362457; e-mail - peter.bright@care4free.net and hardinge@ btinternet.com

Buckies   LAPADA
31 Trinity St. CB2 1TB. (Robin Wilson and Graham Whitehead). NAG. GMC. Est. 1972. Open 9.45-5. CL: Mon. SIZE: Medium. *STOCK: Jewellery, silver, objets*

d'art. PARK: Multi-storey nearby. TEL: 01223 357910. SER: Valuations; restorations; repairs. VAT: Stan/Spec.

Cambridge Fine Art Ltd   LAPADA
Priesthouse, 33 Church St., Little Shelford. CB2 5HG. (R. and J. Lury). Resident. Est. 1972. By appointment. SIZE: Large. *STOCK: British and European paintings, 1780-1900; modern British paintings, 1880-1940; British prints by J.M. Kronheim to the Baxter Process.* LOC: Next to church. PARK: Easy. TEL: 01223 842866/843537. SER: Valuations; restorations; buys at auction. VAT: Stan/Spec.

Gabor Cossa Antiques
34 Trumpington St. CB2 1QY. (D. Theobald). Est. 1948. Open 11-6. *STOCK: English and Chinese ceramics, glass, bijouterie.* LOC: Opposite Fitzwilliam Museum. PARK: 100yds. TEL: 01223 356049; e-mail - gaborcossa@yahoo.co.uk SER: Valuations. FAIRS: Horticultural Hall. VAT: Global.

Peter Crabbe Antiques
3 Pembroke St. CB2 3QY. Open 10-4.30. *STOCK: Furniture and Oriental porcelain and works of art.* TEL: 01223 357117. VAT: Spec.

G. David
16 St. Edward's Passage. CB2 3PJ. (D.C. Asplin, N.T. Adams and B.L. Collings). ABA. PBFA. Est. 1896. Open 9.30-5. *STOCK: Antiquarian books, fine bindings, secondhand and out of print books, selected publishers' remainders.* LOC: 100 yards from Market Sq. PARK: Lion Yard. TEL: 01223 354619.

The Hive
Unit 3, Dales Brewery, Gwydir St. CB1 2LG. (B. Blakemore and A. Morgan). Open 10-5, Sun. 11-5. SIZE: 11 dealers. *STOCK: Victorian and Edwardian furniture, antique pine, kitchenalia, period lighting, ceramics, tiles, jewellery, vintage clothing and Oriental rugs.* LOC: Off Mill Rd. PARK: Opposite. TEL: 01223 300269.

Sarah Key
The Haunted Bookshop, 9 St. Edward's Passage. CB2 3PJ. (Sarah Key and Phil Salin). PBFA. Est. 1987. Open 10-5. *STOCK: Children's and illustrated books, literature and antiquarian.* LOC: City centre. PARK: Lion Yard multi-storey. TEL: 01223 312913; e-mail - sarahkey@hauntedbooks.demon.co.uk SER: Shipping. FAIRS: Major UK.

The Lawson Gallery
7-8 King's Parade. CB2 1SJ. (Leslie J. and Lucinda J. Lawson). FATG. Est. 1967. Open 9.30-5.30. SIZE: Medium. *STOCK: Posters, prints, limited editions, original artwork, specialists in antiquarian and modern prints of Cambridge.* LOC: Opposite King's College. PARK: Lion Yard. TEL: 01223 313970. VAT: Stan.

Solopark Plc
Station Rd., Pampisford. CB2 4HB. (R.J. Bird). SALVO. Est. 1976. Open 8-5, Fri. and Sat. 8-4, Sun. 10-2. *STOCK: Traditional and new building materials, timber and period architectural items.* PARK: Easy. TEL: 01223 834663; fax - 01223 834780; e-mail - info@solopark. co.uk website - www.solopark.co.uk

111

CAMBRIDGESHIRE

CHITTERING, Nr. Cambridge

Simon and Penny Rumble Antiques
Causeway End Farmhouse. CB5 9PW. Open by appointment. *STOCK: Early oak, country furniture, woodcarving and works of art.* LOC: 6 miles north of Cambridge, off A10. TEL: 01223 861831.

COMBERTON

Comberton Antiques and Interiors
5 Green End. CB3 7DY. (Clare and Stuart Tunstall). Est. 2003. Open Thurs. 2-8, Fri. and Sat. 10-5, Sun. 2-5. SIZE: Large. *STOCK: Pine, oak, country and mahogany furniture; lighting, pictures, soft furnishings, rugs, ceramics and kitchenalia.* LOC: 6 miles west of Cambridge, 2 miles junction 12, M11. PARK: In front of premises. TEL: 01223 262674; e-mail - contact@ combertonantiques.co.uk website - www.comberton antiques.co.uk VAT: Margin.

DUXFORD

Riro D. Mooney
4 Moorfield Rd. CB2 4PS. Est. 1946. Open 9-6.30. SIZE: Medium. *STOCK: General antiques, 1780-1920, £5-£2,600.* LOC: 1 mile from M11. PARK: Easy. TEL: 01223 832252; website - www.riromooney-antiques.com SER: Restorations (furniture). VAT: Stan/Spec.

ELY

Cloisters Antiques
1-1B Lynn Rd. CB7 4EG. (Barry Lonsdale). PBFA. Est.

1999. Open 10-4.30, Sun. 12.30-4.30. CL: Tues. SIZE: Medium. *STOCK: Small antiques and collectables, paintings and clocks; antiquarian and secondhand books; postcards and prints.* LOC: Opposite Lamb Inn, close to cathedral. PARK: St Mary's St. TEL: 01353 668558; mobile - 07767 881677. SER: Repairs (clocks); picture framing.

Mrs Mills Antiques
1a St. Mary's St. CB7 4ER. Est. 1968. Open 10-5. CL: Tues. SIZE: Small. *STOCK: China, jewellery, silver.* Not Stocked: Furniture. LOC: Near cathedral. PARK: Nearby. TEL: 01353 664268.

Valued History
9 Market Place. CB7 4NP. (Paul Murawski). Est. 1995. Open 10-5. CL: Mon. SIZE: Small. *STOCK: Antiquities, ancient to Tudor, £25-£1,000+; coins and other artifacts, £5-£1,000.* TEL: 01353 654080. SER: Valuations. FAIRS: Cumberland Coin.

Waterside Antiques Centre
The Wharf. CB7 4AU. Est. 1986. Open 9.30-5.30 including Bank Holidays, Sun. 11.30-5.30. SIZE: Large. *STOCK: General antiques and collectables.* LOC: Waterside area. PARK: Easy. TEL: 01353 667066.

FORDHAM, Nr. Ely

Phoenix Antiques
1 Carter St. CB7 5NG. Est. 1966. Open by appointment. SIZE: Medium. *STOCK: Early European furniture, domestic metalwork, pottery and delft, carpets, scientific instruments, treen and bygones.* LOC: Centre of village. PARK: Own. TEL: 01638 720363. SER: Valuations.

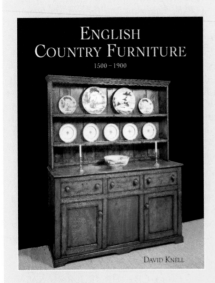

ENGLISH COUNTRY FURNITURE
1500-1900
DAVID KNELL

The literature on English period furniture has largely been dominated by a preoccupation with that of the rich and upper classes, resulting in a neglect of the humbler pieces used in more ordinary homes over the centuries.

This book, the first major production of its kind and now a classic reference work, examines the pieces found in humbler urban and rural homes over a span of some four centuries, throwing fresh light on such aspects as regional variations, dating assessment, construction techniques, stylistic influence and context. Each of the many examples illustrated, most of them previously unpublished in book form, is accompanied by a detailed caption giving timber, a realistic date range and an extensive description, including such information as local characteristics, finish, distinctive decorative features and manufacturing methods.

In this second edition both the format and the text have been thoroughly revised and the number of illustrations greatly increased.

Specifications:
414pp., 108 col. illus.,
625 b.&w. illus.,
11 x 8½in./279 x 216mm.
£45.00 (hardback)

For full details of all ACC publications, log on to our website:
www.antiquecollectorsclub.com
or telephone 01394 389950 for a free catalogue

GREAT SHELFORD, Nr. Cambridge

Storm Fine Arts Ltd
Church Street Barns. CB2 5EL. (Bill and Sue Mason). Resident. Est. 1998. Open by appointment. SIZE: Medium. *STOCK: Paintings and pictures, 1500 to date, £500-£100,000; porcelain, pottery and glass, 1800-1900, £150-£1,500; decorative arts, 1700 to date, £100-£15,000; textiles, 1700-1900, £1,000-£30,000.* PARK: Easy. TEL: 01223 844786; fax - 01223 847871; website - www.stormfinearts.com SER: Valuations; restorations; buys at auction. VAT: Stan.

HOUGHTON, Nr. Huntingdon

Houghton Antiques
Thicket Rd. PE28 2BQ. (Jean Stevens). Est. 2001. Open 1-5.30 every day. SIZE: Small. *STOCK: Ceramics and glass, silver and plate including cutlery, Victorian to 1930s; collectables, some sporting, framed antique prints, small furniture.* LOC: Village square. PARK: Easy. TEL: 01480 461887; home - 01487 813316; mobile - 07803 716842; e-mail - jeanmstevens@btinternet.com FAIRS: Alexandra Palace.

HUNTINGDON

Huntingdon Trading Post
1 St Mary's St. PE29 3PE. (Mrs D. J. A. De'Ath). Est. 1980. Open daily. SIZE: 40+ dealers. *STOCK: Wide range of general antiques, to £10,000.* PARK: Easy.

TEL: 01480 450998/431142; website - www.huntingdontradingpost.co.uk

LANDBEACH

J.V. Pianos and Cambridge Pianola Company
The Limes, 85 High St. CB4 8DR. (F.T. Poole). Est. 1972. Open Mon.-Fri., evenings and weekends by appointment. SIZE: Medium. *STOCK: Pianos, pianolas and pianola rolls.* LOC: First building on right in Landbeach from A10. PARK: Easy. TEL: 01223 861348/861507; home - same; fax - 01223 441276; e-mail - ftpoole@talk21.com website - www.cambridgepianolacompany.co.uk SER: Valuations; restorations. VAT: Stan.

OUTWELL, Nr. Wisbech

A.P. and M.A. Haylett
Glen-Royd, 393 Wisbech Rd. PE14 8PG. Open 9-6 including Sun. *STOCK: Country furniture, pottery, treen and metalware, 1750-1900, £5-£500.* Not Stocked: Firearms. LOC: A1101. PARK: Easy. TEL: 01945 772427; home - same. SER: Buys at auction.

PETERBOROUGH

Antiques & Curios
249 Lincoln Rd., Millfield. PE2 5NZ. (M. and Mrs R. Mason). Est. 1990. Open 10-5. SIZE: Medium. *STOCK: Pine furniture, 19th C, £50-£500; mahogany and oak furniture, 19th to early 20th C, £50-£500; fireplaces,*

19th C, £50-£1,000; collectables, 19th-20th C, £10-£100. LOC: North from city centre. PARK: Easy. TEL: 01733 314948; home - same. SER: Valuations; restorations (furniture stripping and polishing, fireplaces). FAIRS: Peterborough Festival of Antiques.

Francis Bowers Chess Suppliers
1 Marriott Court, Oxney Rd. PE1 5NQ. Resident. Est. 1991. Open by appointment. SIZE: Small. *STOCK: Chess books, boards, sets and timers; clocks.* PARK: Easy. TEL: 01733 897119; e-mail - chessbower@aol.com

Ivor and Patricia Lewis Antique and Fine Art Dealers LAPADA
30 Westwood Park Rd. PE3 6JL. Open by appointment. *STOCK: Decorative English and French furniture, 19th to early 20th C.* TEL: 01733 344567; mobile - 07860 553388.

RAMSEY, Nr. Huntingdon

Abbey Antiques
63 Great Whyte. PE26 1HL. (R. and J. Smith). Est. 1977. Open Tues.-Sat. 10-5. SIZE: Medium. *STOCK: Furniture including pine, 1850-1930, £50-£500; porcelain, glass, Goss and crested china, 1830-1950, £3-£500; Beswick, Fen pottery, Mabel Lucie Attwell, small collectables.* PARK: Easy. TEL: 01487 814753. SER: Mabel Lucie Attwell Museum and Collectors' Club: Memories UK (Enesco Memories of Yesterday figurines). FAIRS: Alexandra Palace.

Antique Barometers
Wingfield, 26 Biggin Lane. PE26 1NB. (William and Helen Rae). Open by appointment. *STOCK: Fine barometers, 18th-19th C, barographs, £400-£8,000.* PARK: Easy. TEL: 01487 814060; home/fax - same; e-mail - antiquebarometers@talk21.com SER: Valuations; restorations. FAIRS: Burnham Market; Putteridge Bury (Luton); Hinchingbrooke.

SOMERSHAM, Nr. Huntingdon

T. W. Pawson - Clocks
31A High St. PE28 3JA. BWCG. Est. 1981. Open by appointment. SIZE: Small. *STOCK: Antique clocks, £150-£5,000; mercury barometers, to mid-19th C.* LOC: Main road through village. PARK: Easy. TEL: 01487 841537; home - same; e-mail - thomas.pawson@

btinternet.com SER: Restorations, overhauls, repairs (clocks and barometers).

ST. IVES

B.R. Knight and Sons
Quay Court, Bull Lane, Bridge St. PE17 4AU. (Michael Knight). Est. 1972. Open Mon., Wed., Fri. 11.30-2.30, Sat. 10.30-4.30 or by appointment. SIZE: Medium. *STOCK: Porcelain, pottery, jewellery, paintings, watercolours, prints, decorative arts.* PARK: Nearby. TEL: 01480 468295/300042; e-mail - michaelknight9@hotmail.com SER: Talks given on 'The Painters of Huntingdonshire' and antiques.

ST. NEOTS

Tavistock Antiques Ltd
Cross Hall Manor, Eaton Ford. PE19 7GB. Open by appointment. *STOCK: Period English furniture.* TEL: 01480 472082. *Trade Only.*

WANSFORD, Nr. Peterborough

Starlight Period Lighting
16 London Rd. PE8 6JB. (Richard P. Rimes and Lynne Ayres). Resident. Est. 1989. Open Tues.-Fri. 9.30-1 and 2.15-5 and most Sats. 10-1 and 2.30-5. SIZE: Medium. *STOCK: Period and new lighting.* LOC: On A1 near A47 junction. PARK: Easy. TEL: 01780 783999; fax - same; e-mail - info@lampsandcandles.co.uk website - www.lampsandcandles.co.uk SER: Restorations (period lighting). FAIRS: Historic Buildings; Parks & Gardens Exhibition. VAT: Stan/Spec.

WISBECH

Antiques & Curios (Steve Carpenter)
95 Norfolk St. PE13 2LF. Est. 1985. Open Tues., Thurs., Fri. and Sat. 9-5. SIZE: Medium. *STOCK: Georgian and Victorian longcase clocks, £1,000-£3,000; Georgian, Victorian and Edwardian furniture, 19th C, £100-£5,000; bygones and collectables, 18th-20th C, £5-£3000.* LOC: Town centre, just off A47. PARK: Easy. TEL: 01945 588441. SER: Valuations; restorations (structural, veneering and polishing); shipping.

Peter A. Crofts BADA
117 High Rd., Elm. PE14 0DN. (Mrs Pat L. Crofts). Est. 1949. Open by appointment. STOCK: General antiques, furniture, porcelain, silver, jewellery. LOC: A1101. TEL: 01945 584614. VAT: Stan/Spec.

Granny's Cupboard
34 Old Market. PE13 1NF. (R.J. Robbs). Est. 1982. Open Tues. and Thurs. 10.30-4, Sat. 10.30-3. SIZE: Medium. *STOCK: China, glass, small furniture, Victorian to 1950s, £5-£500.* PARK: Easy. TEL: 01945 589606; home - 01945 870730. FAIRS: The Maltings, Ely.

R. Wilding
Lanes End, Gadds Lane, Leverington. PE13 5BJ. Resident. Est. 1966. *STOCK: Bamboo furniture and mirrors including reproduction.* PARK: Easy. TEL: 01945 588204; fax - 01945 475712. SER: Veneering; polishing; compo carving; gilding; conversions; bamboo replicas made to order. *Trade Only.*

THE ENGLISH REGIONAL CHAIR

Bernard D. Cotton

This is arguably the most detailed study ever made of any branch of British furniture. Its unique scope embraces the work of hundreds of craftsmen throughout the country, working within the general tradition of their area, yet superimposing their individual design 'signatures'.

Employing a remarkable combination of talents, the author has examined thousands of regional chairs, researched local archives, conducted field studies and collated anecdotal evidence to relate the evolution of known types and makes. The result, far from being a dry research document, is a fascinating living account of the development of hundreds of chair types from all over England and the lives of the craftsmen who produced them.

This book has revolutionised collecting and the study of vernacular furniture. It continues to be studied avidly by collectors as hundreds of new makers' names emerge from the anonymity of generalised terms such as 'Windsor', 'ladder back' and 'spindle back'. This reprint is most welcome.

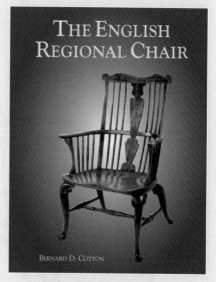

THE ENGLISH REGIONAL CHAIR

BERNARD D. COTTON

Specifications:
512pp., 69 col. illus.,
over 1,400 b.&w. illus.,
11 x 8½in./279 x 216mm.
£49.50 (hardback)

Windsor Chairs Michael Harding-Hill

Windsor Chairs

Michael Harding-Hill

Specifications:
160pp., 183 col. illus.,
196 b.&w. illus.,
9½ x 7½in./240 x 195mm.
£25.00 (hardback)

The Windsor chair, whether simple or complicated in construction, plain or ornate in appearance, has always served its purpose – to be utilitarian, durable, comfortable and even handsome.

Many excellent academic works have been written on the subject, but this book does not attempt to improve on their expertise. The intention rather is to complement them by showing the finest designs in greater detail. The form and construction of the chairs speak for themselves. All the chairs illustrated, although made in different centuries, are in use today. Is there another example of utilitarian furniture made in such numbers that still survives and is in everyday use?

More than 150 colour plates illustrate the very best Windsor chairs from the earliest stick-backs – literally stools with a few sticks added to the back – of the eighteenth century to those mass-produced for offices, schools, public institutions and the armed forces in the nineteenth century. There is a special section on American Windsors and the story of the Windsor chair continues through the twentieth century and concludes by illustrating a 2002 Golden Jubilee chair. This book is a celebration of the beautiful Windsor chair.

For full details of all ACC publications, log on to our website:
www.antiquecollectorsclub.com
or telephone 01394 389950 for a free catalogue

CHESHIRE

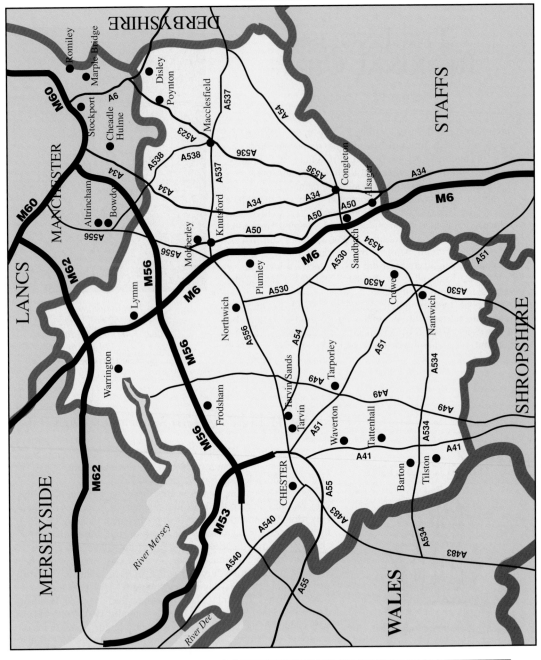

Dealers and Shops in Cheshire

						Stockport	8
Alsager	1	Crewe	1	Mobberley	2	Tarporley	1
Altrincham	3	Disley	2	Nantwich	6	Tarvin	1
Barton	1	Frodsham	1	Northwich	1	Tarvin Sands	1
Bowdon	1	Knutsford	4	Plumley	1	Tattenhall	1
Cheadle Hume	1	Lymm	1	Poynton	1	Tilston	1
Chester	17	Macclesfield	4	Romiley	1	Warrington	1
Congleton	2	Marple Bridge	1	Sandbach	1	Waverton	1

ALSAGER, Nr. Crewe

Trash 'n' Treasure
48 Sandbach Rd. South. ST7 2LP. (G. and D. Ogden). Est. 1979. Open Tues., Thurs., Fri. and Sat. 10-4. SIZE: Medium. *STOCK: Late Georgian to 1930s furniture, pictures, ceramics, £5-£10,000.* LOC: 10 mins. junction 16, M6. PARK: Nearby. TEL: 01270 872972/873246. SER: Valuations; lectures.

ALTRINCHAM

Church Street Antiques   LAPADA
4/4a Old Market Place. WA14 4NP. (Alex Smalley and Nick Stanley). Est. 1991. Open 10-5, Sun. 12-4. CL: Tues. SIZE: Large. *STOCK: Furniture, 18th-19th C, £100-£10,000; paintings, 19th C to contemporary, £100-£10,000.* PARK: Easy. TEL: 0161 929 5196; fax - same; mobile - 07768 318661; e-mail - sales@churchstreet antiques.com website - www.churchstreetantiques.com SER: Valuations; restorations. FAIRS: Tatton; Chester; Arley; Harrogate. VAT: Spec.

Robert Redford Antiques & Interiors
48 New St. WA14 2QS. (S. and R. Redford). Est. 1989. By appointment. *STOCK: General antiques, furniture, small silver, porcelain, glass.* LOC: Town centre. PARK: Easy. TEL: Home - 0161 926 8232; fax - 0161 928 4827.

Squires Antiques
25 Regent Rd. WA14 1RX. (V. Phillips). Est. 1977. Open 10-5. CL: Mon. and Wed. SIZE: Medium. *STOCK: Small furniture, 1800-1930, £60-£1,500; small silver, 1850-1970, £20-£400; brass, copper and bric-a-brac, 1850-1940, £10-£400; jewellery, porcelain, fire accessories, light fittings and interior design items.* Not Stocked: Large furniture, coins and badges. LOC: Adjacent hospital and large car park. PARK: Easy. TEL: 0161 928 0749. SER: Valuations.

BARTON, Nr. Farndon

Derek and Tina Rayment Antiques   BADA
Orchard House, Barton Rd. SY14 7HT. (D.J. and K.M. Rayment). Est. 1960. Open by appointment every day. *STOCK: Barometers, 18th-20th C, from £100.* LOC: A534. PARK: Easy. TEL: 01829 270429; home - same; e-mail - raymentantiques@aol.com website - www.antique-barometers.com SER: Valuations; restorations (barometers only); buys at auction (barometers). FAIRS: Olympia; Chelsea; BADA. VAT: Stan/Spec.

BOWDON

Richmond Antiques
The Hollies, Richmond Rd. WA14 2TT. (Joe and Lesley Freeman). Est. 1992. Open 12-6, Sun. by appointment. CL: Mon. *STOCK: French and English mirrors, 19th C, £300-£2,000.* LOC: Near Manchester airport, junction 7, M56, junction 19, M6. PARK: Easy. TEL: 01619 281229; home - same. SER: Restorations.

CHEADLE HULME

Andrew Foott Antiques
4 Claremont Rd. SK8 6EG. Est. 1985. Open by appointment. SIZE: Small. *STOCK: Barometers, 18th-20th C, £200-£2,500; small furniture, 18th-20th C, £500-£3,000.* LOC: 5 mins. from new A34 by-pass. PARK: Easy. TEL: 0161 485 3559; e-mail - andrew.foott @tesco.net SER: Restorations (barometers and furniture). FAIRS: NEC.

CHESTER

Aldersey Hall Ltd
Town Hall Sq., 47 Northgate St. CH1 2HQ. (Kim Wilding-Welton). Est. 1990. Open 8.30-5.30. SIZE:

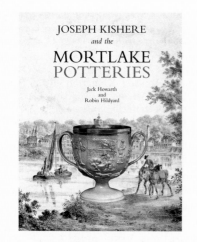

Medium. *STOCK: Art Deco and general British ceramics, £5-£500; small furniture, £50-£200; all 1880-1940.* LOC: Between library and Odeon cinema. PARK: Own 100 yards. TEL: 01244 324885. SER: Valuations; buys at auction (Art Deco ceramics). FAIRS: Alexandra Palace, Loughborough, Ardingly, Newark, Birmingham. VAT: Stan/Spec.

Antique Exporters of Chester
CH3 7RZ. (Michael Kilgannon). Est. 1970. Open 8-8 including Sun. SIZE: Large warehouse. *STOCK: Furniture, 18th-19th C and shipping.* LOC: Waverton. PARK: Easy. TEL: 01829 741001; home - 01244 570069; fax - 01829 749204. SER: Full packing and shipping; cabinet making and polishing. VAT: Stan/Spec.

The Antique Garden
Grosvenor Garden Centre, Wrexham Rd. CH4 9EB. (Maria Hopwood). Est. 1991. Open 10-4.30 including Sun. *STOCK: Garden-related bygones.* LOC: A483. PARK: Easy. TEL: 01244 629191; mobile - 07976 539990. SER: Valuations. VAT: Global.

Architectural Salvage Online
Units 5 & 15 Sealand Farm, Sealand Rd. CH1 6BS. (David and Caroline Lyons). Est. 1998. Open Mon., Wed., Fri, Sat. and Sun. 10.30-5. SIZE: Medium. *STOCK: Interior and exterior doors, £35-£3,000; fireplaces, cast-iron and timber surrounds, slate, marble, £200-£5,000; radiators, £150-£1,000; flooring and architechtural items.* LOC: On route to town centre. PARK: Easy. TEL: 01244 657976; mobile - 07970 698518; e-mail - sales@uksalvageonline.com website - www.uksalvageonline.com SER: Valuations; restorations.

Baron Fine Art   LAPADA
68 Watergate St. CH1 2LA. (S. and R. Baron). Est. 1984. Open 9.30-5.30. *STOCK: Watercolours and oils, some etchings, late 19th to early 20th C, some contemporary, £50-£60,000.* PARK: Easy. TEL: 01244 342520; website - www.baronfineart.com SER: Restorations; framing. FAIRS: Tatton Park; LAPADA; NEC (Jan., April, Aug. and Nov); Watercolours & Drawings (Jan/Feb). VAT: Stan/Spec.

Cameo Antiques
19 Watergate St. CH1 2LB. Est. 1994. Open 9-5, Sat. 9-5.30. SIZE: Small. *STOCK: Jewellery and English silver, 1800-1990, £20-£4,000; English pottery including Moorcroft and Sally Tuffin, Continental porcelain, 1750-1960; small furniture.* LOC: Off Bridge St. PARK: Easy. TEL: 01244 311467; fax - same. SER: Valuations. VAT: Stan/Spec.

Farmhouse Antiques
21-23 Christleton Rd., Boughton. CH3 5UF. (K. Appleby). Est. 1973. Open 9-5. SIZE: Large. *STOCK: Farmhouse furniture, longcase clocks, Staffordshire pottery, country bygones, mechanical music, Manchester United football programmes.* LOC: 1 mile from City centre on A41. PARK: Easy. TEL: 01244 322478; evenings - 01244 318391; e-mail - progsunited@aol.com SER: Export. VAT: Stan/Spec.

Sandra Harris Interiors and Antiques
61 Watergate Row. CH1 6NP. Est. 1978. Open Tues.-Sat. or by appointment. SIZE: Medium. *STOCK: English and Continental furniture, £500-£10,000; oil paintings including portraits, £1,000-£10,000; works of art, £100-£5,000; all 17th-19th C.* PARK: Easy. TEL: 01244 409009; fax - 0151 353 8107; mobile - 07860 560875. SER: Valuations; buys at auction. VAT: Spec.

J. Alan Hulme
Antique Maps & Old Prints, 52 Mount Way, Waverton. CH3 7QF. Est. 1965. Open Mon.-Sat. by appointment. *STOCK: Maps, 16th-19th C; prints, 18th-19th C.* TEL: 01244 336472; e-mail - alanhulme@pssa.freeserve.co.uk FAIRS: Robert Bailey; Cooper; Galloway.

Jamandic Ltd
22 Bridge St. Row. CH1 1NN. Est. 1975. Open 9.30-5.30, Sat. 9.30-1. SIZE: Medium. *STOCK: Decorative furniture, mirrors, lighting, pictures and prints.* TEL: 01244 312822. SER: Interior design and decoration; export. VAT: Stan/Spec.

K D Antiques
11 City Walls. CH1 1LD. (Dorothea Gillett). Est. 1990. Open 10-5. SIZE: Medium. *STOCK: Staffordshire figures, 18th-19th C, £50-£500; wooden boxes, 18th-19th C, £20-£300; collectables, £5-£50; pottery, porcelain and glass, 19th C, £50-£150; pictures and prints, small furniture.* LOC: City centre, next to Eastgate Clock, wall level. TEL: 01244 314208.

Kayes of Chester   LAPADA
9 St. Michaels Row. CH1 1EF. (A.M. Austin-Kaye and N.J. Kaye). NAG. Est. 1948. Open 9-5.30. SIZE: Medium. *STOCK: Diamond rings and jewellery, 1850-1950, £20-£20,000; silver and plate, 1700-1930, £20-£8,000; small objects and ceramics, 19th to early 20th C, £50-£1,000.* PARK: Nearby. TEL: 01244 327149/343638; fax - 01244 318404; e-mail - kayesgem @btopenworld.com website - www.kayesonline.com SER: Valuations; restorations (silver, jewellery and plate); buys at auction. VAT: Stan/Spec.

Lowe and Sons
11 Bridge St. Row. CH1 1PD. Est. 1770. *STOCK: Jewellery and silver, Georgian, Victorian and Edwardian; unusual collectors' items.* TEL: 01244 325850. VAT: Stan/Spec.

Melody's Antiques   LAPADA
The Old School House, Kinnerton Rd., Lower Kinnerton. CH4 9AE. (M. and M. Melody). Est. 1977. Open 10-5.30 by appointment. SIZE: Large. *STOCK: 18th-20th C oak, mahogany, walnut and pine furniture; porcelain, lighting, decorative items.* LOC: 3 miles from Chester. TEL: 01244 660204. SER: Courier; container packing. FAIRS: Newark; NEC. VAT: Stan/Spec.

Moor Hall Antiques
27 Watergate Row. CH1 2LE. (John Murphy). Resident. Est. 1992. Open 10-5.30. SIZE: Large. *STOCK: Furniture, 18th-19th C, £500-£10,000; prints, 19th C, £50-£200; modern decorative items, £2- £1,500.* LOC: City centre. PARK: Easy. TEL: 01244 340095. SER: Restorations (oils, watercolours and furniture). FAIRS: Buxton. VAT: Stan/Spec.

The Old Warehouse Antiques
7 Delamere St. CH1 4DS. (Mr and Mrs M. O'Donnell).

Est. 1990. Open 10-5. SIZE: Large. *STOCK: Victorian and Edwardian furniture, £50-£1,000.* LOC: Opposite Delamere bus station. PARK: Nearby. TEL: 01244 383942; mobile - 07876 633111. SER: French polishing. VAT: Spec.

Stothert Old Books
4 Nicholas St. CH1 2NX. (Alan and Marjory Checkley). PBFA. Est. 1977. Open 10-5 and occasional Bank Hol. SIZE: Medium. *STOCK: Books, 17th-20th C, £2-£1,000.* LOC: At junction with Watergate St. PARK: Nearby. TEL: 01244 340756; e-mail - alancheckley@yahoo.com SER: Valuations. FAIRS: PBFA and north western.

CONGLETON

W. Buckley Antiques Exports
35 Chelford Rd. CW12 4QA. Open 7 days by appointment. *STOCK: Mainly shipping and Victorian furniture.* TEL: 01260 275299. SER: Shipping.

Littles Collectables
8/10 Little St. CW12 1AR. (Mrs J. Storey). Est. 1989. CL: Wed. SIZE: Medium. *STOCK: Pottery and glass, Doulton, pine furniture, French period furniture, lighting, mirrors and objets d'art, £5-£1,000.* LOC: Town centre. PARK: Nearby. TEL: 01260 299098.

CREWE

Copnal Books
18 Meredith St. CW1 2PW. (P. and R. Ollerhead). Est. 1980. Open 9.30-4.30. SIZE: Medium. *STOCK: Books, £1-£50.* LOC: 200 yards north of market. PARK: Easy. TEL: 01270 580470; home - 01270 585622; e-mail - copnalbooks@yahoo.co.uk SER: Valuations; buys at auction.

DISLEY, Nr. Stockport

Michael Allcroft Antiques
203 Buxton Rd., Newmills. SK12 2RA. Est. 1984. Open Tues.-Fri. 10.30-5, Sat. 12-5, other times by appointment. SIZE: Large. *STOCK: Antique, Edwardian and 1930s furniture.* LOC: A6 south of Stockport. TEL: Mobile - 07798 781642; fax - 01663 744014. SER: Container packing.

Mill Farm Antiques
50 Market St. SK12 2DT. (F.E. Berry). Est. 1968. Open every day. SIZE: Medium. *STOCK: Pianos, clocks especially longcase, mechanical music, shipping goods, general antiques, £50-£10,000.* LOC: A6, 7 miles south of Stockport. PARK: Outside premises. TEL: 01663 764045; fax - 01663 762690; website - www.millfarm antiques.co.uk SER: Valuations; restorations (clocks, watches, barometers and music boxes). VAT: Stan/Spec.

FRODSHAM

Sweetbriar Gallery Ltd
3 Collinson Court, Off Church St. WA6 6PN. (Mrs A. Metcalfe). Est. 1986. Open 9.30-5, Sat. by appointment. *STOCK: Antique and modern paperweights, £5-£8,000.* LOC: Off M56, junction 12, left at traffic lights in village centre, up Church St., left at Helter Skelter public house leading to railway car park. Shop up alley next to pub.

PARK: Railway station behind shop. TEL: 01928 730064; fax - 01928 730066; mobile - 07860 907532; e-mail - sales@sweetbriar.co.uk website - www.sweetbriar.co.uk SER: Valuations; buys at auction (paperweights). FAIRS: Glass (May and Nov.); National Motorcycle Museum (Birmingham); Newark; Shepton Mallet; Woking Glass; Cambridge Glass. VAT: Stan/Spec.

KNUTSFORD

B.R.M. Coins
3 Minshull St. WA16 6HG. (Brian Butterworth). Est. 1968. Open 11-3, Sat. 11-1 or by appointment. SIZE: Small. *STOCK: Coins, medals and banknotes, worldwide, BC to date, from 5p; money boxes, coin scales and weights.* LOC: A50. PARK: Nearby. TEL: 01565 651480; home - 01606 74522. SER: Valuations; buys at auction (as stock).

Cranford Galleries
10 King St. WA16 6DL. (M.R. Bentley). Est. 1964. Open 11-5. CL: Wed. SIZE: Small. *STOCK: Pictures and prints.* LOC: Main St. PARK: Easy. TEL: 01565 633646. SER: Framing and mounting. VAT: Stan.

Knutsford Antiques Centre
113 King St. WA16 6EH. (David and Patricia McLeod). Est. 1995. Open 10-5, Sun. 12-5. CL: Mon. SIZE: 20+ dealers. *STOCK: Furniture, 18th C, £100-£2,000; pine, £200-£600; early British porcelain, ceramics and collectables, £10-£2,000; British silver, £10-£1,000; books, £1-£50; glass, £10-£500; jewellery, £25-£500.* LOC: Main street, 5 mins. from junction 19, M6. PARK: Easy. TEL: 01565 654092; website - www.knutsford antiques.com SER: Valuations.

Lion Gallery and Bookshop
15a Minshull St. WA16 6HG. (R.P. Hepner). Est. 1964. Open Fri. 10.30-4.30, Sat. 10-4.30. *STOCK: Antiquarian maps including John Speed, Blaeu, Jansson and Ogilby; prints and books, watercolours and oils, 16th-20th C; O.S. maps and early directories.* LOC: King St. 3 mins. M6. PARK: Nearby. TEL: 01565 652915; fax - 01565 75014; mobile - 07850 270796. SER: Restorations; binding; cleaning; framing; mounting. VAT: Stan.

LYMM

Willow Pool Garden Centre
Burford Lane. WA13 0SH. (S. Brunsveld). Open 9-6, including Sun. *STOCK: Architectural and general antiques.* TEL: 01925 757827; fax - 01925 758101. FAIRS: Newark.

MACCLESFIELD

Gatehouse Antiques
5/7 Chester Rd. SK11 8DG. (W.H. Livesley). Est. 1973. Open 9-5. CL: Sun. except by appointment and Wed. pm. *STOCK: Small furniture, silver and plate, glass, brass, copper, pewter, jewellery, 1650-1880.* PARK: Opposite. TEL: 01625 426476; home - 01625 612841; website - www.gatehouse.com SER: Valuations; repairs; insurance estimates.

Hills Antiques
Indoor Market, Grosvenor Centre. SK11 6SY. (D. Hill).

Est. 1968. Open 9.30-5.30. *STOCK: Small furniture, jewellery, collectors' items, stamps, coins, postcards.* LOC: Town centre. PARK: Easy. TEL: 01625 420777/420467; e-mail - hillsantiques@tinyworld.co.uk website - www.hillsantiques.co.uk

D.J. Massey and Son
47 Chestergate. SK11 6DG. Est. 1900. Open 9.30-5.15. *STOCK: Jewellery, gold and diamonds, all periods; antique silver.* TEL: 01625 616133.

Mereside Books
75 Chestergate. SK11 6DG. (Miss S. Laithwaite and K. S. Kowalski). PBFA. Est. 1996. Open 10-5, Mon. and Tues. by appointment. SIZE: Small. *STOCK: Books - secondhand, 20th C, £2-£100; antiquarian, 19th C, £10-£300; illustrated, 20th C, £10-£1,000.* TEL: 01625 425352; home - 01625 431160. SER: Valuations; restorations (books including re-binding). FAIRS: Buxton Book. PBFA.

MARPLE BRIDGE, Nr. Stockport

Town House Antiques
21 Town St. SK6 5AA. (Paul and Jeri Buxcey). Est. 1982. Open 10-6 most days. *STOCK: Antique pine, French beds and decorative items.* LOC: Village centre. PARK: Forecourt. TEL: 0161 427 2228; home - 0161 427 1343.

MOBBERLEY

David Bedale
WA16 7HR. Est. 1977. By appointment. SIZE: Medium. *STOCK: 18th-19th C furniture, unusual and decorative items.* TEL: 01565 872270; mobile - 07836 623021. FAIRS: Olympia (June and Nov). VAT: Stan/Spec.

WATCH AND CLOCKMAKERS' HANDBOOK DICTIONARY AND GUIDE

FJ. Britten

A reprint of the classic book which ran to 15 editions between 1881 and 1955. Arranged in dictionary format, an outstanding amount of factual illustrated material is contained within a pocket-sized book.

Specifications:
500pp., 460 engravings, 8½ x 5½in./216 x 140mm.
£14.95 (hardback)

Limited Editions
The Barn, Oak Tree Farm, Knutsford Rd. WA16 7PU. (C.W. Fogg). Est. 1978. Open Thurs., Fri. and Sat. 10-5.30, Sun. 12-4. SIZE: Large. *STOCK: Furniture, 19th C, especially dining tables and chairs, £100-£5,000; armchairs and couches for re-upholstery.* LOC: Main road between Knutsford and Wilmslow. PARK: Own. TEL: 01565 874075; e-mail - info@ltd-editions.co.uk website - www.antique-co.com SER: Valuations; restorations (furniture). VAT: Stan/Spec.

NANTWICH

Adams Antiques   BADA LAPADA
Churche's Mansion, Hospital St. CW5 5RY. (Sandy Summers). Resident. Est. 1975. Open 10-5 or by appointment. SIZE: Large, 8 showrooms. *STOCK: Mainly oak, walnut and fruitwood country furniture, especially Welsh dressers, corner cupboards, tables and chairs; longcase clocks, Mason's Ironstone.* LOC: A500 towards town centre, shop on left on main roundabout. PARK: Own large. TEL: 01270 625643; fax - 01270 625609; e-mail - sandy@adams-antiques.net website - www.adams-antiques.net SER: Valuations; restorations (furniture). FAIRS: BADA; LAPADA; NEC; Olympia (Nov). VAT: Stan/Spec.

Barn Antiques
8 The Cocoa Yard, Pillory St. CW5 5BL. (J.B. Lee). Est. 1993. CL: Wed. SIZE: Small. *STOCK: Carltonware, Beswick, Royal Doulton and Shelley china and collectables.* LOC: Town centre. TEL: 01270 627770.

Chapel Antiques
47 Hospital St. CW5 5RL. (Miss D.J. Atkin). Est. 1983. Open 9.30-5.30, Wed. 9.30-1 or by appointment. CL: Mon. SIZE: Medium. *STOCK: Oak, mahogany and pine furniture, Georgian and Victorian, £100-£3,000; longcase clocks, pre-1830, £1,000-£3,000; copper, brass, silver, glass, porcelain, pottery and small items, 19th C, £10-£500.* LOC: Enter town via Pillory St., turn right into Hospital St. PARK: Easy. TEL: 01270 629508; home - same. SER: Valuations; restorations (furniture and clocks).

Roderick Gibson
1 Chapel Court, Hospital St. CW5 5RP. (R. and L. Gibson). Est. 1975. Strictly by appointment. *STOCK: Furniture and decorative collectors' pieces.* PARK: Nearby. TEL: 01270 625301; website - www.goantiques.com/members/roderickgibson SER: Valuations. VAT: Stan/Global.

Love Lane Antiques
Love Lane. CW5 5BH. (M. Simon). Est. 1982. Open 10-5. CL: Wed. SIZE: Small. *STOCK: General antiques, 19th-20th C, £5-£1,000.* LOC: 2 mins. walk from town square. PARK: Nearby. TEL: 01270 626239.

Nantwich Antiques
7A Beam St. CW5 5LR. (A. S. Coupe). Est. 1982. Open 10.30-5. SIZE: Medium. *STOCK: 18th-19th C English furniture, to £1,000; field sports accessories; period and reproduction Indian and Chinese furniture.* LOC: Town centre. PARK: Own. TEL: 01270 610615; website - www.indianfurniture.co.uk SER: Valuations; restorations. FAIRS: CLA Game; Lowther Horse Trials. VAT: Stan/Spec.

NORTHWICH

Northwich Antiques Centre
132 Witton St. CW9 5NP. (F.J. Cockburn). Est. 1990. Open 10-5 including Sun. SIZE: Large. *STOCK: Georgian, Victorian and Edwardian furniture, £50-£1,000+; china, clocks and barometers; Royal Doulton, Beswick, Moorcroft; prints, paintings, books, jewellery.* LOC: Town centre. PARK: Easy. TEL: 01606 47540; fax - same; mobile - 07980 645738; website - www.northwichantiquescentre.com

PLUMLEY

Coppelia Antiques
Holford Lodge, Plumley Moor Rd. WA16 9RS. (V. and R. Clements). Resident. Est. 1970. Open 10-6 including Sun. by appointment. SIZE: Large. *STOCK: Over 500 clocks (mainly longcase and wall), £1,000-£50,000; tables - Georgian mahogany, wine, oak gateleg and side; bureaux, desks, chests of drawers, lowboys, coffers - all stock guaranteed.* LOC: 4 miles junction 19, M6. PARK: Own. TEL: 01565 722197/020 7629 6606; fax - 01565 722744; website - www.pendulumofmayfair.co.uk SER: Restorations. VAT: Spec.

POYNTON, Nr. Stockport

The Attic
96 London Rd. South. SK12 1LQ. (Jonathan and Hazel Hodgson). Est. 1998. Open 10.30-4.30 or by appointment. SIZE: Medium. *STOCK: World-wide pine furniture and kitchenalia, mainly post 1900.* LOC: A523 just outside village. PARK: Easy. TEL: 01625 873229; mobile - 07791 190931; website - www.theatticonline.co.uk SER: Pine stripping, repair, preservation treatment, sand and wax.

Recollections
69 Park Lane. SK12 1RD. (Angela Smith). Open 10-5. SIZE: Medium. *STOCK: Antique, pre-war and secondhand furniture; jewellery and decorative collectables.* PARK: Own at rear and Civic Centre. TEL: 01625 859373.

ROMILEY, Nr. Stockport

Romiley Antiques & Jewellery
42 Stockport Rd. SK6 3AA. (P. Green). Est. 1983. Open Thurs., Fri. and Sat. 9-5. SIZE: Medium. *STOCK: Furniture, 18th-19th C, £100-£3,000; ceramics, 18th-19th C, £5-£1,000; jewellery, 19th C, £5-£1,000.* LOC: 5 miles from Stockport. PARK: Nearby. TEL: 0161 494 6920; home - same. SER: Valuations. VAT: Stan/Spec.

SANDBACH

Saxon Cross Antiques Emporium
Town Mill, High St. CW11 1AH. (John and Christine Jones). Est. 1972. Open 10-5. SIZE: Large - 4 storey Georgian mill. *STOCK: Furniture, 16th to early 20th C, £50-£10,000; glass, silver, china and porcelain, 19th-20th C, £50-£1,000;* LOC: 1 mile off junction 17, M6. PARK: Easy and nearby. TEL: 01270 753005; fax - same. SER: Valuations; restorations; buys at auction. FAIRS: Cheshire Show. VAT: Stan/Spec.

Coppelia Antiques

Valerie and Roy Clements

Holford Lodge, Plumley Moor Road,
Plumley, Nr. Knutsford,
Cheshire WA16 9RS
Telephone: 01565 722197
Fax: 01565 722744
4 miles from J.19, M6

Fine quality mahogany longcase clock, c.1770, London maker, ht. 7ft. 8in. Dial with chapter ring and spandrels with strike-silent in the arch

We currently have one of the finest selections of quality longcase clocks in the U.K. We also stock mantel, bracket, English and Vienna wall clocks. Established 1970, all our clocks are fully restored and guaranteed 1 year. Free delivery U.K. mainland. Why not pay us a visit, you will receive a warm welcome, free coffee and constructive, expert advice.

OPEN 7 DAYS BY APPOINTMENT

STOCKPORT

Antique Furniture Warehouse
Units 3/4 Royal Oak Buildings, Cooper St. SK1 3QJ. Est. 1975. Open 10-4. SIZE: Large. *STOCK: English and Continental mahogany, walnut and inlaid furniture, paintings, clocks, shipping goods, pottery, porcelain and curios, decorative items, architectural.* LOC: 5 mins. off M56 towards town centre, 2 mins. off M60. PARK: Own. TEL: 0161 429 8590; fax - 0161 480 5375; website - www.antiques-atlas.com SER: Courier; packing. VAT: Stan.

Antiques Import Export
20 Buxton Rd., Hevley. SK2 6NU. (Paul, Mark and Adrian Ledger). Est. 1968. Open 9-5.30. SIZE: Large. *STOCK: American and pre-1930 English furniture, to £5,000.* LOC: A6 opposite cemetery. PARK: At side of shop. TEL: 0161 476 4013; fax - 0161 285 2860; e-mail - paul@antiquesimportexport.freeserve.co.uk SER: Valuations; restorations. FAIRS: Newark.

Flintlock Antiques
28 and 30 Bramhall Lane. SK2 6HD. (F. Tomlinson and Son). Est. 1968. Open 9-5. SIZE: Large. *STOCK: Furniture, clocks, pictures, scientific instruments.* PARK: Easy. TEL: 0161 480 9973. VAT: Stan/Spec.

Halcyon Antiques
435/437 Buxton Rd., Great Moor. SK2 7HE. (Mrs Jill A. Coppock and Miss Lesley Coppock). Est. 1980. Open 10-5. SIZE: Large. *STOCK: Porcelain and glass, £1-£2,000 and furniture, £50-£2,000, all 1750-1940. Jewellery, silver and plate, linen and lace.* LOC: A6, 3

miles south of town. PARK: Easy. TEL: 0161 483 5038; home - 0161 439 3524; e-mail - halcyonantiques @tiscali.co.uk

Imperial Antiques LAPADA
295 Buxton Rd., Great Moor. SK2 7NR. (A. Todd). Est. 1972. Open 10-5, Sun. by appointment. SIZE: Large. STOCK: Decorative French and English antiques; silver and plate, 19th-20th C; porcelain especially Japanese and Chinese, 18th-19th C; all £100-£10,000. LOC: A6 Buxton Rd., 1.5 miles south of town centre. PARK: Easy. TEL: 0161 483 3322; fax - 0161 483 3376; e-mail - Alfred@imperialantiques.com website - www.imperial antiques.com SER: Buys at auction (as stock). VAT: Stan/Spec.

Manchester Antique Company
MAC House, St Thomas's Place. SK1 3TZ. Est. 1967. Open 9.30-4.30. SIZE: Very large. STOCK: Antique furniture, English, Continental and shipping goods, mainly walnut and mahogany. LOC: Town centre. PARK: Own. TEL: 0161 355 5566/5577; fax - 0161 355 5588; e-mail - sales@manchesterantique.co.uk website - www.manchester-antique.co.uk SER: Containers packed worldwide. FAIRS: Newark. VAT: Stan/Spec.

Nostalgia Architectural Antiques LAPADA
Holland's Mill, Shaw Heath. SK3 8BH. (D. and E. Durrant). Est. 1975. Open Tues.-Fri. 10-6, Sat. 10-5. SIZE: Large. STOCK: Fireplaces, £200-£50,000; bathroom fittings and architectural items, £50-£2,000; all 18th-19th C. LOC: 5 mins. from junction 1, M60. PARK: At rear. TEL: 0161 477 7706; fax - 0161 477 2267; website - www.nostalgia-uk.com SER: Valuations. VAT: Stan/Spec.

The Old Curiosity Shop
123 Stockport Rd. West, Bredbury. SK6 2AN. (Sandra Crook). Est. 1984. Open 10-6, Sun. 12-5. CL: Wed. SIZE: Medium. STOCK: 1920s, 1930s oak furniture, especially barley twist; brass coal buckets, fire tools. LOC: 2 miles from M60. PARK: Forecourt or opposite. TEL: 0161 494 9469; home - same. SER: Restorations (furniture - hand stripping).

TARPORLEY

Tarporley Antique Centre
76 High St. CW6 0DP. Est. 1992. Open 10-5, Sun. 11-4. SIZE: 9 dealers on two floors. STOCK: Furniture, ceramics, commemoratives, treen, glass, oils, watercolours, prints, silver and plate, Art Deco, dolls and bears, books. LOC: Main road, near Crown public house. PARK: In front of premises and opposite. TEL: 01829 733919.

TARVIN, Nr. Chester

Antique Fireplaces
The Manor House, Church St. CH3 8EB. (Mrs G. O'Toole). Est. 1979. Open Fri., Sat. and Sun. 10-5 or by appointment. SIZE: Medium. STOCK: Fireplaces and ranges, 18th-19th C, £150-£3,000. LOC: At junction of A556 and A51. PARK: Easy. TEL: 01829 740936; home - 01606 46717. SER: Valuations; restorations; installations (fireplaces and ranges); new tiles and

fenders ordered from suppliers on request. FAIRS: Tatton Park, Knutsford.

TARVIN SANDS, Nr. Chester

Cheshire Brick and Slate Co
Brook House Farm, Salters Bridge. CH3 8NR. (Malcolm and Jason Youde). Est. 1978. Open 7.30-5.30, Sat. 8-4.30. SIZE: Large. STOCK: Reclaimed conservation building materials and timber, 16th-20th C; architectural antiques - garden statuary, stonework, lamp posts, gates, fireplaces, bathroom suites, chimney pots and ironwork, 18th-20th C, £50-£1,000; furniture, pews, leaded lights, pottery, 18th-20th C, £5-£1,000. LOC: Directly off A54 just outside Tarvin. PARK: Own. TEL: 01829 740883; fax - 01829 740481; e-mail - enquiries@cheshirebrickandslate.co.uk website - www. cheshirebrickandslate.co.uk SER: Valuations; restorations (fireplaces, timber treatment); building/construction and demolition; renovations; manufactured doors, units and beams etc cut to customers specification on site. VAT: Stan/Global.

TATTENHALL, Nr. Chester

The Great Northern Architectural Antique Company Ltd
New Russia Hall, Chester Rd. CH3 9AH. Open 9.30-5, Sun. 10-4. SIZE: Large. STOCK: Period doors, fire surrounds, stained glass, garden statuary, furniture and curios. LOC: Off A41. PARK: Easy. TEL: 01829 770796; fax - 01829 770971; e-mail - gnaacoltd@ enterprise.net SER: Stripping; restorations (stained glass); repairs (metalwork). VAT: Stan.

TILSTON, Nr. Malpas

Well House Antiques
The Well House. SY14 7DP. (S. French-Greenslade). Est. 1968. Open by appointment. SIZE: Small. STOCK: Collectors' items, china, glass, silver. PARK: Easy. TEL: 01829 250332.

WARRINGTON

The Rocking Chair Antiques
Unit 3, St. Peter's Way. WA2 7BL. (Mike and Jane Barratt). Est. 1976. Open 8.30-5, Sat. 10-4. SIZE: Large. STOCK: Furniture and bric-a-brac. LOC: Off Orford Lane. PARK: Easy. TEL: 01925 652409; fax - same; mobile - 07774 492891. SER: Valuations; packing and shipping. VAT: Stan.

WAVERTON, Nr. Chester

The White House
Whitchurch Rd. CH3 7PB. (Mrs Elizabeth Rideal). Est. 1979. Open 10-5. SIZE: Medium. STOCK: Stripped pine furniture, 19th-20th C, £50-£2,000; Victorian china, 19th C, £5-£100; bric-a-brac. LOC: A41, 2.5 miles south of Sainsbury's roundabout on Whitchurch Rd. PARK: Easy. TEL: 01244 335063; home - same; fax - 01244 335098. VAT: Margin.

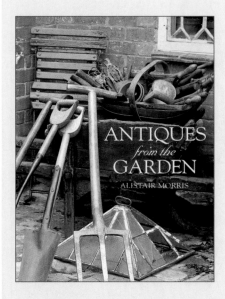

ANTIQUES *from the* GARDEN

ALISTAIR MORRIS

The huge success of the first edition of *Antiques from the Garden* has demonstrated the demand and created the opportunity for a new, enlarged edition. This new revised edition includes a great deal of new content, directly reflecting the interest expressed by the media in their requests for articles, Radio and TV interviews following the original publication. Particular interest has been generated in garden tools and accessory items, terracotta wares, cast-iron containers, garden furniture and all manner of related novelties. The book includes over 200 colour illustrations and 500 black and white images including some early trade advertisements from scarce magazines.

As a collecting area, it is still in its infancy but has all the ingredients a potential collector would choose. There is history, geography, economics, workmanship and engineering. There are makers' marks and trademarks, common, scarce and rare varieties. There are collecting areas within areas and satisfying, attractive objects of varying sizes in various materials. From wrought iron gates to marble urns and asparagus forks to cucumber straighteners, this book will fascinate with its wealth of detail and illustration making the reader aware of a lesser known but intriguing aspect of gardening history.

Specifications:
280pp., 235 col. illus.,
500 b.&w. illus.,
11 x 8½in./279 x 216mm.
£25.00 (hardback)

A History of
English Brickwork

Nathaniel Lloyd

A History of English Brickwork is one of those rare books which covers the whole spectrum of the subject, from the practical problems faced by the craftsman shaping a brick or "manipulating" it to make the glorious decorations found on so many English houses, to the detailed drawings necessary to construct a complicated capital; from the historical aspects of the manufacture to the dating of work by the thickness of the joints. The book features hundreds of black and white photographs from the turn of the century illustrating numerous properties throughout England.

Nathaniel Lloyd (1867-1933), the distinguished architect and author, wrote this great standard work on English bricks and brickwork in 1925. It is a superb photographic record, meticulously annotated, which has never been rivalled and is unlikely ever to be surpassed.

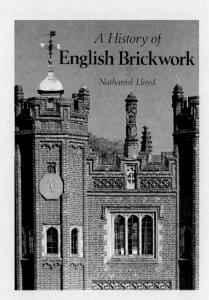

Specifications:
456pp., 374 b.&w. photographs,
35 measured drawings and
profiles of chimney caps.
11 x 8½in./279 x 216mm.
£35.00 (hardback)

For full details of all ACC publications, log on to our website:
www.antiquecollectorsclub.com
or telephone 01394 389950 for a free catalogue

CORNWALL

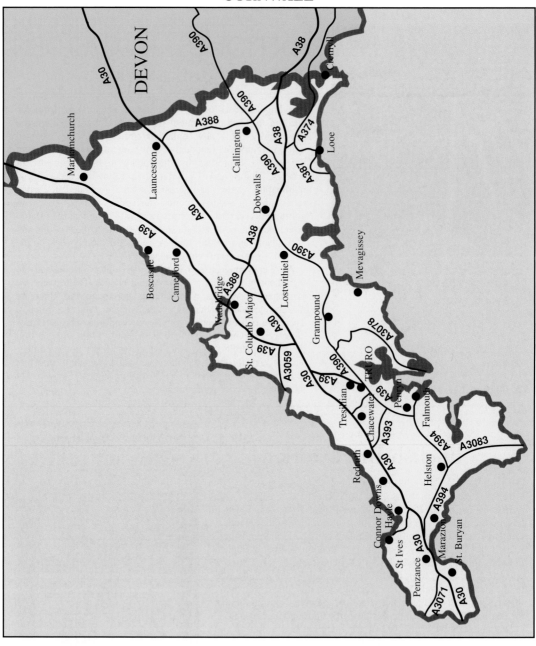

Dealers and Shops in Cornwall					
				Mevagissey	1
				Penryn	2
Boscastle	2	Grampound	1	Penzance	8
Callington	2	Hayle	1	Redruth	2
Camelford	1	Helston	1	St. Buryan	1
Chacewater	1	Launceston	1	St. Columb Major	1
Connor Downs	1	Looe	1	St. Ives	3
Cremyll	1	Lostwithiel	5	Tresillian	1
Dobwalls	1	Marazion	1	Truro	5
Falmouth	3	Marhamchurch	1	Wadebridge	1

BOSCASTLE

Newlyfe Antiques
The Old Mill. PL35 0AQ. (Harry Ruddy). Open seven days a week May-Sept., prior telephone call advisable at other times. *STOCK: Collectables, 18th-19th C furniture, French beds.* LOC: Village centre. PARK: Nearby. TEL: 01840 250230; website - www. boscastleoldmill.com

Pickwick Antiques
The Old Mill, Old Rd. PL35 0AQ. (David Lamond). Est. 1970. Open 11-5. CL: Wed. SIZE: Small. *STOCK: General small antiques including silver and plate, glass, pre-1950, £5-£500+.* PARK: Easy. TEL: 01840 250770; home/fax - 01566 880085; mobile - 07971 648107; e-mail - david-peter@craigmoor.freeserve.co.uk SER: Valuations.

CALLINGTON

Church Street Antiques & Junque
Newport, Church St. PL17 7AS. (Harry Davis). Est. 1990. Open 9-5. SIZE: Medium. *STOCK: Decorative items and furniture, £5-£700.* PARK: Own. TEL: 01579 383491; mobile - 07791 769812; e-mail - harry@ harryskelter.plus.com SER: Decorative painting and murals executed

Country Living Antiques
Weston House, Haye Rd. PL17 7JJ. (Ian Baxter CBE). Resident. Est. 1990. Open 10-6. SIZE: Large - including barn. *STOCK: 19th C oak and pine country furniture, general antiques, £1-£2,000.* LOC: Town centre. PARK: Own. TEL: 01579 382245; fax - same. SER: Valuations; buys at auction.

CAMELFORD

Corner Shop Antiques and Gallery
68 Fore St. PL32 9PG. (P. J. Tillett). Est. 1982. Open 9.30-5.30. SIZE: Small. *STOCK: General antiques including Torquay ware, Victorian watercolours, collector's items and bric-a-brac, £2-£1,000.* LOC: Main road. PARK: Nearby. TEL: 01840 212573; home - same; mobile - 07884 456247; e-mail - tillett18@aol.com *Trade Only.*

CHACEWATER, Nr. Truro

Chacewater Antiques
5 Fore St. TR4 8PS. (Jeanette Bateman). Est. 1991. Open Tues.-Sat. 10-5. *STOCK: Furniture, English silver, fine jewellery, brass and copper, paintings, lamps, china and glass.* LOC: 5 mins. from Truro. From A30 Chiverton roundabout towards Truro. PARK: Free nearby. TEL: 01872 561411.

CONNOR DOWNS, Nr. Hayle

Julie Strachey
Trevaskis Barn, Gwinear Rd. TR27 5JQ. Est. 1975. Open by appointment. SIZE: Medium. *STOCK: Decorative 18th-19th C farm and country furniture, especially tables, dressers, chests, wrought iron and unusual garden items.* TEL: 01209 613750; mobile - 07711

249939. SER: Packing and shipping. FAIRS: NEC. VAT: Stan.

CREMYLL, Nr. Plymouth

Cremyll Antiques
The Cottage, Cremyll Beach, Torpoint. PL10 1HX. (E. Kaszewski). BHI. Est. 1949. SIZE: Small. *STOCK: Clocks and watches, small items, jewellery, Victorian trinkets.* PARK: Own. TEL: 01752 823490. SER: Repairs (barometers, barographs, watches, clocks and jewellery).

DOBWALLS, Nr. Liskeard

Olden Days
Five Lanes. PL14 6JD. (G.M. and Mrs. H.K. Young). Est. 1980. Open 9.30-5.30, Sun. 11-4. SIZE: Medium. *STOCK: Period furniture, £50-£1,500; reclaimed and new pine furniture; bric-a-brac and collectables.* LOC: A38 between Liskeard and Bodmin. PARK: Easy and private behind shop. TEL: 01579 321577; home - same; e-mail - glenyoung@aol.com website - www.oldendays. info SER: Restorations; furniture made to order. VAT: Stan/Spec.

FALMOUTH

John Maggs
54 Church St. TR11 3DS. (C.C. Nunn). Est. 1900. Open 10-5. CL: Wed. SIZE: Medium. *STOCK: Antiquarian prints and maps, exclusive limited editions.* LOC: Main street. PARK: At rear of shop. TEL: 01326 313153; fax - same; e-mail - colin@johnmaggs.co.uk website - www.johnmaggs.co.uk SER: Restorations; framing.

Old Town Hall Antiques
3 High St. TR11 2AB. (Mary P. Sheppard and Terence J. Brandreth). Est. 1986. Open 10-5.30, Sun. 11-4. SIZE: Large + trade store. *STOCK: Furniture including French, beds and mirrors, 19th-20th C, £100-£2,000; country smalls, china and collectables, 19th-20th C, £10-£60.* LOC: From edge of Falmouth follow signs towards marina, shop situated on right under road arch (one-way street). PARK: Easy. TEL: 01326 319437; home - 01326 377489; website - www.oldtownhallantiques.co.uk SER: Storage and delivery. VAT: Global.

Rosina's
4 High St. TR11 2AB. (Mrs R. Gealer). Est. 1977. Open 11-4. *STOCK: Old dolls, bears (including limited edition Steiff and artist bears) toys, dolls' houses and miniatures, linen and lace. Fairies especially designed for Rosina's.* TEL: 01326 219491; mobile - 07791 837658. SER: Restorations.

GRAMPOUND, Nr. Truro

Radnor House
Fore St. TR2 4QT. (P. and G. Hodgson). Est. 1972. Open 10-5. SIZE: Medium. *STOCK: Furniture and accessories, pre-1900.* Not Stocked: Jewellery, coins and weapons. LOC: A390. PARK: Easy. TEL: 01726 882921; home - same; e-mail - radnorantiques@aol.com SER: Valuations; buys at auction.

HAYLE

Copperhouse Gallery - W. Dyer & Sons
14 Fore St. TR27 4DX. (A.P. Dyer). Est. 1900. Open 9-5.30. SIZE: Medium. *STOCK: Watercolours and oils, including Newlyn and St. Ives schools; small antiques, Art Deco and studio pottery.* LOC: Main road. PARK: Easy. TEL: 01736 752787; home - 01736 752960. SER: Framing.

HELSTON

Turners Antiques
Poldark Mine and Heritage Centre, Wendron. TR13 0ER. (Jacqueline and Stuart Smith). Est. 1999. Open Sun.-Fri. 10-4.30 Easter to end Oct; also Sat. April, July and Aug. SIZE: Medium. *STOCK: Jewellery and collectables, 1850-1950, £5-£150; books, postcards and ephemera, from 1750, £1-£75; tools, 1800-1950, £1-£100; small furniture, 1850-1930, £15-£300.* LOC: 2 miles from Helston on B3297, follow brown tourist signs. PARK: Easy. TEL: 01326 573173; fax - 01326 563166; home - 01209 612142; e-mail - turnersantiques@btconnect.com

Antique Chairs and Museum
Colhay Farm, Polson. PL15 9QS. (Tom and Alice Brown). Est. 1988. Open seven days. SIZE: Large. *STOCK: Chairs, 18th to early 20th C.* LOC: Signed from A30. PARK: Easy. TEL: 01566 777485; fax - same; home - same; e-mail - chairs@brown7368.fslife.co.uk website - www.antiquechairscolhay.co.uk SER: Restorations; buys at auction.

LOOE

Tony Martin
Fore St. PL13 1AE. Est. 1965. Open 9.30-1 and 2-5, appointment advisable. SIZE: Medium. *STOCK: Porcelain, 18th C; silver, 18th-19th C, both £20-£200; glass, furniture, oils and watercolours.* LOC: Main street. TEL: 01503 262734; home - 01503 262228.

LOSTWITHIEL

John Bragg Antiques
35 Fore St. PL22 0BN. Open 10-5. CL: Wed. pm. *STOCK: Furniture, mainly period mahogany and Victorian.* LOC: 100yds. off A390. TEL: 01208 872827.

The Higgins Press
South St. PL22 0BZ. (Mrs Doris Roberts). Est. 1982. Open 10-4, Wed. and Sat. 10-1. SIZE: Small. *STOCK: Porcelain, Victorian and collectable, £5-£1,000; clocks and glass, Victorian to Art Deco, £5-£750; furniture, Georgian to 1930s, £10-£3,000.* LOC: Just off A390. PARK: Easy and nearby. TEL: 01208 872755; home - same; mobile - 07729 868875.

The Home Store
8 Queen St. PL22 0AB. (Mrs Amanda Davidge). Est. 1999. Open 10-4. CL: Wed. pm. *STOCK: Kitchen related antiques and collectables, furniture and country ceramics.* LOC: Main road. PARK: Free nearby. TEL: 01208 873228; home - 01208 871127; e-mail - adavidge @yahoo.com

Old Palace Antiques
Old Palace, Quay St. PL22 0BS. (J.S. Askew). Open 9.30-1 and 2-5. *STOCK: Pine, general antiques, collectors' items, Beswick, Beatrix Potter figures, Royal Doulton caricature jugs, crested china and Cornishware; antiquities including Egyptian, Roman and Chinese.* LOC: In the old duchy palace, by the river. PARK: Nearby. TEL: 01208 872909; e-mail - melaniej. askew@virgin.net

Uzella Court Antiques Centre
2 Fore St. PL22 0BP. (Mark and Mandy Royle). Est. 2003. Open Tues.-Sat. 10-5, every 2nd and 3rd Sun. 11-4. SIZE: Small. *STOCK: Furniture, Georgian to Art Deco, £100-£2,000; jewellery - gold, silver, Tiffany and costume, £3-£500; ceramics including Clarice Cliff, Charlotte Rhead, Crown Devon, £10-£1,000; silver, £10-£2,000.* LOC: Central. PARK: 50 metres. TEL: 01208 872255; fax - same; mobile - 07976 522597; e-mail - mark@royle2202.freeserve.co.uk

MARAZION

Antiques
The Shambles, Market Place. TR17 0AR. (Andrew S. Wood). Est. 1988. Open Mon.-Fri. 10.15-5.30, also Sats. 1st Nov.-31st March. SIZE: Medium. *STOCK: General antiques and collectors' items including 19th-20th C pottery and porcelain; Victorian to 20th C glass including pressed; blue and white china, Art Deco ceramics, Devon pottery, commemorative ware, Goss and crested china, '50s-'60's pottery and glass, bottles.* LOC: Main street. PARK: Easy. TEL: 01736 711381; home - same.

MARHAMCHURCH

Marhamchurch Antiques
Blackthorne, Endsleigh Park. EX23 0HL. (Paul Fitzsimmons). Est. 1991. Open 9-5 by appointment only. SIZE: Small. *STOCK: Early oak, 16th-17th C.* PARK: Easy. TEL: 01288 361803; mobile - 07779 038891; website - www.marhamchurchantiques.co.uk

MEVAGISSEY

Cloud Cuckoo Land
12 Fore St. PL26 6UQ (Paul Mulvey and Chris Nguyen-Duc). Est. 1982. Open seven days 11-5. SIZE: Medium. *STOCK: Letters, manuscripts, toys and dolls: Nelson, TV, film and rock 'n' roll memorabilia; ceramics, local interest items.* LOC: Central. PARK: Nearby. TEL: 01726 842364; home - same; website - www.cloud cuckooland.biz

PENRYN

Old School Antiques
Church Rd. TR10 8DA. (J.M. Gavin). Est. 1988. Open 8.30-5.30. *STOCK: General antiques.* PARK: Easy. TEL: 01326 375092. SER: Free delivery within Cornwall.

Neil Willcox & Mark Nightingale
Jobswater, Mabe. TR10 9BT. Open by appointment. *STOCK: Sealed wine and other bottles, British and Continental 1650-1850, and related items.* TEL: 01326 340533; e-mail - nightdes@aol.com website -

www.earlyglass.com SER: Valuations; mail order - catalogue and photos supplied.

PENZANCE

Antiques & Fine Art
1-3 Queens Buildings, The Promenade. TR18 4DL. (Elinor Davies and Geoffrey Mills). Est. 1985. Open 10-4. SIZE: Medium. *STOCK: Furniture, 17th C to Edwardian, to £10,000; some decorative pieces, to £250.* LOC: Next to Queen's Hotel. PARK: Nearby. TEL: 01736 350509; home - 01736 350677; e-mail - enquiries@antiquesfineart.co.uk website - www.antiques fineart.co.uk SER: Valuations; restorations (furniture including upholstery).

Chapel Street Antiques Arcade
61/62 Chapel St. TR18 4AE. Est. 1985. Open 9.30-5. SIZE: Two floors, 30 dealers. *STOCK: Furniture, pottery, porcelain, glass, silver, metalware, kitchenalia, pictures, books, clocks, jewellery, decorative and collectors' items.* TEL: Mobile - 07890 542708.

Daphne's Antiques
17 Chapel St. TR18 4AW. (Daphne Davies). Est. 1976. Open 10-5. SIZE: Medium. *STOCK: Early country furniture, Georgian glass, Delft, pottery and decorative objects.* TEL: 01736 361719.

Peter Johnson
62 Chapel St. TR18 4AE. (Peter Chatfield-Johnson). Est. 1961. Open 9.30-5, Mon. by appointment. SIZE: Small. *STOCK: Lighting, 19th-20th C, £25-£500; Oriental ceramics and furniture, 18th-19th C, £25-£2,000; handmade silk lampshades, 20th C, £25-£250.* LOC: Left at top of Market Jew St. PARK: Easy. TEL: 01736 363267; home - 01736 368088. SER: Valuations; restorations (soft furnishings).

Little Jem's
69 Causewayhead. TR18 2SR. (J. Lagden). Open 9.30-5. *STOCK: Antique and modern jewellery (specialising in opal and amber), gem stones, objets d'art, paintings, clocks and watches.* TEL: 01736 351400. SER: Repairs; commissions.

New Street Bookshop
4 New St. TR18 2LZ. (K.E. Hearn and C.J. Bradley). Open 10-5. *STOCK: Books and ephemera.* LOC: Close to town centre, just off Chapel St. TEL: 01736 362758; e-mail - eankelvin@yahoo.com

Penzance Rare Books
43 Causewayhead. TR18 2SS. (Patricia Johnstone). Est. 1990. Open 10-5. SIZE: Medium. *STOCK: Antiquarian and secondhand books.* LOC: Top of Causewayhead. PARK: Nearby. TEL: 01736 362140; home - 01736 367506; e-mail - patricia.johnstone@blue-earth.co.uk SER: Valuations; search.

Tony Sanders Penzance Gallery and Antiques
14 Chapel St. TR18 4AW. Est. 1972. Open 9-5.30. SIZE: 3 floors. *STOCK: Oils and watercolours, 19th-20th C, £50-£5,000; glass, silver, china and small furniture; specialist in Newlyn and J F Pool of Hayle copper; contemporary art, paintings and bronzes.* TEL: 01736 366620/368461. VAT: Stan.

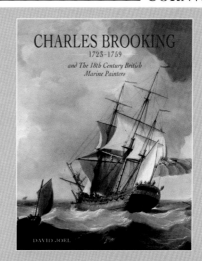

All the known pictures of one of the foremost maritime painters are illustrated and described in this much needed *catalogue raisonné*, together with all his known drawings and engravings. The book also describes the Dutch marine painters in the 17th century and contains biographies of other British marine painters of the 18th century. There is an additional chapter on 18th century London marine engravers by James Taylor.

Specifications: 208pp., 142 col., 193 b.&w. illus., 11 x 8½in./279 x 216mm. **£35.00 (hardback)**

REDRUTH

Evergreen Antiques
38 Fore St. TR15 2AE. (Miss A. Champion and Miss M. Jelf). Est. 1993. Open 10-4.30. SIZE: Medium. *STOCK: Victorian and Edwardian furniture including pine; table lamps, copper and brass.* LOC: Main street, opposite Post Office. PARK: Nearby. TEL: 01209 215634; mobile - 07870 195717.

The Old Steam Bakery
60A Fore St. TR14 7NU. (Stephen J. Phillips). Est. 1986. Open 10.30-5. SIZE: Large. *STOCK: Furniture including oak, 19th to early 20th C, £50-£100+; china and glass, early 20th C.* LOC: Next to main Post Office. PARK: Easy. TEL: 01209 315099; home - 01209 710650. SER: Valuations; restorations (furniture). VAT: Stan.

ST BURYAN, Nr. Penzance

Boathouse Antiques
Churchtown. TR19 6BX. (M.A. and P.A. Cleaver). Resident. Est. 1994. Open in summer Tues.-Sat. 10-5, other times ring or knock at Belmont House; winter - prior telephone advisable. SIZE: Medium. *STOCK: Wide range of general antiques including nautical items, furniture, rugs, jewellery, pictures and ceramics.* LOC: Opposite pub in village centre. PARK: Easy. TEL: 01736 810025; home - same. FAIRS: DCAF.

ALAN BENNETT LTD

18th and 19th century Furniture, Porcelain Silver, Jewellery and Paintings

NEW BRIDGE HOUSE NEW BRIDGE STREET TRURO CORNWALL 01872 273296

ST. COLUMB MAJOR

Stiltskin & Walrus Antiques
61 Fore St. TR9 6RH. (Mrs Janet Prescott). Est. 2000. Open 9.15-4, Wed. 9.15-1. SIZE: Medium. *STOCK: China, glass, books, pictures and prints, postcards, furniture, curios and collectables.* LOC: Central. PARK: Loading only and nearby. TEL: 01841 520182; home - same. SER: Valuations.

ST. IVES

Courtyard Collectables
Cyril Noall Sq., Fore St. TR26 1HE. (Janice Mosedale). Est. 1994. Open June to end Sept. 7 days 10-10; Oct., April and May 7 days 10-6; Nov. to March - Fri., Sat. and Sun. 10.30-4.30. SIZE: Medium. *STOCK: 20th C collectables.* TEL: 01736 798809. SER: Valuations; buys at auction.

Mike Read Antique Sciences
1 Abbey Meadow, Lelant. TR26 3LL. Est. 1974. Open by appointment. SIZE: Small. *STOCK: Scientific instruments - navigational, surveying, mining, barometers, telescopes and microscopes, medical, 18th-19th C, £10-£5,000; maritime works of art and nautical artifacts.* LOC: Turn left on hill in village, heading towards St. Ives. PARK: Easy. TEL: 01736 757237. SER: Valuations; restorations. FAIRS: Scientific & Medical Instrument.

Tremayne Applied Arts
Street-an-Pol. TR26 2DS. (Roger and Anne Tonkinson). Est. 1998. Summer - Open 10.30-4.30, Sat. 10-1.30. CL:

Wed. Winter - Open Mon., Fri. and Sat. mornings. *STOCK: Furniture, china, glass, paintings and prints, late 19th to late 20th C, £50-£3,000.* LOC: Central, close to tourist information office. PARK: Station. TEL: 01736 797779; fax - 01736 793222; home - 01736 753537.

TRESILLIAN, Nr. Truro

Tresillian Antiques
The Elms. TR2 4BA. (Philip and Linda Buddell). Est. 1972. Open 9.30-5.30, Sun. by appointment. SIZE: Small. *STOCK: Oak and mahogany furniture, Georgian, Victorian and Edwardian; collectables including china, ivory, silver and teddy bears; oils and watercolours, mainly landscape and marine.* LOC: A390. PARK: Easy. TEL: 01872 520173; home - same; mobile - 07974 022893; e-mail - lulubudd@aol.com SER: Valuations; restorations (furniture).

TRURO

Alan Bennett Ltd
24 New Bridge St. TR1 2AA. Est. 1954. Open 9-5.30. SIZE: Large. *STOCK: Furniture, £50-£5,000; jewellery and porcelain, to 1900, £5-£1,000; paintings and prints, £20-£2,000.* LOC: Eastern side of cathedral. PARK: 100yds. from shop. TEL: 01872 273296. VAT: Stan/Spec.

Blackwater Pine Antiques
Blackwater. TR4 8ET. (J.S. Terrett). Open 9-6. *STOCK: Pine and country furniture.* TEL: 01872 560919. SER: Restorations; stripping; furniture made to order.

Bonython Bookshop
16 Kenwyn St. TR1 3BU. (Rosemary Carpenter). Est. 1996. Open 10.30-4.30. SIZE: Small. *STOCK: Books especially Cornish, £5-£700; topography and art, £5-£100.* TEL: 01872 262886; e-mail - bonythonbooks@ btconnect.com SER: Valuations; book search.

The Coinage Hall Antiques Centre
1 Boscawen St. TR1 2QU. (Paul Booth). Est. 1994. Open 10-4.30. SIZE: Medium. *STOCK: Fine art, furniture, paintings, sculpture, lighting, architectural items, collectables including postcards.* LOC: City centre. PARK: Easy. TEL: 01872 262520; fax - same; e-mail - pboothantiques@btconnect.com SER: Valuations; restorations (furniture, French polishing, cabinet making, upholstery). FAIRS: Newark, Shepton Mallet, Westpoint.

Collector's Corner
45-46 Pannier Market, Back Quay. TR1 2LL. (Alan McLoughlin and John Lethbridge). Est. 1980. Open 9.30-4.30, Sat. 9-4. SIZE: Small. *STOCK: Stamps, coins, postcards, medals, postal history, militaria, £5-£500.* LOC: City centre. PARK: Nearby. TEL: 01872 272729; home - 01326 573509; mobile - 07815 668551; website - www.militarycollectables.co.uk SER: Valuations.

WADEBRIDGE

Victoria Antiques
21 Molesworth St. PL27 7DQ. (M. and S. Daly). Open Mon.-Sat. SIZE: Large. *STOCK: Furniture, 17th-19th C, £25-£10,000.* LOC: On A39 between Bude and Newquay. PARK: Nearby. TEL: 01208 814160. SER: Valuations; restorations. VAT: Stan/Spec/Global.

François Linke (1855-1946), born in Pankraz, Bohemia, is considered by many as the greatest Parisian cabinetmaker of his day, at a time when the worldwide influence of French fashion was at its height. His exquisitely finished, richly made furniture was produced for potentates and industrial magnates from Paris to New York, London to Buenos Aires, the Far East and the Cameroons. The son of a subsistence gardener, Linke trained under the strict disciplines of the Austro-Hungarian Empire and as a young man, travelled penniless, on foot, via Vienna to Paris in 1876. There he married the daughter of a local innkeeper and started a business in the days before electricity and the motor car, a business that continued, despite the loss of his two sons, through two world wars and the invention of atomic power.

The *ancien régime* has always been the greatest source of inspiration for artistic design in France and, influenced amongst others by the de Goncourt brothers, the Louis XV and Louis XVI styles were revived to wide popular appeal. During the Second Empire these styles were so eclectic that they became debased. Linke wanted to create a fresh new style and his association with the enigmatic sculptor Léon Messagé resulted in a highly original series of designs, based on the rococo style fused with the latest fashion in Paris, *l' art nouveau*.

The book, with 140,000 words of text and over 700 unique photographs, many previously unpublished and drawn from Linke's own archive and private collections, has ten chapters showing the development of this exacting and prolific man's life work. It traces his early life and apprenticeship and his comfortable family life in Paris, culminating with the award of the *Légion d'honneur*. Appendices on Metalwork and Wood add to the technical expertise of this book, giving a unique insight into the workings of any designers recorded to date.

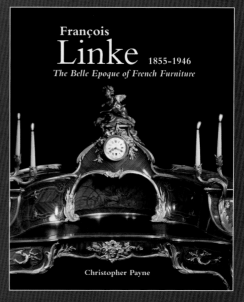

François Linke
1855-1946
The Belle Epoque of French Furniture

Christopher Payne

Specifications: 528pp., 200 col. illus., 500 b.&w. illus., 11¼ x 9¼in./285 x 238mm. **£75.00 (hardback)**

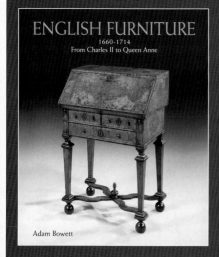

ENGLISH FURNITURE
1660-1714
from Charles II to Queen Anne
Adam Bowett

English Furniture describes the development of fashionable English furniture between the restoration of Charles II in 1660 and the death of Queen Anne in 1714. Based largely on contemporary documents and on original and firmly documented furniture, together with the latest modern scholarship, it provides a closely-reasoned analysis of changing furniture styles, together with much technical information on materials and processes. The author's radical new approach to the stylistic and structural analysis of furniture will change perceptions of English furniture and establish a new chronology for late seventeenth and early eighteenth century English furniture. This extensively illustrated book is the first comprehensive review of the subject for nearly one hundred years.

Part one focuses on Charles II and James II, 1660-1688 with chapters on The Restoration, Case Furniture, Seat Furniture, Tables, Stands and Mirrors and Lacquer, Japanning and Varnish. The second part focuses on William III and Queen Anne, 1689-1714 and includes chapters on Furnishing the Williamite Court, Case Furniture, Seat Furniture, Tables, Stands and Looking Glasses. A full bibliography is included.

Specifications: 328pp., 465 col. illus., 59 b.&w. illus., 11¼ x 9¼in./310 x 234mm. **£45.00 (hardback)**

THE COTSWOLDS

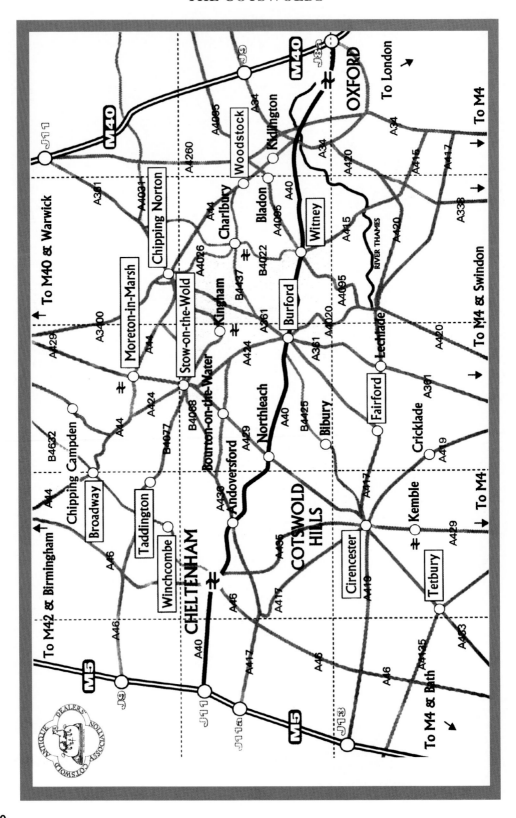

THE COTSWOLD ANTIQUE DEALERS' ASSOCIATION

Buy Fine Antiques and Works of Art at provincial prices in England's lovely and historic countryside

The Cotswolds, one of the finest areas of unspoilt countryside in the land, have been called "the essence and the heart of England." The region has a distinctive character created by the use of honey-coloured stone in its buildings and dry stone walls. Within the locality the towns and villages are admirably compact and close to each other and the area is well supplied with good hotels and reasonably priced inns. The Cotswolds are within easy reach of London (1½ hour by road or rail) and several major airports.

Cotswold sheep – which inspired the logo for the Cotswold Antique Dealers' Association – a quatrefoil device with a sheep in its centre – have played an important part in the region's history with much of its wealth created by the woollen industry. As for antiques, shops and Galleries of the CADA offer a selection of period furniture, pictures, porcelain, metalwork, and collectables unrivalled outside London.

With the use of the CADA directory on the following pages, which lists the names of its members, their specialities and opening times, visitors from all over the world can plan their buying visit to the Cotswolds. CADA members will assist all visiting collectors and dealers in locating antiques and works of art. They will give you advice on where to stay in the area, assistance with packing, shipping and insurance and the exchange of foreign currencies. They can advise private customers on what can realistically be bought on their available budgets, and if the first dealer does not have the piece which you are selecting he will know of several other members who will. The CADA welcomes home and overseas buyers in the certain knowledge that there are at least forty dealers with a good and varied stock, a reputation for fair trading and an annual turnover in excess of £15,000,000.

BROADWAY

Fenwick and Fenwick Antiques
88-90 High St. WR12 7AJ. (George and Jane Fenwick). CADA. Est. 1980. Open 10-6 and by appointment. SIZE: Large. *STOCK: Furniture, oak, mahogany and walnut, 17th to early 19th C; samplers, boxes, treen, Tunbridgeware, Delft, decorative items and corkscrews.* LOC: Upper High St. PARK: Nearby. TEL: 01386 853227; after hours - 01386 841724; fax - 01386 858504. VAT: Spec.

Haynes Fine Art of Broadway   BADA LAPADA
Picton House Galleries, 42 High St. WR12 7DT. (A.C. Haynes). CADA. Open 9-6. SIZE: Large - 12 showrooms. *STOCK: Over 2000 British and European 16th-21st C oil paintings and watercolours.* LOC: From Lygon Arms, 100 yards up High St. on left. PARK: Easy. TEL: 01386 852649; fax - 01386 858187; e-mail - enquiries@haynes-fine-art.co.uk website - www.haynesfineart.com   SER: Valuations; restorations; framing; catalogue available (£10). VAT: Spec.

H.W. Keil Ltd   BADA
Tudor House, High St. WR12 7DP. (John Keil). CADA. Est. 1925. Open 9.30-12.45 and 2.15-5.30, Sat. by appointment. SIZE: Large - 12 showrooms. *STOCK: Walnut, oak, mahogany and rosewood furniture; early pewter, brass and copper, tapestry and works of art, 16th to early 19th C.* LOC: By village clock. PARK: Private by arrangement. TEL: 01386 852408; fax - 01386 852069; e-mail - info@hwkeil.co.uk SER: Restorations. VAT: Spec.

John Noott Galleries   BADA LAPADA
28 High St., 14 Cotswold Court. WR12 7AA. (John, Pamela and Amanda Noott). CADA. Est. 1972. Open 9.30-1 and 2-5. SIZE: Large. *STOCK: Paintings, watercolours and bronzes, 19th C to contemporary.* PARK: Easy. TEL: 01386 854868/858969; fax - 01386 854919; e-mail - info@john-noott.com website - www.john-noott.com SER: Valuations; restorations; framing. VAT: Stan/Spec.

BURFORD

Jonathan Fyson Antiques
50 High St. OX18 4QF. (J.R. Fyson). CADA. Est. 1970. Open 9.30-1 and 2-5.30, Sat. from 10. SIZE: Medium. *STOCK: English and Continental furniture, decorative brass and steel including lighting and fireplace accessories; mirrors, porcelain, table glass, jewellery.* LOC: At junction of A40/A361 between Oxford and Cheltenham. PARK: Easy. TEL: 01993 823204; fax - same; home - 01367 860223; e-mail - j@fyson.co.uk SER: Valuations. VAT: Spec.

Gateway Antiques
Cheltenham Rd., Burford Roundabout. OX18 4JA. (M.C. Ford and P. Brown). CADA. Est. 1986. Open 10-5.30 and Sun. 2-5. SIZE: Large. *STOCK: English and Continental furniture, 18th to early 20th C; decorative accessories.* LOC: On roundabout (A40) Oxford/Cheltenham road, adjacent to the Cotswold Gateway Hotel. PARK: Easy. TEL: 01993 823678/822624; fax - 01993 823857; e-mail - enquiries @gatewayantiques.co.uk website - www.gateway antiques.co.uk SER: Courier (multi-lingual). VAT: Stan/Spec.

David Pickup   BADA
115 High St. OX18 4RG. CADA. Est. 1977. Open 9.30-1 and 2-5.30, Sat. 10-1 and 2-4. SIZE: Medium. *STOCK: Fine furniture, works of art, from £500+; decorative objects, from £100+; all late 17th to mid 20th C, specialising in Arts and Crafts.* PARK: Easy. TEL: 01993 822555. FAIRS: Olympia. VAT: Spec.

Manfred Schotten Antiques
109 High St. OX18 4RG. CADA. Est. 1974. Open 9.30-5.30 or by appointment. SIZE: 3 floors and trade warehouse open by appointment. *STOCK: Sporting antiques and library furniture.* PARK: Easy. TEL: 01993 822302; fax - 01993 822055; e-mail - antiques@schotten.com website - www.schotten.com SER: Restorations; trophies. FAIRS: Olympia (Summer). VAT: Stan/Margin.

Brian Sinfield Gallery Ltd
150 High St. OX18 4QU. CADA. Est. 1972. Open 10-5.30, Mon. by appointment. SIZE: Medium. *STOCK: Mainly contemporary and late 20th C paintings and watercolours.* PARK: Easy. TEL: 01993 824464; e-mail - gallery@briansinfield.com website - www.brian sinfield.com SER: 8 exhibitions annually; art brokers. VAT: Spec.

Swan Gallery
High St. OX18 4RE. (D. Pratt). CADA. Est. 1966. Open 10-5.30. SIZE: Large. *STOCK: Country furniture in oak, yew, walnut and fruitwood, 17th-19th C, £300-£12,000; Staffordshire figures and small decorative items, 18th-20th C, £50-£800.* PARK: Easy. TEL: 01993 822244. VAT: Mainly Spec.

CHIPPING NORTON

Key Antiques
11 Horse Fair. OX7 5AL. (Jane and Keith Riley). CADA. Open 10-5.30 or by appointment. CL: Mon. and Tues. SIZE: Medium. *STOCK: English period oak and country furniture, 17th-19th C; domestic metalware, early portraits, pottery and associated items.* LOC: Main road. PARK: Easy. TEL: 01608 644992/643777; e-mail - info@keyantiques.com website - www.keyantiques.com VAT: Spec.

CIRENCESTER

William H. Stokes   BADA
The Cloisters, 6/8 Dollar St. GL7 2AJ. (W.H. Stokes and P.W. Bontoft). CADA. Est. 1968. Open 9.30-5.30, Sat. 9.30-4.30. *STOCK: Early oak furniture, £1,000-£50,000; brassware, £150-£5,000; all 16th-17th C.* LOC: West of parish church out of Market Place. TEL: 01285 653907; fax - 01285 640533; e-mail - post@williamhstokes.co.uk website - www.williamh stokes.co.uk VAT: Spec.

Patrick Waldron Antiques
18 Dollar St. GL7 2AN. Resident. CADA. Est. 1965. Open 9.30-1 and 2-6, Sun. by appointment. SIZE:

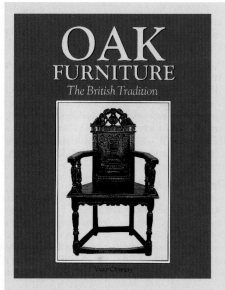
Medium. *STOCK: Town and country furniture, 17th to early 19th C.* LOC: In street behind church. PARK: Easy and public behind shop. TEL: 01285 652880; home - same; workshop - 01285 643479; e-mail - patrick.waldron@virgin.net SER: Restorations (furniture); buys at auction. VAT: Stan/Spec.

FAIRFORD

Blenheim Antiques
Market Place. GL7 4AB. (N. Hurdle). CADA. Resident. Est. 1972. Open 9.30-6. SIZE: Medium. *STOCK: 18th-19th C furniture and accessories.* PARK: Easy. TEL: 01285 712094. VAT: Stan/Spec.

MORETON-IN-MARSH

Astley House - Contemporary   LAPADA
Astley House, London Rd. GL56 0LE. (David, Nanette and Caradoc Glaisyer). CADA. CINOA. Est. 1973. Open 10-1 and 2-5 and by appointment. CL: Wed. SIZE: Large. *STOCK: Oil paintings, 19th-21st C; large decorative oils and portraits, jewellery, ceramics, glass.* LOC: Town centre. PARK: Easy. TEL: 01608 650608; fax - 01608 651777; e-mail - astart333@aol.com website - www.contemporaryart-uk.com SER: Restorations (oils and watercolours); framing (porcelain). VAT: Spec.

Astley House - Fine Art   LAPADA
Astley House, High St. GL56 0LL. (David, Nanette and Caradoc Glaisyer). CADA. CINOA. Est. 1973. Open 9-5.30 and by appointment. SIZE: Medium. *STOCK: Oil paintings, 19th-21st C, £800-£20,000.* LOC: Main street. PARK: Easy. TEL: 01608 650601; fax - 01608 651777;

e-mail - astart333@aol.com website - www.art-uk.com SER: Restorations (oils and watercolours); framing. VAT: Spec.

Jon Fox Antiques
High St. GL56 0AD. CADA. Est. 1983. Open 9.30-5.30, Sun. and Tues. by appointment. SIZE: Large - 2 adjacent shops. *STOCK: 19th C garden items including urns, seats, troughs and tools, £50-£5,000+; 18th -19th C country furniture £300-£3,000; treen, bygones, metalware, fireplace items.* PARK: Easy. TEL: 01608 650325/650714. VAT: Spec.

STOW-ON-THE-WOLD

Duncan J. Baggott   LAPADA
Woolcomber House, Sheep St. GL54 1AA. CADA. Est. 1967. Open 9-5.30 or by appointment. CL: Bank Holidays. SIZE: Large. *STOCK: 17th-20th C English oak, mahogany and walnut furniture, paintings, domestic metalwork and decorative items; garden statuary and ornaments.* PARK: Sheep St. or Market Sq. TEL: 01451 830662; fax - 01451 832174. SER: Worldwide shipping; UK delivery. FAIRS: Exhibition Oct. annually (CADA).

Baggott Church Street Ltd   BADA
Church St. GL54 1BB. (D.J. and C.M. Baggott). CADA. Est. 1978. Open 9.30-5.30 or by appointment. SIZE: Large. *STOCK: 17th-19th C English oak, mahogany and walnut furniture, portrait paintings, metalwork, pottery, treen and decorative items.* LOC: South-west corner of market square. PARK: Market square. TEL: 01451 830370; fax - 01451 832174. SER: Annual exhibition - Oct.

BUYING ANTIQUES IN THE COTSWOLDS

Christopher Clarke Antiques Ltd   LAPADA
The Fosseway. GL54 1JS. (Simon and Sean Clarke). CADA. Est. 1961. Open 9.30-5.30 or by appointment. SIZE: Large. *STOCK: Specialists in campaign furniture and travel items; English furniture, metalware, treen, pictures and decorative items.* LOC: Corner of The Fosseway and Sheep St. PARK: Easy. TEL: 01451 830476; fax - 01451 830300; e-mail - cclarkeantiques @aol.com website - www.campaignfurniture.com FAIRS: Olympia (June, Nov); CADA Exhibition.

Cotswold Galleries
The Square, GL54 1AB. (Richard and Cherry Glaisyer). CADA. FATG. Est. 1961. Open 9-5.30 or by appointment. SIZE: Large. *STOCK: Oil paintings especially 19th-20th C landscape.* PARK: Easy. TEL: 01451 870567; fax - 01451 870678; website - www.cotswoldgalleries.com SER: Restorations; framing.

The John Davies Gallery
Church St. GL54 1BB. CADA. Est. 1977. Open 9.30-1.30 and 2.30-5.30. SIZE: Large. *STOCK: Contemporary and late period paintings; limited edition bronzes.* PARK: In square. TEL: 01451 831698; fax - 01451 832477; e-mail - daviesart@aol.com website - www.the-john-davies-gallery.co.uk SER: Restorations and conservation to museum standard. VAT: Spec/Margin.

Keith Hockin Antiques   BADA
The Square. GL54 1AF. CADA. Est. 1968. Open Thurs., Fri. and Sat. 10-5, other times by appointment or ring the bell. SIZE: Medium. STOCK: Oak furniture, 1600-1750; country furniture in oak, fruitwoods, yew, 1700-1850; pewter, copper, brass, ironwork, all periods. Not Stocked: Mahogany. PARK: Easy. TEL: 01451 831058; e-mail - keithhockin@aol.com SER: Buys at auction (oak, pewter, metalwork). VAT: Stan/Spec.

Huntington Antiques Ltd   LAPADA
Church St. GL54 1BE. (M.F. and S.P. Golding). CADA. CINOA. Resident. Est. 1974. Open 9.30-5.30 or by appointment. SIZE: Large. *STOCK: Early period and fine country furniture, metalware, tapestries and works of art.* LOC: Opposite main gates to church. TEL: 01451 830842; fax - 01451 832211; e-mail - info@huntington-antiques.com website - www.huntington-antiques.com SER: Valuations; buys at auction. VAT: Spec.

Roger Lamb Antiques & Works of Art   LAPADA
The Square. GL54 1AB. CADA. Est. 1993. Open 10-5 or by appointment. SIZE: 3 main showrooms. *STOCK: Fine 18th to early 19th C furniture especially small items, lighting, decorative accessories, oils and watercolours.* LOC: Next to town hall. PARK: Easy. TEL: 01451 831371; fax - 01451 832485; mobile - 07860 391959. SER: Search.

Antony Preston Antiques Ltd   BADA
The Square. GL54 1AB. CADA. CINOA. Est. 1965. Open 9.30-5.30 or by appointment. SIZE: Large. STOCK: 18th-19th C English and Continental furniture and objects; barometers and period lighting. LOC: Town centre. PARK: Easy. TEL: 01451 831586; fax - 01451 831596; mobile - 07785 975599; e-mail - antony@antonypreston.com website - www.antonypreston.com FAIRS: BADA. VAT: Stan/Spec.

Queens Parade Antiques Ltd   BADA
The Square. GL54 1AB. (Sally and Antony Preston). CADA. CINOA. Est. 1985. Open 9.30-5.30. SIZE: Large. STOCK: 18th to early 19th C furniture, decorative objects, needlework, tole and lighting. LOC: Town centre. PARK: Easy. TEL: 01451 831586; fax - 01451 831596; e-mail - antony@antonypreston.com website - www.antonypreston.com FAIRS: BADA. VAT: Stan/Spec.

Ruskin Decorative Arts
5 Talbot Court. GL54 1DP. (Anne and William Morris). CADA. Est. 1990. Open 10-1 and 2-5.30. SIZE: Small. *STOCK: Interesting and unusual decorative objects, Arts and Crafts furniture, Art Nouveau, Art Deco, glass and pottery, metalwork, 1880-1960.* LOC: Between the square and Sheep St. PARK: Nearby. TEL: 01451 832254; home - 01993 831880; e-mail - william.anne @ruskindecarts.co.uk SER: Valuations. FAIRS: NEC.

Stow Antiques   LAPADA
The Square. GL54 1AF. (Mr and Mrs J. and Bruce Hutton-Clarke). CADA. Resident. Est. 1969. Open Mon.-Sat. 10-5.30, other times by appointment. SIZE: Large. *STOCK: Furniture, mainly Georgian and Regency mahogany - dining tables, chairs, bookcases, sideboards and cabinets, £500-£30,000; decorative items, gilded mirrors, £50-£10,000.* PARK: Easy. TEL: 01451 830377; fax - 01451 870018; e-mail - hazel@ stowantiques.demon.co.uk SER: Shipping worldwide.

Talbot Court Galleries
Talbot Court. GL54 1BQ. (J.P. Trevers). CADA. IMCOS. Est. 1988. Open 9.30-1 and 1.30-5.30. SIZE: Medium. *STOCK: Prints and maps, 1580-1880, £10-£5,000.* LOC: Behind Talbot Hotel in precinct between the square and Sheep St. PARK: Nearby. TEL: 01451 832169; fax - 01451 832167. SER: Valuations; restorations; cleaning; colouring; framing; buys at auction (engravings). VAT: Stan.

The Titian Gallery   LAPADA
Sheep St. GL54 1JS. (Ilona Johnson Gibbs). CADA. CINOA. Est. 1978. Open 10-5 and by appointment. SIZE: Medium. *STOCK: Fine 18th-19th C British and European oil paintings and watercolours, £1,000-£40,000.* LOC: Opposite the Unicorn Hotel, near The Fosseway. PARK: Adjacent and nearby. TEL: 01451 830004; fax - 01451 830126; e-mail - ilona@titian gallery.co.uk website - www.titiangallery.co.uk SER: Valuations; buys at auction (oils and watercolours). FAIRS: CADA exhibition. VAT: Spec.

STRETTON-ON-FOSSE

Astley House - Fine Art   LAPADA
The Old School. GL56 9SA. (David, Nanette and Caradoc Glaisyer). CADA. CINOA. Est. 1973. Open by appointment. SIZE: Large. *STOCK: Large decorative oil paintings, 19th-21st C.* LOC: Village centre. PARK: Easy. TEL: 01608 650601; fax - 01608 651777; e-mail -

astart333@aol.com website - www.art-uk.com SER: Exhibitions; mailing list. VAT: Spec.

TADDINGTON, Nr. Cheltenham

Architectural Heritage

Taddington Manor. GL54 5RY. (Adrian, Suzy, and Alex Puddy). CADA. Est. 1978. Open Mon.-Fri. 9.30-5.30, Sat. 10.30-4.30. SIZE: Large. *STOCK: Oak and pine period panelled rooms; stone and marble chimney pieces; stone, marble, bronze and terracotta statuary; garden ornaments, fountains, temples, well-heads, seats, urns, cisterns, sundials and summer houses.* PARK: Easy. TEL: 01386 584414; fax - 01386 584236; e-mail - puddy@architectural-heritage.co.uk website - www.architectural-heritage.co.uk SER: Worldwide delivery; shipping; bespoke ornaments, chimneypieces and panelled rooms. FAIRS: Chelsea Flower Show. VAT: Stan.

TETBURY

Breakspeare Antiques

36 and 57 Long St. GL8 8AQ. (M. and S.E. Breakspeare). CADA. Resident. Est. 1962. Open 10-5 or by appointment. CL: Thurs. SIZE: Medium. *STOCK: English period furniture - early walnut, 1690-1740, mahogany, 1750-1835.* LOC: Main street - four gables building. PARK: Own. TEL: 01666 503122; fax - same. VAT: Spec.

Day Antiques   BADA

5 New Church St. GL8 8DS. CADA. Est. 1975. Open 10-5. SIZE: Medium. *STOCK: Early oak furniture and related items.* **PARK: Easy. TEL: 01666 502413; e-mail - dayantiques@lineone.net website - www.day antiques.com VAT: Spec.**

WINCHCOMBE, Nr. Cheltenham

Prichard Antiques

16 High St. GL54 5LJ. (K.H. and D.Y. Prichard). CADA. Est. 1979. Open 9-5.30, Sun. by appointment. SIZE: Large - six showrooms. *STOCK: Period and decorative furniture, £10-£20,000; treen and metalwork, £5-£5,000; interesting and decorative accessories.* LOC: On B4632 Broadway to Cheltenham road. PARK: Easy. TEL: 01242 603566. VAT: Spec.

WITNEY

Colin Greenway Antiques

90 Corn St. OX28 6BU. CADA Resident. Est. 1975. Open 9.30-5, Sat. 10-4, Sun. by appointment. SIZE: Large. *STOCK: Furniture, 17th-20th C; fireplace implements and baskets, metalware, decorative and unusual items; garden furniture, rocking horses.* PARK: Easy. TEL: 01993 705026; fax - same; mobile - 07831 585014; e-mail - jean_greenway@hotmail.com website - www.greenwayantiques.viewing.at FAIRS: Newark. VAT: Stan/Spec.

W.R. Harvey & Co (Antiques) Ltd   LAPADA

86 Corn St. OX28 6BU. CADA. GMC. CINOA. Est. 1950. Open 9.30-5.30 and by appointment. SIZE: Large. *STOCK: Fine English furniture, £500-£150,000; clocks, mirrors, objets d'art, pictures, £250-£50,000; all 1680-1830.* LOC: 300 yards from Market Place. PARK: Easy.

TEL: 01993 706501; fax - 01993 706601; e-mail - antiques@wrharvey.co.uk website - www.wrharvey. co.uk SER: Valuations; restorations; consultancy. FAIRS: Chelsea (Sept.); Olympia (June). VAT: Stan/Spec.

Witney Antiques   BADA LAPADA

96/100 Corn St. OX28 6BU. (L.S.A. and C.J. Jarrett and R.R. Jarrett-Scott). CADA. Est. 1962. Open 10-5, Mon. and Tues. by appointment. SIZE: Large. *STOCK: English furniture, 17th-18th C; bracket and longcase clocks, mahogany, oak and walnut; early needlework and samplers.* **LOC: From Oxford on old A40 through Witney via High St., turn right at T-junction, 400yds. on right. PARK: Easy. TEL: 01993 703902/703887; fax - 01993 779852; e-mail - witney antiques@community.co.uk website - www. witneyantiques.com SER: Restorations. FAIRS: BADA; Grosvenor House. VAT: Spec.**

WOODSTOCK

John Howard   BADA

Heritage, 6 Market Place. OX20 1TE. TVADA. CADA. Open 10-5.30. SIZE: Medium. *STOCK: 18th-19th C British pottery especially rare Staffordshire animal figures, bocage figures, lustre, 18th C creamware and unusual items.* **PARK: Easy. TEL: 0870 4440678; fax - same; mobile - 07831 850544; e-mail - john@johnhoward.co.uk website - www. antiquepottery.co.uk and www.Staffordshires.com SER: Packing; insurance service to USA. FAIRS: Olympia; BADA. VAT: Spec.**

CUMBRIA

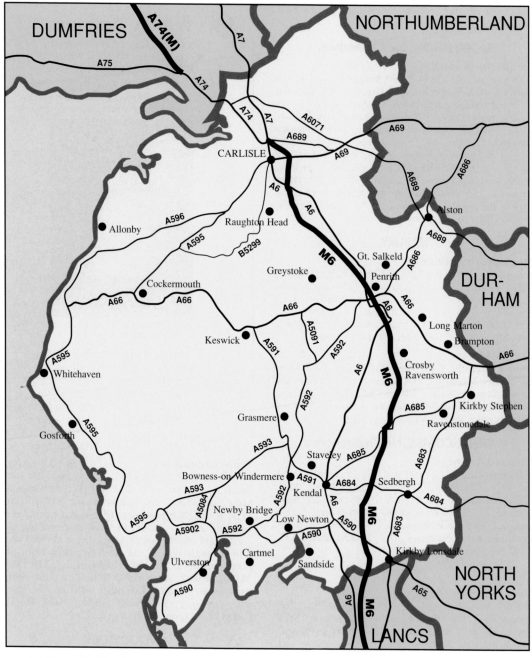

ALLONBY

Cottage Curios
Main St. CA15 6PX. (B. Pickering). Est. 1965. Open Sat. and Sun. 2-5.

ALSTON

Alston Antiques
Front St. CA9 3HU. (Mrs J. Bell). Est. 1976. Open 10-5. CL: Tues. SIZE: Medium. *STOCK: General antiques.* PARK: Easy. TEL: 01434 382129; mobile - 07876 501929.

Just Glass
Cross House, Market Place. CA9 3HS. (M.J. Graham). Est. 1987. Open Wed., Thurs., Sat. 11-4, Sun. 12-4 or by appointment. *STOCK: Glass, 1700-1930s, to £800.* LOC: Town centre. PARK: Easy. TEL: Home - 01434 381263; mobile - 07833 994948. FAIRS: Naworth Castle.

BOWNESS ON WINDERMERE

Something Old, Something New Ltd
(Behind Royal Hotel), St Martin's Parade. LA23 3DY. (Jeff and Marie Waszkiel). Est. 1994. Open 11-5.30 including Sun. SIZE: 3 rooms. *STOCK: Rare vinyl, books, collectables, antiques, cameras and bric-a-brac.* TEL: Mobile - 07859 920703; 01524 781718.

BRAMPTON

The Cumbrian Antiques Centre
St Martin's Hall, Front St. CA8 1NT. (S.T. Summerson-Wright). Est. 1976. Open 10-5, Sun. 12-5. SIZE: Large - 2 floors. *STOCK: Wide range of general antiques from silver and china to longcase clocks and furniture.* LOC: A69 Carlisle to Newcastle road into town centre, premises on right as road forks. PARK: Easy. TEL: 016977 42741; fax - same; home - 07889 924843 and 01697 742515; e-mail - cumbrianantiques@hotmail.com SER: Valuations; restorations.

CARLISLE

Carlisle Antiques Centre
Cecil Hall, Cecil St. CA1 1NT. (Wendy Mitton). Open 9-4. *STOCK: Furniture, porcelain, clocks, silver, jewellery, quilts and textiles.* LOC: M6 junction 43. PARK: Easy. TEL: 01228 536910; fax - same; e-mail - wendymitton @aol.com website - www.carlisle-antiques.co.uk SER: Repairs (clocks). FAIRS: Naworth Castle, Brampton (March and Aug). Below are listed the dealers at this centre.

  It's About Time
  (B. and W. Mitton). 1985. *Fine period furniture, porcelain, jewellery, textiles, glass and silver.* TEL: 01228 536910.

  Warwick Antiques
  (J.T. Wardrope). CMBHI. *Period furniture, wall, bracket and longcase clocks.* SER: Valuations; restorations (clocks); clockmaker.

Saint Nicholas Galleries Ltd. (Antiques and Jewellery)
39 Bank St. CA3 8HJ. (C.J. Carruthers). Open 10-5. CL:

The Antique Shop
Fine English antique furniture, also decorative items

Open 10.00am – 5.00pm every day including Sunday

CARTMEL NEAR GRANGE-OVER-SANDS CUMBRIA
TELEPHONE 015395-36295
MOBILE TELEPHONE 07768 443757
Email: anthemioncartmel@aol.com
www.anthemionantiques.co.uk

Mon. SIZE: Medium. *STOCK: Jewellery, silver, plate, Rolex and pocket watches, clocks; collectables; Royal Doulton; Dux, Oriental vases; pottery, porcelain; watercolours, oil paintings; brass and copper.* LOC: City centre. PARK: Nearby. TEL: 01228 544459.

Souvenir Antiques
Long Lane, Castle St. CA3 8TA. (J. Higham). Est. 1985. Open Wed., Fri. and Sat. 11-3 or later. SIZE: Small. *STOCK: Ceramics and collectables, crested china, local prints, maps, postcards, Roman and medieval coins, antiquities and jewellery.* Not Stocked: Textiles. LOC: City centre, off Castle St. PARK: Castle St. TEL: 01228 401281; mobile - 07803 107429; website - www. souvenirantiques.co.uk and www.cumbriamaps.co.uk

CARTMEL

Anthemion - The Antique Shop BADA LAPADA LA11 6QD. (J. Wood). Est. 1982. Open 10-5 including Sun. SIZE: Large. *STOCK: English period furniture, mainly walnut and mahogany, 17th to early 19th C, £500-£50,000; decorative items, 17th-19th C, £100-£5,000; paintings and prints, 19th-20th C, £400-£8,000.* Not Stocked: Victoriana, bric-a-brac. LOC: Village centre. PARK: Easy. TEL: 01539 536295; mobile - 07768 443757; e-mail - anthemioncartmel@aol.com website - www.anthemionantiques.co.uk FAIRS: NEC (Jan); Olympia (March and June); Harrogate (April and Sept). VAT: Stan/Spec.

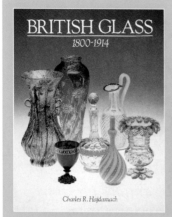

BRITISH GLASS
1800-1914

Specifications:
466pp.,
50 col. illus.,
430 b.&w. illus.,
11 x 8½in./
279 x 216mm.
£29.95
(hardback)

Charles R. Hajdamach

In addition to cut, engraved, cameo and etched glass, the information provided on personalities, working conditions and the operations of the glasshouse gives the collector an all-round view of the subject not available elsewhere in a single publication. A detailed section describes a host of techniques with the help of original patent specifications and drawings.

"…the most comprehensive survey yet of the greatest period in the history of glass." **First Sunday**

BRITISH GLASS
1800-1914
Charles R. Hajdamach

Norman Kerr - Gatehouse Bookshop
The Square. LA11 6PX. (H. and J.M. Kerr). PBFA. Est. 1933. Open Fri. and Sat. or by appointment. *STOCK: Antiquarian and secondhand books.* TEL: 01539 536247; e-mail - enquiries@kerrbooks.co.uk website - www.kerrbooks.co.uk SER: Valuations; book search; antiquarian books bought.

Peter Bain Smith (Bookseller)
Bank Court, Market Sq. LA11 6QB. Est. 1973. Open 1.30-5 including Sun. From mid Nov. to mid Feb open Thurs., Fri., Sat. and Sun. 1.30-4.30. *STOCK: Books including antiquarian, especially children's and local topography.* LOC: A590 from Levens Bridge, off roundabout at Lindale by-pass through Grange-over-Sands. PARK: Nearby. TEL: 01539 536369. SER: Valuations.

Simon Starkie Antiques
Gatehouse Cottage, Cavendish St. LA11 6QA. Est. 1980. Open Wed., Fri. and Sat. 10.30-4.30, Sun. 11.30-4.30 and by appointment. SIZE: Small. *STOCK: Oak furniture, 17th-19th C, £100-£8,000; painted country furniture and clocks, 18th-19th C, £50-£2,500; Delftware and pewter, 18th-19th C, £30-£1,000.* LOC: 10 miles from junction 36 M6, follow signs for Cartmel priory. PARK: Nearby. TEL: 015395 36453; home - 01229 861222. SER: Valuations; buys at auction (furniture and earthenware). VAT: Stan/Spec.

COCKERMOUTH

CG's Curiosity Shop
43 Market Place. CA13 9LT. (Colin Graham). Est. 1985. Open 10-12.30 and 1.30-5. SIZE: Medium. *STOCK: China, glass, collectables, militaria, books, linen, furniture, advertising, radios and unusual items, from 1800, £5-£1,000+.* LOC: End of main street, over the bridge. PARK: Nearby. TEL: 01900 824418; home - 01697 321108; mobile - 07712 206786; e-mail - cgcuriosity@hotmail.com website - www.cgcuriosity shop.fws1.com SER: Valuations; restorations; buys at auction; internet search. FAIRS: Newark.

Cockermouth Antiques
5 Station St. CA13 9QW. (E. Bell and G. Davies). Est. 1983. Open 10-5. SIZE: Large. *STOCK: General antiques especially jewellery, silver, ceramics, furniture, pictures, glass, books, metalware, quilts.* LOC: Just off A66, in town centre. PARK: Easy. TEL: 01900 826746; e-mail - elainebell54@aol.com

Cockermouth Antiques Market
Courthouse, Main St. CA13 9LU. Est. 1979. Open 10-5. SIZE: Large - 4 stallholders. *STOCK: Victorian, Edwardian and Art Deco items, furniture, printed collectables, postcards, books, linen, china, glass, textiles, jewellery and pictures.* LOC: Town centre, just off A66. PARK: 50 yds. TEL: 01900 824346. SER: Restorations (furniture); stripping (pine). VAT: Stan/Spec.

CROSBY RAVENSWORTH, Nr. Penrith

Jennywell Hall Antiques
CA10 3JP. (Mrs M. Macadie). Resident. Est. 1975. Open most days, but telephone call advisable. SIZE: Medium. *STOCK: Oak and mahogany furniture, paintings, interesting objects.* LOC: 5 miles from junction 39, M6. PARK: Easy. TEL: 01931 715288; home - same.

GOSFORTH

Archie Miles Bookshop
Beck Place. CA20 1AT. (Mrs C.M. Linsley). Est. 1971. Open 10-5, Sun. 1-5.30, out of season opening times may vary. CL: Mon. *STOCK: Secondhand, antiquarian and out-of-print books, maps and prints.* LOC: Main street. PARK: Nearby. TEL: 01946 725792. SER: Book search.

GRASMERE

Lakes Crafts & Antiques Gallery
3 Oak Bank, Broadgate. LA22 9TA. (Joe and Sandra Arthy). Est. 1990. Open 15th Mar.-31st Oct. 9.30-6 including Sun., other times 10-4.30. SIZE: Medium. *STOCK: Books, 18th-20th C, £1-£500; collectables and postcards, £1-£100; general antiques, 17th-20th C, £5-£250.* LOC: North side of village, off A591 on Ambleside to Keswick road. PARK: Easy. TEL: 01539 435037; home - 01539 444234. VAT: Stan.

The Stables
College St. LA22 9SW. (J.A. and K.M. Saalmans). Est. 1971. Open daily Easter-November 10-6, other times and in May, telephone call advisable. SIZE: Small. *STOCK:*

Brass and copper items, oil lamps, domestic bygones; pottery, silver, prints, Royal commemoratives, books. Not Stocked: Weapons, furniture. LOC: By the side of Moss Grove Hotel. PARK: Easy. TEL: 01539 435453; home - same; e-mail - a.saalmans@btopenworld.com

GREAT SALKELD, Nr. Penrith

G.K. Hadfield

Beck Bank. CA11 9LN. (G.K. and J.V. Hadfield (Hon. FBHI) and D.W. and N.R. Hadfield-Tilly). Est. 1966. Open 9-5. *STOCK: Clocks - longcase, dial, Act of Parliament, skeleton and carriage; secondhand, new and out of print horological books.* LOC: From M6, junction 40 take A686 towards Alston for 3 miles, left on B6412 signed Great Salkeld, about 1.5 miles, turn left at sign for Salkeld Dykes, 1st house on right. TEL: 01768 870111; fax - same; e-mail - gkhadfield@dial.pipex.com website - www.gkhadfield.tilly.co.uk SER: Restoration materials (antique clocks including hand cut hands and gilding); valuations (clocks and horological books). VAT: Stan/Spec.

GREYSTOKE, Nr. Penrith

Roadside Antiques

Watsons Farm, Greystoke Gill. CA11 0UQ. (K. and R. Sealby). Resident. Est. 1988. Open 10-6 including Sun. SIZE: Medium. *STOCK: Ceramics, longcase clocks, glass, Staffordshire figures, pot-lids, paintings, furniture, small collectables, jewellery, mainly 19th C, £5-£2,000.* LOC: B5288 Penrith/Keswick road to Greystoke, through village, first left then left again, premises second on right. PARK: Easy. TEL: 01768 483279.

KENDAL

Architectural Antiques

146 Highgate. LA9 4HW. (G. Fairclough). Est. 1984. Open 9.30-5. SIZE: Medium. *STOCK: Fireplaces, hobs, grates, marble and wooden chimney pieces, cast iron inserts; Victorian tiles and kitchen ranges, unusual architectural items, Flemish brass chandeliers.* PARK: Easy. TEL: 01539 737147; fax - same; mobile - 07801 440031; e-mail - gordonfairclough@aol.com website - www.architecturalantiques.co.uk SER: Valuations; restorations (cast-iron).

Dower House Antiques

38/40 Kirkland. LA9 5AD. Open 10-6. *STOCK: Pottery, porcelain, paintings, furniture.* TEL: 01539 722778.

Granary Collectables

29 All Hallows Lane. LA9 4JH. (B.J. Cross). Est. 1998. Open 10-4.30. CL: Mon. SIZE: Small. *STOCK: Small collectables, pictures, kitchenalia, pottery, advertising and unusual items, £1-£350.* LOC: 100 yards from town centre, off main road. PARK: Easy. TEL: 01539 740770. SER: Valuations.

Shambles Antiques

17-19 New Shambles. LA9 4TS. (John G. and Janet A. Smyth). Est. 1992. Open Tues.-Sat. 10-5. SIZE: Medium. *STOCK: Arts and Crafts, art pottery, paintings, furniture; English pottery and porcelain, 18th-19th C; 20th C Scandinavian ceramics and glass; collectors'*

items, silver, all £5-£5,000. LOC: Off Market Place. PARK: Multi-storey nearby. TEL: 01539 729947; home - 01539 821590; mobile - 07808 124635; e-mail - j-jsmyth@kencomp.net SER: Valuations.

The Silver Thimble

39 All Hallows Lane. LA9 4JH. (V. Ritchie). Est. 1980. Open 10-4. SIZE: Large. *STOCK: Jewellery, silver, glass, linen and lace, porcelain, copper and brass.* LOC: Turn left at second set of traffic lights on main road into Kendal from south, shop 200yds. on right. PARK: Easy. TEL: 01539 731456; e-mail - gmvritchie@aol.com VAT: Spec.

Sleddall Hall Antiques Centre inc. Kendal Studios Antiques

Wildman St. LA9 6EN. (Robert and Andrew Aindow and Sleddall Hall Antiques Centre). Est. 1950. Open 10.30-4, prior telephone call advisable. SIZE: Medium. *STOCK: Ceramics, maps and prints, paintings, oak furniture, art pottery and clocks.* LOC: Leave M6 at junction 37, follow one-way system, shop on left. PARK: Nearby. TEL: 01539 723291 (24 hrs. answering service). SER: Finder; shipping. VAT: Stan/Spec.

Utopia Antiques Ltd

40 Market Place. LA9 4TN. (P.J. and Mrs. J. Wilkinson). Est. 1970. Open 10-5. *STOCK: Indian Colonial furniture including reproduction, handicrafts and fabrics.* TEL: 01539 722862; e-mail - utopiaantique@utopiaantique.com website - www.utopiaantique.com

Westmorland Clocks

Gillinggate. LA9 4HW. (G. and I. Fairclough). Est. 2002. Open 9.30-5. SIZE: Small. *STOCK: Clocks, especially Lancashire and Lake District longcase.* PARK: Easy. TEL: 01539 737147; website - www.westmorlandclocks.com SER: Valuations; restorations.

KESWICK

The Country Bedroom and En-Suite

Lake Rd. CA12 5BZ. (W.I. Raw). Est. 1981. Open 9.30-5. *STOCK: Brass beds, iron and brass beds, mattress and base sets for antique beds, mirrors, linen, quilts, £150-£2,000; traditional and contemporary bathroom accessories.* LOC: Top of Main St. TEL: 01768 774881; fax - 01768 771424. VAT: Stan.

Keswick Bookshop

4 Station St. CA12 5HT. (Jane and John Kinnaird). PBFA. Est. 1994. Open April to end Oct. 10.30-5, and by appointment in winter. SIZE: Medium. *STOCK: Books, 18th-20th C; prints and maps, 18th-20th C.* LOC: Town centre. PARK: Nearby. TEL: 01768 775535; fax - 01228 528567. VAT: Stan/Spec.

John Young and Son (Antiques)   LAPADA

12-14 Main St. CA12 5JD. Est. 1890. Open 9-5. SIZE: Large. *STOCK: 17th-20th C furniture, clocks and decorative items.* LOC: Town centre. PARK: At rear. TEL: 01768 773434; fax - 01768 773306. VAT: Stan/Spec.

KIRKBY LONSDALE

Architus Antiques

14 Main St. LA6 2AE. (J. Pearson). Est. 1990. Open 10-4.30, Sat. 10-5.30. SIZE: Medium. *STOCK: Victorian oil*

lamps, £100-£250; china and glass, jewellery and silver, Victorian to early 20th C. LOC: First antique shop on left in village from A65 towards Kendal. TEL: 015242 72409; home - 015242 71517. SER: Valuations.

Johnson & Johnson
New Rd. LA6 2AB. (D.J. Johnson). Est. 1989. Open 11-4.30. CL: Wed. SIZE: Medium. *STOCK: Period oak and walnut furniture, portraits, lamps and candlesticks; pewter, 17th-18th C.* LOC: Town centre. PARK: Easy. TEL: 01524 272916; home/fax - 01539 552126; mobile - 07714 146197; e-mail - mail@johnsonandpark.co.uk website - www.johnsonandpark.co.uk

KIRKBY STEPHEN

Haughey Antiques   LAPADA
28/30 Market St. CA17 4QW. (D.M. Haughey). Est. 1969. Open 10-5 or by appointment. SIZE: Large. *STOCK: 17th-19th C oak, walnut and mahogany furniture.* LOC: M6, junction 38, 10 mins. to east. PARK: Own. TEL: 01768 371302; fax - 01768 372423; e-mail - info@haugheyantiques.co.uk website - www.haugheyantiques.co.uk SER: Valuations. FAIRS: Olympia (Summer and Winter). VAT: Stan/Spec.

David Hill
36 Market Sq. CA17 4QT. Est. 1965. Open Thurs., Fri. and Sat. 9.30-4. SIZE: Medium. *STOCK: Country clocks and furniture, 18th-19th C, £10-£1,000; glassware, £5-£75; curios, £5-£50; shipping goods, kitchenalia, iron and brassware.* LOC: On A685; M6 junction 38. PARK: Easy. TEL: 01768 371598.

LONG MARTON, Nr. Appleby

Ben Eggleston Antiques Ltd
The Dovecote. CA16 6BJ. (Ben and Kay Eggleston). Est. 1976. Open by appointment. SIZE: Large. *STOCK: Pine furniture, £5-£2,500.* LOC: 2 miles east of A66 between Appleby and Penrith. PARK: Easy. TEL: 01768 361849; home and fax - same; e-mail - ben@beneggleston antiques.co.uk website - www.beneggletonantiques.co.uk FAIRS: Newark. VAT: Stan/Spec.

LOW NEWTON, Nr. Grange-over-Sands

W.R.S. Architectural Antiques Ltd
Yew Tree Barn. LA11 6JP. (Clive Wilson). Est. 1986. Open 10-5, Sun. 12-6 (winter 10-4.30). SIZE: Large barn. *STOCK: General architectural antiques including fireplaces; period furniture.* PARK: Free. TEL: 01539 531498; e-mail - wrs@yewtreebarn.co.uk website - www.yewtreebarn.co.uk SER: Restorations (furniture); garden design. VAT: Stan/Spec.

NEWBY BRIDGE

Townhead Antiques   LAPADA
LA12 8NP. (C.P. Townley). Est. 1960. Open 10-5, Sun. by appointment. SIZE: Large. *STOCK: 18th-19th C furniture, silver, porcelain, glass, decorative pieces; clocks, pictures.* LOC: A592. 1 mile from Newby Bridge on the Windermere road. PARK: Easy. TEL: 01539 531321; fax - 01539 530019; e-mail - Townhead@ aol.com website - www.Townhead-Antiques.com and www.townhead.com SER: Valuations. VAT: Stan/Spec.

PENRITH

Antiques of Penrith
4 Corney Sq. CA11 7PX. (Sylvia Tiffin and Lilian Cripps). Est. 1964. Open 10-12 and 1.30-5, Sat. 10-12.30. CL: Wed. SIZE: Large. *STOCK: Early oak and mahogany furniture, clocks, brass, copper, glass, china, silver plate, metal, Staffordshire figures, curios, paintings and collectables.* Not Stocked: Jewellery, books, rugs. LOC: Near Town Hall. PARK: Easy. TEL: 01768 862801. VAT: Stan/Spec/Global.

Brunswick Antiques
8 Brunswick Rd. CA11 7LU. (M. and L. Hodgson). Est. 1985. Open 10-5. SIZE: Small. *STOCK: Furniture, clocks, pottery, glass, metalware, 19th-20th C.* LOC: Town centre. PARK: Easy. TEL: 01768 899338; home - 01768 867164; e-mail - brunswickantiques@msn.com VAT: Spec.

Joseph James Antiques
Corney Sq. CA11 7PX. (G.R. Walker). Est. 1970. Open 9-5. CL: Wed. SIZE: Medium. *STOCK: Furniture and upholstery, 18th C and Victorian, £10-£3,000; porcelain and pottery, £5-£1,000; silver and plate, pictures, £2-£800; all 18th-19th C.* LOC: On the one-way system in the town, 100yds. from the main shopping area (Middlegate), 50yds. from the town hall. PARK: Easy and 100yds. TEL: 01768 862065. SER: Re-upholstery; soft furnishings. VAT: Stan.

Penrith Coin and Stamp Centre
37 King St. CA11 7AY. (Mr and Mrs A. Gray). Resident. Est. 1974. Open 9-5.30. CL: Wed. Sept.-May. SIZE: Medium. *STOCK: Coins, B.C. to date, 1p-£500; jewellery, secondhand, £5-£500; Great Britain and Commonwealth stamps.* LOC: Just off town centre. PARK: Behind shop. TEL: 01768 864185; fax - same. SER: Valuations; repairs (jewellery). FAIRS: Many coin and stamp. VAT: Stan.

RAUGHTON HEAD, Nr. Carlisle

Cumbria Architectural Salvage
Birkshill. CA5 7DH. (K. Temple). SALVO. Est. 1988. Open 9-5, Sat. 9-12. SIZE: Medium. *STOCK: Fireplaces, 1700-1930, £150-£2,000; kitchen ranges, cast iron radiators, bathroom fittings, doors, church pews, bricks and granite setts, building materials, sandstone, flags, oak joists and beams, balusters and staircase parts.* LOC: 9 miles SW of Carlisle. PARK: Easy. TEL: 01697 476420; home/fax - same. SER: Valuations; restorations (fireplaces and ranges).

RAVENSTONEDALE, Nr. Kirkby Stephen

The Book House
Fallowfield. CA17 4NG. (C. and M. Irwin). PBFA. Est. 1963. Open 10-5. CL: Tues. *STOCK: Books, mainly 19th-20th C, £1-£1,000; some postcards, 20th C, 25p-£20.* LOC: Off A685. Near top of village street set back on left. PARK: Easy. TEL: 015396 23634; fax - same; e-mail - enquiries@thebookhouse.co.uk SER: Valuations. FAIRS: Northern PBFA. VAT: Stan.

SANDSIDE, Nr. Milnthorpe

Peter Haworth
10 Herons Quay. LA7 7HW. Open by appointment. *STOCK: Scottish and Staithes Group paintings and watercolours, 1850-1950, £100-£30,000.* LOC: 2 miles from Milnthorpe on Arnside road. PARK: Easy. TEL: 01539 562488; fax - same; e-mail - pvhaworth@yahoo.com SER: Valuations; restorations; commissions. VAT: Spec.

SEDBERGH

R. F. G. Hollett and Son
6 Finkle St. LA10 5BZ. (R.F.G. and C.G. Hollett). ABA. Est. 1951. Open by appointment only. SIZE: Large. *STOCK: Antiquarian books, 15th-20th C, £20-£60,000+; maps, prints and paintings, 17th-19th C, £20-£10,000+.* LOC: Town centre. PARK: Free nearby. TEL: 015396 20298; fax - 015396 21396; e-mail - hollett@sedbergh.demon.co.uk website - www.holletts-rarebooks.co.uk SER: Valuations. VAT: Stan.

STAVELEY

Staveley Antiques
27/29 Main St. LA8 9LU. (P. John Corry). Est. 1991. Open 10-5, Sun. by appointment. SIZE: Large. *STOCK: Brass and iron bedsteads, 1830-1930, £200-£1,200; French walnut bedsteads, from 1880, £500-£2,000; lighting, 1880-1935, from £50; fire-irons, kerbs and metalware, from 1850, from £50.* LOC: Between Kendal and Windermere on A591 (now bypassed). PARK: Easy. TEL: 01539 821393; home - 01539 821123; e-mail - john@staveley-antiques.co.uk website - www.staveley-antiques.co.uk SER: Valuations; restorations (brass and iron bedsteads, metalware)

ULVERSTON

Elizabeth and Son
Market Hall. LA12 7LJ. (J.R. Bevins). Est. 1960. Open 9-5. CL: Wed. SIZE: Medium. *STOCK: Victorian and Edwardian glass, silver, brass and copper, gold and silver jewellery, books.* LOC: Town centre. PARK: Easy. TEL: 01229 582763.

WHITEHAVEN

Michael Moon - Antiquarian Booksellers
19 Lowther St. CA28 7AL. SBA. PBFA. Est. 1970. Open 9.30-5. SIZE: Large. *STOCK: Antiquarian books including Cumbrian topography.* LOC: Opposite Clydesdale Bank. PARK: Nearby. TEL: 01946 599010. FAIRS: PBFA Northern. VAT: Stan.

DERBYSHIRE

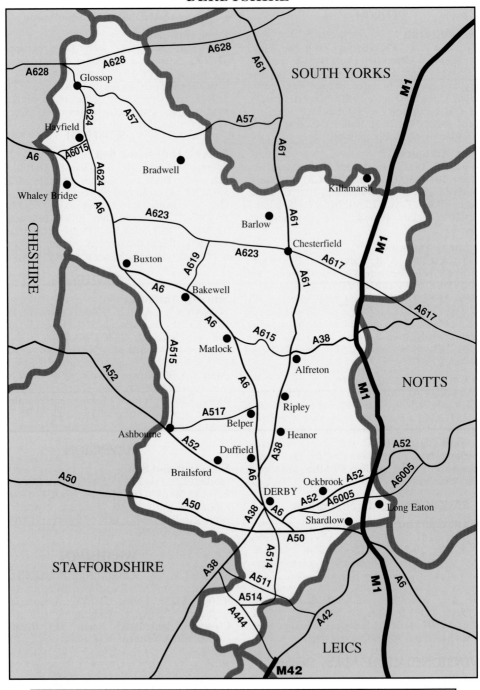

ALFRETON

Alfreton Antiques Centre
11 King St. DE55 7AF. (Helen Dixon). Est. 1996. Open 10-4.30, Sun. 11-4.30. SIZE: Large - 40 dealers. *STOCK: Wide range of furniture, ceramics, books, lighting, metalware, glass, collectables, Deco, jewellery, pictures, militaria, silver, Denby pottery.* LOC: Off junction 28, M1, A38 to Alfreton, King St. is main street up to traffic lights, shop on right before the lights. PARK: Own at rear. TEL: 01773 520781; home - 01773 852695; mobile - 07970 786968; e-mail - sales@alfretonantiquescentre. com website - www.alfretonantiquescentre.com SER: Valuations; Denby replacement service; restorations (ceramics); house clearance. FAIRS: Kedleston.

Steam-models.uk.com
31-32 South St., Riddings. DE55 4EJ. (Richard Evison). Est. 1990. Open 9-5, Sat. by appointment. SIZE: Small. *STOCK: Steam models and advertising figures, 20th C.* LOC: A610 from junction 26, M1 to Codnor. Right at traffic lights, right again to Riddings. PARK: Easy. TEL: 01773 541527; e-mail - raevison@aol.com website - www.steam-models.uk.com SER: Valuations; restorations (steam models); buys at auction (steam models). VAT: Stan.

ASHBOURNE

Ashbourne Antiques Ltd
Warehouse, Blake House, Shirley. DE6 3AS. (Robert Allsebrook). Est. 1977. Open by appointment. SIZE: Small. *STOCK: English furniture, 17th-20th C and hand-made copies.* LOC: A52 Ashbourne/Derby. PARK: Easy. TEL: 01335 361236; mobile - 07970 094883. SER: Restorations; cabinet making; removals; packing and shipping. VAT: Stan.

Daniel Charles Antiques
33 Church St. DE6 1AE. (Keith Phillips-Moul). Est. 2000. Open 10-5 or by appointment. SIZE: Medium. *STOCK: Furniture, decoration and fine art, 17th-20th C, to £1,000+.* PARK: Easy. TEL: 01335 300002; fax - 01335 348200; mobile - 07050 129250; e-mail - keith@danielcharlesantiques.com and k3iths@btinternet.com website - www.danielcharlesantiques.com SER: Restorations (furniture and porcelain); buys at auction. VAT: Stan/Spec.

J H S Antiques Ltd   LAPADA
47 Church St. DE6 1AJ. (Julian Howard Snodin). CINOA. Est. 1972. Open 10-5. CL: Mon. and Wed. SIZE: Medium. *STOCK: 17th C oak, £1,000-£20,000; metalware, 17th to early 19th C, £50-£3,000; carvings, 17th to early 18th C, £300-£3,000.* LOC: A52 from junction 25, M1. PARK: Easy. TEL: 01335 347733; mobile - 07810 122248. VAT: Spec.

Manion Antiques
23 Church St. DE6 1AE. (Mrs V.J. Manion). Est. 1984. Open 10-5.30 or by appointment. SIZE: Small. *STOCK: Jewellery, silver, porcelain, paintings and small furniture.* LOC: Central. PARK: Outside. TEL: 01335 343207; home - same; mobile - 07968 067316. SER: Valuations.

Pine and Decorative Items
38 Church St. DE6 1AJ. (M. and G. Bassett). Est. 1980. Open 10-5. CL: Wed. and Sun. except by appointment; warehouse open 9-5. CL: Sat. SIZE: Small + warehouse. *STOCK: English and French pine and country furniture; garden furniture, ironwork, kitchenalia, 18th C to 1950s, from £10.* TEL: 01335 300061; fax - same; e-mail - mgbassett@aol.com website - www.antiques-atlas.com VAT: Stan.

Rose Antiques
37 Church St. DE6 1AJ. Est. 1982. Open 10-5. SIZE: Medium. *STOCK: Furniture including pine, silver, porcelain, jewellery, copper and brass.* LOC: A52. PARK: Easy. TEL: 01335 343822; home - 01335 324333.

Spurrier-Smith Antiques   LAPADA
28, 30 and 39 Church St. DE6 1AJ. (I. Spurrier-Smith). Est. 1973. Open 10-5, Wed. and Sun. by appointment. SIZE: Large (8 showrooms) + warehouse. *STOCK: Furniture, oils, watercolours, porcelain, pottery, metalware, instruments, Oriental bronzes, collectables, pine, decorative items. Warehouse - pine and American export goods.* PARK: Easy. TEL: 01335 343669/342198; home - 01629 822502; e-mail - ivan@spurrier-smith.fsnet.co.uk website - www.spurrier-smith.co.uk SER: Valuations; restorations (furniture). VAT: Stan/Spec.

BAKEWELL

Peter Bunting Antiques   BADA LAPADA
Harthill Hall, Alport. DE45 1LH. Est. 1980. Open by appointment. SIZE: Medium. *STOCK: Early oak, country furniture, portraits and period decoration.* LOC: On B5056. PARK: Own. TEL: 01629 636203; fax - 01629 636101; mobile - 07860 540870. VAT: Stan/Spec.

Over 30 professional dealers offering quality antique furniture, furnishings, decorative & collectors items from 17th to 20th centuries. Licenced Tea & Coffee House.

CHAPPELLS ANTIQUES CENTRE, BAKEWELL

King Street, Bakewell, Derbyshire
Ring 01629 812496 or visit www.chappellsantiquescentre.com
for brochure - location & parking information.

Open Mon-Sat 10 to 5. Sun 12 to 5. Closed Christmas, Boxing & New Years Days

Chappells Antiques Centre

King St. DE45 1DZ. Est. 1992. Open 10-5, Sun. 12-5. *STOCK: Period furniture, decorative and collectors' items, 17th-20th C - see dealers listed below.* LOC: King St is signposted B5055, Monyash, off the A6. PARK: Agricultural Centre (entrance off A6) and Smith's Island (off Baslow Rd.) 5 mins walk from Centre. TEL: 01629 812496; fax - 01629 814531; website - www. chappellsantiquescentre.com

Allens
20th C ceramics and secondhand books.

Peter and Sonia Allerston
Period furniture, especially French painted, and associated items including unusual and decorative with an interior design theme.

Barbara Austin
Linen, lace and small textile items.

Cambridge Fine Art
(Nicholas Lury). *Period British and Continental paintings.*

Chappell's Antiques & Fine Art
Est. 1940. *17th-19th C English furniture, oil paintings, watercolours and decorative items.*

Cottage Antiques
18th-19th C furniture, glass, treen, textiles, furnishing and decorative items.

Stephanie Davison Antiques   LAPADA
Early English oak and country furniture.

Roger de Ville
19th C pottery and porcelain, specialising in commemoratives.

J. Dickinson
Maps, prints and books.

Elizabeth Ann Antiques
Furniture and decorative items.

Elizabeth Antiques
General antiques and collectables.

G.W. Ford & Son Ltd   LAPADA
(I.G.F. Thomson). Est. 1890. *Mahogany and country furniture, 18th-19th C, £50-£5,000; sculpture, 19th to early 20th C, £50-£3,000; collectable and decorative items, 18th-19th C, £10-£1,200.* TEL: Home - 01246 410512; fax - same. SER: Valuations; restorations (furniture, silver and EP).

Emma Hart
Napoleonic Wars and Nelson memorabilia.

Brian L. Hills
Period furniture, decorative items, paintings, sculpture, works of art.

Ho-Ho-Bird
18th-19th C English furniture and clocks especially English dial

J. Lawrence Antiques
Small 19th-20th C decorative items.

Shirley May Antiques & Collectables
Kitchenalia, Cornish, Denby and textiles.

Millennium Antiques
Fine English silver, Sheffield plate, glass and bijouterie.

Walter Moores & Son   LAPADA
18th-19th C furniture and decorative items.

Paraphernalia Lighting
Antique lighting and decorative arts especially Art & Crafts.

Judy Portway
(Benjamin Henry & Co). *Vintage and designer costume jewelley and accessories.*

Pye Antiques
Early blue and white, ironstone, Dux, wall clocks and barometers.

Renaissance Antiques
Pottery, papier-mâché, metals, glass and objects d'art.

Scarlett Antiques
Victorian to 1930s jewellery, clocks and watches.

Sandra Wallhead Antiques
19th to early 20th C furniture, cranberry glass, dolls, jewellery and objets d'art.

N.I. Wilkinson
19th-20th C collectables.

Martin and Dorothy Harper Antiques   LAPADA
King St. DE45 1DZ. Est. 1973. Open 10-5, Sun. and other times by appointment. CL: Mon. and Thurs. SIZE: Medium. *STOCK: Furniture, £75-£7,500; metalware, £30-£500; glass, £15-£150; all 17th to early 20th C.*

PARK: Easy. TEL: 01629 814757; mobile - 07885 347134 and 07753 819854. SER: Valuations; restorations; buys at auction. VAT: Spec.

Michael Pembery Antiques
Peppercorn House, King St. DE45 1FD. (M. and L. Pembery). Est. 1967. Open 10-5. SIZE: Medium. *STOCK: Furniture, £500-£4,000; metalware, £100-£1,000; objets d'art, £100-£1,500; all 18th-19th C.* PARK: Nearby. TEL: 01629 814161. SER: Valuations; restorations. VAT: Stan/Spec.

BARLOW, Nr. Dronfield

Byethorpe Furniture
Shippen Rural Business Centre, Church Farm. S18 7TR. (Brian Yates and J. and E. Gelsthorpe). Est. 1977. Open 9.30-5.30. SIZE: Medium. *STOCK: Oak, mahogany and pine country and classical furniture, £150-£2,500; interior design items and paintings, £30-£350.* PARK: Easy. TEL: 01142 899111; fax - same; website - www.byethorpe.com SER: Restorations (furniture); specialist woodwork; upholstery; French polishing; hand-made reproductions. VAT: Stan/Spec.

Hackney House Antiques & Clocks
Hackney Lane, S18 7TD. (Mrs J.M. Gorman). Resident. Est. 1984. Open Tues.-Sun. 9-6. SIZE: Small. *STOCK: Longcase and wall clocks, furniture, 18th-19th C; prints, linen, silver.* LOC: B6051 NW of Chesterfield. PARK: Easy. TEL: 01142 890248.

BELPER

Derwentside Antiques
Derwent St. DE56 1WN. Est. 1995. Open 8.30-5.30, Sun. 8.30-5. SIZE: Large - four storey mill. *STOCK: General antiques mainly furniture and collectables.* LOC: Just off A6. PARK: Own. TEL: 01773 828008; fax - 01773 828983; e-mail - enquiries@derwentsidehomecentre.co.uk website - www.derwentsidehomecentre.co.uk SER: Restorations; sourcing of period furniture.

Sweetings (Antiques 'n' Things)
1 & 1a The Butts. DE56 1HX. (K.J. and J.L. Sweeting). Est. 1971. Open daily. SIZE: Large. *STOCK: Pre 1940s furniture including stripped pine, oak, mahogany, satinwood, £20-£1,000.* LOC: Off A6, near Market Place. PARK: Easy. TEL: 01773 825930/822780. SER: Valuations; restorations (pine and satinwood); shipping. VAT: Stan.

Neil Wayne "The Razor Man"
The Cedars (rear of 55 Field Lane), DE56 1DD. Resident. Est. 1969. Open every day 9.30-6 by appointment. SIZE: Medium. *STOCK: Razors and shaving items, 18th to early 19th C, £20-£300.* PARK: Easy. TEL: 01773 824157; fax - 01773 825573; e-mail - neil.wayne@derbyshire-holidays.com

BRADWELL, Hope Valley

Bradwell Antiques Centre
Newburgh Hall, Netherside. S33 9JL. Est. 2000. Open 10-5, Sun. 11-5. SIZE: 30 dealers. *STOCK: Wide range of general antiques, 18th-20th C, £5-£5,000.* LOC: A623 turn by Anchor public house on to B6049. PARK: Own.

TEL: 01433 621000; fax - same; website - www. bradwellantiques.com and www.antiquestrail.com

BRAILSFORD, Nr. Ashbourne

Heldreich Antiques & French Polishers
Home Farm, Ednaston. DE6 3AY. (Neil Heldreich). Est. 1986. Open daily, Sat. by appointment. SIZE: Medium. *STOCK: Furniture, late 17th C to mid 19th C, £250-£10,000; clocks, 18th-19th C, £300-£6,000; smalls, 18th-19th C, £10-£1,000.* LOC: A52 between Derby and Ashbourne, approximately 2 miles out of Brailsford on left towards Ashbourne. TEL: 01335 361676; home - 01283 733617. SER: Valuations; restorations; conservation and French polishing.

BUXTON

The Antiques Warehouse
25 Lightwood Rd. SK17 7BJ. (N.F. Thompson). Est. 1983. Open 10.30-4 or by appointment. SIZE: Large. *STOCK: British furniture, mainly mahogany, rosewood and walnut, 17th-20th C; paintings, silver, metalware, smalls, clocks including longcase, Victorian brass and iron bedsteads.* LOC: Off A6. PARK: Own at rear. TEL: 01298 72967; home/fax - 01298 22603; mobile - 07947 050552. SER: Valuations; restorations; buys at auction.

Maggie Mays
Unit 10, Cavendish Arcade. SK17 6BQ. (Mrs J. Wild). Est. 1993. Open 10.30-5. CL: Mon. *STOCK: Victorian furniture and effects, £35-£800; Art Deco glassware, mirrors, pottery, £20-£500; Edwardian furniture, £100-£800.* LOC: Opposite Turners Memorial on Terrace Road. PARK: Easy. TEL: Mobile - 07831 606003; home - 01663 733935. SER: Valuations; buys at auction.

The Penny Post Antiques
9 Cavendish Circus. SK17 6AT. (D. and R. Hammond). Est. 1978. Open 10-5. SIZE: Small. *STOCK: Pictures, commemoratives, crested china, shaving mugs and other collectables; furniture; general antiques.* LOC: Town centre, opposite Palace Hotel. PARK: Easy. TEL: Home - 01298 25965.

West End Galleries
8 Cavendish Circus. SK17 6AT. (A. and A. Needham). Est. 1955. Open 9-5, Sat. 9-4. SIZE: Medium. *STOCK: French and English furniture; clocks, paintings, works of art, bronzes.* LOC: A6. PARK: Easy. TEL: 01298 24546. FAIRS: Buxton; Tatton. VAT: Spec.

What Now Antiques
Cavendish Arcade, The Crescent. SK17 6BQ. (L. Carruthers). Est. 1987. Open 10-5, Sun. 12-5. CL: Mon. and Thurs. SIZE: Small. *STOCK: General antiques and collectables including Art Deco pottery, small silver items, jewellery, textiles, lighting, clocks, Victorian and Edwardian furniture, £1-£1,000.* LOC: Central. PARK: Easy. TEL: 01298 27178; mobile - 07977 369878; e-mail - ally4antiques@ic24.net SER: Valuations; export; foreign trade.

CHESTERFIELD

Anthony D. Goodlad
26 Fairfield Rd., Brockwell. S40 4TP. Est. 1974. Open by

appointment. SIZE: Small. *STOCK: General militaria, WWI and WWII.* LOC: Close to town centre. PARK: Easy. TEL: 01246 204004. FAIRS: Major UK Arms.

Ian Morris

479 Chatsworth Rd. S40 3AD. Est. 1970. Open by chance or appointment. SIZE: Small. *STOCK: Furniture, 18th-20th C, £50-£2,000; pictures, small items.* LOC: A619 to Baslow and Chatsworth House. PARK: Easy. TEL: 01246 235120.

Marlene Rutherford Antiques

401 Sheffield Rd., Whittington Moor. S41 8LS. Est. 1985. Open Mon. and Tues. 12-4, Thurs. 10-4, Fri. and Sat. 1-4. *STOCK: Furniture, pottery, clocks and lamps, £5-£2,000.* PARK: Easy. TEL: 01426 450209; mobile - 07885 665440. SER: Valuations. FAIRS: Bowman, Newark; Buxton; Jaguar.

DERBY

Finishing Touches

224 Uttoxeter Old Rd., The Rowditch. DE1 1NF. (Lynne Robinson). Est. 1994. Open 10-5.30, Sun. by appointment. CL: Mon. SIZE: Small. *STOCK: Fire surrounds, £200-£800; pine furniture, £50-£500; kitchenalia and pottery, £1-£25; all late 19th to early 20th C.* LOC: Off A38 at junction with A52. PARK: Rear of church. TEL: 01332 721717; website - www.derbyantiques.co.uk SER: Fireplace restoration.

Friargate Pine Company Ltd

The Pump House, Friargate Goods Wharf, Stafford St. Entrance. DE1 1JL. (N.J. Marianski). Open 9-5. *STOCK: Antique and reproduction pine furniture.* TEL: 01332 341215.

DUFFIELD, Nr. Derby

Wayside Antiques

62 Town St. DE56 4GG. (B. and Mrs J. Harding). Est. 1975. Open 10-6 or by appointment. *STOCK: Furniture, 18th-19th C, £50-£5,000; porcelain, pictures, boxes and silver.* PARK: Forecourt. TEL: 01332 840346. SER: Restorations (furniture). VAT: Stan/Spec.

GLOSSOP

Derbyshire Clocks

104 High St. West. SK13 8BB. (J.A. and T.P. Lees). Est. 1975. Open Thurs., Fri. and Sat. or by appointment. *STOCK: Clocks.* PARK: Easy. TEL: 01457 862677. SER: Restorations (clocks and barometers). VAT: Spec.

HAYFIELD, Nr. New Mills

Michael Allcroft Antiques

1 Church St. SK22 2JE. Est. 1984. Open Sat. 2-5, Sun. 1-5, other times by appointment. *STOCK: Pine furniture and decorative items.* TEL: 01663 742684; mobile - 07798 781642; fax - 01663 744014.

Paul Pickford Antiques

Top of the Town, Church St. SK22 2JE. Est. 1975. Open Tues., Thurs. and Sat. 11-4, Sun. 1-5, other times by appointment. SIZE: Medium. *STOCK: 19th C furniture, stripped pine, jewellery, ceramics, glass, lighting and*

general antiques, £50-£1,000. LOC: Off A6 at Newtown, near Disley, take A6015. PARK: Easy. TEL: 01663 747276; home - 01663 743356; e-mail - paul@pickford antiques.co.uk website - www.pickfordantiques.co.uk

HEANOR

Heanor Antiques Centre

1-3 Ilkeston Rd. DE75 7AG. (Jane Richards). Est. 1998. Open 10.30-4.30. SIZE: Large. *STOCK: Wide range of general antiques and collectables.* LOC: Off M1, junction 26 or A38, PARK: Easy. TEL: 01773 531181. SER: Valuations; restorations.

KILLAMARSH

Havenplan's Architectural Emporium

The Old Station, Station Rd. S21 1EN. Est. 1972. Open Tues., Wed., Thurs. and Sat. 10-2.30. SIZE: Large. *STOCK: Architectural fittings and decorative items, church interiors and furnishings, fireplaces, doors, decorative cast ironwork, masonry, bygones, garden ornaments, 18th to early 20th C.* LOC: M1, exit 30. Take A616 towards Sheffield, turn right on to B6053, turn right on to B6058 towards Killamarsh, turn right between two railway bridges. PARK: Easy. TEL: 01142 489972; home - 01246 433315. SER: Hire.

LONG EATON

Miss Elany

2 Salisbury St. NG10 1BA. (D. and Mrs Mottershead). Est. 1977. Open 9-5. SIZE: Medium. *STOCK: Pianos, 1900 to date, £150-£1,000; general antiques, Victorian and Edwardian, £180-£500.* PARK: Easy. TEL: 0115 9734835. VAT: Stan.

MATLOCK

Matlock Antiques and Collectables Centre

7 Dale Rd. DE4 3LT. (W. Shirley). Est. 1995. Open 10-5 including Sun. SIZE: Large - 70 + dealers. *STOCK: Wide range of general antiques including mahogany, oak and pine furniture, pictures and books, kitchenalia, china, clocks, linen, clothing and textiles.* LOC: Town centre. PARK: Easy. TEL: 01629 760808; e-mail - bmatlockantiques@aol.com website - www.matlock-antiques-collectables.cwc.net FAIRS: Chatsworth Country Show.

OCKBROOK

The Good Olde Days

6 Flood St. DE72 3RF. (Mr and Mrs S. Potter). Est. 1992. Open 10-5, Wed. 12-5. CL: Mon. SIZE: Medium. *STOCK: Beswick, Doulton, Wedgwood, Moorcroft, small furniture.* LOC: Village centre. PARK: Rear of shop. TEL: 01332 544244; home - 01332 663586. website - www.houseclearancederby.com SER: Valuations. FAIRS: Coventry, Kettering, Wickstead Park, RAF Swinderby, Ipswich, Norwich.

RIPLEY

A.A. Ambergate Antiques

c/o Upstairs & Downstairs, 8 Derby Rd. DE5 3HR. (C.V.

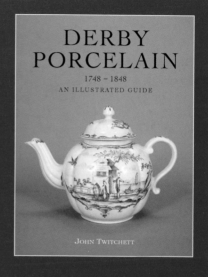
Lawrence). Est. 1972. Open 10-4. SIZE: Medium. *STOCK: Oak and mahogany Victorian and Edwardian furniture including bedroom, sideboards, tables and chairs, display cabinets; pottery, clocks and pictures.* LOC: Town centre. PARK: Easy. TEL: 01773 745201; mobile - 07885 327753. website - www.upstairs downstairsantiques.co.uk SER: Valuations; restorations.

Memory Lane Antiques Centre
1 Nottingham Rd. DE5 3AS. (James Cullen). Est. 1994. Open 10-4, Sun. and Bank Holidays 11-4. SIZE: Large. *STOCK: Victoriana and 20th C collectables, pine furniture, specialist in Denby, Bourne and Langley, lighting.* LOC: Town centre, at junction with Grosvenor Rd. PARK: Easy. TEL: 01773 570184; mobile - 07900 211393. SER: Valuations; old Denby replacement service and plate pattern library, 1940 to date. FAIRS: Derby University; Newark; Abacus; Kedleston Hall; Swinderby.

SHARDLOW, Nr. Derby

Shardlow Antiques Warehouse
24 The Wharf. DE72 2GH. (Nigel Critchlow). Est. 1986. Open 10.30-4.30, Sun. and Fri. 12-4. SIZE: Large. *STOCK: Furniture, Georgian to shipping.* LOC: Off M1, junction 24. PARK: Own. TEL: 01332 792899/662899. VAT: Spec.

SPONDON, Nr. Derby

Spondon Antiques and Collectables
38 Moor St. DE21 7EA. (D. and Mrs C. Rice). Est. 2000.

Open 10-5, Sat. and Sun. 10.30-4.30. CL: Wed. SIZE: Medium. *STOCK: Collectables especially Beswick, Crown Derby, Royal Doulton, Goss, Dinky and Corgi toys, Hornby railways.* LOC: 100 yds from village. PARK: Opposite. TEL: 01332 733761; e-mail - mail@ spondonantiquesandcollectables.co.uk website - www.spondonantiquesandcollectables.co.uk

WHALEY BRIDGE

Richard Glass
Hockerley Old Hall, Hockerley Lane. SK23 7AS. Resident. Est. 1985. Open by appointment. SIZE: Small. *STOCK: Oak furniture, 17th-18th C, £1,000-£5,000; paintings, drawings, metal and stoneware, 17th-19th C, £200-£2,000.* LOC: From town centre towards Stockport, turn left at station car park, up hill and 2nd right into Hockerley Lane, up farm track at the end of the lane, house on left. PARK: Easy. TEL: 0161 236 1520; fax - 0161 237 5174; mobile - 07802 860787. SER: Valuations. VAT: Spec.

Nimbus Antiques
14 Chapel Rd. SK23 7JZ. (L.M. and H.C. Brobbin). Est. 1979. Open 9-5.30, Sun. 2-5.30. SIZE: Large. *STOCK: Furniture, mainly mahogany, walnut and some oak, including desks, dining tables, clocks, chests, 18th-19th C.* LOC: A6, 20 mins. from Stockport. PARK: Own. TEL: 01663 734248; e-mail - nimbusantiques@ tiscali.co.uk website - www.antiques-atlas.com/ nimbus.htm VAT: Stan/Spec.

DEVON

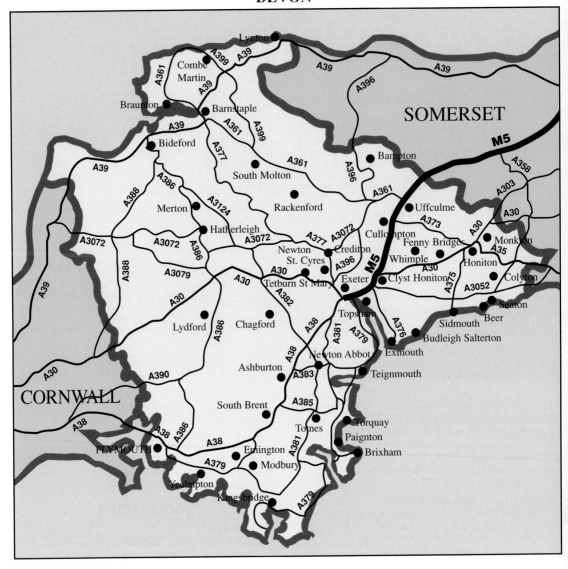

Dealers and Shops in Devonshire

				Paignton	1
Ashburton	8	Ermington	1	Plymouth	5
Bampton	2	Exeter	11	Rackenford	1
Barnstaple	5	Exmouth	2	Seaton	1
Beer	1	Fenny Bridges	1	Sidmouth	2
Bideford	2	Hatherleigh	1	South Brent	1
Braunton	1	Honiton	23	South Molton	3
Brixham	2	Kingsbridge	1	Tedburn St. Mary	1
Budleigh Salterton	2	Lydford	1	Teignmouth	2
Chagford	2	Lynton	2	Topsham	4
Clyst Honiton	1	Merton	1	Torquay	3
Colyton	1	Modbury	3	Totnes	7
Combe Martin	1	Monkton	1	Uffculme	1
Crediton	1	Newton Abbot	2	Whimple	1
Cullompton	5	Newton St. Cyres	1	Yealmpton	1

ASHBURTON

Adrian Ager Ltd
Ashburton Marbles, Great Hall, North St. TQ13 7DU. Est. 1976. Open 8-5, Sat. 10-4. SIZE: Warehouse and showrooms. *STOCK: Marble and wooden fire-surrounds, decorative cast iron inserts; scuttles, fenders, overmantels, 1790-1910; architectural decorative antiques, garden statuary and related items, chandeliers, soft furnishings and furniture; mid-Victorian dining tables and bedroom furniture.* PARK: Easy. TEL: 01364 653189; fax - same; e-mail - sales@adrianager.com website - www.adrianager.com

Antiques Ad Hoc
17 North St. TQ13 7QH. (Helen Harvey). Est. 1994. Open 10-5, Sat. 11-5. CL: Wed. and Mon. SIZE: Small. *STOCK: Period furniture and decorative items, mirrors and lamps, pottery and porcelain, woolwork pictures, line and stipple engravings, copper and brass, English and French, 1770-1910.* LOC: North end of North St. PARK: Loading and nearby. TEL: 01364 654667; mobile - 07778 764424; home - 01752 402130.

Dartmoor Bookshop
2 Kingsbridge Lane. TQ13 7DX. (Paul and Barbara Heatley). PBFA. Est. 1982. Open Wed.-Sat. 9.30-5.30. SIZE: Large. *STOCK: Books - secondhand and antiquarian.* LOC: On lane facing car park. PARK: Easy. TEL: 01364 653356; e-mail - dartmoorbks@aol.com website - www.dartmoorbks.dabsol.co.uk SER: Valuations.

Kessler Ford
9 North St. TQ13 7QJ. (Elisabeth Kessler and Matthew Ford). Est. 1998. Open 10-5. CL: Mon. SIZE: Medium. *STOCK: Period oak and Georgian mahogany furniture; pictures, carvings, bronzes.* LOC: Main street. PARK: Easy. TEL: 01364 654310; fax - 01364 652141; e-mail - antiques@kessler-ford.co.uk SER: Valuations. VAT: Spec.

Mo Logan Antiques
11 North St. TQ13 7AG. (Martin & Mo Logan). Est. 1972. Open Tues., Thurs., Fri. and Sat. 10-4.30. SIZE: Small. *STOCK: Textiles, early 20th C; rugs, gilt furniture and mirrors, lamps, small period furniture, decorative items.* LOC: Town centre. TEL: 01364 654179; mobile - 07967 234129.

Moor Antiques
19a North St. TQ13 7QH. (T. and Mrs D. Gatland). Est. 1984. CL: Wed. pm. SIZE: Small. *STOCK: English porcelain, 1750-1850, £20-£800; small silver, 1720-1920, £20-£500.* LOC: A38 town centre, 100 yards past town hall. PARK: Opposite. TEL: 01364 653767. SER: Valuations.

Pennsylvania Pine Co
18 East St. TQ13 7AZ. (S. F. Robinson and C.A. Tolchard). Est. 1967. Open 10.30-4.30. CL: Wed. SIZE: Medium. *STOCK: Unusual English pine furniture, 18th-20th C, £50-£5,000.* PARK: Easy. TEL: 01364 652244; fax - same; mobile - 07941 891640; home - 01364 652594. SER: Valuations; restorations (pine).

The Shambles
24 North St. TQ13 7QD. Est. 1982. Open 10-5. SIZE: 5

dealers. *STOCK: Country and general antiques and decorative items, £5-£2,000.* LOC: Town centre. PARK: Opposite. TEL: 01364 653848. SER: Valuations. FAIRS: Sandown Park; Westpoint Exeter; Shepton Mallet. VAT: Stan/Spec.

BAMPTON, Nr. Tiverton

Bampton Gallery
2-4 Brook St. EX16 9LY. (Gerald Chidwick). FRICS. Est. 1997. Open Mon., Tues. and Wed. 9.30-3, Thurs. 9.30-5.30, Sat. 9-12, other times by appointment or chance. SIZE: Medium. *STOCK: Porcelain (especially English hard-paste), pottery and glass, 1750-1900, £10-£2,000; pictures and prints, furniture including upholstered, £20-£10,000.* LOC: Main street. PARK: Outside. TEL: 01398 331119; fax - same; home - 01398 331354. e-mail - bampton.gallery@bampton.org.uk website - www.bamptongallery.co.uk SER: Restorations (furniture including traditional upholstery, ceramics); buys at auction (porcelain and furniture).

Robert Byles and Optimum Brasses
7 Castle St. EX16 9NS. (Robert and Rachel Byles). Est. 1966. Open Mon.-Fri. 9-1 and 2-5 or by appointment. SIZE: Medium. *STOCK: Furniture, 16th-18th C; local farmhouse tables and settles, metalwork, pottery, unstripped period pine, architectural items.* PARK: Nearby. TEL: 01398 331515; fax - 01398 331164; website - www.obida.com SER: Restoration materials; replica brass handles for antique furniture. VAT: Stan/Spec.

BARNSTAPLE

Barn Antiques
73 Newport Rd. EX32 9BG. (T. Cusack). Open 9.30-5, Wed. 9.30-1. SIZE: Large. *STOCK: General antiques.* TEL: 01271 323131.

Medina Gallery
80 Boutport St. EX31 1SR. (R. and C.F. Jennings). Est. 1972. Open 9.30-5. SIZE: Medium. *STOCK: Maps, prints, photographs, oils and watercolours, £1-£500.* PARK: Easy. TEL: 01271 371025. SER: Picture framing, mounting. VAT: Stan.

North Devon Antiques Centre
The Old Church, 18 Cross St. EX31 1BD. (P. Broome). Est. 1985. Open 10-4.30. SIZE: Large. *STOCK: Furniture, china, clocks, 18th C to 1960s, £5-£2,500; Victorian and Art Deco fireplaces, £100-£900.* LOC: 40 yards off High St. PARK: Nearby. TEL: 01271 375788. SER: Restorations (woodwork and clocks). FAIRS: Newark, Shepton Mallet, Exeter Westpoint.

Mark Parkhouse Antiques and Jewellery
106 High St. EX31 1HP. Est. 1976. CL: Wed. *STOCK: Jewellery, furniture, silver, paintings, clocks, glass, porcelain, small collectors' items, 18th-19th C, £100-£10,000.* PARK: Nearby. TEL: 01271 374504; fax - 01271 323499. SER: Valuations; buys at auction. VAT: Stan/Spec.

Tudor House
115 Boutport St. EX31 1TD. (C. and D. Pilon). Est. 1980. Open 9.30-3.30, Wed. 9.30-1. SIZE: Large.

STOCK: *Furniture and bric-a-brac, late 18th C and reproduction.* LOC: Off M5, Tiverton link road to town centre. PARK: Easy. TEL: 01271 375370; home - 01271 371750. SER: Valuations; restorations (furniture).

BEER

Dolphin Antiques

Dolphin Courtyard. EX12 3EQ. (L.R. Forkes). Est. 1985. Open 10-5 including Sun. SIZE: Medium. *STOCK: Antique fishing tackle, from £25; jewellery, £50-£2,000; china and smalls, £2-£50.* PARK: Easy. TEL: 01297 24362; home - 01460 65294. SER: Valuations; buys at auction. FAIRS: West country.

BIDEFORD

J. Collins and Son Fine Art   BADA LAPADA

P O Box 119. EX39 1WX. (J. and P. Biggs). CINOA. Est. 1953. By appointment. *STOCK: Georgian and Regency furniture; general antiques including framed and restored 19th-20th C oils and watercolours, £100-£100,000.* TEL: 01237 473103; fax - 01237 475658; home - 01237 476485; e-mail - biggs@collins antiques.co.uk website - www.collinsantiques.co.uk SER: Valuations; cleaning and framing (oils and watercolours). FAIRS: BADA (March). VAT: Spec.

Cooper Gallery

Cooper St. EX39 2DA. (Mrs J. Bruce). Est. 1975. Open 10-4.30, Wed. 10-1.30, Sat. 10-2. SIZE: Small. *STOCK: Watercolours, mainly West Country views, late 19th to early 20th C, £200-£5,000; antique jewellery.* LOC: Just off the quay, opposite HSBC bank. PARK: Nearby. TEL: 01237 477370; fax - same; home - 01237 423415; e-mail - coopergallery@freecall-uk.co.uk SER: Valuations; restorations (watercolours); cleaning; framing. VAT: Spec.

BRAUNTON

Caen Antiques

19 Caen St. EX33 1AA. (J. and C. Owen). Est. 1992. Open 9.30-5. CL: Wed. pm. SIZE: Small. *STOCK: Clocks including longcase and bracket; barometers, Art Nouveau, Victorian oil lamps and spares, small furniture.* LOC: Village centre. PARK: At rear. TEL: 01271 817808; home - same; mobile - 07890 133820; e-mail - jcoa@devon942.fsnet.co.uk website - www.caen antiques.co.uk SER: Longcase clock, oil lamp and barometer repairs.

BRIXHAM

Antique, Electrical & Turret Clocks

Ye Olde Coffin House, King St. TQ5 9TF. (Dr. Paul Strickland). NAWCC. Telephone for opening times. SIZE: Small. *STOCK: Antique, early electric and turret clocks.* PARK: Loading only and nearby. TEL: 01803 856307; e-mail - clocks@forall.fsnet.co.uk website - www.forall.fsnet.co.uk SER: Valuations; restorations.

John Prestige Antiques

1 and 2 Greenswood Court. TQ5 9HN. (John and Patricia Prestige). Est. 1971. Open 8.45-6, appointment advisable. CL: Sat. and Sun. except by appointment.

SIZE: Large + warehouse. *STOCK: Period and Victorian furniture; shipping goods; decorative smalls.* PARK: Own. TEL: 01803 856141; home - 01803 853739; fax - 01803 851649; e-mail - sales@john-prestige.co.uk website - www.john-prestige.co.uk SER: Courier (West Country). VAT: Stan/Spec.

BUDLEIGH SALTERTON

Days of Grace

15 Fore St. EX9 6NH. (L. Duriez). *STOCK: Antique lace, vintage textiles and costume, china, jewellery, furniture, interesting decorating items.* TEL: 01395 443730.

David J. Thorn

2 High St. EX9 6LQ. Est. 1950. Open Tues., Fri. and Sat. 10-1. SIZE: Small. *STOCK: English, Continental and Oriental pottery and porcelain, 1620-1850, £5-£5,000; English furniture, 1680-1870, £20-£5,000; paintings, silver, jewellery, £1-£1,000.* PARK: Easy. TEL: 01395 442448. SER: Valuations. VAT: Stan/Spec.

CHAGFORD

Godolphin

11 The Square. TQ13 8AA. (S. Freeman). Est. 1999. Open 10.15-5.15, Sun. by appointment. SIZE: Medium. *STOCK: Watercolours and oils, 18th-20th C, £200-£35,000; oak and country furniture.* LOC: Turn opposite Easton Court Hotel off A382 Moretonhampstead-Okehampton road. PARK: Easy. TEL: 01647 433999; website - www.godolphinfineart.com VAT: Margin.

Rex Antiques

The Old Rex Cinema. TQ13 8AB. (John Meredith). Est. 1979. Open by appointment. SIZE: Large. *STOCK: Country oak, 16th-19th C, £5-£2,000; Oriental brass and copper, weapons, large unusual items, granite, architectural items, old iron work.* PARK: Easy. TEL: 01647 433405. SER: Buys at auction. *Trade only.*

CLYST HONITON, Nr. Exeter

Home Farm Antiques

EX5 2LX. (Michael Clark). Est. 1975. Open 10-5. SIZE: Large. *STOCK: Antiques and collectables.* LOC: Off A30 Exeter Airport exit. PARK: Easy. TEL: 01392 444491. SER: Restorations; delivery.

COLYTON

Colyton Antiques Centre

Dolphin St. EX24 6LU. (R.C. Hunt and M.J. Conway). Est. 2000. Open 10-5, Sun. 11-4. SIZE: Large. *STOCK: General antiques.* PARK: Easy. TEL: 01297 552339; fax - same.

COMBE MARTIN

Sherbrook Selectables

2 Hangman Path. EX34 0DN. (Trevor and Mrs Lesley Pickard). Est. 1997. Open 10-5.30. CL: Mon.-Wed. SIZE: Small. *STOCK: General antiques and collectables.* LOC: 300 yards from sea front. PARK: Easy. TEL: 01271 889060; mobile - 07887 806493; e-mail - Trevor@sherbrookantiques1.fsbusiness.co.uk SER: Valuations.

CREDITON

Musgrave Bickford Antiques

15 East St. EX17 3AT. (Mr and Mrs D.M. Bickford). Est. 1983. Open by appointment. SIZE: Small. *STOCK: Clocks and barometers, mainly 19th C, from £400.* LOC: From Exeter on A377 on right entering one-way system, towards Tiverton. PARK: Easy and at rear by arrangement. TEL: 01363 775042. SER: Restorations (longcase, mantel, wall clock and barometer movements, dials, cases). VAT: Stan/Spec.

CULLOMPTON

Cobweb Antiques

The Old Tannery, Exeter Rd. EX15 1DT. (R. Holmes). Est. 1980. Open 10-5. SIZE: Large. *STOCK: English oak, pine and country furniture, decorative and general items, 16th-19th C.* LOC: Half a mile from junction 28, M5. PARK: Easy. TEL: 01884 855748. SER: Stripping; restorations; courier.

Cullompton Old Tannery Antiques

Exeter Rd. EX15 1DT. (Cullompton Antiques). Est. 1989. Open 10-5, Sun. by appointment. SIZE: Large. *STOCK: Pine, oak, mahogany and fruitwood country furniture - wardrobes, cupboards, tables and chairs, beds, dressers, coffers, desks, mirrors and decorative items, 17th to early 19th C, £50-£5,000.* LOC: Off M5, junction 28, through town centre, premises on right, approximately 1 mile. PARK: Easy. TEL: 01884 38476; fax - same; e-mail - tannery@cullompton-antiques.co.uk website - www.cullompton-antiques.co.uk

Miller Antiques

The Old Tannery, Exeter Rd. EX15 1DT. (Nick Miller). Open 10-5, Sun. by appointment. SIZE: Large. *STOCK: Furniture, 18th-19th C, £25-£2,000, country, 17th-19th C, £25-£3,000; decorative accessories, £5-£2,000.* LOC: M5 junction 28, bottom of the High St. opposite Somerfield. PARK: Easy. TEL: 01884 38476; fax - same. SER: Valuations; buys at auction.

Mills Antiques

The Old Tannery, Exeter Rd. EX15 1DT. Est. 1979. Open 10-5. *STOCK: 17th C to Edwardian furniture including oak, mahogany and pine - coffers, desks, wardrobes, cupboards, tables and chairs, £50-£3,000.* PARK: Easy. TEL: 01392 860945.

R.C. Associates

The Old Tannery, Exeter Rd. EX15 1DT. Open 10-5. *STOCK: French provincial furniture, various woods - beds, armoires, tables, buffets.* PARK: Easy.

ERMINGTON, Nr. Ivybridge

Mill Gallery

PL21 9NT. (Christopher Trant). Resident. Est. 1984. CL: Sat. SIZE: Small. *STOCK: Oils and watercolours, 18th-20th C, £300-£1,000.* LOC: From A38 take Ivybridge exit, follows signs, 1st premises in village. PARK: Easy. TEL: 01548 830172; website - www.millgallery.com SER: Valuations; restorations (oils). VAT: Spec.

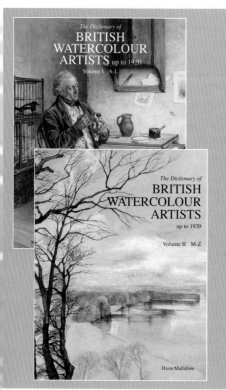

EXETER

The Antique Centre on the Quay
The Quay. EX2 4AP. (Exeter Traders in Collectables Ltd). Est. 1983. Open winter 10-5, Sat. and Sun. 10-5.30; summer 10-6 including Sun. SIZE: 20+ dealers. *STOCK: General antiques - small furniture, clocks, ceramics, glass, jewellery, collectables, books, pictures, coins, cameras, postcards, records, tools and toys.* PARK: Nearby. TEL: 01392 493501.

The Antiques Complex   LAPADA
Exeter Airport Industrial Estate, Westcott Lane. EX5 2BA. Est. 1975. Open 9-5.30, Sat. 10-1. CL: Bank Holiday weekends. SIZE: 4 large warehouses. *STOCK: Over 2,000 items of antique, decorative, Victorian and Edwardian, Arts and Crafts and collectable furniture.* LOC: 3 miles from junction 29, M5. After airport, turn left and follow sign to Westcott for 1 mile. PARK: Easy. TEL: 01392 366261; fax - 01392 365572; e-mail - mcbains@netcomuk.co.uk SER: Container packing and shipping; courier. FAIRS: Newark. VAT: Spec/Global/Export. Below are listed the dealers trading from this address.

Acorn Antiques
Open bookcases, pairs of bedside tables, desks and writing tables.

M. Burbidge Antiques
General antique and shipping furniture.

M. Dunscombe Antiques
Antique and decorative furniture.

J. Durn Antiques
Oak and shipping furniture.

Heritage Green Antiques
Dutch walnut and oak furniture.

J. Huggett Antiques
Georgian and Victorian furniture.

Ian McBain Antiques
Georgian, Victorian and shipping furniture. TEL: 01392 366261; mobile - 07887 737231; e-mail - mcbains@netcomuk.co.uk

McBain Exports
(Martin and Kathy McBain). 1963. *English, French and Belgium and other Continental furniture and garden accessories.* TEL: 01392 466304; mobile - 07831 389236; e-mail - mcbain.exports@zetnet.co.uk SER: Stock details e-mailed on request; full container packing and collection; courier for France available.

Miscellany Antiques
Fine quality and period furniture. TEL: 01684 566671.

P & A
Arts & Crafts, Art Deco and Art Nouveau furniture.

Portobello Antiques
General antique and shipping furniture.

P. Reynolds Antiques
General antique and shipping furniture.

Leon Robertson Antiques
Antique and decorative furniture. TEL: Mobile - 07971 171909.

Tredantiques
(Jonathan Tredant). *Fine Georgian, Victorian and Edwardian furniture and accessories; decorative, architectural and granite items.* TEL: 01392 447082; mobile - 07967 447082; website - www.tredantiques.com

Michael Youll Antiques
French beds, Continental painted and country furniture, 18th-19th C. TEL: 01392 445559; mobile - 07785 232054.

Ivor Doble Ltd
24 Sidwell St. EX4 1AS. Est. 1950. Open 9-5.30. SIZE: Small. *STOCK: Silver and jewellery, £5-£5,000; clocks, including Georgian and Victorian, £25-£3,000.* PARK: Easy. TEL: 01392 272228. SER: Valuations; restorations (silver and jewellery); buys at auction. VAT: Stan.

Eclectique
Cellars 18 & 23, The Quay. EX2 4AP. (E.J. Henson and C. Frank). Est. 1992. Open 7 days 11-5. SIZE: Medium. *STOCK: Mainly Victorian and Edwardian furniture including pine and oak; dining tables, chests of drawers, chairs and pictures.* LOC: Town centre. PARK: Nearby. TEL: 01392 250799; e-mail - sales@eclectique.co.uk website - www.eclectique.co.uk

Exeter Rare Books
Guildhall Shopping Centre. EX4 3HG. (R.C. Parry). ABA. PBFA. Est. 1975. Open 10-1 and 2-5. SIZE: Small. *STOCK: Books, antiquarian, secondhand, out-of-print, 17th-20th C; Devon and West Country topography. £5-£500.* LOC: City centre. PARK: Easy. TEL: 01392 436021. SER: Valuations; buys at auction. FAIRS: ABA Chelsea, Bath.

Fagins Antiques
The Old Whiteways Cider Factory, Hele. EX5 4PW. (C.J. Strong). Open 9.15-5, Sat. 11-5, Sun. 11-4. SIZE: Large. *STOCK: Furniture, decorative items, pictures, porcelain, garden furniture, architectural and shipping items.* LOC: 10 mins. from junction 28, M5 on the B3181 Cullompton - Exeter road. PARK: Easy. TEL: 01392 882062; fax - 01392 882194; e-mail - info@faginsantiques.com website - www.faginsantiques.com SER: Stripping (pine); pine furniture made to order.

The House that Moved
24 West St. EX1 1BA. (L. Duriez). Est. 1980. Open 10-5. SIZE: 3 floors and courtyard. *STOCK: Lace, shawls, babywear, linen, 1920s costume, Victorian and Edwardian bridal wedding dresses.* LOC: West Quarter. PARK: Easy. TEL: 01392 432643.

Mortimers
87 Queen St. EX4 3RP. Est. 1970. Open 9-5. SIZE: Small. *STOCK: Jewellery, silver, clocks, watches and objet d'art.* LOC: City centre. PARK: Easy. TEL: 01392 279994; website - www.mortimers.co.uk SER: Valuations; repairs. VAT: Stan/Spec.

Phantique
47 The Quay. EX2 4AN. (Patsy Bliss). Est. 1996. Open daily - summer 10.30-5.30, winter 10.30-5. SIZE: Several dealers. *STOCK: General antiques, collectables, prints, books, ephemera, militaria, toys, jewellery, small furniture, kitchenalia.* PARK: Nearby. TEL: 01392 498995.

The Quay Gallery Antiques Emporium
43 The Quay. EX2 4AP. (Mark Davis and Danielle Rawstron). Est. 1984. Open 10-5 including Sun. SIZE: Large - 15 dealers. *STOCK: Fine English 18th-20th C oak and mahogany furniture, marine items, porcelain, silver, plate, glass, paintings, prints, antiquities, carpets and decorative items.* LOC: Next to Old Customs House. PARK: Easy. TEL: 01392 213283; e-mail - quayantiques@aol.com SER: Shipping arranged; free UK delivery. VAT: Spec.

Peter Wadham Antiques
3 Crane Cellars, Exeter Quay. EX2 4AN. Est. 1967. Open 10-5, Sun. and Mon. by appointment. SIZE: Small. *STOCK: Small furniture and mirrors, 1780-1880, £100-£1,000; glass, metalwork, topographical prints and local views, 1750-1870, £10-£500.* LOC: Close to Customs House. PARK: Easy. TEL: Home - 01392 255801. SER: Valuations; restorations (small furniture and picture frames). VAT: Spec.

EXMOUTH

Alison Gosling Antiques Studio
Bridge House, 11 North St. EX8 1LF. Est. 1983. Open Tues. and Fri. 10.30-5, other times by appointment. SIZE: Medium. *STOCK: Late 17th to early 19th C furniture, £400-£10,000; sculpture and metalware, 17th to early 20th C, £20-£2,000.* LOC: Opposite library car park, next to the Manor House. PARK: Opposite. TEL: 01395 273758; evenings - 01395 271451. SER: Valuations.

Treasures
34 Exeter Rd. EX8 1PS. (L. Treasure). Open 9-5. *STOCK: General antiques.* TEL: 01395 279512.

FENNY BRIDGES, Nr. Honiton

Alexander Paul Antiques
Unit 2. EX14 3BG. (David Steele and Mathew Yates). Est. 1998. Open 8.30-5.30, Sat. 10-3. SIZE: Small. *STOCK: Furniture including dresser bases, serving, dining, coffee and side tables, chairs, French buffets, chests of drawers and bedside cabinets; decorative mirrors, all mainly 1760-1900, £200-£4,000.* LOC: 3 miles west of Honiton on A30. PARK: Easy. TEL: 01404 850881; fax - 01404 851299; e-mail - sales@alexander paulantiques.com website - www.alexanderpaulantiques. com SER: Restorations (inlay and veneer, re-leathering, turning, French polishing).

HATHERLEIGH

Hatherleigh Antiques   BADA
15 Bridge St. EX20 3HU. (M. Dann). Open by appointment. SIZE: Medium. *STOCK: Collectors' furniture and works of art, pre-1700.* PARK: Easy. TEL: 01837 810159/811101. VAT: Spec.

HONITON

Jane Barnes Antiques & Interiors
Avalon, Upottery. EX14 9PQ. (J.A.C. and S.J. Barnes). By appointment only. SIZE: Medium. *STOCK: General antiques and country pine.* LOC: Off A30. PARK: Easy.

LEIGH EXTENCE
ANTIQUE CLOCKS

Selected stock at:
The Grove, High Street, Honiton, Devon

For a Personal Appointment:
Tel: 01404 549047 Mobile: 07967 802160
Correspondence: PO Box 85, Honiton, Devon. EX14 1ZL

See website for stock and details
www.extence.co.uk
email: clocks@extence.co.uk

TEL: 01404 861300; e-mail - jane@janebarnesantiques. co.uk and john@devonshirehilldesign.co.uk SER: Furniture copies made to order.

Roderick Butler   BADA
Marwood House. EX14 1PY. (Roderick and Valentine Butler). Est. 1948. Open 9.30-5 (during August by appointment only). SIZE: Large. STOCK: 17th-18th C and Regency furniture, curiosities, unusual items, early metalwork. LOC: Adjacent to roundabout at eastern end of High St. PARK: In courtyard. TEL: 01404 42169; e-mail - vfbutler@yahoo.co.uk SER: Restorations (furniture). VAT: Spec.

Collectables
134B High St. EX14 1JP. (Chris Guthrie). Est. 1995. Open 10-1 and 1.30-4.45. CL: Thurs. SIZE: Small. *STOCK: Railwayana, Wade, cigarette and 'phone cards, toys and games, breweriana, commemoratives, militaria.* PARK: Nearby. TEL: 01404 47024; e-mail - chris@ collectableshoniton.co.uk website - www.collectables honiton.co.uk

Evans Emporium
140 High St. EX14 1JP. (Bob Evans). Est. 1992. Open 10-5. SIZE: Medium. *STOCK: General antiques and collectables, sheet music and musical instruments, silver and jewellery, furniture and furnishings, 19th-20th C, £1-£500.* PARK: Nearby. TEL: 01404 47869; mobile - 07790 546495.

Leigh Extence Antique Clocks   LAPADA
The Grove Showroom, 55 High St. EX14 1PW. Est.

1981. Open 10-5. SIZE: Medium. *STOCK: Clocks and barometers, 1710-1880.* PARK: Outside shop. TEL: 01404 549047; mobile - 07967 802160; e-mail - clocks @extence.co.uk and info@tompion.co.uk website - www.extence.co.uk VAT: Spec.

Fountain Antiques
132 High St. EX14 1JP. (J. Palmer and G. York). Est. 1980. Open 9.30-5.30. *STOCK: General antiques including pictures, books and linen.* PARK: Nearby. TEL: 01404 42074; fax - 01404 44993; e-mail - antiques@gyork.co.uk

The Grove Antiques Centre Ltd
55 High St. EX14 1PW. (Lesley V. Phillips). Est. 1998. Open 10-5. SIZE: Large. *STOCK: Fine period and country furniture; antique beds; glass, porcelain, Staffordshire, silver and jewellery, pictures, carpets and rugs; early longcase, bracket and carriage clocks, objets d'art; 20th C decorative design.* PARK: Easy. TEL: 01404 43377; fax - 01404 43390; e-mail - info@ groveantiquescentre.com website - www.groveantiques centre.com SER: Shipping; delivery.

Hermitage Antiques
37 High St. EX14 1PW. (N.R. Kirk). Est. 1993. Open 10-5, Sun. 11-3.30 (June-Jan), Bank Holidays 11-3.30, otherwise by appointment. SIZE: Large. *STOCK: English and French furniture, 18th-20th C, £50-£10,000+; Arts and Crafts furniture, metalware, tiles, art pottery, £5-£7,500+; clocks, barometers, glass, lighting, china and collectables, 18th-20th C, £1-£5,000+.* LOC: M5 junction 28 or A30. TEL: 01404 44406; home/fax - 01884 820944; mobile - 07768 553172; e-mail - raykirk04@aol.com SER: Shipping.

High Street Books
150 High St. EX14 8JB. (G. Tyson). PBFA. Est. 1978. Open 10-5. SIZE: Medium. *STOCK: Books, prints and maps, 18th-20th C, £1-£1,000.* LOC: Opposite police station. PARK: Easy. TEL: 01404 45570; fax - same; home - 01404 41771. SER: Valuations. FAIRS: Major London Book.

Honiton Antique Centre
Abingdon House, 136 High St. EX14 8JP. (N.D.A. and E.K. Thompson). Est. 1985. Open 9.30-5.30. SIZE: Large - 20 dealers. *STOCK: 17th-20th C furniture, metalwork, copper, brass, tools, sporting items, pottery, porcelain, pictures and collectables.* LOC: Exeter end of High St. PARK: Nearby. TEL: 01404 42108; e-mail - tbumble84@aol.com

Honiton Antique Toys
38 High St. EX14 1PJ. (L. and S. Saunders). Est. 1986. Open Wed., Fri. and Sat. 10.30-5. *STOCK: Diecast and tinplate toys, dolls, teddies, lead soldiers.* PARK: Easy. TEL: 01404 41194; e-mail - hattoys@hotmail.com

Honiton Clock Clinic
16 New St. EX14 1EY. (David P. Newton). BHI; BWCG. Est. 1992. Open 9-5, Sat. 9-3. CL: Thurs. SIZE: Small. *STOCK: Clocks - mantel, bracket, carriage and longcase, fully restored, 30 hour and 8 day, painted and brass dial, 1 year guarantee; aneriod and mercurial barometers; clock and watches keys, clock and barometer spares.* LOC: Near town centre. PARK:

Nearby. TEL: 01404 47466; fax - same. SER: Valuations; restorations (clocks and barometers); collection and delivery; home calls.

Honiton Fine Art
189 High St. EX14 8LQ. (C.B. and P.R. Greenberg). Est. 1974. Open 11.30-5. SIZE: Medium. *STOCK: English watercolours and oil paintings, 18th-20th C, £300-£5,000; Old Master drawings, Dutch, Italian and French, 16th-18th C, £300-£1,500.* LOC: Town centre. PARK: Easy. TEL: 01404 45942. SER: Valuations; restorations (oil paintings and watercolours).

The Honiton Lace Shop
44 High St. EX14 8PJ. (Jonathan Page). Est. 1983. Open by appointment only. SIZE: Medium. *STOCK: Lace including wedding veils, specialist and collectors; quilts, shawls and other textiles, bobbins and lace making equipment.* PARK: Easy. TEL: 01404 42416; fax - 01404 47797; e-mail - shop@honitonlace.com website - www. honitonlace.com SER: Valuations; repairs. VAT: Stan.

Honiton Pottery
30 High St. EX14 1PU. (E.H. Stephenson). Open 9-5. SIZE: Large. *STOCK: Honiton pottery, 1908 to date.* PARK: Easy. TEL: 01404 42106; fax - same; home - 01404 831865; e-mail - EricJane@tiscali.co.uk website - www.hpcs.info SER: Valuations; restorations.

Lombard Antiques
14 High St. EX14 8PU. (B. and T. Sabine). Est. 1974. Open 10-5.30. SIZE: Small. *STOCK: 18th-19th C English furniture, porcelain, Clarice Cliff (300+ pieces) and decorative items.* PARK: Easy. TEL: 01404 42140.

Merchant House Antiques
19 High St. EX14 1PR. (C. Giltsoff). Open 10-5, Sun. by appointment. SIZE: Large. *STOCK: English and French fine and provincial furniture, 17th-19th C; works of art, ironstone and later china, collectables and decorative items, upholstery and furnishings, £10-£20,000+.* PARK: Easy. TEL: 01404 42694; fax - 01404 42471; mobile - 07768 960144. SER: Valuations. VAT: Stan/Spec.

Otter Antiques
69 High St. EX14 1PW. (Kate Skailes). Est. 1978. Open 9.30-4.30. CL: Thurs. pm. *STOCK: Fine antique silver, jewellery and plate including flatware; modern silver.* TEL: 01404 42627; e-mail - kate@otterantiques. fsnet.co.uk SER: Silverplating; restorations and repairs (glass, metal, jewellery).

Pilgrim Antiques   LAPADA
145 High St. EX14 8LJ. (G. and J.E. Mills). Est. 1970. Open 9-5.30. SIZE: Large - trade warehouse. *STOCK: Period English and Continental, oak and country furniture.* PARK: Easy. TEL: 01404 41219/45316; fax - 01404 45317; e-mail - pilgrim1@btconnect.com website - www.pilgrimantiques.co.uk SER: Packing and shipping. VAT: Spec.

Jane Strickland & Daughters   LAPADA
71 High St. EX14 1PW. Est. 1977. Open 10-5. SIZE: Medium. *STOCK: 18th-19th C furniture especially 19th C upholstered English and French furniture; 19th C English and French mirrors; lighting, decorative items.*

LOC: 10 miles from M5. PARK: Easy. TEL: 01404 44221; e-mail - JSandDaughtersUK@aol.com website - www.janestricklandanddaughters.co.uk SER: Restorations (upholstery). FAIRS: Decorative Antique Textile, Battersea. VAT: Stan/Spec.

Upstairs, Downstairs
12 High St. EX14 8PU. (T. and B. Sabine). Est. 1975. Open 10-5.30. SIZE: Large - 5 rooms. *STOCK: 18th-19th C furniture, porcelain, metalware, pictures and clocks, Clarice Cliff.* PARK: Easy. TEL: 01404 42140.

Yarrow
155 High St. EX14 1LJ. (James Yarrow and Sarah Wolfe). Open 10-5. SIZE: Large. *STOCK: Architectural features, Chinese furniture.* LOC: Off A303. TEL: 01404 44399; website - www.asianart.co.uk

Graham York Rare Books
225 High St. EX14 1LB. ABA. ILAB. PBFA. Est. 1982. Open 9.30-5. SIZE: Medium. *STOCK: Travel - especially Spain and South Africa; art - fine and applied, especially lace, costume and textiles; literature, natural history, history, biography, children's, British topography especially West Country, gypsies, George Borrow; maps and prints.* LOC: Last shop at west end of High St. PARK: Nearby. TEL: 01404 41727; fax - 01404 44993; mobile - 07831 138011; e-mail - books@gyork. co.uk website - www.gyork.co.uk FAIRS: Monthly (Hotel Russell, Bloomsbury); ABA Chelsea; International Book, Olympia (June); PBFA Bath (April).

KINGSBRIDGE

Avon House Antiques/Hayward's Antiques
13 Church St. TQ7 1BT. (D.H. and M.S. Hayward). Est. 1969. Open 10-1 and 2-5. SIZE: Small. *STOCK: General antiques.* PARK: Limited. TEL: 01548 853718; e-mail - daymor@btopenworld.com SER: Valuations. FAIRS: Devon County.

LYDFORD, Nr. Okehampton

Skeaping Gallery
Townend House. EX20 4AR. Est. 1972. Open by appointment. *STOCK: Oils and watercolours.* TEL: 01822 820383; fax - same. VAT: Spec

LYNTON

Farthings
Churchill House. EX35 6NF. (Mrs L.R. Farthing and Miss I.J. Farthing). Est. 1996. Open 10-4.30 (4pm in winter) including Sun. SIZE: Small. *STOCK: Pictures, 19th-20th C, £50-£5,000; small furniture, Victorian and Edwardian, £50-£1,000; collectibles, 19th-20th C, £5-£2,000.* LOC: Opposite church. PARK: Easy. TEL: 01598 753744; home - 01598 753465; e-mail - jane@farthings1.freeserve.co.uk SER: Valuations; restorations; buys at auction.

Wood's Antiques
29A Lee Rd. EX35 6BS. (Pat and Brian Wood). Est. 1994. Open 9-5.30 incuding Sun. (Sun. 9-2 in winter). CL: Thurs. *STOCK: General antiques including small furniture, mainly Victorian, £10-£8,000.* PARK: Easy. TEL: 01598 752722.

MERTON, Nr. Okehampton

Barometer World Ltd
Quicksilver Barn. EX20 3DS. Est. 1979. Open Tues.-Sat. 9-5. SIZE: Medium. *STOCK: Mercurial wheel and stick barometers, 1780-1900, £650-£12,500; aneroid barometers, 1850-1930, £100-£1,500.* LOC: Between Hatherleigh and Torrington on A386. PARK: Easy. TEL: 01805 603443; fax - 01805 603344; e-mail - enquiries@barometerworld.co.uk website - www. barometerworld.co.uk SER: Valuations; restorations (barometers). VAT: Stan/Spec.

MODBURY, Nr. Ivybridge

Collectors Choice
27 Church St. PL21 0QR. (Allan Jenkins). Resident. Est. 1994. Open 10-5.30. CL: Some Wed. SIZE: Small. *STOCK: Clocks, £20-£1,000; valve radios, ceramics, fountain pens and small furniture, £5-£500; all 19th-20th C; garden urns and statues.* LOC: A379 between Plymouth and Kingsbridge. PARK: Easy. TEL: 01548 831111. SER: Valuations; restorations (clocks and fountain pens); repairs (clocks); cleaning.

Devonshire Fine Art
9 Church St. PL21 0QN. (David and Karen Smith). Est. 1991. Open 10-1 and 2-5.30. CL: Wed. pm. SIZE: Small. *STOCK: Paintings, drawings and watercolours, 18th-19th C, £75-£3,500; maps and charts, 16th-19th C, £20-£1,500; prints, 16th-19th C, £15-£1,000.* LOC: Central. PARK: Easy. TEL: 01548 830872; e-mail - info@ antique-fine-art.com website - www.antique-fine-art. com SER: Restorations (frames).

Wild Goose Antiques
34 Church St. PL21 0QR. (Mr and Mrs T.C. Freeman). Open 10-5.30. *STOCK: Old pine, country furniture, decorative items.* LOC: A379 between Plymouth and Kingsbridge. PARK: Nearby. TEL: 01548 830715. SER: Delivery. VAT: Stan.

MONKTON, Nr. Honiton

Pugh's Farm Antiques
Pugh's Farm. EX14 9QH. (G. Garner and C. Cherry). Est. 1974. Open 9-5.30. SIZE: Large. *STOCK: French furniture, armoires, farm tables, country furniture, neo-rustique, French and Italian wooden beds; Victorian and Edwardian furniture.* LOC: A30 2 miles from Honiton. PARK: Easy. TEL: 01404 42860; home - same; fax - 01404 47792; e-mail - sales@pughsantiques.com and sales@antiquebeds.com website - www.antiquebeds. com and www.pughsantiques.com SER: Importers and exporters. VAT: Stan.

NEWTON ABBOT

The Attic
9 Union St. TQ12 2JX. (G.W. Gillman). Est. 1976. CL: Mon. and Thurs., prior telephone call advisable. SIZE: Medium. *STOCK: General antiques, to £1,000.* LOC: Town centre. PARK: Easy. TEL: 01626 355124. SER: Valuations.

St Leonards Antiques & Craft Centre
Wolborough St. TQ12 1JQ. (Derick Wilson). Est. 1970.
Open 10-4.30 including Sun., Tues. 9.30-4.30. SIZE:
Large. STOCK: General antiques, 19th C, £5-£1,000.
LOC: At start of main road to Totnes. PARK: Adjacent
and opposite. TEL: 01626 335666; fax - same. SER:
Valuations; restorations; buys at auction (furniture,
decorative items). FAIRS: All major.

NEWTON ST. CYRES, Nr. Exeter

Gordon Hepworth Fine Art
Hayne Farm, Sand Down Lane. EX5 5DE. (C.G. and
I.M. Hepworth). Est. 1990. Open by appointment.
STOCK: Modern British paintings, post-war and
contemporary especially West Country - West Cornwall
and St. Ives School, £300-£5,000. LOC: A377, 3 miles
nw. of Exeter turn left by Newton St. Cyres village sign,
into Sand Down Lane, farm entrance on left, after last
white house, called Compass House. PARK: Easy. TEL:
01392 851351; home - same.

PAIGNTON

The Pocket Bookshop
159 Winner St. TQ3 3BP. (L. and A.R. Corrall). Est.
1985. Open Tues.-Sat. 10.30-5.30. SIZE: Small. STOCK:
Books, secondhand and out of print. LOC: Outskirts.
PARK: Nearby. TEL: 01803 529804.

PLYMOUTH

Annterior Antiques
22 Molesworth Rd., Millbridge. PL1 5LZ. (A. Tregenza
and R. Mascaro). Est. 1987. Open 9.30-5.30, Sat. 10-5 or
by appointment. CL: Tues. SIZE: Small. STOCK:
Stripped pine, 18th-19th C, £50-£3,000; some painted,
mahogany and decorative furniture; brass and iron beds,
19th C, £250-£3,000; decorative small items. LOC:
Follow signs to Torpoint Ferry from North Cross
roundabout, turn left at junction of Wilton St. and
Molesworth Rd. PARK: Easy. TEL: 01752 558277; fax -
01752 564471; e-mail - info@annterior.co.uk website -
www.annterior.co.uk SER: Buys at auction; finder. VAT:
Stan/Spec.

Barbican Antiques Centre
82-84 Vauxhall St., Barbican. PL4 0EX. (T. Cremer-
Price). Est. 1971. Open 9.30-5 including Sun. SIZE: 60+
dealers. STOCK: Silver and plate, art pottery, porcelain,
glass, jewellery, furniture, pictures, clocks, collectables.
LOC: Adjacent to the Old Quay. PARK: Own. TEL:
01752 201752; fax - 020 8546 1618; e-mail - tony@
silversales.co.uk

New Street Antique Centre
27 New St., The Barbican. PL1 2LS. (Turner Properties).
Est. 1980. Open 10-5. SIZE: Medium. STOCK: Clocks,
silver, jewellery, weapons, general antiques. PARK:
Nearby. TEL: 01752 661165. VAT: Stan/Spec.

Parade Antiques Market
27 New St., The Barbican. PL1 2NB. (John Cabello).
Est. 1982. Open 10-5 including Sun. SIZE: Medium.
STOCK: Collectables, 19th-20th C, £1-£1,000; militaria,
18th-20th C, £1-£7,000. PARK: Easy. TEL: 01752

221443; mobile - 07765 408063; e-mail -
paradeantiques@hotmail.com

Michael Wood Fine Art
The Gallery, 1 Southside Ope, The Barbican, PL1 2LL.
Est. 1967. Open Tues.-Sat. 10-5, other times by
appointment. SIZE: Medium. STOCK: Oils,
watercolours, original prints, sculptures, ceramics, art
glass and books, contemporary, RA exhibitors, modern
British, Newlyn, St Ives and Victorian, £50-£250,000.
LOC: Harbour front. PARK: Nearby. TEL: 01752
225533; mobiles - 07971 847722 and 07764 377899; e-
mail - michael@michaelwoodfineart.com SER:
Valuations; conservation, presentation and security
advice. VAT: Stan/Spec.

RACKENFORD, Nr. Tiverton

Guy Dennler Antiques & Interiors
The Old Rectory Stables, EX16 8ED. Open Mon.-Fri.
10-4, other times by appointment. STOCK: Fine 18th to
early 19th C English furniture and decorative objects.
TEL: 01884 881250; fax - 01884 881552; e-mail -
guydennler@btconnect.com

SEATON

Etcetera Antiques
12 Beer Rd. EX12 2PA. (Michael and Deborah Rymer).
Est. 1969. Open Mon., Wed. and Fri. 10-1 and 2-5, other
times by appointment. SIZE: Medium. STOCK: General
antique furniture and shipping goods. PARK: Own.
TEL: 01297 21965; mobile - 07780 840507; e-mail -
etceteraantiques@tiscali.co.uk website - www.etcetera
antiques.co.uk VAT: Margin/Global. Trade Only.

SIDMOUTH

Sidmouth Antiques & Collectors Centre
All Saints Rd. EX10 8ES. Open 9.30-4.30, Sun. 1-4
(Easter-end Oct. 10-5.30, Sun. 2-5). SIZE: 10 dealers.
STOCK: Wide range of antiques and collectables,
militaria, antiquarian and out of print books, postcards,
stamps, limited edition plates, pictures and prints, linen,
lace, dolls and teddy bears. PARK: Nearby. TEL: 01395
512588; website - www.sidmouth.ws FAIRS: DCAF
Westpoint, Exeter.

The Vintage Toy and Train Shop
Sidmouth Antiques and Collectors Centre, All Saints Rd.
EX10 8ES. (R.D.N. and J.W. Salisbury). Est. 1995. Open
10-5. STOCK: Hornby Gauge 0 and Dublo trains, Dinky
toys, Meccano and other die-cast and tinplate toys,
wooden jig-saw puzzles. LOC: Near main Post Office.
PARK: Limited and opposite. TEL: 01395 512588; home
- 01395 513399.

SOUTH BRENT

P.M. Pollak
Moorview, Plymouth Rd. TQ10 9HT. (Dr Patrick Pollak
and Mrs Jeanne Pollak). ABA. Est. 1973. Open by
appointment. SIZE: Small. STOCK: Antiquarian books
especially medicine and science; prints, some
instruments, £50-£5,000. LOC: On edge of village, near
London Inn. PARK: Own. TEL: 01364 73457; fax -

01364 649126; e-mail - patrick@rarevols.co.uk website - www.rarevols.co.uk SER: Valuations; buys at auction; catalogues issued, computer searches.

SOUTH MOLTON

The Dragon
77 South St. EX36 3AG. (Mrs J.E. Aker). Est. 1994. Open 9-5. SIZE: Small. *STOCK: Pine and country furniture, from 19th C; bric-a-brac, books and pictures.* LOC: Near town centre. PARK: Limited or nearby. TEL: 01769 572374; mobile - 07712 079818; e-mail - snap dragonantiques@hotmail.com website - www.snap dragondevon.co.uk SER: Restorations (furniture).

The Dragon and the Phoenix
24 East St. EX36 3DB. (Paul Williams and Caroline Bennett). Open 10-4. SIZE: Small. *STOCK: Antique Chinese and Tibetan furniture.* PARK: Easy. TEL: 01769 574104; e-mail - antiques@dragonphoenix.co.uk website - www.antiquechinesefurniture.co.uk

Snap Dragon
80 South St. EX36 3AG. (Mrs J.E. Aker and G. Harris). Est. 1994. Open 9-5. SIZE: Small. *STOCK: Pine and country furniture, kitchenalia and tools, architectural and garden artefacts.* LOC: Near town centre. PARK: Opposite. TEL: 01769 572374; mobile - 07712 079818; e-mail - snapdragonantiques@hotmail.com website - www.snapdragondevon.co.uk SER: Restorations (furniture).

TEDBURN ST MARY, Nr. Exeter

A. E. Wakeman & Sons Ltd
Newhouse Farm. EX6 6AL. (A.P., G.M. and A.A. Wakeman). Est. 1967. Open Mon.-Fri. 9-5.30 or by appointment. SIZE: Large. *STOCK: Mahogany, walnut and rosewood furniture, mainly 19th C, £200-£5,000; some 18th C mahogany and oak, £300-£5,000.* LOC: 6 miles from Exeter. PARK: Easy. TEL: 01647 61254; home/fax - same; mobile - 07836 284765; e-mail - a.e.wakeman@btopenworld.com FAIRS: Newark; Ardingly. VAT: Stan/Spec. *Trade Only.*

TEIGNMOUTH

Extence Antiques
2 Wellington St. TQ14 8HH. (T.E. and L.E. Extence). Est. 1928. Open Tues.-Sat. 10-5. SIZE: Medium. *STOCK: Jewellery, silver, objets d'art.* PARK: Limited. TEL: 01626 773353. VAT: Stan/Spec.

Timepiece
125 Bitton Park Rd. TQ14 9BZ. (Clive and Willow Pople). Est. 1988. Open Tues.-Sat. 9.30-5.30, Sat. 9.30-6. SIZE: Medium. *STOCK: Country furniture, clocks, 19th C, £25-£2,000; collectables, 19th-20th C, £1-£100.* LOC: On A379 next to Bitton Park. TEL: 01626 770275.

TOPSHAM, Nr. Exeter

Bounty Antiques
76 Fore St. EX3 0HQ. (John Harding and John Purves). MADA. Est. 2000. Open 9.30-5. SIZE: Small. *STOCK: Marine, aviation, transport items, to £500; clocks, cameras, ceramics, tools, glass, ephemera, collectables,* *steam engines, to £500.* LOC: Next to Lloyds TSB. PARK: Nearby. TEL: 01392 875007; home - 01395 266077/232397. SER: Valuations. FAIRS: Westpoint; Exeter; Newark.

Domani
48 Fore St. EX3 0HY. (Jonathan Cull and Caro Brewster). Est. 1978. Open Wed.-Sat. 10-5.30 or by appointment. SIZE: Small. *STOCK: English and Continental small decorative furniture, 18th-19th C; contemporary arts.* LOC: Near quay. PARK: Nearby. TEL: 01392 877899; mobile - 07771 657522; e-mail - shop@domani-topsham.com website - www.domani-topsham.com

Mere Antiques   LAPADA
13 Fore St. EX3 0HF. (Marilyn Reed). Resident. Est. 1986. Open 9.30-5.30, Sat. 10-5.30, Sun. by appointment. SIZE: 3 rooms. *STOCK: English porcelain, 18th-19th C, £50-£10,000; furniture, 17th-20th C, £200-£5,000; decorative items and silver; 19th C and contemporary paintings.* PARK: Easy and nearby. TEL: 01392 874224; e-mail - info@mereantiques.com website - www.mereantiques.com FAIRS: NEC; LAPADA. VAT: Spec.

Topsham Quay Antiques Centre
The Quay. EX3 0JA. (Stonewall Ltd). Est. 1993. Open seven days 10-5. SIZE: Large. *STOCK: Furniture, 18th-19th C, £100-£3,000+; ceramics and tools, 18th-20th C, £5-£1,000+; collectables, 20th C, £5-£200; silver and plate, 18th-20th C, £10-£1,500+; textiles, 18th-20th C, £5-£500.* LOC: 4 miles from Exeter, M5 junction 30. PARK: Easy. TEL: 01392 874006; fax - same; e-mail - office@quayantiques.com website - www.quayantiques.com SER: Valuations. FAIRS: Local.

TORQUAY

The Old Cop Shop
Castle Lane. TQ1 3AN. (L. Rolfe). Est. 1971. Open 9-5. SIZE: Medium. *STOCK: General antiques and shipping items.* PARK: Easy. TEL: 01803 294484; fax - 01803 316620. SER: Valuations. FAIRS: Local.

The Schuster Gallery
P O Box 139. TQ1 2XX. (T.E. Schuster). ABA. PBFA. Est. 1973. Open by appointment. *STOCK: Antique prints, maps, medieval manuscripts, fine and rare colour plate books, atlases; children's illustrated books including Beatrix Potter, Kate Greenaway and Alice in Wonderland and related items.* TEL: 01803 211422; fax - 01803 211290. FAIRS: Olympia (June); Penman Chelsea (Sept). VAT: Stan.

Toby's Architectural Antiques
Torre Station, Newton Rd. TQ2 2DD. (Paul and John Norrish). SALVO. Est. 1985. Open 10.30-5 seven days. SIZE: Large. *STOCK: Furniture, £15-£3,000; pianos, fireplaces, lighting, collectables, 19th-20th C, £5-£2,000.* LOC: Main Newton Abbot road, 1 mile from sea front. PARK: Easy. TEL: 01803 212222; fax - 01803 200523; e-mail - paul4tobys@yahoo.co.uk website - www.tobysreclamation.co.uk SER: Valuations; delivery (UK). VAT: Spec.

STARTING TO COLLECT ANTIQUE FURNITURE
John Andrews

This concise yet wide-ranging survey of collectable antique furniture, illustrated throughout in full colour, guides the new collector through almost three centuries of Western Furniture with clarity and authority. Invaluable as a reference tool, it offers collectors the means to identify key features of a wide variety of pieces, ranging from the Gothic and Renaissance period to Art Nouveau, and the beginning of the twentieth century. The book is structured chronologically by century and, within each time period, by country. Existing collectors will find all titles in the series act as a handy and portable reference, and beginners will welcome a reliable, accessible starting point from which their interests can develop.

Specifications: 192pp., Colour throughout
9½ x 7¾in./240 x 195mm. **£12.50 (hardback)**

TOTNES

The Antique Dining Room
93 High St. TQ9 5PB. (P. Gillo). Est. 1983. Open Tues.-Sat. 10-5. SIZE: Small. *STOCK: Victorian and Edwardian furniture especially Victorian wind-out tables.* PARK: Nearby. TEL: 01803 847800. SER: Restorations.

Bogan House Antiques
43-45 High St. TQ9 5NP. (Chris Mitchell). Est. 1977. Open Fri. 10-1 and 2-4, Sat. 10.30-1 and 2-4.30 and some Tues., otherwise by appointment. SIZE: Small. *STOCK: Silver flatware, £5-£200; metalware, Victorian and Delft tiles, £5-£40; Japanese woodblock prints, £20-£400.* LOC: Above arch, under Butterwalk on right. PARK: Nearby. TEL: 01803 862075; home - 01803 865386; mobile - 07989 416518.

Collards Books
4 Castle St. TQ9 5NU. (B. Collard). Est. 1970. Open 10.30-5, restricted opening in winter. *STOCK: Antiquarian and secondhand books.* LOC: Opposite castle. PARK: Nearby. TEL: Home - 01548 550246.

The Exchange
76 High St. TQ9 5SN. (J. and M. Caley). Est. 1997. Open 10-5 (winter), 10-5.30 (summer, June-Sept). SIZE: Small. *STOCK: Antiquarian and secondhand books, papers and ephemera; general antiques and curios.* LOC: Town centre. PARK: Nearby. TEL: 01803 866836; home - 01803 868598; e-mail - bookworm1700@yahoo.co.uk SER: Valuations (books).

Fine Pine Antiques
Woodland Rd., Harbertonford. TQ9 7SX. (Nick and Linda Gildersleve). Est. 1973. Open 9.30-5, Sun. 11-4. SIZE: Large. *STOCK: Stripped pine and country furniture.* LOC: A381. PARK: Easy. TEL: 01803 732465; home - 01548 821360; e-mail - info@fine-pine-antiques.co.uk website - www.fine-pine-antiques.co.uk SER: Restorations; stripping.

Pandora's Box
51/2 High St. TQ9 5NN. (Sarah Mimpriss and Mark and June Anderson). Est. 1989. Open Thurs., Fri. and Sat. 10.30-4.30. SIZE: Small. *STOCK: Etchings, small boxes, small Victorian furniture and trunks; porcelain - Derby,* Worcester, Minton, Limoges, Dresden, Belleek and Royal Copenhagen. PARK: Nearby. TEL: 01803 867799; home - 01803 762112.

Pedlars Pack Books
4 The Plains. TQ9 5DR. (Andy Collins and Brenda Greysmith). Est. 1991. Open 10-5. SIZE: Medium. *STOCK: Books, £5-500.* LOC: Near river. PARK: Nearby. TEL: 01803 866423; e-mail - info@thepedlarspack.co.uk SER: Valuations.

UFFCULME, Nr. Cullompton

English Country Antiques
The Old Brewery, High St. EX15 3AB. (M.C. Mead). Est. 1984. Open 9-5 by appointment/telephone call. SIZE: Large. *STOCK: Country and decorating antiques - furniture - pine including painted, fruitwoods, oak and mahogany, bamboo, bentwood, leather and upholstered; metalware including lighting, brass, copper and iron, gardenalia, architectural; china and glass, mainly 19th-20th C; textiles, leatherwork, bric-a-brac, basketware, wooden items, model yachts, pictures and paintings, mirrors.* LOC: Village centre. PARK: Own. TEL: 01884 841770; fax - same; mobile - 07768 328433; e-mail - mike@englishcountryantiques.co.uk website - www.englishcountryantiques.co.uk SER: Delivery and export by arrangement. FAIRS: NEC.

WHIMPLE, Nr. Exeter

Anthony James Antiques
Brook Cottage, The Square. EX5 2SL. Open by appointment. *STOCK: 17th-19th C furniture and works of art.* LOC: A30 between Exeter and Honiton. PARK: Easy. TEL: 01404 822146. SER: Valuations. VAT: Spec.

YEALMPTON, Nr. Plymouth

Carnegie Paintings & Clocks
15 Fore St. PL9 2JN. (Chris Carnegie). Open Thurs.-Sat. 10-5.30 or by appointment. *STOCK: Clocks, barometers, paintings and small furniture.* PARK: Easy. TEL: 01752 881170; mobile - 07970 968337; website - www.paintingsandclocks.com SER: Restorations (paintings, clocks and barometers).

DORSET

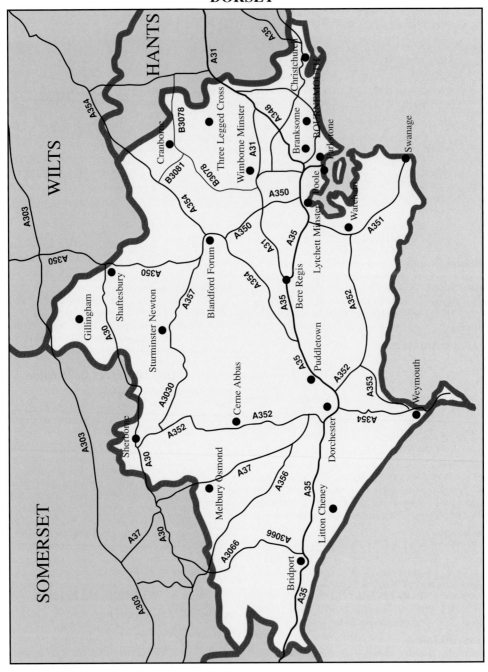

Dealers and Shops in Dorset					
Bere Regis	2	Dorchester	7	Shaftesbury	3
Blandford Forum	1	Gillingham	1	Sherborne	14
Bournemouth	17	Litton Cheney	1	Sturminster Newton	1
Brankstone	3	Lytchett Minster	1	Swanage	2
Bridport	4	Melbury Osmond	1	Three Legged Cross	1
Cerne Abbas	1	Parkstone	1	Wareham	2
Christchurch	4	Poole	4	Weymouth	3
Cranborne	1	Puddletown	1	Wimborne Minster	3

Stocks & Chairs
ANTIQUES

ONE OF THE BEST ANTIQUE SHOPS IN THE SOUTH OF ENGLAND

19th Century marquetry rosewood centre table circa 1840.

Victorian burr walnut stretcher table circa 1870.

George III period mahogany open bookcase circa 1790.

Georgian style hand dyed leather wing back chair made by Stocks & Chairs circa 2004.

visit our website at www.stocksandchairsantiques.com

10/11 Bank Chambers, Penn Hill Avenue, Parkstone, Poole, Dorset BH14 9NB
& associated warehouse of 4,000 square feet
Tel: 01202 718618 Fax: 01202 708666 Mobile: 07970 010512

BERE REGIS, Nr. Wareham

Dorset Reclamation
Cow Drove. BH20 7JZ. (Tessa Pearce). SALVO. Open 8-5, Sat. 9-4. SIZE: Large. *STOCK: Decorative architectural and garden antiques, hard landscaping materials, fireplaces and bathrooms.* TEL: 01929 472200; fax - 01929 472292; e-mail - info@dorset reclamation.co.uk website - www.dorsetreclamation. co.uk SER: Delivery; restorations.

Legg of Dorchester
The Old Mill Antiques, West St. BH20 7HS. (W. and H. Legg & Sons). Est. 1930. Open 9-5 or by appointment. SIZE: Large. *STOCK: General antiques, Regency and decorative furniture, stripped pine.* LOC: On Bournemouth road. PARK: Easy. TEL: 01929 472051; e-mail - jerry@leggofdorchester.co.uk website - www.leggofdorchester.co.uk SER: Restorations (furniture). VAT: Spec.

BLANDFORD FORUM

Milton Antiques
Market Place. DT11 7DX. Est. 1993. Open 9-5, Sat. 9-4. SIZE: Medium. *STOCK: Furniture, 18th-19th C, £50-£5,000; decorative items, 18th-20th C, £5-£200.* LOC: Opposite church, adjacent to town museum. PARK: Easy. TEL: 01258 450100. SER: Valuations; restorations including polishing.

BOURNEMOUTH

Altamiradeco
14 Seamoor Rd. BH4 9AR. (A. Benarroch). Est. 1994. Open Tues.-Sat. 10-5.30. SIZE: Medium. *STOCK: Art Deco - bronzes including Chiparus, Preiss, Colinet and Lorenz; furniture, glass, ceramics.* PARK: Loading only and nearby. TEL: 01202 766444; mobile - 07885 778342; e-mail - gallery@altamiradeco.com website - www.altamiradeco.com SER: Valuations.

Antiques and Furnishings
339 Charminster Rd. BH8 9QR. (P. Neath). Open 10-5.30. *STOCK: Furniture, brass, copper, china, textiles and decorative objects.* TEL: 01202 527976.

Boscombe Militaria
86 Palmerston Rd., Boscombe. BH1 4HU. (E.A. Browne). Est. 1981. Open 10-1 and 2-5, prior telephone call advisable. CL: Wed. SIZE: Small. *STOCK: German militaria, £10-£800; British and Japanese militaria, £5-£500, all 1914-1918 and 1939-1945.* LOC: Just off Christchurch Rd. TEL: 01202 304250; fax - 01202 733696. FAIRS: Farnham; Beltring; major South of England Arms.

Boscombe Models and Collectors Shop
802c Christchurch Rd., Boscombe. BH7 6DD. (Sylvia Hart). Open 10-5. CL: Wed. *STOCK: Collectors' toys, 19th-20th C, £1-£1,000.* TEL: 01202 398884.

Chorley-Burdett Antiques
828-830 Christchurch Rd., Pokesdown. BH7 6DF. (Raymond Burdett). Open 9-5.30. SIZE: Large. *STOCK: Furniture, pine furniture including reclaimed, late 19th to early 20th C, £50-£1,000.* LOC: Corner of Warwick Rd. PARK: Easy. TEL: 01202 423363; fax - same. VAT: Stan/Spec.

Lionel Geneen Ltd   LAPADA
811 Christchurch Rd., Boscombe. BH7 6AP. Est. 1902. Open 9-5, Sat. 9-12, (closed lunchtimes), other times by appointment. SIZE: Large. *STOCK: English, Continental and Oriental furniture, china and works of art including some bronzes, enamels, ivories, jades, all mainly 19th C, Art Nouveau and Art Deco; specialising in tea, dinner and dessert services.* LOC: Main road through Boscombe. PARK: Own. TEL: 01202 422961; home - 01202 520417; mobile - 07770 596781. SER: Valuations. VAT: Stan/Spec.

H.L.B. Antiques
139 Barrack Rd. BH23 2AW. (H.L. Blechman). Est. 1969. SIZE: Large. *STOCK: Collectable items.* PARK: Easy. TEL: 01202 429252/482388.

Hampshire Gallery
18 Lansdowne Rd. BH1 1SD. Est. 1971. Open by appointment. *STOCK: Paintings and watercolours, 17th to early 20th C.* PARK: Easy. TEL: 01202 551211. SER: Valuations. VAT: Spec.

Libra Antiques
916 Christchurch Rd. BH7 6DL. (Andrew Morrish). Est. 1997. Open 10-5, Wed. 10-1. SIZE: Medium. *STOCK: Silver and plate, objects, furniture, metalware, china and glass.* LOC: Near Pokesdown station. PARK: Opposite. TEL: 01202 427615; mobile - 07836 680928. VAT: Stan.

G.B. Mussenden and Son Antiques, Jewellery and Silver
24 Seamoor Rd., Westbourne. BH4 9AR. BJA. Est. 1948. Open 9-4.30. CL: Wed. SIZE: Medium. *STOCK: Antiques, jewellery, silver.* LOC: Central Westbourne, corner of R.L. Stevenson Ave. PARK: Easy. TEL: 01202 764462. SER: Valuations. VAT: Stan/Global/Spec.

R.E. Porter
2-6 Post Office Rd. BH1 1BA. (G.R. Broadway). Est. 1934. Open 9.30-5. SIZE: Medium. *STOCK: Silver including early antique spoons, Georgian, £20-£5,000; jewellery, pot lids, Baxter and Le Blond prints, clocks including second-hand.* Not Stocked: Furniture, arms, armour, carpets. LOC: Walking from the square, take the Old Christchurch Rd., then the first turning on the left. PARK: Opposite Post Office Rd. TEL: 01202 554289. SER: Valuations. VAT: Stan/Spec.

Sainsburys of Bournemouth Ltd   LAPADA
23-25 Abbott Rd. BH9 1EU. Est. 1918. Open 8-1 and 2-6, appointment advisable. CL: Sat. *STOCK: Furniture especially bookcases and dining tables, 18th C, to £20,000; fine Chippendale to Regency replica chairs; replica giltwood.* PARK: Own. TEL: 01202 529271; home - 01202 763616; fax - 01202 510028; e-mail - sales @sainsburys-antiques.com website - www. sainsburys-antiques.com SER: Custom-made furniture from recycled Georgian wood including exceptionally large pieces. VAT: Stan/Spec.

Sandy's Antiques
790-792 Christchurch Rd., Boscombe. BH7 6DD. BDADA. Open 10-5.30. SIZE: 2 large shops +

warehouse. *STOCK: Victorian, Edwardian and shipping goods.* TEL: 01202 301190; fax - same; evenings - 01202 304955; mobile - 07836 367384. VAT: Stan/Spec/Export.

Sterling Coins and Medals

2 Somerset Rd., Boscombe. BH7 6JH. (W.V. Henstridge). Est. 1969. Open 9.30-4. CL: Wed. pm. SIZE: Small. *STOCK: Coins, medals, militaria, World War II German items.* LOC: Next to 806 Christchurch Rd. TEL: 01202 423881. SER: Valuations. VAT: Stan.

M.C. Taylor

995 Christchurch Rd., Boscombe East. BH7 6BB. (Mark Taylor). MAPH, CMBHI. Est. 1982. Open Tues.-Fri. 10-3.30, Sat. 9-1. SIZE: Small. *STOCK: Clocks, barometers, music boxes and turret clocks, £500-£20,000.* LOC: Opposite St. James' School and Kings Park entrance. PARK: Easy. TEL: 01202 429718; website - www.taylorclocks.com SER: Valuations; restorations. VAT: Stan/Spec.

Tregoning Antiques

57 Westover Rd. BH1 2BZ. (Barry Papworth). NAG. Est. 1969. Open Mon.-Sat. SIZE: Small. *STOCK: Fine jewellery, including masonic, 18th-19th C, £50-£24,000; silver, 18th-19th C, £10-£5,000; collectables, 19th C, £10-£200.* LOC: At junction with Bath Rd., opposite Royal Bath Hotel. PARK: Easy. TEL: 01202 312100; fax - same; mobiles - 07813 820624 and 07901 994497; e-mail - jewellers57@hotmail.com SER: Valuations; restorations (jewellery and silver). VAT: Stan/Margin.

Vintage Clobber

920 Christchurch Rd., Boscombe. BH7 6DL. (R.A. Mason). Open 10-5. *STOCK: Clothing and fabrics, from Victorian.* TEL: 01202 429794; website - www. vintageclobber.com

BRANKSOME

Allen's (Branksome) Ltd

447/449 Poole Rd. BH12 1DH. (P.J. D'Ardenne). Est. 1948. Open 9-5.30. SIZE: Large. *STOCK: Furniture.* TEL: 01202 763724; fax - 01202 763724; e-mail - allens@branksome447.fsnet.co.uk VAT: Stan.

Branksome Antiques

370 Poole Rd. BH12 1AW. (B.A. Neal). Est. 1971. Open 10-5. CL: Wed. and Sat. SIZE: Medium. *STOCK: Scientific and marine items, furniture and general small items.* PARK: Easy. TEL: 01202 763324; home - 01202 679932. SER: Buys at auction (as stock). VAT: Stan/Spec.

Derek J. Burgess - Horologist

368 Poole Rd. BH12 1AW. Est. 1980. Open 9.30-3 and some Sat. *STOCK: Clocks, watches, furniture and smalls.* LOC: Opposite Tesco's, near Westbourne. PARK: Street and forecourt. TEL: 01202 751111. SER: Restorations (clocks and watches of all periods); parts made.

BRIDPORT

Batten's Jewellers

26 South St. DT6 3NQ. (R. and G. Batten). BWCG. Est.

1974. Open 9.30-5. *STOCK: Jewellery, silver and clocks.* LOC: Town centre. PARK: Easy and nearby. TEL: 01308 456910. SER: Valuations; repairs.

Benchmark Antiques

Chancery Lane, DT6 3PZ. (Megan Standage). BAFRA. Est. 1992. Open by appointment. SIZE: Small. *STOCK: English furniture and related items, 1700-1880, £100-£15,000.* LOC: Off East St. PARK: Easy. TEL: 01308 420941; home - 01308 428200. e-mail - hohobird@ netscape.net SER: Valuations; restorations; buys at auction. FAIRS: NEC; Olympia.

Bridport Old Books

11 South St. DT6 3NR. PBFA. Est. 1998. Open 10-5. SIZE: Small. *STOCK: Antiquarian and secondhand books and prints.* LOC: Town centre. PARK: Nearby. TEL: 01308 425689. FAIRS: PBFA; Oxford; Bath; Lyme Regis: Glasgow; Edinburgh; Aberdeen; H&D, Royal National, London.

Ann Quested Antiques

59 East St. DT6 3LB. Est. 1980. Open Wed.-Sat. 10.30-5. SIZE: Large. *STOCK: Furniture - pine, oak, country; brass lighting and fenders; fire irons and coal buckets.* PARK: Opposite. TEL: 01308 422576; home - 01308 421551.

CERNE ABBAS

Cerne Antiques

DT2 7LA. (I. Pulliblank). Est. 1972. Open 10-1 and 2-5, Sun. 2-5. CL: Mon. and Fri. SIZE: Medium. *STOCK: Silver, porcelain, furniture including unusual items, mainly 19th C, £1-£400.* LOC: A352. PARK: Easy. TEL: 01300 341490; home - same.

CHRISTCHURCH

J.L. Arditti

20 Twynham Ave. BH23 1QU. Est. 1964. Open by appointment. SIZE: Medium. *STOCK: Oriental carpets and rugs, 18th to early 20th C, £500-£20,000.* LOC: From town centre take road towards Hurn airport, left turn. PARK: Twynham Avenue. TEL: 01202 485414/481500; e-mail - mike@arditti.freeserve.co.uk website - www.arditti.freeserve.co.uk SER: Valuations; restorations; cleaning (Persian rugs). VAT: Stan/Spec.

Christchurch Carpets

55/57 Bargates. BH23 1QE. (J. Sheppard). Est. 1963. Open 9-5.30. SIZE: Large. *STOCK: Persian carpets and rugs, 19th-20th C, £100-£5,000.* LOC: Main road. PARK: Adjacent. TEL: 01202 482712. SER: Valuations; repairs; cleaning. VAT: Stan/Spec.

Hamptons

12 Purewell. BH23 1EP. (G. Hampton). Open 10-6. CL: Sat. am. SIZE: Large. *STOCK: Furniture, 18th-19th C; general antiques, clocks, china, instruments, metalware, oil paintings, Chinese and Persian carpets and rugs.* PARK: Easy. TEL: 01202 484000.

Tudor House Antiques   LAPADA

420 Lymington Rd., Highcliffe, BH23 5HE. (P. Knight and D. Burton). Est. 1940. Open 10-5. CL: Mon. and Wed. SIZE: Medium. *STOCK: General antiques.* LOC:

Main road, A337. PARK: Easy. TEL: 01425 280440. VAT: Stan/Spec.

CRANBORNE, Nr. Wimborne

Tower Antiques
The Square. BH21 5PR. (P.W. Kear and P. White). Est. 1975. Open 8.30-5.30. CL: Sat. *STOCK: Georgian and Victorian furniture.* TEL: 01725 517552.

DORCHESTER

Box of Porcelain Ltd
51d Icen Way. DT1 1EW. (R.J. and Mrs. S.Y. Lunn). Est. 1984. Open 10-5. CL: Thurs. *STOCK: Porcelain including Worcester, Doulton, Spode, Moorcroft, Coalport, Beswick, Lladro.* LOC: Close town centre, near Dinosaur Museum. TEL: 01305 267110; fax - 01305 263201; e-mail - rlunn@boxofporcelain.com website - www.boxofporcelain.com

Colliton Antique Centre
Colliton St. DT1 1XH. Est. 1983. Open 9-4, Sun. by appointment. SIZE: 14 dealers. *STOCK: 18th-20th C furniture, £25-£5,000; brass, bric-a-brac, pictures, china, pine, clocks, jewellery and silver, toys.* LOC: Rear of County Museum. PARK: Easy. TEL: 01305 269398; e-mail - anthonyphilips@tiscali.co.uk SER: Restorations (metalware).

De Danann Antique Centre
25/27 London Rd. DT1 1NF. (J. Burton). Est. 1993. Open 9.30-5, Sun. 10-4. SIZE: Large - 20 dealers. *STOCK: 17th-20th C furniture, bedsteads, ceramics, rugs, clocks, pine, kitchenalia, brass and copper, collectables.* PARK: Easy. TEL: 01305 250066; fax - 01305 250113; e-mail - dedanann@supanet.com website - www.dedanann.co.uk SER: Restorations (furniture including French polishing, cabinet making).

Finesse Fine Art
Empool Cottage, West Knighton. DT2 8PE. (Tony Wraight). Open strictly by appointment. *STOCK: Pre-war motoring accessories - metal mascots and Lalique glassware, including mascots, fine bronzes, automobilia, picnic hampers, £1,000-£50,000.* TEL: 01305 854286; fax - 01305 852888; mobile - 07973 886937.

Michael Legg Antiques
8 Church St. DT1 1JN. (E.M.J. Legg). Open 9-5.30 or any time by appointment. SIZE: Medium. *STOCK: 17th-19th C furniture, clocks, porcelain, pictures, silver, glass.* TEL: 01305 264596. SER: Lectures on the Arts. VAT: Stan/Spec.

Legg of Dorchester
Regency House, 51 High East St. DT1 1HU. (W. and H. Legg & Sons). Est. 1930. Open 10.15-4.30. *STOCK: General antiques, Regency and decorative furniture, stripped pine.* TEL: 01305 264964; e-mail - jerry@leggofdorchester.co.uk website - www.leggofdorchester.co.uk SER: Restorations (furniture). VAT: Stan/Spec.

Words Etcetera
2 Cornhill. DT1 1BA. (Julian Nangle). PBFA. Est. 1974. Open 10-5. SIZE: Medium. *STOCK: Antiquarian and quality second-hand books and prints; remainders on all*

subjects. LOC: Close to museum. TEL: 01305 251919. SER: Buys at auction (books). FAIRS: PBFA London (June).

GILLINGHAM

Talisman
The Old Brewery, Wyke. SP8 4NW. (Kenneth Bolaw). Est. 1980. Open 9-5, Sat. 10-4. SIZE: Large. *STOCK: Unusual and decorative items, garden furniture, architectural fittings, 18th-19th C; English and Continental furniture.* PARK: Easy. TEL: 01747 824423/824222; fax - 01747 823544; e-mail - shop@talismanantiques.com website - www.talismanantiques.com FAIRS: Olympia (June); Palm Beach, Florida. VAT: Stan/Spec.

LITTON CHENEY, Nr. Dorchester

F. Whillock
Court Farm. DT2 9AU. Est. 1979. Open by appointment. *STOCK: Maps and prints.* LOC: Village centre. PARK: Easy. TEL: 01308 482457. SER: Framing.

LYTCHETT MINSTER, Nr. Poole

Old Button Shop Antiques
BH16 6JF. (Thelma Johns). Est. 1970. Open Tues.-Fri. 2-5, Sat 11-1. *STOCK: Small antiques, curios, glass, lace, antique and Dorset buttons.* LOC: 3 miles north-west of Poole. PARK: Adjacent. TEL: 01202 622169; e-mail - info@oldbuttonshop.fsnet.co.uk

MELBURY OSMOND, Nr. Dorchester

Hardy Country
Meadow View. DT2 0NA. (Steven and Caroline Groves). Est. 1980. Open by appointment. SIZE: Large. *STOCK: Georgian, Victorian, Edwardian pine and country furniture, £40-£2,500.* LOC: Off A37. PARK: Easy. TEL: 01935 83440; website - www.hardycountry.com

PARKSTONE, Nr. Poole

Dorset Coin Company
193 Ashley Rd. BH14 9DL. (E.J. and C.P. Parsons). BNTA, IBNS. Est. 1977. Open 9.30-4, Sat. 9.30-1. *STOCK: Coins, 19th-20th C, £1-£50; banknotes, 20th C, £3-£50.* LOC: Main road through Upper Parkstone. PARK: Easy. TEL: 01202 739606; fax - 01202 739230. SER: Valuations. FAIRS: BNTA London. VAT: Stan/Global/Exempt

POOLE

G.D. and S.T. Antiques
(G.D. and S.T. Brown). Open by appointment. *STOCK: General antiques.* TEL: 01202 676340.

Great Expectations
115 Penn Hill Ave., Lower Parkstone. BH14 9LY. (A. Carter). Est. 1999. Open Wed.-Sat. 10.30-4.30. SIZE: Small. *STOCK: Furniture, mahogany, pine, burr walnut, oak and French, from 1800, to £1,250; English pottery - Doulton, Moorcroft, Maling, Crown Devon; English watercolours 1870-1930.* PARK: Nearby. TEL: 01202 740645. SER: Restorations (furniture including upholstery).

Laburnum Antiques
Lonbourne House, 250 Bournemouth Rd. BH14 9HZ. (Doreen Mills). Est. 1998. Open Tues.-Sat. 10-5.30. *STOCK: Fine Georgian and Victorian furniture and artifacts.* LOC: A35. PARK: Forecourt. TEL: 01202 746222; fax - 01202 736777; e-mail - enquiries@laburnumantiques.co.uk SER: Restorations (furniture); soft furnishings. FAIRS: Wilton House.

Stocks and Chairs
10-11 Bank Chambers, Penn Hill Ave. BH14 9NB. (Mrs C.E. Holding-Parsons). Est. 1992. Open Tues.-Sat. 10.30-5 and by appointment. SIZE: Large and trade warehouse. *STOCK: Furniture, 18th to early 20th C, mainly £500-£5,000; specialist in hand-dyed leather chairs and settees.* PARK: Easy. TEL: 01202 718618; mobile - 07970 010512; e-mail - hp@stocksandchairsantiques.com website - www.stocksandchairsantiques.com SER: Restorations (including cabinet work, polishing and upholstery).

PUDDLETOWN, Nr. Dorchester
Antique Map and Bookshop
32 High St. DT2 8RU. (C.D. and H.M. Proctor). ABA. PBFA. Est. 1976. Open 9-5. *STOCK: Antiquarian and secondhand books, maps, prints and engravings.* PARK: Easy. TEL: 01305 848633; e-mail - proctor@puddletown.demon.co.uk website - www.puddletownbookshop.co.uk SER: Postal; catalogues.

SHAFTESBURY
Cartouche
32 Salisbury St. SP7 8EJ. (Mrs S. Comer). Est. 1999. Open 10-6. CL: Wed. SIZE: Medium. *STOCK: Painted cupboards and wardrobes, French upholstered and iron beds, French leather armchairs, mirrors, garden furniture, sofas and armchairs, mainly 1850-1950, £75-£750.* LOC: Continuation of High St., towards Salisbury. TEL: 01747 858700; home - 01749 860472; mobile - 07798 692633; e-mail - cartouche@tiscali.co.uk website - www.cartouchedecorative.co.uk

Mr. Punch's Antique Market
33 Bell St. SP7 8AE. Est. 1994. Open 10-5.30. CL: Mon. SIZE: Large. *STOCK: Wide variety of general antiques, fine art and collectables. Also Punch and Judy collection.* LOC: On corner with Muston's Lane. PARK: Easy 100 yards. TEL: 01747 855775; fax - same; e-mail - admin@mrpunches.co.uk website - www.mrpunches.co.uk SER: Valuations; restorations; repairs (ceramics); delivery.

Shaston Antiques
14 and 16A Bell St. SP7 8AE. (J. D. Hine). Resident. Est. 1996. Open 9-5. CL: Mon. SIZE: Medium. *STOCK: Furniture, 18th-19th C, £300-£5,000.* LOC: From town centre, turn right opposite Grosvenor Hotel into Bell St. TEL: 01747 850405; home - same; website - www.shaston-antiques.co.uk SER: Restorations (furniture).

SHERBORNE
Abbas Antiques
at Sherborne World of Antiques, Long St. DT9 3BS.

(T.F.J. Jeans). Est. 1991. Open 9.30-5. *STOCK: Small collectables and furniture, 18th-19th C.* PARK: Opposite. TEL: 01935 816451. SER: Restorations.

Antiques of Sherborne   LAPADA
1 The Green. DT9 3HZ. (C. and L. Greenslade). CINOA. SAADA. Est. 1988. Open 10-5. *STOCK: 18th-19th C furniture, dining tables and chairs, sofas and armchairs.* LOC: Top of Cheap St., just off A30. PARK: Nearby. TEL: 01935 816549; mobile - 07971 019173; e-mail - clive@antiquesofsherborne.fsnet.co.uk SER: Delivery (overseas); re-upholstery. VAT: Spec.

Chapter House Books
Trendle St. DT9 3NT. (Claire Porter and Tudor Books Ltd). Est. 1988. Open 10-5. SIZE: Large. *STOCK: Out-of-print, secondhand and antiquarian books, to £400.* LOC: Next to Almshouse and Abbey. TEL: 01935 816262; e-mail - chapterhousebooks@tiscali.com website - www.chapterhouse-books.co.uk SER: Valuations; restorations (bookbinding and repair); search.

Dodge and Son   LAPADA
28-33 Cheap St. DT9 3PU. (S. Dodge). Est. 1918. Open 9-5.30, Sun. by appointment. SIZE: Large. *STOCK: Furniture, including dining, all periods.* PARK: At rear. TEL: 01935 815151; e-mail - sales@dodgesherborne.co.uk SER: Restorations; furniture makers; worldwide delivery. VAT: Stan/Spec.

Greystoke Antiques
Swan Yard, Off Cheap St. DT9 3AX. (F.L. and N.E. Butcher). Est. 1970. Open 10-4.30. *STOCK: Silver, Georgian, Victorian and later; early 19th C English blue transfer printed pottery.* LOC: Off main street. PARK: Adjacent to Swan Yard or outside shop. TEL: 01935 812833. VAT: Stan/Margin/Global.

Macintosh Antiques
The Courtyard, Newland. DT9 3JG. (Patrick Macintosh). Est. 1985. Open 10-5. SIZE: Large. *STOCK: 17th-20th C country house furniture and accessories including Arts & Craft movement, £100-£10,000.* LOC: Opposite Somerfield's. PARK: Own. TEL: 01935 815827; home - 01935 815584; mobile - 07768 606811; e-mail - patrick@macintoshantiques.fsnet.co.uk SER: Valuations; restorations. FAIRS: Olympia (Feb., June, Nov); Little Chelsea; Bath. VAT: Spec.

Phoenix Antiques
21 Cheap St. DT9 3PU. (Sally and Neil Brent Jones). Est. 1998. Open 9.30-5.30. SIZE: Medium. *STOCK: Furniture, 17th-20th C; lighting, mirrors, furnishings, decorative and unusual items.* LOC: Town centre. PARK: Easy. TEL: 01935 812788; e-mail - phoenixantique@aol.com SER: Valuations; restorations. VAT: Spec.

Piers Pisani Antiques Ltd
The Courtyard, Newland. DT9 3JG. Est. 1987. Open 10-5. SIZE: Medium. *STOCK: Furniture including sofas and armchairs, dining tables and sets of chairs, English and French country house and reproduction; decorative items.* LOC: Next to Sherborne House. PARK: Own. TEL: 01935 815209; fax - same; mobile - 07973 373753; e-mail - pp@pierspisani.com website - www. pierspisani.

com SER: Valuations; restorations (upholstery, chairs copied, cabinet-making). VAT: Spec.

Renaissance
South St. DT9 3NG. (Malcolm Heygate Browne). Open 10-5. SIZE: Large. *STOCK: 18th-19th C furniture, pottery and porcelain.* LOC: Off Cheap St. towards station. PARK: Easy. TEL: 01935 815487; e-mail - antiquemalcolm@aol.com SER: Valuations; restorations. VAT: Stan/Spec.

Sherborne World of Antiques
Long St. DT9 3BS. (T.F.J. Jeans). Open Tues.-Sat. 9.30-5. SIZE: 40+ dealers. *STOCK: Fine arts, painting, furniture, rugs, objets d'art, jewellery, ceramics, glass.* LOC: From A30 via Greenhill. PARK: Easy - opposite. TEL: 01935 816451; fax - 01935 816240; e-mail - info@sherborneworldantiques.co.uk SER: Restorations; upholstery; delivery.

The Swan Gallery
51 Cheap St. DT9 3AX. (S. and Mrs K. Lamb). Est. 1977. Open 9.30-5, Wed. 9.30-1. SIZE: Large. *STOCK: Watercolours, 18th to early 20th C; oil paintings, antiquarian maps and prints.* PARK: Easy, at rear. TEL: 01935 814465; fax - 01308 868195; website - www. swangallery.co.uk SER: Valuations; restorations (paintings, watercolours and prints); framing. FAIRS: Watercolours and Drawings, Park Lane, London. VAT: Stan/Spec.

Timecraft Clocks
Unit 2, 24 Cheap St. DT9 3PX. (Gordon M. Smith). MBHI. Est. 1993. Open Tues.-Sat. by appointment or

chance. SIZE: Small. *STOCK: Clocks, 18th-20th C, £200-£5,000; barometers, 18th-20th C, £80-£2,000; telephones, 20th C, £80-£250.* PARK: Easy. TEL: 01935 817771. SER: Restorations (clock and barometer movements, cases and dials).

Wessex Antiques
6 Cheap St. DT9 3PX. (Mrs Frances Bryant). Est. 1986. Open Tues.-Sat. 10-5 or by appointment. SIZE: Small. *STOCK: Staffordshire figures, 1800-1900, £100-£3,000; English drinking glasses, 1680-1820, £50-£2,000; small English furniture, 1500-1850, £300-£6,000; Oriental rugs, 1800-1950, £400-£6,000.* PARK: Loading and nearby. TEL: 01935 816816; fax - same; website - www. wessexantiques.com SER: Valuations; restorations (ceramics).

Henry Willis (Antique Silver)
38 Cheap St. DT9 3PX. Est. 1974. Open 10-5. SIZE: Small. *STOCK: Silver, 16th-20th C, £15-£15,000.* LOC: Town centre, just off A30. PARK: Nearby. TEL: 01935 816828. SER: Valuations; restorations (silver); buys at auction (silver). FAIRS: Olympia (June). VAT: Stan/Spec.

STURMINSTER NEWTON

Tom Tribe and Son Ltd
Bridge St. DT10 1BZ. CMBHI. Resident. Open Tues.-Fri. 9-1 and 2-5, Sat. 9-1 or by appointment. *STOCK: Longcase and mantel clocks, barometers.* PARK: At side of shop. TEL: 01258 472311. VAT: Stan/Spec.

SWANAGE

Georgian Gems Antique Jewellers
28 High St. BH19 2NU. (Brian Barker). NAG. Est. 1971. Open 7 days 9.30-1 and 2.30-5 or by appointment. Jan.-Mar. closed Thurs. and Sun. SIZE: Small. *STOCK: Jewellery, £5-£2,000; silver, £5-£500; both from 1700.* LOC: Town centre. PARK: Nearby. TEL: 01929 424697; freephone - 0800 4710 242; fax - 01929 426830; mobile - 07932 794742. SER: Valuations; repairs; gem testing; special search.

Reference Works Ltd.
at The Last Resort, 9 Commercial Rd. BH19 1DF. (B. and J.E. Lamb). Est. 1984. Open 10-4, Sat. 10-1. *STOCK: Reference books and catalogues on ceramics, all subjects, new and out-of-print; small range of ceramics, 18th-20th C.* TEL: 01929 424423; fax - 01929 422597; e-mail - sales@referenceworks.co.uk website - www.referenceworks.co.uk SER: Monthly list of books available; two newsletters each year; ceramic research and consultancy.

THREE LEGGED CROSS, Nr. Wimborne

Minter Reclamation
Lower Common Lane. BH21 6RX. (Michael Minter). Est. 1995. Open 8-6, Sat. 9-5. SIZE: Medium. *STOCK: General reclamation materials, from floorboards to bathrooms.* LOC: B3072. PARK: Easy. TEL: 01202 828873; fax - 01202 828813; mobile - 07889 731851; e-mail - info@minterreclamation.co.uk website - www.minterreclamation.co.uk

WAREHAM

Heirlooms Antique Jewellers and Silversmiths
21 South St. BH20 4LR. (M. and Mrs G. Young). FGA, DGA, RJDip., FNAG. Est. 1986. Open 9.30-5. CL: Wed. SIZE: Medium. *STOCK: Jewellery, £30-£1,000; silver, £20-£500; both Georgian to Edwardian.* LOC: On main thoroughfare. PARK: At rear. TEL: 01929 554207. SER: Valuations; restorations; repairs; gem testing; watch and clock repairs.

Yesterdays
13A North St. BH20 4AB. Est. 1995. Open 9.30-4.30, Wed. 9.30-1.30. *STOCK: Pottery and porcelain - Dennis, Poole, blue and white, Beswick, Isle of Wight, Wade, Carlton and Spode, Jonathan Harris; okra glass.* LOC: Town centre opposite Post Office. PARK: Nearby. TEL: 01929 550505; home - 01929 556381. SER: Valuations; buys at auction. FAIRS: Shepton Mallet, Exeter; Winchester. VAT: Stan.

WEYMOUTH

Books Afloat
66 Park St. DT4 7DE. (J. Ritchie). Est. 1983. Open 9.30-5.30. SIZE: 2 floors. *STOCK: Rare and secondhand books especially nautical; maritime ephemera, liner and naval memorabilia, ship models, paintings, prints.* LOC: Near rail station. PARK: Easy. TEL: 01305 779774.

The Nautical Antiques Centre
3 Cove Passage, off Hope Sq. DT4 8TR. (D.C. Warwick). Est. 1989. Open 10-1 and 2-5 prior telephone call advisable, Sat., Sun. and Mon. by appointment. SIZE: Medium. *STOCK: Exclusively original nautical, including sextants, logs, clocks, flags, blocks, old sails, old rope, bells, ship models, telescopes, ship badges, portholes and memorabilia, also restaurant/pub decorative items, 19th-20th C, £5-£2,000.* LOC: Opposite Brewers Quay, adjacent harbour. PARK: Nearby. TEL: 01305 777838; home - 01305 783180; mobile - 07833 707247; e-mail - info@nauticalantiques.org and ships@nautical-antiques-centre.co.uk website - www.nautical-antiques-centre.co.uk and www.nauticalantiques.org SER: Buys at auction (nautical items).

The Treasure Chest
29 East St. DT4 8BN. (P. Barrett). Open 10-1 and 2.30-5. CL: Wed. pm. *STOCK: Maps, prints, coins, medals; army, RN and RAF badges.* PARK: Next door. TEL: 01305 772757. SER: Lost medals replaced; medal mounting - full size or miniature, brooches and new ribbons.

WIMBORNE MINSTER

J.B. Antiques
10A West Row. BH21 1LA. (J. Beckett). Est. 1978. Open 10-4, Fri. and Sat. 9.30-4. SIZE: Small. *STOCK: Copper, £5-£360; brass, £1-£350; furniture, £30-£1,200; all 18th-20th C.* LOC: 2 mins. from Sq. PARK: Nearby. TEL: Home - 01202 882522; mobile - 07957 863169; e-mail - johnjlbeckett@aol.com SER: Valuations; restorations (metalware). FAIRS: Hinchingbrooke House, Huntingdon.

Minster Books
12 Corn Market. BH21 1HW. (John and Angela Child). Est. 1970. Open 10-5. SIZE: Medium. *STOCK: Books, £5-£100.* LOC: In road at side of Minster. PARK: King St. TEL: 01202 883355; e-mail - minsterbooks@aol.com website - www.minsterbooks.com SER: Valuations; restorations (book binding).

Portique
42 East St. BH21 1DX. (N. and E. Harkness). NAG. Est. 1968. Open Tues.- Fri. 9.30-4.30, Sat. 9.30-4. *STOCK: Silver and jewellery; modern Derby china and clocks.* LOC: A31 westbound, Leigh Rd., turn right at small roundabout, take 1st left into Park Lane, over bridge, premises on left. TEL: 01202 884282; e-mail - portiquethejewellers@hotmail.com SER: Repairs; restorations (silver and jewellery); valuations. VAT: Stan/Spec.

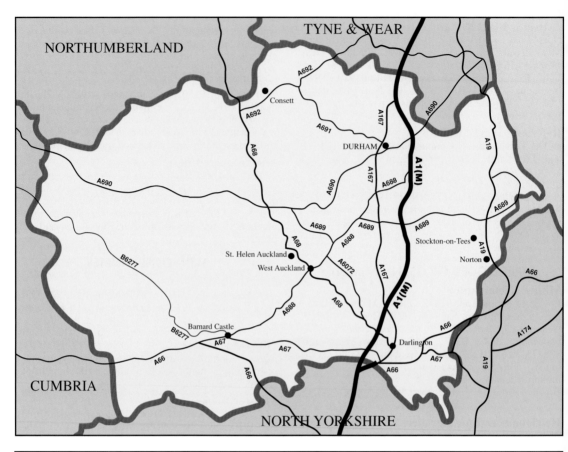

Dealers and Shops in Durham			Darlington	1	St. Helen Auckland	1
			Durham	1	Stockton-on-Tees	2
Barnard Castle	5	Consett	1	Norton	1	West Auckland	1

BARNARD CASTLE

Edward Barrington-Doulby
23 The Bank. DL12 8PH. (M.A. Venus). Est. 1990. Open Wed.-Sat. 11-5.30, Sun.12-5.30. SIZE: Warehouse + shops. *STOCK: 18th-20th C unusual tools, implements, kitchenalia, eccentricities, cast iron, pottery, pictures, £1-£1,000; 17th-20th C pine, oak, mahogany, rustic and provincial furniture; period costume.* PARK: Easy. TEL: 01833 630500; home - 01325 264339; website - www.barnard-castle.co.uk/antiques/edwardbarrington-doulby SER: Delivery; prop hire.

The Collector
Douglas House, The Bank. DL12 8PH. (Robert A. Jordan). Est. 1970. Open Sat. 10-5 or by appointment. SIZE: Medium. *STOCK: Early oak, walnut and country furniture with complementary objects, decorative interior fittings and Eastern rugs.* PARK: Own. TEL: 01833 637783; fax - same; e-mail - TheCollector@onetel.com website - www.barnard-castle.co.uk/antiques SER: Restorations (especially metalwork, early furniture and interiors).

James Hardy Antiques Ltd
12 The Bank. DL12 8PQ. (Alan Hardy). Est. 1993. Open 10-5. CL: Thurs. SIZE: Medium. *STOCK: Furniture, 18th C to Edwardian, £500-£25,000; silver and porcelain, 18th-20th C, £25-£5,000.* PARK: Nearby. TEL: 01833 695135; fax - same; mobile - 07710 162003; e-mail - alan@jameshardyantiques.co.uk website - www.jameshardyantiques.co.uk SER: Restorations (silver and furniture); buys at auction (furniture). FAIRS: Harrogate; NEC. VAT: Spec.

Robson's Antiques
36 The Bank. DL12 8PN. (Anne, David and Dale Robson). Est. 1977. Open 10-5.30, Sun. 1.30-5.30. SIZE: Medium. *STOCK: Smalls including cutlery and canteens; silver perfume bottles, cruets, photograph frames; Victorian and north east glass; pottery including Maling, Carltonware and Losol; Durham and patchwork quilts; Georgian, Victorian and Edwardian fireplaces, ranges, marble and wooden surrounds, inserts.* LOC: Below Market Cross. PARK: Easy. TEL: 01833 690157/638700; mobile - 07977 146584; e-mail - dale. hunter.robson@virgin.net website - www.robsonantiques.co.uk SER: Valuations; restorations (fireplace fitting and stripping). FAIRS: Newark; Birmingham Glass; Manchester Armatage Centre Textile. VAT: Global.

Joan, David and Richard White Antiques
Neville House, 10 The Bank. DL12 8PQ. Est. 1975. Open Tues., Thurs., Fri. and Sat. 11-5. *STOCK: Georgian, Victorian, export and pine furniture, decorative items.* LOC: 100yds. from Market Cross. PARK: Front of shop. TEL: 01833 638329; home - 01325 374303. VAT: Stan/Spec.

CONSETT

Harry Raine Antiques
Kelvinside House, Villa Real Rd. DH8 6BL. Appointment advisable. *STOCK: General antiques.* TEL: 01207 503935.

DARLINGTON

Robin Finnegan (Jeweller)
39 Cornmill Centre. DL1 1LS. NAG. Est. 1974. Open 9-5.30. SIZE: Medium. *STOCK: Jewellery, general antiques, coins, medals, military blazer badges and ties, £1-£10,000.* LOC: Town centre. PARK: Easy. TEL: 01325 489820; fax - 01325 357674; website - www.militarybadges.co.uk SER: Valuations; repairs (jewellery); mounting (medals). VAT: Stan.

DURHAM

Old & Gold
87B Elvet Bridge. DH1 3AG. (Pam Tracey). Est. 1989. SIZE: Small. *STOCK: Jewellery and china, 19th C, £50-£100.* LOC: Next to Marriott Royal County Hotel. PARK: Multi-storey nearby. TEL: 0191 386 0728; mobile - 07831 362252. SER: Valuations; restorations (jewellery). FAIRS: Newark.

NORTON, Nr. Stockton-on-Tees

Paraphernalia
12 Harland Place, High St. TS20 1AA. (Rena Thomas). Est. 1982. Open 9.30-5. SIZE: Large. *STOCK: Mainly 19th C mahogany furniture, to £1,000.* LOC: Next to Red Lion public house. PARK: Easy. TEL: 01642 535940; website - www.antiques2you.com VAT: Stan/Spec.

ST. HELEN AUCKLAND

Something Different
34a Maude Terrace. DL14 9BD. (P. Reeves and M. Holmes). Est. 1968. Open 9.30-5.30, Sun. 10-4.30.

SIZE: Large. *STOCK: Furniture, clocks, decorative items, 19th-20th C.* PARK: Easy. TEL: 01388 664366; e-mail - y.reeves@btinternet.com SER: Repairs (clocks); delivery (UK and Europe).

STOCKTON-ON-TEES

Margaret Bedi Antiques & Fine Art
Est. 1976. Open by appointment. *STOCK: English period furniture, 1720-1920; oils and watercolours, 19th-20th C.* PARK: Easy. TEL: 01642 583247; mobile - 07860 577637. FAIRS: Harrogate; North of England. VAT: Stan/Spec.

T.B. and R. Jordan (Fine Paintings)   LAPADA
Aslak, Eaglescliffe. TS16 0QN. (Tom and Rosamund Jordan). Est. 1974. Open by appointment. *STOCK: Oil paintings and watercolours especially Staithes group, 19th-20th C, £200-£25,000.* LOC: Village centre. PARK: Easy. TEL: 01642 782599; fax - same; e-mail - info@tbrj.co.uk website - www.tbrj.co.uk SER: Commissions. FAIRS: Harrogate. VAT: Spec.

WEST AUCKLAND

Eden House Antiques
10 Staindrop Rd. DL14 9JX. (C.W. Metcalfe). Est. 1978. Open daily including Sun. SIZE: Small. *STOCK: Clocks, furniture, 18th-20th C; collectables, bric-a-brac, oak and mahogany reproductions, Continental furniture.* LOC: A68, approx. 7 miles west of A1M. PARK: Easy. TEL: 01388 833013; e-mail - cchrismetcalfe@aol.com SER: Valuations; restorations; clock repairs.

ESSEX

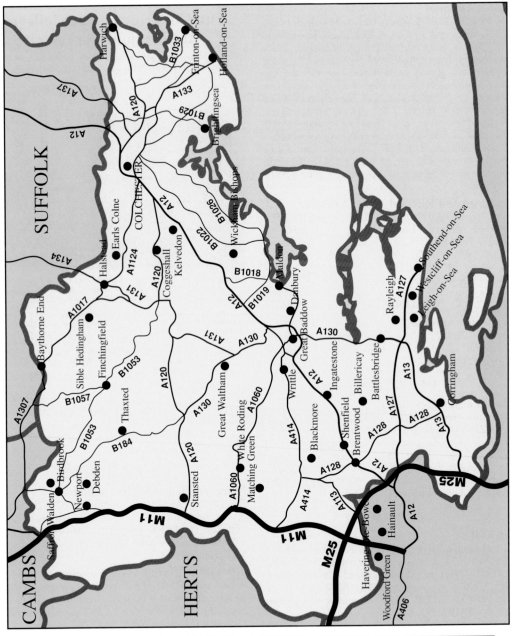

Dealers and Shops in Essex

Battlesbridge	1	Danbury	1	Havering-atte-Bower	1	Shenfield	1
Baythorne End	1	Debden	1	Holland-on-sea	1	Sible Hedingham	3
Billericay	1	Earls Colne	1	Ingatestone	1	Southend-on-Sea	1
Birdbrook	1	Finchingfield	1	Kelvedon	2	Stansted	1
Blackmore	1	Frinton-on-Sea	2	Leigh-on-Sea	5	Thaxted	1
Brentwood	2	Great Baddow	1	Maldon	2	Westcliff-on-Sea	2
Brightlingsea	1	Great Waltham	1	Matching Green	1	White Roding	1
Coggeshall	2	Hainault	1	Newport	1	Wickham Bishops	1
Colchester	4	Halstead	2	Rayleigh	1	Woodford Green	1
Corringham	1	Harwich	2	Saffron Walden	5	Writtle	1

BATTLESBRIDGE

Battlesbridge Antique Centre
SS11 7RF. (Jim and Fraser Gallie and Joseph Pettitt). Est. 1967. Open 7 days 10-5. SIZE: Over 80 units within adjacent premises (see below). *STOCK: Wide range from large furniture to jewellery, all periods with specialist dealers for most items.* LOC: A130, mid-way between Chelmsford and Southend. Junction 29, M25, east on A127 to A130, then north for 3 miles. By rail: Liverpool St.-Southend-on-Sea, change at Wickford for Battlesbridge. PARK: Own. TEL: Fax - 01268 561700; e-mail - info@battlesbridge.com website - www. battlesbridge.com SER: Restorations (furniture); container facilities; delivery (UK and overseas).

> **Cromwell House Antique Centre**
> TEL: Management : John Gallie - 01268 762612; ground floor dealers - 01268 762612; first floor dealers - 01268 734030.

> **Haybarn and Bridgebarn Antique Centres**
> (J.P. Pettitt). TEL: 01268 763500/735884.

> **Muggeridge Farm Buildings**
> (Jim Gallie). TEL: 01268 769000.

> **The Old Granary Antique and Craft Centre**
> (Jim Gallie). TEL: Management - Paul Elliott - 01268 769000; showrooms - 01268 764197.

BAYTHORNE END

Swan Antiques
The Swan. CO9 4AF. (Mr and Mrs K. Mercado). Est. 1983. Open 9.30-6 including Sun. SIZE: Medium. *STOCK: Furniture, 18th-19th C and some Edwardian, £50-£2,000; porcelain, 19th C, £5-£1,000; small silver and collectables, 19th-20th C, £5-£500.* LOC: A1017 (formerly A604) junction with A1092 to Clare and Long Melford. PARK: Easy. TEL: 01440 785306; home - same. SER: Valuations. FAIRS: Newark; Ardingly.

BILLERICAY

Junior Antique Exporters
Longcroft Farm, Dowsetts Lane, Ramsden Heath. CM11 1JN. (Vic Hall). Open 7 days by appointment. *STOCK: Oak, mahogany and walnut furniture including longcase clocks; reproduction stained glass and bars.* LOC: 1 hour from Heathrow and Gatwick airports, 45 mins. from London. TEL: 01268 711777; fax - 01268 711666; e-mail - info@juniorantiques.com website - www.junior antiques.com SER: Packing and shipping.

BIRDBROOK, Nr. Halstead

I. Westrope
The Elms. CO9 4AB. Est. 1958. Open 9-5, Sat. 10-1 or by appointment. *STOCK: Furniture, china, dolls house furniture, garden ornaments including birdbaths, fountains, statues, animals.* LOC: A1017. TEL: 01440 780034; evenings - 01440 730594.

BLACKMORE, Nr. Ingatestone

Megarry's and Forever Summer
Jericho Cottage, The Duckpond Green. CM4 0RR. (Peter

and Judi Wood). EADA. Est. 1986. Open Wed.-Sun. 11-5 or by appointment. SIZE: Medium. *STOCK: Furniture, mainly 18th-19th C, some 20th C, £60-£3,500; ceramics, glass, treen and metalware, 19th-20th C, £5-£200; small silver and plate, jewellery and collectables, 19th-20th C, £5-£200; pine, 19th to early 20th C, £75-£1,000.* LOC: From A12, A414 or A128 into Blackmore, turn at war memorial, premises behind Bull garden on the village green. PARK: Own. TEL: 01277 821031. SER: Valuations.

BRENTWOOD

Brandler Galleries
1 Coptfold Rd. CM14 4BM. (J. Brandler). FATG. Est. 1973. Open 10-5.30, Sun. by appointment. CL: Mon. SIZE: Medium. *STOCK: British pictures, 20th C, £100-£100,000; original artwork for books and comics.* LOC: Near Post Office. PARK: Own at rear. TEL: 01277 222269 (24 hrs); e-mail - john@brandler-galleries.com website - www.noddy-art.com and www.brandler-galleries.com and www.thomas-art.com SER: Valuations (photographs); restorations (watercolour and oil cleaning, relining); framing; buys at auction (pictures); 2-3 free catalogues annually. VAT: Spec.

Neil Graham Gallery
11 Ingrave Rd. CM15 8AP. (Mr and Mrs Neil Graham Firkins). Est. 1977. CL: Mon. SIZE: Large. *STOCK: 19th to early 20th C watercolours, oils and prints, £50-£1,000; Victorian and Edwardian occasional furniture, £100-£1,500; silver, pottery and porcelain, 19th-20th C, £25-£500.* LOC: Near junction of Wilson's Corner, town centre. PARK: Easy and High St. TEL: 01277 215383; fax - same; e-mail - info@neilgrahamgallery.com website - www.neilgrahamgallery.com SER: Valuations; restorations (paintings); buys at auction. VAT: Stan/Spec.

BRIGHTLINGSEA

The Shipwreck
Brightlingsea's Antiques & Collectables Centre, 22e Marshes Yard, Victoria Place. CO7 0BX. (P. Keel). Est. 1994. Open 10-5 including Sun. SIZE: Large. *STOCK: General antiques and collectables including postcards and books, £10-£300+.* LOC: Between High St. and police station. PARK: Free. TEL: 01206 307307; e-mail - info@theshipwreck.net website - www.theshipwreck.net

COGGESHALL

English Rose Antiques
7 Church St. CO6 1TU. (Mark and Iryna Barrett). Est. 1983. Open 10-5.30, Sun. 10.30-5.30. CL: Wed. *STOCK: English and Continental pine including dressers, chests, tables and wardrobes, 18th-19th C, £50-£2,000; fruitwood, ash and elm country furniture and kitchenalia.* LOC: Town centre. PARK: Loading or 50 yds. TEL: 01376 562683; home - same; fax - 01376 563450; mobile - 07770 880790; e-mail - englishroseantiques@hotmail.com website - www.englishroseantiques.co.uk SER: Valuations; restorations; stripping; repairs; finishing. FAIRS: Newark, Swinderby, Ardingly.

Partners in Pine
63/65 West St. CO6 1NS. (W.T. and P.A. Newton). Resident.

BARS & ANTIQUES
Est. 1975
(Only 45 minutes from London. 1 hour from Heathrow/Gatwick Airports)

We hold a large selection of Bars of all sizes

Suitable for homes or commercial use

We can make "Bespoke" to your requirements

Size: 6ft 6in. wide x 7ft 6in. high

Full Packing and Shipping Service to anywhere in the world

Size: 10ft wide x 7ft 6in. high

We hold a large selection of quality antiques for you to view

Grandfather Clocks, Linen Presses, Chests on Chests, Sideboards and much more

STAINED GLASS WINDOWS
Made the traditional way and depicting scenes of 'Old London'. Hundreds to choose from

Good quality oak, mahogany and walnut furniture always in stock

For further information contact JUNIOR ANTIQUES (VIC HALL)
Tel: 01268 711777 Fax: 01268 711666
Email: info@juniorantiques.com Open 7 Days a Week by Appointment

Est. 1982. Open 10-5. CL: Wed. SIZE: Small. *STOCK: Victorian stripped pine.* PARK: Easy. TEL: 01376 561972; fax - same; e-mail - newton65@supanet.com SER: Restorations; bespoke furniture from reclaimed timber.

COLCHESTER

S. Bond and Son
Olivers Orchard, Olivers Lane. CO2 0HH. (R. Bond). Open by appointment. SIZE: Large. *STOCK: Furniture and pictures.* TEL: 01206 331175; mobile - 07710 823800. SER: Valuations; restorations. VAT: Stan/Spec. *Trade only.*

Elizabeth Cannon Antiques
85 Crouch St. CO3 3EZ. (Elizabeth and Brian Cooksey). Est. 1978. Open 10-5. *STOCK: General antiques including jewellery, silver, glass, porcelain and furniture.* PARK: Easy. TEL: 01206 575817. VAT: Spec.

Castle Bookshop
40 Osborne St. CO2 7DB. (J.R. Green). PBFA. Est. 1947. Open 9-5. SIZE: 2 floors. *STOCK: Antiquarian and secondhand books, maps & prints.* PARK: Private - telephone for instructions. TEL: 01206 577520; fax - same. SER: Book search. FAIRS: Some PBFA.

E. J. Markham & Son Ltd
122/3 Priory St. CO1 2PX. (Mrs S. Campbell). NAG, NPA. Est. 1836. Open 8.30-5.30. SIZE: Medium. *STOCK: Jewellery, 19th-20th C, £25-£8,000; porcelain, 18th-20th C, £25-£2,000; furniture, 19th-20th C, £100-£1,500.* LOC: Opposite St Botolph's priory ruins. PARK: NCP Priory St. TEL: 01206 572646. SER: Valuations; restorations (porcelain). VAT: Stan.

CORRINGHAM, Nr. Stanford-le-Hope

Bush House
Church Rd. SS17 9AP. (F. Stephens). Est. 1976. Open by appointment. *STOCK: Staffordshire animals, portrait figures, 1770-1901, £50-£5,000.* LOC: Opposite church. PARK: Own. TEL: 01375 673463; home - same; fax - same; e-mail - francis_j_stephens@hotmail.com website - www. antiquestaffordshire.mysite.wanadoo-members.co.uk and www.staffordshire.mysite.wanadoo-members.co.uk FAIRS: NEC, Birmingham; Kensington Ceramics; Glass. VAT: Spec.

DANBURY

Danbury Antiques
Eves Corner (by the Village Green). CM3 4QF. (Mrs Pam Southgate). EADA. Est. 1983. Open Tues.-Sat. 10-5, Wed. 10-1. SIZE: Medium. *STOCK: Jewellery and silver, ceramics, metalware, furniture, 18th to early 20th C, £5-£3,000.* LOC: M25, A12, A414, on left after 3 miles. PARK: Easy. TEL: 01245 223035. SER: Valuations; restorations (jewellery, upholstery, furniture). VAT: Stan/Spec.

DEBDEN, Nr. Saffron Walden

Debden Antiques
Elder St. CB11 3JY. (Robert Tetlow). EADA. Est. 1995. Open 10-5.30, Sun. and Bank Holidays 11-4. SIZE: Large. *STOCK: Furniture, 17th-19th C, £100-£10,000; pictures, £50-£5,000, jewellery, silver, glass, porcelain, £5-£500, garden furniture, architectural, £50-£1,000; all 19th C.*

LOC: Follow signs to Carver Barracks. PARK: Own. TEL: 01799 543007; fax - 01799 542482; e-mail - info@debden-antiques.co.uk website - www.debden-antiques.co.uk SER: Valuations; restorations. VAT: Stan/Spec.

EARLS COLNE

Totteridge Gallery
74 High St. CO6 2QX. (Janet Clarke). Est. 1985. Open 5 days and by appointment. SIZE: Medium. *STOCK: Oil paintings, £1,000-£25,000; watercolours, £300-£10,000; both 18th-20th C. Limited edition Russell Flint prints, 20th C, £500-£3,000.* PARK: Easy. TEL: 01787 220075; website - www.totteridgegallery.com SER: Valuations; restorations; frame repairs. FAIRS: NEC. VAT: Stan/Spec.

FINCHINGFIELD

Finchingfield Antiques Centre
The Green. CM7 4JX. (Peter Curry). Est. 1992. Open 10-5 including Sun. SIZE: Large - 40 dealers. *STOCK: Wide range of general antiques, clocks and collectables, from 17th C oak to Art Deco.* LOC: From M11, A120 to Gt. Dunmow, then B1057. PARK: Easy. TEL: 01371 810258; fax - 01371 810625; website - www.antiquecentreworldwide.com SER: Shipping arranged.

FRINTON-ON-SEA

Dickens Curios
151 Connaught Ave. CO13 9AH. (Miss M. Wilsher). Est. 1970. Open 10-1 and 2-5.30, Sat. 10-1 and 2-5. CL: Wed. pm. SIZE: Small. *STOCK: Postcards and ephemera, Victorian and later items, £5-£200.* LOC: From Frinton Station quarter of mile down Connaught Ave. PARK: Easy. TEL: 01255 674134.

Number 24 of Frinton
24 Connaught Ave. CO13 9PR. (Chris Pereira). Est. 1993. Open 10-5, Sun. 2-4. CL: Wed. SIZE: Medium. *STOCK: Art Deco and Victorian prints, general antiques, furniture and collectables.* PARK: Easy. TEL: 01255 670505. website - www.artdecoclassics.co.uk

GREAT BADDOW

Baddow Antique Centre
The Bringey, Church St. CM2 7JW. EADA. Est. 1969. Open 10-5, Sun. 11-5. SIZE: 22 dealers. *STOCK: 18th-20th C furniture, porcelain, silver, paintings, Victorian brass bedsteads, shipping goods.* LOC: Near A12/A130 inter-change. PARK: Easy. TEL: 01245 476159. SER: Restorations; upholstery; framing; stripping (pine).

GREAT WALTHAM, Nr. Chelmsford

The Stores
CM3 1DE. (E. Saunders). Est. 1974. Open Wed.-Sat. 10-5, Sun. 11-4. SIZE: Large. *STOCK: Period pine and country furniture.* LOC: Village centre. PARK: At rear. TEL: 01245 360277; home - 01245 360260.

HAINAULT, Nr. Ilford

Gallerie Antiques
62-70 Fowler Rd. IG6 3XE. (M. Johnson). EADA. Est.

1998. Open 10-5.30, Sun. 11-5. SIZE: 80 dealers. *STOCK: Wide range of general antiques including 18th-20th C furniture, £500-£1,000; china, porcelain, glass, linen and lace, books, collectables.* LOC: A12 Eastern Ave. At Moby Dick public house, turn towards Hainault Forest Country Park. PARK: Easy. TEL: 020 8501 2229; fax - 020 8501 2209. SER: Valuations; restorations (furniture, paintings, ceramics, clocks, re-caning); buys at auction. VAT: Stan/Spec.

HALSTEAD

Antique Bed Shop
Napier House, Head St. CO9 2BT. (Veronica McGregor). Est. 1977. Open Thurs.-Sat., other times by appointment. SIZE: Large. *STOCK: Antique wooden bedsteads - 19th C mahogany, rosewood, chestnut, oak, bergere and painted, £1,295-£3,500.* Not Stocked: Brass, iron or pine beds. LOC: On A131 to Sudbury. PARK: Own. TEL: 01787 477346; fax - 01787 478757. SER: Free UK delivery. VAT: Spec.

Townsford Mill Antiques Centre
The Causeway. CO9 1ET. (I. Newman). Open 10-5, Sun. and Bank Holidays 11-5. SIZE: 70 dealers. *STOCK: General antiques and collectables.* LOC: On A131 Braintree/Sudbury road. TEL: 01787 474451.

HARWICH

Peter J. Hadley Bookseller
21 Market St. CO12 3DX. ABA. ILAB. Est. 1982. Open Fri. and Sat. 10-5, Sun. 1-4, other times by chance or appointment. SIZE: Small. *STOCK: Books - architecture, literature, art reference and illustrated.* PARK: Easy. TEL: 01255 551667; e-mail - books@ hadley.co.uk website - www.hadley.co.uk

Harwich Antiques Centre
19 Kings Quay St. CO12 3ER. (Karin Scholz). Est. 1997. Open 10-5, Sun. and Bank Holidays 1-5. CL: Mon. SIZE: Medium. *STOCK: Furniture, porcelain, china, glass, silverware, jewellery, 19th C, £10-£2,000; collectables, 19th-20th C; decorative items.* LOC: Between the Pier and Electric Palace Cinema. PARK: Nearby. TEL: 01255 554719; e-mail - hac@antiques-access-agency.com website - www.antiques-access-agency.com

HAVERING-ATTE-BOWER

Robert Bush Antiques
(Robert and Eleanor Bush). Open by appointment. SIZE: Large warehouse. *STOCK: Quality furniture, all styles, including oak, barley twist and carved; Art Deco and retro; leather and crocodile luggage and effects.* LOC: 10 mins. from M25, 40 mins. from Stansted Airport and central London. TEL: Mobile - 07836 236911; e-mail - bush.antiques@virgin.net website - www.robertbush antiques.co.uk SER: Shipping arranged. FAIRS: Ardingly.

HOLLAND-ON-SEA

Bookworm
100 King's Ave. CO15 5EP. (Andrew M'Garry-Durrant). Est. 1995. Open 9-2.30, Sat. 9-4. SIZE: Small. *STOCK: Modern fiction, first editions, 1930-2001, £10-£500; rare and out-of-print, military history, motor and general*

sport, transport, nautical, £5-£100. LOC: On junction with Holland Rd. PARK: Easy. TEL: 01255 815984; fax - same; e-mail - question@bookwormshop.com website - www.bookwormshop.com SER: Valuations.

INGATESTONE

Kendons
122a High St. CM4 0BA. (Mrs Hilary A. O'Connor). Est. 1978. Open Thurs., Fri. and Sat. 10.30-5. *STOCK: Jewellery, silver, china, small furniture, clocks, medals, coins, stamps.* LOC: 10 mins. from A12. PARK: Easy. TEL: 01277 353625; mobile - 07778 392699. SER: Valuations. FAIRS: Sandown Park; Alexandra Palace.

KELVEDON, Nr. Colchester

Colton Antiques
Station Rd. CO5 9NP. (Gary Colton). Est. 1993. Open 8-5, Sun. by appointment. SIZE: Medium. *STOCK: Furniture, 17th to early 20th C, £300-£15,000; decorative items.* PARK: Own. TEL: 01376 571504; mobile - 07973 797098. SER: Restorations (furniture). VAT: Stan/Spec.

Chris L. Papworth
2 High St. CO5 9AG. (Kelvedon Clocks Ltd). MBHI. BWCG. Est. 1970. Open 9-5, Sat 10-5. CL: Fri. SIZE: Medium. *STOCK: Clocks, watches (including pocket) and barometers.* LOC: Near mainline rail station. PARK: Own. TEL: 01376 573434; home - same; mobile - 07802 615461; e-mail - chrislpapworth@btconnect.com website - www.chrislpapworth.co.uk SER: Repairs. FAIRS: Brunel, Uxbridge, Bracknell; Essex Watch & Clock, Colchester.

LEIGH-ON-SEA

K.S. Buchan
135 The Broadway. SS9 1PJ. Open 10-5. *STOCK: Furniture and general antiques.* TEL: 01702 479440.

Collectors' Paradise
993 London Rd. SS9 3LB. (H.W. and P.E. Smith). Est. 1967. Open 10-5. CL: Fri. SIZE: Small. *STOCK: Clocks, 1830-1930, from £85; bric-a-brac; postcards, 1900-1930s; cigarette cards, 1889-1939.* LOC: On A13. PARK: Easy. TEL: 01702 473077.

Deja Vu Antiques
876 London Rd. SS9 3NQ. (Stuart D. Lewis). Est. 1990. Open 9.30-5.30, Sun. by appointment. SIZE: Large. *STOCK: French furniture, late 18th to 19th C; antique bedsteads, lighting and gilt mirrors.* PARK: Easy. TEL: 01702 470829; e-mail - info@deja-vu-antiques.co.uk website - www.deja-vu-antiques.co.uk SER: Valuations; restorations. FAIRS: Newark; Ardingly.

John Stacey and Sons
86-90 Pall Mall. SS9 1RG. Est. 1946. Open 9-5.30. CL: Sat. pm. *STOCK: General antiques.* TEL: 01702 477051. SER: Valuations; exporters; auctioneers. VAT: Stan.

J. Streamer Antiques
86 Broadway and 212 Leigh Rd. SS9 1AE. Est. 1965. Open 9.30-5.30. CL: Wed. *STOCK: Jewellery, silver, bric-a-brac, small furniture.* TEL: 01702 472895.

WEST ESSEX ANTIQUES
Stonehall

Dealer in English and Continental Furniture 18th – 20th C.

e-mail: chris@essexantiques.demon.co.uk

Tel/Fax: 01279 730609

Down Hall Road
Matching Green
Nr. Harlow ESSEX. CM17 0RA

Mobile: 07702 492111

15 mins. from M11
15 mins. Stansted Airport
45 mins. London

MALDON

The Antique Rooms
104A High St. CM9 7ET. (Mrs E. Hedley). Est. 1966. Open 10-3. CL: Wed. SIZE: Medium. *STOCK: Furniture, pottery, porcelain, glass and silver, costume, linen and lace, jewellery, lace-making equipment, collectors' items.* LOC: Just off High St. PARK: In courtyard. TEL: 01621 856985. SER: Valuations; lectures.

Clive Beardall Restorations Ltd
104B High St. CM9 5ET. BAFRA. EADA. Est. 1982. Open 8-5.30, Sat 8-2. SIZE: Medium. *STOCK: Furniture, 18th-19th C, £100-£5,000.* LOC: Off High St. up alleyway between Just Fabrics and Foulkes Electrical. PARK: Easy. TEL: 01621 857890; fax - 01621 850753; website - www.clivebeardall.co.uk SER: Restorations (furniture). VAT: Stan/Spec.

MATCHING GREEN, Nr. Harlow

West Essex Antiques (Stone Hall)
Downhall Rd. CM17 0RA. Est. 1982. Open 9-5, Sat and Sun. by appointment. SIZE: Warehouse. *STOCK: English and Continental furniture, 18th-20th C, £100-£3,000.* LOC: Turning off A1060 at Hatfield Heath. PARK: Own. TEL: 01279 730609; mobile - 07702 492111; e-mail - chris@essexantiques.demon.co.uk VAT: Stan.

NEWPORT, Nr. Saffron Walden

Omega
High St. CB11 3PF. (Tony Phillips and Sybil Hooper). Est. 1982. Open 10-6, Sat. 10-5.30. CL: Thurs. SIZE: Small. *STOCK: Furniture and lighting, 1880-1960, £20-£1,000; jewellery, objects, 1900-1960, £20-£300.* LOC: B1383. PARK: Easy. TEL: 01799 540720; home - same. SER: Valuations; restorations (furniture including French polishing, repairs and re-veneering). FAIRS: Art Deco - Battersea, Brighton, Tunbridge Wells.

RAYLEIGH

F.G. Bruschweiler (Antiques) Ltd   LAPADA
41-67 Lower Lambricks. SS6 8DA. Est. 1963. Open 9-5, Sat. by appointment. SIZE: Warehouses. *STOCK: Furniture, 18th-19th C.* LOC: A127 to Weir roundabout through Rayleigh High St. and Hockley Rd., first left past cemetery, then second left, warehouse round corner on left. PARK: Easy. TEL: 01268 773761/773932; home - 01621 828152; fax - 01268 773318; e-mail - info@fgbantiques.com website - www.fgbantiques.com VAT: Stan.

SAFFRON WALDEN

Bush Antiques
26-28 Church St. CB10 1JQ. (Mrs J.M. Hosford). EADA. Est. 1962. Open 11-4.30. CL: Thurs. SIZE: Medium. *STOCK: English ceramics including blue and white transfer printed pottery, copper and pink lustre, £25-£250; mahogany and country furniture, to £1,000; copper and brass, to £250; all 1800-1860.* LOC: 300 yards north of Market Sq., on crossroads with Museum St. PARK: Nearby. TEL: 01799 523277.

Ickleton Antiques
4A Gold St. CB10 1EJ. (B. Arbery). Est. 1983. Open 10-4, Mon. 10-3, Sat. 10-5. SIZE: Small. *STOCK: Militaria including badges, medals and weapons; advertising and packaging, postcards.* LOC: Just off centre of town. PARK: Nearby. TEL: 01799 513114; home - 01799 527474. SER: Valuations.

Lankester Antiques and Books
Old Sun Inn, Church St., and Market Hill. CB10 1JW. (P. Lankester). Est. 1965. Open 10-5. SIZE: Large. *STOCK: Furniture, porcelain, pottery, metalwork, general antiques, books, prints and maps.* TEL: 01799 522685. VAT: Stan

Littlebury Antiques - Littlebury Restorations Ltd
58/60 Fairycroft Rd. CB10 1LZ. (N.H. D'Oyly). Est. 1962. Open 9-5. CL: Sat. and Sun. except by appointment. SIZE: Medium. *STOCK: Barometers, marine antiques, chess sets, walking sticks and curios.* PARK: Easy. TEL: 01799 527961; fax - same; home - 01279 771530; e-mail - heather@doyly.fsnet.co.uk SER: Valuations; restorations; buys at auction. VAT: Stan/Spec.

Saffron Walden Antiques Centre
1 Market Row. CB10 1HA. Est. 1996. Open 10-5, Sun. 11-4. SIZE: Large - 50+ dealers. *STOCK: Wide range of general antiques and collectibles; specialist dealers in silver and jewellery, furniture, glass and ceramics, old*

toys. LOC: Town centre. PARK: Nearby. TEL: 01799 524534; website - www.saffronantiques.co.uk

SHENFIELD

The Chart House
33 Spurgate, Hutton Mount. CM13 2JS. (C.C. Crouchman). Est. 1974. Open by appointment. SIZE: Small. *STOCK: Nautical items.* PARK: Easy. TEL: 01277 225012; fax/home - same; e-mail - cccrouchman @aol.com SER: Buys at auction.

SIBLE HEDINGHAM, Nr. Halstead

Hedingham Antiques
100 Swan St. CO9 3HP. (Patricia Patterson). Est. 1978. Open by appointment. SIZE: Small. *STOCK: Mainly silver, some plate, china and glass, small furniture.* LOC: On A1017, village centre. PARK: Forecourt. TEL: 01787 460360; home - same; fax - 01787 469109; e-mail - patricia@patriciapatterson.wanadoo.co.uk website - www.hedinghamantiques.co.uk SER: Repairs and restorations (silver). VAT: Spec/Global/Stan/Export.

Lennard Antiques   LAPADA
c/o W.A. Pinn & Sons, 124 Swan St. CO9 3HP. (Gill Meddings). Est. 1978. Open 9.30-6, Sun. by appointment. SIZE: Medium. *STOCK: Oak and country furniture, 17th to early 19th C; English Delftware and interesting accessories.* LOC: On A1017 opposite Shell garage in village centre. PARK: Easy. TEL: 01787 461127. FAIRS: Chelsea; West London; Olympia (June); Harrogate. VAT: Spec.

W.A. Pinn and Sons   BADA LAPADA
124 Swan St. CO9 3HP. (K.H. and W.J. Pinn). Est. 1943. Open 9.30-6. CL: Sun. except by appointment. SIZE: Medium. STOCK: Furniture, 17th to early 19th C, £250-£5,000; Chinese export porcelain, £25-£1,000; brassware, lighting and interesting items, prior to 1830, £25-£2,500. LOC: On A1017 opposite Shell Garage. PARK: Easy. TEL: 01787 461127. FAIRS: Chelsea (Autumn); Olympia (June and Nov); Harrogate. VAT: Stan/Spec.

SOUTHEND-ON-SEA

Curio City.
Chartwell North, Upper Level, Victoria Plaza Shopping Centre. SS2 5SP. (T.W. Cornforth). Est. 1996. Open 10-5, Sat. 9-5. SIZE: Large - 80 dealers. *STOCK: 18th-20th C furniture, Oriental items, ceramics and collectables.* LOC: Town centre. PARK: Nearby multi-storey. TEL: 01702 611350; fax - 01702 710303; website - www.ridgeweb.co.uk

STANSTED

Valmar Antiques   BADA
The Barn, High Lane. CM24 8LQ. (John and Marina Orpin). Resident. Est. 1960. Open by appointment. SIZE: Large. STOCK: Furniture and decorative items including Arts and Crafts, £50-£10,000. LOC: 2 miles from airport. TEL: 01279 813201; fax - 01279 816962; mobile - 07831 093701; e-mail - valmar-antiques@cwcom.net FAIRS: Major British.

THAXTED

Harris Antiques
24 Town Street. CM6 2LA. (F.A.D., B.D.A., F.J.B. and M. Harris). Resident. BAFRA. EADA. RHI. Est. 1956. Open 9-6, Sun. by appointment. SIZE: Medium. *STOCK: Quality period furniture, barometers and clocks, 16th-19th C, £50-£20,000+.* LOC: Near M11 and Stansted Airport. PARK: Easy. TEL: 01371 832832; home - same. SER: Valuations; restorations. VAT: Spec.

WESTCLIFF-ON-SEA

It's About Time
863 London Rd. SS0 9SZ. (P. Williams). EADA. Est. 1980. Open Tues.-Sat. 9-5.30. SIZE: Large. *STOCK: Clocks, 18th-19th C, £200-£11,000; barometers, Victorian and Edwardian furniture.* LOC: A13. PARK: Easy. TEL: 01702 472574; e-mail - shop@antiqueclock. co.uk website - www.antiqueclock.co.uk

Ridgeway Antiques
66 The Ridgeway. SS0 8NU. (Trevor Cornforth). EADA. Est. 1987. Open 10.30-5. SIZE: Small. *STOCK: General antiques and Oriental, £5-£1,000.* LOC: A13 London road, right at Chalkwell Ave., right to The Ridgeway. PARK: Easy. TEL: 01702 710383. SER: Valuations. FAIRS: Ridgeway; Hallmark.

WHITE RODING, Nr. Dunmow

White Roding Antiques
'Ivydene', Chelmsford Rd. CM6 1RG. (F. and J. Neill). Est. 1971. Open by appointment. SIZE: Medium. *STOCK: Furniture and shipping goods, 18th-19th C, £10-£1,500.* LOC: A1060 between Bishops Stortford and Chelmsford. PARK: Easy. TEL: 01279 876376; home - same. VAT: Stan/Spec.

WICKHAM BISHOPS

Barling Fine Porcelain Ltd   LAPADA
(S. Parish). Open by appointment. *STOCK: English porcelain including Royal Worcester and Royal Crown Derby, £100-£12,000; watercolours, £300-£2,500.* TEL: 01621 890058; e-mail - stuart@barling.uk.com website - www.barling.uk.com FAIRS: NEC; LAPADA.

WOODFORD GREEN

Mill Lane Antiques
29 Mill Lane. IG8 0NG. (Niki Wood and Bonnita Read). Open Tues.-Sun. SIZE: Medium. *STOCK: French lighting, furniture and Venetian mirrors.* TEL: 020 8502 9930; fax - same; mobile - 07980 419956. SER: Valuations; restorations. FAIRS: Kempton Park.

WRITTLE, Nr. Chelmsford

Whichcraft Jewellery
54-56 The Green. CM1 3DU. (A. Turner). EADA. Est. 1978. Open 9.30-5.30. CL: Mon. SIZE: Small. *STOCK: Jewellery, silver and watches, 19th C, £30-£5,000.* PARK: Easy. TEL: 01245 420183. SER: Valuations; restorations (jewellery). VAT: Stan/Spec.

GLOUCESTERSHIRE

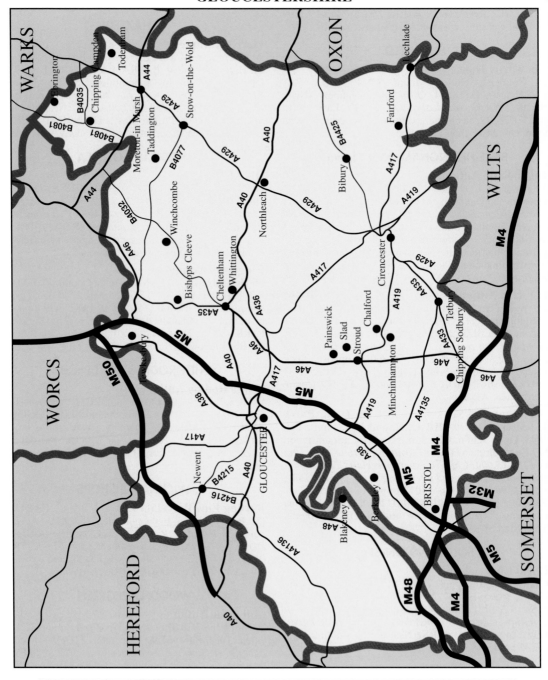

Dealers and Shops in Gloucestershire

Berkeley	2	Chipping Campden	3	Minchinhampton	1	Stroud	1
Bibury	1	Chipping Sodbury	1	Moreton-in-Marsh	15	Taddington	1
Bishops Cleeve	1	Cirencester	9	Newent	1	Tetbury	22
Blakeney	1	Ebrington	1	Northleach	3	Tewkesbury	2
Bristol	25	Fairford	2	Painswick	1	Todenham	1
Chalford	1	Gloucester	2	Slad	1	Whittington	1
Cheltenham	20	Lechade	3	Stow-on-the-Wold	33	Winchcombe	4

BERKELEY

Berkeley Antiques Market
GL13 9BP. Est. 1985. Open 9.30-1 and 2-5. CL: Mon. SIZE: Large - 10 dealers. *STOCK: General antiques, oak, mahogany, pine, linen and smalls, £1-£5,000.* LOC: Village centre, 1 mile from A38. PARK: Easy. TEL: 01453 511032; mobile - 07802 304534. VAT: Spec.

Peter and Penny Proudfoot
16-18 High St. GL13 9BJ. FATG. Est. 1956. Open 9-6, Sun. by appointment. SIZE: Small. *STOCK: Furniture, 1600-1900, £100-£3,000; silver, 1700 to date, £5-£1,000; pictures, 1800 to date, £20-£3,000; jewellery, 1800 to date, £1-£1,000.* LOC: Town centre. PARK: Easy. TEL: 01453 811513; home - same; fax - 01453 511616; e-mail - pclaireproudfoot@aol.com SER: Valuations; restorations (furniture and oil paintings); framing. VAT: Stan/Spec.

BIBURY, Nr. Cirencester

The Swing Riots Collection
Arlington Mill. GL7 5NL. Est. 1999. Open 7 days from 8-6. SIZE: 5 floors - museum and gallery. *STOCK: Antiques, collectables, oils and prints, Beatles memorabilia.* PARK: Easy. TEL: 01285 740199; mobile - 07788 681998. FAIRS: TBA.

BISHOPS CLEEVE, Nr. Cheltenham

Cleeve Picture Framing
Church Rd. GL52 8RL. (J. Gardner). FATG. Est. 1974. Open 9-1 and 2-5.30, Sat. 9-1. *STOCK: Prints and pictures.* TEL: 01242 672785. SER: Framing; cleaning; restorations (oils, watercolours and prints).

BLAKENEY

Lion, Witch and Lampshade
Birmingham House, High St. GL15 4EB. (Mr. and Mrs N. Dixon). Open by appointment. *STOCK: Unusual decorative objects, 18th to early 20th C, £5-£150; lamps, wall brackets, chandeliers and candlesticks, £50-£1,000.* LOC: Opposite Soudley Rd. PARK: Opposite in side road. TEL: 01594 516422/020 7730 1774; fax - 01594 516422. SER: Restorations (porcelain and glass); lamp rewiring.

BRISTOL

Alexander Gallery
122 Whiteladies Rd. BS8 2RP. (P.J. Slade and H.S. Evans). Est. 1971. Open 9-5.30. *STOCK: 19th-20th C paintings, watercolours and prints.* TEL: 01179 734692; fax - 01179 466991; website - www.alexander-gallery.co.uk

Antique Corner with A & C Antique Clocks
86 Bryants Hill, Hanham. BS5 8QT. (D.A. and J.P. Andrews). BWCMG. Est. 1985. Open 10-4. CL: Mon. and Wed. SIZE: Large - 2 floors. *STOCK: Clocks including longcase, wall and mantel; furniture and ceramics, £5-£5,000; aneroid and mercurial barometers; dolls.* LOC: Next to The Trooper public house, A431 Bristol to Bath road. PARK: Easy. TEL: 01179 476141; website - www.antiquecorner.org.uk SER: Repairs (clocks and barometers).

The Antiques Warehouse Ltd
430 Gloucester Rd., Horfield. BS7 8TX. (Chris Winsor). Resident. Est. 1994. Open Tues.-Sat. 10-6, Sun. 12-4. SIZE: Large warehouse. *STOCK: Furniture, especially dining tables, wardrobes, chests, desks and chairs, 18th to early 20th C, £200-£2,500; mirrors, from 19th C, £60-£1,000; rugs, from 19th C, £150-£600; lighting £100-£1,000.* LOC: A38 4 miles from M4/M5 interchange, 2 miles from city centre. PARK: Easy. TEL: 01179 424500; mobile - 07785 532173; website - www.theantiqueswarehouseltd.co.uk SER: Valuations; restorations (furniture, upholstery and lighting). VAT: Stan/Spec.

Arcadia Antiques & Interiors
4 Boyces Ave., Clifton. BS8 4AA. Est. 1993. Open 10-5.30. SIZE: Small. *STOCK: General antiques including sofas and chairs, lighting including chandeliers, jewellery and decorative items, £5-£2,500.* LOC: Near The Mall. TEL: 01179 144479; fax - 01179 239308

Bizarre Antiques
210 Gloucester Rd., Bishopston. BS7 8NZ. (E.J. Parkin). Open 8.15-5. *STOCK: General antiques.* TEL: 01179 427888; home - 01179 503498.

Bristol Brocante
123 St. Georges Rd., College Green, Hotwells. BS1 5UW. (David and Elizabeth Durant). Est. 1966. Open 12-6, Sun. by appointment. SIZE: Small. *STOCK: 19th-20th C French decorative antiques - small furniture, crystal and brass, hanging and wall lights and unusual items, £80-£1,000.* LOC: Junction of Anchor Rd. and Hotwells Rd., 3 mins. walk from library and city centre. PARK: Meters. TEL: 01179 096688; mobile - 07986 612056; mail - daviddurant580@yahoo.co.uk FAIRS: Chelsea Brocante, Newark, Sandown Park, Ardingly, Shepton Mallet.

Bristol Guild of Applied Art Ltd
68/70 Park St. BS1 5JY. Est. 1908. Open Mon.-Fri. 9-5.30, Sat. 9.30-5.30. *STOCK: 20th C furniture.* LOC: West end. PARK: Multi-storey adjacent. TEL: 01179 265548; fax - 01179 255659; e-mail - bristolguild@70parkst.freeserve.co.uk

Bristol Trade Antiques
192 Cheltenham Rd. BS6 5RB. (L. Dike). Est. 1970. SIZE: Large and warehouse. *STOCK: General antiques.* TEL: 01179 422790; e-mail - bristoltradeantiques@yahoo.co.uk

Caledonian Antiques
6 The Mall, Clifton. BS8 4DR. Open 9-5.30. SIZE: Small. *STOCK: Antique and secondhand jewellery, silver and plate; modern classic jewellery.* LOC: Central. PARK: Nearby. TEL: 01179 743582; fax - 01179 667997. SER: Valuations; restorations (jewellery); engraving.

Cotham Antiques
1c Pitville Place, 39 Cotham Hill. BS6 6JZ. (Susan Miller and Cornelius Cummins). Est. 1983. Open Tues.-Sat.10.30-5.30. SIZE: Small. *STOCK: Jewellery, 1800 to*

designer modern, £50-£500; ceramics, 19th C to Art Deco, £100-£500; small furniture, 19th to early 20th C, £100-£700; prints and engravings. LOC: Off Whiteladies Rd from Clifton - turn left at Whiteladies shopping centre. PARK: Limited. TEL: 01179 733326. SER: Valuations.

Flame and Grate
159 Hotwells Rd., Hotwells. BS8 4RU. Open 9-5. STOCK: Original cast iron fireplaces, marble surrounds and fireplace accessories. PARK: Easy. TEL: 01179 252560/292930.

Focus on the Past
25 Waterloo St., Clifton. BS8 4BT. (K. Walker and A. Roylance). Est. 1976. Open 9.30-5.30, Sat. 9.30-6, Sun. 11-5. SIZE: Large. STOCK: 19th-20th C furniture including mahogany, country, pine, French, English; ceramics, kitchenalia, glass, silver, plate, jewellery, advertising and packaging, to £1,000+. LOC: Off Princess Victoria St. PARK: Nearby. TEL: 01179 738080. FAIRS: Shepton Mallet, Newark.

Grey-Harris and Co
12 Princess Victoria St., Clifton. BS8 4BP. Est. 1963. Open 10-5. STOCK: Jewellery, Victorian; silver, old Sheffield plate. TEL: 01179 737365. SER: Valuations. VAT: Stan/Spec.

Chris Grimes Militaria
13 Lower Park Row. BS1 5BN. (Chris and Hazel Grimes). Est. 1968. Open 11-5.30. STOCK: Militaria, scientific instruments, nautical items. PARK: Meters or multi-storey nearby. TEL: 01179 298205. FAIRS: Shepton Mallet.

Kemps
9 Carlton Court, Westbury-on-Trym. BS9 3DF. Open 9-5.30. STOCK: Jewellery. PARK: Free. TEL: 01179 505090.

Robert Mills Architectural Antiques Ltd
Narroways Rd., Eastville. BS2 9XB. SALVO. Est. 1969. Open 9-5. CL: Sat. SIZE: Large. STOCK: Architectural items, panelled rooms, shop interiors, Gothic Revival, stained glass, church woodwork, bar and restaurant fittings, 1600-1950s, £50-£30,000. LOC: Half mile from junction 2, M32. PARK: Easy. TEL: 01179 556542; fax - 01179 558146; e-mail - sales@rmills.co.uk website - www.rmills.co.uk VAT: Stan.

Jan Morrison
3 Victorian Arcade, Boyce's Avenue, Clifton. BS8 4AA. Est. 1982. Open Tues.-Sat. 10-5.30. SIZE: Small. STOCK: Silver, 1750 to date; glass, 18th C to Victorian. PARK: Victoria Square. TEL: 01179 706822; fax - same; home - 01179 247995; mobile - 07789 094428.

Oldwoods
4 Colston Yard. BS1 5BD. (S. Duck). Open 11-5.30, Sat. 11-4. STOCK: Victorian and Edwardian furniture, pine and other woods. TEL: 01179 299023. SER: Restorations.

Pastimes
22 Lower Park Row. BS1 5BN. (A.H. Stevens). Est. 1970. Open 10.30-1.45 and 2.45-5. SIZE: Medium. STOCK: Militaria and military books, £1-£1,000. LOC:

Opposite Christmas Steps, off Colston St. PARK: Meters. TEL: 01179 299330.

Period Fireplaces
The Old Station, Station Rd., Montpelier. BS6 5EE. (John and Rhian Ashton and Martyn Roberts). Est. 1987. Open daily. SIZE: Medium. STOCK: Fireplaces, original and reproduction, £250-£1,000. LOC: Just off Gloucester Rd. PARK: Easy. TEL: 01179 444449; website - www.periodfireplaces.co.uk SER: Restorations; fitting. VAT: Stan.

Porchester Antiques
58 The Mall, Clifton. BS8 4JG. (Devonia Andrews). Est. 1978. Open Tues.-Sat. 10-6. SIZE: Small. STOCK: Moorcroft pottery and enamels, Sally Tuffin, Dennis chinaworks, diamond jewellery, £250-£10,000. PARK: Easy. TEL: 01173 730256; mobile - 07970 970449; website - www.porchester-collectables.co.uk SER: Valuations.

Potter's Antiques and Coins
60 Colston St. BS1 5AZ. (B.C. Potter). Est. 1965. Open 10.30-5.30. SIZE: Small. STOCK: Antiquities, 500 B.C. to 1600 A.D., £5-£500; commemoratives, 1770-1953, £4-£300; coins, 500 B.C. to 1967, £1-£100; drinking glasses, 1770-1953, £3-£200; small furniture, from 1837, £10-£200. LOC: Near top of Christmas Steps, close to city centre. PARK: NCP Park Row. TEL: 01179 262551. SER: Valuations; buys at auction. VAT: Stan/Spec.

Relics - Pine Furniture
109 St. George's Rd., College Green. BS1 5UW. (R. Seville and S. Basey). Est. 1972. Open 10-5.30. SIZE: Large. STOCK: Victorian style, reclaimed pine, hardwood furniture; contemporary oak furniture; nauticalia, mirrors and model yachts. LOC: Near cathedral, 1/2 mile from city centre. PARK: Easy. TEL: 01179 268453; fax - same. VAT: Stan.

St. Nicholas Markets
The Exchange Hall, Corn St. BS1 1JQ. (Steve Morris). Est. 1975. Open 9.30-5, Fri. 7-4. STOCK: Wide range of general antiques and collectors' items. LOC: City centre. TEL: 01179 224014/244037

Tower House Antiques   LAPADA
Almondsbury. BS32 4HA. (Graham Pendrill and Tony Yole Smith). Est. 1968. Open by appointment. SIZE: Large. STOCK: Country house antiques, mainly 19th C Gothic Revival, Arts and Crafts, Aesthetic Movement; exhibition quality furniture, mirrors, paintings and sculpture; baronial items. LOC: 1 minute junction 16, M5. PARK: Easy. TEL: 01454 626233; fax - 01454 619203; mobile - 07971 579350; home - 01453 548912; e-mail - info@towerhouseantiques.com website - www.towerhouseantiques.com

CHALFORD

J. and R. Bateman Antiques   LAPADA
Green Court, High St. GL6 8DS. (Robert Bateman). Est. 1975. Open 9-6 or by appointment. STOCK: Furniture, oak and country, 17th-19th C; decorative items. LOC: Eastern end of High St. PARK: Easy. TEL: 01453 883234. SER: Restorations; cabinet making; rushing and caning. VAT: Stan/Spec.

CHELTENHAM

David Bannister FRGS
26 Kings Rd. GL52 6BG. PBFA. Est. 1963. Open by appointment. SIZE: Medium. *STOCK: Early maps and prints, 1480-1850; decorative and topographical prints; atlases and colour plate books.* TEL: 01242 514287; e-mail - db@antiquemaps.co.uk SER: Valuations; restorations; lectures; buys at auction. VAT: Stan.

Cheltenham Antique Market
54 Suffolk Rd. GL50 2AQ. (K.J. Shave). Est. 1970. Open 10-5. SIZE: 6 dealers. *STOCK: General antiques including chandeliers.* TEL: 01242 529812.

Cocoa
9 Clarence Parade. GL50 3NY. (Cara Wagstaff). Est. 1970. Open 10-5. CL: Wed. SIZE: Small. *STOCK: Lace, antique wedding dresses and accessories, 19th-20th C, £1-£2,000.* LOC: Town centre. TEL: 01242 233588. SER: Wedding dress re-creations; restorations (period textiles). VAT: Stan.

Giltwood Gallery
30/31 Suffolk Parade. GL50 2AE. (Mrs G. Butt). Resident. Est. 1992. Open 9-5.30, Sat. 10-5.30. SIZE: Large. *STOCK: Furniture, £500-£3,000; mirrors, £500, all 18th to early 20th C.* PARK: Easy. TEL: 01242 512482; fax - same. SER: Valuations; restorations (upholstery); buys at auction. VAT: Stan/Spec.

Greens of Cheltenham Ltd
15 Montpellier Walk. GL50 1SD. Est. 1946. Open 9-5. SIZE: Large. *STOCK: Jewels, objets, porcelain and silver.* LOC: Conjunction of Promenade and main shopping centre. PARK: Easy. TEL: 01242 512088; e-mail - steve@greensofcheltenham.co.uk SER: Buys at auction. VAT: Stan/Spec.

The Loquens Gallery
3 Montpellier Avenue. GL50 1SA. (Stephen and Mrs Jean Loquens). Est. 1992. Open 10.15-5. SIZE: Small. *STOCK: 18th-20th C watercolours and some oils.* LOC: Adjacent to The Queens Hotel. PARK: Nearby. TEL: 01242 254313; e-mail - info@ loquensgallery.co.uk website - www.loquensgallery.co.uk SER: Valuations; framing; restorations.

Manor House Gallery
16 Royal Parade, Bayshill Rd. GL50 3AY. (Geoff Hassell). Resident. Open any time by appointment only. *STOCK: British oils and watercolours, £200-£2,000; prints, under £100; all 20th C.* LOC: Central. PARK: Easy. TEL: 01242 228330; home - same; e-mail - geoff@ manorhousegallery.net website - www.manorhouse gallery.net SER: Valuations; restorations (oils). VAT: Stan/spec.

Martin and Co. Ltd
19 The Promenade. GL50 1LP. (I.M. and N.C.S. Dimmer). Est. 1890. Open 9-5.30, Wed. 9-5. *STOCK: Silver, Sheffield plate, jewellery, objets d'art.* TEL: 01242 522821; fax - 01242 570430. VAT: Stan/Spec.

Montpellier Clocks   BADA
13 Rotunda Terrace, Montpellier. GL50 1SW. (B. Bass and T. Birch). Est. 1959. Open 9-5. SIZE: Medium. *STOCK: Clocks, 17th-19th C; barometers.* LOC: Close to Queens Hotel. PARK: Easy. TEL: 01242 242178; e-mail - info@montpellierclocks.com website - www.montpellierclocks.com SER: Repairs and restorations by West Dean/BADA Dip. conservator. VAT: Spec.

Patrick Oliver   LAPADA
4 Tivoli St. GL50 2UW. Est. 1896. SIZE: Large. *STOCK: Furniture and shipping goods.* PARK: Easy. TEL: 01242 519538. VAT: Stan/Spec.

Q & C Militaria
22 Suffolk Rd. GL50 2AQ. (J.F. Wright). OMRS, MCCOFI, BACSEA. Est. 1970. Open 10-5. CL: Mon. SIZE: Medium. *STOCK: Military memorabilia - British orders, decorations and medals; military drums, edged weapons, cap badges.* LOC: A40 ring road. PARK: At rear, off Old Bath Rd. TEL: 01242 519815; fax - same; mobile - 07778 613977; e-mail - qcmilitaria@ btconnect.com website - www.qcmilitaria.com SER: Valuations; restorations (drums and military equipment); framing and mounting (medals); buys at auction. FAIRS: OMRS Convention, Aldershot, Yate, Stratford-upon-Avon; Aldershot Collectors (Farnham); Britannia Medal, London.

Michael Rayner
11 St. Luke's Rd. GL53 7JQ. Est. 1988. Open 10-6, other times by appointment. CL: Mon. and Tues. *STOCK: Books, antiquarian and secondhand.* LOC: Near St Luke's church, 8 mins. walk from The Promenade. PARK: Nearby. TEL: 01242 512806.

Catherine Shinn Decorative Textiles
5/6 Well Walk. GL50 3JX. Open 10-5. SIZE: 3 floors. *STOCK: Antique tapestry cushions, hangings, bell pulls; passe menterie and upholstery pieces, old curtains and table covers, toile.* PARK: Rear of library. TEL: 01242 574546; fax - 01242 578495; website - www.catherine shinn.com SER: Valuations; restorations; buys at auction (European textiles). VAT: Stan.

Sixways Antique Centre
199 London Rd., Charlton Kings. GL52 6HU. (Bob and Jill Sommer). Est. 1984. Open 9.30-5.30, Sun. 11-5. SIZE: Large - 15 dealers. *STOCK: General antiques, pine and painted furniture, china, glass, prints, silver and plate, linen, books, toys, flatware, gardening equipment and collectibles, £5-£5,000.* LOC: A40. PARK: Opposite. TEL: 01242 510672. SER: Restorations (furniture).

Tapestry
33 Suffolk Parade. GL50 2AE. Open 10.30-5.30. SIZE: Medium. *STOCK: Antique and decorative furniture and objects including soft furnishings, garden items, mirrors and lighting.* LOC: 10 mins. walk from The Promenade. PARK: Easy. TEL: 01242 512191.

Julian Tatham-Losh Ltd
Crescent House, 19 Eldorado Crescent. GL50 2PY. (Julian Tatham-Losh (Top Banana Antiques Mall)). Resident. TADA. Est. 1980. Open any time by appointment. SIZE: Medium. *STOCK: 19th C decorative smalls, bamboo and interesting furniture, majolica, flow blue, Staffordshire figures and animals, boxes and*

caddies, candlesticks, decorative glass, primitive and folk art items, kitchenalia, mirrors, desk-related items, brass and copper, luggage, £2-£10,000. LOC: Town centre near railway station. PARK: Own. TEL: 0871 2881100; fax - 0871 2881101; mobile - 07850 574924; e-mail - julian@topbananaantiques.com SER: Antique and decorative items supplied to order, especially repeat bulk shipping items; courier (air-conditioned transport); free storage. FAIRS: Newark. *Trade & Export Only.*

John P. Townsend
Ullenwood Park Farm, Ullenwood. GL53 9QX. (J.P., Mrs. A. and S. Townsend). Est. 1969. Open 9-5. CL: Sat. SIZE: Medium. *STOCK: Country and shipping furniture, to 1940s; books and bric-a-brac.* LOC: 4 miles from Cheltenham. PARK: Easy. TEL: 01242 870169; home - 01242 870223.

Triton Gallery
27 Suffolk Parade. GL50 2AE. (L. Bianco). Resident. Est. 1984. Open 9-5.30, other times by appointment. *STOCK: Period furniture, 18th C paintings, mirrors and lighting.* PARK: Easy. TEL: 01242 510477; e-mail - lorenzo.bianco@btconnect.com VAT: Spec.

Peter Ward Fine Paintings
Nothill Cowley. GL53 9NJ. Est. 1972. Open 9-5. *STOCK: 17th-19th C paintings.* TEL: 01242 870178; mobile - 07979 857347; website - www.corinium finepaintings.co.uk SER: Valuations; restorations; framing. VAT: Spec.

Woodward Antique Clocks   LAPADA
21 Suffolk Parade. GL50 2AE. (Patricia Woodward and Christopher Daines). Est. 1989. Open Tues.-Sat. 10.30-5.30. SIZE: Small. *STOCK: Clocks - longcase, 18th-19th C, £200-£10,000; decorative mantel especially French, 18th-19th C; wall, carriage and bracket.* PARK: Easy. TEL: 01242 245667; mobile - 07745 101081; e-mail - woodwardclocks@onetel.com website - www.woodward clocks.com SER: Valuations; restorations. FAIRS: LAPADA, NEC.

CHIPPING CAMPDEN

Cottage Farm Antiques
Cottage Farm, Aston sub Edge. GL55 6PZ. (A.E. and E.A. Willmore). Est. 1986. Open 9-5 including Sun. SIZE: Large. *STOCK: Furniture including 19th C wardrobes, 18th-19th C dressers and tables, to £3,000.* LOC: Follow brown tourist signs. PARK: Easy. TEL: 01386 438263; fax and home - same; e-mail - info @cottagefarmantiques.co.uk website - www.cottage farmantiques.co.uk SER: Delivery. VAT: Spec.

School House Antiques
School House, High St. GL55 6HB. (G. and M. Hammond). Est. 1895. Open 9.30-5 including Sun. (June-Sept.). CL: Thurs. (Oct.-May). SIZE: Large. *STOCK: Clocks, silver and jewellery, 18th-19th C; Georgian and Victorian furniture; works of art, oils and watercolours.* PARK: At rear. TEL: 01386 841474; e-mail - hamatschoolhouse@aol.com website - www. schoolhouseantiques.co.uk SER: Valuations.

Stuart House Antiques
High St. GL55 6HB. (J. Collett). Est. 1985. Open 10-1

and 2-5.30 including Sun. SIZE: Large. *STOCK: China, 19th C; general antiques, from 18th C; all £1-£1,000.* LOC: Opposite market hall. PARK: Easy. TEL: 01386 840995. SER: Valuations; china search; restorations (ceramics).

CHIPPING SODBURY, Nr. Bristol

Sodbury Antiques
70 Broad St. BS37 6AG. (Millicent Brown). Est. 1986. CL: Wed. SIZE: Small. *STOCK: Porcelain and china, mainly 18th-19th C; antique and secondhand jewellery, £5-£1,000.* PARK: Easy. TEL: 01454 273369.

CIRENCESTER

Walter Bull and Son (Cirencester) Ltd
10 Dyer St. GL7 2PF. NAG. Est. 1815. Open 9-5. SIZE: Small. *STOCK: Silver, from 1700, £50-£3,000; objets d'art.* LOC: Lower end of Market Place. PARK: At rear. TEL: 01285 653875; fax - 01285 641751. VAT: Stan/Spec.

Cirencester Arcade
25 Market Place. GL7 2NX. (M.J. and P.J. Bird). Est. 1995. Open every day. SIZE: 70 dealers. *STOCK: General antiques.* PARK: Opposite. TEL: 01285 644214; website - www.cirencester-arcade.co.uk SER: Shipping.

Corner Cupboard Curios
2 Church St. GL7 1LE. (P. Larner). Est. 1972. Usually open but prior telephone call advisable. SIZE: Small. *STOCK: Collectables including gramophones, radios, records.* LOC: Swindon side of town. PARK: Easy. TEL: 01285 655476; home - same.

Forum Antiques
Springfield Farm, Perrotts Brook. GL7 7DT. (W. Mitchell). Est. 1986. Open Mon.-Fri. 8.30-5.30 by appointment only. SIZE: Small. *STOCK: Period furniture, pre-1850.* TEL: 01285 831821. SER: Valuations; restorations. VAT: Spec.

Fossil Decor   LAPADA
Unit 15 Cirencester Business Estate, Elliott Rd. GL7 1YS. (Paul Nash). Est. 1961. Open by appointment. SIZE: Large. *STOCK: Decorative fossils.* TEL: 01285 650666; mobile - 07785 570701. FAIRS: Olympia (Spring and Summer). VAT: Spec.

Hares
4 Black Jack St. GL7 2AA. (Allan G. Hare). Est. 1972. Open 10-5.30, Sun. by appointment. SIZE: Large.

William H. Stokes

EARLY OAK FURNITURE

THE CLOISTERS, 6/8 DOLLAR STREET, CIRENCESTER, GLOUCESTERSHIRE, GL7 2AJ

W.H. Stokes
P.W. Bontoft
post@williamhstokes.co.uk
www.williamhstokes.co.uk

Telephone
(01285) 653907

Fax
(01285) 640533

Private
(01285) 657101

Early 18c. oak dresser with walnut cross-banding to the drawer fronts, c.1720.

STOCK: *Furniture, especially dining tables and long sets of chairs, 18th to early 19th C, £100-£50,000; Old Howard and other upholstery, pictures, carpets and decorative objects.* LOC: Near market square. PARK: Own. TEL: 01285 640077; fax - 01285 653513; mobile - 07860 350097; e-mail - hares@hares-antiques.com website - www.hares-antiques.com SER: Restorations; traditional upholstery. FAIRS: Olympia. VAT: Spec.

William H. Stokes   **BADA**
The Cloisters, 6/8 Dollar St. GL7 2AJ. (W.H. Stokes and P.W. Bontoft). CADA. Est. 1968. Open 9.30-5.30, Sat. 9.30-4.30. STOCK: Early oak furniture, £1,000-£50,000; brassware, £150-£5,000; all 16th-17th C. LOC: West of parish church out of Market Place. TEL: 01285 653907; fax - 01285 640533; e-mail - post @williamhstokes.co.uk website - www.williamh stokes.co.uk VAT: Spec.

Patrick Waldron Antiques
18 Dollar St. GL7 2AN. Resident. CADA. Est. 1965. Open 9.30-1 and 2-6, Sun. by appointment. SIZE: Medium. STOCK: *Town and country furniture, 17th to early 19th C.* LOC: In street behind church. PARK: Easy and public behind shop. TEL: 01285 652880; home - same; workshop - 01285 643479; e-mail - patrick. waldron@virgin.net SER: Restorations (furniture); buys at auction. VAT: Stan/Spec.

Bernard Weaver Antiques
28 Gloucester St. GL7 2DH. Open by appointment.

SIZE: Medium. STOCK: *Furniture, mahogany and oak, 18th-19th C.* LOC: Continuation of Dollar St. PARK: Easy. TEL: 01285 652055. SER: Valuations; restorations.

EBRINGTON, Nr. Chipping Campden

John Burton Natural Craft Taxidermy
21 Main St. GL55 6NL. Est. 1973. Open by appointment. SIZE: Medium. STOCK: *Taxidermy - Victorian and Edwardian cased fish, birds and mammals, heads, from £65-£2,500; glass domes, sporting trophies.* LOC: Village centre. PARK: Easy. TEL: 01386 593231; home - same; mobile - 07850 356354. SER: Valuations; restorations (taxidermy); buys at auction (taxidermy and natural history items).

FAIRFORD

Blenheim Antiques
Market Place. GL7 4AB. (N. Hurdle). CADA. Resident. Est. 1972. Open 9.30-6. SIZE: Medium. STOCK: *18th-19th C furniture and accessories.* PARK: Easy. TEL: 01285 712094. VAT: Stan/Spec.

Anthony Hazledine
Antique Oriental Carpets, High St. GL7 4AD. Est. 1976. Open 9.30-5. SIZE: Small. STOCK: *Oriental carpets and textiles, 18th-19th C, £150-£4,000.* PARK: Easy. TEL: 01285 713400; home and fax - same. SER: Restorations; cleaning. VAT: Stan/Spec.

GLOUCESTER

Antiques Centre Gloucester Ltd
1 Severn Rd. GL1 2LE. Est. 1979. Open 10-5, Sun. 1-5. SIZE: 100+ dealers. 50p admission charge weekends and Bank Hols. - Trade free. *STOCK: General antiques - furniture and furnishings, jewellery, silver, clocks, ceramics, collectables.* LOC: Within Gloucester Docks area. PARK: Ample within docks. TEL: 01452 529716; fax - 01452 307161.

Arthur S. Lewis
LAPADA
Est. 1969. By appointment. *STOCK: Mechanical music, automata, clocks.* TEL: 01452 780258; website - www.arthurlewisantiques.com

LECHLADE

Jubilee Hall Antiques Centre
Oak St. GL7 3AY. Est. 1997. Open 10-5, Sun. 11-5 or by appointment. SIZE: Large. *STOCK: 18th-19th C furniture, metalwork, prints, pictures, mirrors, pottery and porcelain, rugs, lighting, 19th C and earlier collectables, glass, silver, arts and crafts, textiles, jewellery, treen, Staffordshire.* LOC: On left 350 yards from town centre going north towards Burford. PARK: Own, free. TEL: 01367 253777; website - www.jubileehall.co.uk SER: Shipping; valuations; restorations. Listed below are the dealers at this centre.

Mandy Barnes
Georgian and Victorian furniture, decorative objects, some textiles, prints, jewellery.

Keith and Lin Bawden
18th-19th C English furniture, boxes, mirrors, barometers and objects.

John Calgie
18th-19th C period furniture, mirrors, copper, brass, Staffordshire, collectables, Arts & Crafts, lighting.

Steve Clure
Boxes, lamps, prints and decorative items.

Andrew Crawforth
Antique metalwork, treen, Arts and Crafts, musical instruments, keys, pewter, scientific, tribal and unusual items.

Francoise Daniel
Small silver, ivory, shibayama, tortoiseshell, art objects, Tunbridge ware, jewellery and glass.

Robert Delarey
Country furniture and related items.

Marc Drogin
Antiquities, from 2000 years.

Paul Eisler
18th-19th C ceramics, metalware, treen, small furniture, samplers, prints and maps.

Anita Harris
Porcelain, decorative objects, furniture and soft furnishings.

Colin and Mary Lee
Glass, porcelain, silver, silhouettes, pottery and objects, blue and white, lustreware.

MORETON-IN-MARSH

Colin Morris
Oak and country furniture, early metalware, pewter, carvings, Delft and Staffordshire pottery, horse brasses, garden items in spring and summer.

NAAS Antiques
18th-19th C decorative furnishings, mirrors, pictures, re-upholstered items, Worcester porcelain.

Oak Antiques
(David and Vicky Wilson). *Small country items, metalware and ancient items.*

Mary Pennel
Porcelain, small silver and jewellery.

Judi Pollitt (Times Past)
Blue and white, interesting objects, sewing items, fans, Tunbridgeware, snuff boxes, card cases.

Red Lane Antiques
(Terry Sparks). *Early oak and country furniture; 17th-19th C metalware, treen, Delft, needlework.*

Lindsey Richardson
Glass, Staffordshire, pottery, porcelain, inkwells, Doulton, bamboo furniture, papier mâché.

Jonathan Roan
Clocks, barometers, mechanical items, 17th-19th C.

Keith Robinson
18th-19th C engravings, ceramics, lighting and Japanese and English objects of art.

Susan Shaw
Silver and jewellery, small collectables, objet d'art.

Jackie & Richard Stent
18th-19th C furniture, prints, pottery, porcelain, chrystoleums, Belleek and small items.

Lechlade Arcade
5, 6 and 7 High St. GL7 3AD. (J. Dickson). Est. 1990. Open 9-5 including Sun. SIZE: 20+ dealers. *STOCK: Bric-a-brac, books, furniture (reclaimed pine), collectables, militaria, medals, pistols.* PARK: Riverside boat yard. TEL: 01367 252832; mobile - 07949 130875.

The Old Ironmongers Antiques Centre
Burford St. GL7 3AP. (Mark A. Serle and Geoff Allen). Est. 1999. Open 10-5 including Sun. *STOCK: Old ironmongery, £5-£200; furniture including country, £40-£2,000; textiles, £10-£200; Georgian glass, £20-£250; decorative china, £10-£500; treen, £50-£200; militaria including medals, £5-£300; tools and rural implements, £5-£300; Victorian bottles, £5-£150; gramophones, £80-£500.* LOC: A361. PARK: Easy. TEL: 01367 252397.

MINCHINHAMPTON, Nr. Stroud

Mick and Fanny Wright
The Trumpet. GL6 9JA. Est. 1979. Open Wed.-Sat. 10.30-5.30. SIZE: Medium. *STOCK: General antiques, decorative items, clocks, furniture, china, silver, plate and books, 50p-£2,000.* LOC: 200 yards west of crossroads at bottom of High St. PARK: Nearby. TEL: 01453 883027; e-mail - thetrumpet.antiques@virgin.net SER: Valuations. FAIRS: Kempton Park. VAT: Margin.

Astley House - Contemporary   LAPADA
Astley House, London Rd. GL56 0LE. (David, Nanette and Caradoc Glaisyer). CADA. CINOA. Est. 1973. Open 10-1 and 2-5 and by appointment. CL: Wed. SIZE: Large. *STOCK: Oil paintings, 19th-21st C; large decorative oils and portraits, jewellery, ceramics, glass.* LOC: Town centre. PARK: Easy. TEL: 01608 650608; fax - 01608 651777; e-mail - astart333@aol.com website - www.contemporaryart-uk.com SER: Restorations (oils and watercolours); framing (porcelain). VAT: Spec.

Astley House - Fine Art   LAPADA
Astley House, High St. GL56 0LL. (David, Nanette and Caradoc Glaisyer). CADA. CINOA. Est. 1973. Open 9-5.30 and by appointment. SIZE: Medium. *STOCK: Oil paintings, 19th-21st C, £800-£20,000.* LOC: Main street. PARK: Easy. TEL: 01608 650601; fax - 01608 651777; e-mail - astart333@aol.com website - www.art-uk.com SER: Restorations (oils and watercolours); framing. VAT: Spec.

Benton Fine Art   LAPADA
Regent House, High St. GL56 0AX. (J.G. Benton). Est. 1972. Open 10-5.30, Sun. 11-5.30, Tues. by appointment. SIZE: Large. *STOCK: Paintings, furniture, 18th to early 20th C, £500-£30,000.* PARK: Easy. TEL: 01608 652153; fax - same; mobile - 07885 575139; e-mail - bentonfineart@excite.com FAIRS: LAPADA; Antiques for Everyone.

Berry Antiques Ltd   LAPADA
3 High St. GL56 0AH. (Chris Berry). Est. 1985. Open 10-5.30, Sun. 11-5.30. CL: Tues. SIZE: Medium. *STOCK: Furniture, late 18th to 19th C, £1,000-£15,000; porcelain, £50-£500; paintings, £200-£10,000; both 19th C.* LOC: Near junction with Broadway road. PARK: Easy. TEL: 01608 652929; home - same; e-mail - chris@berryantiques.co.uk website - www.berryantiques.com SER: Valuations. FAIRS: NEC, LAPADA. VAT: Spec.

Cox's Architectural Reclamation Yard
Unit 10, Fosseway Industrial Estate. GL56 9NQ. (P. Watson). SALVO. Est. 1991. Open 9-5, Sun. by appointment. SIZE: Large. *STOCK: Architectural antiques, fire surrounds and fireplaces, £250-£25,000; doors, £50-£3,500; all 19th C; stained glass, £50-£1,000.* LOC: Just off Fosseway, northern end of Moreton-in-Marsh. PARK: Easy. TEL: 01608 652505; fax - 01608 652881; e-mail - info@coxsarchitectural.co.uk website - www.coxsarchitectural.co.uk SER: Valuations. VAT: Stan.

Dale House Antiques
High St. GL56 0AD. (N. and A. Allen). Open 10-5.30, Sun. 11-5. SIZE: Large. *STOCK: 17th-19th C town and country furniture, clocks, barometers, pictures, porcelain and pottery, metalwork, objets.* LOC: Main street. PARK: Easy. TEL: 01608 652950; fax - 01608 652424. VAT: Spec.

Jeffrey Formby Antiques   BADA
Orchard Cottage, East St. GL56 0LQ. Resident. Est. 1994. Open by appointment. SIZE: Small. *STOCK: Fine English clocks, pre 1850, £2,000-£15,000; horological books, old and new, £5-£500.* LOC: 100 yards from High

St. PARK: Easy. TEL: 01608 650558; e-mail - jeff@formby-clocks.co.uk website - www.formby-clocks.co.uk FAIRS: BADA; Olympia. VAT: Spec.

Jon Fox Antiques
High St. GL56 0AD. CADA. Est. 1983. Open 9.30-5.30, Sun. and Tues. by appointment. SIZE: Large - 2 adjacent shops. *STOCK: 19th C garden items including urns, seats, troughs and tools, £50-£5,000+; 18th -19th C country furniture £300-£3,000; treen, bygones, metalware, fireplace items.* PARK: Easy. TEL: 01608 650325/650714. VAT: Spec.

Grimes House Antiques & Fine Art
High St. GL56 0AT. (S. and V. Farnsworth). FATG. Est. 1978. Open 9.30-1 and 2-5, other times by appointment. *STOCK: Old cranberry and antique coloured glass, fine paintings.* LOC: Town centre. PARK: Free nearby. TEL: 01608 651029; e-mail - grimes_house@cix.co.uk website - www.grimeshouse.co.uk and www.cranberry glass.co.uk VAT: Spec/Stan.

Howards of Moreton
1 Old Market Way, High St. GL56 0AX. (Robert Light). Est. 1989. Open 9.30-4.45. SIZE: Small. *STOCK: Jewellery, 1750 to modern; silver, 1700 to modern, both £20-£5,000; objects of vertu, 1700-1900, £50-£500.* PARK: Easy and nearby. TEL: 01608 650583; e-mail - robert.light@talk21.com SER: Valuations; restorations. VAT: Stan/Spec.

London House Antique Centre
London House, High St. GL56 OAH. Est. 1979. Open 10-5 including Sun. (Sun. 11-5 Nov.-March). SIZE: Large. *STOCK: Quality furniture, paintings, watercolours, prints, Doulton Lambeth, Royal Doulton, potlids, porcelain, domestic artifacts, clocks, silver, jewellery and plate, mainly 17th-19th C, £5-£3,000.* LOC: Centre of High St. (A429). PARK: Easy. TEL: 01608 651084; e-mail - londonhouseantiques@msn.com website - www.london-house-antiques.co.uk VAT: Stan/ Spec.

Simply Antiques
at Windsor House Antiques Centre, High St. GL56 0AD. (G. Ellis). Open 10-5, Tues. and Sun. 12-5. *STOCK: Visiting card cases and small period furniture, mainly 18th to early 19th C.* LOC: In large 17th C premises, adjacent town hall. PARK: Easy. TEL: Mobile - 07710 470877; e-mail - info@callingcardcases.com website - www.callingcardcases.com SER: Finder. FAIRS: NEC; Cooper; Penman; Harrogate; Trident, Buxton. VAT: Spec.

The Roger Widdas Gallery   LAPADA
High St. GL56 0AD. Est. 1977. Open 10-5. CL: Tues. SIZE: Medium. *STOCK: 19th C English and European paintings and watercolours including Impressionist art, £2,000-£50,000; 19th C English and European town furniture, £1,000-£20,000.* PARK: Opposite - in New St. TEL: 01608 650618; fax - 01608 652301; e-mail - gallery@widdas.com website - www.widdas.com SER: Restorations (oil paintings).

Windsor House Antiques Centre
High St. GL56 0AD. Est. 1992. Open 10-5, Tues. and Sun. 12-5. SIZE: 48 dealers. *STOCK: Comprehensive selection of mid-range furniture, from 1650-1914; silver,* *portrait miniatures, ivory, visiting card cases, French decorative items, English and European porcelain, pottery and glass, objets de vertu, caddies and boxes, brass, copper and pewter.* LOC: Large 17th C premises, adjacent town hall. PARK: Ample. TEL: 01608 650993; fax - 01858 565438; e-mail - windsorhouse@btinternet. com website - www.windsorhouse.co.uk

Gary Wright Antiques
Unit 5, Fosseway Business Park, Stratford Rd. GL56 9NQ. Est. 1983. Open 9.30-5.30, Sun. by appointment. SIZE: Large. *STOCK: English and Continental furniture, 18th-19th C, £500-£30,000; unusual and decorative objects, 17th-20th C, £200-£4,000.* LOC: Entrance adjacent to railway bridge on north side of Moreton, on Fosseway (A429). PARK: Easy, TEL: 01608 652007; fax - same; mobile - 07831 653843; e-mail - info@gary wrightantiques.co.uk website - www.garywright antiques.co.uk SER: Valuations; restorations; buys at auction (furniture). VAT: Stan/Spec.

NEWENT
Jillings Antiques - Distinctive Antique Clocks
                    BADA LAPADA
Croft House, 17 Church St. GL18 1PU. (Doro and John Jillings). CINOA. Est. 1986. Open Fri. and Sat. 9.30-5, other times by appointment. *STOCK: 18th to early 19th C English and Continental clocks including bronze, ormolu, marble and boulle.* PARK: Easy. TEL: 01531 822100; fax - 01531 822666; mobile - 07973 830110; e-mail - clocks@jillings.com website - www.jillings.com SER: Valuations; restorations; repairs; shipping worldwide; free delivery and set up in UK. FAIRS: BADA (March); Olympia (June). VAT: Margin.

NORTHLEACH, Nr. Cheltenham
The Doll's House
Market Place. GL54 3EJ. (Miss Michal Morse). Est. 1971. Open Thurs., Fri. and Sat. 10-5, other times prior telephone call advisable. SIZE: Small. *STOCK: Handmade doll's houses and miniature furniture in one twelfth scale.* LOC: A40. PARK: Easy. TEL: 01451 860431; home and fax - same. SER: Replica houses and special designs to order.

Keith Harding's World of Mechanical Music
The Oak House, High St. GL54 3ET. (K. Harding, FBHI and C.A. Burnett, CMBHI). Est. 1961. Open 10-6 including Sun. SIZE: Large. *STOCK: Clocks, musical boxes and automata.* PARK: Easy. TEL: 01451 860181; fax - 01451 861133; e-mail - keith@mechanical music.co.uk website - www.mechanicalmusic.co.uk SER: Guided tours, demonstrations and written articles; valuations; restorations (musical boxes and clocks); buys at auction. VAT: Stan/Spec.

Robson Antiques
New Barn Farm, London Rd. GL54 3LX. Est. 1982. Open daily till late. *STOCK: Furniture, from 18th C, £50-£5,000; garden artefacts - reclaimed flagstones, staddle stones, troughs, Cotswold stone tiles.* PARK: Easy. TEL: 01451 861071/861006.

PAINSWICK

Nina Zborowska BADA
Damsels Mill, Paradise. GL6 6UD. Est. 1980. By appointment, except during exhibitions (May-June and Oct.-Nov) 11-5 including Sun. SIZE: Medium. *STOCK: Modern British paintings and drawings, St Ives, Newlyn, NEAC and Bloomsbury schools, 1900-1970, £500-£40,000.* **LOC: From Cheltenham towards Stroud on A46, take first turning on left to Sheepscombe. PARK: Easy. TEL: 01452 812460; fax - 01452 812912; e-mail - enquiries@ninazborowska. com website - www.ninazborowska.com SER: Valuations; restorations. FAIRS: Olympia (Spring); 20th/21st C British Art.**

SLAD, Nr. Stroud

Ian Hodgkins and Co. Ltd
Upper Vatch Mill, The Vatch. GL6 7JY. (G.A. Yablon). ABA. Est. 1973. Open by appointment. STOCK: Antiquarian books including pre-Raphaelites and associates, the Brontës, Jane Austen; 19th C illustrated, children's art and literature books. TEL: 01453 764270; fax - 01453 755233; e-mail - i.hodgkins@dial.pipex.com website - www.ianhodgkins.com

STOW-ON-THE-WOLD

Yvonne Adams Antiques BADA
The Coffee House, 3-4 Church St. GL54 1BB. Est. 1955. Open Tues.-Sat. 9.30-5. SIZE: Small. *STOCK: 18th C Meissen porcelain.* **LOC: Town centre. PARK: In square. TEL: 01451 832015; fax - 01451 833826; mobile - 07971 961101; e-mail - antiques@ adames.demon.co.uk; website - www.antiquemeissen. com SER: Valuations. FAIRS: Olympia (June). VAT: Margin.**

Ashton Gower Antiques LAPADA
9/9A Talbot Court, Market Square. GL54 1BQ. (C. Gower and B. Ashton). Est. 1987. Open 10-5. *STOCK: English and Continental furniture, gilt mirrors and decorative accessories, Lucite furniture, 18th-20th C, £25-£5,000.* LOC: Between the square and Sheep St. PARK: Nearby. TEL: 01451 870699; fax - same; e-mail - ashtongower@aol.com SER: Valuations; restorations; buys at auction. VAT: Stan/Spec.

Duncan J. Baggott LAPADA
Woolcomber House, Sheep St. GL54 1AA. CADA. Est. 1967. Open 9-5.30 or by appointment. CL: Bank Holidays. SIZE: Large. *STOCK: 17th-20th C English oak, mahogany and walnut furniture, paintings, domestic metalwork and decorative items; garden statuary and ornaments.* PARK: Sheep St. or Market Sq. TEL: 01451 830662; fax - 01451 832174. SER: Worldwide shipping; UK delivery. FAIRS: Exhibition Oct. annually (CADA).

Baggott Church Street Ltd BADA
Church St. GL54 1BB. (D.J. and C.M. Baggott). CADA. Est. 1978. Open 9.30-5.30 or by appointment. SIZE: Large. *STOCK: 17th-19th C English oak, mahogany and walnut furniture, portrait paintings, metalwork, pottery, treen and decorative items.* **LOC: South-west corner of market square. PARK: Market**

square. TEL: 01451 830370; fax - 01451 832174. SER: Annual exhibition - Oct.

Black Ink LAPADA
7A Talbot Court. GL54 1BQ. (David Stoddart). Est. 1990. Open 10-4, Sat. 10-5. CL: Tues. SIZE: Small. *STOCK: Artists' original etchings, lithographs, woodcuts and aquatints, especially 1860-1930, with emphasis on the Impressionists - Renoir, Pisarro, Gaugin, Manet, Cezanne; also works of outstanding quality by lesser known artists.* PARK: Free - town square. TEL: 01451 870022; mobile - 07721 454840; e-mail - art@blackinkprints.com website - www.blackinkprints.com FAIRS: NEC.

Annarella Clark Antiques
11 Park St. GL54 1AQ. Est. 1968. Open 10-5 or by appointment. SIZE: Medium. *STOCK: Conservatory and garden, English and French country and painted furniture and textiles.* LOC: Park St. leads from Sheep St., 1st right at lights leading into town. PARK: Easy. TEL: 01451 830535; home - same.

Christopher Clarke Antiques Ltd LAPADA
The Fosseway. GL54 1JS. (Simon and Sean Clarke). CADA. Est. 1961. Open 9.30-5.30 or by appointment. SIZE: Large. *STOCK: Specialists in campaign furniture and travel items; English furniture, metalware, treen, pictures and decorative items.* LOC: Corner of The Fosseway and Sheep St. PARK: Easy. TEL: 01451 830476; fax - 01451 830300; e-mail - cclarkeantiques @aol.com website - www.campaignfurniture.com FAIRS: Olympia (June, Nov); CADA Exhibition.

Cotswold Galleries
The Square, GL54 1AB. (Richard and Cherry Glaisyer). CADA. FATG. Est. 1961. Open 9-5.30 or by appointment. SIZE: Large. *STOCK: Oil paintings especially 19th-20th C landscape.* PARK: Easy. TEL: 01451 870567; fax - 01451 870678; website - www. cotswoldgalleries.com SER: Restorations; framing.

The John Davies Gallery
Church St. GL54 1BB. CADA. Est. 1977. Open 9.30-1.30 and 2.30-5.30. SIZE: Large. *STOCK: Contemporary and late period paintings; limited edition bronzes.* PARK: In square. TEL: 01451 831698; fax - 01451 832477; e-mail - daviesart@aol.com website - www.the-john-davies-gallery.co.uk SER: Restorations and conservation to museum standard. VAT: Spec/Margin

Durham House Antiques Centre
Sheep St. GL54 1AA. (Alan Smith). Open 10-5, Sun. 11-5. SIZE: 30+ dealers. PARK: Easy. TEL: 01451 870404; fax - same; e-mail - DurhamHouseGB@aol.com SER: Buys at auction. FAIRS: NEC (Aug); Newark; Ardingly. Below are listed the dealers at this centre.

> **Acorn Antiques**
> (Stanley Taylor). Est. 1987. *19th C Staffordshire figures and animals.*
>
> **Aldus Antiques**
> (Carrie and David Tarplett). *Steiff and other soft toys, dolls and doll furnishings; samplers and other needleworks.*
>
> **Ancient and Oriental Ltd**
> *Ancient art and archaeological items from many periods, lands and cultures.*

DURHAM HOUSE ANTIQUES
STOW-ON-THE-WOLD

A Quality Antiques Centre in the
Heart of the Cotswolds Over 30
Well Established Trade Dealers
and over 2,000sq.ft. display area

Mon - Sat 10-5 Sun 11-5
Tel/Fax: 01451 870404
email: DurhamHouseGB@aol.com
www.DurhamHouseGB.com

Sheep Street, STOW-ON-THE-WOLD, GL54 1AA

Michael Armson Antiques
Quality 18th-19th C mahogany and oak furniture, Staffordshire and metalware.

Aston Antiques
Arts and Crafts and Art Deco lighting, decanters, drinking glasses and ceramics, metalwork and furniture.

Paula Biggs Antiques
Quality and unusual silver including cutlery and table items.

Judi Bland Antiques
Toby jugs, Staffordshire, pot lids, Prattware, bargeware, country furniture and decorative items.

Peter and Sonia Cashman
18th-19th C portrait miniatures and silhouettes, watercolours, samplers and needlework, objets de vertu.

Simon Clarke Antiques
Oak and mahogany furniture, pictures, prints, metalware and leather items, ceramics, glass and door furniture.

Bryan Collyer
English pottery and Staffordshire figures, corkscrews, prints and pictures, small furniture.

Crockwell Antiques
(Philip Dawes). *18th-19th C oak and mahogany furniture, longcase clocks, silver, brass and copper, ironstone china and fireplace accessories.*

Lee Elliott Antiques
19th-20th C prints and pictures, specialising in rural pastimes.

Tony and Jane Finegan
Traditional English and French furniture, mirrors, lighting, decorative accessories including papier mâché and tole.

Marion Gregg Antiques
19th-20th C Oriental ceramics and cabinet pieces, fabrics and carvings, English furniture and accessories.

Beryl and Brian Harrison
Quality linen, including table and bed, and lace accessories.

Erna Hiscock and John Shepherd
Fine samplers and needlework, early carvings and ceramics, blue and white, country furniture and decorative items.

Dorothy Hyatt
Early English porcelain and pottery (Worcester, creamware, blue and white); 18th-19th C drinking glasses, decanters and objects for the table.

Corrie Jeffery Antiques
Decorative accessories, stitchery and textiles, pictures and prints, sewing ephemera, objets d'art.

Ian Kellam
English and Continental porcelain, silver and jewellery, religious objects and cabinet pieces.

Little Nells
(Helen Middleton).*Coronation commemoratives, automobilia, Staffordshire and majolica, collectibles and small interesting items.*

189

La Chaise Antique

Beauport, Sheep Street, Stow-on-the-Wold, Glos GL54 1AA
Tel: (01451) 830582 Mobile: (07831) 205002 Email: lachaise@tiscali.co.uk

Specialists in leather chairs, upholstery and suppliers of loose leather desk tops. Always available from our new Showroom at Stow-on-the-Wold after 30 years at Faringdon.

Typical example of our leather fully re-upholstered Victorian Chesterfields.

Audrey McConnell
Silver and jewellery, picture frames, ceramics, ivory and micromosaics.

Vicki Mills Antiques
Beadwork and needlework pictures, quilts and bedcovers, blue and white and chintz pottery, bamboo furniture.

Colin Morris
Early oak furniture and carvings, pewter, copper and brass, ceramics, religious imagery and interesting vernacular objects.

Paper Moon Books
Fine 19th-20th C bindings including poetry, prose and history; prayer books and bibles.

Edith and Brian Prosser Antiques
18th-20th C furniture, mirrors, prints and lighting; decorative items including glass and ceramics, metalware and objets de vertu.

Jane Radford Fine Art
Quality mourning and sentimental jewellery, fine portrait miniatures, silhouettes and objets de vertu.

Lindsey Richardson Antiques
19th C ceramics including Staffordshire, blue and white and majolica; glass and small decorative items.

Times Past
(Judy Pollitt). Needlework tools, chatelaines, small silver and objets de vertu

The Fosse Gallery
The Square. GL54 1AF. Est. 1979. Open 10-5.30 prior telephone call advisable. SIZE: Large. *STOCK: English and Scottish painters, many RA, RSA and Royal Glasgow Institute members, including Gore, Howard, Ward, Dunstan, Spear, Weight, Morrocco, Donaldson, McClure, Haig, Devlin and Michael Scott.* LOC: Off Fosseway, A429. PARK: Easy. TEL: 01451 831319; fax - 01451 870309. SER: Valuations.

Fox Cottage Antiques
Digbeth St. GL54 1BN. (Sue London). Est. 1995. Open 10-5. SIZE: 10 dealers. *STOCK: Wide variety of general antiques including pottery and porcelain, silver and plate, metalware, prints, small furniture, country and decorative items, mainly pre 1900, £5-£1,000.* LOC: Left hand side at bottom of narrow street, running down from the square. PARK: Nearby. TEL: 01451 870307; e-mail - info@foxcottageantiques.co.uk website - www.fox cottageantiques.co.uk

Keith Hockin Antiques   BADA
The Square. GL54 1AF. CADA. Est. 1968. Open Thurs., Fri. and Sat. 10-5, other times by appointment or ring the bell. SIZE: Medium. *STOCK: Oak furniture, 1600-1750; country furniture in oak, fruitwoods, yew, 1700-1850; pewter, copper, brass, ironwork, all periods.* Not Stocked: Mahogany. PARK: Easy. TEL: 01451 831058; e-mail - keithhockin@aol.com SER: Buys at auction (oak, pewter, metalwork). VAT: Stan/Spec.

Huntington Antiques Ltd   LAPADA
Church St. GL54 1BE. (M.F. and S.P. Golding). CADA. CINOA. Resident. Est. 1974. Open 9.30-5.30 or by appointment. SIZE: Large. *STOCK: Early period and fine country furniture, metalware, tapestries and works of art.* LOC: Opposite main gates to church. TEL: 01451 830842; fax - 01451 832211; e-mail - info@huntington-antiques.com website - www.huntington-antiques.com SER: Valuations; buys at auction. VAT: Spec.

Kenulf Fine Arts   LAPADA
Digbeth St. GL54 1BN. (E. and J. Ford). Est. 1978. Open 10-5, Sun. 12-5. SIZE: 7 rooms. *STOCK: 19th to early 20th C oils, watercolours and prints; decorative items, fine period walnut and mahogany furniture; bronzes and contemporary paintings.* LOC: Near Barclays Bank. PARK: Easy. TEL: 01451 870878; mobile - 07774 107269; e-mail - kenulf.finearts@virgin.net SER: Valuations; restorations (oils and watercolours, period framing). FAIRS: NEC; LAPADA; Northern; Belgian. VAT: Spec.

T.M. King-Smith & Simon W. Nutter
Wraggs Row, Fosseway. GL54 1JT. Est. 1975. Open 9.30-5.30. *STOCK: 18th-19th C mahogany and oak furniture, £500-£10,000; porcelain, brass, copper and pictures.* LOC: Near traffic lights opposite the Unicorn Hotel. TEL: 01451 830658. SER: Buys at auction. VAT: Spec.

La Chaise Antique
Beauport, Sheep St. GL54 1AA. (Roger Clark). GMC. Est. 1968. Open 9.30-5.30, Sun. 11-4 (prior telephone call advisable). SIZE: Large. *STOCK: Chairs, pre-1860; furniture, 18th-19th C; general antiques, decorators*

items, upholstered library and Victorian arm chairs (leather/fabric). Not Stocked: Silver, porcelain and glass. PARK: Ample. TEL: 01451 830582; mobile - 07831 205002; e-mail - lachaise@tiscali.co.uk SER: Valuations; restorations; upholstery (leather and fabrics); table top liners. FAIRS: NEC (Jan., April, Aug., Nov); LAPADA, London (Oct). VAT: Spec.

Roger Lamb Antiques & Works of Art   LAPADA
The Square. GL54 1AB. CADA. Est. 1993. Open 10-5 or by appointment. SIZE: 3 main showrooms. *STOCK: Fine 18th to early 19th C furniture especially small items, lighting, decorative accessories, oils and watercolours.* LOC: Next to town hall. PARK: Easy. TEL: 01451 831371; fax - 01451 832485; mobile - 07860 391959. SER: Search.

Malt House Antiques
The Malt House, Digbeth St. GL54 1BN. (C.P., K.V. and A.E. Mortimer). Est. 1986. Open 9.30-5.30 (including some Sun.) and by appointment. SIZE: Large (5 showrooms). *STOCK: Fine 17th-19th C furniture; ceramics including Royal Worcester, Staffordshire pot-lids and ware, Wemyss; wine, medical and dental items, paintings and prints; specialist antiques and collecting books.* LOC: Just off The Square. PARK: Easy. TEL: 01451 830592; fax - same; e-mail - Malthousestow@aol.com website - www.malthouseantiques.com VAT: Spec.

Park House Antiques
Park St. GL54 1AQ. (G. and B. Sutton). Est. 1986. Open Wed.- Sat. 10-1 and 2-4.30. By appointment Nov., Dec., Jan. and May. SIZE: Large. *STOCK: Early dolls, teddy bears, toys, Victorian linen and lace, porcelain, collectables, small furniture and pictures.* PARK: Easy. TEL: 01451 830159; home - same; e-mail - info@ thetoymuseum.co.uk website - www.thetoymuseum. co.uk SER: Museum of dolls, teddies, toys, textiles and collectables; teddy bears repaired; antique dolls dressed.

Antony Preston Antiques Ltd   BADA
The Square. GL54 1AB. CADA. CINOA. Est. 1965. Open 9.30-5.30 or by appointment. SIZE: Large. STOCK: 18th-19th C English and Continental furniture and objects; barometers and period lighting. LOC: Town centre. PARK: Easy. TEL: 01451 831586; fax - 01451 831596; mobile - 07785 975599; e-mail - antony@antonypreston.com website - www.antony preston.com FAIRS: BADA. VAT: Stan/Spec.

Queens Parade Antiques Ltd   BADA
The Square. GL54 1AB. (Sally and Antony Preston). CADA. CINOA. Est. 1985. Open 9.30-5.30. SIZE: Large. STOCK: 18th to early 19th C furniture, decorative objects, needlework, tole and lighting. LOC: Town centre. PARK: Easy. TEL: 01451 831586; fax - 01451 831596; e-mail - antony@antonypreston.com website - www.antonypreston.com FAIRS: BADA. VAT: Stan/Spec.

Michael Rowland Antiques
Little Elms, The Square. GL54 1AF. Est. 1991. Open 10.45-5. SIZE: Medium. *STOCK: Furniture including Welsh dressers, farmhouse, gateleg and side tables, bureaux, 17th-18th C, £750-£10,000.* PARK: Easy. TEL: 01451 870089; home - same. VAT: Spec.

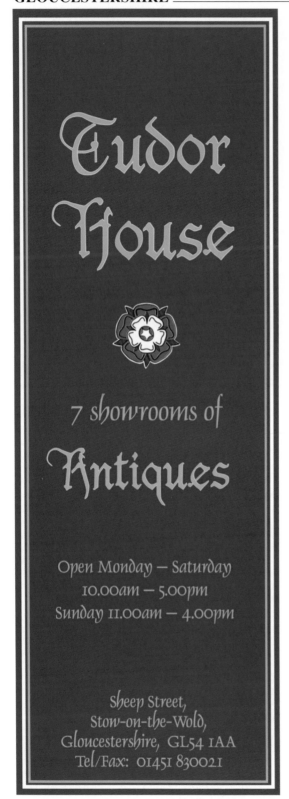

Tudor House

7 showrooms of

Antiques

Open Monday – Saturday
10.00am – 5.00pm
Sunday 11.00am – 4.00pm

Sheep Street,
Stow-on-the-Wold,
Gloucestershire, GL54 1AA
Tel/Fax: 01451 830021

Ruskin Decorative Arts
5 Talbot Court. GL54 1DP. (Anne and William Morris). CADA. Est. 1990. Open 10-1 and 2-5.30. SIZE: Small. *STOCK: Interesting and unusual decorative objects, Arts and Crafts furniture, Art Nouveau, Art Deco, glass and pottery, metalwork, 1880-1960.* LOC: Between the square and Sheep St. PARK: Nearby. TEL: 01451 832254; home - 01993 831880; e-mail - william.anne@ ruskindecarts.co.uk SER: Valuations. FAIRS: NEC.

Arthur Seager Antiques
50 Sheep St. GL54 1AA. Est. 1977. Open Thurs., Fri. and Sat. 11-4. *STOCK: Period oak, carvings and sculpture, £500-£20,000.* TEL: 01451 831605; e-mail - arthur.seager@btconnect.com website - www.arthur seager.co.uk

Stow Antiques   LAPADA
The Square. GL54 1AF. (Mr and Mrs J. and Bruce Hutton-Clarke). CADA. Resident. Est. 1969. Open Mon.-Sat. 10-5.30, other times by appointment. SIZE: Large. *STOCK: Furniture, mainly Georgian and Regency mahogany - dining tables, chairs, bookcases, sideboards and cabinets, £500-£30,000; decorative items, gilded mirrors, £50-£10,000.* PARK: Easy. TEL: 01451 830377; fax - 01451 870018; e-mail - hazel@ stowantiques.demon.co.uk SER: Shipping worldwide.

Styles of Stow
The Little House, Sheep St. GL54 1JS. (Mr and Mrs W.J. Styles). Est. 1981. Open 10-4.30. SIZE: Medium. *STOCK: Longcase (100+) and bracket clocks, barometers, 18th-19th C, £400-£30,000; fine furniture, 18th-19th C, £250-£15,000; oils and watercolours, 19th-20th C, £25-£20,000.* LOC: Opposite post office. PARK: Easy. TEL: 01451 830455; home and fax - same; e-mail - info@stylesofstow.co.uk website - stylesofstow.co.uk SER: Valuations; restorations; buys at auction (longcase and bracket clocks). VAT: Margin.

Talbot Court Galleries
Talbot Court. GL54 1BQ. (J.P. Trevers). CADA. IMCOS. Est. 1988. Open 9.30-1 and 1.30-5.30. SIZE: Medium. *STOCK: Prints and maps, 1580-1880, £10-£5,000.* LOC: Behind Talbot Hotel in precinct between the square and Sheep St. PARK: Nearby. TEL: 01451 832169; fax - 01451 832167. SER: Valuations; restorations; cleaning; colouring; framing; buys at auction (engravings). VAT: Stan.

The Titian Gallery   LAPADA
Sheep St. GL54 1JS. (Ilona Johnson Gibbs). CADA. CINOA. Est. 1978. Open 10-5 and by appointment. SIZE: Medium. *STOCK: Fine 18th-19th C British and European oil paintings and watercolours, £1,000-£40,000.* LOC: Opposite the Unicorn Hotel, near The Fosseway. PARK: Adjacent and nearby. TEL: 01451 830004; fax - 01451 830126; e-mail - ilona@ titiangallery.co.uk website - www.titiangallery.co.uk SER: Valuations; buys at auction (oils and watercolours). FAIRS: CADA exhibition. VAT: Spec.

Tudor House
Sheep St. GL54 1AA. (Peter Collingridge and Roy Hooper). Est. 2001. Open 10-5, Sun. 11-4. SIZE: 7 showrooms. *STOCK: Furniture, £500-£10,000;*

metalware, £50-£2,500; both 1700-1900. Porcelain, 1720-1920, £50-£2,500; silver, 1850-1940, £30-£500. LOC: Turn at traffic lights from A429. PARK: At rear. TEL: 01451 830021; fax - same; mobile - 07860 581858; website - www.tudor-house-antiques.com SER: Valuations. VAT: Spec. Below are listed the dealers trading from this address.

Ashley Antiques
Curios.

Colin Brand
Clocks, porcelain, decorative furniture, militaria.

Jeremy Collingridge
Fountain pens.

Peter Collingridge
Metalware, mirrors, lighting, furniture 1700-1900.

Norma Cordery
19th C brass including fireplace items.

David Cridland and Vivienne King
Lighting, fireside items, porcelain, glass, collectables and furniture.

Vienneta Edwards
18th-19th C pottery, metalware, decorative and collectable items.

Peter Gibbons
Early metalware and carvings.

Maureen Gough
Traditional English furniture and objects.

Roy Hooper
Metalware, Arts & Crafts, Art Nouveau.

Hopeful Fish
Arts & Crafts, metalware especially Newlyn and Keswick schools.

Hugh Jolly
Original signed prints by Snaffles, Cecil Aldin, Lionel Edwards and other sporting artists.

Hazel Kewley
Blue & white pottery, Staffordshire figures and animals, decorative collectables.

Atlanti Meyer
Decorative items including pewter, silver, glass and porcelain.

Tim Olney
18th to early 19th C English porcelain, especially Worcester and Newhall.

Outram Antiques
Mainly country furniture and Mson's Ironstone

Malcolm Potter
Mainly 17th-18th C oak, pewter.

Iris Walker
Decorative and garden furniture, objets d'art.

Elizabeth Watkiss
Silver, 19th C boxes, blue & white transfer printed pottery.

Wooden Bygones
Treen.

Vanbrugh House Antiques
Park St. GL54 1AQ. (J. and M.M. Sands). Resident. Est. 1972. Open 10-5.30 or by appointment. *STOCK: Furniture and decorative items, 17th to early 19th C; early maps, music boxes, clocks and barometers.* LOC: Opposite the Bell Inn. PARK: Easy. TEL: 01451 830797; fax - same; e-mail - johnsands@vanbrughhouse.co.uk website - www.vanbrughhouse.co.uk SER: Valuations. VAT: Stan/Spec.

Wychwood Books
Sheep St. GL54 1AA. (Lucy and Henry Baggott). Est. 2001. Open 9.30-5.30. SIZE: Small. *STOCK: Secondhand and antiquarian books especially architectural, field sports and antiques, £1-£2,000.* LOC: Near Post Office. TEL: 01451 831880; e-mail - wychwoodbooks@btopenworld.com SER: Restorations (books).

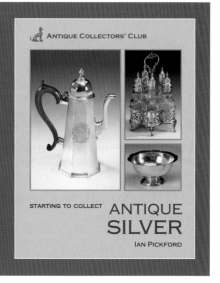

WYNDHAMS

1 Brewery Yard, Sheep Street,
Stow-on-the-Wold,
Gloucestershire

Fine 18th and 19th Century
English Furniture
Decorative Antiques

LAPADA
MEMBER

Tel/Fax: 01451 870067

Wyndhams   **LAPADA**
1 Brewery Yard, Sheep St. GL54 1AA. (Philip Brown and Kevin Quin). Est. 1988. Open 10-5 or by appointment. SIZE: Large - 3 showrooms. *STOCK: Fine mid-18th to early 19th C English exotic wood furniture and barometers; decorative antiques including boxes and caddies; watercolours and prints.* PARK: Nearby. TEL: 01451 870067; fax - same; e-mail - antiques@wyndhams.com   website - www. wyndhams.com SER: Valuations. VAT: Spec.

STROUD

Minchinhampton Architectural
Cirencester Rd., Aston Down. GL6 8PE. (S. Tomlin and D. Kedge). SALVO. Est. 1978. Open 9-5, Sat. 9-3, Sun. 11-2. SIZE: Large. *STOCK: Architectural items, chimneypieces, garden ornaments, stone and wood flooring, landscape and building materials, columns and balustrading, doors and windows, door hardware and accessories.* PARK: Easy. TEL: 01285 760886; fax - 01285 760838; e-mail - masco@catbrain.com website - www.catbrain.com SER: Valuations.

TADDINGTON, Nr. Cheltenham

Architectural Heritage
Taddington Manor. GL54 5RY. (Adrian, Suzy, and Alex Puddy). CADA. Est. 1978. Open Mon.-Fri. 9.30-5.30, Sat. 10.30-4.30. SIZE: Large. *STOCK: Oak and pine period panelled rooms; stone and marble chimney*

pieces; stone, marble, bronze and terracotta statuary; garden ornaments, fountains, temples, well-heads, seats, urns, cisterns, sundials and summer houses. PARK: Easy. TEL: 01386 584414; fax - 01386 584236; e-mail - puddy@architectural-heritage.co.uk   website - www.architectural-heritage.co.uk SER: Worldwide delivery; shipping; bespoke ornaments, chimneypieces and panelled rooms. FAIRS: Chelsea Flower Show. VAT: Stan.

TETBURY

Alchemy Antiques
The Old Chapel, Long St. GL8 8AA. (D. Sayers). TADA. Est. 2004. Open 10-5. SIZE: Large - 12 dealers. *STOCK: Fruitwood and country furniture, fine oak and mahogany, mirrors and decorative porcelain, treen, copper and brass, silver, £1-£5,000. Not Stocked:* Reproductions. PARK: Nearby. TEL: 01666 505281; fax (by prior arrangement) - 01666 505661. SER: Export. VAT: Stan/Spec.

Alderson   **BADA**
58 Long St. GL8 8AQ. (C.J.R. Alderson). CINOA. Est. 1977. Open 10-5. SIZE: Small. *STOCK: British 18th-19th C furniture and works of art; British colonial furniture.* PARK: Easy. TEL: 01666 500888; mobile - 07836 594498; e-mail - kit.alderson@btopenworld. com SER: Valuations. FAIRS: BADA; Olympia.

Artique
Talboys House, Church St. GL8 8JG. (George Bristow).

TADA. Open 10-6, Sun. 12-4. *STOCK: Interiors, textiles, carpets and kelims and objets d'art from the Orient.* TEL: 01666 503597; fax - same; e-mail - george @artique.demon.co.uk website - www.artique.uk.com

Ball and Claw Antiques
45 Long St. GL8 8AA. (Chris Kirkland). TADA. Est. 1994. Open 10-5. SIZE: Medium. *STOCK: 17th-19th C furniture especially Victorian pine kitchen tables; engravings, pictures, ceramics, general antiques and decorative items.* PARK: Easy. TEL: 01666 502440; mobile - 07957 870423; e-mail - chris@ballandclaw.co. uk website - www.ballandclaw.co.uk and www. antiquekitchentables.co.uk SER: Finder.

Breakspeare Antiques
36 and 57 Long St. GL8 8AQ. (M. and S.E. Breakspeare). CADA. Resident. Est. 1962. Open 10-5 or by appointment. CL: Thurs. SIZE: Medium. *STOCK: English period furniture - early walnut, 1690-1740, mahogany, 1750-1835.* LOC: Main street - four gables building. PARK: Own. TEL: 01666 503122; fax - same. VAT: Spec.

The Chest of Drawers
24 Long St. GL8 8AQ. (A. and P. Bristow). TADA. Resident. Est. 1969. Open Tues.-Fri. 9.30-6, Mon. by appointment. SIZE: Medium. *STOCK: Late Georgian and Regency furniture; country pieces, 17th-18th C; walnut and other woods, 18th C; pictures.* LOC: On A433. PARK: Easy. TEL: 01666 502105; home - same. VAT: Spec.

Day Antiques   BADA
5 New Church St. GL8 8DS. CADA. Est. 1975. Open 10-5. SIZE: Medium. *STOCK: Early oak furniture and related items.* PARK: Easy. TEL: 01666 502413; e-mail - dayantiques@lineone.net website - www.day antiques.com VAT: Spec.

The Decorator Source
39a Long St. GL8 8AA. (Colin Gee). TADA. Open 10-5 or by appointment. SIZE: Large. *STOCK: French provincial furniture - armoires, farm tables, buffets; decorative and interior design items.* PARK: Easy. TEL: 01666 505358. VAT: Stan/Spec.

The Heritage Gallery
12 Church St. GL8 8JG. (B. Hulftegger). TADA. Open 10-5. SIZE: Medium. *STOCK: Period and contemporary sporting pictures, engravings, watercolours, oils and associated sporting items.* PARK: Easy. TEL: 01666 500234.

Jester Antiques
10 Church St. GL8 8JG. (Lorna Coles and Peter Bairsto). TADA. Open 10-5 including Sun. *STOCK: Longcase and wall clocks, also oil portraits and pictures, Oriental objects, lamps, furniture, decorative items, outside statuary and architectural.* PARK: Easy. TEL: 01666 505125; e-mail - sales@jesterantiques.co.uk website - www.jesterantiques.co.uk SER: Shipping; delivery. VAT: Margin.

Long Street Antiques
Stamford House, 14 Long St. GL8 8AQ. (Ray and Samantha White). Open 10-5. Sun. and Bank Holidays (excluding Christmas and New Year's day) 12-4. SIZE: Large - 45+ dealers. *STOCK: Fine and country furniture, mirrors, works of art, textiles, silver, kitchenalia, barometers, clocks, glass, collectables, objets d'art, brass and leather goods.* PARK: Easy. TEL: 01666 500850; e-mail - longstantiques@aol.com website - www.longstreetantiques.co.uk

Merlin Antiques
Shops 4 & 5 Chipping Court Shopping Mall. GL8 8ES. (Miriam and Brian Smith). Est. 1990. Open 9.30-5, Sun. by appointment. SIZE: Medium. *STOCK: Furniture, Georgian to date, £50-£2,000; collectables, glass, pictures, china, jewellery - gold, silver and costume, £2-£500; books.* PARK: Nearby. TEL: 01666 505008. SER: Valuations; restorations.

Peter Norden Antiques   LAPADA
61 Long St. GL8 8AA. (Peter and Jenny Norden). TADA. Est. 1960. Open 10-5.30, anytime by appointment. SIZE: Medium. *STOCK: Early oak furniture, 16th-17th C, £250-£20,000; country furniture, 17th-19th C, £75-£10,000; early carvings, metalware, pewter, pottery, treen, 14th-19th C, £10-£10,000.* PARK: Nearby. TEL: 01666 503854; fax - 01666 505595; home - 01666 505877; e-mail - peternorden-antiques@ linone.net website - www.peter-norden-antiques.co.uk SER: Valuations. VAT: Spec.

Porch House Antiques
40/42 Long St. GL8 8AQ. (Anne and Mervyn Woodburn). TADA. Est. 1977. Open 10-5. SIZE: Large. *STOCK: 17th-20th C furniture and decorative items.* LOC: Town centre. TEL: 01666 502687. VAT: Spec.

Sharland & Lewis
52 Long St. GL8 8AQ. (Ali Sharland). TADA. Open 10.30-5, Sat 10-5 or by appointment. SIZE: Medium. *STOCK: Painted furniture, textiles and decorative objects.* PARK: Easy. TEL: 01666 500354; website - www.sharland&lewis.com

Sieff
49 Long St. GL8 8AA. TADA. Est. 1994. Open 10-1 and 2-5.30, Sat. 10-5.30, Sun. by appointment. SIZE: Large. *STOCK: English and French 18th-20th C furniture and objets, £100-£10,000.* PARK: Easy. TEL: 01666 504477; fax - 01666 504478; e-mail - sieff@sieff.co.uk website - www.sieff.co.uk SER: Valuations; buys at auction. FAIRS: Harvey Decorative Antiques & Textile. VAT: Stan/Spec.

Tetbury Old Books
4 The Chipping. GL8 8ET. TADA. Open 10-6, Sun. 11-5. *STOCK: Antiquarian and secondhand books and prints.* TEL: 01666 504330; fax - 01666 504458; e-mail - oldbooks@tetbury.co.uk

Top Banana Antiques Mall 1
1 New Church St. GL8 8DS. (Julian Tatham-Losh). TADA. Est. 2002. Open 10-5.30, Sun. 11-5. SIZE: Large - 50 dealers. *STOCK: Decorative antiques and interior design items, £5-£5,000.* LOC: Beginning of Long St. PARK: Free. TEL: 08712 881102; fax - 08712 881103; e-mail - info@topbananaantiques.com website - www.topbananaantiques.com SER: Packing and shipping. VAT: Stan/Spec. Below are listed the dealers.

Avrick Antiques
(Nick Hughes and Avril Stretton). *Antique firearms and related items, swords; silver and ceramics.*

Bananarama
(Sarah Nunan). *Painted and brown furniture, pictures, kitchenalia, metalware.*

Sue Blacker
Glassware and bronzes

Shaun Bolster
Mirrors and paintings.

Elizabeth Bradwin
Period animal bronzes.

Sheila Briggs
Small collectables, jewellery and games boxes, writing slopes.

Martin Causer
Paintings, French and English furniture.

Cocoa
Antique lace, ribbons, fans and shoes.

Hedley Cullimore
Small collectables.

Rhys Davies
English and French furniture, fenders, lighting and general antiques.

W. and B. Dee
Black Forest and decorative items.

Steve Dix and Amanda Nash
Silver and toys.

Martin Ellis-Jones
Silk top hats and antiquarian books.

Michelle Gazeley-Howitt
Unusual Victorian and Edwardian items.

Philip Gibbons
Prints and pictures.

John and Sally Gormley
English furniture and decorative accessories.

Keith Gormley
Unusual decorative furniture and tribal art.

Judith Harper
Decorative accessories.

Sheena Henderson
Glass, silver and porcelain.

Hopeful Fish
Art Nouveau and Arts and Crafts ceramics, furniture and metalware.

Jennie Horrocks
English Art Nouveau and Edwardian light fittings; Arts and Crafts items.

F. Jarvis
Small collectables, ivory, silver and glass.

Kevin Jenkinson and Ruthie Shelton
Decorative furniture - painted, country pine and bamboo.

Janet Kaulbach
Decorative French painted furniture - mirrors, armoires and dressers; French textiles and linen.

Lansdown Antiques
(Chris and Ann Kemp). *Original painted English furniture, brass, pictures and mirrors.*

Mayfield Antiques
(Terry Cusack). *Large furniture - country, painted and bamboo.*

Judith Miller
Decorative antiques.

Brian Moses
Country oak furniture and small collectables.

Jenny Owen
Folk items with spongeware, wirework, wood and brass, needlework.

Mike Rawlings
Quality brassware, tools and garden items.

John Shaw
Garden items, decorative brown furniture, metal and wire work.

Julian Tatham-Losh
Decorative smalls, Black Forest items, majolica, Staffordshire, 19th C blue and white, bamboo and interesting furniture.

Tawny Owl
(Alison Wilson, Richard Wilkins). *Pictures, glassware, jewellery and small collectables.*

Jenny Turner
Sewing items, Mauchline and tartanware, small collectables.

Gary Wallis and Stuart Badcock
Decorative English and French furniture and accessories; garden items.

John and Sonia Ward
Country furniture, brass, copper and collectables.

Jan Wookey and Mike Loveday
Antique to contemporary jewellery, hatpins, button hooks, dressing table items.

Christine and Alec Yirrell
Silver and plated items, small collectables.

Top Banana Antiques Mall 2
32 Long St. GL8 8AQ. (Julian Tatham-Losh). TADA. Est. 2004. Open 10-5.30, Sun. 11-5. SIZE: 15 dealers. *STOCK: Decorative antiques and interior design, £5-£5,000.* LOC: Halfway along Long St. PARK: Easy. TEL: 08712 881110; fax - 08712 881103; e-mail - info@topbananaantiques.com website - www.topbanana antiques.com SER: Packing and shipping. VAT: Stan/Spec. Below are listed the dealers.

Chris Ashton
Art Deco and decorative furniture, mirrors and lighting.

Cocoa
Painted decorative furniture.

Maureen Elder and Cliff Butler
Traditional furniture and smalls; contemporary chrome.

Graham Fowler
Writing slopes and tea caddies.

Graham and Barbara Hale
Framed period oil portraits and landscapes.

Ines Muir Antiques
Decorative wooden lamps, French linen, 20th C furniture including Art Deco and retro; French mirrors, glass and vases.

John Sotirakis Ioannou
Decorative lighting.

Slade Antiques
17th C oak to 19th C furniture and traditional smalls.

Ashley Wade
Period glass and country furniture.

Sheila Young
Prints, watercolours.

Top Banana Antiques Malls 3 & 4
46-48 Long St. GL8 8AQ. (Julian Tatham-Losh). TADA. Est. 2004. Open 10-5.30, Sun. 11-5. SIZE: 7 dealers. *STOCK: Decorative antiques and interior design including jewellery, kitchenalia, luggage, paintings, decorative and painted furniture, Art Deco, £5-£5,000.* PARK: Free. TEL: 08712 883058; fax - 08712 881103; e-mail - info@topbananaantiques.com website - www.topbananaantiques.com SER: Packing and shipping. VAT: Stan/Spec. Below are listed the dealers.

Philip Biltoft
French country furniture and accessories and garden items.

Ben Cooper
Furniture especially Irish and dressers.

Dray Luggage
Luggage, hat boxes, sporting leather items, bamboo tables.

Raymond Harrison
Jewellery.

Skip and Janey Smithson
Period kitchenalia.

White Leopard Antiques
General antiques especially Staffordshire.

Townsend Bateson
51A Long St. GL8 8AA. (Lynda Townsend Bateson). TADA. Est. 1995. Open 10-5. SIZE: Medium. *STOCK: Mainly French provincial and painted furniture, ceramics and interior design items.* TEL: 01666 505083; e-mail - townsendbateson@btopenworld.com website - www.townsendbatesonantiques.com SER: Shipping. VAT: Global.

Westwood House Antiques
29 Long St. GL8 8AA. (Richard Griffiths). TADA. Resident. Est. 1993. Open 10-5.30 or by appointment. SIZE: Large. *STOCK: Oak, elm and ash country furniture - dressers, dresser bases and tables (especially French farmhouse), 17th-19th C; decorative country pottery.* TEL: 01666 502328; fax - same; mobile - 07774 952909; e-mail - westwoodhouseantiques1@btconnect.com VAT: Spec.

TEWKESBURY

Gainsborough House Antiques
81 Church St. GL20 5RX. (A. and B. Hilson). Open 9.30-5. *STOCK: Furniture, 18th to early 19th C; glass, porcelain.* TEL: 01684 293072. SER: Restorations; conservation.

Tewkesbury Antiques & Collectables Centre
Tolsey Lane (by The Cross). GL20 5AE. Open 10-5, Sun. 11-5. SIZE: 14 units. *STOCK: Furniture, rugs, porcelain, glass, cameras, books, records, textiles, pictures, kitchenalia.* LOC: Town centre. TEL: 01684 294091.

TODENHAM, Nr. Moreton-in-Marsh

Geoffrey Stead   BADA
Wyatts Farm. GL56 9NY. Est. 1963. Open by appointment. STOCK: English and Continental furniture, decorative works of art and sculpture. LOC: 3 miles from Moreton-in-Marsh. PARK: Easy. TEL: 01608 650997; fax - 01608 650597; mobile - 07768 460450; e-mail - geoffreystead@geoffreystead.com SER: Valuations. FAIRS: Olympia. VAT: Spec.

WHITTINGTON, Nr. Cheltenham

Whittington Barn Antiques
GL54 4HD. (Miss Marie Pinchin). Resident. Est. 1982. Open by appointment. SIZE: Medium. *STOCK: 18th-19th C English and French furniture and mirrors, £100-£2,000; 20th C lighting, £100-£1,000.* LOC: A40 Cheltenham to Oxford road. PARK: Easy. TEL: 01242 820164; mobile - 07710 411501. FAIRS: Newark. VAT: Stan/Spec.

WINCHCOMBE

Berkeley Antiques
3 Hailes St. GL54 5HU. (P.S. and S.M. Dennis). *STOCK: Mahogany, oak, walnut, 17th-19th C, £50-£2,000; brass, copper, silver, china and glass.* TEL: 01242 609074; website - www.berkeleyantiques.com SER: Valuations; restorations.

Government House
St Georges House, High St. GL54 5LJ. Est. 1979. Open by appointment. *STOCK: Antique and pre-war lighting and accessories.* LOC: Village centre. PARK: Own. TEL: 01242 604562; mobile - 07970 430684. SER: Spare parts stocked; restorations (period lighting). FAIRS: Newark, Ardingly, Swinderby. VAT: Spec/Global.

In Period Antiques
Queen Anne House, High St. GL54 5LJ. (John Edgeler). Resident. Est. 1999. Open Tues.-Thurs. 10-1, Fri. and Sat. 10-5. SIZE: Medium. *STOCK: Period oak and mahogany furniture, Arts and Crafts, porcelain, glass, silver and metalware and decorative accessories.* PARK: Easy. TEL: 01242 602319; mobile - 07816 193027; website - www.inperiodantiques.co.uk

Prichard Antiques
16 High St. GL54 5LJ. (K.H. and D.Y. Prichard). CADA. Est. 1979. Open 9-5.30, Sun. by appointment. SIZE: Large - six showrooms. *STOCK: Period and decorative furniture, £10-£20,000; treen and metalwork, £5-£5,000; interesting and decorative accessories.* LOC: On B4632 Broadway to Cheltenham road. PARK: Easy. TEL: 01242 603566. VAT: Spec.

HAMPSHIRE

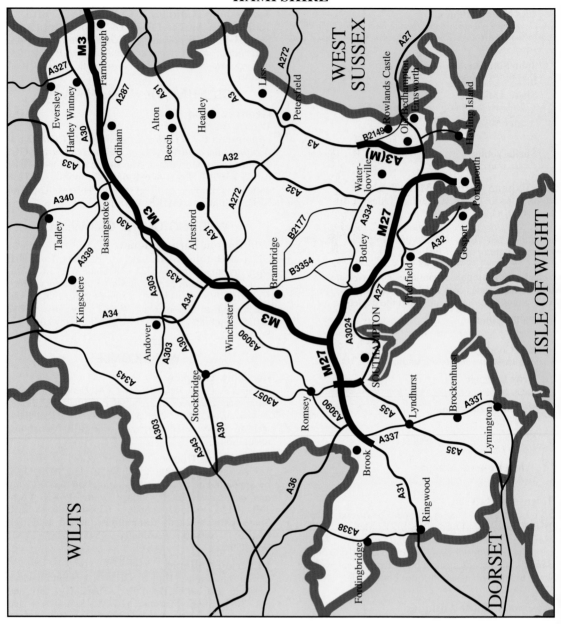

Dealers and Shops in Hampshire

Alresford	3	Brook	1	Headley	1	Ringwood	3
Alton	1	Emsworth	5	Kingsclere	1	Romsey	1
Andover	1	Eversley	1	Liss	1	Rowlands Castle	1
Basingstoke	1	Farnborough	1	Lymington	5	Southampton	5
Beech	1	Fordingbridge	1	Lyndhurst	3	Stockbridge	6
Botley	1	Gosport	3	Odiham	1	Tadley	1
Brambridge	1	Hartley Wintney	9	Old Bedhampton	1	Titchfield	2
Brockenhurst	2	Hayling Island	1	Petersfield	3	Waterlooville	1
				Portsmouth	3	Winchester	11

ALRESFORD, Nr. Winchester

Artemesia
16 West St. SO24 9AT. (D.T.L. Wright). Est. 1972. Open 9.30-5. SIZE: Medium. *STOCK: English and Continental furniture, English, Continental and Oriental porcelain and works of art, £20-£6,000.* LOC: A31. PARK: Nearby. TEL: 01962 732277. SER: Valuations.

Laurence Oxley Ltd
Studio Bookshop and Gallery, 17 Broad St. SO24 9AW. (Anthony Oxley). ABA. FATG. Est. 1951. Open 9-5. SIZE: Large. *STOCK: Antiquarian books, £5-£2,500; topographical prints, £2-£250; maps, £5-£800; watercolours, (specialising in M. Birket Foster, RWS 1825-1899), £100-£30,000.* LOC: B3046. PARK: Easy. TEL: 01962 732188 (books), 01962 732998 (pictures); e-mail - aoxley@freenet.co.uk SER: Valuations; restorations (oil paintings, watercolours, prints and books); framing; book-binding. FAIRS: London ABA (Chelsea). VAT: Stan.

Pineapple House Antiques
49 Broad St. SO24 9AS. (Peter Radford). Est. 1979. Open Thurs., Fri. and Sun. 11-4, Sat. 11-6, other times by appointment. SIZE: Small. *STOCK: Furniture, especially dining tables, chairs, sideboards, chests of drawers and smaller items, 18th-20th C.* PARK: Easy. TEL: 01962 736575; fax - same; mobile - 07973 254749; website - www.pineapplehouseantiques.com SER: Valuations; restorations; repairs; cabinet making.

ALTON

Appleton Eves Ltd
30 Normandy St. GU34 1BX. (Richard Eves and Errin Bale). Est. 2000. Open 10-5. SIZE: Small - 9 dealers. *STOCK: 19th-20th C silver, jewellery, pictures, china, glass and metalwork, £5-£500.* PARK: Nearby. TEL: 01420 84422; fax - same; mobile - 07747 043655; e-mail - richard.eves@carltonhouseantiques.co.uk website - www.appleton-eves.co.uk

ANDOVER

Graylings Antiques
(Nick and Gail Young). Est. 1968. Open by appointment. *STOCK: Staffordshire portrait figures and animals, 1800-1890, £50-£2,500.* PARK: Easy. TEL: 01264 710077; home - same. SER: Valuations; restorations. FAIRS: Newark.

BASINGSTOKE

Squirrel Collectors Centre
9A New St. RG21 1DF. (A.H. Stone). Est. 1981. Open 10-5.30. SIZE: Small. *STOCK: Jewellery and silver, Victorian and Edwardian, £5-£4,500; books, postcards, watches, collectors' items, smalls, china, toys and large furniture showroom.* LOC: Near traffic lights at junction with Winchester St. PARK: Nearby. TEL: 01256 464885; e-mail - ahs@squirrelsuk.fsnet.co.uk SER: Valuations. VAT: Stan.

BEECH, Nr. Alton

Jardinique
Old Park Farm, Abbey Rd. GU34 4AP. (Edward and Sarah Neish). Resident. Est. 1994. Open 10-5. CL: Sun. and Mon. and Jan. and Feb. except by appointment. SIZE: Very large. *STOCK: Garden ornaments, urns, statuary and furniture, from 17th C, £10-£5,000.* LOC: From Alton on the A339 Basingstoke road, take first left signed Beech, after 1.5 miles premises on left opposite Alton Abbey. PARK: Easy. TEL: 01420 560055; fax - 01420 560050; e-mail - enquiries@Jardinique.co.uk website - www.Jardinique.co.uk SER: Valuations; buys at auction (as stock). VAT: Stan/Spec.

BOTLEY, Nr. Southampton

The Furniture Trading Co
Botley Mills. SO30 2GB. (L. Davies). Est. 1986. Open 10-5, Sun. 11-4. SIZE: Medium. *STOCK: Antique and reproduction furniture, including painted and distressed; decorative accessories aand contemporary oak furniture.* LOC: Off M27, exit 7. PARK: Easy. TEL: 01489 788194; fax - 01489 797337. SER: Valuations; restorations (furniture including upholstery, caning and French polishing); furniture made to order - old and new pine and painted; interior decoration. VAT: Stan.

BRAMBRIDGE, Nr. Eastleigh

Brambridge Antiques
The Barn, Bugle Farm, Highbridge Rd. SO50 6HS. (Desmond and Ann May). Est. 1982. Open 10-5. SIZE: Medium. *STOCK: Furniture, including oak and pine, late Georgian to Edwardian.* PARK: Easy. TEL: 01962 714386; home - 02380 269205. SER: Valuations; restorations (furniture including upholstery and re-leathering).

BROCKENHURST

Antiquiteas
37 Brookley Rd. SO42 7RB. (R. Wolstenholme). Resident. Est. 1996. Open 10-5, Sun. 10.30-3. SIZE: Medium. *STOCK: Furniture including pine, £50-£350; china and glass, copper and brass, £10-£100; all 19th-20th C.* LOC: Near watersplash and village post office. PARK: Easy. TEL: 01590 622120. VAT: Stan.

Squirrels
Lyndhurst Rd. SO42 7RL. (Sue Crocket). Est. 1990. Open 10-5 including Sun. - until dusk in winter. CL: Tues. *STOCK: Furniture including stripped pine, china especially blue and white, Victoriana, Art Deco, Art Nouveau, retro and gardenalia, 19th-20th C, to £1,000.* LOC: Opposite Rose and Crown. PARK: Easy. TEL: 01590 622433,

BROOK

F.E.A. Briggs Ltd
Birchenwood Farm. SO43 7JA. Est. 1968. Open by appointment. SIZE: Large warehouse. *STOCK: Antique and Victorian furniture.* LOC: M27 exit 1. PARK: Easy. TEL: 02380 812595; e-mail - feabriggs@aol.com SER: Restorations; valuations. FAIRS: Newark. VAT: Stan/Spec.

EMSWORTH

Antique Bed Company
32 North St. PO10 7DG. (Ian and Judi Trewick). Est. 1993. Open 9-5, Wed. 9-12.30. SIZE: Small. *STOCK: Iron and brass, brass and wooden beds, 19th C, to £1,000.* LOC: From A259 roundabout in Emsworth, turn towards station. PARK: Nearby. TEL: 01243 376074; fax - same; home - 02392 492772. SER: Restorations (beds).

Bookends
7 High St. PO10 7AQ. (Mrs Carol Waldron). Est. 1982. Open 9.30-5, Sun. 10-3. SIZE: Medium. *STOCK: Books, some antiquarian; sheet music and scores, £2-£200.* PARK: Nearby. TEL: 01243 372154; e-mail - cawaldron@tinyworld.co.uk website - www.bookends. me.uk SER: Valuations; book search.

Clockwise
10 South St. PO10 7EH. (D. Judge). AHS. GMC. Est. 1976. Open Wed.-Sat. 10-5. SIZE: Small. *STOCK: Longcase, wall, mantel, bracket and carriage clocks, 18th-19th C, £300-£12,000.* LOC: A259 off A27, head for harbour. PARK: Easy. TEL: 01243 377558; e-mail - judge@clock-wise.fsnet.co.uk website - www.clock-wise.co.uk SER: Valuations; restorations.

Dolphin Quay Antique Centre
Queen St. PO10 7BU. (C. and L. Creamer). Est. 1996. Open 10-5, Sun. and Bank Holidays 10-4. SIZE: Large - 40+ dealers. *STOCK: Fine English, French and country furniture, 18th C to 1939; marine antiques; clocks - bracket, mantel, longcase; wristwatches, fobs, dress watches, vintage pens, conservatory and garden antiques, decorative arts, silver, jewellery, china including Clarice Cliff and Troika, Whitefriars glass, paintings, watercolours, prints.* PARK: Own and in square. TEL: 01243 379994. e-mail - chrisdqantiques@aol.com

Tiffins Antiques
12 Queen St. PO10 7BL. (Phyl Hudson). Est. 1987. Open 9.30-5. CL: Mon. and Tues. SIZE: Small. *STOCK: General antiques, oil lamps and silver.* TEL: 01243 372497; home - same.

EVERSLEY, Nr. Wokingham

Eversley Barn Antiques
Church Lane. RG27 0PX. (H. Craven). Est. 1988. Open 7 days 10-5. SIZE: Large. *STOCK: Regency, Victorian and Edwardian furniture; glass, ceramics, pictures, mirrors, books, rugs, silver, chandeliers, clocks and collectables.* LOC: From M3, junction 4A, A327 to Reading, 1.5 miles from Blackbush airport and Hartley Wintney. PARK: Easy. TEL: 01189 328518; e-mail - eversleybarn@hotmail.com website - www.eversley barnantiques.co.uk

FARNBOROUGH

Martin and Parke   LAPADA
97 Lynchford Rd. GU14 6ET. (J. Martin). Est. 1971. Open 9-5. SIZE: Large. *STOCK: Furniture, shipping goods and books.* PARK: Easy. TEL: 01252 515311. VAT: Stan.

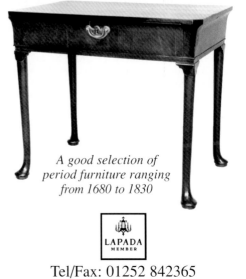

FORDINGBRIDGE

Quatrefoil
Burgate. SP6 1LX. (C.D. and Mrs I. Aston). Resident. Est. 1972. Always open. SIZE: Large. *STOCK: Early oak furniture, 16th-18th C, £50-£15,000; carvings and sculpture, 13th-17th C, £20-£20,000; antiquities and coins, £50-£10,000.* LOC: On A338, adjacent Tudor Rose Inn. PARK: Easy. TEL: 01425 653309. VAT: Stan/Spec.

GOSPORT

Former Glory
49 Whitworth Rd. PO12 3AH. (Les Brannon). Est. 1987. Open 9.30-5. SIZE: Small. *STOCK: Victorian and Edwardian furniture, £120-£400.* LOC: Near town centre. PARK: Easy. TEL: 02392 504869. SER: Valuations; restorations (furniture repairs, refinishing, repolishing, traditional upholstery)

Peter Pan's Bazaar
87 Forton Rd. PO12 4TG. (S.V. Panormo). Est. 1960. CL: Mon., Tues. and Wed. *STOCK: Vintage cameras, early photographica, images, 1850-1950, £5-£1,500.* LOC: Main road into town. PARK: Easy. TEL: 02392 524254. FAIRS: Main south of England.

Peter Pan's of Gosport
87 Forton Rd. PO12 4TG. (J. McClaren). Est. 1965. CL: Mon., Tues. and Wed. *STOCK: Jewellery, dolls, toys and miniatures.* LOC: Main road into town. PARK: Easy. TEL: 02392 524254. FAIRS: Main south of England.

Cedar Antiques Centre
Hartley Wintney, Hampshire, RG27 8NY

Over 40 Individual Dealers offer a wide variety of good quality antiques and collectables. Charming Courtyard Café serves delicious Lunches, Cream Teas and also houses the T.G. Green Pottery Museum. Space for Dealers with high quality stock sometimes available.

Open: Mon to Sat. 10am to 5.30pm Sundays & Bank Holidays 11am to 4pm
Tel: 01252 843222 Fax: 01252 842111
www.cedar-antiques.com e-mail: dg@cedar-ltd.demon.co.uk

HARTLEY WINTNEY

Nicholas Abbott   LAPADA
High St. RG27 8NY. (C.N. Abbott). Est. 1962. Open 9.30-5.30 or by appointment. SIZE: Medium. *STOCK: Walnut and mahogany English furniture, 18th to early 19th C.* LOC: Village centre. PARK: Easy. TEL: 01252 842365; fax - same; e-mail - nicholasabbott@web-hq.com website - www.nicholasabbott.com SER: Restorations; valuations. VAT: Stan/Spec.

Anvil Antiques
The Green. RG27 8PG. (Andrew Pitter). Open 10-5. SIZE: Medium. *STOCK: General antiques.* LOC: A30. PARK: Easy. TEL: 01252 845403; mobile - 07778 934938. SER: Restorations (porcelain).

Cedar Antiques Centre Ltd
High St. RG27 8NY. (Derek and Sally Green). Est. 1998. Open 10-5.30, Sun. and Bank Holidays 11-4. SIZE: Large - 40+ dealers. *STOCK: Quality furniture, glass, porcelain and pottery, paintings, rugs, silver, collectibles from teddy bears to treen; Cornishware museum.* LOC: A30 village centre. PARK: Opposite. TEL: 01252 843222; fax - 01252 842111; e-mail - dg@cedar-ltd.demon.co.uk website - www.cedar-antiques.com SER: Restorations (furniture). VAT: Stan/Spec.

Cedar Antiques Limited
High St. RG27 8NY. (Derek and Sally Green). Est. 1964. Open 10-5.30, Sun. and Bank Holidays 11-4. SIZE: Large. *STOCK: Fine English oak, walnut and country furniture, 17th-18th C, £50-£10,000; French provincial furniture, £800-£5,000; steel and brasswork, £30-£1,000.* Not Stocked: China, glass, silver. LOC: A30. PARK: Opposite. TEL: 01252 843252; fax - 01252 842111; e-mail - dg@cedar-ltd.demon.co.uk website - www.cedar-antiques.com SER: Valuations; restorations (period furniture); interior design and furnishing. VAT: Stan/Spec.

Bryan Clisby Antique Clocks
at Cedar Antiques Centre Ltd., High St. RG27 8NY. Est. 1976. Open 10-5.30. *STOCK: Longcase clocks, 1700-1830, £3,000-£20,000; barometers, 1770-1850, £500-£3,000; bracket, wall and mantel clocks.* LOC: A30 village centre. PARK: Opposite. TEL: 01252 716436; e-mail - bryanclisby@boltblue.com website - www.bryanclisby-antiqueclocks.co.uk SER: Valuations; restorations (clocks and barometers).

Deva Antiques
High St. RG27 8NY. (A. Gratwick). Est. 1987. Open 9-5.30. SIZE: Large. *STOCK: 18th-19th C English mahogany and walnut furniture.* PARK: Easy. TEL: 01252 843538; 01252 842946; fax - same; e-mail - devaants@aol.com website - www.devaantiques.com VAT: Stan/Spec.

David Lazarus Antiques   BADA
High St. RG27 8NS. Resident. Est. 1973. Open 9.30-5.30; some Sundays, other times by appointment. SIZE: Medium. *STOCK: 17th to early 19th C English and Continental furniture; objets d'art.* LOC: Main

street. PARK: Own. TEL: 01252 842272; fax - same. VAT: Stan/Spec.

A.W. Porter and Son

High St. RG27 8NY. (M.A. and S.J. Porter). Est. 1844. Open 9.30-5, Wed. 9.30-4. *STOCK: Clocks, silver, jewellery, glass.* LOC: Opposite Lloyds Bank. TEL: 01252 842676; fax - 01252 842064; e-mail - mark@awporter.fsnet.co.uk SER: Restorations (clocks). VAT: Stan/Spec.

Sheila Revell Antiques

at Deva, High St. RG27 8NY. Est. 1986. Open 9-5.30. *STOCK: 18th-19th C decorative objects, small furniture and collectors' items especially tea caddies and boxes.* PARK: Easy. TEL: 01252 843538.

HAYLING ISLAND

J. Morton Lee   BADA

Cedar House, Bacon Lane. PO11 0DN. (Commander and Mrs J. Morton Lee). Est. 1984. Open by appointment. *STOCK: Watercolours, 18th-20th C, £50-£10,000.* PARK: Easy. TEL: 02392 464444; mobile - 07860 810938; e-mail - j.mortonlee@ btinternet.com SER: Valuations; buys at auction; exhibitions in June and Dec. FAIRS: West London (Jan); Petersfield (Feb., Sept); BADA (March); Losely House (May); Harrogate (Oct). VAT: Stan/Spec.

HEADLEY

Victorian Dreams

The Old Holme School, Village Green, Crabtree Lane. GU35 8QH. (S. Kay). Est. 1990. Open 9-5.30, Sun. 10-4. SIZE: Large. *STOCK: Bedsteads including wooden, brass and iron, brass, caned and upholstered.* PARK: Easy. TEL: 01428 717000; fax - 01428 717111; e-mail - sales@victorian-dreams.co.uk website - www.victorian-dreams.co.uk SER: Valuations; restorations (metalwork and woodwork).

KINGSCLERE, Nr. Newbury

Kingsclere Old Bookshop (Wyseby House Books)

2A George St. RG20 5NQ. (Dr. Tim and Mrs Anne Oldham). PBFA. Est. 1978. Open 9-5. SIZE: Medium. *STOCK: Old, unusual and out-of-print books on fine art, art history, architecture, decorative arts, design, photography, biology, natural history, science, horticulture and gardening; prints: all 19th-20th C, £5-£500.* PARK: Nearby. TEL: 01635 297995; fax - 01635 297677; e-mail - info@wyseby.co.uk website - www.wyseby.co.uk SER: Valuations. FAIRS: PBFA London. VAT: Stan.

LISS

Plestor Barn Antiques

Farnham Rd. GU33 6JQ. (T.P. and C.A. McCarthy). Est. 1982. Open 10-4. CL: Sat. SIZE: Large. *STOCK: Furniture including upholstered, Victorian and Edwardian, shipping goods, pine; china and glass, copper and brass.* LOC: A325, 2 mins from A3 roundabout, near Spread Eagle public house. PARK: Easy. TEL: 01730 893922; mobile - 07850 539998; e-mail - plestor_barn@btopenworld.com.

LYMINGTON

Century Fine Arts

120 High St. SO41 9AQ. (S.A. and V. Roberts). Open 9.15-5.30. SIZE: Large. *STOCK: English furniture, English School watercolours and oil paintings and decorative items.* TEL: 01590 673532; fax - 01590 678855; website - www.centuryfinearts.co.uk VAT: Stan/Spec.

Lymington Antiques Centre

76 High St. SO41 9AL. (Lisa Reeves and Angela Simpson). Est. 1990. Open 10-5, Sat. 9-5. SIZE: 30 dealers. *STOCK: General antiques, books, clocks and watches, jewellery, glass.* PARK: Nearby. TEL: 01590 670934.

Barry Papworth

28 St. Thomas St. SO41 9NE. Est. 1960. Open 9-5.15. SIZE: Small. *STOCK: Diamond jewellery, £50-£10,000; silver, £25-£1,500 both 18th-19th C. Watches, 19th C, £50-£1,000.* LOC: A337 into town, bay window on left. PARK: Easy. TEL: 01590 676422. SER: Valuations (NAG registered); restorations. VAT: Stan/Spec.

Robert Perera Fine Art

19 St. Thomas St. SO41 9NB. (R.J.D. Perera). Open 10-1 and 2-5, Wed. 10-1, lunch-times and Sun. by appointment. SIZE: Small. *STOCK: British paintings, 19th-20th C, £100-£5,000; occasional ceramics and sculpture, 19th-20th C, £50-£1,500; paintings and etchings by W.L. Wyllie.* LOC: Top (west) end of main shopping area. PARK: Easy. TEL: 01590 678230; fax - same; website - www.art-gallery.co.uk SER: Framing. VAT: Margin.

Wick Antiques   LAPADA

Fairlea House, 110-112 Marsh Lane. SO41 9EE. (R.W. and Mrs. C. Wallrock). Est. 1977. Open 9-5, Sat. 10-1. SIZE: Medium. *STOCK: French and English furniture, 18th-19th C, £1,000-£15,000; small items, 19th to early 20th C, £100-£20,000.* LOC: Town outskirts. PARK: Own. TEL: 01590 677558; fax - same; home - 01590 672515; mobile - 07768 877069; e-mail - charles@ wickantiques.co.uk website - www.wickantiques.co.uk SER: Valuations; restorations; furniture polishing; repairs; upholstery; re-gilding; buys at auction. FAIRS: Olympia (June); LAPADA (Jan., April, Oct). VAT: Spec.

LYNDHURST

Forest Antique Centre

17 High St. SO43 7BB. (Jack and Sharon Brown). Est. 1985. Open 7 days 10-5. SIZE: Medium. *STOCK: Wide range of general antiques including furniture, jewellery and silver, clocks, ceramics, toys, postcards and stamps, 18th-21st C.* LOC: Central. PARK: Nearby. TEL: 02380 284545; mobile - 07971 355641; 07929 927252. SER: Valuations.

Lita Kaye of Lyndhurst

13 High St. SO43 7BB. (S. and S. Ferder). Est. 1947. Open 9.30-1 and 2.15-5. SIZE: Large. *STOCK: Furniture, clocks, 1690-1820; decorative porcelain, 19th C.* LOC: A35. PARK: 100yds. in High St. TEL: 02380 282337. VAT: Spec.

Lyndhurst Antiques Centre
19-21 High St. SO43 7BB. (Robert Sparks). Est. 1997. Open 10-5 including Sun. SIZE: Medium on 2 floors. *STOCK: Furniture and clocks, 18th to early 20th C, £50-£5,000; ceramics, 18th to mid 20th C, £5-£1,000; collectables, 20th C, £2-£200.* LOC: Main street by traffic lights. PARK: Public nearby. TEL: 02380 284000; website - www.lyndhurstantiques.com

ODIHAM

The Odiham Gallery
78 High St. RG25 1HJ. (I. Walker). Open 10-5, Sat. 10-1. *STOCK: Decorative and Oriental rugs and carpets.* PARK: Easy. TEL: 01256 703415.

OLD BEDHAMPTON

J F F Fire Brigade & Military Collectables
Ye Olde Coach House, Mill Lane. PO9 3JH. (Johnny Franklin). Resident. Est. 1982. Open by appointment. *STOCK: Brass firemen's helmets and fire related memorabilia; military, police and ambulance items including helmets, cap and collar badges, buttons, uniforms, caps, weapons, equipment, medals and brooches.* PARK: Easy. TEL: 02392 486485; e-mail - jffcollectables@aol.com SER: Valuations; buys at auction. FAIRS: 999 Memorabilia.

PETERSFIELD

The Barn
North Rd. GU31 4AH. (P. Gadsden). Est. 1956. Open 9-5.

STOCK: Victoriana, bric-a-brac; also large store of trade and shipping goods. TEL: 01730 262958.

The Folly Antiques Centre
Folly Market, College St. GU31 4AD. (Red Goblet Ltd). Est. 1980. Open 9.30-5. SIZE: Small. *STOCK: Furniture, 19th-20th C, £25-£1,000; ceramics and silver, 18th-20th C, £5-£100; jewellery, 19th-20th C; pictures, general antiques and collectables.* LOC: Behind Folly Wine Bar. PARK: Opposite - Festival Hall, Heath Rd. TEL: 01730 266650.

The Petersfield Bookshop
16a Chapel St. GU32 3DS. (F. Westwood). ABA. PBFA. Est. 1918. Open 9-5.30. SIZE: Large. *STOCK: Books, old and modern, £1-£500; maps and prints, 1600-1859, £1-£200; oils and watercolours, 19th C, £20-£1,000.* LOC: Chapel St. runs from the square to Station Rd. PARK: Opposite. TEL: 01730 263438; fax - 01730 269426; e-mail - sales@petersfieldbookshop.com website - www.petersfieldbookshop.com SER: Restorations and rebinding of old leather books; picture-framing and mount-cutting. FAIRS: London ABA. VAT: Stan.

PORTSMOUTH

A. Fleming (Southsea) Ltd
The Clock Tower, Castle Rd., Southsea. PO5 3DE. (A.J. and Mrs C. E. Fleming). Est. 1905. Open by appointment only. *STOCK: Furniture, silver, barometers, boxes and general antiques.* LOC: Near seafront and Royal Naval dockyard. PARK: Easy. TEL: 02392 822934; fax - 02392

293501; e-mail - mail@flemingsantiques.fsnet.co.uk website - www.flemingsantiques.com SER: Restorations. FAIRS: Local vetted. VAT: Stan/Spec.

Gray's Antiques
250 Havant Rd., Drayton. PO6 1PA. (Alexandra J. Gray). Est. 1968. Open 10-5, Sun. 12-4. CL: Wed. *STOCK: English and French furniture, £200-£5,000; oil lamps, prints and paintings, china, collectables, decorative items, £25-£3,000; all 19th-20th C.* PARK: Easy and side of shop. TEL: 02392 376379. SER: Restorations (furniture and upholstery).

Oldfield Gallery
76 Elm Grove, Southsea. PO5 1LN. Est. 1970. Open 10-5. CL: Mon. SIZE: Large. *STOCK: Maps and engravings, 16th-19th C, £5-£1,000; decorative prints, 18th-20th C, £5-£350.* PARK: Nearby. TEL: 02392 838042; fax - 02392 838042; e-mail - oldfield-gallery@ntlworld.com website - www.oldfield-antiquemaps.co.uk SER: Valuations; framing. FAIRS: London Map, Rembrant Hotel (occasionally). VAT: Stan.

RINGWOOD

Millers of Chelsea Antiques Ltd   LAPADA
Netherbrook House, 86 Christchurch Rd. BH24 1DR. Est. 1897. Open Mon. 9.30-1.30, Tues.-Fri. 9.30-5, Sat. 10-3, other times by appointment. SIZE: Large. *STOCK: Furniture - English and Continental country, mahogany, gilt and military; decorative items, treen, majolica and faïence, 18th-19th C, £25-£5,000.* LOC: On B3347 towards Christchurch. PARK: Own. TEL: 01425 472062; fax - 01425 472727; e-mail - mail@millers-antiques.co.uk website - www.millers-antiques.co.uk SER: Restorations. FAIRS: Decorative Antiques; Wilton. VAT: Stan/Spec.

New Forest Antiques
90 Christchurch Rd. BH24 1DR. Est. 1984. Open Tues.-Sat. 10-5. SIZE: Small. *STOCK: Militaria and postcards.* LOC: Off A31 into Ringwood, straight over 1st roundabout, left at next roundabout, shop 150yds. on right. PARK: Easy and at rear. TEL: 01425 474620. SER: Valuations; restorations. FAIRS: Yeovil; Woking Postcard. VAT: Stan/Spec.

Lorraine Tarrant Antiques
23 Market Place. BH24 1AN. Est. 1991. Open 10-5. CL: Mon. SIZE: Medium. *STOCK: Victorian furniture, to £1,000; china, glass, collectors items, £5-£100.* LOC: Opposite church. PARK: Easy. TEL: 01425 461123.

ROMSEY

Bell Antiques
8 Bell St. SO51 8GA. (M. and B.M. Gay). FGA. Est. 1979. Open 9.30-5.30. CL: Wed. (winter). SIZE: Large. *STOCK: Jewellery and silver, glass, pottery, porcelain, small furniture, prints and maps, mainly 19th-20th C.* LOC: Near market place. PARK: Town centre. TEL: 01794 514719. VAT: Global/Stan/Spec.

ROWLANDS CASTLE, Nr. Portsmouth

Good Day Antiques and Decor
22 The Green. PO9 6AB. (Gillian Day). Est. 1980. Open 11-5, Sun. 12-4.30. CL: Tues. and Wed. *STOCK: 20th C prints; porcelain and pottery, 1800-1950, £25-£500; jewellery and silver, 1840-1970, £25-£1,000; collectables, 19th-20th C, £5-£50.* LOC: Off junction 2, A3(M). PARK: Easy. TEL: 02392 412924; home - 02392 413221; e-mail - gooddayantiques@aol.com SER: Restorations (silver plating, gilding).

SOUTHAMPTON

Mr. Alfred's "Old Curiosity Shop" and The Morris and Shirley Galleries
280 Shirley Rd., Shirley. SO15 3HL. Est. 1952. Open 9-6 including Sun. SIZE: Very large. *STOCK: Furniture, 18th-20th C; paintings, porcelain, bronzes, brass, glass, books, silver, jewellery and general antiques.* LOC: On left of main Shirley road, 3/4 mile from Southampton central station. PARK: Own. TEL: 02380 774772. SER: Fine art dealer; valuations; auctions; curator; restorations; framing.

Amber Antiques
115 Portswood Rd., Portswood. SO17 2FX. (R. Boyle). Est. 1985. Open 10-5, Sat. 9-5, Sun. 11-3. SIZE: Large. *STOCK: Furniture, late Victorian to 1930s, £100-£1,500.* PARK: Easy. TEL: 02380 583645; fax - same. SER: Restorations; repairs; French polishing. VAT: Stan/Spec.

Meg Campbell
10 Church Lane, Highfield. SO17 1SZ. Est. 1967. Open by appointment. *STOCK: English, Scottish and Irish silver, collectors' pieces, Old Sheffield plate, portrait miniatures.* TEL: 02380 557636; fax - 02380 581070. SER: Mail order; catalogues available. VAT: Spec.

Cobwebs
78 Northam Rd. SO14 0PB. (P.R. and J.M. Boyd-Smith). Est. 1975. Open 10.30-4. CL: Wed. SIZE: Medium. *STOCK: Ocean liner memorabilia, china, silverplate, ephemera, paintings, furniture, ship fittings, 1840-1990, £5-£5,000.* LOC: 20 mins from M27. Main road into city centre from the east (A334). PARK: 20yds. TEL: 02380 227458; fax - same; website - www.cobwebs.uk.com SER: Valuations. FAIRS: Beaulieu Boat & Auto; Ship Show, London.

The Olympic Gallery
80 Northam Rd. SO14 0PB. (J.M. and P.R. Boyd-Smith). Est. 2002. Open 10.30-4. CL: Wed. SIZE: Medium. *STOCK: Prints, paintings, posters, artwork from ocean liners; ships furniture and fittings.* LOC: 20 mins from M27. Main road into city from the east (A334). PARK: Outside. TEL: 02380 227458; fax - same.

STOCKBRIDGE

Antique Eyes
Brookside, High St. SO20 6EY. (Jane and Julian Benson). Est. 1987. Open 10.30-5. SIZE: Medium. *STOCK: English and Continental furniture and decorative items, china and glass, 18th-19th C, £50-£3,000.* PARK: Easy. TEL: 01264 811137; fax - 01264 710447; mobile - 07747 611025; home - 01264 710389; e-mail - oldrecyes@aol.com FAIRS: Decorative Antiques & Textile, Battersea; Little Chelsea.

T.R. Baker
at Stockbridge Antique Centre, Old London Rd. SO20 6EJ. Est. 1962. Open 10-5. CL: Wed. SIZE: Large. *STOCK: General antiques, country furniture.* LOC: On White Hart roundabout. TEL: 01264 811008; fax - same. SER: Stripping; restorations; repairs.

The Bakhtiyar Gallery
High St. SO20 6HF. (Masoud Mazaheri-Asadi). Open 10-5. SIZE: 2 floors. *STOCK: Hand-made Persian carpets, runners, kelims, new, old and antique, nomadic, village and fine city pieces; fine English and European furniture, decorative antiques and mirrors.* PARK: Front of shop. TEL: 01264 811033; fax - 01264 811077; mobile - 07740 333333; e-mail - bakhtiyar@bakhtiyar.com website - www.bakhtiyar.com and www.thebakhtiyargallery.com SER: Valuations; restorations (furniture and carpets). FAIRS: Annual exhibitions, Salisbury

Lane Antiques
High St. SO20 6EU. (Mrs E.K. Lane). Est. 1981. Open 10-5. CL: Mon. SIZE: Small. *STOCK: English and Continental porcelain, 18th-20th C; silver and plate, decorative items, glass, chandeliers, lighting, small furniture, oils and watercolours; boxes, 18th-19th C.* PARK: Easy. TEL: 01264 810435; e-mail - info@ laneantiques.fsnet.uk website - www.stockbridge.org.uk

Fizzy Warren Decorative Antiques
High St. SO20 6EY. Est. 1988. Open 10.30-5. SIZE: Medium. *STOCK: Decorative antique furniture, mirrors, chandeliers, lamps and wall lights, tapestries, small tables, chairs, china and glass, papier mâché, to £2,000.*

LOC: Next to Greyhound public house. PARK: Easy. TEL: 01264 811137; home - 01962 867428; mobile - 07762 201076; e-mail - brymerhouse@aol.com website - www.stockbridge.org.uk

The Wykeham Gallery
High St. SO20 6HE. (Mark Jerram and Gerald Dodson). Est. 1986. Open 10-5. SIZE: Medium. *STOCK: Paintings, sculpture, watercolours, 1890-1940 and contemporary, £150-£15,000.* LOC: Main street. PARK: Easy. TEL: 01264 810364; fax - 01264 810182; e-mail - enquiries@wykehamgallery.co.uk website - www. wykehamgallery.co.uk SER: Valuations; restorations (paintings and works on paper); buys at auction (19th-20th C pictures). VAT: Spec.

TADLEY

Gasson Antiques and Interiors   LAPADA
P O Box 7225. RG26 5IY. (Patricia and Terry Gasson). Open by appointment. *STOCK: Georgian, Victorian and Edwardian furniture, clocks, porcelain and decorative items.* TEL: 01189 813636; mobile - 07860 827651.

TITCHFIELD, Nr. Fareham

Alexanders
13 South St. PO14 4DL. Open Tues.-Sat. 10-5. *STOCK: General antiques including Art Nouveau and Art Deco.* PARK: Easy. TEL: 01329 315962. SER: Restorations (furniture and silver).

Gaylords
75 West St. PO14 4DG. (I. Hebbard). Est. 1970. Open 9-

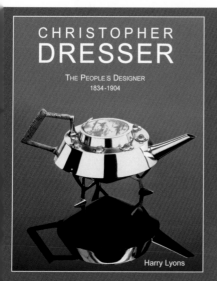

5. CL: Tues. SIZE: Large. *STOCK: Furniture, from 18th C; clocks, £50-£10,000.* LOC: Off junction 9 M27. PARK: Easy. TEL: 01329 843402; home - 01329 847134; website - www.gaylords.co.uk SER: Valuations. VAT: Stan/Spec.

WATERLOOVILLE

Goss and Crested China Centre and Goss Museum
62 Murray Rd., Horndean. PO8 9JL. (L.J. Pine). Est. 1968. Open 9-5. SIZE: Medium. *STOCK: Goss, 1860-1930, £2-£1,000; other heraldic china, Art Deco pottery including Carlton ware, Charlotte Rhead, Chamelion, 1890-1930, £1-£1,000.* LOC: Just off A3(M), junction 2, on to B2149. PARK: Easy. TEL: 02392 597440; fax - 02392 591975; e-mail - info@gosschinaclub.co.uk website - www.gosschinaclub.co.uk SER: Valuations; collections purchased; mail order catalogue; relevant books. VAT: Stan.

WINCHESTER

Bell Fine Art
67b Parchment St. SO23 8AT. (L.E. Bell). FATG. Est. 1977. Open Tues.-Sat. 9.30-5.30. SIZE: Large. *STOCK: Watercolours, oils and prints, 1750-1950, £5-£10,000.* PARK: 2 spaces. TEL: 01962 860439; fax - same; home - 01962 862947; e-mail - sales@bell-fine-art.demon.co. uk website - www.bellfineart.co.uk SER: Valuations; restorations (oils and watercolours); buys at auction. FAIRS: Surrey; Chelsea; Wilton. VAT: Spec.

Burgess Farm Antiques
39 Jewry St. S023 8RY. (N. Spencer-Brayn). Est. 1970. Open 9-5. SIZE: Large. *STOCK: Furniture, especially pine and country, 18th-19th C, £25-£5,000; architectural items - doors, panelling, fire-places.* LOC: One way street, right turn from top of High St. or St. George, shop 100 yards on right. PARK: Easy. TEL: 01962 777546. SER: Stripping; export. VAT: Stan/Spec.

The Clock-Work-Shop (Winchester)
6a Parchment St. SO23 8AT. (P. Ponsford-Jones and K.J. Hurd). BHI. AHS. Est. 1997. Open Mon.-Sat. 9-5. SIZE: Large. *STOCK: Restored longcase, wall, dial, mantel, bracket and carriage clocks, especially English, 18th-19th C, £300-£18,000; barometers, books and tools.* LOC: Central, off main pedestrian precinct, near W.H. Smith. PARK: Easy. TEL: 01962 842331; mobiles - 07885 954302 and 07973 736155; website - www.clock-work-shop.co.uk SER: Valuations; restorations (clocks and barometers). VAT: Margin.

Lacewing Fine Art Gallery
28 St Thomas St. SO23 9HJ. (N. James). Open Tues.-Sat. 10-5. *STOCK: Paintings, watercolours, sculpture, Old Master drawings, 16th-20th C.* LOC: Just off High St., alongside Lloyds TSB. TEL: 01962 878700; e-mail - noeljames@lacewing.co.uk website - www.lacewing. co.uk SER: Fine art restoration; bespoke framing; valuations and advice.

G.E. Marsh Antique Clocks Ltd   BADA
32a The Square. SO23 9EX. BHI. AHS. Est. 1947. Open 9.30-5, Sat. 9.30-1 and 2-5. STOCK: Clocks including longcase, bracket, English, French and

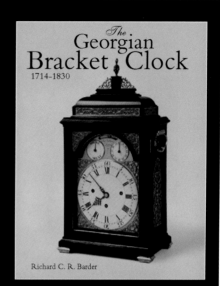
Continental, watches and barometers, 1680-1880. LOC: Near cathedral. PARK: Easy. TEL: **01962 844443**; fax - same; e-mail - gem@marshclocks.co.uk website - www.marshclocks.co.uk SER: Valuations; restorations; commissions.

The Pine Cellars
39 Jewry St. SO23 8RY. (N. Spencer-Brayn). Est. 1970. Open 9.30-5. SIZE: Large and warehouses. *STOCK: Pine and country furniture, 18th-19th C, £10-£5,000; painted furniture, architectural items, panelled rooms, lighting and china.* LOC: One way street, a right turn from top of High St. or St. Georges St., shop 100yds. on right. PARK: Nearby. TEL: 01962 867014/777546/870102. SER: Stripping and export. VAT: Stan/Spec.

Max Rollitt   BADA
27 St. Thomas St. SO23 9HJ. (M. and G. Rollitt). Est. 1971. Open Thurs. and Fri. 9.30-5, Sat. 9.30-1 or by appointment. *STOCK: English furniture, mirrors, period decorative items, 1680-1840; reproduction sofas and chairs; interior decor.* **LOC: Town centre. PARK: At rear. TEL: 01962 853779; fax - 01962 853852; mobile - 07771 960393. SER: Interior design. FAIRS: Olympia (Feb., June, Nov). VAT: Stan/Spec.**

Samuels Spencers Antiques and Decorative Arts Emporium
39 Jewry St. SO23 8RY. (N. Spencer-Brayn). Open 9.30-5. SIZE: 31 dealers. *STOCK: General antiques.* LOC: One way street, right turn from top of High St. or St.

George St., shop 100yds. on right. PARK: Nearby. TEL: 01962 867014/777546.

Todd and Austin Antiques of Winchester
2 Andover Rd. SO23 7BS. (G. Austin). MCIM. Est. 1964. Open Tues.-Fri. 9.30-5, Sat. 9.30-12.30. SIZE: Medium. *STOCK: 19th C glass, paperweights, silver, tea caddies, boxes, objets d'art and decorative items; late 18th-late 19th C pottery and porcelain, some Oriental porcelain; small furniture; hanging lamps, chandeliers and snuff boxes; Victorian and Edwardian jewellery.* LOC: 1 min. from Winchester Station. PARK: Meters. TEL: 01962 869824. SER: Selected range on view at Lainston House Hotel, Sparsholt, Nr Winchester; finder.

Irene S. Trudgett
3 Andover Rd. SO23 7BS. Est. 1964. Open 10-4, Thurs. and Sat. 9.30-12. SIZE: Medium. *STOCK: Cigarette cards, china including Goss, glass; pottery including Doulton, Minton, Wedgwood, Wade; militaria, silver.* LOC: Near station. PARK: Limited or nearby. TEL: 01962 854132.

Webb Fine Arts
38 Jewry St. SO23 8RY. (D.H. Webb). Est. 1955. Open 9-5, Sat. 9-1. SIZE: Large - 4 floors. *STOCK: Oil paintings and furniture.* PARK: Own. TEL: 01962 842273; fax - 01962 880602; website - www. webbfinearts.co.uk SER: Valuations; restorations (oil paintings); lining and framing; buys at auction (paintings). VAT: Stan/Spec.

HEREFORDSHIRE

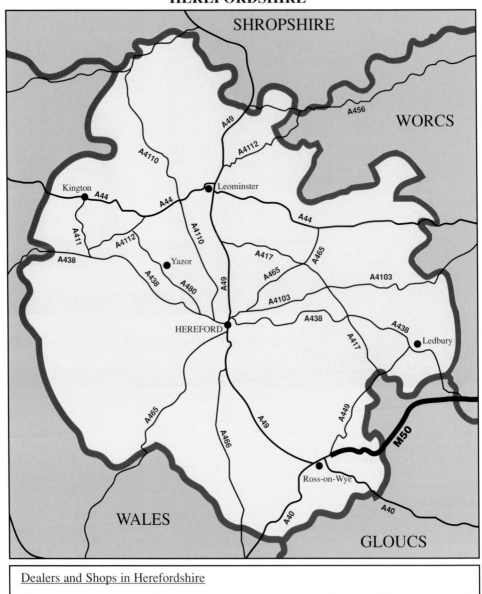

SHROPSHIRE

WORCS

WALES

GLOUCS

Dealers and Shops in Herefordshire

Hereford	3	Ledbury	3	Ross-on-Wye	6
Kington	1	Leominster	11	Yazor	1

HEREFORD

I. and J.L. Brown Ltd

Whitestone Park, Whitestone. HR1 3SE. Open 9-5.30. SIZE: Large. *STOCK: Matched sets of period country chairs, English country, French provincial and reproduction furniture, decorative items.* LOC: A4103, 4 miles from Hereford towards Worcester. PARK: Easy. TEL: 01432 851991; fax - 01432 851994; e-mail - enquiries@brownantiques.com website - www.brown antiques.com SER: Restorations; re-rushing chairs. VAT: Stan/Spec.

Great Brampton House Antiques Ltd   LAPADA

Great Brampton House, Madley. HR2 9NA. (Lady Pidgeon). Est. 1969. Open 9-5, Sat. and Sun. by appointment. SIZE: Large. *STOCK: English and French furniture and fine art.* TEL: 01981 250244; fax - 01981 251333.

Hereford Antique Centre

128 Widemarsh St. HR4 9HN. (G.P. Smith). Est. 1991. Open 10-5, Sun. 12-5. SIZE: 30 dealers. *STOCK: General antiques and collectables.* PARK: Easy. TEL: 01432 266242. SER: Restorations; shipping.

KINGTON

Castle Hill Books
12 Church St. HR5 3AZ. (Peter Newman). Est. 1988. Open 10.30-1, Sat. 10.30-1 and 2-5. *STOCK: Books - out of print, secondhand and antiquarian especially British topography, Herefordshire, Radnorshire, Wales, archaeology.* LOC: Off High St. PARK: Easy. TEL: 01544 231195; fax - 01544 231161; e-mail - sales@castlehillbooks.co.uk website - www.castlehillbooks.co.uk

LEDBURY

John Nash Antiques and Interiors   LAPADA
Tudor House, 17c and 18 High St. HR8 1DS. (J. Nash and L. Calleja). Est. 1972. Open 10-5.30, Sun. by appointment. SIZE: Medium. *STOCK: Mahogany, oak and walnut furniture, 18th-20th C, £300-£10,000; decorative items, fabrics and wallpapers.* PARK: Public nearby. TEL: 01531 635714; fax - 01531 635050; e-mail - louis@johnnash.co.uk website - www.johnnash.co.uk SER: Valuations; restorations; buys at auction (furniture and silver). VAT: Stan/Spec.

Serendipity
The Tythings, Preston Court. HR8 2LL. (Mrs R. Ford). Est. 1967. Open 9-5 or by appointment. SIZE: Large. *STOCK: 17th-20th C furniture especially long dining tables, sets of chairs and four-poster beds; general antiques.* LOC: Take A449 for 3 miles from Ledbury, at roundabout turn left on B4215, premises 800yds. on left behind half-timbered house. TEL: 01531 660245; fax - 01531 660689; e-mail - sales@serendipity-antiques.co.uk website - www.serendipity-antiques.co.uk SER: Restorations (furniture); buys at auction. FAIRS: Kensington; Olympia; Battersea. VAT: Stan/Spec.

Keith Smith Books
78B The Homend. HR8 1BX. Est. 1986. Open 10-5. SIZE: Small. *STOCK: Secondhand and old books.* LOC: Main road. PARK: Easy. TEL: 01531 635336; e-mail - keith@ksbooks.demon.co.uk SER: Valuations. FAIRS: Churchdown Book, Gloucester.

LEOMINSTER

The Barometer Shop Ltd
New St. HR6 8DP. (C.F. and V.J. Jones). MBHI. Open 9-5, Sat. 10-4 or by appointment. *STOCK: Barometers, barographs, clocks, period furniture.* PARK: Own. TEL: 01568 613652/610200; fax - 01568 610200; e-mail - thebarometershop@btconnect.com website - www.thebarometershop.co.uk SER: Valuations; restorations.

Coltsfoot Gallery
Hatfield. HR6 0SF. (Edwin Collins). Est. 1971. Open by appointment. SIZE: Medium. *STOCK: Sporting and wildlife watercolours and prints, £20-£2,000.* PARK: Easy. TEL: 01568 760277. SER: Restoration and conservation of works of art on paper; mounting; framing.

Coromandel
The Pound House, Leysters. HR6 0HS. (P. Lang and B. Leigh). Resident. Open any time by appointment. *STOCK: Boxes, table cabinets and decorative items,*

Anglo-Indian and European Colonial, 17th-19th C, £250-£10,000. PARK: Easy. TEL: 01568 750294; fax - 01568 750237; mobile - 07932 102756; e-mail - info@antiqueboxes.com SER: Restorations (ivory, tortoiseshell, horn, mother of pearl etc). VAT: Stan/Spec.

Courts Miscellany
48A Bridge St. HR6 6DZ. (George Court). Est. 1983. Open 10-5 or by appointment. *STOCK: General curios including corkscrews, social and political history, police, fire brigade and sporting items; tools, horse brasses, enamel signs - advertising, military, brewery; studio pottery and commemoratives.* TEL: 01568 612995.

Farmers Gallery
1 High St. HR6 8LZ. Est. 1987. SIZE: 6 galleries. *STOCK: 18th-19th C furniture, paintings, prints, maps, frames, needlework, porcelain and decorative items.* LOC: Town centre. PARK: Easy. TEL: 01568 611413; fax - 01568 611141. e-mail - info@farmersgallery.com website - www.farmersgallery.com SER: Exhibition gallery available.

Jeffery Hammond Antiques   LAPADA
Shaftesbury House, 38 Broad St. HR6 8BS. (J. and E. Hammond). Resident. Est. 1970. Open 9-6, Sun. by appointment. SIZE: Medium. *STOCK: Furniture and works of art, 18th to early 19th C.* LOC: Town centre. PARK: Own. TEL: 01568 614876; fax - same; mobile - 07971 289367; e-mail - enquiries@jefferyhammond antiques.co.uk website - www.jefferyhammond antiques.co.uk SER: Valuations; buys at auction (furniture). VAT: Stan/Spec.

Leominster Antiques Market
14 Broad St. HR6 8BS. (M. & J. Markets). Est. 1975. Open 10-5. SIZE: 18 units - 3 floors. *STOCK: Mahogany, oak, pine, kitchenalia, collectables, toys, glass, textiles, silver, postcards, Gaudy Welsh, fine china, pictures, jewellery, tools.* PARK: Nearby. TEL: 01568 612189; home - 01584 890013; mobile - 07976 628115. SER: Deliveries arranged. FAIRS: Ludlow.

Linden House Antiques Centre
1 Draper's Lane. HR6 8ND. (C. Scott-Mayfield). Est. 1999. Open 10-1 and 2-5. SIZE: Large - 20 dealers. *STOCK: Furniture, 18th C to Edwardian, £100-£10,000; pictures, 1700s to 1940s, £50-£5,000; silver and jewellery, porcelain and pottery, carvings, objets d'art, textiles, 18th-20th C, £5-£3,000; maps, 1600s to 1800s.* LOC: Town centre. PARK: Easy. TEL: 01568 620350; mobile - 07890 100225. SER: Valuations; restorations (re-upholstery); repairs (jewellery). FAIRS: Bingley Hall; Buith Wells; CC's.

Minster House
Leominster Antiques Centre, 34 Broad St. HR6 8BS. (M. Cramp). Est. 1995. Open 10-5, Sun. 11-4. SIZE: 40 units, 4 floors and gardens. *STOCK: Mahogany, oak, pine, kitchenalia, collectables, toys, glass, textiles, silver, postcards, Gaudy Welsh, fine china, pictures, jewellery and tools.* TEL: 01568 615505; home - 01584 890013; mobile - 07976 628115. FAIRS: Ludlow (1st & 3rd Sun. monthly).

The Old Shoe Box
2 Church St. HR6 8NE. Open 10-5. *STOCK: Furniture, china, prints, watercolours and smalls.* LOC: Opposite Barclays Bank. PARK: Loading only. TEL: 01568 611414. SER: Mount cutting; framing.

Teagowns & Textiles
28-30 Broad St. HR6 8AB. (Annie Townsend). Open 10-1 and 2-5. SIZE: Large. *STOCK: Vintage costume, textiles, shoes and handbags, Victorian to 1960s.* LOC: Main street. PARK: Nearby. TEL: 01568 612999; home - 01982 560422; e-mail - annietownsend@lineone.net website - www.vintage-fabrics.co.uk SER: Valuations; restorations. FAIRS: Own - every 3 months.

ROSS-ON-WYE

Baileys Home & Garden
Whitecross Farm, Bridstow. HR9 6JU. (M. and S. Bailey). Est. 1978. Open 9-5. SIZE: Medium. *STOCK: Garden furniture, tools, orchard ladders, kitchenware, quilts, Welsh blankets, French and English lighting, bathrooms (including copper baths, metal washstands), fireplaces, industrial lamps, factory trolleys, machinists' stools, shoe lasts, baskets, bobbins.* LOC: A49 1 mile from Ross-on-Wye on Hereford Rd. PARK: Easy. TEL: 01989 563015; fax - 01989 768172; e-mail - sales@ baileys-home-garden.co.uk website - www.baileyshome andgarden.com VAT: Stan.

Fritz Fryer Antique Lighting
23 Station St. HR9 7AG. (K. and S. Wallis-Smith). Est. 1981. Open 10-5.30. SIZE: Large. *STOCK: Decorative lighting, chandeliers, lamps, gas brackets and sconces, original shades, Georgian to Art Deco.* PARK: Easy. TEL: 01989 567416; fax - 01989 566742; e-mail - enquiries@fritzfryer.co.uk website - www.fritzfryer.co. uk SER: Restorations; lighting scheme design. VAT: Margin.

Robin Lloyd Antiques
The Elizabethan House, Brookend St. HR9 7EE. Est. 1970. Open 10-5. SIZE: Large - 5 showrooms. *STOCK: Oak, country and traditional furniture including dining tables and Windsor chairs; longcase clocks, beds and brassware.* LOC: 100yds. downhill from Market Hall. PARK: Nearby. TEL: 01989 562123; fax - same; e-mail - robinloyd@aol.com website - www.robinlloydantiques. com SER: Export delivery to shipper; finder; digital imaging before purchase. VAT: Global/Spec/Exp.

Ross Old Book and Print Shop
51 and 52 High St. HR9 5HH. (Phil Thredder and Sarah Miller). PBFA. Est. 1984. Open Wed.-Sat. 10-5. CL: Mid-Jan. to mid-Feb. *STOCK: Antiquarian and secondhand books, prints and maps.* PARK: Behind shop. TEL: 01989 567458; e-mail - enquiries@ rossoldbooks.co.uk website - www.rossoldbooks.co.uk SER: Worldwide postal.

Ross-on-Wye Antiques Gallery   LAPADA
Gloucester Rd. HR9 5BU. (Michael Aslanian). Est. 1996. Open 12-5, Sun. by appointment. CL: Bank Holidays. SIZE: Large. *STOCK: Wide variety of general antiques, furniture and collectables, from 17th to early 20th C.* LOC: Town centre. PARK: At rear. TEL: 01989 762290; fax - 01989 76229; website - www.ross antiquesgallery.com SER: Valuations; buys at auction.

Waterfall Antiques
2 High St. HR9 5HL. (O. McCarthy). Est. 1991. Open 10-4, Wed. and Fri. 9.30-12. SIZE: Medium. *STOCK: Country pine furniture, Victorian and Edwardian; china and general antiques.* PARK: At rear. TEL: 01989 563103; mobile - 07932 105542. SER: Valuations.

YAZOR

M. and J. Russell
The Old Vicarage. HR4 7BA. Est. 1969. Open at all times, appointment advisable. SIZE: Medium. *STOCK: English period oak and country furniture, some garden antiques.* LOC: 7 miles west of Hereford on A480. PARK: Easy. TEL: 01981 590674; mobile - 07889 702556. SER: Valuations. VAT: Spec. *Mainly Trade.*

ARTS AND CRAFTS TO ART DECO: THE JEWELLERY AND SILVER OF H.G. MURPHY

PAUL ATTERBURY
AND JOHN BENJAMIN

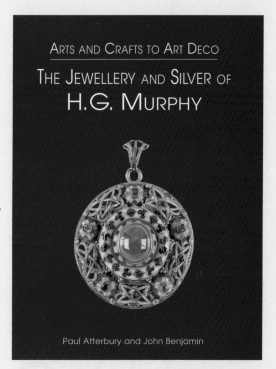

ARTS AND CRAFTS TO ART DECO

THE JEWELLERY AND SILVER OF H.G. MURPHY

Paul Atterbury and John Benjamin

- *The first book to deal with the life and work of HG Murphy in such comprehensive detail, providing a glimpse into the world of silver and jewellery by one of Britain's great but neglected silversmiths*

- *Murphy's work spans both the Art Deco and the Arts & Crafts periods*

- *Published to coincide with the exhibition "At the Sign of the Falcon: HG Murphy: Art Deco Jeweller and Silversmith" at the Goldsmith's Company, London*

With a reputation second to none during his lifetime, Harry Murphy was Britain's leading jewellery designer of the first half of the twentieth century, and one of the most influential and accomplished silversmiths of the Art Deco and Arts & Crafts periods. One of the first to be nominated Royal Designer for Industry, Murphy was a widely revered figure who seemed in his many skills to encapsulate that early twentieth century dream, the successful marriage of art and industry. Yet today, he is little known.

This book, published to coincide with an exhibition of Murphy's work at Goldsmith's Hall in London, redresses the balance and brings Murphy once again to the forefront of the public's attention. Featuring a broad spectrum of Murphy's work - domestic silver and flatware, Church silver, regalia, civic and corporate silver, enamels and a fascinating range of gold and gem-set jewellery - The Jewellery and Silver of H.G. Murphy is the definitive book on the subject.

Paul Atterbury is a lecturer, writer, broadcaster and exhibition curator specialising in art, architecture, design and decorative arts of the nineteenth and twentieth centuries. He has been a member of the BBC Antiques Roadshow team of experts since 1990 and has appeared on many other radio and TV programmes.

Specifications:
204pp., 260 col. illus.,
50 b.&w. illus.,
11 x 8½in./279 x 216mm.
£35.00 (hardback)

For full details of all ACC publications, log on to our website:
www.antiquecollectorsclub.com
or telephone 01394 389950 for a free catalogue

HERTFORDSHIRE

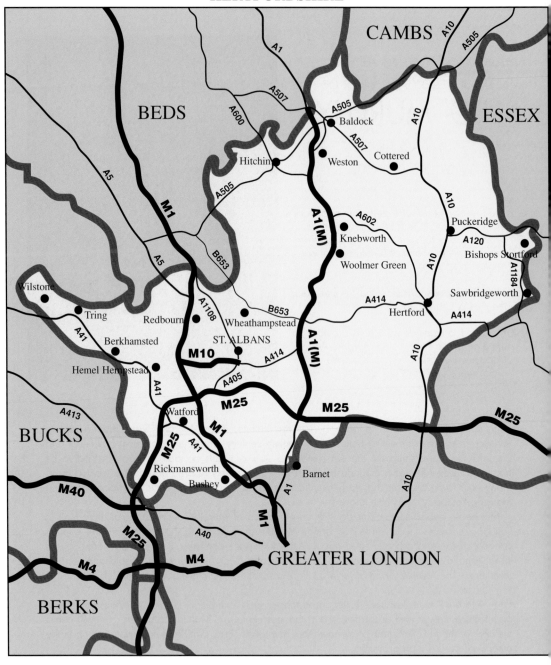

BALDOCK

The Attic
20 Whitehorse St. SG7 6QN. (P. Sheppard). Est. 1977. CL: Thurs. SIZE: Small. *STOCK: Small furniture, china, brass and copper, dolls and teddy bears, £5-£100.* LOC: 3 mins. from A1(M). PARK: Easy. TEL: 01462 893880.

Anthony Butt Antiques
7/9 Church St. SG7 5AE. Resident. Est. 1968. Open by appointment. SIZE: Small. *STOCK: English furniture, 17th-19th C, £500-£5,000; works of art and objects of interest.* Not Stocked: Bric-a-brac, shipping goods. PARK: Easy. TEL: 01462 895272. SER: Valuations. VAT: Spec.

Howards
33 Whitehorse St. SG7 6QF. (D.N. Howard). Est. 1970. Open 9.30-5.00. CL: Mon. *STOCK: Clocks, 18th-19th C, £200-£5,000.* PARK: Easy. TEL: 01462 892385. SER: Valuations; restorations; repairs. VAT: Spec.

BARNET

C. Bellinger Antiques
91 Wood St. EN5 4BX. Est. 1974. Open Thurs., Fri. and Sat. 10-4 or by appointment. SIZE: Medium. *STOCK: Furniture and decorative items.* LOC: Opposite Ravenscroft Park. PARK: Within 100yds. TEL: 020 8449 3467. VAT: Spec.

The Collector Limited
20 Granville Rd. EN5 4DS. (Tom Power). Est. 1973. Open by appointment. SIZE: Large. *STOCK: Decorative ceramics especially Royal Doulton, from 1900, £50-£3,000; Beswick, from 1920, £40-£1,000; Moorcroft, £150-£750; Lladro, Worcester and Spode.* LOC: Near High Barnet underground, B550/A406. PARK: Easy. TEL: 020 8440 2469; fax - 020 8440 4832; e-mail - collector@globalnet.co.uk SER: Valuations. FAIRS: Specialist Decorative Art. VAT: Stan.

Michael Lipitch Ltd   BADA
P O Box 3146. EN4 0BP. Est. 1959. Open by appointment. *STOCK: 18th to early 19th C English furniture, decoration and works of art.* PARK: Meters. TEL: 020 8441 4340; mobile - 07730 954347; e-mail - michaellipitch@hotmail.com SER: Specialist advice. FAIRS: Grosvenor House. VAT: Spec.

BERKHAMSTED

Heritage Antique Centre
24 Castle St. HP4 2DW. Open 10-5.30 including Sun. SIZE: Medium - 24 dealers. *STOCK: Furniture, china, glass, pictures, books, tools and clocks, 18th-20th C.* LOC: Just off High St. PARK: Nearby. TEL: 01442 873819.

Home and Colonial
134 High St. HP4 3AT. (Alison and Graeme Reid-Davies and Liz and Tony Stanton-Kipping). Est. 1997. Open 10-5.30, Sun. 11-5. CL: Wed. SIZE: Large. *STOCK: Period, country, French fruitwood and painted furniture; Arts and Crafts, Art Deco, decorative antiques, clocks and barometers, metalware, pictures, porcelain, silver, glass, jewellery, textiles and costume, antiquarian books,* radios and gramophones, toys and teddy bears, fireplaces, garden antiques and lighting, 60s and 70s design, £10-£10,000. LOC: M25 junction 20; M1 junction 8. PARK: Easy. TEL: 01442 877007; e-mail - homeandcolonial@btinternet.com website - www.home andcolonial.co.uk SER: Design; prop hire; interiors dept; antiques sourcing.

BISHOP'S STORTFORD

David Penney
Grooms Cottage, Elsenham Hall, Elsenham. CM22 6DP. BHI. Est. 1973. Strictly no visitors, no stock held on premises. *STOCK: Watches, 18th-20th C, £500-£50,000; watch movements, 18th-20th C, £50-£5,000; horological books and ephemera, 18th-21st C, £5-£15,000.* TEL: 01279 814946; fax - 01279 814962; e-mail - info@ davidpenney.co.uk website - www.antiquewatchstore. co.uk SER: Valuations; restorations; specialist research; postal auction catalogue; buys at auction (watches, chronometers and all technical horology). VAT: Stan/Spec. *Mail Order Only.*

The Windhill Antiquary
4 High St. CM23 2LT. (G.R. Crozier). Est. 1951. Open 10-1 and 2-4 appointment advisable. CL: Wed. pm. SIZE: Medium. *STOCK: English furniture, 18th C; carved and gilded wall mirrors, 17th-19th C.* LOC: Next to George Hotel. PARK: Up hill - first right. TEL: 01279 651587; home - 01920 821316.

BUSHEY, Nr. Watford

Country Life Interiors
33a High St. WD3 1BD. (Peter Myers). Est. 1981. Open 10-5. SIZE: Large. *STOCK: Victorian and Edwardian, European and Scandinavian original pine, French country oak; kitchenalia, watercolours, china and Art Deco.* PARK: Easy. TEL: 020 8950 8575; fax - 020 8950 6982; e-mail - sales@countrylifeinteriors website - www.countrylifeinteriors.com VAT: Stan.

COTTERED

Wareside Antiques
SG9 9PT. (David Broxup). Est. 1983. Open by appointment. *STOCK: Victorian dining room furniture, especially extending dining tables; sets of 6, 8, and 10 Victorian dining chairs, chiffoniers, buffets etc.* PARK: Easy. TEL: 01763 281234. SER: Restorations.

HEMEL HEMPSTEAD

Abbey Fine Jewellery & Silver
97 High St., Old Town. HP1 3AH. (S. and C. Eames). Est. 1962. Open 9.30-5.30. SIZE: Medium. *STOCK: Jewellery and silver, £10-£5,000.* LOC: M1, junction 8, M25, junction 20, bypass main shopping centre to Old Town. PARK: Easy. TEL: 01442 264667; e-mail - simoneames@abbey.uk.com SER: Valuations; jewellery design and repair; diamond and gemstone specialists. VAT: Stan/Global.

Cherry Antiques
101 High St. HP1 3AH. (A. and R.S. Cullen). Open 9.30-4.30. CL: Wed. pm. SIZE: Medium. *STOCK: Victorian,*

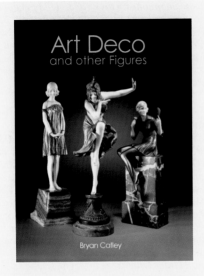
Edwardian and some period furniture, pine, general antiques, collectors' and decorative items, bric-a-brac, needlework tools, dolls, linens, some silver, plate, jewellery, glass, pottery, porcelain, brass, copper, some shipping items. PARK: Easy. TEL: 01442 264358. VAT: Stan/Spec.

Jordans Antiques Centre
63 High St., Old Town. HP1 3AF. (Michal Porter). Est. 1999. Open 10-5 including Sun. SIZE: Medium - 25+ dealers. *STOCK: General antiques, books, china, collectables, commemoratives, ephemera, furniture, glass, jewellery, kitchenalia, prints and treen, mainly from late 19th C, £10-£500+.* PARK: Nearby. TEL: 01442 263451; mobile - 07881 804840; website - www.thecollectorscompanion.co.uk/jordans.html

Off the Wall
52 High St., Old Town. HP1 3AF. (Michelle Smith). Est. 2001. Open 10-5.30, Sun. 11-4. *STOCK: Unusual and decorative items, some furniture.* LOC: Near St. Mary's Church. PARK: Nearby. TEL: 01442 218300. e-mail - off-thewallantiques@hotmail.com SER: Large item delivery.

HERTFORD

Beckwith and Son
St. Nicholas Hall, St. Andrew St. SG14 1HZ. (G.C.M. Gray). Est. 1904. Open 9-5.30. SIZE: Large. *STOCK: General antiques, furniture, silver, pottery, porcelain, prints, weapons, clocks, watches, glass.* LOC:

A414/B158. PARK: Adjacent. TEL: 01992 582079; e-mail - sales@beckwithandsonantiques.co.uk website - www.beckwithandsonantiques.co.uk SER: Valuations; restorations (fine porcelain, furniture, upholstery, silver and clocks). VAT: Spec.

Gillmark Gallery
25 Parliament Sq. SG14 1EX. (Mark Pretlove and Gill Woodhouse). Est. 1997. CL: Mon. and Thurs. pm. SIZE: Medium. *STOCK: Maps and prints, 16th-20th C, £10-£5,000; secondhand books, 18th-20th C, £1-£5,000.* LOC: 15 yards from roundabout at junction of A414 and B158. PARK: Nearby. TEL: 01992 534444; fax - 01992 554734; e-mail - gillmark@btinternet.com website - www.gillmark.com SER: Framing, conservation, restorations, map and print colouring. VAT: Stan.

Robert Horton Antiques
13 Castle St. SG14 1ER. BWCMG. Est. 1972. Open 9-5. *STOCK: Clocks, barometers, furniture.* TEL: 01992 587546; fax - same. SER: Restorations and repairs (clock movements, cases and dials). VAT: Stan/Spec.

Tapestry Antiques
27 St. Andrew St. SG14 1HZ. (D.W. and P. Stokes). Est. 1973. Open 10-1 and 2-5, Sat. 10-5.30, Sun. by appointment. CL: Thurs. SIZE: Medium. *STOCK: Furniture, 18th-19th C, £100-£1,000; porcelain, 19th to early 20th C, £25-£500; brass and copper, 18th-19th C, £50-£300; mirrors.* LOC: Near rail station. PARK: Easy and behind premises. TEL: 01992 587438. SER: Valuations.

HITCHIN

Michael Gander
10-11 Bridge St. SG5 2DE. Est. 1973. Open Mon. 3-6, Wed., Thurs. and Sat. 9-6, other times by appointment. *STOCK: Period furniture, metalware, ceramics, glass, pictures.* TEL: 01462 432678; mobile - 07885 728976.

Eric T. Moore
24 Bridge St. SG5 2DF. Open 8.30-6, Sun. 11-5. SIZE: Large. *STOCK: Secondhand and antiquarian books, maps and prints.* PARK: Easy. TEL: 01462 450497; e-mail - booksales@erictmoore.co.uk website - www.erictmoore.co.uk SER: Free booksearch and mail order.

Phillips of Hitchin (Antiques) Ltd   BADA
The Manor House. SG5 1JW. (J. and B. Phillips). Est. 1884. Open 9-5.30, Sat. by appointment. SIZE: Small. *STOCK: Mahogany furniture, 18th to early 19th C, £500-£20,000; reference books on furniture.* LOC: In Bancroft, main street of Hitchin. PARK: Easy. TEL: 01462 432067; fax - 01462 441368. VAT: Spec.

Tom Salusbury Antiques
7 Nutleigh Grove. SG5 2NH. Est. 1963. Open by appointment. SIZE: Small. *STOCK: Furniture, to 1910, £100-£3,000.* LOC: 3 miles from A1, junction 8. PARK: Easy. TEL: 01462 441520. SER: Valuations; restorations (especially upholstery). VAT: Stan/Spec.

KNEBWORTH

Hamilton Billiards & Games Co.
Park Lane. SG3 6PJ. (H. Hamilton). Est. 1980. Open 9-5, weekends and evenings by appointment. SIZE: Large. *STOCK: Victorian and Edwardian billiard tables, £3,000-£18,000; 19th C convertible billiard/dining tables and accessories, £30-£5,000; indoor and outdoor games.* LOC: Near rail station. PARK: Easy. TEL: 01438 811995; fax - 01438 814939; e-mail - showrooms@hamiltonbilliards.com website - www.hamiltonbilliards.com SER: Valuations; restorations (billiard tables and furniture); buys at auction (as stock). VAT: Stan.

PUCKERIDGE

St. Ouen Antiques
Vintage Corner, Old Cambridge Rd. SG11 1SA. (J., J. and S.T. Blake and Mrs P.B. Francis). Est. 1918. Open 10.30-5. SIZE: Large. *STOCK: English and Continental furniture, decorative items, silver, porcelain, pottery, glass, clocks, barometers, paintings.* PARK: Own. TEL: 01920 821336. SER: Valuations; restorations.

REDBOURN

Antique Print Shop
86 High St. AL3 7BD. (David Tilleke). AIA (Scot). Est. 1982. Open 9-4. SIZE: Small. *STOCK: Prints, all categories, 1650-1930.* PARK: Easy. TEL: 01582 794488; mobile - 07801 682268; home - 01442 397094; e-mail - antiqueprintshop@btinternet.com website - www.antiqueprintshop.co.uk SER: Valuations.

Bushwood Antiques   LAPADA
Stags End Equestrian Centre, Gaddesden Lane. HP2 6HN. (Anthony Bush). CINOA. Est. 1967. Open 8.30-4,

Sat. 10-4. SIZE: Very large. *STOCK: 18th-19th C furniture, accessories and objects of art.* LOC: Telephone for directions. PARK: Easy. TEL: 01582 794700; fax - 01582 792299; e-mail - antiques@bushwood.co.uk website - www.bushwood.co.uk

J.N. Antiques
86 High St. AL3 7BD. (Martin and Jean Brunning). Est. 1975. Open 9-6. SIZE: Medium + barn. *STOCK: Furniture, 18th-20th C, £5-£3,000; brass and copper, porcelain, 19th C, £5-£100; pictures and books, 19th-20th C.* LOC: Close to junction 8, M1. PARK: 50 yds. TEL: 01582 793603; e-mail - jnantiques@btopenworld.com SER: Valuations. VAT: Spec.

Tim Wharton Antiques   LAPADA
24 High St. AL3 7LL. Est. 1970. Open 10-5.30, Sat. 10-4. CL: Mon. and usually Thurs. *STOCK: Oak and country furniture, 17th-19th C; some mahogany, 18th to early 19th C; copper, brass, ironware, decorative items and general small antiques.* LOC: On left entering village from St. Albans on A5183. PARK: Easy. TEL: 01582 794371; mobile - 07850 622880; e-mail - tim@timwhartonantiques.co.uk website - www.timwharton antiques.co.uk VAT: Stan/Spec.

RICKMANSWORTH

Clive A. Burden Ltd
Elmcote House, The Green, Croxley Green. WD3 3HN. (Philip D. Burden). ABA. IMCOS. Est. 1966. Open by appointment. SIZE: Medium. *STOCK: Maps, 1500-1860, £5-£1,500; natural history, botanical and Vanity Fair prints, 1600-1900, £1-£1,000; antiquarian books, pre-1870, £10-£5,000.* TEL: 01923 778097/772387; fax - 01923 896520. SER: Valuations; buys at auction (as stock). VAT: Stan.

SAWBRIDGEWORTH

Charnwood Antiques and Arcane Antiques Centre
Unit E2 Ground Floor, The Maltings, Station Rd. CM21 9JX. (Nigel Hoy and Nicola Smith). EADA. GMC. Open 10-5, Sat. and Sun. 11-5. CL: Mon. SIZE: Large. *STOCK: Furniture, 18th C to Edwardian, £500-£8,000; European and Oriental porcelain, glass, silver and jewellery, longcase clocks, 19th C oils and watercolours.* LOC: From Harlow on A1184, turn right at first mini roundabout into Station Rd., over river bridge, first right into maltings. Shop 100 yards on left. PARK: Easy. TEL: 01279 600562; mobile - 07957 551899. SER: Restorations (furniture including structural and veneer, French polishing, traditional upholstery, desk re-leathering, brass ware supplied and fitted; clock repairs and overhauls; glass and ceramics; jewellery including restringing).

The Herts and Essex Antiques Centre
The Maltings, Station Rd. CM21 9JX. Est. 1982. Open 10-5, Sat. and Sun. 10.30-5.30. SIZE: Large - over 100 dealers. *STOCK: General antiques and collectables, £1-£2,000.* LOC: Opposite B.R. station. PARK: Easy. TEL: 01279 722044; fax - 01279 725445; website - www.antiques-of-britain.co.uk

Riverside Antiques Ltd

The Maltings, Station Rd. CM21 9JX. (Shirley Rowley and John Barrance). EADA. Est. 1998. Open 10-5 including Sun. SIZE: Large - 3 floors. *STOCK: General antiques, furniture, art and collectables.* LOC: Near railway station. PARK: Easy. TEL: 01279 600985; fax - 01279 726398. SER: Valuations; restorations; in house auction room.

ST. ALBANS

By George! Antiques Centre

23 George St. AL3 4ER. Open 10-5, Thurs. 11-5, Sat. 10-5.30, Sun. 1-5. SIZE: 20 dealers. *STOCK: A wide range of general antiques, lighting, jewellery and collectables.* LOC: 100yds. from Clock Tower. PARK: Internal courtyard (loading) and Christopher Place (NCP) nearby. TEL: 01727 853032. SER: Restorations.

James of St Albans

11 George St. AL3 4ER. (S.N. and W. James). Est. 1957. Open 10-5, Thurs. 10-4. *STOCK: Furniture including reproduction; smalls, brass and copper; topographical maps and prints of Hertfordshire.* TEL: 01727 856996. VAT: Stan/Spec.

Magic Lanterns

at By George! Antiques Centre, 23 George St. AL3 4ES. (Josie A. Marsden). Est. 1987. Open 10-5, Thurs. 11-5, Sat. 10-5.30, Sun. 1-5. SIZE: Medium. *STOCK: Lighting - candle, gas and early electric, 1800-1950s, £35-£1,500; small furniture, prints, mirrors, china, metalware, fire accessories, 1850-1950, £25-£1,000.* LOC: Near the abbey. PARK: Multi-storey nearby. TEL: 01727 853032/865680.

Oriental Rug Gallery Ltd

42 Verulam Rd. AL3 4DQ. (R. Mathias and J. Blair). BORDA. Open 9-6. *STOCK: Russian, Afghan, Turkish and Persian carpets, rugs and kelims; Oriental objets d'art.* TEL: 01727 841046; e-mail - rugs@orientalrug gallery.com website - www.orientalruggallery.com

Reg and Philip Remington

23 Homewood Rd. AL1 4BG. Est. 1979. By appointment only. SIZE: Medium. *STOCK: Books on voyages and travels, 17th-20th C, £5-£1,000.* TEL: 01727 893531. SER: Buys at auction. FAIRS: London Book; Olympia. VAT: Stan.

TRING

John Bly
BADA

The Old Billiards Room, Church Yard. HP23 5MW. Est. 1891. Open Wed.-Sat. 9.30-4.30. SIZE: Large. *STOCK: English furniture.* LOC: Next to church. PARK: Easy. TEL: 01442 823030. SER: Valuations; restorations; consultancy. FAIRS: West Palm Beach.

Country Clocks

3 Pendley Bridge Cottages, Tring Station. HP23 5QU. (T. Cartmell). Resident. Est. 1976. Prior telephone call advisable. SIZE: Small. *STOCK: Clocks, 18th-19th C.* LOC: One mile from A41 in village, cottage nearest canal bridge. PARK: Easy. TEL: 01442 825090. SER: Restorations (clocks); valuations.

New England House Antiques

50 High St. HP23 5AG. (Jennifer and Suj Munjee). Est. 1990. Open Tues.-Sat. 10.30-5. SIZE: Large - 6 showrooms on 3 floors. *STOCK: Fine Georgian and Victorian furniture, £100-£10,000; paintings, glass, silver, decorative furnishings specialising in antique table lights and hand-made shades.* LOC: A41 towards Aylesbury. PARK: Next to shop. TEL: 01442 827262; home - 01462 431914; e-mail - enquiries@newengland houseantiques.co.uk website - www.newengland houseantiques.co.uk SER: Valuations; restorations (paintings, metalwork and furniture); searches undertaken. VAT: Stan/Spec.

WATFORD

Thwaites Fine Stringed Instruments

33 Chalk Hill, WD19 4BL. (J.H. and W.J. Pamplin and C.A. Lovell). Open 9-5, Sat. 9.30-3. *STOCK: Stringed instruments, from violins to double basses.* PARK: Own. TEL: 01923 232412; fax - 01923 232463; e-mail - sales@thwaites.com website - www.thwaites.com SER: Restorations.

WESTON, Nr. Hitchin

Weston Antiques

Weston Barns, Hitchin Rd. SG4 7AX. (M.A. Green). BAFRA. BHI. Est. 1974. Open Tues.-Sat. 10.30-5, Mon. by appointment. SIZE: Small. *STOCK: Period furniture, longcase and mantel clocks, mainly 18th-19th C.* LOC: Off B197, near junction 9 A1(M). PARK: Easy. TEL: 01462 790646; fax - 01462 680304; mobile - 07802 403800; e-mail - gxc@freeuk.com website - www. greenrestorers.com SER: Valuations; restorations (furniture and clocks). VAT: Spec.

WHEATHAMPSTEAD

Collins Antiques (F.G. and C. Collins Ltd.)

Corner House. AL4 8AP. (M.C. Collins). Est. 1907. Open 9-1 and 2-5, appointment advisable. SIZE: Medium. *STOCK: Furniture - mahogany, 1730-1920, £100-£8,000; oak, 1600-1800, £50-£5,000; walnut, 1700-1740, £75-£3,000.* LOC: London, A1(M) junction 4 to B653. PARK: Easy. TEL: 01582 833111. VAT: Stan/Spec.

WILSTONE, Nr. Tring

Michael Armson (Antiques) Ltd

The Old Post Office, 34 Tring Rd. HP23 4PB. Est. 1970. Prior telephone call advisable. SIZE: Large. *STOCK: Furniture, 17th-19th C.* PARK: Easy. TEL: 01442 890990; mobile - 07860 910034; e-mail - armson antiques@ic24.net website - www.armsonantiques.com FAIRS: NEC. VAT: Spec.

WOOLMER GREEN, Nr. Knebworth

Redfield Interiors

11 London Rd. SG3 6JE. (Carol-Anne Brunt). Est. 2003. Open 9.30-5.30, Sat. 10-4.30, Sun. 12-4. SIZE: Large. *STOCK: Furniture and accessories.* LOC: B197. PARK: Easy. TEL: 01438 816400; fax - 01438 816644; website - www.redfieldinteriors.co.uk SER: Free local delivery. VAT: Stan.

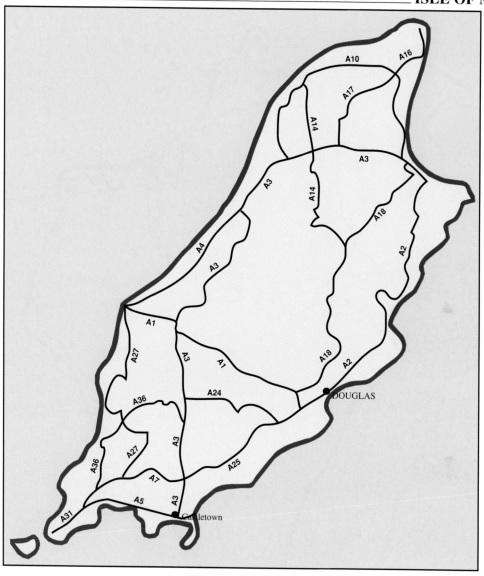

Dealers and Shops on the Isle of Man	
Castletown	1
Douglas	1

CASTLETOWN

J. and H. Bell Antiques

22 Arbory St. IM9 1LJ. Est. 1965. Open Wed., Fri. and Sat. 10-5. SIZE: Medium. *STOCK: Jewellery, silver, china, early metalware, furniture, 18th-20th C, £5-£5,000.* TEL: 01624 823132/822414. VAT: Stan/Spec.

DOUGLAS

John Corrin Antiques

73 Circular Rd. IM1 1AZ. Est. 1972. Open Sat. 10-4.30 otherwise by appointment. SIZE: Medium. *STOCK: Furniture, 18th-19th C, £100-£6,000; clocks, barometers, 19th C.* LOC: From the promenade, travel up Victoria St., this becomes Prospect Hill and Circular Rd. is on left. PARK: Easy. TEL: 01624 629655; home - 01624 621382.

ISLE OF WIGHT

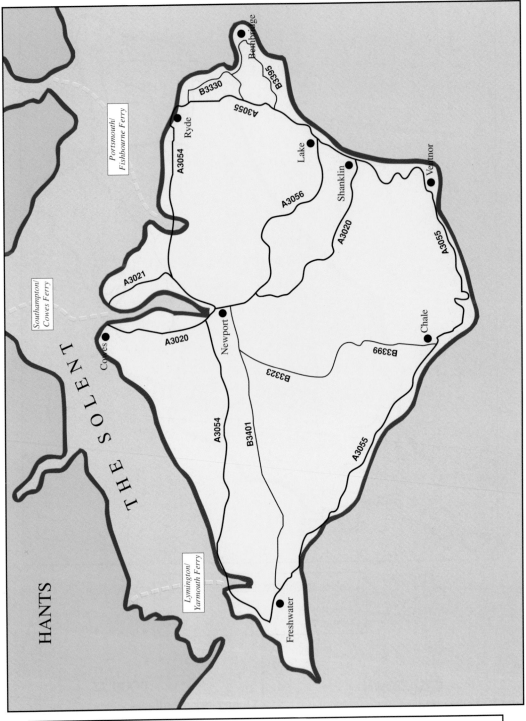

Dealers and Shops on the Isle of Wight					
Bembridge	1	Freshwater	1	Ryde	2
Chale	1	Lake	1	Shanklin	1
Cowes	2	Newport	3	Ventnor	2

BEMBRIDGE

Windmill Antiques
1 Foreland Rd. PO35 5XN. (E.J. de Kort). Est. 1970. Open 10-1 and 2.15-4. CL: Mon. and Thurs. SIZE: Medium. *STOCK: Furniture, silver, porcelain, jewellery.* TEL: 01983 873666. SER: Buys at auction. VAT: Stan/Spec.

CHALE

Curios of Chale
3 Church Place. PO38 2HA. (Michael Gregory). Est. 1983. Open 12-5 including Sun. SIZE: Large. *STOCK: Architectural items, fireplaces, £50-£500; general antiques, curios and taxidermy, £5-£500; mainly 19th C.* LOC: Off Military Rd., near Black-Gang. PARK: Easy. TEL: 01983 730230; mobile - 07811 835159. SER: Valuations.

COWES

Flagstaff Antiques
Tudor House, Bath Rd. PO31 7RH. (T.A.M. Cockram). Est. 1987. Open from 10 am. CL: Wed. SIZE: Small. *STOCK: Jewellery, 19th-20th C, £50-£2,000; porcelain, 19th C, £25-£1,000; pictures, 19th-20th C, £10-£1,000.* LOC: 100 yards from The Parade. PARK: Easy. TEL: 01983 200138. SER: Valuations; restorations (porcelain and silver).

Royal Standard Antiques
70-72 Park Rd. PO31 7LY. (Dennis and Caroline Bradbury). Resident. Est. 1992. Open 10.30-5.30 or any time by appointment. SIZE: Medium. *STOCK: Georgian, Victorian, Edwardian and French provincial furniture, £100-£1,000+; architectural items, £20-£500; pictures, commemoratives, breweriana, £5-£500.* LOC: 5 mins. walk from hydrofoil terminus; corner of Victoria Rd. PARK: Own, behind premises. TEL: 01983 281672; home - same; e-mail - caroline@royalstandardantiques.fsbusiness.co.uk website - www.royalstandardantiques.fsbusiness.co.uk SER: Restorations; upholstery, caning, stained glass.

FRESHWATER

Ye Olde Village Clock Shop
3 Moa Place. PO40 9DS. (Ron and Sandra Tayler). Est. 1970. Open 9.30-1 or by appointment. CL: Mon., Tues and Thurs. SIZE: Small. *STOCK: Clocks - longcase, Vienna, carriage, bracket, French and novelty, 17th-19th C, £300-£6,000; mechanical music.* PARK: Easy. TEL: 01983 754193; home - same. SER: Valuations; restorations (clocks).

LAKE

Lake Antiques
Sandown Rd. PO36 9JP. (P. Burfield). Est. 1982. Open 10-4. CL: Wed. *STOCK: General antiques, Georgian and Victorian furniture, clocks.* LOC: On the main Sandown to Shanklin Road. PARK: On forecourt. TEL: 01983 406888/865005; mobile - 07710 067678.

NEWPORT

Mike Heath Antiques
3-4 Holyrood St. PO30 5AU. (M. and B. Heath). GCF. Est. 1979. Open 10-5. CL: Thurs. SIZE: Medium. *STOCK: General antiques and bric-a-brac, 19th-20th C, £5-£500.* LOC: Off High St. PARK: Nearby. TEL: 01983 525748; home - same. SER: Restorations (copper and brass).

Kitsch 22
3-4 Holyrood St. PO30 5AU. (F. Heath). Est. 2004. Open 10-5. CL: Thurs. SIZE: Small. *STOCK: 20th C - mainly 50s, 60s and 70s items, £2-£200.* LOC: Off High St. PARK: Nearby. TEL: 01983 525748.

Lugley Antiques & Interiors
13 Lugley St. PO30 5HD. (S.J. Gratton). Est. 1992. Open 9.30-5. CL: Thurs. SIZE: Large. *STOCK: Furniture, clocks, some china and unusual collectables, late 18th to early 20th C, £5-£5,000.* LOC: Town centre. PARK: Meters or nearby. TEL: 01983 523348. SER: Valuations; restorations (furniture). VAT: Margin.

RYDE

Nooks & Crannies
60 High St. PO33 2RS. (David and Sally Burnett). Est. 1984. Open 9.30-1.30 and 2.30-5. CL: Thurs. SIZE: Medium. *STOCK: China, glass, collectables, some furniture, gramophones and radios, Victorian to 1950s, £1-£750.* LOC: Near catholic church. PARK: Limited. TEL: 01983 568984; home - 01983 868261. FAIRS: Ardingly.

Victoria Antiques
Royal Victoria Arcade, Union St. PO33 2LQ. (J. Strudwick and C. Beeney). Open 9.30-5 including Sun. CL: Mon. and Tues. *STOCK: General antiques and collectables including furniture, jewellery, porcelain and china.* PARK: Nearby. TEL: 01983 564661; mobile - 07970 175926.

SHANKLIN

The Shanklin Gallery
67 Regent St. PO37 7AE. (Jacqueline and Terry Townsend). FATG. GCF. Est. 1992. Open 9-5. SIZE: Medium. *STOCK: Oils, watercolours, engravings, prints, maps, 17th-20th C, £10-£2,000.* LOC: Town centre near rail station. PARK: Easy. TEL: 01983 863113; e-mail - spaltown@compuserve.com SER: Valuations; restorations (oils, watercolours and prints); framing.

VENTNOR

Ultramarine
40B High St. PO38 1LG. (Milly Stevens). Open Wed.-Sat. 10-2. SIZE: Small. *STOCK: 19th-20th C collectables including jewellery, china, studio pottery, textiles and glass, £5-£500.* LOC: Central. PARK: Nearby. TEL: 01983 854062.

Ventnor Rare Books
32 Pier St. PO38 1SX. (Nigel and Teresa Traylen). ABA. PBFA. Est. 1989. Open 10-5. CL: Wed. *STOCK: Antiquarian and secondhand books, prints.* TEL: 01983 853706; fax - 01983 854706.

KENT

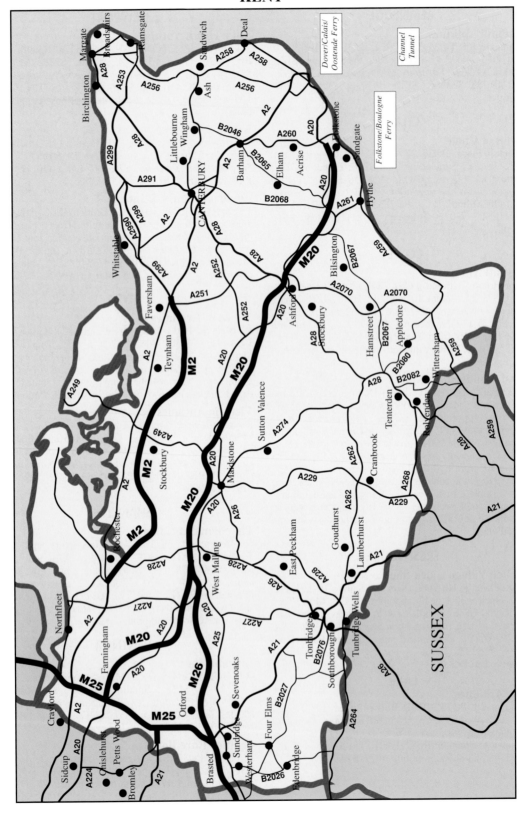

Stablegate Antiques
Barham, Nr Canterbury, Kent
Tel/Fax: 01227 831639 Mobile: 07802 439777

Our showrooms are in a charming C17th farmhouse in the village of Barham, near Canterbury, Kent, just off the A2. We specialise in Georgian & Victorian furniture & also have a selection of good quality porcelain, silver plate, pictures and other items.
We are always happy to purchase any of the above.

Visit us at:
www.stablegate.co.uk

ACRISE, Nr. Folkestone

R. Kirby Antiques
Caroline Farm, Ridge Row. CT18 8JT. (R.D. and M.W. Kirby). Est. 1972. Open by appointment 7 days. *STOCK: Early period oak, 16th-18th C, and works of art.* TEL: 01303 893230; fax - 01303 891478; e-mail - rkirby@antiques8.fsnet.co.uk SER: Valuations.

APPLEDORE, Nr. Ashford

Back 2 Wood
The Old Goods Shed, Station Rd. TN26 2DF. (Steve Fowler). Est. 1987. Open 9-5, Sat. 9-4, Sun. 11-4. *STOCK: Stripped and finished pine furniture.* LOC: Adjacent to station. PARK: Easy. TEL: 01233 758109; mobile - 07971 288869; e-mail - pine@back2wood.com website - www.back2wood.com VAT: Stan/Margin.

ASH, Nr. Canterbury

Henry's of Ash
Darrington, Durlock Rd. CT3 2HU. (P.H. Robinson). Est.

1988. Open by appointment only. SIZE: Small. *STOCK: General antiques, linen, Victorian and Art Deco, £5-100.* LOC: Main road. PARK: Outside. TEL: 01304 812563. SER: Buys at auction (small items). FAIRS: Copthorne; Bromley.

ASHFORD

County Antiques
Old Mill Cottage, Kennett Lane, Stanford North. TN25 6DG. (B. Nilson). Open by appointment. *STOCK: General antiques.* TEL: 01303 813039.

BARHAM, Nr. Canterbury

Stablegate Antiques **LAPADA**
CT4 6QD. (Mr and Mrs M.J. Giuntini). Est. 1989. Open 10-5.30 including Sun. SIZE: Large. *STOCK: Georgian and Victorian dining tables, chairs, sideboards, bureaux, davenports, chests of drawers; silver plate, china, clocks, jewellery, glass, objets d'art, collectables, copper, brass.* LOC: Village just off the A2 to Dover. PARK: Easy. TEL: 01227 831639; mobile - 07802 439777. SER: Valuations. FAIRS: NAFAAF, Claridges; Tatton Park; NEC.

Dealers and Shops in Kent										
Acrise	1	Brasted	12	Deal	6	Goudhurst	1	Ramsgate	2	Sutton Valence	1
Appledore	1	Broadstairs	1	East Peckham	1	Hamstreet	1	Rochester	7	Tenterden	3
Ash	1	Bromley	4	Edenbridge	3	Hythe	4	Rolvenden	2	Teynham	2
Ashford	1	Canterbury	15	Elham	1	Lamberhurst	1	Sandgate	11	Tonbridge	4
Barham	1	Chilham	2	Farningham	1	Littlebourne	1	Sandwich	1	Tunbridge Wells	25
Beckenham	3	Chislehurst	2	Faversham	2	Maidstone	2	Sevenoaks	3	West Malling	2
Bilsington	1	Cranbrook	3	Folkestone	1	Margate	1	Sidcup	1	Westerham	7
Birchington	1	Crayford	1	Four Elms	1	Northfleet	1	Southborough	2	Whitstable	2
						Otford	3	Stockbury	1	Wingham	1
						Petts Wood	1	Sundridge	1	Wittersham	1

BECKENHAM

Beckenham Antiques & Collectors' Market
Public Hall, Bromley Rd. BR3. Est. 1979. Open Wed. 8.30-2. SIZE: 16 stalls. *STOCK: General antiques.* PARK: Nearby. TEL: 020 8660 1369.

Pepys Antiques
9 Kelsey Park Rd. BR3 2LH. (S.P. Elton). Est. 1969. Open 11-1. CL: Wed. *STOCK: Furniture, paintings, clocks, silver, porcelain, copper, brass.* LOC: Central Beckenham. TEL: 020 8650 0994.

Ward Antique Fireplaces Ltd
436 Croydon Rd. BR3 4EP. (Michael and Terry Ward). Open 10-5, Sun. 11-2. *STOCK: Fireplaces, some furniture, Victorian and Edwardian.* TEL: 020 8650 9005. SER: Restorations (fireplaces).

BILSINGTON, Nr. Ashford

Gabrielle De Giles
The Barn at Bilsington, Swanton Lane. TN25 7JR. Open by appointment. *STOCK: Country furniture, mainly French, tables, mirrors, armoires, chairs, to £5,000.* LOC: 5 miles south of Ashford. PARK: Easy. TEL: 01233 720917; fax - 01233 720156; mobile - 07721 015263; e-mail - gabrielle@gabrielledegiles.com website - www.gabrielledegiles.com VAT: Spec.

BIRCHINGTON, Nr. Margate

John Chawner
36 Station Approach. CT7 9RD. Open 10.30-12.30 and 2-5. CL: Tues. *STOCK: Clocks, barometers, smalls and bureaux.* PARK: Easy. TEL: 01843 846943; mobile - 07786 902297. SER: Repairs (clocks and barometers).

BRASTED, Nr. Westerham

David Barrington
The Antique Shop. TN16 1JA. (James and Richard Barrington). Est. 1947. Open 9-6. SIZE: Medium. *STOCK: Furniture, decorative items and mirrors, 18th-19th C.* LOC: A25. PARK: Easy. TEL: 01959 562479. VAT: Stan/Spec.

Bigwood Antiques
High St. TN16 1JA. (S. Bigwood). Est. 1984. Open 10.30-5, Sun. 12.45-4.30. SIZE: Small. *STOCK: Furniture, 19th-20th C, £250-£4,000.* PARK: Easy. TEL: 01959 564458. SER: Restorations. VAT: Stan/Spec.

Cooper Fine Arts Ltd
Swan House, High St. TN16 1JJ. (J. Hill-Reid). Est. 1976. Open 10-6, Sun. 11-5. SIZE: Medium. *STOCK: 17th-19th C furniture, paintings and decorative.* PARK: Easy. TEL: 01959 565818. VAT: Stan/Spec.

Courtyard Antiques incorporating Southdown House
High St. TN16 1JE. (H. La Trobe). Est. 1982. Open 10-5, Sun. and Bank Holidays 12.30-4.30. SIZE: Large. *STOCK: Fine Georgian to Edwardian furniture, silver, jewellery, glass, ceramics, Tunbridge ware, watercolours, oils and prints.* LOC: A25, off M25, junction 5. PARK: Easy - at rear. TEL: 01959 564483/563522; fax - 01732 454726; website - www.courtyardantiques.co.uk SER: Restorations (furniture); French polishing; re-leathering.

G. A. Hill Antiques
5 High St. TN16 1JA. Est. 1999. Open 10-5, Sun. and Mon. by appointment. SIZE: Medium. *STOCK: Fine furniture and mirrors, 18th to early 19th C, £2,000-£15,000.* PARK: Easy. TEL: 01959 565500; mobile - 07774 443455.

Keymer Son & Co. Ltd
Swaylands Place, The Green. TN16 1JY. Est. 1977. Open 10-1 and 2.30-5. CL: Sat. SIZE: Small. *STOCK: 18th-19th C furniture, £100-£3,000.* LOC: A25. PARK: Easy. TEL: 01959 564203; fax - 01959 561138. e-mail - keymer.london@virgin.net

Louisa Francis
High St. TN16 1JB. (Louise Hayward). Est. 1984. Open Tues.-Sat. 10.30-5. SIZE: Small. *STOCK: 18th Worcester, Caughley, Lowestoft and Bow; fine and important signed pieces by Baldwyn, Stinton and Davis etc; 18th C drinking glasses, jewellery and silver.* PARK: Easy. TEL: 01959 561222; fax - same. SER: Valuations. FAIRS: Kensington Ceramics.

Roy Massingham Antiques   LAPADA
The Coach House. TN16 1JJ. Est. 1968. Prior appointment advisable. *STOCK: 18th-19th C furniture, pictures and decorative items.* LOC: 10 mins. from M25. PARK: Easy. TEL: 01959 562408; mobile - 07860 326825. VAT: Spec.

Old Bakery Antiques
High St. TN16 1JA. (P. and M. Dyke). Est. 1977. Open Mon., Fri. and Sat. 10-5, other times by appointment. SIZE: Medium. *STOCK: Furniture, 18th-20th C, £500-£10,000; paintings, 19th-20th C, £500-£1,000+; decorative objects, 18th-20th C, £150-£5,000.* TEL: 01959 565343; mobile - 07776 186819. SER: Valuations; buys at auction. VAT: Spec.

Old Manor House Antiques
The Green. TN16 1JL. (Jane R. Read). Est. 1983. Open Tues.-Sat. *STOCK: Clocks, barometers, lighting, copper and brass, mirrors, furniture and general antiques.* PARK: Easy. TEL: 01959 562536.

S. L. Walker
High St. TN16 1JA. (Sharon Walker). Est. 1994. Open Tues.-Sat. 10.30-5 or by appointment. SIZE: Medium. *STOCK: Quality English and European porcelain especially Royal Worcester, 1860-1970 including Doris Lindner, Freda Doughty and Ruyckevelt; Royal Crown Derby, from 1890; Royal Doulton, Sevres and Meissen; Georgian to Victorian furniture; oil paintings and watercolours.* PARK: Easy. TEL: 01959 565623; mobile - 07879 626721; e-mail - sharon10@talk21.com SER: Valuations.

W.W. Warner (Antiques)   BADA
The Green, High St. TN16 1JL. (C.S. Jowitt). Est. 1957. Open Tues.-Sat. 10-5. STOCK: 18th-19th C English and Continental pottery, porcelain, glass, furniture. LOC: A25. PARK: Easy. TEL: 01959 563698. SER: Valuations; restorations.

BROADSTAIRS

Broadstairs Antiques and Collectables
49 Belvedere Rd. CT10 1PF. (Mrs P. Law). Est. 1980. Open 10-4.30. CL: Mon. in summer. Jan. and Feb. - open Thurs., Fri. and Sat. 10-4.30. *STOCK: General antiques, linen, china and small furniture.* LOC: Road opposite Lloyds TSB. PARK: Easy. TEL: 01843 861965. FAIRS: DMG.

BROMLEY

Patric Capon   BADA
PO Box 581. BR1 2WX. Open by appointment. STOCK: Unusual carriage clocks, 19th C, £2,000-£25,000; 8-day and 2-day marine chronometers, 19th C, £3,500-£18,000; clocks and barometers, 18th-19th C, £2,000-£35,000. TEL: 020 8467 5722; fax - 020 8295 1475; e-mail - patric.capon@sagnet.co.uk SER: Valuations; restorations.

Halstead Antiques
24A Tynley Rd. BR1 2RP. (Roger G. Halstead). Est. 1989. Open 9.30-5.30, Sat. and Sun. by appointment. SIZE: Medium. *STOCK: Dual height snooker, dining, billard tables, 1840-1930, £1,500-£15,000.* LOC: 20 mins. from M25. PARK: Easy. TEL: 020 8289 2240; fax - 020 8289 9903. SER: Restorations (snooker, dining and billiard tables).

Peter Morris
1 Station Concourse, Bromley North BR Station. BR1 4EQ. BNTA. OMRS. ANA. IBNS. BDOS. Open 10-1 and 2-6, Sat. 9-2. CL: Wed. SIZE: Medium. *STOCK: Coins, from 1660s; medals, from 1790; antiquities, Egyptian, Greek and Roman; bank notes, from 1800; all 50p to £1,000.* LOC: Inside station. PARK: Easy. TEL: 020 8313 3410; fax - 020 8466 8502; e-mail - info@petermorris.co.uk website - www.petermorris.co.uk SER: Valuations; buys at auction. FAIRS: BNTA Coinex; OMRS Convention; major UK and European Coin & Medal. VAT: Stan/Spec.

Past and Present
22 Plaistow Lane. BR1 3DQ. (Mrs Jan Sibley). Est. 1992. Open 9-5. SIZE: Small. *STOCK: General antiques and collectables including furniture and garden items.* PARK: Outside shop. TEL: 020 8466 7056; home - 020 8464 0290; mobile - 07961 995303. SER: Valuations.

CANTERBURY

Antique and Design
The Old Oast, Hollow Lane. CT1 3SA. (Steve Couchman). Est. 1988. Open 9-6, Sun. 10-4. SIZE: Large. *STOCK: Pine furniture, decorative items, 1800-1950, £5-£1,500.* LOC: M2 from London, Canterbury exit, straight at first roundabout, right at second and third roundabouts, left at second pedestrian lights, shop 500 yards. PARK: Ample free. TEL: 01227 762871; website - www.antiqueanddesign.co.uk SER: Buys at auction; import and export. VAT: Stan/Spec.

R. J. Baker
16 Palace St. CT1 2DZ. Est. 1979. Open Wed.-Sat. 9.30-5. SIZE: Small. *STOCK: Silver and jewellery, 18th-19th C, £500-£10,000; handmade modern silverware, modern jewellery.* LOC: 5 mins. from cathedral, opposite The King's School. PARK: Easy. TEL: 01227 463224. SER: Valuations; restorations; gold and silversmiths; manufacturers. VAT: Stan/Spec.

Burgate Antique Centre
23A Palace St. CT1 2DZ. (V. Reeves). Est. 1986. Open 10-5. SIZE: 10 dealers. *STOCK: General antiques and collectables, militaria and British war medals.* TEL: 01227 456500.

Bygones Reclamation
Nackington Rd. CT4 7BA. (Bob and Sue Thorpe). SALVO. Est. 1995. Open 8-5.30, Sat. 8.30-6, Sun. 9-5. *STOCK: Victorian fireplaces, cast iron radiators, 19th C, £200-£1,500; garden statuary, 18th-20th C, £300-£1,500.* LOC: B2068 Hythe road, 2 miles from city centre. PARK: Own. TEL: 01227 767453; freephone - 0800 0433012; fax - 01227 762153; e-mail - bob@bygones.net website - www.bygones.net SER: Valuations; restorations. FAIRS: Newark. VAT: Spec.

Canterbury Antiques
2 The Borough. CT1 2DR. (M.D. Patten). Est. 1993. Open 10-5. SIZE: Medium. *STOCK: Clocks and barometers, china, furniture, to Victorian, £50-£10,000.* PARK: Loading only and nearby. TEL: 01227 785755; fax - 01227 766222; mobile - 07711 404231.

The Canterbury Bookshop
37 Northgate. CT1 1BL. (David Miles). ABA. PBFA. Est. 1980. Open 10-5. SIZE: Medium. *STOCK: Antiquarian and secondhand books, children's books, prints.* PARK: Easy. TEL: 01227 464773; fax - 01227 780073; e-mail - canterburybookshop@btconnect.com FAIRS: PBFA and major provincial; ABA; Olympia; Chelsea.

Chaucer Bookshop
6-7 Beer Cart Lane. CT1 2NY. (Sir Robert Sherston-Baker Bt). ABA. PBFA. Est. 1956. Open 10-5. *STOCK: Books and prints, 18th-20th C, £5-£150; maps, 18th-19th C, £50-£1,000.* LOC: 5 mins. walk from cathedral, via Mercery Lane and St. Margaret's St. PARK: Castle St. TEL: 01227 453912; fax - 01227 451893; e-mail - chaucerbooks@btconnect.com SER: Valuations; buys at auction (books, maps and prints). VAT: Stan.

City Pride Ltd
72-73 Northgate. CT1 1BB. (M.D. Patten). Est. 1993. Open 10-5. SIZE: Medium. *STOCK: General antiques, collectables, furniture, Victorian, 1920s, 1930s, £2-£4,000.* TEL: 01227 764255; fax - 01227 766222.

Coach House Antiques Centre
2A Duck Lane, St. Radigunds. CT1 2AE. Est. 1975. Open Tues.-Sat. SIZE: Large. *STOCK: General antiques, small furniture, ceramics, glass, linen, books, collectors' items and bygones.* Not Stocked: Jewellery. PARK: Nearby. TEL: 01227 463117.

Conquest House Antiques
17 Palace St. CT1 2DZ. (C.C. Hill and D.A. Magee). Est. 1975. Open 10-5.30. *STOCK: 18th-19th C furniture, chandeliers and decorative items.* LOC: Near cathedral, King's Mile. PARK: St. Radigunds. TEL: 01227 464587; fax - 01227 451375; e-mail - caroline@empire-antiques.co.uk website - www.conquesthouse.com SER: Restorations; valuations; packing and shipping; delivery.

H.S. Greenfield and Son, Gunmakers (Est. 1805)
The Shooting Grounds, Sturry Hill, Sturry. CT2 0NQ. (T.S. Greenfield). GTA. Est. 1927. Open 9-5.30. *STOCK: English sporting guns, in pairs and singles; Continental sporting guns, firearms.* PARK: Own. TEL: 01227 713222. website - www.greenfieldshooting.co.uk SER: Valuations; restorations (antique firearms). VAT: Stan.

Nan Leith's Brocanterbury
Errol House, 68 Stour St. CT1 2NZ. Resident. Est. 1983. Open Mon., Wed., Fri. and Sat. 1-6 or by appointment. *STOCK: Art Deco, Victoriana, pressed glass, costume jewellery.* LOC: Close to Heritage Museum. TEL: 01227 454519.

Pinetum
25 Oaten Hill. CT1 3HZ. (Alan Pattinson). Est. 1967. Open 9.30-5, Sat. 10-4, Sun. 11-4. SIZE: Medium. *STOCK: 18th-19th C pine and country furniture, £50-£3,000.* LOC: Old Dover road. PARK: Easy. TEL: 01227 780365; home - same. SER: Valuations; restorations (furniture); buys at auction (furniture).

The Saracen's Lantern
9 The Borough. CT1 2DR. (W.J. Christophers). Est. 1970. *STOCK: General antiques, silver, jewellery, clocks, watches, Victorian bottles and pot-lids, prints, porcelain and pottery, plates, Royal commemoratives, post-cards, brass, copper and pewter.* LOC: Near cathedral opposite King's School. PARK: At rear, by way of Northgate and St. Radigund's St. or rear of Sainsbury's, Kingsmead Rd. TEL: 01227 451968.

Victorian Fireplace
Thanet House, 92 Broad St. CT1 2LU. (J.J. Griffith). Est. 1980. Open 10-5.30. CL: Wed. SIZE: Medium. *STOCK: Georgian to Victorian fireplaces.* LOC: Town centre. PARK: Nearby. TEL: 01227 767723. SER: Restorations; fitting. VAT: Stan/Spec.

CHILHAM

Bagham Barn Antiques
Canterbury Rd. CT4 8DU. Open Tues.-Sat. and Bank Holiday Mon. 10-5. SIZE: Large. *STOCK: Wide range of fine antiques, 17th to early 20th C including furniture, clocks, ceramics, silver, books and militaria.* LOC: A28 adjacent to station. PARK: Own large. TEL: 01227 732522; mobile - 07780 675201; e-mail - peggyboyd@ baghambarn.com SER: Restorations (clocks, furniture, ceramics, teddy bears, books and pens); exhibitions.

Alan Lord Antiques
at Bagham Barn Antiques, Canterbury Rd. CT4 8DU. (A.G., J.A. and R.G. Lord). Est. 1952. Open Tues.-Sun. 10-5 and Bank Holiday Mon. *STOCK: 18th-19th C furniture.* LOC: A28 adjacent to station. PARK: Large private. TEL: 01303 253674; fax - same; mobile - 07855 547467. VAT: Stan/Spec.

CHISLEHURST

Chislehurst Antiques   LAPADA
7 Royal Parade. BR7 6NR. (Mrs M. Crawley). Est. 1976. Open Thurs., Fri., Sat., 10-5, Sun. 11-4. SIZE: Large. *STOCK: Furniture, 1760-1910; lighting - oil, gas, electric, 1850-1910; mirrors, 1820-1910.* LOC: Half

mile from A20, 3 miles from M25. PARK: Easy. TEL: 020 8467 1530; mobile - 07773 345266; e-mail - margaret@chislehurstantiques.co.uk website - www. antiquefurnishings.co.uk FAIRS: Olympia; NEC. VAT: Spec.

Michael Sim
1 Royal Parade. BR7 5PG. Est. 1983. Open 9-6 including Sun. SIZE: Medium. *STOCK: English furniture, Georgian and Regency, £500-£50,000; clocks, barometers, globes and scientific instruments, £500-£50,000; Oriental works of art, £50-£5,000; portrait miniatures, £300-£5,000; animalier bronzes, £1,000-£10,000.* LOC: 50yds. from War Memorial at junction of Bromley Rd. and Centre Common Rd. PARK: Easy. TEL: 020 8467 7040; home - same; fax - 020 8857 1313. SER: Valuations; restorations; buys at auction. VAT: Spec.

CRANBROOK

Antiques at Cranbrook
19 High St. TN17 3EE. Est. 1978. Open 10-5. SIZE: 10 dealers. *STOCK: Small general antiques.* PARK: Free nearby. TEL: 01580 712173.

Douglas Bryan   BADA LAPADA
The Old Bakery, St. David's Bridge. TN17 3HN. Est. 1971. Open by appointment. *STOCK: Mainly English oak and country furniture, 17th-18th C; woodcarvings, some metalware.* LOC: Adjacent Tanyard car park - off road towards Windmill. PARK: Adjacent. TEL: 01580 713103; fax - 01580 712407; mobile - 07774 737303; e-mail - douglasbryan@tiscali.co.uk

Cranbrook Gallery
21B Stone St. TN17 3HF. (P.J. and N.A. Rodgers). Est. 1978. Open 9.30-5. CL: Mon. *STOCK: Watercolours, prints and maps, 18th-19th C.* PARK: Free nearby. TEL: 01580 720720; e-mail - cranbrookg@aol.com and info @britishfineart.com website - www.britishfineart.com SER: Framing; restorations; picture search. VAT: Margin.

CRAYFORD

Watling Antiques
139 Crayford Rd. DA1 4AS. Open 10-6.30. *STOCK: General antiques and shipping goods.* TEL: 01322 523620.

DEAL

Nicole Loftus-Potter
67A Beach St. CT14 6HY. Est. 1973. Open by appointment. *STOCK: Decorative items, general antiques and fabrics (including modern).* PARK: Easy. TEL: 01304 368030; fax - same; home - same; e-mail - potter@decorsantiques.com SER: Finder; restorations.

McConnell Fine Books
The Golden Hind, 85 Beach St. CT14 6JB. (Nick McConnell). ABA. PBFA. Est. 1976. Open Wed.-Sun. 11-4, other times by appointment. SIZE: Medium. *STOCK: Leather-bound antiquarian books.* LOC: Seafront opposite Royal Hotel. PARK: Nearby. TEL: 01304 375086; fax - same; mobile - 07966 404164; e-mail - mcconnellbooks@aol.com website - www.

LENNOX CATO
ANTIQUES AND WORKS OF ART

1 THE SQUARE, CHURCH STREET, EDENBRIDGE, KENT, TN8 5BD, ENGLAND
TELEPHONE/FAX: +44 (0) 1732 865 988 MOBILE: 07836 233473
website: www.lennoxcato.com

Pair of oak stools

Open: MONDAY – FRIDAY 9.30 – 5.30 SAT. 10 – 12 *other times by appointment*

---

mcconnellfinebooks.com SER: Valuations. FAIRS: ABA - Olympia, Chelsea Town Hall; monthly PBFA Russell Hotel.

Quill Antiques
12 Alfred Sq. CT14 6LR. (A.J. and A.R. Young). Open 9-5.30. *STOCK: General antiques, porcelain, Oriental items.* TEL: 01304 375958.

Serendipity
125 High St. CT14 6BB. (M. and K. Short). Est. 1976. Open 10-1 and 2-4.30, Sat. 9.30-4.30 or by appointment. SIZE: Medium. *STOCK: Staffordshire figures, ceramics, pictures, furniture.* PARK: Easy. TEL: 01304 369165; home - 01304 366536; e-mail - dipityantiques@aol.com and fivetake@aol.com SER: Valuations; restorations (ceramics and oil paintings).

Toby Jug
South Toll House, Deal Pier, Beach St. CT14 6HZ. (Mrs Sandy Pettit). Est. 1996. Open Tues.-Sat. 11-5.30. SIZE: Small. *STOCK: Toby and character jugs, 1800-2000, £10-£1,000; 20th C ceramics collectables.* LOC: Seafront. PARK: Middle St. TEL: 01304 369917; home - 01304 365617. SER: Valuations. FAIRS: DMG, Detling; The Grand, Folkestone.

Vintage Cameras Ltd
P O Box 359. CT14 8WF. (J. and M. Jenkins). Est. 1959. Open 9-5 by appointment. *STOCK: Vintage and classic cameras, £50-£5,000; general photographica, £5-£500;*

all 1840 to date. TEL: 01304 380218; fax - same; e-mail - i@vintagecameras.co.uk website - www.vintage cameras.co.uk

EAST PECKHAM, Nr.Tonbridge

Desmond and Amanda North
The Orchard, Hale St. TN12 5JB. Est. 1971. Open daily, appointment advisable. SIZE: Medium. *STOCK: Oriental rugs, runners, carpets and cushions, 1800-1939, mostly £100-£4,000.* LOC: On B2015, 400yds south of roundabout at northern end of Hale Street bypass (A228). PARK: Easy. TEL: 01622 871353; home - same; fax - 01622 872998. SER: Valuations; restorations (reweaving, re-edging and patching); cleaning.

EDENBRIDGE

Lennox Cato   BADA LAPADA
1 The Square, Church St. TN8 5BD. (Lennox and Susan Cato). Est. 1975. Open 9.30-5.30, Sat. 10-12 or by appointment. SIZE: Large. *STOCK: 18th-19th C English and Continental furniture and related items, including mirrors, lamps, paintings, ceramics.* LOC: 20 mins from M25, town centre (B2026), next door to Chevertons. PARK: Nearby. TEL: 01732 865988; mobile - 07836 233473; e-mail - cato@lennoxcato.com website - www.lennoxcato.com SER: Valuations; restorations. FAIRS: Olympia (Summer and Winter); BADA (London and Harrogate). VAT: Stan/Spec.

Chevertons of Edenbridge Ltd   BADA LAPADA 71-73 High St. TN8 5AL. (David and Angus Adam). CINOA. Est. 1961. Open 9-5.30. SIZE: 10 showrooms + warehouse. *STOCK: English and Continental furniture and accessories, £500-£40,000.* LOC: From Westerham, on B2026 to Edenbridge. PARK: Nearby. TEL: 01732 863196/863358; fax - 01732 864298; e-mail - chevertons@ msn.com website - www.chevertons.com FAIRS: Olympia (June and Nov); BADA, March. VAT: Spec.

Restall Brown & Clennell
Taylour House, High St. TN8 5AL. Open 9-5, other times by appointment. SIZE: Large. *STOCK: English furniture, 17th-19th C.* PARK: Easy. TEL: 01732 866390; fax - 01932 862178; e-mail - sales@rbc-furniture.co.uk website - www.rbc-furniture.co.uk

ELHAM, Nr. Canterbury

Elham Antiques
New Farmhouse, Cock Lane. CT4 6TL. (Julian and Linda Chambers). Resident. Est. 1990. Open by appointment. SIZE: Large. *STOCK: Fireplaces, 18th-19th C, £500-£1,000; country furniture, late 17th C to late 19th C, £500-£1,000; trains and models, early 20th C, £200-£600.* PARK: Easy. TEL: 01303 840085; home - 01303 840874. SER: Valuations. VAT: Spec.

FARNINGHAM

P.T. Beasley
Forge Yard, High St. DA4 0DB. (P.T. and R. Beasley).

Est. 1964. Open every day, prior telephone call advisable. *STOCK: English furniture, pewter, brass, Delft and woodcarvings.* LOC: Opposite Social Club. PARK: Easy. TEL: 01322 862453.

FAVERSHAM

Squires Antiques (Faversham)
3 Jacob Yard, Preston St. ME13 8NY. (A. Squires). Est. 1985. Open 10-5. CL: Wed. and Thurs. SIZE: Large. *STOCK: General antiques.* PARK: Nearby. TEL: 01795 531503; fax - 01227 750396; e-mail - squiresantiques@ aol.com

FOLKESTONE

Marrin's Bookshop
149 Sandgate Rd. CT20 2DA. (Patrick Marrin). ABA. PBFA. ILABA. Est. 1949. Open 9.30-1 and 2.30-5.30. CL: Mon.   SIZE: Large. *STOCK: Maps, early engravings, topographical and sporting prints, paintings, drawings, books, engravings.* TEL: 01303 253016; fax - 01303 850956; e-mail - marrinbook @clara.co.uk website - www.marrinbook.co.uk SER: Restorations; framing. FAIRS: Olympia, Chelsea Town Hall Book; Russell Hotel. VAT: Stan.

Military History Bookshop
P O Box 590CT20 2WX. (I.H. and G.M. Knight). Est. 1975. Open by appointment. SIZE: Medium. *STOCK: Military books.* TEL: 01303 246500; fax - 01303 245133; e-mail - info@militaryhistorybooks.com website - www.militaryhistorybooks.com. SER: Search.

FOUR ELMS, Nr. Edenbridge

Treasures
The Cross Roads. TN8 7NH. (B. Ward-Lee). Est. 1974. Open 10-5. *STOCK: Copper, brass, glass, porcelain, silver, jewellery, linen, books, toys, pine, small furniture and collectables.* PARK: Forecourt. TEL: 01732 700363.

GOUDHURST

Mill House Antiques
High St. TN17 1AL. Est. 1968. Open 10-5. CL: Wed pm. SIZE: Medium. *STOCK: Oak, pine country and painted furniture and associated items, 18th C to Victorian, £5-£1,000.* LOC: Off A21 on to A262, village about 3 miles. PARK: Easy. TEL: 01580 212476; home - 01892 528223. SER: Valuations.

HAMSTREET, Nr. Ashford

Woodville Antiques
The Street. TN26 2HG. (A.S. MacBean). Est. 1972. Open Tues.-Sun. 10-5.30. SIZE: Small. *STOCK: Woodworking tools, 18th-20th C; 19th C furniture, glass and pictures.* LOC: Village centre. PARK: Easy. TEL: 01233 732981; home - same; e-mail - woodville antique@yahoo.co.uk SER: Valuations.

HYTHE

Alan Lord Antiques
158 High St. CT21 5JR. (R.G. and M. Lord). Open 9.30-5, Wed. 9.30-1. *STOCK: 18th-19th C furniture; books relating to Kent, antiques and architecture, leather bindings.* LOC: Near Waitrose (A259). PARK: Private forecourt. TEL: 01303 264239; mobile - 07855 547467; e-mail - russell@lord8829.fsnet.co.uk VAT: Stan/Spec.

Malthouse Arcade
High St. CT21 5BW. (Mr and Mrs R.M. Maxtone Graham). Est. 1974. Open Fri., Sat. and Bank Holiday Mon. 9.30-5.30. SIZE: Large - 37 stalls. *STOCK: Furniture, jewellery and collectors' items.* LOC: West end of High St. PARK: 50yds. TEL: 01303 260103; home - 01304 613270.

Owlets
99 High St. CT21 5JH. NAG. NGA. Est. 1961. Open 9-5. *STOCK: Antique and estate jewellery and silver.* TEL: 01303 230333: e-mail - alison@owlets.co.uk website - www.owlets.co.uk

Samovar Antiques
158 High St. CT21 5JR. (Mrs F. Rignault). Open 9.30-5, Wed. 9.30-1. *STOCK: 19th C and French provincial furniture, Oriental carpets and rugs, general antiques.* PARK: Own. TEL: 01303 264239.

LAMBERHURST

The China Locker
TN3 8HN. (G. Wilson). Est. 1973. Open by appointment. SIZE: Small. *STOCK: 19th C prints, £5-£40; 19th C porcelain and pottery.* PARK: Outside. TEL: 01892 890555. FAIRS: Local.

LITTLEBOURNE, Nr. Canterbury

Jimmy Warren Antiques
Cedar Lodge, 28 The Hill. CT3 1TA. Est. 1969. Open 10-5 including Sun. SIZE: Small. *STOCK: Decorative antiques and garden ornaments.* LOC: A257. PARK: Own. TEL: 01227 721510; e-mail - enquiries@jimmy warren.co.uk website - www.jimmywarren.co.uk SER: Valuations. VAT: Stan/Spec.

MAIDSTONE

Gem Antiques
10 Gabriels Hill. ME15 6JG. Est. 1969. Open 10-5. SIZE: Small. *STOCK: Jewellery, £5-£10,000.* TEL: 01622 763344. SER: Restorations; repairs. VAT: Spec.

Sutton Valence Antiques
Unit 4 Haslemere Estate, Sutton Rd. ME15 9NL. (T. and N. Mullarkey). Est. 1971. Open 9-5.30, Sun. 11-4. SIZE: Large warehouse. *STOCK: Antique and shipping furniture.* LOC: Approx. 3 miles south of Maidstone, just off A274. PARK: Easy. TEL: 01622 675332; fax - 01622 692593; e-mail - svantiques@aol.com website - www.svantiques.co.uk SER: Container packing and shipping; restorations; courier; buys at auction.

MARGATE

Cottage Antiques
172 Northdown Rd., Cliftonville. CT9 2RB. (D. J. and Mrs L.O. Empsley). Est. 1982. Open 10-5. CL: Wed. SIZE: Large. *STOCK: Furniture, 1700-1930; china, 1800-1950; jewellery, Victorian to Art Deco; general antiques and collectables.* PARK: Easy. TEL: 01843 298214; home - 01843 299166; mobile - 07771 542872; e-mail - davidjempsley@aol.com SER: Valuations; restorations (furniture and china, replating).

Furniture Mart
Bath Place. CT9 2BN. (R.G. Scott). Est. 1971. CL: Wed. SIZE: Large. *STOCK: General antiques £1-£3,000; shipping goods.* LOC: Corner of Bath Place. TEL: 01843 220653. SER: Restorations; restoration materials supplied; container packing. VAT: Global/Stan.

NORTHFLEET

Northfleet Hill Antiques
36 The Hill. DA11 9EX. (Mrs M. Kilby). Est. 1986. Open Mon., Tues., Fri., some Sats. 10-5 and by appointment. SIZE: Small. *STOCK: Furniture, 19th to early 20th C, £50-£800; bygones and collectables, £1-£100.* LOC: A226 near junction with B261 and B2175. PARK: Easy (behind Ye Olde Coach and Horses Inn). TEL: 01474 321521. FAIRS: Chelsea.

OTFORD

Ellenor Antiques and Tea Shop
11a High St. TN14 5PG. (Ellenor Hospice Care). Open 10-5; April-Oct. - 10-4, Sat.10-5. SIZE: Medium. *STOCK: Furniture, ceramics, glass, 18th to early 20th C, £5-£1,500.* LOC: Towards Sevenoaks, 3 miles south of junction 4, M25. PARK: Nearby. TEL: 01959 524322.

Mandarin Gallery - Oriental Art

The Mill Pond, 16 High St. TN14 5PQ. (J. and M.C. Liu). Est. 1984. Open Tues.-Sat. 10-5. SIZE: Medium. *STOCK: Chinese rosewood and lacquer furniture, 18th-19th C; jade and soap stone, ivory and wood carvings.* Not Stocked: Non-Oriental items. LOC: A225. PARK: Easy. TEL: 01959 522778; home - 01732 457399; fax - same; e-mail - mandaringallery@hotmail.com SER: Restorations (Chinese rosewood furniture).

Otford Antiques & Collectors Centre

26-28 High St. TN14 5PQ. (Mr and Mrs David Lowrie). Est. 1997. Open 10-5, Sun. 11-4. SIZE: Large. *STOCK: Furniture and collectables, to £800+.* PARK: Easy. TEL: 01959 522025; fax - 01732 883365; website - www. otfordantiques.co.uk SER: Restorations (upholstery).

PETTS WOOD, Nr. Orpington

Beehive

22 Station Sq. BR5 1NA. Est. 1994. Open 9.30-5, Sat. 9.30-4.30. SIZE: 50 dealers. *STOCK: Collectables, china, glass, jewellery and furniture, 19th-20th C, £1-£500.* PARK: Easy. TEL: 01689 890675. FAIRS: Detling, Ardingly.

RAMSGATE

Granny's Attic

2 Addington St. CT11 9JL. (Penelope J. Warn). Est. 1987. Open 10-5. CL: Thurs. SIZE: Medium. *STOCK: Pre-1940s items, £2-£1,500.* LOC: Left off harbour approach road or right off Westcliffe Rd. PARK: Easy. TEL: 01843 588955; home - 01843 596288; mobile - 07773 155339. SER: Free local delivery, national and Continental delivery by arrangement.

Thanet Antiques

45 Albert St. CT11 9EX. (Mr and Mrs R. Fomison). Est. 1971. Open Mon., Tues. and Wed. 10-1 and 2.15-4. SIZE: Large. *STOCK: Furniture and bric-a-brac, 18th-20th C, £1-£10,000.* LOC: From London Rd. right to seafront. With harbour on right turn first left down Addington St., then last right. PARK: Own. TEL: 01843 597336; e-mail - marytfom@tiscali.co.uk

ROCHESTER

Baggins Book Bazaar - The Largest Secondhand Bookshop in England

19 High St. ME1 1PY. Est. 1986. Open 10-6 including Sun. SIZE: Large. *STOCK: Secondhand and antiquarian books.* LOC: Next to the Guildhall Museum. PARK: Nearby. TEL: 01634 811651; fax - 01634 840591; website - www.bagginsbooks.co.uk SER: Book search; new book ordering.

Cottage Style Antiques

24 Bill Street Rd. ME2 4RB. (W. Miskimmin). Est. 1981. Open 9.30-5.30. *STOCK: General and architectural antiques.* PARK: Easy. TEL: 01634 717623.

Field Staff Antiques

93 High St. ME1 1LX. (Jim Field and Jane Staff). Open 10-5. SIZE: Large - 3 showrooms. *STOCK: Furniture including beds, silver, commemorative and crested china, ephemera.* LOC: Next to visitor centre. TEL: 01634 846144; e-mail - fieldstaffantiques@supanet.com website - www.fieldstaffantiques.com

Francis Iles

Rutland House, La Providence, High St. ME1 1LX. (The Family Iles). Est. 1960. Open 9.30-5.30. SIZE: Large. *STOCK: Over 700 works, all mediums including sculpture, mainly 20th C, £50-£10,000.* PARK: 40yds. TEL: 01634 843081; fax - 01634 846681; e-mail - advice@artycat.com and nettie@francis-iles.com website - www.francis-iles.com and www.artycat.com SER: Restorations; cleaning; relining; framing. FAIRS: Affordable Art (Spring), Battersea and Bristol; RA Watercolour & Drawings. VAT: Stan/Spec.

Kaizen International Ltd

88 High St. ME1 1JT. (Jason Hunt). Est. 1997. Open 10-5. SIZE: Medium. *STOCK: General antiques including antique and secondhand jewellery.* PARK: Nearby. TEL: 01634 814132. SER: Valuations; restorations (jewellery).

Langley Galleries Ltd

143 High St. ME1 1EL. (K.J. Cook). Est. 1978. Open 9-5. *STOCK: Prints, watercolours, oils, 19th-20th C.* TEL: 01634 811802. SER: Framing.

Memories

128 High St. ME1 1JT. (Mrs M. Kilby and C. Allwright). Est. 1985. Open 9.30-5, Sun. 11-4. SIZE: Medium - 12 dealers. *STOCK: Small furniture, £50-£500; china, £5-£200; both 1900-1950; pictures, late Victorian to Edwardian, £20-£70; collectables, bric-a-brac, linen and books.* PARK: Opposite. TEL: 01634 811044. FAIRS: Chelsea; Detling.

ROLVENDEN, Nr. Cranbrook

Falstaff Antiques

63-67 High St. TN17 4LP. (C.M. Booth). Est. 1964. Open 10-5.30, Sun. by appointment. SIZE: Medium. *STOCK: English furniture, £5-£700; china, metal, glass, silver, £1-£200.* Not Stocked: Paintings. LOC: On A28, 3 miles from Tenterden, 1st shop on left in village. PARK: Easy. TEL: 01580 241234. SER: Valuations. Motor Museum. VAT: Stan/Spec.

J.D. and R.M. Walters

10 Regent St. TN17 4PE. Est. 1977. Open 8-6, Sat. 11-4.30 or by appointment. SIZE: Small. *STOCK: Mahogany furniture, 18th-19th C.* LOC: A28 turn left in village centre onto B2086, shop on left. PARK: Easy. TEL: 01580 241563; home - same. SER: Handmade copies of period furniture including chairs; restorations (GMC). VAT: Stan/Spec.

SANDGATE, Nr. Folkestone

Christopher Buck Antiques   BADA

56-60 High St. CT20 3AP. (Christopher and Jane Buck). Est. 1983. Open 10-5. CL: Wed. SIZE: Medium. *STOCK: English furniture, 18th C, £500-£30,000; decorative items, 18th-19th C, £100-£2,000.* LOC: 5 mins. from junction 12, M20 and Channel Tunnel. PARK: Easy. TEL: 01303 221229; fax - 01303 221229. e-mail - cb@christopherbuck.co.uk SER: Valuations; restorations (furniture); buys at auction. FAIRS: Olympia (June, Nov); BADA (March). VAT: Stan/Spec.

Gabrielle de Giles
Antique Country Furniture and Interiors, 21 High St. CT20 3BD. Est. 1987. Open Tues.-Sat. 10.30-5. *STOCK: Country furniture, mainly French, 18th-20th C, to £5,000.* LOC: A259 coast road. PARK: Behind shop. TEL: 01303 255600; fax - 01233 720156; mobile - 07721 015263; e-mail - gabrielle@gabrielledegiles.com website - www.gabrielledegiles.com FAIRS: London.

Finch Antiques
40 High St. CT20 3AP. (Robert and Sylvia Finch). Est. 1978. Open 9.30-6, Sun. 10.30-4. SIZE: Medium. *STOCK: Furniture, 1800-1920, £150-£3,000; silver plate and writing items, £5-£400.* PARK: Easy. TEL: 01303 240725. SER: Restorations (furniture, French polishing).

Michael Fitch Antiques   LAPADA
95-99 High St. CT20 3BY. Est. 1980. Open 10-5.30, Sun. by appointment. SIZE: Large. *STOCK: Georgian, Victorian and Edwardian furniture and clocks.* PARK: Own. TEL: 01303 249600; fax - same; website - www.michaelfitchantiques.co.uk SER: Delivery; shipping advice.

Freeman and Lloyd Antiques   BADA LAPADA
44 High St. CT20 3AP. (K. Freeman and M.R. Lloyd). CINOA. Est. 1968. Open 10-5.30, Mon. and Wed. by appointment only. SIZE: Medium. *STOCK: Fine Georgian and Regency English furniture; clocks, paintings and other period items.* LOC: On main coast road between Hythe and Folkestone (A259). PARK: Easy. TEL: 01303 248986; fax - 01303 241353; mobile - 07860 100073; e-mail - enquiries@freemanandlloyd.com website - www.freemanandlloyd.com SER: Valuations. FAIRS: Olympia (Feb., June, Nov). VAT: Spec.

David Gilbert Antiques
30 High St. CT20 3AP. Est. 1975. Open 9-5. SIZE: Two floors. *STOCK: Furniture, smalls, glass, Arts and Crafts furniture, 1790-1930, £5-£1,000.* LOC: A259 coast road. PARK: Easy. TEL: 01303 850491; home - 01304 812237. SER: Valuations.

Jonathan Greenwall Antiques   LAPADA
61-63 High St. CT20 3AH. Est. 1964. Open 9.30-5. SIZE: Large. *STOCK: Furniture, to 19th C; decorative items, jewellery, oils and watercolours, prints and maps, sculpture and bronzes.* LOC: Folkestone-Brighton road. PARK: Easy. TEL: 01303 248987. SER: Valuations.

J. Luckhurst Antiques
63 High St. CT20 3AH. Est. 1989. Open 9.30-5 and by appointment. SIZE: Small. *STOCK: Furniture - Georgian, Victorian, Edwardian and decorative; gilt mirrors, carpets.* PARK: Nearby. TEL: Home - 01303 891642; mobile - 07786 983231. SER: Valuations; restorations (period furniture). FAIRS: Newark; Ardingly.

Old English Oak
101-102 High St. CT20 3BY. (A. Martin). Est. 1997. Open 10-6. *STOCK: Oak furniture and interesting items.* PARK: 1 hour in front of shop and nearby. TEL: 01303 248560.

Gabrielle de Giles
Antique Country Furniture & Interiors

Specialising in large dining tables, chairs and mirrors

21 High Street, Sandgate, Near Folkestone, Kent, CT20 3BD

 Tel: 01303 255600
Fax: 01233 720156
Mobile: 07721 015263

 Gabrielle@gabrielledegiles.com
www.gabrielledegiles.com

Old English Pine
100 High St. CT20 3BY. (A. Martin). Est. 1986. Open 10-6. SIZE: 15 showrooms. *STOCK: Pine furniture and interesting items.* PARK: 1 hour in front of shop and nearby. TEL: 01303 248560.

Brian West Antiques
Emporium, 31-33 High St. CT20 3AH. Est. 1978. Prior telephone call advisable. CL: Thurs. SIZE: Medium. *STOCK: Arts and Crafts, Art Nouveau, Aesthetic Movement, Gothic Revival and decorative Victorian and Edwardian furniture, £100-£3,000.* LOC: Village centre. PARK: Nearby - free on sea front, next to castle. TEL: Mobile - 07860 149387.

SANDWICH

All Our Yesterdays & Chris Baker Gramophones
3 Cattle Market. CT13 9AE. (Sandie and Chris Baker). Est. 1994. Open 10.30-2.30, Fri. 10.30-2, Sat. 10.30-3.30, Sun. by appointment. CL: Wed. SIZE: Medium. *STOCK: General antiques, gramophones and associated items, £5-£1,000.* LOC: Opposite Guildhall. PARK: Behind Guildhall. TEL: 01304 614756; e-mail - cbgramophones@aol.com website - www.chrisbakergramophones.co.uk SER: Repairs (gramophones, phonographs, etc).

SEVENOAKS

Antiques & Fine Furniture
18 London Rd., Dunton Green. TN13 2UE. (C.E. West). Est. 1977. Open 10-5. SIZE: Large. *STOCK: Clocks and watches, period furniture, porcelain, glass, toys, bric-a-brac.* LOC: London road into town, opposite Whitmore's Vauxhall showroom. PARK: Easy. TEL: 01732 464346; mobile - 07957 110534. SER: Valuations; restorations (clocks, furniture); re-upholstery, curtains and soft furnishings).

Neill Robinson Blaxill   LAPADA
21 St. John's Hill. TN13 3NX. FBHI. Open 9-6, appointment preferred. *STOCK: Clocks, barometers, decorative items, furniture, sundials and garden furniture, 16th-20th C.* LOC: 1 mile from High St. PARK: Easy. TEL: 01732 454179; mobile - 07786 860782; website - www.antiques-clocks.co.uk and www.hyperiondials.co.uk SER: Restorations (fine clocks).

Gem Antiques
122 High St. TN13 1XA. Est. 1969. Open 10-5. SIZE: Small. *STOCK: Jewellery, 18th-20th C, £10-£10,000.* LOC: Next door to Boots. PARK: Nearby. TEL: 01732 743540. SER: Valuations; restorations (as stock). VAT: Spec.

SIDCUP

Ward Antique Fireplaces Ltd
105 Main Rd. DA14 6ND. (T. and M. Ward). Est. 1981. Open 10-5, Sun. 11-2. SIZE: Large. *STOCK: Fireplaces, Victorian and Edwardian furniture, £50-£1000.* LOC: Off A20. PARK: Opposite. TEL: 020 8302 2929.

SOUTHBOROUGH, Nr. Tunbridge Wells

Henry Baines   LAPADA
14 Church Rd. TN4 0RX. (Henry and Anne Baines). Est. 1968. Open Tues.-Fri. 10-5, Sat. 10-4.30, prior telephone call advisable. SIZE: Medium. *STOCK: Early oak and country furniture especially tables and sets of chairs; French provincial furniture and decorative items.* PARK: Easy. TEL: 01892 532099; fax - same; e-mail - henrybaines@onetel.com VAT: Stan/Spec.

Peter Hoare Antiques
35 London Rd. TN4 0PB. Est. 1985. Open 10-5.30. CL: Mon. SIZE: Medium. *STOCK: British Arts and Crafts furniture, Gothic revival, aesthetic movement, 19th-20th C design, £25-£5,000.* LOC: A26. PARK: At rear. TEL: 01892 524623; fax - 01892 619776. SER: Valuations.

STOCKBURY

Steppes Hill Farm Antiques   **BADA**
The Hill Farm, South St. ME9 7RB. (W.F.A. Buck). Est. 1965. Always open, appointment advisable. SIZE: Medium. *STOCK: English porcelain, pottery, pot-lids, 18th-20th C, to £30,000; small silver; caddy spoons, wine labels, silver boxes, furniture, 18th-19th C, to £30,000.* LOC: 5 mins. from M2 on A249. Enquire in village for Steppes Hill Antiques. PARK: Easy. TEL: 01795 842205; e-mail - dwabuck@ btinternet.com SER: Valuations; buys at auction.

FAIRS: BADA; International Ceramics; Olympia (Nov). VAT: Spec.

SUNDRIDGE, Nr. Sevenoaks

Sundridge Gallery
9 Church Rd. TN14 6DT. (T. and M. Tyrer). Est. 1986. Open 10-5.30. *STOCK: Watercolours and oils, 19th-20th C.* LOC: Off M25, junction 5. PARK: Easy. TEL: 01959 564104. SER: Restorations. VAT: Spec.

SUTTON VALENCE, Nr. Maidstone

Sutton Valence Antiques   LAPADA
North St. ME17 3AP. (T., N. and J. Mullarkey and O. Marles). CINOA. Est. 1971. Open 9-5, Sat. 9-4. SIZE: Large. *STOCK: Furniture, porcelain, clocks, silver, metalware, 18th-20th C.* LOC: On A274 Maidstone to Tenterden Rd. PARK: Side of shop. TEL: 01622 843333; fax - 01622 843499; e-mail - svantiques@aol.com SER: Valuations; restorations; container packing and shipping; courier; buys at auction.

TENTERDEN

Flower House Antiques
90 High St. TN30 6JB. (Barry Rayner and Quentin Johnson). Open 9.30-5.30, Sun. by appointment. SIZE: Medium. *STOCK: English and Continental furniture, 16th to early 19th C; Oriental works of art, 16th-19th C; pictures, lighting, mirrors, objets d'art.* LOC: A28. PARK: Easy and private. TEL: 01580 763764. SER: Valuations; restorations. VAT: Spec.

Gaby's Clocks and Things
140 High St. TN30 6HT. (Gaby Gunst). Est. 1972. Open 10.30-5. SIZE: Small. *STOCK: Clocks - longcase and grandmother, regulator wall, English dial, bracket, mantel and skeleton, restored and guaranteed.* PARK: Limited or nearby. TEL: 01580 765818. SER: Valuations; restorations (clocks).

Tenterden Antiques and Silver Vaults
66 High St. TN30 6AU. (T.J. Smith). Open 10-5, Sun. 11-4.30. *STOCK: Clocks, silver, telephones, barometers and general antiques.* PARK: Easy. TEL: 01580 765885.

TEYNHAM, Nr. Sittingbourne

Jackson-Grant Antiques
The Old Chapel, 133 London Rd. ME9 9QJ. (D.M. Jackson-Grant). Est. 1966. Open 10-5, Sun. 1-5. CL: Wed. SIZE: Large. *STOCK: General antiques, French and English furniture, bookcases, buffets, beds, smalls, 18th C to Art Deco, £5-£3,000.* LOC: A2 between Faversham and Sittingbourne. PARK: Easy. TEL: 01795 522027; home - same; mobile - 07831 591881; e-mail - david.jacksongrant@bt.openworld.com SER: Customised tester beds available. VAT: Stan/Spec.

Peggottys
The Old Chapel, 133 London Rd. ME9 9QJ. (B. Smith). Est. 1999. Open 10-5, Sun. 1-5. CL: Wed. SIZE: Large. *STOCK: Beds including wooden, half-testers and four-posters, French, English and Flemish, 1800-1920; Edwardian, Victorian, Georgian, Rococo, Renaissance, Breton and Henri II, £1,150-£5,000.* LOC: A2 Village

centre. PARK: Outside. TEL: 01795 522027; home - same; website - www.peggottysbeds.co.uk

TONBRIDGE

Barden House Antiques
1-3 Priory St. TN9 2AP. (Mrs B.D. Parsons). Open Wed.-Sat. 10-5. SIZE: 3 dealers. *STOCK: General antiques and collectables.* PARK: Nearby. TEL: 01732 350142; evenings - 01732 355718.

Greta May Antiques
7 Tollgate Buildings, Hadlow Rd. TN9 1NX. Est. 1987. Open Tues., Thurs., Fri. and Sat. 10-5. SIZE: Small. *STOCK: General antiques and collectables, from Victorian; old and artist bears.* LOC: A26 off High St. PARK: Mill Lane. TEL: 01732 366730; e-mail - gretamayantiques@hotmail.com SER: Valuations; restorations (teddy bears). FAIRS: Ramada Hotel, Hollingbourne, Maidstone.

Derek Roberts Antiques   BADA
25 Shipbourne Rd. TN10 3DN. (Paul Archard). Est. 1968. Open 9.30-5, Sat. 10-4, other times by appointment. SIZE: Large. *STOCK: Fine restored clocks, mostly £2,000-£100,000.* LOC: From B245 to Tonbridge, left before first lights, left again, shop 50 yards on right. PARK: Easy. TEL: 01732 358986; fax - 01732 771842; e-mail - drclocks@clara.net website - www.qualityantiqueclocks.com. SER: Valuations; restorations (clock repairs and cabinet making). FAIRS: Olympia (Autumn); BADA (Spring); Harrogate (Autumn). VAT: Spec.

B.V.M. Somerset
Stags Head, 9 Stafford Rd. TN9 1HT. Est. 1948. Open 11-6.30. *STOCK: Clocks, £500-£5,000.* LOC: Off High St. beside castle. TEL: 01732 352017; fax - 01732 368343. SER: Valuations; restorations (cabinets, gilt and French polishing); buys at auction (longcase and bracket clocks). VAT: Stan.

TUNBRIDGE WELLS

Aaron Antiques
77 St. Johns Rd. TN4 9TT. (R.J. Goodman). Open 9-5. *STOCK: Clocks and pocket watches, paintings and prints; period and shipping furniture; English, Continental and Oriental porcelain; antiquarian books, postcards, coins and medals.* TEL: 01892 517644. VAT: Stan/Spec.

Amadeus Antiques
32 Mount Ephraim. TN4 8AU. (P.A. Davies). Open 11-5, Sun. by appointment. SIZE: Medium. *STOCK: Unusual furniture, to Art Deco, £50-£5,000; china and bric-a-brac, £25-£500; chandeliers, £100-£1,000.* LOC: Near hospital. PARK: Easy. TEL: 01892 544406; 01892 864884. SER: Valuations.

The Architectural Stores
55 St John's Rd. TN4 9TP. (Nick Bates). SALVO. Est. 1988. Open Tues.-Sat. 10-5.30. SIZE: Medium. *STOCK: Fireplaces, garden statuary, lighting, decorative salvage, Georgian to Edwardian.* LOC: A26 towards Southborough. PARK: John St. TEL: 01892 540368; e-mail - nic@architecturalstores.com website - www. architecturalstores.com VAT: Stan/Spec.

Beau Nash Antiques
29 Lower Walk, The Pantiles. TN2 5TD. (Nicola Mason and David Wrenn). Est. 1992. Open 11-5. CL: Mon. and Fri. SIZE: Medium. *STOCK: Furniture, silver, porcelain and glass, 18th-20th C.* LOC: Behind Tourist Information Centre. PARK: Pantiles. TEL: 01892 537810.

Calverley Antiques
30 Crescent Rd. TN1 2LZ. (P.A. Nimmo). Est. 1995. Open 10-5.30 including Sun. *STOCK: Furniture including European pine, 1920s oak, decorative painted and garden.* LOC: Near police station and Assembly Hall. PARK: Multi-storey next door. TEL: 01892 538254; e-mail - phil@calverleyantiques.com FAIRS: Ardingly.

Chapel Place Antiques
9 Chapel Place. TN1 1YQ. (J. and A. Clare). Est. 1984. Open 9-6. *STOCK: Silver photo frames, antique and modern jewellery, old silver plate, claret jugs, hand-painted Limoges boxes.* LOC: Near The Pantiles. PARK: Nearby. TEL: 01892 546561.

Down Lane Hall Antiques
Culverden Down, St John's. TN4 9SA. (Michael Howlett). Est. 1980. Open 9-5, Sat. 10-5. SIZE: Large. *STOCK: Georgian, Victorian and Edwardian furniture; clocks and barometers.* LOC: Half mile from town centre, on A26. PARK: Easy. TEL: 01892 522440; home - 01892 522425; website - www.downlanehall.co.uk SER: Restorations; French polishing.

Glassdrumman Antiques
7 Union Square, The Pantiles. TN4 8HE. (Graham and Amanda Dyson Rooke). Open Tues.-Sat. 10-5.30. SIZE: Medium. *STOCK: Silver, jewellery, watches, clocks, furniture, decorative items, 18th-20th C.* PARK: Nearby. TEL: 01892 538615; fax - same. VAT: Stan/Spec.

Pamela Goodwin
11 The Pantiles. TN2 5TD. Est. 1980. Open 9.30-5, Sat. 9.30-5.30. SIZE: Medium. *STOCK: Furniture, longcase and wall clocks, mirrors, oil lamps, ceramics including Moorcroft and Royal Doulton, silver and glass, collectibles, Tunbridgeware, music boxes, decorative items, 18th-20th C, £50-£5,000.* LOC: Central. PARK: Nearby. TEL: 01892 618200; fax - same; e-mail - mail@goodwinantiques.co.uk website - www.goodwinantiques.co.uk VAT: Spec.

Hall's Bookshop
20-22 Chapel Place. TN1 1YQ. PBFA. Est. 1898. Open 9.30-5. *STOCK: Antiquarian and secondhand books.* TEL: 01892 527842.

Kentdale Antiques
Motts Farm Estate, Forge Rd., Eridge Green. TN3 9LJ. (C. Bigwood and T. Rayfield). Est. 1981. Open 9-5. CL: Sat. SIZE: Warehouse. *STOCK: Mostly mahogany and walnut furniture.* LOC: Telephone for directions. PARK: Easy. TEL: 01892 863840; fax - same; e-mail - kentdale.antiques@ukgateway.net SER: Restorations (furniture). VAT: Stan/Spec. *Trade only.*

Langton Green Antiques
Langton Rd. TN3 0HP. (Tim and Barbara Cooper). Resident. Est. 1980. Open Thurs., Fri. and Sat. 10-5 or by appointment. SIZE: Small. *STOCK: 18th-19th C furniture, clocks, paintings and ceramics, especially Wedgwood; decorative items.* LOC: A264, 2 miles from Tunbridge Wells. PARK: Easy. TEL: 01892 862004; home - same; mobile - 07708 127731; e-mail - antiques@langtongreen.fsbusiness.co.uk website - www.langtongreenantiques.co.uk SER: Valuations. FAIRS: Lomax - Burnham Market, Langley School, Loddon. Gemsco - Towcester.

Joroen Markies
48A St John's Rd. TN4 9NY. Open 10-5.30. SIZE: Medium. *STOCK: 19th-20th C decorative arts - Art Deco, Art Nouveau, Arts and Crafts.* PARK: Nearby. TEL: 01892 614004; mobile - 07703 328562; e-mail - sales@markies.co.uk website - www.markies.co.uk SER: Valuations; restorations.

Old Colonial
56 St John's Rd., St John's. TN4 9NY. (Dee Martyn and Suzy Rees). Est. 1982. Open Tues.-Sat. 10.30-5.30. SIZE: Small. *STOCK: English and French country and decorative furniture and associated smalls.* LOC: Approximately 1 mile outside Tunbridge Wells. PARK: Opposite. TEL: 01892 533993; fax - 01892 513281. VAT: Spec.

The Pantiles Antiques
31 The Pantiles. TN2 5TD. (Mrs E.M. Blackburn). Est. 1979. Open 10-5. SIZE: Medium. *STOCK: Georgian, Victorian and Edwardian furniture; 19th C porcelain, silver.* LOC: Lower Walk. PARK: Easy. TEL: 01892 531291.

Pantiles Oriental Carpets
31A The Pantiles. TN2 5TD. (Judith Williams). Est. 1980. Open 10-5.30. CL: Wed. SIZE: Small. *STOCK: Oriental carpets, rugs, kelims, cushions and tribal artifacts.* LOC: Lower walk. PARK: Nearby. TEL: 01892 530416; fax - 01892 530416. SER: Restorations and cleaning (carpets, rugs, kelims, tapestries).

Pantiles Spa Antiques
4/5/6 Union Square, The Pantiles. TN4 8HE. (J.A. Cowpland). Est. 1979. Open 9.30-5, Sat. 9.30-5.30. SIZE: Large. *STOCK: Period and Victorian furniture especially dining tables and chairs, £200-£10,000; pictures, £50-£3,000; clocks, £100-£5,000; porcelain, £50-£2,000; silver, £50-£1,000; all 17th-19th C; dolls, bears and toys.* PARK: Nearby. TEL: 01892 541377; fax - 01435 865660; e-mail - janettec@btconnect.com website - www.pantiles-spa-antiques.co.uk SER: Restorations (furniture); 30 mile radius free delivery (large items). VAT: Spec.

Payne & Son (Silversmiths) Ltd
Clock House, 37 High St. TN1 1XL. (E.D., M.D. and A.E. Payne). NAG: FGA. Est. 1790. Open 9-5.30, Mon. 9.30-5.30, Sat. 9-5. SIZE: Medium. *STOCK: English jewellery, Victorian to modern; British silver, Georgian to modern; Swiss watches, to modern; all £50-£10,000+.* LOC: Halfway along High St., marked by projecting clock. PARK: Street and multi-storey near station. TEL: 01892 525874; fax - 01892 535447; e-mail - jewellers@payneandson.com website - www.payneandson.com

SER: Valuations; restorations (jewellery, silver, watches and clocks). VAT: Stan/Spec.

Phoenix Antiques
51-53 St. John's Rd. TN4 9TP. (Peter Janes, Jane Stott and Robert Pilbeam). Est. 1982. Open 10-5.30 or by appointment. SIZE: Large. *STOCK: 18th-19th C French, English, original painted and country furniture, decorative furnishings, original gilt overmantel mirrors, garden statuary.* LOC: On A26 from A21 into town, by St. John's Church. PARK: Easy. TEL: 01892 549099; e-mail - shop@phoenixantiques.co.uk website - www.phoenixantiques.co.uk VAT: Spec.

Redleaf Gallery
1 Castle St. TN1 1XJ. (Nick Hills). Open Tues.-Sat. 10.30-5. *STOCK: 19th-20th C watercolours, modern British and contemporary paintings.* LOC: Off High St. PARK: Nearby. TEL: 01892 526695. VAT: Spec.

Ian Relf Antiques
132/134 Camden Rd. TN1 2QZ. Open 9.30-1.30 and 2.30-5.30. *STOCK: Mainly furniture.* TEL: 01892 538362.

Sporting Antiques
10 Union House, The Pantiles. TN4 8HE. (L.A. Franklin and Mrs Pat Hayes). Est. 1996. Open 10-5.30. SIZE: Small. *STOCK: Firearms - civil and military pistols, civil, military and sporting longarms; edged weapons - swords, bayonets, daggers and knives; fishing tackle - rods, reels, gaffs and nets; marine - telescopes, binoculars, compasses, clocks, sextants; surveying - levels, scopes, theodolites, instruments; sporting - golf, football, rugby, fencing, skiing, croquet; sporting and military prints.* PARK: Nearby. TEL: 01892 522661; fax - same.

John Thompson
27 The Pantiles. TN2 5TD. Est. 1982. Open Tues.-Sat. 11-5. SIZE: Medium. *STOCK: Furniture, late 17th to early 19th C; paintings 17th-20th C; decorative items.* Not Stocked: Jewellery, silver and militaria. PARK: Linden Road or Warwick Park. TEL: 01892 547215. VAT: Spec.

Up Country
The Old Corn Stores, 68 St. John's Rd. TN4 9PE. (G.J. Price and C.M. Springett). Est. 1988. Open 9-5.30. SIZE: Large. *STOCK: British and European country furniture, £50-£5,000; associated decorative and interesting items, £5-£500; all 18th-19th C.* LOC: On main London road to Southborough and A21 trunk road which joins M25 and M26 at Sevenoaks intersection. PARK: Own at rear. TEL: 01892 523341; fax - 01892 530382; e-mail - mail @upcountryantiques.co.uk website - www.upcountry antiques.co.uk VAT: Stan.

The Vintage Watch Co.
The Old Pipe House, 74 High St. TN1 1YB. (F. Lawrence). Open Wed.-Sat. 10-5. *STOCK: Pre-1950's fine wrist watches, pocket watches.* TEL: 01892 616077. SER: Restorations.

WEST MALLING

The Old Clock Shop
63 High St. ME19 6NA. (S.L. Luck). Est. 1970. Open 9-5. SIZE: Large. *STOCK: Grandfather clocks, 17th-19th C; carriage, bracket, wall clocks and barometers.* LOC: Half a mile from M20. PARK: Easy. TEL: 01732 843246; website - www.theoldclockshop.co.uk VAT: Spec.

Rose and Crown Antiques
40 High St. ME19 6QR. (Candy and Julian Lovegrove). GMC. Est. 1995. Open 9.30-5.30. SIZE: Medium. *STOCK: General antiques including furniture, 18th to early 20th C.* PARK: Free. TEL: 01732 872707; fax - 01732 872810; e-mail - candylovegrove@hotmail.com and jlantiques@hotmail.com website - www.antiqueswestmalling.co.uk SER: Restorations (furniture including French polishing and upholstery).

WESTERHAM

Apollo Antique Galleries   LAPADA
19 -21 Market Sq. TN16 1AN. (S.M and R.W. Barr). Est. 1967. Open 9.30-5.30. SIZE: Large. *STOCK: Georgian, Victorian and Edwardian furniture; 19th C oils and watercolours; bronze and marble statuary; clocks, silver.* LOC: Between junctions 5 and 6 of M25, close to Gatwick Airport. PARK: Easy. TEL: 01959 562200; fax - 01959 562600; e-mail - enq@apollogalleries.com website - www.apollogalleries.com SER: Valuations; free delivery. FAIRS: Olympia; LAPADA. VAT: Spec.

Castle Antiques Centre
1 London Rd. TN16 1BB. (Stewart Ward Properties). Est. 1986. Open 10-5 including Sun. SIZE: Small - 8 dealers. *STOCK: General antiques, books, linen, collectables, costume, chandeliers, cat images.* LOC: Just off town centre. PARK: Easy - nearby. TEL: 01959 562492. SER: Valuations; props for stage productions. FAIRS: Ardingly; Alexandra Palace; Detling.

The Design Gallery 1850-1950   LAPADA
5 The Green. TN16 1AS. (John Masters and Chrissie Painell). Est. 2002. Open Tues.-Sat. 10-5.30, Sun. 1-5, Mon. by appointment. SIZE: Medium. *STOCK: Decorative arts, 1850-1950 - Art Deco, Art Nouveau, Arts and Crafts, Aesthetic Movement, Gothic Revival furniture, ceramics, metalware, bronzes, glass, paintings, prints and etchings, books, £50-£20,000.* LOC: 45 mins from London; from junction 5 or 6, M25 on A25. PARK: Easy. TEL: 01959 561234; fax - same; mobile - 07785 503044; e-mail - sales@designgallery.co.uk website - www.designgallery.co.uk VAT: Margin.

London House Antiques
4 Market Sq. TN16 1AW. Est. 1977. Open 10-5, Sun. by appointment. SIZE: Medium. *STOCK: Furniture, 18th-19th C, £500-£10,000; paintings, prints and engravings, 19th-20th C, £100-£2,000; English and German teddy bears and dolls, 19th-20th C, £100-£3,000; clocks and bronzes, 19th C, £300-£5,000; silver and porcelain, 19th-20th C, £50-£1,500.* LOC: Off M25, junction 6 on A25 to Westerham. PARK: Easy. TEL: 01959 564479; e-mail - londonhouseantiques@hotmail.com

Taylor-Smith Antiques   LAPADA
4 The Grange, High St. TN16 1AH. (Ashton Taylor-Smith). Est. 1986. Open 10-5. CL: Wed. *STOCK: Fine 18th-19th C furniture; paintings, porcelain, glass, decorative items; Churchill ephemera.* PARK: Easy. TEL: 01959 563100; e-mail - ashton@ts-antiques.co.uk

Taylor-Smith Books   LAPADA
2 High St. TN16 1RF. Est. 1972. Open by appointment. *STOCK: Books by Sir Winston Churchill and related items.* LOC: A25 on corner with B2048 Croydon road. PARK: Adjacent. TEL: 01959 561561; fax - 01959 561561; e-mail - taylorsmithbooks@aol.com

Vintage Jewels
2 Market Sq. TN16 1AW. (T. Lawrence). Open Wed.-Sat. 11-5. *STOCK: Antique jewellery, fine paintings, portrait miniatures, porcelain.* TEL: 01959 561778. SER: Picture restorations.

WHITSTABLE

Laurens Antiques
2 Harbour St. CT5 1AG. (G. A. Laurens). Est. 1965. Open 9.30-5.30. SIZE: Medium. *STOCK: Furniture, 18th-19th C, £300-£500+.* LOC: Turn off Thanet Way at Whitstable exit, straight down to one-way system in High St. PARK: Easy. TEL: 01227 261940; home - same. SER: Valuations; restorations (cabinet work); buys at auction.

Tankerton Antiques
136 Tankerton Rd. CT5 2AN. (Mrs F. Holland and Paul Wrighton). Est. 1985. Open Thurs., Fri. and Sat. 10.30-5. SIZE: Medium. *STOCK: Furniture, Regency to 1930s, £10-£3,000; glass, clocks and barometers, from 1700, £30-£2,500; French, English and German costume jewellery and contemporary bead and pearl jewellery, £30-£300.* LOC: From A299 Thanet Way take A290/B2205 turn off to Whitstable. Through town and into Tankerton. Shop on right just past roundabout. TEL: 01227 266490; mobile - 07702 244064. SER: Repairs (clocks and barometers). FAIRS: Brunel Clock & Watch.

WINGHAM

Architectural Miscellanea
Waterlock House, Canterbury Rd. CT3 1BH. (Tina Pasco). SALVO. Est. 1993. Open Fri., Sat. and Sun. 10-6. SIZE: Large. *STOCK: Statues, 19th-20th C, £1,000-£60,000; garden urns and planters, 19th-20th C, £500-£5,000; fountains and water troughs, staddle stones; cloches and rhubarb forcers; quality reproduction items.* PARK: Easy. TEL: 01227 722151; home - same; fax - 01227 722652; mobile - 07770 922844; e-mail - tinapasco@tinapasco.com website - www.tinapasco.com SER: Restorations (stonework).

WITTERSHAM

Old Corner House Antiques
6 Poplar Rd. TN30 7PG. (G. and F. Shepherd). Open Wed.-Sat. 10-5 or by appointment. *STOCK: General antiques, country furniture, samplers; 18th-19th C English pottery including blue and white and creamware; watercolours, 19th to early 20th C.* PARK: Easy. TEL: 01797 270236.

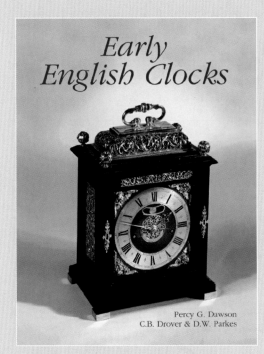

LANCASHIRE

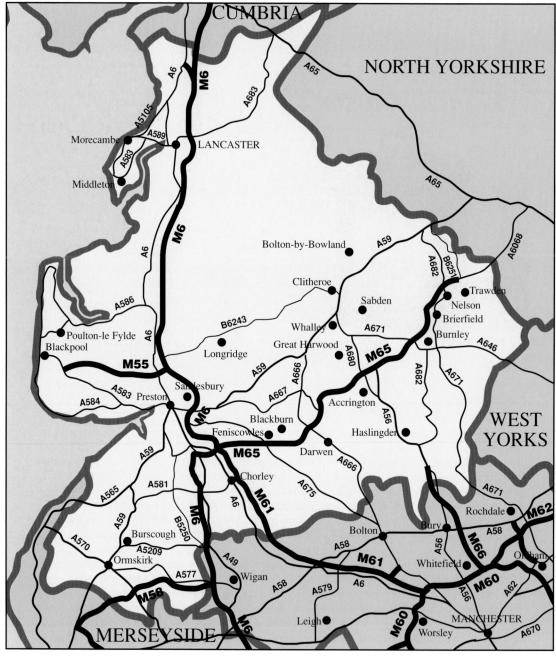

Dealers and Shops in Lancashire

Accrington	1	Bury	1	Leigh	1	Preston	7
Blackburn	2	Chorley	1	Longridge	1	Rochdale	1
Blackpool	2	Clitheroe	3	Manchester	12	Sabden	2
Bolton	2	Darwen	3	Middleton Village	1	Samlesbury	1
Bolton-by-Bowland	2	Feniscowles	1	Morecambe	2	Trawden	1
Brierfield	1	Great Harwood	2	Nelson	1	Whalley	1
Burnley	3	Haslingden	4	Oldham	3	Whitefield	1
Burscough	1	Lancaster	5	Ormskirk	2	Wigan	2
				Poulton-le-Fylde	1	Worsley	1

Understanding Jewellery
David Bennett & Daniela Mascetti

This essentially practical book, *Understanding Jewellery*, now available in a revised and fully updated third edition, is unique in explaining why jewellery values vary and the individual points important for each category. A major section is devoted to the identification of the major gem-stones and the testing methods to assess quality and detect fakes. Explanations are given in a straightforward, uncomplicated manner with a text largely linked directly to specific illustrations. This makes the assimilation of the information much easier than in traditional text dominated books. The authors, both jewellery experts, evaluate many millions of pounds' worth annually and thus handle a complete cross-section of what is available on the market. They have specially selected the hundreds of superb colour illustrations to show what to look for and, equally important, what to avoid.

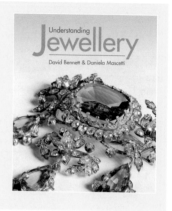

Specifications: 496pp., 960 col. illus., 30 b.&w. illus.,
11¼ x 9¼in./286 x 234mm. **£45.00 (hardback)**

ACCRINGTON
The Coin and Jewellery Shop
129a Blackburn Rd. BB5 0AA. Est. 1977. Open 9.30-5. CL: Wed. *STOCK: Coins, jewellery and small antiques.* TEL: 01254 384757.

BLACKBURN
Ancient and Modern
17 New Market St. BB1 7DR. (Gail and Zachary Coles). NAG. OMRS. Est. 1943. Open 9-5.30. SIZE: Medium. *STOCK: Jewellery, Georgian to date, up to £30,000; clocks, vintage and modern watches including Rolex, Cartier, Patek; militaria and silver; diamond merchants.* LOC: Town centre, opposite side entrance of Marks & Spencer. PARK: Easy. TEL: 01254 677866/668818; fax - 01254 677866. FAIRS: Bangkok; Miami; Beirut. VAT: Stan/Margin/Global.

Mitchell's Antiques
76 Bolton Rd. BB2 3PZ. (S. Mitchell). Est. 1972. Open 9-5. *STOCK: General antiques, gold and silver jewellery, wrist watches.* LOC: Main road. PARK: Easy. TEL: 01254 664663.

BLACKPOOL
Ascot Antiques
106 Holmfield Rd. FY2 9RF. (J.C. Winwood). Est. 1987. Open by appointment. SIZE: Small. *STOCK: Furniture and oil paintings, Georgian to Victorian.* PARK: Easy. TEL: 01253 356383; home - same; mobile - 07816 645716. SER: Valuations.

Chard Coins
521 Lytham Rd. FY4 1RJ. Est. 1965. Open 10-5. SIZE: Large. *STOCK: Paintings and furniture, English and ancient coins, gold bullion coins, jewellery and silver, £50-£20,000+.* LOC: Between Central Promenade south and Blackpool Airport main gates, 1/4 mile from airport. PARK: Easy. TEL: 01253 343081. SER: Valuations. VAT: Stan/Spec.

BOLTON
Drop Dial Antiques
Last Drop Village, Hospital Rd., Bromley Cross. BL7 9PZ. (I.W. and I.E. Roberts). Est. 1975. Open every afternoon except Mon. and Fri. SIZE: Medium. *STOCK: Clocks, mainly English and French, 18th-20th C, £100-£4,000; mercury barometers, 19th-20th C, paintings, silver, furniture and general antiques, £20-£2,000.* PARK: Easy. TEL: 01204 307186; home - 01257 480995. SER: Restorations (clocks and barometers). FAIRS: Galloway and Bailey. VAT: Stan/Spec.

Siri Ellis Books
The Last Drop Village, Hospital Rd., Bromley Cross. BL7 9PZ. PBFA. Est. 1998. Open 12-5, Sat. and Sun. 11-5. CL: Wed. SIZE: Small. *STOCK: Rare and collectable childrens books, 50p to £2,000.* PARK: Easy. TEL: 01204 597511; e-mail - mail@siriellisbooks.co.uk website - www.siriellisbooks.co.uk FAIRS: PBFA; Buxton.

BOLTON-BY-BOWLAND, Nr. Clitheroe
Farmhouse Antiques
23 Main St. BB7 4NW. (K. Sidwick). Est. 1980. Open Easter to end Sept. Fri., Sat., Sun. and Mon. 10.30-5; Winter - Sat.and Sun. 10.30-5 or by appointment. SIZE: Small. *STOCK: Bed and table linen, quilts, christening robes, lace, samplers, embroideries, bags, buttons, trimmings, beads, costume to Victorian jewellery, Victoriana, china, Art Deco, glass and collectables.* LOC: Off A59, past Clitheroe, through Sawley. PARK: Easy. TEL: 01200 445585/447294; fax - 01200 445021; e-mail - info@farmhousecollectables.com website - www.farmhousecollectables.com

Harrop Fold Clocks (F. Robinson)
Harrop Fold, Lane Ends. BB7 4PJ. Est. 1974. Open by appointment. SIZE: Medium. *STOCK: British longcase and wall clocks, barometers, 18th-19th C, £1,000-£10,000.* LOC: Through Clitheroe to Chatburn and Grindleton. Take Slaidburn road, turn left after 3 miles. (Please telephone for more details). PARK: Own. TEL: 01200 447665; home - same; e-mail - robinsonharrop @aol.com SER: Valuations; restorations (clocks).

BRIERFIELD, Nr. Nelson
J.H. Blakey and Sons Ltd
Burnley Rd. BB9 5AD. Est. 1905. Open 8-5.30, Sat. 8-

12. STOCK: Furniture, brass, copper, pewter, clocks, curios. LOC: Main Burnley to Nelson road. PARK: Easy. TEL: 01282 613593; e-mail - sales@blakeys.fsworld. co.uk SER: Restorations (furniture); frames made, renovated, gold-leaf gilded or bronzed. VAT: Stan.

BURNLEY

Brun Lea Antiques
3/5 Standish St. BB11 1AP. Est. 1974. Open 9.30-5.30. SIZE: Large. STOCK: General antiques and shipping goods. LOC: Town centre. PARK: Easy. TEL: 01282 413513; e-mail - jwaite@freenetname.co.uk website - www.antiques-atlas.com/brunlea.htm

Brun Lea Antiques (J. Waite Ltd)
Unit 1, Rear Elm St. Mill, Travis St. BB10 1DG. Est. 1974. Open 8.30-5.30, Fri. and Sat. 9-4, Sun. 12-4. SIZE: Large warehouse. STOCK: Georgian furniture to 1930s shipping goods. PARK: Easy. TEL: 01282 413513; fax - 01282 832769; e-mail - jwaite@freenetname.co.uk website - www.antiques-atlas.com/brunlea.htm

King's Mill Antique Centre
Unit 2 King's Mill, Queen St., Harle Syke. BB10 2HX. (Michael and Linda Heuer). Open 10-5, Thurs. 10-7, Sun. 11-5. SIZE: Large. STOCK: Furniture and bric-a-brac, Edwardian and Victorian, £5-£1,000. LOC: From General Hospital, follow brown tourist signs for Queen's Mill. PARK: Easy. TEL: 01282 431953; fax - 01282 839470; mobile - 07803 153752. SER: Export.

BURSCOUGH, Nr. Ormskirk

West Lancs. Antique Exports   LAPADA
Victoria Mill, Victoria St. L40 0SN. (W. and B. Griffiths). Est. 1959. Open 9-5.30, Sat. and Sun. 10-5. SIZE: Large. STOCK: Shipping furniture. TEL: 01704 894634; fax - 01704 894486. SER: Courier; packing and shipping. VAT: Stan.

BURY

Newtons
151 The Rock. BL9 0ND. (Newtons of Bury). Est. 1900. Open 9-5. SIZE: Small. STOCK: General antiques, 18th-19th C, £5-£500; furniture including reproduction. Not Stocked: Continental furniture. LOC: From Manchester through Bury town centre, shop is on left 200yds. before fire station. PARK: Opposite. TEL: 0161 764 1863; website - www.newtonsofbury.com SER: Valuations; restorations. VAT: Stan.

CHORLEY

Heskin Hall Antiques
Heskin Hall, Wood Lane, Heskin. PR7 5PA. (Harrison Steen Ltd). Est. 1996. Open 10-5.30 seven days. SIZE: Large - 60+ dealers. STOCK: Wide range of general antiques. LOC: B5250. PARK: Easy. TEL: 01257 452044; fax - 01257 450690; e-mail - heskinhall@ aol.com SER: Valuations; restorations.

CLITHEROE

Brittons - Watches and Antiques
4 King St. BB7 2EP. Est. 1970. Open daily. STOCK: Jewellery and collectors' watches. LOC: Town centre opposite main Post Office. PARK: Opposite. TEL: 01200 425555; fax - 01200 424200; website - www.brittons-watches.co.uk SER: Valuations.

Lee's Antiques
59 Whalley Rd. BB7 1EE. (P.A. Lee). Est. 1980. STOCK: General antiques. TEL: 01200 425441; e-mail - alex_lee51@hotmail.com

Past & Present
22 Whalley Rd. BB7 1AW. (D. and Mrs K.J. Hollings). Est. 1988. Open 10.30-5 or by appointment. SIZE: Medium. STOCK: Victorian and Georgian cast-iron fireplaces and ranges, £85-£1,500; Victorian and Edwardian wooden mantels, marble fireplaces, dog grates, coal buckets, brass and cast-iron fenders, fireplace accessories, spare parts, brass and copper, small collectables. LOC: Near town centre. PARK: Easy. TEL: 01200 428678; home - 01200 445373; mobile - 07779 478716. SER: Restorations (repairs, refurbishing, re-tiling cast iron fireplaces).

DARWEN

Belgrave Antique Centre
Britannia Mill 136 Bolton Rd. BB3 1BZ. (Martin and Elaine Cooney). Est. 1998. Open Tues.-Sat. 9.30-5, Sun. 11-4. SIZE: Large - 40 dealers. STOCK: Porcelain, pottery, glass, furniture, architectural, collectables. LOC: Opposite India Mill. PARK: Easy. TEL: 01254

777714. SER: Valuations. FAIRS: Newark, Ardingly, Swinderby.

K.C. Antiques LAPADA
538 Bolton Rd. BB3 2JR. (K. and J. Anderton). Resident. Open 9-6, Sun. 12-5. *STOCK: Georgian, Victorian and Edwardian furniture and decorative items.* LOC: A666. PARK: Easy. TEL: 01254 772252; mobile - 07767 340501. VAT: Stan/Spec.

G. Oakes and Son
The Courtyard, Hampden Mill, Spring Vale Rd. BB3 2ES. Est. 1958. Open 9-5 or by appointment. SIZE: Large. *STOCK: General antiques, furniture and bric-a-brac.* LOC: Off A666 right into Watery Lane (from south); left into Grimshaw St. (from north). PARK: Easy. TEL: 01254 777144/776644; mobile - 07774 284609; e-mail - ycs12@dial.pipex.com website - www.antique-dealeruk.com SER: Valuations; packing and shipping; buys at auction. VAT: Stan.

FENISCOWLES, Nr. Blackburn

Old Smithy
726 Preston Old Rd. BB2 5EP. (R.C. and I.R. Lynch). Est. 1967. Open 9.30-5. SIZE: Large. *STOCK: Period and Victorian fireplaces, pub and architectural items, violins and musical instruments, pictures and prints, furniture, shipping items, brass, copper.* LOC: Opposite Fieldens Arms. PARK: Own or nearby. TEL: 01254 209943/580874. SER: Valuations; restorations (wooden items); buys at auction. FAIRS: Newark, Lincs.

GREAT HARWOOD, Nr. Blackburn

Benny Charlesworth's Snuff Box
51 Blackburn Rd. BB6 7DF. (N. Walsh). Est. 1984. Open 10-5. SIZE: Small. *STOCK: Furniture, china, linen, costume jewellery, teddies and limited editions.* LOC: 200yds. from town centre, off A680. PARK: Next to shop. TEL: 01254 888550. FAIRS: Local.

Jean's Military Memories
32 Queen St. BB6 7QQ. (Len and Jean South). Est. 1994. Open 9-5, Sat. 9-4, other times by appointment. SIZE: Medium. *STOCK: Air weaponry, from 1880, £30-£4,000; deactivated weaponry, £100-£2,000; swords, £50-£1,000; knives, £10-£1,200.* LOC: Main road. PARK: Easy. TEL: 01254 877825; fax - same; mobile - 07713 636069; e-mail - jean.south@btinternet.com

HASLINGDEN

P.J. Brown Antiques
8 Church St. BB4 5QU. Est. 1979. Open 10-5, Sat. 10-4, Sun. by appointment. SIZE: Medium. *STOCK: Georgian, Victorian and Edwardian furniture, shipping goods, old advertising items, bottles and related items.* LOC: Town centre, off Bury Rd./Regent St. PARK: Easy. TEL: 01706 224888. VAT: Stan/Spec.

Fieldings Antiques
176, 178 and 180 Blackburn Rd. BB1 2LG. Est. 1956. Open 9-4.30, Fri. 9-4, Thurs. and other times by appointment. SIZE: Large. *STOCK: Longcase clocks, £30-£2,000; wall clocks, sets of chairs, pine, period oak, French furniture, oil paintings, glass, shipping goods,*

toys, steam engines, veteran cars, vintage and veteran motor cycles. PARK: Easy. TEL: 01706 214254; mobile - 07973 698961; home - 01254 263358.

Holden Wood Antiques Centre
St Stephen's Church, Grane Rd. BB4 4AT. (Peter and Mary Crossley and John Ainscough). Est. 1996. Open 10-5.30 including Sun. SIZE: 35 dealers. *STOCK: Furniture, 18th-19th C, £200-£2,000; ceramics including figures, glass, 19th C, £50-£2,000.* PARK: Own. TEL: 01706 830803; e-mail - john@holdenwood.co.uk website - www.holdenwood.co.uk SER: Valuations; restorations.

P.W. Norgrove - Antique Clocks
38 Bury Rd. BB4 5LR. Est. 1978. Open most days, prior telephone call advisable. *STOCK: Longcase, wall, bracket and mantel clocks.* PARK: Easy. TEL: 01706 211995; mobile - 07788 164621. SER: Repair and restorations (clocks); re-caning Bergere suites and chairs.

LANCASTER

Anything Old & Military Collectables
55 Scotforth Rd. LA1 4SA. (Graham H. Chambers). Est. 1985. Open Wed.-Sat. 1.30-6, Sun. by appointment. SIZE: Medium. *STOCK: WW1 and WW11 British, Imperial German, Third Reich and Commonwealth medals, cap badges, uniforms and head dress, edged weapons and field equipment, £5-£500.* LOC: 1.5 miles south of city centre on A6. PARK: Easy. TEL: 01524 69933; home - same. SER: Valuations; full size and miniature medal mounting.

The Assembly Rooms Market
King St. LA1 1XD. Open Tues.-Sat. 10-4.30. SIZE: Several dealers. *STOCK: General antiques, period and costume jewellery; Victorian to '70s memorabilia, costume and retro fashion, books, memorabilia.* LOC: Town centre. TEL: Market Supervisor - 01524 66627; website - www.lancasterdistrictmarkets.co.uk SER: Costume hire.

G.B. Antiques Ltd
Lancaster Leisure Park, Wyresdale Rd. LA1 3LA. (Mrs G. Blackburn). Open 10-5 including Sun. SIZE: Large. 100+ dealers. *STOCK: Porcelain, glass and silver, late 19th to early 20th C; furniture, Victorian to mid 20th C; collectables, Art Deco and retro items.* LOC: Off M6, junction 33 or 34. PARK: Easy. TEL: 01524 844734; fax - 01524 844735; home - 01772 861593. SER: Valuations; buys at auction. VAT: Stan/Spec.

Lancaster Leisure Park Antiques Centre
Wyresdale Rd. (on site of former Hornsea Pottery Plant). LA1 5LA. Open 10-5 including Sun. SIZE: 140 dealers. *STOCK: Wide range of general antiques and collectables.* LOC: Off M6, junction 33 or 34. PARK: Easy. TEL: 01524 844734.

Lancastrian Antiques & Co
70/72 Penny St. LA1 1XF. (S.P. and H.S. Wilkinson). Open 10-4. CL: Wed. *STOCK: Furniture, lighting, paintings, bric-a-brac, fire surrounds.* LOC: City centre, one block south of Marks and Spencers. TEL: 01524 847004.

LEIGH

Leigh Jewellery
3 Queens St. WN7 4NQ. (R. Bibby). Open 9.30-5.30. CL: Wed. *STOCK: Jewellery.* TEL: 01942 607947/ 722509; mobile - 07802 833467.

LONGRIDGE, Nr. Preston

Berry Antiques & Interiors
61 Berry Lane, Longridge. PR3 3NH. (Mrs Eloise M. Halsall and Mrs Kerry I. Barnet). Est. 1989. Open 10-4, Wed. 10-1. SIZE: Small. *STOCK: Victorian pine furniture - chests of drawers, bedding boxes, small cupboards, shelves; gardening tools, trugs and general garden related items; kitchenalia, enamelware, wooden boxes, lighting, ceramics including blue and white, mirrors, pictures, glass, silver, tapestry cushions, £1-£500.* LOC: Main shopping street. PARK: Easy. TEL: 01772 780476.

MANCHESTER

A.S. Antique Galleries
26 Broad St, Salford. M6 5BY. (A. Sternshine). Est. 1975. Open Thurs., Fri. and Sat. 10-5.30 or by appointment. SIZE: Large. *STOCK: Art Nouveau and Art Deco, bronzes, bronze and ivory figures, silver, glass, ceramics, furniture, jewellery, lighting and general antiques.* Not Stocked: Weapons. LOC: On A6, one mile north of Manchester city centre, next to Salford University College. PARK: Easy. TEL: 0161 737 5938; mobile - 07836 368230; e-mail - as@sternshine.demon. co.uk SER: Valuations; restorations; commission purchasing.

Antique Fireplace Warehouse
1090 Stockport Rd, Levenshulme. M19 2SU. (D. McMullan & Son). Open 9-6, Sun. 11-5. *STOCK: Fireplaces and architectural items.* PARK: Easy. TEL: 0161 431 8075; fax - 0161 431 8084.

Antiques Village
The Old Town Hall, 965 Stockport Rd., Levenshulme. M19 3NP. Est. 1978. Open 10-5.30, Sun. 11-4. SIZE: 40+ dealers. *STOCK: Furniture and clocks, reproduction pine, fireplaces, collectables.* LOC: A6 between Manchester and Stockport. PARK: Own. TEL: 0161 256 4644; fax - same; mobile - 07976 985982. SER: Valuations; restorations; pine stripping. FAIRS: Newark.

Cathedral Jewellers
38 Thomas St. M4 1ER. (Jason Taylor). Open 9.30-5. *STOCK: Jewellery.* TEL: 0161 832 3042.

Empire Exchange
1 Newton St., Piccadilly. M1 1HW. (David Ireland). Est. 1975. Open every day 9-7.30 except Christmas day. SIZE: Large. *STOCK: General small antiques including silver, pottery, clocks and watches, ephemera, autographs, football memorabilia, records, books and comics, 18th-20th C, £5-£10,000.* PARK: Easy. TEL: 0161 236 4445; fax - 0161 273 5007; mobile - 07984 203984. SER: Valuations. VAT: Stan/Spec.

Family Antiques
405/407 Bury New Rd., Prestwich. M25 1AA. (J. and J.

Ditondo). Open daily. *STOCK: General antiques.* TEL: 0161 798 0036.

Fernlea Antiques
Failsworth Mill, Ashton Rd West, Failsworth. M35 0FD. (A.J. and Mrs B. McLaughlin). Est. 1983. Open 10-5. SIZE: Large. *STOCK: General antiques and shipping goods.* PARK: Easy. TEL: 0161 682 0589; e-mail - fernlea@i12.com SER: Container packing (worldwide).

Fulda Gallery Ltd
19 Vine St., Salford. M7 3PG. (M.J. Fulda). Est. 1969. Open by appointment. *STOCK: Oil paintings, 1500-1950, £500-£30,000; watercolours, 1800-1930, £350-£10,000.* LOC: Near Salford police station off Bury New Rd. TEL: 0161 792 1962; mobile - 07836 518313. SER: Valuations; restorations; buys at auction.

In-Situ Manchester
Talbot Mill, 44 Ellesmere St., Hulme. M15 4JY. (Laurence Green). Est. 1983. Open 10-5.30, Sun. 11-5. SIZE: Large. *STOCK: Architectural items including fireplaces, doors, panelling, sanitary ware, radiators, flooring, glass, gardenware, staircasing.* PARK: In front of premises. TEL: 0161 839 5525; fax - 0161 839 2010; mobile - 07780 993773; e-mail - enquiries@insitu manchester.com website - www.insitumanchester.com

Eric J. Morten
6 Warburton St., Didsbury. M20 6WA. Est. 1959. Open 10-5.30. SIZE: Medium. *STOCK: Antiquarian books, 16th-20th C, £5-£5,000.* LOC: Off Wilmslow Rd., near traffic lights in Didsbury village. A34. PARK: Easy. TEL: 0161 445 7629 and 01265 277959; fax - 0161 448 1323. SER: Valuations; buys at auction (antiquarian books). FAIRS: PBFA.

R.J. O'Brien and Son Antiques Ltd
Failsworth Mill, Ashton Rd. West, Failsworth. M35 0FD. Est. 1970. Open 9-5. CL: Sat. SIZE: Very large. *STOCK: Furniture, Victorian, Edwardian and 1930s; shipping goods, general antiques and pianos.* PARK: Own. TEL: 0161 688 4414; mobile - 07710 455489; e-mail - ob.antiques@btconnect.com website - www.Antique-Exports.com SER: Container and courier service.

St. James Antiques
STOCK: Jewellery, silver and paintings. TEL: 0161 773 4662; mobile - 07808 521671.

MIDDLETON VILLAGE, Nr. Morecambe

G G Antique Wholesalers Ltd
Newfield House, Middleton Rd. LA3 3PP. (G. Goulding). Est. 1967. Open any time by appointment. SIZE: Large. *STOCK: Shipping goods, £30-£5,000, English and European furniture.* LOC: On main road between Morecambe promenade and Middleton village. PARK: Easy. TEL: 01524 850757; fax - 01524 851565; e-mail - jay@ggantiques.com website - www.ggantique-wholesalers.com SER: Courier; packing; 40ft containers weekly worldwide. VAT: Stan. *Trade Only.*

MORECAMBE

Tyson's Antiques Ltd
Clark St. LA4 5HT. (George, Andrew and Shirley

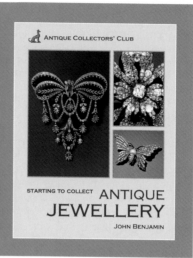
Tyson). Est. 1952. Open Sat. 8-11.30, other times by appointment. SIZE: Large. *STOCK: Georgian, Victorian and Edwardian furniture.* PARK: Easy. TEL: 01524 416763/425235/420098; mobile - 07971 836892; website - www.tysons-antiques.freeserve.co.uk VAT: Stan/Spec. *Trade Only.*

Luigino Vescovi
135 Balmoral Rd. LA3 1HJ. Est. 1970. Open by appointment every day. SIZE: Warehouse. *STOCK: Georgian and Victorian furniture, inlaid Edwardian and plated ware, £50-£10,000.* PARK: Easy. TEL: 01524 416732; mobile - 07860 784856. VAT: Stan/Spec/Export

NELSON

Colin Blakey Fireplaces
115 Manchester Rd. BB10 2LS. Est. 1904. Open 9.30-5, Sun. 12-3.30. SIZE: Large. *STOCK: Fireplaces and hearth furniture, paintings and prints.* LOC: Exit 12, M65. PARK: Opposite. TEL: 01282 614941; fax - 01282 698511; e-mail - cbfireplaces@hotmail.com website - www.colinblakeyfireplaces.co.uk SER: Manufacturers and suppliers of hand-carved marble fireplaces and hardwood mantels. VAT: Stan.

OLDHAM

Charles Howell Jeweller
2 Lord St. OL1 3EY. (N.G. Howell). NAG. Est. 1870. Open 9.15-5.15. SIZE: Small. *STOCK: Edwardian and Victorian jewellery, £25-£2,000; silver, early to mid 20th C, £40-£1,500; watches, Victorian to mid 20th C, £50-£800.* LOC: Town centre, off High St. PARK: Limited or by arrangement. TEL: 0161 624 1479. SER: Valuations; restorations (jewellery and watches); buys at auction. VAT: Stan/Spec.

Marks Jewellers and Antique Dealers
16 Waterloo St. OL1 1SQ. (B.J. and S. Marks). Est. 1969. Open 9.30-5. SIZE: Medium. *STOCK: General antiques, Victorian and Edwardian jewellery, silver and watches.* LOC: Town centre, off Yorkshire St. PARK: Nearby. TEL: 0161 624 5975; fax - same; e-mail - bmarks46@hotmail.com SER: Valuations.

H.C. Simpson and Sons Jewellers (Oldham)Ltd
37 High St. OL1 3BA. Open 9-5.30. *STOCK: Clocks, jewellery, watches.* TEL: 0161 624 7187. SER: Restorations (clocks, watches and jewellery).

ORMSKIRK

Green Lane Antiques
Unit B20 Malthouse Business Centre, 48 Southport Rd. L39 1QR. (J. Swift). Est. 1982. Open seven days 10-4. SIZE: Large. *STOCK: Furniture - pine, mahogany and oak; longcase clocks.* PARK: Easy. TEL: 01695 580731; home - 01704 895444; mobile - 07715 371902. SER: Restorations (longcase clocks).

Alan Grice Antiques
106 Aughton St. L39 3BS. Est. 1946. Open 10-6. *STOCK: Period furniture.* PARK: Easy. TEL: 01695 572007.

POULTON-LE-FYLDE

Ray Wade Antiques
P O Box 39. FY6 9GA. Est. 1978. By appointment or at fairs. *STOCK: Decorative items, sculpture, European and Oriental works of art, paintings.* TEL: 01253 700715; fax - 01253 702342; mobile - 07836 291336; e-mail - antiques@r-wades.demon.co.uk SER: Finder; valuations; buys for export. VAT: Stan/Spec/Global.

PRESTON

The Antique Centre
56 Garstang Rd. PR1 1NA. (Paul Allison). Est. 1966. Open 9-5.30, Sat. 9.30-5.30, Sun. 10.30-4.30. SIZE: Large, 20 dealers. *STOCK: Furniture, including French pine, Georgian-Edwardian; porcelain, silver, clocks, bric-a-brac and pictures.* LOC: A6 into city centre. PARK: Easy and free. TEL: 01772 882078; fax - 01772 252842; e-mail - paul@paulallisonantiques.co.uk website - www.paulallisonantiques.co.uk SER: Nationwide deliveries; worldwide shipping; containers.

European Fine Arts and Antiques
10 Cannon St. PR1 3NR. (B. Beck). Est. 1970. Open 9-5.30. SIZE: 2 floors. *STOCK: Victorian paintings and furniture, to £8,000; English and Louis XV style reproduction.* LOC: City centre - Fishergate. PARK: Loading only and nearby. TEL: 01772 883886; fax - 01772 823888; e-mail - info@european-fine-arts.co.uk website - www.european-fine-arts.co.uk SER: Valuations; buys at auction. VAT: Stan/Spec.

Hackler's Jewellers
6b Lune St. PR1 2NL. (N.E. Oldfield). FBHI. Open 9.30-4.30. CL: Thurs. pm. *STOCK: Silver and clocks.* TEL: 01772 258465. VAT: Stan.

Halewood and Sons
37 Friargate. PR1 2AT. ABA. PBFA. Est. 1867. CL: Thurs. pm. *STOCK: Antiquarian books and maps.* TEL: 01772 252603; e-mail - halewoodandsons@aol.com

Nelson's Antiques
113 New Hall Lane. PR1 5PB. (W. and L. Nelson). Open 10-5 or by appointment. *STOCK: General antiques and collectors' items.* LOC: Half mile from junction 31, M6. PARK: Easy. TEL: 01772 794896/862066. SER: Valuations.

Preston Antique Centre
The Mill, New Hall Lane. PR1 5NX. Open 8.30-5.30, Sat.10-4, Sun. 10-4. SIZE: Large - 40+ dealers. *STOCK: General antiques, Georgian-Edwardian; shipping furniture; shipping, Dutch, Italian and French furniture; collectables and longcase clocks.* LOC: 1 mile from exit 31 M6. PARK: Own. TEL: 01772 794498; fax - 01772 651694; e-mail - prestonantiques@talk21.com website - www.antiquesatlas.com/preston.htm and www.prestonantiquescentre.com

Preston Book Co
68 Friargate. PR1 2ED. (M. Halewood). Est. 1950. Open 10-5.30. *STOCK: Antiquarian books.* LOC: Town centre. PARK: Easy. TEL: 01772 252613. SER: Buys at auction.

ROCHDALE

Antiques and Bygones
100 Drake St. OL16 1PQ. (K. and E. Bonn). Est. 1983. Open 10-3, Sat. 10-2. CL: Mon. and Tues. SIZE: Small. *STOCK: Pottery, coins and medals, jewellery, 19th-20th C, £5-£100.* TEL: 01706 648114.

SABDEN, Nr. Clitheroe

Walter Aspinall Antiques Ltd
Pendle Antiques Centre, Union Mill, Watt St. BB7 9ED. Est. 1964. Open 9-5, Sat. and Sun. 11-4 or by appointment. SIZE: Large. *STOCK: Furniture and bric-a-brac.* LOC: On Pendle Hill between Clitheroe and Padiham. PARK: Easy. TEL: 01282 778642; fax - 01282 778643; e-mail - walter.aspinall@btinternet.com SER: Export; packing; courier; containers; wholesale. VAT: Stan.

Pendle Antiques Centre Ltd
Union Mill, Watt St. BB7 9ED. (B. Seed and J.L. Billington). Est. 1993. Open 10-5, Sun. 11-5 (other times by appointment for Trade). SIZE: 10 dealers. *STOCK: Furniture and bric-a-brac.* LOC: Over Pendle Hill, off the A59 between Clitheroe and Padiham. TEL: 01282 776311; fax - 01282 778643; e-mail - sales@pendleantiquescentre.co.uk website - www.pendleantiquescentre.co.uk

SAMLESBURY, Nr. Preston

Samlesbury Hall
(Dating from 1325). Preston New Rd. PR5 0UP. (Samlesbury Hall Trust). Est. 1969. Open 11-4.30. Admission - adults £3, children £1. CL: Sat. SIZE: Large. *STOCK: General collectable antiques.* LOC: Exit 31, M6 on A677 between Preston and Blackburn. PARK: Easy and free. TEL: 01254 812010/2229. website - www.samlesburyhall.co.uk FAIRS: Craft Exhibitions.

TRAWDEN, Nr. Colne

Jack Moore Antiques and Stained Glass
The Old Rock, Keighley Rd. BB8 8RW. (Jack Moore and Connie Hartley). Est. 1976. Open Wed.-Sat. 9-5 or by appointment. SIZE: Medium. *STOCK: Stained glass and furniture.* PARK: Easy. TEL: 01282 869478; home - same; fax - 01282 865193; mobile - 07802 331594. SER: Restoration and manufacture of stained glass; container packing; courier. VAT: Stan.

WHALLEY, Nr. Blackburn

Edmund Davies & Son Antiques
32 King St. BB7 9SL. (E. and P. Davies). Est. 1960. Open 10-5. SIZE: Medium + trade warehouse. *STOCK: Oak and country furniture, longcase clocks, to £10,000; jewellery, to £500.* Not Stocked: Reproductions. LOC: A59 (11 miles from M6). PARK: Easy. TEL: 01254 823764. SER: Restorations (longcase clocks). VAT: Stan/Spec.

WHITEFIELD, Nr. Manchester

Henry Donn Gallery
138/142 Bury New Rd. M45 6AD. (Henry and Nicholas Donn). FATG. Est. 1954. Open 9.30-5. SIZE: Large. *STOCK: Paintings, 19th-20th C, £20-£100,000.* LOC: Off M60, junction 17 towards Bury. PARK: Own at rear. TEL: 0161 766 8819; fax - same; e-mail - donn@netline uk.net website - www.henrydonngallery.com SER: Valuations; framing; restorations. VAT: Stan/Spec.

WIGAN

Colin de Rouffignac
57 Wigan Lane. WN1 2LF. BNTA. Est. 1972. Open 10-4.30. CL: Wed. *STOCK: Furniture, jewellery, oils and watercolours.* PARK: Easy. TEL: 01942 237927.

John Robinson Antiques
172-176 Manchester Rd., Higher Ince. WN2 2EA. Est. 1965. Open any time. SIZE: Large. *STOCK: General antiques.* LOC: A577 near Ince Bar. PARK: Easy. TEL: 01942 247773/241671. SER: Export packing. VAT: Stan. *Export and Trade Only.*

WORSLEY, Nr. Manchester

Northern Clocks   LAPADA
Boothsbank Farm, Leigh Rd. M28 1LL. (R.M. and M.A. Love). Est. 1998. Open by appointment. SIZE: Large. *STOCK: Longcase, bracket and wall clocks, 17th-19th C.* LOC: Off junction 13, M60. PARK: Easy. TEL: 0161 790 8414; home - same; mobile - 07970 820258; e-mail - info@northernclocks.co.uk website - www.northern clocks.co.uk SER: Valuations; restorations. VAT: Stan.

European Fine Arts & Antiques

Welcome to European Fine Arts and Antiques. We have a selection of works by popular Victorian and European artists to view as well as high quality reproduction French furniture.

Please see our website listed below or call in and see us.

Opening hours 9 - 5:30 or by appointment

European Fine Arts & Antiques
10 Cannon Street, Preston
Lancashire, England PR1 3NR

Tel: (+44) (0)1772 883886
Fax: (+44) (0)1772 823888
Mob: 07967 427710

http://www.european-fine-arts.co.uk
info@european-fine-arts.co.uk

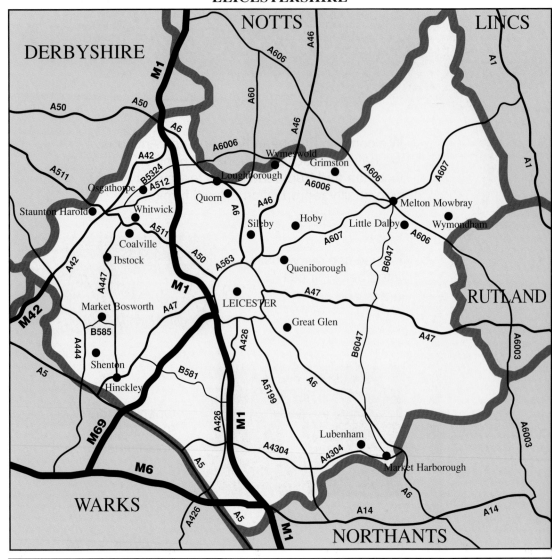

Dealers and Shops in Leicestershire

				Shenton	1
				Sileby	1
Coalville	1	Hoby	1	Loughborough	1	Melton Mowbray	1	Staunton Harold	1
Great Glen	1	Ibstock	1	Lubenham	2	Osgathorpe	2	Whitwick	1
Grimston	1	Leicester	6	Market Bosworth	2	Queniborough	1	Wymeswold	1
Hinckley	2	Little Dalby	1	Market Harborough	4	Quorn	1	Wymondham	1

COALVILLE

Keystone Antiques   **LAPADA**
66 London Rd. LE67 3JA. (I. and H. McPherson). FGA.
Est. 1979. Open Thurs., Fri. and Sat. 10-5, Mon. and Tues.
by appointment. SIZE: Small. *STOCK: Jewellery, Victorian
and Georgian, £25-£1,500; silver, 1700-1920, £20-£500;
small collectable items, 18th-19th C, £15-£300; cranberry,
needlework tools, Victorian and Georgian table glass.* LOC:
A511 outskirts of town. PARK: In front of shop. TEL:
01530 835966; e-mail - keystone@heathermcpherson.co.uk
SER: Valuations (jewellery); gem testing.

GREAT GLEN

Sitting Pretty
45a Main St. LE8 9GH. (Jennifer Jones-Fenleigh). Est.
1979. Open Thurs., Fri. and Sat. 10-5.30, other days by
appointment. *STOCK: Upholstered furniture, 18th-20th
C, £50-£1,000.* LOC: Off A6. PARK: Easy. TEL: 0116
259 3711; home - same. SER: Valuations; restorations
(re-upholstery, French polishing, caning and rushing).
VAT: Spec.

GRIMSTON, Nr. Melton Mowbray

Ancient & Oriental Ltd
69 Main St. LE14 3BZ. (A. Szolin). ADA. Open by appointment. SIZE: Medium. *STOCK: Ancient Egyptian, Greek, Roman, Celtic, Saxon, Pre-Columbian and medieval antiquities.* PARK: Easy. TEL: 01664 812044; fax - 01664 810087; e-mail - alex@antiquities.co.uk website - www.antiquities.co.uk SER: Valuations; illustrated catalogues (4 per year).

HINCKLEY

House Things Antiques
Trinity Lane, 44 Mansion St. LE10 0AU. (P.W. Robertson). Est. 1976. Open 10-6. SIZE: Small. *STOCK: Stripped pine, satinwood, oak and walnut, mainly Victorian and Edwardian, £50-£600; small collectors' items, 1860-1930s, £5-£100; cast-iron fireplaces, brass and iron beds, 1890-1920s, £50-£1,000; garden items.* LOC: Inner ring road. PARK: Easy. TEL: 01455 618518; home - 01455 212797. SER: Valuations; restorations.

Magpie Antiques
126 Castle St. LE10 1DD. (M. Johnson and D. Wassell). Est. 1982. Open 9-5. SIZE: Small. *STOCK: Oak and mahogany furniture, Regency to Edwardian; Staffordshire pottery and porcelain; English and Continental items and collectables.* PARK: Nearby. TEL: 01455 891819; e-mail - michelle@magpieantiques. fsnet.co.uk SER: Valuations. FAIRS: Ardingly, Newark, Swinderby, Kedlestone Hall, Peterborough, Warwick.

HOBY, Nr. Melton Mowbray

Withers of Leicester
The Old Rutland, Church Lane. LE14 3DU. (S. Frings). Est. 1860. Open 9-5.30. CL: Thurs. pm. and Sat. SIZE: Medium. *STOCK: Furniture, 17th-19th C, £50-£3,000; china, 18th-19th C, £10-£300; oil paintings, 19th C, £5-£500.* Not Stocked: Jewellery and coins. PARK: Easy. TEL: 01664 434803. SER: Valuations; restorations (furniture). VAT: Stan/Spec.

IBSTOCK, Nr. Leicester

Mandrake Stevenson Antiques
101 High St. LE67 6LJ. Est. 1979. Open Mon.-Fri. 10-5. SIZE: Small. *STOCK: Furniture, pre 1930s.* PARK: Easy. TEL: 01530 260898/450132; mobile - 07903 602022. SER: Valuations; restorations (furniture). FAIRS: Newark.

LEICESTER

Britain's Heritage Ltd
Shaftesbury Hall, 3 Holy Bones. LE1 4LJ. (Mr and Mrs J. Dennis). Est. 1980. Open 9.30-5.30, Sat. 9.30-5. SIZE: Large. *STOCK: Fireplaces, 18th-21st C, £100-£25,000.* LOC: Off Vaughan Way, 70 yards from Holiday Inn. PARK: Own. TEL: 0116 251 9592; fax - 0116 262 5990; e-mail - britainsheritage@tinyonline.co.uk website - www.britainsheritage.co.uk SER: Valuations; restorations (antique fireplaces). VAT: Stan/Spec.

Clarendon Books
144 Clarendon Park Rd. LE2 3AE. (Julian Smith).

PBFA. Est. 1984. Open 10-5. SIZE: Small. *STOCK: Antiquarian and second-hand books, £1-£1,000.* LOC: Between London Rd. (A6) and Welford Rd. (A50), 2 miles south of city centre. PARK: Easy. TEL: 0116 270 1856; home - 0116 270 1914; mobile - 07803 174139. SER: Valuations; restorations; repairs; binding; buys at auction (books and maps). FAIRS: London HD; PBFA.

Corry's Antiques   LAPADA
24 Francis St., Stoneygate. LE2 2BD. (Mrs E.I. Corry). Est. 1962. Open 10-5. SIZE: Medium. *STOCK: Furniture, 18th-19th C, £500-£10,000; paintings, 19th C, £100-£8,000; silver, porcelain, 18th-20th C, £5-£5,000.* TEL: 0116 270 3794; mobile - 07989 427411; e-mail - customer@corrys-antiques.com website - www. corrys-antiques.com SER: Restorations. FAIRS: NEC; LAPADA, NEC and London. VAT: Spec.

Leicester Antiques Warehouse
Clarkes Rd., Wigston. LE18 2BG. Est. 2002. Open Tues.-Sat. 10-5, Sun. 11-4. SIZE: Large - 80 dealers. *STOCK: Furniture and general antiques.* LOC: B582 towards Wigston, cross railway bridge, turn immediately sharp left into Clarkes Rd., warehouse on left at end of road. PARK: Easy. TEL: 0116 288 1315; e-mail - michael@lawh.icom43.net website - www.antiques-of-britain.co.uk

Oxford Street Antique Centre
16-26 Oxford St. LE1 5XU. (Paul and Linda Giles). Est. 1987. Open 10-5.30, Sat. 10-5, Sun. 2-5. SIZE: Large warehouse, 14 showrooms on 4 floors. *STOCK: Victorian and Edwardian furniture, shipping goods, pine, bric-a-brac and general antiques, 19th to mid-20th C, 50p-£5,000.* LOC: Inner ring road. PARK: Own. TEL: 0116 255 3006; fax - 0116 255 5863. SER: Container loading facilities. VAT: Stan/Spec.

The Rug Gallery
50 Montague Rd., Clarendon Park. LE2 1TH. (Dr. Roy Short). Est. 1987. Open Fri. and Sat. 10-4 or by appointment. SIZE: Medium. *STOCK: Oriental rugs and kilims, £100-£2,000; Swat, Afghan, Indian and Chinese furniture, £50-£1,000; all 19th-20th C.* LOC: From London Rd. A6, take Victoria Park Rd., to Queen's Rd., then Montague Rd. PARK: Easy. TEL: 0116 270 0085; fax - 0116 270 0113.

LITTLE DALBY, Nr. Melton Mowbray

Treedale Antiques
Little Dalby Hall, Pickwell Lane. LE14 2XB. (G.K. Warren and Imogen Wall). GMC. Est. 1972. Open 9-5, Sat. and Sun. by appointment. SIZE: Workshop, showroom and shop. *STOCK: Furniture including walnut, mahogany and oak, from 1680; portraits and paintings, tapestries and chandeliers; all to £20,000.* PARK: Own. TEL: 01664 454535; shop - 01572 757521; home - same. SER: Valuations; restorations (furniture and chandeliers).

LOUGHBOROUGH

Lowe of Loughborough
37-40 Church Gate. LE11 1UE. Est. 1846. Open Mon.-Fri. 9-5.30. SIZE: Large - 16 showrooms. *STOCK:*

Furniture and period upholstery from early oak, 1600 to Edwardian; mahogany, walnut, oak, £20-£8,000; clocks, bracket and longcase, £95-£2,500; maps, copper and brass. Not Stocked: Jewellery. LOC: Opposite parish church. PARK: Own. TEL: 01509 212554/217876. SER: Upholstery; restorations; interior design. VAT: Stan/Spec.

LUBENHAM, Nr. Market Harborough

Oaktree Antiques
The Draper's House, Main St. LE16 9TF. (Gillian Abraham and John Wright). Open Wed.-Sun. 10-6. SIZE: Medium. *STOCK: Town and country furniture, 17th-19th C; longcase clocks and barometers, Georgian to early Victorian; works of art.* LOC: A4304, 1 mile west of Market Harborough. PARK: Opposite on village green. TEL: 01858 410041; mobile - 07710 205696; website - www.oaktreeantiques.co.uk VAT: Spec.

Stevens and Son
61 Main St. LE16 9TF. (M.J. Stevens). Resident. Est. 1977. Open 10-5. *STOCK: General antiques, mainly furniture.* LOC: A4304 via junction 20 M1. TEL: 01858 463521. SER: Restorations (furniture).

MARKET BOSWORTH

Bosworth Antiques
10 Main St. CV13 0JW. (John Thorp). Est. 1986. Open Wed.-Sat. 10-1 and 2-5. *STOCK: General antiques, 19th-*20th C. PARK: Easy. TEL: 01455 292134. SER: Valuations.

P. Stanworth (Fine Arts)
The Grange, 2 Barton Rd. CV13 0LQ. (Mr and Mrs G. and James Stanworth). Resident. Est. 1965. Open by appointment. SIZE: Medium. *STOCK: Oil paintings and watercolours, 18th to early 20th C.* LOC: Road just off town square. PARK: Easy. TEL: 01455 291023; fax - 01455 291767; e-mail - james@stanworth116.freeserve.co.uk VAT: Spec.

MARKET HARBOROUGH

Coughton Galleries Ltd
The Old Manor, Arthingworth. LE16 8JT. (Lady Isabel Throckmorton). Est. 1968. Open Wed., Thurs., Sat., Sun. and Bank Holidays 10.30-5 or by appointment. SIZE: Medium. *STOCK: Modern British and Irish oil paintings and watercolours, mainly Royal Academicians.* PARK: Easy. TEL: 01858 525436; fax - 01858 525535. VAT: Spec.

Graftons of Market Harborough
92 St Mary's Rd. LE16 7DX. (F. Ingall). Est. 1967. Open Mon., Tues., Fri. and Sat. 10-5.30, other times by appointment. *STOCK: Oils, watercolours, etchings and engravings, 18th-19th C.* PARK: Forecourt. TEL: 01858 433557. FAIRS: Royal Show.

Walter Moores and Son LAPADA
P O Box 5338. LE16 7WG. (Peter Moores). Est. 1925.

Open by appointment. *STOCK: Georgian furniture; complementary Victorian items.* TEL: 07071 226202; fax - same; mobile - 07710 019045; e-mail - waltermoores@ btinternet.com website - www.waltermoores.co.uk FAIRS: Most major. VAT: Spec.

J. Stamp and Sons
The Chestnuts, 15 Kettering Rd. LE16 8AN. (M. Stamp). Resident. Est. 1947. Open 8-5.30, Sat. 9-12.30 or by appointment. SIZE: Medium. *STOCK: Mahogany and oak furniture, 18th-19th C, £500-£5,000; Victorian furniture, £250-£2,500; Edwardian furniture, £100-£1,000.* LOC: A6. PARK: Easy. TEL: 01858 462524; fax - 01858 465643; e-mail - jstampandsons@btconnect. com SER: Valuations (furniture); restorations (furniture). VAT: Stan/Spec.

MELTON MOWBRAY

Flagstones Pine & Interiors
24 Burton St. LE13 1AF. (Julie Adcock). Est. 1986. Open Tues.-Sat. 9.30-5.15. SIZE: Medium. *STOCK: English and European pine furniture, 18th-20th C; new and reclaimed wood reproductions, including kitchens; bespoke furniture.* PARK: Easy. TEL: 01664 566438; e-mail - flagstonespine@email.com website - www. flagstonespine.com SER: Restorations; stripping; waxing; re-seating (rush and cane). VAT: Stan.

OSGATHORPE, Nr. Loughborough

David E. Burrows   LAPADA
Manor House Farm. LE12 9SY. Est. 1973. *STOCK: Pine, oak, mahogany and walnut furniture, clocks, £100-£10,000.* LOC: Junction 23, M1, turn right off Ashby road after 4.5 miles, farm next to church or off A42. PARK: Easy. TEL: 01530 222218; mobile - 07702 059030; fax - 01530 223139; e-mail - david. burrows2@virgin.net VAT: Stan/Spec.

QUENIBOROUGH, Nr. Leicester

J. Green and Son
1 Coppice Lane. LE7 3DR. (R. Green). Resident. Est. 1932. Appointment advisable. SIZE: Medium. *STOCK: 18th-19th C English and Continental furniture.* LOC: Off A607 Leicester to Melton Mowbray Rd. PARK: Easy. TEL: 0116 2606682; e-mail - jgreenson.antiques@ btinternet.com SER: Valuations; buys at auction. VAT: Stan/Spec.

QUORN, Nr. Loughborough

Quorn Pine and Decoratives
The New Mills, Leicester Rd. LE12 8ES. (S. Yates). Est. 1982. Open 9-5.30, Sat. 9.30-5.30, Sun. 2-5. SIZE: Large. *STOCK: Pine and country furniture.* PARK: Own. TEL: 01509 416031; website - www.quorn-pine.co.uk SER: Stripping and restorations (pine). VAT: Stan/Spec.

SHENTON, Nr. Market Bosworth

Whitemoors Antiques and Fine Art
Mill Lane. CV13 6BZ. (D. Dolby and P. McGowan). Est. 1987. Open Mon.-Fri. 11-4, (until 5 in summer), Sat. and Sun. 11-5. SIZE: Large - 20+ unitholders. *STOCK:*

Furniture, £25-£2,000; smalls, £5-£200; prints and pictures, Victorian to early 20th C, £40-£400. LOC: A5 onto A444 towards Burton-on-Trent, first right then second left. PARK: Easy. TEL: 01455 212250; 01455 212981 (ansaphone); fax - 01455 213342.

SILEBY, Nr. Loughborough

R. A. James Antiques
Ammonite Gallery, 15a High St. LE12 7RX. *STOCK: Mainly stripped pine, general antiques.* TEL: 01509 812169; mobile - 07713 132650.

STAUNTON HAROLD

Ropers Hill Antiques
Ropers Hill Farm. LE65 1SE. (S. and R. Southworth). Est. 1974. Open by appointment. SIZE: Small. *STOCK: General antiques, silver and metalware.* LOC: On old A453. PARK: Easy. TEL: 01530 413919. SER: Valuations. FAIRS: Donington.

WHITWICK, Nr. Coalville

Charles Antiques
Dial House, 34 Cadman St. LE67 5AE. (Brian Haydon). Est. 1970. Open anytime by appointment. SIZE: Small. *STOCK: Clocks, 18th C, £25-£4,000; furniture, 19th C, £50-£1,000; china.* LOC: A511. PARK: Easy. TEL: 01530 836932; home - same; mobile - 07831 204406; e-mail - charles.antiques@btopenworld.com SER: Buys at auction. VAT: Stan/Spec.

WYMESWOLD, Nr. Loughborough

N. Bryan-Peach Antiques
30 Brook St. LE12 6TU. Resident. Est. 1977. Open by appointment. *STOCK: Clocks, barometers, 18th-19th C furniture, £50-£5,000.* PARK: Easy. TEL: 01509 880425. SER: Valuations; restorations; buys at auction. VAT: Spec.

WYMONDHAM, Nr. Melton Mowbray

Old Bakery Antiques
Main St. LE14 2AG. (Tina Bryan). Est. 1990. Open 10-5.30, Sun. 12-5. CL: Thurs. SIZE: Medium. *STOCK: Cottage, garden, architectural and reclamation items including pine furniture, kitchenalia, advertising items, chimney pots, stained glass, doors and door hardware, tiles, rural and domestic bygones.* PARK: Easy. TEL: 01572 787472; home - same.

LINCOLNSHIRE

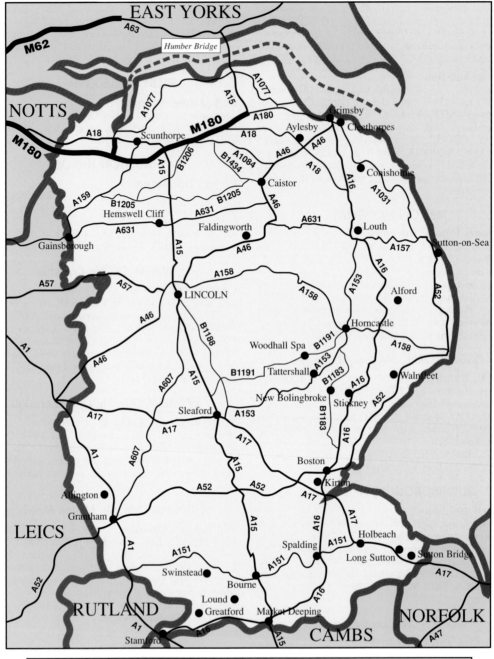

Dealers and Shops in Lincolnshire				
		Kirton	1	Spalding	3
Alford	2	Faldingworth	1	Lincoln	11	Stamford	11
Allington	1	Gainsborough	2	Long Sutton	1	Stickney	1
Aylesby	1	Grantham	6	Lound	1	Sutton Bridge	2
Boston	2	Greatford	1	Louth	1	Sutton-on-Sea	1
Bourne	1	Grimsby	1	Market Deeping	2	Swinstead	1
Caistor	1	Hemswell Cliff	5	New Bolingbroke	1	Tattershall	1
Cleethorpes	1	Holbeach	1	Scunthorpe	1	Wainfleet	1
Conisholme	1	Horncastle	10	Sleaford	2	Woodhall Spa	2

James Usher and Son Ltd

incorporating John Smith & Son, 26 & 27 Guildhall St. LN1 1TR. Open 9-5.30. *STOCK: Silver and jewellery.* TEL: 01522 527547/523120.

LONG SUTTON

The Chapel Emporium Antique Centre

London Rd. PE12 9EA. (J.A. Beck and B. Hill). Est. 1984. Open 10-5 including Sun. CL: Mon. SIZE: Large. *STOCK: Furniture, 18th-19th C, £100-£5,000; collectables, 19th-20th C, 50p-£300; ephemera, 19th C, 50p-£25.* LOC: Opposite playing fields. PARK: Free opposite. TEL: 01406 364808; e-mail - barbara.hill4 @btopenworld.co.uk

LOUND, Nr. Bourne

Antique & Secondhand Traders

Bourne Removals Depot. PE10 0JY. (C.A. and A.L. Thompson). Est. 1962. Open Fri. and Sat. 10-5 or by appointment. SIZE: Warehouse. *STOCK: Furniture - antique, Victorian, Edwardian, shipping, oak, reproduction and modern, £50-£5,000.* PARK: Own. TEL: 01778 394700; mobiles - Alan - 07885 694299, Clyde - 07958 941728. SER: Valuations. FAIRS: Newark; Ardingly. VAT: Spec/Global.

LOUTH

Old Maltings Antique Centre

38 Aswell St. LN11 9HP. (Norman and Margaret Coffey). Est. 1980. Open 10-4.30, Sat. 10-5. SIZE: Large - over 40 cabinets. *STOCK: Furniture including Victorian and Edwardian, collectables, ceramics, glass, jewellery.* LOC: 2 mins. walk from town centre. PARK: Easy. TEL: 01507 600366; e-mail - norman@tomaclincs.fsnet.co.uk website - www.antiques-atlas.com SER: Valuations; restorations; stripping (pine). FAIRS: Swinderby.

MARKET DEEPING

Market Deeping Antiques & Craft Centre

50-56 High St. PE6 8EB. (J. Strutt and C. Stubbins). Resident. Est. 1995. SIZE: Large. *STOCK: General antiques, bric-a-brac and craft items.* LOC: A15. PARK: Easy. TEL: 01778 380238.

Portland House Antiques

23 Church St. PE6 8AN. (G.W. Cree and V.E. Bass). Est. 1987. Open Mon.-Sat. or by appointment. SIZE: Medium. *STOCK: Porcelain, glass, furniture, 18th-19th C, £100-£10,000.* PARK: Easy. TEL: 01778 347129; home - same. SER: Buys at auction. VAT: Stan/Spec.

NEW BOLINGBROKE, Nr. Boston

Junktion

The Old Railway Station. PE22 7LD. (J. Rundle). Est. 1981. Open Wed., Thurs. and Sat. SIZE: Large. *STOCK: Early advertising, decorative and architectural items; toys, automobilia, mechanical antiques and bygones; early slot machines, wireless, telephones, bakelite, 20th C collectables.* Not Stocked: Porcelain and jewellery. LOC: B1183 Boston to Horncastle. PARK: Easy. TEL: 01205 480087/480068.

SCUNTHORPE

Antiques & Collectables & Gun Shop

Rear of 251 Ashby High St. DN16 2SQ. (J.A. Bowden). Est. 1973. Open 9-5. *STOCK: Clocks, furniture, arms and collectables.* TEL: 01724 865445/720606. SER: Restorations; repairs.

SLEAFORD

Mill Antiques

19A Northgate. NG34 7BH. (John Noble and A. Crabtree). Est. 1988. Open 9-5. SIZE: Medium. *STOCK: General antiques including furniture, porcelain and pictures, 18th-20th C, £5-£5,500.* LOC: 100 yards from market square. PARK: Loading only. TEL: 01529 413342; home - 01529 415101. SER: Valuations; restorations (furniture and porcelain).

Marcus Wilkinson

The Little Time House, 13 Southgate. NG34 7SU. (M. and P. Wilkinson). BHI. AHS. NAWCC. Est. 1935. Open 10-4.30. SIZE: Small. *STOCK: Jewellery, watches and silver, £50-£5,000.* LOC: High St. near River Slea. PARK: Nearby. TEL: 01529 413149 and 01476 560400; e-mail - info@thetimehouse.com website - www.thetime house.com SER: Valuations; restorations (including clock and watch movements); buys at auction (rings and watches). VAT: Stan.

SPALDING

Dean's Antiques

"The Walnuts", Weston St. Mary's. PE12 6JB. (Mrs B. Dean). Est. 1969. Open daily. SIZE: Medium. *STOCK: General antiques, farm and country bygones, £2-£200.* LOC: On Spalding to Holbeach main road A151. PARK: Easy. TEL: 01406 370429.

Penman Clockcare (UK) Ltd

Unit 4 & 5 Pied Calf Yard, Sheepmarket. PE11 1BE. (Michael Strutt). BWCMG. Est. 1998. Open 9-5, Sat. 9-4. *STOCK: Clocks 18th-20th C; watches, 19th-20th C; jewellery.* LOC: In yard behind Pied Calf public house, opposite PO. PARK: Nearby. TEL: 01755 714900; 01755 840955 (ansaphone); website - www.penman clockcare.co.uk SER: Valuations; restorations (clocks and watches).

Spalding Antiques

1 Abbey Path, The Crescent. PE11 1AY. (John Mumford). Est. 1980. Open 10-5, Thurs. 10-12 and 1.30-5, Sat. 10-4. SIZE: Medium. *STOCK: Clocks, furniture and smalls, 19th C, £10-£3,000.* LOC: Opposite Sessions House. PARK: Victoria St. TEL: 01775 713185. SER: Valuations.

STAMFORD

Norman Blackburn

Old Print Shop, 7 Red Lion Sq. PE9 2AJ. Est. 1974. Open 10-5, Tues. by appointment; CL: Mon. SIZE: Large. *STOCK: Prints in period frames - decorative, stipple and mezzotints, botanical, sporting, marine, portraits and views, pre-1860.* LOC: Top end of town. PARK: On riverside. TEL: 01780 489151; fax - same; mobile - 07714 721846; e-mail - oldprints@norman blackburn.com website - www.normanblackburn.com SER: Valuations.

Dawson of Stamford Ltd
6 Red Lion Sq. PE9 2AJ. (J. Dawson and S.E. Davies). Est. 1974. Open 9-5.30. SIZE: Large. *STOCK: Fine antique furniture, jewellery and silver.* LOC: Town centre between St. John's Church and All Saint's Church. TEL: 01780 754166; fax - 01780 764231; e-mail - dawsonofstamford@hotmail.com SER: Valuations; repairs. VAT: Stan/Spec.

The Forge Antiques & Collectibles
5 St. Mary's St. PE9 2DE. (Mrs Tessa Easton). Est. 1998. Open 9.30-5, Sun. and Bank Holidays 10-4. SIZE: Large. *STOCK: 19th C samplers and quilts, £95-£1,000; china and glass, from 17th C, £5-£500; brass and copper, 18th-19th C, £15-£200; jewellery, Victorian to date, £5-£1,000; collectibles and memorabilia, modern sculpture; clocks and watches, £50-£6,000.* PARK: Nearby - The Meadows. TEL: 01780 767874; mobile - 07763 934703; e-mail - theforgeantiques@fsmail.net SER: Search; reference library. FAIRS: Swinderby.

Hunters Antiques & Interior Design
9a St. Mary's Hill. PE9 2DP. (Jill Hunter). Est. 2000. Open 9.30-5.30. SIZE: Medium. *STOCK: Period mahogany and country furniture, decorative items.* LOC: Just over town bridge, on the left. PARK: George Hotel. TEL: 01780 757946; fax - same; mobile - 07976 796969. SER: Restorations (furniture, clocks and barometers); interior design. VAT: Stan/Spec.

Graham Pickett Antiques
7 High St., St Martins. PE9 2LF. (G.R. Pickett). Est. 1990. Open 10-5.30, Sun. by appointment. SIZE: Medium. *STOCK: Furniture - country, 1650-1900, French provincial, 1700-1900, both £50-£3,000; French and English beds, 1750-1900, £350-£4,000; silver, £10-£500; decorative items and mirrors, 1800-1900, £200-£2,500.* LOC: From A1 north into town, on right by 1st lights opposite George Hotel. PARK: Easy. TEL: 01780 481064; home - 01780 764502; mobile - 07710 936948; e-mail - graham@pickettantiques.demon.co.uk website - www.pickettantiques.demon.co.uk VAT: Stan/Spec.

Sinclair's
11/12 St. Mary's St. PE9 2DE. (J.S. Sinclair). Est. 1970. Open 9-5.30. SIZE: Large. *STOCK: Oak country furniture, 18th C, £200-£3,000; Victorian mahogany furniture, £100-£1,000; Edwardian furniture.* LOC: Near A1. PARK: George Hotel. TEL: 01780 765421. VAT: Stan/Spec.

St. George's Antiques
1 St. George's Sq. PE9 2BN. (G.H. Burns). Est. 1974. Open 9-1 and 2-4.30. CL: Sat. SIZE: Shop + trade only warehouse. *STOCK: Period and Victorian furniture, some small items.* TEL: 01780 754117; home - 01780 460456. VAT: Stan/Spec.

St. Martins Antiques Centre
23a High St., St. Martin's. PE9 2LF. (P. B. Light). Est. 1993. Open 10-5 including Sun. SIZE: 70 dealers. *STOCK: Georgian, Victorian and Edwardian furniture, country pine, Art Deco and Arts and Crafts furniture, porcelain, glass, copper, brass, clocks and watches, silver, jewellery, military books, leather and willow, paintings, prints, textiles, fireplaces, surrounds and grates, 20th C lighting and other artefacts, collectables and ephemera including Roman and Chinese.* LOC: 1 mile from Carpenters Lodge roundabout on A1. PARK: At rear. TEL: 01780 481158; fax - 01780 764742; e-mail - peter@st-martins-antiques.co.uk website - www.st-martins-antiques.co.uk

Staniland (Booksellers)
4/5 St. George's St. PE9 2BJ. (V.A. and B.J. Valentine-Ketchum). PBFA. Est. 1973. Open 10-5. CL: Thurs. SIZE: Large. *STOCK: Books, mainly 19th-20th C, £1-£2,000.* LOC: High St. PARK: St. Leonard's St. TEL: 01780 755800; e-mail - stanilandbooksellers@btinternet.com

Andrew Thomas
Old Granary, 10 North St. PE9 2YN. Est. 1970. Open 9-6. SIZE: Large. *STOCK: Pine and country furniture in original paint; ironware.* LOC: From south take old A1 through Stamford. Turn right at second set of traffic lights, warehouse on right. PARK: Opposite. TEL: 01780 762236; home - 01780 410627. VAT: Stan.

Vaughan Antiques   LAPADA
45 Broad St. PE9 1PX. (Barry and Lindy Vaughan). Est. 1993. Open 10-5, Fri. 10-3. SIZE: Large. *STOCK: 18th-19th C furniture, decorative items, clocks, paintings, metalware, mirrors, jewellery.* PARK: Easy. TEL: 01780 765888; e-mail - vaughanantiques@aol.com FAIRS: NEC. VAT: Spec.

STICKNEY, Nr. Boston

B and B Antiques
Main Rd. PE22 8AD. (B.J. Whittaker). Open by appointment. *STOCK: General antiques.* LOC: A16 north of Boston. PARK: Easy. TEL: 01205 480204.

SUTTON BRIDGE

The Antique Shop
100 Bridge Rd. PE12 9SA. (R. Gittins). Est. 1973. Open 9-5.30, Sun. 11-5. SIZE: Large - 8 showrooms. *STOCK: Victorian furniture, glass, china, oil lamps and clocks.* Not Stocked: Pine. LOC: On old A17 opposite church. PARK: Easy. TEL: 01406 350535. VAT: Spec.

Old Barn Antiques & Furnishings
48-50 Bridge Rd. PE12 9UA. (S. and Mrs T.J. Jackson). Est. 1984. Open 9-5, Sat. 10-5, Sun. 11-4. SIZE: Large + trade warehouse. *STOCK: 19th-20th C furniture - oak, mahogany, walnut, pine and upholstered.* LOC: 200 yards from swing-bridge. PARK: Easy. TEL: 01406 359123; fax - same; mobile - 07956 677228. SER: Shipping; storage and packing. VAT: Spec.

SUTTON-ON-SEA

Knicks Knacks Emporium
41 High St. LN12 2EY. (Mr and Mrs R.A. Nicholson). Est. 1983. Open 10.30-1 and 2-5, including Sun. CL: Mon. SIZE: Medium + small warehouse. *STOCK: Victorian gas lights, lights and lamps, brass and iron beds, cast-iron fireplaces, bygones, curios, tools, collectables, pottery, porcelain, Art Deco, Art Nouveau, advertising items, furniture and shipping goods, £1-£1,000.* LOC: A52. PARK: Easy. TEL: 01507 441916; home - 01507 441657; mobile - 07800 958438; e-mail - knicksknacks@tiscali.co.uk website - www.knicksknacks.com

SWINSTEAD

Robin Shield Antiques　　　　　　**LAPADA**
Tyton House, 11 Park Rd. NG33 4PH. Est. 1974. Open by appointment any time. SIZE: Medium. *STOCK: Furniture and paintings, £200-£20,000; works of art, £100-£5,000; all 17th-19th C.* PARK: Easy. TEL: 01476 550892; mobile - 07860 520391; e-mail - robinshield@fsmail.net SER: Valuations; buys at auction. VAT: Stan/Spec.

TATTERSHALL

Wayside Antiques
Market Place. LN4 4LQ. (G. Ball). Est. 1969. Open any time by appointment. *STOCK: General antiques.* LOC: A158. PARK: Easy. TEL: 01526 342436.

WAINFLEET, Nr. Skegness

Haven Antiques
Bank House, 36 High St. PE24 4BJ. (Julie Crowson). Est. 1980. Open Fri. or by appointment. SIZE: Small. *STOCK: General antiques, jewellery, porcelain and collectibles.* LOC: A52. PARK: Easy and opposite. TEL: 01754 880661; home - same. SER: Valuations.

WOODHALL SPA

Underwoodhall Antiques
5 The Broadway. LN10 6ST. (G. Underwood). Est. 1987. Open 10-5, Sun. 1-4.30, prior telephone call advisable. SIZE: Medium. *STOCK: Furniture, £10-£1,000; porcelain and china, £5-£500; general antiques, £1-£500; pictures, £5-£500, all 1750 to date.* LOC: B1191. PARK: Easy. TEL: 01526 353815; e-mail - underwoodhall@supanet.com SER: Framing. FAIRS: Newark.

V.O.C. Antiques　　　　　　**LAPADA**
27 Witham Rd. LN10 6RW. (D.J. and C.J. Leyland). Resident. Est. 1970. Open 9.30-5.30, Sun. 2-5. SIZE: Medium. *STOCK: 17th-19th C furniture, to £5,000; period brass and copper, pottery, porcelain and pictures.* LOC: B1191. PARK: Easy. TEL: 01526 352753; fax - same; home - same. SER: Valuations.

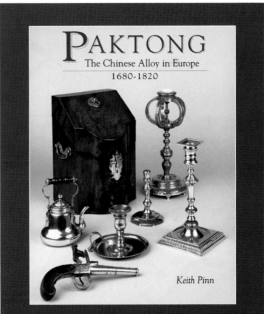

PAKTONG
The Chinese Alloy in Europe
1680-1820

Keith Pinn

Paktong, a rare Chinese alloy, imported in small quantities during the eighteenth century, was used by European craftsmen to make domestic objects in imitation of silverware. This metal has been shrouded in mystery since it was first recorded by Western travellers in the seventeenth century. The vital silver-coloured ingredient, nickel, was not identified in the West until the second half of the eighteenth century, and it was to be a further fifty years before scientists were able to perfect a viable imitation of paktong.

In more recent times the mystery of paktong has lain in the lack of documentary evidence concerning its use in the Georgian period. This has given rise to many myths and speculative theories about the metal. Now, at last, the author's research among contemporary records has enabled the history of paktong in eighteenth century England to be pieced together.

Specifications:
204pp., 30 col. illus., 115 b.&w. illus.,
11 x 8½in./279 x 216mm. **£45.00 (hardback)**

MERSEYSIDE

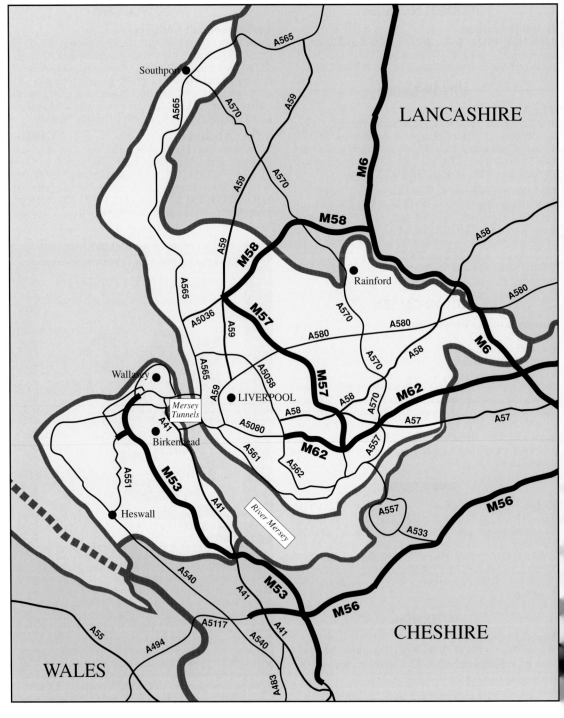

Dealers and Shops on Merseyside					
Birkenhead	2	Liverpool	9	Wallasey	2
Heswell	1	Rainford	1	West Kirby	1
Hoylake	1	Southport	10		

BIRKENHEAD

Architectural Salvage Online
219 Church Rd., Higher Tranmere. CH42 0LD. (David and Caroline Lyons). Est. 1998. Open Wed., Fri. and Sat. 10-5, other times by appointment. SIZE: Medium. *STOCK: Interior and exterior doors, £35-£3,000; fireplaces, cast-iron and timber surrounds, slate, marble, £200-£5,000; radiators, £150-£1,000; flooring and architectural items.* LOC: Town centre. TEL: 0151 670 0058; mobile - 07970 698518. e-mail - sales@uksalvage online.com website - www.uksalvageonline.com SER: Valuations; restorations.

Bodhouse Antiques
379 New Chester Rd., Rock Ferry. CH42 1LB. (G. and F.M. Antonini). Open by appointment. SIZE: Large. *STOCK: Furniture, 19th C; ceramics, from 19th C; silver plate, 18th-20th C; all £5-£1,000+; prints and pictures, 19th C, £35£5,000.* PARK: Easy. TEL: 0151 644 9494; mobiles - 07802 608357 and 07710 561199; e-mail - antonini@btinternet.com website - www.antiques-atlas.co.uk SER: Packing; courier; regular containers to Italy and Spain. FAIRS: Newark; Bailey. VAT: Stan/Spec.

HESWALL

C. Rosenberg
The Antique Shop, 120-122 Telegraph Rd. CH60 0AQ. Est. 1960. Open Fri. and Sat. 10-5, other times by appointment. *STOCK: Jewellery, silver, porcelain, objets d'art.* TEL: 0151 342 1053.

HOYLAKE

Mansell Antiques and Collectables
Mulberry House, 128-130 Market St. CH47 3BH. (Gary Mansell and David Williamson). Est. 1979. Open 9-5.30, Sun. and other times by appointment. CL: Wed. SIZE: Large plus courtyard. *STOCK: Furniture, pine, china, decorative arts, architectural items and gardenalia.* LOC: A540 in town centre. PARK: Own. TEL: 0151 632 0892; mobile - 07944 883021; fax - 0151 632 6137. SER: Free local deliveries, national and international transport arranged. FAIRS: Chester Art Deco; Birmingham Bull Ring. VAT: Margin.

LIVERPOOL

Antique Fireplaces
109 Liverpool Rd., Crosby. L23 5TD. (J. Toole). Est. 1978. Open 10-5, Sat. 10-5.30. SIZE: Medium. *STOCK: Fireplaces, 18th-19th C, £100-£1,000+; doors, 19th C, from £35.* PARK: Easy. TEL: 0151 949 0819. SER: Valuations; restorations. VAT: Stan.

The Boydell Galleries   BADA
(Paul Breen). Est. 1851. Open by appointment. SIZE: Small. STOCK: English watercolours, 18th-19th C, £1,000-£20,000. LOC: Blundellsands. PARK: Easy. TEL: 0151 932 9220; fax - 0151 924 0199; e-mail - boydellgalleries@btinternet.com website - www. boydellgalleries.co.uk VAT: Stan/Spec/Global.

Circa 1900
11-13 Holts Arcade, India Buildings, Water St. L2 0RR.

(Wayne Colquhoun). Est. 1989. Open 10-2.30 and 3.30-6, Sat. and Sun. by appointment. SIZE: Small. *STOCK: Art Nouveau, classic Art Deco, decorative and applied arts, 1860-1940, £10-£1,000+.* LOC: 100 yards from Liver Buildings. PARK: Easy. TEL: 0151 236 1282; fax - same; e-mail - classicartdeco@aol.com website - www. classicartdeco.com SER: Valuations.

Edward's Jewellers
45a Whitechapel. LI 6DT. (R.A. Lewis). FGA. Est. 1967. Open by appointment. CL: Sat. SIZE: Small. *STOCK: Jewellery, silver and plate, 19th-20th C, £50-£1,000.* LOC: City centre. TEL: 0151 236 2909. SER: Valuations.

Maggs Shipping Ltd
66-68 St Anne St. L3 3DY. (G. Webster). Est. 1965. Open 9-5, weekends by appointment. *STOCK: General antiques, period and shipping smalls, £1-£1,000.* LOC: By Central station. PARK: Meters. TEL: 0151 207 2555; evenings - 01928 564958. SER: Restorations; container packing, courier.

Pryors of Liverpool
110 London Rd. L3 5NL. (Mr Levey). Est. 1876. Open 9-5.30. *STOCK: General antiques, jewellery, Georgian and Victorian silver, pottery, porcelain, coins and medals, clocks, paintings, ivory and carvings.* LOC: 400 yards from St. Georges Hall, Walker Art Gallery. PARK: Nearby Pay & Display. TEL: 0151 709 1361; e-mail - nickbolton@msn.com VAT: Stan.

Ryan-Wood Antiques
102 Seel St. L1 4BL. Est. 1972. Open 10-5. CL: Some Bank Holiday weekends. SIZE: Large. *STOCK: Furniture, paintings, china, silver, curios, bric-a-brac, Georgiana, Victoriana, Edwardiana, Art Deco, architectural.* LOC: City centre, close to Anglican cathedral. PARK: Easy. TEL: 0151 709 7776; home/fax - 0151 709 3203; mobile - 07050 094779; e-mail - pdw@ ryan-wood.freeserve.co.uk website - www.ryan-wood. freeserve.co.uk SER: Restorations; valuations. VAT: Stan/Spec.

Stefani Antiques
497 Smithdown Rd. L15 5AE. (T. Stefani). Est. 1969. Open 10-5. CL: Wed. SIZE: Medium. *STOCK: Furniture, to 1910, £200-£2,000; jewellery, £25-£2,000; pottery, silver, old Sheffield plate, porcelain, bronzes.* LOC: On main road, near Penny Lane. PARK: Easy. TEL: 0151 734 1933; home - 0151 425 4889; mobile - 07946 646395. SER: Valuations; restorations (furniture including French polishing and upholstery).

Swainbanks Ltd
50-56 Fox St. L3 3BQ. Open 9-5 or by appointment. CL: Sat. SIZE: Large. *STOCK: Shipping goods and general antiques.* LOC: Half a mile from city centre. TEL: 0151 207 9466; fax - 0151 284 9466; website - www. swainbanks.co.uk SER: Containers. VAT: Stan.

RAINFORD, Nr. St. Helens

Colin Stock   BADA
8 Mossborough Rd. WA11 8QN. Est. 1895. Open by appointment. STOCK: Furniture, 18th-19th C. TEL: 0174 488 2246.

SOUTHPORT

Birkdale Antiques

119a Upper Aughton Rd., Birkdale. PR8 5NH. (John Napp). Est. 1996. CL: Tues. SIZE: Medium. *STOCK: English and Continental items, £200-£2,000; bedroom suites, chandeliers, lighting including European chandeliers.* LOC: From Lord St. West into Lulworth Rd., first left into Aughton Rd., over railway crossing into Upper Aughton Rd. PARK: Easy. TEL: 01704 550117; home - 01704 567680; website - www.birkdale antiques.co.uk SER: Valuations; restorations (furniture including polishing); buys at auction. FAIRS: Stafford, Newark, Swinderby.

C.K. Broadhurst and Co Ltd

5-7 Market St. PR8 1HD. (Laurens R. Hardman). ABA. ILAB. PBFA. Est. 1926. Open 9-5.30. SIZE: 4 floors. *STOCK: 18th-20th C literature, children's illustrated, private press, natural history, general and antiquarian.* LOC: Town centre, off Lord St. by Victorian band-stand. TEL: 01704 532064/534110; fax - 01704 542009; e-mail - litereria@aol.com website - www.ckbroadhurst.com SER: Book search; valuations; restorations; rebinding. FAIRS: Olympia; Chelsea; some provincial.

Molloys Furnishers Ltd

6-8 St. James St. PR8 5AE. (P. Molloy). Est. 1955. Open daily. SIZE: Large. *STOCK: Mahogany and oak, shipping and Edwardian furniture.* LOC: Off A570 Scarisbrick New Rd. PARK: Easy. TEL: 01704 535204; fax - 01704 548101. VAT: Stan.

John Nolan - King Street Antiques

29 King St. PR8 1LH. Est. 1972. Open Mon.-Sat. SIZE: Medium. *STOCK: Furniture and decorative items.* LOC: Town centre. PARK: Easy. TEL: 01704 540808; mobile - 07714 322252. SER: Courier; packing and shipping. VAT: Stan/Spec.

The Original British American Antiques

Kings House, 27 King St. PR8 1LH. (John Nolan). Est. 1976. Open 10-5, evenings by appointment. SIZE: Medium + warehouse. *STOCK: Export items, especially for US decorator market.* LOC: Town centre. PARK: Easy. TEL: 01704 540808; mobile - 07714 322252. SER: Courier; packing and shipping. VAT: Stan/Spec. *Trade only.*

Osiris Antiques

Royal Arcade, 131A Lord St. PR8 1NT. (C. and P. Wood). Est. 1983. Open 10.45-5.30, Sun. 12-5. SIZE: Small. *STOCK: Art Nouveau and Art Deco, Arts and Crafts, £10-£5,000; jewellery, 1880-1960, to £150.* LOC: Town centre. PARK: Easy. TEL: 01704 500991; mobile - 07802 818500; home - 01704 560418. SER: Valuations; buys at auction (Art Nouveau, Art Deco); lectures given on Decorative Arts 1895-1930.

David M. Regan

25 Hoghton St. PR9 0NS. Est. 1983. Open Mon., Wed., Fri. and Sat. 10-5. SIZE: Small. *STOCK: Roman and English coins, £3-£300; postcards and cigarette cards, small collectables.* TEL: 01704 531266. SER: Valuations.

The Southport Antiques Centre

27/29 King St. PR8 1LH. (J. Nolan). Open 10-5. SIZE: Large, 11 rooms + warehouse. LOC: Town centre. PARK: Easy. TEL: 01704 540808; mobile - 07714 322252. Below are listed the dealers at this centre. VAT: Stan/Spec.

Antiques and Interiors

British-American Antiques
Shipping goods.

The China Shop
China and pottery.

Collectors Corner
Collectables from 1930, including porcelain and pottery, Royal Doulton and Beswick.

Halsall Hall Antiques
Country furniture.

King St. Antiques
General antiques.

John Nolan
Period furniture.

Pine Country Antiques
Country pine furniture.

Quest
General antiques.

S.M. Collectors Items
Doulton and pressed glass.

Tony and Anne Sutcliffe Antiques

130 Cemetery Rd. and warehouse - 37A Linaker St. PR8 6RP. Est. 1969. Open 8.30-5 including Sun. or by appointment. SIZE: Large. *STOCK: Shipping goods, Victorian and period furniture.* LOC: Town centre. TEL: 01704 537068; home - 01704 533465; mobile - 07860 949516/480376. SER: Containers; courier. VAT: Stan/Spec.

Weldons Jewellery and Antiques

567 Lord St. PR9 0BB. (N.C. Weldon). Est. 1914. Open 9.30-5.30. SIZE: Medium. *STOCK: Furniture, clocks, watches, jewellery, silver, coins.* Not Stocked: Militaria. PARK: Easy. TEL: 01704 532191; fax - 01704 500091; e-mail - weldongemsuk@aol.com SER: Valuations; restorations. VAT: Stan/Spec.

WALLASEY

Arbiter

10 Atherton St., New Brighton. CH45 2NY. (W.D.L. Scobie and P.D. Ferrett). Resident. Est. 1983. Open Wed.-Sat. 1-5 or by appointment. *STOCK: Decorative arts, 1850-1980; base metal and treen, £20-£2,000; Oriental, ethnographic and antiquities, £40-£1,500; original prints and drawings, £80-£500.* LOC: Opposite New Brighton station. PARK: Easy. TEL: 0151 639 1159. SER: Valuations; buys at auction; consultant.

Victoria Antiques/City Strippers

155-157 Brighton St. CH44 8DU. (J.M. Colyer). Est. 1978. Open 9.30-5.30. SIZE: Large. *STOCK: Furniture.* PARK: Easy. TEL: 0151 639 0080. SER: Restorations.

WEST KIRBY

Helen Horswill Antiques and Decorative Arts

62 Grange Rd. CH48 4EG. Est. 1977. Open 10-5.30. CL: Mon. and Wed. SIZE: Medium. *STOCK: Furniture 17th-19th C; decorative items.* LOC: A540. PARK: Easy TEL: 0151 625 2803; mobile - 07879 456244.

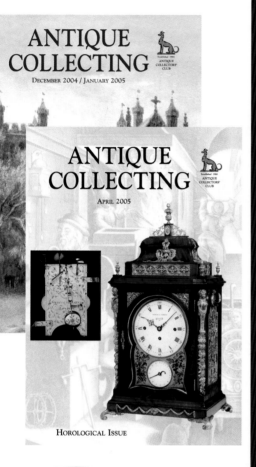

MIDDLESEX

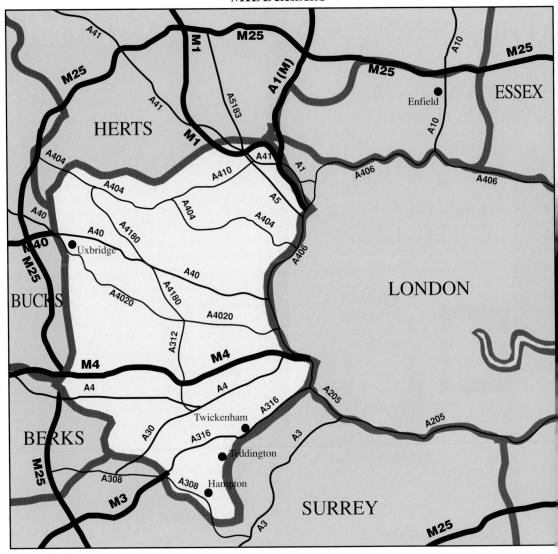

Dealers and Shops in Middlesex					
Enfield	2	Teddington	1	Uxbridge	1
Hampton	2	Twickenham	6		

ENFIELD

Gallerie Veronique
66 Chase Side. EN2 6NJ. (Veronica Aslangul). Est. 1993. Open 10-3, Sat. 10-5. CL: Sun (except by appointment) and Wed. SIZE: Medium. *STOCK: Furniture including decorative, 1820-1970, £50-£1,000.* LOC: Near junction A10 and M25. PARK: Easy. TEL: 020 8342 1005; mobile - 07770 410041. SER: Restorations (French polishing and upholstery).

Period Style Lighting
8-11 Antiques Village, East Lodge Lane, Botany Bay. EN2 8AS. (Gillian and Geoff Day). Est. 1992. Open 10-5 including Sun. CL: Mon. SIZE: Medium. *STOCK: Lighting - period, Victorian and Edwardian, French and Italian chandeliers, £150-£1,000; period style wall and centre lights, Tiffany lamps, glass shades.* LOC: North London. PARK: Easy. TEL: 020 8363 9789; fax - 020 8363 2369; e-mail - sales@period-style-lighting.com website - www.period-style-lighting.com SER: Lighting design for cottages and country houses; restorations; repairs. VAT: Global.

HAMPTON

Peco
139 Station Rd. TW12 2BT. (C.D. Taylor). Est. 1969. Open 8.15-5. SIZE: Large. *STOCK: Doors, 18th-20th C, £75-£250; fireplaces including French and marble, 18th-19th C, £495-£5,500; stoves.* LOC: 1.5 miles from Hampton Court. Turning off Hampton Court/Sunbury Rd. PARK: Own. TEL: 020 8979 8310. SER: Restorations (marble, stained glass, cast-iron fireplaces, doors); stained glass made to order. VAT: Stan.

Ian Sheridan's Bookshop
Thames Villa, 34 Thames St. TW12 2DX. Est. 1960. Open 11-5 (dusk in winter), including Sun. SIZE: Large. *STOCK: Antiquarian and secondhand books.* LOC: 1 mile from Hampton Court Palace. PARK: Riverside. TEL: 020 8979 1704.

TEDDINGTON

Chris Hollingshead Horticultural Books
10 Linden Grove. TW11 8LT. PBFA. Resident. Est. 1994. Open 10-6 by appointment only. SIZE: Small. *STOCK: Antiquarian, scarce and out-of-print books, specialising in landscape architecture, garden history, finely illustrated, botanical and horticultural, £5-£5,000.* PARK: Easy. TEL: 020 8977 6051; e-mail - chris. hollingshead@onetel.net SER: Booksearch.

TWICKENHAM

Anthony C. Hall
30 Staines Rd. TW2 5AH. Est. 1966. Open Mon., Thurs. and Fri. 10-5. SIZE: Medium. *STOCK: Antiquarian books.* PARK: Easy. TEL: 020 8898 2638; fax - 020 8893 8855; e-mail - achallbooks@intonet.co.uk website - www.hallbooks.co.uk

John Ives Bookseller
5 Normanhurst Drive, St. Margarets. TW1 1NA. PBFA. Resident. Est. 1977. Open by appointment at any time. SIZE: Medium. *STOCK: Scarce and out of print books*

on antiques and collecting, £1-£500. LOC: Off St. Margarets Rd. near its junction with Chertsey Rd. PARK: Easy. TEL: 020 8892 6265; fax - 020 8744 3944; e-mail - jives@btconnect.com website - www.ukbookworld.com/members/johnives SER: Valuations (as stock).

Tobias Jellinek Antiques
20 Park Rd. TW1 2PX. (Mrs D.L. and T.P. Jellinek). Est. 1963. Open by appointment. SIZE: Small. *STOCK: Fine early furniture and objects, 16th-17th C or earlier, £500-£5,000+.* LOC: East of town centre near Richmond Bridge. PARK: Easy. TEL: 020 8892 6892; home - same; fax - 020 8744 9298; mobile - 07831 523 671; e-mail - toby@jellinek.com SER: Valuations; buys at auction (as stock). VAT: Stan/Spec.

Marble Hill Gallery
70/72 Richmond Rd. TW1 3BE. (D. and L. Newson). Est. 1974. Open 10-5.30. *STOCK: English and French marble and natural stone, pine and white Adam-style mantels.* PARK: Easy. TEL: 020 8892 1488; website - www.marblehill.co.uk VAT: Stan/Spec.

Rita Shenton
142 Percy Rd. TW2 6JG. Est. 1973. Open by appointment. SIZE: Medium. *STOCK: Clocks, watches, barometers, sundials, scientific instruments, automata and ornamental turning books, £1-£1,000.* LOC: Continuation of Whitton High St. PARK: Easy. TEL: 020 8894 6888; fax - 020 8893 8766; e-mail - rita@shentonbooks.com website - www.shentonbooks.com SER: Valuations; buys at auction (horological books); catalogues available. FAIRS: Midland and Brunel Clock and Watch. *International postal service.*

Twickenham Antiques Warehouse
80 Colne Rd. TW2 6QE. (A. Clubb). Est. 1985. Open 9.30-1 and 2-5, Sat. 10-4, Sun. 10-2. SIZE: Medium. *STOCK: European furniture, 1700-1920, £50-£2,000.* LOC: Off London Rd. PARK: Easy. TEL: 020 8894 5555; mobile - 07973 132847; e-mail - andclubb@aol.com website - www.twickenhamantiques.com SER: Valuations; restorations (French polishing, cabinet work, carving). VAT: Spec.

UXBRIDGE

Antiques Warehouse (Uxbridge)
34-35 Rockingham Rd. UB8 2TZ. (Mike, Sue and Ben Allenby and Simon Phillips). Est. 1977. Open 10-5. SIZE: Large. *STOCK: General antiques, shipping items, £1-£4,000.* PARK: Easy. TEL: 01895 256963/271012; fax - 01895 252157; e-mail - info@uxbridgeantiques.co.uk website - www.uxbridgeantiques.co.uk SER: Restorations; French polishing; re-upholstery; VAT: Stan/Global.

NORFOLK

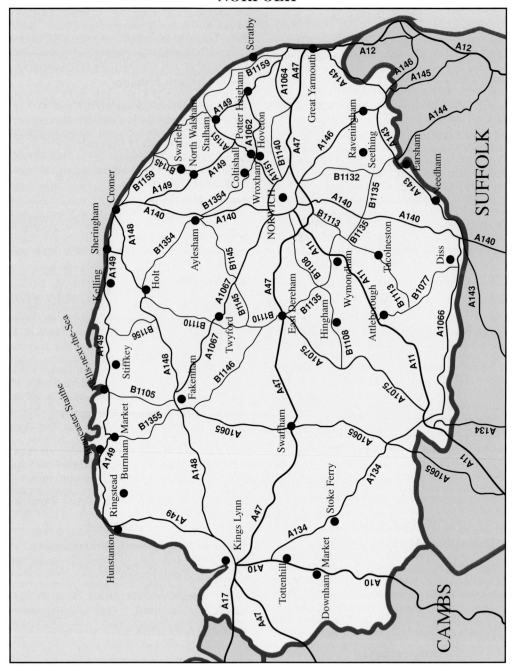

Dealers and Shops in Norfolk

		Hoveton	1	Raveningham	1	Swaffham	1
Attleborough	1	Downham Market 2	Hunstanton	3	Ringstead	2	Swafield	1
Aylsham	1	Earsham	1	Kelling	1	Scratby	1	Tacolneston	1
Brancaster Staithe	1	East Dereham	1	King's Lynn	4	Seething	1	Tottenhill	1
Burnham Market	3	Fakenham	2	Needham	1	Sheringham	2	Twyford	1
Coltishall	2	Great Yarmouth	6	North Walsham	1	Stalham	1	Wells-next-the-Sea 1
Cromer	3	Hingham	2	Norwich	23	Stiffkey	2	Wroxham	1
Diss	2	Holt	11	Potter Heigham	1	Stoke Ferry	1	Wymondham	3

ATTLEBOROUGH

A.E. Bush and Partners
Vineyards Antiques Gallery, Leys Lane. NR17 1NE. (A.G., M.S. and J.A. Becker). Est. 1940. Open 9-1 and 2-5.30. SIZE: Large. *STOCK: Walnut and mahogany, 18th-19th C.* LOC: Town outskirts. PARK: Easy. TEL: 01953 454239/452175. SER: Restorations; wholesale antiques and export; storage; buys at auction. VAT: Stan/Spec.

AYLSHAM

Pearse Lukies
The Old Vicarage. NR11 6HE. Est. 1975. Open preferably by appointment. *STOCK: Period oak, sculpture, objects, 18th C furniture.* TEL: 01263 734137. *Trade Only.*

BRANCASTER STAITHE, Nr. King's Lynn

Staithe Antiques
Main Rd. PE31 8BJ. (Martin Allen). Est. 1994. Open seven days. SIZE: Small. *STOCK: 18th-19th C furniture, china, glass and pictures.* PARK: Easy. TEL: 01485 210600. SER: Delivery.

BURNHAM MARKET

The Brazen Head Bookshop & Gallery
Market Place. PE31 8HD. (David S. Kenyon). Est. 1997. Open 9.30-5. SIZE: Large. *STOCK: Rare, out-of-print and secondhand books; paintings, prints and ceramics.* LOC: On green, opposite PO. PARK: Easy. TEL: 01328 730700; fax - 01328 730929; e-mail - brazenheadbook@ aol.com SER: Valuations.

M. and A. Cringle
The Old Black Horse. PE31 8HD. Est. 1965. Open 10-1 and 2-5. CL: Wed. SIZE: Medium. *STOCK: 18th to early 19th C furniture, £50-£2,000; china, glass, pottery, prints, maps, £10-£500; modern china and decorative items.* Not Stocked: Large furniture. LOC: In village centre. PARK: Easy. TEL: 01328 738456; e-mail - pmcringle@aol.com

Hamilton Antiques
North St. PE31 8HG. (A. Hudson). Open 10-1 and 2-5. SIZE: Medium. *STOCK: Georgian furniture; porcelain, decorative items.* LOC: 20yds. from village green towards coast. PARK: Easy. TEL: 01328 738187; fax - same. VAT: Stan/Spec.

COLTISHALL

Roger Bradbury Antiques
Church St. NR12 7DJ. Est. 1967. Open daily by appointment. SIZE: Medium. *STOCK: Oriental shipwreck porcelain cargoes including Nanking, Tek Sing, Vung Tau, Hoi An.* LOC: Close to village centre. PARK: Easy. TEL: 01603 737444; fax - 01603 737018; e-mail - rogerbradbury@btinternet.com SER: Valuations. VAT: Stan.

Village Clocks
9 High St. NR12 7AA. (Mike Darley). Open Tues.-Sat., other days by appointment. *STOCK: Clocks - 17th-19th C longcase, bracket, English wall and regulators.* LOC: Main Norwich to North Walsham road. PARK: Easy.

TEL: 01603 736047; fax - same; mobile - 07050 229758; website - www.village-clocks.co.uk SER: Valuations; restorations (cases and movements).

CROMER

Bond Street Antiques
6 Bond St. and 38 Church St. NR27 9DA. (M.R.T., J.A. and M.L. Jones). NAG. FGA. GMC. Est. 1970. Open 9-1 and 2-5. SIZE: Medium. *STOCK: Jewellery, silver, porcelain, china, glass, 18th-20th C, £50-£15,000.* LOC: From Church St. bear right to Post Office, shop on opposite side on street further along. PARK: Easy. TEL: 01263 513134; home - same. SER: Valuations; repairs (jewellery); gem testing. VAT: Stan.

Books Etc.
15A Church St. NR27 9ES. (Kevin Reynor). UACC. Est. 1996. Open 1st June to end Sept. 10-4. 1st Oct. to end May - Tues.-Sat. 10-4 or by appointment. SIZE: Large. *STOCK: Books, football programmes, memorabilia and autographs.* LOC: Town centre. PARK: Nearby. TEL: 01263 515501; e-mail - bookskcr@aol.com SER: Valuations.

Collectors World
6 New Parade, Church St. NR27 9EP. (John and Irene Nockels). Est. 1988. Open 10-1 and 2-4, Sat. 10-1 and 2-5, Sun. 2.30-5. CL: Mon. SIZE: Small. *STOCK: Collectables, 19th-20th C, £5-£100.* LOC: Near traffic lights on Norwich road. PARK: Limited at rear. TEL: 01263 515330; home - 01263 514174. FAIRS: Norfolk Showground; Newark.

DISS

The Antiques & Collectors Centre (Diss)
3 Cobbs Yard, St Nicholas St. IP22 4LB. (Martin Moye). Est. 1997. Open 9-4.30. SIZE: Large. *STOCK: Furniture, 18th-20th C; porcelain, Victorian to 1960s; glassware, Georgian to 1930s; silver, paintings, prints, jewellery, Georgian to modern, £10-£300; rustic bygones, £20-£200; clocks, £50-£500.* LOC: Next to Diss Ironworks, off St. Nicholas St. PARK: Easy. TEL: 01379 644472. VAT: Spec.

Diss Antiques & Interiors   LAPADA
2 & 3 Market Place. IP22 4JT. (B. Wimshurst). GMC. Est. 1973. Open 9-5. SIZE: Large. *STOCK: Furniture, barometers, clocks, jewellery, porcelain, copper, brass.* PARK: Nearby. TEL: 01379 642213; e-mail - sales@ dissantiques.co.uk website - www.dissantiques.co.uk SER: Repairs (furniture, jewellery and china). VAT: Stan/Spec.

DOWNHAM MARKET

Antiques & Gifts
47 Bridge St. PE38 9DW. (B. and T. Addrison). Est. 1980. Usually open 10-5. SIZE: Medium. *STOCK: Furniture - pine, oak, mahogany; brass and iron beds, bric-a-brac and smalls, Victorian to 1930.* PARK: Free nearby. TEL: 01366 387700. SER: Free local delivery.

Castle Antiques
1 Paradise Rd. PE38 9HS. (Margaret Goodwin). Est. 1987. Open 10-4.30. SIZE: Large. *STOCK: Furniture*

including 18th C oak coffers, £750-£950; clocks, mirrors, silver tea services, Royal Dux, Royal Worcester, cranberry glass and lamps. LOC: Town centre. PARK: Nearby. TEL: 01366 388324; fax - same; mobile - 07946 201911.

EARSHAM, Nr. Bungay

Earsham Hall Pine
Earsham Hall. NR35 2AN. (R. Derham). Est. 1976. Open 9-5, Sun. 10.30-5. SIZE: Large. *STOCK: Pine furniture.* LOC: On Earsham to Hedenham road. PARK: Easy. TEL: 01986 893423; fax - 01986 895656; website - www.earshamhallpine.co.uk

EAST DEREHAM

Village Books
20A High St. NR19 1DR. (J.A.R. and J.W. James). Est. 1996. Open 9.30-4.30, Wed. 9.30-3, Sat. 9.30-5. SIZE: Medium. *STOCK: Books, 19th-20th C, £1-£150.* PARK: Nearby. TEL: 01362 853066; fax - same; e-mail - VillageBkDereham@aol.com SER: Book binding; book search. VAT: Stan.

FAKENHAM

Fakenham Antique Centre
Old Congregational Church, 14 Norwich Rd. NR21 8AZ. (Julie Hunt and Mandy Allen). Est. 1984. Open 10-4.30. SIZE: 27 dealers. *STOCK: Furniture, glass, ceramics, books, pens, oil lamps, kitchenalia, memorabilia, clocks, paintings and prints.* LOC: Turn off A148 at roundabout to town, at traffic lights turn up Queens Rd., left at second mini-roundabout, centre 50yds. on right opposite Godfrey DIY. PARK: Easy. TEL: 01328 862941. SER: Restorations (furniture); polishing; replacement handles; cane and rush seating repairs.

Sue Rivett Antiques and Bygones
6 Norwich Rd. NR21 8AX. (Mrs S. Rivett). Est. 1969. Open 10-1. *STOCK: General antiques and bygones.* LOC: On Norwich Rd. into Fakenham. PARK: Easy. TEL: 01328 862924; home - 01263 860462; mobile - 07778 819965. SER: Valuations.

GREAT YARMOUTH

Barry's Antiques
35 King St. NR30 2PN. Est. 1979. Open 9.30-5. SIZE: Large. *STOCK: Jewellery, porcelain, clocks, glass, pictures.* LOC: Main shopping street. PARK: Opposite. TEL: 01493 842713. VAT: Stan/Spec.

David Ferrow
77 Howard St. South. NR30 1LN. ABA. PBFA. Est. 1940. Open 10-4.30. CL: Thurs. SIZE: Large. *STOCK: Books, some antiquarian maps, local prints, manuscripts.* LOC: From London, sign before river bridge to The Docks, keep to nearside, turn left and then right to car park. PARK: Easy. TEL: 01493 843800. SER: Valuations; restorations (books and prints). VAT: Stan.

Folkes Antiques and Jewellers
74 Victoria Arcade. NR30 2NU. (Mrs J. Baldry). Est. 1946. Open 10-4. *STOCK: General antiques especially jewellery and collectables.* LOC: From A47 into town centre, shop on right of Victoria Arcade, opposite Regent Rd. to seafront. PARK: Easy. TEL: 01493 851354. SER: Valuations; repairs. FAIRS: Local collectors.

Gold and Silver Exchange
Theatre Plain. NR30 2BE. (C. Birch). Open 9.30-5.15. *STOCK: Coins, medals and secondhand jewellery.* TEL: 01493 859430.

Peter and Valerie Howkins Jewellers
135 King St. NR30 2PQ. NAG. Est. 1945. Open 9.30-4.45. SIZE: Medium. *STOCK: Jewellery, silver, crystal, porcelain, pottery, Georgian to present day.* LOC: South of Market Place. PARK: Limited and nearby. TEL: 01493 844639; fax - 01493 844857. SER: Valuations; restorations; repairs. VAT: Spec.

Wheatleys
16 Northgate St., White Horse Plain and Fullers Hill. NR30 1BA. Est. 1971. Open 9.30-5, Thurs. 9.30-1. SIZE: Large. *STOCK: Jewellery and general antiques.* LOC: 2 mins. walk from Market Place. PARK: Easy. TEL: 01493 857219. VAT: Stan.

HINGHAM, Nr. Norwich

Mongers
15 Market Place. NR9 4AF. (Sam Coster). SALVO. Est. 1997. Open 9.30-5.30. SIZE: Large. *STOCK: Fireplaces, 1700-1930, £400-£3,000; sanitaryware, 1870-1950, £250-£1,000; Victorian and Edwardian garden antiques, £50-£2,000; door furniture, from 1800 to date, £20-£100.* LOC: B1108. PARK: Easy. TEL: 01953 851868; fax - 01953 851870; e-mail - mongers@mongersof hingham.co.uk website - www.mongersofhingham.co.uk SER: Restorations (bath re-surfacing, fireplaces); stripping (pine). VAT: Stan/Spec.

Past & Present
16a The Fairland. NR9 4HN. (C. George). Est. 1970. Open Tues.-Sun. 10-5. SIZE: Medium. *STOCK: Furniture, £25-£1,500; smalls, 18th-19th C, £10-£500; lighting - lamps and chandeliers.* LOC: B1108. PARK: Easy. TEL: 01953 851471; home - 01953 851400. SER: Valuations. FAIRS: Swinderby, Newark, Staffordshire. VAT: Stan.

HOLT

Baron Art
9 & 17 Chapel Yard, Albert St. NR25 6HG. (Anthony R. Baron and Michael J. Bellis). Est. 1992. Open 9.30-5.30. SIZE: Medium. *STOCK: Paintings, 19th-20th C, £50-£5,000; prints and lithographs, 19th-20th C, £5-£500; collectables, 1830-1940, £5-£500; books and Art Deco.* PARK: Easy. TEL: 01263 713906 (No. 9); 01263 713430 (No. 17); fax - 01263 711670; e-mail - baronholt@ aol.com SER: Valuations; buys at auction (paintings); framing. VAT: Stan/Spec.

Baskerville Bindings
3-5 Fish Hill. NR25 6BD. ABA. ILAB. Open 10-5. SIZE: 10 rooms. *STOCK: Antique leatherbound books for decoration and library furnishing.* TEL: 01263 711143; fax - 01263 711153; e-mail - antique@leather boundbooks.com website - www.leatherboundbooks. com

Cottage Collectables
8 Fish Hill and 3 Chapel Yard. NR25 6BD. (Philip and Linda Morris). Est. 1984. Open 10-5, Sun. 11-5. SIZE: Medium. *STOCK: Collectables, 18th-20th C, £5-£250; furniture, 18th-20th C, £50-£300; jewellery, from Victorian, £5-£50; linen.* PARK: Easy. TEL: 01263 711707/712920; e-mail - cottcoll@aol.com SER: Valuations; restorations (furniture and ceramics); buys at auction (furniture and collectables). FAIRS: Swinderby, Peterborough, Newark and others.

Anthony Fell   BADA LAPADA
Chester House, 47 Bull St. NR25 6HP. (A.J. and C.R. Austin-Fell). CINOA. Est. 1996. Open 9.30-1 and 2-5, prior telephone call advisable if travelling long distance. SIZE: Medium. STOCK: English and Continental furniture, 16th-18th C, £1,000-£50,000; works of art, 16th C to contemporary, £1,000-£20,000. LOC: Near Post Office. PARK: Easy. TEL: 01263 712912; fax - same; e-mail - afellantiques@tiscali. co.uk website - www.anthonyfell.com SER: Valuations; restorations. FAIRS: Olympia (June, Nov). VAT: Spec.

Simon Finch Norfolk
3-5 Fish Hill. NR25 6BD. ABA. Est. 1976. Open 10-5. SIZE: 10 rooms. *STOCK: Antiquarian and secondhand books; bindings.* TEL: 01263 712650; website - www.simonfinch.com and www.simonfinchnorfolk.com

Heathfield Antiques & Country Pine
Candlestick Lane, Thornage Rd. NR25 6SU. (S.M. Heathfield). Est. 1989. Open 8.30-5. SIZE: Large. *STOCK: Pine furniture, £15-£3,500.* LOC: From Holt roundabout junction of A148/B1149, take the Dereham/Thornage road, business half a mile on left hand side. PARK: Own. TEL: 01263 711609; website - www.antique-pine.net SER: Restorations; painted furniture. VAT: Stan/Global.

Judy Hines of Holt - The Gallery
3 Fish Hill. NR25 6BD. Est. 1973. Open 11-5. CL: Mon. *STOCK: Modern British paintings; sculptures; British prints 1900-1980.* TEL: 01263 713000; fax - same; e-mail - judyhines@btinternet.com website - www.judy hines.com

Holt Antique Centre
Albert Hall, Albert St. NR25 6HY. (David Attfield). Est. 1980. Open 10-5, Sat. 10-5.30 (Sun. Easter-October). SIZE: Large. *STOCK: Pine and country furniture, china, glass, lighting, silver plate and kitchenalia, jewellery, clothes, soft furnishings, 18th-20th C, £1-£1,500.* LOC: Turn right from Chapel Yard car park, 100 yards. PARK: Easy. TEL: 01263 712097; home - 01263 860347.

Mews Antique Emporium
17B High St. NR25 6BH. Est. 1998. Open 10-5. SIZE: Large - 12 dealers. *STOCK: 18th-20th C furniture, collectables, £1-£1,000.* LOC: Rear of 17 High St. PARK: Nearby. TEL: 01263 713224.

Past Caring Vintage Clothing
6 Chapel Yard. NR25 6HG. (L. Mossman). Est. 1988. Open 11-5. SIZE: Medium. *STOCK: Period clothes, linen and textiles, Victorian to 1950, £5-£200; jewellery and accessories, Victorian to 1960, £5-£125.* PARK:

Easy. TEL: 01263 713771; home - 01362 683363; fax - 01362 680078. e-mail - mossmlyn@aol.com SER: Valuations; restorations (christening gowns and some beadwork). FAIRS: Alexandra Palace.

Richard Scott Antiques
30 High St. NR25 6BH. Est. 1967. Open 10-5. SIZE: Large. *STOCK: Pottery, porcelain, glass, furniture, general antiques.* LOC: On A148. PARK: Easy. TEL: 01263 712479; e-mail - lukescott@richardscottantiques. co.uk SER: Valuations; conservation advice.

HOVETON, Nr. Wroxham

Eric Bates and Sons Ltd.
Horning Road West. NR12 8QJ. (Eric, Graham and James Bates). Est. 1973. Open 9-5. SIZE: Large. *STOCK: Victorian and Edwardian furniture.* LOC: Opposite rail station. PARK: Easy. TEL: 01603 781771; fax - 01603 781773; e-mail - furniture@ebates.fsnet.co. uk website - www.batesfurniture.co.uk SER: Restorations (furniture); manufacturer of period-style furniture; upholstery; container packing and shipping. VAT: Stan/Spec.

HUNSTANTON

Delawood Antiques
10 Westgate. PE36 5AL. (R.C. Woodhouse). Resident. Est. 1975. Open Mon., Wed., Fri. and Sat. 10-5 and most Sun. afternoons, other times by chance or appointment. SIZE: Small. *STOCK: General antiques, furniture, jewellery, collectors' items, books, £1-£1,000.* LOC: Near town centre and bus station. PARK: Easy. TEL: 01485 532903; home and fax - same. SER: Valuations; commission sales.

Le Strange Old Barns Antiques, Arts & Craft Centre
Golf Course Rd., Old Hunstanton. PE36 6JG. (E. Maloney and R.M. Weller). Est. 1994. Open 10-6, (10-5 winter), including Sun. SIZE: Large. *STOCK: General antiques, collectables, arts and crafts.* LOC: Opposite Mariner Inn. PARK: Easy. TEL: 01485 533402.

R.C. Woodhouse (Antiquarian Horologist)
10 Westgate. PE36 5AL. BWCG. Resident. Est. 1975. Open Mon., Wed., Fri., and Sat. 10-5 and usually Sun. afternoons, other times by chance or appointment. SIZE: Small. *STOCK: Georgian, Victorian and Edwardian longcase, dial, wall and mantel clocks; some watches and barometers.* LOC: Near town centre and bus station. PARK: Easy. TEL: 01485 532903; home and fax - same. SER: Restorations (longcase, bracket, chiming, carriage, French, wall clocks, dials, barometers); small locks repaired and lost keys made - postal service if required; valuations.

KELLING, Nr. Holt

The Old Reading Room Gallery and Tea Room
NR25 7EL. (B.R. Taylor). Est. 1994. Open 9.30-4.30 including Sun. SIZE: Large. *STOCK: Paintings and prints, wood carvings, books, postcards and collectables.* LOC: A149 coast road between Weybourne and Cley, at war memorial in village. PARK: Easy. TEL: 01263

588227; home - 01263 588435. SER: Restorations; framing. VAT: Stan/Spec.

KING'S LYNN

Tim Clayton Jewellery Ltd
21-23 Chapel St. PE30 1EG. (Tim and Sue Clayton). NAG. Est. 1975. Open 9-5. SIZE: Large. *STOCK: Silver, jewellery, clocks, furniture and pictures.* LOC: Town centre. PARK: Nearby. TEL: 01553 772329; fax - 01553 776583; website - www.timclaytonjewellery.com SER: Bespoke jewellery; repairs; picture framing. VAT: Global/Margin.

James K. Lee
Nicholson House, 29 Church St. PE30 5EB. (A.J. and J.K. Lee). Est. 1950. Open 9-6 including Sun. SIZE: Small. *STOCK: Furniture including desks, chests of drawers and tables, 18th-19th C, £800-£4,500.* LOC: In old town, through Southgates, by mini roundabout. PARK: Easy and NCP opposite. TEL: 01553 810681; fax - 01553 760128; home - 01553 811522. SER: Valuations; restorations including polishing; buys at auction (furniture).

Old Curiosity Shop
25 St. James St. PE30 5DA. (Mrs R.S. Wright). Est. 1980. Open Mon., Thurs., Fri. and Sat. 11-5. SIZE: Small. *STOCK: General collectable smalls, glass, clothing, linen, jewellery, lighting, Art Deco and Art Nouveau, furniture, prints, stripped pine and paintings, pre 1930, £1-£500.* LOC: Off Saturday market place towards London Rd. PARK: At rear or nearby. TEL: 01553 766591. SER: Restorations (teddy bears); repairs (clocks). FAIRS: Alexandra Palace, Newark; local.

The Old Granary Antiques and Collectors Centre
King Staithe Lane, Off Queen St. PE30 1LZ. Est. 1977. Open 10-5. *STOCK: China, coins, glass, books, stamps, silver, jewellery, brass, copper, postcards, linen, some furniture and general antiques.* LOC: Close to Customs House. PARK: Easy. TEL: 01553 775509.

NEEDHAM, Nr. Harleston

Jennifer and Raymond Norman Antiques
Henstead Lodge. IP20 9LA. Resident. Est. 1974. Open by appointment. *STOCK: Clocks, 1780-1900, £100-£5,000; longcase, 1720-1830, £1,000-£8,000; stereoscopic views and viewers.* LOC: A143 Harleston by-pass. At Harleston/Needham roundabout turn towards Harleston. Entrance to Henstead Lodge immediately on right. PARK: Easy. TEL: 01379 855124; fax - 01379 855134; mobile - 07774 887045; e-mail - rjn@longcase.co.uk website - www.worldofstereoviews.com SER: Valuations; restorations (longcase clocks - cases and movements); buys at auction. VAT: Stan/Spec.

NORTH WALSHAM

The Angel Bookshop
4 Aylsham Rd. NR28 0BH. (O.D., M.E. and W.T.E. Green). PBFA. ABA. Est. 1980. Open Thurs. and Fri. 9.30-5, Sat. 9.30-3.30. SIZE: Medium. *STOCK: Books, 1700 to date, £3-£500.* LOC: Short walk from town centre. PARK: Nearby. TEL: 01692 404054; e-mail - angelbooks@onetel.net.uk SER: Valuations; buys at auction. FAIRS: East Anglia PBFA.

NORWICH

3A Antiques
2 and 3A Wrights Court, Elm Hill. NR3 1HQ. (Philip and Julie Milne). Est. 1983. Open 9-5. SIZE: Small. *STOCK: General antiques and collectables, curios and bric-a-brac.* LOC: City centre. TEL: 01603 667441.

Albrow and Sons Family Jewellers
10 All Saints Green. NR1 3NA. (R. Albrow). NAG Registered Valuer. Open 9.30-4.30. *STOCK: Jewellery, silver, plate, china, glass, furniture.* LOC: Opposite John Lewis'. PARK: Behind John Lewis'. TEL: 01603 622569; fax - 01603 766158. SER: Valuations; repairs.

Liz Allport-Lomax
t/a Corner Antiques. Est. 1971. *STOCK: Porcelain, glass, silver, objects de vertue, sewing accessories, small furniture and collectors' items - card cases, lace bobbins, snuff boxes, scent bottles.* TEL: 01603 737631; mobile - 07747 843074; e-mail - info@lomaxantiquesfairs.co.uk website - www.lomaxantiquesfairs.co.uk FAIRS: Organiser of Lomax Antiques Fairs at Langley School (May and Oct.); North Norfolk, Burnham Market (Easter).

Antiques & Interiors
31-35 Elm Hill. NR3 1HG. (P.S. Russell-Davis). Est. 1976. Open 10-5. CL: Thurs. *STOCK: 19th-20th C furniture; Art Deco, Arts & Crafts and modern design; pictures, lighting, decorative objects.* PARK: Nearby. TEL: 01603 622695; home - 01603 632446; fax - same; e-mail - patrick.russelldavis@btopenworld.com website - www.englishartdeco.com

The Bank House Gallery   LAPADA
Newmarket Rd. NR2 2HW. (R.S. Mitchell). Resident. Est. 1979. Open by appointment. *STOCK: English oil paintings especially Norwich and Suffolk schools, 19th C, £1,000-£50,000.* LOC: On A11 between City centre and ring road. PARK: Own. TEL: 01603 633380; e-mail - paintings@bankart.com website - www.bankart.com SER: Valuations; restorations. VAT: Stan/Spec.

James Brett   BADA
42 St. Giles St. NR2 1LW. Est. 1870. Open 9.30-1 and 2-5, Sat. by appointment. SIZE: Large. STOCK: Antique furniture, mahogany, walnut and oak; sculpture and metalwork. LOC: Near City Hall. PARK: Easy. TEL: 01603 628171; fax - 01603 630245. FAIRS: Olympia. VAT: Stan/Spec.

Cloisters Antique & Collectors Fair
St. Andrew's and Blackfriars Hall, St. Andrew's Plain. NR3 1AU. (Norwich City Council). Est. 1976. Open Wed. 9-3. SIZE: 21 dealers. *STOCK: Wide range of antiques and collectables.* LOC: City centre. PARK: Easy. TEL: 01603 628477; fax - 01603 762182; bookings - 01493 750981.

Country and Eastern Ltd.
Old Skating Rink Gallery, 34-36 Bethel St. NR2 1NR. (J. Millward). Est. 1978. Open 10-5. SIZE: Very

large. *STOCK: Oriental rugs, kelims and textiles; Indian and S.E. Asian antiques - furniture, objects, ceramics and metalwork.* LOC: Near The Forum. PARK: Easy. TEL: 01603 663890; fax - 01603 758108; website - www.countryandeastern.co.uk SER: Export. VAT: Stan.

Crome Gallery and Frame Shop
34 Elm Hill. NR3 1HG. (J. Willis). UKIC. Est. 1971. Open 9.30-5. SIZE: Large. *STOCK: Watercolours, oils and prints, mainly 20th C, some 19th C; wood carvings and sculpture.* LOC: Near cathedral. PARK: Easy. TEL: 01603 622827; e-mail - jwillis@elmhillgallery.com SER: Crome Gallery Conservation (oils, watercolours, prints, frames); framing.

Clive Dennett Coins
66 St. Benedicts St. NR2 4AR. BNTA. Est. 1970. CL: Thurs. and lunchtime. SIZE: Small. *STOCK: Coins and medals, ancient Greek to date, £5-£5,000; jewellery, 19th-20th C; banknotes, 20th C; both £5-£1,000.* PARK: Easy. TEL: 01603 624315. SER: Valuations; buys at auction (as stock). FAIRS: London Coin; International Banknote, London; Maastricht.

The Fairhurst Gallery
Bedford St. NR2 1AR. Est. 1951. Open 9-5. CL: Sat. pm. SIZE: Medium. *STOCK: Oil paintings, £5-£5,000; watercolours, £5-£2,000, both 19th-20th C; frames, 18th-20th C; furniture, £500-£10,000; mirrors.* LOC: Behind Travel Centre. TEL: 01603 614214. SER: Valuations; restorations; cleaning; framemakers; gold leafing. VAT: Spec.

Nicholas Fowle Antiques   BADA
Websdale Court, Bedford St. NR2 1AR. Est. 1965. Open 9-5, Sat. by appointment. SIZE: Medium. STOCK: Furniture, £500-£20,000; works of art, £5-£1,000; both 17th-19th C. LOC: City centre pedestrian area (limited access for loading and unloading). PARK: St Andrews multi-storey. TEL: 01603 219964; fax - 01692 630378; e-mail - nicholas @nicholasfowleantiques.com website - www.nicholas fowleantiques.com SER: Restorations (furniture). FAIRS: BADA. VAT: Stan/Spec.

Leona Levine Silver Specialist
2 Fisher's Lane. NR2 1ET. (Leona Levine and Bruce Thompson). Est. 1865. Open Tues., Wed. and Fri. 9.15-4.30. *STOCK: Silver and Sheffield plate.* LOC: Off St Giles St., 150 yards from City Hall. PARK: Multi-storey. TEL: 01603 628709; fax - same. SER: Valuations; engraving; restorations. VAT: Stan/Spec.

Maddermarket Antiques
18c Lower Goat Lane. NR2 1EL. (Mr and Mrs H. Tagg). NAG. Est. 1978. Open 9-5. *STOCK: Antique, secondhand and modern jewellery and silver, £10-£10,000.* PARK: St Giles multi-storey. TEL: 01603 620610; fax - same.

Mandell's Gallery   BADA
Elm Hill. NR3 1HN. Est. 1964. Open 9-5. SIZE: Large. STOCK: Oils and watercolours, especially English and Continental works and Norwich and Suffolk painters, 19th-20th C. LOC: Near shopping centre, close to cathedral. PARK: Easy. TEL: 01603

626892/629180; fax - 01603 767471. SER: Conservation; framing. FAIRS: Snape. VAT: Spec.

The Movie Shop
Antiquarian and Nostalgia Centre, 11 St. Gregory's Alley. NR2 1ER. (Peter Cossey). Open 11-5. SIZE: Large. *STOCK: Books, magazines and movie ephemera; telephones, collectables and general antiques.* TEL: 01603 615239; e-mail - peter.cossey@ntlworld.com website - www.thenorwichmovieshop.com

Norwich Collectors Toyshop
Tombland Antique Centre, Augustine Stewart House, 14 Tombland. NR3 1HF. (S. Marshall). Est. 1985. Open 9.30-5. *STOCK: Dinky and Corgi toys, 1940-1990, £5-£150; trains and soldiers, 1910-1980, £5-£500; teddies and tin toys, 1920-1980, £5-£200.* TEL: 01603 457761. SER: Valuations. FAIRS: Sandown Park, NEC, Donington Park, Doncaster Racecourse, Norfolk Showground.

Oswald Sebley
20 Lower Goat Lane. NR2 1EL. (P.H. Knights). Est. 1895. Open 9-5.15. CL: Thurs. SIZE: Small. *STOCK: Silver, 18th-20th C, £15-£2,000; jewellery, Victorian, £10-£4,000.* LOC: 150yds. to right of City Hall, down paved street. PARK: Nearby. TEL: 01603 626504. SER: Valuations; restorations (silver and gold jewellery). VAT: Stan/Spec.

Stiffkey Bathrooms
89 Upper St. Giles St. NR2 1AB. (Brown and Hyde). Est. 1985. Open 10-5. *STOCK: Victorian, Edwardian and French bathroom fittings.* PARK: Easy. TEL: 01603 627850; fax - 01603 619775; website - www.stiffkey bathrooms.com SER: Mail order period bathroom accessories.

Timgems
30 Elm Hill. NR3 1HG. (Tim Snelling). Open Tues., Wed., Fri. and Sat. 11-4. SIZE: Small. *STOCK: Jewellery and silver, £10-£3,000; small objects, £10-£1,000.* PARK: Monastery Court. TEL: 01603 623296; e-mail - tim.snelling@btinternet.com SER: Valuations; restorations.

Tombland Antiques Centre
Augustine Steward House, 14 Tombland. NR3 1HF. (Mrs Joan Gale). Est. 1974. Open 10-5. SIZE: Large. *STOCK: Furniture, 18th-20th C, £50-£2,000; china, porcelain, antiquities, dolls, Art Deco, Art Nouveau, collectables, curios, militaria, silver, pictures, postcards, jewellery, cranberry and other glass, toys, kitchenalia, linen, needlework tools.* LOC: City centre, opposite cathedral. PARK: Elm Hill. TEL: 01603 619129. SER: Valuations.

The Tombland Bookshop
8 Tombland. NR3 1HF. (J.G. and A.H. Freeman). Open 9.30-5. *STOCK: Antiquarian and secondhand books.* LOC: Opposite the Cathedral. TEL: 01603 490000; fax - 01603 760610; e-mail - tombland.bookshop@virgin.net

Tombland Jewellers & Silversmiths
12/13 Tombland. NR3 1HF. NAG. Est. 1972. Open 9-5, Sat. 9-4. *STOCK: English silver, flatware and jewellery, from 17th C; mustard pots, collectors' items, barometers,*

barographs, from 18th C. LOC: Opposite Erpingham Gate, Norwich cathedral and Maid's Head Hotel. TEL: 01603 624914; fax - 01603 764310. SER: Valuations; restorations; export facilities. VAT: Stan/Spec.

POTTER HEIGHAM

Times Past Antiques
Station Rd. NR29 5AD. (P. Dellar). Open Wed.-Sun. 10-5. *STOCK: Barometers, clocks, furniture including reproduction, china, pictures, glass, militaria, collectables, bric-a-brac.* LOC: A149 village centre. PARK: Easy. TEL: 01692 670898.

RAVENINGHAM

M.D. Cannell Antiques
Castell Farm, Beccles Rd. NR14 6NU. Resident. Est. 1982. Open Fri., Sat., Sun. and Mon. 10-6 or by appointment. SIZE: Large. *STOCK: Oriental rugs, carpets, kilims, furniture, metalwork and decorative items.* LOC: On B1140. PARK: Easy. TEL: 01508 548441. website - www.raveningham.demon.co.uk VAT: Stan/Spec.

RINGSTEAD

Priests Antiques Ltd
17 Chapel Lane. PE36 5JX. Est. 1978. Open by appointment. SIZE: Medium. *STOCK: 17th-18th C oak and walnut furniture, £500-£20,000+; some 18th-19th C mahogany.* LOC: Just off High St. PARK: Easy. TEL: 01485 525121; mobile - 07899 994304; e-mail - priestsantiques@freenet.co.uk SER: Buys at auction.

Ringstead Village Antique Centre
41 High St. PE36 5JU. (Tim and Cathy Roberts). Est. 1997. Open 8-5.30 including Sun; Tues., Wed. and Sat. 8-1. SIZE: 12 rooms including 2 courtyards. *STOCK: Furniture including pine, Edwardian and period, £50-£2,000; porcelain, curios, kitchenalia, books and magazines, paintings and prints.* LOC: 3 miles from Hunstanton. PARK: Easy. TEL: 01485 525270.

SCRATBY, Nr. Gt. Yarmouth

Keith Lawson Antique Clocks
Scratby Garden Centre, Beach Rd. NR29 3AJ. LBHI. Est. 1979. Open seven days 2-6. SIZE: Large. *STOCK: Clocks and barometers.* LOC: B1159. PARK: Easy. TEL: 01493 730950; website - www.antiqueclocks.co.uk SER: Valuations; restorations. VAT: Stan/Spec.

SEETHING, Nr. Brooke

Country House Antiques
NR15 1AL. (Geoff and Glenda Searle). Est. 1979. Open by appointment. SIZE: Large trade warehouses. *STOCK: Mahogany, oak, walnut furniture, 17th-19th C; interesting china and porcelain.* LOC: Village centre. PARK: Easy. TEL: 01508 558144; mobile - 07860 595658. *Trade only.*

SHERINGHAM

Parriss
20 Station Rd. NR26 8RE. (J.H. Parriss). Est. 1947. Open 9-1 and 2.15-5. CL: Wed. SIZE: Medium. *STOCK:*

Jewellery, £30-£5,000; silver, £40-£4,000; clocks, £100-£3,000. LOC: A1082, in main street. PARK: Within 150yds. TEL: 01263 822661. SER: Valuations; restorations (jewellery, silver, clocks). VAT: Stan.

The Westcliffe Gallery
2-8 Augusta St. NR26 8LA. (Richard and Sheila Parks). Resident. Est. 1979. Open 9.30-1 and 2-5.30, Sat. 9.30-5.30; (Sun. 10-4 summer only). SIZE: Medium. *STOCK: Oils, watercolours and drawings, 19th-20th C, £100-£15,000; furniture.* LOC: Town centre. PARK: Easy. TEL: 01263 824320; e-mail - sparks@westcliffegallery. co.uk SER: Valuations; restorations (oils, watercolours, prints); gilding. VAT: Stan/Spec.

STALHAM

Stalham Antique Gallery   LAPADA
29 High St. NR12 9AH. (Mike Hicks). CINOA. Est. 1970. Open 9-1 and 2-5. CL: Sat pm. SIZE: Medium. *STOCK: Furniture, 17th C to 19th C; pictures, china, glass, brass. Not Stocked: Reproductions.* LOC: 20 mins. from Norwich. PARK: Easy. TEL: 01692 580636; fax - same; e-mail - mbhickslink@btinternet.com SER: Valuations; restorations. FAIRS: Langley (Oct). VAT: Spec.

STIFFKEY

Stiffkey Antiques
The Old Methodist Chapel. NR23 1AJ. Est. 1976. Open 10-5 including Sun. CL: Wed. and Thurs. 1st Oct. to Easter. *STOCK: Door furniture, window fittings, fireplaces and accessories, 1800-1920; carpets, bric-a-brac, bronze garden statuary and water features.* PARK: Easy. TEL: 01328 830690; fax - 01328 830005.

The Stiffkey Lamp Shop
Townshend Arms. NR23 1AJ. (R. Belsten and D. Mann). Est. 1976. Open 10-5 including Sun. CL: Wed. and Thurs. 1st Oct. to Easter. SIZE: Medium. *STOCK: Lamps including rare, hanging, wall and table and fittings, electric, converted gas and oil, 1800-1920, £100-£3,000.* LOC: Coast road near Wells-next-the-Sea. PARK: Easy. TEL: 01328 830460; fax - 01328 830005; website - www.stiffkeylampshop.co.uk VAT: Stan.

STOKE FERRY, Nr. King's Lynn

Farmhouse Antiques
White's Farmhouse, Barker's Drove. PE33 9TA. (P. Philpot). Resident. Est. 1969. Open by appointment. *STOCK: General antiques.* PARK: Easy. TEL: 01366 500588. SER: Restorations; furniture made to order in old timber.

SWAFFHAM

Cranglegate Antiques
Market Place. PE37 7LE. (Mrs R.D. Buckie). Resident. Est. 1965. Open Tues., Thurs. and Sat. 10-1 and 2-5.30. SIZE: Small. *STOCK: Small furniture, general antiques and collectors items, 17th-20th C.* LOC: A47. PARK: In square opposite or in passage at rear. TEL: Home - 01760 721052; e-mail - rbuckie@buckie-antiques.com website - www.buckie-antiques.com

SWAFIELD, Nr. North Walsham

Staithe Lodge Gallery
Staithe Lodge. NR28 0RQ. (M.C.A. Foster). Resident. Est. 1976. Open 9-5. CL: Wed. SIZE: Large. *STOCK: Watercolours, paintings and prints, 1800-1950, £50-£500; furniture including reproduction.* LOC: On B1145 at the Mundesley end of the North Walsham by-pass. PARK: Easy. TEL: 01692 402669. SER: Restorations; framing; buys at auction (mainly watercolours).

TACOLNESTON, Nr. Norwich

Freya Antiques
St. Mary's Farm, Cheneys Lane. NR16 1DB. Usually open but appointment advisable; evenings by appointment. SIZE: Large. *STOCK: General antiques, especially pine and country furniture; upholstery, secondhand and antiquarian books.* PARK: Own large. TEL: 01508 489252; mobile - 07799 401067; e-mail - freyaantiques@btinternet.com website - www.freya antiques.co.uk and www.antiquesbarn.co.uk SER: Valuations; restorations; re-upholstery. FAIRS: Own (see website for details)

TOTTENHILL, Nr. King's Lynn

Jubilee Antiques
Coach House, Whin Common Rd. PE33 0RS. (A.J. Lee). Est. 1953. Open daily including Sun. SIZE: Medium. *STOCK: Georgian and Victorian furniture, £50-£4,000; interesting items.* LOC: Between King's Lynn and Downham Market, adjacent to A10. PARK: Easy. TEL: 01553 810681; home - same; fax - 01553 760128. SER: Valuations; restorations (furniture).

TWYFORD, Nr. Fakenham

Norton Antiques
NR20 5LZ. (T. and N. Hepburn). Est. 1966. Open by appointment. *STOCK: Furniture, 1680-1900, £25-£8,000; oils and watercolours, 19th to early 20th C, £25-£5,000; clocks, 18th-19th C, £50-£6,000; woodworking and craftsman's hand tools.* PARK: Easy. TEL: 01362 683331. SER: Valuations.

WELLS-NEXT-THE-SEA

Wells Antique Centre
The Old Mill, Maryland. NR23 1LY. Est. 1986. Open 10-5 (10-4 winter) including Sun. SIZE: 15 dealers. *STOCK: General antiques and collectables.* PARK: Easy. TEL: 01328 711433.

WROXHAM

T.C.S. Brooke BADA
incorporating The Ruth Lowe Gallery of Contemporary Art, The Grange. NR12 8RX. (S.T. Brooke). Est. 1952. Open 9.30-1 and 2.15-5.30. CL: Mon. SIZE: 2 large showrooms and gallery. STOCK: English porcelain, 18th C; furniture, mainly Georgian; silver, glass, works of art, Oriental rugs. LOC: On main Norwich road. PARK: Easy. TEL: 01603 782644. SER: Valuations. VAT: Spec.

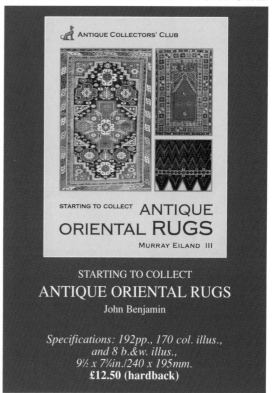
WYMONDHAM

King
Market Place. NR18 0AX. (M. King). Est. 1969. Open 9-4. CL: Thurs., Fri and Sat. except by appointment. SIZE: 5 rooms. *STOCK: General antiques, furniture, copper, brass, silver, jewellery, porcelain.* PARK: Easy. TEL: 01953 604758; evenings - 01953 602427. FAIRS: Lomax.

Turret House
27 Middleton St. NR18 0AB. (Dr and Mrs D.H. Morgan). PBFA. Resident. Est. 1972. SIZE: Small. *STOCK: Antiquarian books especially science and medical; occasional scientific instruments.* LOC: Corner of Vicar St., adjacent to War Memorial. TEL: 01953 603462. SER: Buys at auction. FAIRS: London Scientific & Medical Instrument; PBFA (London and York). VAT: Stan/Spec.

Wymondham Antique and Collectors Centre
3 Town Green. NR18 0PN. (Charles White). Est. 1983. Open 10-5 including Sun. SIZE: 2 floors, 22 dealers. *STOCK: China including crested, Beswick, Moorcroft, Royal Doulton, Coalport, Victorian to 1960s; jewellery, postcards, books, glass including cranberry, toys, furniture, clocks, pine, prints, oils and watercolours.* PARK: Easy. TEL: 01953 604817; fax - 01603 811112; home - same; mobile - 07771 970112. SER: Valuations. FAIRS: Norwich; Swinderby; Crystal Palace; Newark; Peterborough - Easton Sports Centre.

NORTHAMPTONSHIRE

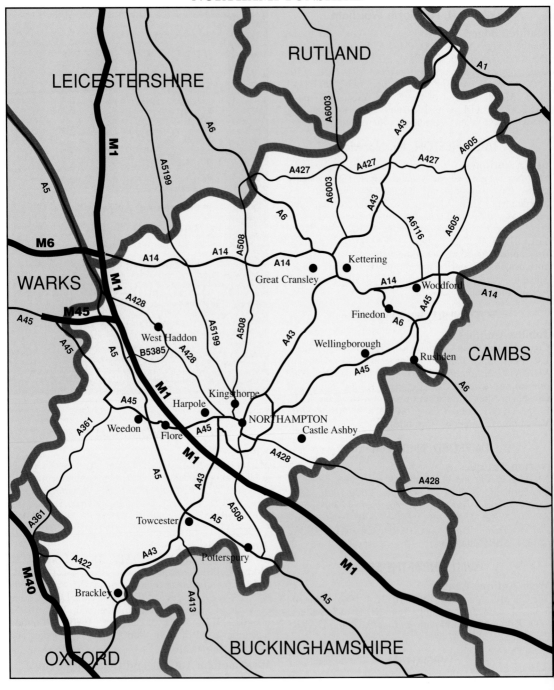

Dealers and Shops in Northamptonshire

Brackley	3	Great Cransley	1	Northampton	3	Weedon	4
Castle Ashby	1	Harpole	1	Potterspury	2	Wellingborough	2
Finedon	4	Kettering	1	Rushden	2	West Haddon	2
Flore	2	Kingsthorpe	2	Towcester	3	Woodford	1

BRACKLEY

Brackley Antique Cellar
Manor Rd. NN13 6DF. (Jim Broomfield). Est. 2000. Open 10-5 including Sun. SIZE: Large, over 100 dealers. *STOCK: Wide range of general antiques.* LOC: Below Co-op Superstore. PARK: Easy. TEL: 01280 841841; fax - 01280 841851.

The Old Hall Bookshop
32 Market Place. NN13 7DP. (John and Juliet Townsend). ABA. PBFA. ILAB. Est. 1977. Open 9.30-5.30. SIZE: Large. *STOCK: Antiquarian, secondhand and new books and maps.* LOC: Town centre on east side of Market Place. PARK: Easy. TEL: 01280 704146; fax - 01280 705131; e-mail - books@oldhallbooks.com website - www.oldhallbooks.com SER: Book search. FAIRS: Occasional PBFA/ABA. VAT: Stan.

Right Angle
24 Manor Rd. NN13 6AJ. (Chris and Val Pendleton). FATG. Est. 1981. Open Tues.-Fri. 9-5, Sat. 9.30-1. *STOCK: Antique maps and topographical engravings, natural history and art books, ceramics.* PARK: Opposite. TEL: 01280 702462; e-mail - chris@right anglegallery.co.uk website - www.rightanglegallery.co.uk SER: Framing (museum standard).

CASTLE ASHBY

Castle Ashby Gallery
The Old Farmyard. NN7 1LF. (Geoffrey S. Wright & Son (Fine Paintings)). Est. 1987. Open 10-5 including Sun. CL: Mon. *STOCK: 19th-20th C oil paintings and watercolours, furniture and decorative furnishings.* LOC: Adjacent to Castle Ashby House. PARK: Easy. TEL: 01604 696787; e-mail - sales@castleashbygallery.com SER: Valuations; restorations (oils). VAT: Spec.

FINEDON

Simon Banks Antiques
28 Church St. NN9 5NA. Est. 1984. Open every day. SIZE: Large. *STOCK: 17th-20th C furniture, £50-£5,000; glass, silver, ceramics, prints, copper, decorative and collectable items, clocks including longcase, wall and mantel.* LOC: Near church. PARK: Easy. TEL: 01933 680371; mobile - 07976 787539; e-mail - simon@banksantiques.com website - www.banks antiques.com SER: Valuations; search; nationwide delivery. VAT: Stan/Spec.

M.C. Chapman   LAPADA
NN9 5ND. Est. 1967. Open 9-5.30, Sun. 11-5 by prior appointment. SIZE: Large. *STOCK: Furniture, clocks, decorative items, 18th-20th C, £100-£4,000.* LOC: 400 yards off A510. PARK: Easy. TEL: Mobile - 07771 883060; e-mail - sales@finedonantiques.com SER: Container facilities. VAT: Stan/Spec/Global.

Robert Cheney Antiques
11-13 High St. NN9 5JN. Est. 1992. Open 9-5.30, Sun. 11-4. SIZE: Medium. *STOCK: 18th-20th C furniture, china and glass, £5-£5,000.* LOC: A6. PARK: Easy. TEL: 01933 681048; home - 01933 680085. SER: Valuations.

E.K. Antiques
37 High St. NN9 5JN. (Edward Kubacki). Est. 1991. Open 9.30-5, Sun. 11-4. SIZE: Medium - several dealers. *STOCK: Furniture, china, silver, glass, pictures, needlework, clocks and decorative items, 1680-1950, £5-£8,000.* PARK: Easy. TEL: 01933 681882; home - 01933 410245. SER: Restorations (furniture); French polishing; valuations. FAIRS: Huntingdon; Kimbolton Castle; Wicksteed Park, Kettering.

FLORE, Nr. Weedon

Blockheads and Granary Antiques
The Huntershields. NN7 4LZ. (Mrs C. Madeira and Richard Sear). Est. 1968. Open 9.30-6, Sun. and other times by appointment. SIZE: Large. *STOCK: Furniture, 17th-19th C, £50-£5,000; early metalware specialist; decorative and period items, 19th C, £50-£2,000; wooden hat makers' blocks, brims and complete models.* LOC: Off M1, junction 16, into Flore, last turning on left at bollard, premises on right at bottom of lane. PARK: Easy. TEL: 01327 340718; home - same; fax - 01327 349263. FAIRS: Newark.

Christopher Jones Antiques
Flore House, The Avenue. NN7 4LZ. Est. 1977. Open 10-5, Sat. 11-4.30, Sun. by appointment. SIZE: Large. *STOCK: Period and decorative furniture, lighting, porcelain, glass and objects, 18th-20th C.* PARK: Easy. TEL: 01327 342165; e-mail - florehouse@msn.com SER: Interior decor advice. FAIRS: Olympia. VAT: Spec.

GREAT CRANSLEY, Nr. Kettering

Bryan Perkins Antiques
The Old Chicken Farm. NN14 1PX. (J., B.H. and S.C. Perkins). Est. 1971. Open 9-5. CL: Sat. pm. SIZE: Large. *STOCK: Furniture and paintings, 19th C, £200-£5,000; small items.* LOC: Just off A43 south of Kettering. PARK: Easy. TEL: Mobile - 07780 850531; home - 01536 790259. SER: Valuations; restorations (furniture). VAT: Spec. *Trade Only.*

HARPOLE

Inglenook Antiques
23 High St. NN7 4DH. (T. and P. Havard). Est. 1971. Open 9-7. SIZE: Small. *STOCK: General antiques, £1-£500.* LOC: Main street. PARK: Easy. TEL: 01604 830007. SER: Restorations (longcase clocks).

KETTERING

Dragon Antiques
85 Rockingham Rd. NN16 8LA. Est. 1982. Open 10-4. CL: Thurs. *STOCK: Pictures, Oriental items, militaria and general antiques.* PARK: Easy. TEL: 01536 517017. SER: Framing.

KINGSTHORPE, Nr. Northampton

Laila Gray Antiques
25 Welford Rd. NN2 8AQ. Open 9-5.30. *STOCK: Pine.* TEL: 01604 715277. SER: Waxing; stripping.

The Old Brigade
10a Harborough Rd. NN2 7AZ. (S.C. Wilson). Est. 1978.

Cave's

111, KETTERING ROAD
NORTHAMPTON
(TEL: 01604 - 638278)

Hidden away in our Basement showroom
is a large stock full of delightful surprises,
mainly 18th and 19th Century Furniture in
all woods and in condition worthy of
high-class homes.

DEALERS SHOW CARD AND
ASK FOR TRADE FACILITIES

*Loop off M1 Exits 15 and 16 or short
detour from A5*

OPEN MON/TUES/WED/FRI/SAT
9AM – 5.30PM.

Open by appointment. SIZE: Medium. *STOCK: Military items, especially German Third Reich, 1850s to 1945, £5-£5,000.* LOC: Junction 15, M1. PARK: Easy. TEL: 01604 719389; fax - 01604 712489; e-mail - theoldbrigade@btconnect.com and stewart@theoldbrigade.co.uk website - www.theoldbrigade.co.uk SER: Valuations. VAT: Stan/Spec.

NORTHAMPTON

F. and C.H. Cave
111 Kettering Rd. NN1 4BA. Est. 1879. Open 9-5.30. CL: Thurs. SIZE: Large. *STOCK: Furniture - Georgian, Victorian and decorative; general antiques.* LOC: Near town centre, quarter mile outside pedestrianised area. PARK: Adjoining side streets. TEL: 01604 638278. VAT: Spec.

Michael Jones Jeweller
Gold St. NN1 1SA. NAG. Est. 1919. Open 9-5.30. *STOCK: Silver, gold and gem jewellery, French carriage clocks.* TEL: 01604 632548; fax - 01604 233813; e-mail - enquiries@michaeljonesjeweller.co.uk website - www. michaeljonesjeweller.co.uk VAT: Margin.

Occultique
30 St Michael's Ave. NN1 4JQ. (Michael J. Lovett). Est. 1973. Open by appointment only. SIZE: Small. *STOCK: Books and artifacts, 50p-£500.* PARK: Easy. TEL: 01604 527727; fax - 01604 603860; e-mail - enquiries@ occultique.co.uk website - www.occultique.co.uk SER: Catalogue available. VAT: Stan.

POTTERSPURY, Nr. Towcester

The Reindeer Antiques Centre
43 Watling St. NN12 7QD. Open 10-5 including Sun. and Bank Holidays. *STOCK: Furniture, porcelain, glass, silver, clocks, paintings, bronzes and needlework.* TEL: 01908 543704; e-mail - sales@reindeer-antiques.co.uk

Reindeer Antiques Ltd BADA LAPADA
43 Watling St. NN12 7QD. (John Butterworth and Nicholas Fuller). Est. 1959. Open 9-6, Sat., Sun. and other times by appointment. SIZE: Large. *STOCK: Fine English furniture, 17th-19th C; caddies, clocks, smalls, paintings.* LOC: A5. PARK: Own. TEL: 01908 542407/542200; fax - 01908 542121. FAIRS: BADA. LAPADA. VAT: Stan/Spec.

RUSHDEN

Magpies
1 East Grove. NN10 0AP. (Jim and Janet Ward). Est. 1993. Open 10-5, Nov.-Feb. 10-4, Sun. 12-4. SIZE: Large. *STOCK: Furniture, £20-£1,000; china, glass, kitchenalia and bric-a-brac, postcards, clocks, 78 records, £1-£100, all 19th-20th C.* LOC: A6 south on one-way system, first left after passing old station. PARK: Easy. TEL: 01933 411404.

D.W. Sherwood Antiques Ltd
59 Little St. NN10 0LS. Est. 1960. Open Tues., Wed., Fri. and Sat. 11-5. *STOCK: General antiques.* PARK: Easy. TEL: 01933 353265; e-mail - rosebud@ 10duckend.freeserve.co.uk

TOWCESTER

Clark Galleries
215 Watling St. NN12 6BX. (A. and S.D. Clark). FBAPCR. Est. 1963. Open 9-5, Sat. 9-4. SIZE: Large. *STOCK: Landscape, portrait and marine oil paintings, 18th-19th C, £500-£20,000.* LOC: M1, junction 15A, on A5. PARK: Easy and at rear. TEL: 01327 352957; e-mail - sales@clarkgalleries.co.uk website - www.victorian-pictures.co.uk SER: Restorations (oils, watercolours and frames); re-lining, valuations, picture hire. VAT: Stan/Spec.

Ron Green
227-239 Watling St. West. NN12 6DD. (Nicholas and Christopher Green). Est. 1952. Open 9-6, Sun. by appointment. SIZE: Large. *STOCK: English and Continental furniture, paintings and decorative items, £30-£30,000.* PARK: Easy. TEL: 01327 350387/350615; fax - 01327 350387; e-mail - ron@green227.freeserve. co.uk website - www.rongreenantiques.com SER: Valuations; restorations.

Lorraine Spooner Antiques
211 Watling Street West. NN12 6BX. Est. 1996. Open 9.30-5.30, Wed. 9.30-1.30, Sun. and Mon. by appointment. SIZE: Medium. *STOCK: Furniture, clocks, silver, porcelain, glass, paintings and prints, treen and metalware, linens, books, 1790-1940, £1-£10,000.* LOC: Main street. PARK: Nearby. TEL: 01327 358777; fax - same; mobile - 07855 828962; e-mail - lorraine@ lsantiques.com website - wwww.lsantiques.com

18TH CENTURY ENGLISH FURNITURE
The Norman Adams Collection

Christopher Claxton Stevens and Stewart Whittington

The 18th century was a period when British design and craftsmanship reached its pinnacle. Based on some of the finest pieces which passed through one of Britain's leading furniture dealers, Norman Adams, this book provides a unique source of picture reference and informed comment and analysis concentrating principally on the mahogany for which the period is renowned.

Specifications: 492pp., 46 col. illus., 475 b.&w. illus., 11 x 8½in./279 x 216mm. **£45.00 (hardback)**

WEEDON

Helios & Co (Antiques)
25/27 High St. NN7 4QD. (J. Skiba and B. Walters). Est. 1976. Open 9.30-5.30, Sat. and Sun. 10-5. CL: Mon. SIZE: 20 showrooms. STOCK: *English and Continental furniture especially dining tables and sets of chairs; decorative accessories, longcase clocks and pianos.* LOC: 4 miles from junction 16, M1 towards Daventry. PARK: Easy. TEL: 01327 340264; fax - 01327 342235; e-mail - john@skiba.net website - www.heliosantiques. com SER: Suppliers and restorers to H. M. Govt. VAT: Spec.

Rococo Antiques, Architectural Goods and Furnishings
The Former Wesleyan Chapel, 1 Bridge St., Lower Weedon. NN7 4PN. (N.K. Griffiths). Resident. Open 10-5, Sun. by appointment. STOCK: *Architectural goods and furnishings, general antiques.* TEL: 01327 341288; mobile - 07939 212542; e-mail - neville@neville griffiths.co.uk website - www.nevillegriffiths.co.uk VAT: Stan/Spec.

The Village Antique Market
62 High St. NN7 4QD. (E.A. and J.M. Saunders). Est. 1967. Open 10.30-5.15 including Sun. and Bank Holidays. SIZE: Large - 40 dealers. STOCK: *General antiques and interesting items.* LOC: Off junction 16, M1. PARK: In front yard. TEL: 01327 342015.

Weedon Antiques
23 High St. NN7 4QD. (N.L. Tillman). Est. 2000. Open 10-5, Sun. and Bank Holidays 10.30-4.30. CL: Mon. and Tues. SIZE: Medium. STOCK: *Porcelain including Royal Worcester, Coalport, Derby, Noritake, George Jones, Clarice Cliff, Aynsley and Limoges; silver including Georgian, all £15-£1,000; glass including cranberry, vaseline, rummers, 17th-20th C, £15-£500; pictures, £50-£1,000; furniture, £200-£3,000.* LOC: A45, 2 miles from junction 16, M1. PARK: Easy. TEL: 01327 349777; mobile - 07711 570798. e-mail - weedon antiques@tiscali.co.uk SER: Valuations. FAIRS: NEC; Milton Keynes; Stafford (Bowman). VAT: Global.

WELLINGBOROUGH

Antiques and Bric-a-Brac Market
Market Sq. NN8 1AF. Open Tues. 9-4. SIZE: 135 stalls. STOCK: *General antiques and collectables.* LOC: Town centre. PARK: Easy. TEL: 01933 231739; mobile - 07786 522407.

Park Gallery & Bookshop
16 Cannon St. NN8 5DJ. (Mrs J.A. Foster). Est. 1979. Open 10-5.30. SIZE: Medium. STOCK: *Books, maps and prints, 18th-19th C, £2-£500.* LOC: Continuation of A510 into town. PARK: Easy. TEL: 01933 222592; e-mail - judy@parkbookshop.freeserve.co.uk website - www.ukbookworld.com/members/parkbookshop SER: Framing; book search.

WEST HADDON

The Country Pine Shop
The Romney Building, Northampton Rd. NN6 7AS (Ryan Dodd and G.L. Cooksey). Est. 1985. Open 10-5. SIZE: Large. STOCK: *English and Continental stripped pine, £30-£1,200.* LOC: A428. TEL: 01788 510430.

Paul Hopwell Antiques   BADA LAPADA
30 High St. NN6 7AP. Est. 1974. Open 10-6, Sun. by appointment. SIZE: Large. STOCK: *17th-18th C oak and walnut country furniture, longcase clocks, metalware: oil paintings and prints, mainly sporting and country pursuits.* **LOC: A428. PARK: Easy. TEL: 01788 510636; fax - 01788 510044; e-mail - paul hopwell@antiqueoak.co.uk website - www.antique oak.co.uk SER: Valuations; restorations (furniture and metalware); buys at auction. VAT: Spec.**

WOODFORD, Nr. Thrapston

Granary Antiques
The Old Granary, Manor House Farm, Addington Rd. NN14 4ES. (A.H. Cox). Est. 1974. Open 10-5.30 including Sun. CL: Thurs. SIZE: Large. STOCK: *Georgian and Victorian pine furniture, £100-£1,000; Georgian country oak, Georgian-Edwardian mahogany £100-£1,500; Victorian-Edwardian walnut, £200-£1,500; Georgian-Edwardian clocks, £150-£2,500; general antiques, china, glass, collectors' items, shipping furniture.* LOC: First property on left from Gt. Addington village. PARK: Easy. TEL: 01832 732535; home - 01933 652557; mobile - 07732 169884. SER: Valuations; restorations (furniture).

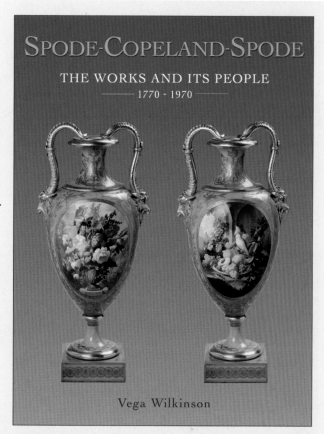

SPODE-COPELAND-SPODE

THE WORKS AND ITS PEOPLE
1770 - 1970

Vega Wilkinson

- Unpublished research from the Copeland family archives at Trelissick the home of Spencer Copeland

- Unpublished original pen and ink drawings of the Factory site by Harold Holdway, late Art Director of Spode, created especially for this book

- New research of the artists and gilders employed at the Factory and examples of their work

- Detailed plans of the Spode works showing its development on the nine-acre site

SPODE-COPELAND-SPODE
THE WORKS AND ITS PEOPLE 1770-1970

Vega Wilkinson

Spode-Copeland-Spode is the story of a manufactory, two families, generations of artists, gilders, modellers and their products. Begun by Josiah Spode I and continued by his son Josiah II, the business and works passed to the Copeland family who for five generations continued the traditions of quality and fine potting started by the Spodes. When the business was sold in 1970 and its products reverted to the original name Spode. The book contains illustrations showing the range of products, including commissions for Royalty and the nobility not forgetting examples of the everyday wares of two centuries. There is new unpublished information, drawings and plans showing the many changes which have taken place at the Spode works. This is the fascinating story of a Pottery that has survived for over two centuries and today still produces many fine innovative wares.

Vega Wilkinson is married with two children. She was born in the West Riding of Yorkshire but has lived in the Potteries for the last twenty-eight years, – the ideal place to pursue her collecting. Her love of fine china, especially landscape decoration, led to research in the archives of Spode and the Copeland family at Trelissick, Cornwall. She has published articles on Copeland and Minton, *Copeland* (Shire book); written the guide book to the Copeland China collection at Trelissick, and is now preparing another book: *A Century of Ceramic Artists 1800-1900.*

Specifications:
288pp., 161 col. illus., 146 b.&w. illus.,
11 x 8½in./279 x 216mm.
£45.00 (hardback)

For full details of all ACC publications, log on to our website:
www.antiquecollectorsclub.com
or telephone 01394 389950 for a free catalogue

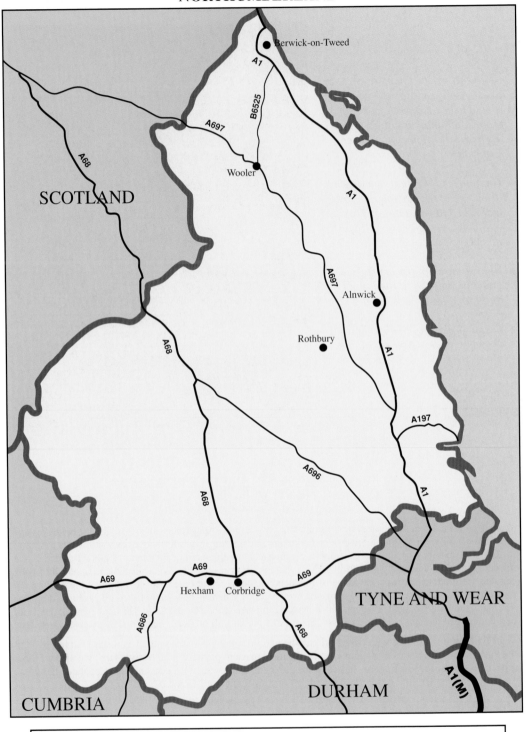

NORTHUMBERLAND

Berwick-on-Tweed

SCOTLAND

Wooler

Alnwick

Rothbury

Hexham   Corbridge

TYNE AND WEAR

CUMBRIA

DURHAM

Dealers and Shops in Northumberland					
Alnwick	5	Corbridge	3	Rothbury	2
Berwick-on-Tweed	2	Hexham	3	Wooler	2

ALNWICK

G.M. Athey
Castle Corner, Narrowgate. NE66 0NP. Est. 1980. Open 8.30-4.30. SIZE: 3 floors. *STOCK: English oak and mahogany furniture, glass, china and brass, 18th-19th C.* LOC: Part of Alnwick Castle. PARK: Easy. TEL: 01665 604229; mobile - 07836 718350; e-mail - gm.athey @alncom.net SER: Restorations (furniture including upholstery). FAIRS: Newark.

Bailiffgate Antique Pine
22 Bailiffgate. NE66 1LX. (S. Aston). Est. 1994. Open Thurs.-Sat. 10-4.30. SIZE: Large. *STOCK: Country pine furniture.* LOC: Opposite the castle. PARK: Easy. TEL: 01665 603616. SER: Valuations; buys at auction.

Barter Books
Alnwick Station. NE66 2NP. (Stuart & Mary Manley). IABA. Est. 1990. Open daily including Sun. SIZE: Large. *STOCK: Antiquarian books, £10-£5,000.* LOC: Off A1, on left on town approach. PARK: Easy. TEL: 01665 604888; fax - 01665 604444; e-mail - webquery@ barterbooks.co.uk website - www.barterbooks.co.uk

Gordon Caris
30 Fenkle St. NE66 1HR. Open Thurs. and Fri. 10-4. *STOCK: Clocks and watches.* TEL: 01665 510820. SER: Restorations (clocks and watches).

Tamblyn
12 Bondgate Without. NE66 1PP. (Mrs S.M. Hirst and Prof. B.E. Hirst). Est. 1981. Open 10-4.30. SIZE: Medium. *STOCK: General antiques including country furniture, pottery, pictures; antiquities, Scandinavian glass, to 20th C, £5-£1,500.* LOC: Diagonally opposite war memorial at southern entrance to town. PARK: Easy. TEL: 01665 603024; home - same; e-mail - profbehirst@tamblynant.fsnet.co.uk SER: Valuations.

BERWICK-UPON-TWEED

Treasure Chest
53 West St. TD15 2DX. (Y. Scott and K. Russell). Est. 1988. Open 11-4. CL: Tues. and Thurs. SIZE: Medium. *STOCK: China, jewellery, glass, clothes, linen, silver plate and small furniture, from 1860, £1-£400.* LOC: Approximately 1 mile from A1. PARK: Easy. TEL: Home - 01289 307736/305675. SER: Restorations (china). FAIRS: Local; Newark.

Woodside Reclamation (Architectural Antiques)
Woodside, Scremerston. TD15 2SY. (Keith Allan and Lynne Gray). SALVO. Est. 1990. Open Tues.-Sat. 9-5. SIZE: Large. *STOCK: Architectural salvage including fireplaces, baths, kitchen pine, 19th C.* LOC: Adjacent A1, just south of town. PARK: Easy. TEL: 01289 331211; fax - 01289 330274; home - 01289 302658; website - www.redbaths.co.uk SER: Restorations (stripping and finishing).

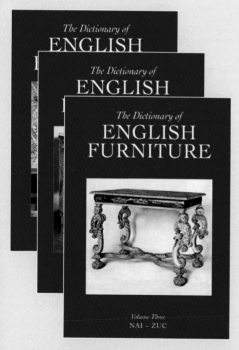

CORBRIDGE

Hedley's of Corbridge
Bishop's Yard, Main St. NE45 5LA. (P. Torday). Open Tues.-Sat. 10-5; Sun. 11-4 (prior telephone call advisable). *STOCK: Furniture including Arts and Crafts, glass, china including Moorcroft and studio pottery, Limoges boxes, jewellery and silver, pictures and prints, longcase and mantel clocks.* LOC: To rear of Shell garage. PARK: Own at rear. TEL: 01434 634936; e-mail - hedleys@torday96.fsnet.co.uk SER: Valuations.

Judith Michael
20A Watling St. NE45 5AH. (Judith Troldahl and Gillian Anderson). Est. 1970. Open 10-5. CL: Mon. SIZE: Medium. *STOCK: China, glass, silver, furniture, mirrors, light fittings and jewellery.* LOC: Just off A69.

PARK: Easy. TEL: 01434 633165; fax - same. SER: Valuations.

Renney Antiques
Bishops Court, Main St. NE45 5LA. Est. 1987. Open 10-5 or by appointment. CL: Mon. SIZE: Large. *STOCK: Decorative lighting, English and French furniture, garden, architectural and decorative items, textiles, china and glass.* TEL: 01434 633663. SER: Buys at auction.

HEXHAM

Gordon Caris
16 Market Place. NE46 1XQ. Est. 1972. Open 9-5. CL: Thurs. *STOCK: Clocks and watches.* TEL: 01434 602106; website - www.caris-clocks.com SER: Restorations (clocks and watches).

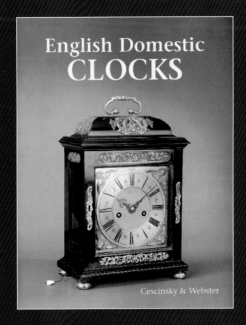

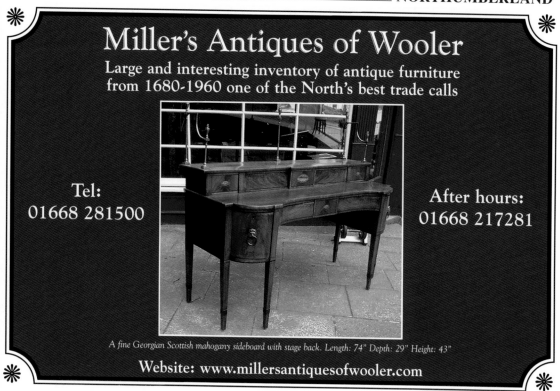
Priest Popple Books
9B Priest Popple. NE46 1PF. (John B. Patterson). Est. 1997. Open 9-5. SIZE: Medium. *STOCK: Books - second-hand non-fiction, first editions, antiquarian, £5-£1,500; sheet music, LPs.* LOC: From A69 to town centre, premises top of bus station. PARK: Easy. TEL: 01434 607773; e-mail - priestpopple.books@tinyworld.co.uk SER: Valuations; book-binding; booksearch.

The Violin Shop
27 Hencotes. NE46 2EQ. (D. Mann). Est. 1970. Open 10-5 or by appointment. *STOCK: Violins, violas, cellos, basses and bows.* TEL: 01434 607897; e-mail - davehexviolins@aol.com website - www.hexham-violins.co.uk SER: Repairs; restorations; bow re-hairing; new instruments made.

ROTHBURY

Bridgedale Antiques
Bridgedale House. Bridge St. NE65 7SE. (Peter, Paul and Susan Leatherland). Est. 1970. Open 10-5. SIZE: Medium. *STOCK: Furniture, 18th C to 1920s; decorative china, clocks, metalware, mirrors and pictures, £5-£4,000.* LOC: Opposite Post Office. PARK: Easy. TEL: 01669 621117. FAIRS: Newark. VAT: Margin.

Golfark International
5 Tollgate Crescent. NE65 7RE. (Michael Arkle). Est. 1997. *STOCK: Golf clubs and bags.* LOC: 2 mins. from centre. PARK: Easy. TEL: 01669 620487; fax/home - same; mobile - 07710 693860; e-mail - michael@golfark.freeserve.co.uk

WOOLER

Hamish Dunn Antiques
17 High St. NE71 6BU. Est. 1986. Open 9.30-12 and 1-4.30. CL: Thurs. SIZE: Medium. *STOCK: Curios and collectables, 19th-20th C, £5-£500; antiquarian and secondhand books, 18th-20th C, £1-£200; small furniture, 19th-20th C, £15-£1,000.* LOC: Off A697. PARK: Easy. TEL: 01668 281341; fax - same; home - 01668 282013; e-mail - hamishoscr@aol.com

James Miller Antiques LAPADA
1-5 Church St. NE71 6BZ. Est. 1947. Open Mon.-Fri. 9.30-5, trade anytime by appointment. SIZE: Large and warehouses. *STOCK: Georgian-Edwardian furniture and clocks.* LOC: A697. PARK: Nearby. TEL: 01668 281500; fax - 01668 282383; home - 01668 217281; website - www.millersantiquesofwooler.com FAIRS: Newark. VAT: Stan/Spec.

NOTTINGHAMSHIRE

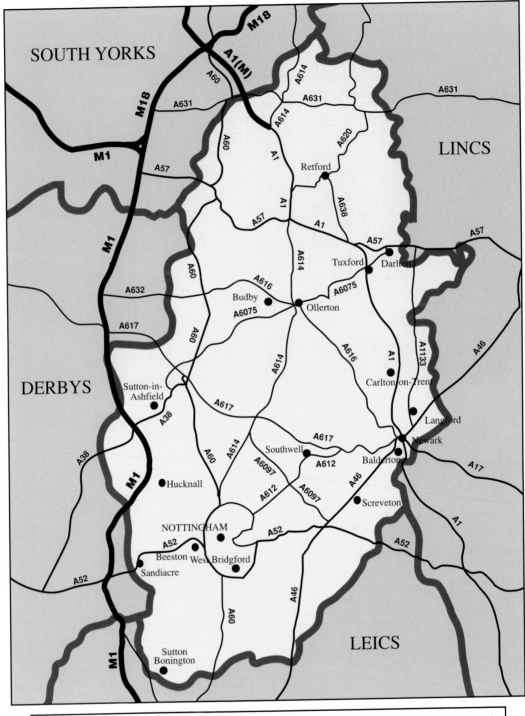

BALDERTON, Nr. Newark

Anthony W. Laywood
Kercheval House, 79 Main St. NG24 3NN. Est. 1967. Open by appointment. SIZE: Medium. *STOCK: Antiquarian books, pre-1850, £20-£8,000.* LOC: 2 miles south of Newark. PARK: Easy. TEL: 01636 659031; fax - 01636 659219; e-mail - books@anthonylaywood.co.uk SER: Valuations; buys at auction.

BEESTON

S. & E.M. Turner Violins
1-5 Lily Grove. NG9 1QL. (Steve and Liz Turner). Est. 1987. Open 9-6, Sat. 9-5. *STOCK: 18th-20th C violins, violas, cellos, basses, bows; old flutes, clarinets, concertinas, guitars, harps, oboes and saxophones.* PARK: Easy. TEL: 0115 943 0333; fax - 0115 943 0444; mobile - 07831 265272; e-mail - info@turnerviolins.co.uk website - www.turnerviolins.co.uk SER: Valuations; restorations.

BUDBY, Nr. Newark

Dukeries Antiques Centre
Thoresby Park. NG22 9EX. (J.A. and J.E. Coupe). Est. 1967. Open 10-5 including Sun. SIZE: Large. *STOCK: Furniture, £25-£8,000; porcelain, £10-£500; pictures, £50-£5,000; all 18th to early 20th C.* LOC: From A1 take A614 towards Nottingham to Ollerton, turn right on to A616. PARK: Easy. TEL: 01623 822252; fax - 01623 822209; e-mail - dukeriesantiques@aol.com SER: Valuations; restorations (furniture). VAT: Stan/Spec.

CARLTON-ON-TRENT, Nr. Newark

Tudor Rose Antiques
Yew Tree Farm. NG23 6NL. (D.H. and C. Rose). Est. 1984. Open by appointment. SIZE: Medium. *STOCK: Furniture, including oak, country, pine, mahogany and walnut; interesting and decorative items, treen.* LOC: Off A1. PARK: Easy. TEL: 01636 821841. FAIRS: Local.

DARLTON

A.J. O'Sullivan Antiques
Whimpton House, Dunham Rd. NG22 0TA. Resident. Est. 1977. Open 9-5, Sat. 9-1. SIZE: Medium. *STOCK: Furniture, 18th-19th C, £200-£4,000: decorative items.* LOC: From A1 take A57 (Lincoln road) at Markham Moor roundabout through Darlton, premises 1/4 mile on left. PARK: Easy. TEL: 01777 228626; fax - same; e-mail - tonyos@btconnect.com SER: Valuations; restorations (furniture). FAIRS: Newark. VAT: Stan/Spec/Global.

HUCKNALL

Ivory Gate
Curiosity Corner, 86 Watnall Rd. NG15 7JW. (B. Orridge and H. Clayton). Est. 1975. Open 9.30-4. CL: Wed. SIZE: Large. *STOCK: Furniture, 18th-19th C, £200-£4,000; porcelain and glass, 18th-20th C, £10-£1,500; general antiques, £5-£500.* LOC: Next to police station. PARK: Easy. TEL: 0115 963 2734; home - 0115 963 0789; mobile - 07799 533272; e-mail - ivorygateantique@aol.com SER: Restorations (furniture including upholstery). FAIRS: Kedleston Hall, Lamport; Derby University; Sandringham; Belvoir Castle.

LANGFORD, Nr. Newark

T. Baker
Langford House Farm. NG23 7RR. Est. 1966. CL: Sun. except by appointment and Sat. SIZE: Medium. *STOCK: Victoriana, period furniture and oak.* LOC: A1133. PARK: Own. TEL: 01636 704026. *Trade Only.*

NEWARK

Castle Gate Antiques Centre
55 Castle Gate. NG24 1BE. Est. 1985. Open 9.30-5. SIZE: Large. *STOCK: Wide variety of general antiques, dealers listed below.* LOC: A46 through town, 250yds. from castle. PARK: Easy. TEL: 01636 700076. SER: Restorations.

Tom Alexander

& Barrington
Fine antique and modern silver. TEL: Mobile - 07850 577724.

Richard Byron-White

Sylvie Collett

Robin Dean

John Dench
Period furniture.

John Harman

Sinclair Antiques
Furniture, pottery, decorative items.

David Walsh
Early pottery.

R.R. Limb Antiques
31-35 Northgate. NG24 1HD. Open 9-6. *STOCK: General antiques and pianos.* TEL: 01636 674546.

M B G Antiques, Fine Art & Jewellery
41B Castlegate. NG24 1BE. (Margaret Begley-Gray). DGA. Est. 1982. Open Wed., Fri. and Sat. 11-4. SIZE: Small. *STOCK: Jewellery, paintings, miniatures, 19th to early 20th C, to £4,000.* PARK: Nearby. TEL: 01636 650790; fax - 01636 679586; mobile - 07702 209808; e-mail - mbegleygray@aol.com SER: Valuations; restorations (jewellery and paintings). FAIRS: NEC; Robert Bailey.

Newark Antiques Centre
Regent House, Lombard St. NG24 1XP. (Marks Tinsley). Est. 1988. Open 9.30-4.30, Sun. 11-4. SIZE: 55 units and 58 cabinets. *STOCK: Georgian, Victorian and period furniture, pottery, porcelain, glass, textiles, militaria, clocks, pictures, books, silver, antiquities, jewellery, paintings, coins, Oriental, pine, oil lamps.* LOC: Opposite bus station. PARK: Own. TEL: 01636 605504; fax - 01636 605101; website - www.newarkantiquescentre.com SER: Upholstery; fabrics; cleaning (metal); valuations; restorations.

Newark Antiques Warehouse   **LAPADA**
Old Kelham Rd. NG24 1BX. Est. 1984. Open 9-5.30,
Sat. and Sun. 10-4. Extended opening during Swinderby
and Newark fairs. SIZE: 30+ dealers, 80+ cabinets.
*STOCK: Mainly 17th-20th C furniture and decorative
items, smalls and collectables.* LOC: Just off A1. PARK:
Easy. TEL: 01636 674869; fax - 01636 612933; e-mail -
enquiries@newarkantiques.co.uk website - www.newark
antiques.co.uk SER: Valuations. FAIRS: Newark
(Sundays).

No. 1 Castlegate Antiques
1-3 Castlegate. NG24 1AZ. (Christine Kavanagh). Est.
1998. Open 9.30-5, Sat. 9.30-5.30. SIZE: Large - 8
dealers. *STOCK: 18th-19th C English mahogany
furniture; 17th-19th C English oak furniture and
decorative objects; all £100-£10,000.* LOC: Town
centre. PARK: Opposite. TEL: 01636 701877; website -
www.castlegateantiques.com SER: Valuations. VAT:
Stan/Spec.

Pearman Antiques & Interiors
9 Castle Gate. NG24 1AZ. (Jan and Stan Parnham and
Sally Moulds). Est. 1996. Open Tues.-Sat. 10-4.30.
SIZE: Medium. *STOCK: Chairs, single and sets,
upholstered, oak, mahogany and walnut, £150-£1,500;
oak, mahogany and walnut chests of drawers, oak mule
and Lancashire chests, chiffoniers, small and side tables,
£350-£3,750, all 18th-19th C. English and Continental
beds, half testers, carved, decorative and brass,*

mahogany, oak and walnut, 19th C, £850-£1,500; LOC:
Opposite castle. PARK: 50 metres. TEL: 01636 679158.

Jack Spratt Antiques
Unit 5 George St. NG24 1LU. Open 8-5.30, Sat. 8-4,
Sun. 10.30-3.30. SIZE: Warehouse. *STOCK: Pine and
oak.* LOC: Near main line railway station, A17 and A1.
PARK: Easy. TEL: 01636 681666/7; fax - 01636 681670.
VAT: Stan.

NOTTINGHAM

**Acanthus Antiques & Collectables
incorporating Dutton & Smith Medals**
140 Derby Rd., Off Canning Circus. NG7 1LR. (Trak E.
and Mrs Smith). Est. 1980. Open 10.30-2.30, Sat. 12.30-
4. SIZE: Small. *STOCK: Ceramics and glass, 19th-20th
C, £5-£1,000; collectors' items, mainly 20th C, £5-£800;
period furniture, 18th-19th C, £200-£1,500; militaria,
medals and badges.* LOC: Derby Rd. exit from Queens
Medical Centre traffic island, continue for 1 mile, shop
on left. PARK: Nearby. TEL: 0115 924 3226; e-mail -
trak.e.smith83@ntlworld.com website - www.acanthus
antiques.co.uk SER: Valuations; restorations (furniture
and ceramics); buys at auction. FAIRS: Newark,
Swinderby, Donington.

Castle Antiques
78 Derby Rd. NG1 5FD. (L. Adamson). Open 9.30-5.
SIZE: 2 floors. *STOCK: General antiques, vintage
lighting, maps and prints.* LOC: City centre. PARK:

Meters. TEL: 0115 947 3913; e-mail - lezadamson @btinternet.com website - www.castleantiques-nottm.co.uk

Cathay Antiques

74 Derby Rd. NG1 5FD. (Paul Shum). Est. 1999. Open 10-5. SIZE: Large. *STOCK: Fine Oriental antiques - furniture, from Qing dynasty, £50-£2,000; porcelain, late 19th to 20th C, £30-£300; ceramics, from AD 800, £90-£2,000; wood craft, 18th-19th C, £20-£400; embroidery, 19th C, £10-£50; Tibetan furniture and thangka, 19th-20th C, £200-£700.* PARK: In front of shop. TEL: 0115 988 1216; fax - same; home - 01664 480633; mobile - 07977 282866; e-mail - jennybu8@hotmail.com FAIRS: Local.

Collectors World

188 Wollaton Rd., Wollaton. NG8 1HJ. (M.T. Ray). Est. 1975. Open 10.30-5. CL: Mon. SIZE: Small. *STOCK: Ancient and modern coins and banknotes, 20th C cigarette and postcards, 19th C medals and accessories, all £1-£100.* LOC: Ring road at A609 Crown Island/Raleigh Island. PARK: Easy. TEL: 0115 928 0347; fax - same. SER: Valuations; buys at auction (coins and banknotes). FAIRS: Newark, Birmingham MSCF; various specialist.

Harlequin Antiques

79-81 Mansfield Rd., Daybrook. NG5 6BE. (Paul Kimche). Est. 1992. Open 9.30-5. SIZE: Large. *STOCK: 18th-19th C pine furniture, £300-£1,200.* LOC: A60 Mansfield road, north from Nottingham. PARK: Easy. TEL: 0115 967 4590; website - www.antiquepine.net SER: Valuations; restorations (pine). VAT: Global/Margin.

D.D. and A. Ingle

380 Carlton Hill. NG4 1JA. Est. 1968. Open 9-5. SIZE: Small. *STOCK: Coins and medals, from Roman, £50-£100; jewellery and watches, £50-£1,000.* PARK: Nearby. TEL: 0115 987 3325; e-mail - ddaingle@talk21.com SER: Valuations; restorations.

Melville Kemp Ltd   LAPADA

79-81 Derby Rd. NG1 5BA. Est. 1900. Open Mon., Wed. and Fri. 10-4. SIZE: Small. *STOCK: Jewellery, Victorian; silver, Georgian and Victorian, both £5-£10,000; ornate English and Continental porcelain, Sheffield plate.* LOC: From Nottingham on main Derby Rd. PARK: Easy. TEL: 0115 941 7055; fax - 0115 941 3075. SER: Valuations; restorations (silver, china, jewellery); buys at auction. VAT: Stan/Spec.

Lights, Camera, Action UK Ltd.

6 Western Gardens, Western Boulevard, Aspley. NG8 5GP. UACC. Est. 1996. Open by appointment. SIZE: Small. *STOCK: Autographs - film, television, sport, historical; Titanic memorabilia.* LOC: Off Nutall Rd. PARK: Easy. TEL: 0115 913 1116; mobile - 07970 342363; e-mail - nickstraw@ntlbusiness.com and lcaukltd@aol.com website - www.lca-autographs.co.uk SER: Valuations; buys at auction. FAIRS: NEC; local.

Michael D. Long

96-98 Derby Rd. NG1 5FB. Est. 1970. Open 9.30-5, Sat. 10-4. SIZE: Large. *STOCK: Arms and armour of all ages and nations.* LOC: From city centre take main Derby Rd., shop on right. PARK: Easy. TEL: 0115 941 3307/947 4137; fax - 0115 941 4199; e-mail - sales @michaeldlong.com website - www.michaeldlong.com VAT: Stan/Spec.

Luna

23 George St. NG1 3BH. (Paul Rose). Est. 1994. Open 10-5.30. SIZE: Small. *STOCK: Design items - glass, ceramics, furniture, telephones, post-war, from £5.* LOC: Near Market Sq. Hockley. PARK: Easy. TEL: 0115 924 3267; e-mail - paul@luna-online.co.uk website - www.luna-online.co.uk VAT: Global.

Anthony Mitchell Fine Paintings

Sunnymede House, 11 Albemarle Rd., Woodthorpe. NG5 4FE. (M. Mitchell). Est. 1965. Open by appointment. *STOCK: Oil paintings, £2,000-£100,000; watercolours, £500-£30,000.* LOC: North on Nottingham ring road to junction with Mansfield road, turn right, then 3rd left. PARK: Easy. TEL: 0115 962 3865; fax - same. SER: Valuations; restorations. VAT: Spec.

Nottingham Architectural Antiques & Reclamation

St. Albans Works, 181 Hartley Rd., Radford. NG7 3DW. (J. Sanders and L. Baldwin). Open 9-6. *STOCK: Georgian, Victorian and Edwardian pine, oak, cast-iron, marble, slate and stone fireplaces; doors, stained and leaded glass, door handles and other door furniture; sanitaryware, gates and railings, reclaimed building materials, flooring and timber.* LOC: Close to city centre. PARK: Easy. TEL: 0115 979 0666; fax - 0115 979 1607; e-mail - admin.naar@ntlworld.com website - www.naar.co.uk SER: Restorations (door stripping, fireplaces and furniture polishing). FAIRS: SALVO Newark and Swinderby.

NSE Medal Dept.

97 Derby Rd. NG1 5BB. (Jeremy Chandler). Est. 2005. Open Tues.-Fri. 10-4, Sat. 10-2. SIZE: Medium. *STOCK: Medals, badges and coins, £5-£1,000+.* LOC: Canning Circus. PARK: Easy. TEL: 0115 950 1882; e-mail - jeremy.chandler@ntlworld.com SER: Valuations; medal mounting and framing.

Top Hat Antiques

62 Derby Rd. NG1 5FD. Est. 1978. Open 10-5. SIZE: 3 floors. *STOCK: Furniture, Georgian to Edwardian; metalware, silver, porcelain, prints, watercolours, oil paintings, glass and collectables.* LOC: A52 town centre. PARK: Meters. TEL: 0115 941 9143; e-mail - info@tophat-antiques.co.uk website - www.tophat-antiques.co.uk VAT: Stan/Spec.

Vintage Wireless Shop

The Hewarths, Sandiacre. NG10 5NQ. (Mr Yates). Est. 1977. Open by appointment. *STOCK: Early wireless and pre-war televisions, crystal sets, horn speakers, valves, books and magazines.* PARK: Easy. TEL: 0115 939 3139; fax - 0115 949 0180; mobile - 07980 912686; e-mail - vintagewireless@aol.com SER: Valuations; repairs; finder.

OLLERTON

Hamlyn Lodge

Station Rd. NG22 9BN. (N. and J.S. Barrows). Est. 1975. Open 10-5. SIZE: Small. *STOCK: General antiques, 18th-20th C, £100-£3,000.* LOC: Off A614. PARK: Easy. TEL: 01623 823600; e-mail - enquiries@hamlynlodge.co.uk website - www.hamlynlodge.co.uk SER: Restorations (furniture).

RETFORD

Stanley Hunt Jewellers

22 The Square. DN22 6DQ. *STOCK: Jewellery and silver including modern.* TEL: 01777 703144.

Ranby Hall   LAPADA

Barnby Moor. DN22 8JQ. (Paul Wyatt). Est. 1980. Open Sat. and Sun. 10-6, other days by appointment. SIZE: Large. *STOCK: Furniture, 18th-20th C, £300-£25,000; mirrors, 19th C to 1930, £500-£15,000; oil paintings, 17th-20th C, £1,500-£10,000; garden urns and furniture, from 19th C, £500-£8,000.* LOC: Take Barnby Moor turning off A1, travel 1/4 mile - drive to house on right. PARK: Easy. TEL: 01777 860696; fax - 01777 701317; e-mail - paul.wyatt@ranbyhall.com website - www.ranbyhall.com SER: Buys at auction (furniture and oils). FAIRS: DMG Newark, LAPADA; Bailey, Tatton Park; RDS Dublin. VAT: Stan/Spec.

SANDIACRE

The Glory Hole

14-16 Station Rd. NG10 5BG. (Colin and Debbie Reid). Est. 1984. Open 10-5.30. CL: Wed. pm. SIZE: Large - 2 floors. *STOCK: Victorian pine, walnut, oak and mahogany furniture; bespoke kitchens; restored fireplaces and reproductions.* PARK: Opposite. TEL: 0115 939 4081; fax - 0115 939 4085. SER: Restorations; stripping; polishing; repairs; reproduction cabinet fittings; fitting.

SCREVETON

Red Lodge Antiques

Fosseway. NG13 8JJ. (L. Bradford). Resident. Est. 1999. Open Mon.-Fri. 9-5, Sat. and Sun. by appointment and prior Newark Fair. SIZE: Large. *STOCK: Shipping furniture, 1900-1930s, £25-£1,000.* LOC: A46 approx. 10 miles from Nottingham and 5 miles from Newark. PARK: Own. TEL: 01949 20244; home - same; e-mail - redlodgeantiques@tradeexport.fsnet.co.uk SER: Container facilites available. *Trade & Export Only.*

SOUTHWELL

Westhorpe Antiques

Old Grapes Inn, Westhorpe. NG25 0NB. (Ralph Downing). Est. 1974. Open 10-5.30, Sun. until 4 - ring bell to gain admittance. SIZE: Small. *STOCK: Furniture, mainly oak, 17th to mid 19th C, £50-£500; brass, copper and pewter, 17th to late 19th C, £10-£200; vintage fishing tackle including reels and rods, stuffed fish, sporting items, £10-£300.* LOC: 15 mins. from Newark. PARK: Easy. TEL: 01636 814095; home - same. SER: Valuations; restorations (furniture). FAIRS: Newark.

SUTTON BONINGTON

Goodacre Engraving

The Dial House, 120 Main St. LE12 5PF. BHI. Est. 1948. Open Mon.-Fri. 9-5 or by appointment. *STOCK: Longcase and bracket clock movements, parts and castings.* LOC: 10 mins. from junction 24, M1. PARK: Easy. TEL: 01509 673082, fax - same; e-mail - goodacre @postmaster.co.uk website - www.ndirect.co.uk/~goodacre SER: Hand engraving; silvering and dial repainting; new hand-made dials. VAT: Stan.

SUTTON-IN-ASHFIELD

Yesterday and Today

82 Station Rd. NG17 5HB. (John and Chris Turner). Resident. Est. 1990. Open Wed.-Sat. 9.30-5.30, Sun. 11-4. SIZE: Medium. *STOCK: Furniture, 1920s-1930s oak and walnut, £50-£500; clocks, 19th C, £100-£2,000; collectables.* LOC: 3 miles from junction 28, M1, take A38 towards Mansfield. PARK: Easy. TEL: 01623 442215; mobile - 07957 552753. FAIRS: Swinderby.

TUXFORD

Sally Mitchell's Gallery

9 Eldon St. NG22 0LB. FATG. Est. 1976. Open Tues.-Sat. 10-5, Sun. and Mon. by appointment. SIZE: Medium. *STOCK: Contemporary sporting and animal paintings, £200-£5,000; limited edition sporting and animal prints, 20th C, £20-£350.* LOC: 1 min. from A1, 14 miles north of Newark. PARK: Easy. TEL: 01777 838 234/198; e-mail - info@sallymitchell.com website - www.sallymitchell.com FAIRS: CLA Game and Burghley Horse Trials. VAT: Stan/Spec.

WEST BRIDGFORD

Portland Antiques & Curios

5 Portland Rd. NG2 6DN. (Brendan and Carole Sprakes). Est. 1999. Open Wed.-Sat. 10-5, other days by appointment. SIZE: Small. *STOCK: Furniture, £50-£750; china, £5-£150; jewellery, £10-£300; mainly 19th-20th C.* LOC: Off Melton Rd. PARK: Easy. TEL: 0115 914 2123; fax - same; home - 0115 914 8614. SER: Delivery. VAT: Stan.

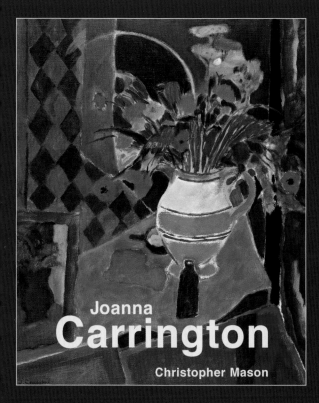

Joanna
Carrington

Christopher Mason

- *The first overview of Joanna Carrington's pictorial output*

- *Published to coincide with an exhibition of Carrington's work at the Thackeray Gallery*

- *Including previously unpublished letters and illustrations*

- *Features over 70 illustrations and line drawings*

"An artist born" is the phrase which introduces the painter Joanna Carrington (1931-2003) in this fully illustrated survey of her life. Joanna was the daughter of Noel Carrington who created Puffin books and niece of the famous Bloomsbury artist Dora Carrington, who committed suicide following the death of Lytton Strachey. At just seventeen years old she was described by Cedric Morris as "really exceptional and a born painter. I have never had a student who showed so much promise". Joanna later studied under Léger in Paris.

Joanna wrote and illustrated hundreds of letters, which together with photographs of the artist and witty caricatures of her friends, provided the author, her husband Christopher Mason, with material for this memoir.

The chief glory of this beautiful book is in the sixty colour illustrations of Joanna Carrington's still lifes, interiors and landscapes from different periods of her life. The book also deals with her *alter ego* Reginald Pepper, whose naïve art was exhibited for a number of years without anybody being aware of the identity of the real artist.

Christopher Mason studied painting at the Chelsea Art School, and in 1951, won a £100 grant which took him to Paris. He survived there, as painter, book jacket designer and English teacher, for ten years, marrying Joanna Carrington in 1966.

Returning to England he began a twelve-year career as a film maker – producing and directing films on architecture and painting for The Arts Council of Great Britain. He made films with Yehudi Menuhin, a comedy with Spike Milligan, a feature film shown at the Cannes Film Festival in 1973 and a film portrait of the artist Duncan Grant. More recently, he has written a novel, an opera libretto and much poetry, including the words for two song cycles.

Specifications:
104pp., 60 col. illus., 14 b.&w. illus.,
9½ x 7½in./240 x 195mm.
£16.50 (hardback)

For full details of all ACC publications, log on to our website:
www.antiquecollectorsclub.com
or telephone 01394 389950 for a free catalogue

OXFORDSHIRE

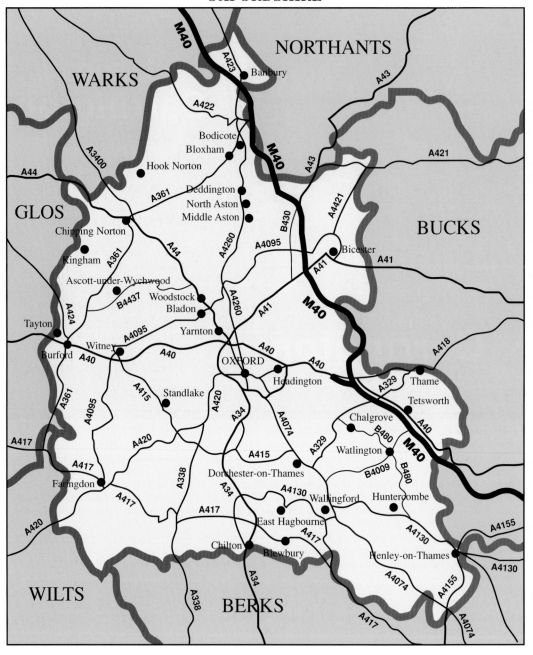

Dealers and Shops in Oxfordshire

Ascott-under-Wychwood	1	Chalgrove	1	Henley-on-Thames	10	Taynton	1
Banbury	1	Chilton	1	Hook Norton	1	Tetsworth	2
Bicester	1	Chipping Norton	9	Huntercombe	1	Thame	1
Bladon	1	Deddington	2	Kingham	1	Wallingford	8
Blewbury	1	Dorchester-on-Thames	2	Middle Aston	1	Watlington	1
Bloxham	1	East Hagbourne	2	North Aston	1	Witney	4
Bodicote	1	Faringdon	3	Oxford	13	Woodstock	7
Burford	13	Headington	1	Standlake	1	Yarnton	1

ASCOTT-UNDER-WYCHWOOD

William Antiques
Manor Farm. OX7 6AL. (Robert Gripper). Est. 1982. Open Mon.-Fri. 9-5. SIZE: Medium. *STOCK: Victorian and Georgian furniture, mainly mahogany.* LOC: Between river bridge and level crossing. PARK: Easy. TEL: 01993 831960; home - same; fax - 01993 830395; e-mail - robgripper@aol.com SER: Valuations; restorations. VAT: Margin.

BANBURY

Banbury Antique Centre
18 Southam Rd. OX16 2EG. (Angela Walsham and Veronica Hammond). Open 10-5, Sun. 11-4. SIZE: 3 floors, 40 dealers. *STOCK: Georgian-Edwardian furniture, gold, silver and platinum jewellery, books, militaria, glass, lighting, mirrors, pottery and porcelain, pictures and paintings.* PARK: Easy and Castle St. TEL: 01295 267800; mobile - 07968 870019. SER: Valuations.

BICESTER

R.A. Barnes   LAPADA
PO Box 82. OX25 1RA. Open by appointment. *STOCK: English, Oriental and Continental porcelain, antiques and collectables; Wedgwood, ironstone, china, glass, copper, domestic brass and other metals, 19th C; Bohemian and art glass, primitive paintings.* TEL: 01844 237388. VAT: Stan/Spec.

BLADON, Nr. Woodstock

Park House Antiques Ltd
26 Park St. OX20 1RW. (T. Thomas). Resident. Est. 1996. Open daily including Sun. SIZE: Medium. *STOCK: Furniture and decorative smalls.* LOC: On A4095 Woodstock to Witney road. PARK: Own. TEL: 01993 813888; e-mail - info@parkhouseantiques.co.uk website - www.parkhouseantiques.co.uk SER: Valuations; restorations; buys at auction.

BLEWBURY

Blewbury Antiques
London Rd. OX11 9NX. (E. Richardson). Est. 1971. Open 10-6 including weekends. CL: Tues. and Wed. *STOCK: General antiques, books, bric-a-brac, country and garden items, oil lamps and oil lamp parts.* PARK: Own. TEL: 01235 850366.

BLOXHAM, Nr. Banbury

H.C. Dickins
High St. OX15 4LT. (P. and H.R. Dickins). Open 10-5.30, Sat. 10-1. *STOCK: 19th-20th C British sporting and landscape paintings, watercolours, drawings and prints.* TEL: 01295 721949; website - www. hcdickins.co.uk

BODICOTE, Nr. Banbury

Cotefield Antiques
Cotefield Farm, Oxford Rd. OX15 4AQ. (Joseph Smith). Open 12-4 or by appointment. SIZE: Large. STOCK: General antiques especially furniture (including upholstered); oils and watercolours. LOC: Banbury-Oxford road, opposite Banbury Rugby Club. PARK: Own. TEL: 01295 254754. e-mail - antiques@greatenglishimports.co.uk

BURFORD

Antiques @ The George
104 High St. OX18 4QJ. (C. Oswald and A. Palmer). Est. 1992. Open 10-5, Sun. 12-5. SIZE: Large. STOCK: General antiques including china, furniture, textiles, silver, plate, books, glass, pictures, early 18th C to 1930s. LOC: Main road. PARK: Around corner. TEL: 01993 823319; e-mail - ask@antiquesatthegeorge.com website - www.antiquesatthegeorge.com SER: Shipping arranged.

Burford Antique Centre
Cheltenham Rd., At the Roundabout. OX18 4JA. (G. Viventi). Est. 1979. Open 10-6 including Sun. SIZE: Large. STOCK: Furniture, 18th-19th C, £100-£5,000; china and pictures. LOC: A40. PARK: Easy. TEL: 01993 823227. SER: Restorations (furniture including re-leathering).

Bygones
29 High St. OX18 4RN. (C.B. Jenkins). Est. 1986. Open 10-1 and 2-5, Sat. 10-5, Sun. 12-5. SIZE: Small. STOCK: Prints and pictures, 1900s, £5-£50; china and glass, curios, 1880-1950, £5-£250. LOC: A40. PARK: Easy. TEL: 01993 823588; fax - 01993 704338; e-mail - sales@bygones-of-burford.co.uk

Jonathan Fyson Antiques
50 High St. OX18 4QF. (J.R. Fyson). CADA. Est. 1970. Open 9.30-1 and 2-5.30, Sat. from 10. SIZE: Medium. STOCK: English and Continental furniture, decorative brass and steel including lighting and fireplace accessories; mirrors, porcelain, table glass, jewellery. LOC: At junction of A40/A361 between Oxford and Cheltenham. PARK: Easy. TEL: 01993 823204; fax - same; home - 01367 860223; e-mail - j@fyson.co.uk SER: Valuations. VAT: Spec.

Gateway Antiques
Cheltenham Rd., Burford Roundabout. OX18 4JA. (M.C. Ford and P. Brown). CADA. Est. 1986. Open 10-5.30 and Sun. 2-5. SIZE: Large. STOCK: English and Continental furniture, 18th to early 20th C; decorative accessories. LOC: On roundabout (A40) Oxford/Cheltenham road, adjacent to the Cotswold Gateway Hotel. PARK: Easy. TEL: 01993 823678; fax - 01993 823857; e-mail - enquiries@gatewayantiques. co.uk website - www.gatewayantiques.co.uk SER: Courier (multi-lingual). VAT: Stan/Spec.

Horseshoe Antiques and Gallery
97 High St. OX18 4QA. (B. Evans). Open 9-5.30, Sun. by appointment. SIZE: Medium. STOCK: Clocks including longcase (all fully restored); early oak and country furniture; oil paintings and watercolours;

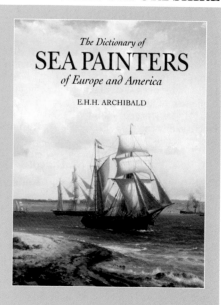
copper and brass, horse brasses. LOC: East side of High St. PARK: Easy. TEL: 01993 823244; fax - 01993 822429. VAT: Spec.

Hubert's Antiques
Burford Roundabout, Cheltenham Rd. OX18 4JA. (A.L. Mollere). Est. 1987. Open 10-5.30. SIZE: Medium. *STOCK: Furniture, £150-£15,000; oils, £50-£10,000; clocks, £250-£12,000; all 17th C onwards.* LOC: A40 halfway between Oxford and Cheltenham. PARK: Easy. TEL: 01993 822151; fax - same; e-mail - hubertsantiques @onetel.com SER: Shipping. VAT: Spec.

David Pickup   BADA
115 High St. OX18 4RG. CADA. Est. 1977. Open 9.30-1 and 2-5.30, Sat. 10-1 and 2-4. SIZE: Medium. STOCK: Fine furniture, works of art, from £500+; decorative objects, from £100+; all late 17th to mid 20th C, specialising in Arts and Crafts. PARK: Easy. TEL: 01993 822555. FAIRS: Olympia. VAT: Spec.

Manfred Schotten Antiques
109 High St. OX18 4RG. CADA. Est. 1974. Open 9.30-5.30 or by appointment. SIZE: 3 floors and trade warehouse open by appointment. *STOCK: Sporting antiques and library furniture.* PARK: Easy. TEL: 01993 822302; fax - 01993 822055; e-mail - antiques@schotten.com website - www.schotten.com SER: Restorations; trophies. FAIRS: Olympia (Summer). VAT: Stan/Margin.

Brian Sinfield Gallery Ltd
150 High St. OX18 4QU. CADA. Est. 1972. Open 10-5.30, Mon. by appointment. SIZE: Medium. *STOCK: Mainly contemporary and late 20th C paintings and watercolours.* PARK: Easy. TEL: 01993 824464; e-mail - gallery@briansinfield.com website - www.brian sinfield.com SER: 8 exhibitions annually; art brokers. VAT: Spec.

The Stone Gallery
93 High St. OX18 4QA. (Mrs Phyllis M. and Simon Marshall). Est. 1918. Open 9.15-6. SIZE: Medium. *STOCK: Pre-Raphaelite and modern British pictures, 1840-1980, £120-£30,000; paperweights, from 1840, £50-£15,000; enamel boxes, from 1760, £50-£1,000; designer jewellery.* LOC: Halfway down High St. PARK: Easy. TEL: 01993 823302; fax/home - same; e-mail - mail@stonegallery.co.uk website - www.stonegallery. co.uk SER: Valuations (paperweights); buys at auction (pictures and paperweights). VAT: Stan/Spec.

Swan Gallery
High St. OX18 4RE. (D. Pratt). CADA. Est. 1966. Open 10-5.30. SIZE: Large. *STOCK: Country furniture in oak, yew, walnut and fruitwood, 17th-19th C, £300-£12,000; Staffordshire figures and small decorative items, 18th-20th C, £50-£800.* PARK: Easy. TEL: 01993 822244. VAT: Mainly Spec.

Wren Gallery
34 Lower High St. OX18 4RR. (S. Hall and G. Mitchell). Est. 1986. Open 10-5.30. SIZE: Medium. *STOCK: 19th-20th C watercolours and drawings.* TEL: 01993 823495. SER: Valuations; restorations (watercolours); buys at auction (watercolours). VAT: Spec.

CHALGROVE, Nr. Oxford

Rupert Hitchcox Antiques
Warpsgrove Lane. OX44 7RW. (P. and R. Hitchcox). Est. 1957. Open Tues.-Sat. 10-5 or by appointment. SIZE: Large - 6 barns. *STOCK: 17th-20th C furniture.* LOC: Halfway between Oxford and Henley, just off the B480, 6 miles from junction 6, M40. PARK: Easy. TEL: 01865 890241; fax - same; mobile - 07710 561505; e-mail - rupertsantiques@aol.com website - www.ruperthitchcox antiques.co.uk VAT: Stan/Spec.

CHILTON, Nr. Didcot

Country Markets Antiques and Collectables
at Country Gardens Garden Centre, Newbury Rd. OX11 0QN. (G.W. Vaughan). Est. 1991. Open 10-5, Mon. 10.30-5, Sun. 10.30-4.30. SIZE: Large - 30 dealers. *STOCK: Wide variety of general antiques including furniture, books, jewellery, porcelain, militaria, cased fish and fishing tackle, £5-£5,000.* LOC: Off A34 near Harwell, 10 mins. from junction 13, M4, 20 mins. from Oxford. PARK: Easy. TEL: 01235 835125; fax - 01235 833068; e-mail - country.markets.antiques@breathemail.net website - www.countrymarkets.co.uk SER: Restorations (furniture and ceramics).

CHIPPING NORTON

Chipping Norton Antique Centre
Ivy House, 1 Market Place and 21/44 West St. OX7 5NH. (G. Wissinger). Open 10-5.30 including Sun. SIZE: 20 dealers. *STOCK: A wide variety of smalls and furniture.* PARK: Own. TEL: 01608 644212.

Georgian House Antiques   LAPADA
21 West St. OX7 5EU. (Georg and Sheila Wissinger). Est. 1974. Open 9-6. *STOCK: 17th-19th C furniture and paintings.* LOC: West end of town. PARK: Easy. TEL: 01608 641369. SER: Restorations. VAT: Stan.

Jonathan Howard
21 Market Place. OX7 5NA. (J.G. Howard). Est. 1979. Open by appointment or ring bell. SIZE: Small. *STOCK: Clocks - longcase, wall and carriage, 18th-19th C.* TEL: 01608 643065. SER: Valuations; restorations (movement, dials and cases).

Key Antiques
11 Horse Fair. OX7 5AL. (Jane and Keith Riley). CADA. Open 10-5.30 or by appointment. CL: Mon. and Tues. SIZE: Medium. *STOCK: English period oak and country furniture, 17th-19th C; domestic metalware, early portraits, pottery and associated items.* LOC: Main road. PARK: Easy. TEL: 01608 644992/643777; e-mail - info@keyantiques.com website - www.keyantiques.com VAT: Spec.

Manchester House Antiques Centre
5a Market Place. OX7 5NA. (Mrs M. Shepherd). Est. 1997. Open 7 days 10-5. SIZE: Medium - 5 dealers. *STOCK: Wide range of general antiques including furniture, china, kitchenalia, copper and brass.* LOC: Town centre. PARK: Nearby. TEL: 01608 646412; e-mail - mshepherd@onetel.com website - www. chippingnorton.net

The Quiet Woman Antiques Centre
Southcombe. OX7 5QH. (David Belcher and Ann Marriott). Est. 1998. Open 10-5.30, Sun. 11-5. SIZE: Large - several dealers. *STOCK: Wide variety of general antiques.* PARK: Own. TEL: 01608 646262; fax - same; e-mail - quietwomanantiq@aol.com

Station Mill Antiques Centre
Station Rd. OX7 5HX. (M.T. Langer). Est. 1994. Open 10-5 including Sun. SIZE: Large. *STOCK: Furniture, fine art, bric-a-brac and collectables, 17th-20th C, £2-£2,000.* LOC: Just out of town off A44 towards Moreton-in-Marsh. PARK: Easy. TEL: 01608 644563; e-mail - info@stationmill.com website - www.stationmill.com

TRADA
21 High St. OX7 5AD. (Valerie Perkins). Est. 1978. Open 9-5. CL: Mon. SIZE: Small. *STOCK: Antiquarian maps and engravings, 1600-1900.* PARK: Nearby. TEL: 01608 644325; e-mail - val_perkins@hotmail.com SER: Print renovation; colouring; picture frame making.

Peter Wiggins
Raffles Farm, Southcombe. OX7 5QH. Est. 1969. Usually available. *STOCK: Barometers.* LOC: 1 mile from Chipping Norton on A34. TEL: 01608 642652; home - same. SER: Valuations; restorations (barometers, clocks, automata); repairs (clocks); buys at auction.

DEDDINGTON

Castle Antiques Ltd   LAPADA
Manor Farm, Clifton. OX15 0PA. (J. and J. Vaughan). Est. 1968. Open Thurs., Fri. and Sat. 10-5 or by appointment. SIZE: Large. *STOCK: Furniture, £25-£3,000; silver, metalware, £10-£1,000; pottery, porcelain, £10-£2,000; kitchenalia.* LOC: B4031, 6 miles from junction 10, M40. PARK: Own. TEL: 01869 338688. VAT: Stan/Spec.

Deddington Antiques Centre
Laurel House, Bull Ring, Market Sq. OX15 0TT. (Mrs B. J. Haller). TVADA. Est. 1972. Open 10-5, Sun. 11-5. SIZE: 11 rooms on 4 floors. *STOCK: Furniture, Georgian to 1930s, £100-£4,000; porcelain, glass, silver, pictures, linen, books, jewellery, 1700-1930, £5-£5,000; collectables, £10-£200.* LOC: 10 mins. junction 10 M40. PARK: Easy and free. TEL: 01869 338968; fax - 01869 338916. SER: Valuations; shipping. FAIRS: TVADA.

DORCHESTER-ON-THAMES

Dorchester Antiques   LAPADA
The Barn, 3 High St. OX10 7HH. (J. and S. Hearnden). TVADA. Est. 1992. Open Tues.-Sat. 10-5. SIZE: Medium. *STOCK: Furniture including chairs and decorative country pieces, 18th-19th C.* LOC: Opposite Abbey. PARK: Easy. TEL: 01865 341373. SER: Restorations; finder. FAIRS: TVADA.

Hallidays (Fine Antiques) Ltd   LAPADA
The Old College, High St. OX10 7HL. TVADA. CINOA. Est. 1950. Open 9-5, Sat. 10-1 and 2-4. SIZE: Large. *STOCK: English and Continental furniture, 17th-19th C; paintings, decorative and small items, 18th-19th C; pine and marble mantelpieces, firegrates, fenders, 18th-20th; bespoke room panelling.* LOC: 8 miles south-

east of Oxford. PARK: At rear. TEL: 01865 340028/68; fax - 01865 341149; e-mail - antiques@ hallidays.com website - www.hallidays.com FAIRS: LAPADA; International Antiques, Chicago. VAT: Stan/Spec.

EAST HAGBOURNE

Craig Barfoot
Tudor House. OX11 9LR. Est. 1993. Open any time by appointment. SIZE: Medium. *STOCK: Longcase clocks, £3,000-£20,000; bracket and lantern clocks.* LOC: Just off A34 halfway between Oxford and Newbury. PARK: Easy. TEL: 01235 818968; home - same; mobile - 07710 858158; e-mail - craig.barfoot@tiscali.co.uk SER: Restorations (clocks); buys at auction (clocks, English oak furniture). VAT: Spec.

E.M. Lawson and Co
Kingsholm. OX11 9LN. (W.J. and K.M. Lawson MBE). ABA. Est. 1921. Usually open 10-5 but appointment preferred. CL: Sat. *STOCK: Antiquarian and rare books, 1500-1900.* PARK: Easy. TEL: 01235 812033. VAT: Stan.

FARINGDON

Aston Pine Antiques
16-18 London St. SN7 7AA. (P. O'Gara). Est. 1982. Open Wed.-Sat. 9-5. *STOCK: Victorian and Continental pine; Victorian fireplaces, doors and bathrooms.* TEL: 01367 243840. SER: Stripping (pine).

Brushwood Antiques
29 Marlborough St. SN7 7JL. (Nathan Sherriff). TVADA. Est. 1989. Open Tues.-Sat. 10-5.30 appointment advisable. SIZE: Small. *STOCK: Fine British and French 18th-19th C furniture and works of art, £100-£15,000.* LOC: Edge of town centre. PARK: Easy. TEL: 01367 244269; mobile - 07768 360350; e-mail - nathan@brushwoodantiques.com website - www.brushwoodantiques.com SER: Valuations; restorations (furniture). FAIRS: TVADA.

Oxford Architectural Antiques
16-18 London St. SN7 7AA. (M. O'Gara). Open Wed.-Sat. 9-5. *STOCK: Fireplaces, fixtures and fittings, doors.* TEL: 01367 242268; mobile - 07973 922393. SER: Packing and container. VAT: Margin.

HEADINGTON, Nr. Oxford

Barclay Antiques
107 Windmill Rd. OX3 7BT. (C. Barclay). Est. 1979. Open 10-5.30. CL: Wed. SIZE: Small. *STOCK: Porcelain, silver, furniture and metalware, 18th-19th C, £50-£100; period lamps, 20th C, £50-£500.* PARK: Own at rear. TEL: 01865 769551; e-mail - barclay_antiques@yahoo.com SER: Valuations.

HENLEY-ON-THAMES

Friday Street Antique Centre (The Ferret)
4 Friday St. RG9 1AH. (D. Etherington and C. Fentum). Est. 1985. Open 10-5.30, Sun. 12-5.30. SIZE: 6 dealers. *STOCK: Furniture, china, silver, books, pictures,*

musical instruments, unusual items. LOC: Second left after Henley bridge, then first left, business on right. PARK: Easy. TEL: 01491 574104.

Jonkers Rare Books
24 Hart St. RG9 2AU. (Christiaan Jonkers). ABA. ILAB. PBFA. Est. 1990. Open 10-5.30. SIZE: Medium. *STOCK: Fine and rare books, 1800-1950, £50-£50,000.* LOC: Main road. PARK: Easy. TEL: 01491 576427; fax - 01491 573805; e-mail - info@jonkers.co.uk website - www.jonkers.co.uk SER: Valuations; buys at auction (rare books). FAIRS: Olympia.

The Barry Keene Gallery
12 Thameside. RG9 1BH. (B.M. and J.S. Keene). FATG. Est. 1971. Open 9.30-5.30 and by appointment. *STOCK: Antique, modern and contemporary art, paintings, watercolours, drawings, etchings, prints and sculpture.* LOC: Junction 8/9 M4, over Henley bridge, left along riverside, 5th building on right. TEL: 01491 577119; e-mail - barrykeene@fsbdial.co.uk website - www.barrykeenegallery.com SER: Restorations; conservation; framing; cleaning; relining; gilding; export. VAT: Stan/Spec.

Richard J. Kingston
BADA
95 Bell St. RG9 2BD. Open 9.30-5 or by appointment. SIZE: Medium. *STOCK: Furniture, 17th to early 19th C; silver, porcelain, glass, paintings, antiquarian and secondhand books.* PARK: Easy. TEL: 01491 574535; home - 01491 573133. SER: Restorations. FAIRS: Surrey. VAT: Stan/Spec.

Knights Antiques
5 Friday St. RG9 1AN. (S.J. and M.L. Knight). Est. 1988. Open 9.30-5.30, Sun. 11.30-5.30. SIZE: Small. *STOCK: English country furniture, 1600-1800, £500-£10,000; pewter, 1600-1900, £10-£1,000; Persian tribal and village carpets and rugs, pre-1900 to modern, £200-£5,000.* LOC: Town centre. PARK: Easy. TEL: 01491 414124; fax - 01491 414117; mobile - 07774 644478; e-mail - simon@knightsantiques.co.uk website - www.knightsantiques.co.uk FAIRS: Cleaning and restorations (carpets and rugs).

The Old French Mirror Co Ltd
Unit 2 Hernes Estate. RG9 4NT. (Roger and Bridget Johnson). Resident. Est. 1999. Open by appointment. SIZE: Large. *STOCK: French mirrors, 19th to early 20th C.* LOC: 3 miles from Henley-on-Thames. PARK: Easy. TEL: 01189 482444; fax - same; e-mail - info@oldfrenchmirrors.com website - www.oldfrenchmirrors.com SER: Shipping. FAIRS: House and Garden; Olympia (June); local. VAT: Spec.

Stephen Orton Antiques
By appointment only. *STOCK: 18th-19th C furniture, some decorative items.* TEL: 01189 402660; mobile - 07788 444144; e-mail - Orton.Antiques@aol.com SER: Supply and pack containers; buying agent. VAT: Stan/Spec.

Thames Oriental Rug Co
Thames Carpet Cleaners Ltd, Newtown Rd. RG9 1HG. (B. and Mrs A. Javadi-Babreh). Resident. Est. 1955. Open 9-12.30 and 1.30-5, Sat. 9-12.30. SIZE: Large *STOCK: Oriental rugs, mid-19th C to modern.* PARK

Easy. TEL: 01491 574676/577877. SER: Valuations; restorations; cleaning. VAT: Stan.

Tudor House Antiques
49 Duke St. RG9 1UR. (David and Linda Potter). Open 10-5 including Sun. *STOCK: Furniture, garden ornaments, architectural items, brass, copper, tools, glass, china, silver and plate, 1750s to 1950s.* LOC: Town centre. PARK: Nearby. TEL: 01491 573680; home - 01491 577808. SER: Valuations.

Richard Way Bookseller
54 Friday St. RG9 1AH. (Diana Cook and Richard Way). ABA. Est. 1977. Open 10-5.30. SIZE: Small. *STOCK: Rare and secondhand books, £5-£1,000.* LOC: Over Henley bridge, turn immediately left behind Angel public house, follow river, turn right, shop past Anchor public house. PARK: At rear. TEL: 01491 576663; fax - 01491 576663. SER: Valuations; restorations. VAT: Stan.

HOOK NORTON

James Holiday Ltd
Wychford Lodge Farmhouse. OX15 5BX. (James and Nicky Holiday). Est. 1865. Open Mon.-Fri. 10-4. SIZE: Medium. *STOCK: Furniture, pottery, porcelain, paintings and decorative items.* LOC: Just outside village on Whichford Rd. PARK: Easy. TEL: 01608 730101; fax - 01608 737537; mobile - 07771 825466; e-mail - jamesgholiday@hotmail.com FAIRS: Swinderby, Ardingly, Newark.

HUNTERCOMBE

The Country Seat   LAPADA
Huntercombe Manor Barn. RG9 5RY. (Harvey Ferry and William Clegg). TVADA. Est. 1965. Open 9-5.30, Sat. 10-5, Sun. by appointment. SIZE: Large. *STOCK: Furniture - signed and designed, 1700-1970; garden and architectural/panelling; art pottery and metalwork, lighting and Whitefriars glass.* LOC: Signed off A4130. PARK: Easy. TEL: 01491 641349; fax - 01491 641533; e-mail - ferry&clegg@thecountryseat.com website - www.thecountryseat.com and www.whitefriarsglass.com SER: Restorations; exhibitions. FAIRS: TVADA; Radley. VAT: Spec.

KINGHAM, Nr. Chipping Norton

Winston Antiques
Clive Payne Restorations, Unit 11 Langston Priory Workshops. OX7 6UR. Open 8-6, Sat. 9-1 or by appointment. *STOCK: 17th-19th C furniture, Mason's ironstone.* TEL: 01608 658856; e-mail - clive.payne@virgin.net website - www.clive.payne.co.uk SER: Restorations.

MIDDLE ASTON, Nr. Bicester

Cotswold Pine & Associates
The Old Poultry Farm. OX25 5QL. (R.J. Prancks). Est. 1980. Open 9-6, Sun. 10-4.30. SIZE: Large. *STOCK: Furniture, 18th-20th C.* LOC: Off A4260, 15 mins. from M40. PARK: Easy. TEL: 01869 340963. SER: Restorations; stripping; polishing; repairs. VAT: Stan/Spec.

NORTH ASTON

Elizabeth Harvey-Lee
1 West Cottages, Middle Aston Lane. OX25 5QB. Est. 1986. Open by appointment. *STOCK: Original prints, 15th-20th C; artists' etchings, engravings, lithographs, £100-£6,000.* LOC: 6 miles from junction 10, M40, 15 miles north of Oxford. TEL: 01869 34716; e-mail - north.aston@btinternet.com SER: Illustrated catalogue available twice yearly (£16 p.a.). FAIRS: London Original Print, Royal Academy; Olympia (June, Nov); Le Salon de l'Estampe, Paris. VAT: Spec.

OXFORD

Antiques on High Ltd
85 High St. OX1 4BG. (Paul Lipson and Sally Young). TVADA. Est. 1982. Open 10-5, Sun. and Bank Holidays 11-5. SIZE: Large - 35 dealers. *STOCK: Small antiques and collectables including jewellery, silver and plate, ceramics, glass, antiquities, watches, books and coins, 17th-20th C.* LOC: Opposite Queen's Lane. PARK: St Clements, Westgate, Seacourt/Thornhill Park and Ride. TEL: 01865 251075; e-mail - antiquesonhigh@aol.com SER: Valuations; restorations (jewellery, silver including replating). FAIRS: TVADA.

Blackwell's Rare Books
48-51 Broad St. OX1 3BQ. ABA. ILAB. PBFA. Est. 1879. Open 9-6, Tues. 9.30-6. SIZE: Large. *STOCK: Antiquarian and rare modern books.* PARK: Easy. TEL: 01865 333555; fax - 01865 794143; e-mail - rarebooks@blackwell.co.uk website - www.rarebooks.blackwell.co.uk SER: Buys at auction; 3-4 catalogues annually. FAIRS: ABA (Olympia); PBFA (Oxford). VAT: Stan/Spec.

The Corner Shop
29 Walton St. OX2 6AA. (P. Hitchcox and D. Florey). Est. 1978. Open 10-5. *STOCK: Pictures, china, glass, silver, small furniture and general items.* LOC: Central north Oxford. TEL: 01865 553364.

Reginald Davis Ltd   BADA
34 High St. OX1 4AN. Est. 1941. Open Tues.-Fri. 9-5, Sat. 10-6. *STOCK: Silver, English and Continental, 17th to early 19th C; jewellery, Sheffield plate, Georgian and Victorian.* LOC: On A40. PARK: Nearby. TEL: 01865 248347. SER: Valuations; restorations (silver, jewellery). VAT: Stan/Spec.

Jeremy's (Oxford Stamp Centre)
98 Cowley Rd. OX4 1JE. Open 10-12.30 and 2-5. *STOCK: Stamps and postcards.* TEL: 01865 241011; website - www.postcard.co.uk/jeremys

Jericho Books
48 Walton St. OX2 6AD. (Frank Stringer). PBFA. Est. 1980. Open 10.30-6, Sun. 12-5. SIZE: Medium. *STOCK: Secondhand and antiquarian books.* PARK: Easy. TEL: 01865 511992; e-mail - shop@jerichobooks.com website - www.jerichobooks.com SER: Valuations; buys at auction (antiquarian books). FAIRS: Royal National Hotel. VAT: Stan.

Christopher Legge Oriental Carpets
25 Oakthorpe Rd., Summertown. OX2 7BD. (C.T. Legge).

Est. 1970. Open 9.30-5. SIZE: Medium. *STOCK: Rugs, various sizes, 19th to early 20th C, £300-£15,000.* LOC: Near shopping parade. PARK: Easy. TEL: 01865 557572; fax - 01865 554877; e-mail - orientalcarpets@btclick.com SER: Valuations; restorations; re-weaving; handcleaning. VAT: Stan/ Margin.

Laurie Leigh Antiques   LAPADA
36 High St. OX1 4AN. (L. and D. Leigh). Est. 1963. Open 10.30-5.30. CL: Thurs. *STOCK: Glass; keyboard musical instruments.* TEL: 01865 244197; e-mail - laurie leigh@hotmail.com; website - www.laurieleighantiques. com and www.davidleigh.com SER: Restorations (keyboards). VAT: Stan/Spec.

Oriental Rug Gallery Ltd
15 Woodstock Rd. OX2 6HA. (Richard Mathias, Julian Blair and Christopher Mould). BORDA. Est. 1989. Open 10-5.30. *STOCK: Russian, Afghan, Turkish and Persian, antique, decorative, classic and Art Deco carpets, rugs and kelims; Oriental objets d'art;* TEL: +44 (0) 1865 316333; fax - same; e-mail - rugs@orientalruggallery. com website - www.orientalruggallery.com SER: Cleaning, repairs and valuations.

Payne and Son (Goldsmiths) Ltd   **BADA**
131 High St. OX1 4DH. (E.P., G.N. and J.D. Payne, P.J. Coppock, A. Salmon and D. Thornton). Est. 1790. Open Mon.-Fri. 9.30-5.30. SIZE: Medium. *STOCK: British silver, antique, modern and secondhand; jewellery, all £50-£10,000+.* LOC: Town centre near Carfax traffic lights. PARK: 800yds. TEL: 01865 243787; fax - 01865 793241; e-mail - silver@payneandson.co.uk website - www.payneandson.co.uk SER: Restorations (English silver). FAIRS: BADA; Chelsea (Spring); Olympia (Autumn). VAT: Stan/Spec.

Sanders of Oxford Ltd
Salutation House, 104 High St. OX1 4BW. Open 10-6. SIZE: Large. *STOCK: Prints, especially Oxford; maps and Japanese woodcuts.* TEL: 01865 242590; fax - 01865 721748; e-mail - soxinfo@btclick.com website - www.sandersofoxford.com SER: Restorations; framing. FAIRS: PBFA (Russell Hotel London); London Original Print. VAT: Margin/Global.

St. Clements Antiques
93 St. Clements St. OX4 1AR. (Giles Power). Est. 1998. Open 10.30-5. SIZE: Medium. *STOCK: Oak and country items, 18th-19th C, £50-£5,000; interesting curios, 18th-20th C, £5-£500.* LOC: Close to city centre, next to Magdalen Bridge. PARK: Easy, opposite. TEL: 01865 727010; home - 01865 200359. SER: Valuations. VAT: Stan/Spec.

Waterfield's
52 High St. OX1 4AS. ABA. PBFA. Est. 1973. Open 9.45-5.45. *STOCK: Antiquarian and secondhand books, all subjects, especially academic in the humanities; literature, history, philosophy, 17th-18th C English.* TEL: 01865 721809.

STANDLAKE, Nr. Witney

Manor Farm Antiques
Manor Farm. OX29 7RL. (C.W. Leveson-Gower). Est. 1964. Open daily, Sun. by appointment. SIZE: Large. *STOCK: Victorian brass and iron beds.* PARK: Easy, in farmyard. TEL: 01865 300303.

TAYNTON, Nr. Burford

Wychwood Antiques
Upper Farm Cottage. OX18 4UH. (R.K. Walker). Open by appointment. *STOCK: English country furniture, Mason's Ironstone, treen, metalware and decorative items.* TEL: 01993 822860. VAT: Spec.

TETSWORTH, Nr. Thame

Quillon Antiques of Tetsworth
The Old Stores, 42a High St. OX9 7AS. (P.W. Magrath). Est. 1993. Open Tues.-Thurs. 10-5, Sat. 10-6, Sun. 12-5. SIZE: Medium. *STOCK: 17th-19th C oak and country furniture, refectory tables and coffers; armour, 15th-19th C; muskets, pistols, armourial items; big game, taxidermy, large bore sporting guns; equestrian paintings and decorative items.* LOC: A40 between exits 6 and 7, M40. PARK: Easy. TEL: 01844 281636. SER: Valuations; restorations. FAIRS: TVADA, Oxford.

The Swan at Tetsworth
High St. OX9 7AB. TVADA. Est. 1995. Open 7 days 10-6. SIZE: 40+ rooms. LOC: A40, 5 mins. from junctions 6 and 8, M40. PARK: Own large. TEL: 01844 281777; fax - 01844 281770; e-mail - antiques@theswan.co.uk website - www.theswan.co.uk SER: Restorations (clocks); cabinet work; delivery and shipping. Below are listed the dealers at this centre.

Deborah Abbot
Jewellery and objets d'art.

Jason Abbot
Sporting guns.

Acanthus Design
Arts & Crafts and Art Nouveau furniture and accessories.

S.J. Allison
Decorative ceramics, small furniture and silver.

Aquila Fine Art
19th to early 20th C watercolours, oils and etchings.

Robin Barnes
Fine 19th-20th C watercolours and etchings.

Sue Barrance
Books.

Oonagh Black   LAPADA
TVADA. *Continental and English furniture and associated decorative items.*

Peter Bond
Prints, watercolours. SER: Gilding

S. Bond & Sons
Fine period furniture.

Ursula Breese
Silver, ceramics, glass and collectables.

Ann Casey
Antique textiles, ceramics, fashion accessories and small furniture.

Caversham Antiques
Furniture and collectables.

Jenny Corkhill-Callin
Textiles including cushions, curtains, braids and quilts.

Jane de Albuquerque
Continental and English furniture and associated decorative items.

Jacqueline Ding
Oriental antiques.

Richard and Deby Earls
Textiles, cushions, small decorative French furniture.

Elisabeth James Ltd
(Chris Millard). TVADA. *Fine furniture, 17th-19th C; gilt mirrors, boxes and caddies.* TEL: 01234 826688; mobile - 07887 834888; website - www.elisabethjames.co.uk

Paul Farrelly Antiques Ltd
TVADA. *Fine 18th-19th C furniture and mirrors.*

Sally Forster
Costume jewellery, vintage fashion and accessories.

Mavis Foster-Abbott
20th C glass, specialising in Latticinio.

Grate Expectations
Fireplaces, Cornish ranges, tiles, garden items and architectural salvage.

Stephen Guth
Framed antiquarian prints and maps.

Mary-Louise Hawkins
Fine English and Continental silver.

Invogue Antiques
(Martin and Shelagh Lister). TVADA. *Georgian and 19th C furniture especially 19th C cherry, oak and pine farmhouse tables and chairs, English and French.* TEL: 01189 341443; mobile - 07773 786103; e-mail - invogueantiques@aol.com

Ross Jennens
Painted decorative furniture, mirrors and accessories.

Nigel Johnston
Furniture and clocks.

Tricia Kent
Gentlemens' jewellery and associated items.

Russell Lane
Jewellery.

Susan Ling
Small furniture, brass and copper.

Rosemary Livingston
Fine silver and plate.

Graham McCarthy
Watercolours and oils.

J. MacNaughton-Smith
TVADA. *Mainly 18th-19th C English furniture including desks, writing tables, chiffoniers, chests of drawers; small decorative items, 19th C watercolours.*

Mark Milkowski
English furniture and decorative items.

Tim and Chris Millard
TVADA. *18th-19th C furniture and mirrors.*

Millroyal Antiques
Fine furniture and smalls.

Nicholas Mitchell
Unusual period furniture and smalls.

The Lamb Arcade Antique Centre

High Street, Wallingford, Oxon. Tel: (01491) 835166

10am-5pm daily, Saturday til 5.30pm (Closed Sundays)

*Furniture · Silver · Glass · Jewellery · Old Tin Toys · Coins
Boxes · Samplers · Antiquarian Documents · Oriental Rugs · Pictures
Porcelain · Militaria · Lighting · Sporting & Fishing items
Decorative & Ornamental pieces · Custom made Dolls
Furniture · Furniture Restoration & Picture Framing*

To Birmingham

Oxford

WALLINGFORD

Henley

Reading

To London

*Coffee Shop & Wine Bar – A fascinating place to visit for trade and public alike
Dealers on hand to give personal service*

John and Gilly Mott
Art Deco furniture and collectables.

Nazaré Antiques
Antique furniture and collectables.

Old Chair Company
Upholstered furniture.

Margi O'Neill
Fine furniture and decorative objects.

Orchard House Antiques
18th-19th C town and country English furniture.

Orient Carpets
Persian rugs, kelims and textiles.

Peter Phillips
Ceramics, especially blue & white transferware; small period furniture.

Alistair Price
Fine period furniture.

Tim Ratcliff
Glass and Art Nouveau jewellery and objets d'art.

Guy Roe
Period furniture and decorative items.

Jane Smithson
Kitchenalia.

Gail Spence Antiques
Small decorative, collectables and gift antiques.

E. Stone Associates
Antique and secondhand jewellery. SER: Restorations.

Tartan Antiques
Objets d'art, pictures and toys.

Paul Templeton
Silver, jewellery and objets d'art.

Tessier
Fine quality jewellery.

S. and S. Timms Antiques Ltd   **LAPADA**
(Martin Murray). TVADA. *Fine English and decorative furniture, especially childrens' chairs and apprentice pieces.*

Touchwood Antiques
English country furniture, especially oak; brass, door furniture, fireplaces and garden items.

Cathy Turner   **LAPADA**
Art Nouveau originals.

Anthony Vingoe
Glass, sporting, leather and metalware items, porcelain.

Cherry Warren
Jewellery, silver and objets d'art.

Sue West and Pauline Sommerville
TVADA. *Small furniture, textiles and ceramics.*

Jinny Wright
French country furniture including garden and kitchen.

Wright Associates
Jewellery, glass, silver, boxes and small furniture.

THAME

Rosemary and Time
42 Park St. OX9 3HR. (Tom Fletcher). Est. 1983. Open 9-6. *STOCK: Clocks and barometers.* TEL: 01844 216923. SER: Valuations; restorations; old spare parts. VAT: Stan/Spec.

WALLINGFORD

de Albuquerque Antiques
12 High St. OX10 0BP. Est. 1982. Open by appointment. SIZE: Medium. *STOCK: Furniture and objects, 18th-19th C.* PARK: At rear. TEL: 01491 832322; fax - same; e-mail - janedealb@tiscali.co.uk SER: Framing; gilding. VAT: Spec.

Toby English
10 St Mary's St. OX10 0EL. (Toby and Chris English). PBFA. Est. 1980. Open 9.30-5. SIZE: Medium. *STOCK: Books including art and antiques reference, 19th-20th C, £5-£1,000; prints, 19th-20th C, £20-£200; maps, 18th-19th C, £30-£1,000.* LOC: Town centre. PARK: Cattle Market. TEL: 01491 836389; fax - same; e-mail - toby@tobyenglish.com website - www.tobyenglish.com SER: Valuations; restorations; buys at auction; catalogues issued. FAIRS: PBFA London, Oxford, York.

The Lamb Arcade
83 High St. OX10 0BX. TVADA. Est. 1979. Open 10-5, Sat. 10-5.30. *STOCK: See dealers listed below.* PARK: Nearby. TEL: 01491 835166; e-mail - patriciantique @aol.com website - www.thelambarcade.co.uk SER: Restorations (furniture); picture framing.

Alicia Antiques
(A. Collins). *China, silver, collectors' items and glassware.* TEL: 01491 833737.

- *Contains a comprehensive list of all the many manufacturers who worked in the Staffordshire Potteries between 1781 and 1900*

- *A new standard reference work for all interested in British ceramics*

- *Contains new information unavailable in existing literature*

- *Includes a useful selection of marks employed by many of the lesser potters*

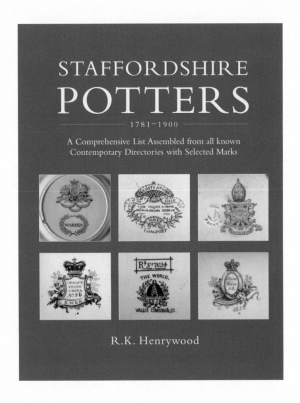

STAFFORDSHIRE
POTTERS
1781-1900

R.K. Henrywood

This book presents a comprehensive list of manufacturers working in the Staffordshire Potteries in the period between 1781 and 1900. This area produced some ninety per cent of the pots made in England and is of prime importance in the study of British ceramics. The list has been assembled by extracting the data contained in directories published in the period, covering more than 10,000 entries from some sixty-one volumes. The book itself consists of introductory chapters covering historical aspects of the survey, a fascinating evaluation of the area under review and the directory of authors and publishers, followed by two major chapters — the assembled alphabetical list of over 3,000 potters and listings of all the original directory entries in date order. This is the most comprehensive list of Staffordshire potters ever published and includes much information unavailable in existing literature. The work covers all potters, regardless of their products, working between 1781, the date of the earliest surviving directory, and the beginning of the twentieth century, by far the most popular period for collectors. The book will easily become a standard reference work for all who are interested in British pottery and porcelain, collected throughout the world.

Dick Henrywood was an aeronautical engineer with a long list of technical papers to his credit and he worked for many years as a business manager. He moved away from engineering and now works as a freelance author and lecturer on antiques and related subjects. He was a founder member of the Friends of Blue and first Keeper of the Records and also wrote the ACC *Dictionary of Blue and White Pottery 1780-1880,* and cover subjects as diverse as jugs, bookmarkers and cat names.

Specifications:
408pp., 420 b.&w. illus.,
11 x 8½in./279 x 216mm.
£65.00 (hardback)

For full details of all ACC publications, log on to our website:
www.antiquecollectorsclub.com
or telephone 01394 389950 for a free catalogue

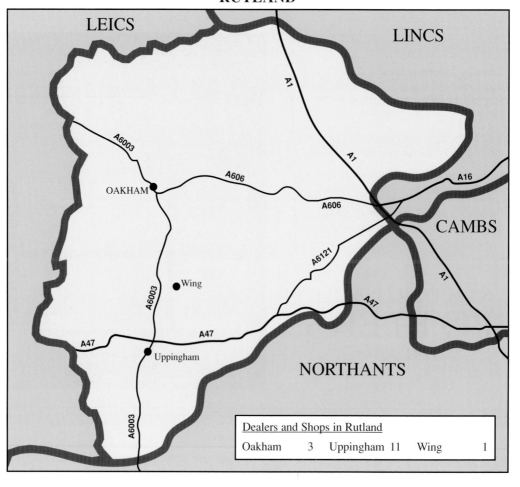

RUTLAND

LEICS

LINCS

A1

A6003

A606

A1

A16

OAKHAM

A606

CAMBS

A6121

A1

Wing

A6003

A47

A47

A47

A47

A6003

Uppingham

NORTHANTS

Dealers and Shops in Rutland

Oakham   3   Uppingham 11   Wing   1

OAKHAM

C. Reynolds Antiques
The East Lodge, Burley Mansion House, Burley-on-the-Hill. LE15 7TE. Est. 1972. Resident. Usually available but telephone call advisable. SIZE: Large. *STOCK: Early verge watches, repeater and other unusual clocks and watches.* LOC: Next to Rutland Water. TEL: 01572 771551. SER: Verge glasses fitted; valuations. FAIRS: Birmingham Clock.

Swans
17 Mill St. LE15 6EA(P.W. Jones). Est. 1988. Open 9-5.30, Sun. and evenings by appointment. SIZE: Large. *STOCK: French and English beds and associated furniture; 18th-19th C antiques, mainly decorative and upholstered.* LOC: 150yds. from High St. PARK: Easy. TEL: 01572 724364; fax - 01572 755094; e-mail - info@swansofoakham.co.uk website - www.swansofoakham.co.uk SER: Manufactures new bases and mattresses; valuations; restorations; delivery (to and from France). VAT: Stan/Spec.

Treedale Antiques
10b Mill St. LE15 6AE. (G.K. Warren). GMC. Est. 1994. Open 9-5, Sun. 2-5. *STOCK: Furniture including walnut, mahogany and oak, from 1680, to £3,000; portraits, paintings, tapestries and chandeliers.* TEL: 01572 757521; home - 01664 454535. SER: Valuations; restorations (furniture).

UPPINGHAM

Aspidistra
5 Queen St. LE15 9QR. (Mike J. Sanderson). Est. 1989. Open Tues.-Sat. 10-5. SIZE: Small. *STOCK: General antiques especially Victorian, Edwardian and painted furniture, decorative items, china, glass, pictures, to £700.* LOC: Off High St. PARK: Easy. TEL: 01572 822757; home - 01572 823105.

Curiosity Shop
3 Queen St. LE15 9QR. (Mrs E. Parsons). Est. 1992. Usually open 9-3. SIZE: Medium. *STOCK: Small furniture, bric-a-brac, Turkish rugs, jewellery.* PARK: Easy.

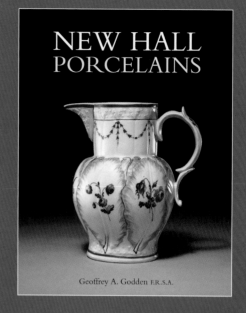

John Garner   LAPADA
51-53 High St. East. LE15 9PY. FATG. Est. 1966. Open 9-5.30, Sun. 2-5, prior telephone call advisable. SIZE: 12 showrooms + warehouse. *STOCK: 17th-19th C furniture, paintings, prints, clocks, bronzes, mirrors, garden statuary, some 20th C furniture.* LOC: Just off A47, 80 yards from market place. PARK: Easy. TEL: 01572 823607; fax - 01572 821654; mobile - 07850 596556; e-mail - sales@johngarnerantiques.com website - www.johngarnerantiques.com SER: Valuations; restorations (furniture, paintings, prints); framing (trade); courier; export. FAIRS: Newark; Miami. VAT: Stan/Spec.

M. Gilbert Antiques & Old Furniture
8 Ayston Rd. LE15 9RL. Est. 1964. Open 9.30-5, Mon. and Tues. 9.30-1 and 2-5. SIZE: Small. *STOCK: General antiques.* PARK: Easy. TEL: 01572 821975; mobile - 07990 573338.

Harvey Art and Antiques
14 Orange St. LE15 9SQ. (Stephen H. Craik). Open Fri. 10-4, Sat. 10-5, Sun. 10-2, other times by appointment. *STOCK: 18th-19th C furniture; clocks, including longcase, bracket and wall, late 17th to early 18th C; contemporary art.* TEL: 01572 822385; mobile - 07766 505818; e-mail - enquiries@harveyantiques.co.uk website - www.harveyantiques.co.uk SER: Door-to-door shipping.

Marc Oxley Fine Art
Resident. Est. 1981. Open by appointment. *STOCK: Original watercolours and drawings, 1700-1950, £5-£850; oils, 19th-20th C, £100-£1,500; prints, mainly 19th C, £5-£50; maps, 17th-19th C, £10-£850.* TEL: 01572 822334; home - same; e-mail - marc@19thC

watercolours.com website - www.marcoxleyfineart.com SER: Valuations; restorations (oils).

T.J. Roberts
39/41 High St. East. LE15 9PY. Resident. Est. 1973. Open 9.30-5.30. *STOCK: Furniture, porcelain and pottery, 18th-19th C; Staffordshire figures, general antiques.* PARK: Easy. TEL: 01572 821493. VAT: Stan/Spec.

Rutland Antiques Centre
Crown Passage. LE15 9NB. (Wendy Foster Grindley). Est. 2001. Open 10-5.30, Sun. 11-5. SIZE: Large. *STOCK: Wide range of general antiques, £5-£3,000.* LOC: Behind Crown Hotel, High St. PARK: Easy. TEL: 01572 824011.

Secondhand Bookshop
7 High Street West. LE15 9QB. (David Siddons). Est. 1986. Open 10.30-5, most Suns. 1.30-4.30. SIZE: Small. *STOCK: Secondhand books, all periods.* PARK: Easy. TEL: 01572 821173; fax - 08701 326314; e-mail - forestbooks@rutlanduk.fsnet.co.uk website - www.http:/homepages.primex.co.uk/~forest

Tattersall's
14b Orange St. LE15 9SQ. (J. Tattersall). Est. 1985. Open 9.30-5. CL: Mon. SIZE: Small. *STOCK: Persian rugs, 19th-20th C.* PARK: Easy, 200yds. TEL: 01572 821171; e-mail - janice_tattersall@hotmail.com SER: Restorations (rugs, carpets).

Woodman's House Antiques
35 High St. East. LE15 9PY. (Mr and Mrs James Collie). Est. 1991. SIZE: Small. *STOCK: Furniture, 17th-18th C.* PARK: Easy. TEL: 01572 821799; fax - same; SER: Valuations; restorations; buys at auction.

WING, Nr. Oakham

Robert Bingley Antiques   LAPADA
Home Farm, Church St. LE15 8RS. (Robert and Elizabeth Bingley). Open 10-5, Sun. by appointment. SIZE: Very large. *STOCK: Furniture and clocks, 17th-19th C, £50-£5,000.* LOC: Next to church. PARK: Own. TEL: 01572 737725; fax - 01572 737284; mobile - 07909 585285; e-mail - robertbingley@tiscali.co.uk website - www.robertbingley.com SER: Valuations; restorations. VAT: Spec.

- *A reprint of the revised edition of this popular title*

- *Deals with the hundreds of types of affordable clocks, often dismissed by the purists as being of no horological interest*

- *Hundreds of photographs are supported by a detailed and highly informative text*

- *A 'must' for any collector or horological student interested in later examples*

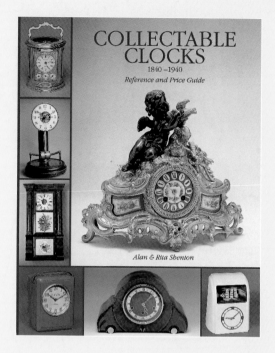

COLLECTABLE CLOCKS
1840-1940
Reference and Price Guide
(Revised Edition)

Alan and Rita Shenton

The majority of books about clocks tend to focus upon the earlier types, or at least the high quality clocks, made before the middle of the nineteenth century. This is a book, however, for those who enjoy later clocks and are keen to learn more about the hundreds of examples which are often available at an attainable price, especially for the collector who knows what to look for and what to avoid. This book covers areas of study, hitherto largely ignored, such as Victorian inventiveness, decorative clocks of the 1920s and technical clocks of the early twentieth century. In short, *Collectable Clocks* is much more than a mere collection of photographs accompanied by auctioneers' descriptions and prices. The authors are keen, experienced horologists and well aware of the questions that need answers – What is quality? What should one look for? What date is this clock?

An impressive amount of original research has gone into the production of this book and the range of examples included is both extensive and impressive. Virtually every known type of clock is illustrated and discussed from alarm, bracket and carriage to skeleton, tension and wall. Specimen pages from actual trade journals plus a useful glossary and bibliography further contribute to the great value of this book as a continuous work of reference and an indispensable guide to all with an interest in horology.

Alan Shenton is a long-standing member of the Antiquarian Horological Society, the British Horological Institute and the American National Association of Watch and Clock Collectors. His interest in horology ranges from research to the practical application of workshop techniques in the field of restoration.

Rita Shenton contributed regular articles on horology to numerous journals and periodicals. She ran a specialist horological book business and was also a member of the British Horological Institute and the American National Association of Watch and Clock Collectors. She served on the Council of the Antiquarian Horological Society for many years.

Specifications:
480pp., 34 col. illus., 700 b.&w. illus., 11 x 8½in./279 x 216mm.
£29.95 (hardback)

For full details of all ACC publications, log on to our website:
www.antiquecollectorsclub.com
or telephone 01394 389950 for a free catalogue

SHROPSHIRE

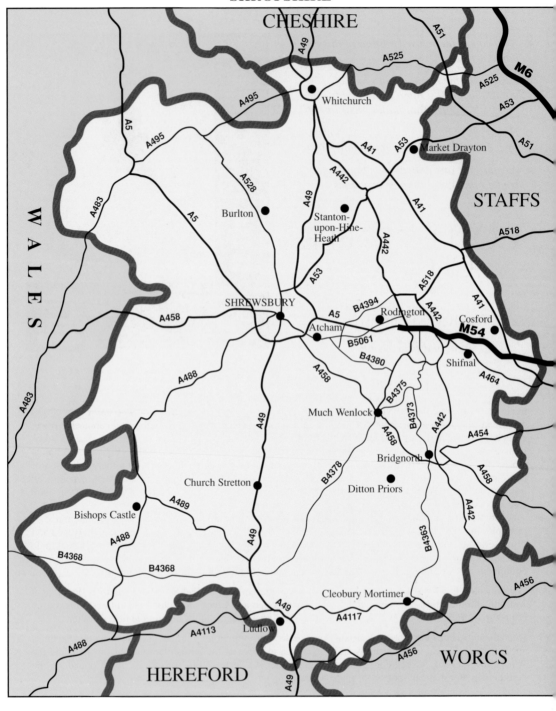

ATCHAM, Nr. Shrewsbury

Mytton Antiques
Norton Cross Roads. SY4 4UH. (M.A., E.A., J.M. and S. Nares). Est. 1972. Open 10-5 or by appointment. SIZE: Medium. *STOCK: General antiques, furniture, 1700-1900, £50-£5,000; clocks, £35-£4,000; smalls, £15-£2,000.* LOC: On B5061 (the old A5) between Shrewsbury and Wellington. PARK: Own. TEL: 01952 740229 (24hrs.); fax - same; mobile - 07860 575639; e-mail - nares@myttonantiques.co.uk website - www. myttonantiques.co.uk SER: Buys at auction; restorations: reference books supplied; restoration materials and equipment; shipping. FAIRS: Newark, Ardingly. VAT: Stan/Spec.

BISHOP'S CASTLE

Decorative Antiques
47 Church St. SY9 5AD. (Evelyn Bowles and Richard Moulson). Est. 1996. Open Mon.-Sat. CL: Wed. pm. SIZE: Small. *STOCK: Ceramics and glass, jewellery and metalware, small furniture, 20th C, £5-£1,000.* PARK: Easy. TEL: 01588 638851; fax/home - same; e-mail - enquiries@decorative-antiques.co.uk website - www. decorative-antiques.co.uk SER: Valuations.

BRIDGNORTH

Bridgnorth Antiques Centre
Whitburn St. WV16 4QT. (Mrs S. Coppen and Miss G.M. Gibbons). Est. 1992. Open 10-5, Sun. 10.30-4.30. SIZE: Large. *STOCK: Clocks, furniture, collectables.* PARK: Easy. TEL: 01746 768055; website - www. bridgnorthantiquecentre.co.uk SER: Restorations (clocks).

English Heritage
2 Whitburn St., High Town. WV16 4QN. (P.J. Wainwright). Est. 1988. Open 10-5. CL: Thurs. SIZE: Medium. *STOCK: Jewellery, silverware and general antiques, militaria, coins, collectibles, glassware.* LOC: Just off High St. PARK: Nearby. TEL: 01746 762097. VAT: Stan/Spec.

Malthouse Antiques
The Old Malthouse, 6 Underhill St. WV16 4BB. (Susan and William Mantle). Est. 1980. Open 10-6, Sun. by appointment. CL: Wed. SIZE: Medium. *STOCK: Victorian and Edwardian furniture, French beds and armoires, £100-£1,500; upholstered chairs and sofas, from 19th C, £300-£1,800; china and decorative items, 19th-20th C, £5-£150; French chandeliers.* LOC: Main road into town from Wolverhampton. PARK: Nearby. TEL: 01746 763054; fax/home - same. SER: Valuations; restorations (furniture).

Micawber Antiques
64 St. Mary's St. WV16 4DR. (N. Berthoud). Est. 1989. Open 10-5, other times by appointment. CL: Mon. and Thurs. SIZE: Medium. *STOCK: English porcelain and pottery, decorative items, £5-£500; small furniture, £100-£1,000.* LOC: 100yds. west of town hall in High St. PARK: Easy. TEL: 01746 763254; home - same.

Old Mill Antique Centre
Mill St. WV15 5AG. (D.A. and J.A. Ridgeway). Est. 1996. Open 10-5 including Sun. SIZE: Large - 90 dealers. *STOCK: Wide range of general antiques including period furniture, porcelain and silver, jewellery, prints and watercolours, collectables.* LOC: Main road. PARK: Own. TEL: 01746 768778; fax - 01746 768944; SER: Valuations; restorations. VAT: Stan.

BURLTON, Nr. Shrewsbury

North Shropshire Reclamation
Wackley Lodge Farm. SY4 5TD. (A. and J. Powell). SALVO. Est. 1997. Open 7 days 9-5. SIZE: Large. *STOCK: Wide range of reclaimed materials.* LOC: A528. PARK: Easy. TEL: 01939 270719; home/fax - 01939 270895; website - www.old&new.uk.com

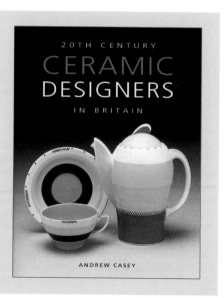

CHURCH STRETTON

Cardingmill Antiques
1 Burway Rd. SY6 6DL. (Mrs P. A. Benton). NHBS. Est. 1976. Open Thurs., Fri. and Sat. 11-4 or by appointment. SIZE: Medium. *STOCK: 18th-19th C longcase and wall clocks, furniture, £250-£3,000; Measham teapots, £90-£450; original horsebrasses and martingales (NHB Soc.); Victorian oil lamps with original shades, £200-£650; 18th-19th C metalware.* LOC: A49. PARK: Easy. TEL: 01694 724555; home - 01584 877880; mobile - 07802 194253; website - www.churchstretton.co.uk

Stretton Antiques Market
36 Sandford Ave. SY6 6BH. (T. and L. Elvins). Est. 1986. Open 9.30-5.30, Sun. and Bank Holidays 10.30-4.30. SIZE: Large - 55 dealers. *STOCK: General antiques, shipping items and collectables.* LOC: Town centre. PARK: Easy. TEL: 01694 723718.

CLEOBURY MORTIMER, Nr. Kidderminster

Antique Centre
Childe Rd. DY14 8PA. Open 10-5, Sun. by appointment. SIZE: Large. *STOCK: Georgian, Victorian, Edwardian, old pine and French furniture, period beds, garden statuary and architectural items.* LOC: Between Kidderminster and Ludlow. PARK: Own. TEL: 01299 270513; fax - 01299 270513; e-mail - antiquecenter@supanet.com

M. and M. Baldwin
24 High St. DY14 8BY. Est. 1978. Open Wed. 2-6, Fri. (Easter-Oct) and Sat. 10-1 and 2-6. SIZE: Medium. *STOCK: 19th-20th C books, to £500.* LOC: A4117. PARK: Easy. TEL: 01299 270110; fax/home - same; e-mail - books@mbaldwin.free-online.co.uk SER: Valuations; buys at auction (books). FAIRS: Crick Boat Show; IWA National Festival. VAT: Stan.

COSFORD

Martin Quick Antiques
Unit E2, Long Lane. TF11 8PJ. (C.R. Quick). Est. 1965. Open every day by appointment or by chance. SIZE: Large. *STOCK: English and Continental furniture and decorative items including farmhouse tables, buffets, armoires.* LOC: Signposted Neachley off A41. PARK: Easy. TEL: 01902 754703; home - 01902 752908; mobile - 07774 124859; e-mail - cqantiques@aol.com SER: Packing and shipping. FAIRS: Newark. VAT: Stan/Spec. *Trade Only.*

DITTON PRIORS

Priors Reclamation
Unit 65 Ditton Priors Industrial Estate. WV16 6SS. (Vicki Bale and Martin Foley). SALVO. Est. 1996. Open by appointment. *STOCK: Flooring, period doors and door furniture, reclaimed and made to order.* PARK: Easy. TEL: 01746 712450; home - same; e-mail - vicki@priorsrec.co.uk website - www.priorsrec.co.uk FAIRS: Burwarton.

LUDLOW

Bayliss Antiques
22-24 Old St. SY8 1NP. (D., A.B. and N. Bayliss).

Resident. Est. 1966. Open 10-6 or by appointment. SIZE: Medium. *STOCK: 18th-19th C furniture.* TEL: 01584 873634; fax - same. SER: Valuations. VAT: Spec.

Bebb Fine Art   LAPADA
1 Church St. SY8 1AP. (Roger Bebb). CINOA. Est. 1978. Open 10-5.30 or by appointment. CL: Thurs. SIZE: Small. *STOCK: Oils, screen prints and lithographs including W. Kay Blacklock, John Piper, Sir Terry Frost, W. Lee-Hankey, mainly 20th C, £200-£8,000.* LOC: Town centre. PARK: Nearby. TEL: 01584 879612; fax/home - same; e-mail - bebbfineart@aol.com website - www.bebbfineart.co.uk SER: Valuations; restorations (oils). VAT: Stan/spec.

R.G. Cave and Sons Ltd   BADA LAPADA
17 Broad St. SY8 1NG. (Mrs M.C., R.G., J.R. and T.G. Cave). Resident. Est. 1962. Open 10-5.30. SIZE: Medium. STOCK: Furniture, 1630-1830; clocks, barometers, metalwork, fine art and collectors' items. LOC: Old town. PARK: Easy. TEL: 01584 873568; fax - 01584 875050. SER: Valuations. VAT: Spec.

Corve Street Antiques
141A Corve St. SY8 2PG. (Mike McAvoy and David Jones). Est. 1990. Open 10-5. SIZE: Medium. *STOCK: Oak, mahogany and pine furniture, clocks, pocket watches, china, glass, prints and pictures, £5-£5,000.* PARK: Easy. TEL: 01584 879100.

Garrard Antiques
139a Corve St. SY8 2PG. (Caroline Garrard). Est. 1985. Open 10-1 and 2-5, Sat. 10-5. SIZE: Large - 7 rooms. *STOCK: Pine and country furniture, 18th-19th C, to £3,000; books, linen, textiles, silver and treen, Staffordshire pottery.* LOC: 200 yards below Feathers Hotel. PARK: Opposite. TEL: 01584 876727. SER: Valuations. VAT: Spec.

G. & D. Ginger Antiques
5 Corve St. SY8 1DA. Resident. Est. 1978. Open 9-5. SIZE: Large. *STOCK: 17th-18th C English and Welsh furniture, mainly oak and fruitwood, farmhouse tables, food cupboards, presses, corner cupboards, decorative and associated items.* TEL: 01584 876939; mobile - 07970 666437; e-mail - gdgingerantiques@aol.com VAT: Spec.

Holloways of Ludlow
140 Corve St. SY8 2PG. (Mark Holloway). Open 9.30-5.30, Sun. 11-4. *STOCK: Bathroom fittings, 1800-1950; fireplaces and surrounds, from 1700; lighting and light fittings, from 1880; ranges and stoves, doors, door and window furniture, rim and box locks, leaded lights, stained glass, general fixtures and fittings.* LOC: Central. PARK: Easy. TEL: 01584 876207; fax - 020 7602 6561; mobile - 07786 802302; e-mail - mark@hollowaysof ludlow.com website - www.hollowaysofludlow.com SER: Restorations (lighting and fireplaces); keys cut for old locks.

Mitre House Antiques
Corve Bridge. SY8 1DY. (L. Jones). Est. 1972. Open 9-5.30. SIZE: Shop + trade warehouse. *STOCK: Clocks, pine and general antiques. Warehouse - unstripped pine and shipping goods.* TEL: 01584 872138; mobile - 07976 549013. FAIRS: Newark; Ardingly.

G & D GINGER ANTIQUES

Dealers in Antique Oak and Country Furniture
5 Corve Street, Ludlow, Shropshire. SY8 1DA

Telephone and Fax: 01584 876939. Mobile: 07970 666437
E-mail: Gdgingerantiques@aol.com

Valentyne Dawes Gallery
Church St. SY8 1AP. (B.S. McCreddie). Open 10-5.30.
SIZE: Medium. *STOCK: Paintings, 19th-21st C, £200-£40,000.* LOC: Town centre near Buttercross. PARK:
Nearby. TEL: 01584 874160; fax - 01384 455576; e-mail
- sales@gallery.wyenet.co.uk website - www.starmark.
co.uk/valentyne-dawes/ SER: Valuations; restorations
(oil paintings, watercolours, furniture). VAT: Spec.

Zani Lady Decorative Antiques
15 Corve St. SY8 1DA. (Susan Humphries). Open 10-5,
Thurs. by appointment. SIZE: 3 floors - 7 dealers.
*STOCK: Wide range of decorative antiques, kitchenalia,
mirrors, lighting, French linen, architectural items and
ironwork, vintage fabrics and cushions.* LOC: Bottom of
Corve St. PARK: Limited and private at rear. TEL:
01584 877200; mobile - 07974 363516.

MARKET DRAYTON

Richard Midwinter Antiques
TF9 4EF. (Richard and Susannah Midwinter). Resident.
Est. 1983. Open any time by appointment. SIZE:
Medium. *STOCK: 17th-19th C town and country
furniture, clocks, textiles and decorative items.* LOC: Off
M6, junction 14 to Eccleshall onto High St., 4+ miles to
Loggerheads, turn right towards Newcastle on A53.
TEL: 01630 673901; mobile - 07836 617361; e-mail -
mail@richardmidwinterantiques.co.uk website - www.
richardmidwinterantiques.co.uk SER: Restorations.
FAIRS: Olympia (June and Nov); Penman, Chester (Feb.
and Oct); NEC (Jan., April and Nov).

MUCH WENLOCK

Raynalds Mansion BADA
High St. TF13 6AE. (John King). Resident. Est. 1970.
Open Mon., Tues. and Fri. 10-2, prior telephone call
advisable. SIZE: Medium. *STOCK: Period furniture
and associated items, £500-£45,000.* PARK: Easy.
TEL: 01952 727456; fax/home - same. VAT: Spec.

Wenlock Fine Art
3 The Square. TF13 6LX. (P. Cotterill). Est. 1990. Open
Wed.-Sat. 10-5. SIZE: Medium. *STOCK: Modern British
paintings, mainly 20th C, some late 19th C.* PARK:
Nearby. TEL: 01952 728232. SER: Valuations;
restorations; cleaning; mounting; framing; buys at
auction (as stock). VAT: Spec.

RODINGTON Nr. Shrewsbury

Brian James Antiques
Unit 9 Rodenhurst Business Park. SY4 4QU. Est. 1985.
Open 9-6, Sat. 9.30-12.30, Sun. by appointment.
STOCK: Chests of drawers, Georgian to Victorian, £50-£1,500. LOC: Off M54, junction 6. Follow signs for
Telford Hospital, Shawbirch, B5063, B5062, between
Telford and Shrewsbury. PARK: Easy. TEL: 01952
770856/243906; e-mail - brianjamesantiques@
yahoo.co.uk SER: Restorations (inlay, veneering,
polishing); conversions; linen presses, sideboards,
cabinets and chests made to order. VAT: Stan.

SHIFNAL

Corner Farm Antiques

Weston Heath, Sheriffhales. TF11 8RY. (Tim Dams). GMC. Est. 1994. Open 10-5 including Sun. SIZE: Large. *STOCK: Georgian to Edwardian furniture, especially dining room extending tables and sets of chairs; longcase and wall clocks, barometers; Victorian fireplaces, lighting, soft furnishings and collectables, £5-£500.* LOC: A41 between Tong and Newport. PARK: Own large. TEL: 01952 691543; home/fax - same. website - www. antiquesclocks.com SER: Valuations; restorations (furniture and clocks); buys at auction. VAT: Stan.

SHREWSBURY

Bear Steps Antiques

2 Bear Steps, Fish St. SY1 1UR. (John and Sally Wyatt). Open 9-5, prior telephone call advisable. SIZE: Small. *STOCK: 18th C English porcelain.* LOC: Town centre. PARK: Limited. TEL: 01743 344298; e-mail - englishporcelain@aol.com website - www.bear-steps-antiques.co.uk FAIRS: NEC.

Candle Lane Books

28-29 Princess St. SY1 1LW. (J. Thornhill). Est. 1974. Open 9.30-4.30. SIZE: Large. *STOCK: Antiquarian and secondhand books.* LOC: Town centre. PARK: Nearby. TEL: 01743 365301.

Juliet Chilton Antiques and Interiors

69 Wyle Cop. SY1 1UX. Open 9.30-6. SIZE: Large. *STOCK: Furniture and smalls, mainly 1700's-1920's and some reproduction.* TEL: 01743 358699; fax - same. SER: Packing and shipping.

Collectors' Place

29a Princess St., The Square. SY1 1LW. (Keith Jones). Open 10-4, Sat. 9.30-5. *STOCK: Collectables especially Prattware potlids and bottles, 1700-1900; ceramics including Wade, Beswick, Carltonware, early 20th C; Art Deco, eyebaths.* LOC: Opposite Shrewsbury Antique Centre. TEL: 01743 246150; e-mail - darren.bec@virgin.net

Adrian Donnelly Antique Clocks

7 The Parade, St Mary's Place. SY1 1DL. BHI. BWCG. Est. 1985. Open 10-5, Sat. 10-1. SIZE: Medium. *STOCK: Longcase and bracket clocks and barometers, 17th-19th C, £250-£12,000.* LOC: Town centre. PARK: Easy. TEL: 01743 361388; fax - same; e-mail - clockshopshrewsbury@hotmail.com SER: Restorations (clocks and barometers). VAT: Stan/Spec.

Expressions

17 Princess St. SY1 1LP. Open 10.30-4.30. *STOCK: Art Deco originals, ceramics, furniture, jewellery, lighting, mirrors, prints.* TEL: 01743 351731.

A Little Furniture Shop

1A Wyle Cop. SY1 1UT. (Heather Maskill and Mark Swain). Est. 2000. Tues.-Sat. 10-4. SIZE: Small. *STOCK: Victorian wing and tub chairs, Edwardian armchairs, Victorian and Edwardian chaises, sofas and dining chairs, 1920s drop arm sofas.* LOC: Town centre. PARK: Nearby. TEL: 01743 352102; mobile - 07714 205660; e-mail - heather@ furniture.fslife.co.uk website - www.alittlefurniture shop.co.uk SER: Restorations (upholstered furniture).

Mansers Antiques   LAPADA

Coleham Head. SY3 7BJ. Est. 1944. Open 9-5. SIZE: Large. *STOCK: Furniture, 18th-20th C, £250-£50,000; silver, porcelain, glass, mirrors, decorative items, £50-£10,000. Not Stocked: Coins, books.* LOC: 150yds. from English bridge away from town centre. PARK: Own. TEL: 01743 351120; fax - 01743 271047; e-mail - mansers@theantiquedealers.com website - www. theantiquedealers.com SER: Valuations; restorations. VAT: Stan/Spec.

Princess Antique Centre

14a The Square. SY1 1LH. (J. Langford). Open 9.30-5. SIZE: 35 dealers. *STOCK: General antiques and collectables.* PARK: Nearby. TEL: 01743 343701.

Quayside Antiques

9 Frankwell. SY3 8JY. (Jean and Chris Winter). Open Tues. and Wed. 10-4, Fri. and Sat. 10-5. SIZE: Large. *STOCK: Victorian and Edwardian furniture, especially dining tables and sets of chairs, desks, bookcases, wardrobes.* LOC: Near Halls Saleroom. PARK: Own. TEL: 01743 360490; workshop - 01948 665838; home - 01948 830363; website - www.quaysideantiques.co.uk SER: Restorations (furniture). FAIRS: NEC.

Shrewsbury Antique Centre

15 Princess House, The Square. SY1 1JZ. (J. Langford). Est. 1978. Open 9.30-5.30. SIZE: Large - 50 dealers. *STOCK: General antiques and collectables.* LOC: Town centre just off the square. PARK: Nearby. TEL: 01743 247704.

STANTON UPON HINE HEATH, Nr. Shrewsbury

Marcus Moore Antiques

Booley House, Booley. SY4 4LY. (M.G.J. and M.P. Moore). Est. 1980. Usually open but prior telephone call advisable. SIZE: Large. *STOCK: Oak and country furniture, late 17th to 18th C; Georgian mahogany furniture, 18th to early 19th C; all £50-£7,000; some Victorian furniture; associated items.* LOC: Half a mile north of Stanton on right. PARK: Easy. TEL: 01939 200333; website - www.marcusmoore-antiques.com SER: Restorations (furniture); polishing; search; shipping. VAT: Stan/Spec.

WHITCHURCH

Age of Elegance

54 High St. SY13 1BB. (Mike and Janet Proudlove). Est. 1988. Open 10-4. CL: Wed. SIZE: Small. *STOCK: Collectables including china and glass; Victorian and Edwardian furniture.* LOC: Midway between Shrewsbury and Chester. PARK: Easy. TEL: 01948 666145; fax - same.

Dodington Antiques

7 Sherrymill Hill. SY13 1BN. (G. MacGillivray). Resident. Est. 1978. By appointment. SIZE: Large. *STOCK: Oak, fruitwood, walnut country and 18th to early 19th C mahogany furniture, longcase clocks, barometers, £10-£6,000.* LOC: On fringe of town centre. PARK: Easy. TEL: 01948 663399. SER: Buys at auction. VAT: Stan/Spec.

THE ANTIQUE COLLECTORS' CLUB LTD

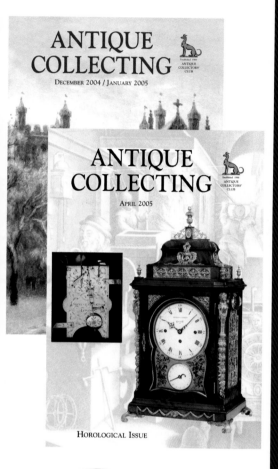

Renowned for over thirty-five years as the very best specialist publishers and distributors of books on antiques and collectables, the Antique Collectors' Club also produces the respected *Antique Collecting* magazine, offering a wealth of knowledge and practical information on all aspects of collecting. It is available only by subscription directly from its publisher, The Antique Collectors' Club.

Subscribe today to *Antique Collecting* for only £25 p.a. (UK), £30 (Overseas) and receive 10 copies of this well respected journal; privileged access to pre-publication book offers at reduced prices, and a £10 money-off book voucher for use on any Antiques Collectors' Club titles.

With almost 1,000 books, the Antique Collectors' Club sells only the best on all aspects of antiques, decorative arts and interiors.

For full details of all ACC publications, log on to our website:
www.antiquecollectorsclub.com
or telephone 01394 389950 for a free catalogue

For Collectors – By Collectors – About Collecting

SOMERSET

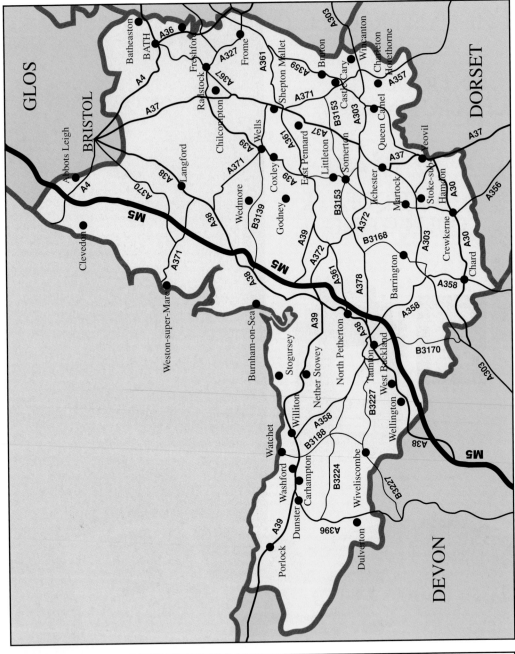

Dealers and Shops in Somerset

Abbots Leigh	1	Charlton Horethorne	1	Frome	2	Queen Camel	1	Wedmore	1
Barrington	2	Chilcompton	1	Godney	1	Radstock	1	Wellington	1
Bath	37	Clevedon	1	Ilchester	1	Shepton Mallet	1	Wells	3
Batheaston	1	Coxley	2	Langford	1	Somerton	3	West Buckland	1
Bruton	3	Crewkerne	5	Littleton	1	Stogursey	1	Weston-Super-Mare	2
Burnham-on-Sea	3	Dulverton	3	Martock	1	Stoke-sub-Hamdon	1	Williton	1
Carhampton	1	Dunster	1	Nether Stowey	1	Taunton	5	Wincanton	4
Castle Cary	1	East Pennard	1	North Petherton	1	Washford	1	Wiveliscombe	3
Chard	1	Freshford	2	Porlock	2	Watchet	2	Yeovil	1

ABBOTS LEIGH, Nr. Bristol

David and Sally March Antiques   LAPADA
Oak Wood Lodge, Stoke Leigh Woods. BS8 3QB. (D. and S. March). Est. 1981. Open by appointment. *STOCK: 18th to early 19th C English porcelain especially figures, Bristol and Plymouth.* PARK: Easy. TEL: 01275 372422; fax - same; mobile - 07774 838376; e-mail - david.march@lineone.net website - www. davidandsallymarch.com SER: Valuations; buys at auction (as stock). FAIRS: Olympia; NEC; LAPADA. VAT: Spec.

BARRINGTON, Nr. Ilminster

Rostrum Antiques
3 Barrington Court, TA19 0NQ. Est. 1988. Open by appointment. SIZE: Medium. *STOCK: Fine tea caddies, collectors' boxes and objets d'art, £100-£5,000.* LOC: Near A303. PARK: Easy. TEL: 01460 241612; e-mail - rostrum.uk@virgin.net SER: Valuations; gilding; French polishing; restorations (antique furniture and musical instruments only). VAT: Spec.

Stuart Interiors Ltd   LAPADA
Barrington Court. TA19 0NG. Open 9-5, Sat. 10-5. SIZE: Large. *STOCK: Oak furniture, £100-£10,000; accessories, £50-£2,500; both pre-1720.* LOC: Between A303 and M5, 5 miles north-east of Ilminster. National Trust property, signposted in area. PARK: Easy. TEL: 01460 240349. SER: Valuations. VAT: Spec.

BATH

Adam Gallery Ltd
13 John St. BA1 2JL. (Paul and Philip Dye). Open 9.30-5.30 or by appointment. *STOCK: 20th C British and international paintings and prints, especially St. Ives, Bacon, Nicholson, Francis, Piper, Debuffet, Kandinsky, Lanyon, Moore, Picasso, Delaunay, Hitchens, Hilton, Heron and Scott, British contemporary, £500-£50,000.* TEL: 01225 480406; fax - same; e-mail - enquiries@adamgallery.com website - www.adamgallery.com SER: Contemporary exhibitions.

The Antique Map Shop Ltd
9/10 Pulteney Bridge. BA2 4AY. (David Gardner). BABAADA. Est. 1984. Open 10-5, Sun. and Bank Holidays 11-4. *STOCK: Antique maps.* PARK: Nearby. TEL: 01225 446097; mobile - 07850 746090; e-mail - dave@dg-maps.com website - www.dg-maps.com SER: Post free worldwide mailing.

Antique Textiles & Lighting
34 Belvedere, Lansdown Rd. BA1 5BN. (Joanna Proops). BABAADA. Open Tues.-Sat. 10-5 or by appointment. *STOCK: Chandeliers, wall lights, tapestries, paisleys, beadwork, fans, samplers, bellpulls, linen and lace.* LOC: 5 mins. walk from city centre. PARK: Easy. TEL: 01225 310795; website - www. antiquetextilesandlighting.co.uk FAIRS: Bath.

Bartlett Street Antiques Centre
5-10 Bartlett St. BA1 2QZ. Open 9.30-5, Wed. 8-5. *STOCK: Wide range of general antiques.* TEL: 01225 466689; stallholders - 01225 446322; fax - 01225

444146; e-mail - info@antiques-centre.co.uk website - www.antiques-centre.co.uk

Bath Galleries
33 Broad St. BA1 5LP. (J. Griffiths). Est. 1973. Open 10-4.45. CL: Thurs. SIZE: Medium. *STOCK: Clocks, furniture, paintings, porcelain, barometers, silver.* LOC: 50yds. from central Post Office. PARK: Walcot St. multi-storey, 30yds. TEL: 01225 462946. SER: Valuations; restorations; buys at auction. VAT: Stan/Spec.

Bath Stamp and Coin Shop
Pulteney Bridge. BA2 4AY. (M.A. Swindells). Est. 1946. Open 9.30-5.30. *STOCK: Coins - Roman, hammered, early milled, G.B. gold, silver and copper, some foreign; literature and accessories; banknotes, medals, stamps and postal history.* PARK: Laura Place; Walcot multi-storey. TEL: 01225 463073; e-mail - m7swindells@hotmail.com SER: Valuations. VAT: Stan.

George Bayntun
Manvers St. BA1 1JW. (E.W.G. Bayntun-Coward). ABA. Est. 1894. Open 9-1 and 2-5.30, Sat. 9.30-1. SIZE: Large. *STOCK: Rare books. First or fine editions of English literature, standard sets, illustrated and sporting books, poetry, biography and travel, mainly in new leather bindings; antiquarian books in original bindings.* LOC: By rail and bus stations. PARK: 50 yds. by station. TEL: 01225 466000; fax - 01225 482122; e-mail - ebc@georgebayntun.com website - www.georgebayntun.com SER: Binding; restorations. VAT: Stan.

Bedsteads
2 Walcot Buildings, London Rd. BA1 6AD. (Mark and Nikki Ashton). Est. 1991. Open Tues.-Sat. 10-5.30. *STOCK: Brass, iron and wooden bedsteads, 1840-1920, £500-£4,500; bedroom suites, 1880-1920, £2,000-£5,500.* LOC: 200 yards before traffic lights, end of London Road. PARK: Weymouth St. TEL: 01225 339182; fax - same; home - 01275 464114. SER: Valuations; restorations (bedsteads). VAT: Stan/Spec.

Lawrence Brass
Apple Studio, Ashley. BA1 3SD. Est. 1973. Open by appointment. SIZE: Small. *STOCK: Furniture, 16th-19th C, to £50,000.* Not Stocked: Ceramics, silver, glass. LOC: A4 towards Chippenham. PARK: Easy. TEL: 01225 852222; fax - 01225 851050; website - www. lawrencebrass.com SER: Restorations (furniture, clocks and barometers). VAT: Stan/Spec.

David Bridgwater
Heather Cottage, Lansdown. BA1 9BL. Est. 1984. Open by appointment. *STOCK: Architectural items and sculpture, including garden, decorative and practical items for the period garden.* PARK: Easy. TEL: 01225 463435; e-mail - davidj.bridgwater@btinternet.com SER: Search. VAT: Spec.

Chomé Fine Art   LAPADA
4 George St. BA1 2EH. (Douglas Chomé and Catherine Wilson). BABAADA. CINOA. Open 10-6, Sat. 11-4, other times by appointment. SIZE: Three galleries. *STOCK: 18th-20th C paintings, drawings and watercolours; regular contemporary exhibitions.* LOC: Central. PARK: Nearby. TEL: 01225 466100; fax - 01225 466150; e-mail - info@chomefineart.co.uk

website - www.chomefineart.com SER: Valuations; restorations; framing; marble and stone conservation.

Brian and Caroline Craik Ltd
8 Margaret's Buildings. BA1 2LP. Est. 1963. Open 10-4. *STOCK: Decorative items, mainly 19th C; metalwork, treen, glass and pewter.* LOC: Between Royal Crescent and the Circus, off Brock St. PARK: Nearby. TEL: 01225 337161.

Mary Cruz   LAPADA
5 Broad St. BA1 5LJ. BABAADA. CINOA. Est. 1974. Open 10-6.30, Sun. by appointment. SIZE: Medium. *STOCK: 18th-19th C furniture, including country; 18th C to date paintings and sculpture; decorative items.* LOC: City centre. PARK: Easy. TEL: 01225 334174; fax - 01225 423300; e-mail - mary.cruz@bt.connect.com SER: Valuations; restorations; finder (Latin American Art). VAT: Stan/Spec.

Frank Dux Antiques
33 Belvedere, Lansdown Rd. BA1 5HR. (F. Dux and M. Hopkins). Resident. Est. 1988. Open Tues.-Sat. 10-5. SIZE: Medium. *STOCK: 18th-19th C glass - drinking, decanters, curiosities and tableware; Venetian glass; Murano, occasionally 19th C, mostly 1950s.* LOC: From Broad St. up Lansdown Hill, on right 100yds. past Guinea Lane. PARK: Easy. TEL: 01225 312367; fax - same; e-mail - m.hopkins@antique-glass.co.uk website - www.antique-glass.co.uk SER: Postal deliveries worldwide.

George Street Antiques Centre
8 Edgar Buildings. BA1 2EE. BABAADA. Est. 1993. Open 9.30-5. SIZE: Small. *STOCK: Clocks, barometers, pocket watches; antique and modern jewellery; paintings, silver, porcelain and Staffordshire, general antiques.* LOC: City centre. PARK: Nearby. TEL: 01225 422322; e-mail - kembery@antiquecentre.gb.com website - www.antiquecentre.gb.com SER: Valuations; restorations (clocks, barometers and jewellery).

George Gregory
Manvers St. BA1 1JW. (C.A.W. Bayntun-Coward). Est. 1845. Open 9-1 and 2-5.30, Sat. 9.30-1. SIZE: Large. *STOCK: Secondhand books, engraved views and portraits.* LOC: By rail station. PARK: By rail station. TEL: 01225 466000; fax - 01225 482122; e-mail - julie@georgebayntun.com website - www.georgebayntun.com

Haliden Oriental Rug Shop
98 Walcot St. BA1 5BG. (Andrew Lloyd, Craig Bale and Owen Parry). Est. 1963. Open 10-5. SIZE: Medium. *STOCK: Caucasian, Turkish, Persian, Chinese, Afghan, Turcoman and tribal rugs and carpets, 19th C, £50-£3,000; some Oriental textiles - coats, embroideries, wall hangings, 19th C, £50-£750.* LOC: Off main London road, into town by Walcot Reclamation. PARK: Walcot St. or multi-storey. TEL: 01225 469240. SER: Valuations; cleaning; restorations; buys at auction.

Anthony Hepworth Fine Art Dealers
3 Margaret's Buildings, Brock St. BA1 2LP. Est. 1989. Open during exhibitions Tues.-Sat. 11-5 other times by appointment. *STOCK: Mainly 20th C British paintings and sculpture; African tribal art and large stock of artists' monographs.* LOC: Off Brock St. between Royal Crescent

and Circus. PARK: Brock St./Catherine Place. TEL: 01225 447480; fax - 01225 442917; mobile - 07970 480650 (during fairs only). SER: Exhibitions Bath and London. FAIRS: Olympia; 20th/21st C British Art; London Art.

Jadis Ltd
14 and 15 Walcot Buildings, London Rd. BA1 6AD. (S.H. Creese-Parsons and N.A. Mackay). BABAADA. Est. 1970. Open 9.30-6, Sun. by appointment. SIZE: Medium. *STOCK: English and European furniture, 18th-19th C; decorative items.* LOC: On left hand side of A4 London Rd. entering Bath. PARK: At rear. TEL: 01225 333130; fax - same; mobiles - 07768 232133 and 07879 692371; e-mail - Jadpalad@aol.com and scp.Jadis@aol.com website - www.Jadis-Ltd.com SER: Design service, murals and trompe l'oeil. VAT: Stan/Spec.

Kembery Antique Clocks Ltd
8 Edgar Buildings, George St. BA1 2EE. (P. and E. Kembery). BABAADA. BWCMG. Est. 1993. Open 10-5. *STOCK: Longcase, bracket, mantel, wall and carriage clocks and barometers, 18th-19th C, £200-£10,000.* TEL: 01179 565281; website - www.kdclocks.co.uk SER: Valuations; restorations. VAT: Spec.

Ann King
38 Belvedere, Lansdown Rd. BA1 5HR. Est. 1977. Open 10-5. SIZE: Small. *STOCK: Period clothes, 19th C to 1970; baby clothes, shawls, bead dresses, linen, lace, curtains, cushions, quilts and textiles.* PARK: Easy. TEL: 01225 336245.

Looking Glass of Bath
94-96 Walcot St. BA1 5BG. (Anthony Reed). Est. 1972. Open 9-6. SIZE: Medium. *STOCK: Large mirrors and picture frames, 18th-19th C, £50-£5,000; decorative prints, 18th-20th C.* PARK: Easy. TEL: 01225 461969; fax - 01225 316191; home - 01275 333595; e-mail - info@lookingglassofbath.co.uk website - www.lookingglassofbath.co.uk SER: Valuations; restorations (re-gilding, gesso and compo work, re-silvering and bevelling glass); manufactures arched top overmantel, pier, convex and triptych mirrors; old mirror plates supplied; simulated mercury silvered mirror glass; buys at auction (mirrors and pictures). VAT: Stan/Spec.

Lopburi Art & Antiques
5 Saville Row. BA1 2QP. (Simon and Mee Ling Roper). BABAADA. Est. 1998. Open 10-5. SIZE: Large. *STOCK: 12th-19th C Buddhist art from Thailand, Cambodia and Burma, in bronze, stone and wood, £500-£35,000; 17th-19th C Tibetan painted wooden chests, £900-£7,000; Chinese furniture, carpets and Nepalese contemporary sculpture.* LOC: City centre. PARK: Meters. TEL: 01225 322947; fax - same; e-mail - mail@lopburi.co.uk website - www.lopburi.co.uk SER: Valuations.

E.P. Mallory and Son Ltd   BADA
1-4 Bridge St. and 5 Old Bond St. BA2 4AP. BABAADA. Est. 1898. Open 10-5. *STOCK: Antique and estate silver, jewellery, objets de vertu, £50-£10,000.* **TEL: (0044) 0 1225 788800; fax - (0044) 0 1225 442210; e-mail - mail@mallory-jewellers.com website - www.mallory-jewellers.com VAT: Stan/Spec.**

OLD BANK ANTIQUES CENTRE

16-17 Walcot Buildings, London Road, Bath, BA1 6AD (Also at 5 & 20, Walcot Buildings.)

Tel: 01225 469282/338813   Email: alexatmontague@aol.com

BABAADA Member. Website: www.oldbankantiquescentre.com

How antique shops used to look, but with a modern twist: A hoarder's paradise to suit all pockets.
16 showrooms, in four shops; home to ten dealers, offering a wide selection of English and
continental furniture, ceramics, glass, metalwork and decorative items.

Own parking at rear, via Bedford Street. Open Daily: 10am - 6pm.
Also open Sundays & most Bank Holidays: 11am-4pm.

Old Bank Antiques Centre

16-17 and 20 Walcot Buildings, London Rd. BA1 6AD. (A.R. Schlesinger and D.K. Moore). BABAADA. Est. 1987. Open 10-6, Sun. 11-4. SIZE: 16 showrooms. *STOCK: English, Continental, pine and country furniture, glass, ceramics, rugs, metalwork, interior design items, lighting.* LOC: A4 London Road, 1/2 mile from city centre near Safeway. PARK: Rear of premises, via Bedford St. TEL: 01225 469282; home - same; e-mail - alexatmontague@aol.com website - www. oldbankantiquescentre.com SER: Valuations. Below are listed the dealers at this centre.

AJ Antiques

Choice Antiques
General antiques and decorative items, 18th-19th C, £25-£2,000.

Gerard Coles

Owen Hirst

Simon Jackson

Norman Kemp

Manor House Old Pine

Montague Antiques

Taylor Wootten

David Zienkiewitz
English furniture.

Paragon Antiques and Collectors Market

3 Bladud Buildings, The Paragon. BA1 5LS. (T.J. Clifford and Son Ltd). Est. 1978. Open Wed. 6.30-3. SIZE: Large. LOC: Milsom St./Broad St. PARK: 50yds. TEL: 01225 463715.

Patterson Liddle

10 Margaret's Buildings, Brock St. BA1 2LP. ABA. PBFA. ILAB. Open 10-5.30. *STOCK: Antiquarian books and prints especially art and architecture, illustrated and transport history, travel, English literature, maps.* PARK: Nearby. TEL: 01225 426722; fax - same; e-mail - mail@pattersonliddle.com website - www.patterson liddle.com SER: Transport History catalogues issued.

Quiet Street Antiques

3 Quiet St. and 14/15 John St. BA1 2JS. (K. Hastings-Spital). BABAADA. Est. 1985. Open 10-6. SIZE: Large - 8 showrooms. *STOCK: Furniture especially English mahogany, 1750-1870, £250-£12,000; objects including bronzes, caddies, boxes, mirrors, £50-£2,000; Royal Worcester porcelain, £30-£2,000; clocks including longcase, wall, bracket and carriage, barometers, 1750-1900, £150-£8,000.* LOC: 25yds. from Milsom St. PARK: Nearby. TEL: 01225 315727; fax - 01225 448300; e-mail - kerry@quietstreetantiques.co.uk website - www. quietstreetantiques.co.uk SER: Buys at auction (furniture and clocks); free delivery 100 mile radius of Bath and weekly delivery to London. Export facilities. VAT: Spec.

Roland Gallery

33 Monmouth St. BA1 2AN. (Michael J. Pettitt). Est. 1982. Open Wed.-Sat. 11-4 or by appointment. SIZE: Small. *STOCK: Decorative arts, 1880-1940; silver and plate, bronzes, glass, luggage, jewellery, unusual,*

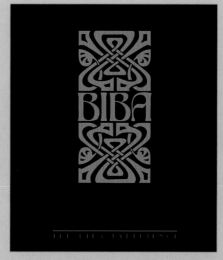
---

decorative and novelty items, £50-£2,000. LOC: Town city. PARK: Pay and Display. TEL: 01225 312330; mobile - 07889 723272; e-mail - therolandgallery@ aol.com FAIRS: NEC; Sandown Park; Newark.

Sarah Russell Antiquarian Prints
5 Margaret's Buildings, Brock St. BA1 2LP. ABA. Open Tues.-Sat. 10-5. *STOCK: Unusual antiquarian prints - architecture, flowers, portraits, landscapes and Bath views, many in original frames.* TEL: 01225 466335; fax - same; e-mail - bathprint@aol.com

Michael and Jo Saffell
3 Walcot Buildings, London Rd. BA1 6AD. BABAADA. Est. 1975. Open 9.30-5, Sat. and other times by appointment. SIZE: Small. *STOCK: British tins and other advertising material including showcards and enamels, 1870-1939; decorative items; all £5-£5,000.* LOC: A4 - main road into city from M4. PARK: Side streets opposite. TEL: 01225 315857; fax - same; home - same; mobile - 07941 158049; e-mail - michael.saffell@ virgin.net SER: Postal. FAIRS: Newark, Winternational, Castle Donington Collectors', Bath Decorative.

Susannah
25 Broad St. BA1 5LW. (Sue Holley). BABAADA. Est. 1985. Open 10-5. *STOCK: Textiles and decorative antiques.* PARK: Opposite. TEL: 01225 445069; fax - 01225 339004; e-mail - sueholley@btopenworld.com FAIRS: Bath Decorative (March).

James Townshend Antiques
1 Saville Row. BA1 2QP. Est. 1992. Open 10-5. SIZE: Large. *STOCK: Trade furniture, china, unusual decorative items and clocks.* LOC: City centre. PARK: Easy. TEL: 01225 332290; website - www. jtownshendantiques.co.uk SER: Delivery. VAT: Spec/Global.

Trimbridge Galleries
Trimbridge. BA1 1HE. (Mr and Mrs A. Anderson). Est. 1973. SIZE: Medium. *STOCK: Watercolours and drawings, £50-£3,000; prints and oil paintings; all 18th-20th C. Annual exhibition in November.* LOC: Just off lower end of Milsom St. PARK: Easy. TEL: 01225 466390; e-mail - info@trimbridgegalleries.com website - www.trimbridgegalleries.com

Vintage to Vogue
28 Milsom St. BA1 1DG. (Mrs Teresa Langton). BABAADA. Est. 1995. Open Tues.-Sat. 10.30-5. SIZE: Medium. *STOCK: Vintage clothing - women's, gentlemen's, children's - including hats, bags, shoes, gloves, scarves and formal wear, 1850-1950s; buttons, trimmings, costume jewellery, costume and antique lace, fashion and needlework books and magazines; all £1-£500.* LOC: In passage from Broad St. car park. PARK: Public at rear of shop. TEL: 01225 337323; website - www.vintagetovogue.com

Walcot Reclamation
108 Walcot St. BA1 5BG. (Mr and Mrs R. Knapp). BABAADA. Est. 1977. Open 8.30-5.30, Sat. 9-5. SIZE: Large. *STOCK: Architectural items - chimney pieces, ironwork, doors, fireplaces, garden statuary, period baths and fittings and traditional building materials.*

PICCADILLY ANTIQUES

1 MILE EAST OF BATH CITY CENTRE
7 MILES M4 MOTORWAY J18

Well established group
dealing in formal and country
furniture and decorative accessories.

**JOHN DAVIES, ROBIN COLEMAN,
GRIERSON GOWER, DAVID ADAMS.**

Over 100 years' combined experience
in dealing with the American
export market

280 High Street, Batheaston,
Bath, BA1 7RA
Tel: 01225 851494
Fax: 01225 851120
Email: piccadillyantiques@ukonline.co.uk

*AN ECLECTIC SELECTION OF THE
RARE AND UNUSUAL*

LOC: Central. PARK: Own and multi-storey nearby. TEL: 01225 444404/448163; e-mail - rick@walcot.com website - www.walcot.com SER: Valuations; restorations. VAT: Stan.

Waterfall Antiques
57 Walcot St. BA1 5BN. BABAADA. Est. 1991. Open 10.30-5.30. SIZE: Medium. *STOCK: 19th C mahogany furniture, especially wardrobes; decorative objects, £20-£500.* LOC: From A4 veer left at 1st mini-roundabout. PARK: Easy. TEL: 01225 444201; mobile - 07990 690240; website - www.waterfallantiques.com VAT: Stan/Spec.

BATHEASTON, Nr. Bath

Piccadilly Antiques
280 High St. BA1 7RA. BABAADA. Est. 1990. Open 9.30-5.30 or by appointment. SIZE: Large. *STOCK: Country, some mahogany, furniture and decorative accessories, £100-£5,000.* LOC: Off junction 17, M4 on old A4. PARK: Easy. TEL: 01225 851494; fax - 01225 851120; e-mail - piccadillyantiques@ukonline.co.uk website - www.babaada.com SER: Restorations (country furniture). FAIRS: Bath Decorative. VAT: Stan/Spec. Below are listed the dealers trading from these premises.

David Adams
BABAADA. *Boxes and globes; contemporary furniture, decorative accessories.*

Robin Coleman Antiques
BABAADA. *Interesting and decorative items, small furniture.*

John Davies
18th-19th C furniture and decorative items. TEL: Home - 01225 852103.

Grierson Gower
Architectural, naive and popular art, toys, models, pub and trade signs.

BRUTON

The Antique Shop
5 High St. BA10 0AB. (D.L. Gwilliam and M.J. Wren). Est. 1976. Open Thurs.-Sat. 10-5.30 or by appointment. SIZE: Medium. *STOCK: Furniture, jewellery, silver, china, copper, brass, general collectables, decorative art and antiques, Georgian to Art Deco, £5-£4,000.* PARK: Easy. TEL: 01749 813264. SER: Repairs (clock, watch and jewellery); re-stringing pearls and beads.

Michael Lewis Gallery - Antiquarian Maps & Prints
17 High St. BA10 0AB. (Leo and Mrs J. L. Lewis). Est. 1980. Open 9.30-5.30 or by appointment. SIZE: Large. *STOCK: Prints and maps, 18th-19th C.* LOC: A359. PARK: Easy. TEL: 01749 813557; home - same. SER: Framing.

M.G.R. Exports
Station Rd. BA10 0EH. Est. 1980. Open Mon.-Fri. 8.30-5.30 or by appointment. SIZE: Large. *STOCK:*

Georgian, Victorian, Edwardian and decorative items, carved oak, barley twist and shipping goods, Continental furniture. PARK: Easy. TEL: 01749 812460; fax - 01749 812882; e-mail - antiques@mgr.exports.co.uk SER: Packing and shipping.

BURNHAM-ON-SEA

Burnham Model & Collectors Shop
3 College Court, College St., TA8 1AR. (W.I. Loudon). Est. 1994. Open 9.30-5 (including Sun. between 13th July to 31st Aug). CL: Wed. SIZE: Medium. *STOCK: Postcards, pre-1945, cigarette cards, medals and banknotes, 50p-£100; Corgi, Dinky, train models, football programmes and comics.* LOC: Seafront, opposite Pavilion Amusements. TEL: 01278 780066; fax - same; e-mail - williamloudon@hotmail.com SER: Valuations.

Castle Antiques
TA8 1AL. (T.C. Germain). NAG. Est. 1953. Open 10-5.30. CL: Wed. *STOCK: Jewellery, silver, 18th-19th C furniture, porcelain, clocks.* LOC: Victoria Court, Victoria St. TEL: 01278 785031; e-mail - castle.antiques@virgin.net website - www.castleantiques.org.uk SER: Restorations.

Heape's Antiques
39 Victoria St. TA8 1AN. (Mrs M.M. Heap). Est. 1987. Open 10-1 and 2.30-4.30. *STOCK: Small furniture, fine arts, porcelain, glass, memorabilia.* LOC: Town centre. PARK: Easy. TEL: 01278 782131. SER: Picture framing, cleaning and restoration.

CARHAMPTON, Nr. Minehead

Chris's Crackers
Townsend Garage. TA24 6NH. (P. Marshall). Est. 1995. Open 11-5.30 including Sun. SIZE: Large warehouses. *STOCK: Mainly 18th-19th C furniture, stripped pine, architectural antiques, iron and stone-work, general building reclamation materials and country artefacts.* LOC: A39 coast road. PARK: Easy. TEL: 01643 821873. SER: Pine stripping.

CASTLE CARY

Antiquus
West Country House, Woodcock St. BA7 7BJ. (Gerald Davison). FRSA. Est. 1962. Open Tues., Wed., Fri. and Sat. 10-5. SIZE: Small. *STOCK: Chinese porcelain and pottery, all dynasties, £25-£2,000; Chinese furniture and works of art, £75-£2,500; English furniture, 18th-20th C, £500-£2,500; English silver, 19th C, £25-£400; boxes, 18th-19th C, £100-£500; English and European pottery and porcelain, 18th-19th C, £35-£500.* PARK: Nearby. TEL: 01963 351246; mobile - 07968 810092; e-mail - gerald.davison@lineone.net website - www.chinesemarks.com SER: Valuations; restorations (ceramics).

CHARD

Chard Antique Centre
23 High St. TA20 1QF. (A.W.E. and Mrs J. Smith). Est. 1994. Open 10-5, other times by appointment. SIZE: Medium. *STOCK: Furniture, 19th C to Edwardian; pine,* *decorative items, pictures and collectables.* PARK: Nearby. TEL: 01460 63517; website - www.chard antiques.co.uk

CHARLTON HORETHORNE, Nr. Sherborne

On-Reflection Mirrors Ltd
Bullen Farmhouse. DT9 4NL. (Alison and Alan Roelich). Est. 1999. By appointment at any time. SIZE: Large. *STOCK: Fine quality English, French and Italian gilt mirrors, mainly 19th C, £50-£5,000.* PARK: Easy. TEL: 01963 220723; home/fax - same; mobile - 07971 889093; e-mail - info@on-reflection.co.uk; website - www.on-reflection.co.uk SER: Valuations; finder. FAIRS: DMG Shepton Mallet; Earls Court; Antiques for Everyone, NEC.

CHILCOMPTON, Nr. Bath

Billiard Room Antiques   LAPADA
The Old School, Church Lane. BA3 4HP. (Mrs J. McKeivor). Est. 1992. Open by appointment. SIZE: Medium. *STOCK: Billiard, snooker and pool tables and accessories, 19th C, £100-£40,000.* PARK: Easy. TEL: 01761 232839; home and fax - same. SER: Valuations; restorations; buys at auction; search.

CLEVEDON

The Collector
14 The Beach. BS21 7QU. (Mrs Tina Simmonds). Est. 1993. Open 10-5, Sun. 12-5. CL: Thurs. (Jan.-Feb. open weekends only). SIZE: Small. *STOCK: Small items and collectables, from 1880, £5-£200; postcards and ephemera, 1900-1960, £1-£30; Beatrix Potter and Bunnykins figures, from 1960, £16-£300.* LOC: On sea front, near pier. PARK: Easy. TEL: 01275 875066; home - same. FAIRS: Malvern 3 Counties.

COXLEY, Nr. Wells

Courtyard Antiques
Main Rd. BA5 1QZ. (Mr and Mrs M. J. Mitchell). Est. 1985. Open 9-5, Sun by appointment. SIZE: Medium. *STOCK: Furniture, £100-£300; smalls, £10-£50; both 19th-20th C.* TEL: 01749 679533. SER: Valuations; restorations (upholstery, cane and rush work, china and furniture).

Wells Reclamation Company
BA5 1RQ. (H. Davies). Est. 1984. Open 8.30-5.30, Sat. 9-4. SIZE: Large including barns and grounds. *STOCK: Architectural items, 18th-19th C.* LOC: A39 towards Glastonbury from Wells. PARK: Easy. TEL: 01749 677087; website - www.wellsreclamation.com SER: Valuations. VAT: Stan.

CREWKERNE

Antiques and Country Pine
14 East St. TA18 7AG. (M.J. Wheeler). Est. 1980. Open Tues.-Sat. 10-5 or by appointment. *STOCK: Country pine and decorative items.* PARK: Own. TEL: 01460 75623.

Julian Armytage
TA18 8QG. Open by appointment. *STOCK: Fine sporting, marine and decorative prints, 18th-19th C.* TEL: 01460 73449; fax - same. VAT: Spec.

Crewkerne Antique Centre
16 Market St. TA18 7LA. (E. Blewden). Est. 1987. Open 9.30-4.30. SIZE: Large, 50 dealers. *STOCK: Furniture, £25-£3,000; collectables, £5-£1,000; pictures, £5-£2,000; all 18th-20th C.* LOC: A303 westward, A359 to Crewkerne, Chard road through town. PARK: Easy. TEL: 01460 77111. SER: Valuations; restorations.

Gresham Books
31 Market St. TA18 7JU. (J. and A. Hine). ABA. PBFA. Est. 1972. Open 10-5. SIZE: Medium. *STOCK: Books, 50p to £1,000.* LOC: A30. PARK: Nearby. TEL: 01460 77726; fax - 01460 52479; e-mail - jameshine@gresham -books.demon.co.uk website - www.greshambooks.co.uk SER: Valuations.

Noahs
41 Market Sq. TA18 7LP. (Mrs. Edmonds and Michael Polirer). Est. 1967. Open Tues.-Sat. 10-4.30. SIZE: Medium. *STOCK: General antiques including silver and jewellery.* LOC: Town centre. PARK: Nearby. TEL: 01460 77786. SER: Valuations; restorations.

DULVERTON

Acorn Antiques
39 High St. TA22 9DW. (P. Hounslow). Est. 1988. Open 9.30-5.30. SIZE: Medium. *STOCK: Decorative antique furniture, period and reproduction upholstery, sofas, fine art, textiles, country furniture.* LOC: Town centre. PARK: Nearby. TEL: 01398 323286; home - same; e-mail - peter@exmoorantiques.co.uk website - www. exmoorantiques.co.uk SER: Interior design.

Rothwell and Dunworth
2 Bridge St. TA22 9HJ. (Mrs C. Rothwell and M. Rothwell). ABA. Est. 1975. Open 10.30-1 and 2.15-5, including Sun. (excluding Nov-Feb). SIZE: Medium. *STOCK: Antiquarian and secondhand books especially on hunting, horses and military history.* LOC: 1st shop in village over River Barle. PARK: 100yds. TEL: 01398 323169; fax - 01398 331161; e-mail - rothwellm@ aol.com SER: Valuations.

Anthony Sampson Antiques
Holland House, Bridge St. TA22 9HJ. Est. 1968. Open 9.30-5.30, Sun. by appointment. SIZE: Medium. *STOCK: Town and country furniture, 17th to early 19th C, £500-£10,000+; porcelain, pottery, silver, glass, pictures, garden ornaments and decorative items.* LOC: Main road, prominent position near bridge. PARK: Nearby. TEL: 01398 324247; e-mail - jenny.sampson@ virgin.net SER: Valuations. VAT: Spec.

DUNSTER

The Crooked Window
7 High St. TA24 6SF. (Robert Ricketts). Est. 1984. SIZE: Small. *STOCK: Chinese ceramics and jade, 3000BC to 19th C, £50-£50,000; English furniture, 16th-18th C, £500-£50,000; maps and prints, 16th-18th C, £50-£2,000; antique jewellery.* PARK: Easy. TEL: 01643 821606; home - same; mobile - 07787 722606; e-mail - icthus-fine-art@supanet.com and enquiries@antiquities. uk.com website - www.antiquities.uk.com SER: Valuations; lectures. FAIRS: Wilton House.

EAST PENNARD, Nr. Shepton Mallet

Pennard House Antiques   LAPADA
BA4 6TP. (Martin Dearden). BABAADA. Est. 1979. Open 9.30-5.30 or by appointment. SIZE: Large. *STOCK: French and English country furniture, £300-£5,000.* LOC: From Shepton Mallet, 4 miles south off A37. One hour from Bath. PARK: Easy. TEL: 01749 860731; home - 01749 860266; fax - 01749 860700; e-mail - pennardantiques@ukonline.co.uk SER: Valuations; restorations; export. VAT: Stan/Spec.

FRESHFORD, Nr. Bath

Janet Clarke
3 Woodside Cottages. BA2 7WJ. *STOCK: Antiquarian books on gastronomy, cookery and wine.* TEL: 01225 723186; fax - 01225 722063; e-mail - janetclarke@ ukgateway.net SER: Catalogue issued. *Mail Order Only.*

Freshfords   LAPADA
High St. BA2 7WF. (Simon Powell). CINOA. BABAADA. Est. 1973. Open by appointment. SIZE: Large. *STOCK: English Regency furniture, 18th-19th C, £2,000-£50,000; Victorian oil paintings, £2,000-£12,000; decorative accessories, 18th-19th C, £2,000-£5,000.* LOC: 4 miles from Bath towards Warminster, just off A36. PARK: Easy. TEL: 01225 722111; fax - 01225 722991; mobile - 07720 838877; e-mail - antiques @freshfords.com website - www.freshfords.com. SER: Valuations; restorations; buys at auction. FAIRS: Olympia; Armoury, New York. VAT: Spec.

FROME

Antiques & Country Living
43-44 Vallis Way, Badcox. BA11 3BA. (Mrs D.M. Williams). Open 9.30-5.30 including Sun. SIZE: Medium. *STOCK: Furniture including country, 19th-20th C, £15-£1,000; porcelain, 18th-19th C, £5-£500; books; lighting.* LOC: A362 Frome to Radstock road. PARK: Free opposite. TEL: 01373 463015; books - 01373 467125; mobile - 07808 933076.

Frome Reclamation
Station Approach. BA11 1RE. (S.J., K.R., R.L. and J.B. Horler). Est. 1987. Open 8-5, Sat. 8-4.30. SIZE: Large + yard. *STOCK: Architectural reclamation.* LOC: From A361 follow signs for rail station. PARK: Easy. TEL: 01373 463919/453122; fax - 01373 453122; e-mail - info@fromerec.co.uk website - www.fromerec.co.uk SER: Valuations. VAT: Stan.

GODNEY, Nr. Wells

Country Brocante
Fir Tree Farm. BA5 1RZ. (Tim and Nicky Ovel). BABAADA. Est. 1993. Open by appointment. SIZE: Medium. *STOCK: 18th-19th C French farmhouse tables and early mirrors; 19th-20th C decorative lighting and chandeliers; interesting objects and furniture.* LOC: Village centre. PARK: Easy. TEL: 01458 833052; home - same; fax - 01458 835611; mobile - 07970 719708; e-mail - ovel@compuserve.com FAIRS: Shepton Mallet; Newark. *Trade Only.*

PENNARD HOUSE ANTIQUES
Martin and Susie Dearden with five guest dealers

Major source of English and French
country furniture and decorative
accessories
Set in splendid country house forty-five
minutes south of Bath off A37

*Open 6 days a week or by
appointment
Shipping and restoration services
on site
Courier services and
accommodation arranged*

Established 25 years
LAPADA and BABAADA member

Pennard House Antiques, East Pennard, Shepton Mallet, Somerset, BA4 6TP
Telephone: **(01749) 860731** Fax: **(01749) 860700** Mobile: **(07802) 243569** Email: pennardantiques@ukonline.co.uk

ILCHESTER

Gilbert & Dale
The Old Chapel, Church St. BA22 8LN. (Roy Gilbert and Joan Dale). Est. 1965. Open 9-5.30 or by appointment. SIZE: Large. *STOCK: English and French country furniture and accessories.* LOC: Village centre on A37. PARK: Easy. TEL: 01935 840464; fax - 01935 841599; e-mail - roy@roygilbert.com

LANGFORD, Nr. Bristol

Richard Essex Antiques
BS40 5BP. (B.R. and C.L. Essex). Est. 1969. *STOCK: General antiques from mid-18th C.* TEL: 01934 863302.

LITTLETON, Nr. Somerton

Westville House Antiques
TA11 6NP. (D. and M. Stacey). Est. 1986. Open daily, Sun. by appointment. SIZE: Large. *STOCK: 18th-19th C pine, mahogany and oak furniture;* LOC: B3151 approximately 1.5 miles north of Somerton. PARK: Own. TEL: 01458 273376; fax - same; e-mail - info@westville.co.uk website - www.westville.co.uk SER: Valuations; buys at auction. VAT: Stan/Spec.

MARTOCK

Castle Reclamation
Parrett Works. TA12 6AE. (T.A.B. Dance and A.J. Wills). Est. 1986. Open daily, Sat. 10-1. SIZE: Large. *STOCK: Architectural antiques.* LOC: 2 miles off A303

between Martock and South Petherton. PARK: Easy. TEL: 01935 826483; fax - 01935 826791; website - www.castlereclamation.com SER: Restorations (stone). FAIRS: Bath and West. VAT: Stan.

NETHER STOWEY, Nr. Bridgwater

House of Antiquity
St. Mary St. TA5 1LJ. (M.S. Todd). Est. 1967. Open 10-5 or by appointment. SIZE: Medium. *STOCK: Philatelic literature, world topographical, maps, handbooks, postcards, ephemera, postal history.* LOC: A39. PARK: Easy. TEL: 01278 732426; fax - same; e-mail - mstodd@lineone.net SER: Valuations; buys at auction. VAT: Stan.

NORTH PETHERTON

Jay's Antiques and Collectables
121A Fore St. TA6 6SA. (Mr and Mrs Jose Alba). Est. 1982. Open 10-4.30, Mon. 10-1. CL: Wed. *STOCK: Clocks including Victorian, mantel and wall, £50-£400; pressed and coloured glass, £15-£45; china, £10-£85.* LOC: Main street. PARK: Easy. TEL: Home - 01278 662508; mobile - 07815 734965. SER: Repairs (clocks). FAIRS: Talisman.

PORLOCK

Magpie Antiques & Collectables
High St. TA24 8PT. (Glenys Battams). Est. 1980. Open Thurs., Fri. and Sat. 10-5 and some Sun, prior telephone call advisable. SIZE: Medium. *STOCK: Jewellery and*

silver; 19th C glass including scent bottles, decorative objects; 18th-19th C pottery and porcelain; Viennese bronzes, objets de vertu. LOC: Opposite Lorna Doone Hotel. PARK: Nearby. TEL: 01271 850669; fax - same; mobile - 07721 679020. SER: Valuations. FAIRS: Westpoint, Shepton Mallet.

Rare Books and Berry
High St. TA24 8PT. (Helen and Michael Berry). Est. 1983. Open 9.30-5. SIZE: Medium. *STOCK: Secondhand and antiquarian books.* PARK: Nearby. TEL: 01643 863255; fax - 01643 863092; e-mail - info@ rarebooksandberry.co.uk website - www.rarebooks andberry.co.uk

QUEEN CAMEL, Nr. Yeovil

Steven Ferdinando
The Old Vicarage. BA22 7NG. PBFA. Est. 1978. Open by appointment. *STOCK: Antiquarian and secondhand books.* PARK: Own. TEL: 01935 850210; e-mail - stevenferdinando@onetel.com SER: Valuations. FAIRS: Shepton Mallet; PBFA.

RADSTOCK

Notts Pine
Old Redhouse Farm, Stratton-on-the-Fosse. BA3 4QE. (Jeffery Nott). Est. 1978. Open Mon.-Fri. 9-5.30. SIZE: Medium. *STOCK: Pine furniture including wardrobes, boxes, pot cupboards and dressers, mainly 19th-20th C.* PARK: Easy. TEL: 01761 419911; home - 01761 471614; mobile - 07968 111553. SER: Valuations; restorations (pine furniture). FAIRS: Newark.

SHEPTON MALLET

Edward Marnier Antiques
Old Bowlish House, Forum Lane, Bowlish. BA4 5JA. (E.F. Marnier). Resident. BABAADA. Est. 1989. Open 7 days, prior telephone call advisable. *STOCK: English and Continental furniture, pictures, rugs, carpets and interesting decorative objects, 17th-20th C, £5-£10,000.* LOC: Quarter mile from Shepton Mallet on A371 Wells Rd., turn right into Forum Lane. PARK: Easy. TEL: 01749 343340; mobile - 07785 110122; e-mail - emarnier@ukonline.co.uk SER: Valuations; buys at auction. VAT: Spec.

SOMERTON

John Gardiner Antiques
Monteclefe House. TA11 7NL. Est. 1974. Appointment advisable. *STOCK: General antiques; decorative Edwardian, Georgian and quality old reproduction furnishings.* LOC: A303, close to M5. TEL: 01458 272238; fax/answerphone - 01458 274329; mobile - 07831 274427; e-mail - rpash@fsbdial.co.uk

The London Cigarette Card Co. Ltd
West St. TA11 6NB. (I.A. and E.K. Laker, F.C. Doggett and Y. Berktay). Est. 1927. Open daily. SIZE: Medium. *STOCK: Cigarette and trade cards, 1885 to date; sets from £2; other cards, from 15p; frames for mounting cards and special albums.* PARK: Easy. TEL: 01458 273452/274148; e-mail - cards@londoncigcard.co.uk

website - www.londoncigcard.co.uk SER: Publishers of catalogues, reference books and monthly magazine; mail order; monthly auctions.

Somerton Antiques Centre
Market Place. TA11 7NB. Est. 1998. Open 10-5. SIZE: Large - 46 dealers. *STOCK: General antiques, £5-£1,800.* PARK: Own. TEL: 01458 274423. SER: Valuations; repairs; restorations (furniture). FAIRS: Shepton Mallet.

STOGURSEY, Nr. Bridgwater

Pride of the Forest
24 High St. TA5 1TA. (Paul, Jayne, Roxanne and Kenzie Farnham). Est. 1974. Usually open. SIZE: Medium. *STOCK: Furniture, art, books and objects, £2-£2,000; rustic furniture, antler art, screens.* LOC: Central High St. PARK: Easy. TEL: 01278 732009; home/fax - same; e-mail - prideoftheforest@aol.com website - www.prideoftheforest.com

STOKE-SUB-HAMDON

Wessex Antique Bedsteads
The Old Glove Works, Percombe. TA14 6RD. (Jeremy Peachell). Est. 1991. Open 9-5, Sat. 10-5, Sun. and other times by appointment. SIZE: Large. *STOCK: Brass, iron and wooden bedsteads, including four-poster and half-tester, mainly Victorian and Edwardian.* LOC: Adjacent A303, north of Yeovil. PARK: Easy. TEL: 01935 829147; home - same; fax - 01935 829148; mobile - 07973 884079; e-mail - info@wessexbeds.com website - www.wessexbeds.com SER: Restorations (wooden and metal beds); bespoke mattresses and bases; delivery and shipping.

TAUNTON

T. J. Atkins
East Criddles Farm, Tolland, Lydeard St. Lawrence. TA4 3PW. Est. 1958. Open by appointment. SIZE: Medium. *STOCK: Porcelain and pottery including Prattware, 18th-19th C.* TEL: 01984 667310.

Cider Press Antiques Centre
58 Bridge St. TA1 1UD. (Norman D.J. Clarke and Mark W.J. Blake). Est. 1998. Open 10-5, Sun. 11-4. SIZE: Medium - 10 dealers. *STOCK: Furniture, Georgian to Victorian, £100-£2,000; jewellery, silver and plate, ceramics, glass, collectables, stamps, postcards, records and books; reclamation items.* LOC: Near town centre. PARK: Nearby. TEL: 01823 283050; fax - same; mobile - 07764 212520; home - 01823 661354. SER: Valuations; restorations (furniture).

Selwoods
Queen Anne Cottage, Mary St. TA1 3PE. Est. 1927. Open 9.30-5. SIZE: Very large. *STOCK: Furniture, including Victorian and Edwardian.* PARK: Own at rear. TEL: 01823 272780.

Taunton Antiques Market - Silver Street
25/29 Silver St. TA1 3DH. (Bath Antiques Market Ltd.). Est. 1978. Open Mon. 9-4 including Bank Holidays. SIZE: 100+ dealers. *STOCK: General antiques and collectables, including specialists in most fields.* LOC: 2

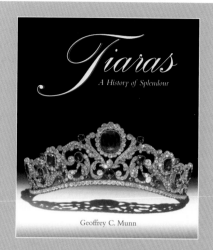
miles from M5, junction 25, to town centre, 100yds. from Sainsburys car park across lights. PARK: Easy - Sainsburys (town centre branch). TEL: 01823 289327; fax - same; enquiries - 020 7351 5353. SER: Valuations.

M.G. Welch Jeweller
1 Corporation St. TA1 4AJ. (Mark and Liz Welch). NAG. Est. 1985. Open 9.30-5. SIZE: Medium. *STOCK: Antique and secondhand jewellery, £100-£10,000; antique and secondhand silver, £100-£1,000; early 20th C masters including Cartier, Tiffany, Georg Jensen, Chaumet.* LOC: Town centre, corner of High St. PARK: Nearby. TEL: 01823 270456; fax - same; e-mail - sales@mgwelch.com SER: Valuations; restorations (jewellery). VAT: Stan/Spec.

WASHFORD

Courtyard Antiques
Rock Cottage, Torre. TA23 0LA. (Nick Wass and Liz Cain). Est. 1997. Open Tues.-Sat. 9-4. SIZE: Small. *STOCK: English vernacular furniture - oak, elm and pine, upholstered chairs, mostly 19th-20th C, £100-£2,000.* LOC: Off the A39. PARK: Easy. TEL: 01984 641619; e-mail - sales@courtyardantiques.net website - www.courtyardantiques.net

WATCHET

Clarence House Antiques
41 Swain St. TA23 0AE. Est. 1970. Open 11.30-5.30. CL: Sun. in winter. SIZE: Medium. *STOCK: General antiques, pine, brass, copper, bric-a-brac, collectables and books (including specialist and antiquarian).* PARK: Nearby. TEL: 01984 631389. VAT: Stan.

Nick Cotton Fine Art
Beachstone House, 46/47 Swain St. TA23 0AG. (Nick

and Lynda Cotton). Est. 1970. Open 10-6. SIZE: Large. *STOCK: Paintings, 1850-2000; some period furniture.* PARK: Adjacent. TEL: 01984 631814; website - www.thelyndacottongallery.co.uk SER: Restorations; conservation; research. VAT: Spec.

WEDMORE

The Walnut Tree
1 King Alfred Mews, Church St. BS28 4AB. (Mrs Stella Littlewood). Est. 2003. Open Tues.-Sat. 9.30-3. SIZE: Small. *STOCK: French country furniture including farmhouse tables, painted armoires and linen presses, dressers, mainly 19th C, to £1,200; small painted pieces - chairs, chests of drawers, shelves; mirrors, linen, enamelware and garden furniture.* LOC: Opposite George Hotel. PARK: Easy. TEL: 01934 710360

WELLINGTON

Michael and Amanda Lewis Oriental Carpets and Rugs   LAPADA
8 North St. TA21 8LT. UKIC. Est. 1982. Open 10-1 and 2-5.30, Mon. and weekends by appointment. SIZE: Medium. *STOCK: Oriental carpets and rugs, mainly 19th-20th C, £25-£25,000.* LOC: 1 mile from junction 26, M5. PARK: 100yds. TEL: 01823 667430; e-mail - rugmike@btopenworld.com SER: Valuations; repairs; restorations; cleaning; restoration and conservation (tapestry).

WELLS

Bernard G. House
Market Place. BA5 2RF. Est. 1963. Open 10-5.30. SIZE: Medium. *STOCK: Barometers and scientific instruments, barographs, telescopes, tripod and hand*

held; furniture, 18th-19th C; longcase and bracket clocks, metalware, decorative and architectural items. PARK: Opposite shop. TEL: 01749 672607; e-mail - info@antiquebarometers.com website - www.antique clocksandbarometers.co.uk SER: Repairs; restorations. VAT: Stan/Spec.

Marshalls of Wells
7 Mill St. BA5 2AS. (Trevor Marshall). Est. 1959. Open 10-5 or by appointment. SIZE: Large. *STOCK: General antiques, antique and reproduction pine, rugs and carpets.* LOC: Town centre. PARK: Easy. TEL: 01749 672489; e-mail - info@marshalls-uk.com website - www.marshalls-uk.com SER: French polishing.

The Sadler Street Gallery
23 Market Place. BA5 2RF. (Jill Swale). Est. 1993. Open 10-5. SIZE: 3 floors. *STOCK: 18th to early 20th C watercolours, oils and etchings; contemporary watercolours and oils mainly by West Country artists.* LOC: City centre. TEL: 01749 670220; website - www.thesadlerstreetgallery.co.uk

WEST BUCKLAND, Nr. Taunton

Everett Fine Art Ltd
Budleigh Studios, Budleigh. TA21 9LW. (Tim and Karen Everett). Open by appointment. *STOCK: Fine paintings and furniture, £1,000-£10,000+.* LOC: 3 miles from junction 26, M5. PARK: Easy. TEL: 01823 421710; e-mail - info@everett-art.co.uk website - www.everett-art.co.uk SER: Restorations; conservation (paintings and frames); framemakers. VAT: Stan/Spec.

WESTON-SUPER-MARE

D.M. Restorations
3 Laburnum Rd. BS23 3LL. (D. Pike). Est. 1983. Open 9-5. *STOCK: Small mahogany furniture.* PARK: Easy. TEL: 01934 811120.

Sterling Books
43A Locking Rd. BS23 3DG. ABA. PBFA. ILAB. Est. 1966. Open 10-5.30. CL: Mon. and Thurs. pm. SIZE: Large. *STOCK: Books, antiquarian and secondhand, some new; ephemera and prints.* PARK: Easy. TEL: 01934 625056; e-mail - sterling.books@talk21.com SER: Bookbinding; picture framing.

WILLITON

Edward Venn
Unit 3, 52 Long St. TA4 4QU. Est. 1979. Open 10-5. *STOCK: Furniture, clocks.* PARK: Easy. TEL: 01984 632631; website - www.vennantiquesrestoration.co.uk SER: Restorations (furniture, barometers and clocks).

WINCANTON

Green Dragon Antiques Centre
24 High St. BA9 9JF. (Mrs Sally Denning). Est. 1991. Open 10-5 including Sun. SIZE: 112 dealers. *STOCK: Wide variety of general antiques and collectables, £1-£1,000.* PARK: Own. TEL: 01963 34111/34702; fax - 01963 34111; website - www.greendragonantiques.com SER: Valuations.

The Old Schoolrooms Antiques
16 Mill St. BA9 9AP. (P.L. Broomfield). Open 9-4 or by appointment. CL: Mon and Thurs. SIZE: Large. *STOCK: Georgian and Edwardian furniture, £50-£7,000+.* LOC: Left towards Bruton, left around side of post office, premises 100 yards on right. PARK: Easy. TEL: 01963 824259; mobile - 07768 726276; e-mail - info@old schoolroomsantiques.com SER: Valuations; restorations (furniture). FAIRS: Newark.

Ottery Antique Restorers   LAPADA
Wessex Way, Wincanton Business Park. BA9 9RR. (C.J. James). BABAADA. Est. 1986. Open 8-5, Sat. 9-2. SIZE: Small. *STOCK: 17th-18th C furniture.* LOC: Outskirts of town, just off A303. PARK: Easy. TEL: 01963 34572; fax - same; mobile - 07770 923955; e-mail - charles@otteryantiques.co.uk website - www.ottery antiques.com SER: Valuations; restorations (see entry in Services section, under Furniture). FAIRS: Bath.

Wincanton Antiques
London House, 12 High St. BA9 9JL. (Tony Kimber). Est. 1997. Open 9.30-5. SIZE: Large. *STOCK: Georgian, Victorian and Edwardian furniture, decorative items, £25-£7,000+.* PARK: Nearby. TEL: 01963 32223; e-mail - old schoolrooms@aol.com SER: Upholstery. FAIRS: Newark.

WIVELISCOMBE

J.C. Giddings
TA4 2SN. Est. 1969. Open by appointment. SIZE: Large warehouses. *STOCK: Mainly 18th-19th C furniture, iron-work and reclamation timber.* PARK: Easy. TEL: 01984 623703. *Mainly Trade.*

Heads 'n' Tails
Bournes House, 41 Church St. TA4 2LT. (D. McKinley). Resident. Open by appointment. *STOCK: Taxidermy including Victorian cased and uncased birds, mammals and fish, £5-£2,000; decorative items, glass domes.* LOC: Opposite church. PARK: Easy. TEL: 01984 623097; fax - 01984 624445; e-mail - mac@taxidermy uk.com website - www.taxidermyuk.com SER: Taxidermy; restorations; commissions; hire. VAT: Spec.

Yew Tree Antiques Warehouse
Old Brewery, Golden Hill. TA4 2NA. (Nigel and Sheila Nation). Est. 1997. Open Tues.-Fri. 10-4.30, Sat. 10-5. SIZE: Large - 2 floors. *STOCK: English and French furniture, mainly Victorian and Edwardian, some Georgian including French beds, armoires, buffets, chairs, tables, mirrors, pot cupboards, wash stands, over mantels, desks, piano stools, £25-£750; china, glass and pictures, £3-£100.* PARK: Easy. TEL: 01984 623950; home - 01984 623914; mobile - 07714 266667; e-mail - yewtreeantiques@btopenworld.com website - www.yewtreeantiques.co.uk

YEOVIL

John Hamblin
Unit 6, 15 Oxford Rd., Penn Mill Trading Estate. BA21 5HR. (J. and M. A. Hamblin). Est. 1980. Open 8.30-5. CL: Sat. SIZE: Small. *STOCK: Furniture, 1750-1900, £300-£3,000.* PARK: Easy. TEL: 01935 471154; home - 01935 476673. SER: Restorations (furniture); cabinet work; French polishing. VAT: Stan.

- *Digitally enhanced photographs*

- *A wealth of illustrations which facilitate identification of individual pieces*

- *The standard work on the subject, long out of print, and much sought after*

- *Comprehensive bibliography*

EIGHTEENTH CENTURY ENGLISH

DRINKING GLASSES

AN ILLUSTRATED HISTORY

L.M. BICKERTON

Firmly established as the standard textbook on its subject, this important work has been out of print for some time and much sought after by dealers and collectors throughout the antiquarian book trade. L.M. Bickerton's book was unique for two reasons, its wealth of illustrations and its extensive bibliography by Robert Elleray. Interest in eighteenth century drinking glasses continues to be very strong and collectors are encouraged by the enormous variety of bowls and stems which are an eloquent testimony to the ingenuity and craftsmanship of glass workers of the time. In the last revision the author had extended the illustrations to over one thousand. This made the book particularly valuable, since it was obviously impossible to show every minor variation although the sheer number of examples included provided a very good representation of what collectors were likely to find. A chapter was also included giving much fuller definitions of the classes of drinking glasses, avoiding the necessity of constant reference to other authorities. Special coverage of baluster-stemmed and engraved glasses was also included. Robert Elleray contributed the superb bibliography of English glass, the most detailed ever produced on the subject. Collectors, dealers, auction houses and anyone interested in this fascinating facet of the eighteenth century decorative arts will welcome this timely reprint.

Specifications: 432pp.,
1,220 b.&w. illus.,
11 x 8½in./279 x 216mm.
£49.50 (hardback)

For full details of all ACC publications, log on to our website:
www.antiquecollectorsclub.com
or telephone 01394 389950 for a free catalogue

STAFFORDSHIRE

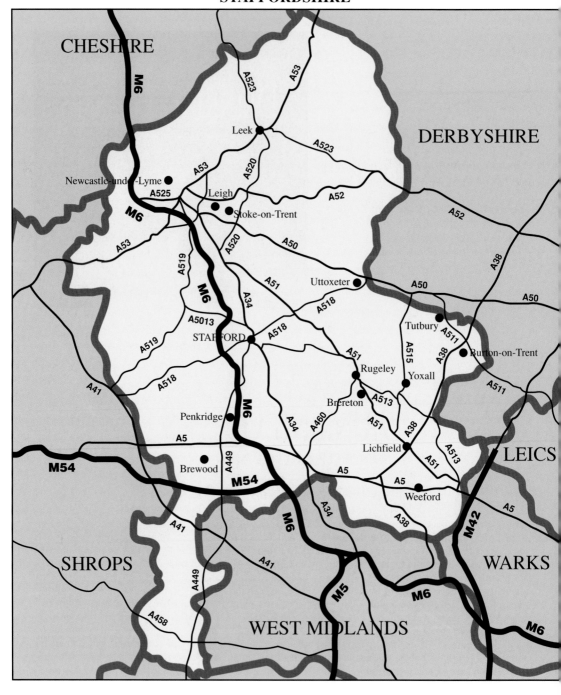

PAINTED DIAL CLOCKS

Brian Loomes

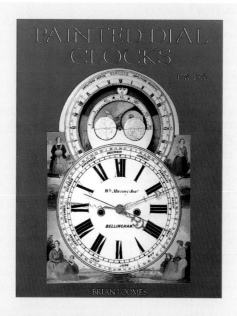

This is a complete re-write of the author's earlier book *White Dial Clocks* which became the standard work on the subject. This new edition, written to take account of the latest research findings, contains additional black and white illustrations and new colour material. The painted dial type of clock is important to the collector or student in Britain in the sense that it is more readily available then many other types of clock. This greater availability often also means that painted dial clocks fall into a lower price category and so are more affordable for the potential buyer. For the collector or student in America, these clocks assume an even greater importance. Of those clocks actually made in North America few were made with brass dials, and those with painted dials were often made using dials imported from Britain by the clockmakers. The same also applies to clocks made in Canada, Australia and New Zealand. For all these countries, therefore, a knowledge of British painted dial clockmaking is essential.

Specifications: 280pp., 44 col. illus., 275 b.&w. illus., 11 x 8½in./279 x 216mm.
£29.95 (hardback)

For full details of all ACC publications, log on to our website:
www.antiquecollectorsclub.com
or telephone 01394 389950 for a free catalogue

BRERETON, Nr. Rugeley

Rugeley Antique Centre
161/3 Main Rd. WS15 1DX. (D. and N. Edwards). Est. 1979. Open Tues. and Sun. 10-4.30, Fri. and Sat. 10-5. SIZE: Large - 40 units. *STOCK: China, glass, pottery, pictures, furniture, pine, treen, linen and shipping goods.* LOC: A51, one mile south of Rugeley town, opposite Cedar Tree Hotel. PARK: Own. TEL: 01889 577166; e-mail - info@rugeleyantiquecentre.co.uk website - www.rugeleyantiquecentre.co.uk VAT: Stan/Spec.

BREWOOD

Passiflora
25 Stafford St. ST19 9DX. (David and Paula Whitfield). Est. 1988. Flexible opening - usually 10-4ish, prior telephone call advisable. SIZE: Medium. *STOCK: General antiques, collectables, curios, copper, brass, Mabel Lucie Attwell corner, Victorian to 1950s, £1-£300.* LOC: Off A5 and A449 near Gailey roundabout, village on Shropshire Union canal. PARK: Free opposite. TEL: 01902 851557 (answerphone); mobile - 07711 682216; e-mail - paula.whitfield@ukonline.co.uk and whitfield@passiflora25.fsnet.co.uk SER: Valuations. FAIRS: Bingley Hall; Stafford.

BURTON-UPON-TRENT

Burton Antiques
1-2 Horninglow Rd. DE14 2PR. (C.H. Armett). Est. 1977. Open 9-5, Sun. 11-3. SIZE: Large. *STOCK: Pine furniture.* LOC: A511. PARK: Nearby. TEL: 01283 542331. SER: Valuations; stripping (pine); buys at auction.

M.A.J. Morris
Weavers Green, Needwood. DE13 9PQ. Est. 1993. Open by appointment only. SIZE: Small. *STOCK: Maps, plans, charts and prints, atlases, county histories, documents and paintings, 1550-1950, £5-£1,000.* LOC: Telephone for directions. PARK: Easy. TEL: 01283 575344. SER: Valuations. VAT: Stan. *Mainly Trade.*

LEEK

Antiques Within Ltd
Ground Floor, Compton Mill. ST13 5NJ. (R. and K. Hicks). Est. 1992. Open 10-5.30. Sun. (Oct. to April) 1-5.30. *STOCK: Pine, oak and mahogany, £50-£3,000; bric-a-brac, £5-£500.* LOC: A520 towards Cheddleton, opposite Catholic church. PARK: Easy. TEL: 01538 387848; e-mail - antiques.within@virgin.net website - www.antiques-within.com SER: Restorations; courier, packing and shipping. FAIRS: Newark; Swinderby. VAT: Stan.

Anvil Antiques Ltd
Antiques Trade Centre, Pretty Polly Mill, Buxton Rd. ST13 6EJ. (J.S. Spooner and N.M. Sullivan). Est. 1975. Open 9-5, Sat. 10-5, Sun. 12-4. SIZE: Large. *STOCK: Stripped pine, old and reproduction; oak, mahogany, bric-a-brac and decorative items, architectural items.* LOC: Ashbourne Rd., from town centre roundabout, turn first left, Victorian mill on right. PARK: Easy. TEL: 01538 384522. VAT: Stan.

England's Gallery
Ball Haye House, 1 Ball Haye Terrace. ST13 6AP. (F.J. and S.J. England). Est. 1968. Open 10-1 and 2-5, Mon. and other times by appointment. SIZE: Large. STOCK: Oils and watercolours, 18th-19th C, £500-£10,000; etchings, engravings, lithographs, mezzotints, £50-£4,000. LOC: Towards Ball Haye Green from A523 turn at lights. PARK: Nearby. TEL: 01538 373451. SER: Valuations; restorations; cleaning; relining; regilding; framing; mount cutting; buys at auction (paintings). VAT: Stan.

Gemini Trading
Limes Mill, Abbotts Rd. ST13 6EY. (T.J. Lancaster and Mrs Y.A. Goldstraw). Est. 1981. Open Mon.-Fri. 9-5, other times by appointment. SIZE: Large. STOCK: Antique pine, £25-£1,500; decorative items, £10-£200. LOC: Turn off A53 along Abbotts Rd. before town centre. PARK: Easy. TEL: 01538 387834; fax - 01538 399819; e-mail - geminitrading@lineone.net VAT: Stan.

Gilligans Antiques
59 St. Edward St. ST13 5DN. (M.T. Gilligan). Est. 1977. Open 9-5.30. STOCK: Victorian and Edwardian furniture. TEL: 01538 384174.

Roger Haynes - Antique Finder
54 Shoobridge St. ST13 5JZ. Est. 1960. Open by appointment. SIZE: Large. STOCK: Pine, smalls and decorative items. TEL: 01538 385161; fax - same; e-mail - info@rogerhaynesantiquefinder.com

Jewel Antiques
'Whitegates', 63 Basford Bridge Lane, Cheddleton. ST13 7EQ. (B. and D. Jeacott-Smith). Est. 1967. Open by appointment. STOCK: Paintings, prints, jewellery, oil lamps, small furniture and clocks, 18th-19th C, £25-£2,000. PARK: Easy. TEL: 01538 360744; fax - same.

Johnsons
Chorley Mill, 1 West St. ST13 8AF. (P.M. and Mrs. J.H. Johnson). Est. 1976. Open 9-5, Sat. and Sun by appointment. SIZE: Large. STOCK: 18th-19th C English, Eastern European and French country furniture, £50-£2,000; decorative accessories, £10-£500. LOC: Opposite Pentecostal church. PARK: Own. TEL: 01538 386745; fax - 01538 388375; e-mail - johnsons antiques@btconnnect.com

The Leek Antiques Centre (Barclay House)
4-6 Brook St. ST13 5JE. Est. 1977. Open 10.30-5, Sun. by appointment. SIZE: 3 floors - 17 showrooms. STOCK: Extending dining tables, sets of chairs, chests of drawers, bedroom furniture, pine, pottery, watercolours and oils, upholstered furniture. TEL: 01538 398475. SER: Valuations; restorations (furniture). FAIRS: Bowman's and West Midland, Staffordshire Showground. VAT: Stan/Spec.

Moorland Antique Mirrors
2 Duke St. ST13 5LG. (Carmen Hargreaves and Ruth Tappin). Est. 1980. Open 8-5. SIZE: Medium. STOCK: Mirrors - gilt, painted and wooden, 19th C, £350-£4,000. LOC: On A53 from Stoke-on-Trent, right at 1st traffic lights, shop 200 yards on left. PARK: Easy. TEL: 01538 372553. SER: Export packing; restorations; special commissions. FAIRS: NEC. VAT: Stan/Spec. Mainly Trade.

Odeon Antiques
76-78 St. Edward St. ST13 5DL. (Steve Ford). Est. 1990. Open 11-5. STOCK: Lighting, beds, pine, country furniture, free-standing kitchens and decorative collectables. TEL: 01538 387188; fax - 01538 384235; e-mail - odeonantiques@hotmail.com website - www. odeonantiques.co.uk SER: Restorations (lighting); free-standing kitchen design.

Page Antiques
Ground Floor, Compton Mill. ST13 5NJ. (Denis and Alma Page). Est. 1974. Open 10-5.30, Sun. 1-5 (winter only). SIZE: Medium. STOCK: Georgian to Edwardian furniture, stripped pine and decorative items. LOC: Town centre. PARK: Easy. TEL: Mobile - 07966 154993; home - 01663 732358. SER: Courier. FAIRS: Newark; Swinderby; Buxton. VAT: Stan/Spec.

LEIGH, Nr. Stoke-on-Trent

John Nicholls
Open by appointment. STOCK: Oak furniture and related items, 17th-18th C. TEL: 01538 702339; mobile - 07836 244024.

LICHFIELD

Mike Abrahams Books
14 Meadowbrook Rd. WS13 7RW. Est. 1975. Open by appointment. SIZE: Large. STOCK: Books and ephemera especially Midlands topography, sport, transport, children's, illustrated, military and antiquarian, 17th C to date, £2-£1,000. LOC: Off A5127 on to Eastern Ave., left at Samuel Johnson public house, immediately right into Purcell Ave., past church and right turn into Meadowbrook Rd. PARK: Easy. TEL: 01543 256200; home - same. SER: Valuations. FAIRS: Stafford, Bingley Hall and Pavilion; Midland Antiquarian Book (organiser).

The Essence of Time
Unit 2 Curborough Hall Farm Antiques & Craft Centre, Watery Lane, Off Eastern Ave. WS13 8ES. (M.T.O. Hinton). Est. 1990. Open Wed.-Sun. 11-5. SIZE: Medium. STOCK: Clocks - 30 hour and 8 day longcase, 1700-1900; Vienna regulator wall, English and French wall; mantel and novelty. LOC: North of Lichfield. PARK: Own large. TEL: 01543 418239; home - 01902 764900; mobile - 07944 245064.

James A. Jordan
7 The Corn Exchange. WS13 6JU. CMBHI. Open 9-5. CL: Wed. STOCK: Clocks, longcase, barometers, jewellery and small furniture. LOC: Market Sq. city centre. PARK: Nearby. TEL: 01543 416221. SER: Restorations (clocks and chronometers).

Milestone Antiques   LAPADA
5 Main St., Whittington. WS14 9JU. (Humphrey and Elsa Crawshaw). Resident. Est. 1988. Open Thurs.-Sat. 10-6, Sun. 11-3, other times by appointment. SIZE: Medium. STOCK: Georgian and Victorian British furniture, ceramics (especially Coalport), copper and other decorative items. LOC: A51 Lichfield/Tamworth road, turn north at Whittington Barracks, shop 50yds. past crossroads in village centre. PARK: Easy. TEL: 01543 432248. VAT: Spec.

Winders
—oOo—
Fine Art and Antiques

Telephone: (01782) 712483 Mobile: 07881 652425

The market town of Newcastle, in North Staffordshire, is home to Winders, a well organised antique and fine art shop. Famous for it's Doulton, Minton and Lambeth, it is equally well known for it's 18th Century furniture. Well worth a visit, a warm welcome to be expected.

Opening Hours: 10.00 am until 5.00 pm
                      Monday to Saturday
                      Thursday by appt. only

31 Bridge Street, Newcastle-under-Lyme, Staffordshire, ST5 2RY.

L. Royden Smith
Church View, Farewell Lane, Burntwood. WS7 9DP. Est. 1972. Open Sat. and Sun. 10-4 or by appointment. *STOCK: General antiques, bric-a-brac.* PARK: Nearby. TEL: 01543 682217.

Brett Wilkins Ltd
Cranebrook Farm, Cranebrook Lane, Hilton. WS14 0EY. Est. 1983. Open by appointment. SIZE: Large. *STOCK: Shipping, export and French furniture.* PARK: Easy. TEL: 01543 483662; mobile - 07860 541260. FAIRS: Newark. VAT: Stan. *Export Only.*

NEWCASTLE-UNDER-LYME

Winder's Fine Art and Antiques
31 Bridge St. ST5 2RY. (S. Winder). Est. 1996. Open 10-5, Thurs. by appointment. SIZE: Medium. *STOCK: Furniture, oak, walnut, mahogany, 17th-19th C, £50-£10,000; longcase, mantel and wall clocks, £150-£4,000; paintings, £35-£3,000, both 18th-19th C; ceramics, especially Doulton Lambeth, and watercolours, 19th C, £15-£1,500; silver, £50-£2,000.* Not Stocked: Pine and ephemera. LOC: Close to Sainsburys and the Magistrates Courts. TEL: 01782 712483; mobile - 07881 652425. SER: Valuations; restorations; gilding; repairs (clocks). VAT: Spec.

PENKRIDGE, Nr. Stafford

Golden Oldies
1 and 5 Crown Bridge. ST19 5AA. (W.A. and M.A. Knowles). Est. 1980. Open Mon. 9.30-1.30, Tues-Sat.

9.30-5.30. *STOCK: Victorian, Edwardian and later furniture; paintings, decorative items.* LOC: 2 miles south junction 13, M6. PARK: Easy. TEL: 01785 714722. FAIRS: Newark. VAT: Global.

RUGELEY

Cawarden Brick Co Ltd
Cawarden Springs Farm, Blithbury Rd. WS15 3HL. (R.G. Parrott). SALVO. Est. 1987. Open 8-5, Sat. 8-4, Sun. 10-4. *STOCK: Architectural salvage and antiques - bricks, tiles, beams, cobbles and York stone; furniture, sanitaryware, fireplaces, radiators, leaded glass panels and garden items.* LOC: 1.5 miles from town, in rural setting. PARK: Easy. TEL: 01889 574066; fax - 01889 575695; e-mail - sales@cawardenreclaim.co.uk website - www.cawardenreclaim.co.uk

Eveline Winter
1 Wolseley Rd. WS15 2QH. (Mrs E. Winter). Est. 1962.

Open 10.30-5 appointment advisable. CL: Wed. SIZE: Small. *STOCK: Staffordshire figures, pre-Victorian, from £90; Victorian, £30-£500; copper, brass, glass and general antiques.* Not Stocked: Coins and weapons. LOC: Coming from Lichfield or Stafford stay on A51 and avoid town by-pass. PARK: Easy and at side of shop. TEL: 01889 583259.

STAFFORD

Windmill Antiques
9 Castle Hill, Broadeye. ST16 2QB. Est. 1990. Open 10-5. SIZE: Medium - several dealers. *STOCK: General antiques and decorative items.* LOC: Opposite Sainsbury's. PARK: Easy. TEL: 01785 228505; website - www.windmill-antiques-stafford.com SER: Valuations; restorations (ceramics).

STOKE-ON-TRENT

Ann's Antiques
26 Leek Rd., Stockton Brook. ST9 9NN. (Ann Byatte). Est. 1980. Open Fri. and Sat. 10-5 and by appointment. SIZE: Small. *STOCK: Victorian and Edwardian glass, porcelain, furniture, brass, copper, jewellery, paintings, pottery and unusual items; toys, rocking horses, teddies, dolls and doll's houses.* LOC: A53 main road between Hanley and Leek. PARK: Opposite. TEL: 01782 503991. SER: Valuations. VAT: Stan.

Burslem Antiques & Collectables
11 Market Place, Burslem. ST6 3AA. (D. Bradbury). Est. 1972. Open 9.30-5.30, Sun. and Bank Holidays 10-4. SIZE: Large. *STOCK: Pottery and porcelain including Minton, Doulton, Wedgwood, Worcester, Goss, Spode, Copeland, S Allcock, George Jones, Carlton, MacIntyre, Moorcroft, Moor Bros., Cauldon, Shelley, Paragon, Royal Stanley, 1750s to date.* LOC: Main road. At rear and town centre. TEL: 01782 577855; fax - 01782 577222; mobile - 07801 473524; home - 01782 710711; e-mail - info@burslemantiques.co.uk website - www.burslemantiques.co.uk and www.burslemantiques.com SER: Valuations; packing and shipping worldwide.

The Potteries Antique Centre Ltd
271 Waterloo Rd., Cobridge. ST6 3HR. (W. Buckley). Est. 1990. Open 9-5.30. SIZE: Large + trade and export warehouse. *STOCK: Pottery and porcelain including Doulton, Moorcroft, Beswick, Wedgwood, Coalport, Shelley, 19th and especially 20th C British; collectors' items, silver plate, clocks, brass, jewellery, pictures, furniture, 18th-20th C, £1-£5,000.* LOC: Off M6, junction 15 or 16 on to A500, follow signs for Festival Park or Potteries Shopping Centre. PARK: Easy. TEL: 01782 201455; fax - 01782 201518; 01782 286622 (auctions); e-mail - sales@potteriesantiquecentre.com website - www.potteriesantiquecentre.com SER: Valuations; export facilities - supply and packing; buys at auction (pottery and collectors' items); pottery auctions held on site. FAIRS: Newark; Doulton and Beswick. VAT: Stan/Spec.

The Pottery Buying Centre
535 Etruria Rd., Basford. ST4 6HT. (Paul Hume). Est. 1989. Open 10-4. SIZE: 2 floors. *STOCK: Pottery and porcelain, 19th-20th C; collectables, 20th C; furniture, 18th-20th C; all £10-£1,000.* PARK: Easy. TEL: 01782 635453; home - same; e-mail - potbuyingcentre@aol.com SER: Valuations; restorations.

TUTBURY, Nr. Burton-on-Trent

R.A. James - The Clock Shop
1 High St. DE13 9LP. (Rob and Alison James). MBHI. Est. 1988. Open 8.30-4. SIZE: Medium. *STOCK: Longcase, bracket and wall clocks, £500-£10,000.* LOC: 2 miles from A38/A50 junction. PARK: Easy. TEL: 01283 814596; fax - 01283 814594; mobile - 07710 161949; e-mail - sales@antique-clocks-watches.co.uk website - www.antique-clocks-watches.co.uk SER: Valuations; restorations (clocks, watches and barometers). VAT: Stan/Spec.

Old Chapel Antique & Collectables Centre
High St. DE13 9LP. (Roger Clarke). OCS. Est. 1996. Open 10-5 including Sun., other times by appointment. SIZE: Large. *STOCK: China, glass, furniture.* PARK: Easy. TEL: 01283 815255; mobile - 07774 238775; e-mail - rocla@supanet.com SER: Mail order. FAIRS: Swinderby.

UTTOXETER

White House Antiques
50-52 Bridge St. ST14 8AP. (Christopher White). Est. 1983. Open 10-4.30. CL: Mon. SIZE: Medium. *STOCK: Victorian and Edwardian furniture, £100-£500; Beswick pottery including horse riders and cattle, £10-£700; Beatrix Potter figures, £15-£450; Wedgwood, Royal Doulton and Coalport.* LOC: Next to Wheatsheaf public house, on Market Sq. PARK: Nearby. TEL: 01889 569344; home/fax - 01889 560685. SER: Valuations; restorations (pottery); buys at auction (Beswick, furniture).

WEEFORD, Nr. Lichfield

Blackbrook Antiques Village
London Rd. WS14 0PS. Open Tues.-Sun. and Bank Holidays 10-5.30. SIZE: 6 large showrooms. *STOCK: Architectural antiques including fireplaces, lighting, garden statuary, stained glass, furniture.* LOC: A38. PARK: Large forecourt. TEL: 01543 481450; fax - 01543 480275; e-mail - info@blackbrook.co.uk SER: Delivery and installation. VAT: Margin.

YOXALL, Nr. Burton-on-Trent

H.W. Heron and Son Ltd   LAPADA
The Antique Shop, 1 King St. DE13 8NF. (H.N.M. and J. Heron). Est. 1949. Open 9-6, Sat. 9-5.30, Bank Holidays 10.30-5.30, Sun. by appointment. SIZE: Medium. *STOCK: 18th-19th C furniture, ceramics and decorative items.* LOC: A515 village centre, opposite church. PARK: Easy. TEL: 01543 472266; home - same; fax - 01543 473800; e-mail - shop@hwheronantiques.com website - www.hwheronantiques.com SER: Valuations. VAT: Spec.

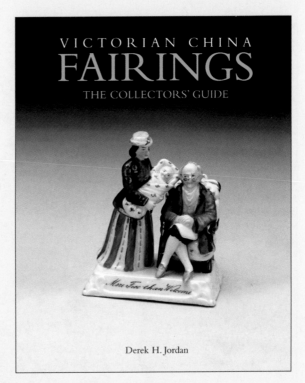

SUFFOLK

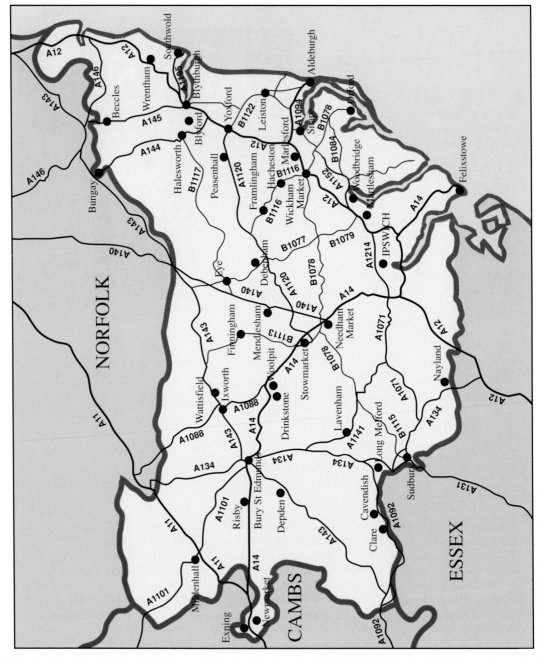

Dealers and Shops in Suffolk

				Hacheston	1	Mendlesham	1	Southwold	5
Aldeburgh	2	Debenham	4	Halesworth	1	Mildenhall	1	Stowmarket	1
Beccles	3	Depden	1	Ipswich	8	Nayland	1	Sudbury	2
Blyford	1	Drinkstone	1	Ixworth	1	Needham Market	3	Wattisfield	1
Blythburgh	1	Exning	1	Lavenham	2	Newmarket	1	Wickham Market	2
Bungay	3	Eye	3	Leiston	3	Orford	1	Woodbridge	9
Bury St. Edmunds	2	Felixstowe	2	Long Melford	11	Peasenhall	1	Woolpit	
Cavendish	1	Finningham	1	Marlesford	1	Risby	1	Wrentham	1
Clare	4	Framlingham	5	Martlesham	2	Snape	1	Yoxford	3

HAMILTON ANTIQUES

5 CHURCH STREET, WOODBRIDGE,
SUFFOLK IP12 1DH

Tel: (01394) 387222

LAPADA
MEMBER

Website: www.hamiltonantiques.co.uk
Email: enquiries@hamiltonantiques.co.uk

Members of LAPADA, The Association of Art and Antique Dealers, Rosemary and Hamilton Ferguson have been trading in Woodbridge since 1977. They have restored this superb 15th century building in Church Street to provide an imposing backcloth for a range of beautiful furniture.

The furniture includes pieces from the Edwardian, Victorian, William IV & Georgian period in mahogany, walnut, rosewood and occasionally oak. The furniture ranges from lovely inlaid items, smaller decorative pieces, sets of chairs, to larger items such as dining tables.

ALDEBURGH

Mole Hall Antiques
102 High St. IP15 5AB. (Peter Weaver). Est. 1976. Open 10-5, Sun. by appointment. SIZE: Small. STOCK: *Paintings, prints, unusual decorative items and country furniture.* PARK: Easy. TEL: 01728 452361; home - same.

Thompson's Gallery
175 High St. IP15 5AN. (J. and S. Thompson). Est. 1982. Open 10-5 or by appointment. SIZE: Large - 6 rooms. STOCK: *19th-20th C paintings; contemporary paintings and sculptures.* PARK: Easy. TEL: 01728 453743; e-mail - john@thompsonsgallery.co.uk website - www. thompsonsgallery.co.uk VAT: Spec.

BECCLES

Besleys Books
4 Blyburgate. NR34 9TA. (P.A. and P.F. Besley). ABA. PBFA. Est. 1978. Open 9.30-1 and 2-5. CL: Wed. SIZE: Medium. STOCK: *Books, 50p-£1,000; prints, £7-£50; maps, £3-£100; all 17th-20th C.* LOC: Town centre. PARK: Nearby. TEL: 01502 715762; home/fax - 01502 675649; e-mail - piers@besleysbooks.demon.co.uk website - www.besleysbooks.demon.co.uk SER: Valuations; restorations (book binding); buys at auction (books). FAIRS: Various ABA and PBFA.

Blyburgate Antiques
27-29 Blyburgate. NR34 9TB. (Mrs K. Lee). Resident. Est. 1997. Open 10-4.30. CL: Mon., Tues. and Wed. SIZE: Small. STOCK: *19th-20th C china, jewellery, furniture and metalware, £5-£1,000.* PARK: Rainbow supermarket at rear. SER: Valuations; restorations (china). FAIRS: Alexandra Palace; Newmarket.

Fauconberges
8 Smallgate. NR34 9AD. (Richard D. Howard and Richard J. Crozier). Est. 1977. Open 10-5. SIZE: Large. STOCK: *Furniture, 1700-1900; pictures, clocks, glass, porcelain, silver.* LOC: Town centre. PARK: Easy. TEL: 01502 716147. SER: Valuations; delivery. FAIRS: Lomax, Langley (Autumn and Spring); Burnham Market; Long Melford.

BLYFORD, Nr. Halesworth

Bly Valley Antiques
Serpentine House, IP19 9JR. Open by appointment only. STOCK: *18th-19th C furniture, ceramics, silver and plate, pictures, objets d'art.* TEL: 01986 875543; e-mail - e.r.ward@btopenworld.com

BLYTHBURGH, Nr. Halesworth

E.T. Webster
Westwood Lodge. IP19 9NB. Est. 1974. Open 7.30-5. SIZE: Large. STOCK: *Ancient oak beams, oak ceilings, panelling, quality reproduction oak furniture, doors, mullioned windows, oak framed barns.* TEL: 01502 478539; fax - 01502 478164.

BUNGAY

Black Dog Antiques
51 Earsham St. NR35 2PB. (K. Button). Est. 1986. Open seven days a week. STOCK: *General antiques including oak, mahogany and stripped pine, china, linen and collectables, antiquities, Saxon and Roman, £1-£1000.* LOC: Opposite Post Office. PARK: Easy. TEL: 01986 895554. SER: Valuations.

Cork Brick Antiques
6 Earsham St. NR35 1AG. (G. and K. Skipper). Open 10.30-5.30. CL: Mon. STOCK: *Country and decorative antiques; architectural decoration.* PARK: Easy. TEL: 01986 894873; home - 01502 712646.

One Step Back
4a Earsham St. NR35 1AQ. (Ian and Diane Wells). Est. 1970. Open 10-5. CL: Wed. SIZE: Medium. STOCK: *Furniture, from 17th C; porcelain and rugs, from 18th C; both £50-£3,000.* TEL: 01986 896626; home - 01508 550988. SER: Valuations; restorations. FAIRS: Halesworth, Bungay, Norwich.

BURY ST. EDMUNDS

The Enchanted Aviary
Lapwings, Rushbrooke Lane. IP33 2RS. (C.C. Frost). Est. 1970. Open by appointment. STOCK: *Cased and uncased mounted birds, animals and fish, mostly late Victorian, £15-£800.* PARK: Easy. TEL: 01284 725430. SER: Restorations.

Winston Mac (Silversmith)
65 St. John's St. IP33 1SJ. (E.W. McKnight). Est. 1978. Open 9-5. CL: Sun. except by appointment, and Sat. SIZE: Small. STOCK: *Silver tea services, creamers, salts, sugar casters, candlesticks, flatware.* PARK: Easy. TEL: 01284 767910. SER: Restorations (silver and plating). VAT: Stan/Spec.

CAVENDISH

Seabrook Antiques and Suffolk Antiques Centre
Lower Rd. (J. Tanner). Est. 1965. Open 9.30-5.30, Sun. 11-4. SIZE: Very large. STOCK: *Furniture, £500-£15,000; objects, £100-£2,000; both 17th-18th C.* LOC: From Long Melford, 1/2 mile before Cavendish on left. PARK: Easy. TEL: 01787 281911; mobile - 07767 242181; home - 01787 311788. SER: Valuations; restorations (17th-18th C furniture); buys at auction (17th-18th C furniture). FAIRS: International. VAT: Spec.

CLARE, Nr. Sudbury

Robin Butler
The Old Bank House, Market Hill. CO10 8NN. Est. 1963. Open by appointment. SIZE: Large. STOCK: *Wine associated antiques, 17th-20th C, £50-£5,000; furniture, 18th-19th C, £200-£20,000; silver, 18th C, £80-£8,000; glass, 18th C, £20-£5,000.* LOC: Town centre. PARK: Easy. TEL: 01787 279111; mobile - 07831 194997; e-mail - robin.butler@btconnect.com SER: Valuations. VAT: Spec.

Clare Antique Warehouse
The Mill, Malting Lane. CO10 8NW. Est. 1989. Open 9.30-5, Sun. 1-5. SIZE: Large - over 80 dealers. STOCK: *17th-20th C furniture, textiles, pictures, porcelain, glass,*

silver, decorative items. LOC: 100yds. from High St. Follow signs for Clare Castle, Country Park. PARK: Easy. TEL: 01787 278449. SER: Valuations; restorations. VAT: Stan/Spec.

F.D. Salter Antiques
1-2 Church St. CO10 8NN. Est. 1959. Open 9-5. CL: Wed. pm. SIZE: Medium. *STOCK: 18th to early 19th C English furniture, porcelain and glass.* LOC: A1092. PARK: Easy. TEL: 01787 277693. SER: Valuations; restorations (furniture). FAIRS: West London. VAT: Stan/Spec.

Trinders' Fine Tools
Malting Lane. CO10 8NW. (P. and R. Trinder). PBFA. Est. 1975. Open 10-1 and 2-5, Wed. 10-12. CL: Sat., prior telephone call advisable. SIZE: Medium. *STOCK: Hand tools for craftsmen, engineers and collectors, woodworking and metalworking books including furniture reference and clocks, other art and antiques reference books.* PARK: Easy. TEL: 01787 277130; home - same; fax - 01787 277677; e-mail - peter@trindersfinetools.co.uk website - www.trindersfinetools.co.uk/ SER: Internet sales.

DEBENHAM

Edward Bigden Fine Art
48 High St. IP14 6QW. Est. 2001. Open by appointment. SIZE: Small. *STOCK: Fine paintings, drawings and sculpture, 16th-21st C; early furniture.* LOC: Opposite church. PARK: Easy. TEL: 01728 862065; home - same; fax - 01728 862066; mobile - 07876 745228; e-mail - edwardbigden.antiques@virgin.net website - www.edwardbigdenantiques.com

Debenham Antiques
73 High St. IP14 6QS. (Chris Bigden). Est. 1969. Open 9.15-5.30. SIZE: Large. *STOCK: 17th-19th C furniture and paintings, £50-£10,000.* PARK: Easy. TEL: 01728 860707; fax - 01728 860333. VAT: Stan/Spec.

Josh Antiques
2a Chancery Lane. IP14 6RN. (John W. Etheridge). Est. 1990. Usually open seven days 9.30-3.30, some days until 4.30. SIZE: Small. *STOCK: Oil lamps, Victorian to 1950s, £20-£200; pictures, £5-£150; metalware, china, glass, £2-100; cigarette and phone cards; kitchenalia, fire related items; crested china.* LOC: Just off High St. PARK: Easy. TEL: 01728 861680; home - same; e-mail - shirley.etheridge@virgin.net SER: Valuations.

Quercus
The Old Toll House, 2 High St. IP14 6QH. (Peter Horsman and Bill Bristow-Jones). Resident. Est. 1972. Open by appointment. SIZE: Medium. *STOCK: Oak furniture, 17th-18th C, £1,000-£5,000.* PARK: Easy. TEL: 01728 860262; home - same. SER: Valuations; restorations (17th C oak furniture). VAT: Spec.

DEPDEN, Nr. Bury St. Edmunds

Coblands Farm Antiques
Bury Rd. IP29 4BT. (Mrs Janet Harding). Open 10-5.30, Sun. in summer 2-5. SIZE: Large. *STOCK: Antique pine and other furniture, especially wing chairs and sofas, £5-£2,000.* LOC: A143 between Haverhill and Bury St.

Edmunds. PARK: Easy. TEL: 01440 820007; home - same; fax - 01440 821165. SER: Restorations (upholstery).

DRINKSTONE, Nr. Bury St. Edmunds

Denzil Grant Antiques   BADA LAPADA
Drinkstone House. IP30 9TG. Est. 1979. Open any time by appointment. STOCK: Furniture, especially French farm tables, 16th to early 19th C. LOC: Off A14 between Bury St. Edmunds and Ipswich. PARK: Easy. TEL: 01449 736576; fax - 01449 737679; e-mail - denzil@fish.co.uk website - www.denzilgrant.com

EXNING, Nr. Newmarket

Exning Antiques & Interiors
14-16 Oxford St. CB8 7EW. (Geoffrey Tabbron). Est. 1982. Open 9-5. SIZE: Medium. *STOCK: Period lighting, gasoliers and electroliers, table and standing lamps; drapes and decorative items.* PARK: Easy. TEL: 01638 600015; fax - 01638 600073; home - 01638 602337. SER: Restorations, conversions, cleaning and re-wiring.

EYE

Bramley Antiques
4 Broad St. 1P23 7AF. (C. Grater). Est. 1987. Open Wed. and Sat. 9.30-5, other times by appointment. SIZE: Medium. *STOCK: Glass, £5-£500; furniture, £20-£1,000; boxes, pictures, general antiques, all 18th to early 20th C.* LOC: Town centre. PARK: Easy. TEL: 01379 871386. SER: Valuations; restorations.

English and Continental Antiques
1 Broad St. IP23 7AF. (Steve Harmer). Est. 1977. Open Wed.-Sat. 11-5. SIZE: Medium. *STOCK: Furniture, 17th-19th C, £10-£20,000.* LOC: Opposite town hall. PARK: Easy. TEL: 01379 871199; e-mail - englishantiques@onetel.com website - www.englishandcontinentalantiques.com SER: Restorations; upholstery.

Laburnum Cottage Antiques
Laburnum Cottage, 2 Broad St. IP23 7AF. (S. Grater). Resident. Est. 1978. Open Wed.-Sat. 9.30-5, other times by appointment. SIZE: Small. *STOCK: Porcelain and glass, £5-£250; linen, silver and plate, jewellery, £2.50-£100; all 18th-20th C.* LOC: Facing the Town Hall. PARK: Easy. TEL: 01379 871386. SER: Valuations.

FELIXSTOWE

John McCulloch Antiques
1a Hamilton Rd. IP11 7HN. Est. 1984. Open 10-4.30. CL: Wed. *STOCK: Furniture, copper, brass, pictures, clocks and bric-a-brac.* LOC: Main street, sea front end at top of Bent Hill. PARK: Around corner. TEL: 01394 283126.

Tea & Antiques
109 High Rd. East. IP11 9PS. (D. George). Est. 1999. Open Thurs.-Sun. and Bank Holidays 10-5. SIZE: Small + outbuildings. *STOCK: General antiques and collectables, bygones and furniture, £5-£500.* LOC: Main road to Felistowe ferry. PARK: Easy. TEL: 01394 277789; e-mail - david.george25@btopenworld.com

FINNINGHAM

Abington Books
Primrose Cottage, Westhorpe Rd. IP14 4TW. (J. Haldane). Est. 1971. Open by appointment. SIZE: Small. *STOCK: Books on Oriental rugs, from 1877, £1-£5,000; books on classical tapestries, 17th-19th C, £1-£3,000.* LOC: At bottom of private drive, about 150m. west of intersection with B1113. PARK: Easy. TEL: 01449 780303; fax - 01449 780202. SER: Valuations; book binding.

FRAMLINGHAM

Bed Bazaar
The Old Station, Station Rd. IP13 9EE. (B.J. Goodbrey). GMC. Est. 1980. Open 10-5, Sun. and Bank Holidays, 11-4. SIZE: Large. *STOCK: Wooden and metal bedsteads.* PARK: Own. TEL: 01728 723756; fax - 01728 724626; e-mail - bengoodbrey@bedbazaar.co.uk website - www.bedbazaar. co.uk SER: Restorations (beds); Sleeping Partners - mattresses and bases made-to-measure. VAT: Stan/Spec.

Dix-Sept
17 Station Rd. IP13 9EE. (S. Goodbrey and M. Cluzan). Est. 1996. Open Sat. 10-1 and 2-5, other times by appointment. *STOCK: French furniture and decoration, pottery, garden furniture, mirrors and textiles.* LOC: On approach road from A12. PARK: Easy. TEL: 01728 621505; fax - 01728 724884. FAIRS: Newark. VAT: Global.

Goodbreys
29 Double St. IP13 9BN. (R. and M. Goodbrey). Est. 1965. Open Sat. 9.30-1 and 2-5.30 or by appointment. SIZE: Large. *STOCK: Decorative items including sleighbeds, upholstery, Biedermeier, simulated bamboo, painted cupboards, garden furniture, country pieces; pottery, glass, textiles, mirrors, bric-a-brac.* LOC: Up Church St. towards Framlingham Castle, opposite church gates turn right into Double St. PARK: Easy. TEL: 01728 621191; fax - 01728 724727. SER: Restorations. FAIRS: Newark; Ardingly. VAT: Mainly Spec. *Mainly Trade.*

Honeycombe Antiques
8 Market Hill. IP13 9AN. (K. Honeycombe). Est. 1997. Open 9.30-5, Sun. during summer and special events. SIZE: Medium. *STOCK: Silver, Georgian to 1950, £10-£1,000; furniture - small tables, chairs, plant stands, Georgian to Edwardian, £30-£600; ceramics, glass and pictures, £10-£300; jewellery, £30-£500; boxes, caddies and writing slopes, £100-£400.* LOC: Market Sq. PARK: Market Sq. and nearby. TEL: 01728 622011; e-mail - kfh@honeycombeantiques.co.uk SER: Valuations; silver cutlery matching and replacement.

The Theatre Antiques Centre
10 Church St. IP13 9BH. (W. Darby). Est. 2001. Open 9.30-5.30. SIZE: Large. *STOCK: Furniture, 18th-20th C, £40-£2,000; French country, 18th-19th C, £500-£1,000; country pine, 19th C, £100-£500; objets d'art, £50-£100.* TEL: 01728 621069. SER: Valuations. VAT: Spec.

HACHESTON, Nr. Wickham Market

Hardy's
IP13 0DS. Resident. Open Tues.-Sat. 10-6. *STOCK: Pine - dressers, corner cupboards, butcher's blocks, old French farmhouse tables, wardrobes and chests of drawers.* LOC: B1116, Framlingham Rd. PARK: At rear. TEL: 01728 746485.

HALESWORTH

P & R Antiques Ltd
Fairstead Farm Buildings, Wash Lane, Spexhall. IP19 0RF. (Pauline and Robert Lewis). Est. 1997. Open by appointment. SIZE: Large. *STOCK: Chests of drawers, £900-£3,000; dining and drawing room furniture, £500-£4,000; all 18th-19th C.* LOC: From A12, take Halesworth turning, through town, turn left into Wissett Road, then right after half mile into Wash Lane, farm is half mile on right. PARK: Easy. TEL: 01986 873232; home - same; fax - 01986 874682; e-mail - pauline@prantiques.com website - www.prantiques.com SER: Worldwide delivery. FAIRS: Snape. VAT: Spec.

IPSWICH

A. Abbott Antiques Ltd
757 Woodbridge Rd. IP4 4NE. (C. Lillistone). Est. 1965. Open 10.30-5. CL: Wed. SIZE: Medium. *STOCK: Small items, especially clocks and jewellery; Victorian, Edwardian and shipping furniture, £5-£5,000.* PARK: Easy. TEL: 01473 728900; fax - same; mobile - 07771 533413; e-mail - abbott_antiques@hotmail.com FAIRS: Newark; Ardingly. VAT: Global.

Claude Cox at College Gateway Bookshop
3 Silent St. IP1 1TF. (Anthony Cox). ABA. PBFA. Est.

1944. Open Wed.-Sat. 10-5. SIZE: Medium. *STOCK: Books, from 1470; some local maps and prints.* LOC: Leave inner ring road at Novotel double roundabout, turn into St. Peters St. PARK: Cromwell Square and Buttermarket Centre. TEL: 01473 254776; fax - same; e-mail - books@ claudecox.co.uk website - www.claudecox.co.uk SER: Valuations; restorations (rebinding); buys at auction; catalogue available.

The Edwardian Shop
556 Spring Rd. IP4 4NT. Est. 1979. Open 9-5. *STOCK: Victorian, Edwardian and 1920s shipping goods, £10-£400.* LOC: Half-mile from hospital. PARK: Own. TEL: 01473 716576.

Hubbard Antiques
16-18 St. Margarets Green. IP4 2BS. Est. 1964. Open 10-5.30 and by appointment. SIZE: Large. *STOCK: Furniture and decorative items, 18th-19th C.* PARK: Easy. TEL: 01473 226033/233034; fax - 01473 253639; e-mail - sales@hubbard-antiques.com SER: Valuations; restorations; desk re-leathering; upholstery; lacquer repairs. VAT: Stan/Spec. *Trade & Export.*

Maud's Attic
25 St. Peter's St. IP1 1XF. (Wendy Childs). Est. 1996. Open Tues.-Sat. 10-5. SIZE: Small *STOCK: General antiques, collectables and reproduction including porcelain, lamps, glass, jewellery, furniture, linen and mirrors.* LOC: Town centre. PARK: Easy. TEL: 01473 221057; fax - 01473 221056; e-mail - maudsattic@hotmail.com SER: Valuations.

Merchant House Antiques & Interiors
27-29 St. Peter's St. IP1 1XF. (Graham and Wendy

Childs). Est. 1999. Open Tues.-Sat. 10-5. SIZE: Small. *STOCK: Furniture including pine, mahogany and oak, fire surrounds and inserts, garden ornaments and furniture, lighting and mirrors, copper and brass.* LOC: Town centre. PARK: Easy. TEL: 01473 221054; fax - 01473 221056; mobile - 07768 068575.

Orwell Furniture For Life
Halifax Mill, 427 Wherstead Rd. IP2 8LH. (M. Weiner). Open 8.30-5.30, Sat. 8.30-4. *STOCK: Pine.* TEL: 01473 680091. SER: Restorations; stripping; pine furniture and kitchens made to order from old wood; manufacturers of bespoke furniture in oak, maple, cherry, painted etc.

Richard A. Rush Antiques
Unit 5 Penny Corner, Farthing Rd. IP1 5AP. Est. 1987. Open 8-5.30, Sat. 9-2. SIZE: Medium. *STOCK: Furniture and decorative items, 18th-19th C.* LOC: Just off A14 at Sproughton Industrial Estate. PARK: Easy. TEL: 01473 464609. SER: Valuations; restorations (furniture); buys at auction.

IXWORTH, Nr. Bury St. Edmunds

E.W. Cousins and Son   LAPADA
27 High St. and The Old School. IP31 2HJ. (E.J.A., J.E. and R.W. Cousins). Est. 1920. CL: Sat. pm. SIZE: Large and warehouse. *STOCK: General antiques, 18th-19th C, £50-£20,000; shipping items.* LOC: A143. PARK: Easy. TEL: 01359 230254; fax - 01359 232370; e-mail - john@ewcousins.co.uk website - www.ewcousins.co.uk SER: Restorations. VAT: Stan/Spec.

LAVENHAM, Nr. Sudbury

J. and J. Baker
12-14 Water St. and 3a High St. CO10 9RW. (Mrs B.A.J. Baker). Est. 1960. Open 10-5.30. SIZE: Medium. *STOCK: Oak and mahogany furniture, 1680-1900, £100-£10,000; oils and watercolours, 19th C, £150-£5,000; English porcelain and metalware, 18th-19th C, £20-£1,000; collectors' items, £20-£1,000.* LOC: Below Swan Hotel at T junction of A1141 and B1071. PARK: Easy. TEL: 01787 247610. e-mail - info@jandjbaker. co.uk website - www.jandjbaker.co.uk VAT: Stan/Spec.

The Timbers Antique & Collectables Centre
High St. CO1 9PY. (Tom and Jeni White). Resident. Est. 1996. Open 9.30-5 every day including Bank Holidays. SIZE: Medium. *STOCK: Smalls and furniture, to £5,000.* PARK: Easy. TEL: 01787 247218; website - www. timbersantiques.com

LEISTON

Leiston Trading Post
Frederick House, 17 High St. IP16 4EL. (L.K. Smith). Est. 1967. Open 10-1 and 2-5, other times by appointment. CL: Wed. pm. SIZE: Large. *STOCK: Bric-a-brac, Victoriana, Victorian and Edwardian furniture, collectables.* LOC: 4 miles from Aldeburgh, Snape, and Saxmundham. PARK: Easy. TEL: 01728 830081; home - 01728 831488; e-mail - lisa@renaultsuffolk.co.uk website - www.leiston tradingpost.co.uk SER: Valuations. VAT: Stan.

Michael Lewis
5 Highbury Cottages, Waterloo Ave. IP16 4TW. Open by appointment. *STOCK: Pine and country furniture, British and Irish, 18th-19th C, £100-£6,500.* PARK: Easy. TEL: 020 7359 7733; 01728 833276; mobile - 07976 307056.

Warrens Antiques Warehouse
High St. IP16 4EL. (J.R. and J.J. Warren). Est. 1980. CL: Wed. and Sat. pm. except by appointment. SIZE: Medium. *STOCK: Furniture, Georgian-Edwardian, £20-£2,000.* LOC: Off High St., driveway beside Geaters Florists. PARK: Easy. TEL: 01728 831414; home - same; mobile - 07989 865598. e-mail - jrwantiques@aol.com website - www.warrenantiques.co.uk SER: Valuations; restorations (furniture). FAIRS: Newark; Ardingly. VAT: Stan/Spec.

LONG MELFORD

Sandy Cooke Antiques
Hall St. CO10 9JQ. Est. 1982. Open Fri., Sat. and Mon. 10-5. SIZE: Large. *STOCK: Furniture, 17th to early 19th C, £500-£40,000. Not Stocked: Silver and glass.* LOC: A134. PARK: Easy. TEL: 01787 378265; fax - 01284 830935; mobile - 07860 206787; e-mail - sandycooke @englishfurniture.co.uk website - www.english furniture.co.uk SER: Valuations; restorations; buys at auction (furniture). VAT: Stan/Spec.

Country Antiques
10 Westgate St. CO10 9DS. (Mr and Mrs G. Pink). Est. 1984. By appointment only. SIZE: Small. *STOCK: Objects, metalware and small furniture, £50-£2,000; unusual objects, £50-£500; watercolours and prints, 18th-19th C, £100-£2,000.* LOC: Outskirts of village, on Clare road. PARK: Easy. TEL: 01787 310617; fax - same; e-mail - countrypink@supanet.com website - www.countrypink.co.uk

Long Melford Antiques Centre
Chapel Maltings. CO10 9HX. (Baroness V. von Dahlen). Est. 1984. Open 9.30-5.30 or by appointment. SIZE: Large - 42 dealers. *STOCK: Furniture - oak, Georgian, Edwardian and Victorian; silver, china, glass, clocks and decorators' items.* LOC: A134, Sudbury end of village. TEL: 01787 379287. SER: Packing and shipping. VAT: Stan/Spec.

Alexander Lyall Antiques
Belmont House, Hall St. CO10 9JF. (A.J. Lyall). Est. 1977. Open 10-5.30. SIZE: Medium. *STOCK: Furniture, 18th-19th C.* LOC: A134 opposite Crown Hotel. PARK: Easy. TEL: 01787 375434; home - same; e-mail - alex@ lyallantiques.com website - www.lyallantiques.com SER: Restorations (furniture); buys at auction (English furniture). VAT: Stan/Spec.

Magpie Antiques
Hall St. CO10 9JT. (Mrs P. Coll). Est. 1985. Open 10.30-1 and 2.15-5, Sat. 11-5. CL: Mon. and Wed. SIZE: Small. *STOCK: Smalls including hand-painted china; furniture, Victorian and stripped pine.* LOC: Main street. PARK: Easy. TEL: 01787 310581; home - same.

Patrick Marney
The Gate House, Melford Hall. CO10 9AA. Est. 1964. Open by appointment. SIZE: Small. *STOCK: Fine barometers, 18th-19th C, £1,000-£5,000; pocket aneroids, 19th C, £150-£1,000; scientific instruments, 18th-19th C, £250-£2,000; all fully restored.* LOC: A134. PARK: Easy. TEL: 01787 880533; e-mail - patrick.marney@virgin.net website - www.patrickmarney.co.uk SER: Valuations; restorations (mercury barometers). VAT: Stan.

Mayflower Antiques
Chapel Maltings. CO10 9HX. (J.W. Odgers). Est. 1970. Open 10-5. SIZE: Medium. *STOCK: Clocks, mechanical music, scientific and marine instruments, general antiques.* PARK: Easy. TEL: Mobile - 07860 843569; e-mail - mayflower@johnodgers.com and mail@ johnodgers.co.uk website - www.oldjunk.co.uk FAIRS: Newark; London Scientific and Medical Instrument.

Melford Antique Warehouse
Hall St. CO10 9JG. (D. Edwards, J. Tanner and P. Scholz). Open 9.30-5, Sun. 1-5. SIZE: 150 dealers exhibiting. *STOCK: 18th-20th C furniture and decorative items.* PARK: Easy. TEL: 01787 379638; e-mail - patrick@worldwideantiques.co.uk website - www.antiques-access-agency.com

Noel Mercer Antiques
Aurora House, Hall St. CO10 9RJ. Est. 1990. Open 10-5 or by appointment. SIZE: Large. *STOCK: Early oak, walnut and country furniture, including refectory and gateleg tables, sets of chairs and dressers; works of art, £500-£30,000.* LOC: Centre of Hall St. PARK: Easy. TEL: 01787 311882; mobile - 07984 643223. e-mail - info@noelmercer antiques.com website - www.noelmercerantiques.com SER: Valuations; restorations. VAT: Stan/Spec.

The Persian Carpet Studio Ltd
The Old White Hart. CO10 9HX. (Sara Barber). Est.

1990. Open 10-5.30. SIZE: Medium. *STOCK: Antique and decorative Oriental carpets and rugs, from 1860, from £50.* LOC: Sudbury end of Long Melford. PARK: Own. TEL: 01787 882214; fax - 01787 882213; e-mail - sarabarber@persian-carpet-studio.net website - www.persian-carpet-studio.net SER: Valuations; repairs and hand-cleaning (Oriental rugs); buys at auction (Oriental carpets, rugs and textiles). Exhibitions held. VAT: Stan/Margin.

Matthew Tyler Antiques
Hall St. CO10 9JL. (Matthew and Catherine Tyler). Open Mon., Fri. and Sat. 10-5, other times by appointment. SIZE: Medium. *STOCK: Quality English furniture, 1690-1837; works of art, mainly late 17th to late 19th C.* PARK: Easy. TEL: 01787 377523; home - 01799 599866; fax - 01799 599978; mobile - 07770 496350; e-mail - m.tyler1@btopenworld.com SER: Valuations; restorations (furniture). FAIRS: Snape.

MARLESFORD

Antiques Warehouse (incorporating The Woodbridge Trading Co.)
The Old Mill, Main Rd. IP13 0AG. (John M. Ball). Est. 1989. Open 8-4.30, Sat. 10-4.30, Sun. 11-4.30. SIZE: Large. *STOCK: Furniture including fine country, 18th-20th C, £50-£5,000; mirrors and decorative items, 18th-20th C, £10-£2,000.* LOC: A12, 7 miles north of Woodbridge. PARK: Easy. TEL: 01728 747438; fax - 01728 747627; home - 01394 382426. SER: Valuations; buys at auction.

MARTLESHAM, Nr. Woodbridge
Martlesham Antiques
The Thatched Roadhouse. IP12 4RJ. (R.F. Frost). Est. 1973. Open Mon.-Sat., Sun. by appointment. SIZE: Large. *STOCK: Furniture and decorative items, 17th-20th C, £25-£3,000.* LOC: A1214 opposite Red Lion public house. PARK: Own. TEL: 01394 386732; fax - 01394 382959.

John Read Antiques
29 Lark Rise, Martlesham Heath. IP5 3SA. Est. 1992. By appointment. *STOCK: Pre 1840 Staffordshire figures, animals and English pottery, including Delft, salt glaze, creamware and pearlware, coloured glazed, underglazed (Pratt) and enamel decoration, 1750-1840, £100-£8,000.* LOC: A12 Ipswich bypass, opposite BT tower. PARK: Easy. TEL: 01473 624897; home - same. SER: Valuations; restorations (as stock). FAIRS: Chelsea; NEC.

MENDLESHAM
Tower Reclaim
Tower Farm, Norwich Rd. IP14 5NE. (James Webster). SALVO. Est. 1974. Open by appointment or chance. *STOCK: Architectural antiques, 16th C to date; garden statuary, stone items and paving, reclaimed building materials.* PARK: Easy. TEL: 01449 766095; website - www.architecturalsalvageuk.com

MILDENHALL
Mildenhall Antique Furniture
10 North Terrace. IP28 7AA. (Gary Bunker). Est. 1979.

Open Tues.-Sat. 11-5. SIZE: Large. *STOCK: Victorian and 1920s oak furniture.* LOC: Near fire station, opposite Jet garage. PARK: Own at rear. TEL: Mobile - 07885 662106; e-mail - moc1oak@aol.com SER: Packing and shipping.

NAYLAND

Maria Cass Antiques
15 High St. CO6 4JF. (Mrs B. M. Stevens). Resident. Est. 1998. Open Tues.-Fri. 10-3, Sat. 9-1, Sun. by appointment. SIZE: Small. *STOCK: 18th-19th C furniture; clocks and pocket watches; mirrors, glass, china and porcelain; art gallery.* LOC: Village centre, on A134 towards Sudbury. PARK: Easy. TEL: 01206 263929; fax - same; e-mail - mariacassantiques@ hotpop.com FAIRS: Newark.

NEEDHAM MARKET

Roy Arnold
77 High St. IP6 8AN. Est. 1974. Open 10-5.30, appointment advisable, Sun. by appointment. SIZE: Medium. *STOCK: Woodworkers' and craftsmen's tools; scientific instruments; books - new, secondhand and antiquarian - on tools and trades, trade catalogues; all £10-£5,000.* LOC: Off A14, centre of High St. PARK: Easy. TEL: 01449 720110; fax - 01449 722498; e-mail - ra@royarnold.com website - www.royarnold.com VAT: Stan.

Old Town Hall Antique & Collectors Centre
High St. IP6 8AL. (Rod Harrison). Est. 1980. Open 10-5 including Bank Holiday Sun. and Mon. SIZE: 30+ cabinets and stalls. *STOCK: Antiques and collectables, bric-a-brac, jewellery, books and ephemera.* LOC: Main street. PARK: Easy. TEL: 01449 720773.

The Tool Shop   LAPADA
78 High St. IP6 8AW. (Tony Murland). Est. 1988. Open 10-5. SIZE: Small. *STOCK: Antique and usable woodworking tools, from 19th C.* PARK: Easy. TEL: 01449 722992; fax - 01449 722683; e-mail - tony@antiquetools.co.uk website - www.antiquetools. co.uk SER: Valuations; buys at auction; tool auctions held. FAIRS: All major Woodworking Shows, Woodmex, Axminster, Harrogate. VAT: Stan.

NEWMARKET

R.E. and G.B. Way
Brettons, Burrough Green. CB8 9NA. (Gregory Way). ABA. PBFA. Est. 1964. Open 8.30-5 appointment advisable. *STOCK: Antiquarian and secondhand books on shooting, fishing, horses, racing and hunting and small general section.* TEL: 01638 507217; fax - 01638 508058; e-mail - greg@waybooks.demon.co.uk

ORFORD

Castle Antiques
Market Sq. IP12 2LH. (S. Simpkin). Est. 1969. Open daily including Sun. 11-4. SIZE: Medium. *STOCK: Furniture, general small antiques, bric-a-brac, glass, china, clocks.* PARK: Easy. TEL: 01394 450100; website - www.castle-antiques.co.uk

PEASENHALL, Nr. Saxmundham

Peasenhall Art and Antiques Gallery
The Street. IP17 2HJ. (A. and M. Wickins). Resident. Est. 1972. Open every day. *STOCK: 19th to early 20th C watercolours and oils; some furniture; walking sticks.* PARK: Easy. TEL: 01728 660224; home - same. SER: Restorations (oils, watercolours, furniture). FAIRS: Snape.

RISBY, Nr. Bury St. Edmunds

The Risby Barn
IP28 6QU. (R. and S. Martin). Est. 1986. Open 9-5.30, Sun. and Bank Holidays 10-5. SIZE: Large - 24 dealers. *STOCK: Furniture, porcelain, metalware, tools, pine, Art Deco, oil lamps.* LOC: Just off A14 west of Bury St. Edmunds. PARK: Own. TEL: 01284 811126; fax - 01284 810783; website - www.risbybarn.co.uk

SNAPE

Snape Antiques and Collectors Centre
Snape Maltings. IP17 1SR. Est. 1992. Open 7 days 10-5 or until dusk in winter. SIZE: 45 dealers. *STOCK: Antiques and collectables, especially smalls - cutlery, pens, sewing, silver, jewellery, ceramics from 18th C, Doulton, Deco, Studio, glass, maps, prints, paintings, textiles, country, decorative and useful furniture, stamps, costume jewellery, drinking glasses, antiquities, coins, advertising, books; clothing, from Victorian to 1970's.* LOC: Next to the Concert Hall. PARK: Easy. TEL: 01728 688038.

SOUTHWOLD

Farleigh House Antiques
Basement, 39 High St. IP18 6AB. (Sharon Munday). Est. 1996. Open 10-4, Sun. by appointment. CL: Wed. SIZE: Small. *STOCK: Porcelain - Lowestoft, Worcester, etc; glass and silver, jewellery, coins, medals, militaria, brass, copper and antiquities, decorative furniture.* PARK: Easy. TEL: 01502 722630; e-mail - sharon@farleighhouse.fsnet.co.uk website - www.antiquesinsouthwold.com

Puritan Values at the Dome
The Dome Art and Antiques Centre, Southwold Business Centre, St. Edmunds Rd. IP18 6BZ. (A.F. Geering). Resident. Est. 1984. Open 10-6, Sun. 11-5. SIZE: Large. *STOCK: Arts and Crafts, Gothic Revival, Aesthetic, decorative arts and Art Nouveau, £50-£20,000.* PARK: Easy. TEL: 01502 722211; mobile - 07966 371676; e-mail - sales@puritanvalues.com website - www. puritanvalues.com SER: Valuations; restorations. FAIRS: Earls Court; Newark; NEC; Scottish Exhibition Centre. VAT: Stan/Spec.

T. Schotte Antiques
The Old Bakehouse, Black Mill Rd. IP18 6AQ. (T. and J. Schotte). Open 10-1 and 2-4. CL: Wed. SIZE: Small. *STOCK: Small furniture, £25-£500; decorative objects, £5-£250; both 18th-19th C. Unusual collectables, £5-£100.* LOC: Turn right at the King's Head, then first left. TEL: 01502 722083. FAIRS: Long Melford monthly; Adams, Horticultural Hall, London.

Southwold Antiques Centre
Buckenham Mews, 83 High St. IP18 6DS. (Anne

Stolliday). Open 10-4.30, Wed. 10-1, Sun. 12-4. SIZE: Medium. *STOCK: General antiques and collectables; replacement china.* LOC: Off High St. PARK: Nearby. TEL: 01502 723060

S. J. Webster-Speakman   BADA
(F.P. and S.J. Webster-Speakman). Open by appointment. STOCK: English furniture, clocks, Staffordshire pottery, general antiques. PARK: Easy. TEL: 01502 722252. SER: Valuations; restorations (clocks, furniture and ceramics). FAIRS: Various.

STOWMARKET

Trench Puzzles
Three Cow Green, Bacton. IP14 4HJ. (Kevin Holmes). Est. 1984. Open by appointment. *STOCK: Antique to pre-WWII jigsaws and mechanical puzzles.* PARK: Limited. TEL: 01449 781178. SER: Mail order; search.

SUDBURY

Napier House Antiques
Church St. CO10 6BJ. (Veronica McGregor). Est. 1977. Open 10-4.30 and by appointment. SIZE: Large. *STOCK: 18th-19th C mahogany furniture, especially larger items - linen presses, wardrobes, desks, bureaux, bookcases, dining tables, sideboards, wing chairs, £350-£5,000.* PARK: Easy. TEL: 01787 375280; fax - 01787 478757. SER: Free UK delivery. VAT: Spec.

Neate Militaria & Antiques
P O Box 3794, Preston St Mary. CO10 9PX. (Gary C. Neate). OMRS, OMSA, MMSSA. MCCofC. Est. 1983. Open Mon.-Fri. 9-6. *STOCK: Orders, decorations and medals of the world, £5-£15,000.* TEL: 01787 248168; fax - 01787 248363; e-mail - gary@neatemedals.co.uk website - www.neatemedals.co.uk SER: Valuations; 4 catalogues p.a. FAIRS: Brittania Medal; Aldershot Medal & Militaria. VAT: Spec. *Mail order only.*

WATTISFIELD, Nr. Diss

Peppers Period Pieces
Park Farm, The Street. IP22 1NT. (M.E. Pepper). Est. 1975. Open by appointment. *STOCK: Furniture, oak, elm, yew, fruitwood, mahogany, 16th-19th C; English domestic implements in brass, copper, lead, tin, iron, pewter and treen, 16th to early 20th C; some pottery and porcelain, bygones and collectables, late 19th to early 20th C. Not Stocked: Reproductions.* LOC: Village centre A143, at top of street before pond. PARK: Easy. TEL: 01359 250606; fax - same. SER: Valuations; repairs and polishing.

WICKHAM MARKET

Ashe Antiques Warehouse
The Old Engine Shed, Station Rd., Campsea Ashe. IP13 0PT. (Graham Laffling). Est. 1986. Open 10-5 including Sun. SIZE: Large. *STOCK: Furniture, 18th-20th C, £100-£5,000; collectables, pictures and prints, 19th C, £50-£500.* LOC: 1.5 miles from A12 Wickham Market by-pass, signposted Orford and Tunstall. PARK: Easy. TEL: 01728 747255; 01394 460490. SER: Valuations; restorations (ceramics); repairs (furniture); re-polishing; upholstery; buys at auction. FAIRS: Newark.

Roy Webb
179 & 181 High St. IP13 0RQ. Open Mon., Thurs. and Sat. 10-6 or by appointment. SIZE: Large warehouse. *STOCK: 17th-20th C furniture, including shipping, and clocks.* LOC: Just off A12. PARK: Own large. TEL: 01728 746077; evenings - 01394 382697. SER: Shipping arranged. VAT: Stan/Spec.

WOODBRIDGE

Church Street Centre
6E Church St. IP12 1DH. (David Sycamore). Est. 1994. Open 10-5, Sat. 10-5.30. CL: Wed. pm. SIZE: Medium - 10+ dealers. *STOCK: 18th-19th C general antiques; 20th C collectables, jewellery, silver, pictures, linen, diecast toys, dolls, railway and topographical books.* LOC: Town centre, just off Thoroughfare, next to Barclays Bank. PARK: Nearby. TEL: 01394 388887; mobile - 07909 623439. FAIRS: Woodbridge Community Centre monthly.

David Gibbins Antiques   BADA
The White House, 14 Market Hill. IP12 4LU. Est. 1964. Open by appointment. STOCK: English furniture, late 16th to early 19th C, £300-£40,000; English pottery and porcelain, metalwork. PARK: Own in Theatre St. TEL: 01394 383531; home - 01394 382685; mobile - 07702 306914; e-mail - david@gibbinsantiques.co.uk website - www.gibbinsantiques.co.uk SER: Valuations; buys at auction. FAIRS: BADA; Harrogate (Autumn). VAT: Spec.

Hamilton Antiques   LAPADA
5 Church St. IP12 1DH. (H.T. and R.E. Ferguson). CINOA. Est. 1976. Open 8.30-5, Sat. 10-5. *STOCK: Furniture - mahogany and walnut, especially inlaid, rosewood and some oak; prints.* TEL: 01394 387222; e-mail - enquiries@hamiltonantiques.co.uk website - www.hamiltonantiques.co.uk SER: Restorations; polishing. VAT: Stan/Spec.

Anthony Hurst Antiques
13 Church St. IP12 1DS. (C.G.B. Hurst). Est. 1957. Open 10-1 and 2-5. CL: Wed. and Sat. pm. SIZE: Large. *STOCK: English furniture, oak, walnut and mahogany, 1600-1900, £100-£5,000.* PARK: Easy. TEL: 01394 382500. SER: Valuations; restorations (furniture); buys at auction. VAT: Spec.

R.A and S.M. Lambert and Son
The Bull Ride, 70A New St. IP12 1DX. Est. 1963. Open 9.30-1 and 2-5. SIZE: Large. *STOCK: 19th-20th C furniture.* LOC: 2 minutes from Market Hill. TEL: 01394 382380; e-mail - mary@lambert667.fsnet.co.uk VAT: Stan/Spec.

Edward Manson (Clocks)
8 Market Hill. IP12 4LU. Open Sat. 10-5 and by appointment. *STOCK: Clocks.* TEL: 01394 380235; e-mail - edwardmanson@hotmail.com SER: Restorations (clocks); dial painting.

Melton Antiques
Kingdom Hall, Melton Rd., Melton. IP12 1NZ. (A. Harvey-Jones). Est. 1975. Open 9.30-5. CL: Wed. SIZE: Small. *STOCK: Silver, collector's items, £5-£500; decorative items and furniture, £15-£500; both 18th-19th*

C; Victoriana and general antiques, 19th C, £5-£500; sewing items. LOC: On right hand-side coming from Woodbridge. PARK: Outside shop. TEL: 01394 386232. FAIRS: Sandown Park. VAT: Global.

Sarah Meysey-Thompson Antiques
10 Church St. IP12 1DH. Est. 1962. Open 10.30-4 or by appointment any time. SIZE: Medium. *STOCK: Small furniture, late 18th-20th C; unusual and decorative items.* PARK: Easy. TEL: 01394 382144. FAIRS: Decorative Antiques & Textile, London. VAT: Spec.

Isobel Rhodes
10-12 Market Hill. IP12 4LU. *STOCK: Furniture, oak, country, mahogany; brassware.* PARK: Easy. TEL: 01394 382763. VAT: Spec.

WOOLPIT, Nr. Bury St. Edmunds

J.C. Heather
The Old Crown. IP30 9SA. Est. 1946. Open 9-8 including Sun. SIZE: Medium. *STOCK: Furniture, 18th-19th C, £20-£1,000.* Not Stocked: China. LOC: Near centre of village on right. PARK: Easy. TEL: 01359 240297; e-mail - john@johnheather.co.uk SER: Restorations.

WRENTHAM, Nr. Beccles

Wren House Antiques
1 High St. NR34 7HD. (Valerie and Tony Kemp). Open Thurs.-Sat. 10.30-5, Sun. 11-4 or by appointment. SIZE: Medium. *STOCK: Furniture, china and collectables.*

LOC: A12 village centre, Fiveways junction. TEL: 01502 675276.

YOXFORD

Garden House Antiques
High St. IP17 3ER. (Janet Hyde-Smith and Anne Gray). Est. 1979. Open 10-5. CL: Wed. SIZE: Medium. *STOCK: Small decorative antiques including furniture, 18th-20th C, £1-£500.* LOC: Opposite church. PARK: Easy. TEL: 01728 668044; home - 01986 874685; mobile - 07767 896401. Free delivery within 15 miles.

Suffolk House Antiques   BADA
High St. IP17 3EP. (A. Singleton). Est. 1990. Open 10-1 and 2.15-5.15. CL: Wed. SIZE: Large. *STOCK: 17th-18th C oak and country furniture, works of art, paintings, delftware and metalware.* LOC: A1120, just off A12. PARK: Easy. TEL: 01728 668122; fax - same; mobile - 07860 521583; e-mail - andrew.singleton @suffolk-house-antiques.co.uk website - www. suffolk-house-antiques.co.uk SER: Advice on interiors. FAIRS: BADA; Snape.

Yoxford Antique Centre & Gardens
Askers Hill. IP17 3JW. (Malcolm and June Purvis). Open 9.30-5.30, Sun. and Bank Holidays 10-4. SIZE: Large. *STOCK: Wide range of general antiques including oak, mahogany and pine furniture, longcase clocks, ceramics and smalls, 17th to early 20th C, £5-£15,000.* LOC: A1120, 1 mile from A12 towards Sibton. PARK: Own. TEL: 01728 668844. e-mail - malcolm@purvis193. fsnet.co.uk

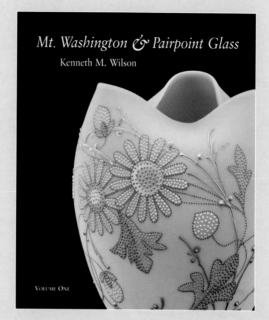

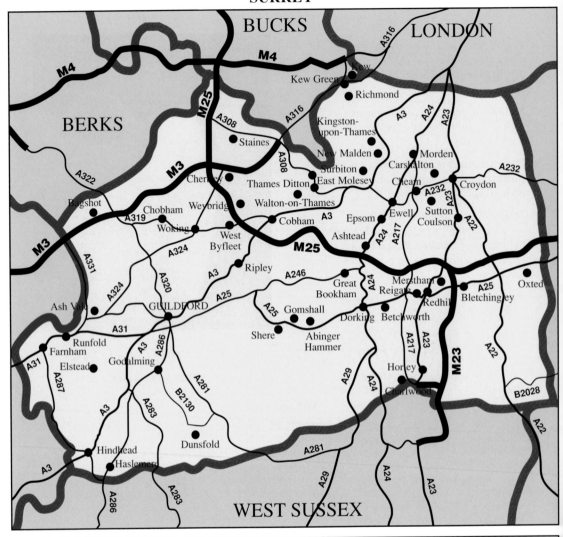

Dealers and Shops in Surrey

Abinger Hammer	1	Chobham	2	Farnham	7	Thames	3	Shere	2
Ash Vale	1	Cobham	1	Godalming	3	Merstham	1	Staines	2
Ashtead	2	Coulsdon	2	Gomshall	1	Morden	1	Surbiton	3
Bagshot	1	Croydon	1	Great Bookham	1	New Malden	1	Sutton	1
Betchworth	1	Dorking	20	Guildford	3	Oxted	1	Thames Ditton	1
Bletchingley	3	Dunsfold	1	Haslemere	3	Redhill	2	Walton-on-Thames	2
Carshalton	3	East Molesey	5	Hindhead	2	Reigate	3	West Byfleet	1
Charlwood	1	Elstead	1	Horley	1	Richmond	7	Weybridge	6
Cheam	1	Epsom	1	Kew Green	1	Ripley	5	Woking	2
Chertsey	2	Ewell	1	Kingston-upon-		Runfold	1		

ABINGER HAMMER

Stirling Antiques
Aberdeen House. RH5 6RY. (V.S. Burrell). Est. 1968. Open 9.30-6.30. CL: Thurs. *STOCK: Stained glass, furniture, copper, brass, jewellery, silver, curios, dolls.* PARK: Easy. TEL: 01306 730706; fax - 01306 731575. VAT: Stan.

ASH VALE, Nr. Aldershot (Hants)

House of Christian
5-7 Vale Rd. GU12 5HH. (A. Bail). Est. 1978. Open 10-5, Sat. 12.30-3. SIZE: Medium. *STOCK: Pine, oak, mahogany and walnut furniture, 19th-21st C; small items, 18th-21st C.* LOC: On B3411 between Ash and Ash Vale railway stations. From Ash Wharf over canal bridge, shop

(bright green) on left on hill. PARK: Easy - opposite. TEL: 01252 314478; fax - 01252 310311. SER: Valuations; restorations (including waxing and staining); cabinet making; stockists of Briwax and Liberon products.

ASHTEAD

Bumbles
90 The Street. KT21 1AW. (Barbara Kay). Est. 1992. Open 10.30-5.30. *STOCK: Cigarette cards.* PARK: Easy. TEL: 01372 276219. SER: Furniture restoration; oil lamp spare parts.

Temptations
88 The Street. KT21 1AW. (Pauline Watson). FGA, NAG. Open 10-5. *STOCK: Jewellery and silver.* LOC: Main street. PARK: Easy. TEL: 01372 277713. SER: NAG registered valuer; security photography; lecturer. VAT: Stan/Spec.

BAGSHOT

Country & Town Antiques
Pantiles, 20 London Rd. GU19 5HN. (S. Sommers and C. Martin). Est. 1990. Open 10-5 including Sun. SIZE: Large. *STOCK: Victorian and Edwardian, some Georgian, furniture, £50-£3,000; china and glass, collectables including lace and prints, Victorian to 1930s, £2-£100.* LOC: A30. PARK: Easy. TEL: 01276 489499.

BETCHWORTH, Nr. Dorking

Stoneycroft Farm   LAPADA
Chalkpit Lane, Reigate Rd. RH3 7EY. (J.G. Elias). Est. 1970. Open 8-5.30, Sat. 10.30-5. SIZE: Large. *STOCK: Large oak and country furniture, library bookcases, dining tables and chairs, special writing furniture, cupboards and wardrobes.* LOC: North of A25. 2 miles east of Dorking. PARK: Own, TEL: 01737 845215; e-mail - dorkingdesks@aol.com website - www.desk. uk.com SER: Search; shipping.

BLETCHINGLEY

Cider House Galleries Ltd   LAPADA
Norfolk House, 80 High St. RH1 4PA. (T. Roberts). Est. 1967. Open 10-5.30. CL: Sat. pm, Sun. and Mon. except by appointment. SIZE: Large. *STOCK: Paintings, 17th-20th C, from £450.* LOC: A25, behind Lawrence Auctioneers. PARK: Own. TEL: 01883 742198; fax - 01883 744014; e-mail - tony.roberts@virgin.net website - www.ciderhousegalleries.com SER: Valuations. FAIRS: Olympia. VAT: Stan/Spec.

John Anthony Antiques
71 High St. RH1 4LJ. (J.A. and N. Hart). Resident. Est. 1973. Open by appointment. *STOCK: 18th to early 19th C furniture.* LOC: A25 between Redhill and Godstone. PARK: Easy. TEL: 01883 743197; fax - 01883 742108. VAT: Spec/Margin.

Post House Antiques
32 High St. RH1 4PE. (P. and V. Bradley). Open daily, Sun. by appointment. *STOCK: Antique lighting, fenders, mirrors.* LOC: A25. PARK: Easy. TEL: 01883 743317; website - www.antiquelightinguk.co.uk VAT: Stan/Spec.

CARSHALTON

Carshalton Antique Galleries
5 High St. SM5 3AP. (B.A. Gough). Est. 1968. Open 9-4. CL: Wed. SIZE: Large. *STOCK: General antiques, furniture, clocks, glass, china, pictures and collectables.* LOC: Carshalton Ponds. PARK: Nearby. TEL: 020 8647 5664; home - 01306 887187. VAT: Stan/Spec.

Cherub Antiques
312 Carshalton Rd. SM5 3QB. (M. Wisdom). Open 9-5.30, Sat. 10-6. *STOCK: Pine, decorative items and general antiques.* LOC: Corner of Oxford Rd. PARK: Easy. TEL: 020 8643 0028. SER: Pine stripping. FAIRS: Hampton Court Palace; Royal Star & Garter. VAT: Spec.

Collectors Corner
3 The Square. SM5 3BN. (A.J. and B.M. Wilton). Est. 1975. Open 11.30-3.30, Sat. 10-5.30. CL: Wed. SIZE: Small. *STOCK: Collectors items, china, glass, 1780-1980, £50-£500; stamps, coins, medals, postcards, 19th-20th C, £5-£250.* LOC: Carshalton Ponds. PARK: Easy. TEL: 020 8669 7377. SER: Valuations; restorations.

CHARLWOOD

G. D. Blay Antiques   BADA
The Old Dairy, Charlwood Place, Norwood Hill Rd., RH6 0EB. By appointment. SIZE: Medium. *STOCK: Fine 18th to early 19th C furniture, £500-£50,000.* PARK: Easy. TEL: Mobile - 07785 767718; e-mail - gdblay@gdblayantiques.com website - www. gdblayantiques.com FAIRS: Olympia (summer, winter); BADA Chelsea (spring); Harrogate (autumn). VAT: Spec.

CHEAM

Cheam Village Antiques
16 Malden Rd. SM3 8QF. (Martyn K. Reed). Est. 1975. Open Mon., Fri. and Sat. 10-6. SIZE: Medium. *STOCK: General antiques and decorative items, from 19th C.* LOC: 10 mins. off A3 towards Worcester Park. PARK: Easy. TEL: 020 8644 4422; mobile - 07949 136499; e-mail - mrantiques@hotmail.com

CHERTSEY

Chertsey Antiques
10 Windsor St. KT16 8AS. (Leandro Ulisse). Open 8-5. SIZE: Medium. *STOCK: Furniture, jewellery, glass, pottery and porcelain, silver, silver plate, pictures, kitchenalia, memorabilia, books, linen, clocks.* PARK: Easy. TEL: 01932 563313; fax - 01753 685538; e-mail - antiques@ulisse.co.uk SER: Local free delivery.

D'Eyncourt
21 Windsor St. KT16 8AY. (Mr and Mrs Davies). Est. 1968. Open 10-5.15, Sat. 7-5.30, Sun. 11-4. SIZE: Medium. *STOCK: Furniture, Victorian to Art Deco, £50-£1,500; china, £5-£250; lighting and fireplaces, Victorian to present day, £25-£500.* LOC: Town centre. PARK: Easy and Guildford St. TEL: 01932 563411; e-mail - deyncourt@bushinternet.com SER: Valuations; restorations. FAIRS: London Photograph (Bonnington Hotel, Southampton Row). VAT: Stan.

CHOBHAM

Greengrass Antiques LAPADA
Hookstone Farm, Hookstone Lane, West End. GU24 9QP. (D. Greengrass). Est. 1970. Open by appointment. *STOCK: Decorative items; furniture, 19th C; works of art; shipping goods.* PARK: Easy. TEL: 01276 857582; fax - 01276 855289; mobile - 07860 399686. VAT: Spec/Global.

Mimbridge Antiques Centre
Mimbridge Garden Centre, Station Rd. GU24 8AS. (Jo Monteath Scott). Est. 1998. Open 10-5 including Sun. SIZE: Medium. *STOCK: Collectors' items, furniture, prints, watercolours, maps, books and garden antiques, 18th-20th C, £5-£2,500.* LOC: Main road. PARK: Easy. TEL: 01276 855736; mobile - 07771 862284. SER: Consultants; fine art installation. FAIRS: Kempton.

COBHAM

Village Antiques
38 Portsmouth Rd. KT11 1HZ. (N. Tsangari & Son). Resident. Est. 1965. Open 10-6, Sat. and Sun. by appointment. SIZE: Small. *STOCK: Oil paintings, watercolours, chairs, brass, wood, mainly 19th C.* LOC: Just off A3. PARK: Easy. TEL: 01932 589841. SER: Restorations (oil paintings). VAT: Stan.

COULSDON

Decodream
233 Chipstead Valley Rd. CR5 3BY. Open by appointment. *STOCK: Pottery - Clarice Cliff, Shorter, Shelley, Foley, F. and C. Rhead and Carlton ware.* LOC: Off junction 7, M25. PARK: Free. TEL: 020 8668 5534.

D. Potashnick Antiques
7 Stoats Nest Parade, 73 Stoats Nest Rd. CR5 2JJ. Est. 1974. Open 9-5.30, Sat. 9-12 or by appointment. *STOCK: Furniture.* LOC: Close to M23/M25. PARK: Easy. TEL: 020 8660 8403. SER: Restorations (furniture).

CROYDON

Oscar Dahling Antiques
87 Cherry Orchard Rd. CR0 6BE. Est. 1988. Open Tues., Wed., Thurs. 10.30-6, Sat. 10.30-4.30, other times by appointment. SIZE: Medium. *STOCK: Furniture, £50-£2,500; ceramics, £10-£250; jewellery and costume, £10-£1,000; all 18th-20th C.* LOC: First left after leaving East Croydon B.R. station. shop 300 yards, near Grouse and Claret public house. PARK: Easy. TEL: 020 8681 8090; home - same; e-mail - oscar.dahling@ virgin.net SER: Valuations; restorations.

DORKING

Adams Room Antiques
within Great Grooms of Dorking, 50/52 West St. RH4 1BU. Est. 1971. Open 9.30-5.30, Sun. 10-4. SIZE: Two large showrooms. *STOCK: 18th-19th C English and French furniture especially dining; decorative Regency and objects.* PARK: Rear of premises. TEL: 01306 887076; fax - 01306 881029; e-mail - dorking@ greatgrooms.co.uk website - www.greatgrooms.co.uk SER: Export orders arranged. VAT: Spec.

Antique Clocks by Patrick Thomas
62A West St. RH4 1BS. Est. 1992. Open 9.30-5.30, Sun. 11-4. SIZE: Medium. *STOCK: Clocks, 18th-19th C, £50-£5,000; optical antiques, 19th-20th C, £50-£3,000; sporting memorabilia, 19th-20th C, £50-£1,000.* PARK: Easy. TEL: 01306 743661; fax - 01483 762801; e-mail - patrickthomas@btconnect.com website - www. antiqueclockshop.co.uk SER: Valuations; restorations (clock and furniture). VAT: Spec.

Arkell Antiques Ltd LAPADA
64-65 West St. RH4 1BS. (Nicholas Arkell and Margaret Monk). CINOA. Est. 2001. Open 10-5. SIZE: Large. *STOCK: Georgian furniture, dining tables, chairs, Edwardian satinwood, £500-£50,000.* TEL: 01306 742152; fax - same; mobile - 07973 819783; e-mail - nick@arkellantiques.co.uk website - www.arkell antiques.com and www.arkellantiques.co.uk FAIRS: Olympia.

J. and M. Coombes
44 West St. RH4 1BU. Est. 1965. Open 9-5, Sun. 11-4. *STOCK: General antiques.* TEL: 01306 885479. VAT: Stan.

Dolphin Square Antiques
42 West St. RH4 1BU. (Mr and Mrs N. James). Est. 1995. Open 10-5. *STOCK: Furniture, clocks, china and glass, bronzes, Staffordshire, 17th to early 20th C, £50-£30,000.* LOC: Western end of High St. PARK: Nearby. TEL: 01306 887901. SER: Valuations; shipping.

The Dorking Desk Shop LAPADA
J.G.Elias Antiques Ltd., 41 West St. RH4 1BU. (J.G. and G.B. Elias). Est. 1969. Open 8-1 and 2-5.30, Sat. 10.30-1 and 2-5. SIZE: Large. *STOCK: Desks, dining tables, bookcases, chairs, wardrobes, oak and country furniture, 18th to late 19th C, £100-£60,000.* PARK: Nearby. TEL: 01306 883327; fax - 01306 875363; e-mail - dorking desks@aol.com website - www.desk.uk.com VAT: Stan/Spec.

Dorking House Antiques
17/18 West St. RH4 1BS. (Mrs G.D. Emburey). Est. 1989. Open 10-5. SIZE: 30 dealers. *STOCK: Period and pine furniture, silver, porcelain, longcase, wall and table clocks, treen, jewellery, copper and brass, pictures and prints, decorative and collectors' items.* LOC: Continuation of High St. into one-way system. PARK: Opposite. TEL: 01306 740915. SER: Restorations.

Great Grooms of Dorking
50-52 West St. RH4 1BU. (J. Podger). Open 9.30-5.30, Sun. and Bank Holidays 10-4. SIZE: 15 showrooms over 3 floors. *STOCK: Wide variety of fine English furniture, glass, ceramics, pictures, jewellery and silver, collectors' items and lighting.* PARK: Free at rear of premises. TEL: 01306 887076; fax - 01306 881029; e-mail - dorking@ greatgrooms.co.uk website - www.greatgrooms.co.uk SER: Valuations; shipping advice.

Harman's
19 West St. RH4 1QH. (Paul and Nicholas Harman). Est. 1956. Open 10-5. SIZE: Large. *STOCK: English mahogany and walnut furniture including tables and chairs, linen presses, sideboards, bookcases, 18th-19th C, £100-£15,000; Moorcroft, mirrors and lamps.* PARK: Nearby. TEL: 01306 743330; home - same; fax - 01306

742593; e-mail - enquiries@harmans.uk.com website - www.harmans.uk.com SER: Restorations; polishing; repairs; upholstery; valuations. VAT: Stan/Spec.

Holmwood Antiques
Norfolk Rd., South Holmwood. RH5 4LA. (R. Dewdney). Open 9-6.30, evenings and weekends by appointment. *STOCK: Georgian and Victorian furniture.* TEL: 01306 888174/888468.

The Howard Gallery   LAPADA
5 West St. RH4 1BL. (Felicity Howard). CINOA. Est. 1992. Open Tues.-Sat. 11-5, Mon. by appointment. SIZE: Medium. *STOCK: Oak, mahogany and walnut furniture, 1680-1750, walnut marquetry, Regency, satinwood, period longcase clocks, £700-£15,000; Continental porcelain mainly figure groups, 19th C.* PARK: Nearby. TEL: 01306 880022; fax - same; e-mail - howard.gallery@virgin.net website - www.thehoward gallery.co.uk SER: Valuations; restorations (period furniture and upholstery). VAT: Spec.

King's Court Galleries
54 West St. RH4 1BS. (Mrs J. Joel). Open 9.30-5.30. *STOCK: Antique maps, engravings, decorative and sporting prints.* TEL: 01306 881757; website - www.kingscourtgalleries.co.uk SER: Framing.

Malthouse Antiques
49 West St. RH4 1BU. (Colin Waters). Est. 1988. Open 10-5, Sat. 10-5.30, Sun. 11-4. SIZE: Large. *STOCK: 18th-19th C mahogany, rosewood and walnut, 17th-19th C oak and country, £100-£10,000; giltwood mirrors, 18th-19th C, £300-£5,000.* PARK: Pay and display behind shop. TEL: 01306 886169. VAT: Spec.

Norfolk House Galleries
48 West St. RH4 1BU. Est. 1979. Open 10-5. SIZE: 5 showrooms. *STOCK: 18th-19th C furniture, especially dining tables and sets of chairs.* PARK: Public behind showrooms. TEL: 01306 881028.

Pilgrims Antique Centre
7 West St. RH4 1BL. Est. 1974. Open 10-5. SIZE: 10 dealers. *STOCK: Furniture, 19th-20th C; china and glass, silver and plate, copper and brass, telephones and collectables.* LOC: A25 through town, just off High St. PARK: Easy. TEL: 01306 875028.

The Refectory
38 West St. RH4 1BU. (Christopher R. Marks). Est. 1964. Open 10.30-5, Sun. by appointment. *STOCK: Refectory tables, coffers, Windsor chairs, early oak and country furniture, 16th-18th C; pewter, brass, iron, copper and treen.* LOC: Town centre. PARK: Opposite and nearby. TEL: 01306 742111; home - 01483 729646. website - www.therefectory.co.uk SER: Valuations. FAIRS: Galloways; Baileys.

Scotts of Dorking
70 High St. RH4 1AY. Open 9-5.15. SIZE: Medium. *STOCK: Jewellery.* LOC: Opposite Boots chemist. PARK: Behind shop. TEL: 01306 880790.

Temptations, Antique Jewellery & Silver
4 Old King's Head Court. RH4 1AR. (Pauline Watson). FGA, NAG. Est. 1960. Open 9.30-5. SIZE: Small. *STOCK: Jewellery and silver especially Victorian.* LOC:

Off 11 High St. at the top of West St. PARK: Behind shop in North St. TEL: 01306 885452. SER: NAG registered valuer; lecturer; photographer. VAT: Stan/Spec.

West Street Antiques
63 West St. RH4 1BS. (J.G. Spooner, R.A. Ratner and P.J. Spooner). Est. 1986. Open 9.30-1 and 2.15-5.30. SIZE: Medium. *STOCK: Arms and armour, 17th-19th C, £500-£30,000; paintings.* LOC: A25, one-way system. PARK: Nearby. TEL: 01306 883487; fax - same; home - 01306 730182 or 01372 452877; e-mail - weststant @aol.com website - www.antiquearmsandarmour.com VAT: Spec.

The Westcott Gallery
4 Guildford Rd., Westcott. RH4 3NR. (Anthony Wakefield). Est. 1989. Open by appointment only. *STOCK: Specialist in contemporary paintings and ceramics by Surrey artists.* LOC: Village centre, opposite the green. TEL: 01306 734100/876261; fax - 01306 740770; e-mail - info@westcottgallery.co.uk website - www.westcottgallery.co.uk SER: Pictures by post (see website).

DUNSFOLD, Nr. Godalming

Antique Buildings Ltd
GU8 4NP. (Peter Barker). Resident. Est. 1975. Open daily, Sat. and Sun. by appointment. SIZE: Large. *STOCK: Oak timbers, 17th C, £25-£1,000; architectural items, 15th-18th C, £25-£500; barn frames, 17th C, £2,000-£50,000.* LOC: From Sun public house 500 yards down Alfold road, row of white posts on left hand side, premises up tarmac drive between last two. PARK: Easy. TEL: 01483 200477; fax - 01483 200752. SER: Valuations; restorations (ancient oak framed buildings); buys at auction (buildings and architectural items). VAT: Stan.

EAST MOLESEY

Bridge Road Antiques Centre
77 Bridge Rd., Hampton Court. KT8 9HH. Open 10.30-5.30, Sun. 12-5. SIZE: 10 dealers. *STOCK: 18th to early 20th C furniture, silver, ceramics, glass, prints, jewellery and decorative antiques.* LOC: Turn down Creek Rd., opposite Hampton Court station, into Bridge Rd. TEL: 020 8979 7954.

Elizabeth R. Antiques
39 Bridge Rd., Hampton Court. KT8 9ER. Est. 1988. Open 10-4.30, Sun. 11-3.30. SIZE: Large. *STOCK: Furniture, 19th C and Art Deco, £500-£2,000; silver, 18th-20th C, £75-£300; toys, 20th C, £35-£600; jewellery, 19th-20th C, £40-£700; porcelain, 18th-19th C; Art Deco, Arts and Crafts porcelain and glass.* PARK: Easy. TEL: 020 8979 4004; fax - same. SER: Valuations; restorations (French polishing and waxing); repairs (clock, glass and china). FAIRS: Sandown; Alexandra Palace.

Hampton Court Emporium
52-54 Bridge Rd., Hampton Court. KT8 9HA. (A.J. Smith). Est. 1992. Open 10-5.30, Sun 11-5.30. SIZE: Medium. *STOCK: Furniture, paintings, silver, jewellery, mirrors, books, clocks, brass and copper, objets d'art, lamps, china*

and porcelain, collectors' cameras, Art Deco. PARK: Palace Rd. station. TEL: 020 8941 8876; e-mail - info@ hamptoncourtemporium.com website - www.hamptoncourt emporium.com SER: Valuations; restorations.

Nostradamus II
53 Bridge Rd., Hampton Court. KT8 9HA. (Heather Ferri). Est. 1998. Open 10-5.30, Sun. 11-6. CL: Mon. SIZE: Medium. *STOCK: Furniture, 18th-19th C; Art Deco, £25-£1,000; Victorian jewellery and silver, £100-£1,000; brass, lighting, cameras.* LOC: 5 mins. walk from Hampton Court rail station, 10 mins from the Palace. PARK: Easy. TEL: 020 8783 0595. SER: Valuations; restorations. VAT: Stan.

A.F.J. Turner Antiques
144A Bridge Rd. KT8 9HW. Est. 1992. Open by appointment only. SIZE: Small. *STOCK: Victorian and Edwardian natural history and taxidermy and associated curiosities, pre 1945, £10-£10,000.* LOC: Near Hampton Court Palace. PARK: In road opposite. TEL: Mobile - 07770 880960.

ELSTEAD

Honeypot Antiques Ltd
Milford Rd. GU8 6HP. Est. 2002. Open 10-5, Sun.11-5. SIZE: Medium. *STOCK: Furniture, books, paintings, prints, tools, jewellery, silver, boxes, lighting, china, architectural fittings, telephones and clocks.* LOC: Main road. PARK: Easy. TEL: 01252 703614; e-mail - sales@ honeypotantiques.co.uk

EPSOM

Vandeleur Antiquarian Books
6 Seaforth Gdns., Stoneleigh. KT19 0NR. (E.H. Bryant). PBFA. Est. 1971. Open by appointment. *STOCK: Antiquarian and secondhand books on all subjects, including Africana, big game hunting and mountaineering; prints including rowing, and maps; Indian Mogul-style paintings.* TEL: 020 8393 7752; fax - same. SER: Subject lists quoted on request. FAIRS: Various book. VAT: Stan.

EWELL

J.W. McKenzie
12 Stoneleigh Park Rd. KT19 0QT. Est. 1971. Appointment advisable. *STOCK: Old and new books and memorabilia on cricket.* TEL: 020 8393 7700; e-mail - jwmck@netcomuk.co.uk website - www.mckenzie-cricket.co.uk

FARNHAM

Annie's Antiques
1 Ridgway Parade, Frensham Rd. GU9 8UZ. Est. 1982. Open 9.30-5.30, Fri. 10.30-5.30, Sun. by appointment. SIZE: Medium. *STOCK: Furniture, bric-a-brac, jewellery, 19th to early 20th C, £5-£1,000; general antiques.* LOC: 1 mile out of Farnham on A287 towards Hindhead. PARK: Easy. TEL: 01252 713447; home - 01252 723217.

The Antiques Warehouse
Badshot Farm, St George's Rd., Runfold. GU9 9HR. (Hilary Burroughs). Est. 1995. Open 10-5.30, including Sun. SIZE: Large - 2 barns, 30 dealers. *STOCK: Furniture, 17th C to 1940s, £75-£10,000; china, glass, silver, jewellery, paintings, prints and interesting collectables, 18th C to 1960s, £5-£2,000.* LOC: A31 from Farnham towards Guildford, 1st exit (signed Runfold), left at end of slip road towards Badshot Lea, premises 200 yards on left. PARK: Own large. TEL: 01252 317590; website - www.theantiqueswarehouse.com. SER: Restorations (furniture); shipping.

Bourne Mill Antiques
39-43 Guildford Rd. GU9 9PY. (G. Evans). Est. 1960. Open 10-5.30 including Sun. SIZE: Large - 83 dealers. *STOCK: Antique and reproduction furniture in oak, walnut, mahogany, yew and pine; china, glass, pictures, jewellery, fireplaces, beds, kitchenalia, bespoke furniture, collectors' items, books, bric-a-brac; garden ornaments, furniture and buildings.* LOC: Eastern outskirts of Farnham. PARK: Own. TEL: 01252 716663. SER: Shipping.

Casque and Gauntlet Militaria
55/59 Badshot Lea Rd., Badshot Lea. GU9 9LP. (R. Colt). Est. 1957. Open 11-5. SIZE: Large. *STOCK: Militaria, arms, armour.* LOC: A324 Aldershot to Farnham road. PARK: Easy. TEL: 01252 320745; e-mail - ann.colt@ntlworld.com SER: Restorations (metals); re-gilding.

Christopher's Antiques
Sandford Lodge, 39a West St. GU9 7DX. (Mr and Mrs C.M. Booth). Resident. Est. 1972. Open 8-1 and 2-5.30, weekends by appointment. SIZE: Large. *STOCK: Fruitwood country furniture, 18th-19th C; walnut furniture, 17th-18th C.* LOC: From Guildford on the A31, turn right at second roundabout. PARK: Easy. TEL: 01252 713794; fax - 01252 713266; e-mail - cbooth7956 @aol.com SER: Valuations; restorations (furniture). VAT: Stan/Spec.

Heytesbury Antiques   BADA LAPADA
P.O. Box 222. GU10 5HN. (Ivor and Sally Ingall). Est. 1974. Open by appointment. SIZE: Medium. **STOCK: 18th-19th C Continental and English furniture, statuary, bronzes and decorative items, £1,000-£15,000. LOC: 5 miles west of Farnham. TEL: 01252 850893; fax - 01252 850828; mobile - 07836 675727; e-mail - ingall@heytesbury.demon.co.uk FAIRS: Olympia; Decorative Antiques & Textile. VAT: Spec.**

Karel Weijand Fine Oriental Carpets   BADA LAPADA
Lion and Lamb Courtyard. GU9 7LL. Est. 1975. Open 9.30-5.30. SIZE: Large. STOCK: Fine antique and contemporary Oriental rugs and carpets, from £150. LOC: Off West St. PARK: Easy. TEL: 01252 726215; e-mail - carpets@karelweijand.com website - www.karelweijand.com SER: Valuations; restorations; cleaning. FAIRS: BADA; LAPADA. VAT: Stan/Spec.

GODALMING

The Antique Shop
72 Ockford Rd. GU7 1RF. (G. Jones). Open 10.30-4.30, Sat. 11-5. SIZE: 6 dealers. *STOCK: General antiques including furniture and light fittings.* PARK: Opposite. TEL: 01483 414428. FAIRS: Clandon.

Heath-Bullocks   **BADA**
8 Meadrow. GU7 3HN. (Roger, Mary and Charlotte Heath-Bullock). Est. 1926. Open 10-4 (winter), 10-4.30 (summer). SIZE: Large. *STOCK: English and Continental furniture.* LOC: A3100. From Guildford on the left side approaching Godalming. PARK: Own. TEL: 01483 422562; fax - 01483 426077; e-mail - heathbullocks@aol.com website - www.heath-bullocks.com and www.AntiquesCare.com and www.sheridanwolf.com SER: Valuations; restorations. **FAIRS: BADA.**

Priory Antiques
29 Church St. GU7 1EL. (P. Rotchell). Open 10-4. CL: Wed. *STOCK: General antiques.* TEL: 01483 421804.

GOMSHALL, Nr. Guildford

The Coach House Antiques
60 Station Rd. GU5 9NP. (P.W. and L. Reeves). Resident. Est. 1985. Open Mon.-Fri. 9-5.30. SIZE: Medium. *STOCK: Longcase clocks, 1780 to 19th C, £4,000-£20,000; furniture, 1790 to late 19th C, £1,000-£20,000.* LOC: Between Guildford and Dorking on the Shere by-pass. PARK: Easy. TEL: 01483 203838; fax - 01483 202999; e-mail - coach_house.antiques@virgin.net website - www.coachhouseantiques.com SER: Restorations (clocks and furniture). VAT: Spec.

GREAT BOOKHAM

Memory Lane Antiques
30 Church Rd. KT23 3PW. (J. Westwood). Est. 1984. Open 10-5. CL: Wed. *STOCK: Toys and general antiques, pre-1920, £5-£1,000.* PARK: Easy. TEL: 01372 459908.

GUILDFORD

Cry for the Moon
17 Tunsgate. GU1 3QT. (Jonathan Owen and Harry Diamond). Est. 1977. Open 10-5.30. SIZE: Medium. *STOCK: Mainly jewellery, £30-£50,000; silver and objets d'art.* TEL: 01483 306600. SER: Valuations; repairs; jewellery commissions undertaken. VAT: Stan/Margin.

Horological Workshops   **BADA**
204 Worplesdon Rd. GU2 9UY. (M.D. Tooke). Est. 1968. Open Tues.-Fri. 8.30-5.30, Sat. 9-12.30 or by appointment. SIZE: Large. *STOCK: Clocks, watches, barometers.* PARK: Easy. TEL: 01483 576496; fax - 01483 452212; e-mail - enquiries@horological workshops.com website - www.horologicalworkshops.com SER: Restorations; collection and delivery.

Oriental Rug Gallery
230 Upper High St. GU1 3JD. (R. Mathias and J. Blair). Est. 1989. Open 10-5.30. *STOCK: Russian, Afghan, Turkish and Persian carpets, rugs and kelims; Oriental objets d'art.* TEL: + 4 (0) 1483 457600; fax - same; e-mail - rugs@orientalruggallery.com website - www.orientalruggallery.com

HASLEMERE

Haslemere Antique Market
1A Causewayside, High St. GU27 2JZ. Est. 1990. Open 9.30-5. SIZE: Large. *STOCK: Wide variety of general antiques.* LOC: Off High St. (A286). PARK: Easy. TEL: 01428 643959. SER: Valuations; restorations; buys at auction.

Surrey Clock Centre
3 Lower St. GU27 2NY. (J.P. Ingrams and S. Haw). Est. 1962. Open 9-1 and 2-5. SIZE: Large. *STOCK: Clocks and barometers.* PARK: Easy. TEL: 01428 651313; website - www.surreyclockcentre.co.uk SER: Restorations; hand-made parts; shipping orders; clocks made to order. VAT: Stan/Spec.

West Street Antiques   **LAPADA**
8-10 West St. GU27 2AB. (Mark Holden). Est. 1998. Open 9.30-5 or by appointment. SIZE: Small. *STOCK: Furniture, pre-1900 but mainly pre-1820, £300-£10,000; longcase and bracket clocks, pre-1900, £600-£7,000; silver, mainly 19th to early 20th C, £25-£500; prints and paintings, mainly 19th to early 20th C, £30-£1,500.* LOC: Opposite PO. PARK: Easy and nearby. TEL: 01428 644911; fax - 01428 645201; e-mail - mfjholden@hotmail.com website - www.weststreetantiques.co.uk SER: Restorations (furniture and clocks).

HINDHEAD

Albany Antiques Ltd
8-10 London Rd. GU26 6AF. (T. Winstanley). Est. 1965. Open 9-6. CL: Sun. except by appointment. *STOCK: Furniture, 17th-18th C, £20-£400; china including Chinese, £5-£400; metalware, £7-£50; both 18th-19th C.* Not Stocked: Silver. LOC: A3. PARK: Easy. TEL: 01428 605528. VAT: Stan/Spec.

Drummonds Architectural Antiques
The Kirkpatrick Buildings, 25 London Rd. GU26 6AB. SALVO. Est. 1988. Open 9-6, Sat. 10-5. SIZE: Large. *STOCK: Architectural and decorative antiques, garden statuary and furniture, period bathrooms, reclaimed flooring, door furniture.* LOC: West side of A3, 50 yards north of traffic lights. PARK: Own. TEL: 01428 609444; fax - 01428 609445; e-mail - sales@drummonds-arch.co.uk website - www.drummonds-arch.co.uk SER: Restorations (stonework and gates); handmade cast iron baths and fittings, cast iron conservatories; vitreous re-enamelling of baths. VAT: Stan/Spec.

HORLEY

Surrey Antiques
3 Central Parade, Massetts Rd. RH6 7PP. (Michael Bradnum). Est. 1990. Open 10-5. SIZE: Medium. *STOCK: China, pottery and glass, furniture, pictures, mirrors, collectables, 19th-20th C.* LOC: On left by traffic lights, almost opposite police station. PARK: Public behind shop. TEL: 01293 775522. e-mail - mike.bradnum@btopenworld.com FAIRS: Ardingly; Copthorne; Effingham Park Hotel.

KEW GREEN

Andrew Davis
6 Mortlake Terrace. TW9 3DT. (Andrew and Glynis Davis). Resident. Est. 1969. Most days by appointment. *STOCK: Mainly pictures - oil, watercolours and prints, 18th-20th C;*

decorative and functional items including furniture, ceramics, glass, clocks, garden and architectural items, £10-£5,000. LOC: South end of Kew Green on South Circular Rd. PARK: Easy - side road or Kew Green. TEL: 020 8948 4911. SER: Valuations and advice.

KINGSTON-UPON-THAMES

Glencorse Antiques   LAPADA
321 Richmond Rd., Ham Parade, Ham Common. KT2 5QU. (M. Igel and B.S. Prydal). Est. 1983. Open 10-5.30. STOCK: 18th-19th C furniture; traditional modern British art, oils and watercolours, 20th-21st C. PARK: Own. TEL: 020 8541 0871 and 020 7229 6770.

Glydon and Guess Ltd
14 Apple Market. KT1 1JE. NAG; GMC. Est. 1940. Open 9.30-5. STOCK: Jewellery, small silver, £100-£5,000. LOC: Town centre. TEL: 020 8546 3758. SER: Valuations; restorations.

Kingston Antique Market
29-31 Old London Rd. KT2 6ND. Est. 1995. Open 10-6, Sat. 9.30-6, Sun. 10-5. SIZE: 100 dealers. STOCK: General antiques including period furniture, porcelain, collectables and jewellery. LOC: Off Clarence St. PARK: Easy. TEL: 020 8549 2004; e-mail - webmaster@ antiquesmarket.co.uk website - www.antiquemarket. co.uk FAIRS: Newark; Ardingly; Shepton Mallet.

MERSTHAM

Geoffrey Van-Hay Antiques
The Old Smithy, 7 High St. RH1 3BA. Open 9-5. SIZE: Medium. STOCK: 18th-19th C furniture, £500-£5,000. PARK: Easy. TEL: 01737 645131; fax - same; e-mail - vanhayanatiques@supanet.com SER: Valuations; restorations. VAT: Spec.

MORDEN

A. Burton-Garbett
35 The Green. SM4 4HJ. Est. 1959. Open by appointment. Prospective clients met (at either Morden or Wimbledon tube station) by car. STOCK: Books on Latin American and Caribbean travel, arts and antiquities. TEL: 020 8540 2367; fax - 020 8540 4594. SER: Buys at auction (books, pictures, fine arts, ethnographica). VAT: Stan.

NEW MALDEN

Coombe Antiques
25 Coombe Rd. KT3 4PX. (Sandra Sephton). Est. 1985. Open 10-5.30. SIZE: Large. STOCK: Georgian, Victorian and Edwardian furniture including chests of drawers, bookcases and wardrobes, to £1,200; cutlery, china, glass and jewellery. PARK: Easy. TEL: 020 8949 4238; mobile - 07970 718214. SER: Restorations.

OXTED

Secondhand Bookshop
27 Station Rd. West. RH8 9EU. (David Neal). Est. 1985. Open 10-5. SIZE: Small. STOCK: Books, 18th C to present day, £1-£500. LOC: Adjacent to station. TEL: 01883 715755; home - 01883 723131. SER: Valuations;

buys at auction (books). FAIRS: Book - in south-east. VAT: Stan.

REDHILL

F.G. Lawrence and Sons
89 Brighton Rd. RH1 6PS. (Chris Lawrence). Est. 1891. Open 9-5, Sat. 9-1. SIZE: Large. STOCK: 1920s, Edwardian, Victorian, Georgian and reproduction furniture. LOC: A23. PARK: Own. TEL: 01737 764196; fax - 01737 240446; e-mail - fglawrence@btinternet.com SER: Valuations. FAIRS: Newark. VAT: Stan.

Lawrence House Antiques
87-89 Brighton Rd. RH1 6PS. (Mrs. Sheila Lawrence). Est. 2004. Open 10-5. SIZE: Large. STOCK: General antiques, collectables and garden statuary. LOC: A23. PARK: At rear. TEL: 01737 779169; fax - same; e-mail - slawrence@sweethaven.uk.net SER: Valuations.

REIGATE

Bourne Gallery Ltd   BADA LAPADA
31/33 Lesbourne Rd. RH2 7JS. (John Robertson). Est. 1970. Open 10-1 and 2-5. CL: Mon. SIZE: Large. STOCK: 19th-20th C oils and watercolours, £250-£50,000; contemporary works, £250-£5,000. LOC: Side street. PARK: Easy. TEL: 01737 241614; e-mail - bournegallery@aol.com website - www.bourne gallery.com FAIRS: Olympia; Chelsea; Watercolours & Drawings. VAT: Spec.

Bertram Noller (Reigate)
14a London Rd. RH2 9HY. (A.M. Noller). Est. 1970. Open Tues., Thurs., Sat. 9.30-1 and 2-5.30. SIZE: Small. STOCK: Collectors' items, furniture, grates, fenders, mantels, copper, brass, glass, pewter, £1-£500. LOC: West side of one-way traffic system. Opposite Upper West St. car park. PARK: Opposite. TEL: 01737 242548. SER: Valuations; restorations (furniture, clocks, bronzes, brass and copper, marble).

M. & M. White Antique & Reproduction Centre
57 High St. RH2 9AE. Est. 1993. Open 10-5. SIZE: Medium. STOCK: Mahogany, £100-£2,500, pine, £60-£1,500, both 18th C; reproduction, 1920-1970, £40-£1,000. PARK: Easy. TEL: 01737 222331; fax - 01737 215702. FAIRS: Newark; Ardingly; Kempton Park. VAT: Spec.

RICHMOND

The Gooday Gallery
14 Richmond Hill. TW10 6QX. (Debbie Gooday). Est. 1971. Open Thurs.-Sat. 11-5 or any time by appointment. SIZE: Medium. STOCK: Decorative and applied design, 1880-1980, Arts and Crafts, Art Nouveau, Art Deco, furniture, pictures, ceramics, metalwork, jewellery; African and oceanic tribal artefacts; 1950s and 1960s designer items, all £100-£5,000. LOC: 100yds. from Richmond Bridge. PARK: Easy. TEL: 020 8940 8652; mobile - 07710 124540; e-mail - Goodaygallery@ aol.com SER: Valuations; buys at auction.

Roland Goslett Gallery
139 Kew Rd. TW9 2PN. Est. 1974. Open Thurs. and Fri.

10-6, Sat. 10-2 or by appointment. SIZE: Medium. *STOCK: English watercolours and oil paintings, 19th to early 20th C, £100-£5,000.* PARK: Meters. TEL: 020 8940 4009; e-mail - rolandgoslett@btconnect.com website - www.rolandgoslettgallery.co.uk SER: Valuations; restorations (oils, watercolours and frames); framing. VAT: Spec.

Horton   LAPADA
2 Paved Court, The Green. TW9 1LZ. (D. Horton). FGA. Est. 1978. Open 10-5. SIZE: Small. *STOCK: Jewellery and silver, 18th-20th C, £500-£5,000.* LOC: Off The Green, behind Dickens & Jones. PARK: Easy. TEL: 020 8332 1775; fax - 020 8332 1994; website - www. hortonlondon.co.uk

Robin Kennedy
P.O Box 265. TW9 1UB. Est. 1971. Open by appointment. *STOCK: Japanese prints, £50-£5,000.* TEL: 020 8940 5346; fax - same; e-mail - robin@ japaneseprints.co.uk website - www.japaneseprints.co.uk FAIRS: Arts of Pacific Asia (New York, San Francisco, Santa Monica).

F. and T. Lawson Antiques
13 Hill Rise. TW10 6UQ. Resident. Est. 1965. Open 10-5.30, Sat. 10-5. CL: Wed. and Sun. am. SIZE: Medium. *STOCK: Furniture, 1680-1870; paintings and watercolours; both £30-£1,500; clocks, 1650-1930, £50-£2,000; bric-a-brac, £5-£300.* LOC: Near Richmond Bridge at bottom of Hill Rise on the river side, overlooking river. PARK: Limited and further up Hill Rise. TEL: 020 8940 0461. SER: Valuations; buys at auction.

Marryat   LAPADA
88 Sheen Rd. TW9 1AJ. (Marryat (Richmond) Ltd). Est. 1990. Open 10-5.30, Sat. 9.30-5.30. SIZE: Large. *STOCK: English and Continental furniture, watercolours and oils, £100-£5,000; porcelain, pottery, glass, silver, objets and decorative antiques, £2-£1,000; mainly 18th-19th C.* LOC: Follow M3/A316 towards Richmond, first left into Church Rd. then left again. Close to underground station. PARK: Easy. TEL: 020 8332 0262. SER: Restorations. VAT: Stan/Spec.

Vellantiques
127 Kew Rd. TW9 2PN. (Saviour Vella). Est. 1984. Open 10-6. SIZE: Medium. *STOCK: Furniture, gold and silver, porcelain, paintings and curios, £50-£3,000.* TEL: 020 8940 5392; fax - same; mobile - 07960 897075. SER: Valuations. FAIRS: Ardingly.

RIPLEY

J. Hartley Antiques Ltd   LAPADA
186 High St. GU23 6BB. Est. 1949. Open 8.45-5.45, Sat. 9.45-4.45. *STOCK: Queen Anne, Georgian and Edwardian furniture.* TEL: 01483 224318. VAT: Stan.

Sage Antiques and Interiors   LAPADA
High St. GU23 6BB. (H. and C. Sage). GMC. Est. 1971. Open 9.30-5.30. SIZE: Large. *STOCK: Furniture, mahogany, oak, walnut, 1600-1900, £150-£8,000; oil paintings, £100-£5,000; watercolours, £50-£1,000, china, £2-£500, all 18th-19th C; silver, Sheffield plate, brass, pewter, decorative items, 18th-19th C, £50-*

£1,000. LOC: Village centre, on main road. PARK: Easy. TEL: 01483 224396; fax - 01483 211996. SER: Restorations (furniture); interior furnishing. VAT: Stan.

Sweerts de Landas   BADA
Dunsborough Park, Newark Lane. GU23 6AL. (A.J.H. and A.C. Sweerts de Landas). SALCO. Est. 1979. Open by appointment. SIZE: Large. *STOCK: Garden ornaments and statuary, 17th-20th C, £500-£250,000.* **LOC: From High St. turn into Newark Lane (between estate agent and Suzuki garage), continue 400 yards, through archway on right, follow drive to gate. PARK: Easy. TEL: 01483 225366; home - same. SER: Valuations; restorations (stone, lead, cast iron, marble); buys at auction (as stock). VAT: Stan/Spec.**

Talbot Walk Antique Centre
The Talbot Hotel, High St. GU23 6BB. (I. and J. Picken). Est. 1999. Open 10-5, Sun. 11-4. SIZE: Large - 30 dealers. *STOCK: English furniture, 1750-1930, £50-£5,000+; glass and ceramics, 1800-1940, £10-£3,000+; lighting, 1850-1940, £50-£2,000+; general antiques including mirrors and clocks, £10-£1,000+.* LOC: 1 mile south of A3/M25, junction 10, take the B2215 to Ripley, 400yds on left after entering village. PARK: Own at rear. TEL: 01483 211724; fax - same. VAT: Stan/Spec. Below are listed some of the dealers at this centre.

Argyll Antiques
(K. Deszberg). *Victorian furniture, Oriental ceramics and objects.*

R. Arnot
19th to early 20th C English furniture including upholstered; clocks and Doulton.

Jane Aspinall
English furniture, 1800-1920; upholstery, lighting and decorative items.

Richard Barnes
Silver.

P. Crowder
Prints and maps.

Draper Antiques
(Dave and Sheena Draper). *Victorian, Edwardian and 1920s dining room furniture.* TEL: 01483 211724; mobile - 07768 213491; e-mail - davedraper@yahoo.co.uk

Carol Dudley
Oak furniture, 1650-1900.

Every Cloud
(A. Machen). *Furniture, jewellery, glass and decorative antiques.*

Colleen Francis
French country copper, kitchenalia and decorative items.

Deidre Geer
Decorative French provincial antiques and mirrors.

D. Harman
Kitchenalia, stoneware and advertising.

Hayloft Antiques
(N. Thomas). *Oak furniture, 1700-1930.*

Heirloom Restorations
(Hazel Bigwood). *Victorian and Edwardian furniture.*

Nick Hill
19th C furniture and works of art.

The Lamp Gallery
(Graham Jones). *Interior lighting, 1860-1940 including Arts & Crafts, Art Deco and Art Nouveau.*

H. Loveland
19th C European ceramics.

Carol Martin
Victorian furniture and objects.

Valerie Swan
Silver, jewellery, coins and general antiques.

Richard Tinson
18th to early 20th C glass.

Sheila Webber
Furniture, 1840-1920.

John Wood
English furniture, clocks and barometers.

Anthony Welling Antiques   **BADA**
Broadway Barn, High St. GU23 6AQ. Est. 1970. Open 9.30-1 and 2-5. Sun. and evenings by appointment. SIZE: Large. STOCK: English oak, 17th-18th C, £250-£8,000; country furniture, 18th C, £200-£6,000; brass, copper, pewter, 18th C, £100-£750. Not Stocked: Glass, china, silver. LOC: Turn off A3 at Ripley, shop in village centre on service road. PARK: Easy. TEL: 01483 225384; fax - same; e-mail - ant@awelling. freeserve.co.uk website - www.antique-oak-furniture.co.uk SER: Restoration (furniture). VAT: Spec.

RUNFOLD, Nr. Farnham

The Packhouse
Hewetts Kilns, Tongham Rd. GU10 1PQ. (A.J. Hougham). Est. 1991. Open 10.30-5.30, Sat. and Sun. 10-5.30. SIZE: Large. *STOCK: Furniture including period, 1930s and country pine; garden statuary, architectural items.* LOC: Off A31 (Hogs Back). PARK: Easy. TEL: 01252 781010; fax - 01252 783876; e-mail - info@packhouse.com website - www.packhouse.com SER: UK delivery

SHERE, Nr. Guildford

Helena's Collectables
Shops 1 and 2, Middle St. GU5 9HF. (Mrs K. White and Mrs H. Lee). Est. 1995. Open 9.30-4.30, Sat. 10-4.30, Sun. 11-4. SIZE: Medium. *STOCK: Royal Doulton, from 1930s, £100-£2,500; Beswick, from 1950s, from £50+; Walt Disney classics, Border Fine Art, Bunnykins and Beatrix Potter, Royal Crown Derby.* LOC: A24. PARK: Behind sports ground. TEL: 01483 203039; fax - same; e-mail - helen@collectables.demon.co.uk website - www.collectables.demon.co.uk SER: Valuations; restorations; search; buys at auction. FAIRS: DMG. VAT: Stan.

Shere Antiques Centre
Middle St. GU5 9HL. (Jean Watson). Est. 1986. Open 11-5 including Sun. SIZE: 4 large showrooms. *STOCK: Mid-Georgian, Victorian and Edwardian clocks, silver,*

copper, brass, English and Continental porcelain, lighting, Victorian garden tools and associated items. LOC: A25 - between Dorking and Guildford. PARK: Easy. TEL: 01483 202846; fax - 01483 830761; e-mail - jean.watson@shereantiques.com website - www. shereantiques.com SER: Restorations; collection and delivery. VAT: Stan/Spec.

STAINES

K.W. Dunster Antiques
23 Church St. TW18 4EN. (Keith and Cynthia Dunster). Est. 1972. Open 9-4.30. CL: Thurs. SIZE: Medium. *STOCK: Clocks, furniture, general antiques, interior decor, jewellery, nautical items.* PARK: Easy. TEL: 01784 453297; fax - 01784 483146; e-mail - kdunsterantiques@aol.com SER: Valuations. VAT: Stan/Spec.

Clive Rogers Oriental Rugs
PO Box 234. TW19 5PE. TVADA. PADA. Est. 1974. Open by appointment. SIZE: Medium. *STOCK: Oriental rugs, carpets, textiles; Near and Central Asian and Islamic works of art.* LOC: On B376, 15 mins. from Heathrow Airport. PARK: Own. TEL: 01784 481177/481100; fax - 01784 481144; e-mail - info@orient-rug.com website - www.orient-rug.com SER: Valuations; restorations (as stock); historical analysis commission agents; buys at auction. FAIRS: TVADA; ICOC; Hali; San Francisco. VAT: Stan/Spec.

SURBITON

Cockrell Antiques
278 Ewell Rd. KT6 7AG. (Sheila and Peter Cockrell). Resident. Est. 1982. Open most Fri., Sat., Sun. and evenings, prior telephone call advisable. SIZE: Medium. *STOCK: Furniture including Art Deco, from 18th C, £50-£3,000+; decorative items, £50-£500.* LOC: Off A3 at Tolworth Tower on A240. PARK: Easy. TEL: 020 8390 8290; home - same; e-mail - antiques@cockrell.co.uk website - www.cockrell.co.uk FAIRS: DMG; Kempton Park. VAT: Stan/Spec.

B. M. and E. Newlove
139-141 Ewell Rd. KT6 6AL. Est. 1958. Open 9.30-5.30, Sat. by appointment. CL: Wed. SIZE: Medium and store. *STOCK: Furniture especially early oak and Georgian mahogany, 17th-19th C, £500-£10,000; china, 18th-19th C, £75-£200; paintings, all periods, £50-£2,000; longcase clocks, Georgian barometers.* Not Stocked: Pot-lids, fairings. LOC: Down Kingston by-pass at Tolworth underpass, turn right into Tolworth Broadway, then into Ewell Rd., shop 1 mile. PARK: Easy. TEL: 020 8399 8857. SER: Gilding. VAT: Stan/Spec.

Laurence Tauber Antiques
131 Ewell Rd. KT6 6AL. Open 10-5. CL: Wed. pm. *STOCK: General antiques, especially lighting, mainly for Trade.* PARK: Easy. TEL: 020 8390 0020; mobile - 07710 443293. VAT: Stan/Spec.

SUTTON

S. Warrender and Co
4 and 6 Cheam Rd. SM1 1SR. (F.R. Warrender). Est.

1947. Open 9-5.30. SIZE: Medium. *STOCK: Jewellery, 1790 to date, £10-£1,500; silver, 1762 to date, £10-£1,000; carriage clocks, 1860-1900, £115-£800.* TEL: 020 8643 4381; e-mail - s.warrender@btconnect.com SER: Valuations; restorations (jewellery, silver, quality clocks). VAT: Stan.

THAMES DITTON

Clifford and Roger Dade
Boldre House, Weston Green. KT7 0JP. Resident. Est. 1937. Open 9.30-6. SIZE: Large. *STOCK: Mahogany furniture, 18th to early 19th C, £500-£5,000.* LOC: A309 between Esher and Hampton Court, near Sandown Park Racecourse. PARK: Outside shop. TEL: 020 8398 6293; fax - same; mobile - 07932 158949. VAT: Spec.

WALTON-ON-THAMES

Antique Church Furnishings
Rivernook Farm, Sunnyside. KT12 2ET. (L. Skilling and S. Williams). Est. 1989. Open Mon.-Fri. 10-6. SIZE: Large. *STOCK: Church chairs and pews, £10-£750; altar tables and screens, pulpits, lecterns, reredos, pine and architectural items, £20-£2,000; all late 19th C to early 20th C.* LOC: Between A3050 and River Thames. PARK: Easy. TEL: 01932 252736; fax - same; website - www.churchantiques.com SER: Valuations; buys at auction (church fixtures and furnishings, stained glass). VAT: Stan/Spec.

S. & H. Jewell
17 Wolsey Dr. KT12 3AY. (Geoffrey Boyes Korkis). Est. 1830. Open by appointment. *STOCK: Small and decorative furniture.* TEL: 01932 222690; mobile - 07973 406255; e-mail - geoff@bkwalton.freeserve.co.uk SER: Valuations; restorations; finder. VAT: Stan/Spec.

WEST BYFLEET

Academy Billiard Company
5 Camphill Industrial Estate. KT14 6EW. (R.W. Donnachie). Est. 1975. Open any time by appointment. SIZE: Large warehouse and showroom. *STOCK: Period and antique billiard/snooker tables, all sizes, 1830-1920; combined billiard/dining tables, period accessories including other games-room equipment and lighting.* LOC: On A245, 2 miles from M25/A3 junction. PARK: Easy. TEL: 01932 352067; fax - 01932 353904; mobile - 07860 523757; e-mail - academygames@fsbdial.co.uk website - www.games-room.com SER: Valuations; restorations; removals; structural advice. VAT: Stan/Spec.

WEYBRIDGE

Brocante
120 Oatlands Drive, Oatlands Village. KT13 9HL. (Barry Dean and Ray Gwilliams). Est. 1988. Open 10-4.30. CL: Mon. and Wed. SIZE: Small. *STOCK: Furniture, 19th C, £300-£1,500; porcelain, 19th C, £10-£250; Sheffield plate, 18th-19th C, £10-£300; silver 1750-1950.* PARK: Easy. TEL: 01932 857807; home - 01932 345524; e-mail - ray@raygwilliams.co.uk website - www.raygwilliams.co.uk SER: Valuations.

Church House Antiques
42 Church St. KT13 8DP. (M.I. Foster). Est. 1886. Open Thurs., Fri., Sat. 10-5.30. SIZE: Medium. *STOCK: Furniture, 18th-19th C, £95-£7,000; jewellery, 18th-19th C, some modern, £30-£5,000; pictures, silver, plate, decorative items.* Not Stocked: Coins and stamps. PARK: Behind library. TEL: 01932 842190. VAT: Stan/Spec.

The Clock Shop Weybridge
64 Church St. KT13 8DL. Est. 1970. Open 10-6. CL: Wed. SIZE: Medium. *STOCK: Clocks, 1685-1900, from £500; French carriage clocks, from £300.* LOC: Opposite HSBC bank on corner. PARK: Easy. TEL: 01932 840407/855503; website - www.theclockshopweybridge.co.uk SER: Valuations; restorations (clocks). VAT: Stan/Spec.

Edward Cross - Fine Paintings
128 Oatlands Drive. KT13 9HL. Est. 1973. Open Fri. 10-1, Sat. 10-12. SIZE: Medium. *STOCK: Fine paintings and bronzes, 18th-20th C, £500-£30,000.* LOC: A3050. PARK: Opposite. TEL: 01932 851093. SER: Valuations; restorations (watercolours and oil paintings); buys at auction (pictures). VAT: Spec.

Not Just Silver
16 York Rd. KT13 9DT. (Mrs S. Hughes). BJA. NAG. Est. 1969. Open 9.30-6, Sun. by appointment. *STOCK: Silver, Georgian to modern.* LOC: Opposite car park, just off Queens Rd. PARK: Opposite. TEL: 01932 842468; fax - 01932 830054; mobile - 07774 298151; e-mail - info@not-just-silver.com website - www.not-just-silver.com SER: Valuations; repairs; silver plating.

Willow Gallery   BADA LAPADA
75 Queens Rd. KT13 9UQ. (Andrew and Jean Stevens and Alick Forrester). Est. 1987. Open 10-6, Sun. by appointment. SIZE: Large. *STOCK: British and European oil paintings, 19th C, £3,000-£200,000.* LOC: Near town centre. PARK: Easy and nearby. TEL: 01932 846095/6; e-mail - enquiries@ willowgallery.com website - www.willowgallery.com SER: Valuations; restorations; conservation; framing; catalogue available. FAIRS: BADA; LAPADA; New York; Olympia; Palm Beach. VAT: Spec.

WOKING

Aspidistra Antiques
Wych Hill. GU22 0EU. (Mrs P. Caswell). Open 10-4.30. SIZE: Medium. *STOCK: Furniture, 19th C to Art Deco, £100-£3,000; china and glass, 18th C to Art Deco, £50-£1,000; silver and jewellery, 19th C to Art Deco, £50-£1,500.* LOC: Just off A320 Guildford-Woking road. PARK: Easy. TEL: 01483 771117; fax - same; website - www.aspidistra-antiques.co.uk SER: Restorations.

Keith Baker
42 Arnold Rd. GU21 5JU. (K.R. Baker). Open Wed.-Sat. 9-4.30. *STOCK: General antiques.* PARK: Easy. TEL: 01483 767425.

SUSSEX EAST

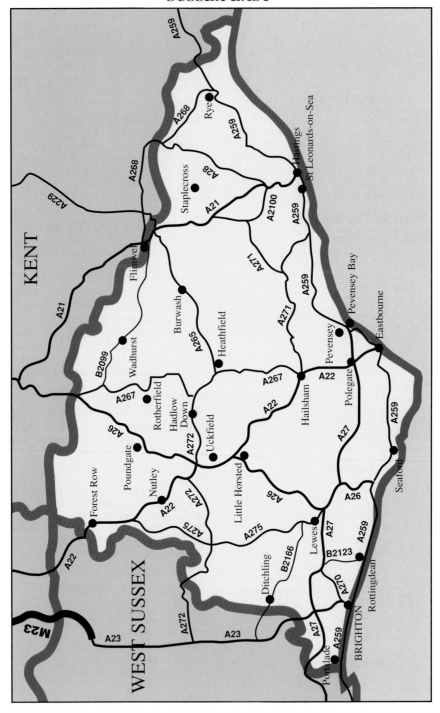

BRIGHTON

Alexandria Antiques
3 Hanover Place, Lewes Rd. BN2 2SD. (A.H. Ahmed). Est. 1978. Open 9.30-6, Sat. by appointment. SIZE: 3 showrooms. *STOCK: Georgian and Victorian furniture; Oriental and European porcelain; oil and watercolour paintings; Oriental carpets, objets d'art.* PARK: Own. TEL: 01273 688793; fax - same. FAIRS: Ardingly; Newark; Sandown.

Ashton's Antiques
1-3 Clyde Rd., Preston Circus. BN1 4NN. (R. and P. Ashton). Est. 1970. Open Thurs., Fri. and Sat. 9.30-5. SIZE: 4 showrooms. *STOCK: Victorian and Edwardian furniture, upholstery and decorative items.* TEL: 01273 605253; fax - same. VAT: Stan/Spec.

Brighton Architectural Salvage
33-34 Gloucester Rd. BN1 4AQ. (R.L. Legendre). Open Tues.-Sat. 10-5. *STOCK: Restored architectural items including pine furniture; fireplaces and surrounds in stone, marble, pine, mahogany, cast-iron, Victorian tiled and cast inserts and over-mantels; doors, stained glass, panelling; cast iron balcony and street railings, gas coal fires, light fittings; garden seats and ornaments, reclaimed flooring.* TEL: 01273 681656.

Brighton Flea Market
31A Upper St. James's St. BN2 1JN. (A. Wilkinson). Est. 1990. Open seven days. SIZE: Large. *STOCK: Bric-a-brac, furniture and collectables, 19th-20th C, £5-£1,000.* LOC: 50 yards from coast road, Kemp Town. TEL: 01273 624006/328665.

Brighton Lanes Antique Centre
12 Meeting House Lane. BN1 1HB. (Peter Brynin). Est. 1967. Open 10-5.30, Sun. 12-4. SIZE: Medium. *STOCK: Furniture, clocks, silver, glass, jewellery, lighting, pens, porcelain, watches and bronzes.* LOC: North entrance to The Lanes. PARK: Loading and nearby. TEL: 01273 823121; fax - 01273 726328; website - www. brightonlanes.antiquecentre.co.uk SER: Valuations; shipping.

Tony Broadfoot
39 Upper Gardner St. BN1 4AN. Est. 1985. Open 9-5.30. SIZE: Large. *STOCK: Furniture, from 17th C.* LOC: Off North Rd. PARK: Easy. TEL: 01273 695457; fax - 01273 620365. SER: Restorations.

C.A.R.S. (Classic Automobilia & Regalia Specialists)
The White Lion Garage, Clarendon Place, Kemp Town. BN2 1JA. (G.G. Weiner and A.P. Gayler). Est. 1976. Open by appointment only. *STOCK: Collectors' car badges, mascots (including Lalique) and associated automobilia and related motoring memorabilia; children's pedal cars, electric cars, collectors' veteran and vintage pedal cars, 1930s-1970s.* PARK: Easy. TEL: 01273 622722 (office hours); 01273 601960; fax - same; mobile - 07890 836734; e-mail - cars@kemptownbrighton.freeserve.co.uk website - www.brmmbrmm.com/pedalcars and www.barcc.co.uk and www.carsofbrighton.co.uk SER: SAE for catalogue/price list; mail order suppliers. FAIRS: NEC; Alexandra Palace; Ardingly; Brighton Classic Car.

Campbell Wilson
1 Brunswick Sq., Hove. BN3 1EG. (Neil Wilson). Est. 1996. Open by appointment. *STOCK: Paintings especially Pre-Raphaelite and Romantic British, 1845-1903; modern British, to 1945.* LOC: On seafront. TEL: 01273 777087; website - www.campbell-wilson. demon.co.uk SER: Buys at auction (Victorian and Modern British paintings). FAIRS: Olympia; Watercolours and Drawings; Antiques for Everyone (Birmingham). '

Harry Diamond and Son
9 Union St., The Lanes. BN1 1HA. (H. and C. Diamond). Est. 1937. Open 10-4.30. *STOCK: Diamond jewellery, £500-£15,000.* Not Stocked: Coins, furniture. TEL: 01273 329696. VAT: Stan/Spec.

Faques Gallery
29 Upper St James's St., BN2 1JN. Est. 1962. Open 10-5.30. SIZE: Large. *STOCK: Reproduction oil paintings.* LOC: Kemp Town area. PARK: Side roads. TEL: 01273 624432; fax - 01273 683692. VAT: Stan.

Paul Goble Jewellers
44 Meeting House Lane, The Lanes. BN1 1HB. NAG. Est. 1965. Open 9-5.30, Sat. 9-6, Sun. 10-6. *STOCK: Jewellery, watches, silver, pictures and prints, teddy bears and dolls.* TEL: 01273 202801; fax - 01273 202736; e-mail - paulgoble@btinternet.com SER: Trade/export; valuations. VAT: Stan/Margin/Export.

Douglas Hall Ltd
23 Meeting House Lane. BN1 1HB. (K.J. and G.J. Draper). Est. 1968. Open 9.30-5. *STOCK: Silver, jewellery.* TEL: 01273 325323. VAT: Stan.

Hallmark Jewellers
4 Union St., The Lanes. BN1 1HA. (J. Hersheson). Est. 1966. Open 9-5. SIZE: Small. *STOCK: Diamond and gem set jewellery; antique and modern silver.* TEL: 01273 725477; fax - same. VAT: Stan/Spec.

Heritage Antiques   BADA LAPADA
P O Box 2974. BN1 3QG. (Anjula Daniel). CINOA. Est. 1975. Open by appointment. SIZE: Large. *STOCK: Metalware, £50-£5,000; interesting and decorative items.* PARK: Easy. TEL: 01273 326850; fax - same; e-mail - ahd@heritage-antiques.com website - www.heritage-antiques.com FAIRS: Olympia; BADA. VAT: Stan/Spec.

The Lanes Armoury
26 Meeting House Lane, The Lanes. BN1 1HB. (Mark and David Hawkins). Est. 1972. Open 10-5.15. *STOCK: Militaria, arms especially Japanese samurai swords, armour and books, from 500BC to WWII.* PARK: By arrangement. TEL: 01273 321357; website - www.thelanesarmoury.co.uk

Leoframes
70 North Rd. BN1 1YD. (S. Round). Est. 1985. Open 9.30-5.20. *STOCK: Prints and maps.* TEL: 01273 695862; e-mail - info@leoframes.com SER: Restorations; framing.

Harry Mason
P O Box 687, Hove. BN3 6JY. Est. 1954. Open by appointment. *STOCK: Silver and plate, 18th-20th C; jewellery, 19th-20th C.* TEL: 01273 500330; fax - 01273 553300; e-mail - mason@fastnet.co.uk SER: Valuations; restorations (silver and jewellery); buys at auction (as

stock); buyers of scrap silver and gold. FAIRS: Sunday London Hotel. VAT: Stan/Spec.

Patrick Moorhead Antiques
Spring Gardens, 76 Church St. BN1 1RL. (Patrick and Heather Moorhead). Est. 1984. Open 9.30-5.30, Sat. and other times by appointment. SIZE: Large trade warehouse. *STOCK: Quality Victorian, Georgian and Continental furniture; Oriental, Continental and English porcelain, clocks, pictures, decorative objects and bronzes.* PARK: Easy. TEL: 01273 779696; fax - 01273 220196; e-mail - patrick.moorhead@virgin.net SER: Collection from local station and Gatwick airport.

Michael Norman Antiques Ltd   BADA
61 Holland Rd., Hove. BN3 1JN. (Michael P. Keehan). Est. 1965. Open 9-1 and 2-5.30, other times by appointment. STOCK: 18th-19th C English furniture. LOC: Close to Hove station and seafront. PARK: Easy. TEL: 01273 329253 or 01273 326712; fax - 01273 206556; e-mail - antiques@michaelnorman.com website - www.michaelnorman.com SER: Restorations; upholstery. VAT: Spec.

The North Laine Antiques Market, incorporating Alan Fitchett Antiques
5-5A Upper Gardner St. BN1 4AN. (Alan and Heidi Fitchett). Est. 1969. Open 10-5.30, Sat. 9-5.30, Sun. 10-4. SIZE: Large. *STOCK: Furniture, 18th-20th C, £50-£10,000; works of art, silver, ceramics, books, jewellery, paintings, prints, collectables, £1-£2,000.* LOC: North Laine (station area). PARK: Easy. TEL: 01273 600894; fax - same. SER: Valuations; restorations.

Odin Antiques
43 Preston St. BN1 2HP. (Audun Sjovold). Resident. Est. 1981. Open 10.30-5.30. SIZE: Medium. *STOCK: Furniture, 18th-19th C; telescopes, scientific instruments, 19th-20th C, £500-£1,500; maritime instruments, 19th-20th C, £500-£1,000.* LOC: Off Kings Rd. (seafront) near West Pier. PARK: Regency Sq. TEL: 01273 732738; home - same. VAT: Stan/Spec.

Colin Page Antiquarian Books
36 Duke St. BN1 1AG. (John Loska). Est. 1969. Open 9.30-5.30. *STOCK: Antiquarian and secondhand books, especially topography, travel, natural history, illustrated and leather bindings, 16th-20th C, £1-£30,000.* LOC: Town centre. PARK: Multi-storey nearby. TEL: 01273 325954.

Brian Page Antiques
18 Regent Arcade, East St. BN1 1HR. Open 10-5. *STOCK: Oriental antiques, Neolithic to 19th C; Chinese antiquities.* LOC: Adjacent to Town Hall. TEL: 01273 723956; e-mail - mail@brianpage.co.uk website - www.brianpage.co.uk VAT: Spec.

Dermot and Jill Palmer Antiques   LAPADA
7-8 Union St., The Lanes. BN1 1HA. Resident. Est. 1968. Open 9.30-5.30, Sun. by appointment. SIZE: Large + warehouse. *STOCK: French and English furniture, objects, pictures, mirrors, screens, garden furniture and ornamental pieces, textiles, £50-£5,000.* PARK: NCP. TEL: 01273 328669 (2 lines); fax - 01273 777641; e-mail - jillpalmer@macunlimited.net website - www.jillpalmerantiques.co.uk FAIRS: Olympia; Decorative Antiques & Textile. VAT: Stan/Spec.

Sue Pearson
18 Brighton Square, The Lanes. BN1 1HD. Est. 1982. Open 10-5 including Sun. SIZE: Large. *STOCK: Antique dolls, teddy bears, dolls' house miniatures.* PARK: NCP. TEL: 01273 329247. SER: Valuations; restorations; buys at auction (dolls and bears). FAIRS: Major London Doll and Bear. VAT: Stan/Spec.

Pure Design Classics
20-21 Chatham Place, Off Seven Dials. BN1 3TN. (Rachel Gander). Est. 2002. Open Tues.-Sat. 10-6. SIZE: Medium. *STOCK: Furniture including Verner Panton, Arné Jacobsen, Eames, Robin Day, 1950-1980, £50-£1,500+; ceramics, fabrics and glass, 1940-1980, £20-£300; lighting, 1940-1980.* LOC: 5 minutes north of Churchill Sq., off Seven Dials roundabout. PARK: Easy. TEL: 01273 735331; fax - 01273 734229; mobile - 07808 003547; home - 01273 494665; e-mail - info@pure2k.com website - www.pure2k.com. SER: Valuations; search; rental.

Savery Antiques
257 Ditchling Rd., (Fiveways). BN1 6JH. (A. and M. Savery). Resident. Est. 1968. Open Mon., Thurs., Fri. and Sat. 10-4, Tues. and Wed. 10-2. *STOCK: China, glass, metalware and collectables.* LOC: Near HSBC Bank. TEL: 01273 564899. FAIRS: Ardingly; Sandown Park.

Valentina Antique Beds
212 Church Rd., Hove. BN3 2DT. (Mrs Flechas). Est. 2003. Open 10-5. SIZE: Medium. *STOCK: Brass, iron and French wooden beds, 19th C, £500-£3,500.* LOC: Continuation of Western Rd. PARK: Nearby. TEL: 01273 735035; home - same; e-mail - info@antiquebeds.com website - www.antiquebeds.com SER: Valuations; restorations; buys at auction (beds).

Wardrobe
51 Upper North St. BN1 3FH. (Clive Parks and Philip Parfitt). Est. 1984. Open Wed.-Sat. 10-5, other times by appointment. SIZE: Small. *STOCK: Vintage clothing, '20s to '30s, £150-£1,500; bakelite, especially jewellery, £20-£300.* PARK: On street - vouchers. TEL: 01273 202201; fax - same; website - www.decoratif.co.uk FAIRS: Alexandra Palace; Sandown Park; Royal Horticultural Hall, Vincent Square.

E. and B. White
43 & 47 Upper North St. BN1 3FH. (Elizabeth and Ben White). Est. 1962. Open 9.30-5. CL: Sat. pm. SIZE: Medium. *STOCK: Country furniture and decorative items, £50-£2,000.* LOC: Upper North St. runs parallel to and north of Western Rd. (main shopping street). TEL: 01273 328706; fax - 01273 207035. VAT: Spec.

Yellow Lantern Antiques Ltd   LAPADA
34 & 34B Holland Rd., Hove. BN3 1JL. (B.R. and E.A. Higgins). Est. 1950. Open 10-1 and 2.15-5.30, Sat. 10-4. SIZE: Medium. *STOCK: Mainly English furniture, £200-£10,000; French and English clocks; both to 1850; bronzes, 19th C, £100-£5,000; Continental porcelain, 1820-1860, £50-£1,000.* LOC: From Brighton seafront to Hove, turn right after parade of Regency houses, shop 100yds. on left past traffic lights. PARK: Easy. TEL: 01273 771572; fax - 01273 455476; mobile - 07860 342976. SER: Valuations; restorations; buys at auction. FAIRS: Buxton; Harrogate; NEC; Olympia; Chester. VAT: Spec.

BURWASH, Nr. Etchingham

Chateaubriand Antiques
High St. TN19 7ES. (William Vincent and Rosalind Chislett). Est. 1985. Open 10-5. SIZE: 3 showrooms. *STOCK: Furniture, paintings, maps and engravings, porcelain, decorative items and linen.* PARK: Nearby. TEL: 01435 882535; website - www.chateaubriand antiques.co.uk SER: Valuations; local deliveries, shipping, picture framing.

DITCHLING

Dycheling Antiques
34 High St. BN6 8TA. (E.A. Hudson). Est. 1977. Open Sat. 10.30-5, other days by appointment. SIZE: Large. *STOCK: Georgian, Victorian and Edwardian furniture, especially dining and armchairs, £25-£5,000.* LOC: Off A23 on A273-B2112 north of Brighton. PARK: Easy. TEL: 01273 842929; home - same; fax - 01273 841929; mobile - 07885 456341; website - www.antiquechairmatching.com VAT: Spec.

EASTBOURNE

W. Bruford
11/13 Cornfield Rd. BN21 3NA. Est. 1883. Open 9.30-5.15. SIZE: Medium. *STOCK: Jewellery, Victorian, late Georgian; some silver, clocks (bracket and carriage).* Not Stocked: China, glass, brass, pewter, furniture. TEL: 01323 725452. SER: Valuations; restorations (clocks and silver). VAT: Stan/Spec.

Camilla's Bookshop
57 Grove Rd. BN21 4TX. (C. Francombe and S. Broad). Est. 1976. Open 10-5.30. SIZE: Large, 3 floors. *STOCK: Books including antiquarian, art, antiques and collectables, naval, military, aviation, technical, needlework, broadcasting, literature, biography and history.* LOC: Next to police station, 5 mins. from rail station. PARK: Nearby. TEL: 01323 736001; e-mail - camillasbooks@tiscali.co.uk SER: Valuations; postal service; own book tokens.

John Cowderoy Antiques Ltd   LAPADA
The Clock and Musical Box Centre, 42 South St. BN21 4XB. (D.J. and R.A. Cowderoy). GMC. Est. 1973. Open 8.30-5.30. CL: Wed. pm. SIZE: Large. *STOCK: Clocks, musical boxes, furniture, porcelain, silver and plate, jewellery, copper, brass.* LOC: 150yds. from town hall. PARK: Easy. TEL: 01323 720058; e-mail - david@ cowderoyantiques.co.uk website - www.cowderoy antiques.co.uk SER: Restorations (clocks, barometers, music boxes and furniture). VAT: Stan/Margin.

John Day of Eastbourne Fine Art
9 Meads St. BN20 7QY. Est. 1964. Open during exhibitions 11-1 and 2-5, otherwise by appointment. SIZE: Medium. *STOCK: English, especially East Anglian, and Continental paintings and watercolours, 19th-20th C.* LOC: Meads village, west end of Eastbourne, near Beachy Head. PARK: Easy. TEL: 01323 725634; mobile - 07960 274139. SER: Restorations; framing (oils and watercolours).

Roderick Dew
10 Furness Rd. BN21 4EZ. Est. 1971. Open by appointment. *STOCK: Antiquarian books, especially on

art and antiques.* LOC: Town centre. PARK: Easy. TEL: 01323 720239. SER: Search; catalogues available.

Eastbourne Antiques Market
80 Seaside. BN22 7QP. Est. 1969. Open 10-5.30, Sat. 10-5. SIZE: Large - 30+ stalls. *STOCK: A wide selection of general antiques and collectables.* PARK: Easy. TEL: 01323 642233.

Enterprise Collectors Market
The Enterprise Centre, Station Parade. BN21 1BE. Est. 1989. Open 9.30-5. SIZE: Medium. *STOCK: Wide range of general antiques and collectables.* LOC: Next to rail station. PARK: Easy. TEL: 01323 732690. SER: Valuations.

A. & T. Gibbard
1-2 Calverley Walk. BN21 4UB. PBFA. Est. 1993. Open 9.30-5.30. SIZE: Medium. *STOCK: Secondhand and antiquarian books, 16th-20th C, £1-£1,000.* LOC: 200yds. east of Town Hall. TEL: 01323 734128. SER: Valuations. VAT: Stan.

Timothy Partridge Antiques
44 Ocklynge Rd. BN21 1PP. Open 10-1. *STOCK: Victorian, Edwardian and 1920s furniture.* LOC: In old town, near St. Mary's Church. PARK: Easy. TEL: Mobile - 07860 864709.

Seaquel Antique & Collectors Market
37 Seaside Rd. BN21 3PP. (Mrs P. Mornington-West). Open 10-5, Sun. 11-4. SIZE: Small. *STOCK: General antiques, collectables and bric-a-brac.* LOC: Just off main shopping area. PARK: Nearby. TEL: 01323 645032.

FLIMWELL

Graham Lower
Stonecrouch Farmhouse. TN5 7QB. (Graham and Penny Lower). Est. 1972. Open by appointment. SIZE: Small. *STOCK: English and Continental 17th-18th C oak furniture.* LOC: A21. PARK: Own. TEL: 01580 879535. SER: Valuations. VAT: Spec.

FOREST ROW

Brookes-Smith Antiques
16 Hartfield Rd. RH18 5HE. (Richard and Kate Brookes-Smith). Est. 1980. Open Tues.-Sat. 9.30-5.30. *STOCK: Fine furniture, objects, works of art, silver and glass, £50-£20,000.* LOC: 3 miles south of East Grinstead on A22, left at roundabout down Hartfield Rd. PARK: Behind shop. TEL: 01342 826622; fax - 01342 826634; e-mail - rick@brookes-smith.com SER: Valuations.

HADLOW DOWN, Nr. Uckfield

Hadlow Down Antiques
Hastingford Farm, School Lane. TN22 4DY. (Adrian Butler and Caroline Knight). Est. 1989. Open Thurs., Fri. and Sat. 10-5, other times by appointment. SIZE: Large. *STOCK: General and decorative antiques, country and formal furniture, 18th C to date, £25-£2,500; English and French decorative accessories, £5-£500.* LOC: 2 mins. down School Lane from A272 in village. PARK: Easy. TEL: 01825 830707; home - same; mobile - 07951 817615; e-mail - verandah@tesco.net SER: Valuations; restorations (furniture); courier. FAIRS: Ardingly DMG.

HAILSHAM

Golden Cross Antiques
Fiveways House, Golden Cross. BN27 4AN. (Ian and Rhoda Buchan). Est. 1970. Open 9.30-5.30, Sun. 10-5 or by appointment. SIZE: Medium. *STOCK: Copper, brass, pewter and iron ware, especially fireside equipment and lamps, furniture including pine, 18th-20th C; silver, 19th to early 20th C; collectables and china.* LOC: A22. PARK: Easy. TEL: 01825 872144; home - same; fax - 01825 873408; mobile - 07957 224165; e-mail - antiques @goldencross.fsbusiness.co.uk SER: Valuations.

HASTINGS

Coach House Antiques
42 George St. TN34 3EA. (R.J. Luck). Est. 1972. Open 10-5 including Sun. SIZE: Medium. *STOCK: Longcase clocks, 18th-19th C, £1,000+; furniture, 19th C, £100+; collectables including Dinky toys, trains, dolls' houses.* PARK: Nearby. TEL: 01424 461849. SER: Valuations; restorations (clocks and furniture); buys at auction (clocks and furniture). VAT: Spec.

George Street Antiques Centre
47 George St. TN34 3EA. (F. Stanley-McKay and H. Stallybrass). Est. 1969. Open 11-4 including Sun. SIZE: Medium - 10 dealers. *STOCK: Small items, antique jewellery, 19th-20th C, £5-£1,000.* LOC: In old town, parallel to seafront. PARK: Seafront. TEL: 01424 429339; home - 01424 813526/428105.

Howes Bookshop
Trinity Hall, Braybrooke Terrace. TN34 1HQ. (Miles Bartley). ABA. PBFA. Est. 1920. Open Mon.-Fri. 9.30-1 and 2-5. *STOCK: Antiquarian and academic books in literature, history, arts, bibliography.* LOC: Near rail station. PARK: Own. TEL: 01424 423437; fax - 01424 460620; e-mail - rarebooks@howes.co.uk FAIRS: ABA; PBFA.

Nakota Curios
12 Courthouse St. TN35 3AU. (D.H. Brant). Est. 1964. Open 10.30-1 and 2-5. SIZE: Medium. *STOCK: General trade items, decorative china, Victoriana, jewellery, pictures, lighting.* Not Stocked: Coins, medals. PARK: Easy. TEL: 01424 438900.

Spice
Samphire House, 75 High St., Old Town. TN34 3EL. (S. Dix). Open by appointment. *STOCK: Early furniture and decorative items.* TEL: Mobile - 07710 209556.

HEATHFIELD

Graham Price Antiques Ltd
Unit 14, Satinstown Farm, Burwash Rd., Broad Oak. TN21 8RU. Est. 1979. Open 9-5. *STOCK: Mainly furniture - country, decorative, French, Irish, painted, some formal and shipping.* PARK: Ample. TEL: 01892 523341; fax - 01892 530382; website - www.grahampriceantiques.co.uk SER: Export; packing and shipping; courier; restorations.

LEWES

Bow Windows Book Shop
175 High St. BN7 1YE. (A. and J. Shelley). ABA. PBFA.

Est. 1964. Open 9.30-5. SIZE: Large. *STOCK: Books including natural history, English literature, travel, topography.* LOC: Off A27. TEL: 01273 480780; fax - 01273 486686; e-mail - rarebooks@bowwindows.com FAIRS: ABA.

Church-Hill Antiques Centre
6 Station St. BN7 2DA. (S. Ramm). Est. 1970. Open 9.30-5. SIZE: 60 stalls and cabinets. *STOCK: Wide range of general antiques including furniture, china, silver, jewellery, clocks, lighting, paintings and decorative items.* LOC: From rail station, in town centre. PARK: Easy, own. TEL: 01273 474842; e-mail - churchhilllewes@aol.com website - www.church-hillantiques.com

Cliffe Antiques Centre
47 Cliffe High St. BN7 2AN. Est. 1984. Open 9.30-5. SIZE: Medium - 16 dealers. *STOCK: General antiques, £5-£1,000.* LOC: Follow town centre signs, turning left 200 yards past Safeways. PARK: Easy. TEL: 01273 473266.

A. & Y. Cumming
84 High St. BN7 1XN. ABA. Est. 1976. Open 10-5, Sat. 10-5.30. *STOCK: Antiquarian and out of print books.* TEL: 01273 472319; fax - 01273 486364; e-mail - a.y.cumming@ukgateway.net SER: Buys at auction. FAIRS: Chelsea; Olympia.

The Emporium Antique Centre
42 Cliffe High St. BN7 2AN. (Doyle and Madigan). Est. 1990. Open 9.30-5, Sun. 12-4. SIZE: 60 dealers. *STOCK: Furniture, pictures, clocks, collectables, books, jewellery, Art Nouveau and Deco, decorative arts, vintage and collectors' toys.* LOC: Town centre. TEL: 01273 486866; e-mail - steve@smadigan.fsnet.co.uk

The Fifteenth Century Bookshop
99/100 High St. BN7 1XH. (Mrs S. Mirabaud). PBFA. Est. 1938. Open 10-5.30, Sun. 10.30-4. *STOCK: Antiquarian and general secondhand books, especially children's and illustrated; prints, teddies and china.* LOC: At top of cobbled lane, just beyond the castle. PARK: Opposite. TEL: 01273 474160. SER: Postal.

Lewes Antique Centre
20 Cliffe High St. BN7 2AH. (Jamie Pettit). Est. 1968. Open 9.30-5, Sun. 12-4. SIZE: Large - 125 stallholders. *STOCK: Furniture, china, copper and metalware, glass, clocks, architectural salvage, books and collectables.* LOC: A27 from Brighton, 2nd roundabout into Lewes, end of tunnel turn left, then next left, next right into Phoenix car park. 100m. walk to Cliffe High St. PARK: Easy. TEL: 01273 476148. SER: Shipping; stripping; restorations; valuations.

Lewes Clock Shop
5 North St. BN7 2PA. (W.F. Bruce). Est. 1982. Open 10-4. CL: Wed. SIZE: Medium. *STOCK: Clocks.* PARK: Nearby. TEL: 01273 473123; fax - same; e-mail - lewesclocks@btopenworld.com SER: Valuations; restorations.

Lewes Flea Market
14a Market St. BN7 2NB. Est. 1995. Open daily including Sun. SIZE: Large. *STOCK: Bric-a-brac, furniture, collectables, 18th-20th C, £5-£1,000.* LOC: 50 metres north of monument. PARK: Nearby. TEL: 01273 480328.

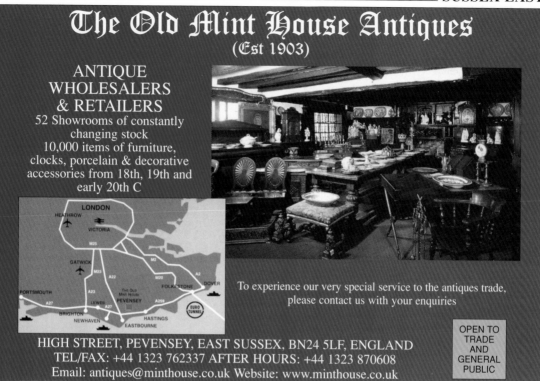
Pastorale Antiques
15 Malling St. BN7 2RA. (O. Soucek). Est. 1984. Open 9.30-6 or by appointment. SIZE: Large. *STOCK: Pine and European country furniture, Georgian and Victorian mahogany and decorative items and garden items.* TEL: 01273 473259; home - 01435 863044; fax - 01273 473259; e-mail - pastorale@btinternet.com website - www.pastorale.cz SER: Delivery (Europe).

Southdown Antiques
48 Cliffe High St. BN7 2AN. (Miss P.I. and K.A. Foster). Est. 1969. Open by appointment. SIZE: Medium. *STOCK: Small antiques, especially 18th-19th C English, Continental and Oriental porcelain, objets d'art, works of art, glass, papier mâché trays, silver plate, £50-£350,000; reproduction and interior decor items.* LOC: A27. One-way street north. PARK: Easy. TEL: 01273 472439. VAT: Stan/Spec.

LITTLE HORSTED, Nr. Uckfield

Pianos Galore
Worth Farm. TN22 5TT. Est. 1922. Open Sat. 9-5 or by appointment. SIZE: Large. *STOCK: Pianos, upright and grands especially Steinway and Bechstein grands, £250-£20,000; also piano stools.* LOC: From A22 Uckfield by-pass take A26 at Little Horsted roundabout. After 1 mile, opposite Wicklands Residential Home, turn right (opposite piano shop), down lane. PARK: Easy. TEL: 01825 750567; fax - 01825 750566. SER: Valuations; restorations (piano repolishing and reconditioning); buys at auction (pianos). VAT: Margin/Stan.

NUTLEY

Nutley Antiques
Libra House, High St. TN22 3NF. (Liza Hall). Open 10-5, Sun. and Bank Holidays 1.30-5. SIZE: Small. *STOCK: Country and cottage furniture, £10-£1,000; decorative items, £1-£400; prints, oils, watercolours, £5-£500; all 19th C to 1930.* LOC: A22 between East Grinstead and Uckfield. PARK: Easy. TEL: 01825 713220. VAT: Stan.

PEVENSEY

The Old Mint House
High St. BN24 5LF. (J.C., A.J. and P.G. Nicholson). Est. 1903. Open 9-5.30, Sat. 10.30-4.30, otherwise by appointment. SIZE: Large + export warehouse. *STOCK: Furniture - Georgian, Victorian, Edwardian; porcelain, clocks, barometers and decorative items, 18th C to 1920s, £50-£10,000.* LOC: A27, 1 mile from Eastbourne. PARK: Easy. TEL: 01323 762337; fax - same; e-mail - antiques@minthouse.co.uk website - www.minthouse.co.uk SER: London trains met at local station (Polegate). VAT: Stan/Spec.

PEVENSEY BAY

Murray Brown
The Studio, Norman Rd. BN24 6JE. (G. Murray-Brown). Open by appointment. *STOCK: Paintings and prints.* TEL: 01323 764298. SER: Valuations; restorations; cleaning; conservation.

DOG PAINTING 1840-1940
A Social History of the Dog in Art
WILLIAM SECORD

William Secord is the first author to explore the presentation of the dog, from its origins in Greek, Roman and later European art, to the remarkable paintings of the eighteenth and nineteenth centuries up to modern times. In this splendid work he traces the evolution of some fifty breeds, using carefully selected illustrations by outstanding nineteenth and twentieth century artists, ranging from depictions of Hounds and sporting dogs in the field to Victorian portraits of pampered pets and highly-bred favourites. From the diminutive Chihuahua to the massive St. Bernard, this fascinating account of most of the popular breeds provides an original and penetrating artistic record of mankind's faithful companions.

Specifications: 368pp., 150 col. illus., 317 b.&w. illus., 11 x 8½in./279 x 216mm. **£35.00 (hardback)**

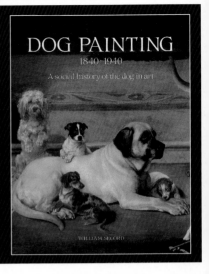

POLEGATE

E. Stacy-Marks Limited   BADA LAPADA
**The Flint Rooms, P O Box 808. BN26 5ST. Est. 1889.
SIZE: Large. STOCK: Paintings, English, Dutch and Continental schools, 18th-20th C. TEL: 01323 482156; fax - 01323 482513. VAT: Stan.**

Summer Antiques
87 High St. BN26 6AE. (R. Millis). Est. 1992. Open 9-5, Sat. 9-12. SIZE: Small. *STOCK: General antiques including silver, china, furniture, brass and copper.* LOC: 250 yards from station. PARK: Easy. TEL: 01323 483834; mobile - 07762 309870. SER: Valuations. FAIRS: Ardingly.

PORTSLADE

Craftsmen in Wood
524 Mile Oak Rd. BN41 2RF. (Victor Potter and Jeffrey Short). GADAR. Est. 1963. *STOCK: Furniture and objets d'art.* PARK: Easy. TEL: 01273 423730; fax - 01273 418853; mobile - 07768 274461; e-mail - cvpotter@aol.com website - www.craftsmen-in-wood.com SER: Restorations (furniture and architectural woodwork).

POUNDGATE, Nr. Crowborough

Nicholas Bowlby
Owl House, TN22 4DE. Est. 1981. Open by appointment. SIZE: Medium. *STOCK: 19th-20th C watercolours, contemporary paintings and sculpture, £200-£20,000.* TEL: 01892 667809; e-mail - nicholas bowlby@hotmail.com website - www.nicholasbowlby.co.uk SER: Valuations; restorations; buys at auction (watercolours and drawings); framing. VAT: Stan/Spec.

ROTHERFIELD

Forge Interiors
South St. TN6 3LN. (Douglas Masham). Est. 1998. Open Tues.-Sat. 10-1 and 2-5. SIZE: Medium. *STOCK: Asian and English antiques and decorative items, furniture, pictures and lighting; Tansu, Hibatchi and Ranma.* PARK: Easy. TEL: 01892 853000; home/fax - 01892 853122; e-mail - asiandecor@forgeinteriors.com website - www.forgeinteriors.com SER: Restorations; caning and rushing.

ROTTINGDEAN

Trade Wind
15A Little Crescent. BN2 7GF. (R. Morley Smith). Est. 1974. Open by appointment. *STOCK: Caddy and sifter spoons, wine labels (80+ instock) and other interesting items, including coloured glass, Bristol blue, green and amethyst; early 18th-19th C white glass including folded foot and engraved items, 1710-1830.* TEL: 01273 301177.

RYE

Bragge and Sons
Landgate House. TN31 7LH. (J.R. Bragge). Est. 1840. Open 9-5. CL: Tues. and Sat. pm. *STOCK: 18th C English furniture and works of art.* LOC: Entrance to town - Landgate. TEL: 01797 223358. SER: Valuations; restorations.

Chapter & Verse Booksellers
105 High St. TN31 7JE. (Spencer J. Rogers). Est. 1990. Open Tues. to Sun. 10-5. SIZE: Medium. *STOCK: Rare and antiquarian books - single items to large collections, £50-£3,000.* PARK: Loading only or nearby. TEL: 01797 222692; mobile - 07970 386905; e-mail - chapterand verse@btconnect.com SER: Valuations; search.

East Street Antiques
Apothecary House, 1 East St. TN31 7JY. (Mr and Mrs Bloomfield). Est. 1988. Open 10.30-5 including Sun. SIZE: Medium. *STOCK: Provincial English and French furniture, 18th-19th C, £500-£3,000.* LOC: Just off High St. PARK: Easy. TEL: 01797 229157; mobile - 07718 732312. SER: Buys at auction. FAIRS: Newark; Ardingly.

Herbert Gordon Gasson

The Lion Galleries, Lion St. TN31 7LB. (T.J. Booth). Est. 1909. Open 10-5, Tues. and Sun. by appointment. SIZE: Large. *STOCK: 17th-19th C oak, walnut and mahogany furniture; decorative items.* Not Stocked: Silver and glass. LOC: Town centre. PARK: Easy. TEL: 01797 222208; e-mail - hggassonantiques@hotmail.com website - www.antiquesrye.co.uk SER: Restorations. VAT: Spec.

Strand Quay Antiques

1 and 2 The Strand. TN31 7BD. (A.M. Sutherland). Est. 1984. Open seven days 10-5. SIZE: Medium. *STOCK: Victorian, Edwardian and shipping furniture, paintings and porcelain; French furniture, Georgian to 1960s, £5-£1,200.* PARK: Easy. TEL: 01797 226790; mobile - 07775 602598. FAIRS: Ardingly.

Wish Barn Antiques

Wish St. TN31 7DA. (Joe Dearden and Robert Wheeler). Est. 1993. Open 10-5, Sun. 12-5. SIZE: Medium. *STOCK: 19th C furniture including oak, mahogany and pine, £50-£3,000; silver plate.* LOC: Just off A259. PARK: Easy. TEL: 01797 226797; home - 01580 881485.

SEAFORD

The Old House

18 High St. BN25 1PG. (S.M. Barrett). Est. 1928. Open 9-5, Wed. 9-1. SIZE: Large. *STOCK: 18th-20th C furniture, china and glass, £5-£5,000.* LOC: Near rail station. PARK: Opposite in Pelham Yard. TEL: 01323 892091/893795. SER: Valuations; restorations (furniture); shippers. VAT: Stan/Spec.

ST. LEONARDS-ON-SEA

The Book Jungle

24 North St. TN38 0EX. (M. Gowen). Est. 1988. Open 10-4 (prior telephone call advised). CL: Mon. and Wed. SIZE: Medium. *STOCK: Secondhand books.* LOC: Just off seafront. PARK: Nearby. TEL: 01424 421187.

Gensing Antiques

70 Norman Rd. TN38 0EJ. (Peter Cawson). Open normal shop hours and by appointment. *STOCK: General antiques especially early Chinese furniture and other Oriental items.* TEL: 01424 424145/714981.

The Hastings Antique Centre

59-61 Norman Rd. TN38 0EG. (R.J. Amstad). Open 10-5.30, Sun. by appointment. SIZE: Large. TEL: 01424 428561. Below are listed some of the dealers at this centre.

R.J. Amstad
Furniture.

Fred Bourne
French decorative antiques.

Pascal Bourne
French furniture.

Jenny Brown
Decorative wares.

Bruno Antiques
French furniture.

P. Few
Decorative French items.

K. Gumbrell
Decorative items.

Bridget Howett
Decorative items.

Clare Kinloch
Dolls.

G. Mennis
Sporting, leather goods.

Mick Neale
Oak.

Pat Robbins
Furniture.

Glen and Linda Simmonds
French interiors.

Swallow Interiors

Monarch Antiques

371 Bexhill Rd. TN38 8AJ. (J.H. King). Est. 1983. Open Mon.-Fri. 8.30-5 or by appointment. SIZE: Warehouse. *STOCK: General furniture, especially 1930s oak furniture for the Japanese, Korean, American and European markets.* LOC: A259. PARK: Own. TEL: 01424 204141; fax - 01424 204142; home - 01424 214158/720821; mobiles - 07802 217842/213081 and 07809 027930; e-mail - monarch.antiques@virgin.net website - www.monarch-antiques.co.uk SER: Packing and shipping; courier; restorations. FAIRS: Newark.

STAPLECROSS, Nr. Robertsbridge

Claremont Antiques

Stockwood Farm, Ellenwhorne Lane. TN32 5RR. (Anthony Broad). SIZE: Warehouse. *STOCK: British, French and Continental original painted pine country furniture, fruitwood farm tables, 18th-19th C; some decorative items; all £10-£5,000.* PARK: Easy. TEL: 01580 830650; mobile - 07786 262843; e-mail - antclaremont@aol.com website - www.claremont antiques.com SER: Import and export.

UCKFIELD

Ringles Cross Antiques

Ringles Cross. TN22 1HF. (J. Dunford). Resident. Est. 1965. Open 10-5 or by appointment. *STOCK: English furniture, mainly oak and country, 17th-18th C; accessories.* LOC: 1 mile north of Uckfield. PARK: Own. TEL: 01825 762909.

WADHURST

Park View Antiques

High St., Durgates. TN5 6DE. (B. Ross). Est. 1985. Open 10-4. CL: Wed. except by appointment. SIZE: Medium. *STOCK: Pine, oak and country furniture, 17th-19th C, £100-£1,500; decorative items, 1930s, £25-£150; iron and metalware, 17th-19th C, £25-£250.* LOC: On B2099 Frant-Hurst Green road. PARK: Easy. TEL: 01892 783630; fax - 01892 740264; home - 01892 740264; website - www.parkviewantiques.co.uk SER: Valuations; restorations (furniture).

SUSSEX WEST

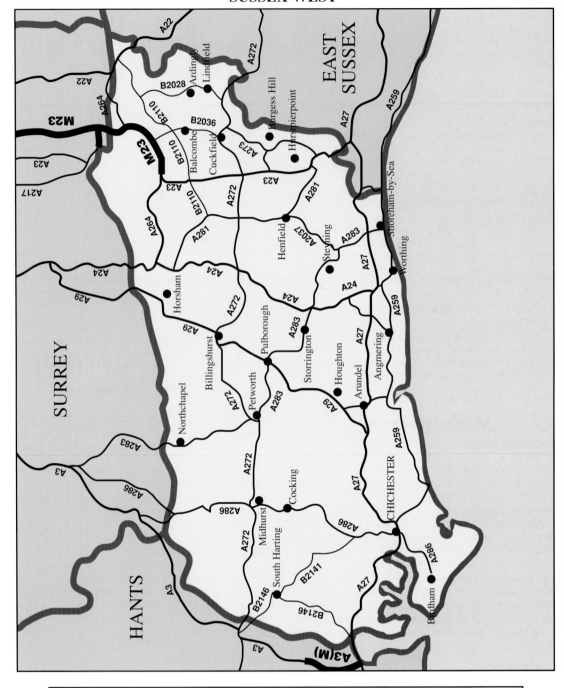

Dealers and Shops in West Sussex							
Angmering	1	Burgess Hill	1	Houghton	1	Pulborough	2
Ardingly	1	Chichester	10	Hurstpierpoint	2	Shoreham-by-Sea	1
Arundel	5	Cocking	1	Lindfield	2	South Harting	1
Balcombe	1	Cuckfield	1	Midhurst	1	Steyning	1
Billingshurst	1	Henfield	1	Northchapel	1	Storrington	1
Birdham	1	Horsham	1	Petworth	29	Worthing	4

ANGMERING

Bygones
The Square. BN16 4EQ. (R.A. and Mrs L.R. Whittaker). Est. 1965. Open Tues. and Thurs. 10-1 and 2.15-5, Sat. 10-12. SIZE: Medium. *STOCK: Furniture, £50-£2,500; china, £5-£750; silver, £10-£250; linen, £5-£75; all 1790-1940.* LOC: A280. PARK: Easy. TEL: 01903 786152; home - same. SER: Valuations; buys at auction (furniture).

ARDINGLY

Rocking Horse Antique Market
16 High St. RH17 6TD. (Peter and Mrs Joy Livett). Est. 1993. Open 9.30-5.30, Sun. 10-5.30 (winter until 5 every day). SIZE: Small. *STOCK: General antiques.* PARK: Rear of village hall. TEL: 01444 892205. FAIRS: Ardingly.

ARUNDEL

Antiquities
5/7 Tarrant St. BN18 9DG. (Ian and Christina Fenwick). Est. 1990. Open 10-5, other times by appointment. SIZE: Large + displayed warehouses. *STOCK: Decorative and unusual - including 19th C English and French furniture, mahogany and fruitwood, painted items, Staffordshire, majolica, metalware, French mirrors, pond yachts, luggage, garden, architectural items, tole.* LOC: Just off town square. PARK: Nearby. TEL: 01903 884355; fax - same; e-mail - antiquities@btconnect.com SER: Shipping. VAT: Stan/Spec.

Baynton-Williams
1st Floor, 37A High St. BN18 9AG. (R.H. and S.C. Baynton-Williams). Est. 1946. Open 10-6. SIZE: Medium. *STOCK: Maps, views, sporting, marine and decorative prints.* PARK: Nearby. TEL: 01903 883588; fax - same; e-mail - gallery@baynton-williams. freeserve.co.uk website - www.baynton-williams.com SER: Valuations; cataloguing. VAT: Stan/Spec.

The Old Cornstore Antiques
31 High St. BN18 9AG. (Timeless Toys). Est. 1982. Open 9.30-4.30, Sun. and Bank Holidays 10.30-4.30. CL: Wed. and 2nd Sun. each month. SIZE: Large - 30 dealers. *STOCK: Wide range of general antiques and collectable toys, £10-£5,000.* PARK: Easy. TEL: 01903 885456; e-mail - theoldcornstore@aol.com

Spencer Swaffer   LAPADA
30 High St. BN18 9AB. Est. 1974. Open 9-6, other times by appointment. SIZE: Large. *STOCK: Quirky decorative and traditional items, English, French, brown and painted furniture, dinner services, chandeliers, lighting, marble tables, iron low tables, bamboo, shop fittings, majolica, garden furniture.* PARK: Easy. TEL: 01903 882132; fax - 01903 884564; e-mail - spencerswaffer@btconnect.com website - www. spencerswaffer.com VAT: Stan/Spec.

The Walking Stick Shop
8/9 The Old Printing Works, Tarrant St. BN18 9JH. (S. Thompson). Est. 1981. Open 8.30-5.30, Wed. 8.30-1, Sun. pm. by appointment. SIZE: Large. *STOCK: Walking sticks and canes, 1620 to date, £10-£2,000.* LOC: Off High St. PARK: Easy. TEL: 01903 883796; fax - 01903

884491; e-mail - stuart.walkingsticks@btinternet.com website - www.walkingstickshop.co.uk VAT: Stan.

BALCOMBE

Woodall and Emery Ltd
Haywards Heath Rd. RH17 6PG. (R.A. Emery and Mrs M.S.E. Chinn). Est. 1884. Open 10-5. *STOCK: Period and decorative lighting including chandeliers, wall brackets, table lights.* LOC: 10 mins. from Gatwick, 1 hour London. PARK: Easy. TEL: 01444 811608/819365; e-mail - enquiries@woodallandemery.co.uk website - www.woodallandemery.co.uk SER: Restorations (including re-wiring); cleaning (chandeliers). VAT: Stan.

BILLINGSHURST

Michael Wakelin and Helen Linfield   BADA
                                          LAPADA
P.O Box 48. RH14 0YZ. CINOA. Est. 1968. Open any time by appointment. *STOCK: Fine English and Continental formal and country furniture - walnut, fruitwoods, faded mahogany and other exotic woods; early brass, bronze, iron and steel; wood carvings, treen, needlework, naïve pictures and lighting.* LOC: Wisborough Green. PARK: Easy. TEL: 01403 700004; fax - 01403 701173; e-mail - wakelin_linfield @btinternet.com website - www.wakelin-linfield.com SER: Shipping; valuations; interior and landscape design. FAIRS: Olympia; BADA; LAPADA; Chelsea. VAT: Stan/Spec.

BIRDHAM, Nr. Chichester

Whitestone Farm Antiques
Whitestone Farm, Main Rd. PO20 7HU. (C.L. Mordue). Open 10-5.30. SIZE: Medium. *STOCK: Town and country furniture, including pine and oak, £50-£2,000; books, £3-£200; gardenalia, £5-£250; china, glass and collectables.* PARK: Easy. TEL: 01243 513706; fax - same; e-mail - antiques@whitestonefarm.F9.co.uk website - www.whitestonefarm.F9.co.uk SER: Valuations; country furniture polishing and repairs.

BURGESS HILL

Recollect Dolls Hospital
17 Junction Rd. RH15 0HR. (P. Jago). Est. 1970. Open 10-4. CL: Mon. and Sat. *STOCK: Dolls and supplies, doll restoration materials.* TEL: 01444 871052; e-mail - dollshopuk@aol.com SER: Restorations (dolls); catalogues available (£3 stamps).

CHICHESTER

Almshouses Arcade
19 The Hornet. PO19 4JL. (Mrs V. Barnet). Est. 1983. Open 9.30-4.30. LOC: 200yds. from Cattle Market at eastern end of city. On one-way system (A286) just before traffic lights at Market Ave. PARK: Easy. TEL: 01243 528089. Below are listed the dealers at these premises.

Antics
(P. German). *General antiques and collectables.*

Autodrome
Motoring, tin plate and ephemera. TEL: 01243 778126.

363

R .K. Barnett
Antiques and collectables, furniture. TEL: 01243 528089.

Collectors Corner
Small collectables and antiques. TEL: 01243 778126

Decographic
Toys, wirelesses, cameras, gramophones. TEL: 01243 787391.

The Delightful Muddle
Unit 3. (Mrs Marjorie Storey). *China, glass, objets d'art, Victorian and Edwardian, £1-£100; linen, general antiques and bric-a-brac, cutlery, £3-£65.*

East Side Records
Records. TEL: 01243 782786.

Yesteryears
(J.A. Cook). *Lighting (oil), general antiques and collectables.* TEL: 01243 771994.

Chichester Antiques Centre
46-48 The Hornet. PO19 4JG. (Mike Carter). Est. 1994. Open 10-5, Sun. 11-4. SIZE: 50 stalls. *STOCK: General antiques and collectables, 50p to £10,000.* LOC: M27, A27 east of town centre. PARK: Loading only and nearby. TEL: 01243 530100; e-mail - mcarter@cwcom.net SER: Restorations (clocks).

Chichester Gallery
8 The Hornet. PO19 4JG. (Tom and Mary McHale). Est. 1997. Open Tues., Wed. and Fri. 10-1 and 2-4. SIZE: 5 rooms. *STOCK: Victorian oils, watercolours, etchings and engravings, £250-£7,000; fine prints, contemporary paintings, including local views.* PARK: Cattlemarket at rear of gallery. TEL: 01243 779821. SER: Cleaning; restorations; commission sales; inventories; valuations.

Frensham House Antiques
Hunston. PO20 1NX. (J. and M. Riley). Est. 1966. Open 9-6. *STOCK: English furniture, 1700-1830, £500-£6,000; clocks, paintings, copper.* LOC: One mile south of Chichester by-pass on B2145. PARK: Easy. TEL: 01243 782660.

Gems Antiques
39 West St. PO19 1RP. (M.L. Hancock). Open 10-1 and 2.30-5.30. CL: Mon. *STOCK: Period furniture, Staffordshire and porcelain figures, glass and pictures.* PARK: Easy. TEL: 01243 786173.

Peter Hancock Antiques
40-41 West St. PO19 1RP. Articles on coins. Est. 1950. Open 10.30-1 and 2.30-5.30. CL: Mon. SIZE: Medium. *STOCK: Silver, jewellery, porcelain, furniture, £20-£2,000; pictures, glass, clocks, books, £5-£500; all 18th-19th C; enthnographica, Art Nouveau, Art Deco, 19th-20th C, £5-£500.* LOC: From Chichester Cross, 17 doors past cathedral. PARK: Easy. TEL: 01243 786173. SER: Valuations; repairs. VAT: Stan/Spec.

Heritage Antiques
84 St. Pancras. PO19 7NL. (D.R. Grover). Est. 1987. Open 9.30-5. *STOCK: Furniture and decorative items.* TEL: 01243 783796.

Rathbone Law
59 North St. PO19 1NB. (Mr and Mrs R. Law). NAG. Est. 1902. Open 9.30-5. CL: Some Mon. *STOCK: Victorian and Edwardian fine jewellery, silver, designer pieces in gold and silver, objets d'art, fine gems.* PARK: Nearby. TEL: 01243 787881; e-mail - info@rathbonelaw.com website - www.rathbonelaw.com SER: Valuations.

W.D. Priddy Antiques
Unit 6 Terminus Mill, Terminus Rd. Industrial Estate. PO19 8UN. Open 10-5, Sun. 11-4 or by appointment. SIZE: Large. *STOCK: Oak, mahogany, walnut and pine furniture, mid-19th C to pre-war and shipping, £20-£7,000.* LOC: Runs off A27 Chichester bypass. PARK: Easy. TEL: 01243 783960; fax - same; e-mail - bill@priddyantiques.fsnet.co.uk website - www.priddy antiques.co.uk VAT: Stan/Spec.

St. Pancras Antiques
150 St. Pancras. PO19 7SH. (R.F. and M. Willatt). Est. 1980. Open 9.30-1 and 2-5. CL: Thurs. pm. SIZE: Small. *STOCK: Arms and armour, militaria, medals, documents, uniforms and maps, 1600-1914, £5-£3,000; china, pottery and ceramics, 1800-1930, £2-£500; small furniture, 17th-19th C, £20-£1,000; coins, ancient to date.* Not Stocked: Silver and carpets. TEL: 01243 787645; e-mail - ralph.willatt@virgin.net SER: Valuations; restorations (arms and armour); buys at auction (militaria).

COCKING, Nr. Midhurst

The Victorian Brass Bedstead Company
Hoe Copse. GU29 0HL. (David Woolley). Resident. Est. 1970. Open by appointment. SIZE: Large. *STOCK: Victorian and Edwardian brass and iron bedsteads, bases and mattresses, 19th-20th C, £300-£3,500.* LOC: Right behind village Post Office, 3/4 mile left turning to Hoe Copse. PARK: Easy. TEL: 01730 812287; e-mail - toria@netcomuk.co.uk website - www.vbbeds.com SER: Valuations; restorations (brass and iron bedsteads). VAT: Stan.

CUCKFIELD

David Foord-Brown Antiques · BADA
High St. RH17 5JU. (David Foord-Brown and Sean Barry). Est. 1988. Open 10-5.30. SIZE: Medium. *STOCK: Furniture, 1750-1880, £500-£25,000; old Sheffield plate and period accessories.* Not Stocked: Country furniture. LOC: A272, east of A23. PARK: Easy. TEL: 01444 414418; e-mail - antiques@davidfoord-brown.com website - www.davidfoord-brown.com FAIRS: BADA (March); Olympia (June and Nov). VAT: Spec.

HENFIELD

Ashcombe Coach House · BADA
P O Box 2527. BN5 9SU. CINOA. Est. 1954. Open by appointment only. *STOCK: Furniture and objects, 17th to early 19th C.* PARK: Own. TEL: 01273 491630; fax - 01273 492681; mobile - 07803 180098. FAIRS: Olympia; BADA.

HORSHAM

Queen Street Antiques Centre
39 Queen St. RH13 5AA. (Jonathan Dick). Est. 2003.

Open Tues.-Sat. 10-5. *STOCK: General antiques - especially furniture, and collectables.* LOC: A281 east of town centre. PARK: On street in afternoons and public nearby. TEL: 01403 756644.

HOUGHTON, Nr. Arundel

Stable Antiques at Houghton
The Old Church, Main Rd. BN18 9LW. (Ian. J. Wadey). Est. 1993. Open Tues.-Sat. 11-4. *STOCK: General antiques and furniture, £20-£1,000.* LOC: B2139 between Storrington and Arundel. PARK: Own. TEL: 01798 839555; 01903 740555; fax - same; website - www.stableantiques.co.uk

HURSTPIERPOINT

The Clock Shop
34-36 High St. BN6 9RG. (Samuel Orr). Est. 1968. Open 9-6 including Sun., or by appointment. *STOCK: 18th-19th longcase, table and wall clocks.* PARK: Easy. TEL: 01273 832081; mobile - 07860 230888; e-mail - clocks@samorr.co.uk website - www.samorr.co.uk SER: Restorations (clocks and furniture).

Julian Antiques
124 High St. BN6 9PX. (Julian and Carol Ingram). Est. 1964. Open by appointment. *STOCK: French 19th C mirrors, fireplaces, fenders, furniture.* PARK: Easy. TEL: 01273 832145.

LINDFIELD

Lindfield Galleries - David Adam   BADA
62 High St. RH16 2HL. Est. 1972. Open Tues.-Fri. 9.30-5, Sat. 9.30-4.30. SIZE: Large. *STOCK: Antique and contemporary Oriental carpets and rugs.* PARK: Easy. TEL: 01444 483817; fax - 01444 484682; e-mail - david@lindfieldgalleries.fsnet.co.uk website - www. orientalandantiquerugs.com SER: Restorations; cleaning. VAT: Stan/Spec.

Stable Antiques
98A High St. RH16 2HP. (Adrian Hoyle). Est. 1987. Open 10-5.30, Sun. 2-5.30. SIZE: Large. *STOCK: Regency and mahogany Victorian furniture including extending tables, bookcases and chests of drawers; pine and country furniture; silver and china.* LOC: Off A272 on B2028, 2 miles south of Ardingly. PARK: Easy and free. TEL: 01444 483662; mobile - 07768 900331; e-mail - adrianhoyle@msn.com SER: Valuations.

MIDHURST

Churchill Clocks
Rumbolds Hill. GU29 9BZ. (W.P. and Dr. E. Tyrrell). Open 9-5, Wed. 9-1. *STOCK: Clocks and furniture.* LOC: Main street. TEL: 01730 813891; website - www.churchillclocks.co.uk SER: Restorations (clocks).

NORTHCHAPEL, Nr. Petworth

Callingham Antiques
GU28 9HL. Est. 1979. Open Mon., Thurs. and Sat. 9.30-5.30 or by appointment. SIZE: Medium. *STOCK: Furniture, 1700-1900, £10-£10,000.* LOC: London Road

5 miles north of Petworth. PARK: Easy. TEL: 01428 707379; e-mail - antiques@callinghamfreeserve.co.uk SER: Valuations; restorations.

PETWORTH

Angel Antiques   LAPADA
Lombard St. GU28 0AG. (Nick and Barbara Swanson). PAADA. Est. 1993. Open 10-5.30, Sun. by appointment. SIZE: Medium. *STOCK: English and French period country furniture, ceramics and decorative items, £50-£15,000.* LOC: Top of Lombard St., opposite church. TEL: 01798 343306; fax - 01798 342665; e-mail - swansonantiques@aol.com website - www.angel-antiques.co.uk VAT: Spec.

Antiquated
10 New St. GU28 0AS. (Vicki Emery). PAADA. Est. 1989. Open 10-5.30 or by appointment. *STOCK: 18th-19th C original painted furniture, decorative items, garden furniture; 19th C rocking horses.* TEL: 01798 344011; fax - same; e-mail - info@antiquated.co.uk website - www.antiquated.co.uk VAT: Spec.

Baskerville Antiques   BADA
Saddlers House, Saddlers Row. GU28 0AN. (A. and B. Baskerville). PAADA. Est. 1978. Open Wed.-Sat. 10-5.30 or by appointment. SIZE: Medium. *STOCK: English clocks and barometers, £1,000-£40,000; decorative items and instruments, £500-£10,000; all 17th-19th C.* LOC: Town centre. PARK: Public, adjoining shop. TEL: 01798 342067; home - same; e-mail - brianbaskerville@aol.com VAT: Spec.

John Bird
High St. GU28 0AU. PAADA. Open 10.15-5.15. SIZE: Medium. *STOCK: Furniture - country, pine, oak, fruitwood, mahogany, painted, architectural, garden and upholstered.* PARK: Easy. TEL: 01798 343250/865143; mobile - 07970 683949; e-mail - bird.puttnam@virgin. net FAIRS: Olympia (Spring, Summer and Winter); Bath Decorative. VAT: Spec.

Bradley's Past & Present
21 High St. GU28 0AU. (M. and A. Bradley). Est. 1975. CL: Mon. SIZE: Small. *STOCK: Furniture, 19th-20th C, £50-£500; china and decorative items, £5-£100; metalware, phonographs, gramophones and records.* PARK: Nearby. TEL: 01798 343533. SER: Restorations and repairs (gramophones).

Brownrigg @ Home
1 Pound St. GU28 0DX. (George Perez Martin). PAADA. Est. 1999. Open 10-5.30, Sun. by appointment. *STOCK: General antiques including Continental furniture, 13th C to 1920s; lighting, luggage, ceramics, decorative items.* PARK: Easy. TEL: 01798 344321; fax - same; mobile - 07751 542149; e-mail - info@ brownrigg-interiors.com website - www.brownrigg-interiors.com SER: Interior design.

The Canon Gallery   BADA
New St. GU28 0AS. (Jeremy Green and James Fergusson). PAADA. Est. 1987. Open 10-1 and 2-5.30. SIZE: Medium. *STOCK: Oils and watercolours, 18th-20th C, £500-£100,000.* LOC: Main road. PARK: Easy. TEL: 01798 344422; e-mail - enquiries@

canongallery.co.uk website - www.thecanongallery.co.uk SER: Valuations; restorations; framing. FAIRS: World of Watercolours; Harrogate; Olympia; New York; BADA. VAT: Spec.

Ronald G. Chambers Fine Antiques   LAPADA
Market Sq. GU28 0AH. (Ronald G. Chambers and Jacqueline F. Tudor). CINOA. PAADA. Est. 1985. Open 10-5.30, Sun. 10-4.30. SIZE: 5 showrooms. *STOCK: Fine 18th-19th C furniture and objets d' art.* PARK: Free. TEL: 01798 342305; fax - 01798 342724; mobile - 07932 161968; e-mail - Jackie@ronaldchambers.com website - www.ronaldchambers.com SER: Search; valuations; shipping; storage.

Cleall Antiques
2 Leppards, High St. GU28 0AU. (Damian Cleall). PAADA. Est. 1994. Open 10.15-5.15, Sun. by appointment. SIZE: Medium. *STOCK: Eclectic and decorative items including painted furniture, majolica, lighting including chandeliers, period furniture including fruitwood, 1800-1950s.* PARK: Easy. TEL: 01798 343933; fax - same; mobile - 07831 869955; e-mail - damiancleall@hotmail.com website - www.paada.com SER: Courier. FAIRS: Arundel Castle; Battersea Decorative.

Cosby Antiques
19-21 East St. GU28 0AB. (Peter Cosby). PAADA. Est. 1992. Open 10-6. SIZE: Large. *STOCK: 17th-18th C English oak country furniture, clocks, mirrors, pictures, decorative items.* PARK: Easy. TEL: 01798 345212; fax - same; mobile - 07816 916480; e-mail - cosbyantiques @btopenworld.com website - www.cosbyantiques.com SER: Valuations; restorations.

Cyrus Antiques & Decorative Interiors
Old Bank House, Market Sq. GU28 0AH. (G. Hazell). PAADA. Open 10-5. SIZE: Medium. *STOCK: French and English furniture, objets d'art and antiques for the garden.* TEL: 01798 344176; e-mail - info@cyrus antiques.co.uk website - www.cyrusantiques.co.uk

Heather Denham Antiques
6 High St. GU28 0AU. PAADA. Est. 1965. Open 10-5.30. SIZE: Medium. *STOCK: 18th-19th C English and Continental decorative furniture, mirrors and chandeliers.* LOC: Near main square. PARK: Easy and nearby. TEL: 01798 344622; fax - 01798 343436. VAT: Stan/Spec.

Elliott's
88A New St. GU28 0AS. (P.V. Elliott). PAADA. Est. 1990. Open Thurs., Fri. and Sat. 10-5. *STOCK: 18th-20th C furniture, fine art and decorative items.* TEL: 01798 343408

Fu Jen Ni Ltd
1st Floor Newlands House, Pound St. GU28 0DX. (Jenni Foster). PAADA. Open Tues.-Sat. 10-5.30. SIZE: Small. *STOCK: Chinese furniture and accessories from Shan-Xi province, Qing dynasty (200-350 years old), £600-£12,000; late Qing Chinese porcelain, £10-£1,500; also Chinese style textiles and wallcoverings.* LOC: Edge of Petworth, entrance off main free car park. PARK: Easy. TEL: 01798 343458; fax - same; mobile - 07733 320488; e-mail - fujenni@btinternet.com website - www.fujenni.com SER: Valuations; restorations.

Richard Gardner Antiques   LAPADA
Swan House, Market Sq. GU28 0AN. (Richard and Janice Gardner). PAADA. Resident. Est. 1992. Open 10-5.30. SIZE: Large. *STOCK: Fine period furniture and works of art, to £250,000; English and Continental porcelain, Victorian Staffordshire figures, bronzes, silver, paintings, 17th-19th C; associated items; globes.* PARK: 50 yards. TEL: 01798 343411; website - www.richardgardnerantiques.co.uk VAT: Spec.

John Giles   LAPADA
High St. GU28 0AU. PAADA. Est. 1980. Open 10-5.30. SIZE: Medium. *STOCK: Furniture - formal, painted and country, £300-£5,000; lamps, mirrors, objects and pottery.* PARK: Easy and free nearby. TEL: 01798 342136; mobile - 07770 873689; e-mail - gilesandhart @btinternet.com

Granville Antiques   BADA
5 High St. GU28 0AU. (I.E.G. Miller). CINOA. Est. 1979. Open 10-5.30 or by appointment. *STOCK: Period furniture, mainly pre-1840, £50-£15,000; accessories and pictures.* PARK: Easy. TEL: 01798 342312; mobile - 07966 279761; website - www.granvilleantiques.com SER: Valuations; restorations (furniture). FAIRS: BADA. VAT: Spec.

William Hockley Antiques   LAPADA
East St. GU28 0AB. (D. and V. Thrower). PAADA. Est. 1974. Open 10-5.30. *STOCK: Fine 18th to early 19th C furniture and decorative items, fabrics, carpets and related items.* PARK: Easy. TEL: 01798 343172; 01403 701917. SER: Interior design. VAT: Stan/Spec.

Muttonchop Manuscripts
The Playhouse Gallery, Lombard St. GU28 0AG. (Roger S. Clarke). PBFA. PAADA. IBA. Est. 1992. Open Wed.-Sat. 10-4. SIZE: Small. *STOCK: Non-fiction antiquarian books, 15th-19th C; collectable, collectors and antiques reference books; maps, prints and ephemera; fiction classic sets and bindings; specialist in Sussex books and collectables.* LOC: Cobbled street from Market Square. PARK: Free nearby. TEL: 01798 344471; fax - same; e-mail - rogmutton@aol.com website - www.mrmuttonchops.com and www.thesussexshop.co.uk SER: Valuations. FAIRS: PBFA - Haywards Heath, Eltham College, Chichester.

Octavia Antiques
East St. GU28 0AB. (Aline Bell). PAADA. Est. 1973. Open 10.30-5.30. CL: Fri. SIZE: Small. *STOCK: Decorative items - blue and white china, lamps, mirrors, chairs, small sofas, mainly 19th C.* PARK: Easy. TEL: 01798 342771.

Oliver Charles Antiques
Lombard St. GU28 0AG. (Allan and Deborah Gardner). PAADA. Est. 1987. Open 10-5.30 (including Sun. from April to Sept) or by appointment. SIZE: Medium. *STOCK: Georgian, Regency and selected French furniture, 1700-1850, £1,000-£25,000; Victorian paintings, £750-£100,000.* LOC: Opposite church. PARK: Easy. TEL: 01798 344443; fax - 01798 343916; e-mail - olivercharles1@aol.com website - www.olivercharles.co.uk SER: Valuations.

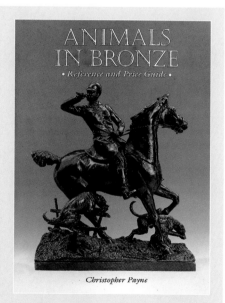
367

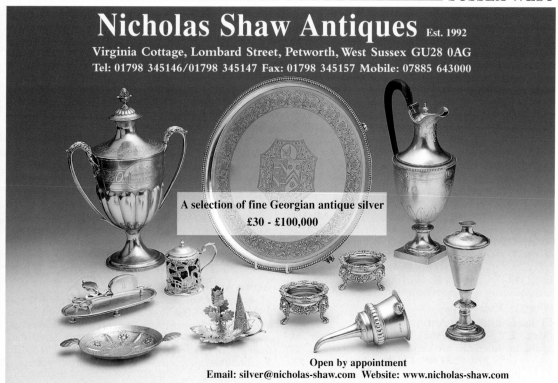

Persian Carpet Gallery
Church St. GU28 0AD. (Dr. Ali Mandegaran). PAADA. Est. 1973. Open 10-5.30. *STOCK: Old and new Persian, Turkish, Indian, Pakistani and Afghan rugs and carpets.* LOC: A272. PARK: Nearby. TEL: 01798 343344; fax - 01798 342673; e-mail - pcg1973@yahoo.co.uk website - www.persiancarpetgallery.co.uk SER: Valuations; restorations; hand cleaning; insurance claims.

Petworth Antique Centre
East St. GU28 0AB. (D.M. Rayment). PAADA. Est. 1967. Open 10-5.30. SIZE: Large - 36 dealers. *STOCK: General antiques, books, furniture, brass, copper, pictures, textiles.* LOC: Near church. PARK: Adjoining. TEL: 01798 342073; fax - 01798 344566; e-mail - info@petworthantiquecentre.co.uk website - www.petworthantiquecentre.co.uk VAT: Stan/Spec.

Riverbank
High St. GU28 0AU. (Linda Burke-White). PAADA. Open 10-5.30. *STOCK: Antiques for the house and garden.* TEL: 01798 344401; fax - 01798 343135.

Nicholas Shaw Antiques   **BADA LAPADA**
Virginia Cottage, Lombard St. GU28 0AG. CINOA. PAADA. Est. 1992. Open Sat. 10-5.30, Tues.-Fri. by appointment. SIZE: Small. *STOCK: Fine and rare English, Scottish and Irish silver, 16th to mid 20th C, £30-£50,000.* LOC: Town centre. PARK: Nearby. TEL: 01798 345146/345147; fax - 01798 345157; mobile - 07885 643000; e-mail - silver@nicholas-shaw.com website - www.nicholas-shaw.com SER:

Valuations; restorations. FAIRS: BADA; Olympia; Harrogate; NEC.

David Swanson Antiques
Lombard St. GU28 0AG. PAADA. Est. 1980. Open 10-5. SIZE: Medium. *STOCK: 17th-18th C oak and walnut country furniture; decorative items.* LOC: Just off main square. PARK: Nearby. TEL: 01798 344111; fax - same; e-mail - david@davidswanson.com website - www.davidswansonantiques.com SER: Valuations.

Thakeham Furniture Ltd   **LAPADA**
Golden Square. GU28 0AP. (T. and B. Chavasse). PAADA. Est. 1988. Open 10-5. SIZE: Large. *STOCK: 18th-19th C English furniture, £100-£8,000; clocks.* PARK: Easy. TEL: 01798 342333; e-mail - enquiries @thakehamfurniture.com website - www.thakehamfurniture.com SER: Restorations (furniture). VAT: Spec.

Tudor Rose Antiques

East St. GU28 0AB. (Mrs E.J. Lee). PAADA. Est. 2001. Open 10-5.15, Sun. 11-4.15. SIZE: Large. *STOCK: General antiques.* LOC: Town centre. PARK: Free nearby. TEL: 01798 343621; mobile - 07980 927331; e-mail - info@tudor-rose-antiques.co.uk website - www.tudor-rose-antiques.co.uk SER: Shipping.

T.G. Wilkinson Antiques Ltd. BADA

Market Sq. GU28 0AH. (Tony Wilkinson). PAADA. Est. 1973. Open 10-5.30. SIZE: Medium. *STOCK: English furniture - mahogany, rosewood and walnut, 1720-1840; mirrors and pictures; all £100-£45,000.* PARK: Nearby. TEL: 01798 343638.

PULBOROUGH

Georgia Antiques LAPADA

The Barn, Broomershill Farm. RH20 2HZ. (Georgia Hicks). CINOA. Est. 1979. Open by appointment. SIZE: Medium. *STOCK: English furniture, pictures and fine art, 18th-19th C; decorative lighting, 19th C.* PARK: Easy. TEL: 01798 872348; fax - 01798 875200; e-mail - georgia@georgia-antiques.com website - www.georgia-antiques.com VAT: Spec.

Elaine Saunderson Antiques BADA

(Mrs. E.C. Saunderson). Est. 1988. Open by appointment. SIZE: Medium. *STOCK: Furniture, late 18th to early 19th C, £1,000-£25,000; decorative items.* TEL: 01798 875528; fax - 01798 872860; mobile - 07836 597485; e-mail - elaine.saunderson@lineone.net SER: Valuations; restorations (furniture). FAIRS: BADA; Olympia (June). VAT: Spec.

SHOREHAM-BY-SEA

Rodney Arthur Classics

Unit 5 Riverbank Business Centre, Old Shoreham Rd. BN43 5FL. (Rodney Oliver). Est. 1979. Open 9.30-5, Sat. and Sun. by appointment. SIZE: Large. *STOCK: Furniture, 1800-1920, £100-£2,500.* LOC: From A27 take A283 exit near Shoreham Airport, then south towards sea, shop opposite Swiss Cottage pub. TEL: 01273 441606; fax - 01273 441977. SER: Restorations; French polishing. VAT: Stan/Spec.

SOUTH HARTING, Nr. Petersfield

Julia Holmes Antique Maps and Prints

South Gardens Cottage. GU31 5QJ. FATG. Est. 1971. Open by appointment. SIZE: Medium. *STOCK: Maps, mainly British Isles, 1600-1850, £25-£2,000; prints, especially sporting, 1740 to date, to £500.* LOC: End of main street, on the Chichester road. PARK: Opposite. TEL: 01730 825040; e-mail - southgardens@beeb.net website - www.juliamaps.co.uk SER: Valuations; restorations; cleaning; colouring maps and prints; framing; buys at auction. FAIRS: Local and major sporting events.

STEYNING

David R. Fileman

Squirrels, Bayards. BN44 3AA. Open daily. *STOCK: Table glass, £20-£1,000; chandeliers, candelabra, £500-£20,000; all 18th-19th C. Collectors' items, 17th-19th C, £25-£2,000; paperweights, 19th C, £50-£5,000.* LOC: A283 to north of Steyning village. TEL: 01903 813229. SER: Valuations; restorations (chandeliers and candelabra). VAT: Stan/Spec.

STORRINGTON

Stable Antiques

46 West St. RH20 4EE. (Ian J. Wadey). Est. 1993. Open 10-6 including Sun. SIZE: Large. *STOCK: General antiques, furniture and bric-a-brac, £1-£1,000.* LOC: A283 west of A24 towards Pulborough, just before Amberley turn. PARK: Easy. TEL: 01903 740555; fax - 01903 740441; website - www.stableantiques.co.uk

WORTHING

Acorn Antiques

91 Rowlands Rd. BN11 3JX. (Henry Nicholls). Est. 1992. Open 9-5.30, Mon. and Wed. 9-4. SIZE: Large. *STOCK: Furniture, china and porcelain, silver and jewellery, 18th-20th C.* LOC: Off Heene Road near seafront. PARK: Easy. TEL: 01903 216926. SER: Restorations; polishing. FAIRS: Ardingly; Kempton Park.

Chloe Antiques

61 Brighton Rd. BN11 3EE. (Mrs D. Peters). Est. 1960. Open 10-4.30. CL: Wed. SIZE: Small. *STOCK: General antiques, jewellery, china, glass, bric-a-brac.* LOC: From Brighton, on main road just past Beach House Park on corner. PARK: Opposite. TEL: 01903 202697.

Corner Antiques

9/10 Havercroft Buildings, North St. BN11 1DY. (R.A. Mihok). Est. 1992. Open 10-5. SIZE: Small. *STOCK: Pine and country furniture, 19th C, £200-£500; objets d'art, 50p-£150; furniture, £100-£1,000; all 19th-20th C.* LOC: Top end of Chapel Rd. turn right at the roundabout. PARK: Loading only, otherwise Connaught NCP. TEL: 01903 537669. SER: Restorations (furniture including French polishing, upholstering and repairs); buys at auction.

Wilsons Antiques LAPADA

45-47 New Broadway, Tarring Rd. BN11 4HS. (F. and K.P. Wilson). Est. 1936. Open Mon.-Fri. 10-4.30, other times by appointment. SIZE: Large. *STOCK: Period furniture, 18th-19th C, £100-£10,000; Edwardian furniture, £50-£4,000; decorative items, 19th C, £10-£750; watercolours and oil paintings, 19th-20th C.* Not Stocked: Pine. LOC: Near West Worthing railway station. PARK: Easy. TEL: 01903 202059; fax - 01903 206300; mobile - 07778 813395; e-mail - Frank@Wilsons-Antiques.com website - www.wilsons-antiques.com SER: Valuations. FAIRS: Goodwood House; Petersfield; West London. VAT: Stan/Spec/Global.

SUSSEX WEST

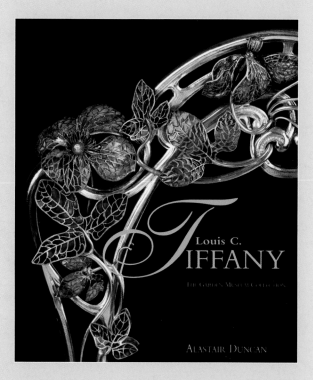

LOUIS C.
TIFFANY
GARDEN MUSEUM COLLECTION
ALASTAIR DUNCAN

- *Every artistic discipline mastered by Tiffany is illustrated here, making this the book for the collector or enthusiast*

- *Examines the Tiffany workshops, the methods of production and the exhibitions*

- *Also features reproductions of oil paintings and watercolours executed by Tiffany himself*

- *Many of the pieces featured are complemented by extracts from contemporary media - such as articles, reviews, catalogues and price lists*

- *Showcases pieces from the Louis C. Tiffany Garden Museum - every piece is illustrated in colour*

Alastair Duncan, the world-renowned authority on Louis C. Tiffany, has produced the definitive work on America's premier artist-designer, examining every facet of Tiffany's unrivalled achievements in a lifetime consecrated, in his own words, to 'The Quest of Beauty'. As Tiffany's wares have continued to rise in popularity since their resurgence in the market-place in the 1950s, many collectors have focused solely on lamps, others on glassware, while others again have assembled collections encompassing several Tiffany disciplines, for example, a handful of lamps, vases, fancy goods, and a window or painting or two. Only Takeo Horiuchi, however, has set out to build a comprehensive collection that incorporates masterworks in each and every artistic discipline to which Tiffany applied himself: Paintings, Furniture, Windows, Mosaics, Art Glass, Lamps, Fancy Goods, Metalware, Enamelware, Silver, Pottery and Jewellery. This book, based on the superlative Louis C. Tiffany Garden Museum Collection formed by Mr. Horiuchi, presents a unique overview of every aspect of Tiffany's talent. For the first time it is possible to see, gathered together 'under one roof', the range of Louis C. Tiffany's creativity – from his famous lamps and windows to his lesser-known paintings and furniture. Every piece in the collection is reproduced in colour, often complemented by extracts from contemporary art revues and the Tiffany firm's sales catalogues, advertisements and price lists, while photographs show them in their original domestic settings, or in the firm's showrooms or international expositions at which they made their debuts. Tiffany's workshops are also illustrated, as well as the logbook entries of its artisans and annotated sketches of its designers. This wealth of illustrative material is accompanied by Alastair Duncan's detailed and evocative descriptions of the workshops, materials, manufacturing processes, the rich and famous who patronised Tiffany, their commissions, and the colourful personalities of the team of artist-craftsmen with whom Tiffany surrounded himself. This book provides a beautiful and comprehensive picture of every artistic discipline to which Tiffany applied himself, a true testament to his extraordinary talent.

Specifications: 672pp., 675 col. illus., 514 b.&w. illus., 12¼ x 10½in./310 x 270mm.
£95.00 (hardback)

For full details of all ACC publications, log on to our website:
www.antiquecollectorsclub.com
or telephone 01394 389950 for a free catalogue

371

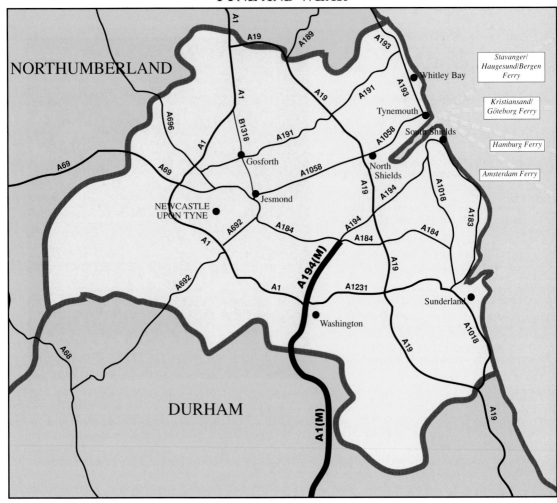

Dealers and Shops in Tyne and Wear					
Gosforth	2	North Shields	1	Tynemouth	4
Jesmond	5	South Shields	1	Washington	1
Newcastle-upon-Tyne	6	Sunderland	1	Whitley Bay	3

GOSFORTH, Nr. Newcastle-upon-Tyne

Jane Kirsopp-Reed Antiques

Harewood House, 49 Great North Rd. NE3 2HH. Open 9-5, Sat. 10-5, Sun. and other times by appointment. SIZE: Large. *STOCK: Fine English furniture and porcelain; oils and watercolours.* LOC: 3 miles north of Newcastle city centre, near Regent Centre. PARK: Forecourt and rear of shop. TEL: 0191 284 3202; website - www.janekirsoppreedantiques.co.uk SER: Restorations. VAT: Stan/Spec.

MacDonald Fine Art

6 Ashburton Rd. NE3 4XN. (T. and C. MacDonald). Est. 1976. Open 10-1 and 2.30-5.30. CL: Wed. SIZE: Medium. *STOCK: Watercolours and oils, mainly north-eastern artists, English and Scottish, 18th-20th C.* LOC: 1 mile west of A1. PARK: Easy. TEL: 0191 284 4214; home - 0191 285 6188. SER: Valuations; restorations (watercolours and oils); framing; buys at auction (watercolours and oils).

JESMOND, Nr. Newcastle-upon-Tyne

Little Theatre Antiques Centre

75-79 Fern Ave. NE2 2RA. (Louise Bennett and John Bell). Est. 1994. Open 10-5.30. SIZE: Large. *STOCK: Victorian and Edwardian British furniture, £200-£3,000; north-east England pressed glass, 1860-1930, £20-£250; Chinese furniture 19th C, £500-£2,000; ceramics, 1880-*

1990; European pine furniture, to £1,000. LOC: Follow city centre motorway to Jesmond exit, north up Osborne Rd. then right into Fern Ave. PARK: Own. TEL: 0191 209 4321; mobile - 07951 035038; website - www. littletheatreantiques.co.uk

Shiners of Jesmond
81 Fern Avenue, NE2 2RA. (M. Nolan and B. Gibbons). SALVO. Est. 2003. Open 10-5. SIZE: Large. *STOCK: Antique and period fireplaces, fires, door furniture, pine and vestibule doors, lighting, fenders.* LOC: Near city centre next to Little Theatre Antiques Centre. PARK: Easy. TEL: 0191 281 6474; fax - 0191 281 9041; e-mail - contactus@shinersofjesmond.com website - www. shinersofjesmond.com SER: Fireplace fitting; brass polishing. VAT: Stan.

A.C. Silver   LAPADA
at Graham Smith Antiques, 83 Fern Avenue. NE2 2RA. (Andrew Campbell). Est. 1976. Open 10-5. *STOCK: Silver, 17th-20th C, £100-£10,000; silver plate, 19th-20th C, £50-£4,000; jewellery, £100-£10,,000.* PARK: Easy. TEL: 0191 281 5065; mobile - 07836 286218; e-mail - andrewcampbell@acsilver.biz website - www. acsilver.biz SER: Valuations. VAT: Stan/Spec.

Graham Smith Antiques   LAPADA
83 Fern Avenue. NE2 2RA. Est. 1999. Open 10-5. SIZE: Large. *STOCK: Furniture, 18th-20th C, £50-£8,000; works of art, 18th-19th C, £100-£10,000; smalls, 18th-20th C, £10-£2,000.* LOC: Follow signs to Fern Avenue Antiques Village off Osborne Rd. PARK: Easy. TEL: 0191 281 5065; mobile - 07836 251873; e-mail - gsmith antiques@aol.com website - www.grahamsmith antiques.co.uk SER: Valuations. FAIRS: Newark; Mansion House, Newcastle. VAT: Stan/Spec.

Turnburrys
257 Jesmond Rd. NE2 1LB. Est. 1995. Open 9-6, Sun. 12-3. SIZE: Large. *STOCK: Period, antique and bespoke fireplaces; original and bespoke vestibule doors: radiators, Victorian to 1920s, £100-£500; over mantel mirrors.* LOC: Off Cradlewell by-pass, next to Jesmond Dene. PARK: Easy. TEL: 0191 281 1770; fax - 0191 240 2569; website - www.turnburrys.co.uk SER: Valuations; restorations (doors, furniture and fireplaces). FAIRS: Traditional Homes & Period Living, London. VAT: Stan.

NEWCASTLE-UPON-TYNE

Corbitt Stamps Ltd
5 Mosley St. NE1 1YE. (David McMonagle). PTS: BNTA: ASDA (New York). Est. 1962. Open 9-5, Sat. 9.30-4. *STOCK: Worldwide stamps, some coins and medals, post and cigarette cards, bank notes.* LOC: Near Tyne bridge. PARK: Opposite. TEL: 0191 232 7268; fax - 0191 261 4130; e-mail - info@corbitts.com website - www.corbitts.com SER: Valuations; regular stamp and coin auctions.

Davidson's The Jewellers Ltd
94 and 96 Grey St. NE1 6AG. (Anthony and Helen Davidson). NAG. Est. 1898. Open 9-5.30. *STOCK: Jewellery, silver.* TEL: 0191 232 2551/232 2895; fax - 0191 232 0714.

Intercoin
103 Clayton St. NE1 5PZ. Est. 1968. Open 9-4.30. *STOCK: Coins and items of numismatic interest; jewellery, silver.* LOC: City centre. TEL: 0191 232 2064.

Steve Johnson Medals & Militaria
PO Box 1SP. NE99 1SP. *STOCK: Medals and militaria.*

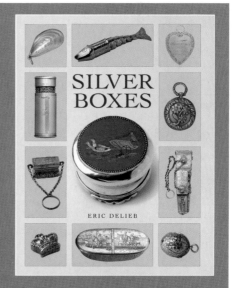

TEL: Fax - 01207 547073; e-mail - steve@wwmeinc. com website - www.wwmeinc.com *Mail Order and Online*.

Newcastle Antique Centre
2nd Floor, 142 Northumberland St. NE1 7DQ. (L. Ingham, D. King and C. Parkin). Est. 1972. Open 10-5. SIZE: Small. *STOCK: Art Deco, Arts & Crafts, Art Nouveau, Maling, militaria, stamps, coins and postcards; railway items, tinplate, watches, Georgian and Victorian silver, glass, gold, silver, jewellery; football memorabilia.* LOC: Opposite Haymarket Metro. PARK: NCP nearby. TEL: 0191 232 9832; mobile - 07885 060155; e-mail - time-antiques@btconnect.com SER: Valuations; restorations (china and jewellery); repairs (clocks). FAIRS: Newark; NEC; Swinderby; Edinburgh.

R.D. Steedman
9 Grey St. NE1 6EE. (David Steedman). ABA. Est. 1907. Open 9-5. CL: Sat. pm. *STOCK: Rare and secondhand books.* LOC: Central. TEL: 0191 232 6561. FAIRS: Olympia Book; Edinburgh.

NORTH SHIELDS

Keel Row Books
11 Fenwick Terrace. NE29 0LU. (Bob and Brenda Cook). Est. 1980. Open 10-4.30, Sun. 11-4. CL: Wed. SIZE: Medium. *STOCK: Books - military, cinema, theatre, local history, art, railways, children's, topography, sci-fi, crime fiction, Penguin aircraft, maritime, antiquarian, £1-£1,000.* LOC: Off Preston Rd. PARK: Nearby. TEL: 0191 296 0664; home - 0191 287 3914. SER: Valuations; restorations.

SOUTH SHIELDS

The Curiosity Shop
16 Frederick St. NE33 5EA. (G.D. Davies). Est. 1969. CL: Wed. SIZE: Large. *STOCK: General antiques, paintings, jewellery, furniture, Royal Doulton.* PARK: Free. TEL: 0191 456 5560; fax - same. FAIRS: Newark.

SUNDERLAND

Peter Smith Antiques   LAPADA
12-14 Borough Rd. SR1 1EP. Est. 1968. Open 9.30-4.30, Sat. 10-1, other times by appointment. SIZE: Warehouse. *STOCK: Georgian, Victorian, Edwardian longcase clocks, shipping goods, £5-£15,000.* LOC: 10 miles from A1(M); towards docks/Hendon from town centre. PARK: Easy. TEL: 0191 567 3537/567 7842; fax - 0191 514 2286; home - 0191 514 0008; e-mail - petersmithantiques@btinternet.co.uk website - www. petersmithantiques.com SER: Valuations; restorations; some shipping; containers packed; buys at auction. VAT: Stan/Spec.

TYNEMOUTH

Curio Corner
Unit 5/6 The Land of Green Ginger, Front St. NE30 4BP. (S. Welton). Est. 1988. Open 10.30-4.30. SIZE: Medium. *STOCK: Period furniture including Dutch oak and English.* LOC: Converted church. PARK: Easy. TEL:

0191 296 3316; fax - 0191 296 3319; mobile - 07831 339906; e-mail - susanwelton@msn.com website - www. curiocorner.co.uk

L.O.G.G. Lights
Unit 3 The Land of Green Ginger, Front St. NE30 4BP. (S. Smyth). Est. 2001. Open 10.30-4.30. SIZE: Medium. *STOCK: French, Dutch and crystal chandeliers; brass, china.* TEL: 0191 296 3316; fax - 0191 296 3319; mobile - 07831 339906.

Ian Sharp Antiques Ltd   LAPADA
23 Front St. NE30 4DX. Est. 1988. Open 10-1 and 1.30-5 or by appointment. SIZE: Small. *STOCK: Furniture, 19th to early 20th C; British pottery including northern especially Maling and Sunderland lustreware, 18th to early 20th C; paintings by north eastern artists, 19th-20th C.* PARK: Easy. TEL: 0191 296 0656; fax - same; e-mail - iansharp@sharpantiques.com website - www. sharpantiques.com FAIRS: Newark. VAT: Global/Spec.

Tynemouth Architectural Salvage
Correction House, 28 Tynemouth Rd. NE30 4AA. (Robin S. Archer). Est. 1998. Open 9-5, Sat. 10-5. SIZE: Large. *STOCK: Antique bathrooms - cast-iron roll top baths with ball and claw feet, English and French pedestal basins, taps, showers, curtain rails, high and low level cisterns, toilets, bathroom accessories; cast-iron radiators, fires, wooden, stone, marble and slate surrounds, doors and door furniture, pews, panelling; cinema seats, coats of arms, staircases.* LOC: Short walk from Tynemouth Metro station, opposite Tanners Bank. PARK: Easy. TEL: 0191 296 6070; fax - 0191 296 6097; e-mail - robin@tynarcsal.demon.co.uk website - www. tynemoutharchitecturalsalvage.com SER: Polishing.

WASHINGTON

Harold J. Carr Antiques
Field House, Rickleton. NE38 9HQ. Est. 1970. Open by appointment. *STOCK: General antiques and furniture.* TEL: 0191 388 6442. SER: Shippers.

WHITLEY BAY

Northumbria Pine
54 Whitley Rd. NE26 2NF. (C. and V. Dowland). Est. 1979. Open 9.15-4.30. SIZE: Small. *STOCK: Reproduction, stripped, reclaimed and made to order pine items.* LOC: Cullercoats end of Whitley Rd. behind sea front. PARK: Easy. TEL: 0191 252 4550; website - www.northumbria-pine.co.uk SER: Free local delivery; restorations (table tops). VAT: Stan.

Olivers Bookshop
48A Whitley Rd. NE26 2NF. (J. Oliver). Est. 1986. Open 11-5. CL: Tues. and Wed. SIZE: Medium. *STOCK: Antiquarian and secondhand books, 50p to £500.* PARK: Easy. TEL: 0191 251 3552. SER: Valuations. FAIRS: Tynemouth Book.

Treasure Chest
2 and 4 Norham Rd. NE26 2SB. Est. 1974. Open 10.30-1 and 2-4. CL: Wed. and Thurs. SIZE: Small. *STOCK: General antiques.* LOC: Just off main shopping area of Park View, leading to Monkseaton rail station. PARK: Easy. TEL: 0191 251 2052.

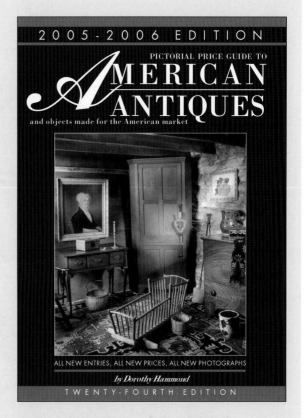

- *Full colour illustrations throughout*

- *Illustrates and prices more than 4,000 objects made for the American market achieved at auction in the US*

- *Includes sections on glass, furniture, ceramics, clocks, toys and dolls and sporting memorabilia*

- *All new entries, all new prices, all new photographs*

PICTORIAL PRICE GUIDE TO
AMERICAN ANTIQUES
and objects made for the American Market
2005-2006 EDITION

Dorothy Hammond

"*Anyone interested in antiques, whether collector or dealer, will find this guide fascinating and helpful*" **The Antique Trader Weekly**

In the highly volatile and uncertain market for antiques, art and collectables it is important to have an up-to-date source of information - this book provides just that. The relevance of the highs and lows of the American market is becoming ever more pertinent for antique dealers and collectors in the UK and the rest of Europe. The 2005-2006 edition of *The Pictorial Price Guide to American Antiques* showcases a selection of approximately 4,000 individual objects in full colour sold recently in the United States at auction. The objects included date from the seventeenth century to the mid-1950s, and range from the relatively common to the rare, from clocks and watches to toys and textiles. The format provides an accurate market value of items sold at auction throughout a twelve month period. Prices realised have been based on actual sales records from a variety of the most highly respected auction houses in America. This visual method of pricing makes the book indispensable to anyone interested in the field of antiques and collectables; it is recognised as one of the most authoritative and up-to-date references on the market.

Dorothy Hammond is among America's foremost authorities on antiques and collectables. Her writing career has spanned over three decades, beginning in 1970. She wrote a weekly nationally syndicated column for Columbia Features, Inc. for fifteen years, before joining Hearst magazines in 1980, as a contributing editor to *Colonial Homes Magazine*, and later *Classic American Homes*. Her first pictorial price guide was published in 1977... and twenty-three editions followed.

Specifications: 288pp.,
Colour throughout,
11½ x 8½in./292 x 218mm.
£17.50 (hardback)

For full details of all ACC publications, log on to our website:
www.antiquecollectorsclub.com
or telephone 01394 389950 for a free catalogue

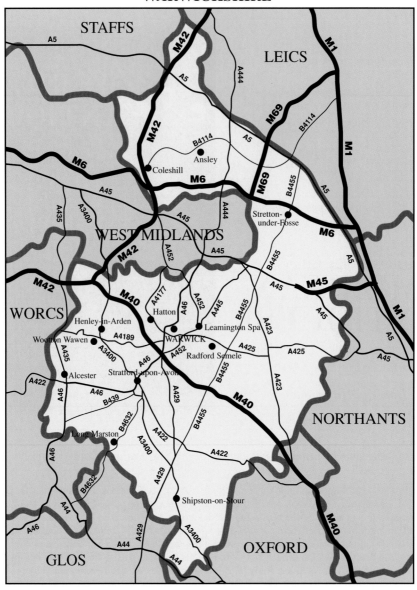

Dealers and Shops in Warwickshire						Stratford-upon-Avon	7
						Stretton-on-Fosse	1
Alcester	2	Hatton	1	Long Marston	1	Warwick	12
Ansley	1	Henley-in-Arden	3	Radford Semele	1	Wootten Wawen	1
Coleshill	1	Leamington Spa	1	Shipston-on-Stour	3		

ALCESTER

High St. Antiques

11A High St. B49 5AE. (V.F.S. and J.F. Baldwin). Est. 1979. Open Fri. 12-5 and Sat. 10-5 or by appointment. SIZE: Small. *STOCK: Glass and china, 18th-20th C, £5-£200; postcards, books, brass and copper, silver and jewellery.* LOC: On left-hand side near church coming from Stratford-on-Avon road. PARK: Rear of High St. TEL: 01789 764009; fax - 01789 766325.

Malthouse Antiques Centre

Market Place. B49 5AE. (J. and P. Allcock). Est. 1982. Open 10-5, Sun. 1-4. SIZE: Large. *STOCK: Furniture, china, silver, collectables and objets d'art, 18th-20th C, £1-£2,000.* LOC: Adjacent to town car park. TEL: 01789 764032.

ANSLEY, Nr. Nuneaton

Granary Antiques
Hoar Park Craft Centre. CV10 0QU. (G. Stockdale). Est. 1987. Open 10-5 including Sun. CL: Mon. except Bank Holidays. SIZE: Medium. *STOCK: Furniture, china, glass, books and collectables.* PARK: Easy. TEL: 02476 395551. FAIRS: Newark.

COLESHILL

Coleshill Antiques and Interiors Ltd
12 and 14 High St. B46 1AZ. (A.J. Webster). Est. 1958. Open Tues.-Fri. 9.30-5 or by appointment. SIZE: Large. *STOCK: Continental porcelain, furniture, jewellery, bronzes, lighting, mirrors and decorative items.* LOC: 1 mile from NEC. PARK: Easy. TEL: 01675 467416; fax - 01675 462931; e-mail - enq@coleshillantiques.com website - www.coleshillantiques.com SER: Valuations; restorations; repairs; interior design. VAT: Stan/Spec.

HATTON, Nr. Warwick

The Stables Antique Centre
Hatton Country World, Dark Lane. CV35 8XA. (John and Margaret Colledge). Est. 1990. Open 10-5 including Sun. SIZE: Large - 25 units. *STOCK: Furniture, 18th-19th C, £50-£3,000; china, 19th-20th C, £5-£200; clocks, 18th-19th C, £200-£4,000; linen, glass, brass and copper, paintings and prints, jewellery and telephones.* LOC: Just off A4177 Solihull-Warwick road, 5 mins. from junction 15, M40. PARK: Own. TEL: 01926 842405. SER: Valuations.

HENLEY-IN-ARDEN

Arden Gallery
54 High St. B95 5AN. (G.B. Horton). Est. 1963. Open 1-6. CL: Sat. SIZE: Medium. *STOCK: Victorian oil paintings, £20-£1,000; watercolours, all periods, to £1,500; portrait miniatures.* LOC: A3400. PARK: Easy. TEL: 01564 792520. VAT: Spec.

Henley Antiques Centre
92 High St. B95 5BY. (Mrs Rosie Montague and Mrs Gill Rayson). Est. 2001. Open 10.30-5, Sun and Bank Holidays 11-4. SIZE: Large. *STOCK: Furniture, porcelain and collectables, 19th to early 20th C, £20-£2,000; art gallery.* LOC: Behind bakery at pedestrian crossing lights. PARK: Easy. TEL: 01564 795979; mobile - 07950 324376. SER: Valuations. FAIRS: NEC.

The Purple Antique Shop
86B High St. B93 9EQ. (Chris and Barbara Davison). Est. 2000. Open 9.30-5, Sun. 11-4.30. SIZE: Medium. *STOCK: China including Beswick, Moorcroft, Royal Doulton and Crown Derby, from 1900, from £20; kitchenalia, collectables, jewellery, small furniture, militaria and toys.* LOC: Opposite The Cross. PARK: Nearby. TEL: 01564 795131; e-mail - thepurpleantique shop@blueyonder.co.uk

LEAMINGTON SPA

King's Cottage Antiques　　　　　　　**LAPADA**
4 Windsor St. CV32 5EB. (G. and A. Jackson). Est. 1993.

Open 9-4, Sat. by appointment. SIZE: Large. *STOCK: Early oak and country furniture, 16th-18th C.* TEL: 01926 422927.

LONG MARSTON, Nr. Stratford-upon-Avon

Barn Antiques Centre
Station Rd. CV37 8RB. (Bev and Graham Simpson). Est. 1978. Open Mon.-Fri. 10-5, Sun. 12-6. SIZE: Large - 50+ dealers. *STOCK: Georgian, Victorian, Edwardian and later furniture, collectables, silver, porcelain, china, kitchenalia, fireplaces, linen, pictures, 18th C to 1950, £5-£2,000.* LOC: Approx. 5 miles from Stratford. PARK: Own. TEL: 01789 721399; fax - 01789 721390; e-mail - info@barnantique.co.uk website - www.barnantique. co.uk

RADFORD SEMELE, Nr. Leamington Spa

Arcadia Antiques
Westfield Farm, Fosse Way. CV31 1XL. (Jack Harness). Est. 1981. Open 7 days by appointment. *STOCK: Pine and country furniture, especially period pine and original painted French provincial.* TEL: 01926 611923; fax - 01926 611924; mobile - 07768 666833; e-mail - jackharness@aol.com website - www.arcadiaantiques. co.uk. SER: Restorations; courier. VAT: Stan/Spec.

SHIPSTON-ON-STOUR

Fine-Lines (Fine Art)　　　　　　　**LAPADA**
The Old Rectory Lodge, West St. CV36 4HD. Est. 1975. Open every day by appointment. SIZE: Medium.

STOCK: British and European watercolours, pastels, drawings and selected oils, from 1850, £300-£20,000. LOC: 2 mins. from town centre. PARK: Easy and nearby. TEL: 01608 662323 (answerphone); e-mail - enquiries@fine-lines-fineart.co.uk SER: Valuations; advice (restoration and framing). VAT: Spec.

Pine and Things
Portobello Farm, Campden Rd. CV36 4PY. (Richard Wood). Est. 1991. Open 9-5. SIZE: Large - 6 showrooms. STOCK: Pine, 18th-19th C, £50-£2,000. LOC: A429/B4035. PARK: Ample. TEL: 01608 663849; home - same; website - www.pinethings.co.uk VAT: Stan/Spec.

Time in Hand
11 Church St. CV36 4AP. (F.R. Bennett). Est. 1979. Open 9-1 and 2-5.30 or by appointment. SIZE: Large. STOCK: Longcase, carriage, mantel and wall clocks, barometers. LOC: Opposite church on main road. PARK: Free - Banbury Road. TEL: 01608 662578; e-mail - timeinhand1@aol.com website - www.timeinhand.co.uk SER: Restorations (clocks, watches, barometers and mechanical instruments).

STRATFORD-UPON-AVON

Burman Antiques
34 College St. CV37 6BW. (J. and J. Burman Holtom). Est. 1973. Open by appointment. STOCK: Ruskin ware, pot-lids, fishing tackle. TEL: 01789 295164.

Thomas Crapper & Co
The Stable Yard, Alscot Park. CV37 8BL. (S.P.J. Kirby). SALVO. Est. 1861. Open Mon.-Fri. 9.30-5 by appointment. SIZE: Medium. STOCK: Hand-made replicas of Crapper's original fittings; some antique decorated WC's, basins and cast-iron baths. PARK: Easy. TEL: 01789 450522; fax - 01789 450523; e-mail - wc@thomas-crapper.com website - www.thomas-crapper.com SER: Valuations; restorations (bathroom fittings).

Howards Jewellers
44a Wood St. CV37 6JG. (Howards of Stratford Ltd). NAG. Est. 1985. Open 9.30-5.30. STOCK: Jewellery, silver, objets d'art, 19th C. LOC: Town centre. PARK: Nearby. TEL: 01789 205404. SER: Valuations; restorations (as stock). VAT: Stan/Spec.

George Pragnell Ltd
5 & 6 Wood St. CV37 6JA. (Jeremy Pragnell). NAG. Est. 1954. Open 9.30-5.30. SIZE: Large. STOCK: Fine jewellery, silver, clocks and watches. LOC: Town centre. PARK: Nearby. TEL: 01789 267072; fax - 01789 415131; e-mail - enquiries@pragnell.co.uk website - www.pragnell.co.uk SER: Valuations; repairs; re-modelling. FAIRS: NEC. VAT: Stan/Spec.

Stratford Antique Centre
60 Ely St. CV37 6LN. (Cyril Waterman). Open 10-5 including Sun. SIZE: 40 dealers. STOCK: General antiques. TEL: 01789 204180.

The Stratford Antiques and Interiors Centre Ltd
Dodwell Industrial Park, Evesham Rd. CV37 9ST. (Andrew and Suzanna Kerr). Est. 1980. Open 10-5 including Sun. SIZE: 25+ dealers. STOCK: Georgian, Victorian, Edwardian and shipping furniture, £100-£10,000; china and smalls, 19th-20th C, £5-£2,000; reclaimed pine, £50-£10,000. LOC: B439. PARK: Easy. TEL: 01789 297729; fax - 01789 297710; website - www.stratfordantiques.co.uk SER: Valuations; restorations. FAIRS: Newark; Ardingly; NEC; Earls Court.

The Stratford Bookshop
45A Rother St. CV37 6LT. (J. and S. Hill). Est. 1993. Open 10-6. SIZE: Medium. STOCK: Secondhand and out-of-print books. LOC: From island in town centre follow Wood St., left into Rother St., shop on corner of Ely St. PARK: Easy. TEL: 01789 298362; e-mail - thestratfordbookshop@btopenworld.com

STRETTON-ON-FOSSE

Astley House - Fine Art   LAPADA
The Old School. GL56 9SA. (David, Nanette and Caradoc Glaisyer). CADA. CINOA. Est. 1973. Open by appointment. SIZE: Large. STOCK: Large decorative oil paintings, 19th-21st C. LOC: Village centre. PARK: Easy. TEL: 01608 650601; fax - 01608 651777; e-mail - astart333@aol.com website - www.art-uk.com SER: Exhibitions; mailing list. VAT: Spec.

WARWICK

Duncan M. Allsop
68 Smith St. CV34 4HS. ABA. Est. 1965. Open 10-4.30. CL: Mon. SIZE: Medium. STOCK: Antiquarian and modern books. LOC: East Gate, opposite Roebuck Inn. PARK: Nearby. TEL: 01926 493266; fax - same; mobile - 07770 895924. FAIRS: Royal National Hotel.

Apollo Antiques   LAPADA
1A St Johns. CV34 4NR. (J. Mynott). Est. 1968. Usually

PRATT WARE

English and Scottish relief decorated and underglaze coloured earthenware

1780-1840

Nelson

John and Griselda Lewis
with an introduction by
Jonathan Horne

Specifications: 304pp.,
colour and b.&w.,
9½ x 7¾in./240 x 195mm.
£25.00 (hardback)

open Mon.-Fri., prior telephone call advisable. SIZE: Large. *STOCK: English furniture, 17th-20th C; Arts and Crafts and decorative items.* PARK: Easy. TEL: 01926 494666; fax - 01926 401477; e-mail - mynott@ apolloantiques.com website - www.apolloantiques.com VAT: Stan/Spec

William J. Casey Antiques   **LAPADA**
9 High St. CV34 4AP. (William and Pat Casey). Est. 1970. Open 10-5, Sun. by appointment. SIZE: Large. *STOCK: Furniture, 18th-20th C, £750-£7,500.* LOC: Town centre. PARK: Nearby. TEL: 01926 499199; home - 01562 777507. VAT: Spec.

Castle Antiques
24 Swan St. CV34 4BJ. (Julia Reynolds). Est. 1979. Open 10-5, Sun. by appointment. SIZE: Medium. *STOCK: China including Shelley, linen, silver, jewellery, furniture, 19th to early 20th C, £100-£3,000.* LOC: Town centre. PARK: Easy - at rear. TEL: 01926 401511; fax - 01926 492469. SER: Restorations (ceramics). VAT: Spec.

Entente Cordiale
9 High St. CV34 4AP. (Mrs C.M. Robson). Est. 2000. Open 10-5, Sun. by appointment. SIZE: Large. *STOCK: English and French furniture, especially small decorative and occasional, pairs of tables and upholstery.* LOC: Town centre. PARK: Nearby. TEL: 01926 499199; mobile - 07754 774491. VAT: Spec.

Russell Lane Antiques
2-4 High St. CV34 4AP. (R.G.H. Lane). Open 10-5. *STOCK: Fine jewellery and silver.* TEL: 01926 494494; fax - 01926 492972; e-mail - russell.laneantiques@ virgin.net

Patrick and Gillian Morley Antiques   **LAPADA**
62 West St. CV34 6AW. Est. 1968. Open Tues.-Fri. 10-5 or by appointment. SIZE: Large. *STOCK: Furniture, 17th to late 19th C; unusual and decorative items, sculpture, carvings; all £250-£100,000.* PARK: Easy. TEL: 01926 494464; mobile - 07768 835040; e-mail - morleyantiques@tinyworld.co.uk VAT: Spec.

James Reeve
at Quinneys of Warwick, 9 Church St. CV34 4AB. (J.C. and D.J. Reeve). Est. 1865. Open 9.30-5.30. CL: Sat. pm. *STOCK: Furniture, mahogany, oak, and rosewood, 17th-18th C, £80-£30,000; furniture, 19th C, £50-£10,000; glass, copper, brass, pewter, china.* LOC: Town centre. PARK: Easy. TEL: 01926 498113. SER: Restorations; re-polishing. VAT: Stan/Spec.

Summersons
172 Emscote Rd. CV34 5QN. (Peter Lightfoot). BHI. Est. 1969. Open 10-5, Sat. 10-1. SIZE: Small. *STOCK: Clocks and barometers.* LOC: A445 Rugby Rd. PARK: Free. TEL: 01926 400630; fax - same; mobile - 07770 300695; e-mail - clocks@summersons.com website - www.summersons.com SER: Restorations; repairs; materials and parts. VAT: Spec.

Tango Antiques
46 Brook St. CV34 4BL. (Jenny and Martin Wills). Open Thurs., Fri. and Sat. 10-5. SIZE: Medium. *STOCK: 19th-20th C furniture and accessories, pottery including*

ℐAMES REEVE

9 Church Street, Warwick, CV34 4AB Tel 01926-498113 Email: jamesreeve@callnetuk.com

Antique English furniture of the 17th, 18th and 19th centuries. All items are sold in the finest condition.

Established over 150 years

Clarice Cliff, £20-£2,000. LOC: Town centre. PARK: Free nearby. TEL: 01926 496999; home - 0121 704 4969; e-mail - info@tango-artdeco.co.uk website - www.tango-artdeco.co.uk

Vintage Antiques Centre
36 Market Place. CV34 4SH. (Peter Sellors). Est. 1977. Open 10-5.30, Sun. 11.30-4.30. SIZE: 15 dealers + cabinets. *STOCK: Ceramics, glass, collectables and small furniture, 19th-20th C.* LOC: Town centre. PARK: Easy. TEL: 01926 491527; e-mail - vintage@globalnet. co.uk FAIRS: NEC; National Glass.

The Warwick Antique Centre
20-22 High St. CV34 4AP. (P.E. Viola). BNTA. Est. 1973. Open 10-5. SIZE: 25 dealers. *STOCK: Porcelain, silver and plate, jewellery, coins, militaria, books, furniture, stamps, metalware, toys, collectables, postcards, glass.* PARK: Easy. TEL: 01926 491382/495704.

WOOTTON WAWEN, Nr. Henley-in-Arden

Le Grenier Antiques
Yew Tree Craft Centre, Stratford Rd. B95 6BY. (Joyce Ellis and Clive Evans). Est. 1991. Open 9-5, Sat. and Sun. 10-5. CL: Mon. SIZE: Medium. *STOCK: French furniture, mainly beds, bedroom furniture, tables, chairs, armoires and buffet cabinets. Made to measure bases and mattresses.* LOC: A34. PARK: Easy. TEL: 01564 795401; mobile - 07712 126048; e-mail - info@ legrenierantiques.com website - www.legrenierantiques. com SER: Valuations; restorations.

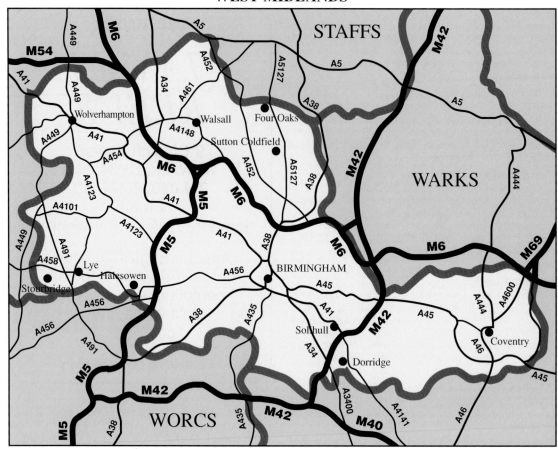

Dealers and Shops in the West Midlands

Birmingham	16	Four Oaks	1	Solihull	3	Walsall	2
Coventry	1	Halesowen	2	Stourbridge	3	Wolverhampton	5
Dorridge	1	Lye	1	Sutton Coldfield	2		

BIRMINGHAM

Peter Asbury Antiques
Greenfield House Farm, 6 Hales Lane, Smethwick, Warley. B67 6RS. (Mrs Susan Asbury). Est. 1986. Open 9.30-5. *STOCK: General antiques.* PARK: Limited. TEL: 0121 558 0579. SER: Repairs (dolls, teddy bears).

Paul Baxter
B47 6LS. Open by appointment. *STOCK: Oriental ceramics and general antiques.* TEL: 01564 824920.

The Birmingham Antique Centre
1403-1407 Pershore Rd., Stirchley. B30 2JR. (David Baldock and Sandra Arblaster). Est. 1960. Open 9-5, Sun. 10-4. SIZE: 3 showrooms, 60 cabinets. *STOCK: General antiques, collectables, jewellery, Clarice Cliff, Royal Doulton, Oriental art, toys.* LOC: Corner with Maryvale Rd. PARK: Free at rear. TEL: 0121 459 4587. e-mail - bhamantiquecent@aol.com website - www.birminghamantiquecentre.co.uk

Chesterfield Antiques
181 Gravelly Lane. B23 5SG. (Mara Cirjanic). Est. 1977. Open 9.30-5.30. *STOCK: General antiques and fine art.* TEL: 0121 373 3876.

Peter Clark Antiques   LAPADA
36 St. Mary's Row, Moseley. B13 8JG. Est. 1969. Open 9-5.30. SIZE: Medium. *STOCK: Furniture, 18th C to mid 19th C, £500-£15,000.* LOC: Centre of Moseley. PARK: At rear. TEL: 0121 449 8245; e-mail - peterclarkantiques@btopenworld.com website - www.peterclarkantiques.com SER: Valuations; restorations (furniture). VAT: Stan/Spec.

R. Collyer
185 New Rd., Rubery. B45 9JP. Est. 1947. Open 9.15-5.30. *STOCK: Secondhand jewellery.* LOC: 1 mile from junction 4, M5. PARK: Free. TEL: 0121 453 2332. SER: Valuations; restorations.

Dolly Mixtures
B68 0AU. Est. 1979. Open by appointment. *STOCK: Dolls and teddies.* TEL: 0121 422 6959. SER: Restorations.

Maurice Fellows
21 Vyse St., Hockley. B18 6LE. *STOCK: Objets d'art, jewellery.* TEL: 0121 554 0211. SER: Valuations; restorations.

Format of Birmingham Ltd
18 Bennetts Hill. B2 5QJ. (G. Charman and D. Vice). Open 9.30-5. CL: Sat. *STOCK: Coins, medals.* PARK: New St. station. TEL: 0121 643 2058. VAT: Stan/Spec.

A.W. Hone and Son Oriental Carpets
1486 Stratford Rd., Hall Green. B28 9ET. (Ian Hone). BORDA. Est. 1949. Open 9.30-5.30, Sun. 11-4. SIZE: Medium. *STOCK: Persian rugs and carpets, late 19th C to date.* LOC: A34 south of city on Robin Hood Island. PARK: Own forecourt. TEL: 0121 744 1001; fax - same; e-mail - honerugs@btopenworld.com website - www.honerugs.co.uk SER: Valuations; restorations; finder. VAT: Stan.

Rex Johnson and Sons
8 Corporation St. B2 4RN. (D. Johnson). Open 9.15-5.15. *STOCK: Gold, silver, jewellery, porcelain and glass.* TEL: 0121 643 9674; website - www.rexjohnson.com

F. Meeks & Co
197 Warstone Lane, Hockley. B18 6JR. (M.L. and S.R. Durham). Open 9-5, Sat. 9-12. *STOCK: Clocks especially longcase, mantel and wall; vintage wrist watches and antique pocket watches; all £100-£10,000.* TEL: 0121 236 9058. SER: Valuations; restorations (clocks); clock and watch parts supplied. VAT: Stan/Spec.

Moseley Emporium
116 Alcester Rd., Moseley. B13 3EF. (G. Dorney). Est. 1982. Open 10-6. SIZE: Medium. *STOCK: Georgian to 1930s furniture, £75-£3,800.* PARK: Easy. TEL: 0121 449 3441; mobile - 07973 156902. SER: Restorations (stripping, polishing, finishing furniture). FAIRS: Newark.

Piccadilly Jewellers
105 New St. B2 4HD. (R. and R. Johnson). Open 10-5. *STOCK: Jewellery, silver and objects.* TEL: 0121 643 5791.

David Temperley Fine and Antiquarian Books
19 Rotton Park Rd., Edgbaston. B16 9JH. (D. and R.A. Temperley). Resident. Est. 1967. Open 9.30-5.30 by appointment. SIZE: Small. *STOCK: Fine antiquarian and rare books, 16th-20th C especially fine bindings, illustrated and private press; fine colour plate books - natural history, costume, travel; British topography and atlases; children's books, especially moveable and pop-up; early and rare English and European playing cards.* LOC: 150 yards off Hagley Rd. (A456) and under 2 miles from city centre. 4 miles junction 3, M5. PARK: Easy. TEL: 0121 454 0135; fax - 0121 454 1124. SER: Valuations; restorations (book binding and paper); buys at auction (antiquarian books).

S. and E.M. Turner Violins
1 Gibb St., Digbeth. B9 4AA. (Steve and Liz Turner). Est. 1987. Open 9-6. *STOCK: 18th-20th C violins, violas, cellos, basses, bows; old flutes, clarinets, concertinas, guitars, harps, oboes and saxophones.* TEL: 0121 772 7708; fax - 0121 772 6796; mobile - 07831 265272; e-mail - info@turnerviolins.co.uk website - www.turnerviolins.co.uk SER: Valuations; restorations.

COVENTRY

Antiques Adventure
Rugby Rd., Binley Woods. CV3 2AW. (N. and J. Green). Est. 1969. Open 10-5 including Sun. SIZE: Large. *STOCK: Georgian, Victorian, Edwardian, contemporary, 1950s and 1960s furniture and effects; French and Chinese furniture, jewellery.* LOC: Just off A46 eastern bypass, entrance off A428 Rugby road. PARK: Easy. TEL: 02476 453878; fax - 02476 445847; e-mail - sales@antiquesadventure.com website - www.antiquesadventure.com SER: Delivery (UK); shipping advice. VAT: Global/Spec/Stan.

DORRIDGE, Nr. Solihull

Dorridge Antiques & Collectables
7 Forest Court. B93 8HN. (Colleen Swift). Est. 1995. Open 11-5.30. SIZE: 2 floors. *STOCK: Furniture, ceramics, silver, militaria, paintings and prints, glass, general antiques and collectables.* LOC: Between Birmingham and Stratford, 10 mins. from NEC. PARK: Free. TEL: 01564 779336 and 01564 779768 (ansaphone).

FOUR OAKS, Nr. Sutton Coldfield

M. Allen Watch and Clockmaker
76A Walsall Rd. B74 4QY. (M.A. Allen). Est. 1969. Open 9-5.30, Sun. by appointment. SIZE: Small. *STOCK: Vintage wristwatches - Omega, Longines, Girard, Perregaux and Jaeger le Coultre; clocks - Vienna regulators, 1820-1880, mantel and wall clocks.* LOC: By Sutton Park, close to television mast. PARK: Easy. TEL: 0121 308 6117; home - 0121 308 8134. SER: Valuations; restorations (clocks and watches). VAT: Stan/Spec.

HALESOWEN

S.R. Furnishing and Antiques
Unit 1, Eagle Trading Estate, Stourbridge Rd. B63 3UA. (S. Wildder). Est. 1975. *STOCK: General antiques and shipping furniture.* TEL: Mobile - 07860 820221.

Tudor House Antiques
68 Long Lane. B62 9LS. (D. Taylor). Open 9.30-5.30. *STOCK: Doors, fireplaces, pine including kitchens and furniture.* TEL: 0121 561 5563.

LYE, Nr. Stourbridge

Lye Antique Furnishings
206 High St. DY9 8JY. (P. Smith). Est. 1979. Open 9-5. SIZE: Medium. *STOCK: Furniture, china, glass, metalware, jewellery and collectors' items.* PARK: Easy. TEL: 01384 897513; mobile - 07976 765142. SER: Valuations.

SOLIHULL

Renaissance
18 Marshall Lake Rd., Shirley. B90 4PL. (S.K. Macrow).
GMC. Est. 1981. Open 9-5. SIZE: Small. *STOCK: General antiques.* LOC: Near Stratford Rd. TEL: 0121 745 5140.
SER: Restorations (repairs, re-upholstery and polishing).

Tilleys Antiques
B91 2ES. (S.A. Alpren). GADAR. Est. 1970. Open by appointment. *STOCK: British glass, Oriental pottery, porcelain, shipping goods; silver, 19th C; Worcester.*
TEL: 0121 704 1813. SER: Valuations; restorations (jewellery, silver); repairs (clocks and watches).

Yoxall Antiques
68 Yoxall Rd. B90 3RP. (Paul Burrows). Est. 1984. Open 9.30-5. SIZE: Medium. *STOCK: Georgian and Regency furniture including mahogany, walnut and rosewood; clocks and barometers, glass and china; desks, tea caddies, figures.* LOC: Just outside town centre. PARK: Easy. TEL: 0121 744 1744; mobile - 07860 168078; e-mail - sales@yoxallantiques.co.uk website - www.yoxallantiques.co.uk SER: Valuations; restorations (furniture). FAIRS: NEC.

STOURBRIDGE

Oldswinford Gallery
106 Hagley Rd., Oldswinford. DY8 1QU. (A.R. Harris). Open 9.30-5. CL: Mon. and Sat. p.m. *STOCK: 18th-20th C oil paintings, watercolours, antiquarian prints and maps.* TEL: 01384 395577. SER: Restorations; framing.

Regency Antique Trading Ltd.
116 Stourbridge Rd. DY9 7BU. (D. Bevan). Open 9.30-5. SIZE: 2 floors. *STOCK: General antiques and collectables, fireplaces and pine.* PARK: Free. TEL: 01384 868778; fax - 01384 825466; e-mail - regency tradingltd@blueyonder.co.uk website - www.regency-antiques.co.uk SER: Stripping; container shipping; fireplaces and kitchens from reclaimed pine.

Retro
48 Worcester St. DY8 1AS. (M. McHugo). Est. 1978. Open 9.30-5. *STOCK: Furniture and architectural items.* TEL: 01384 442065; mobile - 07929 082076; e-mail - info@retroantiques.co.uk website - www.retroantiques.co.uk

SUTTON COLDFIELD

Thomas Coulborn and Sons BADA
Vesey Manor, 64 Birmingham Rd. B72 1QP. (Peter, Alison, Jonathan and James Coulborn). Est. 1939. Open 9.30-1 and 2-5.30, Sat. 10-1 and 2-4, other times by appointment. SIZE: Large. *STOCK: General antiques, 1600-1830; fine English and Continental furniture, 17th-18th C; paintings and clocks.* **LOC: 3 miles from Spaghetti Junction. From Birmingham A5127 through Erdington, premises on main road opposite cinema. PARK: Easy. TEL: 0121 354 3974; fax - 0121 354 4614; e-mail - jc@coulborn.com website - www.coulborn.com SER: Valuations; restorations (furniture and paintings); buys on commission. VAT: Spec.**

Driffold Gallery
78 Birmingham Rd. B72 1QR. (David Gilbert). Est.

1974. Open 10.30-6. SIZE: Medium. *STOCK: Oil paintings and watercolours, 19th C to contemporary.* LOC: Town centre approach. PARK: Own. TEL: 0121 355 5433. SER: Valuations; restorations.

WALSALL

The Doghouse (Antiques)
309 Bloxwich Rd. WS2 7BD. (John and Kate Rutter). Est. 1971. Open 9-5.30, Sun. (Oct.-March) 2-5.30. SIZE: Large. *STOCK: General antiques, fireplaces, architectural items.* LOC: B4210. PARK: At rear. TEL: 01922 630829; fax - 01922 631236; website - www. doghouseantiques.co.uk VAT: Stan/Spec/Global.

L.P. Furniture Ltd
The Old Brewery, Short Acre St. WS2 8HW. (Pierre Farouz). Est. 1982. Open daily, Sun. by appointment. SIZE: Warehouse. *STOCK: French, Spanish and Continental including French and Spanish decorative furniture - armoires, buffets, beds, mirrors; French style reproduction mirrors, consoles, tables, chairs and Deco furniture.* LOC: Junction 10, M6, A454 towards town centre, left on A34 towards Cannock. PARK: Own. TEL: 01922 746764; fax - 01922 611316; e-mail - pierre. farouz@btconnect.com website - www.lpfurniture.co.uk and www.lpantiques.net and www.somethingfrench.net FAIRS: Swinderby. VAT: Stan.

WOLVERHAMPTON

Antiquities
75-76 Dudley Rd. WV2 3BY. Est. 1968. Open 10-6. *STOCK: General antiques.* TEL: 01902 459800.

No 9 Antiques
9 Upper Green, Tettenhall. WV6 8QQ. 1995. Open 10-5.30. CL: Mon. and Tues. SIZE: Medium. *STOCK: Furniture, 18th-19th C, £200-£1,000; ceramics, silver and prints, 19th C, £25-£500; works of art, £25-£100.* LOC: Corner of the Green. PARK: Easy. TEL: 01902 755333.

The Red Shop
7 Hollybush Lane, Penn. WV4 4JJ. (B. Savage). Open 9.30-5.30. *STOCK: Furniture including pine.* TEL: 01902 342915.

Martin Taylor Antiques LAPADA
140b and 323 Tettenhall Rd. WV6 0BQ. Est. 1976. Open 8.30-5.30, Sat. 10-5 or by appointment. SIZE: Large + showroom. *STOCK: Furniture, mainly 1800-1930, for the UK, USA, Japanese and Italian markets, £50-£10,000.* LOC: One mile from town centre on A41. PARK: Easy. TEL: 01902 751166; showroom - 01902 751122; fax - 01902 746502; mobile - 07836 636524; home - 01785 284539; e-mail - enquiries@mtaylor-antiques.co.uk website - www.martintaylorantiques.com SER: Restorations; French polishing. VAT: Stan/Spec

Wolverhampton Antiques and Collectors Market
Basement of Retail Market, Salop St. WV3 0SF. Est. 1984. Open 9-4. CL: Mon. and Thurs. SIZE: 20 units. *STOCK: China, glass, jewellery, militaria, books and comics, linen, football memorabilia, 19th-20th C, £5-£1,000.* LOC: Wolverhampton ring road, exit Chapel Ash island, market signposted. PARK: Easy - Peel St. and Pitt St. TEL: 01902 555212.

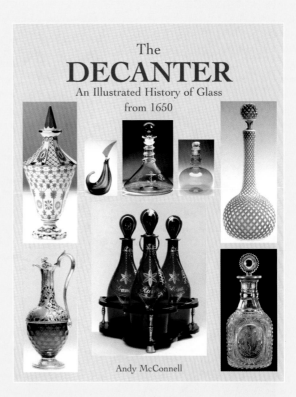

WILTSHIRE

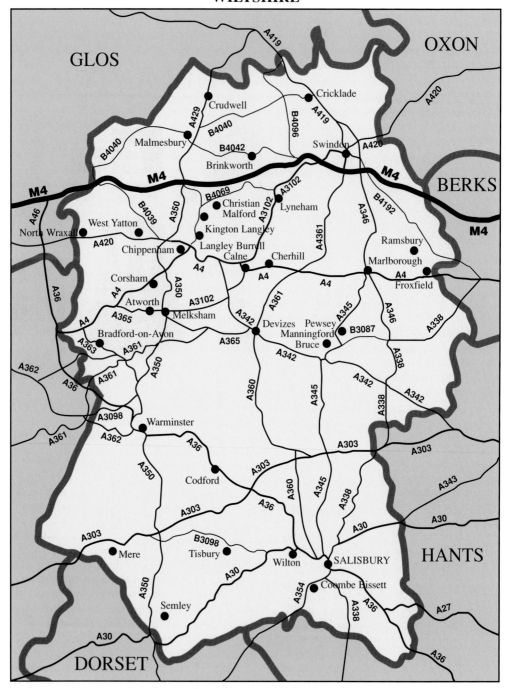

Dealers and Shops in Wiltshire

					Manningford Bruce	1	Salisbury	11
Atworth	1	Christian Malford	1	Devizes	3	Marlborough	4	Semley	1
Bradford-on-Avon	5	Codford	1	Froxfield	1	Melksham	4	Swindon	3
Brinkworth	1	Coombe Bissett	1	Kington Langley	1	Mere	1	Tisbury	1
Calne	3	Corsham	1	Langley Burrell	1	North Wraxhall	1	Warminster	8
Cherhill	1	Cricklade	1	Lyneham	1	Pewsey	1	West Yatton	1
Chippenham	1	Crudwell	1	Malmesbury	1	Ramsbury	2	Wilton	3

ATWORTH, Nr. Melksham

Peter Campbell Antiques
59 Bath Rd. SN12 8JY. (P.R. Campbell). Est. 1976. Open 10-5, Sun. and Mon. by appointment. SIZE: Medium. *STOCK: General antiques and decorative items, 18th-19th C.* Not Stocked: Silver and jewellery. LOC: Between Bath and Melksham on A365. PARK: Easy. TEL: 01225 709742; home - same. VAT: Stan/Spec.

BRADFORD-ON-AVON

Avon Antiques   BADA
25, 26 and 27 Market St. BA15 1LL. (V. and A. Jenkins BA). BABAADA. Est. 1963. Open 9.45-5.30, Sun. by appointment. SIZE: Large. *STOCK: English and some Continental furniture, 1600-1880; metalwork, treen, some clocks, barometers, textiles, painted furniture; English naive pictures.* LOC: A363, main street of town. PARK: Ask at shop for key to private parking opposite. TEL: 01225 862052; fax - 01225 868763; e-mail - avonantiques@aol.com website - www.avon-antiques.co.uk FAIRS: Grosvenor House; Olympia (winter). VAT: Spec.

Andrew Dando   BADA
34 Market St. BA15 1LL. (A.P. and J.M. Dando). BABAADA. Est. 1915. Open Tues.-Sat. 10-5, appointment recommended. SIZE: Medium. *STOCK: English (including Staffordshire), Continental and Oriental porcelain and pottery, 17th to mid-19th C; local topographical and decorative antique prints.* LOC: Town centre. PARK: Nearby. TEL: 01225 865444; e-mail - andrew@andrewdando.co.uk website - www.andrewdando.co.uk SER: Valuations. FAIRS: Olympia (June). VAT: Stan/Spec.

Mac Humble Antiques   BADA
7-9 Woolley St. BA15 1AD. (W. Mc. A. and B.J. Humble). BABAADA. Est. 1979. Open 9.30-5.30, Sat. 9.30-1. SIZE: Medium. *STOCK: 17th-19th C oak, mahogany, fruitwoods, metalware, treen, samplers, silkwork pictures, decorative objects.* PARK: Nearby. TEL: 01225 866329; fax - same; e-mail - mac.humble @virgin.net website - www.machumbleantiques. co.uk SER: Valuations; restorations. FAIRS: BADA (March); Olympia (Nov). VAT: Stan/Spec.

Moxhams Antiques   LAPADA
17 Silver St. BA15 1JZ. (R., J. and N. Bichard). BABAADA. Est. 1967. Open 9-5.30 or by appointment. SIZE: Large + store. *STOCK: English and Continental furniture, clocks, 1650-1850; European and Oriental pottery and porcelain, 1700-1850; decorative items, 1600-1900, all £50-£50,000.* LOC: Near town centre on B3107 towards Melksham. PARK: Own, at rear. TEL: 01225 862789; fax - 01225 867844; home - 01225 755026/01380 828677; e-mail - info@moxhams-antiques.demon.co.uk SER: Restorations. FAIRS: Olympia (June, Nov). VAT: Spec.

Trevor Waddington Antique Clocks
5 Trowbridge Rd. BA15 1EE. MBHI. BABAADA. Est. 1996. Strictly by appointment. SIZE: Small. *STOCK: 17th-19th C clocks - longcase, £3,000-£30,000; wall, £1,500-£7,000; carriage, bracket and mantel, £1,000-*

Trevor Waddington OBE
ANTIQUE CLOCKS

★ Offering quality antique clocks, restored and fully guaranteed   ★ Showroom open by appointment   ★ Stock details on request/website

Founded 1858
MEMBER OF THE
BRITISH HOROLOGICAL
INSTITUTE

5 TROWBRIDGE RD., BRADFORD ON AVON
Tel: 01225 862351
www.clocks-antique.co.uk

£9,000. LOC: Quarter mile south of town bridge on A363. PARK: Easy. TEL: 01225 862351; home/fax - same; e-mail - twclocks@aol.com website - www. clocks-antique.co.uk SER: Valuations; restorations (BADA/West Dean Dip. conservator).

BRINKWORTH, Nr. Malmesbury

North Wilts Exporters
Farm Hill House. SN15 5AJ. (M. Thornbury). Est. 1972. Open Mon.-Sat. or by appointment. *STOCK: Imported Continental pine, 18th-19th C; shipping goods.* LOC: Off M4, junction 16 Malmesbury road. TEL: 01666 510876; mobile - 07836 260730; e-mail - mike@ northwilts.demon.co.uk website - www.northwilts antiqueexporters.com SER: Valuations; shipping; import and export. VAT: Stan/Global.

CALNE

Calne Antiques
London Rd. SN11 0AB. (M. Blackford). GMC. Est. 1981. Open 10-5 seven days. *STOCK: Antique pine and country furniture, Victorian to 1930s; mahogany, oak and walnut.* LOC: A4, next to White Hart Hotel. PARK: Own. TEL: 01249 816311; fax - same. SER: Furniture made to order; free-standing kitchens.

Clive Farahar and Sophie Dupré - Rare Books, Autographs and Manuscripts
Horsebrook House, 15 The Green. SN11 8DQ. ABA. ILAB. PADA. UACC. Manuscript Society. Est. 1980. Open by appointment. SIZE: Medium. *STOCK: Rare books on voyages and travels, autograph letters and manuscripts, 15th-20th C, £5-£5,000+.* LOC: Off A4 in town centre. PARK: Easy. TEL: 01249 821121; fax - 01249 821202; e-mail - post@farahardupre.co.uk website - www.farahardupre.co.uk SER: Valuations; buys at auction (as stock). FAIRS: Universal Autograph Collectors' Club; Olympia (June). VAT: Stan.

Hilmarton Manor Press
Hilmarton Manor. SN11 8SB. (H. Baile de Laperriere). Est. 1967. Open 9-6. SIZE: Medium. *STOCK: New, out-of-print and antiquarian art related books including fine, applied, dictionaries and reference.* LOC: 3 miles from Calne on A3102 towards Swindon. PARK: Easy. TEL: 01249 760208; fax - 01249 760379. SER: Buys at auction; publishers of 'Who's Who in Art'.

CHERHILL, Nr. Calne

P.A. Oxley Antique Clocks and Barometers
LAPADA
The Old Rectory, Main Rd. SN11 8UX. BABAADA. Est. 1971. Open 9.30-5, other times by appointment. CL: Wed. SIZE: Large. *STOCK: Longcase, bracket, carriage clocks and barometers, 17th-19th C, £500-£30,000.* LOC: A4, not in village. PARK: Easy. TEL: 01249 816227; fax - 01249 821285; e-mail - info@paoxley.com website - www.british-antiqueclocks.com VAT: Spec.

CHIPPENHAM

Cross Hayes Antiques
LAPADA
Unit 6 Westbrook Farm, Draycot Cerne. SN15 5LH. (D. Brooks). BABAADA. Est. 1975. Open Mon.-Fri. 9-5, other times by appointment. SIZE: Warehouse. *STOCK: Furniture, 1850-1930, Victorian, Edwardian and shipping oak.* LOC: Off M4, junction 17 on B4122, premises 800 yards. PARK: Own. TEL: 01249 720033; fax - same; home - 01666 822062; e-mail - david@crosshayes.co.uk website - www.crosshayes.co.uk SER: Packing and shipping; courier (UK and France). VAT: Stan/Spec.

CHRISTIAN MALFORD, Nr. Chippenham

Harley Antiques
The Comedy. SN15 4BS. (G.J. Harley). Est. 1959. Open 9-6 including Sun. or later by appointment. SIZE: Large. *STOCK: Furniture, 18th-19th C, £250-£6,000; decorative objects, £30-£8,000.* LOC: B4069, 4 miles off M4, junction 17. PARK: Own. TEL: 01249 720112; home - same; fax - 01249 720553; e-mail - thecomedy.wilts@ukonline.co.uk website - www.harleyantiques.co.uk SER: Colour brochure available (export only). VAT: Stan. *Trade Only.*

CODFORD, Nr. Warminster

Tina's Antiques
75 High St. BA12 0ND. (T.A. Alder). Open 9-6, Sat. 9-4. *STOCK: General antiques.* PARK: Ample. TEL: 01985 850828.

COOMBE BISSETT, Nr. Salisbury

Edward Hurst
The Battery, Rockbourne Rd. SP5 4LP. Est. 1983. Usually open. SIZE: Medium. *STOCK: English furniture*

P.A.Oxley

Antique Clocks & Barometers
Established 1971

**The Old Rectory · Cherhill · Near Calne
Wiltshire SN11 8UX**
Telephone (01249) 816227 Fax (01249) 821285
**Visit our Web site - Full stock & prices
www.british-antiqueclocks.com
E-mail: info@paoxley.com**

Established in 1971, P.A. Oxley is one of the
largest quality antique clock and barometer
dealers in the U.K. Current stock includes over
30 quality restored **longcase clocks** ranging in
price from £3,500 to £30,000. In addition we
have a fine selection of **bracket clocks,
carriage clocks** and **barometers**.

We do not exhibit at antique fairs, and
therefore our extensive stock can only be viewed
at our large showrooms on the main A4 London
to Bath road at Cherhill or on our website
address shown above.

**Full shipping facilities are available to any
country in the world.** U.K. customers are
provided with a free delivery and setting up service
combined with a twelve month guarantee.

**If your desire is for a genuine antique clock
or barometer** then please visit us at Cherhill
where you can examine our large stock and
discuss your exact requirement. If time is short
and you cannot visit us we will send you a
selection of colour photographs from which you
can buy with confidence.

**Hours of opening are 9.30-5.00 every day
except Wednesday.** Sunday and evening
appointments can easily be arranged. We look
forward to welcoming you to our establishment.

The Association of Art and Antique Dealers

and associated works of art, 1650-1820. LOC: Just west of Salisbury. PARK: Easy. TEL: 01722 718859; mobile - 07768 255557. FAIRS: Olympia (June, Nov). VAT: Spec.

CORSHAM

Matthew Eden
Pickwick End. SN13 0JB. Resident. Est. 1951. SIZE: Large. *STOCK: Country house furniture and garden items, 17th-19th C.* LOC: A4 between Chippenham and Bath. TEL: 01249 713335; fax - 01249 713644. SER: Shipping. FAIRS: Chelsea Flower Show. VAT: Spec.

CRICKLADE, Nr. Swindon

Edred A.F. Gwilliam
Candletree House, Bath Rd. SN6 6AX. Est. 1976. Open by appointment. SIZE: Medium. *STOCK: Arms and armour, swords, pistols, long guns, £50-£20,000+.* PARK: Easy. TEL: 01793 750241; fax - 01793 750359. SER: Valuations; buys at auction. FAIRS: Major arms. VAT: Stan/Spec.

CRUDWELL

Philip A. Ruttleigh Antiques incorporating Crudwell Furniture
Odd Penny Farm. SN16 9SJ. Est. 1990. Open 9-5 and by appointment. CL: Sat. SIZE: Small. *STOCK: Furniture including pine in the paint, and decorative items, £10-£3,000.* LOC: Next to RAF Kemble on A429, 5 minutes from Cirencester, 15 mins. from junction 17, M4. PARK: Easy. TEL: 01285 770970; website - www.crudwell furniture.co.uk SER: Furniture restoration, including stripping; bead blasting for architectural antiques.

DEVIZES

Cross Keys Jewellers
The Ginnel, Market Pl. SN10 1HN. (D. and D. Pullen). Est. 1967. Open 9-5. *STOCK: Jewellery, silver.* LOC: Alley adjacent Nationwide Building Society. PARK: Easy. TEL: 01380 726293. SER: Valuations; repairs; restringing (pearls). VAT: Stan.

St Mary's Chapel Antiques
Northgate St. SN10 1JL. (Richard Sankey). Est. 1971. Open 10-6, Wed. by appointment. SIZE: Large. *STOCK: Original painted and Continental furniture, decorative accessories, garden items.* LOC: Just off market square. PARK: Easy. TEL: 01380 721399; e-mail - richard@ rsankey.freeserve.co.uk SER: Restorations. FAIRS: BABAADA.

Upstairs, Downstairs Collectors Centre
40 Market Place. SN10 3DL. (J. Coom). Est. 2002. Open 9.30-4.30, Sun. 9.30-3. CL: Wed. SIZE: Large. *STOCK: Oak, mahogany and pine furniture, toys, dolls and teddies, postcards, records, china, glass, prints, militaria, clocks and books.* LOC: Next to Lloyds TSB. PARK: Free, 1 hr. TEL: 01380 730266; fax - same; e-mail - devizesantiques@btconnect.com SER: Valuations; restorations (dolls and teddies); clock repairs. FAIRS: Newark, Ardingly, Kensington, Carmarthen, NEC, Sandown.

FROXFIELD, Nr. Marlborough

Blanchard   LAPADA
Bath Rd. SN8 3LD. Est. 1940. Open 9.30-5.30. SIZE: Large. *STOCK: 18th-20th C antiques and decorative pieces including garden furniture.* PARK: Easy. TEL: 01488 680666; fax - 01488 680668. FAIRS: Olympia (June).

KINGTON LANGLEY

Willow UK
Church Farm, Middle Common. SN15 5NN. (Willow Bicknell). Resident. Est. 1990. Open by appointment. SIZE: Medium. *STOCK: Furniture, objects and art for home and garden, 1770-1970; contemporary designed furniture and home wares.* LOC: Junction 17, M4. A350 to Chippenham, within mile of traffic lights, turn left. Church Farm on right, opposite church. PARK: Easy. TEL: 01249 758333; fax - same; mobile - 07770 554559; e-mail - willow@willowuk.com website - www. willowuk.com SER: Finder; copy and design; interior and exterior design. FAIRS: TVADA. VAT: Spec.

LANGLEY BURRELL, Nr. Chippenham

Harriet Fairfax Fireplaces and General Antiques
Langley Green. SN15 4LL. Est. 1971. Open by appointment. *STOCK: China, glass, dolls, furniture, fabrics and needlework; architectural items and fittings, brass and iron knobs, knockers; fireplaces, pine and iron, 1780-1950.* TEL: 01249 655889. SER: Design consultancy.

LYNEHAM, Nr. Chippenham

Pillars Antiques
10 The Banks. SN15 4NS. (K. Clifford). Resident. Est. 1986. Open 10-5, including Sun. CL: Wed. and Thurs. SIZE: Large. *STOCK: Victorian and Edwardian pine, shipping oak.* LOC: B4069 Chippenham road, 1 mile from village. PARK: Easy. TEL: 01249 890632; home - same; e-mail - enquiries@pillarsantiques.com website - www.pillarsantiques.com VAT: Global.

MALMESBURY

Antiques - Rene Nicholls
56 High St. SN16 9AT. (Mrs R. Nicholls). Est. 1980. Open 10-5.30, Sun. by appointment. SIZE: Small. *STOCK: English pottery and porcelain, 18th to early 19th C, £50-£900; small furniture.* PARK: Opposite. TEL: 01666 823089; home - same.

MANNINGFORD BRUCE

Indigo
Dairy Barn. SN9 6JW. (Richard Lightbown and Marion Bender). Est. 1982. Open 10-5, Sat. 10-4. SIZE: Large. *STOCK: Furniture and architectural items, decorative accessories from India, China, Japan and Tibet, from early 19th C, £10-£5,000.* LOC: A345 2 miles from Pewsey. PARK: Forecourt. TEL: 01672 564722; fax - 01672 564733; e-mail - antiques@indigo-uk.com website - www.indigo-uk.com SER: Collection from Pewsey station by arrangement; importers; restorers. VAT: Stan.

MARLBOROUGH

William Cook (Marlborough)   **LAPADA**
High Trees House, Savernake Forest. SN8 4NE. (W.J. Cook). BAFRA. Est. 1963. Open by appointment. SIZE: Medium. *STOCK: Furniture, 18th to early 19th C; objets d'art, 18th-19th C.* LOC: 1.5 miles from Marlborough on A346 towards Burbage. PARK: Easy. TEL: 01672 513017; fax - 01672 514455. SER: Valuations; restorations (furniture including polishing and gilding); buys at auction (furniture). FAIRS: Olympia; Harrogate; Claridges; Chester; Tatton Park. VAT: Stan/Spec.

Katharine House Gallery
Katharine House, The Parade. SN8 1NE. (C.C. Gange). Est. 1983. Open 10-5.30. SIZE: Medium. *STOCK: Furniture, 18th-19th C, £200-£2,000; decorative items, £100-£1,000; Chinese, Roman and Greek antiquities, 2000BC-1000AD, £100-£1,000; 20th C British paintings and prints, £50-£5,000; books, £5-£500.* PARK: Easy. TEL: 01672 514040; home - same. VAT: Spec.

The Marlborough Parade Antique Centre
The Parade. SN8 1NE. (G. Wilkinson and P. Morgan). Est. 1985. Open 10-5 including Sun. SIZE: 40 dealers. *STOCK: Furniture, paintings, silver, porcelain, glass, clocks, jewellery, copper, brass and pewter, £5-£5,000.* LOC: Adjacent A4 in town centre. PARK: Easy. TEL: 01672 515331. SER: Valuations; restorations (furniture, porcelain, copper, brass). VAT: Spec.

The Military Parade Bookshop
The Parade. SN8 1NE. (G. and P. Kent). Est. 1988. Open 10.30-1 and 2-5. *STOCK: Military history books especially regimental histories and the World Wars.* LOC: Next to The Lamb. TEL: 01672 515470; fax - 01980 630150; e-mail - enquiry@militaryparadebooks.com website - www.militaryparadebooks.com

MELKSHAM

Dann Antiques Ltd
Unit 1, Avonside Enterprise Park, New Broughton Rd. SN12 8BS. (G. Low). BABAADA. Est. 1983. Open 9-5.30, Sat. 9.30-3.30. SIZE: Large. *STOCK: 18th-19th C English furniture; French and decorative pieces, lighting, fenders, mirrors, pottery, porcelain.* PARK: Own. TEL: 01225 707329; fax - 01225 790120; e-mail - sales@dannantiques.com website - www.dannantiques. com. SER: Restorations. VAT: Stan/Spec.

Alan Jaffray
16 Market Place. SN12 6EX. BABAADA. Est. 1956. Open Mon.-Fri. 9-5. SIZE: Large. *STOCK: Furniture and smalls, 18th-19th C, £50-£2,000.* LOC: Main Bath to Devizes Road. PARK: On premises. TEL: 01225 702269; fax - 01225 790413; e-mail - jaffrayantiques@ fsmail.net VAT: Stan/Spec.

Andrew Jennings Antiques
1 Farmhouse Court, Bowerhill Park. SN12 6FG. Est. 2003. Open by appointment. SIZE: Small. *STOCK: Carvings and corkscrews, some early oak.* PARK: Easy. TEL: 01225 707400; mobile - 07957 121740; website - www. antiquecarvings.co.uk and www.antiquecorkscrews.co.uk

King Street Curios

8 King St. SN12 6HD. Est. 1991. Open 10-5. SIZE: 20 units. *STOCK: China, discontinued Denby, USSR, glass, jewellery, Art Deco, kitchenalia, furniture.* LOC: A350. PARK: Own at rear. TEL: 01225 790623. FAIRS: Oasis, Swindon; Neeld Hall, Chippenham; Templemeads (Brunel), Bristol; DMG.

MERE, Nr. Warminster

Louis Stanton   BADA
Woodlands Farm, Woodlands Rd. BA12 6BY. (L.R. and S.A. Stanton). CINOA. Est. 1965. Open by appointment. *STOCK: Early English oak furniture, medieval sculpture and works of art, metalware, unusual decorative items.* **TEL: 01747 860747; fax - same. SER: Valuations; buys at auction.**

NORTH WRAXALL, Nr. Chippenham

Delomosne and Son Ltd   BADA
Court Close. SN14 7AD. (T.N.M. Osborne and M.C.F. Mortimer). BABAADA. Articles on chandeliers, glass and porcelain. Est. 1905. Open Mon.-Fri. 9.30-5.30, other times by appointment. SIZE: Large. *STOCK: English and Irish glass, pre-1830, £20-£20,000; glass chandeliers, English and European porcelain, needlework, papier mâché and treen.* **LOC: Off A420 between Bristol and Chippenham. PARK: Easy. TEL: 01225 891505; fax - 01225 891907; website - www.delomosne.co.uk SER: Valuations; buys at auction. FAIRS: Winter Olympia; Grosvenor House. VAT: Spec.**

PEWSEY

Time Restored Ltd
18-20 High St. SN9 5AQ. (J.H. Bowler-Reed and D.I. Rider). Est. 1975. Open 10-6. SIZE: Small. *STOCK: Clocks, barometers and musical boxes.* LOC: Village centre. PARK: Free at rear of premises. TEL: 01672 563544; e-mail - time.restored@btopenworld.com website - www.timerestored.co.uk SER: Valuations; restorations.

RAMSBURY, Nr. Marlborough

Heraldry Today
Parliament Piece. SN8 2QH. (Mrs Rosemary Pinches). ABA. ILAB. Est. 1954. Open 9.30-4.30. CL: Sat. SIZE: Medium. *STOCK: Heraldic and genealogical books and manuscripts, £3-£10,000.* PARK: Own. TEL: 01672 520617; fax - 01672 520183; e-mail - heraldry@ heraldrytoday.co.uk website - www.heraldrytoday.co.uk SER: Book search; catalogues.

Inglenook Antiques
59 High St. SN8 2QN. (Dennis White). Est. 1969. Open 10-1 and 2-5, prior telephone call advisable. CL: Mon. and Wed. except by appointment. SIZE: Small. *STOCK: Oil lamps, £50-£850; clocks, barometers and spare parts, £150-£4,000; some furniture.* LOC: 3 miles from A4 between Hungerford and Marlborough. PARK: Easy. TEL: 01672 520261; home - same. SER: Restorations (longcase clock movements only).

SALISBURY

21st Century Antics
13 Brown St. SP1 1HE. (David, Geraldine, Jonathan and Ben Scott). Est. 1988. Open 9-5.30. SIZE: Large. *STOCK: Furniture, Georgian to date, £30-£3,000; small collectables, £2-£250.* PARK: Own. TEL: 01722 337421; fax - same; e-mail - Dave.21stcenturyantics@ virgin.net website - www.21stcenturyantics.co.uk

Antique and Collectors Market
37 Catherine St. SP1 2DH. (Peter Beck). Est. 1977. Open 10-5. SIZE: Large. *STOCK: Silver, plate, china, glass, toys, books, prints, pens, furniture, Art Deco, antiquities.* LOC: City centre. PARK: Nearby. TEL: 01722 326033/338487; website - www.salisburyantiques.com SER: Silver plating; repairs.

The Avonbridge Antiques and Collectors Market
United Reformed Church Hall, Fisherton St. SP2 7RG. Open Tues. 9-3.30. SIZE: 15 dealers. *STOCK: General antiques.* LOC: Opposite old hospital. PARK: Nearby. TEL: 01202 669061.

Boston Antiques
223 Wilton Rd. SP2 7JY. Est. 1964. Open by appointment any time. SIZE: Medium. *STOCK: Fine rare world furniture, 16th-19th C.* LOC: Main A36 at Skew Bridge, on edge of city. PARK: Nearby. TEL: 01722 322682; mobile - 07713 756439; e-mail - daboston@gotadsl.co.uk VAT: Stan/Spec.

Robert Bradley Antiques
71 Brown St. SP1 2BA. Est. 1970. Open 9.30-5.30. CL: Sat. *STOCK: Furniture, 17th-18th C; decorative items.* TEL: 01722 333677; fax - 01722 339922. VAT: Spec.

Ronald Carr
6 St. Francis Rd. SP1 3QS. (R.G. Carr). Est. 1983. Open by appointment. SIZE: Small. *STOCK: Modern British etchings, wood engravings and colour wood cuts, £5-£1,000.* LOC: 1 mile north of city on A345. PARK: Easy. TEL: 01722 328892; home - same. SER: Buys at auction.

Castle Galleries
81 Castle St. SP1 3SP. (John C. Lodge). Est. 1971. Open 9-4.30, Sat. 9-1. CL: Mon. and Wed. *STOCK: Coins and medals, jewellery and objets d'art.* PARK: Easy. TEL: 01722 333734; mobile - 07709 203745; e-mail - john.lodge1@tesco.net SER: Medal mounting and framing; miniature medals supplied and mounted.

Myriad
48-54 Milford St. SP1 2BP. (Karen Montlake and Stuart Hardy). Est. 1982. Open 9.30-5, Sat. 10-5, other times by appointment. SIZE: Large. *STOCK: Georgian mahogany, oak and pine - chairs, corner cupboards, wardrobes, dressers, tables, chests of drawers, coffers; Victorian mahogany, pine and fruitwood - chests of drawers, wardrobes, chairs, dressing tables and dressing chests, boxes, kitchen and dining tables.* LOC: Near town centre. PARK: Culver St. TEL: 01722 413595; fax - 01722 416395; home - 01722 718203; mobile - 07775 627662; e-mail - karen@myriad-antiques.co.uk website - www.myriad-antiques.co.uk SER: Restorations (furniture); free collection/delivery (30 mile radius). VAT: Spec.

Salisbury Antiques Warehouse Ltd   LAPADA
94 Wilton Rd. SP2 7JJ. (R.W. and Mrs C. Wallrock). Est. 1964. Open 9-5.30, Fri. 9-5, Sat.10-4, Sun. by appointment. SIZE: Large. *STOCK: 18th-19th C English and Continental furniture, decorative works of art, clocks and pictures, £1,000-£15,000; small items, £100-£1,000.* LOC: A36 Warminster-Southampton road. PARK: Easy. TEL: 01722 410634; fax - 01722 410635; mobile - 07768 877069; home - 01590 672515; e-mail - kevin@salisbury-antiques.co.uk SER: Restorations (gilding). VAT: Stan/Spec.

Mike Scott Repair & Restoration
Old Stables Workshop, 30 St. Edmunds Church St. SP1 1EF. Est. 1993. Open 9-5.30. SIZE: Small. *STOCK: Country furniture including Windsor arm chairs, 18th to early 20th C, £50-£1,000.* PARK: Own. TEL: 01722 323526; mobile - 07778 300316. SER: Restorations (furniture).

Chris Wadge Clocks
83 Fisherton St. SP2 7ST. (Patrick Wadge). Open 9-4. CL: Mon. *STOCK: Clocks and spare parts for 400 day clocks.* TEL: 01722 334467; e-mail - cwclocks@aol.com SER: 400 day clock specialist; repairs (antique/mechanical clocks).

SEMLEY

Dairy House Antiques
Station Rd. SP7 9AN. (A. Stevenson). Est. 1998. Open 9-5. SIZE: Large. *STOCK: Furniture, paintings, decorative items, 1600-1960.* LOC: Just off the A350, 2 miles north of Shaftesbury. PARK: Easy. TEL: 01747 853317. SER: Valuations. VAT: Spec.

SWINDON

Penny Farthing Antiques Arcade
Victoria Centre, 138/9 Victoria Rd., Old Town. SN1 3BU. (Ann Farthing). Est. 1999. Open 10-5. SIZE: Large. *STOCK: Furniture, silver, porcelain, watches, clocks.* LOC: On left on hill between Old Town and college. PARK: Prospect Place. TEL: 01793 536668. VAT: Stan.

Sambourne House Antiques Ltd
50-51 The Arcade, Brunel Shopping Centre. SN1 1LL. (T. and Mrs K. Cove). Est. 1984. Open 10-5, Sun. 10-4. SIZE: Large. *STOCK: Restored 19th C pine, £120-£2,000; reclaimed 19th C pine, £50-£1,500; reproduction smalls, £2-£90.* LOC: 1.5 miles from junction 16, M4. PARK: Easy. TEL: 01793 610855; fax - same. SER: Importer (antique pine); deliveries (S. England and Midlands). VAT: Stan.

Allan Smith Antique Clocks
162 Beechcroft Rd., Upper Stratton. SN2 7QE. Est. 1988. Open any time by appointment. SIZE: Large. *STOCK: 50-60 longcase clocks including automata, moonphase, painted dial, brass dial, 30 hour, 8 day, London and provincial, £1,950-£39,500; occasionally stick and banjo barometers, mantel, wall, bracket, Vienna and lantern clocks.* LOC: Near Bakers Arms Inn. PARK: Own. TEL: 01793 822977; fax - same; mobile - 07778 834342; e-mail - allansmithclocks@lineone.net website - www. allansmithantiqueclocks.co.uk VAT: Spec.

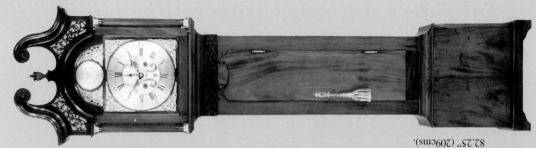

TISBURY, Nr. Salisbury

Heatons
2-3 High St. SP3 6PS. (Ros King). Open Mon., Fri. and Sat. 9-4 or by appointment. SIZE: Large. *STOCK: Original maps, prints, etchings and engravings, from 1600; furniture and decorative items, to 1960s designer pieces; modern art glass from Daum to Liskeard.* LOC: Top of hill. PARK: Limited and nearby. TEL: 01747 873025; fax - 01747 870059; evenings - 01747 870048; e-mail - rosking@freenetname.co.uk website - www.heatons-of-tisbury.co.uk SER: Valuations.

WARMINSTER

Cassidy's Antiques
7 Silver St. BA12 8PS. (M. Cassidy). BABAADA. Est. 1989. Open 9-5, Sat. 10-5. SIZE: Large - 2 floors. *STOCK: Furniture, 17th-19th C, £200-£5,000.* PARK: Outside shop. TEL: 01985 213313; e-mail - mat_cassidy @yahoo.co.uk website - www.cassidyantiques.com SER: Restorations (furniture and cabinet making).

Chloe
4 Silver St. BA12 8PS. (Chloe Cyphus). BABAADA. Est. 1977. Open Wed.-Sat. 10-5, other times by arrangement. SIZE: Medium. *STOCK: Decorative French and Swedish painted furniture; accessories including textiles and garden items, mainly 19th C, £10-£1,000.* PARK: Easy. TEL: 01985 218924; home - 01985 212767; mobile - 07977 127862; e-mail - cywoodjoinery @btconnect.com SER: Sewing commissions; sourcing. FAIRS: Bath Decorative; Brocante, Kensington.

Annabelle Giltsoff
3 Silver St. BA12 8PS. Est. 1983. Open 10-5. SIZE: Small. *STOCK: 18th-19th C gilt mirrors.* LOC: Main road through town. PARK: Easy. TEL: 01985 218933; e-mail - isabellaantiques@aol.com website - www. isabellaantiques.co.uk SER: Restorations (mirrors, frames and furniture gilding; oil paintings).

Isabella Antiques
3 Silver St. BA12 8PS. (B.W. Semke). BABAADA. Est. 1990. Open 10-5. SIZE: Medium. *STOCK: Furniture, late 18th C to late 19th C, £100-£5,000; boxes and mirrors, 19th C, £50-£1,000.* LOC: Main road. PARK: Easy. TEL: 01985 218933; e-mail - isabellaantiques @aol.com website - www.isabellaantiques.co.uk SER: Buys at auction (furniture). VAT: Spec.

Lewis Antiques & Interiors
9 Silver St. BA12 8PS. (Sandie Lewis). BABAADA. Est. 1985. Open Wed.-Sat. 10-5, or by appointment. SIZE: Small. *STOCK: Silver, glass, ceramics, textiles, jewellery, prints, metalware and painted furniture, 1800-1930s, £1-£1,000.* LOC: Town centre. PARK: Easy and nearby. TEL: 01985 846222; mobile - 07764 576106; e-mail - sandie.lewis@blueyonder.co.uk SER: Valuations; restorations (ceramics and furniture). FAIRS: BABAADA Bath.

Maxfield House Antiques
Maxfield House, 16 Silver St. BA12 8PS. (Rosemary Reynolds). Est. 1992. Open 10-5 or by appointment. SIZE: Small. *STOCK: Mainly English oak and mahogany, some painted, 18th-20th C; town and country furniture; pictures and decorative objects; all £50-£2,000.* LOC: Main Bath road leading into Silver St. PARK: Outside premises. TEL: 01985 212121; home - same; mobile - 07747 654244. e-mail - maxfield@x-router.com website - www.maxfield-antiques.com

Obelisk Antiques   LAPADA
2 Silver St. BA12 8PS. (P. Tanswell). BABAADA. Est. 1980. Open 10-1 and 2-5.30. SIZE: Large. *STOCK: English and Continental furniture, 18th-19th C; decorative items, objets d'art.* PARK: Easy. TEL: 01985 846646; fax - 01985 219901; e-mail - all@ obeliskantiques.com website - www.obeliskantiques. com VAT: Spec.

Warminster Antiques Centre
6 Silver St. BA12 8PT. (Peter Walton). BABAADA. Est. 1970. Open 10-5. SIZE: 15 dealers. *STOCK: Furniture, home embellishments, textiles, silver, jewellery, collectors' items.* PARK: Easy. TEL: 01985 847269; fax - 01985 211778; mobile - 07860 584193; e-mail - phwalton@btconnect.com website - www.warminster antiques.co.uk FAIRS: Newark.

WEST YATTON, Nr. Chippenham

Heirloom & Howard Limited
Manor Farm. SN14 7EU. (D.S. Howard). BABAADA. Est. 1972. Open by appointment. SIZE: Medium. *STOCK: Porcelain mainly Chinese armorial and export, 18th C, £100-£5,000; heraldic items, 18th-19th C, £10-£1,000; portrait engravings, 17th-19th C, £10-£50.* LOC: 10 miles from Bath, 1/4 mile off A420 Chippenham/Bristol road. Transport from Chippenham station (4 miles) if required. PARK: Own. TEL: 01249 783038; fax - 01249 783039; website - www.chinese-armorial-porcelain.co.uk SER: Valuations; buys at auction (Chinese porcelain). VAT: Spec.

WILTON, Nr. Salisbury

Bay Tree Antiques
26 North St. SP2 0HJ. Open 9-5.30 or by appointment. SIZE: Medium. *STOCK: General antiques, specialising in period English furniture and decorative items.* TEL: 01722 743392.

Hingstons of Wilton
36 North St. SP2 0HJ. Est. 1976. Open 9-5, Sat. 10-4. SIZE: Large. *STOCK: 18th-20th C furniture, clocks, pictures and objects.* PARK: Easy. TEL: 01722 742263; home - 01722 714742; mobile - 07887 870569; website - www.hingstons-antiques.co.uk

A.J. Romain and Sons
The Old House, 11 and 13 North St. SP2 0HA. Est. 1954. Open 9-5. CL: Wed. pm. *STOCK: Furniture, mainly 17th-18th C; early oak, walnut and marquetry; clocks, copper, brass and miscellanea.* PARK: Market Sq. TEL: 01722 743350. VAT: Stan/Spec.

WORCESTERSHIRE

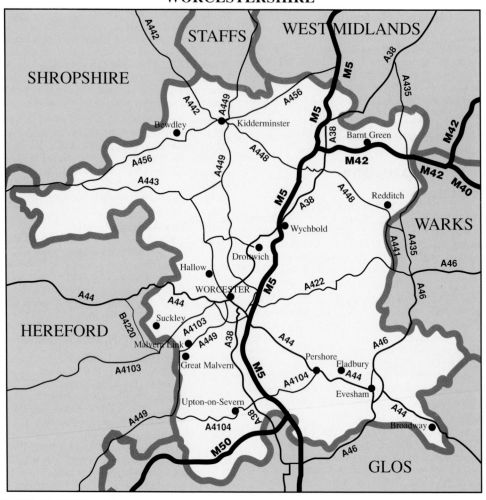

Dealers and Shops in Worcestershire

Barnt Green	1	Evesham	2	Kidderminster	2	Suckley	1
Bewdley	1	Fladbury	1	Malvern Link	2	Upton-upon-Severn	1
Broadway	7	Great Malvern	7	Pershore	3	Worcester	11
Droitwich	2	Hallow	1	Redditch	2	Wychbold	1

BARNT GREEN, Nr. Birmingham

Barnt Green Antiques
93 Hewell Rd. B45 8NL. (N. Slater). BAFRA. Est. 1977. Open 9-5.30, Sat. 9.30-1. SIZE: Medium. *STOCK: Furniture, 17th-19th C, £100-£5,000.* PARK: Easy. TEL: 0121 445 4942. SER: Restorations (furniture, gilt frames, clocks and oils). VAT: Stan/Spec.

BEWDLEY

Bewdley Antiques
62A Load St. DY12 2AP. Est. 1999. Open 10-5.30. SIZE: Small. *STOCK: 25 cabinets displaying 19th-20th C collectables and decorative furniture.* LOC: A456 town centre. PARK: Easy. TEL: 01299 405636.

BROADWAY

Stephen Cook Antiques   BADA
58 High St. WR12 7DP. Est. 1987. Open 10-5.30. SIZE: Large. *STOCK: 17th-18th C oak, walnut and mahogany, treen and paintings.* PARK: Easy. TEL: 01386 854716; fax - 01386 859360; mobile - 07973 814656; e-mail - stephen@scookantiques.com website - www.scookantiques.com SER: Valuations; restorations (cabinet and polishing furniture).

Fenwick and Fenwick Antiques
88-90 High St. WR12 7AJ. (George and Jane Fenwick). CADA. Est. 1980. Open 10-6 and by appointment. SIZE: Large. *STOCK: Furniture, oak, mahogany and walnut, 17th to early 19th C; samplers, boxes, treen, Tunbridgeware,*

Delft, decorative items and corkscrews. LOC: Upper High St. PARK: Nearby. TEL: 01386 853227; after hours - 01386 841724; fax - 01386 858504. VAT: Spec.

Gallimaufry
51A High St. WR12 7DP. (Chris Stone). Est. 1993. Open Mon. 10-1 and Thurs.-Sat. 11-4. SIZE: Medium. *STOCK: Victorian and later furniture, £150-£5,000; watercolours and oils, silver, £50-£500; china especially Crown Derby and Royal Worcester, £50-£3,000.* PARK: Nearby. TEL: 01386 852898; fax - 01386 858120.

Richard Hagen
Stable Lodge, 55-57 High St. WR12 7DP. Est. 1972. Open 9.30-5, Sun. by appointment. *STOCK: 20th-21st C oils, watercolours and bronzes.* TEL: 01386 853624/858561; fax - 01386 852172; e-mail - fineart@richardhagen.com website - www.richardhagen.com VAT: Spec.

Haynes Fine Art of Broadway   BADA LAPADA
Picton House Galleries, 42 High St. WR12 7DT. (A.C. Haynes). CADA. Open 9-6. SIZE: Large - 12 showrooms. *STOCK: Over 2000 British and European 16th-21st C oil paintings and watercolours.* LOC: From Lygon Arms, 100 yards up High St. on left. PARK: Easy. TEL: 01386 852649; fax - 01386 858187; e-mail - enquiries@haynes-fine-art.co.uk website - www. haynesfineart.com SER: Valuations; restorations; framing; catalogue available (£10). VAT: Spec.

H.W. Keil Ltd   BADA
Tudor House, High St. WR12 7DP. (John Keil). CADA. Est. 1925. Open 9.30-12.45 and 2.15-5.30, Sat. by appointment. SIZE: Large - 12 showrooms. *STOCK: Walnut, oak, mahogany and rosewood furniture; early pewter, brass and copper, tapestry and works of art, 16th to early 19th C.* LOC: By village clock. PARK: Private by arrangement. TEL: 01386 852408; fax - 01386 852069; e-mail - info@ hwkeil.co.uk SER: Restorations. VAT: Spec.

John Noott Galleries   BADA LAPADA
28 High St., 14 Cotswold Court. WR12 7AA. (John, Pamela and Amanda Noott). CADA. Est. 1972. Open 9.30-1 and 2-5. SIZE: Large. *STOCK: Paintings, watercolours and bronzes, 19th C to contemporary.* PARK: Easy. TEL: 01386 854868/858969; fax - 01386 854919; e-mail - info@john-noott.com website - www. john-noott.com SER: Valuations; restorations; framing. VAT: Stan/Spec.

DROITWICH

Robert Belcher Antiques
128 Worcester Rd. WR9 8AN. (Robert & Wendy Belcher). Est. 1986. Open Tues.-Fri. 9-5.30, Sat. 10-5.30, Sun. by appointment. SIZE: Large. *STOCK: Furniture, 18th-19th C, £500-£10,000; ceramics, silver, glass, paintings and prints, 19th-20th C, £50-£1,000.* PARK: Easy. TEL: 01905 772320. SER: Valuations; restorations; picture framing. FAIRS: NEC. VAT: Spec.

Grant Books
The Coach House, New Rd., Cutnall Green. WR9 0PQ. PBFA. Est. 1971. Open 9-5 or by appointment. CL: Sat. SIZE: Small. *STOCK: Books, prints, pictures, clubs, golfiana, £5-£1,000.* LOC: A442 Droitwich to

Kidderminster road. PARK: Easy. TEL: 01299 851588; fax - 01299 851446; e-mail - golf@grantbooks.co.uk website - www.golfbooks-memorabilia.com

EVESHAM

Bookworms of Evesham
81 Port St. WR11 6AF. (T.J. Sims). PBFA. Est. 1971. Open 10-5, Mon. by appointment. SIZE: Small. *STOCK: Books - Gloucestershire and Worcestershire, 18th-20th C, £5-£1,200; John Moore, 20th C, £5-£75; general books, 19th-20th C, from 50p.* PARK: Behind premises. TEL: 01386 45509; fax - same. SER: Valuations; restorations; buys at auction. FAIRS: PBFA - Bath, Cheltenham, Cirencester, Churchdown. VAT: Stan.

Magpie Jewellers and Antiques and Magpie Arms & Armour
Manchester House 1 High St. WR11 4DA. (R.J. and E.R. Bunn). Est. 1975. Open 9-5.30. SIZE: Large. *STOCK: Silver, jewellery, furniture, general antiques, arms and armour, books, stamps and coins.* LOC: Town centre. TEL: 01386 41631; e-mail - magpie2500@aol.com website - www.magpieantiques.co.uk

FLADBURY

The Hayloft Antique Centre
Craycombe Farm, Evesham Rd. WR10 2QS. (Mrs Susan Pryse-Jones). Est. 1994. Open 7 days - summer 10.30-5, winter 10.30-4. SIZE: 10 dealers. *STOCK: Furniture - oak, mahogany, elm, stripped pine; collectables, paintings and prints, jet jewellery, reproduction pine, linen and textiles, mirrors and books.* LOC: Just outside village. PARK: Easy. TEL: 01386 861166; home - 01684 563926; fax - same; mobile - 07782 244145; e-mail - prysejones@supanet.com SER: Restorations (furniture stripping, French polishing and repairs).

GREAT MALVERN

Carlton Antiques
43 Worcester Rd. WR14 4RB. (Dave Roberts). Open 10-5. *STOCK: Edwardian postcards and cigarette cards; Victorian and Edwardian furniture, stripped pine; oil paintings, watercolours and prints.* TEL: 01684 573092; e-mail - dave@carlton-antiques.com website - www. carlton-antiques.com SER: Valuations.

Foley House Antiques
28 Worcester Rd. WR14 4QW. (Trevor Guiver, Roger Hales and Kimber & Son). Open 10-5.30, Sun. 11-5. SIZE: Large. *STOCK: General furnishings, 19th to early 20th C, £100-£2,000; collectables, china, £5-£100.* LOC: A449. PARK: Easy. TEL: 01684 575750; home - 01684 575904/572491. SER: Restorations; French polishing; buys at auction. VAT: Stan/Spec.

Malvern Bookshop
7 Abbey Rd. WR14 3ES. (Howard and Julie Hudson). Est. 1955. Open 10-5. SIZE: 5 rooms. *STOCK: Antiquarian, secondhand books and sheet music.* LOC: By priory church steps. PARK: Short stay on road above. TEL: 01684 575915; e-mail - browse@malvernbookshop.co.uk

Malvern Studios
56 Cowleigh Rd. WR14 1QD. (L.M. Hall). BAFRA.

Open 9-5.15, Fri. and Sat. 9-4.45. CL: Wed. *STOCK: Period, Edwardian painted and inlaid furniture, general furnishings.* TEL: 01684 574913; fax - 01684 569475. SER: Restorations; woodcarving; polishing; interior design. VAT: Stan/Spec.

Miscellany Antiques
20 Cowleigh Rd. WR14 1QD. (Ray and Liz Hunaban). Resident. Est. 1974. SIZE: Medium + trade warehouse. *STOCK: Victorian, Edwardian and Georgian furniture, including shipping goods, £300-£20,000; some porcelain, silver, bronzes and jewellery.* LOC: B4219 to Bromyard. PARK: Own. TEL: 01684 566671; fax - 01684 560562; e-mail - liz.hunaban@virgin.net VAT: Stan/Spec.

Promenade Antiques
41 Worcester Rd. WR14 4RB. (Mark Selvester). Open 10-5.30, Sun. 12-5. *STOCK: General antiques including Victorian and Edwardian furniture, lamps, bric-a-brac and books.* TEL: 01684 566876; e-mail - promant@aol.com

Whitmore
Teynham Lodge, Chase Rd., Upper Colwall. WR13 6DT. (John and Stella Whitmore). BNTA. Est. 1965. *STOCK: British and foreign coins, 1700-1950; trade tokens, 1650-1900; commemorative medallions, 1600-1950; all £1-£500.* TEL: 01684 540651; 01684 541417; e-mail - teynham@aol.com *Postal Only.*

HALLOW

Antique Map and Print Gallery
April Cottage, Main Rd. WR2 6LS. (M.A. and G.P. Nichols). Est. 1969. By appointment only. *STOCK: Antiquarian maps (including Speed and Blaeu) of every country; prints including Baxter and Le Blond, and books.* LOC: Approx. 4 miles from Worcester on the Tenbury Wells Rd. PARK: Easy. TEL: 01905 641300; e-mail - antiqmap@aol.com website - www.ampgworcester.com SER: Greetings cards reproduced from original prints.

KIDDERMINSTER

The Antique Centre
5-8 Lion St. DY10 1PT. (Vivien and Robin Lapham). Est. 1980. Open 10-5. SIZE: Large. *STOCK: Furniture, early 18th C to 1930s, £10-£2,000; collectables, to 1930s, £1-£1,000; Victorian, Edwardian and reproduction fireplaces; jewellery, silver, lighting, pictures, prints, mirrors, architectural items.* LOC: Off Bromsgrove St. PARK: Easy. TEL: 01562 740389; fax - same; mobile - 07980 300660; e-mail - theantiquecentre @btconnect.com website - www.theantiquecentre.co.uk SER: Valuations; restorations (furniture); door stripping; jewellery repairs and commissions.

B.B.M. Coins.
1st Floor, 9 & 10 Lion St. DY10 1PT. (W.V. and A. Crook). BJA. Est. 1977. Open Wed., Thurs., Fri. and Sat. 10-5. SIZE: Medium. *STOCK: Coins, £5-£1,000; coin and stamp accessories, jewellery including modern, £5-£10,000.* LOC: Adjacent Youth Centre, off ring road. PARK: Easy. TEL: 01562 744118/515007; fax - 01562 829444. SER: Valuations. VAT: Stan/Spec/Global.

MALVERN LINK

Kimber & Son
6 Lower Howsell Rd. WR14 1EF. (E.M. and M.E. Kimber). Est. 1956. Open 9-5.30, Sat. 9-1. *STOCK: 18th-20th C antiques for English, Continental and American markets.* TEL: 01684 574339; home - 01684 572000; mobile - 07792 115941. VAT: Stan/Spec.

Timeless Beds
Lower Quest Hills Rd. WR14 1RP. (S.D. Forrest). Est. 1992. Open 10-5, Sat. 10-4. SIZE: Small. *STOCK: Restored bedsteads, 1840s to 1910; hand-made mattresses, upholstered bases and bed linen.* PARK: Easy. TEL: 01684 561380; fax - same; mobile - 07932 007403; e-mail - info@timelessbeds.co.uk website - www.timelessbeds.co.uk SER: Valuations; restorations.

PERSHORE

The Drawing Room - Interiors & Antiques
9 Bridge St. WR10 1AJ. (Janet Davie). IDS. Est. 1980. Open 9.30-5, Sat. 9.30-1. CL: Thurs. SIZE: Medium. *STOCK: Decorative pieces including antique and reproduction furniture, lighting, mirrors, framed prints and engravings, £50-£20,000.* PARK: Easy (in main square or opposite). TEL: 01386 555747; fax - 01386 555071. SER: Valuations; interior design. VAT: Stan/Spec.

Hansen Chard Antiques
126 High St. WR10 1EA. (P.W. Ridler). BSc LBHI. Est. 1984. Open Fri. and Sat. 10-4 or by appointment. SIZE: Large. *STOCK: Clocks, barometers, models, tools, books, antique and secondhand, £5-£10,000.* LOC: On B4084. PARK: Easy. TEL: 01386 553423; home - same. SER: Valuations; restorations (as stock); buys at auction (as stock). FAIRS: Brunel, Midlands. VAT: Spec.

S.W. Antiques   LAPADA
Abbey Showrooms, Newlands. WR10 1BP. (A.M. Whiteside). CINOA. Est. 1978. Open 9-5. SIZE: Large. *STOCK: 19th-20th C furniture including beds and bedroom furniture, to £4,000. Not Stocked: Jewellery, small items.* LOC: 2 mins. from Abbey. PARK: Own. TEL: 01386 555580; fax - 01386 556205; e-mail - catchall@s.w.antiques.co.uk website - www.swantiques.co.uk VAT: Stan/Spec.

REDDITCH

Angel Antiques
211 Mount Pleasant, Southcrest. B97 4JG. (Carol Manners and David Foreman). Est. 1982. Open 10-3.30, Wed. 10-1.30, Sat. 9.30-5. SIZE: Medium. *STOCK: Georgian, Victorian and Edwardian furniture and collectable, £5-£1,000.* PARK: Easy. TEL: 01527 545041; mobile - 07855 162542. SER: Valuations; restorations.

Lower House Fine Antiques
Lower House, Far Moor Lane, Winyates Green. B98 0QX. (Mrs J.B. Hudson). Est. 1987. Prior telephone call advisable. SIZE: Small. *STOCK: Furniture, 17th to early 20th C, £100-£4,000; silver and plate, 18th to early 20th C, £10-£1,000; oil lamps, 19th C, £50-£500. Not*

Stocked: Pine furniture. LOC: 3 miles due east Redditch town centre and half a mile from Coventry Highway island, close to A435. PARK: Own. TEL: 01527 525117; home - same; e-mail - LWSE.antiques@Tesco.net SER: Valuations; restorations (including porcelain).

SUCKLEY

Holloways
Lower Court. WR6 5DE. (Edward and Diana Holloway). Est. 1989. Open 9-5, Sun. (April-August) 11-4. SIZE: Large. *STOCK: Antique and period garden ornaments and furniture, £5-£20,000.* LOC: A44 from Worcester towards Leominster, left at Knightwick, 3.5 miles on right close to village church. PARK: Easy. TEL: 01886 884665; website - www.agos.co.uk SER: Valuations; restorations; buys at auction. FAIRS: RHS Chelsea. VAT: Stan/Spec.

UPTON-UPON-SEVERN

The Highway Gallery
40 Old St. WR8 0HW. (J. Daniell). Est. 1969. Open 10.30-5, appointment advisable. CL: Thurs. and Mon. SIZE: Small. *STOCK: Oils, watercolours, 19th-20th C, £100-£10,000.* LOC: 100yds. from crossroads towards Malvern. PARK: Easy. TEL: 01684 592645; home - 01684 592909; fax - 01684 592909; e-mail - mr.daniell@ukonline.co.uk SER: Valuations; restorations; relining; cleaning; buys at auction (pictures).

WORCESTER

Antique Warehouse
Rear of 74 Droitwich Rd, Barbourne. WR3 8BW. (D. Venn). Open 9-5, Sat. 10-4.30. SIZE: Large. *STOCK: General antiques, shipping, restored pine and satin walnut, Victorian doors and fireplaces.* PARK: Easy. TEL: 01905 27493. SER: Stripping (wood and metalwork).

The Barber's Clock
37 Droitwich Rd. WR3 7LG. (Graham Gopsill). Est. 1990. Open 9-5, Mon. 10-5, Sun. 1-4. SIZE: Medium. *STOCK: Clocks, 19th C to Art Deco, £35-£1,000; gramophones and phonographs, 20th C, £250-£475+.* PARK: Own. TEL: 01905 29022; home - 01905 779011; e-mail - graham@barbersclock37.fsnet.com SER: Valuations; restorations (clocks and gramophones).

Bygones by the Cathedral   LAPADA
Cathedral Sq. WR1 2JD. (Gabrielle Doherty Bullock). FGA. DGA. Gemmological Assn of GB. Est. 1946. Open 9.30-5.30, Sat. 9.30-1 and 2-5.30. SIZE: Medium. *STOCK: Furniture, 17th-19th C; silver, jewellery, paintings, glass; English and Continental pottery and porcelain especially Royal Worcester; 20th C collectables.* LOC: Adjacent main entrance to cathedral. PARK: NCP opposite cathedral. TEL: 01905 25388/23132. SER: Valuations. VAT: Spec.

Bygones of Worcester   LAPADA
55 Sidbury. WR1 2HU. (Gabrielle Bullock). FGA. DGA. Gemmological Assn of GB. Est. 1946. Open 9.30-1 and 2-5.30. *STOCK: 17th-20th C walnut, oak, mahogany and exotic wood furniture, brass and copper, oil paintings, porcelain, pottery and glass and decorative objects.*

LOC: Opposite car park near approach to cathedral. PARK: Opposite. TEL: 01905 23132/25388. SER: Valuations. VAT: Stan/Spec.

Gray's Antiques
29 The Tything. WR1 1JL. (David Gray). Open 8.30-5.30. *STOCK: General antiques, soft furnishings, chandeliers.* TEL: 01905 724456; fax - 01905 723433; e-mail - enqs@grays-interiors.com

Gray's Interiors
35 The Tything. WR1 1JL. Open 8.30-5.30. *STOCK: Chandeliers, chairs, sofas, soft furnishings.* PARK: Limited. TEL: 01905 21209; e-mail - enqs@grays-interiors.com website - www.gray.interior.com

Heirlooms
46 Upper Tything. WR1 1JZ. (L. Rumford). Open 9.30-4.30. *STOCK: General antiques, objets d'art, Royal Worcester porcelain and prints.* TEL: 01905 23332.

Sarah Hodge
Peachley Manor, Hallow Lane, Lower Broadheath. WR2 6QL. Resident. Est. 1985. By appointment only. SIZE: Medium. *STOCK: General antiques, country bygones, pine and kitchenalia.* LOC: Off B4204, 3 miles N.W. Worcester. PARK: Easy. TEL: 01905 640255.

Juro Antiques
Bromyard Rd., Whitbourne. WR6 5SF. (Roy Hughes and Judy George). Open 9-1 and 2-5. *STOCK: Cider mills, stone troughs, staddle stones, fountains, statuary, vintage farm machinery, bronzes, mill wheels and unusual items.* LOC: A44. PARK: Easy. TEL: 01886 821261; fax - same; e-mail - info@juro.co.uk website - www.juro.co.uk FAIRS: Spring and Autumn Garden, Malvern; Royal Show, Stoneleigh.

M. Lees and Sons   LAPADA
Tower House, Severn St. WR1 2NB. Resident. Est. 1955. Open 9.15-5.15, Sat. by appointment. CL: Thurs. pm. SIZE: Medium. *STOCK: Furniture, 1780-1880; porcelain, 1750-1920; mirrors, Oriental and decorative.* LOC: At southern end of Worcester cathedral adjacent to Edgar Tower; near Royal Worcester Porcelain Museum and factory. PARK: Easy. TEL: 01905 26620; mobile - 07860 826218. VAT: Stan/Spec.

Worcester Antiques Centre
15 Reindeer Court, Mealcheapen St. WR1 4DF. (Stephen Zacaroli). Est. 1992. Open 10-5. *STOCK: Pottery and porcelain, 1750-1950, £10-£4,000; silver, 1750-1940, £10-£5,000; jewellery, 1800-1940, £5-£5,000; furniture, 1650-1930, £50-£10,000.* PARK: Loading only or 50 yards. TEL: 01905 610680/1; e-mail - worcesantiques@aol.com SER: Valuations; restorations (furniture, ceramics and metalware). FAIRS: East Berkshire (May and Oct).

WYCHBOLD

D & J Lines Antiques
Papermill Lane. WR9 0DE. (Derek and Jill Lines). Open by appointment. SIZE: Medium. *STOCK: Oak and country furniture, 17th-18th C, £500-£8,000; metalware, 18th-19th C, £50-£500; Persian carpets, 19th-20th C, £50-£1,000; pearls, diamond set jewellery.* TEL: 01527 861282. SER: Valuations; restorations; desk re-leathering.

YORKSHIRE EAST

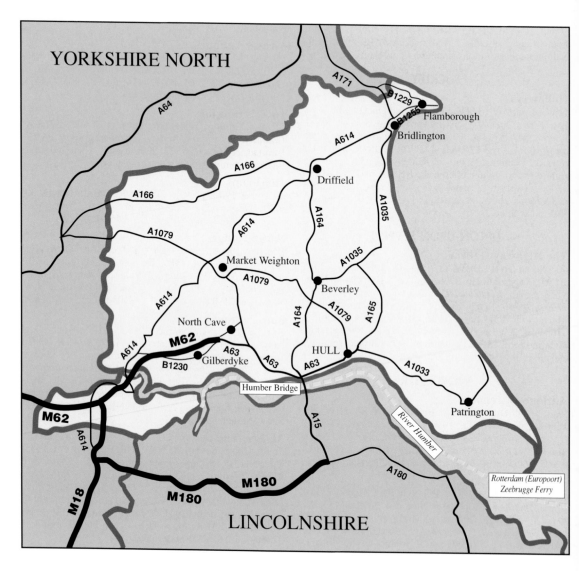

BEVERLEY

Guest & Philips
24 Saturday Market Place. HU17 8BB. (Karen and Philip Guest). NAG registered Valuer and Jeweller. HRD Dip. of Diamond Grading. Est. 1966. Open 9.15-5. SIZE: Medium. *STOCK: Jewellery and silver, 18th-20th C, £50-£20,000.* PARK: Easy. TEL: 01482 882334; fax - 01482 866485. SER: Valuations; restorations. VAT: Stan/Spec.

David Hakeney Antiques
P O Box 171. HU17 8GX. Est. 1970. Open by appointment. *STOCK: Porcelain, silver, clocks and watches, 19th C and Edwardian furniture, decorative items.* TEL: 01482 677006; mobile - 07860 507774. FAIRS: NEC(April, Aug. and Dec); Newark; Harrogate.

Hawley Antiques   LAPADA
5 North Bar Within. HU17 8AP. Est. 1966. Open by appointment. *STOCK: General antiques, furniture, pottery, porcelain, glass, oil paintings, watercolours, silver.* LOC: Town centre. TEL: 01430 470654; mobile - 07850 225805; e-mail - info@hawleys.info website - www.hawleys.info SER: Restorations (fine furniture); valuations; buys at auction. VAT: Stan/Spec.

St Crispin Antique Centre
11 Butcher Row. HU17 0AA. (Chris Fowler and Jill Northgraves). Est. 1971. Open 10-5, Sun. 10.30-4.30. SIZE: 70+ dealers. *STOCK: Ceramics, glass, furniture, books, jewellery.* TEL: 01482 869583. SER: Valuations.

James H. Starkey Galleries
49 Highgate. HU17 0DN. Est. 1968. Open Mon.-Fri. 9.30-4.30 by appointment only. SIZE: Medium. *STOCK: Oil paintings, 16th-19th C; drawings and watercolours, 17th-19th C.* LOC: Opposite Minster. PARK: Easy. TEL: 01482 881179; fax - 01482 861644. SER: Valuations; restorations (paintings); buys at auction. VAT: Stan/Spec.

Time and Motion
1 Beckside. HU17 0PB. (Peter A. Lancaster). FBHI. Est. 1977. Open 10-5. CL: Thurs. SIZE: Large. *STOCK: English longcase clocks, 18th-19th C, £2,000-£10,000; English, German and French mantel and wall clocks, 19th C, £300-£3,500; aneroid and mercurial barometers, 18th-19th C, £150-£3,000.* LOC: 1 mile from town centre and Minster, 300 yards from Leisure Centre. PARK: Easy. TEL: 01482 881574; home - same. SER: Valuations; restorations (clocks and barometers). VAT: Stan/Spec.

Vicar Lane Antique Centre
The Old Granary, Vicar Lane, North Bar Within. HU17 8DF. (Chris Fowler and Jill Northgraves). Est. 2002. Open 10-5, Sun. 10.30-4.30. SIZE: Large, 20+ dealers. *STOCK: Date-lined (1945) furniture and small items.* TEL: 01482 888088. SER: Valuations.

BRIDLINGTON

C.J. and A.J. Dixon Ltd
1st Floor, 23 Prospect St. YO15 2AE. Est. 1969. Open 9.30-5. SIZE: Large. *STOCK: British war medals and decorations.* LOC: Town centre. PARK: Easy. TEL: 01262 676877/603348; fax - 01262 606600; e-mail -

chris@dixonsmedals.co.uk website - www.dixons medals.co.uk SER: Valuations; renovations. VAT: Stan/Spec.

The Georgian Rooms
56 High St., Old Town. YO16 4QA. (Karen Peacock and Diane Davison). Est. 1999. Open 10-5 including Sun. SIZE: 10 showrooms. *STOCK: Wide range of general antiques and collectables, Georgian to modern, £1-£13,000.* PARK: Free nearby. TEL: 01262 608600; website - www.georgianrooms.co.uk SER: Restorations.

Priory Antiques
47-49 High St. YO16 4PR. (P.R. Rogerson). Est. 1979. Open Tues. and Fri. 10-5, Sat. 10-12. SIZE: Large. *STOCK: Georgian and Victorian furniture.* TEL: 01262 601365.

Sedman Antiques
106 Cardigan Rd. YO15 3LR. (R.H.S. and M.A. Sedman). Est. 1971. Open 10-5.30, Sun. by appointment. *STOCK: General antiques, period and shipping furniture, Oriental porcelain, Victorian collectors' items.* PARK: Easy. TEL: 01262 675671.

DRIFFIELD

The Crested China Co
Highfield, Windmill Hill. YO25 5YP. (D. Taylor). Est. 1978. Open by appointment. *STOCK: Goss and crested china.* PARK: Easy. TEL: 01377 257042 (24 hr.); e-mail - dt@thecrestedchinacompany.com website - www.the crestedchinacompany.com SER: Sales catalogues. FAIRS: Goss.

Karen Guest Antiques
80A Middle St. South. YO25 6QE. NAG. HRD Diploma of Diamond Grading. Est. 1989. Open 9.30-5. SIZE: Small. *STOCK: Jewellery and silver, 18th-20th C, £50-£5,000.* TEL: 01377 241467; website - www. michaelphilips.com SER: Valuations; restorations. VAT: Stan/Spec.

Smith & Smith Designs
58A Middle St. North. YO25 6SU. (D.A. Smith). Est. 1977. Open 9.30-5.30, Sat. 9.30-5, Sun. by appointment. SIZE: Medium + warehouse. *STOCK: Furniture including pine and country, 18th to early 20th C, £50-£2,000; furniture designed and made to order, from £50+.* LOC: Main street. PARK: Easy. TEL: 01377 256321; home - same; e-mail - dave@pine-on-line.com website - www.pine-on-line.com SER: Restorations.

FLAMBOROUGH, Nr. Bridlington

Lesley Berry Antiques
The Manor House. YO15 1PD. (Mrs L. Berry). Resident. Est. 1972. Open 9.30-5.30, other times by appointment. SIZE: Small. *STOCK: Furniture, silver, jewellery, amber, Whitby jet, oils, watercolours, prints, copper, brass, textiles, secondhand and antiquarian books on-line.* LOC: On corner of Tower St. and Lighthouse Rd. PARK: Easy. TEL: 01262 850943; e-mail - lb@flamborough manor.co.uk website - www.flamboroughmanor.co.uk SER: Buys at auction.

GILBERDYKE

Lewis E. Hickson FBHI
Antiquarian Horologist, Sober Hill Farm. HU15 2TB. Est. 1965. Open by appointment. SIZE: Small. *STOCK: Longcase, bracket clocks, barometers and instruments.* TEL: 01430 449113. SER: Restorations; repairs.

HULL

Grannie's Parlour
33 Anlaby Rd. HU1 2PG. (A. and Mrs. N. Pye). Est. 1974. Open 11-5. CL: Thurs. *STOCK: General antiques, ephemera, Victoriana, dolls, toys, kitchenalia.* LOC: Near rail and bus station. PARK: Nearby. TEL: 01482 228258; home - 01482 341020.

Grannie's Treasures
1st Floor, 33 Anlaby Rd. HU1 2PG. (Mrs N. Pye). Est. 1974. Open 11-5. CL:Thurs. *STOCK: Advertising items, dolls' prams, toys, small furniture, china and pre-1940s clothing.* LOC: Near rail and bus station. PARK: Nearby. TEL: 01482 228258; home - 01482 341020.

Imperial Antiques
397 Hessle Rd. HU3 4EH. (M. Langton). Est. 1982. Open 9-5.30. *STOCK: British stripped pine furniture, antique, old and reproduction.* LOC: Main road. PARK: Easy. TEL: 01482 327439. FAIRS: Newark, Swinderby. VAT: Stan/Global.

Kevin Marshall's Antiques Warehouse
17-20A Wilton St., Holderness Rd. HU8 7LG. Est. 1981. Open 10-5 including Sun. SIZE: Large. *STOCK: Bathroom ware, architectural items, fires, lighting, furniture and reproductions, 19th C, £5-£5,000.* LOC: 1st right off Dansom Lane South. PARK: Easy. TEL: 01482 326559; fax - same; e-mail - kevinmarshall@antiquewarehouse.karoo.co.uk SER: Valuations; restorations; boardroom tables made to order. VAT: Stan/Spec.

Pine-Apple Antiques
321-327 Beverley Rd. HU5 1LD. (Diane C. Todd). Est. 1981. Open 9-5.30, Sun. 11-4. SIZE: Large. *STOCK: Pine, oak and beech furniture, bathrooms, bespoke kitchens, curios, gifts and jewellery, mirrors, pictures and clocks, architectural items, fireplaces, lighting including reproduction.* PARK: Easy. TEL: 01482 441384; fax - 01482 441073; mobile - 07860 874480; e-mail - diane@pine-apple.co.uk website - www.pine-apple.co.uk

MARKET WEIGHTON, Nr. York

Houghton Hall Antiques
Cliffe/North Cave Rd. YO43 3RE. (M.E. Watson). Est. 1965. Open daily 8-4, Sun. 11-4. SIZE: Large. *STOCK: Furniture, 17th-19th C, £5-£18,000; china, 19th C, £1-£2,000; paintings and prints, £20-£5,000; objets d'art.* Not Stocked: Coins, guns. LOC: Turn right on new by-pass from York (left coming from Beverley), 3/4 mile, signposted North Cave - sign on entrance. PARK: Easy. TEL: 01430 873234. SER: Valuations; restorations (furniture); buys at auction. FAIRS: New York. VAT: Stan/Spec.

Mount Pleasant Antiques Centre
46 Cliffe Rd. YO43 3BP. (Linda and John Sirrs). Est. 1974. Open 9.30-5 including Sun. SIZE: Large - 27 dealers. *STOCK: Georgian and Victorian furniture including large dining tables, bureaux, display cabinets, £200-£4,500; clocks, £80-£4,000; side and tilt top tables, silver, pottery and porcelain, jewellery, copper and books.* LOC: A1079 Market Weighton by-pass. PARK: Easy. TEL: 01430 872872; home - same. website - www.mountpleasantantiquescentre.co.uk SER: Restorations (furniture); cabinet making.

NORTH CAVE

Penny Farthing Antiques
Albion House, 18 Westgate. HU15 2NJ. (C.E. Dennett). Est. 1987. Open by appointment only. SIZE: Medium. *STOCK: 19th-20th C furniture, Victorian brass and iron bedsteads, £25-£2,000; linen, textiles and samplers, 18th-20th C, £5-£500; general collectables, china and glass, 19th-20th C, £5-£500.* LOC: Main road (B1230). PARK: Easy. TEL: 01430 422958; mobile - 07980 624583. SER: Valuations; buys at auction. FAIRS: Newark.

PATRINGTON

Clyde Antiques
12 Market Place. HU12 0RB. (S.M. Nettleton). Est. 1978. Open 10-5. CL: Sun., Mon. and Wed. except by appointment. SIZE: Medium. *STOCK: General antiques.* PARK: Easy. TEL: 01964 630650; home - 01964 612471. SER: Valuations. VAT: Stan.

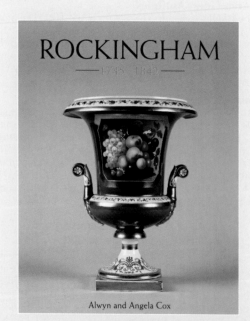

ROCKINGHAM
——1745-1842——

Alwyn and Angela Cox

Specifications: 432pp., 146 col. illus., 386 b.&w. illus., 67 marks & stamps 11 x 8½in./279 x 216mm.
£45.00 (hardback)

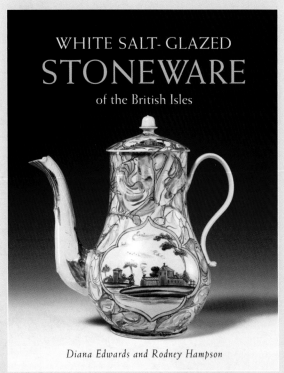

YORKSHIRE NORTH

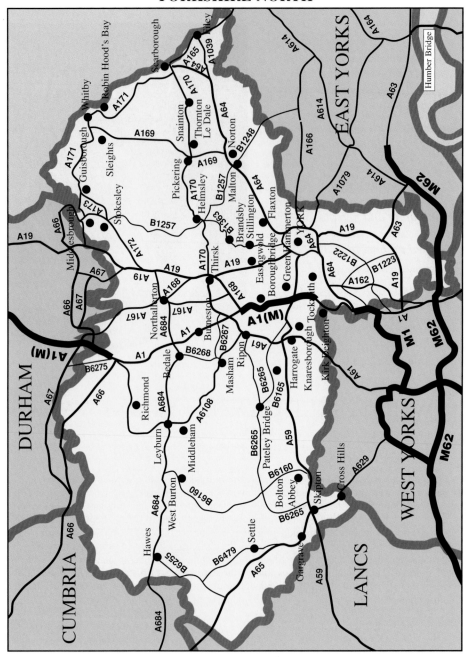

Dealers and Shops in North Yorkshire

							Pateley Bridge	2	Snainton	1
Bedale	1	Flaxton	2	Knaresborough	5	Pickering	3	Stillington	1
Bolton Abbey	1	Gargrave	4	Leyburn	2	Richmond	1	Stokesley	1
Boroughbridge	2	Green Hammerton	1	Malton	1	Ripon	4	Thirsk	4
Brandsby	1	Guisborough	1	Masham	1	Robin Hood's Bay	1	Thornton le Dale	1
Burneston	1	Harrogate	26	Middleham	2	Scarborough	3	Tockwith	1
Cross Hills	1	Hawes	2	Middlesbrough	1	Settle	4	West Burton	1
Easingwold	5	Helmsley	4	Northallerton	1	Skipton	3	Whitby	4
Filey	1	Kirk Deighton	1	Norton	1	Sleights	2	York	18

BEDALE

Bennett's Antiques & Collectables
7 Market Place. DL8 1ED. (Paul and Kim Bennett). Est. 1996. Open 9-5, Sun. by appointment. SIZE: Large. *STOCK: Furniture, 18th to early 20th C, £200-£15,000; fine art, 19th to early 20th C, £100-£10,000; clocks, 19th to early 20th C, £200-£6,000; collectables, 19th-20th C, £50-£2,000; local works of art, 20th C, £100-£1,000.* LOC: 5 mins. from A1, Leeming Bar junction. PARK: Easy and free. TEL: 01677 427900; fax - 01677 426858; mobile - 07711 054219; e-mail - info@bennetts.uk.com website - www.bennetts.uk.com SER: Restorations; clock repairs; exhibitions of Yorkshire artists; worldwide shipping; weekly deliveries (London and the South). VAT: Spec.

BOLTON ABBEY, Nr. Skipton

Grove Rare Books
The Old Post Office. BD23 6EX. (Andrew and Janet Sharpe). ABA. PBFA. Est. 1984. Open Tues.-Sat. 10-5. SIZE: Medium. *STOCK: Antiquarian books and maps; topographical and sporting prints.* LOC: 1 mile from A59. PARK: At rear. TEL: 01756 710717; fax - 01756 711098; e-mail - antiquarian@groverarebooks.co.uk website - www.groverarebooks.co.uk SER: Valuations; restorations; buys at auction (as stock).

BOROUGHBRIDGE

John Wilson
St James House, St. James Sq. YO51 9AR. Est. 1989. Open 9-5.30, prior telephone call advisable. SIZE: Small. *STOCK: Period and later furniture, brass, copper and china.* LOC: Town centre. PARK: Own. TEL: 01423 322508; home - same; fax - 01423 326690; mobile - 07720 544926. SER: Valuations; restorations; upholstery.

R.S. Wilson and Sons
PO Box 41. YO51 9WY. (G. Richard Wilson). Est. 1917. Open by appointment only. SIZE: Small. *STOCK: 17th-19th C furniture and accessories.* TEL: 01423 322417; fax - same; mobile - 07711 794801; e-mail - richard. wilsonantiques@virgin.net

BRANDSBY

L.L. Ward and Son
Bar House. YO61 4RQ. (R. Ward). Est. 1970. Open 8.30-5. *STOCK: Antique pine.* LOC: Midway between York and Helmsley. PARK: Easy. TEL: 01347 888651; e-mail - pine@brandsby1.freeserve.co.uk website - www.brandsbypine.co.uk

BURNESTON, Nr. Bedale

W. Greenwood (Fine Art)
Oak Dene, Church Wynd. DL8 2JE. Est. 1978. Open by appointment. SIZE: Small. *STOCK: Paintings and watercolours, 19th-20th C, £100-£5,000; frames, £20-£500; mirrors.* LOC: Take B6285 left off A1 northbound, house 1/4 mile on right. PARK: Easy. TEL: 01677 424830; home - 01677 423217; mobile - 07885 175279. SER: Valuations; restorations (paintings and frames); framing.

CROSS HILLS, Nr. Keighley

Heathcote Antiques
Skipton Rd. Junction. BD20 7DS. (M.H. and S.A. Webster Ltd). Resident. Est. 1979. Open 10-5.30, Sun. 12.30-4.30. CL: Mon. and Tues. SIZE: Very large showroom + trade warehouse. *STOCK: Furniture, clocks, barometers, unstripped English pine, pottery, porcelain, brass and metal wares.* PARK: Own large. TEL: 01535 635250; fax - 01535 637205; mobile - 07836 259640.

EASINGWOLD

Milestone Antiques
Farnley House, 101 Long St. YO61 3HY. (A.B. and S.J. Streetley). Est. 1982. Open daily, Sun. by appointment. SIZE: Medium. *STOCK: Mahogany and oak furniture especially dining tables, upholstered armchairs and sofas; longcase and wall clocks; all 18th to early 20th C.* LOC: Old A19, village centre. PARK: Easy. TEL: 01347 821608; home - same; e-mail - milestoneantiques-easingwold@fsmail.net website - www.milestone antiques.co.uk SER: Valuations. VAT: Stan/ Spec.

Old Flames
30 Long St. YO61 3HT. (P. Lynas and J.J. Thompson). Est. 1988. Open 10-5. SIZE: Medium. *STOCK: Fireplaces, 18th-19th C, £100-£4,000; lighting, 19th C, £100-£5,000; architectural items, 18th-19th C, £50-£2,000.* PARK: Easy. TEL: 01347 821188; fax - same; e-mail - philiplynas@ aol.com website - www.oldflames.co.uk SER: Valuations. FAIRS: Newark. VAT: Stan/ Spec.

Mrs B.A.S. Reynolds
42 Long St. YO61 3HT. *STOCK: General antiques, Victorian.* TEL: 01347 821078.

Vale Antiques
Mooracres, North Moor. YO61 3NB. (J.M., C.M. and D.N. Leach). GADAR. Est. 1986. Open 9-5. SIZE: Medium. *STOCK: Furniture, 18th-20th C, £20-£1,500; china, brass and copper, £5-£100; prints and paintings, £15-£100.* LOC: Outskirts, just off Thirsk Rd. PARK: Easy. TEL: 01347 821298; home/fax - same; e-mail - valeantiques@ mooracres.co.uk website - www.mooracres.co.uk SER: Restorations (furniture repair and re-polishing).

The White House Antiques & Architectural Reclamation
Thirsk Rd. YO61 3NF. (G. Hood). Resident. Est. 1960. Usually open but prior telephone call advisable. *STOCK: Rural and domestic bygones, stone troughs, architectural reclamation and garden ornaments.* LOC: 1 mile north of Easingwold, 200 yards from northern junction of bypass (A19). PARK: Easy. TEL: 01347 821479; e-mail - info@grahamhood.co.uk

FILEY

Cairncross and Sons
31 Bellevue St. YO14 9HU. (G. Cairncross). Open 9.30-12.45 and 2-4.30. CL: Wed. (Nov.-Mar); Wed. pm. (April-Oct). *STOCK: Medals, uniforms, insignia, cap badges, general militaria.* Not Stocked: Weapons. TEL: 01723 513287; e-mail - george@cairnxson.freeserve.co.uk website - www.cairnxson.freeserve.co.uk

FLAXTON, Nr. York

Elm Tree Antiques
YO60 7RJ. (R. and J. Jackson). Est. 1975. Open 9-5, (winter - 4.30) Sun. 10-5 (winter - Sat. and Sun. 10-4). SIZE: Large. *STOCK: Furniture, 17th C to Edwardian; small items, £5-£5,000, Staffordshire figures.* LOC: 1 mile off A64. PARK: Easy. TEL: 01904 468462; home - same; website - www.elmtreeantiques.co.uk SER: Valuations; restorations (cabinet making, polishing and upholstery). FAIRS: Newark.

Flaxton Antique Gardens
Glebe Farm. YO60 7RU. (Tim and Heather Richardson). SALVO. Est. 1992. Open summer 10-4 including Sun. Winter by appointment. CL: Tues. SIZE: Large. *STOCK: Stone troughs, staddle stones, sundials, bird baths, urns, pedestals; statues - lead, stone, reconstituted stone; chimney pots, agricultural implements, cartwheels, Victorian edging tiles, old terracotta oil jars from Morocco, Portugal and Greece.* PARK: Easy. TEL: 01904 468468; fax - same; website - www.salvo.co.uk/dealers/flaxton SER: Valuations. FAIRS: Harrogate Flower Show.

GARGRAVE, Nr. Skipton

Antiques at Forge Cottage
22A High St. BD23 3RB. Est. 1979. Open Wed.- Sat. 10-5. SIZE: Medium. *STOCK: Pottery and porcelain.* LOC: A65. PARK: Easy. TEL: 01756 748272; mobile - 07860 525579; e-mail - philina@carrol.fsnet.co.uk SER: Restorations; valuations. FAIRS: NEC; Newark. VAT: Spec.

Dickinson's Antiques Ltd
Estate Yard, West St. BD23 3PH. Est. 1958. Open 9-5.30 or by appointment. *STOCK: Early English furniture.* LOC: Just off A65 Skipton-Settle road. PARK: Easy. TEL: 01756 748257. SER: Restorations. VAT: Spec.

Gargrave Gallery
48 High St. BD23 3RB. (B. Herrington). Est. 1975. Appointment advisable. *STOCK: General antiques, oak, mahogany, metal, paintings, 18th to early 20th C.* LOC: A65. PARK: Easy. TEL: 01756 749641.

R.N. Myers and Son BADA
Endsleigh House, High St. BD23 3LX. (Jean M. and Simon Myers). Est. 1890. Open 9-5.30 or by appointment. SIZE: Medium. STOCK: Furniture, oak, mahogany, 17th to early 19th C; pottery, porcelain and metalware. Not Stocked: Victoriana, weapons, coins, jewellery. LOC: A65. Skipton-Settle road. PARK: Behind shop and opposite. TEL: 01756 749587; fax - 01756 749322; e-mail - rnmyersson@aol.com SER: Valuations. VAT: Spec.

GREEN HAMMERTON, Nr. York

The Main Pine Co
Grangewood, The Green. YO26 8BQ. (C. and K.M. Main). Est. 1976. Open 9-5. SIZE: Large. *STOCK: Pine furniture, 18th-19th C, £100-£1,500; reproductions from reclaimed pine.* LOC: Just off A59. PARK: Easy. TEL: 01423 330451; home - 01423 331078; fax - 01423 331278; e-mail - sales@mainpinecompany.com website - www.mainpinecompany.com SER: Export; containers packed. VAT: Stan.

GUISBOROUGH

Period Interiors
179 Westgate. TS14 6ND. (D.J. Crowther). Est. 1983. Open 9-4.30 including Sun. CL: Wed. SIZE: Large. *STOCK: Victorian and Edwardian fireplaces, Victorian 4-panel pine doors, wide range of architectural antiques.* TEL: 01287 634000; mobile - 07774 639754.

HARROGATE

Nigel Adamson
Flat 1, 19 Park View. HG1 5LY. (N.J.G. Adamson). Est. 1863. Open by appointment. *STOCK: Furniture, 17th to early 19th C; porcelain, Chinese, English and Continental .* PARK: Easy. TEL: 01423 528924; mobile - 07957 686493; e-mail - nigeladamson@harrogate antiques.com SER: Valuations; restorations (furniture and porcelain). VAT: Spec.

Armstrong BADA
10-11 Montpellier Parade. HG1 2TJ. (M.A. Armstrong). Est. 1983. Open 10-5.30. SIZE: Medium. STOCK: Fine English furniture, 18th to early 19th C; works of art, 18th C. PARK: Easy. TEL: 01423 506843; e-mail - armsantiques@aol.com FAIRS: Olympia (June, Nov). VAT: Spec.

Bryan Bowden
Oakleigh, 1 Spacey View, Leeds Rd., Pannal. HG3 1LQ. (Bryan and Elizabeth Bowden). Est. 1969. Open by appointment. SIZE: Small. *STOCK: English pottery and porcelain, 1750-1850; small Georgian furniture.* LOC: 2.5 miles south of Harrogate on Leeds road. PARK: Easy. TEL: 01423 870007; home - same. SER: Valuations; restorations (pottery and porcelain); buys at auction (English pottery and porcelain). FAIRS: Northern; Buxton. VAT: Spec.

Derbyshire Antiques Ltd
4 Montpellier Mews. Montpellier St. HG1 2TQ. (R.C. Derbyshire). Est. 1960. Open 10-5. SIZE: Small. *STOCK: Early oak, 16th-18th C; pewter.* PARK: Nearby. TEL: 01423 503115; fax - same; e-mail - r-derbyshire@bt.com website - www.thepewtershop.co.uk

Dragon Antiques
10 Dragon Rd. HG1 5DF. (P.F. Broadbelt). Resident. Est. 1954. Open 11-6. Always available. SIZE: Small. *STOCK: Victorian art glass, art pottery, British and foreign postcards.* LOC: 5 mins. from town centre, opposite Dragon Rd. car park. PARK: Easy. TEL: 01423 562037.

Garth Antiques LAPADA
16 Montpellier Parade. HG1 2TG. (J. and I. Chapman). Est. 1978. Open 10-5.30. SIZE: Large. *STOCK: Furniture, 18th-19th C, £500-£12,000; oils and watercolours, £200-£5,000.* PARK: Easy and nearby. TEL: 01423 530573; fax - 01423 564084; e-mail - irenechapman@btconnect.com SER: Restorations; upholstery. VAT: Stan/Spec.

The Ginnel Antiques Centre
The Ginnel. HG1 2RB. (Pauline Stephenson). Est. 1986. Open 9.30-5.30. SIZE: Large. *STOCK: All date-lined and vetted - see individual entries.* LOC: Off Parliament St. opposite Debenhams. PARK: Nearby. TEL: 01423 508857;

website - www.ginnel.co.uk and www.ginnel.com SER: Courier. Below are listed the specialist dealers at this centre.

Abbot Antiques
Fine antique silver.

Acomb Antiques
19th C furniture and objets d'art.

Appleton Antiques
19th-20th pottery including Carlton, Moorcroft, Linthorpe, Poole and crested china; drinking glasses, paintings, small furniture.

Art-iques & Design
Silver especially Georg Jenson.

Fiona Aston
Objets d'art including porcelain and miniatures.

Margaret Bedi Antiques & Fine Art
English period furniture, 1720-1920; oils and watercolours, 19th-20th C. TEL: Home - 01642 583247; mobile - 07860 577637.

Brackmoor Antiques
Silver, porcelain and objets d'art.

Murray Burgess
Collectables and sporting memorabilia especially golf.

Catkins Jewellery and Antiques
Jewellery.

Cedar House Antiques
18th to early 20th C silver.

Joyce Chatterton
Chinese artifacts and objets d'art.

J.E. Chew
19th to early 20th C silver and plate.

The Clock Inn
(R.K. Mayes). Clocks. SER: Repairs; restorations.

B.J. Coltman
19th C furniture.

Cook's Cottage Antiques
Furniture and collectables.

Mary Cooper
Antique costumes and textiles, to 1929, including lace, fans, shawls, linen, quilts, samplers, wool and beadwork.

Helena Francis
Victorian jewellery, porcelain and silver.

Garden House
Prints and maps.

Jeffrey and Pauline Glass
Porcelain and glass, objets d'art, 19th to early 20th C.

Emilia Greenwood
Jewellery.

James Hardy (Antiques) Lrd
Decorative silver, glass and porcelain.

R. Himsworth
Silver and jewellery.

Historic Gems
Jewellery.

Holyome
Porcelain especially Belleek.

Hug and Plum
19th to early 20th C furniture and objets d'art.

G. Kendall
Furniture and collectables.

Kismet
Art Deco Jewellery.

Brian Loomes
Longcase clocks, small period furniture.

March Antiques
Victorian and early 20th C porcelain; mantle clocks.

Sheila Morgan
Victorian collectables.

Ann Morton
19th C furniture, oil paintings and watercolours.

Odyssey Antiquities
Ancient artifacts and coins.

S. Ogley
19th-20th C collectables.

Parker Gallery
19th to early 20th C oils and watercolours, £100-£3,000.

Paul Raine
19th C silver.

G. Rhodes
19th C furniture and objets d'art.

Jane Robson
Collectables.

Alan Sharp
English pottery and porcelain, 1750-1850.

Silver Thimble
Glass, porcelain, collectables.

Elisa Silverton
Silver, furniture and paintings.

Time Antiques
Porcelain and jewellery.

C.E. Tweedale *V*
Victorian and Edwardian pottery.

Ann Wilkinson
Silver, porcelain and jewellery.

J. Wood Antiques
19th C oils and watercolours, Oriental porcelain.

Michael Green Pine & Country Antiques
Library House, Regent Parade. HG1 5AN. Est. 1976. Open 8.30-5.30, Sat. 8.45-4, Sun. by appointment. SIZE: Medium. *STOCK: Oak, mahogany and pine furniture, from 17th C, £5-£3,000; treen, kitchenalia, collectors treasures, lamps and decorative items.* LOC: Overlooking the Stray. PARK: Easy. TEL: 01423 560452. SER: Valuations; restorations; stripping. VAT: Stan/Spec.

Havelocks
13-17 Westmoreland St. HG1 5AY. (Philip Adam). Est. 1989. Open 10-5. SIZE: Large. *STOCK: Original pine, oak, general antique furniture.* LOC: A59 towards Skipton, turn left into Westmoreland St. PARK: Free. TEL: 01423 506721. SER: Valuations; restorations; stripping and finishing.

Carlton Hollis Ltd
9 Montpellier Mews. HG1 2TQ. (Paul and Beverley Hollis). Est. 1952. Open Tues.-Sat. 10-5. *STOCK: Antique silver and jewellery.* TEL: 01423 500216; fax - 01423 500283; mobile - 07711 188565; e-mail - carltonhollis@btconnect.com SER: Valuations; restorations. FAIRS: NEC; HTAF. Bailey.

London House Oriental Rugs and Carpets
9 Montpellier Parade. HG1 2TJ. Est. 1981. Open 10-5. SIZE: Medium. *STOCK: Persian, Turkish, Indian, Tibetan, Nepalese and Afghan rugs and carpets, 19th-20th C, £25-£5,000; kelims and camel bags, 19th-20th C, £25-£2,000.* LOC: Town centre on The Stray. PARK: Easy. TEL: 01423 567167. SER: Valuations; restorations (handmade rugs). VAT: Stan.

David Love   BADA
10 Royal Parade. HG1 2SZ. Est. 1969. Open 9-1 and 2-5.30. SIZE: Large. *STOCK: Furniture, English, 17th-19th C; pottery and porcelain, English and Continental; decorative items, all periods.* LOC: Opposite Pump Room Museum. PARK: Easy. TEL: 01423 565797/525567. SER: Valuations; buys at auction. VAT: Stan/Spec.

Charles Lumb and Sons Ltd   BADA
2 Montpellier Gardens. HG1 2TF. (A.R. and Mrs C.M. Lumb). Est. 1920. Open 10-1 and 2-6, Sat. 10-1 or by appointment. SIZE: Medium. *STOCK: Furniture, 17th to early 19th C; metalware, period accessories.* PARK: 20yds. immediately opposite. TEL: 01423 503776; home - 01423 863281; fax - 01423 530074. VAT: Spec.

McTague of Harrogate
17/19 Cheltenham Mount. HG1 1DW. (P. McTague). Open 11-5. CL: Mon. SIZE: Medium. *STOCK: Prints, watercolours, oil paintings, mainly 18th to early 20th C.* LOC: From Conference Centre on Kings Rd., go up Cheltenham Parade and turn first left. PARK: Easy. TEL: 01423 567086; mobile - 07885 108190. e-mail - paul@mctague.co.uk website - www.mctague.co.uk VAT: Stan/Spec.

Montpellier Mews Antique Centre
Montpellier St. HG1 2TG. Open 10-5. SIZE: Various dealers. *STOCK: General antiques - porcelain, jewellery, furniture, paintings, interior decor, golf memorabilia, linen, glass and silver.* LOC: Behind Weatherells Antiques. TEL: 01423 530484.

Ogden Harrogate Ltd   BADA
38 James St. HG1 1RQ. (G.M. Ogden). Est. 1893. Open 9.15-5. SIZE: Large. *STOCK: Jewellery, English silver and plate.* LOC: Town centre. PARK: Easy. TEL: 01423 504123; fax - 01423 522283; e-mail - sales @ogden-of-harrogate.co.uk website - www. ogden-of-harrogate.co.uk SER: Repairs; restorations; valuations. VAT: Stan/Spec.

Paraphernalia
38A Cold Bath Rd. HG2 0NA. (Peter F. Hacker). Est. 1986. Open 10-5. SIZE: Medium. *STOCK: Wallplates, crested and commemorative china, cutlery, glass including carnival, Mauchlineware, bric-a-brac, furniture and collectables.* LOC: Adjacent Lancaster Home Bakery. PARK: Free for 1 hr. with free disc from

shop. TEL: Evenings - 01423 567968; fax - same. SER: Free local delivery. FAIRS: Harrogate Showground.

Paul M. Peters Fine Art Ltd   LAPADA
15a Bower Rd. HG1 1BE. Est. 1967. Open 10-5. CL: Sat. SIZE: Medium. *STOCK: Chinese and Japanese ceramics and works of art, 17th-19th C; European ceramics and glass, 18th-19th C; European metalware, scientific instruments and unusual objects.* LOC: Town centre, at bottom of Station Parade. PARK: Easy. TEL: 01423 560118. SER: Valuations. FAIRS: Olympia (June). VAT: Stan/Spec.

Elaine Phillips Antiques Ltd   BADA
1 and 2 Royal Parade. HG1 2SZ. (Colin, Elaine and Louise Phillips). Est. 1968. Open 9.30-5.30, other times by appointment. SIZE: Large. *STOCK: Oak furniture, 1600-1800; country furniture, 1700-1840; some mahogany, 18th to early 19th C; period metalwork and decoration.* LOC: Opposite Crown Hotel, Montpellier Quarter. PARK: Nearby. TEL: 01423 569745. SER: Interior design. FAIRS: Harrogate (Spring, Autumn). VAT: Spec.

Smith's (The Rink) Ltd
Dragon Rd. HG1 5DR. Est. 1906. Open 9-5.30, Sun. 11-4.30. SIZE: Large. *STOCK: General antiques, 1750-1820; Victoriana, 1830-1900.* LOC: From Leeds, right at Prince of Wales roundabout, left at next roundabout, 1/2 mile on Skipton Rd., left into Dragon Rd. PARK: Easy. TEL: 01423 567890. VAT: Stan/Spec.

Sutcliffe Galleries   BADA
5 Royal Parade. HG1 2SZ. Est. 1947. Open 10-5. *STOCK: Paintings, 19th C.* LOC: Opposite Crown Hotel. TEL: 01423 562976; fax - 01423 528729; e-mail - enquiries@sutcliffegalleries.co.uk website - www. sutcliffegalleries.co.uk SER: Valuations; restorations; framing. FAIRS: Harrogate. VAT: Spec.

Thorntons of Harrogate   LAPADA
1 Montpellier Gdns. HG1 2TF. (R.H. and R.J. Thornton). Est. 1971. Open 9.30-5.30. SIZE: Medium. *STOCK: 17th-19th C furniture, barometers, decorative items, clocks, paintings, porcelain, scientific instruments.* PARK: Easy. TEL: 01423 504118; fax - 01423 528400; e-mail - info@harrogateantiques.com website - www. harrogateantiques.com SER: Valuations. FAIRS: Harrogate (Spring). VAT: Spec.

Walker Galleries Ltd   BADA LAPADA
6 Montpellier Gdns. HG1 2TF. Est. 1972. Open 9.30-1 and 2-5.30. SIZE: Medium. *STOCK: Oil paintings and watercolours, 18th C furniture.* TEL: 01423 567933; fax - 01423 536664; e-mail - wgltd@aol.com website - www.walkergalleries.com and www. walkerfineart.co.uk SER: Valuations; restorations; framing. FAIRS: BADA, London; Harrogate: Olympia. VAT: Spec.

Paul Weatherell Antiques   LAPADA
30-31 Montpellier Parade. HG1 2TG. Est. 2004. Open 9-5.30. SIZE: Large. *STOCK: Period and fine decorative furniture; lighting, pictures, mirrors, garden items.* LOC: Opposite Crown Hotel. PARK: Nearby. TEL: 01423 507810; fax - 01423 520005; website - www. weatherells.com VAT: Spec.

Weatherell's of Harrogate Antiques & Fine Arts **LAPADA**
10-11 Montpellier Mews, Montpellier St. HG1 2TQ. Open 10-5.30. SIZE: Two showrooms. *STOCK: Period and decorative furniture.* TEL: 01423 525004; fax - 01423 520005.

Chris Wilde Antiques **LAPADA**
134 King's Rd. HG1 5HY. (C.B. Wilde). Est. 1996. Open 10-5 or by appointment. CL: Wed. SIZE: Large. *STOCK: Furniture, 1680-1920, £300-£10,000; longcase clocks, 1720-1920, £500-£10,000; ceramics, glass and pictures.* LOC: North side of town. PARK: Easy. TEL: 01423 525855; mobile - 07831 543268; e-mail - chris@harrogate.com website - www.antiques.harrogate.com and www.antiquescourses.co.uk SER: Valuations; restorations; courses. FAIRS: Antiques For Everyone (NEC); Harrogate. VAT: Stan/Spec.

HAWES

Cellar Antiques
Bridge St. DL8 3QL. (Ian Milton Iveson). Est. 1987. Open 10-5, Sun. 11-5. SIZE: Large. *STOCK: 17th-19th C oak and country furniture, longcase clocks, metalware and pottery.* LOC: Cobbled street near bridge. PARK: Rear of shop. TEL: 01969 667224; home - 01969 667132. SER: Valuations.

Sturman's Antiques **LAPADA**
Main St. DL8 3QW. (P.J. Sturman). Est. 1985. Open 10-5 including Sun. *STOCK: Georgian and Victorian furniture; porcelain and pottery including Moorcroft; longcase, wall and mantel clocks and barometers.* PARK: Opposite. TEL: 01969 667742; website - www.sturmansantiques.co.uk VAT: Spec.

HELMSLEY

Castle Gate Antiques
14 Castle Gate. YO62 5AB. (D. Hartshorne). Open 10-5. SIZE: Medium. *STOCK: Silver, from 17th C; early English glass, Georgian drinking glasses, pottery and china; paintings, mainly sporting and Yorkshire interest; furniture.* LOC: Off Market Place, down side of town hall and across beck. PARK: Easy. TEL: 01439 770370; fax - same. SER: Valuations.

E. Stacy-Marks Limited **LAPADA**
10 Castlegate. YO62 5AB. Est. 1889. Open Tues.-Sat. 10-5. *STOCK: Paintings, English, Dutch and Continental schools, 18th-20th C.* TEL: 01439 771950; fax - 01439 771859.

Westway Pine
Carlton Lane. YO62 5HB. (J. and J. Dzierzek). Est. 1987. Open 10-5, Sun. 1-5. CL: Tues. SIZE: Medium. *STOCK: Pine furniture, 19th C, £20-£2,000.* LOC: From A170 from Scarborough, first right into town, first left, then left again 100m. PARK: Easy. TEL: 01439 771399/771401; e-mail - westway.pine@btopenworld.com website - www.westwaypine.com SER: Valuations; restorations (pine).

York Cottage Antiques
7 Church St. YO62 5AD. (G. and E.M. Thornley). Est. 1976. Open 10-5. SIZE: Small. *STOCK: Early oak and country furniture.* LOC: Opposite church, within 'The Rievaulx Collection'. PARK: Adjacent.

KIRK DEIGHTON, Nr. Wetherby

Elden Antiques
23 Ashdale View. LS22 4DS. (E. and D. Broadley). Est. 1970. Open 9-5, Sat. 12-5, Sun. 10-4. SIZE: Medium. *STOCK: General antiques including furniture.* LOC: Main road between Wetherby and Knaresborough. PARK: Easy. TEL: 01937 584770; home - same; e-mail - dennis.broadley@virgin.net

KNARESBOROUGH

Robert Aagaard & Co
Frogmire House, Stockwell Rd. HG5 0JP. GMC. Est. 1961. Open 9-5, Sat. 10-4. SIZE: Medium. *STOCK: Chimney pieces, marble fire surrounds, stone and wood fireplaces, fire baskets and cast-iron inserts.* LOC: Town centre. PARK: Own. TEL: 01423 864805; fax - 01423 869356; e-mail - robertaagaardco@btinternet.com SER: Fireplace restoration and design. VAT: Stan.

Early Oak
8 High St. HG5 0ES. (A.D. Gora). Est. 1995. Open any time by appointment. SIZE: Large. *STOCK: Oak and country furniture, 17th-18th C, £100-£10,000; longcase clocks, £1,000-£3,000; metalware including copper and pewter, 17th-19th C, £30-£500.* PARK: Private. TEL: 01904 627823; e-mail - info@earlyoak.co.uk website - www.earlyoak.co.uk

Omar (Harrogate) Ltd
21 Boroughbridge Rd. HG5 0LY. (P. McCormick). Est. 1946. Open by appointment. *STOCK: Persian, Turkish, Caucasian rugs and carpets.* PARK: Easy. TEL: 01423 863199; fax - same; e-mail - philipmccormick@hotmail.com SER: Cleaning; restorations. VAT: Stan.

Starkie/Bowkett
9 Abbey Rd. HG5 8HY. (E.S. Starkie). Resident. Est. 1919. Open 9-6. SIZE: Medium. *STOCK: Chairs, small furniture, books, pottery and collectables.* LOC: By the river at the lower road bridge. PARK: Easy. TEL: 01423 866112.

John Thompson Antiques **LAPADA**
Swadforth House, Gracious St. HG5 8DT. Est. 1968. *STOCK: 18th-19th C furniture and related decorative objects.* PARK: Easy. TEL: 01423 864698. FAIRS: Olympia. VAT: Spec.

LEYBURN

Leyburn Antiques Centre
Harmby Rd. DL8 5NS. (Paul Ashford). Est. 1984. Open 9.30-4.30 including Sun. SIZE: Large - 40 dealers. *STOCK: Fine Georgian, Victorian and Edwardian furniture, pine, pottery and porcelain, glass, lighting, silver and jewellery, oil paintings, prints, taxidermy, books, garden reclamation items and bygones.* LOC: 300 yards from Tennants Auctioneers. PARK: Easy. TEL: 01969 625555; e-mail - leyburnantiques@aol.com website - www.leyburnantiques.com SER: Valuations; restorations.

Thirkill Antiques
Newlands, Worton. DL8 3ET. Est. 1963. *STOCK: Musicals, pottery, porcelain, small furniture, 18th-19th C.* PARK: Easy. TEL: 01969 650725. SER: Restorations.

MALTON

Magpie Antiques
9-13 The Shambles. YO17 7LZ. (G.M. Warren). Est. 1972. Open 10-4. CL: Thurs. SIZE: Small. *STOCK: General antiques and collectables, 19th-20th C, £5-£50; kitchenalia, £5-£100; some furniture.* LOC: Town centre, near Cattle Market. PARK: Nearby. TEL: Home - 01653 658335; mobile - 07969 852849. FAIRS: Newark.

MASHAM, Nr. Ripon

Aura Antiques
1-3 Silver St. HG4 4DX. (R. and R. Sutcliffe). Est. 1985. Open 9.30-4.30, Sun. by appointment. SIZE: Medium. *STOCK: Furniture especially period mahogany and oak, 17th to mid-19th C, £50-£5,000; metalware - brass and copper, fenders, £5-£250; china, glass, silver and decorative objects, £5-£1,000; all 18th-19th C.* LOC: Corner of Market Sq. PARK: Easy. TEL: 01765 689315; home - 01765 658192; e-mail - Robert@aura-antiques.co.uk website - www.aura-antiques.co.uk SER: Valuations; UK delivery. VAT: Spec.

MIDDLEHAM

Middleham Antiques
The Corner Shop, Kirkgate. DL8 4PF. (Angela Walton). Est. 1984. Usually open 10-5.30 - prior telephone call always advisable. *STOCK: Victorian, Edwardian and decorative curios and ceramics, to £1,500.* PARK: Easy. TEL: 01969 622982.

MIDDLESBROUGH

Appleton Antiques
Marton. TS7 8NF. (James Appleton). Est. 1993. Open by appointment only. SIZE: Small. *STOCK: Pottery - Moorcroft, Carltonware, Linthorpe, Poole, from late 19th C, £15-£4,000; glass, especially 19th C drinking, 1760-1930, £2-£300; crested china, 1900-1920s, £2-£60; postcards, 1900-1960, £1-£30; modern Lise Moorcroft and Sally Tuffin (Dennis china), £140-£650; paintings and drawings, late 19th to 20th C, £10-£1,800.* LOC: South side of town. PARK: Easy. TEL: 01642 316417; home - same; e-mail - info@appletonantiques.co.uk website - www.appletonantiques.co.uk SER: Valuations; restorations arranged(pottery).

NORTHALLERTON

Collectors Corner
145/6 High St. DL7 8SL. (J. Wetherill). Est. 1972. Open 10-4 or by appointment. CL: Thurs. *STOCK: General antiques, collectors' items.* LOC: Opposite GPO. TEL: 01609 777623; home - 01609 775199.

NORTON, Nr. Malton

Northern Antiques Company
2 Parliament St., Scarborough Rd. YO17 9HE. (Sara Ashby-Arnold). Est. 1991. Open 9-1 and 2-5, Sat. 9.30-12.30, Sun. and evenings by appointment. SIZE: Medium. *STOCK: Country oak furniture, from 17th C, £200-£2,000; pine, Georgian to Victorian, to £1,000; upholstered sofas and chairs, cast-iron and wooden beds, decorative items and prints, from 19th C, to £800; some contemporary interior design items.* LOC: From Malton town centre on old Scarborough Rd., through Norton, shop on right above Aga shop. PARK: Easy. TEL: 01653 697520.

PATELEY BRIDGE

Country Oak Antiques
Yorkshire Country Wines, The Mill, Glasshouses. HG3 5QH. (Richard Brown). Est. 1980. Open Wed.-Sun. 11.30-4.30, (reduced hours Jan. and Feb) - most times by appointment. SIZE: Medium. *STOCK: Oak and country furniture, 17th-19th C, £50-£5,000.* LOC: 1/4 mile from crossroads of B6165. PARK: Easy. TEL: 01423 711947; fax - same; home - 01423 711223; e-mail - info@countryoakantiques.co.uk website - www.countryoakantiques.co.uk.

Brian Loomes
Calf Haugh Farm. HG3 5HW. (Brian and Joy Loomes). (Author of clock reference books). Est. 1966. Open strictly by appointment. SIZE: Medium. *STOCK: British clocks especially longcase, wall, bracket and lantern, pre-1840, £2,000-£20,000.* Not Stocked: Foreign clocks. LOC: From Pateley Bridge, first private lane on left on Grassington Rd. (B6265). PARK: Own. TEL: 01423 711163; e-mail - clocks@brianloomes.com website - www.brianloomes.com VAT: Spec.

PICKERING

Country Collector
11-12 Birdgate. Y018 7AL. (G. and M. Berney). Est. 1991. Open 10-5. CL: Wed. SIZE: Small. *STOCK: Ceramics, including blue and white and Art Deco pottery, and collectables, 1800-1940, £10-£1,000.* LOC: Top of the Market Place, at crossroads of A169 and A170. PARK: Eastgate. TEL: 01751 477481; website - www.country-collector.co.uk SER: Valuations; buys at auction (ceramics). VAT: Stan.

Pickering Antique Centre
Southgate. YO18 8BL. (Tina and Jim Vance). Est. 1972. Open 10-5. SIZE: Large. *STOCK: Bedsteads, from 1840; Victorian and Edwardian furniture; pictures and prints, pottery and porcelain, books, collectables, glass, clocks, jewellery, silver and plate, postcards, lighting and metalware.* LOC: Next to traffic lights on A170 Helmsley road. PARK: Own at rear. TEL: 01751 477210; mobile - 07899 872309; e-mail - sales@pickantiques.freeserve.co.uk website - www.pickeringantiquecentre.co.uk SER: Valuations; restorations (metalware including bedsteads, furniture).

C.H. Reynolds Antiques
The Old Curiosity Shop, 122 Eastgate. YO18 7DW. (C.H. and D.M. Reynolds). Est. 1947. Open 9.30-5.30, Sun. by arrangement. *STOCK: Furniture, glass, china.* LOC: A170. PARK: Free, outside shop. TEL: 01751 472785.

RICHMOND

York House (Antiques)
York House, 60 Market Place. DL10 4JQ. (Christine Swift). Est. 1986. Open 9.30-5.30, Sun. 12-4. SIZE: Medium.

BRIAN LOOMES

Specialist dealer in antique British clocks. Internationally recognised authority and author of numerous books on antique clocks. Large stock of longcase clocks with a number of lantern clocks and bracket clocks.

Restoration work undertaken

EST'D 39 YEARS (2005)

Resident on premises. Available six days a week but strictly by prior telephone appointment.

Copies of my current books always in stock.

CALF HAUGH FARMHOUSE, PATELEY BRIDGE, NORTH YORKS. (On B6265 Pateley-Grassington road.)
Tel: (01423) 711163   www.brianloomes.com

STOCK: Furniture, mainly Victorian and Edwardian including pine, £500-£1,000; china, lamps, figures, Victorian to 1930s, £20-£500; kitchenalia, garden artifacts, French and English fires and fireplaces, Victorian and later, to £800. PARK: Loading bay or nearby. TEL: 01748 850338; fax - same; home - 01748 850126; mobile - 07711 307045; e-mail - christina.swift@tiscali.com SER: Interior design; 'layaway' scheme.

RIPON

Milton Holgate   **BADA**
P O Box 77. HG4 3XX. Est. 1972. Open by appointment. *STOCK: Fine English furniture and accessories, 17th-19th C.* TEL: 01765 620225; e-mail - miltonholgate@hotmail.com

Hornsey's of Ripon
3 Kirkgate. HG4 1PA. (Bruce, Susan and Daniel Hornsey). Est. 1976. Open 9-5.30. SIZE: Medium. *STOCK: Textiles, bric-a-brac, rare and secondhand books.* PARK: Market Square. TEL: 01765 602878; e-mail - hornseys@ripon-internet.co.uk

Sigma Antiques and Fine Art
The Old Opera House, Water Skellgate. HG4 1BH. (D. Thomson). Est. 1963. Open 10.30-5, other times by appointment. SIZE: Large. *STOCK: 17th-20th C furniture, furnishing items, pottery, porcelain, objets d'art, paintings, jewellery and collectors' items.* LOC: Near town centre. PARK: Nearby. TEL: 01765 603163; fax - same; e-mail - sigmaantiques@aol.com SER: Restorations (furniture); repairs (jewellery and silver); valuations. VAT: Spec.

Skellgate Curios
2 Low Skellgate. HG4 1BE. (J.I. Wain and P.S. Gyte). Est. 1974. Open 11-5. CL: Wed. *STOCK: Furniture, decorative antiques, period jewellery, silver, brass, copper and collectors items.* TEL: 01765 601290; home - 01765 635336/635332.

ROBIN HOOD'S BAY

John Gilbert Antiques
King St. YO22 4SH. Est. 1990. Open Sat. 10-1 and 2-5, Sun. 11-4, other days by appointment. SIZE: Small. *STOCK: Country furniture, 18th-19th C, £100-£1,500; oak furniture from 1650, £250-£1,500; Victorian furniture, £50-£1,000; treen, £5-£500.* LOC: At bottom of old village, between Bay and Dolphin Hotels. PARK: Top of hill. TEL: Home - 01947 880528; mobile - 07969 004320. SER: Valuations; restorations (furniture).

SCARBOROUGH

Antiques & Collectors Centre
35, St. Nicholas Cliff. YO11 2ES. Est. 1965. Open 9.30-4.30. *STOCK: Collectables and accessories including postcards, coins, cigarette cards, stamps, military items and jewellery.* TEL: 01723 365221; mobile - 07730 202405. e-mail - sales@collectors.demon.co.uk

Hanover Antiques & Collectables
33 St Nicolas Cliff. YO11 2ES. (R.E. and P.J. Baldwin). Est. 1976. Open 10-4. *STOCK: Small collectables, medals, badges, militaria, toys, 50p-£500.* LOC: Close to Grand Hotel. PARK: Nearby. TEL: 01723 374175.

St. Nicholas Antiques
34, St Nicholas Cliff. YO11 2ES. Open 10-4. *STOCK: General antiques including furniture, clocks, porcelain and pottery, paintings, silver and collectables.*

SETTLE

Mary Milnthorpe and Daughters Antique Shop
Market Place. BD24 9DX. (Judith Milnthorpe). Est. 1958. Open 9.30-5. CL: Wed. SIZE: Small. *STOCK: Antique and 19th C jewellery and English silver.* LOC: Opposite Town Hall. PARK: Easy. TEL: 01729 822331. VAT: Stan/Spec.

Nanbooks
Roundabout, 41 Duke St. BD24 9DJ. (J.L. and N.M. Midgley). Resident. Est. 1955. Open Tues., Fri. and Sat. 11-12.30 and 2-5.30, other times by appointment. SIZE: Small. *STOCK: English pottery, porcelain including Oriental, glass, general small antiques, 17th-19th C, to £500.* Not Stocked: Jewellery. LOC: A65. PARK: Easy. TEL: 01729 823324; e-mail - midglui@aol.com

Anderson Slater Antiques
6 Duke St. BD24 7DW. (K.C. Slater). Est. 1962. Open 10-1 and 2-5. SIZE: Medium. *STOCK: Furniture, 18th-19th C, £200-£6,000; porcelain, 18th-19th C, £25-£500; pictures, 19th-20th C, £200-£1,500.* LOC: Main street out of Market Place. PARK: Nearby. TEL: 01729 822051. SER: Valuations; restorations (furniture and porcelain); buys at auction. VAT: Stan/Spec.

E. Thistlethwaite
The Antique Shop, Market Sq. BD24 9EF. Est. 1972.

Open 9-5. CL: Wed. SIZE: Medium. *STOCK: Country furniture and metalware, 18th-19th C.* LOC: Town centre, A65. PARK: Forecourt. TEL: 01729 822460. VAT: Stan/Spec.

SKIPTON

J.K. Adamson - Adamson Armoury
70 Otley St. BD23 1ET. Est. 1975. Open by appointment. SIZE: Medium. *STOCK: Weapons, 17th-19th C, £10-£1,000.* LOC: A65, 200yds. from town centre. PARK: At rear. TEL: 01756 791355. SER: Valuations.

Manor Barn
Providence Mill, The Old Foundry Yard, Cross St. BD23 2AE. (Manor Barn Furniture Ltd). Est. 1972. Open 9-5. *STOCK: Pine, 17th-19th C and reproduction; oak.* PARK: Easy. TEL: 01756 798584; fax - 01756 798536; e-mail - info@manorbarnpine.co.uk website - www. manorbarnpine.co.uk VAT: Stan/Spec.

Skipton Antiques Centre
The Old Foundry, Cavendish St. BD23 2AB. (Andrew Tapsell). Est. 1994. Open 10.30-4.30, Sun. 11-4. SIZE: Large - 30 dealers. *STOCK: Wide range of general antiques and collectables, Georgian to Art Deco, £5-£1,500.* LOC: West side of town off A59. PARK: Loading and nearby. TEL: 01756 797667.

SLEIGHTS, Nr. Whitby

Coach House Antiques
75 Coach Rd. YO22 5BT. (C.J. Rea). Resident. Est. 1973. Open Sat. from 10 and by appointment. SIZE: Small. *STOCK: Furniture, especially oak and country; metalware, paintings, pottery, textiles, unusual and decorative items.* LOC: On A169, 3 miles south west of Whitby. PARK: Easy, opposite. TEL: 01947 810313.

Eskdale Antiques
164 Coach Rd. YO22 4BH. (Philip Smith). Est. 1978. Open 9-5.30 including Sun. SIZE: Medium. *STOCK: Pine furniture and farm bygones, 19th-20th C, £50-£500.* LOC: Main Pickering road. PARK: Easy. TEL: 01947 810297; home - same. SER: Valuations; buys at auction.

SNAINTON, Nr. Scarborough

Antony, David & Ann Shackleton
19 & 72 High St. YO13 9AE. Resident. Est. 1984. CL: Fri. SIZE: Medium. *STOCK: Longcase clocks, Victorian rocking horses, Georgian and Victorian furniture, collectables, £1-£3,500.* LOC: A170, equidistant Scarborough and Pickering. PARK: Easy. TEL: 01723 859577/850172. SER: Restorations (furniture, longcase clocks, rocking horses).

STILLINGTON

Pond Cottage Antiques
Brandsby Rd. YO61 1NY. (C.M. and D. Thurstans). Resident. Est. 1970. Open seven days 9-5. SIZE: Medium. *STOCK: Pine, kitchenalia, country furniture, treen, metalware, brass, copper.* LOC: B1363 York to Helmsley road. PARK: Own. TEL: 01347 810796. SER: Re-polishing. VAT: Global.

STOKESLEY, Nr. Middlesborough

Alan Ramsey Antiques LAPADA
7 Wainstones Court, Stokesley Industrial Park. TS9 5JY. Est. 1973. Open by appointment only. SIZE: Warehouse. *STOCK: Victorian, Edwardian and Georgian furniture; longcase, wall and bracket clocks; interesting pine.* PARK: Easy. TEL: 01642 711311/713008; mobile - 07702 523246; 07762 049848; e-mail - a.ramsey antiques@btinternet.com website - www.alanramsey antiques.co.uk VAT: Stan/Spec.

THIRSK

Classic Rocking Horses
from Windmill Antiques. (B. and J. Tildesley). Est. 1980. Open by appointment. *STOCK: Restored antique rocking horses and authentic replicas of Victorian rocking horses, £1,500-£5,000.* TEL: 01845 501330; fax - 01845 501700; e-mail - info@classicrockinghorses.co.uk website - www.classicrockinghorses.co.uk

Kirkgate Fine Art & Conservation
The Studio, 3 Gillings Yard. YO7 1SY. (Richard Bennett). BAPCR. UKIC. Est. 1979. Open by appointment. SIZE: Small. *STOCK: Oil paintings, £50-£2,000; watercolours, £50-£500; both 19th to mid-20th C.* LOC: Joins Market Place. PARK: Nearby. TEL: 01845 524085; home - same; e-mail - reb@vetscapes.fsnet.co.uk website - www. kirkgateconservation.co.uk SER: Restorations (oil paintings and framing); buys at auction.

Millgate Pine & Antiques
Abel Grange Farm, Newsham Rd. YO7 4DB. (T.D. and M. Parvin). Est. 1990. Open 8.30-5. SIZE: Large + warehouse. *STOCK: English and European pine especially doors.* LOC: 2.5 miles north of Thirsk. PARK: Easy. TEL: 01845 523878; e-mail - babs.jenkins @btinternet.com SER: Repairs; stripping; restorations.

Potterton Books
The Old Rectory, Sessay. YO7 3LZ. (Clare Jameson). Est. 1980. Open 9-5. SIZE: Large. *STOCK: Classic reference works on art, architecture, interior design, antiques and collecting.* PARK: Easy. TEL: 01845 501218; fax - 01845 501439; website - www. pottertonbooks.co.uk SER: Book search; catalogues. FAIRS: London; Frankfurt; Paris; New York; Milan; Dubai.

THORNTON-LE-DALE

Cobweb Books
1 Pickering Rd. YO18 7LG. (Robin and Sue Buckler). Est. 1990. Open every day June-Oct. 10-5. CL: Mon. in winter. SIZE: Medium. *STOCK: Books - leather bindings, illustrated, modern first editions, literature, military, poetry, history.* PARK: Nearby. TEL: 01751 476638; home - 01751 474402; e-mail - sales@ cobwebbooks.co.uk website - www.cobwebbooks.co.uk

TOCKWITH, Nr. York

Tomlinsons LAPADA
Moorside. YO26 7QG. Est. 1977. Open Mon-Fri. 8-5 or by appointment. Fine Furniture Club members - open 8-5, Sat. 9-5, Sun. 10-4. SIZE: Very large. *STOCK:*

Furniture, antique, upholstered and reproduction, £10-£20,000; clocks, porcelain, silver plate and decorative items, £10-£5,000. LOC: A1 Wetherby take B1224 towards York. After 3 miles turn left on to Rudgate. At end of this road turn left, business 200m on left. PARK: Easy. TEL: 01423 358833; fax - 01423 358188; e-mail - ffc@antique-furniture.co.uk website - www.antique-furniture.co.uk SER: Export; restorations; container packing, delivery, desk leathering; bespoke reproductions. VAT: Stan/Spec.

WEST BURTON, Nr. Leyburn

The Old Smithy
DL8 4JL. (Bill Woodbridge, Lynn Watkinson and Pete and Elaine Dobbing). Est. 2000. Open 10-4, prior telephone call advisable for winter opening. SIZE: Small. *STOCK: General antiques, silver and jewellery, collectables, £5-£300; clocks and small furniture, £50-£1,000; all 18th-20th C.* LOC: Between Leyburn and Hawes, take Kettlewell road. PARK: Easy. TEL: 01969 663999; mobile - 07881 985555. SER: Valuations; buys at auction. *Trade Only.*

WHITBY

The Bazaar
7 Skinner St. YO21 3AH. (F.A. Doyle). Est. 1970. Open 10.30-5.30. *STOCK: Jewellery, furniture, general antiques and collectables, 19th C.* LOC: Town centre. TEL: 01947 602281.

Bobbins Wool, Crafts, Antiques
Wesley Hall, Church St. YO22 4DE. (Dick and Pam Hoyle). Est. 1984. Open 10-5 including Sun. SIZE: Small. *STOCK: General antiques especially oil lamps, bric-a-brac, 78 records and postcards, kitchenalia and fireplaces, 19th-20th C.* LOC: Between Market Place and steps to Abbey on cobbled East Side. PARK: Nearby (part of Church St. is pedestrianised). TEL: 01947 600585 (answerphone); e-mail - bobbins@globalnet.co.uk SER: Repairs and spares (oil lamps). VAT: Stan.

Caedmon House
14 Station Sq. YO21 1DU. (E.M. Stanforth). Est. 1977. Open 11-4.30. SIZE: Medium. *STOCK: General, mainly small, antiques including jewellery, dolls, Disney and china, especially Dresden, to £1,200.* PARK: Easy. TEL: 01947 602120; home - 01947 603930. SER: Valuations; restorations (china); repairs (jewellery). VAT: Stan/Spec.

Eskdale Antiques Ltd
85 Church St. YO22 4BH. (P.E. and P.A. Smith). Est. 1983. Open 10.30-12.30 and 1-5 (Sat. and Sun. only Nov. to Mar.). SIZE: Medium. *STOCK: Clarice Cliff, £100-£3,000; English transfer print creamware and general antiques.* LOC: A174. PARK: Nearby. TEL: 01947 600512. SER: Valuations; buys at auction (Clarice Cliff). VAT: Margin/Global.

YORK

Antiques Centre York
Allenby House, 41 Stonegate. YO1 8AW. (David Waggott). Est. 2003. Open seven days 9-6. SIZE: Large. *STOCK: Wide range of general antiques, from £1-* £7,000. LOC: In pedestrianised thoroughfare between Minster and main shopping area, 10 mins. from station. PARK: Nearby. TEL: 01904 635888; fax - 01904 676342; website - www.theantiquescentreyork.co.uk VAT: Stan.

Barbican Bookshop
24 Fossgate. YO1 9TA. PBFA. Est. 1961. Open 9.15-5.30. SIZE: Large. *STOCK: Books - antiquarian, secondhand and new.* LOC: City centre. PARK: Multi-storey nearby. TEL: 01904 653643; fax - 01904 653643; e-mail - mail@barbicanbookshop.co.uk website - www.barbicanbookshop.co.uk SER: Mail order. FAIRS: PBFA. VAT: Stan.

Bishopsgate Antiques
23/24 Bishopsgate St. YO2 1JH. (R. Wetherill). Est. 1965. Open 9.15-6. *STOCK: General antiques.* TEL: 01904 623893; fax - 01904 626511.

Barbara Cattle   BADA
45 Stonegate. YO1 8AW. Open 9-5.30. *STOCK: Jewellery and silver, Georgian to date.* TEL: 01904 623862; fax - 01904 651675; e-mail - info@ barbaracattle.co.uk website - www.barbaracattle. co.uk SER: Valuations; repairs; restorations.

Cavendish Antiques & Collectors Centre
44 Stonegate. YO1 8AS. (Debbie and Mark Smith). Est. 1996. Open seven days 9-6. SIZE: Large. *STOCK: Wide range of general antiques, £1-£7,000.* LOC: In pedestrianised thoroughfare between Minster and main shopping area. PARK: Nearby. TEL: 01904 621666; fax - 01904 675747. VAT: Stan.

Coulter Galleries
Open by appointment. *STOCK: Watercolours and oils, pre-1900; frames.* TEL: 07850 665144; fax - 01904 792285; e-mail - rober.coulter@btinternet.com

Ruth Ford Antiques
39 Fossgate. YO1 9TF. Est. 1976. Open 11.30-4.30. CL: Wed. SIZE: Small. *STOCK: 18th-19th C country furniture, pine, treen and collectables, £5-£1,000.* LOC: Near Merchant Adventurers Hall. PARK: Nearby. TEL: Home - 01904 632864.

Fossgate Books
36 Fossgate. YO1 9TF. (Alex Helstrip). Est. 1992. Open 10-5.30. SIZE: Large. *STOCK: Out-of-print and antiquarian books.* LOC: City centre. PARK: Nearby. TEL: 01904 641389.

The French House (Antiques) Ltd.
74 Micklegate. YO1 6LF. (S.B. and M.J. Hazell). Est. 1995. Open 9.30-5.30. SIZE: Large. *STOCK: Wooden beds, 18th-19th C, £900-£2,500; gilt mirrors, 19th C, £300-£2,000; lighting, 19th-20th C, £200-£1,000; all French.* LOC: Main entry to city from A64. PARK: Side streets. TEL: 01904 624465; fax - 01904 629965; website - www.thefrenchhouse.co.uk VAT: Margin.

Golden Memories of York
14 Newgate. YO1 7LA. (M.S. and D.J.Smith). NAG. Est. 1991. Open Tues.-Sat. 9-5.30. SIZE: Small. *STOCK: Antique and secondhand jewellery and silver, £5-£6,000.* LOC: Adjacent York market, off Parliament St. PARK: Multi-storey. TEL: 01904 655883; fax - 01904 623925;

e-mail - goldenmemories@compuserve.com SER: Repairs; valuations. VAT: Stan/Spec/Global/Margin.

Harpers Jewellers
2-6 Minster Gates. YO1 7HL. (J. Saffer and N. Wiseman). Open 9-5.30. SIZE: Small. *STOCK: Vintage watches, from 1900, especially unusual, quirky and very rare - Omega, Longines, Eterna specialising in Heuer and military pieces.* LOC: Near the Minster. PARK: Mary Gate. TEL: 01904 632634; fax - 01904 673370; e-mail - harpersYork@btopenworld.com website - www.vintage-watches.co.uk SER: Valuations; restorations (watches).

Minster Gate Bookshop
8 Minster Gates. YO1 7HL. (N. Wallace). PBFA. Est. 1970. Open 10-5.30. SIZE: Large. *STOCK: Antiquarian and secondhand books; old maps and prints.* LOC: Opposite south door of Minster. PARK: Nearby. TEL: 01904 621812; fax - 01904 622960; e-mail - rarebooks@minstergatebooks.co.uk SER: Valuations; restorations; book finding.

Janette Ray Rare and Out of Print Books
8 Bootham. YO30 7BL. PBFA. ABA. Est. 1987. Open Fri. and Sat. 9.30-5.30 or by appointment. SIZE: Small. *STOCK: Out of print books on design, architecture and gardens.* LOC: City centre. PARK: Opposite. TEL: 01904 623088; fax - 01904 620814; e-mail - books@janetteray.co.uk website - www.janetteray.co.uk SER: Valuations; catalogues issued; finder. FAIRS: ABA Olympia.

The Red House Antiques Centre
Duncombe Place. YO1 7ED. (Ginnel Antiques Centres - P. Stephenson). Open Mon.-Sat. 9.30-5.30, (June-Sept. 9.30-8), Sun. 10.30-5.30. LOC: 200 yards from Minster. TEL: 01904 637000; e-mail - enquiries@redhouseyork. co.uk website - www.redhouseyork.co.uk SER: Packing and shipping; arts and antiques lectures. Below are listed the specialist dealers at this centre.

Aldholme Antiques
18th-19th C ceramics.

April Antiques
18th-19th C ceramics.

Art Decoration
Art Deco furniture.

Fiona Aston
19th C porcelain, silver and objets d'art.

Automotive Art
Chinese antiquities.

413

Edward Bacon
Fine longcase, wall and mantel clocks.

Margaret Bedi Antiques & Fine Art
English period furniture, 1720-1920; oils and watercolours, 19th-20th C. TEL: Home - 01642 583247; mobile - 07860 577637.

Bootham Antiques
19th C silver, porcelain, glass and curios.

Brackmoor Antiques
Silver.

Bygones
Jewellery and dolls.

Charleston Antiques
Art Deco ceramics.

Jocelyn Chatterton
Fine Oriental textiles.

J.E. Chew
Silver.

Pauline Conway
19th C furniture, Carltonware, Maling.

Cornucopia
Jewellery and coins.

Garden House Antiques
19th C prints and maps.

G. Gardiner
19th C ceramics.

Graham and Dianne
Militaria.

James Hardy (Antiques) Ltd
18th-19th C silver.

Roy Harris
Coins.

Hogarth Antiques
Silver, plate, porcelain and treen.

Jean Linford
Deco chrome, clocks, jewellery and accessories.

Lycurgus Glass
19th-20th C decorative art glass and mirrors.

Stella Mar Antiques
19th C furniture and furnishings, porcelain, metalware, treen and objets d'art.

March Antiques
Art Nouveau silver and metalware.

Olivia Meyler
Jewellery and Russian artefacts.

Mick's Antiques
Militaria and railwayana.

John Moor
Ancient art and antiques.

Nichola
General antiques.

F. O'Flynn
Antique prints, maps and books.

Osiris
Art Nouveau metalware and jewellery.

Anne Powell
18th-19th C ceramics, Tunbridgeware and silver.

Alan Price
17th-18th C oak furniture, brass and copper.

Pure Imagination
Scandinavian Deco furniture, metalware and ceramics.

P.W. Raine
Silver, pewter, metalware and ceramics.

G. Rhodes
19th C furniture and paintings.

Janice Scanlon
Art Deco ceramics and jewellery.

Small Fish Antiques
19th C furniture, mirrors, glass, pottery, toys, advertising materials and ephemera.

Station Road Antiques
Silver and jewellery.

Topaz Antiques
Victorian and Edwardian jewellery.

C.E. Tweedale
Victorian and Edwardian pottery and porcelain.

Willow and Urn
American jewellery.

Gwen Wood
Belleek.

Jack Yarwood
18th-19th C wood, metalware and objets d'art.

York Decorative Antiques
Boxes, caddies and Oriental decoratives.

J. Smith
47 The Shambles. YO1 7LX. BNTA. Est. 1963. Open Tues.-Sat. 9.30-4. SIZE: Small. *STOCK: Numismatic items, mainly English coins.* LOC: City centre. TEL: 01904 654769; fax - 01904 677988. VAT: Stan/Spec.

Ken Spelman
70 Micklegate. YO1 6LF. (Peter Miller and Tony Fothergill). ABA. PBFA. Est. 1948. Open 9-5.30. SIZE: Large. *STOCK: Secondhand and antiquarian books especially fine arts and literature, 50p-£20,000.* LOC: City centre. PARK: Easy. TEL: 01904 624414; fax - 01904 626276; e-mail - rarebooks@kenspelman.com website - www.kenspelman.com SER: Valuations; buys at auction (books); catalogues issued. FAIRS: Bath, Oxford, York, Harrogate, Cambridge, Edinburgh and London PBFA and ABA. VAT: Spec.

St. John Antiques
26 Lord Mayor's Walk. YO31 7HA. (R. and N. Bell). Est. 1985. Open Sat. 10-5 or any time by appointment. *STOCK: Victorian stripped pine, curios, blue and white pottery.* LOC: Near Minster. PARK: At rear. TEL: 01904 644263. SER: Stripping and finishing.

York Antiques Centre
2a Lendal. YO1 8AA. Est. 1984. Open 10-5. SIZE: 25 dealers. *STOCK: Antiques and collectable items, 18th-20th C.* LOC: Opposite the museum gardens. PARK: Easy. TEL: 01904 641445.

- *The first comprehensive study of needlework tools and accessories made in Holland between 1400 and the twentieth century*

- *Features approximately 500 photographs, most of which have never before been published*

- *Unique information on makers of needlework tools and their marks*

- *Also includes a comprehensive study of knitting tools and accessories*

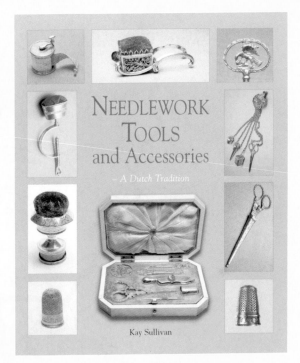

NEEDLEWORK TOOLS
and Accessories

A Dutch Tradition

Kay Sullivan

> *"… as comprehensive a study as one would ever need… for collectors of sewing accoutrement, small metalwork or those interested in Dutch history, it is a fascinating, clearly written history"* **Antiques Magazine**

This book, with 400 colour and almost 100 black and white illustrations, is the result of years of research. It is the first published history of the tools and accessories used by needlewomen in Holland, from the Middle Ages to the twentieth century, describing how they were used and also who would have used them. Many of these tools were beautifully made by craftsmen from precious metals, treasured by their owners and handed down through generations. Others were very simply crafted out of wood, individually carved and decorated by the artisan. Thimble collectors will be delighted with the abundance of illustrations of thimbles, from those simply made of brass, to gold ones decorated with gemstones. Collectors of other sewing tools will welcome the inclusion of chapters on sewing sets, chatelaines, scissors, needle cases, pin-cushions, tape measures, thread holders and winders, tambour tools and knitting accessories. The final chapter is particularly useful for collectors, as it contains a unique list of the makers of Dutch silver and gold needlework tools, with drawings of their marks to aid identification. The book will be especially interesting to collectors outside Holland, as many of the beautiful sewing tools made there have found their way to other parts of the world. They were exported to the Dutch colonies in America and South Africa, and in the nineteenth and twentieth centuries families took all their household chattels with them, including family heirlooms, when they emigrated to America, Canada or Australasia. Overseas collectors may well discover that some of their treasures were in fact made in Holland. This comprehensive book will be an indispensable addition to the library of the needlework tool enthusiast, as all other books on this subject are lacking in this particular area. It contains much new information encompassing the breadth of her expertise, and most of the illustrations are published here for the first time.

Specifications: 224pp.,
458 col. illus., 94 b.&w. illus.,
11¼ x 9½in./285 x 242mm.
£29.50 (hardback)

For full details of all ACC publications, log on to our website:
www.antiquecollectorsclub.com
or telephone 01394 389950 for a free catalogue

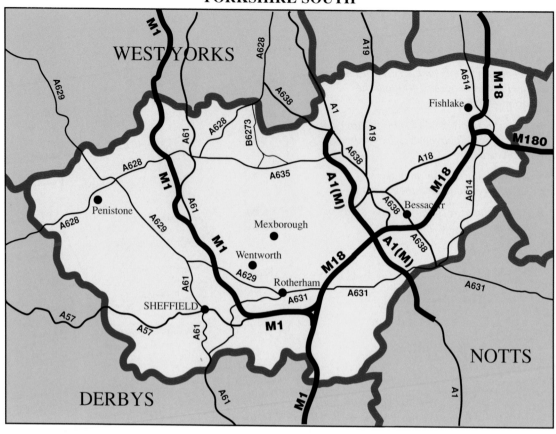

BESSACARR, Nr. Doncaster

Keith Stones Grandfather Clocks

5 Ellers Drive. DN4 7DL. Est. 1988. Open by appointment. SIZE: Small. *STOCK: Grandfather clocks, especially painted dials 30 hour and 8 day movements, Georgian to early 19th C, £1,250-£3,750.* LOC: Take A638 Bawtry road off racecourse roundabout, through traffic lights after 3/4 mile, take second right into Ellers Rd. then second left. PARK: Easy. TEL: 01302 535258; home - same; e-mail - clocks@kstones.fsnet.co.uk website - www.kstones.fsnet.co.uk SER: Valuations.

FISHLAKE

Fishlake Antiques

Pinfold Lane. DN7 5LA. Resident. Est. 1972. Open Sun. 1-5 and by appointment. SIZE: Medium. *STOCK: Rural furniture especially stripped pine; clocks including longcase and wall clocks, garden and small architectural*

items, Victorian to mid-19th C, £30-£2,000; smalls, £3-£70. LOC: Off A63. PARK: Own. TEL: 01302 841411.

MEXBOROUGH

Roger Appleyard Ltd   LAPADA

The Gent Building, Whitelea Grove, Whitelea Industrial Estate. S64 9QL. Open Mon.-Fri. 8-5. SIZE: Large. *STOCK: General antiques, £5-£10,000.* TEL: 01709 590404; fax - same; e-mail - roger@rogerappleyard.com SER: Packing and shipping. VAT: Stan/Spec. *Trade Only.*

PENISTONE, Nr. Sheffield

Penistone Pine and Antiques

Units 2 and 3 Penistone Court, Sheffield Rd. S36 6HP. (Peter Lucas). Est. 1984. Open 9-5. SIZE: Large. *STOCK: Stripped and finished pine, 1800-1920.* PARK: Easy. TEL: 01226 370018; home - 01226 791330; mobile - 07891 193828; e-mail - barrie@lucas165. freeserve.co.uk SER: Restorations.

ROTHERHAM

Foster's Antique Centre
Foster's Garden Centre, Doncaster Rd., Thrybergh. S65 4BE. (The Foster Family). Est. 1996. Open 10-4.30, Sun. 11-5. SIZE: 20 dealers. STOCK: Wide range of general antiques and collectables including furniture, jewellery, Rockingham china. LOC: A630 between Rotherham and Doncaster. PARK: Own large. TEL: 01709 850337; fax - 01709 850402.

Holly Farm Antiques
Holly Farm, Harley Rd., Harley. S62 7UD. (Trevor and Linda Hardwick). Resident. Est. 1988. Open Sat. and Sun. 10-5, other days by appointment. SIZE: Small. STOCK: Rockingham porcelain, 1830-1842; porcelain, pottery, clocks and watches, lamps, glass, silver, furniture. LOC: B6090 quarter mile off A6135 Sheffield to Barnsley, between junctions 35/36 M1. PARK: Own. TEL: 01226 744077; home - same; e-mail - hollyfarm antique@btclick.com SER: Valuations; buys at auction.

Philip Turnor Antiques
94a Broad St., Parkgate. S62 6EG. Est. 1980. Open 9-5, Sat. 10-4. STOCK: Shipping furniture including oak, 1880-1940. LOC: Main road. PARK: Easy. TEL: 01709 524640; e-mail - philipsfurniture@turnorfreeserve.co.uk SER: Export (Japan and USA). FAIRS: Swinderby.

SHEFFIELD

Acorn Antiques
298-300 Abbeydale Rd. S7 1FL. (R.C. and B.C. Priest). Est. 1984. Open 10-5. SIZE: Medium. STOCK: Furniture, 19th-20th C, £20-£500; bronzes, sculptural and unusual items. LOC: A625 to Bakewell. PARK: Easy. TEL: 0114 255 5348; home - same.

Barmouth Court Antiques Centre
Unit 2 Barmouth Rd., Off Abbeydale Rd. S7 2DH. Open 10-5, Sun. 11-4. SIZE: 50 dealers on 2 floors. STOCK: General antiques and collectables. TEL: 0114 255 2711; fax - 0114 258 2672.

Beech House
361 Abbeydale Rd. S7 1FS. (J.M. and A.J. Beech). Est. 1996. Open 10-5. CL: Thurs. SIZE: Small. STOCK: Pine furniture, £100-£2,500; art and ceramics including contemporary, £50-£5,000. LOC: 1 mile from city centre. PARK: Easy. TEL: 0114 250 1004; fax - same; mobile - 07970 196126. SER: Furniture made to order from reclaimed pine.

Chapel Antiques Centre
99 Broadfield Rd. S8 0XH. Open 10-5, Sun. and Bank Holidays 11-5. SIZE: 20+ dealers. STOCK: Furniture, textiles and accessories. LOC: From city centre, 1 mile along A61 Chesterfield Rd., turn right. PARK: Easy. TEL: 0114 258 8288; fax - same; website - www. antiquesinsheffield.com SER: Upholstery and furniture stripping; paint effects; interior design.

Court House Antique Centre
2-6 Town End Rd., Ecclesfield. S35 9YY. (J.P. & K.E. Owram). Open 10.30-5, Sun. 11.30-5. SIZE: Large - 35+ dealers. STOCK: Town and country furniture, French bedroom furniture, antiquarian maps, decorative items,

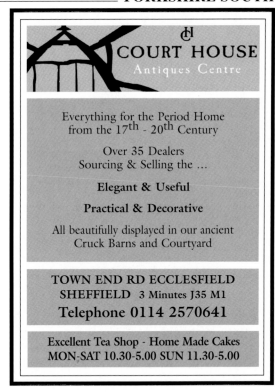
ceramics, glass, clocks, barometers, kitchenalia, books, silver, jewellery, lighting, mirrors, collectables, £5-£5,000. LOC: 2 miles from M1, junction 35. Down hill, bear left into Nether Lane, through lights to church, turn left 250 yards on right. PARK: Easy. TEL: 0114 257 0641; e-mail - courthouseantiques@email.com

Dovetail Antiques
336 Abbeydale Rd. S7 1FN. (D.W. Beedle). Est. 1980. Open 9.30-4.30. SIZE: Medium. STOCK: Georgian, Victorian and Edwardian mahogany, walnut, oak and pine furniture. PARK: Easy. TEL: 0114 255 1554; mobile - 07801 278257; e-mail - dovetailantiques @tiscali.co.uk SER: Restorations.

Dronfield Antiques
375-377 Abbeydale Rd. S7 1FS. (H.J. Greaves). Est. 1968. Open 10.30-5.30 or by appointment. CL: Mon. and Thurs. SIZE: Large + warehouses. STOCK: Trade and shipping goods, Victoriana, glass, china. LOC: A621, 1 mile south of city centre. PARK: Easy. TEL: 0114 255 0172/258 1821; home and fax - 0114 255 6024. SER: Container packing facilities. VAT: Stan.

F S Antiques
Court House Antiques Centre, 2-6 Town End Rd., Ecclesfield. S35 9YY. Open 10.30-5, Sun. 11.30-4.30. SIZE: Small. STOCK: Longcase, wall and mantel clocks, £150-£3,000. LOC: 2 miles from M1, junction 35. PARK: Easy. TEL: 0114 257 0641; home - 01226 382805; mobile - 07949 399481; e-mail - antique@ clocksforall.f9.co.uk website - www.antiqueclocksforall. co.uk SER: Restorations.

THE DICTIONARY OF
20th Century
BRITISH BOOK
ILLUSTRATORS

ALAN HORNE

"Finely produced and generously illustrated" **The Art Newspaper**

Specifications: 224pp., 458 col. illus., 94 b.&w. illus., 11¼ x 9½in./285 x 242mm.
£29.50 (hardback)

Alan Hill Books
Unit 4, Meersbrook Works, Valley Rd. S8 9FT. Est. 1980. Open by appointment. *STOCK: Antiquarian books, maps and prints.* TEL: 0114 255 6242; e-mail - alanhillbooks@supanet.com

Kelly Lighting
679 Ecclesall Rd. S11 8TG. (Frank R. Kelly). Est. 1982. Open Fri. 9-5, Sat. 10.30-5, other days by appointment. SIZE: 2 showrooms. *STOCK: Lighting - ceiling, wall, table and floor, Edwardian and Victorian, £160-£10,000.* LOC: Half mile from Sheffield Parkway End. PARK: Easy. TEL: 0114 267 8500; fax - 0114 268 3242; e-mail - sales@kellyantiquelighting.co.uk website - www.kellyantiquelighting.co.uk SER: Restorations (polishing, lacquering, re-wiring).

Langtons Antiques & Collectables
443 London Rd./Courtyard, 100 Guernsey Rd., Heeley Bottom. S2 4HJ. (Langton Family). Est. 1999. Open 10-5. Sun. 10.30-4.30. SIZE: Large, 70+ dealers. *STOCK: Furniture, architectural items, military, china, porcelain, jewellery, clocks, Art Deco, from 1850, £5-£3,000.* LOC: M1, exit 33, A61 to city centre. PARK: Easy. TEL: 0114 258 1791. FAIRS: Newark. VAT: Stan.

Nichols Antique Centre
The Nichols Building, Shalesmoor. S3 8UJ. (T. and M. Vickers). Est. 1994. Open 10-5, Sat. and Sun. 10.30-4.30. SIZE: Large. *STOCK: Ceramics, fine furniture, clocks and collectables, mainly 19th-20th C, £50-£3,000.* LOC: A61, half mile from city centre. PARK: Easy. TEL: 0114 281 2811; fax - 0114 281 2812. SER: Valuations; restorations; re-upholstery. VAT: Stan.

The Oriental Rug Shop
763 Abbeydale Rd. S7 2BG. (Kian A. Hezaveh). Est. 1880. Open 10-5. SIZE: Large. *STOCK: Handmade rugs and carpets especially large carpets.* LOC: A621. TEL: 0114 255 2240; fax - 0114 250 9088; e-mail - kian@btinternet.com website - www.rugs.btinternet.co.uk SER: Restorations.

Paraphernalia
66/68 Abbeydale Rd. S7 1FD. (W.K. Keller). Est. 1972. Open 9.30-5. *STOCK: General antiques, stripped pine, lighting, brass and iron beds.* LOC: Main road. PARK: Easy. TEL: 0114 255 0203.

N.P. and A. Salt Antiques   LAPADA
Abbeydale House, Barmouth Rd. S7 2DH. Open 10-5, Sun. 11-4. SIZE: Large. *STOCK: Victorian furniture, shipping goods, smalls and toys.* TEL: 0114 258 2672/255 2711. SER: Valuations; packing and shipping; courier.

Sarah Scott Antiques   LAPADA
6 Hutcliffe Wood Rd. S8 0EX. Open Tues.-Sat. 10-5. *STOCK: Furniture, 1760-1910; lighting - oil, gas, electric, 1850-1910; mirrors, 1820-1910.* LOC: 2 minutes from A61. PARK: Easy. TEL: 0114 236 3100; mobile - 07970 050661; e-mail - sarahscottantiques @tiscali.co.uk .website - www.antiquefurnishings.co.uk

Tilley's Vintage Magazine Shop
281 Shoreham St. S1 4SS. (A.G.J. and A.A.J.C. Tilley). Est. 1978. Open Tues.-Sat. 9.30-4.30, other times by appointment. SIZE: Large. *STOCK: Magazines, comics, newspapers, books, postcards, programmes, posters, cigarette cards, prints, ephemera.* LOC: Opposite Sheffield United F.C. PARK: Easy. TEL: 0114 275 2442; fax - same; e-mail - tilleys281@aol.com website - www.tilleysmagazines.com SER: Mail order; valuations.

Paul Ward Antiques
Owl House, 8 Burnell Rd., Owlerton. S6 2AX. Resident. Est. 1976. Open by appointment. SIZE: Large. *STOCK: Matched sets of Victorian dining and kitchen chairs, country chairs, general antiques.* LOC: 2 miles north of city on A61. PARK: Easy. TEL: 0114 233 5980. VAT: Stan/Global.

WENTWORTH, Nr. Rotherham

Wentworth Arts, Crafts and Antiques Ltd
The Old Builders Yard, Cortworth Lane. S62 7SB. (Mrs Jan Sweeting). Est. 1999. Open 10-5 including Sun. SIZE: Large - 50 dealers. *STOCK: Furniture, to £2,500; Royal Doulton, Crown Devon and collectables.* LOC: 5 mins. from junctions 35 and 36, M1. PARK: Easy. TEL: 01226 744333; website - www.wentworthartscraftsandantiques.co.uk

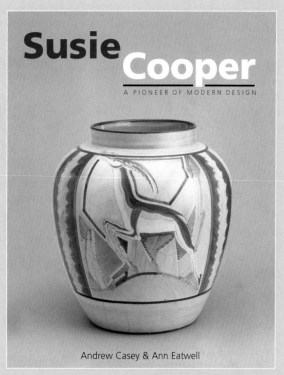

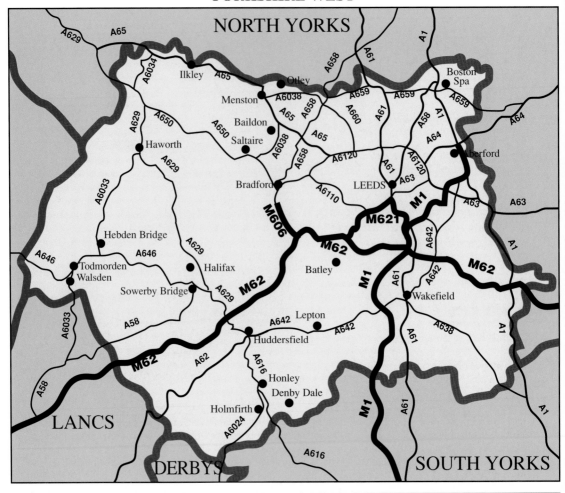

ABERFORD

Aberford Antiques Ltd t/a Aberford Country Furniture

Hicklam House. LS25 3DP. (J.W.H. Long and C.A. Robinson). Est. 1973. Open 9.30-5, Sun. 10.30-5. CL: Mon. SIZE: Large. *STOCK: French oak and painted furniture, occasional English mahogany and accessories.* LOC: Large detached property at south end of village. PARK: Easy. TEL: 0113 281 3209; fax - 0113 281 3121; e-mail - enquiries@aberfordinteriors.co.uk website - www.aberfordinteriors.co.uk VAT: Stan/Spec.

BAILDON, Nr. Shipley

The Baildon Furniture Co. Ltd

Spring Mills, Otley Rd. BD17 6AD. (Richard Parker).

Est. 1972. Open 9.30-5, Sat. 10.30-5, Sun. by appointment. SIZE: Large. *STOCK: Furniture, architectural fitments, pottery and metalware, 17th-20th C, £5-£5,000.* PARK: Easy. TEL: 01274 414345; fax - same; e-mail - baildonfurniture@aol.com SER: Valuations; restorations (cabinet work, repolishing, upholstery, pottery). VAT: Stan/Spec.

Browgate Antiques

13 Browgate. BD17 6BP. (Dianne and David Shaw). Est. 1992. Open 10.30-5 including Sun. CL: Thurs. SIZE: Medium. *STOCK: Georgian, Victorian and Edwardian furniture, £500-£5,000.* PARK: Easy. TEL: 01274 597494; mobile - 07950 638166; website - www. browgateantiques.co.uk

BATLEY

Tansu Oriental Antiques
Redbrick Mill, 218 Bradford Rd, Batley Carr. WF17 6JF. (Stephen P. and C.J. Battye). Est. 1993. Open 9.30-5.30, Sat. 9-6, Sun. 11-5. SIZE: Medium. *STOCK: Japanese and Chinese furniture, chests including staircase and shop display, wheeled trunks, calligraphy boxes, granite lanterns, 1850-1900, £100-£20,000; kimono, 1930-1960, £20-£200.* LOC: Close to M1 and M62. PARK: Own large. TEL: 01924 460044/459441; fax - 01924 462844. SER: Valuations; restorations (Japanese antique furniture). VAT: Spec/Margin.

BOSTON SPA, By Wetherby

London House Oriental Rugs and Carpets
London House, High St. LS23 6AD. (M.J.S. Roe). Open 10-5.30. SIZE: Large. *STOCK: Caucasian, Turkish, Afghan and Persian rugs, runners and carpets, £50-£10,000; kelims and textiles.* LOC: Off A1, south of Wetherby. PARK: Easy. TEL: 01937 845123; home - same. SER: Restorations (Oriental carpets and rugs); buys at auction (Oriental carpets and rugs). VAT: Stan.

BRADFORD

The Corner Shop
89 Oak Lane. BD9 4QU. (Miss Badland). Est. 1961. Open Tues. and Thurs. 2-5.30, Sat. 11-5.30. *STOCK: Pottery, small furniture, clocks and general items.*

Heaton Antiques
1 Hammond Place, Emm Lane, Heaton. BD9 4AN. (T. Steward). Est. 1991. Open 10-5. CL: Mon. SIZE: Medium. *STOCK: Furniture, silver plate and bric-a-brac, pre 1930, £10-£1,000.* LOC: Near A650. PARK: Easy. TEL: 01274 480630. SER: Valuations. FAIRS: Harrogate.

DENBY DALE, Nr. Huddersfield

Worlds Apart
Unit 6A Springfield Mill, Norman Rd. HD8 8TH. (Sharon Dawson). Est. 1995. Open Tues.-Sat. 10-4.30, Sun. 12-4. SIZE: Medium. *STOCK: General antiques, including furniture, and collectables - Denby Dale pie memorabilia, bakelite dial telephones, giftware and jewellery.* LOC: Just off main Huddersfield/Wakefield road (A628). PARK: Easy. TEL: 01484 866713; home - 01226 380093; mobile - 07801 349960; e-mail - shaz@chris216.fsnet.co.uk SER: Restorations and conversions (bakelite dial telephones). *Trade Only.*

HALIFAX

Collectors Old Toy Shop and Antiques
89 Northgate. HX1 1XF. (S. Haley). Est. 1983. Open Tues., Wed., Fri. and Sat. 10.30-4.30. SIZE: 2 floors. *STOCK: Collectors toys, clocks and antiques.* PARK: Nearby. TEL: 01422 360434/822148; e-mail - collectorsoldtoy@aol.com website - www.collectors oldtoyshop.com SER: Valuations; TV hire.

Halifax Antiques Centre
Queens Rd. HX1 4LR. (M. and A. Carroll). Est. 1981.

Open Tues.-Sat. 10-4.30. SIZE: Large - 30 dealers. *STOCK: Art Deco, jewellery, porcelain, linen, costume, pine, oak, mahogany, French and English furniture, kitchenalia, decorative collectables.* LOC: A58 to King Cross, turn at Trafalgar Inn into Queens Rd. corner, 3rd set of lights. PARK: Own. TEL: 01422 366657.

Muir Hewitt Art Deco Originals
Halifax Antiques Centre, Queens Rd. Mills. HX1 4LR. Est. 1982. Open Tues.-Fri. 11-4.30, Sat. 11-5. *STOCK: 20th C ceramics including Clarice Cliff, Susie Cooper, Charlotte Rhead, Shelley; furniture, metalware, lighting and mirrors.* LOC: 1 mile west of town centre off A58 (A646) Aachen Way/Burnley Rochdale road. Turn right at Trafalgar Inn traffic lights. Centre at 3rd set of traffic lights at junction of Queens Rd. and Gibbet St. PARK: Easy. TEL: 01422 347377; fax - same; e-mail - muir. hewitt@virgin.net website - www.muirhewitt.com SER: Valuations. FAIRS: Ann Zierold Art Deco at Leeds and Chester. VAT: Spec.

Andy Thornton Ltd
Victoria Mills, Stainland Rd., Greetland. HX4 8AD. SALVO. Est. 1976. Open 8.30-5.30, Sat. 9-5. SIZE: Large. *STOCK: Architectural antiques - doors, stained glass, fireplaces, panelling, garden statuary, furniture, light fittings, decor items, church interiors including pews.* LOC: Off junction 24, M62. PARK: Easy. TEL: 01422 377314; fax - 01422 310372; e-mail - antiques @ataa.co.uk website - www.andythornton.com SER: Delivery; worldwide shipping. VAT: Stan.

HAWORTH, Nr. Keighley

Bingley Antiques
Springfield Farm Estate, Flappit. BD21 5PT. (J.B. and J. Poole). Est. 1965. Open Tues.-Sat. 8.45-5 or by appointment. SIZE: 3 warehouses. *STOCK: Furniture, 18th-19th C; shipping goods, porcelain, architectural antiques, stained glass and doors.* LOC: Near Haworth. PARK: Easy. TEL: 01535 646666. e-mail - john@ bingleyantiques.com website - www.bingleyantiques. com VAT: Stan/Spec.

Clock House Antiques
2 Janet St. BD22 9ET. (P.A. Langham). Open Tues., Wed. and Thurs. 1-4, Sat. 11-4. SIZE: Medium. *STOCK: Clocks, porcelain and small furniture.* PARK: Easy. TEL: 01535 648777; mobile - 07759 503699. SER: Valuations; repairs (clocks).

HEBDEN BRIDGE, Nr. Halifax

Cornucopia Antiques
9 West End. HX7 8JP. (Noel Strophair). Open Fri.-Sun. 12-5. *STOCK: Furniture, Art Deco, lighting, mirrors, stoves, bric-a-brac, garden furniture and accessories.* LOC: Town centre behind Pennine Information Centre. PARK: Easy. TEL: 01422 845844.

HOLMFIRTH

Bruton Gallery
PO Box 145. HD9 1YU. (Helen Robinson). Est. 1969. Open by appointment. *STOCK: French sculpture, 19th-20th C, from £1,000+; contemporary British art, to*

£10,000. PARK: Limited. TEL: Mobile - 0870 747 1800; e-mail - art@BrutonGallery.co.uk website - www. BrutonGallery.co.uk. SER: Valuations; buys at auction; corporate hire; presentations and lectures. FAIRS: Glasgow; Oxford; London; Bristol; Kingston-upon-Thames; Edinburgh; Yorkshire. VAT: Stan/Spec.

Chapel House Fireplaces
Netherfield House, St. Georges Rd., Scholes. HD9 1UH. (J. and M. Forster). Est. 1979. Open strictly by appointment Tues.-Sat. 9-5. SIZE: Large. STOCK: Georgian, Victorian and Edwardian grates and mantels; French chimneypieces. PARK: Own. TEL: 01484 682275; e-mail - info@chapelhousefireplaces.co.uk website - www.chapelhousefireplaces.co.uk SER: Restorations.

The Toll House Bookshop
32/34 Huddersfield Rd. HD9 2JS. (Elaine V. Beardsell). PBFA. ABA. Est. 1977. Open 9-5. SIZE: Large. STOCK: Books including antiquarian. LOC: Town centre. PARK: Nearby. TEL: 01484 686541/688406; e-mail - tollhouse.bookshop@virgin.net website - www.toll-house.co.uk SER: Valuations; commission bidding. FAIRS: Major PBFA.

HONLEY, Nr. Holmfirth

A. and Y.M. Frost Antique Clocks
Honey Head Farm, Meltham Rd. HD9 6RG. (Alan and Yvonne Frost). Est. 1979. Open by appointment only. SIZE: Small. STOCK: 17th-18th C bracket, wall and longcase clocks, £5,000-£100,000. LOC: Edge of village. PARK: Easy. TEL: 01484 661361; website - www.aymfrostantiqueclocks.com

HUDDERSFIELD

D.W. Dyson (Antique Weapons)
Wood Lea, Shepley. HD8 8ES. Est. 1974. Open by appointment. STOCK: Antique weapons including cased duelling pistols, armour, miniature arms, cigar and smoking related accessories, rare and unusual items. LOC: Off A629. PARK: Easy. TEL: 01484 607331; home - same; fax - 01484 604114; website - www.dwdhallmark.com SER: Valuations; buys at auction (antique weapons); special presentation items made to order in precious metals; restorations; interior design; finder (film props). FAIRS: Dorchester Hotel, London; Dortmund, Stuttgart and other major foreign. VAT: Spec.

Huddersfield Picture Framing Co
Cloth Hall Chambers, Cloth Hall St. HD1 2EG. (Miss Pamela Ward). Est. 1962. Open 9-5, Wed. 9-1, Sat. 9-4. SIZE: Large. STOCK: Watercolours, picture mouldings, swept frames, ovals and circles. LOC: Between Market St. and New St. PARK: Meters or nearby. TEL: 01484 546075; home - 01484 687598. SER: Valuations; restorations (especially oil paintings). VAT: Stan.

Geoff Neary (incorporating Fillans Antiques Ltd)
2 Market Walk. HD1 2QA. NAG, FGA. Est. 1852. Open 9.30-5.15. SIZE: Small. STOCK: English silver, 1700-1980; Sheffield plate, 1760-1840, jewellery, 1800-1980,

£50-£20,000. LOC: Town centre. PARK: Multi-storey. TEL: 01484 531609; fax - 01484 432688; website - www.geoffneary-jewellers.co.uk SER: Valuations; restorations. VAT: Stan/Spec.

ILKLEY

Coopers of Ilkley   LAPADA
46-50 Leeds Rd. LS29 8EQ. (Charles and Jane Cooper). Est. 1910. Open 9-1 and 2-5.30. SIZE: Large. STOCK: English and Continental furniture, pre-1900, £100-£10,000; porcelain and metalware. LOC: A65. PARK: Own. TEL: 01943 608020; fax - 01943 604321; e-mail - enquiries@cooperantiquesilkley.co.uk website - www.cooperantiquesilkley.co.uk SER: Valuations; furniture restorations and repairs, upholstery and polishing. VAT: Stan/Spec.

Jack Shaw and Co
The Old Grammar School, Skipton Rd. LS29 9EJ. Est. 1945. Open Thurs., Fri. and Sat. 9.30-12.45 and 2-5.30. STOCK: Silver especially cutlery and 18th C domestic. TEL: 01943 609467; mobile - 07711 679836. VAT: Spec.

LEEDS

Aladdin's Cave
19 Queens Arcade. LS1 6LF. (R. Spencer). Est. 1954. SIZE: Small. STOCK: Jewellery, £15-£5,000; collectors' items. LOC: Town centre. PARK: 100 yards. TEL: 01132 457903. SER: Valuations; repairs. VAT: Stan.

Geary Antiques
LS28 5QQ. (J.A. Geary). Est. 1933. Open by appointment. STOCK: Furniture, Georgian, Victorian and Edwardian; copper and brass. TEL: 0113 256 4122; fax - 08700 511346; e-mail - jag@t-nlbi.demon.co.uk and jag@gearyantiquefurniture.co.uk website - www.gearyantiquefurniture.co.uk SER: Restorations (furniture); interior design. VAT: Stan/Spec.

Headrow Antiques Centre
Level 3 Headrow Shopping Centre, The Headrow. LS1 6JE. (Sally Hurrell). Est. 1991. Open 10-5, Sun.11-4 (Dec). SIZE: 25 dealers. STOCK: Ceramics, jewellery, specialist buttons, radios, cameras, railwayana and furniture, £5-£2,000. LOC: City centre. PARK: NCP Albion St. TEL: 0113 245 5344; home - 0113 274 9494; website - www.headrowantiques.co.uk

J. Howorth Antiques/Swiss Cottage Furniture
85 Westfield Crescent, Burley. LS3 1DJ. Est. 1986. Open 10-5.30. CL: Tues. SIZE: Warehouse. STOCK: Collectables, furniture, architectural items, £5-£3,000. LOC: Town hall to Burley Rd., road opposite YTV. PARK: Easy. TEL: 0113 242 9994. SER: Prop. hire for film and TV. FAIRS: Newark. VAT: Stan/Spec.

Oakwood Gallery
613 Roundhay Rd., Oakwood. LS8 4AR. Open 9-6. STOCK: Fine paintings and prints. PARK: Easy. TEL: 0113 240 1348. SER: Framing; restorations; conservation.

The Piano Shop
39 Holbeck Lane. LS11 9UL. (B. Seals). Open 9-5. SIZE: 2 floors. STOCK: Pianos, especially decorated

cased grand. LOC: 5 mins. from City centre. TEL: 0113 244 3685; e-mail - thepianoshop@freenet.co.uk website - www.thepianoshop.co.uk SER: Restorations; French polishing; hire.

Year Dot
41 The Headrow. LS1 6PU. (A. Glithro). Est. 1977. Open 9.30-5. *STOCK: Jewellery, watches, silver, pottery, porcelain, glass, clocks, prints, paintings, bric-a-brac.* TEL: 0113 246 0860.

LEPTON, Nr. Huddersfield

K.L.M. & Co. Antiques
The Antique Shop, Wakefield Rd. HD8 0EL. (K.L. & J. Millington). Est. 1980. Open 10.30-5, other times by appointment. SIZE: 8 showrooms and warehouse. *STOCK: Furniture including stripped pine, satin walnut, to 1940s; pianos, all £25-£1,500.* LOC: A642 Wakefield road from Huddersfield, shop opposite church. PARK: Easy and at rear. TEL: 01484 607763; home - 01484 607548. VAT: Stan.

MENSTON

Antiques
101 Bradford Rd. LS29 6BU. (W. and J. Hanlon). Est. 1974. Open Thurs.-Sat. 2.30-5. *STOCK: Handworked linen, textiles, pottery, porcelain, Art Nouveau, Art Deco, silver, plate, jewellery, small furniture, collectors items.* LOC: A65 near Harry Ramsden. PARK: Forecourt. TEL: 01943 877634; home - 01943 463693. FAIRS: Newark.

Park Antiques
2 North View, Main St. LS29 6JU. (Brian O'Connell). Resident. Est. 1975. Open Wed.-Fri. 10.30-4.30, Sat. 9.30-5.30, Sun. 12-5. SIZE: Medium. *STOCK: Furniture, Georgian to Edwardian, £200-£5,000; decorative items, £50-£1,000; porcelain and ceramics, £10-£1,000; paintings, £100-£5,000.* LOC: Opposite the park. PARK: Easy. TEL: 01943 872392; mobile - 07887 812858; website - www.parkantiques.com and www.beacon-antiques.co.uk SER: Furniture repairs, restorations and French polishing.

OTLEY

Monkman Antiques
6 Bondgate. LS21 3AB. (A. Monkman). Est. 1991. Open by appointment. SIZE: *STOCK: Watercolours, oils, prints and period frames.* LOC: Top of High St., opposite parish church on Leeds road. PARK: Free next to church. TEL: 01943 850342.

SALTAIRE, Nr Shipley

Victoria Antiques
3-4 Victoria Rd. BD18 3LA. (Andrew Draper). Est. 1995. Open Tues.-Sun. 10.30-5. SIZE: Large - 40+ dealers. *STOCK: Wide range of general antiques including fine furniture, paintings, silver, clocks, porcelain, pine and collectables, £5-£10,000.* LOC: In World Heritage village. PARK: Nearby. TEL: 01274 530611; fax - 01274 533722; e-mail - info@victoria-antiques.co.uk SER: Valuations; restorations (furniture and pictures). VAT: Stan/Spec.

SOWERBY BRIDGE, Nr. Halifax

Memory Lane
69 Wakefield Rd. HX6 2UX. (L. Robinson). Est. 1978. Open 10.30-5, Sun. 12-4. SIZE: Warehouse + showroom. *STOCK: Pine, oak and teddy bears.* PARK: Easy. TEL: 01422 833223; fax - 01422 835230; website - www.memorylaneantiques.co.uk and www.memorylanebears.co.uk

Talking Point Antiques
66 West St. HX6 3AP. (Paul Austwick). Est. 1986. Usually open Thurs., Fri., Sat. 10.30-5.30, prior telephone call advisable. *STOCK: Restored gramophones and phonographs, 78rpm records, gramophone accessories and related items.* LOC: From Haliax, on A58 through village, last row of shops. PARK: Nearby. TEL: 01422 834126; e-mail - tpagrams@aol.com website - www.talkingpointgramophones.co.uk SER: Restorations (gramophones). FAIRS: National Vintage Communications (NEC); Leeds Vintage Audio; Yorks. and Lancs. general.

TODMORDEN

Echoes
650a Halifax Rd., Eastwood. OL14 6DW. (P. Oldman). Est. 1980. CL: Mon. and Tues. SIZE: Medium. *STOCK: Costume, textiles, linen and lace, £5-£500; jewellery, £5-£150; all 19th-20th C.* LOC: A646. PARK: Easy. TEL: 01706 817505; home - same. SER: Valuations; restorations (costume); buys at auction (as stock).

WAKEFIELD

Robin Taylor Fine Arts
36 Carter St. WF1 1XJ. Est. 1981. Open 9.30-5.30. *STOCK: Oils and watercolours.* LOC: Off Westgate. TEL: 01924 381809; website - www.picturerestoration.co.uk

WALSDEN, Nr. Todmorden

Cottage Antiques (1984) Ltd
788 Rochdale Rd. OL14 7UA. (G. Slater). Resident. Est. 1978. Open Tues.-Sun. SIZE: Medium. *STOCK: Pine, country and decorative painted furniture, kitchenalia; collectables, garden items and accessories.* LOC: A6033 Todmorden to Littleborough road. PARK: Easy. TEL: 01706 813612. SER: Restorations; stripping (pine); import/export of European pine and collectables.

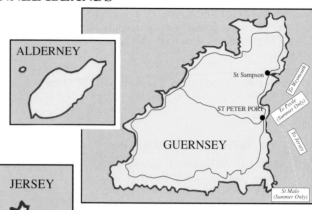

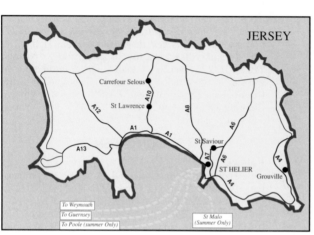

ALDERNEY

Beverley J. Pyke - Fine British Watercolours
22 Victoria St. GY9 3TA. Est. 1988. Open by appointment. *STOCK: 20th C watercolours, £150-£2,000.* TEL: 01481 824092.

Victoria Antiques
St. Catherine's, Victoria St. GY9 3TA. (P.A. Nightingale). Open 10-12.30 or by appointment. *STOCK: Period and Victorian furniture, glass, silver, china, jewellery, small objets d'art.* TEL: 01481 823260. SER: Valuations.

GUERNSEY

ST PETER PORT

Stephen Andrews Gallery
5 College Terrace, Grange. GY1 2PX. (J. Geddes and S. Wilkowski). Est. 1984. Open 9.30-5. SIZE: Medium. *STOCK: Furniture, pottery and porcelain, paintings, 19th-20th C.* LOC: Main road. PARK: Adjacent. TEL: 01481 710380. SER: Buys at auction. FAIRS: Local.

Channel Islands Galleries Ltd
Trinity Square Centre, Trinity Sq. GY1 1LX. (G.P. and Mrs C. Gavey). Est. 1970. Open 10-5. SIZE: Medium. *STOCK: Antique maps, sea charts, prints, oil paintings and watercolours; books, illustrated, historical, social, geographical and natural history; banknotes and coins; all Channel Islands.* LOC: Near town centre. PARK: Easy. TEL: 01481 723247; home - 01481 247337; fax - 01481 714669; e-mail - geoff.gavey@cigalleries.f9.co.uk website - www.cigalleries.f9.co.uk SER: Framing.

The Collectors Centre
1 Sausmarez St. GY1 2PT. (Andrew Rundle). Est. 1984. Open 11-6. SIZE: Small. *STOCK: Prints, engravings, maps, coins, banknotes, stamps, postcards, books and ephemera.* PARK: Opposite. TEL: 01481 725209. SER: Valuations.

W. De la Rue Antiques
29 Mill St. GY1 1HG. Est. 1972. Open 10-12.30 and 2-4. CL: Thurs. pm. SIZE: Small. *STOCK: General antiques and collectors' items.* PARK: Nearby. TEL: 01481 723177.

N. St. J. Paint & Sons Ltd
26-29 The Pollet. GY1 1WQ. (Michael St John Paint). NAG. Est. 1947. Open 9-5. SIZE: Large. *STOCK: Jewellery, silver and objets d'art, 18th-20th C, £10-£75,000.* LOC: Town centre. TEL: 01481 721096; fax - 01481 710241; e-mail - paint@guernsey.net SER: Valuations; restorations (silver and jewellery).

The Pine Collection
La Route de la Garenne, Pitronnerie Road Industrial Estate. GY1 2RL. (P. Head). Est. 1986. Open 9.30-5.30. *STOCK: Pine.* TEL: 01481 726891.

ST. SAMPSON

The Curiosity Shop
Commercial Rd. GY2 4QP. (Mike Vermeulen and Diana Walker). Est. 1978. Open 10-2. CL: Thurs. *STOCK: Books, prints, postcards, ephemera, paintings, small furniture, china, glass, silver, jewellery, brass, £1-£5,000.* TEL: 01481 245324. SER: Picture framing. FAIRS: Organiser.

Ray & Scott Ltd

The Bridge. GY2 4QN. (M. J. Search). NAG. Est. 1962. Open 9-5.15, Sat. 9-5. SIZE: Medium. *STOCK: Jewellery and watches, 19th C, £500-£1,000+.* PARK: Easy. TEL: 01481 244610; fax - 01481 247843; e-mail - rayscott@cwgsy.net SER: Valuations; restorations (jewellery and engraving).

JERSEY

CARREFOUR SELOUS, ST. LAWRENCE

David Hick Interiors

Alexandra House. JE3 1GL. (David and Rosemary Hick). Est. 1977. Open Fri. and Sat. 9.30-5, Thurs. 4.30-7.30 or by appointment. SIZE: Large and warehouse. *STOCK: Furniture and objets d'art.* PARK: Own. TEL: 01534 865965; fax - 01534 865448; e-mail - hickantiques@localdial.com SER: Shipping (UK and overseas).

GROUVILLE

Atelier Ltd   LAPADA

Le Bourg Farm, Le Grand Bourg. JE3 9UY. (Jonathan Voak). Est. 1997. Open by appointment only. SIZE: Small. *STOCK: 17th to early 20th C oil paintings, watercolours and drawings especially early marine paintings and views of the Channel Islands and London - especially the Thames, £200-£25,000+.* LOC: Half mile from Grouville church. PARK: Easy. TEL: 01534 855728; fax - 01534 852099; mobile - 07797 729231; e-mail - art@atelierlimited.com website - www.atelierlimited.com SER: Valuations; conservation of oil paintings, watercolours, prints and drawings. FAIRS: LAPADA; Cheltenham; annual exhibitions.

ST. HELIER

John Blench & Son

50 Don St. JE2 4TR. (W. and J. Blench). Est. 1972. Open 9.30-5, Thurs. and Sat. 9.30-12.30. SIZE: Medium. *STOCK: Fine books, bindings, local maps, prints and paintings.* LOC: Town centre. PARK: Nearby. TEL: 01534 725281; fax - 01534 758789; e-mail - segart@itl.net website - www.selectiveeye.com SER: Valuations; restorations.

John Cooper Antiques

16 The Market. JE2 4WL. (John M. Cooper and Antonio de Lemos). *STOCK: General antiques.* TEL: 01534 723600.

Falle Fine Art Limited   LAPADA

94 Halkett Place. JE2 4WH. (John Falle). Est. 1993. Open 11-5, Sat. 9.30-1. SIZE: Large. *STOCK: 20th C paintings, watercolours and bronzes.* LOC: Opposite public library. PARK: Limited and multi-storey nearby. TEL: 01534 887877; fax - 01534 723459; e-mail - gallery@fallefineart.com website - www.fallefineart.com SER: Valuations; restorations; exhibitions.

David Hick Antiques

45 Halkett Place. JE2 4WQ. (David and Rosemary Hick). Open 10-5. *STOCK: Furniture and smalls.* TEL: 01534 721162; fax - same; e-mail - hickantiques@localdial.com

Peter Le Vesconte's Collectables

62 Stopford Rd. JE2 4LZ. Est. 1979. Open 10-1. CL: Thurs. SIZE: Medium. *STOCK: Toys, 1920-1999, £5-£500; militaria, 1900-1945, £1-£500; small items, 1900-1970, £5-£300.* LOC: Road opposite Hotel de France. PARK: Easy. TEL: 01534 732481; fax - same. SER: Valuations; buys at auction (toys and militaria).

A. & R. Ritchie

7 Duhamel Place. JE2 4TP. Est. 1973. Open 9.30-4.30. SIZE: Medium. *STOCK: Silver, militaria, jewellery, small items.* LOC: Behind central library. PARK: Opposite. TEL: 01534 873805.

Robert's Antiques

14 York St. JE2 3RQ. (Robert Michieli). Est. 1975. Open 9.30-4.45. SIZE: Medium. *STOCK: English silver, ceramics, clocks, glass, jewellery, 19th C, £50-£10,000.* LOC: Opposite town hall. PARK: Easy. TEL: 01534 509071; home - 01534 865005; mobile - 07798 876553: e-mail - count.roberto@jerseymail.co.uk SER: Valuations; buys at auction (as stock).

The Selective Eye Gallery

50 Don St. JE2 4TR. (John and Warwick Blench). Est. 1958. Open 9-5. CL: Thurs. and Sat. pm. SIZE: Medium. *STOCK: Oil paintings, 19th-20th C; maps, prints and antiquarian books, 16th-20th C. Not Stocked: General antiques.* LOC: Town centre. PARK: Multi-storey 100yds. TEL: 01534 725281; fax - 01534 758789; e-mail - segart@itl.net website - www.selectiveeye.com SER: Valuations; restorations (pictures). FAIRS: Jersey.

Thesaurus (Jersey) Ltd

3 Burrard St. JE2 4TT. (I. Creaton). Est. 1973. Open 9-5.30. SIZE: Small. *STOCK: Antiquarian and out of print books, £1-£2,000; maps and prints.* LOC: Town centre. PARK: 100yds. TEL: 01534 737045. SER: Buys at auction. VAT: Spec.

Thomson's

60 Kensington Place and 10 Waterloo St. JE2 3PA. (R.N. Thomson). Est. 1967. Open 10-6. SIZE: Large. *STOCK: General antiques and collectors' items, mainly furniture.* LOC: 60 Kensington Place at the side of Grand Hotel; 10 Waterloo St. opposite Bonhams. PARK: Easy. TEL: 01534 723673/618673; mobile - 07797 826414. SER: Valuations.

ST. LAWRENCE

I.G.A. Old Masters Ltd

5 Kimberley Grove, Rue de Haut. JE3 1JR. (I.G. and Mrs C.B.V. Appleby). Est. 1953. Open by appointment. *STOCK: Old Master and 19th C paintings.* LOC: Near glass church. PARK: Easy. TEL: 01534 724226; home - same.

ST. SAVIOUR

Grange Gallery - Fine Arts Ltd

10 Victoria Rd. JE2 7QG. (G.J. Morris). Est. 1973. Open 9-5.30. SIZE: Medium. *STOCK: 19th-20th C oil paintings and watercolours, local items, £10-£10,000.* LOC: 1 mile east of St Helier. PARK: Forecourt. TEL: 01534 720077; e-mail - cassy@localdial.com SER: Valuations; restorations (paintings); framing.

NORTHERN IRELAND

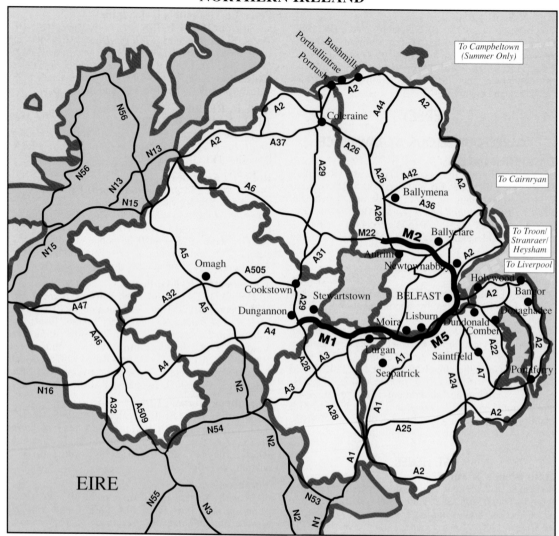

Bushmills
Portballintrae
Portrush
To Campbeltown
(Summer Only)
A2
Coleraine
A2
A44
A2
N56
A2
A37
A26
N13
A29
A42
A2
To Cairnryan
N56
N13
A26
A2
A6
Ballymena
A36
N15
A26
N15
M22
M2
Ballyclare
To Troon/
Stranraer/
Heysham
A5
Antrim
A2
To Liverpool
Omagh
A505
A31
Newtownabbey
Holywood
A2
Bangor
A32
Cookstown
A29
Stewartstown
BELFAST
A2
Donaghadee
Dungannon
Lisburn
Dundonald
Comber
A2
A47
A5
Moira
M5
A22
A46
A4
M1
Lurgan
Saintfield
A7
Portaferry
N16
A3
A1
A24
A4
A28
A3
Seapatrick
A2
A32
A509
N2
A28
A1
A2
N54
N2
A25
EIRE
N55
N3
N53
N2
N1

LONDONDERRY
ANTRIM
TYRONE
FERMANAGH
ARMAGH
DOWN

NORTHERN IRELAND		Co Down	
		Bangor	1
		Donaghadee	1
Co Antrim		Dundonald	1
Antrim	1	Holywood	1
Ballyclare	1	Saintfield	4
Ballymena	1	Seapatrick	1
Belfast	5		
Bushmills	1	Co Londonderry	
Lisburn	1	Coleraine	2
Newtownabbey	1	Londonderry	2
Portballintrae	1		
Portrush	2	Co Tyrone	
		Cookstown	2
Co Armagh		Dungannon	1
Lurgan	1	Omagh	1
Moira	1	Stewartstown	1

CO. ANTRIM

ANTRIM

David Wolfenden Antiques   LAPADA
219B Lisnevenagh Rd. BT41 2JT. IADA. Est. 1984. Open 10-6. SIZE: Large. *STOCK: Furniture, £200-£10,000; porcelain, £100-£3,000; all 19th C.* LOC: Main Antrim-Ballymena line. PARK: Easy. TEL: 028 9442 9498; e-mail - antiquewolfirl@aol.com website - www.country-antiques-wolfenden.co.uk and www.david wolfendenantiques.com SER: Valuations; restorations. FAIRS: Dublin; Belfast. VAT: Stan/Spec.

BALLYCLARE

Robert Christie Antiques
20 Calhame Rd. BT39 9NA. IADA. Est. 1976. Open 11-5. SIZE: Medium. *STOCK: Furniture, 1750-1900, £200-£3,000; clocks, 1750-1900, £500-£2,000; decorative objects, 1800-1900, £50-£500.* LOC: Just off A8 Belfast-Larne road. PARK: Easy. TEL: 02893 341149; mobile - 07802 968846. SER: Valuations. FAIRS: Kings Hall, Belfast; all RDS fairs.

BALLYMENA

Once upon a Time Antiques
The Old Mill, 2 Parkfield Rd., Ahoghill. BT42 2QS. (Ronan McLaughlin). Est. 1971. Open 10-5.30, Thurs. 10-8. SIZE: Large. *STOCK: Furniture, porcelain, art, silver and jewellery, 18th-20th C; Art Nouveau, Art Deco.* LOC: Edge of village. PARK: Large free. TEL: 028 2587 1244; fax - 028 2587 9295; mobile - 07703 360447. SER: Valuations; restorations (jewellery, furniture, brass and copper, pictures and frames). FAIRS: Galgorm Manor, Ballymena; King's Hall, Belfast; RDS, Dublin.

BELFAST

Archives Antiques
88 Donegall Pass. BT7 1BX. (L. Johnston). Est. 1992. Open 10.30-5.30 or by appointment. SIZE: Medium. *STOCK: Irish silver, light fittings, porcelain, glass, coins and medals, collectables, bottles, advertising signs, pharmacy.* PARK: Easy. TEL: 028 9023 2383; mobile - 07889 104719. SER: Valuations; restorations (copper and brass polishing and repairs, re-wiring). FAIRS: Kings Hall, Belfast.

The Bell Gallery
13 Adelaide Park. BT9 6FX. (J.N. Bell). Est. 1964. Open Mon.-Thurs. 10-6 or by appointment. SIZE: Medium. *STOCK: British and Irish art, 19th-20th C.* LOC: Off Malone Rd. PARK: Easy. TEL: 028 9066 2998; e-mail - bellgallery@btinternet.com website - www.bellgallery.com SER: Valuations; restorations (paintings); buys at auction. VAT: Stan/Spec.

T.H. Kearney & Sons
Treasure House, 123 University St. BT7 1HP. Resident. *STOCK: Small antiques.* TEL: 028 9023 1055. SER: Restorations and upholstery. VAT: Stan.

Oakland Antiques
135 Donegall Pass. BT7 1DS. (Alberta and Donald McCluskey). Est. 1977. *STOCK: Furniture, Georgian to Edwardian, £100-£25,000; silver, porcelain, glass, bronze and pictures, 18th-20th C, £20-£5,000.* LOC: Near city centre. PARK: Easy. TEL: 028 9023 0176; fax - 028 9024 8144; home - 028 9047 1146; mobile - 07831 176438; e-mail - sales@oaklandni.com website - www.oaklandni.com SER: Valuations.

Past & Present
58-60 Donegall Pass. BT7 1BU. (Trevor McNally). Est. 1987. Open Tues.-Sat. 10.30-5. SIZE: Medium. *STOCK: Art & Crafts, Art Nouveau, Victorian and Edwardian furniture; collectables, paintings and prints.* PARK: Easy. TEL: 028 9033 3137. SER: Framing.

BUSHMILLS

Dunluce Antiques
33 Ballytober Rd. BT57 8UU. (Mrs C. Ross). Est. 1978. Open 10-6 or by appointment. CL: Fri. SIZE: Small. *STOCK: Furniture, £100-£5,000; porcelain and glass, £10-£2,000; silver, £10-£2,000; all Georgian to 1930s; paintings, mainly Irish, £100-£25,000.* LOC: 1.5 miles off Antrim coast road, at Dunluce Castle. PARK: Easy. TEL: 028 2073 1140; e-mail - dunluceantiques@btinternet.com website - www.dunlucegallery.com SER: Restorations (porcelain).

LISBURN

Parvis Sigaroudinia
Mountainview House, 40 Sandy Lane, Ballyskeagh. BT27 5TL. IADA. Est. 1974. Open any time by appointment and 11-8 during quarterly exhibitions. *STOCK: Oriental and European carpets and tapestries; cushions, lamps, furniture, architectural items, William Yeoward crystal, bronze sculpture by David Williams-Ellis and Anthony Scott, Irish art, hand-crafted furniture by Richard Reade.* LOC: Take Malone Road from Belfast, then Upper Malone Road towards Lisburn, cross Ballyskeagh bridge over M1, 1st left into Sandy Lane. PARK: Easy. TEL: 02890 621824; home - same; fax - 02890 623311; mobile - 07801 347358; e-mail - parvissig@aol.com website - www.parvis.co.uk SER: Valuations; buys at auction; exhibitions held in Belfast. FAIRS: IADA in RDS Dublin and King's Hall, Belfast. VAT: Stan.

NEWTOWNABBEY

MacHenry Antiques
Caragh Lodge, Glen Rd., Jordanstown. BT37 0RY. (R. and A. MacHenry). IADA. Est. 1964. Open Fri. and Sat. 12-6 or by appointment. SIZE: Medium. *STOCK: Georgian and Victorian furniture and objects.* LOC: 6 miles from Belfast on M2/M5 to Whiteabbey village, left at traffic lights at Woody's, then left into Old Manse Rd. and continue straight into Glen Rd. PARK: Easy. TEL: 028 9086 2036; fax - 028 9085 3281; mobile - 07831 135226; e-mail - rupert.machenry@ntlworld.com SER: Valuations. FAIRS: Dublin, Belfast and Irish. VAT: Stan/Spec.

PORTBALLINTRAE, Nr. Bushmills

Brian R. Bolt Antiques
88 Ballaghmore Rd. BT57 8RL. (Brian and Helen Bolt).

Est. 1977. Open 11-5.30 and by appointment. CL: Wed. am and Fri. am. SIZE: Small. *STOCK: Silver - small and unusual items, objects of vertu, snuff boxes, vesta cases, table, Scottish and Irish provincial; treen; English and Continental glass, antique and 20th C; art and studio glass and ceramics; Arts and Crafts, Art Nouveau and Art Deco jewellery and metalwork; vintage fountain pens.* LOC: 1 mile from Bushmills. PARK: Nearby. TEL: 028 2073 1129; fax - same; mobile - 07712 579802; e-mail - brianbolt@antiques88.freeserve.co.uk SER: Search; illustrated catalogues available; worldwide postal service; valuations. FAIRS: Local.

PORTRUSH

Alexander Antiques
108 Dunluce Rd. BT56 8NB. (Mrs M. and D. Alexander). Est. 1974. Open 10-5.30. CL: Sun. except by appointment. SIZE: Large. *STOCK: Furniture, silver, porcelain, fine art, 18th-20th C; oils and watercolours, 19th-20th C.* LOC: 1 mile from Portrush on A2 to Bushmills. PARK: Easy. TEL: 028 7082 2783; fax - 028 7082 2364; e-mail - sales@alexanderantiques.com SER: Valuations; buys at auction. VAT: Stan/Spec.

Kennedy Wolfenden
86 Main St. BT56 8BN. (Eleanor Wolfenden-Orr). Est. 1977. Open 10-5.30 - later in summer. SIZE: Medium. *STOCK: Furniture, porcelain, paintings, antique and modern jewellery.* TEL: 028 7082 5587/822995; mobile - 07831 453038; e-mail - eleanorwolfenden@hotmail.com website - www.antiquesni.co.uk and www.kwauctions. co.uk. SER: Valuations; restorations (silver and furniture including upholstery).

CO. ARMAGH

LURGAN

Charles Gardiner Antiques
48 High St. BT66 8AU. Est. 1968. Open 9-1 and 2-6. CL: Wed. *STOCK: Clocks, furniture and general antiques.* PARK: Own. TEL: 028 3832 3934.

MOIRA

Fourwinds Antiques
96 Main St. BT67 0LH. (John and Tina Cairns). Est. 1997. Open 10-5. *STOCK: Quality longcase and bracket clocks; Georgian to Edwardian furniture, porcelain and paintings.* LOC: Village centre. PARK: Beside premises. TEL: 028 9261 2226; fax - same; home - 028 3833 6352; mobile - 07713 081748; e-mail - fourwindsantiques@ freeserve.co.uk SER: Valuations. FAIRS: Bohill House Hotel, Coleraine; King's Hall, Belfast.

CO. DOWN

BANGOR

Balloo Moon
Unit 30 Balloo Drive. BT19 7QY. (Marie Erwin). Est. 2001. Open 10-5.30. SIZE: Large. *STOCK: Furniture, Victorian to 1970s; ceramics, collectables and costume jewellery.* LOC: Industrial estate. PARK: Easy. TEL: 028 9145 6886.

DONAGHADEE

Phyllis Arnold Gallery Antiques
4A Shore St. BT21 0DG. Est. 1968. Open Wed. to Sat. 11-5. *STOCK: General antiques, jewellery, small furniture, Irish paintings and watercolours, portrait miniatures, maps and engravings of Ireland.* LOC: On promenade. PARK: Easy. TEL: 028 9188 8199; home - 028 9185 3322; fax - same; website - www.antiquesni. com SER: Restorations (maps, prints, watercolours, portrait miniatures); conservation framing. FAIRS: Belfast International.

DUNDONALD, Nr. Belfast

Stacks Bookshop
67 Comber Rd. BT16 2AA. (Jim Tollerton). Est. 1992. Open 10-6. SIZE: Medium. *STOCK: Books - paperback fiction; military, religious, ancient and modern Irish, Arts & Crafts, travel, educational text.* LOC: Near Stormont. PARK: Easy. TEL: 028 9048 6880. SER: Valuations.

HOLYWOOD

Jacquart Antiques
10-12 Hibernia St. BT18 9JE. (Daniel Uprichard). Est. 1992. Open 10-5.30, Sun. and other times by appointment. SIZE: Medium. *STOCK: Town and country French antiques including fruitwood, walnut, oak and rosewood dining tables, chairs, beds, sideboards and occasional furniture; mirrors, chandeliers, kitchenalia and champagne memorabilia, mainly 1820-1939.* LOC: Just off High St. PARK: Nearby. TEL: 028 9042 6642; mobile - 07831 548803; e-mail - jacquart@nireland.com website - www.jacquart.co.uk SER: Advice; interior designers and architects supplier; minor repairs. FAIRS: Belfast (King's Hall).

SAINTFIELD

Agar Antiques
92 Main St. BT24 7AD. (Rosie Agar). Est. 1990. Open Tues.-Sat. 11-5. SIZE: Medium. *STOCK: Furniture, mainly Victorian, some Georgian and Edwardian, £30-£1,000; light fittings, Victorian and Edwardian, £15-£650; general small items, £1-£500; jewellery, Victorian and Edwardian, £10-£350: French beds and armoires, £100-£1,000.* PARK: Nearby. TEL: 028 9751 1214. SER: Valuations.

Attic Antiques & Pine
88 Main St. BT24 7AB. (Reuben Doyle). Est. 1992. Open 10-5, Sat. 10-5.30. SIZE: Large. *STOCK: Victorian and Edwardian furniture, £50-£2,000; Victorian jewellery, £5-£1,000; bric-a-brac, to £100. (+ Irish, European and reclaimed pine, £30-£1,000 at Attic Pine).* PARK: Easy. TEL: 028 9751 1057. SER: Valuations.

Peter Francis Antiques
92 Main St. BT24 7AD. Est. 1998. Open Tues.-Sat. 11-5. SIZE: Medium. *STOCK: English, Irish and Oriental ceramics, 18th-20th C; English and Irish glass, mainly 18th-19th, some 20th C; smalls including ethnographic, Indian, European, bronzes, metalwork, treen and prints; all £5-£500.* PARK: Nearby. TEL: 028 9751 1214; e-mail - irishantiq@aol.com SER: Valuations.

Town & Country Antiques
92 Main St. BT24 7AB. (Patricia Keller). Est. 1997. Open Wed.-Sat. 10.30-5. SIZE: Medium. *STOCK: Prints, botanical, ornithological and sporting, £100-£400; 18th-19th C French tapestries, £600-£1,500; French chandeliers £300-£600; Venetian, French and Victorian mirrors, £400-£700; Georgian, Victorian and Edwardian small mahogany furniture, £500-£1,000; table lamps, rugs and equestrian items, desks.* PARK: Easy. TEL: 028 4461 4721; home - same; fax - 028 4461 9716; mobile - 07710 840090; e-mail - l.w.k@btinternet. com SER: Restorations (furniture, prints and tapestries). VAT: Stan.

SEAPATRICK, Nr. Banbridge

Millcourt Antiques
99 Lurgan Rd. BT32 4NE. (Gillian Close). Est. 1982. Open 11-5.30. CL: Thurs. SIZE: Small. *STOCK: Furniture, 18th-19th C, £30-£4,000; work and writing boxes, clocks; china, glass and collectables, to Art Deco, to £1,000; linen, quilts and textiles; jewellery, Victorian and 20th C, £20-£500.* PARK: Easy. TEL: 028 4066 2909. SER: Valuations.

CO. LONDONDERRY

COLERAINE

The Forge Antiques
24 Long Commons. BT52 1LH. (M.W. and R.G.C. Walker). Est. 1977. Open 10-5.30. CL: Thurs. SIZE: Medium. *STOCK: General antiques, silver, clocks, jewellery, porcelain, paintings.* PARK: Easy. TEL: 028 7035 1339. VAT: Stan.

Homes, Pubs and Clubs
1-5 Portrush Rd. BT52 1RL. (McNulty Wholesalers). Resident. Est. 1983. Open 9-6, Sun. 2.30-6. SIZE: Large. *STOCK: Pine and mahogany, small interesting items.* LOC: Main Portrush road, near traffic lights. PARK: At rear. TEL: 028 7035 5733. SER: Valuations; restorations. FAIRS: Newark. VAT: Stan.

LONDONDERRY

Foyle Antiques/Whitehouse Furniture
16 Whitehouse Rd. BT48 0NE. (John Helferty). Est. 1982. Open 9.30-5.30, Sun. 3-6. SIZE: Large. *STOCK: Victorian and Edwardian furniture, £200-£3,000; lamps, pictures, ornaments, prints, clocks and decorative items, £30-£300; reproduction furniture, four-poster beds, bedroom and dining suites, £1,000-£5,000.* LOC: Buncrana Rd., just out of Londonderry. PARK: Own. TEL: 028 7126 7626; fax - same; e-mail - John@ foyleantiques.com website - www.foyleantiques.com SER: Restorations (furniture including upholstery).

Foyle Books
12 Magazine St. BT48 6HH. (A. Byrne and K. Thatcher). Est. 1982. Open 11-5. SIZE: Medium. *STOCK: Antiquarian books on Ireland, Derry, Donegal, theology, French and general.* LOC: Town centre. PARK: Quayside. TEL: 028 7137 2530; e-mail - ken@ thatcher30.freeserve.co.uk SER: Valuations.

CO. TYRONE

COOKSTOWN

Cookstown Antiques
16 Oldtown St. BT80 8EF. (G. Jebb). Est. 1976. Open Thurs. and Fri. 2-5.30, Sat. 10.30-5.30. SIZE: Small. *STOCK: Jewellery, silver, £10-£2,000; coins, £25-£200; pictures, ceramics and militaria, £5-£1,000; general antiques, all 19th-20th C.* LOC: Going north, through both sets of traffic lights, on left at rear of estate agency. PARK: Easy. TEL: 028 8676 5279; fax - 028 8676 2946; home - 028 8676 2926. SER: Valuations; buys at auction.

The Saddle Room Antiques
4 Coagh St. BT80 8NG. (C.J. Leitch). Est. 1968. Open 10-5.30. CL: Mon. and Wed. SIZE: Medium. *STOCK: China, silver, furniture, glass, jewellery.* TEL: 028 8676 4045.

DUNGANNON

Moy Antiques
12 The Square, Moy. BT71 7SG. (Laurence MacNeice). Est. 1970. Open 9.30-5.30 or by appointment. SIZE: Large. *STOCK: Georgian to pre-1940's furniture, paintings, clocks, mirrors, objets d'art and fireplaces; cast-iron, marble and bronze garden statuary; Irish pine furniture.* LOC: Village centre. PARK: Easy. TEL: 028 8778 4755; home - same; fax - 028 8778 4895; mobile - 07778 373509; e-mail - macneice@moyantiques.fsnet. co.uk website - www.moyantiques.com SER: Valuations; restorations. FAIRS: IDA, Dublin.

OMAGH

Kelly Antiques
Mullaghmore House, Old Mountfield Rd. BT79 7EX. (Louis Kelly). IPRCA. Est. 1932. Open 9-7, Sat. 10-5.30. SIZE: Large. *STOCK: Fireplaces, from early Adam inlaid to Edwardian slate, European chimney pieces, £80-£125,000; hardwood furniture including dining and bedroom, Georgian to early Victorian, £150-£40,000; early architectural salvage, £10-£10,000.* LOC: One mile from town centre. PARK: Easy. TEL: 028 8224 2314; home - same; fax - 028 8225 0262; e-mail - mullaghmorehouse@aol.com website - www.kelly antiques.com SER: Valuations; restorations (Elizabethan to Edwardian furniture; fireplaces); short and full time courses for conservation, heritage and restoration. Bi-annual private auctions.

STEWARTSTOWN

P. J. Smith (Antiques)
1 North St. BT71 5JE. Est. 1977. Open 10.30-1 and 2-6, Thurs. until 9, Sat. 10.30-6. SIZE: Large. *STOCK: Fireplaces, from early Georgian - marble, £1,500-£60,000; metal, £250-£10,000; wooden, £950-£20,000; slate, £1,150-£5,000; antique leaded and stained glass, brass and brass and iron beds.* LOC: Town centre. PARK: Town square. TEL: 028 8773 8071; fax - 028 8773 8059; website - www.antique-fireplaces.com SER: Valuations; restorations (fireplaces).

SCOTLAND

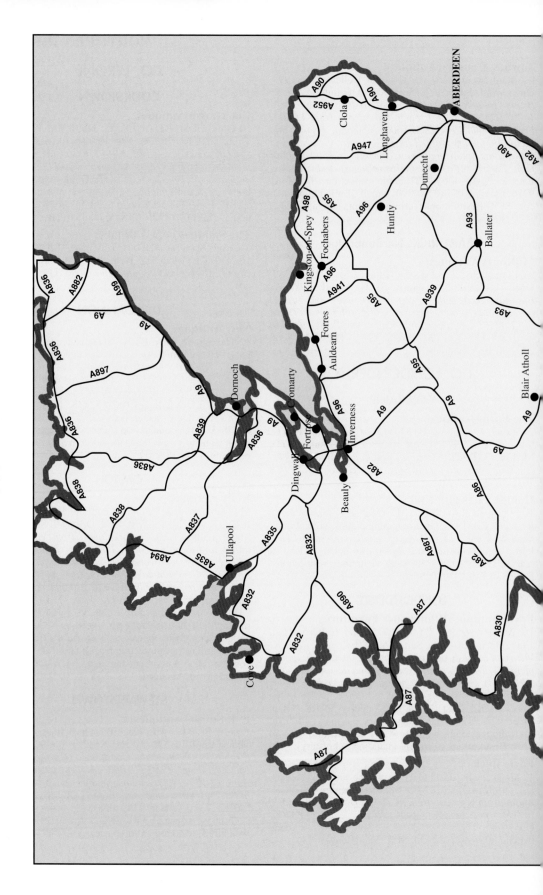

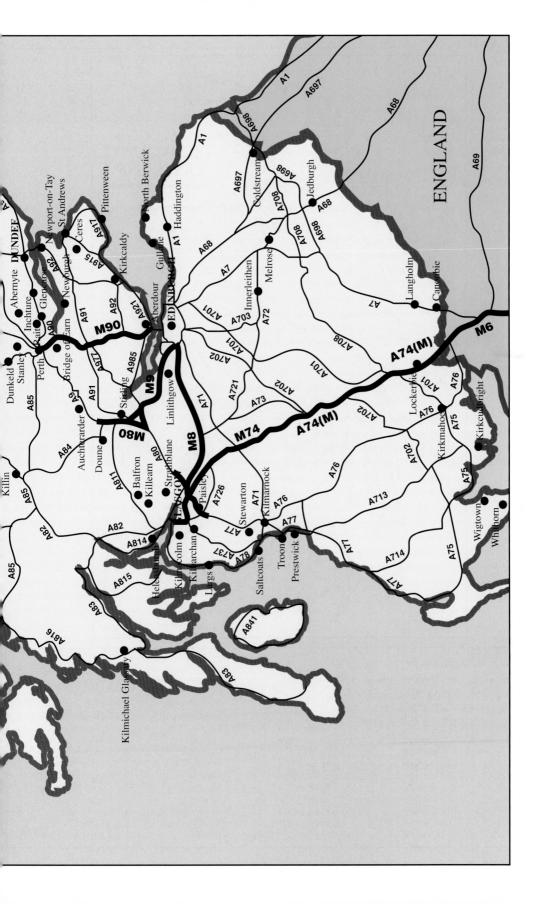

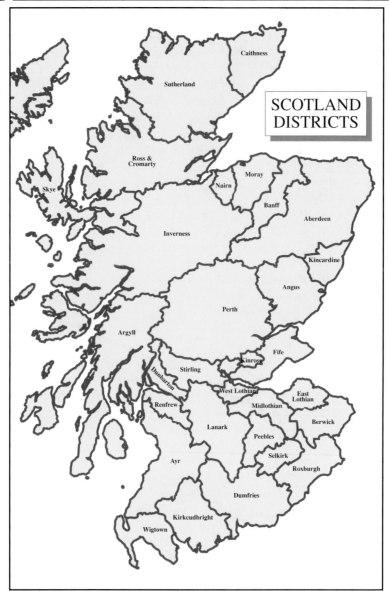

SCOTLAND
DISTRICTS

Dealers and Shops in Scotland

								Perth	4
Aberdeen	9	Clola by Mintlaw	1	Glencarse	1	Kingston-on-Spey	1	Pittenweem	1
Aberdour	1	Coldstream	3	Gullane	1	Kirkcaldy	2	Prestwick	1
Aberfeldy	1	Cromarty	1	Haddington	2	Kirkcudbright	2	Rait	1
Abernyte	1	Dornoch	2	Huntly	1	Langholm	1	Saltcoats	1
Auchterarder	4	Doune	1	Inchture	2	Largs	1	St. Andrews	2
Auldearn	1	Dundee	2	Innerleithen	1	Linlithgow	2	Stanley	1
Balfron	1	Dunecht	1	Inverness	1	Lockerbie	1	Stewarton	1
Ballater	2	Dunkeld	1	Jedburgh	2	Longhaven	1	Stirling	1
Beauly	1	Edinburgh	50	Kilbarchan	2	Melrose	2	Strathblane	1
Blair Atholl	2	Fochabers	1	Killearn	1	Montrose	1	Troon	2
Blairgowrie	2	Forfar	1	Killin	2	Newburgh	2	Ullapool	1
Bridge of Earn	1	Forres	1	Kilmacolm	1	Newport-on-Tay	1	Upper Largo	1
Canonbie	1	Fortrose	1	Kilmarnock	1	North Berwick	3	Whithorn	1
Ceres	1	Glasgow	13	Kilmichael Glassary	1	Paisley	1	Wigtown	1

ABERDEEN

Atholl Antiques
322 Great Western Rd. AB10 6PL. (Gordon Murray). Est. 1971. Open 10.30-1 and 2.30-6 or by appointment. SIZE: Small. *STOCK: Scottish paintings and furniture.* LOC: Central. PARK: Easy. TEL: 01224 593547. VAT: Stan/Spec.

Burning Embers
165-167 King St. AB2 3AE. (J. Bruce). Est. 1988. Open 10-5. SIZE: Medium. *STOCK: Fireplaces, bric-a-brac and pine.* LOC: Off Union St. TEL: 01224 624664. SER: Installations.

Gallery
239 George St. AB25 1ED. (M. Gray). Est. 1981. Open 9-5.30. SIZE: Large. *STOCK: Jewellery, post 1850; curios and Victoriana, paintings and prints, post 1800.* TEL: 01224 632522. SER: Valuations; repairs (jewellery and clocks).

McCalls (Aberdeen)
90 King St. AB1 2JH. (B. McCall). Est. 1948. Open 10-5.30. *STOCK: Jewellery.* PARK: Nearby. TEL: 01224 641916.

McCalls Limited
11 Bridge St. AB11 6JL. (Iain Hawthorne). Est. 1887. Open 9.30-5.30, Thurs. 9.30-8. *STOCK: Victorian, Edwardian, Art Deco and modern jewellery; small silver.* LOC: Town centre, just off Union St. PARK: Trinity centre adjacent. TEL: 01224 405303; e-mail - jewellery@mccalls.co.uk website - www.mccalls.co.uk

The Odd Lot
18 Adelphi, Union St. AB11 5BL. (George Knight-Mudie). Est. 1995. Open 10-5.30. SIZE: Medium. *STOCK: Furniture, £30-£1,000; jewellery and china, £5-£750; all 19th-20th C.* LOC: 2 mins. from Tourist Information Office. PARK: Easy. TEL: 01224 592551; mobile - 07833 773772; e-mail - info@theoddlot.com website - www.theoddlot.com SER: Valuations; restorations (furniture and china).

The Rendezvous Gallery
100 Forest Ave. AB15 4TL. Est. 1973. Open 10-1 and 2.30-6. CL: Fri. SIZE: Medium. *STOCK: Art Nouveau, Art Deco, glass, jewellery, bronzes, furniture, £100-£5,000; paintings, watercolours, Scottish School, £200-£10,000.* LOC: Just off Great Western Rd. to Braemar. PARK: Easy. TEL: 01224 323247; fax - 01224 326029; e-mail - info@rendezvous-gallery.co.uk website - www.rendezvous-gallery.co.uk VAT: Stan/Spec.

Thistle Antiques *LAPADA*
28 Esslemont Ave. AB25 1SN. (P. and Mrs M. Bursill). Est. 1967. Open 10-5, Sat. 10-1. CL: Wed. SIZE: Medium. *STOCK: General antiques, Georgian and Victorian furniture, period lighting.* LOC: City centre. PARK: Easy. TEL: 01224 634692. VAT: Spec.

Colin Wood (Antiques) Ltd
25 Rose St. AB10 1TX. Est. 1968. Open 9.30-5, Wed. and Thurs. 10-5. SIZE: Medium. *STOCK: Furniture, 17th-19th C; works of art, Scottish paintings, prints and silver; specialist in maps of Scotland, 16th-19th C.* PARK: Multi-storey in Chapel St. TEL: 01224 644786 (answerphone); fax - same. VAT: Stan/Spec.

ABERDOUR

Antiques and Gifts
26 High St. KY3 0SW. Est. 1976. CL: Mon., Tues. am. and Wed. pm. SIZE: Small. *STOCK: China, pottery, glass and collectables.* LOC: A921. PARK: Nearby. TEL: 01383 860523. SER: Restorations (china).

ABERFELDY

Sonia Cooper
19 Bridgend. PH15 2DF. Est. 1983. Open Thurs.-Sat. 11-4, Mon. in summer. SIZE: Medium. *STOCK: China, glass, cutlery, wood and metal, from 18th C, £1-£100.* LOC: 10 miles from A9. PARK: Easy. TEL: 01887 820266. SER: Buys at auction.

ABERNYTE

Scottish Antique & Arts Centre
PH14 9SJ. (Templemans). Open 10-5 including Sun. SIZE: Very large - 100 dealers. *STOCK: Furniture, £50-£5,000; accessories, £5-£2,000; collectibles, £5-£50; all 18th-19th C.* LOC: A90 Perth-Dundee road, Inchture junction. PARK: Own. TEL: 01828 686401; fax - 01828 686199. website - www.scottish-antiques.com SER: Valuations; restorations. VAT: Stan/Spec/Global.

AUCHTERARDER

Ian Burton Antique Clocks
at The Antique Galleries, 125 High St. PH3 1AA. Open 9-5, Sat. 10-5. *STOCK: Clocks.* TEL: Mobile - 07785 114800; e-mail - ian@ianburton.com website - www.ianburton.com

Times Past Antiques

Broadfold Farm. PH3 1DR. (J.M. and A.M. Brown). Est. 1970. Open 8-4.30, weekends and holidays 10-3. SIZE: Large. *STOCK: Stripped pine, 19th-20th C, from £50; shipping goods, £5-£500.* LOC: From town centre take Abbey Rd. to flyover A9 at T junction. Turn left, 1st farm on left. PARK: Easy. TEL: 01764 663166; fax - same. SER: Restorations (pine); courier; container-packing.

John Whitelaw and Sons Antiques   LAPADA

125 High St. PH3 1AA. Open 9-5, Sat. 9-1 and 2-5. *STOCK: General antiques; furniture, 17th-19th C.* PARK: Easy. TEL: 01764 662482; fax - 01764 663577; e-mail - jwsantique@aol.com website - www.whitelaw antiques.com. SER: Repairs (furniture). FAIRS: SEEC Glasgow; NEC (Jan). VAT: Stan/Spec.

Ian Whitelaw Antiques   LAPADA

87 Feus. PH3 1DG. Est. 1974. Open 8.30-5, Sat. 10-5, other times by appointment. SIZE: Medium. *STOCK: Furniture and accessories, 18th to early 20th C.* PARK: Easy. TEL: 01764 664781; fax - 01764 663730; mobile - 07836 725559; e-mail - ian@ianwhitelawantiques.co.uk website - www.ianwhitelawantiques.co.uk SER: Restorations (period furniture). FAIRS: NEC; Glasgow.

AULDEARN, Nr. Nairn

Auldearn Antiques

Dalmore Manse, Lethen Rd. IV12 5HZ. Est. 1980. Open 9.30-5.30 including Sun. SIZE: Medium. *STOCK: Victorian linen and lace, kitchenalia, china, furniture, architectural items.* LOC: 1 mile from village. TEL: 01667 453087; home - same; e-mail - rogermiltonrj@aol.com

BALFRON

Amphora Galleries

16-18 Buchanan St. G63 0TT. (L. Ruglen). Resident. Est. 1961. Open 10-5.30 and by appointment. SIZE: Large. *STOCK: General antiques, furniture, decorative items.* LOC: A81. PARK: Easy. TEL: 01360 440329. SER: Polishing; repairs.

BALLATER

The McEwan Gallery   LAPADA

Bridge of Gairn. AB35 5UB. (D., P. and R. McEwan). Est. 1968. Open 11-5, Sun. 2-5, prior telephone call advisable during winter. SIZE: Medium. *STOCK: 18th-20th C British and European paintings, specialising in Scottish; rare and elusive polar, Scottish, sporting, including large stock on golf, and natural history books.* LOC: First house on the east side of A939 after its junction with A93 outside Ballater. PARK: Easy. TEL: 01339 755429; fax - 01339 755995; e-mail - pjmm@easynet.co.uk website - www.mcewangallery.com SER: Valuations; restorations; framing; buys at auction (paintings, watercolours, books); golf catalogues. VAT: Spec.

Treasures of Ballater & Rowan Antiques

1, 5 & 7 Victoria Rd. AB35 5QQ. (Mrs Nichola L. Henderson). Est. 1982. Open 10.30-5.30 (including Sun. April-Oct). SIZE: 2 shops + store. *STOCK: Victorian furniture, porcelain and pottery, Scottish silver and jewellery, antique, fine and estate jewellery, paintings*

and engravings, £10-£3,000. LOC: Village centre. PARK: Easy. TEL: 01339 755122; home - 01339 755676; e-mail - nikki.rowan@lineone.net SER: Valuations; restorations (jewellery); upholstery; shipping. FAIRS: Treetops Hotel, Aberdeen (monthly).

BEAULY

Iain Marr Antiques   LAPADA

3 Mid St. IV4 7DP. (I. and A. Marr). HADA. Est. 1975. Open 10.30-1 and 2-5.30. CL: Thurs. *STOCK: Silver, jewellery, clocks, porcelain, scientific instruments, arms, oils, watercolours, small furniture, Scottish regalia.* LOC: Off the square, on left going north (next to Coffee Shop). PARK: Easy. TEL: 01463 782372; fax - 01463 783623; home - 01463 831609; e-mail - info@iain-marr-antiques.com website - www.iain-marr-antiques.com VAT: Stan/Spec/Global.

BLAIR ATHOLL, Nr. Pitlochry

Blair Antiques

By Bruar Falls. PH18 5TW. (Duncan Huie). Est. 1976. Open 9-5. SIZE: Medium. *STOCK: Period furniture, Scottish oil paintings, silver - some provincial, curios, clocks, pottery and porcelain.* LOC: Opposite House of Bruar. PARK: Easy. TEL: 01796 483264. SER: Valuations; buys at auction. VAT: Stan/Spec.

The Gallery (Nigel Stacy-Marks Ltd)   LAPADA

House of Bruar. PH18 5TW. (Nigel and Ginny Stacy-Marks). Open 10-5 every day. *STOCK: Oils and watercolours, 19th-20th C, £250-£30,000; British etchings, late 19th C to mid 20th C, £100-£5,000; contemporary art, fine furniture.* LOC: A9, 5 miles north of Pitlochry. PARK: Easy. TEL: 01796 483710; fax - 01796 483712; e-mail - thegallery@houseofbruar.com website - www.stacy-marks.com SER: Valuations; restorations; framing; regular exhibitions (catalogues on request). FAIRS: Antiques For Everyone, SECC, Glasgow. VAT: Stan/Spec.

BLAIRGOWRIE

Blairgowrie Books

3 Meadow Place, Wellmeadow. PH10 6NQ. (Marlene Hughes). Est. 1982. Open 10.30-1 and 2-5, Sat. 10.30-5, Sun. by appointment. CL: Tues. SIZE: Medium. *STOCK: Books - mainly on Scottish fishing, shooting, hunting and climbing, £2.50-£150; children's and general.* LOC: Next to River Ericht, town centre. PARK: Easy. TEL: 01250 875855. SER: Valuations.

Roy Sim Antiques

The Granary Warehouse, Lower Mill St. PH10 6AQ. (Roy and Ann Sim). Est. 1977. Open 9-5.30, Sun. 12-5. SIZE: Large. *STOCK: Furniture, clocks, silver, EPNS, collectables, decorative and furnishing items.* LOC: Town centre. PARK: Own. TEL: 01250 873860. SER: Shipping. VAT: Spec.

BRIDGE OF EARN

Imrie Antiques

Back St. PH2 9AE. (Mr and Mrs I. Imrie). Est. 1969. Open 10-1 and 2-5.30. SIZE: Large. *STOCK: Victorian and 18th C shipping goods.* PARK: Easy. TEL: 01738 812784. VAT: Stan.

CANONBIE, Nr. Carlisle

The Clock Showrooms
DG14 0SY. (John R. Mann). MCWG. Est. 1987. Open by
appointment. SIZE: Large. *STOCK: Clocks - over 80
restored longcase, 17th-19th C, £2,500-£90,000; bracket,
17th-19th C, £3,500-£35,000; wall, 19th C, £500-£6,000;
small antiques and collectables.* LOC: Leave M6, junction
44, A7 north through Longtown, follow sign to village,
premises next to Cross Keys Hotel. PARK: Easy. TEL:
01387 371337/71827; fax - 01387 371337; mobile - 07850
606147; e-mail - jmannclock@aol.com website -
www.johnmannantiqueclocks.co.uk SER: Valuations;
restorations (clock movements, cases and dials); buys at
auction (clocks). VAT: Stan.

CERES

Ceres Antiques
1 High St. KY15 5NF. (Mrs E. Norrie). SIZE: Medium.
STOCK: General antiques, china and linen. PARK:
Easy. TEL: 01334 828384.

CLOLA BY MINTLAW, Nr. Peterhead

Clola Antiques Centre
Shannas School House. AB42 5AE. (Joan and David
Blackburn). Est. 1985. Open 10-5, Sun. 11-5 or by
appointment. SIZE: Large - 10 dealers. *STOCK:
Victorian and Edwardian furniture, antique and modern
jewellery, collectables, china and militaria.* LOC: 3
miles south of Mintlaw and 25 miles north of Aberdeen
on A952. PARK: Own. TEL: 01771 624584; fax - 01771
624751; e-mail - clolaantique@aol.com VAT: Margin.

COLDSTREAM

Coldstream Antiques
42B High St. TD12 4AS. (Mr and Mrs J. Trinder). Open
by appointment. SIZE: Small. *STOCK: Furniture, 17th-
20th C; general antiques, clocks.* LOC: A697. PARK:
Easy. TEL: 01890 830334. VAT: Stan/Spec.

Fraser Antiques
65 High St. TD12 4DL. (R. Fleming). Est. 1968. Open
Tues.-Fri. 10-5, Sat. 9.30-5, other times by appointment.
SIZE: Medium. *STOCK: Porcelain, glass, pictures, silver,
small furniture, general antiques.* PARK: Easy. TEL: 01890
882450; fax - 01890 882451; e-mail - m13border@aol.com
SER: Valuations; restorations. VAT: Spec.

Hand in Hand
Hirsel Law Schoolhouse. TD12 4HX. (Mrs Ruth Hand).
Est. 1969. Open by appointment. SIZE: Small. *STOCK:
Paisley shawls, period costume, fine linens, quilts,
curtains and interesting textiles.* PARK: Own. TEL:
01890 883496; e-mail - ruth.hand@virgin.net website -
www.ruthhandinhand.com SER: Restorations;
valuations. FAIRS: Textile (London, Manchester).

CROMARTY

Cromarty Antiques
24 Church St. IV11 8XA. (Jean and Jenny Henderson).
Est. 2000. Open Tues.-Sat. 10-5 in summer, other days and
winter by appointment. SIZE: Large. *STOCK: Georgian,
Victorian and Edwardian fine furniture, especially dining
room tables; porcelain, glass, metalware, silver including
Scottish provincial.* LOC: On the Black Isle (just north of
Inverness), follow signs for Cromarty from A9. PARK:
Easy. TEL: 01381 600404; fax - 01381 610408; home -
01381 610269. FAIRS: Hopetoun House, Edinburgh;
Scone Palace, Perth; Newton Hotel, Nairn. VAT: Spec.

DORNOCH

Castle Close Antiques
Castle Close. IV25 3SN. (Mrs J. Maclean). Est. 1982.
Open 10-1 and 2-5. CL: Thurs. pm. SIZE: Medium.
*STOCK: General antiques including furniture, stripped
pine, porcelain, jewellery and silver, paintings.* PARK:
Easy. TEL: 01862 810405; home - 01862 81057; e-mail
- enquiries@castle-close-antiques.com VAT: Spec.

Little Treasures
Shore Rd. IV25 3LS. (Allison Taylor). Est. 1993. Open
10-5, Sun. 12-4 (summer only). SIZE: Small. *STOCK:
Jewellery, ceramics and glass, 19th-20th C, £5-£1,000.*
LOC: Just off cathedral square, road opposite Tourist
Information. PARK: Easy. TEL: 01862 811175; e-mail -
alliandtrev@aol.com website - www.littletreasures
dornoch.co.uk SER: Valuations.

DOUNE

Scottish Antique & Arts Centre
FK16 6HE. (Robert Templeman). Est. 1999. Open 10-5
including Sun. SIZE: Very large. *STOCK: General
antiques, collectables, Georgian and Victorian furniture,
jewellery, glass, paintings, books.* LOC: A84 Stirling to
Callander road, 1 mile north of Doune. PARK: Own
large. TEL: 01786 841203; fax - 01786 842561; e-mail -
info@scottish-antiques.com website - www.scottish-
antiques.com VAT: Stan/Spec.

DUNDEE

Angus Antiques
4 St. Andrews St. DD1 2EX. (Stanley Paget and John Czerek).
Est. 1964. Open Mon.-Fri. 10-4, other times by appointment.
*STOCK: Militaria, badges, medals, swords, jewellery, silver,
gold, collectors' items, Art Nouveau, Art Deco, advertising and
decorative items, tins, toys, teddy bears.* LOC: City centre.
PARK: Nearby. TEL: 01382 322128.

Neil Livingstone   LAPADA
3 Old Hawkhill. DD2 1LS. Est. 1976. Open any time by
appointment. SIZE: Small. *STOCK: French and Italian
furniture and decorative items, 17th-20th C.* TEL: 01382
907788/221751; fax - 01382 566332; mobile - 07775 877715;
e-mail - npl88@onetel.com SER: Shipping worldwide.

DUNECHT

The Magic Lantern
Nether Corskie. AB32 7EL. (Mr and Mrs P. Whyte). Est.
1978. SIZE: Medium. *STOCK: Georgian and Victorian
furniture, £500-£2,000; silver and plate Victorian
cutlery, £50-£100; china, porcelain, Scottish pottery,
candlesticks, £25-£200.* LOC: A944, turn towards
Kintore. PARK: Easy. TEL: 01330 860678; home - same.
SER: Restorations (china).

435

DUNKELD

Dunkeld Antiques   LAPADA

Tay Terrace. PH8 0AQ. (D. Dytch). Est. 1986. Open 10-5, Sun. 12-5. Jan. and Feb. - Fri and Sat. only. CL: Thurs (Nov.-June). SIZE: Large. *STOCK: 18th-19th C furniture, clocks, paintings, decorative items, out-of-print and antiquarian books.* LOC: Converted church, overlooking River Tay. PARK: Easy. TEL: 01350 728832; fax - 01350 727008; e-mail - sales@dunkeldantiques.com website - www.dunkeldantiques.com SER: Valuations. VAT: Spec.

EDINBURGH

Antiques

48 Thistle St. EH2 1EN. (E. Humphrey). Est. 1946. Open mornings or by appointment. *STOCK: Paintings, etchings, china and glass.* TEL: 0131 226 3625.

Armchair Books

72-74 West Port. EH1 2LE. (David Govan and William Lytle). Est. 1993. Open 10-6 inluding Sun. SIZE: 2 shops. *STOCK: Books, secondhand and Victorian, £2-£1,000.* LOC: West from Grassmarket. PARK: Nearby. TEL: 0131 229 5927; e-mail - armchairbooks @hotmail.com website - www.armchairbooks.co.uk SER: Valuations; restorations (books).

Bebes et Jouets

c/o Lochend Post Office. 165 Restalrig Rd. EH7 6HW. Est. 1988. Open by appointment. SIZE: Small. *STOCK: Fine French and German dolls, vintage teddy bears, dolls' houses and miniature doll-related items, dolls' clothing and accessories.* LOC: 1/2 mile from Princes St. PARK: Easy. TEL: 0131 332 5650; e-mail - bebesetjouets@tiscali.co.uk SER: Photographs and videos of stock available.

Berland's of Edinburgh

143 Gilmore Place. EH3 9PW. (R. Melvin). GMC. Open 9-4.45. CL: Wed. *STOCK: Restored antique light fittings.* TEL: 0131 228 6760. e-mail - melvinlighting@fsbdial.co.uk SER: Lighting restorations; stockist of old style braided flex.

Joseph Bonnar, Jewellers

72 Thistle St. EH2 1EN. Open 10.30-5 or by appointment. SIZE: Medium. *STOCK: Antique and period jewellery.* LOC: Parallel with Princes St. TEL: 0131 226 2811; fax - 0131 225 9438. VAT: Stan/Spec.

Bourne Fine Art Ltd

6 Dundas St. EH3 6HZ. (P. Bourne). Est. 1978. Open 10-6, Sat. 11-4. SIZE: Medium. *STOCK: Scottish paintings, 1700 to date.* LOC: New Town. PARK: Easy. TEL: 0131 557 4050; e-mail - art@bournefineart.com website - www.bournefineart.com SER: Valuations; restorations; buys at auction; framing. VAT: Stan/Spec.

Bow-well Antiques

103-105 West Bow. EH1 2JP. (Murdoch J. McLeod). Est. 1984. Open 10-5 or by appointment. SIZE: Medium. *STOCK: Scottish items - jewellery, dress items, weapons, ceramics and glass, silver, £50-£10,000; clocks and barometers, £200-£8,000; prints, some paintings, £50-£3,000; furniture, £100-£10,000; all mainly 18th-19th C. Scientific and medical items, 19th C, £10-£2,000.* LOC: Grassmarket area of old town. PARK: Grassmarket.

TEL: 0131 225 3335; fax - 0131 226 1259; mobile - 07710 600431; e-mail - murdoch.mcleod@virgin.net SER: Valuations.

Broughton Books

2A Broughton Place. EH1 3RX. (P. Galinsky). Est. 1964. Open Tues.-Fri. 12-6, Sat. 10.30-5.30. SIZE: Medium. *STOCK: Books, secondhand and antiquarian, £2.50-£250.* LOC: Off Broughton St, close to Waverley station and top of Leith Walk. TEL: 0131 557 8010; home - 0131 478 0614.

Cabaret

37 Grassmarket. EH1 2HS. (T. Cavers). Est. 1990. Open 10.30-5.30 including Sun. SIZE: Medium. *STOCK: Collectors' items - jewellery, books, glass, Art Deco, silver, ceramics, Scottish paperweights, compacts.* PARK: Easy. TEL: 0131 225 8618.

Calton Gallery   BADA

6A Regent Terrace. EH7 5BN. (A.G. Whitfield). Est. 1979. Open by appointment. SIZE: Medium. STOCK: Paintings, especially Scottish, marine and watercolours, £100-£100,000; prints, £10-£1,000; sculpture, to £20,000; all 19th to early 20th C. LOC: East end of Princes St. PARK: Pay & Display. TEL: 0131 556 1010; home - same; fax - 0131 558 1150; mobile - 07887 793781; e-mail - mail@caltongallery.com website - www.caltongallery.com SER: Valuations; restorations (oils, watercolours, prints); buys at auction (paintings). VAT: Stan/Spec.

Castle Antiques

330 Lawnmarket. EH1 2PN. (H. Parry). *STOCK: Silver, porcelain, English and Continental furniture, clocks.* TEL: 0131 225 7615.

The Carson Clark Gallery - Scotland's Map Heritage Centre

181-183 Canongate, The Royal Mile. EH8 8BN. (A. Carson Clark). FRGS. FBCartS. Est. 1969. Open 10.30-5.30. *STOCK: Maps, sea charts and prints.* TEL: 0131 556 4710; fax - same; e-mail - scotmap@aol.com website - www.carson-clark-gallery.co.uk SER: Collections valued and purchased.

The Collectors Shop

49 Cockburn St. EH1 1BS. (D. Cavanagh). Est. 1970. Open 11-5. *STOCK: Coins, medals, militaria, cigarette and postcards, small collectors' items, jewellery, silver and plate. Not Stocked: Postage stamps.* TEL: 0131 226 3391. SER: Buys at auction.

Craiglea Clocks

88 Comiston Rd. EH10 5QJ. (R.J. Rafter). Est. 1977. Open 10-5. SIZE: Small. *STOCK: Antique clocks and barometers.* LOC: On Biggar road from Morningside. PARK: Adjacent streets. TEL: 0131 452 8568; website - www.craiglea clocks.com SER: Restorations (clocks and barometers).

Da Capo Antiques

68 Henderson Row. EH3 5BJ. (Nick Carter). Est. 1975. Open Tues.-Sat. 10.30-5.30. SIZE: Medium. *STOCK: Furniture, including brass bedsteads, and accessories; lighting, 18th to early 20th C, £100-£5,000.* LOC: Off Dundas St. PARK: Easy. TEL: 0131 557 1918; home - 0131 557 3621. SER: Valuations; restorations (furniture including upholstery). VAT: Spec.*

Alan Day Antiques LAPADA
25A Moray Place. EH3 6DA. Est. 1973. Open by appointment. *STOCK: Furniture and paintings, 18th-19th C; general antiques.* LOC: City centre. PARK: Nearby. TEL: 0131 225 2590.

Duncan & Reid Books & Antiques
5 Tanfield, Inverleith. EH3 5DA. (Margaret Duncan, Susie Reid and Pippa Scott). Est. 1992. Open Tues.-Sat. 11-5. SIZE: Small. *STOCK: 18th-19th C English, Chinese and Continental ceramics, glass and decorative objects; books including sets, modern and antiquarian.* LOC: Near Royal Botanic Gardens. TEL: 0131 556 4591.

EASY - Edinburgh Architectural Salvage Yard
31 West Bowling Green St. EH6 5NX. Est. 1985. Open 9-5, Sat. 12-5. SIZE: Large. *STOCK: Fireplaces, stained glass, roll-top baths, carriage gates, panelled doors, cast-iron radiators.* TEL: 0131 554 7077; fax - 0131 554 3070; e-mail - enquiries@easy-arch-salv.co.uk website - www.easy-arch-salv.co.uk

Edinburgh Coin Shop
11 West Crosscauseway. EH8 9JW. (T.D. Brown). Open 10-5. *STOCK: Coins, medals, badges, militaria, postcards, cigarette cards, stamps, jewellery, clocks and watches, general antiques; bullion dealers.* TEL: 0131 668 2928/667 9095; fax - 0131 668 2926. VAT: Stan.

Donald Ellis incorporating Bruntsfield Clocks
7 Bruntsfield Place. EH10 4HN. (D.G. and C.M. Ellis). Est. 1970. Open 9.30-5.30. CL: Wed. pm. SIZE: Medium. *STOCK: Clocks and general antiques.* LOC: Opposite Links Garage at Bruntsfield Links. PARK: Nearby. TEL: 0131 229 4720. SER: Repairs (clocks). FAIRS: Buxton (May).

Georgian Antiques LAPADA
10 Pattison St., Leith Links. EH6 7HF. Est. 1976. Open 8.30-5.30, Sat. 10-2. SIZE: 2 large warehouses. *STOCK: Furniture, Georgian, Victorian, inlaid, Edwardian; shipping goods, smalls, £10-£10,000.* LOC: Off Leith Links. PARK: Easy. TEL: 0131 553 7286 (24 hrs.); fax - 0131 553 6299; e-mail - info@georgianantiques.net website - www.georgianantiques.net SER: Valuations; restorations; buys at auction; packing and shipping; courier. VAT: Stan/Spec.

Goodwin's Antiques Ltd
15-16 Queensferry St. and 106A-108 Rose St. EH2 4QW. Est. 1952. Open 9-5.30, Sat. 9-5. SIZE: Medium. *STOCK: Antique and modern silver and jewellery.* LOC: Off Princes St., west end. TEL: 0131 225 4717; fax - 0131 220 1412; Rose St. - 0131 220 1230. VAT: Stan/Spec.

Harlequin Antiques
30 Bruntsfield Place. EH10 4HJ. (C.S. Harkness). Est. 1995. Open 10-5 and Sun. (Dec. only) 12-4. SIZE: Small. *STOCK: Clocks and watches, silver, ceramics, small furniture, £10-£4,000.* LOC: 2 miles south of Princes St. (west end). PARK: Easy. TEL: 0131 228 9446. SER: Valuations; restorations (clocks); buys at auction (clocks).

Hawkins & Hawkins BADA
9 Atholl Crescent. EH3 8HA. (Emma H. Hawkins). Resident. Est. 1994. Open by appointment. SIZE: Medium. *STOCK: Taxidermy, 1890-1920, £100-£10,000; English furniture, 1800-1910, £500-£100,000.* LOC: Off Princess St. PARK: Easy. TEL: 0131 229 2828; fax - 0131 229 2128; mobile - 07831 093198; e-mail - emma@emmahawkins.co.uk website - www.emmahawkins.demon.co.uk FAIRS: Olympia (June). VAT: Spec/Stan.

Holyrood Architectural Salvage
Holyrood Business Park, 146 Duddingston Rd. West. EH16 4AP. (Ken Fowler). Est. 1993. Open 9-5. SIZE: Very large. *STOCK: Original and reproduction fireplaces, rolltop baths, doors, radiators, pews, brassware, flooring.* LOC: 5 minutes drive from Holyrood Palace, 2 mins. from Duddingston village - telephone for directions. PARK: Easy and free. TEL: 0131 661 9305; fax - 0131 656 9404; website - www.holyroodarchitecturalsalvage.com SER: Fireplace fitting. VAT: Stan/Global.

Allan K. L. Jackson
67 Causewayside. EH9 1QF. Est. 1974. Open 10-6. SIZE: Medium. *STOCK: General small antiques, from Victorian, £5-100.* PARK: Easy. TEL: 0131 668 4532; mobile - 07989 236443. SER: Valuations.

Kaimes Smithy Antiques
79 Howdenhall Rd. EH16 6PW. (J. Lynch). Est. 1972. Open 1.30-5. CL: Mon. and Thurs. SIZE: Medium. *STOCK: Furniture, clocks, porcelain, glass, paintings, curios, 18th-20th C, £10-£3,000.* LOC: From City bypass take A701 (at Straiton junction) into city centre, located at 1st set of traffic lights. PARK: Easy. TEL: 0131 441 2076/664 0124; e-mail - john@jlynch.freeserve.co.uk SER: Valuations; restorations.

London Road Antiques
15 Earlston Place, London Rd. EH7 5SU. (Randall Forrest and Tim Hardie). Est. 1990. Open 10-5, Sun. 1-5 or by appointment. SIZE: Large + trade store. *STOCK: Georgian, Victorian and stripped pine furniture.* LOC: 2 mins. from Princes St. PARK: Easy. TEL: 0131 652 2790; e-mail - shop@19thC.com website - www.19thC.com SER: Shipping arranged.

J. Martinez Antiques
17 Brandon Terrace. EH3 5DZ. Est. 1975. Open 11-5. SIZE: Small. *STOCK: Clocks, jewellery and general antiques, mainly Victorian, £50-£1,000.* LOC: Off Dundas St. PARK: Easy. TEL: 0131 558 8720; fax - same. SER: Valuations; restorations (porcelain, clocks and watches); buys at auction. FAIRS: Midland Clock & Watch, NEC; Antique Clock & Watch, Haydock Park; Ingliston, Edinburgh; Freemasons Hall, Edinburgh.

McNaughtan's Bookshop
3a and 4a Haddington Place. EH7 4AE. (Elizabeth Strong). ABA. ILAB. Est. 1957. Open 9.30-5.30. CL: Mon. SIZE: Large. *STOCK: Antiquarian books.* LOC: Leith Walk. PARK: Limited. TEL: 0131 556 5897; fax - 0131 556 8220; e-mail - mcnbooks@btconnect.com website - www.mcnaughtansbookshop.com SER: Book search; valuations. FAIRS: ABA; Olympia; Chelsea; Edinburgh.

The Meadows Lamp Gallery
48 Warrender Park Rd. EH9 1HH. (Scott Robertson).

Est. 1992. Open Tues., Thurs. and Sat. 10-6. SIZE: Small. *STOCK: Old glass lampshades, table lamps, brass light fittings and accessories, especially Art Nouveau.* LOC: 10 minutes walk from city centre. PARK: Easy. TEL: 0131 221 1212; mobile - 07836 223311; e-mail - s4sarok@aol.com SER: Restorations (cleaning, polishing, lacquering, silver plating).

Neilsons Ltd
56 Bankhead Crossway South. EH11 4EP. (J. and A. Neilson). NFA. Est. 1932. Open 9.30-5, Sat. 12-5. SIZE: Large. *STOCK: Fireplaces, 18th-20th C, £100-£20,000; interiors, stoves, fenders, fire irons; marble (including French), wood and stone chimney pieces.* LOC: Sight Hill Industrial Estate, near by-pass. PARK: Easy. TEL: 0131 453 5820; e-mail - info@chimneypiece.co.uk website - www.chimneypiece.co.uk VAT: Stan.

The Old Town Bookshop
8 Victoria St. EH1 2HG. (Ronald Wilson). Est. 1982. Open 10.30-5.45. SIZE: Medium. *STOCK: Books, 16th-20th C; prints, from 1450's to 19th C.* LOC: Centre of old town. PARK: Nearby. TEL: 0131 225 9237; fax - 0131 229 1503; website - www.oldtownbookshop.com SER: Valuations. FAIRS: Book - London, York, Oxford, Cambridge, Edinburgh and Glasgow.

Open Eye Gallery Ltd
34 Abercromby Place. EH3 6QE. (T. and P. Wilson). Est. 1976. Open 10-6, Sat. 10-4. SIZE: Medium. *STOCK: Early 20th C etchings, contemporary paintings, ceramics and jewellery.* LOC: Corner of Dundas St. PARK: Easy. TEL: 0131 557 1020; fax - same; e-mail - open.eye@virgin.net website - www.openeyegallery.co.uk SER: Valuations; restorations (paintings and ceramics); buys at auction. VAT: Mainly Spec.

R.L. Rose Oriental Carpets Ltd
8 Howe St. EH3 6TD. GMC. Est. 1919. Open 9.30-5.30 including Sun. *STOCK: Antique, decorative, modern and fine old Oriental rugs and carpets.* PARK: Nearby. TEL: 0131 225 8785; fax - 0131 226 7827; e-mail - roger@rlroseltd.com website - www.rlroseltd.com SER: Valuations; repairs; cleaning.

Royal Mile Curios
363 High St. EH1 1PW. (L. Bosi and R. Eprile). Est. 1875. Open 10.30-5. *STOCK: Jewellery and silver.* TEL: 0131 226 4050; e-mail - info@antique-jewelry.cc website - www.antique-jewelry.cc

Royal Mile Gallery
272 Canongate, Royal Mile. EH8 8AA. (J. A. Smith). Est. 1970. Open 11.30-5. SIZE: Medium. *STOCK: Maps, engravings, etchings and lithographs.* LOC: Between castle and Holyrood Palace. PARK: New Street. TEL: 0131 558 1702; home - 0131 668 4007; e-mail - james@royalmilegallery.com website - www.royalmile gallery.com SER: Valuations; restorations; framing; buys at auction.

Samarkand Galleries
16 Howe St. EH3 6TD. (Brian MacDonald). Est. 1979. Open 10-6, Sun. 11-4. SIZE: Small. *STOCK: Tribal and village rugs and artefacts, 19th C, £100-£10,000; fine decorative carpets, 19th-20th C, £1,000-£10,000+; kelims, 19th-20th C, £200-£2,000; also unique contemporary rugs and carpets.* LOC: Corner of Jamaica St. PARK: Heriot Row. TEL: 0131 225 2010; fax - same; e-mail - howe@samarkand.co.uk and mac@samarkand.co.uk website - www.samarkand.co.uk SER: Exhibitions. FAIRS: Hali, Olympia. VAT: Stan/Spec.

James Scott
43 Dundas St. EH3 6JN. Est. 1964. Open 11-1 and 2-5.30. CL: Thurs. pm. *STOCK: Curiosities, unusual items, silver, jewellery, small furniture.* TEL: 0131 556 8260; mobile - 07714 004370. VAT: Stan.

The Scottish Gallery
16 Dundas St. EH3 6HZ. (Aitken Dott Ltd). Est. 1842. Open 10-6, Sat. 10-4. *STOCK: 20th C and contemporary Scottish paintings and contemporary British and international applied art.* LOC: New Town. TEL: 0131 558 1200; fax - 0131 558 3900; e-mail - mail@scottish-gallery.co.uk website - www.scottish-gallery.co.uk VAT: Stan/Spec.

Second Edition
9 Howard St. EH3 5JP. (Mr and Mrs W.A. Smith). Est. 1978. Open 10.30-5.30, Sat. 9.30-5.30. SIZE: Medium. *STOCK: Antiquarian and secondhand books, £10-£1,000; late 19th to early 20th C maps and prints, £7-£75.* LOC: 200 yards south of Royal Botanical Gardens. PARK: Nearby. TEL: 0131 556 9403; home - 0131 552 1850; website - www.secondeditionbookshop.com SER: Valuations; book-binding.

Still Life
54 Candlemaker Row. EH1 2QE. (Ewan Lamont). Est. 1984. Open 12-5. SIZE: Small. *STOCK: Small antiques and collectables.* LOC: City centre. PARK: Crichton St. TEL: 0131 225 8524; e-mail - ewanlamont@mac.com website - www.homepage.mac.com/ewanlamont/ PhotoAlbum14 SER: Valuations.

The Talish Gallery
168 Canongate. EH8 8DF. (John R. Martin). Est. 1970. Open 11-3. SIZE: Medium. *STOCK: Silver, plate, collectors' items, rugs, pictures, small furniture, £10-£10,000.* LOC: Bottom of Royal Mile, opposite clock. PARK: Easy. TEL: 0131 557 8435. SER: Valuations. VAT: Spec.

The Thrie Estaits
49 Dundas St. EH3 6RS. (Peter D.R. Powell). Est. 1970. Open Tues.-Sat. 11-5. *STOCK: Pottery, porcelain, glass, contemporary and period paintings and prints, unusual and decorative items, some early oak and country furniture.* TEL: 0131 556 7084; e-mail - TheThrieEstaits@aol.com

Trinity Curios
4-6 Stanley Rd.,Trinity. EH6 4SJ. (Alan Ferguson). Resident. Est. 1987. Open Tues., Thurs. and Fri. 10-5, Wed. and Sat. 12-6. SIZE: Medium. *STOCK: Furniture, ceramics and silver, 19th C, £50-£1,000.* LOC: From Ferry Rd. turn north on to Newhaven Rd., shop 300 yards on left. PARK: Easy. TEL: 0131 552 8481. SER: Restorations (furniture including upholstery). VAT: Stan.

Unicorn Antiques
65 Dundas St. EH3 6RS. (N. Duncan). Est. 1967. Usually open 10.30-7. SIZE: Medium. *STOCK: Architectural and domestic brassware, lights, mirrors, glass, china, cutlery and bric-a-brac. Not Stocked:*

Weapons, coins, jewellery. LOC: From Princes St. turn into Hanover St. - Dundas St. is a continuation. PARK: Meters. TEL: 0131 556 7176; home - 0131 332 9135.

John Whyte
116b Rose St. EH2 3JF. Est. 1928. Open 9.30-5, Sat. 9.30-5. STOCK: Jewellery, watches, clocks and silver. TEL: 0131 225 2140; e-mail - whytejohnj@aol.com VAT: Stan.

Richard Wood Antiques
66 Westport. EH1 2LD. Est. 1972. Open 10-5.30. SIZE: Small. STOCK: Small collectable silver and Oriental objects, art glass, Art Deco, Art Nouveau, Arts and Crafts, pottery and porcelain, Scottish items, bayonets, daggers, pistols; ivory, pewter, Scottish jewellery. LOC: Central. PARK: Grassmarket (meters). TEL: 0131 229 6344. FAIRS: Ingliston.

Anthony Woodd Gallery Ltd
4 Dundas St. EH3 6HZ. Est. 1978. Open 10-6, Sat. 11-4. Medium. STOCK: Scottish natural history and sporting pictures, 1750 to date. PARK: Easy. TEL: 0131 558 9544; fax - 0131 558 9525; home - 01721 740278; mobile - 07717 744014; e-mail - sales@anthonywoodd. com website - www.anthonywoodd.com SER: Valuations; restorations; framing. VAT: Spec.

Young Antiques
185 Bruntsfield Place. EH10 4DG. (T.C. Young). Est. 1979. Open 10.30-1.30 and from 2.30. CL: Wed. pm. SIZE: Medium. STOCK: Victorian and Edwardian furniture, £50-£1,000; ceramics, £20-£2,000; oils and watercolours, £50-£1,500. PARK: Easy. TEL: 0131 229 1361. SER: Valuations.

FOCHABERS

Marianne Simpson
61/63 High St. IV32 7DU. (M.R. Simpson). Est. 1990. Open Easter-Oct: Mon.-Sat. 10-1 and 2-4; Oct.-Easter: Tues., Thurs., Sat. 10-1 and 2-4, or by appointment. SIZE: Small. STOCK: Books and ephemera, 19th-20th C, £1-£100. LOC: A96. PARK: Easy. TEL: 01343 821192; home - same.

FORFAR

Gow Antiques
Pitscandly Farm. DD8 3NZ. (Jeremy Gow). BAFRA. Resident. Est. 1986. Appointment advisable. SIZE: Medium. STOCK: Fine Continental and British furniture, 17th-19th C, £50-£20,000. LOC: 3 miles off A90, take B9134 out of Forfar, through Lunenhead, first right at sign Myreside, premises next left, in farmyard. PARK: Easy. TEL: 01307 465342; mobile - 07711 416786; e-mail - jeremy@knowyourantiques.com website - www.knowyourantiques.com SER: Restorations; valuations; disaster management; 3 day antique furniture recognition courses. FAIRS: Antiques For Everyone, Glasgow (Aug.); LAPADA; NEC.

FORRES

Michael Low Antiques
45 High St. IV36 2PB. Est. 1967. Open 10-1 and 2-5. STOCK: Small antiques. TEL: 01309 673696.

FORTROSE

Cathedral Antiques
45 High St. IV10 8SU. (Patricia MacColl). Est. 1996. Open Fri. and Sat. March to Dec. (extra days in summer months). CL: Jan. and Feb. except by appointment. SIZE: Medium - 2 showrooms. STOCK: Fine furniture, 1780-1920, £100-£5,000; silver and plate, 1780-1940, £5-£1,000; porcelain and Scottish pottery, glass, 1820-1940, £5-£500. LOC: 20 mins. from Inverness. PARK: Easy. TEL: 01381 620161; home - same; mobile - 07778 817074; e-mail - cathant@hotmail.com SER: Valuations. FAIRS: Hopetoun House, Edinburgh; Blair Castle, Perthshire; Highland, Nairn; Scone Palace, Perth.

GLASGOW

All Our Yesterdays
6 Park Rd., Kelvinbridge. G4 9JG. (Susie Robinson). Est. 1989. Open 11.30-5.30, flexible and by appointment. SIZE: Small. STOCK: Kitchenalia, mainly 1850-1949, £5-£500; smalls, especially decorative arts, advertising related items, books, etchings and postcards, mechanical items, crystals and minerals, smokers sundries and oddities, to £500. LOC: Near junction with Gt. Western Rd. and university. PARK: Easy. TEL: 0141 334 7788; answerphone/fax - 0141 339 8994; e-mail - antiques@allouryesterdays.fsnet.co.uk website - www. healingroom.org SER: Valuations; buys at auction; search and hire.

The Antiques Warehouse
Unit 3b, Yorkhill Quay Estate. G3 8QE. (P. Mangan). Open 9-5, Sat. 10-5, Sun. 12-5. SIZE: 30 dealers. STOCK: Antique pine, Oriental rugs and carpets, general antiques, furnishings, smalls and fine arts. TEL: 0141 334 4924. SER: Import and export worldwide.

The Roger Billcliffe Fine Art
134 Blythswood St. G2 4EL. Est. 1992. Open 9.30-5.30, Sat. 10-1. SIZE: Large. STOCK: British paintings, watercolours, drawings, sculpture, especially Scottish, from 1850; jewellery, metalwork, glass and woodwork. TEL: 0141 332 4027; fax - 0141 332 6573; e-mail - roger @rbfa.demon.co.uk website - www.billcliffegallery.com VAT: Spec.

Butler's Furniture Galleries
39 Camelon St., Carntyne Industrial Estate. G32 6AF. (Laurence Butler). Est. 1951. Open 10-5 or by appointment. CL: Sat. SIZE: Large. STOCK: Georgian, Victorian and Edwardian furniture, £200-£5,000. LOC: From M8 to Edinburgh, off at Stepps Cutoff, right at traffic lights down to bottom of road. Left on to dual carriageway, right at first traffic lights and straight down to sign for industrial estate, turn right. PARK: Easy. TEL: 0141 778 5720; home - 0141 639 3396; mobile - 07950 312355; website - www.butlersfurnituregalleries.co.uk SER: Valuations; restorations; repolishing. VAT: Spec.

A.D. Hamilton and Co
7 St. Vincent Place. G1 2DW. (Jeffrey Lee Fineman). Est. 1890. Open 9.30-5. SIZE: Small. STOCK: Jewellery and silver, 19th to early 20th C, £100-£3,000; British coins, medals and banknotes, £10-£1,000. LOC: City centre, next to George square. PARK: Meters. TEL: 0141

221 5423; fax - 0141 248 6019; website - www. adhamilton.co.uk SER: Valuations. VAT: Stan/Spec.

Ewan Mundy Fine Art Ltd
Lower Ground Floor, 211 West George St. G2 2LW. Est. 1981. Open Mon.-Fri. SIZE: Medium. *STOCK: Fine Scottish, English and French oils and watercolours, 19th-20th C, from £250; Scottish and English etchings and lithographs, 19th-20th C, from £100; Scottish contemporary paintings, from £50.* LOC: City centre. PARK: Nearby. TEL: 0141 248 9755. FAIRS: New York. VAT: Stan/Spec.

Pastimes Vintage Toys
126 Maryhill Rd. G20 7QS. (Gordon and Anne Brown). Est. 1980. Open Tues.-Sat. 10-5. SIZE: Medium. *STOCK: Vintage toys, die-cast, railways and dolls' houses, from 1910, £1-£300.* LOC: From the west off junction 17, M8; from the east junction 16, M8. PARK: Easy. TEL: 0141 331 1008; website - www. dinkydoll.com SER: Valuations. VAT: Stan.

R.L. Rose Oriental Carpets Ltd
Unit 3b, Yorkhill Quay. G3 8QE. Open 10.5. *STOCK: Oriental and decorative carpets.* TEL: 0141 339 7290; fax - 0141 334 1499. SER: Repairs; cleaning.

Jeremy Sniders Antiques
158 Bath St. G2 4TB. Est. 1983. Open 9-5. SIZE: Medium. *STOCK: British decorative arts including furniture, 1850-1960; Scandinavian decorative arts including furniture, silver and jewellery, 1800 to date; silver, mainly 19th-20th C; all £30-£5,000.* PARK: Nearby - Sauchiehall St. Centre. TEL: 0141 332 0043; fax - 0141 332 5505; e-mail - snidersantiques@aol.com website - www.jeremysnidersantiques.com and www. jeremysnidersantiques.co.uk SER: Will source Scandinavian articles - eg. Georg Jensen, Royal Copenhagen. VAT: Spec.

Strachan Antiques
40 Darnley St., Pollokshields. G41 2SE. (Alex and Lorna Strachan and Saranne Jenkins). Est. 1990. Open 10-6, Sun. 10-5. SIZE: Warehouse. *STOCK: Furniture especially Arts and Crafts, Art Nouveau and Glasgow Style, £50-£5,000; some decorative items.* LOC: 2 mins. from M8, junction 20 westbound, junction 21 eastbound. PARK: Own. TEL: 0141 429 4411; e-mail - alex. strachan@btconnect.com website - www.strachan antiques.co.uk FAIRS: SECC Glasgow. VAT: Stan/Spec.

The Victorian Village Antiques
93 West Regent St. G2 2BA . Est. 1978. Open 10-5.

IS YOUR ENTRY CORRECT?
If there is even the slightest inaccuracy in your entry, please let us know before
1st January 2006

GUIDE TO THE ANTIQUE SHOPS OF BRITAIN
Sandy Lane, Old Martlesham,
Woodbridge, Suffolk IP12 4SD, UK.

Tel: **01394 389968** or Fax: **01394 389999**
Email: editorial@antique-acc.com
Website: www.antiquecollectorsclub.com

SIZE: 3 floors. LOC: Between Renfield St and Wellington St. PARK: At rear and meters. TEL: 0141 332 0808/9808. VAT: Stan/Spec. Below are listed the dealers at these premises.

Golden Oldies
Jewellery. SER: Repairs; commissions.

Putting-on-the-Ritz
Art Deco, china, jewellery, 1920's curios. TEL: 0141 332 9808.

Rosamond Rutherford
Victorian jewellery, Scottish agate, silver, Sheffield plate. TEL: 0141 332 9808.

Victoria
Silverware.

Voltaire & Rousseau
12-14 Otago Lane. G12 8PB. (Joseph McGonigle). Est. 1972. Open 10-6. SIZE: Medium. *STOCK: Books - classic, literature, foreign, literature, Scottish, some rare and first editions; student textbooks.* PARK: Gibson St. TEL: 0141 339 1811. SER: Valuations (books).

Tim Wright Antiques   LAPADA
147 Bath St. G2 4SQ. (T. and J. Wright). Est. 1971. Open 9.45-5, Sat. 10.30-4 or by appointment. SIZE: 6 showrooms. *STOCK: Furniture, European and Oriental ceramics and glass, decorative items, silver and plate, brass and copper, mirrors and prints, textiles, samplers, all £50-£6,000.* LOC: On opposite corner to Christie's. PARK: Multi-storey opposite and meters. TEL: 0141 221 0364; fax - same; e-mail - tim@timwright-antiques.com website - www. timwright-antiques.com VAT: Mainly Spec.

GLENCARSE, Nr. Perth

Michael Young Antiques at Glencarse
PH2 7LX. Est. 1887. Open 10.30-5.30 and by appointment SIZE: Large. *STOCK: 17th-19th C furniture, paintings and silver.* LOC: A90 3 miles east of Perth. PARK: Easy. TEL: 01738 860001; fax - same. SER: Valuations; restorations.

GULLANE

Gullane Antiques
5 Rosebery Place. EH31 2AN. (E.A. Lindsey). Est. 1981. Open 10.30-1 and 2.30-5. CL: Wed. and Thurs. SIZE: Medium. *STOCK: China and glass, 1850-1930, £5-£150; prints and watercolours, early 20th C, £25-£100; metalwork, 1900's, £5-£150; jewellery, £5-£200.* LOC: 6 miles north of Haddington, off A1. PARK: Easy. TEL: 01620 842994.

HADDINGTON

Leslie and Leslie
EH41 3JJ. (R. Skea). Est. 1920. Open 9-1 and 2-5. CL: Sat. *STOCK: General antiques.* PARK: Nearby. TEL: 01620 822241; fax - same. VAT: Stan.

Yester-Days
79 High St. EH41 8ET. (Betty Logan). Est. 1992. Open Tues., Wed., Fri. and Sat. 11-4.30. *STOCK: General antiques and collectables.* TEL: 01620 824543.

HUNTLY

Bygones
1 Bogie St. AB54 8DX. (Sue and Bruce Watts). Est. 1996. Open Wed. and Sat. 10-2, other days by appointment. SIZE: Medium. *STOCK: Clocks and pocket watches, £50-£3,000; furniture, barometers, Victoriana, curios and collectables, 19th-20th C, £10-£3,000.* LOC: Off Duke St. towards rail station. PARK: Nearby. TEL: 01466 794412. FAIRS: Swinderby; Newark.

INCHTURE

Inchmartine Fine Art
Inchmartine House. PH14 9QQ. (P.M. Stephens). Est. 1998. Open 9-5.30. SIZE: Medium. *STOCK: Mainly Scottish oils and watercolours, £150-£2,500.* LOC: Take A90 Perth/Dundee road, entrance on left at Lodge. PARK: Easy. TEL: 01828 686412; home - same; fax - 01828 686748; mobile - 07702 190128; e-mail - fineart @inchmartine.freeserve.co.uk SER: Cleaning; restorations; framing. FAIRS: Chester; Scone; Naworth. VAT: Spec.

C.S. Moreton (Antiques)
Inchmartine House. PH14 9QQ. (P.M. and Mrs M. Stephens). Est. 1922. Open 9-5.30. SIZE: Large. *STOCK: Furniture, £100-£10,000; carpets and rugs, £50-£3,000; ceramics, metalware; all 16th C to 1860; old cabinet makers' tools.* LOC: Take A90 Perth/Dundee road, entrance on left at Lodge. PARK: Easy. TEL: 01828 686412; home - same; fax - 01828 686748; mobile - 07702 190128; e-mail - moreton@inchmartine. freeserve.co.uk SER: Valuations; cabinet making and repairs. FAIRS: Chester; Scone; Naworth. VAT: Mainly Spec.

INNERLEITHEN

Keepsakes
96 High St. EH44 6HF. (Margaret Maxwell). CL: Tues., Wed. and lunchtimes. SIZE: Small. *STOCK: Ceramics and glass, £50-£800; dolls, teddies and toys, £100-£500; books, post and cigarette cards, £5-£25; jewellery, £5-£100; some 19th C but mainly 20th C.* LOC: A72. PARK: Easy. TEL: 01896 831369; home - 01896 830701. FAIRS: Ingliston; some Border.

INVERNESS

Gallery Persia
By Aird House, Upper Myrtlefield, Nairnside. IV2 5BX. (G. MacDonald). *STOCK: Persian, Turkoman, Afghanistan, Caucasus, Tibetan, Anatolian rugs and carpets, late 19th C to 1940, £500-£2,000+; quality contemporary pieces, £100+.* LOC: From A9 1st left after flyover, 1st left at roundabout, then 2.25 miles on B9006, then 1st right, 1st left. PARK: Easy. TEL: 01463 798500; home - 01463 792198; fax - same; e-mail - mac@gallerypersia.co.uk website - www.gallerypersia. co.uk SER: Valuations; restorations; cleaning; repairs. FAIRS: Game, Scone Palace, Perth (July).

JEDBURGH

Mainhill Gallery
Ancrum. TD8 6XA. (Diana Bruce). Est. 1981. Open by prior telephone call. SIZE: Medium. *STOCK: Oil paintings, watercolours, etchings, some sculpture and ceramics, 19th C to contemporary, £35-£7,000.* LOC: Just off A68, 3 miles north of Jedburgh, centre of Ancrum. PARK: Easy. TEL: 01835 830545; fax - 01835 830518. SER: Exhibitions; valuations. FAIRS: Glasgow; London; Edinburgh. VAT: Spec.

R. and M. Turner (Antiques Ltd)   LAPADA
34-36 High St. TD8 6AG. (R.J. Turner). Est. 1965. Open 9.30-5.30, Sat. 10-5. SIZE: 6 large showrooms and warehouse. *STOCK: Furniture, clocks, porcelain, paintings, silver, jewellery, 17th-20th C and fine reproductions.* LOC: On A68 to Edinburgh. PARK: Own. TEL: 01835 863445; fax - 01835 863349; e-mail - turner.antiques@virgin.net SER: Valuations; packing and shipping. VAT: Stan/Spec.

KILBARCHAN

Gardner's The Antique Shop   LAPADA
Wardend House, Kibbleston Rd. PA10 2PN. (G.D., R.K.F. and D.D. Gardner). Est. 1950. Open to Trade 7 days, retail 9-6, Sat. 10-5. SIZE: 11 showrooms. *STOCK: Smalls, furniture, general antiques.* LOC: 12 miles from Glasgow, at far end of Tandlehill Rd. 10 mins. from Glasgow Airport. PARK: Easy. TEL: 01505 702292; e-mail - gardantiques@cqm.co.uk website - www. gardnersantiques.co.uk SER: Valuations. VAT: Spec.

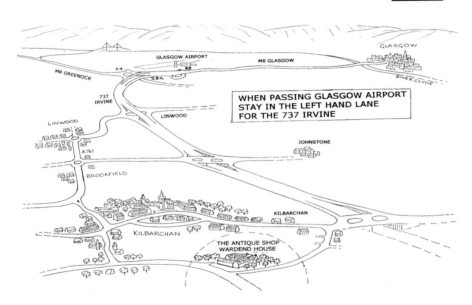

McQuade Antiques
7 Shuttle St. PA10 2JN. (W. G. & W. J. McQuade). Est. 1975. Open 10-5.30, Sun. 2-5.30. CL: Sat. SIZE: Large. *STOCK: Furniture, porcelain, clocks, brass and silver, 19th-20th C.* LOC: Next to Weavers Cottage. PARK: Easy. TEL: 01505 704249; e-mail – walterjmcquadeantiques@supanet.com SER: Valuations. FAIRS: Newark. VAT: Spec.

KILLEARN, Nr. Glasgow

Country Antiques
G63 9AJ. (Lady J. Edmonstone). Est. 1975. Open Mon.-Sat. *STOCK: Small antiques and decorative items.* Not Stocked: Reproduction. LOC: A81. In main street. PARK: Easy. TEL: Home – 01360 770215. SER: Interior decoration.

KILLIN

Maureen H. Gauld
Craiglea, Main St. FK21 8UN. Est. 1975. Open March-Oct. 10-5, Nov.-Feb. Thurs., Fri., Sat. SIZE: Medium. *STOCK: General antiques, furniture, silver, paintings and etchings, £5-£3,500.* PARK: Easy. TEL: 01567 820475; home – 01567 820605; e-mail – killingallery @btopenworld.com website – www.killingallery.co.uk

Killin Gallery
Craiglea, Main St. FK21 8UN. (J.A. Gauld). Est. 1992. Open 10-5, Sun. by appointment. SIZE: Medium. *STOCK: Etchings and drypoints, £100-£1,000; paintings, £300-£3,000; furniture, £100-£2,000; all 1860-1960.* LOC: Village centre. PARK: Easy. TEL: 01567 820475; home – 01567 820605; e-mail – killin gallery@btopenworld.com website – www.killingallery. co.uk SER: Valuations.

KILMACOLM

Kilmacolm Antiques Ltd
Stewart Place. PA13 4AF. (H. Maclean). Est. 1973. Open 10-1 and 2.30-5.30. CL: Sun. except by appointment. SIZE: Medium. *STOCK: Furniture, 18th-19th C, £100-£8,000; objets d'art, 19th C; jewellery, £5-£5,000; paintings, £100-£5,000.* LOC: First shop on right when travelling from Bridge of Weir. PARK: Easy. TEL: 01505 873149. SER: Restorations (furniture, silver, jewellery, porcelain). FAIRS: Hopetoun, Pollock House, Edinburgh, Inverness. VAT: Stan/Spec/Global.

KILMARNOCK

QS Antiques and Cabinetmakers
Moorfield Industrial Estate. KA2 0DP. (J.R. Cunningham and D.A. Johnson). Est. 1980. Open 9-5.30, Sat. 9-5. SIZE: Large. *STOCK: Furniture including stripped pine, 18th-19th C; shipping goods, architectural and collectors' items.* PARK: Easy. TEL: 01563 571071. SER: Restorations; stripping; custom-built kitchens and furniture. VAT: Stan.

KILMICHAEL GLASSARY, By Lochgilphead

Rhudle Mill
PA31 8QE. (D. Murray). Est. 1979. Open daily, weekends by appointment. SIZE: Medium. *STOCK: Furniture, 18th C to Art Deco, £30-£3,000; small items and bric-a-brac, £5-£500.* LOC: Signposted 3 miles south of Kilmartin on A816 Oban to Lochgilphead road. PARK: Easy. TEL:

01546 605284; home – same; fax – 01546 606173. SER: Restorations (furniture); French polishing; buys at auction.

KINGSTON-ON-SPEY

Collectables
Lein Rd. IV32 7NW. (J. Penman and B. Taylor). Est. 1987. Open daily including most weekends by appointment. SIZE: Small. *STOCK: Militaria, jewellery, lap desks, china, collectables, small silver, £5-£1,000.* LOC: On B9105. PARK: Easy. TEL: 01343 870462. SER: Valuations. FAIRS: Newton Hotel, Nairn; Treetops Hotel, Aberdeen.

KIRKCALDY

A. K. Campbell & Sons
277 High St. KY1 1LA. Est. 1977. SIZE: Small. *STOCK: Coins, medals, old banknotes, militaria, china and porcelain, pictures, small furniture, die-cast models, postcards.* PARK: Easy. TEL: 01592 597022. SER: Valuations.

Second Notions Antiques
2 Normand Rd., Dysart. KY1 2XJ. (James Sinclair). Est. 1995. Open by appointment. SIZE: Medium. *STOCK: General antiques especially furniture and longcase clocks, £2-£3000; shipping furniture.* LOC: A92. PARK: Easy. TEL: 01592 650505; home – 01592 573341; fax – same; e-mail – james@sinclair1155.freeserve.co.uk website – www.secondnotions.co.uk SER: Valuations. FAIRS: Swinderby; Newark.

KIRKCUDBRIGHT

The Antique Shop
67 St Mary St. DG6 4DU. (Paul and Marisa Mairs). Est. 1993. Open 10-5. *STOCK: General antiques, collectors' items, linen and lace, kichenalia, furniture, bric-a-brac, 18th-20th C, to £1,500.* LOC: Near entrance of town, at junction to Gatehouse of Fleet. PARK: Easy. TEL: 01557 332400; e-mail – mjmantiques@hotmail.com

Osborne Antiques   LAPADA
41 Castle St. and 63 High St. DG6 4JD. (David Mitchell). Est. 1949. Open 9-12.30 and 1.30-5 or by appointment. SIZE: Large. *STOCK: Georgian and Victorian furniture, smalls.* PARK: Easy. TEL: 01557 330441; e-mail – mitch0106@hotmail.com SER: Free UK delivery. VAT: Stan/Spec.

LANGHOLM

The Antique Shop
High St. DG13 0DH. (R. and V. Baird). Est. 1970. Open 10.30-5. CL: Wed. pm. SIZE: Small. *STOCK: China, glass, pictures, 18th-20th C; jewellery, rugs, 19th-20th C; trade warehouse – furniture, shipping goods and antiquarian books.* LOC: 20 miles north of Carlisle on A7. PARK: 100yds. TEL: 01387 380238. SER: Restorations (furniture).

LARGS

Narducci Antiques
11 Waterside St. KA30 9LN. (G. Narducci). Open Tues., Thurs. and Sat. 2.30-5.30 or by appointment – trade any time. SIZE: Warehouse. *STOCK: General antiques and shipping goods.* TEL: 01475 672612; 01294 461687; fax – 01294 470002; mobile – 07771 577777; website – www.

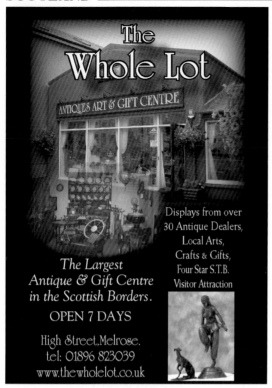

20th C. LOC: A90 6 miles south of Peterhead. PARK: Own. TEL: 01779 813223; fax/home - same; e-mail - jacqui@grannieusedto.co.uk website - www.grannieused to.co.uk SER: Valuations; buys at auction; worldwide shipping. FAIRS: Hopetoun House, Edinburgh; Scone Palace, Perth; Blair Castle, Pitlochry.

MELROSE

Michael Vee Design - Birch House Antiques
High St. TD6 9PB. (Michael Vee and Enid Cranston). Est. 1990. Open 9.30-12.30 and 1.30-5, Sat. 9.30-4, Sun. by appointment. SIZE: Medium. *STOCK: Mirrors and lighting, French, English, decorative and some garden furniture, 1850-1920, £20-£5,000.* LOC: 1.5 miles off A68. PARK: Easy. TEL: 01896 822116; home - 01896 822835. SER: Interior design; upholstery; specialist paint finishes. VAT: Margin.

The Whole Lot
Melrose Antique, Art and Gift Centre, St Dunstans, High St. TD6 9RU. (I. Purves). Est. 2002. Open 9.30-5, Sat. 9.30-5.30, Sun. 12-5. SIZE: Medium - 30 dealers. *STOCK: Wide range of general antiques including furniture, silver, china, glass, jewellery, curios and collectables, smalls.* LOC: Edge of town centre. PARK: Easy and public behind building. TEL: 01896 823039; fax - 01896 823484; website - www.thewholelot.co.uk SER: Valuations.

MONTROSE

Harper-James
25-27 Baltic St. DD10 8EX. (J. Philp). Est. 1990. Open 9-5, Sat. 10-4, other times by appointment. SIZE: Large. *STOCK: Furniture, clocks, silver, 1690-1910, £50-£15,000; ceramics and pottery, 1800-1945, £10-£650+; general antiques and curios, £2-£750.* LOC: From south turn right at Peel statue, then first left. PARK: Easy. TEL: 01674 671307; mobile - 07903 055457; e-mail - antiques@telco4u.net website - www.harperjames antiques.com SER: Valuations; restorations (furniture and upholstery); French polishing; export. FAIRS: Major UK. VAT: Stan/Spec.

NEWBURGH

Newburgh Antiques
222 High St. KY14 6DZ. (Dorothy Fraser). Est. 1991. Open by appoinment. SIZE: Small. *STOCK: Wemyss ware, 1882-1930, £100-£2,000; Scottish watercolours and oil paintings, 1800-1950s, £100-£1,500; furniture, 1750-1900, £200-£2,000.* LOC: A913. PARK: Easy. TEL: 01337 841026; home - 01337 827158; mobile - 07850 013191; e-mail - antiques@wemyssware.net website - www.wemyssware.net SER: Valuations.

NEWPORT-ON-TAY

Mair Wilkes Books
3 St. Mary's Lane. DD6 8AH. (James Mair and Alan Wilkes). PBFA. Est. 1969. Open Tues.-Fri. 10-12.30 and 2-4.30, Sat. 10-5. SIZE: Medium. *STOCK: Books, all subjects, from 16th C to date, £1-£1,000.* PARK: Nearby. TEL: 01382 542260; fax - same; e-mail - mairwilkes. books@zoom.co.uk SER: Valuations.

narducci-antiques.co.uk SER: Packing and shipping; road haulage (Europe). *Mainly Trade and Export.*

LINLITHGOW

County Antiques
30 High St. EH49 7AE. (Mrs M. Flynn). Est. 1987. Open 10-5. SIZE: Small. *STOCK: Jewellery and small antiques.* LOC: East end High St. PARK: Nearby. TEL: 01506 671201. SER: Valuations; jewellery repairs.

Town & County
20 High St. EH49 7AE. (Mrs M. Flynn). Est. 1987. Open 10-5. *STOCK: Furniture and general antiques.* PARK: Nearby. TEL: 01506 845509. SER: Valuations.

LOCKERBIE

Cobwebs of Lockerbie Ltd
30 Townhead St. DG11 2AE. (Irene M. Beck). Est. 1992. Open 9-5. SIZE: Medium. *STOCK: Victorian furniture and china, collectables, to £650.* LOC: Outskirts of town. PARK: Easy. TEL: 01576 202554; fax - 01576 203737; home - 01387 811284; e-mail - sales@cobwebsantiques. co.uk website - www.cobwebs-antiques.co.uk VAT: Global.

LONGHAVEN, Nr Peterhead

Grannie Used To Have One
Sanderling. AB42 0NX. (Mrs Jacqui Harvey). Est. 1991. Open Thurs. and Fri. 1-5, Sat. and Sun. 11-5, Mon., Tues. and other times by appointment. SIZE: Large. *STOCK: Pottery including Scottish, 18th-19th C, £5-£2,000; porcelain, glass, wooden items, curios, furniture, 18th-*

NORTH BERWICK

Kirk Ports Gallery
49A Kirk Ports. EH39 4HL. (Alan Lindsey). Est. 1995. Open 10-5. CL: Thurs. SIZE: Medium. *STOCK: Oil paintings, £100-£1,000; watercolours, £50-£600; etchings and prints, £30-£100; all 19th C to 1940.* LOC: Behind main street. PARK: Own. TEL: 01620 894114. SER: Valuations.

Lindsey Antiques
49a Kirk Ports. EH39 4HL. (Stephen Lindsey). Est. 1995. Open 10-1 and 2-5. CL: Thurs. SIZE: Medium. *STOCK: Ceramics and glass, 1800-1935, £20-£500; furniture, 1750-1910, £150-£2,000.* LOC: Behind main street. PARK: Own. TEL: 01620 894114. SER: Valuations.

Penny Farthing
23 Quality St. EH39 4HR. (S. Tait). Est. 1981. Open 9.30-5.30, Sun. 2.30-5.30. SIZE: Medium. *STOCK: Secondhand books, collectables, 20th C, £5-£500.* LOC: On corner with High St. PARK: Easy. TEL: 01620 890114; fax - same; mobile - 07817 721928; e-mail - pennyfarthing@amserve.net SER: Valuations; buys at auction. FAIRS: Scot, Meadowbank, Edinburgh.

PAISLEY

Corrigan Antiques
Woodlands, High Calside. PA2 6BY. Open by appointment. SIZE: Small. *STOCK: Furniture and accessories.* LOC: 5 mins. from Glasgow Airport. TEL: 01418 896653; fax - 0141 848 9700; mobile - 07802 631110.

PERTH

Design Interiors and Perth Antiques
46-50 South St. PH2 8PD. (Margaret J.S. and Robert J. Blane). Est. 1990. Open 10.30-6. SIZE: Medium. *STOCK: Victorian and Edwardian furniture, £40-£1,000; paintings and etchings, paperweights, silver, porcelain and pottery, mainly 18th-20th C, £20-£600.* PARK: Easy. TEL: 01738 635360/440888; e-mail - robert.blane@btconnect.com SER: Valuations; restorations (clocks and china).

Hardie Antiques
25 St. John St. PH1 5SH. (T.G. Hardie). PADA. Est. 1980. Open 9.30-5, Sat. 10-4.30. SIZE: Medium. *STOCK: Jewellery and silver, 18th-20th C, £5-£5,000.* PARK: Nearby. TEL: 01738 633127; fax - same; home - 01738 551764; e-mail - info@timothyhardie.co.uk SER: Valuations. VAT: Stan/Spec.

Henderson
5 North Methven St. PH1 5PN. (S.G. Henderson). Est. 1938. Open 9.15-5.15. SIZE: Small. *STOCK: Silver, jewellery, £5-£2,000.* LOC: A9. PARK: Easy. TEL: 01738 624836; e-mail - wtg.henderson@virgin.net SER: Valuations; repairs. VAT: Stan/Margin.

Yesterdays Today
267 High St. PH1 5QN. (Bill and Nora MacGregor). Est. 1996. Open 9-5. SIZE: Small. *STOCK: General collectables especially china, £25-£1,000.* LOC: Follow signs for Tourist Information Centre. PARK: Nearby.

TEL: 01738 443534; e-mail - macgregor-5@hotmail.com SER: Valuations; buys at auction. VAT: Global.

PITTENWEEM

The Little Gallery
20 High St. KY10 2LA. (Dr. Ursula Ditchburn-Bosch). Est. 1988. Open 10-5, Sun. 2-5. CL: Mon. and Tues. SIZE: Small. *STOCK: China, 18th C to 1950s, £5-£100; small furniture, mainly Victorian, £30-£500; rustica, £5-£150; contemporary paintings, £40-£2,500.* LOC: From Market Sq. towards church, on right. PARK: Easy. TEL: 01333 311227; home - same. SER: Valuations.

PRESTWICK

Crossroads Antiques
7 The Cross. KA9 1AJ. (Timothy Okeeffe). Est. 1989. Open 9-5. SIZE: Medium. *STOCK: Furniture, 18th-20th C, £5-£1,000+; china and silver, 19th-20th C, £5-£500+.* PARK: Nearby. TEL: 01292 474004. SER: Valuations; buys at auction.

RAIT

Rait Village Antiques Centre
PH2 7RT. Est. 1985. Open 10-5, Sun. 12.30-4.30. SIZE: 16 showrooms. *STOCK: General antiques, furniture, paintings, clocks and Wemyssware.* LOC: Midway between Perth and Dundee, 1 mile north of A90. PARK: Easy. Below are listed the dealers at this centre. TEL: 01821 670379; e-mail - lynda.templeman@btopenworld.com

Abernethy Antiques

The Bothy Antiques & Collectables
Agricultural and farming memorabilia.

L. Christie Campbell Fine Art

Fair Finds
(Lynda Templeman). *Large stock of antique and early 20th C country house furnishings, pictures, rugs, silver and clocks, £50-£10,000.* TEL: 01821 670379.

Forget-me-Not

Kaeleigh International

Gordon Loraine Antiques
(Liane and Gordon Loraine). *Georgian, Victorian and Edwardian furniture, decorative items and collectables.* TEL: 01821 670760.

The Luckenbooth

Now and Then

Old Timers

Rait Interiors

St Michael Antiques
Furniture and furnishings.

Thistle & Rose

Tickety Boo Antiques

The Undercroft
Farming memorabilia.

Whimsical Wemyss
(Lynda Templeman, Chris Comben). *Wemyssware, £50-£3,000.* TEL: 01821 67039.

SALTCOATS

Narducci Antiques
Factory Place. KA21 5LA. (G. Narducci). Est. 1972. Open by appointment. *STOCK: Furniture, general antiques and shipping goods.* PARK: Easy. TEL: 01294 461687 and 01475 672612; fax - 01294 470002; mobile - 07771 577777. SER: Packing, export, shipping and European haulage. *Mainly Trade and Export.*

ST. ANDREWS

The David Brown (St. Andrews) Gallery
9 Albany Place. KY16 9HH. (Mr and Mrs D.R. Brown). Est. 1973. CL: 1-2 daily. SIZE: Medium. *STOCK: Golf memorabilia, 19th C, £100-£20,000; silver, jewellery especially Scottish, 18th-20th C, £100-£10,000; general antiques, from 18th C, £50-£5,000.* LOC: Main street. PARK: Easy. TEL: 01334 477840; fax - 01334 476915. SER: Valuations; restorations (jewellery, silver); buys at auction (golf memorabilia). VAT: Stan.

St. Andrews Fine Art
84 Market St. KY16 9PA. (J. Carruthers). Open 10-5.30. *STOCK: Scottish oils, watercolours and drawings, 19th-20th C.* PARK: Easy. TEL: 01334 474080; e-mail - info @st-andrewsfineart.co.uk website - www.st-andrewsfine art.co.uk

STANLEY

Coach House Antiques Ltd
Charleston. PH1 4PN. (John Walker). Est. 1971. Open by appointment. SIZE: Medium. *STOCK: Period furniture, decorative items, 18th-19th C; garden furniture.* LOC: 9 miles north of Perth off A9. Take B9099 to Luncarty and Stanley, continue 2 miles through village, sign at end of road Charleston. PARK: Easy. TEL: 01738 828627; home - same; mobile - 07710 122244; e-mail - john walkerantiques@btopenworld.com SER: Valuations; restorations; buys at auction (furniture). VAT: Spec.

STEWARTON

Woolfsons of James Street Ltd t/a Past & Present
3 Lainshaw St. KA3 5BY. Est. 1983. Open 9.30-5.30, Sun. 12-5.30. SIZE: Medium. *STOCK: Furniture, £100-£500; porcelain, £25-£500; bric-a-brac, £5-£50; all from 1800.* LOC: Stewarton Cross. PARK: Easy. TEL: 01560 484113; fax - same. SER: Valuations; restorations (French polishing, upholstery, wood). VAT: Stan/Spec.

STIRLING

Abbey Antiques
4 Friars St. FK8 1HA. (S. Campbell). Resident. Est. 1980. Open 9-5. SIZE: Small. *STOCK: Jewellery, £10-£5,000; silver and plate, £5-£1,000; furniture including pine, £20-£1,000; paintings, £50-£2,500; bric-a-brac, £1-£100; coins and medals, £1-£1,000; all 18th-20th C; china, porcelain, collectables.* LOC: Off Murray Place, part of main thoroughfare. PARK: Nearby. TEL: 01786 447840. SER: Valuations.

STRATHBLANE

Whatnots
16 Milngavie Rd. G63 9EH. (F. Bruce). Est. 1965. *STOCK: Furniture, paintings, jewellery, silver and plate, clocks, small items and shipping goods.* LOC: A81, 10 miles NW of Glasgow. PARK: Easy. TEL: 01360 770310.

TROON

Old Troon Sporting Antiques
49 Ayr St. KA10 6EB. (R.S. Pringle). Est. 1984. Open 9-12.30 and 2-5. CL: Wed. pm. and Sat. SIZE: Medium. *STOCK: Golf items, 19th C, to £500+.* LOC: 5 mins. from A77. PARK: Easy. TEL: 01292 311822; home - 01292 313744; fax - 01292 313111. SER: Valuations; buys at auction (golf items). VAT: Stan.

Tantalus Antiques
79 Templehill. KA10 6BQ. (Iain D. Sutherland). BWCMG. Open 10-5, Sun. by appointment. SIZE: Medium. *STOCK: Furniture, clocks and watches, pictures and paintings, silverware, jewellery, ceramics.* LOC: Town centre, main road to the harbour. PARK: Easy. TEL: 01292 315999; fax - 01292 316611; e-mail - idsantique@aol.com website - www.scottishantiques. com SER: Valuations; restorations.

ULLAPOOL

Wishing Well Antiques
Shore St. IV26 2UB. (Simon and Eileen Calder). Est. 1988. Open 10-6. SIZE: Medium. *STOCK: China, glass, silver, pottery, furniture, country artefacts, curiosities; books, prints and paintings; stone garden architectural.* LOC: Village centre. PARK: Easy. TEL: 01854 613265; mobile - 07884 294926. e-mail - tocalder@aol.com SER: Valuations; restorations; wood stripping.

UPPER LARGO

D.V. & C.A. St. Clair
13 Main St. KY8 6EL. Est. 1958. Open 10.30-5.30, Sun. by appointment. SIZE: Medium. *STOCK: Pictures, furniture, china, pottery, glass and works of art.* LOC: Coast road from Leven to St. Andrews. PARK: Easy. TEL: 01333 360437; home - same. SER: Valuations.

WHITHORN

Priory Antiques
29 George St. DG8 8NS. (Mary Arnott). Est. 1988. Open most days 11-4, prior telephone call advisable. CL: Thurs. SIZE: Small. *STOCK: Silver, ceramics and furniture, pre 1940, £5-£500.* LOC: Town centre. PARK: Easy. TEL: 01988 500517; home - same. SER: Valuations.

WIGTOWN, Nr. Newton Stewart

Ming Books
Beechwood House, Acre Place. DG8 9DU. (Marion and Robin Richmond). Est. 1982. Open 10-6 in summer, by appointment in winter. SIZE: Small. *STOCK: Books.* PARK: Easy. TEL: 01988 402653; home - same; e-mail - mingbooks@aol.com website - www.mingbooks. supanet.com SER: Valuations. FAIRS: Belfast Book.

WALES

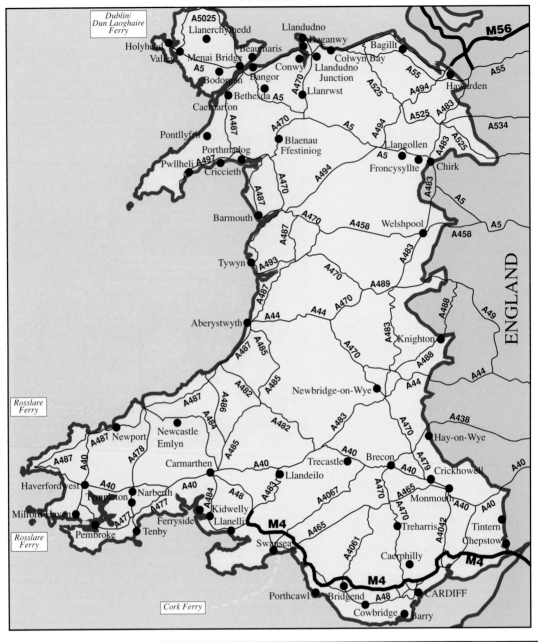

Dealers and Shops in Wales

Aberystwyth	1	Caerphilly	1	Froncysyllte	1	Llangollen	2	Porthmadog	1
Bagillt	1	Cardiff	9	Haverfordwest	2	Llanrwst	2	Pwllheli	1
Bangor	1	Carmarthen	3	Hawarden	1	Menai Bridge	2	Swansea	3
Barmouth	2	Chepstow	2	Hay-on-Wye	4	Milford Haven	1	Templeton	1
Barry	1	Chirk	1	Holyhead	1	Monmouth	2	Tenby	1
Beaumaris	1	Colwyn Bay	1	Kidwelly	2	Narberth	1	Tintern	1
Bethesda	1	Conwy	1	Knighton	2	Newbridge-on-Wye	1	Trecastle	1
Blaenau Ffestiniog	1	Cowbridge	3	Llandeilo	2	Newcastle Emlyn	1	Treharris	1
Bodorgan	1	Criccieth	2	Llandudno	1	Newport	1	Tywyn	1
Brecon	2	Crickhowell	1	Llandudno Junction	2	Pembroke	1	Valley	1
Bridgend	2	Deganwy	2	Llanelli	1	Pontllyfrii	1	Welshpool	2
Caernarfon	1	Ferryside	1	Llanerchymedd	1	Porthcawl	1		

ABERYSTWYTH

The Furniture Cave
33 Cambrian St. SY23 1NZ. (P. David). Est. 1975. Open 9-5, Sat. 10-5. *STOCK: Pine, 1700-1930, from £100; general antiques, Victorian and Edwardian, £30-£3,000; small items, 19th C, £10-£500; maps.* LOC: First right off Terrace Rd., at rail station end. PARK: Nearby. TEL: 01970 611234; e-mail - thecave@btconnect.com website - www.furniture-cave.co.uk SER: Restorations. VAT: Spec.

BAGILLT

King's House Antiques
High St. CH6 6ED. (Mr and Mrs George Baynham). Open 10-5. SIZE: Large. *STOCK: Furniture, mainly Victorian.* LOC: Opposite post office. PARK: Easy. TEL: 01352 733323; home - same; e-mail - nippjune@aol.com

BANGOR

David Windsor Gallery
173 High St. LL57 1NU. FATG. Est. 1970. Open 10-5. CL: Wed. *STOCK: Oils and watercolours, 18th-20th C; maps, engravings, lithographs.* TEL: 01248 364639. SER: Restorations; framing; mounting. VAT: Stan/Spec.

BARMOUTH

Chapel Antiques Centre
High St. LL42 1DS. (Danny Jones and Brenda Evans). Est. 1985. Open 10.30-5. CL: Wed. SIZE: Medium. *STOCK: General antiques including furniture and glass, 18th-20th C, £5-£2,000.* PARK: Nearby. TEL: 01341 281377.

Fronhouse Antiques
Jubilee Rd. LL42 1EE. (Tony and Barbara Howard). Est. 1967. Open seven days 10-5. CL: Wed. and Sun. Dec to Mar. SIZE: Small. *STOCK: Nautical items, 19th C £5-£250; oil lamps, bric-a-brac and small furniture, £5-£200.* LOC: On corner of Church St. PARK: Easy. TEL: 01341 280649; home/fax - same. SER: Valuations; restorations (nautical items). FAIRS: Swinderby, Newark.

BARRY

Flame 'n' Grate
99-100 High St. CF6 8DS. (A. Galsworthy). Open 9-5.30. *STOCK: Antique and reproduction fireplaces and surrounds.* TEL: 01446 744788.

BEAUMARIS (Anglesey)

Museum of Childhood Memories
1 Castle St. LL58 8AP. (R. and J. Brown). Est. 1973. Open 10.30-5. CL: Jan. and Feb. *STOCK: Children's toys and memorabilia collectables.* LOC: Opposite castle. PARK: Nearby. TEL: 01248 712498; website - www.aboutbritain.com/museumofchildhoodmemories.htm

BETHESDA

A.E. Morris (Books)
40 High St. LL57 3AN. Est. 1980. Open 10-5. SIZE: Medium. *STOCK: Antiquarian and secondhand books.* PARK: Easy. TEL: 01248 602533.

BLAENAU FFESTINIOG

The Antique Shop
Bryn Marian. LL41 3HD. (Mrs R. Roberts). Est. 1971. *STOCK: Victoriana, furniture, brass and copper, oil lamps, clocks and watches.* TEL: 01766 830629/830041.

BODORGAN, (Anglesey)

Michael Webb Fine Art   LAPADA
Cefn-Llwyn. LL62 5DN. Est. 1972. Open by appointment. *STOCK: Victorian and 20th C oil paintings and watercolours.* TEL: 01407 840336. SER: Valuations; restorations; framing. FAIRS: Chester; Carmarthen; Anglesey; Cowbridge. VAT: Spec.

BRECON

Books, Maps and Prints
7 The Struet. LD3 7LL. (Andrew Wakley). ABA. Est. 1961. Open 9-5, Wed. 9-1. SIZE: Medium. *STOCK: Books, maps and prints, from 17th C, £10-£1,000.* LOC: A438, opposite Somerfield. PARK: Opposite. TEL: 01874 622714. SER: Conservation framing. VAT: Stan.

Hazel of Brecon & Silvertime
6 The Bulwark. LD3 7LB. (H.Hillman). Est. 1969. Open 10-5.30. CL: Wed. SIZE: Medium. *STOCK: Jewellery and silver 19th-20th C, £20-£10,000.* LOC: Main square, town centre. PARK: Easy. TEL: 01874 625274 (24 hr. answering service). SER: Valuations; repairs.

BRIDGEND

J. & A. Antiques
1 Prince Rd., Kenfig Hill. CF33 6ED. (Jennifer Lawson). Est. 1990. Open 10-12.30 and 2-4.30, Sat. CL: Sat. pm.and Wed. SIZE: Small. *STOCK: Furniture, china and clocks, 19th to early 20th C, £10-£800.* LOC: From A48 Pyle take B4281. PARK: Easy. TEL: 01656 746681; home - 01656 744709.

Nolton Antiques
66 Nolton St. CF31 3BP. (Gittins and Beynon). Est. 1997. Open 10-4. CL: Wed. SIZE: Large. *STOCK: General antiques including Clarice Cliff, majolica and Victorian furniture.* LOC: Off M4, junction 35. PARK: Nearby. TEL: 01656 667774; 07855 958461; website - www.welsh-antiques.com SER: Valuations; buys at auction (named china).

CAERNARFON

Days Gone By Antiques
6 Palace St. LL55 1RR. (Geraint and Sue Prytherch). Est. 1992. Open 10-5.30 including Sun. *STOCK: Furniture, jewellery, china especially Royal Doulton, glass, collectables, silver, Staffordshire, new Brambly Hedge and Beswick; art gallery.* LOC: Within walled town. PARK: Easy. TEL: 01286 678010; fax - 01286 678554; home - 01286 672526; e-mail - sue@daysgoneby antiques.demon.co.uk SER: Valuations.

CAERPHILLY

Yesterday's Future - G.J. Gittins and Son
10 Clive St. CF8 1GE. Est. 1930s. Open 9-4, Sat. 10-5.

CL: Wed. *STOCK: General antiques, jewellery, shipping goods, collectables.* TEL: 02920 868835; e-mail - gittinsantiques@supanet.com

CARDIFF

Cardiff Antiques Centre
10/12 Royal Arcade. CF1 2AE. Open 10-5.30. SIZE: 3 floors. *STOCK: Antiques, collectables and classic clothing.* LOC: Town centre. TEL: 02920 398891.

Cardiff Reclamation
Site 7 Tremorfa Industrial Estate, Rover Way. CF24 5SD. (Jeff and John Evans). Est. 1990. Open 9-5, Sat. 9-1, Sun. 10-1. SIZE: Large. *STOCK: Architectural antiques, fireplaces, doors, wood flooring, stained glass, bathrooms, church fittings, flagstones, chimney pots, £10-£3,000.* PARK: Easy. TEL: 02920 458995; fax - same; mobile - 07855 038629. SER: Restorations.

Jacobs Antique Centre
West Canal Wharf. CF10 5DB. Open Thurs.-Sat. 9.30-5. SIZE: Large - 50 dealers. *STOCK: General antiques and collectables.* LOC: 2 mins. from main rail and bus stations. PARK: 100yds. TEL: 02920 390939. SER: Valuations; restorations.

Kings Fireplaces, Antiques and Interiors
The Old Church, Adamsdown Sq., Adamsdown. CF24 0EZ. (B. Quinn). Est. 1984. Open 10-5. SIZE: Medium. *STOCK: Period fireplaces (working fireplaces on display), mirrors and lighting.* PARK: At rear of premises. TEL: 02920 492439; fax - 02920 472224. SER: Fireplace restoration, installation and spares. VAT: Stan.

Llanishen Antiques
26 Crwys Rd., Cathays. CF2 4NL. (Mrs J. Boalch). Open 10.30-4.30. CL: Wed. except by appointment. *STOCK: Furniture, silver, china, glass, bric-a-brac.* TEL: 02920 397244.

Riverside Antiques (Wales) Ltd
The Pumping Station, Penarth Rd. CF11 8TT. (Mrs Patricia Brownhill). Est. 1988. Open 9.30-5.30 including Sun. SIZE: Large. *STOCK: Victoria and Edwardian furniture, £100-£6,500; Art Deco furniture, £100-£15,000; ceramics, 1750-1960, £75-£2,500; Art Deco lighting, £145-£650.* LOC: Edge of town. PARK: Easy. TEL: 02920 231308; fax - 02920 232588; mobile - 07967 264325.

Roberts Emporium
58-60 Salisbury Rd. CF24 4AD. (I. Roberts). Est. 1980. Open 11-5. SIZE: Large. *STOCK: General antiques, Victorian, £5-£1,000; collectables, '50s, '60s, '70s.* LOC: In road near Museum of Wales. PARK: Easy. TEL: 02920 235630; mobile - 07891 080714; e-mail - info@ cheapaschips.cc website - www.cheapaschips.cc SER: Valuations; restorations (ceramics and furniture); buys at auction; prop. hire. FAIRS: Newark.

San Domenico Stringed Instruments
175 Kings Rd., Pontcanna. CF1 9DF. (H.W. Morgan). Est. 1978. Open 10-4, Sat. 10-1. SIZE: Small. *STOCK: Fine violins, violas, cellos and bows, mainly 18th-19th C, £300-£20,000.* LOC: Off Cathedral Rd. or Cowbridge Rd. PARK: Easy. TEL: 02920 235881; fax - 02920 344510; home - 02920 777156; e-mail - HWM@san-domenico.co.uk website - www.san-domenico.co.uk SER: Valuations; restorations; buys at auction. FAIRS: Mondomusica, Cremona, Italy. VAT: Stan/Spec.

Ty-Llwyd Antiques
Lisvane Rd., Lisvane. CF14 0SF. (G.H. Rowsell). Est. 1981. Open by appointment only. SIZE: Medium. *STOCK: Longcase clocks, some period furniture.* LOC: North Cardiff, near Griffin public house. PARK: Easy. TEL: 02920 754109; fax - same; mobile - 07778 117624; e-mail - ghrowsell@supanet.com SER: Valuations; restorations (clocks). FAIRS: Carmarthen; Motorcycle Museum.

CARMARTHEN

Audrey Bull
2 Jacksons Lane. SA31 1QD. (Jonathan and Jane Bull). Open 10-5. *STOCK: Period and Welsh country furniture, general antiques especially jewellery and silver.* TEL: 01267 222655; home - 01834 813425. VAT: Spec.

Merlins Antiques
Market Hall. SA31 1QY. (Mrs J.R. Perry). Est. 1984. Open Wed.-Sat. 9.30-4.30. *STOCK: Small items - porcelain, pottery, glass, silver and plate, postcards.* PARK: Opposite. TEL: 01267 233814; mobile - 07967 131109.

The Mount Antiques Centre
1 and 2 The Mount, Castle Hill. SA31 1JW. (R. Lickley). Est. 1987. Open 10-5.30, Sun. 11-3 (summer only). SIZE: Large. *STOCK: Fine furniture including country, 18th-19th C, £500-£1,000+; china and collectables, 19th-20th C, £50-£500; architectural salvage, musical instruments, 19th C, £50-£1,500.* LOC: A40 near county hall. PARK: Easy. TEL: 01267 220005. SER: Valuations; restorations (furniture and china). FAIRS: Towy - Cowbridge, Bristol; Cardiff.

CHEPSTOW

Foxgloves
20 St. Mary St. NP16 5EW. (Lesley Brain). Est. 1994. Open 10ish-5. CL: Wed. SIZE: Medium. *STOCK: Period and antique furniture; pictures, china and objet d'art.* LOC: Central. PARK: Nearby. TEL: 01291 622386. SER: Restorations.

Intaglio
(John Harrison). Est. 1995. Open by appointment. SIZE: Small. *STOCK: Sculpture, marble, 19th to early 20th C, £500-£20,000.* PARK: Easy. TEL: 01291 621476 or 01873 810036; fax - 01291 621476; e-mail - intaglio@tiscali.co.uk website - authorised seller on - www.Sothebys.com SER: Valuations; restorations; cleaning; conservation; buys at auction (bronze and marble sculpture). FAIRS: NEC; Bailey.

CHIRK

Seventh Heaven
Chirk Mill. LL14 5BU. Est. 1971. Open 9-5, Sat. 10-4. SIZE: Large. *STOCK: Brass, iron and wooden beds including half-tester, four-poster and canopied, mainly 19th C.* LOC: B5070, below village, off A5 bypass. PARK: Easy. TEL: 01691 777622; fax - 01691 777313; e-mail - requests@seventh-heaven.co.uk website - www.seventh-heaven.co.uk VAT: Stan.

COLWYN BAY

North Wales Antiques - Colwyn Bay
58 Abergele Rd. LL29 7PP. (F. Robinson). Est. 1958. Open 9-5. SIZE: Large warehouse. *STOCK: Shipping items, Victorian, early oak, mahogany and pine.* LOC: On A55. PARK: Easy. TEL: 01492 530521; evenings - 01352 720253. VAT: Stan.

CONWY

Teapot World
25 Castle St. LL32 8AY. Open every day Easter to end Oct. *STOCK: Traditional and novelty teapots and tea-related items.* TEL: 01492 596533; 01492 593429; fax - same; website - www.teapotworld.co.uk

COWBRIDGE

Eastgate Antiques
6 High St. CF7 7AG. (Liz Herbert). Est. 1984. Open 10-1 and 2-5.30. CL: Mon. SIZE: Medium. *STOCK: Furniture, silver, jewellery, 18th C to Edwardian.* LOC: Off A48. PARK: Nearby. TEL: 01446 775; home - 01446 773505. SER: Buys at auction (furniture). VAT: Stan/Spec.

Havard and Havard LAPADA
59 Eastgate. CF71 7EL. (Philip and Christine Havard). Est. 1992. Open 10.30-1 and 2-5. CL: Mon. and Wed. SIZE: Small. *STOCK: Oak, mahogany and walnut furniture especially provincial, £100-£10,000; metalware and samplers, £25-£1,000; all 18th-19th C.* LOC: Main street, 500 yards after lights on right. PARK: Easy. TEL: 01446 775021; e-mail - cphavard@aol.com SER: Valuations. FAIRS: NEC Antiques for Everyone; Margam Park. VAT: Stan/Spec.

Renaissance Antiques - The Vale of Glamorgan Antiques Centre
Ebenezer Chapel, 48A Eastgate. CF71 7AB. (R.W. and J.A. Barnicott). Est. 1984. Open 10-5. SIZE: Small. *STOCK: Brass, copper, plate, decorative ceramics, Staffordshire figures, objets d'art, 18th to 20th C, £5-£500. Not Stocked: Coins, militaria, reproductions.* LOC: Main street. PARK: Nearby. TEL: 01446 771190.

CRICCIETH

Capel Mawr Collectors Centre
21 High St. LL52 0BS. (Alun and Dee Turner). Resident. Est. 1998. Open in summer 10-5; winter - Tues., Fri. and Sat. only. SIZE: Large. *STOCK: Books, from 18th C, £1-£500; postcards, 1894-1960, £1-£50; Sylvac, £5-£100.* LOC: A497. PARK: Nearby. TEL: 01766 523600; home - 01766 523435; e-mail - capelmawr@aol.com SER: Valuations. VAT: Stan.

Criccieth Gallery
London House, High St. LL52 0RN. (Mrs Anita Evens). Est. 1972. Open 9-5.30. CL: Wed pm. Nov-Feb. SIZE: Small. *STOCK: General antiques, Staffordshire figures, china and porcelain, paintings and prints, clocks and watches (mainly pocket), small furniture, mainly 19th C, £5-£250+.* PARK: Easy. TEL: 01766 522836. SER: Valuations; restorations (china, watch and clock repairs). FAIRS: Newark; Mona, Anglesey; Builth Wells.

CRICKHOWELL

Gallop and Rivers Architectural Antiques
Ty'r Ash, Brecon Rd. NP8 1SF. (G.P. Gallop). Open 9.30-5. *STOCK: Architectural items, pine and country furniture.* TEL: 01873 811084; website - www.gallopandrivers.co.uk VAT: Stan.

DEGANWY

Acorn Antiques
Castle Buildings. LL31 9EJ. (K.S. Bowers-Jones). Open 10-5. *STOCK: Ceramics, glass, furniture, pictures, brass and copper, 19th C.* PARK: Opposite. TEL: 01492 584083.

Castle Antiques
71 Station Rd. LL31 9DF. (J. and D. Nickson Ltd). Est. 1977. Open 10-5. SIZE: Medium. *STOCK: Mainly 19th C furniture, jewellery, copper and brass, watercolours and silver.* LOC: Opposite Castle Hotel. PARK: Nearby. TEL: 01492 583021; fax - 01492 596664; home - 01492 582586. SER: Valuations.

FERRYSIDE

Tim Bowen Antiques LAPADA
Ivy House. SA17 5SS. (Tim and Betsan Bowen). Resident. Est. 1987. Open by chance or appointment. SIZE: Medium. *STOCK: Oak and country furniture, 1650-1900, £100-£10,000; spongeware and country pottery, 19th C, £20-£500; longcase clocks, 18th-19th C, £2,000-£4,000; folk art, 18th-19th C, £40-£1,000.* LOC: Main road, near Poachers Rest Hotel. PARK: Easy. TEL:

01267 267122; home - same; fax - 01267 267045; mobile - 07967 728515; e-mail - info@timbowen antiques.co.uk website - www.tim-bowen-antiques.com SER: Valuations. FAIRS: Carmarthen, Margam, Anglesey, NEC. VAT: Stan/Spec.

FRONCYSYLLTE, Nr. Llangollen

Romantiques
Methodist Chapel, Holyhead Rd. LL20 7RA. (Miss S.E. Atkin). Est. 1994. Open 10-5 including Sun., or by appointment. SIZE: Large. *STOCK: Furniture, £50-£4,000; collectables, £1-£1,000; clocks and barometers, £50-£3,000.* LOC: On A5 and off A539 Llangollen roads. PARK: Easy. TEL: 01691 774567; mobile - 07778 279614; e-mail - satkin1057@aol.com website - www.romantiques.co.uk SER: Valuations; restorations (furniture, upholstery and clocks); courier. VAT: Stan/Spec.

HAVERFORDWEST

Dyfed Antiques and Architectural Salvage
The Wesleyan Chapel, Perrots Rd. SA61 2JD. (Giles Chaplin). SALVO. Est. 1968. Open 10-5. SIZE: Large. *STOCK: Fireplaces including restored Georgian and Victorian tiled, £200-£2,000; reclaimed doors, £25-£500; flooring including slate slabs and quarry tiles; pine farmhouse furniture, general antiques.* PARK: Opposite. TEL: 01437 760496; fax - same; mobile - 07775 915237; home - 01994 419260; website - www.dyfedantiques.com SER: Furniture stripping; hand-made bespoke furniture.

Kent House Antiques
Kent House, Market St. SA61 1NF. (G. Fanstone and P. Thorpe). Est. 1987. Open 10-5. CL: Mon. SIZE: Medium. *STOCK: Victoriana, decorative items, hand-made rugs, £5-£500+.* LOC: Town centre. PARK: Easy. TEL: 01437 768175; home - same. SER: Valuations; restorations (furniture, some china).

HAWARDEN

On the Air Ltd
The Vintage Technology Centre, The Highway. CH5 3DN. (Steve Harris). Est. 1990. Open by appointment only. SIZE: Small. *STOCK: Vintage wireless, gramophones and telephones, £50-£500.* LOC: Near St. David's Park, Ewloe, opposite Crown & Liver public house. PARK: Rear of premises. TEL: 01244 530300; fax - same; e-mail - info@vintageradio.co.uk website - www.vintageradio.co.uk SER: Valuations; restorations (vintage wireless and gramophones). FAIRS: National Vintage Communications, NEC.

HAY-ON-WYE

Richard Booth's Bookshop Ltd
44 Lion St. and Hay Castle. HR3 5AA. (Richard and Hope Booth). WBA. Est. 1974. Open 7 days 9-5.30, later at weekends and during summer. SIZE: Very large. *STOCK: Books, magazines, photographs, records, postcards, leather bindings.* LOC: Town centre. PARK: Nearby. TEL: 01497 820322; fax - 01497 821150; Hay Castle - 01497

820503; e-mail - postmaster@richard booth.demon.co.uk website - www.richardbooth.demon.co.uk

Hay Antique Market
6 Market St. HR3 5AF. Est. 1990. Open 10-5, Sun. 11-5. SIZE: 17 units. *STOCK: Antiques and collectables.* LOC: By the Butter Market. PARK: Easy. TEL: 01497 820175.

Rose's Books
14 Broad St. HR3 5DB. (Maria Goddard). Resident. Est. 1982. Open 7 days. SIZE: Large. *STOCK: Children's books, 1900-1960, £5-£25.* TEL: 01497 820013; fax - 01497 820031; e-mail - enquiry@rosesbooks.com website - www.rosesbooks.com

Mark Westwood Antiquarian Books
High Town. HR3 5AE. ABA. PBFA. Est. 1976. Open 10.30-5.30 including Sun., prior telephone call advisable in winter months. *STOCK: Antiquarian and secondhand books on most subjects, £2-£1,000.* TEL: 01497 820068; fax - 01497 821641; e-mail - books@markwestwood.co.uk SER: Valuations; buys at auction (antiquarian books). VAT: Stan.

HOLYHEAD (Anglesey)

Gwynfair Antiques
74 Market St. LL65 1UW. (Mrs A.D. McCann). Est. 1984. Open Mon., Wed., Fri. and Sat. 10.30-4.30. SIZE: Small. *STOCK: China, ornaments, £5-£250, furniture, £20-£1,000; all 1860-1950's.* PARK: Loading outside shop, parking 100 yds. TEL: 01407 763740; home - same; e-mail - anwenholyhead@aol.com SER: Valuations.

KIDWELLY

Antiques in Wales
31 Bridge St. SA17 4UU. (R. Bebb). Est. 1971. Open by appointment. SIZE: Medium. *STOCK: Country, Georgian and Victorian furniture; pottery and collectables.* LOC: Leave bypass (A484), into centre of village, castle side of bridge. PARK: Opposite shop. TEL: 01554 890534; e-mail - info@antiquesinwales.fsnet.co.uk website - www.antiquesinwales.com VAT: Stan/Spec.

Country Antiques (Wales) Ltd BADA
Castle Mill. SA17 4UU. (Richard Bebb). Est. 1971. Open Fri. and Sat. 10-5, other times by appointment. SIZE: Large. STOCK: Welsh oak furniture and folk art; Welsh dressers, cupboards, clocks, pottery and treen. LOC: Leave bypass (A484), into centre of village, turn opposite war memorial, turn right by Boot and Shoe public house. PARK: Own. TEL: 01554 890534; e-mail - info@welshantiques.com website - www.welshantiques.com SER: Valuations; lectures; research. VAT: Stan/Spec.

KNIGHTON

Offa's Dyke Antique Centre
4 High St. LD7 1AT. (Mrs H. Hood and I. Watkins). Est. 1985. Open 10-1 and 2-5. SIZE: Medium - 16 dealers. *STOCK: Pottery, glass, bijouterie, 18th-19th C furniture, £5-£1,000.* LOC: Near town clock. PARK: Easy. TEL: 01547 528635; evenings - 01547 528940/560272.

Islwyn Watkins
4 High St. LD7 1AT. Est. 1978. Open 10-1 and 2-5. SIZE: Small. *STOCK: Pottery including studio, 18th-20th C, £25-£1,000; country and domestic bygones, treen, 18th-20th C, £5-£200; small country furniture, 18th-19th C, £20-£600.* Not Stocked: Jewellery, silver, militaria. LOC: By town clock. PARK: Easy. TEL: 01547 520145; home - 01547 528940. SER: Valuations.

LLANDEILO

Jim and Pat Ash
The Warehouse, 5 Station Rd. SA19 6NG. Est. 1977. Open 10.30-5, other times by appointment. SIZE: Large. *STOCK: Victorian and antique furniture, Welsh country, oak, mahogany, walnut.* LOC: 50yds. off A40. PARK: Easy. TEL: 01558 823726/822130; fax - same. SER: Valuations. VAT: Stan/Margin/Export.

The Works Antiques Centre
Station Rd. SA19 6NH. (Steve Watts and Jon Storey). Est. 2000. Open Tues.-Sat. 10-6, Sun. 10-5. SIZE: Large. *STOCK: Period furniture including country oak and Welsh country; china, treen, books, jewellery, architectural salvage, clocks, brass and copper, dolls and toys, musical instruments, lighting, textiles and clothing.* LOC: On outskirts of village, near A40 roundabout. PARK: Easy. TEL: 01558 823964; e-mail - theworks@storeyj.clara.co.uk website - www.works-antiques.co.uk SER: Restorations (furniture repair and renovation, picture framing and upholstery).

LLANDUDNO

The Antique Shop
24 Vaughan St. LL30 1AH. (C.G. Lee). Est. 1938. Open 10-5. SIZE: Medium. *STOCK: Jewellery, silver, porcelain, glass, ivories, metalware, from 1700; period furniture, shipping goods.* LOC: Near promenade. PARK: Easy. TEL: 01492 875575.

Drew Pritchard Ltd
St George's Church, Church Walks. LL30 2HL. (A.T. Pritchard). SALVO. Est. 1987. Open 9-5, Sat. 10-4. SIZE: Medium. *STOCK: English decorative architectural antiques, to 1950s; antique stained glass.* PARK: Easy. TEL: 01492 874004; fax - 01492 874003; mobile - 07740 289099; e-mail - enquiries@ drewpritchard.co.uk website - www.drewpritchard.co.uk SER: Valuations; restorations (stained and leaded glass, door furniture and metal polishing). Online catalogue. FAIRS: Swinderby; Newark, SALVO; Cheshire and Staffordshire shows.

LLANDUDNO JUNCTION

Collinge Antiques
Old Fyffes Warehouse, Conwy Rd. LL31 9LU. (Nicky Collinge). Est. 1978. Open seven days. SIZE: Large. *STOCK: General antiques including Welsh dressers, dining, drawing and bedroom furniture, clocks, porcelain and pottery, silver, copper and brass, paintings, prints, glass and collectables, mainly Victorian and Edwardian.* LOC: Just off A55, Deganwy exit (A546). PARK: Easy. TEL: 01492 580022; fax - same; e-mail - sales@collinge-antiques.co.uk website - www.collinge-antiques.co.uk SER: Valuations; restorations including French polishing; buys at auction. VAT: Stan/Spec.

The Country Seat
35 Conwy Rd. LL31 9LU. (Steve and Helen Roberts). Est. 1994. Open Tues., Thurs. and Fri. 11-4.30, Sat. 10-5. SIZE: Small. *STOCK: Old and interesting items including paintings, pottery and porcelain, jewellery, furniture, linen, ephemera and bric-a-brac; decorative arts, 19th-20th C.* LOC: Just off A55. PARK: Easy. TEL: 01492 573256; e-mail - hkjroberts@hotmail.com website - www.thecountryseat.co.uk FAIRS: Newark; Birmingham Rag; Chester Northgate.

LLANELLI

John Carpenter
SA14 7HA. Resident. Est. 1973. Open by appointment. SIZE: Large. *STOCK: Musical instruments, furniture, general antiques and shipping goods.* LOC: 5 mins. from Cross Hands. PARK: Easy. TEL: 01269 831094; e-mail - sales@cjcantiques.co.uk SER: Repairs (musical instruments); container packing.

LLANERCHYMEDD (Anglesey)

Two Dragons Oriental Antiques
8 High St. LL71 8EA. (Tony Andrew). Est. 1976. Open by appointment. SIZE: Large + warehouse. *STOCK: Chinese country furniture, signed prints by C.F. Tunnicliffe.* PARK: Easy. TEL: 01248 470204/470100; fax - 01248 470040; mobile - 07811 101290. FAIRS: Newark.

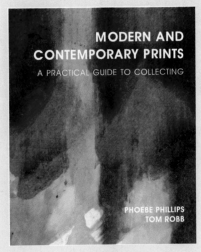

MODERN AND CONTEMPORARY PRINTS
A PRACTICAL GUIDE TO COLLECTING

PHOEBE PHILLIPS
TOM ROBB

Specifications:
192pp., 130 col. illus., 50 b.&w. illus.,
9¾ x 8in./250 x 205mm.
£25.00 (hardback)

LLANGOLLEN

J. and R. Langford
10 Bridge St. LL20 8PF. (P. and M. Silverston). Est. 1960. Open Tues., Fri. and Sat. 10-5. SIZE: Medium. *STOCK: Furniture, £100-£7,000; pottery and porcelain, £50-£2,000; silver, general antiques, clocks, paintings, £20-£4,000; all 18th-20th C.* LOC: Turn right at Royal Hotel, shop on right. PARK: Easy. TEL: 01978 860182; home - 01978 860493. SER: Valuations.

Passers Buy (Marie Evans)
Oak St/Chapel St. LL20 8NR. (Mrs M. Evans). Est. 1970. Open 11-5 always on Tues., Fri. and Sat., often on Mon., Wed. and Thurs., prior telephone call advisable, Sun. by appointment. SIZE: Medium. *STOCK: Furniture, Staffordshire figures, Gaudy Welsh, fairings, general antiques, copper and brass and fenders.* LOC: Just off A5. Junction of Chapel St. and Oak St. PARK: Easy. TEL: 01978 860861/757385. FAIRS: Anglesey (June and Oct.)

LLANRWST

Carrington House
26 Ancaster Sq. LL26 0LD. (Richard Newstead). Est. 1975. Open 10.30-1.30 and 2.30-5, Mon. pm. and Sun. by appointment. SIZE: Medium. *STOCK: 19th C pine, £200-£1,000; oak and mahogany, 19th-20th C, £150-£2,000.* LOC: From A55 take A470 towards Betws-y-Coed. PARK: Easy. TEL: 01492 642500; fax - same; home - 01492 641279; e-mail - richard@carringtonhouse.co.uk SER: Valuations. VAT: Spec.

Snowdonia Antiques
LL26 0EP. (J. Collins). Est. 1961. Open 9-5.30, Sun. by appointment. SIZE: Medium. *STOCK: Period furniture especially longcase clocks.* LOC: Turn off A5 just before Betws-y-Coed on to A496 for 4 miles. PARK: Easy.

TEL: 01492 640789. SER: Restorations (furniture); repairs (grandfather clocks).

MENAI BRIDGE (Anglesey)

Better Days

The Basement, 31 High St. LL59 5EF. (A. and Mrs E. Rutter). Est. 1988. Open 10.30-4.30, Wed. 11-1, Sat. 10.30-5. CL: Mon. SIZE: Small. *STOCK: Decorative smalls, early 19th to mid 20th C, £5-£200; furniture, late 19th to mid 20th C, £50-£1,000; metal and miscellaneous, mid 19th C to early 20th C, £10-£150.* PARK: Rear of premises. TEL: 01248 716657; e-mail - elaine@andytoo.freeserve.co.uk SER: Buys at auction. FAIRS: Mona Showground, Anglesey.

Peter Wain

44 High St. LL59 5EF. (Peter and Susan Wain). Est. 1980. Open by appointment. SIZE: Small. *STOCK: Chinese ceramics and works of art, over 1000 years, £100-£10,000.* PARK: Opposite. TEL: 01407 710077; fax - 01407 710294; mobile - 07860 302945; e-mail - peterwain@supanet.com SER: Valuations. VAT: Spec.

MILFORD HAVEN

Milford Haven Antiques

Robert St. SA73 2JQ. Est. 1968. Open 10-5. *STOCK: General antiques.* TEL: 01646 692152.

MONMOUTH

Frost Antiques & Pine

8 Priory St. NP25 3BR. (Nicholas Frost). GMC. Resident. Est. 1960. Open 9-5, Sun. and other times by appointment. SIZE: Small. *STOCK: Pine furniture and Staffordshire pottery, 19th C, £100-£1,500.* LOC: When entering town from east - first shop on left. PARK: Easy. TEL: 01600 716687; website - www.frostantiques.com SER: Valuations; restorations (furniture); buys at auction (Victorian furniture and ceramics).

The House 1860-1925

6-8 St. James St. NP25 3DL. (Nick Wheatley). Open Tues.-Sat. 11-5. SIZE: Medium. *STOCK: Arts & Crafts furniture, Gothic Revival, Aesthetic movement, Art Nouveau, Art Deco, post-war.* PARK: In courtyard and nearby. TEL: 01600 772721; e-mail - nick@thehouse 1860-1925.com website - www.thehouse1860-1925.com SER: Valuations.

NARBERTH

Malt House Antiques

Back Lane. SA67 7AR. (P. Griffiths). Est. 1995. Open 10-5.30. SIZE: Large. *STOCK: Country furniture, 18th-20th C, £5-£5,000; pine, oak, Persian carpets, prints and paintings, collectables and china.* LOC: Village centre. PARK: Easy. TEL: 01834 860303.

NEWBRIDGE-ON-WYE, Nr. Llandrindod Wells

Allam Antiques

Old Village Hall. LD1 6HL. (Paul Allam). Est. 1985. Open Sat. 10-5. SIZE: Medium. *STOCK: Furniture, 1700-1930, £50-£3,000.* LOC: A470. PARK: Easy. TEL: 01597 860455. SER: Valuations; paint stripping.

NEWCASTLE EMLYN

The Old Saddlers Antiques

Bridge St. SA38 9DU. (P.C. and E. Coomber). Est. 1982. Open 10-5. CL: Wed. SIZE: Large. *STOCK: Country furniture, ceramics, pictures and prints, textiles, country bygones, kitchenalia, collectables and decorative items.* LOC: Lower end of High St., last shop before bridge. PARK: Own. TEL: 01239 711615. FAIRS: Towy, Carmarthen.

NEWPORT (Pembs.)

The Carningli Centre

East St. SA42 05Y. (Ann Gent and Graham Coles). Est. 1994. Open 10-5.30, Sun. by appointment. SIZE: Medium. *STOCK: Furniture, 17th-19th C, £50-£5,000; railwayana, nautical items, country collectables including oil lamps and tools, £1-£500; secondhand books, fine art gallery.* LOC: A487, town centre. PARK: Free in Long St. TEL: 01239 820724; website - www.carningli.co.uk SER: Valuations; restorations (furniture); polishing; turning; buys at auction (railwayana). VAT: Spec.

PEMBROKE

Pembroke Antiques Centre

Wesley Chapel, Main St. SA71 4DE. (Michael Blake). Est. 1986. Open 10-5. SIZE: Large. *STOCK: Pine, oak, mahogany and shipping furniture; china, rugs, paintings, Art Deco enamel signs, kitchenalia, pottery, toys, curios, collectables, postcards, advertising and decorative items.* LOC: Opposite end of Main St. to the castle. PARK: Free. TEL: 01646 687017. SER: Valuations; restorations; delivery.

PONTLLYFRII, Nr. Caernarfon

Sea View Antiques

LL54 5EF. (David A. Ramsell). Resident. Est. 1995. Open daily. SIZE: Small. *STOCK: General antiques and collectables, 18th-20th C, £5-£1,500.* LOC: Main Caernarfon to Pwllheli road. PARK: Easy. TEL: 01286 660436; e-mail - david@ramsell-antiques.freeserve.co.uk

PORTHCAWL

Harlequin Antiques

Dock St. CF36 3BL. (Ann and John Ball). Est. 1974. Open 10-4. *STOCK: General antiques, textiles, early 19th to 20th C books.* PARK: Easy. TEL: 01656 785910; mobile - 07980 837844.

PORTHMADOG

Huw Williams Antiques

Madoc St. LL49 9LR. Est. 1993. Open 10-5, Mon. 12-5. CL: Wed. SIZE: Small. *STOCK: Weapons, 18th-19th C, £50-£5,000; country furniture, 18th-19th C, £100-£1,000; general antiques, 19th-20th C, to £300.* LOC: Opposite entrance to main car park. PARK: Opposite. TEL: 01766 514741; mobile - 07785 747561; e-mail - huwantiques@aol.com website - www.antiqueguns wales.co.uk FAIRS: Stockport Arms; International Arms, Motorcycle Museum, Birmingham; Big Brum (Rag Market); London Arms, Heathrow.

PWLLHELI

Rodney Adams Antiques
Hall Place, Old Town Hall, Penlan St. and 62 High St. LL53 5DH. (R. and C. Adams). Resident. Est. 1965. Open 9-5. CL: Sun. except by appointment. *STOCK: Longcase clocks, country oak and period furniture.* PARK: At rear. TEL: 01758 613173; evenings - 01758 614337; website - www.rodneyadams.com SER: Delivery; export. VAT: Stan/Spec.

SWANSEA

Keith Chugg Antiques
Gwydr Lane, Uplands. SA2 0HJ. Open 9-5.30, Sat. 9-1. *STOCK: Pianos and general antiques including furniture.* TEL: 01792 472477.

Dylan's Bookstore
Salubrious House, 23 King Edward Rd. SA3 4LL. (J.M. Towns). ABA. PBFA. Est. 1971. Open 10-5, prior telephone call advisable. *STOCK: Antiquarian books on Welsh history and topography, Anglo/Welsh literature and general books.* TEL: 01792 655255; fax - same; mobile - 07850 759199; e-mail - jefftowns@dylans.com website - www.dylans.com FAIRS: London; Boston; Los Angeles; San Francisco.

Magpie Antiques
57 St. Helens Rd. SA1 4BH. (H. Hallesy). Est. 1984. Open 10-5. CL: Thurs. *STOCK: Ceramics including Swansea and other Welsh potteries; oak, pine and mahogany furniture; small antiques.* PARK: Opposite. TEL: 01792 648722; e-mail - helen@hallesy. wanadoo.co.uk SER: Valuations; restorations (furniture).

TEMPLETON, Nr. Narberth

Barn Court Antiques, Crafts & Tearoom
Barn Court. SA67 8SL. (D., A. and M. Evans). Est. 1989. Open 10-5. SIZE: Medium. *STOCK: Mahogany, walnut, rosewood and oak furniture, Georgian to late Edwardian, £10-£2,000; china, glass, and decorative items, £10-£500.* LOC: Off A40 on A478 Narberth to Tenby road, follow brown signs. PARK: Easy. TEL: 01834 861224; e-mail - info@barncourtantiques.com website - www.barncourtantiques.com VAT: Margin.

TENBY

Audrey Bull
15 Upper Frog St. SA70 7DJ. Est. 1945. Open 9.30-5. *STOCK: Period and Welsh country furniture, paintings, general antiques especially jewellery and silver; secondhand and designer jewellery.* TEL: 01834 843114; workshop - 01834 871873; home - 01834 813425. VAT: Spec.

TINTERN

Tintern Antiques
The Old Bakehouse. NP6 6SE. (Dawn Floyd). Open 9.30-5.30. *STOCK: Antique jewellery and general antiques.* TEL: 01291 689705.

TRECASTLE, Nr. Brecon

Trecastle Antiques Centre
The Old School. LD3 8YA. (A. Perry). Est. 1980. Open 10-5 including Sun. SIZE: Large. *STOCK: General antiques, £5-£1,500.* LOC: A40. PARK: Easy. TEL: 01874 638007. SER: Valuations; restorations. FAIRS: Newark, Shepton Mallet.

TREHARRIS

Treharris Antiques & Collectables
18 Perrott St. CF46 5ER. (Mrs Janet Barker). Est. 1974. Open 9.30-5. SIZE: Medium. *STOCK: Local mining memorablia - lamp checks and miners' lamps, twist boxes; tokens, English coins, banknotes, medals, military and civil badges, local maps and history books and artifacts, general collectors' items.* LOC: Opposite police station. PARK: Easy. TEL: 01443 413081; home - same. SER: Valuation and indentification (coins and antiquities).

TYWYN

Welsh Art
(Miles Wynn Cato). Est. 1989. Open by appointment (also in London). *STOCK: Welsh paintings, 1550-1950; Welsh portraits of all periods and historical Welsh material.* TEL: 020 7259 0306 and 01654 711715; mobile - 07766 460127; e-mail - wynncato@welshart.co.uk SER: Consultancy (Welsh art).

VALLEY, Nr. Holyhead (Anglesey)

Ann Evans LAPADA
Carna Shop, Station Rd. LL65 3HB. Est. 1990. Open Thurs.-Sat. 10-4.30, other days by appointment. SIZE: Medium. *STOCK: Welsh oak dressers and pottery; 18th-19th C cranberry glass, Staffordshire figures, silver and jewellery.* LOC: Just off junction 3, A55, 100 yards from traffic lights, turn left towards Trearddur Bay. PARK: Easy. TEL: 01407 741733; mobile - 07753 650376. SER: Valuations. VAT: Spec.

WELSHPOOL

F.E. Anderson and Son LAPADA
5 High St. SY21 7JF. (I. Anderson). Est. 1842. Open 9-5. SIZE: 3 large showrooms. *STOCK: Furniture, 17th-19th C; mirrors, paintings and decorative items.* TEL: 01938 553340; home - 01938 590509; fax - 01938 555998; mobile - 07773 795931; e-mail - antiques@feanderson. fsnet.co.uk FAIRS: Olympia; LAPADA. VAT: Margin.

Rowles Fine Art LAPADA
The Old Brewery, Brook St. SY21 7LF. (Mark and Glenn Rowles). CINOA. Est. 1978. Open 9.30-5.30, Sat. 9.30-3, other times by appointment. SIZE: Large. *STOCK: Victorian paintings and watercolours, some contemporary; small furniture.* PARK: Own. TEL: 01938 558811; fax - 01938 558822; mobiles - 07836 348688; 07802 303506; e-mail - enquiries@ rowlesfineart.co.uk website - www.rowlesfineart.co.uk SER: Valuations; restorations (paintings). FAIRS: NEC; LAPADA; Olympia (June); Chester; Harrogate.

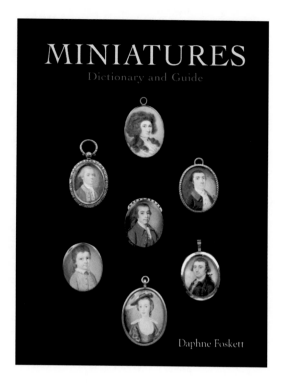

- *The standard work of reference on Miniatures.*

- *Helpful advice for the collector*

- *Written by the twentieth century's leading authority on the subject*

- *Comprehensively illustrated*

MINIATURES
Dictionary and Guide

Daphne Foskett

The art of a painting in miniature has a long history dating back to Tudor times. The medium attracted many skilled and famous artists whose works have been treasured by successive generations, not only as delightful portraits of loved ones, but also as fascinating small works of art generally sought after by discerning collectors. This substantial work of reference combines the author's two previous great books on the subject: the classic *Collecting Miniatures* (1979) with the revised and updated biographical details of some 4,400 artists from her celebrated *Dictionary of British Miniature Painters* (1972) which has long been accepted as the standard reference book. This scholarly but eminently readable book answers in a practical fashion all the difficult questions that arise for the collector; on the crucial matter of dating by costume; the idiosyncracies of individual artists and their methods of working; the restoration of paintings, and of course, the delicate matter of fakes, forgeries and 'improvements'.

The late Daphne Foskett, F.R.S.A., Hon. R.M.S. had a life-long interest in collecting and gained a deep knowledge in several fields, such as pottery, porcelain and ivories but developed a special interest in miniature painting. In 1983 she was involved in a consultant capacity with the exhibition *Artists of the Tudor Court* at the Victoria and Albert Museum. The author was made an Honorary Member of the Royal Miniature Society in 1987. She died in 1998

*Specifications: 704pp.,
165 col. illus., 860 b.&w. illus.,
11 x 8½in./279 x 216mm.*
£49.50 (hardback)

For full details of all ACC publications, log on to our website:
www.antiquecollectorsclub.com
or telephone 01394 389950 for a free catalogue

Index of
Packers and Shippers:
Exporters of Antiques (Containers)

ANGLO PACIFIC INTERNATIONAL
SPECIALIST PACKERS AND WORLDWIDE SHIPPERS OF BESPOKE FURNITURE, ANTIQUES AND FINE ART

FOR ADVICE ON SHIPPING OR FOR AN IMMEDIATE SHIPPING QUOTATION PLEASE CONTACT OUR EXPERIENCED SALES TEAM

Anglo Pacific Int.
Units 1 & 2 Bush Industrial Estate
Standard Road
London NW10 6DF
Tel: +44 (0) 208 838 8008
Fax: +44 (0) 208 453 0225
Email: antiques@anglopacific.co.uk

LONDON

Air-Sea Packing Group Ltd.
See under Middlesex.

Anglo Pacific International plc   LAPADA
Units 1 and 2 Bush Industrial Estate, Standard Rd.
NW10 6DF. Tel: 020 8838 8008; fax - 020 8453 0225;
e-mail - antiques@anglopacific.co.uk website - www.
anglopacific.co.uk *Specialist antique and fine art
packers and shippers serving worldwide destinations by
land, sea or air. Free estimates and advice. Courier
services available.*

AR. GS International Transport Ltd
North London Freight Centre, York Way, King's Cross. N1
0BB. Tel: 020 7833 3955; fax - 020 7837 8672;
e-mail - sales@args.co.uk website - www.args.co.uk *Fine
art and antiques removals by road transport, Europe,
especially Italy, door-to-door service. Documentation.*

Art Logistics Ltd
Unit 1, Victoria Industrial Estate, Victoria Rd. W3 6UU.
Tel: 020 8993 8811; fax - 020 8993 8833; e-mail - mail@
artlogistics.co.uk *Fine art packing, freight forwarding.*

AR · GS International Transport Ltd.

SHIPPERS & PACKERS OF ANTIQUES, FINE ART & REMOVALS TO **ITALY**

Tel: 020 7833 3955 or 07836 612376
Fax: 020 7837 8672
Email: sales@args.co.uk   www.args.co.uk

North London Freight Centre,
York Way, King's Cross, London N1 OBB

BBF Shipping Ltd
12 Ashmead Business Centre, North Crescent, Cody Rd. E16 4TG. Tel: 020 7511 6107; fax - 020 7511 6109; e-mail - bbfshipping@aol.com *Fine art packers, worldwide shippers by sea, air and road.*

Robert Boys Shipping   **LAPADA**
North London Freight Centre, York Way, King's Cross. N1 0AU. Tel: 020 7837 4806; fax - 020 7837 4815; e-mail - info@robertboysshipping.co.uk *Worldwide shipping. Air and sea cargo. Specialists in fine art and furniture packing.*

Cadogan Tate Fine Art Logistics Ltd   LAPADA
6-12 Ponton Rd. SW8 5BA. Tel: 020 7498 3255; fax - 020 7498 9017. e-mail - fineart@cadogantate.com website - www.cadogantate.com *Fine art and antiques export packed. World-wide shipping, scheduled European vehicles, New York weekly consols. International exhibitions. High security bonded storage. New York office and warehouse.*

Davies Turner Worldwide Movers Ltd
London Headquarters : 49 Wates Way, Mitcham. CR4 4HR. Tel: 020 7622 4393; fax - 020 7720 3897; e-mail - antiques@daviesturner.co.uk website - www.davies turner.co.uk *Fine art and antiques packers and shippers. Courier and finder service. Full container L.C.L. and groupage service worldwide. Offices countrywide.*

Robert Boys Shipping

North London Freight Centre,
York Way, King's Cross,
London N1 0AU.
Tel: 020 7837 4806
Fax: 020 7837 4815
Email: info@robertboysshipping.co.uk

International Fine Art Packers & Shippers

Founded in London in 1933, Gander & White has established a reputation as one of the world's leading packers and shippers of antiques and works of art. A family owned business with staff of over 100, we pride ourselves on our skills at combining the traditional standards of service with the modern skills and expertise needed to meet the requirements of museums, dealers and individuals for the packing, shipping and storage of antiques and fine art.

London   –   Unit 1, St Martin's Way
                   Wimbledon, London SW17 0JH
                   Tel: (020) 8971 7171 Fax: (020) 8946 8062

Sussex   –   Newpound, Wisborough Green, Nr. Billingshurst
                   West Sussex, RH14 0AZ
                   Tel: (01403) 700044 Fax: (01403) 700814

Paris   –   2 Boulevard de la Liberation
                   93200 Saint Denis, Paris
                   Tel: 00 33 1 55 87 67 10 Fax: 00 33 1 42 43 20 18

New York   –   21-44 44th Road, Long Island City, New York 11101
                   Tel: (718) 784 8444 Fax: (718) 784 9337

Palm Beach   –   2206 Mercer Avenue
                   West Palm Beach, Florida 33401
                   Tel: (561) 655 4204 Fax: (561) 655 4224

Esthers Shipping Ltd

Unit 64 Faraday Way, Westminster Industrial Estate. SE18 5TR. Tel: 020 8331 0321; fax - 020 8331 0421; e-mail - info@estership.com and antique@estership.com website - www.estership.com *Expert packing and worldwide shipping of antiques and fine art.*

Focus Packing Services Ltd

37-39 Peckham Rd. SE5 8UH. Tel: 020 7703 4715; fax - same; e-mail - focuspacking@aol.com *Specialist packers of antiques and works of art. Premises in Portobello Rd. and Camden Passage for on-the-spot quotations; drop-off service available.*

Gander and White Shipping Ltd   LAPADA

Unit 1 St Martin's Way, Wimbledon. SW17 0JH. Tel: 020 8971 7171; fax - 020 8946 8062; website - www.ganderandwhite.com *Specialist packers and shippers of antiques and works of art. Offices in Paris, New York and Palm Beach.*

Hedleys Humpers Ltd   LAPADA

3 St Leonard's Rd., North Acton. NW10 6SX. IATA. BAR (overseas group). RMA. Tel: 020 8965 8733; fax - 020 8965 0249; e-mail - gasb@hedleyshumpers.com website - www.hedleyshumpers.com *Weekly collection services in Europe for consolidation and onward shipment worldwide. Offices in Paris, Avignon and New York.*

Interdean Interconex

Central Way, Park Royal. NW10 7XW. Tel: 020 8961 4141; telex - 922119; fax - 020 8965 4484. *Antiques and fine art packed, shipped and airfreighted worldwide. Storage and international removals. Full container L.C.L. and groupage service worldwide.*

Kuwahara Ltd   LAPADA

6 McNicol Drive, NW10 7AW. Tel: 020 8963 5995; fax - 020 8963 0100; e-mail - info@kuwahara.co.uk website - www.kuwahara.co.uk *Specialist packers and shippers of antiques and works of art. Regular groupage service to Japan.*

Locksons Services Ltd

See entry under Essex.

Stephen Morris Shipping plc   LAPADA

Unit 4, Brent Trading Estate, 390 North Circular Rd. NW10 0JF. Tel: 020 8830 1919; fax - 020 8830 1999; e-mail - enquiries@shipsms.co.uk website - www.stemo.co.uk *Specialist packers and shippers of antiques and fine art worldwide. Weekly European services.*

Nelson Shipping

Unit C3, Six Bridges Trading Estate, Marlborough Grove. SE1 5JT. Tel: 020 7394 7770; fax - 020 7394 7707. *Expert export and packing service.*

Robinsons International   LAPADA

The Gateway, Staples Corner. NW2 7AJ. Tel: 020 8208 8484; fax - 020 8208 8488; website - www.robinsons-intl.com *Specialist packers and shippers of antiques and fine art worldwide. Established over 100 years.*

T. Rogers and Co. Ltd

PO Box No. 8, 1A Broughton St. SW8 3QL. Tel: 020 7622 9151; fax - 020 7627 3318; e-mail - trogersco@ukonline.co.uk *Specialists in storage, packing, removal, shipping and forwarding antiques and works of art. Insurance.*

BUCKINGHAMSHIRE

Clark's of Amersham
Higham Mead, Higham Rd., Chesham. HP5 2AH. Tel: 01494 774186; fax - 01494 774196; e-mail - enquiries@clarksofamersham.com website - www.bluelorry.com *Removals and storage, domestic and commercial; export packing and shipping - worldwide door to door.*

CHESHIRE

The Rocking Chair Antiques
Unit 3, St. Peters Way, Warrington. WA27 7BL. Tel: 01925 652409; fax - same; mobile - 07774 492891. *Exporters and packers.*

DEVON

Barnstaple Removal
14/15 Meadow Way, Tree Beech Rural Enterprise Park, Gunn, Barnstaple. EX32 7NZ. Tel: 01271 831164; fax - 01271 831165; e-mail - sales@barnstapleremovals.com and info@barnstapleremovals.com website - www.barnstapleremovals.co.uk *Overseas freight and shipping, full or part loads, worldwide door to door. Export packing and documentation. Regular European services. Storage facilities.*

Bishop's Blatchpack
Kestrel Way, Sowton Industrial Estate, Exeter. EX2 7PA. Tel: 01392 202040; fax - 01392 201251. *International fine art packers and shippers.*

DORSET

Alan Franklin Transport Ltd   LAPADA
26 Blackmoor Rd., Ebblake Industrial Estate, Verwood. BH31 6BB. Tel: 01202 826539; fax - 01202 827337; e-mail - enquiries@afteurope.co.uk website - www.alanfranklintransport.co.uk *Worldwide container packing and shipping. Weekly door-to-door European service. Paris office - 2 Rue Etienne Dolet, 93400 St. Ouen, Paris. Tel: 00 33140 115000; fax - 00 33140 114821. South of France office - Quartier La Tour de Sabran, 84440 Robion (Vaucluse). Tel: 00 33490 764900; fax - 00 33490 764902. Belgian office - De Klerckstraat 41, B8300, Knokke. Tel: 00 3250 623579; fax - 00 3250 620747.*

ESSEX

Geo. Copsey and Co. Ltd
178 Crow Lane, Romford. RM7 0ES. Tel: 01708 740714 or 020 8592 1003; e-mail - htebutt@copsey.org.uk *Worldwide packers and shippers.*

Lockson Services Ltd   LAPADA
Unit 1, Heath Park Industrial Estate, Freshwater Rd., Chadwell Heath. RM8 1RX. BIFA. Tel: 020 8597 2889; fax - 020 8597 5265; mobile (weekends) - 07831 621428; e-mail - bob@lockson.co.uk New Jersey office - 201 392 9800; fax - 201 392 8830; e-mail - locksoninc @aol.com website - www.lockson.co.uk *Specialist packers and shippers of fine art and antiques by air, sea and road to the USA, Japan, Far East, Canada and other*

SOME ARE MORE EQUAL THAN OTHERS

ALAN FRANKLIN TRANSPORT LTD
Specialist Carriers to the Continent

England
26 Black Moor Road, Verwood, Dorset BH31 6BB
Tel: +44 1202 826539 Fax: +44 1202 827337

France
2 Rue Etienne Dolet, 93400 St. Ouen, Paris
Tel: +33 1 40 11 50 00 Fax: +33 1 40 11 48 21

France
Quartier La Tour de Sabran, 84440 Robion (Vaucluse)
Tel: +33 4 90 76 49 00 Fax: +33 4 90 76 49 02

Belgium
De Klerckstraat 41, B8300 Knokke
Tel: +32 50 623 579 Fax: +32 50 620 747

Our door to door weekly service throughout
Europe is well known and very reliable.
Visit our Paris warehouse and offices located
within the famous Paris flea market area.
Container and Air Freight Services Worldwide.

LOCKSON

Leading specialists
in packing and
shipping of fine art
and antiques,
worldwide.

UK
T: 0208 597 2889
F: 0208 597 5265
E: shipping@lockson.co.uk

USA
T: 201 392 9800
F: 201 392 8830
E: locksoninc@aol.com

www.lockson.co.uk

*a moving
experience...*

PACKERS AND SHIPPERS

worldwide destinations. A complete personalised service. At Olympia, Newark and Ardingly fairs. Shipping to all major US fairs.

GLOUCESTERSHIRE

The Removal Company - Loveday & Loveday
2 Wilkinson Rd., Cirencester. GL7 1YT. Tel: 01285 651505; e-mail - cirencester@int-moving.com website - www.int-moving.com *Shipping and packing.*

Robinsons International   LAPADA
Aldermoor Way, Longwell Green, Bristol. BS30 7DA. Tel: 0117 980 5858; fax - 0117 980 5830; e-mail - antiques@robinsons-intl.com website - www.robinsons-intl.com *Specialist packers and shippers of antiques and fine art worldwide. Established over 100 years.*

The Shipping Company Ltd
Bourton Industrial Park, Bourton-on-the-Water. GL54 2HQ. Tel: 01451 822451; fax - 01451 810985; website - www.theshippingcompanyltd.com *Export packers and shippers specialising in the antique, fine art and interior design markets worldwide. Single, consolidated and full container shipments by air and sea. All risks insurance offered.*

HAMPSHIRE

Robinsons International   LAPADA
Atlantic House, Oakley Rd., Shirley, Southampton. SO16 4LL. Tel: 02380 515111; fax - 02380 515112; e-mail - southampton@robinsons-intl.com website - www.robinsons-intl.com *Specialist packers and shippers of antiques and fine art worldwide. Established over 100 years.*

Robinsons International   LAPADA
1 Hamilton Close, Houndmills Industrial Estate, Basingstoke. RG21 6YU. Tel: 01256 465533; fax - 01256 324959; website - www.robinsons-intl.com *Specialist packers and shippers of antiques and fine art worldwide. Established over 100 years.*

KENT

Sutton Valence Antiques
Unit 4, Haslemere Estate, Sutton Rd., Maidstone. ME15 9NL. Tel: 01622 675332; fax - 01622 692593; e-mail - svantiques@aol.com website - www.svantiques.co.uk *Antique and shipping furniture. Container packing and shipping. Facilities for 20ft. and 40ft. containers, all documentation. Worldwide service.*

IS YOUR ENTRY CORRECT?
If there is even the slightest inaccuracy in your entry, please let us know before
1st January 2006

GUIDE TO THE ANTIQUE SHOPS OF BRITAIN
Sandy Lane, Old Martlesham,
Woodbridge, Suffolk IP12 4SD, UK.

Tel: **01394 389968** or Fax: **01394 389999**
Email: editorial@antique-acc.com
Website: www.antiquecollectorsclub.com

LANCASHIRE

Robinsons International   LAPADA
32 Stanley Rd., Manchester. M45 8QX. Tel: 0161 766 8414; fax - 0161 767 9057; website - www.robinsons-intl.com *Specialist packers and shippers of antiques and fine art worldwide. Established over 100 years.*

MIDDLESEX

Air-Sea Packing Group Ltd   LAPADA
Air-Sea House, Third Cross Rd., Twickenham. TW2 5EB. Tel: 020 8893 3303; fax - 020 8893 3068; e-mail - antiques@airseapacking.com website - www. airsea packing.com *Specialist packers and shippers.*

Crown Relocations
19 Stonefield Way, South Ruislip. HA4 0BJ. Tel: 020 8839 8000; fax - 020 8839 8001; website - www. crownrelo.com *Packers and shippers - 12 offices throughout U.K.*

The Holt Group
Beaconsfield Rd., Hayes. UB4 0SL. Tel: 020 7278 5585; fax - 020 8848 1273. *Packers and shippers of antiques and fine art. Shipping, forwarding and airfreight agents. Comprehensive service provided for visiting antique dealers. Insurance arranged.*

Nippon Express (UK) Ltd
Ocean Freight Division, Unit 7, Parkway Trading Estate, Cranford Lane, Heston, Hounslow. TW5 9NE. Tel: Commercial (Export) - 020 8737 4240; fax - 020 8737 4249; (Import) - 020 8737 4260; fax - 020 8737 4269; Removal (Cargo) - 020 8737 4200; fax - 020 8737 4209. *Mainly Japanese imports/exports, both commercial and removals. Also import/export all other Far East countries.*

PDQ-Art Move   LAPADA
Unit 4, Court 1, Challenge Rd., Ashford, TW15 1AX. CINOA. GTA. IATA. Tel:01784 243695; fax - 01784 242237; e-mail - art@pdq.uk.com website - www.pdq.uk.com *Fine art air freight packers and shippers, including firearms.*

Sovereign International Freight Ltd
Sovereign House, 8-10 St. Dunstans Rd., Feltham. TW13 4JU. Tel: 020 8751 3131; fax - 020 8751 4517; e-mail - info@sovereignlondon.co.uk *Heathrow Airport based shippers and packers registered to ISO 9002 quality. Holders of the Queen's Award for Export and National Training Award. Specialist in antiques and the fine art trades.*

OXFORDSHIRE

Cotswold Carriers
Unit 2 The Walk, Hook Norton Rd., Chipping Norton. OX7 5TG. Tel: 01608 730500; fax - 01608 730600; e-mail - info@cotswoldcarriers.com website - www. cotswoldcarriers.com*Removals, storage, shipping, door-to-door Continental deliveries.*

Robinsons International   LAPADA
Nuffield Way, Abingdon. OX14 1TN. Tel: 01179 805858; fax - 01179 805830; e-mail - antiques@ robinsons-intl.com website - www.robinsons-intl.com *Specialist packers and shippers of antiques and fine art worldwide. Established over 100 years.*

A.J. Williams (Shipping)

ANTIQUES & FINE ART PACKERS & SHIPPERS

LAPADA
MEMBER

Tel: +44(0) 1761 413976
Fax: +44(0) 1761 410868
Email: **ajw_4@hotmail.com**

Unit 32, Fourth Avenue, Westfield Trading Estate, Midsomer Norton, Radstock BA3 4XE

SOMERSET

Mark Chudley Ltd
The Old Station, Gt. Western Rd., Chard. TA20 1EQ.
Tel:01460 62800; website - www.markchudley.com
International shipping.

A.J. Williams (Shipping)   LAPADA
Unit 32 Fourth Ave., Westfield Trading Estate, Radstock,
Bath. BA3 4XE. Tel: 01761 413976; fax - 01761
410868; mobile - 07732 681754; e-mail -
ajw_4@hotmail.com *Packing and shipping of antiques
and fine art.*

STAFFORDSHIRE

Acorn G.D.S Ltd
183 Queen's Rd., Penkhull, Stoke-on-Trent. ST4 7LF.
RHA. Tel: 01782 817700; e-mail - acorn@acorn-

freight.co.uk website - www.acorn-freight.co.uk
*Container packing and export documentation. Freight
forwarding; UK furniture transport and storage.*

Crown Relocations
Crown House, Unit 1 Ninian Way, Tame Valley
Industrial Estate, Wilnecote, Tamworth. B77 5ES. Tel:
01827 264100; fax - 01827 264101; mobile - 07740
747664; e-mail - birmingham@crownrelo.com website -
www.crownrelo.com *UK, Europe and worldwide
removal and relocation services.*

SURREY

W. Ede & Co
The Edes Business Park, Restmor Way, Wallington. SM2
5AA. Tel: 020 8773 9933; fax - 020 8773 9011; e-mail -
blair@edes-removals.co.uk website - www.edes.com
*Worldwide packing and shipping, complete docu-
mentation and removals service, container packing.*

Traders Delivery Service
105 King's Rd., Long Ditton, Surbiton. KT6 5JE. Tel: 020
8398 3681. *Removals and carriers; courier, part loads.*

WEST SUSSEX

Gander and White Shipping Ltd   LAPADA
Newpound, Wisborough Green, Billingshurst. RH14
0AZ. Tel: 01403 700044; fax - 01403 700814; e-mail -
ukinfo@ganderandwhite.com *Specialist packers and
shippers of fine art and antiques. Offices in London,
Paris, New York and Palm Beach.*

467

Martells International
Units 3-4 Charlwoods Rd. East Grinstead. RH19 2HG. Tel: 01342 321303; fax - 01342 302145. *National and international removers, export packers and shippers.*

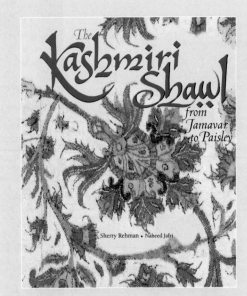

The Kashmiri shawl is rooted in a complex tradition of craft that dates back at least five hundred years. Its uniqueness lies in a combination of factors that have made it virtually impossible to duplicate anywhere else. *The Kashmiri Shawl* is the story of this textile, re-told through a South Asian perspective. This book realigns the design symbolism and technical evolution of the shawl to indigenous sources by emphasising on areas previously ignored in earlier histories. The shawl's origins in Kashmir, the rich vein of patronage it thrived on, its changing ornamental face, its regional variations in Persia and the Punjab, its enormous impact on the European imagination, all combine to form a narrative shaped to engage the reader.

Specifications: 374pp., 430 col. and 7 b.&w., 12 x 10in./304 x 254mm. **£45.00 (hardback)**

WEST MIDLANDS

The British Shop - Shipping U.S.A
Old Sandwell House, Sandwell St., Walsall. WS1 3DR. Tel: 01922 721088; fax - 01922 723123; (USA - 336 434 4645; fax - 336 434 7765) *Weekly container from Birmingham to High Point, North Carolina, USA. Pickup and pack, no minimums.*

Clentons Removals Ltd
94 Caldmore Rd., Walsall. WS1 3PD. Tel; 01922 624431; fax - 01922 613053; e-mail - clentons@yahoo. co.uk website - www.clentonsremovals.com *Collections arranged in UK and Europe for clients' goods. Storage available. Packing and wrapping of all goods for container shipments. All paperwork done for containers. Packing of containers and shipment of containers.*

Robinsons International   LAPADA
22A Bartleet Rd., Washford, Redditch. B98 0DG. Tel: 01527 830860; fax - 01527 500777; website - www.robinsons-intl.com *Specialist packers and shippers of antiques and fine art worldwide. Established over 100 years.*

WILTSHIRE

Martin Bros Ltd
The Old Sawmills, The Street, Kilmington, Nr. Warminster. BA12 6RG. Tel: 01985 844144; fax - 01985 844113; website - www.martinbrosltd.com *Specialist carriers of fine art and furniture throughout mainland UK.*

WORCESTERSHIRE

Simon Hall Ltd   LAPADA
Willersey Industrial Estate, Willersey, Nr. Broadway. WR12 7RR. Tel: 01386 858555; fax - 01386 858501; e-mail - enquiries@simonhalllimited.com *Specialist packers and shippers for fine art and antiques world wide. UK collections and deliveries. Humidity controlled containerised and conventional storage.*

SCOTLAND

Crown Worldwide Ltd
Cullen Square, Deans Rd. Industrial Estate, Livingstone EH54 8SJ. Tel: 01506 468150; fax - 01506 468151. *Packers and shippers.*

Martin Bros. Ltd

The Old Sawmills, The Street,
Kilmington, Nr Warminster, Wilts. BA12 6RG
Tel: 01985 844 144, 112,
Fax: 01985 844 113
Specialist Carriers of
Fine Art and Furniture
throughout mainland UK.

INDEX OF
AUCTIONEERS

LONDON

Bloomsbury Auctions
Bloomsbury House, 24 Maddox St., Mayfair. W1S 1PP. Tel: 020 7495 9494; fax - 020 7495 9499; e-mail - info @bloomsburyauctions.com website - www.bloomsbury-book-auctions.com *Twenty-four sales a year of books on all subjects and of all values, manuscripts, autograph letters, prints and paintings, maps, drawings, photographs, posters and ephemera. Valuations. Collection service.*

Bonhams
101 New Bond St., W1S 1SR. Est. 1793. Tel: 020 7447 7447; fax - 020 7447 7400; e-mail - info@bonhams.com website - www.bonhams.com *Extensive network of international and UK salerooms and offices. Regular auctions of vintage motor cars, automobilia, sporting items, watercolours, Old Masters, European and modern pictures, portrait miniatures, prints, carved frames, furniture, clocks and watches, decorative arts, European porcelain and glass, Oriental and contemporary ceramics, objects of art, tribal art and antiquities, silver, jewellery, objects of vertu, books and manuscripts, antique and modern guns, musical instruments, Oriental carpets and rugs. Viewing Mon.-Fri. 9-4.30, Sun. 11-3.*

Christie's
8 King St., St.James's, SW1Y 6QT. Est. 1766. Tel: 020 7839 9060; fax - 020 7839 1611; website - www.christies.com *Porcelain, pottery, objets d'art and miniatures, pictures including Old Masters, English, Victorian, Continental, Impressionist, contemporary, prints, drawings, watercolours, Art Deco, Art Nouveau; Japanese and Chinese, Islamic and Persian works of art; glass, silver, jewellery, books, modern guns, furniture, carpets, tapestries, clocks and watches, garden statuary, photographs, Russian works of art, sculpture, wine, house sales (contents only).*

Christie's South Kensington Ltd
85 Old Brompton Rd., SW7 3LD. Tel: 020 7581 7611; fax - 020 7321 3311. *Sales of jewellery, silver, pictures, watercolours, drawings and prints; furniture and carpets, ceramics and works of art, printed books; costume, textiles and embroidery; toys and games, dolls, wines, Art Nouveau, Art Deco, cameras. Periodic sales of automata, mechanical music and vintage machines, motoring and aeronautical items including car mascots; Staffordshire portrait figures, miniatures.*

Criterion Auctioneers
53 Essex Rd., Islington. N1 2BN. Tel: 020 7359 5707; fax - 020 7354 9843; e-mail - info@criterion-auctioneers.co.uk website - www.criterion-auctioneers.co.uk *Sales every Mon. at 4 pm of general antiques, reproduction and contemporary furniture, glass, china, rugs and smalls. Viewing Fri. 4-8, Sat. and Sun. 10-6, Mon. prior to sale.*

Stanley Gibbons Auctions
399 Strand, WC2R 0LX. Est. 1901. Tel: 020 7836 8444; fax - 020 7836 7342; e-mail - auctions@stanleygibbons.co.uk website - www.stanleygibbons.com *Regular auctions throughout the year.*

Harmers of London Stamp Auctioneers Ltd
Unit 11, 111 Power Rd., Chiswick. W4 5PY. Est. 1918. Tel: 020 8747 6100; fax - 020 8996 0649; e-mail - auctions@harmers.demon.co.uk website - www.harmers.com *Monthly auctions of Great Britain, British Commonwealth, foreign countries, airmail stamps, also postal history and literature, stamp boxes, postal scales and related ephemera. Fully illustrated catalogues. Valuations for sale, probate or insurance.*

Hornsey Auctions Ltd
54-56 High St., Hornsey. N8 7NX. Tel: 020 8340 5334; fax - same. *Sales weekly on Wed. at 6.30. Viewing Tues. 5-7 and Wed. from 10 am. Open Thurs., Fri. 10-5.30 and Sat. 10-4 to take in for next auction.*

Lloyds International Auction Galleries Ltd
9 Lydden Rd., Earlsfield, SW18 4LT. Tel: 020 8788 7777; fax - 020 8874 5390; e-mail - valuations@lloyds-auction.co.uk website - www.lloyds-auction.co.uk *Fortnightly Sat. sales of antique and modern furniture, china, glassware, pictures and collectables. Website catalogue.*

Lots Road Auctions
71-73 Lots Rd., Chelsea, SW10 0RN. Est. 1978. Tel: 020 7376 6800; fax - 020 7376 6899; e-mail - info@lotsroad.com website - www.lotsroad.com *Auctions every Sunday at 2 pm (modern and reproduction) and 4.30 pm (antique), approx. 600 lots of antique, traditional and decorative furniture, Oriental carpets, paintings, prints, ceramics, clocks, glass, silver, objets d'art and soft furnishings. On view Thurs. 10-7, Fri. and Sat. 10-4, Sun. from 10 am. Goods accepted Mon.-Fri. Payment by direct credit 10 days after the sale. Catalogue details and auction results by fax, telephone or on website. Valuers, consultants and carriers. VAT registered.*

Rippon Boswell and Co
The Arcade, South Kensington Station. SW7 2NA. Tel:

020 7589 4242. *International specialist auctioneers of old and antique Oriental carpets. Periodical auctions in London. Also in Germany, Switzerland, USA and Far East.*

Rosebery's

74-76 Knights Hill, West Norwood. SE27 0JD. Est. 1987. Tel: 020 8761 2522; fax - 020 8761 2524; e-mail - auctions@roseberys.co.uk website - www.roseberys. co.uk *Quarterly selected and monthly antique and collectors auctions on Tues. and Wed. Monthly Mon. general auctions. Specialist auctions of toys and collectors' items, decorative arts, modern design, musical instruments, books and textiles held periodically.*

Sotheby's

34-35 New Bond St., W1A 2AA. Tel: 020 7293 5000. *Open for free valuations Mon.-Fri. 9-5. Daily sales of paintings, drawings, watercolours, prints, books and manuscripts, European sculpture and works of art, antiquities, silver, ceramics, glass, jewellery, Oriental works of art, furniture, musical instruments, clocks and watches, vintage cars, wine, postage stamps, coins, medals, toys and dolls and other collectors' items.*

Sotheby's Olympia

Hammersmith Rd., W14 8UX. Tel: 020 7293 5555; e-mail - olympia@sothebys.com *Sales of antique arms and armour, ceramics and glass, silver and vertu, furniture and interior decor items, decorative arts, paintings and sporting guns. Viewing Mon. 9-8, Tues.-Fri. 9-5, Sun. 12-5. CL: Sat.*

Southgate Auction Rooms

55 High St., Southgate. N14 6LD. Est. 1977. Tel: 020 8886 7888; website - www.southgateauctionrooms.com *Weekly Mon. sales at 4 pm of jewellery, silver, china, porcelain, paintings, furniture. Viewing Sat. 9-12 noon and from 9 am on day of sale.*

BEDFORDSHIRE

W. & H. Peacock

The Auction Centre, 26 Newnham St., Bedford. MK40 3JR. Est. 1901. Tel: 01234 266366; e-mail - info@ peacockauction.co.uk website - www.peacockauction. co.uk *Antiques sales first Fri. monthly. Viewing Fri. prior 9 am-8 pm. General sales every Sat. at 9.30 am.*

Douglas Ross (Auctioneers)

The Old Town Hall, Woburn. MK17 9PZ. Tel: 01525 290502; fax - 01525 290864; e-mail - info@charles-ross.co.uk website - www.douglasross.co.uk *Sales every four weeks on Thurs.*

BERKSHIRE

Dreweatt Neate

Donnington Priory Salerooms, Donnington, Nr. Newbury. RG14 2JE. Est. 1759. Tel: 01635 553553; fax - 01635 553599; e-mail - donnington@dnfa.com website - www.dnfa.com *Open Mon.-Fri. 9-5. Sales of ceramics, glass, pictures and books, silver and jewellery, wine, furniture and works of art, clocks. Fortnightly sales of Victorian and later furniture and furnishings. Commission 15% and 10% plus VAT. Catalogues available by post or on website. Valuations. Part of The Fine Art Auction Group.*

Law Fine Art Ltd

Ash Cottage, Ashmore Green, Newbury. RG18 9ER. Est. 2000. Tel: 01635 860033; fax - 01635 860036; e-mail - info@lawfineart.co.uk website - www.lawfineart.co.uk *Three sales per annum of furniture, pictures, silver, jewellery and works of art. Three major sales of ceramics and glass per annum. All sales held at Littlecote House, Hungerford, Berks. Viewing Sat., Sun. and Mon. prior to sales.*

Martin and Pole

The Auction House, 10 Milton Rd., Wokingham. RG40 1DB. Tel: 0118 979 0460; fax - 0118 977 6166; e-mail - a@martinpole.co.uk website - www.martinpole.co.uk *Sale of antiques and collectables held every month at above address.*

Thimbleby & Shorland

Market House, PO Box 175, 31 Great Knollys St., Reading. RG1 7HU. Est. 1901. Tel: 01189 508611; fax - 01189 505896; mobile - 07778 766172; e-mail - sarah.needham@thimbleby-shorland.co.uk website - www.tsauction.co.uk *Collective sales of antique and modern furniture held monthly at Reading Auction Market. Also sales and valuations of horse-drawn carriages and driving equipment with four sales annually in Reading.*

BUCKINGHAMSHIRE

Amersham Auction Rooms

125 Station Rd., Amersham. HP7 0AH. RICS. CFAAS. Est. 1877. Tel: 08700 460606; fax - 08700 460607; e-mail - info@amershamauctionrooms.co.uk website - www.amershamauctionrooms.co.uk *Weekly general and monthly selected antique sales held on Thurs. at 10.30 am.*

CAMBRIDGESHIRE

Bonhams

The Golden Rose, 17 Emmanuel Rd., Cambridge. CB1 1JW. Tel: 01223 366523; fax - 01223 300208; website - www.bonhams.com *Regular sales of good furniture, pictures, silver, ceramics and Victoriana. Enquiries to Clodagh Sapsford.*

Cheffins

Clifton House, 1 and 2 Clifton Rd., Cambridge. CB1 7EA. Est. 1825. Tel: 01223 213343 (10 lines); e-mail - fine.art@cheffins.co.uk website - www.cheffins.co.uk *Regular fine art and general auction sales including pictures, furniture, works of art, silver and jewellery, ceramics and collectors' items.*

Hyperion Auctions Ltd

Station Rd., St. Ives. PE27 5BH. Est. 1995. Tel: 01480 464140; fax - 01480 497552; e-mail - enquiries@ hyperionauctions.co.uk website - www.hyperion auctions.co.uk *Regular sales of antiques and collectables.*

W. & H. Peacock

The Auction Centre, 75 New St., St Neots. PE19 1AJ. Tel: 01480 474550; fax - 01480 470104; e-mail - info@ peacockauction.co.uk *General sales every Thurs. at 11 am.*

Rowley Fine Art Auctioneers & Valuers
8 Downham Rd., Ely. CB6 1AH. Est. 2001. Tel: 01353 653020; fax - 01353 653022; e-mail - mail@rowley fineart.com website - www.rowleyfineart.com *Monthly general sales held on the 2nd Sat. Quarterly film poster sales. Regular sales of fine art and antiques at Tattersalls Sale Ring, Newmarket. Valuations. Bi-annual toy auctions.*

Willingham Auctions
25 High St., Willingham. CB4 5ES. Tel: 01954 261252; fax - 01954 201396; website - www.willinghamauctions. com *Sales every three weeks of antique and fine furniture, silver, ceramics and clocks.*

CHESHIRE

Andrew, Hilditch and Son Ltd
Hanover House, 1A The Square, Sandbach. CW11 0AP. Est. 1866. Tel: 01270 767246/762048. *Quarterly sales of fine pictures and period furnishings. General and Edwardian furniture sales held weekly.*

Bonhams
New House, 150 Christleton Rd., Chester. CH3 5TD. Est. 1793. Tel: 01244 313936; fax - 01244 340028; website - www.bonhams.com *14 salerooms countrywide including Chester, New Bond Street, Knightsbridge and Chelsea.*

Byrne's Auctioneers and Valuers
Booth Mansion, 30 Watergate St., Chester. CH1 2LA. RICS. Est. 2003. Tel: 01244 312300; fax - 01244 312112; e-mail - auctions@byrnesauctioneers.co.uk *Quarterly antique sales. Fortnightly general antiques and later effects. Collectors sales 3 times a year. Valuation day Thurs. 10-1 and 2-4. Home visits by appointment. Office open Mon.-Fri. 10-4*

Cheyne's Auctions
38 Hale Rd., Altrincham. WA14 2EX. RICS. Est. 1983. Tel: 0161 941 4879; e-mail - patrickcheyne@aol.com website - www.antiquestradegazette.com/patrickcheyne *Bi-monthly sales held at St Peter's Assembly Rooms, Cecil Road, Hale. Viewing day prior 2-4.30 and 6-8 and sale morning 9-10.30.*

Frank R. Marshall and Co
Marshall House, Church Hill, Knutsford. WA16 6DH. Est. 1948. Tel: 01565 653284; fax - 01565 652341; e-mail - antiques@frankmarshall.co.uk website - www. frankmarshall.co.uk *Regular sales of antique furniture, objets d'art, silver, pewter, glass, porcelain, musical instruments, pictures, brass and copper. Fortnightly general collective sales including bric-a-brac. Specialised sales at The Knutsford Auction Salerooms.*

Peter Wilson Fine Art Auctioneers
Victoria Gallery, Market St., Nantwich. CW5 5DG. SOFAA. NAVA. Est. 1955. Tel: 01270 623878; fax - 01270 610508; e-mail - auctions@peterwilson.co.uk website - www.peterwilson.co.uk *Five catalogued (illustrated in colour) two-day sales each year. Uncatalogued auctions every Thurs., shipping goods and household effects (500+ lots).*

Wright Manley Auctioneers
Beeston Castle Salerooms, Tarporley. CW6 9NZ. Est. 1861. Tel: 01829 262150; fax - 01829 261829; e-mail - wendymiller@wrightmanley.co.uk website - www. wrightmanley.co.uk *Fortnightly Victoriana and household sales and quarterly catalogued fine art and furniture sales.*

CORNWALL

Bonhams Cornwall
Cornubia Hall, Eastcliffe Rd., Par. PL24 2AQ. Tel: 01726 814047; fax - 01726 817979; e-mail - par@ bonhams.com website - www.bonhams.com *Monthly sales of antiques, Victorian and later furnishings, silver, jewellery, pictures and collectors' items.*

Jefferys
The Auction Rooms, 5 Fore St., Lostwithiel. PL22 0BP. RICS. Est. 1865. Tel: Office - 01208 872245; auction rooms - 012908 871947; fax - 01208 873260; e-mail - lostwithiel@jefferys.uk.com website - www.jefferys. uk.com *Fortnightly sales of antique furniture, ceramics, glass, jewellery, silver and plate, pictures, prints and collectors' items, on Wed. at 10 am. Viewing Tues. prior 10-1 and 2-5. Specialist sales at Royal Cornwall Showground on Sat. at 10 am., viewing from 9 am prior to sale.*

Lambrays
Polmorla Walk Galleries, The Platt, Wadebridge. PL27 7AE. Est. 1983. Tel: 0120 881 3593. e-mail - lambrays@freeuk.com *Fortnightly sales of antiques and pine. Quarterly auctions of antiques and objets d'art. Illustrated catalogues.*

W. H. Lane & Son
Jubilee House, Lower Queen St., Penzance. TR18 4DF. Est. 1934. Tel: 01736 361447; fax - 01736 350097; e-mail - info@whlane.co.uk website - www.invaluable. com/whlane *Six picture sales annually (specialists in the Newlyn and St. Ives Schools). Valuations for insurance, probate and family division.*

David Lay FRICS
The Penzance Auction House, Alverton, Penzance. TR18 4RE. Tel: 01736 361414; fax - 01736 360035; e-mail - david.lays@btopenworld.com *Regular sales of fine art, antiques, collectors' items, books and studio pottery. Three-weekly general household sales.*

Martyn Rowe Auctioneers and Valuers
Triplets Business Park, Poldice Valley, Nr Chacewater, Truro. TR16 5PZ. Est. 1990. Tel: 01209 822266; fax - 01209 821782; e-mail - mroweauctioneer@aol.com *Weekly on Thurs. at 10 am - Victorian, Edwardian and general sales. Viewing morning of sale and Wed. prior 2-6. Antique and picture sales every 6-8 weeks. Collectors and sporting sales - every 6-8 weeks. Quarterly sales of vintage and classic motorcycles, cars and automobilia. House, commercial, industrial and receivership sales on site or at auction centre.*

CUMBRIA

H. & H. King
Cumbria Auction Rooms, 12 Lowther St., Carlisle. CA3 8DA. Tel: 01228 525259. *Weekly sales of antiques, Victorian and later furnishings, collectors' items and*

Gilding's Ltd Auctioneers and Valuers
Roman Way, Market Harborough. LE16 7PQ. Tel: 01858 410414; fax - 01858 432956; e-mail - sales@gildings. co.uk website - www.gildings.co.uk *Quarterly fine art sales, weekly (excluding Bank Holidays) antiques and collectors' sales. Free valuations by appointment each Thurs.*

LINCOLNSHIRE

Batemans Auctioneers & Valuers
The Exchange Hall, Broad St., Stamford. PE9 1PX. Tel: 01780 766466; fax - 01780 765071; e-mail - info@ batemans-auctions.co.uk website - www.batemans-auctions.co.uk *1st Sat. monthly fine art, antiques and collectables auctions at 10.30am. Viewing Thurs. prior 10-5, Fri. 10-7 and from 9am on sale day. All auctions catalogued and on-line.*

DDM Auction Rooms
Old Court Rd., Brigg. DN20 8JJ. Tel: 01652 650172; fax - 01652 650085; e-mail - auctions@ddauctionrooms. co.uk website - www.ddauctionrooms.co.uk *Fine art & antiques auctions every seven weeks. General, household and shipping goods auctions fortnightly. Valuations for insurance, probate and divorce and free on for sale items. Valuation clinic Thurs. 9.30-12 noon.*

Thomas Mawer & Son Ltd
Dunston House, Portland St., Lincoln. LN5 7NN. Est. 1864. Tel: 01522 524984; fax - 01522 535600; e-mail - auctions@thosmawer.co.uk website - www.thosmawer. com *Sales on first Sat. every month at 10 am. Viewing Fri. prior 12-4 and sale morning from 8.30. Catalogue sales quarterly.*

Richardsons
Bourne Auction Rooms, Spalding Rd., Bourne. PE10 9LE. Tel: 01778 422686; fax - 01778 425726; e-mail - enquiries@richardsonsauctions.co.uk website - www. richardsonsauctions.co.uk *Antiques sales every month. Antique and modern sales every other Sat. Various specific sales periodically, eg silver, clocks, bygones, transport.*

Marilyn Swain
The Old Barracks, Sandon Rd., Grantham. NG31 9AS. SOFAA. Est. 1989. Tel: 01476 568861; fax - 01476 576100; e-mail - marilynswain@btconnect.com website - www.marilynswainauctions.co.uk *Bi-monthly antique, fine art and collectable sales. Fortnightly sales of Victorian and later furniture, general effects and collectables. Specialist toy and collectable sales. Valuations.*

MERSEYSIDE

Cato Crane & Co
6 Stanhope St., Liverpool. L8 5RF. Tel: 0151 709 5559; fax - 0151 707 2454; e-mail - johncrane@cato-crane.co.uk website - www.cato-crane.co.uk *Fine art and antiques sales 1st Mon. monthly. Collectors' sales weekly on Tues. and Thus.*

Kingsley Auctions Ltd.
3/4 The Quadrant, Hoylake. L47 2EE. Tel: 0151 632 5821; fax - 0151 632 5823. *Sales every Tues. at 10 am.,*

of antiques, fine art, general chattels. Viewing Sat. 9-12.30, Mon. 9-5 and Tues. 9-10.

Outhwaite and Litherland
Kingsway Galleries, Fontenoy St., Liverpool. L3 2BE. SOFAA. Est. 1907. Tel: 0151 236 6561; fax - 0151 236 1070; e-mail - auction@lots.uk.com website - www. lots.uk.com *Victorian, Edwardian and later furnishings - weekly Tues. Collectors cavalcade sale of general antiques and collectibles - monthly Tues. Fine art and antiques - quarterly Wed. Clocks, watches, scientific instruments - bi-annually Wed. Specialist sales of books, wines, stamps etc. periodically. Branch office at Southport and representatives covering the north-west.*

MIDDLESEX

Bainbridge's
The Auction Room, Ickenham Rd., Ruislip. HA4 7DL. Est. 1979. Tel: 01895 621991; fax - 01895 623622; website - www.thecollectorscompanion.co.uk *Monthly sales on Thurs. at 11 am. Viewing on sale day from 9.30 and day before 1-7.*

NORFOLK

James Beck Auctions
The Cornhall, Cattle Market St., Fakenham. NR21 9AW. Tel: 01328 851557; e-mail - jamesbeck@auctions18. fsnet.co.uk website - www.jamesbeckauctions.co.uk *Weekly sales of antique furniture and collectables every Thurs. at 11 am.*

Clowes Nash Auctions
Norwich Livestock & Commercial Centre, Hall Rd., Norwich. NR4 6EQ. Tel: 01603 504488. *Antiques and general furniture weekly sales.*

Ewings
Market Place, Reepham, Norwich. NR10 4JJ. Tel: 01603 870473; e-mail - mail@ewings.co.uk website - www. ewings.co.uk *Periodic sales of antiques and modern furniture and effects.*

Thos. Wm. Gaze and Son
Diss Auction Rooms, Roydon Rd., Diss. IP22 4LN. RICS. AFAF. Est. 1857. Tel: 01379 650306; fax - 01379 644313; e-mail - sales@dissauctionrooms.co.uk website - www.twgaze.com *Weekly Fri. auctions (over 2,000 lots) including antiques and collectables, Victorian pine and country furniture. Regular specialist sales including special antiques, decorative arts, modern design, toys and nostalgia, rural bygones, architectural salvage and statuary etc. Online catalogues.*

Horners Auctioneers
Acle Salerooms, Norwich Rd., Acle. NR13 3BY. Est. 1890. Tel: 01493 750225; fax - 01493 750506; e-mail - auction@horners.co.uk website - www.horners.co.uk *Special monthly (Sat.) auctions of antiques and collectables held at Acle. Viewing Fri. prior 10-8. Weekly Thurs. general sales. Details and catalogue on website.*

Keys - Aylsham Salerooms
Auctioneers & Valuers, 8 Market Place, Aylsham. NR11 6EH. Est. 1953. Tel: 01263 733195; fax - 01263 732140; e-mail - mail@aylshamsalerooms.co.uk website - www.

aylshamsalerooms.co.uk *Three-weekly sales of period, antique and Victorian furniture, silver, porcelain etc. Bimonthly picture sales - oils, watercolours and prints etc. Six book sales annually and regular collectors sales. Weekly sales of modern and secondhand furniture.*

NORTHAMPTONSHIRE

Goldsmiths
15 Market Place, Oundle. PE8 4BA. Est. 1964. Tel: 01832 272349. *Sales approximately bi-monthly.*

Wilfords Ltd
76 Midland Rd., Wellingborough. NN8 1NB. Tel: 01933 222760/222762. *Weekly antique and general sales on Thurs. from 9.30 am (1400 lots).*

NORTHUMBERLAND

Jack Dudgeon
76 Ravensdowne, Berwick-upon-Tweed. TD15 1DQ. Tel: 01289 332700; fax - 01289 332701; e-mail - jack@ jackdudgeon.co.uk website - www.jackdudgeon.co.uk *Antiques and fine art, collectables every two months on Mon. Viewing Wed., Thurs., Fri. and Sat. prior.*

NOTTINGHAMSHIRE

Arthur Johnson and Sons (Auctioneers)
The Nottingham Auction Centre, Meadow Lane, Nottingham. NG2 3GY. Tel: 0115 986 9128; fax - 0115 986 2139; e-mail - arthurjohnson@btconnect.com *Approximately 1,800 lots weekly on Sat. at 10 am. of antique and shipping furniture, silver, gold, porcelain, metalware and collectables.*

Mellors & Kirk Fine Art Auctioneers
Gregory St., Nottingham. NG7 2NL. RICS. Est. 1993. Tel: 0115 979 0000; fax - 0115 978 1111; e-mail - enquiries@ mellorsandkirk.com website - www.mellorsandkirk.com *Specialist sales of Beswick and collectable ceramics and specialist sales of medals, orders and decorations twice a year. Two-day fine art sales every six weeks of antique furniture, clocks, pictures, ceramics, Oriental works of art, books and ephemera, collectors' toys and dolls, coins and medals and other specialist items. Weekly general sales of 500-800 lots on Tues. 10.30 am. Viewing Sat. 9-12 and Mon. 9-5.*

Neales
192-194 Mansfield Rd., Nottingham. NG1 3HU. Tel: 0115 962 4141; fax - 0115 985 6890; e-mail - fineart @neales-auctions.com website - www.neales-auctions. com *Part of The Fine Art Auction Group. Bi-monthly specialist sales of paintings, drawings, prints and books; silver, jewellery, bijouterie and watches; European and Oriental ceramics and works of art, glass; furniture and decoration; clocks, barometers and mechanical music; metalwork, fabrics, needlework, carpets and rugs; collectors' toys and dolls; stamps, coins and medals, post and cigarette cards; autographs and collectors' items. Weekly collective sales (Mon.) of general antique and later furnishings, shipping goods and reproduction furnishings. Period and later ceramics, glass and decorative effects. Contents sales on the premises of town and country properties.*

Northgate Auction Rooms Ltd
17 Northgate, Newark. NG24 1EX. Tel: 01636 605905; fax - 01636 640051; e-mail - auctions@northgateauction roomsnewark.co.uk website - www.northgate auctionroomsnewark.co.uk *Monthly sales of antique and Victorian furniture, oil paintings, silver etc. Weekly sales of early 20th C and general household furniture.*

OXFORDSHIRE

Bonhams Auctioneers
39 Park End St., Oxford. OX1 1JD. Est. 1793. Tel: 01865 723524; fax - 01865 791064; e-mail - oxford@ bonhams.com website - www.bonhams.com *Regular county sales of antiques and general effects. Specialist sales of fine furniture, rugs, works of art, silver, jewellery, paintings and militaria throughout the year.*

Holloway's Ltd
49 Parsons St., Banbury. OX16 5NB. Tel: 01295 817777; fax - 01295 817701; e-mail - enquiries@holloways auctioneers.co.uk website - www.hollowaysauctioneers. co.uk *General or specialist sales on own premises every other week.*

Mallams Fine Art Auctioneers
Bocardo House, 24 St. Michael's St., Oxford. OX1 2EB. SOFAA. Est. 1788. Tel: 01865 241358; fax - 01865 725483; e-mail - oxford@mallams.co.uk website - www. mallams.co.uk/fineart *Frequent sales of furniture, silver, paintings and works of art. House sales arranged on the premises.*

Simmons and Sons
32 Bell St., Henley-on-Thames. RG9 2BH. Est. 1802. Tel: 01491 571111; fax - 01491 579833; website - www. simmonsandsons.com *Eight antique and eight general sales per year held at The Saleroom Watcombe Manor, Ingham Lane, Watlington, Oxon. Sales start 10.30 am. Viewing Sat. previous 9.30-12.30, Mon. prior 2-7, Tues. prior 10-6 and morning of sale.*

RUTLAND

Tennants Auctioneers
Mill House, South St. Oakham. LE15 6BG. Est. 1977. Tel: 01572 724666; fax - 01572 724422; e-mail - oakham @tennants-ltd.co.uk *Weekly sales.*

SHROPSHIRE

Halls Fine Art
Welsh Bridge Salerooms, 1 Frankwell, Shrewsbury. SY3 8LA. Tel: 01743 231212; fax - 01743 246191; e-mail - welshbridge@hallsestateagents.co.uk *Weekly Fri. household and Victoriana sales. Monthly catalogued antique sales.*

Perry and Phillips
Auction Rooms, Old Mill Antique Centre, Mill St., Bridgnorth. WV15 5AG. Est. 1853. Tel: 01746 762248; fax - 01746 768994; e-mail - denisridgway@hotmail. com website - www.oldmill.com *Monthly Tues. antiques and collectables sales.*

Walker Barnett and Hill
Cosford Auction Rooms, Long Lane, Cosford. TF11 8PJ.

Tel: 01902 375555; fax - 01902 375556; website - www.walker-barnett-hill.co.uk *Monthly sales of Victoriana, reproduction, shipping, modern furniture and effects on Tues. 10.30. Fine art and antiques sales every 6-8 weeks.*

SOMERSET

Adam Auctions
28 Adam St., Burnham-on-Sea. TA8 1PQ. Est. 1973. Tel: 01278 783193/793709. *Monthly sales of general antiques usually held on Wed. Telephone for details.*

Aldridges of Bath
Newark House, 26-45 Cheltenham St., Bath. BA2 3EX. Est. 1976. Tel: 01225 462830; fax - 01225 311319. *Fortnightly Tues. sales, broken down into specialist categories:- antique furniture to include clocks and Oriental carpets; silver and porcelain, glass and metalware; paintings and prints; collector's sales; Victorian and general furniture. Viewing Sat. 9-12 and Mon. 9-6. Catalogues available upon annual subscription.*

Bonhams
1 Old King St., Bath. BA1 2JT. Est. 1793. Tel: 01225 788988; fax - 01225 446675; e-mail - bath@bonhams.com website - www.bonhams.com/bath *Regular county sales including antiques, furniture and decorative objects; Specialist sales of fine antiques and furniture, clocks, rugs, ceramics including contemporary ceramics, books, maps and atlases, paintings, silver and jewellery.*

Clevedon Salerooms
The Auction Centre, Kenn Rd., Kenn, Clevedon. BS21 6TT. Est. 1885. Tel: 01934 830111; fax - 01934 832538; e-mail - info@clevedon-salerooms.com website - www.clevedon-salerooms.com *Quarterly auctions of antique furniture, fine art and collectors' items. Fortnightly sales of Victorian, Edwardian and general furniture and effects. Occasional specialist sales and sales held on vendors' property. Valuations.*

Cooper & Tanner Chartered Surveyors
The Agricultural Centre, Standerwick, Frome. BA11 2QB. Est. 1890. Tel: 01373 831010. *Weekly sales of antiques and general household chattels on Wed. at 10.30 am. Viewing morning of sale. Haulage service.*

Dreweatt Neate Wells Auction Rooms
66/68 Southover, Wells. BA5 1UH. Tel: 01749 678094; e-mail - bristol@dnfa.com website - www.dfna.com *Open Mon.-Fri. 9-5. Monthly sales of antique and modern furniture and effects. Catalogues, fully illustrated, available at saleroom. Commission 15% and 10% plus VAT. Valuations. Part of The Fine Art Auction Group.*

Greenslade Taylor Hunt Fine Art
Magdalene House, Church Square, Taunton. TA1 1SB. Tel: 01823 332525; fax - 01823 353120; e-mail - fine.art@gth.net website - www.gth.net *Last Thurs.monthly sales of antique furniture, ceramics, glass, metalwork, paintings and prints. Specialist sales of silver and jewellery; collectors' items, printed books, clocks and watches, sporting. Fortnightly Thurs. sales of antique and shipping furniture, china, glass and effects.*

Hosegood Ford
3 Fore St., Williton, Taunton. TA4 4PX. Tel: 01984 632040; fax - 01984 633898; e-mail - mail@exmoorproperties.co.uk *Sales approximately every two months.*

Lawrence Fine Art Auctioneers Ltd
South St., Crewkerne. TA18 8AB. SOFAA. RICS. ARVA. Tel: 01460 73041; fax - 01460 270799; e-mail - enquiries@lawrences.co.uk website - www.lawrences.co.uk *Specialist auctioneers and valuers. Quarterly sales of antiques and fine art. General sales every Wed. (uncatalogued). collectors' section first Wed. monthly. Bi-annual book sales (Jan. and July); bi-annual militaria sales (April and Oct). Catalogue on website.*

The London Cigarette Card Co. Ltd
Sutton Rd., Somerton. TA11 6QP. Est. 1927. Tel: 01458 273452; fax - 01458 273515; e-mail - cards@londoncigcard.co.uk website - www.londoncigcard.co.uk *Suppliers of thousands of different series of cigarette and trade cards and special albums. Publishers of catalogues, reference books and monthly magazine. Regular auctions in London and Somerset. S.A.E. for details. Showroom in West St. open Mon-Sat. or mail order.*

STAFFORDSHIRE

John German
1 Lichfield St., Burton-on-Trent. DE14 3QZ. Tel: 01283 512244; fax - 01283 517896; e-mail - burton@johngerman.co.uk website - www.johngerman.co.uk *Occasional sales of major house contents.*

Potteries Specialist Auctions
271 Waterloo Rd., Cobridge, Stoke-on-Trent. ST6 3HR. Tel: 01782 286622; fax - 01782 201518; e-mail - enquiries@potteriesauctions.com website - www.potteriesauctions.com *Specialist auctions every month, usually Wed. at 11 am. Viewing Tues. prior 10-4.*

Louis Taylor Fine Art Auctioneers
Britannia House, 10 Town Rd., Hanley, Stoke-on-Trent. ST1 2QG. RICS. Est. 1877. Tel: 01782 214111; fax - 01782 215283. *Quarterly fine art sales including furniture, pictures, pottery, porcelain, silver and works of art. Specialist Royal Doulton and Beswick auctions. General Victoriana auctions held every two weeks. Fine art auctions through www.auction-net.co.uk and antiquestradegazette.com*

Wintertons Fine Arts
Uttoxeter Auction Rooms, 8 Short St., Uttoxeter. ST14 7LH. Est. 1864. Tel: 01889 564385; fax - same. *Monthly sales of Victorian and general household furniture and effects.*

Wintertons Fine Arts
Lichfield Auction Centre, Fradley Park, Fradley, Lichfield. WS13 8NF. SOFAA. RICS. Est. 1864. Tel: 01543 263256; fax - 01543 415348; e-mail - enquiries@wintertons.co.uk website - www.wintertons.co.uk *Bi-monthly sales of antiques and fine art and sales of Victorian and general furniture every two weeks. Quarterly sales jewellery and antiques at the Agricultural Business Centre, Bakewell; monthly sales of*

Victorian and general antiques and quarterly toy sales at Uttoxeter (01889 562811). Fine arts manager, Charles Hanson MRICS.

SUFFOLK

Abbotts Auction Rooms
Campsea Ashe, Woodbridge. IP13 0PS. Tel: 01728 746323; fax - 01728 748173; e-mail - info@abbotts auctionrooms.co.uk website - www.abbottsauction rooms.co.uk *Extensive calendar of fine art and antique auctions held on Wed. Sales calendar and catalogues available. Weekly sales of Victoriana & household furniture held on Mon. Viewing Sat. 9-11.*

Boardman - Fine Art Auctioneers
PO Box 99, Haverhill. CB9 7YS. Tel: 01440 730414. *Large occasional sales held specialising in selected fine furniture (particularly oak), clocks, paintings and early metalware.*

Bonhams Auctioneers
32 Boss Hall Rd., Ipswich. IP1 5DJ. Tel: 01473 740494; e-mail - ipswich@bonhams.com website - www. bonhams.com *Five two-day specialist sales annually at Bury St. Edmunds. Eight mixed sales in Ipswich.*

Diamond Mills and Co. Fine Art Auctioneers
117 Hamilton Rd., Felixstowe. IP11 7BL. Tel: 01394 282281 (4 lines). Ipswich office - 01473 218600. *Periodic fine art sales. Monthly general sales. Auctions at The Orwell Hall, Orwell Rd., Felixstowe.*

Durrant's
The Auction Rooms, Gresham Rd., Beccles. NR34 9QN. Est. 1854. Tel: 01502 713490; e-mail - infobeccles@ durrants.com website - www.durrants.com *Antique and general furniture auctions every Fri; fine antiques sales every six weeks.*

Dyson & Son
The Auction Room, Church St., Clare. CO10 8PD. Est. 1978. Tel: 01787 277993; fax - 01787 277996; e-mail - info@dyson-auctioneers.co.uk website - www.dyson-auctioneers.co.uk *Sales of antiques and chattels every three weeks on Sat. at 11 am. Viewing Fri. 9-9, Sat. from 9 am.*

Lacy Scott and Knight Fine Art & Furniture
10 Risbygate St., Bury St. Edmunds. IP33 3AA. SOFAA. Est. 1868. Tel: 01284 748600; fax - 01284 748620; e-mail - fineart@lsk.co.uk website - www.lsk.co.uk *Quarterly sales of fine art including antique and decorative furniture, silver, pictures, ceramics etc. on behalf of executors and private vendors. Regular (every three weeks) sales of Victoriana and general household contents. Also quarterly sales of live steam models, scale models, diecast and tinplate toys.*

Neal Sons and Fletcher
26 Church St., Woodbridge. IP12 1DP. Tel: 01394 382263; fax - 01394 383030; e-mail - enquiries@ nsf.co.uk website - www.nsf.co.uk *Two special mixed antiques sales annually. Individual specialised sales and complete house contents sales as required. Household furniture sales monthly on Wed.*

Olivers
The Saleroom, Burkitts Lane, Sudbury. CO10 1HB.

SOFAA. Est. 1766. Tel: 01787 880305; fax - 01787 883107; e-mail - oliversauctions@btconnect.com *Fortnightly sales of Victorian and later furniture and household effects. Regular sales of antiques and works of art. Enquiries to James Fletcher FRICS, ASFAV.*

SURREY

Clarke Gammon Wellers
The Guildford Auction Rooms, Bedford Rd., Guildford. GU1 4SJ. Est. 1919. Tel: 01483 880915; fax - 01483 880918; website - www.invaluable.com/clarkegammon

Croydon Auction Rooms (Rosan and Co.) (incorporating E. Reeves Auctions)
145/151 London Rd., Croydon. CR0 2RG. Tel: 020 8688 1123. *Fortnightly Sat. collective sales at 10 am. Viewing Fri. prior.*

Ewbank Auctioneers
Burnt Common Auction Rooms, London Rd., Send, Woking. GU23 7LN. SOFAA. RICS. Est. 1990. Tel: 01483 223101; fax - 01483 222171; e-mail - antiques@ ewbankauctions.co.uk website - www.ewbank auctions.co.uk *Quarterly antique and fine art sales. General sales every 2-3 weeks.*

Hamptons International Auctioneers & Valuers
Baverstock House, 93 High St., Godalming. GU7 1AL. Tel: 01483 423567; fax - 01483 426392; e-mail - fineartauctions@hamptons-int.com website - www. hamptonsauctioneers.com *Four selected fine art sales a year supported by fortnightly Sat. sales.*

Kew Auctions
The Old Railway Parcels Depot, Kew Rd., Richmond. TW9 2NA. Est. 1992. Tel: 020 8948 6677; fax - 020 8948 2021. *Auctioneers, valuers and consultants. Sales every Thurs. at 6 pm of fine antique and modern furniture, jewellery, rugs, glass, silver, porcelain, paintings. Viewing Mon.-Fri. 10-8, Sat. 10-4, Sun. 11-4.*

Lawrences' - Auctioneers Limited
Norfolk House, 80 High St., Bletchingley. RH1 4PA. Tel: 01883 743323; fax - 01883 744578; e-mail - enquiries @lawrencesbletchingley.co.uk website - www.lawrences bletchingley.co.uk *Six-weekly antique and reproduction furniture and effects.*

P.F. Windibank Auctioneers
The Dorking Halls, Reigate Rd., Dorking. RH4 1SG. Est. 1945. Tel: 01306 884556/876280; fax - 01306 884669; e-mail - sjw@windibank.co.uk website - www.windibank. co.uk *Antique auctions held every 4-5 weeks on Sat. at 10.30 am. Viewing Thurs. evening prior 5-9, Fri. prior 9-5 and morning of sale 8.15-10.15. Catalogues available 1 week before. 10% buyers premium.*

EAST SUSSEX

Burstow and Hewett
Abbey Auction Galleries and Granary Sale Rooms, Battle. TN33 0AT. Tel: 01424 772374; website - www. burstowandhewett.co.uk *Monthly sales of antique furniture, silver, jewellery, porcelain, brass, rugs etc. at the Abbey Auction Galleries. Also monthly evening sales of fine oil paintings, watercolours, prints, and*

engravings. At the Granary Sale Rooms - monthly sales of furniture, china, silver, brass, etc.

Dreweatt Neate
46-50 South St., Eastbourne. BN21 4XB. Tel: 01323 410419; fax - 01323 416450; e-mail - eastbourne@dnfa.com website - www.dnfa.com *Open Mon.-Fri. 9-5. Fortnightly sales of general antiques and effects. Catalogues, fully illustrated, available by post or on website. Commission 15% and 10% plus VAT. Valuations. Part of The Fine Art Auction Group.*

Eastbourne Auction Rooms
Auction House, Finmere Rd., Eastbourne. BN22 8QL. Tel: 01323 431444; fax - 01323 417638; e-mail - enquiries@eastbourneauction.com website - www.eastbourneauction.com *Sales held fortnightly, usually Fri. and Sat. at 10 am.*

Gorringes inc. Julian Dawson
Terminus Rd., Bexhill-on-Sea. TN39 3LR. Tel: 01424 212994; fax - 01424 224035; e-mail - bexhill@gorringes.co.uk website - www.gorringes.co.uk *Fine art and antique sales held every six weeks.*

Gorringes inc. Julian Dawson
15 North St., Lewes. BN7 2PD. Tel: 01273 472503; fax - 01273 479559; e-mail - clientservices@gorringes.co.uk website - www.gorringes.co.uk *Fine art and antique sales held every six weeks.*

Gorringes inc. Julian Dawson
Garden St., Lewes. BN7 1XE. Tel: 01273 478221; fax - 01273 487369; website - www.gorringes.co.uk *General sales held weekly on Mon. at 10.30 am.*

Raymond P. Inman
The Auction Galleries, 98a Coleridge St. Hove. BN3 5AA. Est. 1929. Tel: 01273 774777; fax - 01273 735660; e-mail - r.p.inman@talk21.com website - www.invaluable.com/raymondinman *Monthly sales of antiques, furniture, china, glass, pictures, silver, jewellery, collectables, etc.*

Scarborough Perry Fine Arts
Hove Auction Room, Hove St., Hove. BN3 2GL. Est. 1896. Tel: 01273 735266; fax - 01273 723813; e-mail - enquiries@scarboroughperry.co.uk website - www.scarboroughperry.co.uk *Monthly sales of fine art including antique furniture, pictures, silver, Oriental carpets and rugs and ornamental items. Specialised sales of primitive art, coins, books and jewellery.*

Wallis and Wallis
West Street Auction Galleries, Lewes. BN7 2NJ. Est. 1928. Tel: 01273 480208; fax - 01273 476562; e-mail - auctions@wallisandwallis.co.uk website - www.wallisandwallis.co.uk *Nine annual sales of arms and armour, militaria and medals. Two connoisseur collectors' sales spring and autumn. Specimen catalogue £3.50. Current catalogues £8.50. Die-cast and tin plate toys and models - catalogue £6.50. Commission bids (without charge) accepted. Valuations.*

WEST SUSSEX

Henry Adams Fine Art Auctioneers
Baffins Hall, Baffins Lane, Chichester. PO19 1UA.

SOFAA. ARVA. Tel: 01243 532223; fax - 01243 532299; e-mail - enquiries@henryadamsfineart.co.uk website - www.henryadamsfineart.co.uk *Monthly catalogue specialist sales, usually on Wed. at 10.30. Viewing Sat. morning, Mon. and Tues. prior. Valuations for sales, insurance and probate.*

John Bellman Ltd
New Pound, Wisborough Green, Billingshurst. RH14 0AZ. Tel: 01403 700858; fax - 01403 700059; e-mail - enquiries@bellmans.co.uk website - www.bellmans.co.uk *Three-day sale once a month; Wed. pm ceramics and Oriental; Thurs. am furniture; Thurs. pm silver, vertu, jewellery, clocks; Fri. am collectors' items, works of art, paintings, textiles. Viewing Sat. 9-12, Mon. 9-4, Tues. 9-7, Wed. 9-1. Book sales three times a year.*

Denham's
The Auction Galleries, Warnham, Horsham. RH12 3RZ. Est. 1884. Tel: 01403 255699/253837; fax - 01403 253837; e-mail - enquiries@denhams.com website - www.denhams.com *Monthly sales of antique furniture, clocks, scientific instruments, metalware, collectors' items, ceramics, glassware, paintings, silver and jewellery.*

King & Chasemore
Midhurst Auction Rooms, West St., Midhurst. GU29 9NQ. Est. 1840. Tel: 01730 812456; fax - 01730 814514. *General sales of antique and modern furniture and effects every six weeks.*

Stride and Son
Southdown House, St. John's St., Chichester. PO19 1XQ. Est. 1890. Tel: 01243 780207; fax - 01243 786713; e-mail - enquiries@stridesauctions.co.uk website - www.stridesauctions.co.uk *Sales last Fri. monthly - antiques and general; periodic book and document sales.*

Worthing Auction Galleries
Fleet House, Teville Gate, Worthing. BN11 1UA. Tel: 01903 205565. *Monthly sales of antique, 20th C and reproduction furniture, ceramics, glass, silver, silver plate, jewellery, pictures and collectables. View Sat. prior 9-12, Fri. and Mon. prior 9-1 and 2-4. Sale Tues. and Wed. both days commencing at 10 am.*

TYNE AND WEAR

Anderson and Garland
Anderson House, Crispin Court, Newbiggin Lane, Westerhope. NE5 1BF. Est. 1840. Tel: 0191 430 3000; fax - 0191 430 3001; e-mail - info@andersonandgarland.com website - www.andersonandgarland.com *Regular sales of paintings, prints, antique furniture, silver and collectors' items. Fortnightly sales of Victorian and later furnishing and collectables.*

Boldon Auction Galleries
24a Front St., East Boldon. NE36 0SJ. Est. 1981. Tel: 0191 537 2630; fax - 0191 536 3875; e-mail - boldon@btconnect.com website - www.boldonauctions.co.uk *Quarterly antique auctions.*

Thomas N. Miller Auctioneers
Algernon Rd., Byker, Newcastle-upon-Tyne. NE6 2UN. Est. 1902. Tel: 0191 265 8080; fax - 0191 265 5050;

e-mail - info@millersauctioneers.co.uk website - www. millersauctioneers.co.uk *China and glass auctions every Tues. at 10 am. Antique auctions every Wed. at 10 am.*

WARWICKSHIRE

Bigwood Auctioneers Ltd
The Old School, Tiddington, Stratford-upon-Avon. CV37 7AW. SOFAA. Est. 1974. Tel: 01789 269415; fax - 01789 294168; e-mail - enquiries@bigwood auctioneers.co.uk website - www.bigwoodauctioneers. co.uk and www.bigwood.uk.com *Sales Friday weekly of general furnishings and house contents. Monthly antiques and selected collectables. Quarterly fine furniture, paintings and works of art. Also special interest sales - sporting items and taxidermy, toys and wine.*

Henley-in-Arden Auction Sales Ltd
The Estate Office, Warwick Rd., Henley-in-Arden. B95 5BH. Tel: 01564 792154; fax - 01564 794916. *Sales of antique and modern furniture and effects, second and fourth Sat. each month.*

Locke & England
18 Guy St., Leamington Spa. CV32 4RT. Est. 1834. Tel: 01926 889100; e-mail - info@leauction.co.uk website - www.leauction.co.uk *Regular sales of antique furniture and effects, collectors' items and general household items.*

Warwick and Warwick Ltd
Chalon House, Scar Bank, Millers Rd., Warwick. CV34 5DB. Est. 1958. Tel: 01926 499031; fax - 01926 491906; e-mail - info@warwickandwarwick.com website - www. warwickandwarwick.com *Philatelic auctioneers and private treaty specialists. Stamp auctions held monthly. Postcards, cigarette cards, autographs, ephemera, medals, militaria, coins, banknotes, sports memorabilia, and other collectables sold by auction periodically.*

WEST MIDLANDS

Biddle & Webb
Ladywood Middleway, Birmingham. B16 0PP. Tel: 0121 455 8042; e-mail - bids@biddleandwebb.com website - www.biddleandwebb.com *Fine art and antiques sales first Tues. and Fri. each month; silver, jewellery, medals, coins, watches first Fri. each month; toys, dolls, model railways and juvenilia sales on Fri. alternate months. All sales commence at 11am. Collectors' sales Sat. am of Victorian and later furnishings, glassware, etc; periodic decorative art and 20th C ceramic sales.*

Bonhams
The Old House, Station Rd., Knowle, Solihull. B93 0HT. Tel: 01564 776151; fax - 01564 778069; e-mail - knowle @bonhams.com website - www.bonhams.com *Specialist sales weekly of furniture, paintings, works of art, clocks, carpets, silver and jewellery, ceramics, 19th-20th C decorative arts, collectors' items, toys, cameras, mechanical music, textiles and books. Valuation day every Fri. 10-4. Subscription available. Free sales programmes on request.*

Fellows and Sons
Augusta House, 19 Augusta St., Hockley, Birmingham.

B18 6JA. BJA. Est. 1876. Tel: 0121 212 2131; fax - 0121 212 1249; e-mail - info@fellows.co.uk website - www. fellows.co.uk *Auctioneers and valuers of jewels, silver, fine art.*

Weller and Dufty Ltd
141 Bromsgrove St., Birmingham. B5 6RQ. Tel: 0121 692 1414; fax - 0121 622 5605; e-mail - sales@ welleranddufty.co.uk website - www.welleranddufty. co.uk *Ten sales annually, approximately every five weeks, of antique and modern firearms, edged weapons, militaria etc. Periodic sales of specialist items - military vehicles and associated military equipment. Six fine art and antiques sales per year Postal bids accepted. Illustrated catalogue available.*

WILTSHIRE

Gardiner Houlgate
9 Leafield Way, Corsham SN13 9SW. Tel: 01225 812912; fax - 01225 811777; e-mail - auctions@ gardiner-houlgate.co.uk *Regular sales of antique furniture, works of art, Clarice Cliff and decorative arts. Frequent sales of Victorian and later furnishings. Fortnightly jewellery sales, quarterly musical instrument sales, specialist painting and clocks and watches sales. Valuations.*

May and Son
Units 1, 3 and 4 Delta Works, Salisbury Rd., Shipton Bellinger. SP9 7UN. Est. 1925. Tel: 01980 846000; fax - 01980 846600; on viewing and auction day - 07710 001660; e-mail - office@mayandson.com website - www.mayandson.com *Monthly sales on 3rd Wed. of antique furniture and collectables at 10. (Lots from private sources only). Also general and specialist sales. Viewing previous day 8.30-6, and morning of sale from 8.30 am. Buyers premium 12% + VAT.*

Woolley and Wallis
Salisbury Salerooms Ltd 51-61 Castle St., Salisbury. SP1 3SU. SOFAA. RICS. Est. 1884. Tel: 01722 424500; fax - 01722 424508; e-mail - enquiries@woolleyand wallis.co.uk website - www.woolleyandwallis.co.uk *Specialist sales of antique furniture, ceramics, pictures, silver, jewellery and 20th C decorative arts. Fortnightly general sales. Written valuations for probate and insurance.*

WORCESTERSHIRE

Andrew Grant Fine Art
St Mark's House, St Mark's Court, Cherry Orchard, Worcester. WR5 3DJ. RICS. Tel: 01905 357547; fax - 01905 763942; e-mail - fineart@andrew-grant.co.uk website - www.andrew-grant.co.uk *Victoriana and collectables sales held monthly; fine art and antique sales quarterly; transport collectables, 3 sales annually. Viewing day before sale.*

Griffiths & Charles
57 Foregate St., Worcester. WR1 1DZ. Est. 1870. Tel: 01905 720160; e-mail - info@griffiths-charles.co.uk website - www.griffiths-charles.co.uk *General auctioneers.*

Philip Laney - FRICS - Fine Art
Malvern Auction Centre, Portland Rd., off Victoria Rd.,

Malvern. WR14 2TA. Tel: 01684 893933; e-mail - philiplaney@aol.com website - www.invaluable.com/philiplaney *Monthly sales of antiques and collectors' items.*

Phipps and Pritchard
31 Worcester St., Kidderminster. DY10 1EQ. Est. 1848. Tel: 01562 822244; fax - 01562 825401; website - www.phippsandpritchard.co.uk *Regular eight-weekly sales of antique furniture, clocks and watches, watercolours and oil paintings, copper, brass, glass, china and porcelain, stamps and coins, silver. Private house sales also conducted.*

Philip Serrell - Auctioneers & Valuers
The Malvern Sale Room, Barnards Green Rd., Malvern. WR14 3LW. Est. 1996. Tel: 01684 892314; fax - 01684 569832; e-mail - serrell.auctions@virgin.net website - www.serrell.com *Bi-monthly catalogued antique and fine art auctions. Fortnightly general sales. Specialist on the premises sales. Free sales estimates.*

EAST YORKSHIRE

Gilbert Baitson
The Edwardian Auction Galleries, Wiltshire Rd, Hull. HU4 6PG. Est. 1935. Tel: 01482 500500; after hours - 01482 645241; fax - 01482 500501; e-mail - info@gilbert-baitson.co.uk website - www.gilbert-baitson.co.uk *Sales of antique and modern furnishings every sixth Wed. at 10.30 am. Viewing day prior until 7 pm.*

Dee Atkinson & Harrison - Agricultural and Fine Arts
The Exchange Saleroom, Driffield. YO25 6LD. Tel: 01377 253151; fax - 01377 241041; e-mail - info@dahauctions.com website - www.dahauctions.com *Regular bi-monthly sales of antiques, Victorian and Edwardian furniture, paintings, silver, jewellery etc. Viewing two days prior. Fortnightly general sales. Bi-annual collectors' toys and sporting sales.*

Haller Evans - Auctioneers and Valuers
1 Parliament St., Hull. HU1 2AR. Est. 1889. Tel: 01482 323033; fax - 01482 211954; e-mail - hallerevans@hull24.com website - www.hallerevans.com *Regular auctions of antiques and modern furniture and effects.*

Spencers Auctions
The Imperial and Repository Salerooms, Olivers Lane, Bridlington. YO15 2AS. Est. 1892. Tel: 01262 676724; fax - 01262 673617. *General auctions every Thurs. Regular sales of antiques and fine art.*

NORTH YORKSHIRE

Boulton and Cooper Ltd
St. Michaels House, Market Place, Malton. YO17 0LR. SOFAA. Tel: 01653 696151; e-mail - antiques@boultonandcooper.com website - www.boultonandcooper.com *Alternating monthly antique sales at Malton and York. Fortnightly general sales at Pickering.*

David Duggleby Fine Art Auctioneers
The Paddock Salerooms, Whitby. YO21 3DB. SOFAA. Tel: 01947 820033; fax - 01947 825680; e-mail - auctions@davidduggleby.com website - www.david

duggleby.com *Special picture sales, Staithes Group, marine and Yorkshire artists. Annual nautical sales. 12.5% buyers premium excluding VAT.*

David Duggleby Fine Art Auctioneers
The Vine Street Salerooms, Scarborough. YO11 1XN. SOFAA. Tel: 01723 507111; fax - 01723 507222; e-mail - auctions@davidduggleby.com website - www.davidduggleby.com *Special picture sales - Staithes group, marine and Yorkshire artists. Annual nautical sale. Buyers premium 12.5% excluding VAT.*

Hutchinson-Scott
The Grange, Marton-le-Moor, Ripon. HG4 5AT. Est. 1976. Tel: 01423 326236; fax - 01423 324264; e-mail - hutchinson-scott@totalise.co.uk *Periodic general sales plus two or three catalogue sales annually. Specialist in fine antiques and works of art.*

Morphets of Harrogate
6 Albert St., Harrogate. HG1 1JL. Est. 1895. Tel: 01423 530030; fax - 01423 500717; website - www.morphets.co.uk *Sales of antiques and works of art, interspersed with regular sales of general furniture and effects. Catalogue subscription scheme.*

Scarthingwell Auction Centre
Scarthingwell, Tadcaster. LS24 9PG. Tel: 01937 557955; fax - same; e-mail - scarthingwell@lineone.net website - www.scarthingwellauctions.co.uk *Evening antique and general sales held twice-monthly on Mon. and Tues. evenings, approx 1,000 lots. Viewing on prior Sun. 12-5 and sale days Mon. from 2 pm and Tues. from 4 pm.*

Summersgill Auctioneers
8 Front St., Acomb, York. YO24 3BZ. Est. 1967. Tel: 01904 791131; e-mail - summersgills@supanet.com *Auctions of antiques and collectors' items.*

Tennants Auctioneers
The Auction Centre, Leyburn. DL8 5SG. Tel: 01969 623780; fax - 01969 624281. e-mail - enquiry@tennants-ltd.co.uk website - www.tennants.co.uk *Minimum of three 1000 lot non-catalogue sales each month of antiques and later house contents, mainly on Sat. at 9.30 am. Viewing Fri. 9-7. Three fine art sales each year. Catalogue subscription service. Specialist sales of collectors' items, books, etc. Offices at 34 Montpellier Parade, Harrogate. Tel : 01423 531661; fax - 01423 530990; e-mail - harrogate@tennants-ltd.co.uk and Mill House, South St., Oakham, Rutland. LE15 6BG. Tel: 01572 724666; fax - 01572 724422; e-mail - oakham@tennants-ltd.co.uk*

SOUTH YORKSHIRE

Paul Beighton Auctioneers Ltd
Woodhouse Green, Thurcroft, Rotherham. S66 9AQ. Est. 1982. Tel: 01709 700005; website - www.paulbeightonauctioneers.co.uk *Antique furniture and fine art sales every two weeks on Sun. from 11 am. Viewing Fri. 11-4 and sale day from 9 am. Quarterly specialist sales of antique furniture and fine art.*

A.E. Dowse and Son
Cornwall Galleries, Scotland St., Sheffield. S3 7DE. Est. 1915. Tel: 0114 2725858; fax - 0114 2490550; e-mail -

aedowse@talk21.com website - www.aedowseand son.com *Monthly Sat. sales of antiques. Quarterly fine art and antique sales. Quarterly sales of diecast, tin plate and collectors' toys. Monthly sales of modern furniture and shipping goods.*

Wilkinson's Auctioneers Ltd
28 Netherhall Rd. Doncaster. DN1 2PW. Est. 1997. Tel: 01302 814884; fax - 01302 814883; e-mail - sid@ wilkinsons-auctioneers.co.uk website - www.wilkinsons-auctioneers.co.uk *Catalogue sales every two months, alternating between fine furniture, paintings, bronzes and effects and period oak, country furniture and carvings.*

WEST YORKSHIRE

Bonhams Auctioneers
Hepper House, 17a East Parade, Leeds. LS1 2BH. Tel: 0113 2448011; fax - 0113 2429875; e-mail - leeds@ bonhams.com website - www.bonhams.com *Quarterly fine sales of pictures, silver and jewellery, ceramics and furniture. Monthly general sales. Sales calendars sent on request.*

De Rome
12 New John St., Westgate, Bradford. BD1 2QY. Tel: 01274 734116/9; e-mail - deromes2000@yahoo.com *Regular sales.*

Andrew Hartley Fine Arts
Victoria Hall Salerooms, Little Lane, Ilkley. LS29 8EA. Est. 1906. Tel: 01943 816363; fax- 01943 817610; e-mail - info@andrewhartleyfinearts.co.uk website - www. andrewhartleyfinearts.co.uk *Fifty sales annually including six good antique and fine art and other specialist sales.*

John H. Raby & Son
Salem Auction Rooms, 21 St. Mary's Rd., Bradford. BD8 7QL. Tel: 01274 491121; e-mail - jhraby@ tiscali.co.uk *Sales of antique furniture and pictures every 4-6 weeks, shipping goods and collectables every week.*

CHANNEL ISLANDS

Bonhams Auctioneers
Westaway Chambers, Don St., St. Helier, Jersey. JE2 4TR. Tel: 01534 722441; fax - 01534 759354; website - www.bonhams.com *Regular antique and specialised auctions, general sales on Wed.*

SCOTLAND

Auction Rooms
Castle Laurie, Bankside, Falkirk. FK2 7XF. Tel: 01324 623000; fax - 01324 630343; e-mail - robert@ auctionroomsfalkirk.co.uk website - www.auctionrooms falkirk.co.uk *Weekly, Wed., sales at 6 pm. Mixed sale of antique, general household and new furniture. Specialised sales are held, details available on website. Viewing Tues. 8-8, Wed. 8-6.*

Bonhams Scotland
65 George St., Edinburgh, Midlothian. EH2 2JL. Tel: 0131 225 2266; e-mail - edinburgh@bonhams.com website - www.bonhams.com *Regular specialist sales of*

oils and watercolours, furniture, clocks, rugs and works of art, silver and jewellery, Oriental and European ceramics and books. Decorative arts, post war, garden and dolls and textiles sales are also held. Monthly general sales. Annual Scottish Sale, held during the Edinburgh Festival, includes important Scottish furniture, paintings, silver, books and sporting memorabilia.

Frasers (Auctioneers)
8a Harbour Rd., Inverness. IV1 1SY. Tel: 01463 232395; fax - 01463 233634. *Weekly sales on Wed. at 6 pm.*

Leslie and Leslie
Haddington, East Lothian. EH41 3JJ. Est. 1920. Tel: 01620 822241; fax - same. *Antique auctions every three months.*

Lindsay Burns & Co
6 King St., Perth. PH2 8JA. Tel: 01738 633888; fax - 01738 441322; e-mail - lindsayburns@btconnect.com website - www.lburns.co.uk *General sales bi-weekly on Thurs. at 10.30 am., viewing day prior 9-5. Quarterly fine art sales (illustrated colour catalogues available on website) held on Tues. Viewing previous Sat. 9-1 and Mon. 9-6.*

Loves Auction Rooms
52-54 Canal St., Perth. PH2 8LF. SOFAA. Est. 1869. Tel: 01738 633337; fax - 01738 629830; e-mail - enquiries @lovesauctions.co.uk website - www.lovesauctions. co.uk *Regular sales of antique and decorative furniture, jewellery, silver and plate, ceramics, works of art, metalware, glass, pictures, clocks, mirrors, pianos, Eastern carpets and rugs, garden furniture, architectural items. Weekly Fri. sales of Victoriana and household effects at 10.30 am. Specialist sales of books and collectors' items. Valuations.*

Lyon & Turnbull
33 Broughton Place, Edinburgh. EH1 3RR. SOFAA. Est. 1826. Tel: 0131 557 8844; fax - 0131 557 8668; e-mail - info@lyonandturnbull.com website - www.lyonand turnbull.com *Open Mon.-Fri. 8.30-5.30. Twenty four sales annually including pictures, books, decorative arts, furniture and works of art, jewellery and silver. Valuations.*

McTear's
Skypark, 8 Elliot Place, Glasgow. G3 8EP. Est. 1842. Tel: 0141 221 4456; fax - 0141 204 5035; e-mail - enquiries@mctears.co.uk website - www.mctears.co.uk *Weekly Fri. sales at 10.30 am. of antique, reproduction and shipping furniture, jewellery, silver, porcelain and paintings. Viewing Thurs. prior 10-7. Monthly auctions of fine art and antiques. Quarterly auctions of militaria and medals, rare whisky, decorative arts and pictures. Annual auctions of sports memorabilia.*

John Milne
9 North Silver St., Aberdeen. AB1 1RJ. Est. 1867. Tel: 01224 639336; website - www.johnmilne-auctioneers. com *Weekly general sales, regular catalogue sales of antiques, silver, paintings, books, jewellery and collectors' items.*

Paterson's

8 Orchard St., Paisley. PA1 1UZ. Est. 1848. Tel: 0141 889 2435. *Fortnightly Tues. sales.*

L.S. Smellie and Sons Ltd

The Furniture Market, Lower Auchingramont Rd., Hamilton. ML10 6BE. Tel: 01698 282007; e-mail - hamiltonauction@btconnect.com website - hamilton auctionmarket.com *Fine antiques auctions on third Thurs. in Feb., May, Aug. and Nov. Weekly sales every Mon. at 9.30 am. (600 lots) household furniture, porcelain and jewellery.*

Taylor's Auction Rooms

11 Panmure Row, Montrose. DD10 8HH. Tel: 01674 672775; fax - 01674 672479; e-mail - jonathan@taylors-auctions.demon.co.uk website - www.scotlandstreasures. co.uk *Antiques sales held every second Sat.*

Thomson, Roddick & Medcalf Ltd

60 Whitesands, Dumfries. DG1 2RS. Est. 1880. Tel: 01387 279879; fax - 01387 266236; e-mail - trmdumfries @btconnect.com *Quarterly catalogued antique and collectors sales including art pottery, silver and jewellery. Monthly general sales.*

Thomson Roddick & Medcalf Ltd

44/3 Hardengreen Business Park, Eskbank, Edinburgh. EH22 3NX. Tel: 0131 454 9090; fax - 0131 454 9191; e-mail - antiquestrm@btconnect.com *Weekly auctions of antiques and general furnishings, regular specialist sales, particularly Scottish provincial silver, quarterly catalogued fine art and antique sales; also quarterly sales in Dumfries and bi-monthly general sales in Annan.*

WALES

Dodds Property World

Victoria Auction Galleries, Chester St., Mold. CH7 1EB. Est. 1952. Tel: 01352 755705; fax - 01352 752542; e-mail - auctions@door-key.com website - www.door-key.com *Weekly Wed. auctions of general furniture and shipping goods at 10.30 am. Bi-monthly auctions of antique furniture, silver, porcelain and pictures etc. at 10.30 am on Sat. Catalogues available.*

Peter Francis

Curiosity Salerooms, 19 King St., Carmarthen. SA31 1BH. Tel: 01267 233456; fax - 01267 233458; e-mail - enquiries@peterfrancis.co.uk website - www.peter francis.co.uk *Catalogued antiques and fine art sales every six weeks. Regular general sales.*

Walter Lloyd Jones Saleroom

Glan-y-Don, High St., Barmouth, LL42 1DW. Est. 1905. Tel: 01341 281527; e-mail - staff@w-lloydjones.com website - www.w-lloydjones.com *Open in summer 10-5.30, Sat. 10-4.30; winter - Mon., Thurs. and Fri. 10-5.30, Sat. 10-4.30.*

Harry Ray & Co

37 Broad St., Welshpool. SY21 7RR. Est. 1946. Tel: 01938 552555; fax - 01938 554678; e-mail - info@ harryray.com website - www.harryray.com *Monthly country sales.*

Services

This section has been included to enable us to list those businesses which do not sell antiques but are in associated trades, mainly restorations. The following categories are included: Art, Books, Carpets & Rugs, Ceramics, Clocks & Barometers, Consultancy, Courier, Enamel, Engraving, Framing, Furniture, Glass, Insurance & Finance, Ivory, Jewellery & Silver, Locks & Keys, Metalwork, Musical Instruments, Photography, Reproduction Stonework, Suppliers, Textiles, Tortoiseshell, Toys. We would point out that the majority of dealers also restore and can give advice in this field.

Below are listed the trade associations mentioned within this section.

BAFRA - British Antique Furniture Restorers' Assn
FATG - Fine Art Trade Guild
GADAR - Guild of Antique Dealers & Restorers
GMC - Guild of Master Craftsmen
MBHI - Member of British Horological Institute
UKIC - UK Institute for Conservation
CGCG - Ceramic & Glass Conservation Group

BTCM - British Traditional Cabinet Makers
BFMA - British Furniture Manufacturers' Assn
BCFA - British Contract Furniture Assn
ASFI - Assn of Suppliers to Furniture Industry
GAI - Guild of Architectural Ironmongers
MBWCG - Member British Watch & Clockmakers Guild

ART

The Antique Restoration Studio
See entry under Furniture.

Armor Paper Conservation Ltd
Glebe Cottage, 2 The Green, Garsington, Oxon. OX44 9DF. Tel: 01865 361741; fax - 01865 361815; e-mail - paper@armor.co.uk website - www.armor.co.uk/paper TVADA. *Conservation and restoration of drawings, prints, watercolour paintings, documents and archive material.*

Paul Congdon-Clelford
The Conservation Studio, 59 Peverells Wood Ave., Chandler's Ford, Hants. SO53 2FX. Est. 1894. Tel: 02380 268167; fax - same; e-mail - winstudio@aol.com website - www.conservationstudio.org IPC. ABPR. FATG. GADAR. Open by appointment. *Conservators of oil paintings and western art on paper; home and business consultations. Collection and delivery. All areas. Conservators to museums, institutions, dealers and private owners.*

Kirkgate Fine Art & Conservation
The Studio, 3 Gillings Yard, Thirsk, Yorks North. YO7 1SY. (Richard Bennett). Est. 1979. Tel: 01845 524085; home - same; e-mail - reb@vetscapes.fsnet.co.uk website - www.kirkgateconservation.co.uk UKIC. BAPCR. Open by appointment. *Oil paintings cleaned and lined on the premises; gilt/gesso frames restored and repaired; framing.* LOC: 100 yards from Market Place, off Kirkgate.

Manor House Fine Arts
73 Pontcanna St. Cardiff, CF11 9HS. (S.K. Denley-Hill). Est. 1976. Tel: 02920 227787; fax - 02920 641132; e-mail - services@manorhousefinearts.co.uk website - www.manorhousefinearts.co.uk NAVA. Open by appointment. *Auctioneers, valuers, restorers, fine arts, antiques and general chattels.*

Stephen Messer Picture Restoration
Tarifa, Millstream Moorings, Mill Lane, Clewer, Windsor, Berks. SL4 5JH. Tel: 01753 622335. Associate member ABPR. *Restorations - paintings, mainly oils including re-lining, frames including gilding.*

Claudio Moscatelli Oil Painting Restoration
46 Cambridge St., London SW1V 4QH. Tel: 020 7828 1304; e-mail - claudio4@btinternet.com website - www. claudiomoscatelli.com BPR. Open 10-6. *Oil paintings cleaned, relined, retouched and varnished.*

The Picture Restoration Studios
The Old Coach House, 16A Tarrant St., Arundel, West Sussex. BN18 9DJ. (Garve Hessenberg). Tel: 01903 885775; fax - 01903 889649; mobile - 07971 184477; e-mail - picturerestoration@hotmail.com website - www. picturerestoration.net UKIC. Open by appointment only. *Cleaning and restoration of oil paintings, watercolours, prints and old gilded frames. Antique, traditional and contemporary framing. Also in Oxford - 01865 200289; Guildford - 01483 479666; Haslemere 01428 641010; Chichester - 01243 778785.*

Plowden & Smith Ltd
190 St Ann's Hill, London SW18 2RT. Tel: 020 8874 4005; fax - 020 8874 7248; e-mail - Info@plowden-smith.co.uk website - www.plowden-smith.co.uk *Conservation and restoration of fine art and antiques. Specialist departments for furniture, ceramics, paintings, metal, stone, decorative arts, mounting/display.* VAT: Stan.

Mrs. C. Reason
Tandridge Priory Lodge, Godstone Rd., Oxted, Surrey. RH8 9JU. Tel: 01883 717010; fax - 01883 713411; mobile - 07711 485486; e-mail - chris@camr.fsnet.co.uk FATG. IPC. Open by appointment. *Valuations; restoration and cleaning of watercolours, prints and oils; gilt frame repair; watercolours bought and sold.*

Colin A. Scott
1st Floor Studio, Anthony Hurst Antiques, 13 Church St., Woodbridge, Suffolk. IP12 1DS. Tel: 01394 388528; home - 01473 622127. Open 9-5.30, Sat. 9-1. *Picture restoration and framing.*

BOOKS

Brignell Bookbinders
25 Gwydir St., Cambridge, Cambs. CB1 2LG. Est. 1982. Tel: 01223 321280; fax - same; website - www. brignellbookbinders.com SOBB. GMC. Open 8.30-4.45,

Fri. 7.30-4. CL: Sat. *Book restoration, conservation including paper, leather photo albums, journal and thesis bindings, boxes and limited editions. Initialling leather goods.* VAT: Stan.

The Manor Bindery Ltd
Calshot Rd., Fawley, Southampton, Hants. SO4 1BB. Est. 1977. Tel: 023 8089 4488; fax - 023 8089 9418; e-mail - manorbindery@btconnect.com website - www. manorbindery.co.uk *Manufacturers of false books, either to use as a display or for cabinet makers to apply to doors and cupboards. Also decorative objects and accessories, various decorative replica book boxes. Leather library shelf edging.*

CARPETS AND RUGS

Barin Carpets Restoration
57a New Kings Rd., London SW6 4SE. (Harout Barin). Est. 1976. Tel: 020 7731 0546; fax - 020 7384 1620. GMC. Conservation Register Museums and Galleries Commission. UKIC. *Oriental carpets, rugs, European tapestries, Aubussons expertly cleaned, restored and lined. Expert advice, free estimates.*

The Restoration Studio
Unit 11 Kolbe House, 63 Jeddo Rd., London W12 9EE. (Ela Sosmowska). Est. 1987. Tel: 020 8740 4977; website - www.restorationstudio.co.uk Member Rug Restorers Assn. Open 8-5. CL: Sat. *Restoration, cleaning, lining and mounting of tapestries, Aubusson carpets, kilims and all kinds of needlework.*

CERAMICS

The Antique Restoration Studio
See entry under Furniture.

China Repair by Roger Carter
15 High St., Metheringham, Lincoln, Lincs. LN4 3DZ. (Roger and Angela Carter). Est. 1990. Tel: 01522 792888; fax - 01522 792777; mobile - 07799 896350; e-mail - rogercarter@enterprise.net website - www. ceramicrepair.com Open Tues.-Fri. 10-4. *Repairs, restoration and conservation of all china and related items including ivory and papier maché - similar items for sale. Attendance at Peterborough, Newark and Lincoln antiques fairs for delivery and collection.* VAT: Stan.

China Repairers
The Old Coach House, King's Mews, off King Street, East Finchley, London N2 8DY. (V. Baron). Est. 1952. Tel: 020 8444 3030; website - www.chinarepairers.co.uk Open 10-4. CL: Fri. and Sat. *Specialised restoration of all pottery and porcelain; restoration courses.*

The China Repairers
1 Street Farm Workshops, Doughton, Tetbury, Glos. GL8 8TH. (Mrs. Amanda Chalmers). Est. 1990. Tel: 01666 503551. TADA. Open 9-4.30. CL: Sat. *Specialised restoration of porcelain and pottery, mirror frame gilding.* LOC: Entrance to Highgrove House.

Porcelain Repairs Ltd
240 Stockport Rd., Cheadle Heath, Stockport, Cheshire. SK3 0LX. Est. 1970. Tel: 0161 428 9599; fax - 0161 286 6702; e-mail - porcelain@repairs999.fsnet.co.uk CGCG. UKIC. Open Mon.-Fri. 9-5. *Highest standard restorations of European and Oriental ceramics, especially under glaze blue and white, museum repairs, carat gilding and modelling. Cracks and crazing removed without any overpainting or glazing.*

CLOCKS AND BAROMETERS

Albion Clocks
4 Grove End, Grove Hill, South Woodford, London E18 2LE. (C.D. Bent). Tel: 020 8530 5570; mobile - 07860 487830; website - www.albionclocks.com and www. albionclocks.info CMBHI. On register of Museum and Galleries Commission conservation unit. Open 9-7, Sun. by appointment. *Full restoration of clocks and watches - movements, dials cases. Full cabinet work, French polishing, gold leaf and lacquer work a speciality. Clocks made on commission, copies of Georgian library globes and globe stands. Showroom of restored decorative clocks and furniture for sale; free estimates and collection, delivery and setting up service nationwide.* LOC: Edge of M11, collection from South Woodford station by arrangement. PARK: Free.

Brown's Clocks
13 Radnor St., Kelvingrove, Glasgow. G3 7UA. (J. Cairns). Est. 1933. Tel: 0141 334 6308. Open Mon.-Fri. 10-5. *Clock and barometer restorations.*

The Clock Gallery
Clarke's Rd., North Killingholme, Lincs. DN40 3JQ. Tel: 01469 540901; fax - 01469 541512. Guild of Lincolnshire Craftsmen. *Clock movements and dials, brass work. Agent for several German clock movement makers.* VAT: Stan.

Clive and Lesley Cobb
3 Pembroke Crescent, Hove, East Sussex. BN3 5DH. Est. 1972. Tel: 01273 772649; e-mail - londinifecit@ aol.com Listed by the Conservation Unit of the Museum and Galleries Commission. *Quality, sympathetic restoration of lacquer clock cases and furniture, and painted clock dials.*

Edmund Czajkowski and Son
See entry under Furniture.

Richard Higgins (Conservation)
See entry under Furniture.

E. Hollander   BADA
1 Bennetts Castle, 89 The Street, Capel, Dorking, Surrey. RH5 5JX. (D.J. and B. Pay). Est. 1886. Tel: 01306 713377; fax - 01306 712013; e-mail - davidpay36@aol.com BWCG. Open Mon.-Fri. 8-4.30, or by appointment. *Restoration of all forms of clocks, mechanisms, cases, dials and barometers.* LOC: Midway between Dorking and Horsham.

Robert B. Loomes
3 St Leonard's Street, Stamford, Lincs. PE9 1HD. Est. 1966. Tel: 01780 481319; website - www.dialrestorer. co.uk MBWCG. MBHI. Open 9-5. *Restoration of longcase, lantern, French and bracket clocks, specialist painted dial restoration.* PARK: NCP opposite. VAT: Stan.

William Mansell
24 Connaught St., Marble Arch, London W2 2AF. (Bill Salisbury). Est. 1864. Tel: 020 7723 4154; fax - 020 7724 2273; e-mail - mail@williammansell.co.uk website - www.williammansell.co.uk MBHI. NAG. BWCG. Open 9-6, Sat. 10-1. *Repair/restoration/sales of all types of clocks, watches and barometers etc., also antique jewellery and silverware. Online catalogue of antique, vintage and modern watches, clocks, jewellery and silverware.*

Meadows and Passmore Ltd
1 Ellen Street, Portslade, Brighton, East Sussex. BN41 1EU. Tel: 01273 421321; fax - 01273 421322; e-mail - sales@m-p.co.uk website - www.m-p.co.uk *Clock and barometer parts, tools and materials.*

Menim Restorations
Bow St., Langport, Somerset. Est. 1830. Tel: 01458 252157. GMC. *Specialists in English clocks, full cabinet making and horological service; French polishing.*

Repton Clocks
Acton Cottage,48 High St., Repton, Derbys. DE65 6GF. (P. Shrouder). Tel: 01283 703657; fax - 01283 702367; e-mail - paul@pshrouder.freeserve.co.uk MBWCMG. MBHI. Open by appointment 9-6. CL: Sat. *Antique and modern watch and clock restoration; musical box repairs; gear cutting; clocks made to order.*

Kevin Sheehan
15 Market Place, Tetbury, Glos. GL8 8DD. Est. 1978. Tel: 01666 503099. Open 9-4.30, Sat. 10-12. *Specialist repairer of English and French 18th-19th C clocks. Written estimates given, all work guaranteed. Awarded Royal Warrant.*

Time Products (UK) Ltd
Alexander House, Chartwell Drive, Wigston, Leics. LE18 2EZ. Tel: 08708 508200. BJA. MBWCG. Jewellery Industry Distributors Assn. *Watch and clock replacement and restoration materials; specialised tools for the horological trade.* VAT: Stan. *Trade Only.*

CONSULTANCY

Athena Antiques of Fleet
59 Elvetham Rd., Fleet, Hants. GU13 8HH. (Richard Briant). Est. 1975. Tel: 01252 615526; home - same; mobile - 07881 541748. Available seven days by appointment. *Consultancy; valuations (jewellery, silver, clocks and furniture); restorations (clocks and furniture); buys at auction on commission; militaria.* LOC: Near Fleet railway station.

Geoffrey Godden   BADA
3 The Square, Findon, West Sussex. BN14 0TE. Tel: 01903 873456. Consultant, author and lecturer in ceramics. Study days and ceramics 'house parties' arranged.

Gerald Sattin   BADA
P O Box 20627, London NW6 7GA. (G. and M.S. Sattin). Est. 1967. Tel: 020 8451 3295; fax - same; e-mail - gsattin@compuserve.com CINOA. Open by appointment. Consultants and commission agents for the purchase of English and Continental porcelain, *1720-1900; English glass, 1700-1900; English collectible silver, 1680-1920.* VAT: Stan/Spec.

COURIER

Antique Tours & Conrad Chauffeur Hire
11 Farleigh Rise, Monkton Farleigh, Nr. Bradford-on-Avon, Wilts. BA15 2QP. (John Veal). Est. 1988. Tel: 01225 858527 (answerphone); fax - same; mobile - 07860 489831; e-mail - conradveal@hotmail.com website - www.conradchauffeurhire.co.uk *Chauffeur service for up to four persons; tours of antique shops, fairs, dealers and warehouses in and around the West Country, (other areas as requested); packing and shipping arranged; air and sea port transfers.*

ENGRAVING

Eastbourne Engraving
12 North Street, Eastbourne, East Sussex. BN21 3HG. (D. Ricketts). Est. 1882. Tel: 01323 723592. Open Tues.-Fri. 9.15-4.45. *Engraving trophies, polishing, silver plating, repairs, hardwood plinths, etc.*

FRAMING

Sebastian D'Orsai Ltd
39 Theobalds Rd., Holborn, London WC1X 8NW. (A. Brooks). Est. 1967. Tel: 020 7405 6663; fax - 020 7831 3300. Open Mon.-Fri. 9.30-4.30. *Framing, traditional to museum standard including hand-coloured finishing to suit individual pictures.* VAT: Stan.

Natural Wood Framing
Eight Bells Gallery, 14 Church St., Tetbury, Glos. GL8 8JG. Tel: 01666 505070. FATG. *Bespoke framing specialising in antiques, textiles and restorations. Contemporary and sporting art stocked.*

FURNITURE

Abbey Antiques & Furnishings Ltd
Plot 1 Maldon Rd., Danes Road Industrial Estate, Off Crow Lane, Romford, Essex. RM7 0JB. Est. 1992. Tel: 01708 741135; fax - 01708 746419; home - 01708 343103; e-mail - info@abbeyantiques.net website - www.abbeyantiques.net Open 8-5, Fri. 8-1, Sat. and Sun. by appointment. *Copies of Victorian and Edwardian four door breakfront bookcases, bureau bookcases, partners and pedestal desks, walnut or mahogany, old or new timber. Furniture repairs - glazing, leathering, gilding, turnings, inlays, veneering.* LOC: Near Oldchurch Hospital. VAT: Stan.

Timothy Akers - Antique Furniture Restorations
The Forge, 39 Chancery Lane, Beckenham, Kent. BR3 2NR. Est. 1978. Tel: 020 8650 9179; website - www.akersofantiques.com BAFRA. *Restorer of and dealer in 17th-19th C English furniture; dealer of objets d'art.*

Alan's Antique Restorations
PO Box 355. Woking, Surrey. GU22 9QE. (A.V. Wellstead). Tel: 01483 724666; fax - 01483 750366. GMC. Open by appointment. *Restoration work including clocks, pictures, cane and rush replacement, gilding, turning, carving, polishing.*

Anthony Allen Antique Restorers
Old Wharf Workshop, Redmoor Lane, New Mills, High Peak, Derbys. SK22 3JL. Tel: 01663 745274. BAFRA. UKIC. Listed on Register of Conservation Unit Museums and Galleries Commission. *Early oak and walnut furniture; conservation; clocks, cases, and movements; artifacts and metalwork.*

Antique Leathers   LAPADA
Lower Rock House, South Cheriton, Templecombe. Somerset. BA8 0BB. (R.A. Holliday and Mrs F. Crisp). Est. 1968. Tel: 01963 370126; fax - same; website - www.antique-leathers.co.uk Open 9.30-4.30. *Table lining with gold tooling; traditional upholstery, leather covered; bookshelf edging; leather restoration.* VAT: Stan. *Trade Only.*

The Antique Restoration Centre
14 Suffolk Rd., Cheltenham, Glos. GL50 2AQ. (M.H. Smith-Wood). Est. 1974. Tel: 01242 262549. Open Mon-Fri 9.30-5. *All types of restoration - all restorers BADA qualified.*

The Antique Restoration Studio
The Stable Block, Milwich Rd. Stafford, Staffs. ST18 0EG. (P. Albright). Est. 1980. Tel: 01889 505544; fax - 01889 505543; e-mail - ars@uk-hq.demon.co.uk website - www.uk-hq.demon.co.uk Open 9-5. *Repairs and restoration (furniture, rush and cane, French polishing, leatherwork and upholstery, ceramics, glassware, paintings, clocks and watches, rare books, documents and photographs). Five year guarantee on all work. Collection and delivery service.* LOC: 4 miles NE of Stafford.

Antom Ltd t/a Antiques of Tomorrow
The Glue Pot, Kyles, Stockinish, Isle of Harris, Scotland. HS3 3EN. (Dr. Carole Green and Simon Burke). Tel: 01859 530300; fax - 01859 502777; mobile - 07769 721428. Open by appointment. *Wholesale and mail order of reproduction chairs, stools and armchairs - unpolished or polished frames or fully upholstered.* VAT: Stan.

Michael Barrington
The Old Rectory, Warmwell, Dorchester, Dorset. DT2 8HQ. Est. 1983. Tel: 01305 852104; fax - 01305 854822; e-mail - headoffice@bafra.org.uk BAFRA. UKIC. Open 9-5. *Conservator and restorer of 17th-20th C furniture, clocks, barometers, gilding, upholstery, metalwork, music boxes and barrel pianos, automatons and rocking horses, historic lighting eg. Colza Oil and Argand.*

Batheaston
20 Leafield Way, Corsham, Wilts. SN13 9SW. Tel: 01225 811295; fax - 01225 810501; website - www.batheaston.co.uk BFMA. BCFA. *Oak reproduction furniture made from solid kiln dried timbers, antique hand finish. Extensive range of Windsor, ladderback and country Hepplewhite chairs; refectory, gateleg and other extendable tables, Welsh dressers, sideboards and other cabinet models. Trade Only.*

David Battle
Brightley Pound, Umberleigh, Devon. EX37 9AL. Est. 1984. Tel: 01769 540483. website - www.brightley.clara.net BAFRA. Open by appointment. *Cabinet*

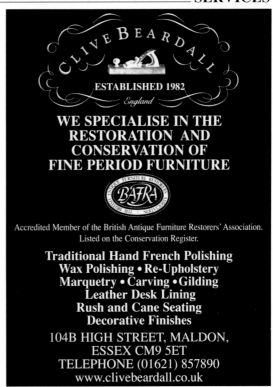
making, restoration and conservation work; polishing, clock cases, veneer and marquetry work, woodturning. Specialists in 17th-19th C English and Continental furniture. Collections and deliveries.

Keith Bawden - Restorer of Antiques
Mews Workshops, Montpellier Retreat, Cheltenham, Glos. GL50 2XG. Tel: 01242 230320. BAFRA. *All period furniture, plus restoration of items made from wood, metals, porcelain, pottery, fabrics, leather, ivory, papier-mâché, etc.*

Clive Beardall Restorations Ltd
104b High St., Maldon, Essex. CM9 5ET. Est. 1982. Tel: 01621 857890; fax - 01621 850753; e-mail - info@clivebeardall.co.uk website - www.clivebeardall.co.uk BAFRA. Conservation Register. *Comprehensive restoration and conservation services to all types of English and Continental period furniture.*

Belvedere Reproductions
11 Dove St., Ipswich, Suffolk. IP4 1NG. (S.M. Curtis). Est. 1984. Tel: 01473 214573; fax - 01473 253229; mobile - 07860 782888; e-mail - stuartcurtis@btopenworld.com website - www.belvederereproductions.co.uk Open 8-5. *Suppliers of traditionally constructed and hand polished oak and fruitwood country furniture.* VAT: Stan.

Berry & Crowther
The Workshops, Nine Whitestones, Stocksmoor, Huddersfield, West Yorks. HD4 6XQ. (Peter N. Berry and David Crowther). Est. 1979. Tel: 01484 609800; fax - same; e-mail - peternberry@aol.com Open 9-6.30. *Fine*

antique restorers and conservators; restoration with traditional methods to highest standards on fine furniture and clocks. Insurance work approved. LOC: 10 miles junction 39, M1; 6 miles south of Huddersfield from M62. Location map available on request. PARK: Own.

Rupert Bevan
40 Fulham High St., London SW6 3LQ. Tel: 020 7731 1919; fax - same. *Gilding, carving and painting.* VAT: Stan.

Peter Binnington
Barn Studio, Botany Farm, East Lulworth, Wareham, Dorset. BH20 5QH. Est. 1979. Tel: 01929 400224; fax - 01929 400744; e-mail - p.binnington@virgin.net website - www.freespace.virgin.net/p.binnington BAFRA. SOG. Open 9-5.30. CL: Sat. *Restoration of verre églomisé, giltwork, decorated surfaces, period furniture.*

Martin Body - Giltwood Restoration
7 Addington Sq., London SE5 7JZ. Est. 1988. Tel: 020 7703 4351; fax - 020 7703 1047; e-mail - giltwooduk@aol.com Open 9-5. *Specialist conservation of fine gilded furniture and frames.* LOC:

David Booth
Panborough Batch House, Panborough, Wells, Somerset, BA5 1PN. Tel: 01934 712769. *Restoration and re-building of antique furniture.*

A.E. Booth & Son
300 Hook Rd., Hook, Nr. Chessington, Surrey. KT9 1NY. Est. 1934. Tel: 020 8397 7675; fax - same; e-mail - aebrestore@talk21.com Open 9-5 by appointment. *Furniture restorations, polishing and upholstery.* LOC: A243 towards A3. PARK: Own.

Stuart Bradbury - M & S Bradbury
The Barn, Hanham Lane, Paulton, Bristol BS39 7PF. Est. 1988. Tel: 01761 418910; e-mail - enquiries@mandsbradbury.co.uk website - www.mandsbradbury.co.uk BAFRA. Open 8-5. *All aspects of antique furniture restoration.*

Lawrence Brass
154 Sutherland Avenue, Maida Vale, London W9. Tel: 0122 585 2222; website - www.lawrencebrass.com UKIC. Approved by the Museums and Galleries Commission. *Conservation and restoration of fine antiques, metal work, gilding and upholstery.*

A. J. Brett & Co Ltd
168c Marlborough Rd., London N19 4NP. Est. 1965. Tel: 020 7272 8462; fax - 020 7272 5102; e-mail - ajbretts@aol.com website - www.ajbrett.co.uk GMC. Open 7-3.30. *Restorers of antique furniture and upholstery; French polishing and gilding; free estimates.*

British Antique Replicas
School Close, Queen Elizabeth Avenue., Burgess Hill, West Sussex. RH15 9RX. Est. 1963. Tel: 01444 245577; e-mail - office@british-antique-replicas website - www.british-antique-replicas.co.uk Open 9-5.30. *Replica and bespoke furniture.* LOC: 3 miles west of A23. PARK: Easy. VAT: Stan.

Bruton Classic Furniture Company Ltd
Unit 1 Station Road Industrial Estate, Bruton, Somerset.

BA10 0EH. Tel: 01749 813266; fax - same; mobile - 07973 342047. *Quality antique replica furniture - mahogany, teak and pine.*

Peter Campion Restorations
The Old Dairy, Rushley Lane, Winchcombe, Glos. GL54 5JE. Est. 1959. Tel: 01242 604403; fax - same; website - www.petercampion.co.uk BAFRA. Open Mon.-Fri. 9-5.30 or by appointment. *Furniture restoration, conservation, polishing, insurance work, furniture designed and made to order.* LOC: Opposite the exit of Sudeley Castle car park.

Cane & Able Antiques - Cane & Rush Furniture Restoration
The Limes, 22 The Street, Beck Row, Bury St. Edmunds, Suffolk. IP28 8AD. Est. 1991. Tel: 01638 515529; fax - 01638 583905; e-mail - bobcaneandable@yahoo.co.uk website - www.caneandableantiques.co.uk *Specialists in antique and designer cane, upholstery and rush seating, furniture and architectural restoration and copying, pianos renovated.*

John B. Carr - Charles Perry Restorations Ltd
Praewood Farm, Hemel Hempstead Rd., St. Albans, Herts. AL3 6AA. Tel: 01727 853487; fax - 01727 846668; e-mail - cperry@praewood.freeserve.co.uk BAFRA.

Carvers & Gilders Ltd
9 Charterhouse Works, Eltringham St., London SW18 1TD. Est. 1979. Tel: 020 8870 7047; fax - 020 8874 0470; e-mail - acc@carversandgilders.com website - www.carversandgilders.com UKIC. Master Carver's Assn. Furniture History Society. GMC. *Design, make, restore and conserve fine decorative woodcarving and giltwood furniture, mirror frames etc. Specialists in water gilding.* VAT: Stan.

Peter G. Casebow
Pilgrims, Mill Lane, Worthing, West Sussex. BN13 3DE. Est. 1987. Tel: 01903 264045; e-mail - pcasebow@hotmail.com BAFRA. Open 9-5.30. *Period furniture, turning, marquetry, metalwork, fretwork, polishing, keyboard instrument cases.*

Castle House Antique Restoration Limited
1 Bennetts Field Estate, Wincanton, Somerset. BA9 9DT. (Michael Durkee). Est. 1975. Tel: 01963 33884; fax - 01963 31278; e-mail - m.durkee@tiscali.com BAFRA. Conservation register. Open 8.30-5.30. CL: Sat. *Restoration, conservation and finishing of all styles of period furniture. Boulle and inlay work.*

Graham Childs - Alpha (Antique) Restorations
Compton, Newbury, Berks. RG20 6NL. Est. 1972. Tel: 01635 578245; mobile - 07880 557557. BAFRA. *Fine oak, walnut and mahogany. Traditional hand finishes. Veneering and inlaying. Clock cases.*

Clare Hall Company
The Barns, Clare Hall, Cavendish Rd., Clare, Nr. Sudbury, Suffolk. CO10 8PJ. (Michael Moore). Est. 1970. Tel: 01787 278445; fax - 01787 278803; 01787 277510 (ansaphone); website - www.clarehallcompany.com and www.clarehallglobes.com Open 8-4.30. *Replicas of 18th and 19th C floor standing and*

table globes. Full cabinet making especially four poster beds; restoration of all antiques and upholstery. VAT: Stan/Spec.

Benedict Clegg
Rear of 20 Camden Rd., Tunbridge Wells, Kent. TN1 2PT. Tel: 01892 548095. BAFRA.

Compton & Schuster Ltd
Studio A133 Riverside Business Centre, Haldane Place, London SW18 4UQ. (Lucinda Compton and Dominic Schuster). Est. 1990. Tel: 020 8874 0762; fax - 020 8870 8060; website - www.comptonandschuster.com BAFRA. UKIC. ICOM. York Consortium. *Conservation and restoration - lacquer, gilding, painted and japanned furniture, paper-mâché, tôle, architectural gilding.*

William Cook
167 Battersea High St., London SW11 3JS. Tel: 020 7736 5329 or 01672 513017. BAFRA. *18th C and English period furniture.*

William Cook
High Trees House, Savernake Forest, Marlborough, Wilts. SN8 4NE. Tel: 01672 513017. BAFRA.

Crawley Studios
39 Woodvale, London SE23 3DS. Est. 1985. Tel: 020 8516 0002; fax - same. BAFRA. *Painted furniture, papier-mâché, tôle ware, lacquer and gilding.*

J.W. Crisp Antiques
1-9 Tennyson Rd., Wimbledon, London SW19 8SH. (Michael Murren). Est. 1926. Tel: 020 8543 1118; fax - same. Open by appointment. *Restoration of antique furniture and French polishing.*

Michael Czajkowski - Edmund Czajkowski and Son
96 Tor-o-Moor Rd., Woodhall Spa, Lincs. LN10 6SB. Est. 1951. Tel: 01526 352895; e-mail - michael. czajkowski@ntlworld.com BAFRA. UKIC. *Furniture, clocks (including church) and barometers restored. Veneering, marquetry, English lacquer and boulle work, carving, gilding, polishing and upholstery.*

D.H.R. Limited
8/10 Lea Lane, Thame Rd., Long Crendon, Aylesbury, Bucks. HP18 9RN. Tel: 01844 202213; fax - 01844 202214. BAFRA. *Boulle, cabinetwork, carving, gilding, lacquer, leather, marble, marquetry, ormolu, upholstery.*

Michael Dolling
Church Farm Barns, Glandford, Holt, Norfolk. NR25 7JR. Also at White Hart St., East Harling, Norfolk. NR16 2NE. Est. 1984. Tel: 01263 741115. BAFRA. Open by appointment. *Furniture repairs; veneering; marquetry; French polishing.*

Brian Duffy - Hope & Piaget
12 and 13 Burmarsh Workshops, Marsden St., London NW5 3JA. Tel: 020 7267 6040; fax - same; e-mail - mail@hope-piaget.co.uk website - www.hopepiaget.co.uk BAFRA. UKIC. *Conservation and restoration of fine furniture.*

EFMA
4 Northgate Close, Rottingdean, Brighton, East Sussex. BN2 7DZ. (Anthony and Patrick Hoole). Est. 1973. Tel: 01273 495002; fax - 01273 495022; e-mail - info@ efma.co.uk website - www.efma.co.uk Fed. of Sussex Industries. IDDA. Inst. of Export. Inst. of Linguists. *Hand-finished reproductions in walnut, elm, myrtle, yew, mahogany, satinwood. Custom-work and bespoke polishing - 18th C, Biedermeier, Victorian, mahogany dining tables. Country furniture - distressed oak and cherry refectory, gateleg and coffee tables, Windsor chairs. Tables reproduced from old timber.* VAT: Stan.

C.S. Embling - The Cabinet Repair Shop
Woodlands Farm, Blacknest, Alton, Hants. GU34 4QB. Est. 1977. Tel: 01420 23090; 01252 794260; e-mail - embling@f2s.com website - www.embling.f2s.com C&G London Inst. GMC. League of Professional Craftsmen. Open 8-5, Sat. by appointment. *Antique and modern furniture restoration and repair including marquetry and veneering, French polishing, modern finishes. Parts made, wood turning, collection and delivery; insurance claim repairs.*

English Home Antiques
Bartholomews Hall, Chancery Lane, Bridport, Dorset. DT6 3TX. Tel: 01308 420941; fax - same. Open Mon.-Fri. 9-5.30. *Full restoration of furniture and furniture related items.*

Everitt and Rogers
Dawsnest Workshop, Grove Rd., Tiptree, Essex. CO5 0JE. Est. 1969. Tel: 01621 816508; fax - 01621 814685. GADAR. *Expert antique furniture restoration.*

Duncan Everitt - D.M.E. Restorations Ltd
11 Church St., Ampthill, Beds. MK45 2PL. Est. 1986. Tel: 01525 405819; fax - 01525 756177; e-mail - info@ dmerestorations.com website - www.dmerestorations. com BAFRA. *Restoration of English and European furniture.*

John Farbrother Furniture Restoration
Ivy House, Main St., Shipton-by-Beningbrough, York, North Yorks. YO30 1AB. Est. 1987. Tel: 01904 470187; fax - 01904 470187; e-mail - jb_farbrother@yahoo.co.uk website - www.johnfarbrother.co.uk GADAR. *All repairs undertaken, refinishing process from complete strip to reviving existing finish. French polishing, oil, wax and lacquers. Pressurised fluid application woodworm treatment.*

Fauld Town and Country Furniture
Whitestone Park, Whitestone, Hereford, Herefs. HR1 3SE. Est. 1972. Tel: 01432 851992; fax - 01432 851994; e-mail - enquiries@fauld.com website - www.fauld.com Open 8-5, appointment advisable. *Windsor chairs, extensive range of farmhouse tables, dressers and racks and many other case pieces. Bespoke work a speciality to traditional styles and methods.* VAT: Stan.

Fenlan
17B Stilebrook Rd., Yardley Road Industrial Estate, Olney, Bucks. MK46 5EA. (Brian Harrison and Stephen Bryden). Est. 1982. Tel: 01234 711799; fax - same; e-mail - fenlan2000@aol.com Open Mon.-Fri. 9-5. *Furniture restoration. Restoration products and fittings supplied; cabinet making and non-caustic stripping.* LOC: 8 miles from junction 14, M1. VAT: Stan.

THE BRITISH ANTIQUE FURNITURE RESTORERS' ASSOCIATION

The Association is nationally recognised as upholding and promoting the highest standards of conservation and restoration. Thereby members' clients are assured of the highest standards of service. Accredited members have undergone a rigorous examination to prove their skills, competence and knowledge and BAFRA actively encourages them to maintain and extend these levels.

To discuss your requirements or make enquiries please telephone or fax
01305 854822
BAFRA Head Office
The Old Rectory, Warmwell
Dorchester, Dorset DT2 8HQ
e-mail:
headoffice@bafra.org.uk
Website: **www.bafra.org.uk**

Image courtesy of Hy Duke & Sons

Andrew Foott
4 Claremont Rd., Cheadle Hulme, Cheshire. SK8 6EG. Est. 1985. Tel: 0161 485 3559. *Sympathetic restoration and conservation of antique furniture and mercurial barometers; free advice and estimates; quality items occasionally for sale.*

Forge Studio Workshops
Stour St., Manningtree, Essex. CO11 1BE. Tel: 01206 396222. BAFRA. *Carving, general restoration, copying and bespoke cabinet making.*

Glen Fraser-Sinclair - G. and R. Fraser-Sinclair
Hays Bridge Farm, Brickhouse Lane, South Godstone, Surrey. RH9 8JW. Est. 1978. Tel: 01342 844112. BAFRA. Open 8-6. *18th C furniture.*

Alistair J. Frayling-Cork
2 Mill Lane, Wallingford, Oxon. OX10 0DH. Est. 1979. Tel: 01491 826221; website - www.frayling-cork.co.uk BAFRA. Open 10-6 or by appointment. *Antique and period furniture, clock cases, ebonising, wood turning, stringed instruments and brass fittings repaired.*

Furniture Studio Ltd
1 Eagle Trading Estate, Stourbridge Rd., Halesowen, West Midlands. B63 3UA. Est. 1987. Tel: 0121 550 8228; fax - 0121 585 5611. *Furniture manufacturers. Special orders undertaken.* VAT: Stan.

Georgian Cabinets Manufacturers Ltd
Unit 4 Fountayne House, 2-8 Fountayne Rd., London N15 4QL. Est. 1964. Tel: 020 8885 1293; fax - 020 8365 1114. *Manufacturers, restorers and polishers. Large*

stock of inlaid furniture. Container services worldwide. LOC: Near Seven Sisters underground, Tottenham. PARK: Free. VAT: Stan.

Michael Goater - Antique Furniture Restoration
15 Red Barn Yards, Thornham Magna, Eye, Suffolk. IP23 8HH. Est. 1987. Tel: 01379 788722; fax - same; mobile - 07791 543955; website - www.michaelgoater. co.uk BAFRA (executive committee member). Open 9-5, Sat. by appointment. *Full furniture restoration and conservation service including upholstery; period picture frames and historic stringed musical instrument restoration; cleaning and restoration of stone sculptures especially marble. Collection and delivery arranged. Lecturer - talks given on care and history of antique furniture.* LOC: Off A140 - follow signs to Thornham Walks. PARK: Easy.

Gow Antiques & Restoration
Pitscandly Farm, Forfar, by Lunanhead, Angus, Scotland. DD8 3NZ. (Jeremy Gow). Est. 1993. Tel: 01307 465342; mobile - 07711 416786; e-mail - jeremy@knowyour antiques.com website - www.knowyourantiques.com Accredited by BAFRA and listed in the Conservation Register run by UKIC in association with Historic Scotland. Appointment advisable. *17th-19th C English and Continental furniture. Specialist in marquetry, tortoiseshell and fine furniture. Three day courses on antique furniture recognition.*

Jeffrey Hall - Malvern Studios
56 Cowleigh Rd., Malvern, Worcs. WR14 1QD. (L.M., D.D. and J. Hall). Est. 1961. Tel: 01684 574913; fax -

01684 569475. BAFRA. Open 9-5.15, Fri. and Sat. 9-4.45. CL: Wed. *Antique furniture restoration.*

Peter Hall & Son
Danes Rd., Staveley, Kendal, Cumbria. LA8 9PL. (Jeremy Hall). Est. 1972. Tel: 01539 821633; fax - 01539 821905; e-mail - info@peter-hall.co.uk website - www. peter-hall.co.uk UKIC. Open 9-5, Sat. 10-4 (closing 1 pm in winter) and by appointment. *Antique furniture restoration and conservation, traditional upholstery, furniture maker, interior design consultants.* LOC: Off A591 Kendal to Windermere road.

John Hartley
Johnson's Barns, Waterworks Rd., Sheet, Petersfield, Hants. GU32 2BY. Est. 1977. Tel: 01730 233792; fax - 01730 233922; e-mail - mail@tankerdale.co.uk website - www.tankerdale.co.uk BAFRA. UKIC. Open 8-5.30. CL: Sat. *Comprehensive restoration and conservation service, including carving, gilding, painted furniture, lacquer, marquetry, boulle and architectural woodwork. Adviser to The National Trust.*

Philip Hawkins
Glebe Workshop, Semley, Shaftesbury, Dorset. SP7 9AP. Tel: 01747 830830; e-mail - hawkinssemley@ hotmail.com BAFRA. *16th to early 18th C oak furniture restoration.*

Roland Haycraft
The Lamb Arcade, Wallingford, Oxon. OX10 0BX. Est. 1980. Tel: 01491 839622; e-mail - roland.haycraft@ fsbdial.co.uk website - www.Diva-ID.com and www.IASA-Online.com GADAR. LPC. *All aspects of antique restorations; one-off reproductions and copying service. Fine furniture designed and made to traditional standards. Antique archiving (DIVA - Digital Inventory & Visual Archive) - museum cataloguing and digital photography combine to produce a modern inventory system designed to combat theft.*

Hedgecoe and Freeland   LAPADA.
21 Burrow Hill Green, Chobham, Surrey. GU24 8QS. Tel: 01276 858206; fax - 01276 857352. BAFRA. *General restorations, cabinet work, polishing, upholstery, chair making.*

Heritage Antiques
Unit 2 Trench Farm, Tilley Green, Wem, Shrops. SY4 5PJ. (M.R. Nelms). Est. 1989. Tel: 01939 235463; fax - 01939 235416; e-mail - heritageantiques@ btconnect.com website - www.heritageantiques.co.uk GADAR. Open 9-5, Sat. (24 hour notice) by appointment. *Furniture, including antique and fitted, full restoration service, antique boxes and clock cases a speciality.*

Alan Hessel
The Old Town Workshop, St. George's Close, Moreton-in-Marsh, Glos. GL56 0LP. Est. 1976. Tel: 01608 650026; fax - same; e-mail - alan.hessel@virgin.net BAFRA. Open Mon.- Fri. 9-5 or by appointment. *Comprehensive restoration service. English and Continental fine period furniture.*

Richard Higgins (Conservation)
The Old School, Longnor, Nr. Shrewsbury, Shrops. SY5 7PP. Est. 1988. Tel: 01743 718162; fax - 01743 718022; e-mail - richardhigginsco@aol.com BAFRA. LBHI. Conservation Register Museums and Galleries Commission. UKIC. Open by appointment. *Comprehensive restoration of all fine furniture and clocks, including movements and dials; specialist work to boulle, marquetry, carving, turning, cabinet and veneer work, lacquer, ormolu, metalwork, casting, glazing, polishing, upholstery, cane and rush seating. Stocks of old timber, veneers, tortoiseshell etc. held to ensure sympathetic restoration.*

Stuart Hobbs Antique Furniture Restoration
Meath Paddock, Meath Green Lane, Horley, Surrey. RH6 8HZ. Tel: 01293 782349. GMC. BAFRA. *Full restoration service for period furniture.*

John Hubbard Antique Restorations   LAPADA
Castle Ash, Birmingham Rd., Blakedown, Worcs. DY10 3SE. Est. 1968. Tel: 01562 701020; e-mail - jhantiques @aol.com website - www.antiquesbulletin.com/ JohnHubbardAntiques CINOA. GMC. Open by appointment. *Restorations of furniture including French polishing, desk leathers and upholstery.* LOC: A456. VAT: Stan.

Christian Macduff Hunt - Hunt and Lomas
Village Farm Workshops, Preston Village, Cirencester, Glos. GL7 5PR. Est. 1985. Tel: 01285 640111. BAFRA. Open 8-5. *17th-19th C oak, mahogany, walnut, satinwood, carving.*

Donald Hunter
The Old School Room, Shipton Oliffe, Cheltenham, Glos. GL54 4JB. Tel: 01242 820755. *Restoration of fine antiques, cabinet making, water gilding, lacquer work, decorative finishes.*

D. Hurst Restoration
4 Gleneldon Mews, London SW16 2AZ. (Deborah Hurst). Est. 1996. Tel: 020 8696 0315; e-mail - deborah.h @ukgateway.net website - www.dhrestoration.co.uk Open 9-6. *French polishing, gilding, wood carving, restoration.*

George Justice
12A Market St., Lewes, East Sussex. BN7 2HE. (J.C., C.C. and S.M. Tompsett). Est. 1910. Tel: 01273 474174; e-mail - geo.justice@virgin.net website - www. lewesartisans.com GMC. Open 8-1 and 2-5. CL: Sat. *Furniture restorations, cabinet making, upholstery, French polishing, caning and rushing, leather re-lining.* LOC: 1 minute from war memorial.

Kingsley & Co.   LAPADA
Unit 10 Stainton Grove Industrial Estate, Barnard Castle, Durham DL12 8UH. (David Harper). Est. 1992. Tel: 01833 695959; fax - 01833 630891; e-mail - info@ kingsleysofas.co.uk website - www.kingsleyantiques. co.uk Open Mon.-Fri. 9-4.30. *Makers of replica furniture.*

Katie Lamb Gilding Restoration
The Square, Long Crendon, Aylesbury, Bucks. HP18 9AA. Tel: 01844 201509; fax - 01296 651652; e-mail - pollicott.lamb@tinyworld.co.uk FATG; UKIC; TVADA. Open Mon.-Fri. 10-4 by appointment. *Gilding and*

restorations of decorative gilt mirrors, frames and furniture; restoration of papier maché, painted furniture and screens.

Roderick Larwood
The Oaks, Station Rd., Larling, Norfolk. NR16 2QS. Est. 1983. Tel: 01953 717937; fax - same; e-mail - rodlar@tinyworld.co.uk BAFRA. Open 8-5.30. CL: Sat. *Brass inlay, 18th to early 19th C furniture; French polishing; traditional finishes; Tunbridgeware.*

E.C. Legg and Son
3 College Farm Buildings, Tetbury Rd., Cirencester, Glos. GL7 6PY. (C. Legg). Est. 1902. Tel: 01285 650695. Open 9-5. CL: Sat. *Restoration of furniture including rushing, caning and re-leathering desk tops.*

John Lloyd
Bankside Farm, Ditchling Common, West Sussex. RH15 0SJ. Est. 1990. Tel: 01444 480388; fax - same; mobile - 07941 124772; e-mail - info@johnlloydfine furniture.co.uk website - www.johnlloydfinefurniture. co.uk BAFRA. Open 9-5. *Sympathetic restoration and conservation of English and Continental furniture; traditional hand finishing, veneering, marquetry and inlay work, carving and turning, gilding, upholstery, rush/cane work, leather lining and tooling, lock repairs and keys. Antique furniture copied, furniture designed and made to order. Regular delivery/collection service to London. Short courses in furniture restoration, cabinet making and gilding.* LOC: 12 miles north of Brighton.

Lomas Pigeon & Co. Ltd
37 Beehive Lane, Great Baddow, Chelmsford, Essex. CM2 9TQ. Est. 1938. Tel: 01245 353708; fax - 01245 355211; e-mail - wpigeon@compuserve.com website - www.lomas-pigeon.co.uk BAFRA. AMU. Open 10-4, Sat. 9-12. CL: Wed. *Antique restoration, French polishing, traditional and modern upholstery. Retailers and makers of fine furniture and rocking horses. Curtains and soft furnishings made to order. Leather table top linings.*

Timothy Long Restoration
St. John's Church, London Rd., Dunton Green, Sevenoaks, Kent. TN13 2 TE. Est. 1987. Tel: 01732 743368; fax - 01732 742206; e-mail - info@timlong. co.uk BAFRA. Open 8-5. CL: Sat. *Cabinet restoration, French polishing, upholstery.*

Bruce Luckhurst
The Little Surrenden Workshops, Ashford Rd., Bethersden, Kent. TN26 3BG. Est. 1976. Tel: 01233 820589; e-mail - woodwise@tiscali.co.uk website - www.bruceluckhurst.co.uk BAFRA. *Conservation and restoration training plus comprehensive restoration service.*

Mackenzie & Smith Restoration
4 Bull Ring, Ludlow, Shropshire. SY8 1AD. (Tim Smith). Est. 1998. Tel: 01584 877133. UKIC. Open 9-5, Sat. 10-1. *Restoration of furniture, especially oak and country; door locks and fittings supplied.*

Oliver Manning Press
Shalmsford St., Chartham, Canterbury, Kent. CT4 7BX. Tel: 01227 731765; mobile - 07808 001844; e-mail - omanningpress@yahoo.co.uk AF RF; Dip European Centre of Conservation, Venice; Dip Conservation Antique Furniture. Open by appointment only. *Antique furniture restoration - insurance and museum work. Cabinet making; wax finishing; French polishing. Small stock quality items and 'breakers'.*

Timothy Naylor
24 Bridge Rd., Chertsey, Surrey. KT16 8JN. Est. 1990. Tel: 01932 567129; fax - 01932 564948; e-mail - timbonaylor@aol.com BAFRA. *Antique furniture restoration.*

Nicholas J. Newman
22 Eastcroft Rd., West Ewell, Surrey. KT19 9TX. Est. 1983. Tel: 020 8224 3347. Open by appointment. *Comprehensive restorations including exterior woodwork and locks.*

Ben Norris & Co
Knowl Hill Farm, Knowl Hill, Kingsclere, Newbury, Berks. RG20 4NY. Tel: 01635 297950; fax - 01635 299851. BAFRA. *All aspects of furniture restoration including carving, gilding, copy chair making and architectural woodwork. Excellent storage facilities.* VAT: Stan.

Nigel Northeast Cabinet Makers
Furniture Workshops, Back Drove, West Winterslow, Salisbury, Wilts. SP5 1RY. Est. 1982. Tel: 01980 862051; fax - 01980 863986; e-mail - nigel@nigelnortheast.co.uk website - www.nigelnortheast.co.uk GADAR. *Antique restoration and French polishing. New furniture made to order, chairs made to complete sets. Cane and rush seating; fire and flood damage service.* VAT: Stan.

Ottery Antique Restorers   LAPADA
Wessex Way, Wincanton Business Park, Wincanton, Somerset. BA9 9RR. (C.J. James). Est. 1986. Tel: 01963 34572; fax - same; mobile - 07770 923955; e-mail - charles@otteryantiques.co.uk website - www.ottery antiques.co.uk BABAADA. Open 8-5, Sat. 9-2. *Marquetry, inlay and veneering repairs and cutting; carving, desk leathers and baize replacement; lead linings to cellarettes and wine coolers; handle repair, matching and replacement; lock repair and period keys cut; brass casting for mounts, castors and handles etc. Cabinet and furniture making, French polishing and wax finishing; upholstery, cane and rush seating. 17th-18th C furniture bought and sold.* LOC: Outskirts of town, just off A303. PARK: Easy.

Simon Paterson Fine Furniture Restoration
Whitelands, West Dean, Chichester, West Sussex. PO18 0RL. Est. 1993. Tel: 01243 811900; e-mail - hotglue@tiscali.co.uk BAFRA. Open 9-6. *Boule, marquetry, frets, tortoiseshell and general furniture restoration.*

Clive Payne Restorations   LAPADA
Unit 11 Langston Priory Workshops, Kingham, Chipping Norton, Oxon. OX7 6UR. Est. 1987. Tel: 01608 658856; fax - same; mobile - 07764 476776; e-mail - clive. payne@virgin.net website - www.clive.payne.co.uk BAFRA. Open 8-6, Sat. 9-1 or by appointment. *17th-19th furniture restoration.*

Noel Pepperall
Dairy Lane Cottage, Walberton, Arundel, West Sussex. BN18 0PT. Tel: 01243 551282; e-mail - pepperall @amserve.net website - www.pepperall.co.uk BAFRA. *Antique furniture restoration.*

Eva-Louise Pepperall
Dairy Lane Cottage, Walberton, Arundel, West Sussex. BN18 0PT. Tel: 01243 551282; e-mail - pepperall@ amserve.net website - www.pepperall.co.uk BAFRA. *Gilding and japanning.*

T. L. Phelps - Fine Furniture Restoration
15A Nidd Valley Business Park, Market Flat Lane, Scotton, Knaresborough, North Yorks. HG5 9JA. Est. 1984. Tel: 01423 862752; e-mail - phelps@ furniturerestoration.fsnet.co.uk Accredited member of UKIC and BAFRA; listed in the Conservation Register. Open Mon.-Fri. 8.30-6 by appointment only. *Specialist restoration (especially water damaged surfaces), and conservation services; all cabinet work, including dining tables, breakfront bookcases; all veneer work; architectural woodwork; traditional hand polishing, colouring and waxed finishes. Condition and treatment reports, reports for insurance loss adjustors;* LOC: Map available on request. PARK: Easy. VAT: Stan.

Plain Farm Workshop
The Old Dairy, Plain Farm, East Tisted, Alton, Hants. GU34 3RT. (Simon Worte). Est. 1990. Tel: 01420 588362; e-mail - simonworte@fsmail.net Open 10-5.30. *18th to 19th C English furniture restoration.* LOC: 4 miles south of Alton and near to A32.

Plowden & Smith Ltd
See entry under Art.

A.J. Ponsford Antiques at Decora
Northbrook Rd., off Eastern Ave., Barnwood, Glos. GL4 3DP. (A.J. and R.L. Ponsford). Est. 1962. Tel: 01452 307700. Open 8-5. CL: Sat. *Restorations (furniture); rushing; caning; upholstery; manufacturers of period book simulations and decorative accessories.* LOC: Off junction 11A, M5. VAT: Stan.

Neil Postons Restorations
29 South St., Leominster, Herefs. HR6 8JQ. Est. 1988. Tel: 01568 616677; fax - same; mobile - 07710 297602. UKIC. Registered with the Museums and Galleries Commission. Open 8.45-5.30, Sat. and other times by appointment. *Antique and fine furniture restorations including re-construction, veneering, carving, turning, French and wax polishing, re-upholstery, rush and cane seating.*

Ludovic Potts Restorations
Unit 1/1A, Haddenham Business Park, Station Rd., Haddenham, Ely, Cambs. CB6 3XD. Est. 1986. Tel: 01353 741537; fax - 01353 741822; London Office - 020 7655 0810. e-mail - mail@restorers.co.uk website - www.restorers.co.uk BAFRA. *Comprehensive restorations and conservation of furniture and effects. London office: 10 Artillery Passage, Bishop's Gate, London E1 7LJ.*

The Real Wood Furniture Company
London House, 16 Oxford St, Woodstock, Oxon. OX20 1TS. (Chris Baylis). Tel: 01993 813887; fax - 01993 812379; e-mail - info@realwoodfurniture.co.uk website - www.realwoodfurniture.co.uk Open Tues.-Sat. 10.30-5.30, Sun. 11-5. *Large stock of superb hand crafted country furniture in traditional antique styles - solid oak, ash and cherry. Tables, dressers etc made to order. Large range of rush seated, Windsor and kitchen style chairs.* VAT: Stan.

Rectory Bungalow Workshop
Station Rd., Elton, Bingham, Notts. NG13 9LF. (E.M. Mackie). Est. 1981. Tel: 01949 850878. Open by appointment. *Restorations - cane and rush seating, painted furniture.*

Riches Upholstery Ltd
Wixamtree, 69 Wood Lane, Cottonend, Beds. MK45 3AP. (R.J. Jennings). Est. 1980. Tel: 01234 742121; e-mail - jennings@wixamtree.wanadoo.co.uk *Re-upholstery, repairs and re-caning.*

Raymond Robertson - Tolpuddle Antique Restorers
The Stables, Southover Yard, Tolpuddle, Dorchester, Dorset. DT2 7HE. Est. 1979. Tel: 01305 848739; home - 01305 267799. West Dean/BADA Award Winner. RFS. Open 9-5.30. *Furniture, clock and barometer cases, marquetry, veneering and boulle work, japanning and gilding, insurance work undertaken.*

David A. Sayer - Courtlands Restorations
Courtlands, Park Rd., Banstead, Surrey. SM7 3EF. Est. 1985. Tel: 01737 352429; fax - 01737 373255. BAFRA. Open 8-5, Sat. and Sun. by appointment. *Comprehensive restoration service including repairs, polishing, carving, turning, veneering, gilding. Metal parts - replacement or repair.*

Michael Schryver Antiques Ltd
The Granary, 10 North Street, Dorking, Surrey. RH4 1DN. Est. 1970. Tel: 01306 881110. Open 8.30-5.30, Sat. 8-12. *Cabinet work, polishing, upholstery, metal work.* VAT: Stan/Spec.

Phillip Slater
93 Hewell Rd., Barnt Green, Worcs. B45 8NL. Est. 1977. Tel: 0121 445 4942. BAFRA. Open 9-5.30, Sat. 9.30-1. *Antique furniture restoration, conservation, sales and valuations.*

Alun Courtney Smith
45 Windmill Rd., Brentford, Middx. TW8 0QQ. Tel: 020 8568 5249; fax - same. BAFRA.

Eric Smith - Antique Furniture Restorations
The Old Church, Park Rd., Darwen, Lancs. BB3 2LD. Tel: 01254 776222; e-mail - workshop@ericsmith restorations.co.uk website - www.ericsmithrestorations. co.uk BAFRA. UKIC. Conservation Register Museums & Galleries Commission. Open 9-6. *Restoration of longcase clocks and furniture. Comprehensive conservation and restoration of fine furniture.*

Julian Stanley Woodcarving - Furniture
1 Caeflwyn, Ewyas Harold Common, Ewyas Harold, Hereford. HR2 0JD. Est. 1983. Tel: 01981 241411; fax - same; e-mail - julian@julianstanley-woodcarving furniture.co.uk website - www.julianstanley-

woodcarvingfurniture.co.uk MCA. Open 9-5. *Carved furniture - the classical work of the 18th C is re-created alongside contemporary designs, figure work and architectural pieces. Showroom on site includes contemporary paintings and sculpture.* VAT: Stan/Spec.

Robert Tandy Restoration
Lake House Barn, Lake Farm, Colehouse Lane, Kenn, Clevedon. Somerset. BS21 6TQ. Est. 1987. Tel: 01275 875014; e-mail - robertptandy@hotmail.com BAFRA. *Furniture restoration especially 17th-19th C longcase clock cases; French polishing and traditional oil and wax finishing.* VAT: Stan.

Titian Studio
32 Warple Way, Acton, London W3 0DJ (Rodrigo and Rosaria Titian). Est. 1963. Tel: 020 8222 6600; fax - 020 8749 2220; e-mail - enquiries@titianstudios.co.uk website - www.titianstudios.co.uk BAFRA. Open 8.30-5.30. *Carving, gilding, lacquer, painted furniture, French polishing, japanning.*

Treen Antiques
Treen House, 72 Park Rd., Prestwich, Manchester, Lancs. M25 0FA. (Simon J Feingold). Est. 1988. Tel: 0161 720 7244; fax - same; mobile - 07973 471185; e-mail - simonfeingold@hotmail.com website - www.treenantiques.com GADAR. RFS. FHS. UKIC. Open by appointment. *Conservation and restoration of all antique furniture (including vernacular) and woodwork, with emphasis on preserving original finish. Research undertaken, housekeeping advice, environmental monitoring and all aspects of conservation. Furniture assessment and advice on purchase and sales. Courses in restoration work held on request.* Listed in Bonham's Directory.

Tony Vernon
15 Follett Rd., Topsham, Devon. EX3 0JP. Est. 1975. Tel: 01392 874635; e-mail - tonyvernon@antiquewood.co.uk website - www.antiquewood.co.uk BAFRA. *Furniture, cabinet making, upholstery, gilding, veneering, inlay and French polishing.*

E.F. Wall
32 Church St. Woodbridge, Suffolk. IP12 1DH. (Libby Wall). Tel: 01394 610511; fax - same; mobile - 07885 374917; e-mail - e.f.wall@btinternet.co.uk website - www.efwall.co.uk Open 10-5.30. CL: Wed. *Makers of fine furniture.* VAT: Stan/Spec.

Barry J. Wateridge
Padouk, Portsmouth Rd., Bramshott Chase, Hindhead, Surrey. GU26 6DB. Tel: 01428 607235. *French polishing and antique furniture restorations.*

Weaver Neave and Daughter
17 Lifford St. Putney, London SW15 1NY. Est. 1977. Tel: 020 8785 2464. *Re-caning and re-rushing of antique furniture in traditional manner with traditional materials.*

Gerald Weir Antiques
Unit 1, Riverside Industrial Park, Wherstead Rd., Ipswich, Suffolk. 1PZ 8JX. Tel: 01473 692300; fax - 01473 692333; e-mail - geraldweirantiques@btinternet.com Open by appointment. *Suppliers of reproduction oak and cherry country furniture, mainly for European and American markets.*

Wick Antiques
LAPADA

Fairlea House, 110-112 Marsh Lane, Lymington, Hants. SO41 8EE. Tel: 01590 677558; fax - same. *Furniture polishing, repairs, upholstery and re-gilding.*

Jonathan Wilbye
Blue Bell Farm, North Stainmore, Kirkby Stephen, Cumbria. CA17 4DY. Est. 1983. Tel: 01768 341715. Open by appointment. *Full restoration service including all carving, inlay, turning and polishing. Longcase clock cases a speciality. Free delivery in Cumbria, Yorkshire and Lancashire.*

GLASS

F.W. Aldridge Ltd
Unit 3 St John's Industrial Estate, Dunmow Rd., Takeley, Essex. CM22 6SP. (J.L. Garwood). Tel: 01279 874000/874001; fex - 01279 874002; e-mail - angela@fwaldridge.abel.co.uk website - www.fwaldridgeglass.com Open 9-5. *Antique glass restoration including removing chips; suppliers of Bristol blue glass liners and stoppers; makers of stems for glasses and claret jugs.*

The Antique Restoration Studio
See entry under Furniture.

INSURANCE AND FINANCE

Shearwater Insurance Services Ltd incorporating Allen Flindall & Assoc.Ltd
Shearwater House, 8 Regent Gate, High St., Waltham Cross, Herts. EN8 7AE. Tel: 08700 718666; fax - 08700 750043; e-mail - enquiries@shearwater-insurance.co.uk *Specialist insurance scheme for antique and fine art dealers, collectors, household and all risks insurance.*

T & R (Insurance Services) Ltd
3 Chichester House, 45 Chichester Rd., Southend-on-Sea, Essex. SS1 2JU. (Trevor and Rita Raye). Tel: 01702 613526; fax - 01702 616835; mobile - 07913 348623; e-mail - insurance@btconnect.com website - www.cargoinsurancecouk.com Open 9-1 and 2-5. *Insurance providers approved by the British International Freight Association. Insurance of fine arts and antiques, mechanical music, military memorabilia, books and collectables. Authorised and regulated by the Financial Services Authority.*

Anthony Wakefield & Company Ltd
Suite C, South House, 21-37 South St., Dorking, Surrey. RH4 2JZ. Est. 1983. Tel: 01306 740555; fax - 01306 740770; e-mail - info@anthonywakefield.com and info@connoisseurpolicies.com website - www.anthonywakefield.com and www.connoisseurpolicies.com Members IIB. Authorised and regulated by the Financial Services Authority. *Fine art and household insurance brokers; special terms for collectors; exclusive antique and fine art dealers policy with Axa Insurance UK plc; exclusive Connoisseur household policy with dealers/fairs extension. Connoisseur online policy for collections between £5,000 and £50,000 (see website).*

Windsor Insurance Brokers
America House, 2 America Square, London EC3 2LU. Tel: 020 7133 1200; fax - 020 7133 1500. Lloyds Insurance Brokers. *Specialist Lloyd's brokers in antique*

SERVICES

and fine art dealers, fine art galleries, contemporary art galleries, restorers and conservators, antique centres, auctioneers and valuers "Heirloom" designed for dealers' own collections and household and all risks insurance brokers. Official brokers to LAPADA, BAFRA, The Fine Art Trade Guild, IDDA.

IVORY

Coromandel
Leominster, Herefs. HR6 0HS. *See entry under Leominster, Herefs. in dealer listing.*

E. and C. Royall Antiques
See entry under Metalwork.

JEWELLERY AND SILVER

Eastbourne Engraving
See entry under Engraving.

Goldcare
5 Bedford St., Middlesborough, TS1 2LL. Tel: 01642 231343; website - www.goldcarerepairs.co.uk *Jewellery repair, engraving, re-stringing, stone cutting. Restoration of silver and cutlery; brass, copper, pinchbeck restoration.* VAT: Stan.

LOCKS & KEYS

Bramah Security Centres Ltd
31 Oldbury Place, London W1U 5PT. Est. 1784. Tel: 020 7935 7147; fax - 020 7935 2779; e-mail - lock.sales@ bramah.co.uk website - www.bramah.co.uk MLA. Open 8.30-5.30, Sat. 9-1. *Keys cut to old locks; old locks opened; repair of old locks; new locks made to an old design; original Bramah locks dated. Quotation provided. Overseas work undertaken.* LOC: Near Baker Street tube station. VAT: Stan.

METALWORK

Rupert Harris Conservation
Studio 5c, 1 Fawe St., London E14 6PD. Est. 1982. Tel: 020 7987 6231/7515 2020; fax - 020 7987 7994; e-mail - enquiries@rupertharris.com website - www.rupertharris. com UKIC. IIC. NACE. SPAB. ICOM. Open by appointment. *Conservation of fine metalwork and sculpture including bronze, lead, zinc and electrotype; chandeliers, lanterns, gold and silver, fine ironwork, arms and armour, ecclesiastical metalwork, casting, replication and gilding; consultancy and maintenance. Appointed metalwork advisors to the National Trust for England and Wales.*

Raymond Konyn Antique Restorations
Brass Foundry Castings Ltd, P O Box 151, Westerham, Kent. TN16 1YF. Est. 1979. Tel: 01959 563863; fax - 01959 561262; e-mail - info@brasscastings.co.uk website - www.brasscastings.co.uk BAFRA. Open by appointment. *Furniture fittings and mounts, brass casting.* VAT: Spec.

Optimum Brasses
7 Castle St., Bampton, Devon. EX16 9NS. (Robert and Rachel Byles). Est. 1981. Tel: 01398 331515; fax - 01398 331164; e-mail - brass@obida.com website - www.obida.com Open 9-1 and 2-4, Sat. and other times by appointment. *Over 5,000 replica brass handles etc. for antique furniture. Copying service.* LOC: On Wiveliscombe road. VAT: Stan.

Plowden & Smith Ltd
See entry under Art.

E. and C. Royall Antiques
10 Waterfall Way, Medbourne, Leics. LE16 8EE. Est. 1981. Tel: 01858 565744. Open 9-5. *Restorations - English and Oriental furniture, bronzes, ivories, brass including inlay work, metalware, woodcarving, French polishing.* VAT: Stan.

H.E. Savill Period Furniture Fittings
9-12 St Martin's Place, Scarborough, North Yorks. YO11 2QH. Tel: 01723 373032; fax - 01723 376984. Open 9-5.30. *Period brass cabinet fittings.* VAT: Stan. *Trade Only.*

Shawlan Antiques Metal Restorers   LAPADA
Croydon/South London area. (Shawn Parmakis). Est. 1976. Tel: 020 8684 5082; fax - same; e-mail - shawlan antiques@aol.com website - www.shawlanantiques.com Open 9-9. *High quality restoration of metalware, using traditional methods and materials. Over 25 years experience.*

MUSICAL INSTRUMENTS

J V Pianos & Cambridge Pianola
85 High St.,Landbeach, Cambridge, Cambs. CB4 8DR. (Tom Poole). Est. 1972. Tel: 01223 861348/861408; fax - 01223 441276; e-mail - ftpoole@talk21.com website - www.cambridgepianolacompany.co.uk Open Mon.-Fri. prior telephone call advisable, or by appointment. *Restoration and sales of period pianos, pianolas and player pianos; music rolls, repair materials, books and accessories.*

PHOTOGRAPHY

Gerry Clist Photography
Unit 235 Webheath Workshops, Netherwood St. London NW6 2JX. Est. 1991. Tel: 020 7691 3200; mobile - 07798 838839; e-mail - gerry@gerryclist.biz website - www.gerryclist.biz MPA. Open 10-6. *Specialising in sculptures, antiques and works of art photography - studio and location.*

REPRODUCTION STONEWORK

Hampshire Gardencraft
Rake Industries, Rake, Nr. Petersfield, Hants. GU31 5DR. Est. 1984. Tel: 01730 895182; fax - 01730 893216; e-mail - sales@hampshire-gardencraft.com website - www.hampshire-gardencraft.com *Manufacturers of antiqued garden ornaments, troughs and pots in reconstituted stone in an old Cotswold stone finish. Many designs, catalogue available.*

Lucas Garden Statuary
Firsland Park Estate, Henfield Road, Albourne, West Sussex. BN6 9JJ. Est. 1970. Tel: 01273 494931; fax - 01273 495125; e-mail - trade@lucasstone.com website - www.lucasstone.com Open Mon.-Fri. 9-5. *Manufacturers of Lucas Stone since 1970, huge range of unusual aged reconstituted stone statuary. Available in*

498

two unique finishes, original classical and contempory designs. Large full colour catalogue available.

SUPPLIERS

C. and A.J. Barmby
140 Lavender Hill, Tonbridge, Kent. TA9 2NJ. (Chris and Angela Barmby). Est. 1980. Tel: 01732 771590; fax - same; e-mail - Bookpilot@aol.com Open by appointment. *Suppliers of display stands in wire; reference books and catalogues on antiques and antiquarian books. Mail order service.* VAT: Stan.

Dauphin Museum Services Ltd
PO Box 602, Oxford, Oxon. OX44 9LU. (John Harrison-Banfield). Est. 1985. Tel: 01865 343542; fax - 01865 343307; e-mail - sales@dauphin.co.uk website - www.dauphin.co.uk Open 9-5, Sat. by appointment. Please telephone for directions. *Design and manufacture of stands, mounts, cabinets and environmental cases. Mounting service. Acrylic display stands - other materials utilised include glass, wood, metal, stone, marble, brass and bronze. Free mail order catalogue available.*

Just Bros. and Co
Roeder House, Vale Rd., London N4 1QA. Tel: 020 8880 2505; fax - 020 8802 0062; e-mail - info@justbros.co.uk Member British Jewellery and Giftware Federation Ltd. Open 9-5, Fri. 9-12.30. *One of the largest suppliers of quality jewellery and presentation cases in Europe. Catalogue on request.*

Marshall Brass
Keeling Hall Rd., Foulsham, Norfolk. NR20 5PR. (Andrew and Tracey Marshall). Est. 1985. Tel: 01362 684105; fax - 01362 684280; e-mail - admin@marshall-brass.com website - www.marshall-brass.com GMC. *Suppliers of quality period furniture fittings in brass and iron. 320 page catalogue available £12.*

Martin and Co. Ltd
160 Dollman St., Duddeston, Birmingham, West Midlands. B7 4RS. Est. 1950. Tel: 0121 233 2111; fax - 0121 236 0488; website - www.martin.co.uk-onlinecatalogue ASFI. GAI. Open Mon.-Fri. 8-5. *Cabinet hardware supplied - handles, locks, hinges, castors etc. Trade Only.*

Alan Morris Wholesale
Stonecourt, Townsend, Nympsfield, Glos. GL10 3UF. Tel: 01453 861069. *Display stands - coated wire, plastic, acrylic and wood for plates, cups, saucers, bowls etc; wire and disc; jewellery boxes, polishing and cleaning cloths, peelable white labels and strung tickets. Mail order available.* VAT: Stan.

Relics of Witney Ltd
35 Bridge St., Witney, Oxon. OX28 1DA. Est. 1987. Tel: 01993 704611; website - www.tryrelics.co.uk Open 9-5. *Suppliers of furniture restoration materials, brass castors, handles, locks, waxes and polish, upholstery and caning requisites, Farrow & Ball and reproduction paints, stencils etc. Mail order also. Online catalogue.* LOC: Main road.

J. Shiner and Sons Ltd
33 Windmill St., London W1T 2JW. Tel: 020 7636 0740;

fax - 020 7580 0740. *Suppliers of brass handles, castors, locks, brass grills and leathers.*

Suffolk Brass
2 & 3 Victoria Way, Exmouth, Devon. EX8 1EW. (Trevor Ford and Steve Lendon). Est. 1975. Tel: 01395 272846; fax - 01395 276688; e-mail - trevor@devonmetalcrafts.co.uk website - www.devonmetalcrafts.co.uk Open Mon.-Fri. 8.30-5. *Period replica cabinet fittings. Catalogue £5.* VAT: Stan. *Trade Only.*

The Victorian Ring Box Company
Unit 1, Fleetside, Gatehouse of Fleet, Kirkcudbright - shire, Scotland. DG7 2JY. (The Franca Bruno Company). Est. 1990. Tel: 01557 814466/814054; fax - same; e-mail - francambruno@hotmail.com Open by appointment. *Manufacturers and distributors of high quality antique style presentation boxes; also available with sterling silver tops and in tartan.*

TEXTILES

The Textile Conservancy Company Ltd
Unit 3A Pickhill Business Centre, Smallhythe Road, Tenterden, Kent. TN30 7LZ. (Alexandra Seth-Smith). Est. 1997. Tel: 01580 761600; fax - same; e-mail - alex@textile-conservation.co.uk website - www.textile-conservation.co.uk UKIC. *Cleaning and repair of historic textiles, tapestries and rugs. Professional advice on correct storage and display. Collection surveys and condition reports.*

The Textile Restoration Studio
2 Talbot Rd., Bowdon, Altrincham, Cheshire. WA14 3JD. (Jacqueline and Michael Hyman). Est. 1982. Tel: 0161 928 0020; fax - same; e-mail - studio@textilerestoration.co.uk website - www.textilerestoration.co.uk and www.conservationconsortium.com Conservation Register. UK Institute for Conservation. *Cleaning and repair of all antique textiles including tapestries, samplers, canvas work, beadwork, lace, costume, ecclesiastical vestments and furnishings, dolls and fans. Mail order catalogue of specialist textile conservation materials (free with large stamped addressed envelope).*

TOYS

Robert Mullis Restoration Services Ltd
55 Berkeley Rd., Wroughton, Swindon, Wilts. SN4 9BN. Tel: 01793 813583; fax - 01793 813577; e-mail - robert@rockinghorses.freeserve.co.uk website - www.restorationservices.co.uk BTG. Strictly by appointment. *Full or partial restorations of antique horses, some wooden toy restoration. Traditional methods and materials used. Collection and delivery. New rocking horses made in five sizes, commissions undertaken.*

Tobilane Designs
The Toyworks, Holly House, Askham, Penrith, Cumbria. CA10 2PG. (Paul and Elaine Commander). Est. 1985. Tel: 01931 712077; e-mail - info@thetoyworks.co.uk website - www.thetoyworks.co.uk Open Wed - Sat. 10-5, Sun. 11-4. *Traditional toymakers and restorers of old toys including rocking horses and teddies. Identification and valuation service.* LOC: Opposite Queen's Head public house, village centre, 5 miles south of Penrith. VAT: Stan.

ALPHABETICAL LIST OF TOWNS AND VILLAGES AND COUNTIES UNDER WHICH THEY ARE LISTED.

A

Abbots Leigh, Somerset.
Aberdeen, Scotland.
Aberdour, Scotland.
Aberfeldy, Scotland.
Aberford, Yorks. West.
Abernyte, Scotland.
Aberystwyth, Wales.
Abinger Hammer, Surrey.
Accrington, Lancs.
Acrise, Kent.
Alcester, Warks.
Aldeburgh, Suffolk.
Aldermaston, Berks.
Alderney, C.I.
Alford, Lincs.
Alfreton, Derbys.
Allington, Lincs.
Allonby, Cumbria.
Alnwick, Northumbs.
Alresford, Hants.
Alsager, Cheshire.
Alston, Cumbria.
Alton, Hants.
Altrincham, Cheshire.
Amersham, Bucks.
Ampthill, Beds.
Andover, Hants.
Angmering, Sussex West.
Ansley, Warks.
Antrim, Co. Antrim, N. Ireland.
Appledore, Kent.
Ardingly, Sussex West.
Arundel, Sussex West.
Ascot, Berks.
Ascott-under-Wychwood, Oxon.
Ash, Kent.
Ash Vale, Surrey.
Ashbourne, Derbys.
Ashburton, Devon.
Ashford, Kent.
Ashtead, Surrey.
Aston Clinton, Bucks.
Atcham, Shrops.
Attleborough, Norfolk.
Atworth, Wilts.
Auchterarder, Scotland.
Auldearn, Scotland.
Aylesby, Lincs.
Aylsham, Norfolk.

B

Bagillt, Wales.
Bagshot, Surrey.
Baildon, Yorks. West.
Bakewell, Derbys.
Balcombe, Sussex West.
Balderton, Notts.
Baldock, Herts.
Balfron, Scotland.
Ballater, Scotland.
Ballyclare, Co. Antrim, N. Ireland.
Ballymena, Co. Antrim, N. Ireland.
Balsham, Cambs.
Bampton, Devon.
Banbury, Oxon.
Bangor, Co. Down, N. Ireland.
Bangor, Wales.
Barham, Kent.
Barkham, Berks.
Barlow, Derbys.
Barmouth, Wales.
Barnard Castle, Durham.
Barnet, Herts.

Barnstaple, Devon.
Barnt Green, Worcs.
Barrington, Somerset.
Barry, Wales.
Barton, Cheshire.
Basingstoke, Hants.
Bath, Somerset.
Batheaston, Somerset.
Batley, Yorks. West.
Battlesbridge, Essex.
Baythorne End, Essex.
Beaconsfield, Bucks.
Beauly, Scotland.
Beaumaris, Wales.
Beccles, Suffolk.
Beckenham, Kent.
Bedale, Yorks. North.
Bedford, Beds.
Beech, Hants.
Beer, Devon.
Beeston, Notts.
Belfast, Co. Antrim, N. Ireland.
Belper, Derbys.
Bembridge, Isle of Wight.
Bere Regis, Dorset.
Berkeley, Glos.
Berkhamsted, Herts.
Berwick-upon-Tweed, Northumbs.
Bessacarr, Yorks. South.
Betchworth, Surrey.
Bethesda, Wales.
Beverley, Yorks. East.
Bewdley, Worcs.
Bibury, Glos.
Bicester, Oxon.
Bideford, Devon.
Biggleswade, Beds.
Billericay, Essex.
Billingshurst, Sussex West.
Bilsington, Kent.
Birchington, Kent.
Birdbrook, Essex.
Birdham, Sussex West.
Birkenhead, Merseyside.
Birmingham, West Mids..
Bishop's Castle, Shrops.
Bishop's Stortford, Herts.
Bishops Cleeve, Glos.
Blackburn, Lancs.
Blackmore, Essex.
Blackpool, Lancs.
Bladon, Oxon.
Blaenau Ffestiniog, Wales.
Blair Atholl, Scotland.
Blairgowrie, Scotland.
Blakeney, Glos.
Blandford Forum, Dorset.
Bletchingley, Surrey.
Blewbury, Oxon.
Bloxham, Oxon.
Blyford, Suffolk.
Blythburgh, Suffolk.
Bodicote, Oxon.
Bodorgan, Wales.
Bolton, Lancs.
Bolton Abbey, Yorks. North.
Bolton-by-Bowland, Lancs.
Boroughbridge, Yorks. North.
Boscastle, Cornwall.
Boston, Lincs.
Boston Spa, Yorks. West.
Botley, Hants.
Bottisham, Cambs.
Bourne, Lincs.
Bourne End, Bucks.

Bournemouth, Dorset.
Bowdon, Cheshire.
Bowness on Windermere, Cumbria.
Brackley, Northants.
Bradford, Yorks. West.
Bradford-on-Avon, Wilts.
Bradwell, Derbys.
Brailsford, Derbys..
Brambridge, Hants.
Brampton, Cumbria.
Brancaster Staithe, Norfolk.
Brandsby, Yorks. North.
Branksome, Dorset.
Brasted, Kent.
Braunton, Devon.
Brecon, Wales.
Brentwood, Essex.
Brereton, Staffs.
Brewood, Staffs.
Bridge of Earn, Scotland.
Bridgend, Wales.
Bridgnorth, Shrops.
Bridlington, Yorks. East.
Bridport, Dorset.
Brierfield, Lancs.
Brightlingsea, Essex.
Brighton, Sussex East.
Brinkworth, Wilts.
Bristol, Glos.
Brixham, Devon.
Broadstairs, Kent.
Broadway, Worcs.
Brockenhurst, Hants.
Bromley, Kent.
Brook, Hants.
Bruton, Somerset.
Buckingham, Bucks.
Budby, Notts.
Budleigh Salterton, Devon.
Bungay, Suffolk.
Burford, Oxon.
Burgess Hill, Sussex West.
Burghfield Common, Berks.
Burlton, Shrops.
Burneston, Yorks. North.
Burnham Market, Norfolk.
Burnham-on-Sea, Somerset.
Burnley, Lancs.
Burscough, Lancs.
Burton-upon-Trent, Staffs.
Burwash, Sussex East.
Burwell, Cambs.
Bury, Lancs.
Bury St. Edmunds, Suffolk.
Bushey, Herts.
Bushmills, Co. Antrim, N. Ireland.
Buxton, Derbys.

C

Caernarfon, Wales.
Caerphilly, Wales.
Caistor, Lincs.
Callington, Cornwall.
Calne, Wilts.
Cambridge, Cambs.
Camelford, Cornwall.
Canonbie, Scotland.
Canterbury, Kent.
Cardiff, Wales.
Carhampton, Somerset.
Carlisle, Cumbria.
Carlton-on-Trent, Notts.
Carmarthen, Wales.
Carrefour Selous, St. Lawrence,

Jersey, C.I .
Carshalton, Surrey.
Cartmel, Cumbria.
Castle Ashby, Northants.
Castle Cary, Somerset.
Castletown, Isle of Man.
Cavendish, Suffolk.
Caversham, Berks.
Ceres, Scotland.
Cerne Abbas, Dorset.
Chacewater, Cornwall.
Chagford, Devon.
Chale, Isle of Wight.
Chalfont St. Giles, Bucks.
Chalford, Glos.
Chalgrove, Oxon.
Chard, Somerset.
Charlton Horethorne, Somerset.
Charlwood, Surrey.
Cheadle Hulme, Cheshire.
Cheam, Surrey.
Cheltenham, Glos.
Chepstow, Wales.
Cherhill, Wilts.
Chertsey, Surrey.
Chesham, Bucks.
Chester, Cheshire.
Chesterfield, Derbys.
Chichester, Sussex West.
Chilcompton, Somerset.
Chilham, Kent.
Chilton, Oxon.
Chippenham, Wilts.
Chipping Campden, Glos.
Chipping Norton, Oxon.
Chipping Sodbury,, Glos.
Chirk, Wales.
Chislehurst, Kent.
Chittering, Cambs.
Chobham, Surrey.
Chorley, Lancs.
Christchurch, Dorset.
Christian Malford, Wilts.
Church Stretton, Shrops.
Cirencester, Glos.
Clare, Suffolk.
Cleethorpes, Lincs.
Cleobury Mortimer, Shrops.
Clevedon, Somerset.
Clitheroe, Lancs.
Clola by Mintlaw, Scotland.
Clyst Honiton, Devon.
Coalville, Leics.
Cobham, Surrey.
Cockermouth, Cumbria.
Cocking, Sussex West.
Codford, Wilts.
Coggeshall, Essex.
Colchester, Essex.
Coldstream, Scotland.
Coleraine, Co. Londonderry, N. Ireland.
Coleshill, Warks.
Coltishall, Norfolk.
Colwyn Bay, Wales.
Colyton, Devon.
Combe Martin, Devon.
Comberton, Cambs.
Congleton, Cheshire.
Conisholme, Lincs.
Connor Downs, Cornwall.
Consett, Durham.
Conwy, Wales.
Cookham Rise, Berks.
Cookstown, Co. Tyrone, N. Ireland.

Coombe Bissett, Wilts.
Corbridge, Northumbs.
Corringham, Essex.
Corsham, Wilts.
Cosford, Shrops.
Cottered, Herts.
Coulsdon, Surrey.
Coventry, West Mids..
Cowbridge, Wales.
Cowes, Isle of Wight.
Coxley, Somerset.
Cranborne, Dorset.
Cranbrook, Kent.
Crayford, Kent.
Crediton, Devon.
Cremyll, Cornwall.
Crewe, Cheshire.
Crewkerne, Somerset.
Criccieth, Wales.
Crickhowell, Wales.
Cricklade, Wilts.
Cromarty, Scotland.
Cromer, Norfolk.
Crosby Ravensworth, Cumbria.
Cross Hills, Yorks. North.
Croydon, Surrey.
Crudwell, Wilts.
Cuckfield, Sussex West.
Cullompton, Devon.

D

Danbury, Essex.
Darlington, Durham.
Darlton, Notts.
Darwen, Lancs.
Datchet, Berks.
Deal, Kent.
Debden, Essex.
Debenham, Suffolk.
Deddington, Oxon.
Deganwy, Wales.
Denby Dale, Yorks. West.
Depden, Suffolk.
Derby, Derbys.
Devizes, Wilts.
Disley, Cheshire.
Diss, Norfolk.
Ditchling, Sussex East.
Ditton Priors, Shrops.
Dobwalls, Cornwall.
Donaghadee, Co. Down, N. Ireland.
Dorchester, Dorset.
Dorchester-on-Thames, Oxon.
Dorking, Surrey.
Dornoch, Scotland.
Dorridge, West Mids..
Douglas, Isle of Man.
Doune, Scotland.
Downham Market, Norfolk.
Driffield, Yorks. East.
Drinkstone, Suffolk.
Droitwich, Worcs.
Duffield, Derbys.
Dulverton, Somerset.
Dundee, Scotland.
Dundonald, Co. Down, N. Ireland.
Dunecht, Scotland.
Dungannon, Co. Tyrone, N. Ireland.
Dunkeld, Scotland.
Dunsfold, Surrey.
Dunster, Somerset.
Durham, Durham.
Duxford, Cambs.

E

Earls Colne, Essex.
Earsham, Norfolk.
Easingwold, Yorks. North.
East Dereham, Norfolk.

East Hagbourne, Oxon.
East Molesey, Surrey.
East Peckham, Kent.
East Pennard, Somerset.
Eastbourne, Sussex East.
Ebrington, Glos.
Edenbridge, Kent.
Edinburgh, Scotland.
Elham, Kent.
Elstead, Surrey.
Ely, Cambs.
Emsworth, Hants.
Enfield, Middx.
Epsom, Surrey.
Ermington, Devon.
Eversley, Hants.
Evesham, Worcs.
Ewell, Surrey.
Exeter, Devon.
Exmouth, Devon.
Exning, Suffolk.
Eye, Suffolk.

F

Fairford, Glos.
Fakenham, Norfolk.
Faldingworth, Lincs.
Falmouth, Cornwall.
Faringdon, Oxon.
Farnborough, Hants.
Farnham, Surrey.
Farningham, Kent.
Faversham, Kent.
Felixstowe, Suffolk.
Feniscowles, Lancs.
Fenny Bridges, Devon.
Ferryside,Wales.
Filey, Yorks. North.
Finchingfield, Essex.
Finedon, Northants.
Finningham, Suffolk.
Fishlake, Yorks. South.
Fladbury, Worcs.
Flamborough, Yorks. East.
Flaxton, Yorks. North.
Flimwell, Sussex East.
Flore, Northants.
Fochabers, Scotland.
Folkestone, Kent.
Fordham, Cambs.
Fordingbridge, Hants.
Forest Row, Sussex East.
Forfar, Scotland.
Forres, Scotland.
Fortrose, Scotland.
Four Elms, Kent.
Four Oaks, West Mids..
Framlingham, Suffolk.
Freshford, Somerset.
Freshwater, Isle of Wight.
Frinton-on-Sea, Essex.
Frodsham, Cheshire.
Frome, Somerset.
Froncysyllte, Wales.
Froxfield, Wilts.

G

Gainsborough, Lincs.
Gargrave, Yorks. North.
Gilberdyke, Yorks. East.
Gillingham, Dorset.
Glasgow, Scotland.
Glencarse, Scotland.
Glossop, Derbys.
Gloucester, Glos.
Godalming, Surrey.
Godney, Somerset.
Gomshall, Surrey.
Gosforth, Cumbria.
Gosforth, Tyne and Wear.
Gosport, Hants.
Goudhurst, Kent.

Grampound, Cornwall.
Grantham, Lincs.
Grasmere, Cumbria.
Great Baddow, Essex.
Great Bookham, Surrey.
Great Cransley, Northants.
Great Glen, Leics.
Great Harwood, Lancs.
Great Malvern, Worcs.
Great Missenden, Bucks.
Great Salkeld, Cumbria.
Great Shefford, Berks.
Great Shelford, Cambs.
Great Waltham, Essex.
Great Yarmouth, Norfolk.
Greatford, Lincs.
Green Hammerton, Yorks. North.
Greystoke, Cumbria.
Grimsby, Lincs.
Grimston, Leics.
GrouvilleJersey, C.I .
Guildford, Surrey.
Guisborough, Yorks. North.
Gullane, Scotland.

H

Hacheston, Suffolk.
Haddenham, Bucks.
Haddington, Scotland.
Hadlow Down, Sussex East.
Hailsham, Sussex East.
Hainault, Essex.
Halesowen, West Mids..
Halesworth, Suffolk.
Halfway, Berks.
Halifax, Yorks. West.
Hallow, Worcs.
Halstead, Essex.
Hampton, Middx.
Hamstreet, Kent.
Harpole, Northants.
Harrogate, Yorks. North.
Hartley Wintney, Hants.
Harwich, Essex.
Haslemere, Surrey.
Haslingden, Lancs.
Hastings, Sussex East.
Hatherleigh, Devon.
Hatton, Warks.
Haverfordwest, Wales.
Havering-atte-Bower, Essex.
Hawarden, Wales.
Hawes, Yorks. North.
Haworth, Yorks. West.
Hay-on-Wye, Wales.
Hayfield, Derbys..
Hayle, Cornwall.
Hayling Island, Hants.
Headington, Oxon.
Headley, Hants.
Heanor, Derbys.
Heathfield, Sussex East.
Hebden Bridge, Yorks. West.
Helmsley, Yorks. North.
Helston, Cornwall.
Hemel Hempstead, Herts.
Hemswell Cliff, Lincs.
Henfield, Sussex West.
Henley-in-Arden, Warks.
Henley-on-Thames, Oxon.
Henlow, Beds.
Hereford, Herefs.
Hertford, Herts.
Heswall, Merseyside.
Hexham, Northumbs.
High Wycombe, Bucks.
Hinckley, Leics.
Hindhead, Surrey.
Hingham, Norfolk.
Hitchin, Herts.
Hoby, Leics.

Holbeach, Lincs.
Holland-on-Sea, Essex.
Holmfirth, Yorks. West.
Holt, Norfolk.
Holyhead, Wales.
Holywood, Co. Down, N. Ireland.
Honiton, Devon.
Honley, Yorks. West.
Hook Norton Oxon.
Horley, Surrey.
Horncastle, Lincs.
Horsham, Sussex West.
Horton, Berks.
Houghton, Cambs.
Houghton, Sussex West.
Hoveton, Norfolk.
Hoylake, Merseyside.
Hucknall, Notts.
Huddersfield, Yorks. West.
Hull, Yorks. East.
Hungerford, Berks.
Hunstanton, Norfolk.
Huntercombe, Oxon.
Huntingdon, Cambs.
Huntly, Scotland.
Hurst, Berks.
Hurstpierpoint, Sussex West.
Hythe, Kent.

I

Ibstock, Leics.
Ilchester, Somerset.
Ilkley, Yorks. West.
Inchture, Scotland.
Ingatestone, Essex.
Innerleithen, Scotland.
Inverness, Scotland.
Ipswich, Suffolk.
Iver, Bucks.
Ixworth, Suffolk.

J

Jedburgh, Scotland.
Jesmond, Tyne and Wear.

K

Kelling, Norfolk.
Kelvedon, Essex.
Kendal, Cumbria.
Keswick, Cumbria.
Kettering, Northants.
Kew Green, Surrey.
Kidderminster, Worcs.
Kidwelly, Wales.
Kilbarchan, Scotland.
Killamarsh, Derbys.
Killearn, Scotland.
Killin, Scotland.
Kilmacolm, Scotland.
Kilmarnock, Scotland.
Kilmichael Glassary, Scotland.
King's Lynn, Norfolk.
Kingham, Oxon.
Kingsbridge, Devon.
Kingsclere, Hants.
Kingsthorpe, Northants.
Kingston-on-Spey, Scotland.
Kingston-upon-Thames, Surrey.
Kington, Herefs.
Kington Langley, Wilts.
Kirk Deighton, Yorks. North.
Kirkby Lonsdale, Cumbria.
Kirkby Stephen, Cumbria.
Kirkcaldy, Scotland.
Kirkcudbright, Scotland.
Kirton, Lincs.
Knaresborough, Yorks. North.
Knebworth, Herts.
Knighton, Wales.
Knutsford, Cheshire.

L
Lake, Isle of Wight.
Lamberhurst, Kent.
Lancaster, Lancs.
Landbeach, Cambs.
Langford, Notts.
Langford, Somerset.
Langholm, Scotland.
Langley Burrell, Wilts.
Largs, Scotland.
Launceston, Cornwall.
Lavenham,, Suffolk.
Leagrave, Beds.
Leamington Spa, Warks.
Lechlade, Glos.
Leckhampstead, Berks.
Ledbury, Herefs.
Leeds, Yorks. West.
Leek, Staffs.
Leicester, Leics.
Leigh, Lancs.
Leigh, Staffs.
Leigh-on-Sea, Essex.
Leighton Buzzard, Beds.
Leiston, Suffolk.
Leominster, Herefs.
Lepton, Yorks. West.
Lewes, Sussex East.
Leyburn, Yorks. North.
Lichfield, Staffs.
Lincoln, Lincs.
Lindfield, Sussex West.
Linlithgow, Scotland.
Lisburn, Co. Antrim, N. Ireland.
Liss, Hants.
Little Dalby, Leics.
Little Horsted, Sussex East.
Littlebourne, Kent.
Littleton, Somerset.
Litton Cheney, Dorset.
Liverpool, Merseyside.
Llandeilo, Wales.
Llandudno, Wales.
Llandudno Junction, Wales.
Llanelli, Wales.
Llanerchymedd, Wales.
Llangollen, Wales.
Llanrwst, Wales.
Lockerbie, Scotland.
Londonderry, Co. Londonderry, N. Ireland.
Long Eaton, Derbys.
Long Marston, Warks.
Long Marton, Cumbria.
Long Melford, Suffolk.
Long Sutton, Lincs.
Longhaven, Scotland.
Longridge, Lancs.
Looe, Cornwall.
Lostwithiel, Cornwall.
Loughborough, Leics.
Lound, Lincs.
Low Newton, Cumbria.
Lower Stondon, Beds.
Lubenham, Leics.
Ludlow, Shrops.
Lurgan, Co. Armagh, N. Ireland.
Luton, Beds.
Lydford, Devon.
Lye, West Mids..
Lymington, Hants.
Lymm, Cheshire.
Lyndhurst, Hants.
Lyneham, Wilts.
Lynton, Devon.
Lytchett Minster, Dorset.

M
Macclesfield, Cheshire.
Maidenhead, Berks.
Maidstone, Kent.
Maldon, Essex.

Malmesbury, Wilts.
Malton, Yorks. North.
Malvern Link, Worcs.
Manchester, Lancs.
Manningford Bruce, Wilts.
Marazion, Cornwall.
Margate, Kent.
Marhamchurch, Cornwall.
Market Bosworth, Leics.
Market Deeping, Lincs.
Market Drayton, Shrops.
Market Harborough, Leics.
Market Weighton, Yorks. East.
Marlborough, Wilts.
Marlesford, Suffolk.
Marlow, Bucks.
Marple Bridge, Cheshire.
Martlesham, Suffolk.
Martock, Somerset.
Masham, Yorks. North.
Matching Green, Essex.
Matlock, Derbys.
Melbury Osmond, Dorset.
Melksham, Wilts.
Melrose, Scotland.
Melton Mowbray, Leics.
Menai Bridge, Wales.
Mendlesham, Suffolk.
Menston, Yorks. West.
Mere, Wilts.
Merstham, Surrey.
Merton, Devon.
Mevagissey, Cornwall.
Mexborough, Yorks. South.
Middle Aston, Oxon.
Middleham, Yorks. North.
Middlesbrough, Yorks.North.
Middleton Village, Lancs.
Midhurst, Sussex West.
Mildenhall, Suffolk.
Milford Haven, Wales.
Minchinhampton, Glos.
Mobberley, Cheshire.
Modbury, Devon.
Modbury, Devon.
Moira, Co. Armagh, N. Ireland.
Monkton, Devon.
Monmouth, Wales.
Montrose, Scotland.
Morden, Surrey.
Morecambe, Lancs.
Moreton-in-Marsh, Glos.
Much Wenlock, Shrops.

N
Nantwich, Cheshire.
Narberth, Wales.
Nayland, Suffolk.
Needham, Norfolk.
Needham Market, Suffolk.
Nelson, Lancs.
Nether Stowey, Somerset.
New Bolingbroke, Lincs.
New Malden Surrey.
Newark, Notts.
Newbridge-on-Wye, Wales.
Newburgh, Scotland.
Newby Bridge, Cumbria.
Newcastle Emlyn, Wales.
Newcastle-under-Lyme, Staffs.
Newcastle-upon-Tyne, Tyne and Wear.
Newent, Glos.
Newmarket, Suffolk.
Newport, Essex.
Newport, Isle of Wight.
Newport, Wales.
Newport-on-Tay, Scotland.
Newton Abbot, Devon.
Newton St. Cyres, Devon.
Newtownabbey, Co. Antrim, N. Ireland.

North Aston, Oxon.
North Berwick, Scotland.
North Cave, Yorks. East.
North Petherton, Somerset.
North Shields, Tyne and Wear.
North Walsham, Norfolk.
North Wraxall, Wilts.
Northallerton, Yorks. North.
Northampton, Northants.
Northchapel, Sussex West.
Northfleet, Kent.
Northleach, Glos.
Northwich, Cheshire.
Norton, Durham.
Norton, Yorks. North.
Norwich, Norfolk.
Nottingham, Notts.
Nutley, Sussex East.

O
Oakham, Rutland.
Ockbrook, Derbys.
Odiham, Hants.
Old Bedhampton, Hants.
Oldham, Lancs.
Ollerton, Notts.
Olney, Bucks.
Omagh, Co. Tyrone, N. Ireland.
Orford, Suffolk.
Ormskirk, Lancs.
Osgathorpe, Leics.
Otford, Kent.
Otley, Yorks. West.
Outwell, Cambs.
Oxford, Oxon.
Oxted, Surrey.

P
Paignton, Devon.
Painswick, Glos.
Paisley, Scotland.
Pangbourne, Berks.
Parkstone, Dorset.
Pateley Bridge, Yorks. North.
Patrington, Yorks. East.
Peasenhall, Suffolk.
Pembroke, Wales.
Penistone, Yorks. South.
Penkridge, Staffs.
Penn, Bucks.
Penrith, Cumbria.
Penryn, Cornwall.
Penzance, Cornwall.
Pershore, Worcs.
Perth, Scotland.
Peterborough, Cambs.
Petersfield, Hants.
Petts Wood, Kent.
Petworth, Sussex West.
Pevensey, Sussex East.
Pewsey, Wilts.
Pickering, Yorks. North.
Pittenweem, Scotland.
Plumley, Cheshire.
Plymouth, Devon.
Polegate, Sussex East.
Pontllyfrii, Wales.
Poole, Dorset.
Porlock, Somerset.
Porlock, Somerset.
Portballintrae, Co. Antrim, N. Ireland.
Porthcawl, Wales.
Pórthmadog, Wales.
Portrush, Co. Antrim, N. Ireland.
Portslade, Sussex East.
Portsmouth, Hants.
Potter Heigham, Norfolk.
Potterspury, Northants.
Potton, Beds.
Poulton-le-Fylde, Lancs.

Poundgate, Sussex East.
Poynton, Cheshire.
Preston, Lancs.
Prestwick, Scotland.
Puckeridge, Herts.
Puddletown, Dorset.
Pulborough, Sussex West.
Pwllheli, Wales.

Q
Queen Camel, Somerset.
Queniborough,, Leics.
Quorn, Leics.

R
Rackenford, Devon.
Radford Semele, Warks.
Radstock, Somerset.
Rainford, Merseyside.
Rait, Scotland.
Ramsbury, Wilts.
Ramsey, Cambs.
Ramsgate, Kent.
Raughton Head, Cumbria.
Raveningham, Norfolk.
Ravenstonedale, Cumbria.
Rayleigh, Essex.
Reading, Berks.
Redbourn, Herts.
Redditch, Worcs.
Redhill, Surrey.
Redruth, Cornwall.
Reigate, Surrey.
Retford, Notts.
Richmond, Surrey.
Richmond, Yorks. North.
Rickmansworth, Herts.
Ringstead, Norfolk.
Ringwood, Hants.
Ripley, Derbys.
Ripley, Surrey.
Ripon, Yorks. North.
Risby, Suffolk.
Robin Hood's Bay, Yorks. North.
Rochdale, Lancs.
Rochester, Kent.
Rodington, Shrops.
Rolvenden, Kent.
Romiley, Cheshire.
Romsey, Hants.
Ross-on-Wye, Herefs.
Rothbury, Northumbs..
Rotherfield, Sussex East.
Rotherham, Yorks. South.
Rottingdean, Sussex East.
Rowlands Castle, Hants.
Rugeley, Staffs.
Runfold, Surrey.
Rushden, Northants.
Ryde, Isle of Wight.
Rye, Sussex East.

S
Sabden, Lancs.
Saffron Walden, Essex.
Saintfield, Co. Down, N. Ireland.
Salisbury, Wilts.
Saltaire, Yorks. West.
Saltcoats, Scotland.
Samlesbury, Lancs.
Sandbach, Cheshire.
Sandgate, Kent.
Sandiacre, Notts.
Sandside, Cumbria.
Sandwich, Kent.
Sawbridgeworth, Herts.
Scarborough, Yorks. North.
Scratby, Norfolk.
Screveton, Notts.
Scunthorpe, Lincs.

Seaford, Sussex East.
Seapatrick, Co. Down, N. Ireland.
Seaton, Devon.
Sedbergh, Cumbria.
Seething, Norfolk.
Semley, Wilts.
Settle, Yorks. North.
Sevenoaks, Kent.
Shaftesbury, Dorset.
Shanklin, Isle of Wight.
Shardlow, Derbys.
Sheffield, Yorks. South.
Shefford, Beds.
Shenfield, Essex.
Shenton, Leics.
Shepton Mallet, Somerset.
Sherborne, Dorset.
Shere, Surrey.
Sheringham, Norfolk.
Shifnal, Shrops.
Shipston-on-Stour, Warks.
Shoreham-by-Sea, Sussex West.
Shrewsbury, Shrops.
Sible Hedingham, Essex.
Sidcup, Kent.
Sidmouth, Devon.
Sileby, Leics.
Skipton, Yorks. North.
Slad, Glos.
Sleaford, Lincs.
Sleights, Yorks. North.
Snainton, Yorks. North.
Snape, Suffolk.
Solihull, West Mids..
Somersham, Cambs.
Somerton, Somerset.
Sonning-on-Thames, Berks.
South Brent, Devon.
South Harting, Sussex West.
South Molton, Devon.
South Shields, Tyne and Wear.
Southampton, Hants.
Southborough, Kent.
Southend-on-Sea, Essex.
Southport, Merseyside.
Southwell, Notts.
Southwold, Suffolk.
Sowerby Bridge, Yorks. West.
Spalding, Lincs.
Spondon, Derbys.
St. Albans, Herts.
St. Andrews, Scotland.
St. Buryan, Cornwall.
St. Columb Major, Cornwall.
St. Helen Auckland, Durham.
St. Helier, Jersey, C.I .
St. Ives, Cambs.
St. Ives, Cornwall.
St. Lawrence, Jersey, C.I .
St. Leonards-on-Sea, Sussex East.
St. Neots, Cambs.
St. Peter Port, Guernsey, C.I .
St. Sampson, Guernsey, C.I .
St. Saviour, Jersey, C.I .
Stafford, Staffs.
Staines, Surrey.
Stalham, Norfolk.
Stamford, Lincs.
Standlake, Oxon.
Stanley, Scotland.
Stansted, Essex.
Stanton upon Hine Heath, Shrops.
Staplecross, Sussex East.
Staunton Harold, Leics.
Staveley, Cumbria.
Stewarton, Scotland.
Stewartstown, Co. Tyrone, N. Ireland.
Steyning, Sussex West.

Stickney, Lincs.
Stiffkey, Norfolk.
Stillington, Yorks. North.
Stirling, Scotland.
Stockbridge, Hants.
Stockbury, Kent.
Stockport, Cheshire.
Stockton-on-Tees, Durham.
Stogursey, Somerset.
Stoke Ferry, Norfolk.
Stoke-on-Trent, Staffs.
Stoke-sub-Hamdon, Somerset.
Stokesley, Yorks. North.
Stony Stratford, Bucks.
Storrington, Sussex West.
Stourbridge, West Mids..
Stow-on-the-Wold, Glos.
Stowmarket, Suffolk.
Stratford-upon-Avon, Warks.
Strathblane, Scotland.
Stretton-on-Fosse, Warks.
Stroud, Glos.
Sturminster Newton, Dorset.
Suckley, Worcs.
Sudbury, Suffolk.
Sunderland, Tyne and Wear.
Sundridge, Kent.
Surbiton, Surrey.
Sutton, Surrey.
Sutton Bonington, Notts.
Sutton Bridge, Lincs.
Sutton Coldfield, West Mids..
Sutton Valence, Kent.
Sutton-in-Ashfield, Notts.
Sutton-on-Sea, Lincs.
Swaffham, Norfolk.
Swafield, Norfolk.
Swanage, Dorset.
Swansea, Wales.
Swindon, Wilts.
Swinstead, Lincs.

T

Tacolneston, Norfolk.
Taddington, Glos.
Tadley, Hants.
Tarporley, Cheshire.
Tarvin, Cheshire.
Tarvin Sands, Cheshire.
Tattenhall, Cheshire.
Tattershall, Lincs.
Taunton, Somerset.
Taynton, Oxon.
Tedburn St Mary, Devon.
Teddington, Middx.
Teignmouth, Devon.
Templeton, Wales.
Tenby, Wales.
Tenterden, Kent.
Tetbury, Glos.
Tetsworth, Oxon.
Tewkesbury, Glos.
Teynham, Kent.
Thame, Oxon.
Thames Ditton, Surrey.
Thaxted, Essex.
Thirsk, Yorks. North.
Thornton-le-Dale, Yorks. North.
Three Legged Cross, Dorset.
Tilston, Cheshire.
Tintern, Wales.
TisburyWilts.
Titchfield, Hants.
Tockwith, Yorks. North.
Todenham, Glos.
Todmorden, Yorks. West.
Tonbridge, Kent.
Topsham, Devon.
Torquay, Devon.
Totnes, Devon.
Tottenhill, Norfolk.
Towcester, Northants.

Trawden, Lancs.
Trecastle, Wales.
Treharris, Wales.
Tresillian, Cornwall.
Tring, Herts.
Troon, Scotland.
Truro, Cornwall.
Tunbridge Wells, Kent.
Tutbury, Staffs.
Tuxford, Notts.
Twickenham, Middx.
Twyford, Berks.
Twyford, Norfolk.
Tynemouth, Tyne and Wear.
Tywyn, Wales.

U

Uckfield, Sussex East.
Uffculme, Devon.
Ullapool, Scotland.
Ulverston, Cumbria.
Upper Largo, Scotland.
Uppingham, Rutland.
Upton-upon-Severn, Worcs.
Uttoxeter, Staffs.
Uxbridge, Middx.

V

Valley, Wales.
Ventnor, Isle of Wight.

W

Waddesdon, Bucks.
Wadebridge, Cornwall.
Wadhurst, Sussex East.
Wainfleet, Lincs.
Wakefield, Yorks. West.
Wallasey, Merseyside.
Wallingford, Oxon.
Walsall, West Mids..
Walsden, Yorks. West.
Walton-on-Thames, Surrey.
Wansford, Cambs.
Wareham, Dorset.
Warfield, Berks.
Wargrave, Berks.
Warminster, Wilts.
Warrington, Cheshire.
Warwick, Warks.
Washford, Somerset.
Washington, Tyne and Wear.
Watchet, Somerset.
Waterlooville, Hants.
Watford, Herts.
Watlington, Oxon.
Wattisfield, Suffolk.
Waverton, Cheshire.
Wedmore, Somerset.
Weedon, Northants.
Weeford, Staffs.
Wellingborough, Northants.
Wellington, Somerset.
Wells, Somerset.
Wells-next-the-Sea, Norfolk.
Welshpool, Wales.
Wendover, Bucks.
Wentworth, Yorks. South.
West Auckland, Durham.
West Bridgford, Notts..
West Buckland, Somerset.
West Burton, Yorks. North.
West Byfleet, Surrey.
West Haddon, Northants.
West Kirby, Merseyside.
West Malling, Kent.
West Yatton, Wilts.
Westcliff-on-Sea, Essex.
Westerham, Kent.
Weston, Herts.
Weston-Super-Mare, Somerset.
Weybridge, Surrey.
Weymouth, Dorset.

Whaley Bridge, Derbys.
Whalley, Lancs.
Wheathampstead, Herts.
Whimple, Devon.
Whitby, Yorks. North.
Whitchurch, Bucks.
Whitchurch, Shrops.
White Roding, Essex.
Whitefield, Lancs.
Whitehaven, Cumbria.
Whithorn, Scotland.
Whitley Bay, Tyne and Wear.
Whitstable, Kent.
Whittington, Glos.
Whitwick, Leics.
Wickham Bishops, Essex.
Wickham Market, Suffolk.
Wigan, Lancs.
Wigtown, Scotland.
Williton, Somerset.
Wilstead (Wilshamstead), Beds.
Wilstone, Herts.
Wilton, Wilts.
Wimborne Minster, Dorset.
Wincanton, Somerset.
Winchcombe, Glos.
Winchester, Hants.
Windsor, Berks.
Wing, Rutland.
Wingham, Kent.
Winslow, Bucks.
Wisbech, Cambs.
Witney, Oxon.
Wittersham, Kent.
Wiveliscombe, Somerset.
Woburn, Beds.
Woking, Surrey.
Wolverhampton, West Mids..
Woodbridge, Suffolk.
Woodford, Northants.
Woodford Green, Essex.
Woodhall Spa, Lincs.
Woodstock, Oxon.
Wooler, Northumbs.
Woolhampton, Berks.
Woolmer Green, Herts.
Woolpit, Suffolk.
Wootton WawenWarks.
Worcester, Worcs.
Worsley, Lancs.
Worthing, Sussex West.
Wraysbury, Berks.
Wrentham, Suffolk.
Writtle, Essex.
Wroxham, Norfolk.
Wychbold, Worcs.
Wymeswold, Leics.
Wymondham, Leics.
Wymondham, Norfolk.

Y

Yarnton, Oxon.
Yazor, Herefs.
Yealmpton, Devon.
Yeovil, Somerset.
York, Yorks. North.
Yoxall, Staffs.
Yoxford, Suffolk.

Specialist Dealers' Index

Most antique dealers in Britain sell a wide range of goods from furniture, through porcelain and pottery, to pictures, prints and clocks. Much of the interest in visting antiques shops comes from this diversity. However, there are a number of dealers who specialise and the following is a list of these dealers. Most of them will stock a representative selection of the items found under their classification.

The name of the business, together with the area of London or the town and county under which the detailed entry can be found are given in the listing. Again we would like to repeat the advice given in the introduction that, if readers are looking for a particular item, they are advised to telephone first, before making a long journey.

CLASSIFICATIONS

Antiques Centres and Markets
Antiquarian Books
Antiquities
Architectural Items
Arms & Armour
Art Deco & Art Nouveau
Barometers - see also Clock Dealers
Beds
Brass (see Metalwork)
Bronzes
Carpets & Rugs
Cars & Carriages
Chinese Art - see Oriental
Church Furniture & Furnishings
Clocks & Watches
Coins & Medals
Dolls & Toys
Etchings & Engravings
Fire Related Items
Frames
Furniture-
   Continental (mainly French)
   Country
   Georgian
   Oak

Pine
Victorian
Garden Furniture, Ornaments &
   Statuary
Glass - see also Glass Domes &
   Paperweights
Glass Domes
Icons - see Russian Art
Islamic Art
Japanese Art - see Oriental
Jewellery - see Silver & Jewellery
Lighting
Maps & Prints
Metalware/work
Miniatures
Mirrors
Musical Boxes, Instruments &
   Literature
Nautical Instruments - see Scientific
Needlework - see Tapestries
Netsuke - see Oriental
Oil Paintings
Oriental Items
Paperweights
Photographs & Equipment

Porcelain & Pottery
Prints - see Maps
Rugs - see Carpets
Russian/Soviet Art
Scientific Instruments
Sculpture
Shipping Goods & Period Furniture
   for the Trade
Silver and Jewellery
Sporting Items & Associated
   Memorabilia
Sporting Paintings & Prints
Stamps
Tapestries, Textiles & Needlework
Taxidermy
Tools - including Needlework &
   Sewing
Toys - see Dolls
Trade Dealers - see Shipping Goods
Treen
Vintage Cars - see Carriages & Cars
Watercolours
Wholesale Dealers - see Shipping
   Goods
Wine Related Items

Antique Centres & Markets
Collectors Centre - Antique City, London E17.
The Angel Arcade, London N1.
Camden Passage Antiques Market and Pierrepont
   Arcade Antiques Centre, London N1.
The Fleamarket, London N1.
London Militaria Market, London N1.
The Mall Antiques Arcade, London N1.
Palmers Green Antiques Centre, London N13.
Hampstead Antique and Craft Emporium, London
   NW3.
Alfies Antique Market, London NW8.
Greenwich Antiques Market, London SE10.
Sydenham Antiques Centre, London SE26.
Northcote Road Antiques Market, London SW11.
Antiquarius, London SW3.
Bourbon-Hanby Antiques Centre, London SW3.
Bond Street Antiques Centre, London W1.
Grays Antique Markets, London W1.
Admiral Vernon Antiques Market, London W11.

Arbras Gallery, London W11.
Central Gallery (Portobello), London W11.
The Corner Portobello Antiques Supermarket, London
   W11.
Crown Arcade, London W11.
The Harris's Arcade, London W11.
The Red Lion Antiques Arcade, London W11.
Roger's Antiques Gallery, London W11.
The Silver Fox Gallery (Portobello), London W11.
World Famous Portobello Market, London W11.
The Old Cinema Antique Department Store, London
   W4.
Kensington Church Street Antiques Centre, London
   W8.
Apple Market Stalls, London WC2.
Covent Garden Flea Market, London WC2.
The London Silver Vaults, London WC2.
Ampthill Antiques Emporium, Ampthill, Beds.
The Woburn Abbey Antiques Centre, Woburn, Beds.
Barkham Antique Centre, Barkham, Berks.

Great Grooms of Hungerford, Hungerford, Berks.
Hungerford Arcade, Hungerford, Berks.
Moss End Antique Centre, Warfield, Berks.
Buck House Antiques, Beaconsfield, Bucks.
Buckingham Antiques Centre, Buckingham, Bucks.
Marlow Antique Centre, Marlow, Bucks.
The Antiques Centre at Olney, Olney, Bucks.
Antiques at .. .Wendover Antiques Centre, Wendover,
  Bucks.
Winslow Antiques Centre, Winslow, Bucks.
The Hive, Cambridge, Cambs.
Waterside Antiques Centre, Ely, Cambs.
Huntingdon Trading Post, Huntingdon, Cambs.
Knutsford Antiques Centre, Knutsford, Cheshire.
Northwich Antiques Centre, Northwich, Cheshire.
Tarporley Antique Centre, Tarporley, Cheshire.
Chapel Street Antiques Arcade, Penzance, Cornwall.
The Coinage Hall Antiques Centre, Truro, Cornwall.
The Cumbrian Antiques Centre, Brampton, Cumbria.
Carlisle Antiques Centre, Carlisle, Cumbria.
Cockermouth Antiques Market, Cockermouth,
  Cumbria.
Alfreton Antiques Centre, Alfreton, Derbys.
Chappells Antiques Centre, Bakewell, Derbys.
Bradwell Antiques Centre, Bradwell, Derbys.
Heanor Antiques Centre, Heanor, Derbys.
Matlock Antiques and Collectables Centre, Matlock,
  Derbys.
Memory Lane Antiques Centre, Ripley, Derbys.
The Shambles, Ashburton, Devon.
North Devon Antiques Centre, Barnstaple, Devon.
Colyton Antiques Centre, Colyton, Devon.
The Antique Centre on the Quay, Exeter, Devon.
The Antiques Complex, Exeter, Devon.
Phantique, Exeter, Devon.
The Quay Gallery Antiques Emporium, Exeter, Devon.
Honiton Antique Centre, Honiton, Devon.
St Leonards Antiques & Craft Centre, Newton Abbot,
  Devon.
Barbican Antiques Centre, Plymouth, Devon.
New Street Antique Centre, Plymouth, Devon.
Parade Antiques Market, Plymouth, Devon.
Sidmouth Antiques & Collectors Centre, Sidmouth,
  Devon.
Topsham Quay Antiques Centre, Topsham, Devon.
Colliton Antique Centre, Dorchester, Dorset.
De Danann Antique Centre, Dorchester, Dorset.
Mr. Punch's Antique Market, Shaftesbury, Dorset.
Sherborne World of Antiques, Sherborne, Dorset.
Battlesbridge Antique Centre, Battlesbridge, Essex.
The Shipwreck, Brightlingsea, Essex.
Finchingfield Antiques Centre, Finchingfield, Essex.
Baddow Antique Centre, Great Baddow, Essex.
Gallerie Antiques, Hainault, Essex.
Townsford Mill Antiques Centre, Halstead, Essex.
Harwich Antiques Centre, Harwich, Essex.
Saffron Walden Antiques Centre, Saffron Walden,
  Essex.
Curio City., Southend-on-Sea, Essex.

Berkeley Antiques Market, Berkeley, Glos.
St. Nicholas Markets, Bristol, Glos.
Cheltenham Antique Market, Cheltenham, Glos.
Sixways Antique Centre, Cheltenham, Glos.
Cirencester Arcade, Cirencester, Glos.
Antiques Centre Gloucester Ltd, Gloucester, Glos.
Jubilee Hall Antiques Centre, Lechlade, Glos.
Lechlade Arcade, Lechlade, Glos.
The Old Ironmongers Antiques Centre, Lechlade, Glos.
London House Antique Centre, Moreton-in-Marsh,
  Glos.
Windsor House Antiques Centre, Moreton-in-Marsh,
  Glos.
Durham House Antiques Centre, Stow-on-the-Wold,
  Glos.
Fox Cottage Antiques, Stow-on-the-Wold, Glos.
Tudor House, Stow-on-the-Wold, Glos.
Alchemy Antiques, Tetbury, Glos.
Long Street Antiques, Tetbury, Glos.
Top Banana Antiques Mall 1, Tetbury, Glos.
Top Banana Antiques Mall 2, Tetbury, Glos.
Top Banana Antiques Mall 3 and 4, Tetbury, Glos.
Tewkesbury Antiques & Collectables Centre,
  Tewkesbury, Glos.
Appleton Eves Ltd, Alton, Hants.
Squirrel Collectors Centre, Basingstoke, Hants.
Dolphin Quay Antique Centre, Emsworth, Hants.
Cedar Antiques Centre Ltd, Hartley Wintney, Hants.
Lymington Antiques Centre, Lymington, Hants.
Forest Antique Centre, Lyndhurst, Hants.
Lyndhurst Antiques Centre, Lyndhurst, Hants.
The Folly Antiques Centre, Petersfield, Hants.
Samuels Spencers Antiques and Decorative Arts
  Emporium, Winchester, Hants.
Hereford Antique Centre, Hereford, Herefs.
Leominster Antiques Market, Leominster, Herefs.
Linden House Antiques Centre, Leominster, Herefs.
Minster House, LeominsterHerefs.
Ross-on-Wye Antiques Gallery, Ross-on-Wye, Herefs.
Heritage Antique Centre, Berkhamsted, Herts.
Jordans Antiques Centre, Hemel Hempstead, Herts.
The Herts and Essex Antiques Centre, Sawbridgeworth,
  Herts.
By George! Antiques Centre, St. Albans, Herts.
Beckenham Antiques & Collectors' Market,
  Beckenham, Kent.
Burgate Antique Centre, Canterbury, Kent.
Bagham Barn Antiques, Chilham, Kent.
Antiques at Cranbrook, Cranbrook, Kent.
Malthouse Arcade, Hythe, Kent.
Beehive, Petts Wood, Kent.
Memories, Rochester, Kent.
Barden House Antiques, Tonbridge, Kent.
Castle Antiques Centre, Westerham, Kent.
King's Mill Antique Centre, Burnley, Lancs.
Heskin Hall Antiques, Chorley, Lancs.
Belgrave Antique Centre, Darwen, Lancs.
Holden Wood Antiques Centre, Haslingden, Lancs.
The Assembly Rooms Market, Lancaster, Lancs.

SPECIALIST DEALERS

G.B. Antiques Ltd, Lancaster, Lancs.
Lancaster Leisure Park Antiques Centre, Lancaster, Lancs.
Antiques Village, Manchester, Lancs.
The Antique Centre, Preston, Lancs.
Preston Antique Centre, Preston, Lancs.
Walter Aspinall Antiques Ltd, Sabden, Lancs.
Pendle Antiques Centre Ltd, Sabden, Lancs.
Leicester Antiques Warehouse, Leicester, Leics.
Oxford Street Antique Centre, Leicester, Leics.
Whitemoors Antiques and Fine Art, Shenton, Leics.
Town & Country Antiques Centre, Alford, Lincs.
Portobello Row Antique & Collectors' Centre, Boston, Lincs.
Bourne Antiques & Art, Bourne, Lincs.
Pilgrims Antiques Centre, Gainsborough, Lincs.
Notions Antiques Centre, Grantham, Lincs.
Astra House Antiques Centre, Hemswell Cliff, Lincs.
Hemswell Antique Centres, Hemswell Cliff, Lincs.
Great Expectations, Horncastle, Lincs.
The Horncastle Antiques Centre, Horncastle, Lincs.
The Trinity Centre, Horncastle, Lincs.
Dorrian Lambert Antiques Centre, Lincoln, Lincs.
The Chapel Emporium Antique Centre, Long Sutton, Lincs.
Old Maltings Antique Centre, Louth, Lincs.
St. Martins Antiques Centre, Stamford, Lincs.
The Southport Antiques Centre, Southport, Merseyside.
The Antiques & Collectors Centre (Diss), Diss, Norfolk.
Fakenham Antique Centre, Fakenham, Norfolk.
Holt Antique Centre, Holt, Norfolk.
Mews Antique Emporium, Holt, Norfolk.
Le Strange Old Barns Antiques, Arts & Craft Centre, Hunstanton, Norfolk.
The Old Granary Antiques and Collectors Centre, King's Lynn, Norfolk.
Cloisters Antique & Collectors Fair, Norwich, Norfolk.
Tombland Antiques Centre, Norwich, Norfolk.
Ringstead Village Antique Centre, Ringstead, Norfolk.
Wells Antique Centre, Wells-next-the-Sea, Norfolk.
Wymondham Antique and Collectors Centre, Wymondham, Norfolk.
Brackley Antique Cellar, Brackley, Northants.
E.K. Antiques, Finedon, Northants.
The Reindeer Antiques Centre, Potterspury, Northants.
The Village Antique Market, Weedon, Northants.
Antiques and Bric-a-Brac Market, Wellingborough, Northants.
Castle Gate Antiques Centre, Newark, Notts.
Newark Antiques Centre, Newark, Notts.
Newark Antiques Warehouse, Newark, Notts.
Top Hat Antiques, Nottingham, Notts.
Banbury Antique Centre, Banbury, Oxon.
Antiques @ The George, Burford, Oxon.
Country Markets Antiques and Collectables, Chilton, Oxon.
Chipping Norton Antique Centre, Chipping Norton, Oxon.

Manchester House Antiques Centre, Chipping Norton, Oxon.
The Quiet Woman Antiques Centre, Chipping Norton, Oxon.
Station Mill Antiques Centre, Chipping Norton, Oxon.
Deddington Antiques Centre, Deddington, Oxon.
Friday Street Antique Centre (The Ferret), Henley-on-Thames, Oxon.
Antiques on High Ltd, Oxford, Oxon.
The Swan at Tetsworth, Tetsworth, Oxon.
The Lamb Arcade, Wallingford, Oxon.
Antiques at Heritage, Woodstock, Oxon.
Yarnton Antiques Centre, Yarnton, Oxon.
Rutland Antiques Centre, Uppingham, Rutland.
Bridgnorth Antiques Centre, Bridgnorth, Shrops.
Old Mill Antique Centre, Bridgnorth, Shrops.
Stretton Antiques Market, Church Stretton, Shrops.
Antique Centre, Cleobury Mortimer, Shrops.
Zani Lady Decorative Antiques, Ludlow, Shrops.
Princess Antique Centre, Shrewsbury, Shrops.
Shrewsbury Antique Centre, Shrewsbury, Shrops.
Bartlett Street Antiques Centre, Bath, Somerset.
George Street Antiques Centre, Bath, Somerset.
Old Bank Antiques Centre, Bath, Somerset.
Paragon Antiques and Collectors Market, Bath, Somerset.
Piccadilly Antiques, Batheaston, Somerset.
Chard Antique Centre, Chard, Somerset.
Crewkerne Antique Centre, Crewkerne, Somerset.
Somerton Antiques Centre, Somerton, Somerset.
Cider Press Antiques Centre, Taunton, Somerset.
Taunton Antiques Market - Silver Street, Taunton, Somerset.
Green Dragon Antiques Centre, Wincanton, Somerset.
Rugeley Antique Centre, Brereton, Staffs.
The Leek Antiques Centre (Barclay House), Leek, Staffs.
Windmill Antiques, Stafford, Staffs.
Old Chapel Antique & Collectables Centre, Tutbury, Staffs.
Clare Antique Warehouse, Clare, Suffolk.
Long Melford Antiques Centre, Long Melford, Suffolk.
Old Town Hall Antique & Collectors Centre, Needham Market, Suffolk.
The Risby Barn, Risby, Suffolk.
Snape Antiques and Collectors Centre, Snape, Suffolk.
Southwold Antiques Centre, Southwold, Suffolk.
Church Street Centre, Woodbridge, Suffolk.
Yoxford Antique Centre & Gardens, Yoxford, Suffolk.
Mimbridge Antiques Centre, Chobham, Surrey.
Dorking House Antiques, Dorking, Surrey.
Great Grooms of Dorking, Dorking, Surrey.
Pilgrims Antique Centre, Dorking, Surrey.
Bridge Road Antiques Centre, East Molesey, Surrey.
Nostradamus II, East Molesey, Surrey.
Bourne Mill Antiques, Farnham, Surrey.
Haslemere Antique Market, Haslemere, Surrey.
Kingston Antique Market, Kingston-upon-Thames, Surrey.
Lawrence House Antiques, Redhill, Surrey.
Talbot Walk Antique Centre, Ripley, Surrey.

Shere Antiques Centre, Shere, Surrey.
Brighton Flea Market, Brighton, Sussex East.
Brighton Lanes Antique Centre, Brighton, Sussex East.
Eastbourne Antiques Market, Eastbourne, Sussex East.
Enterprise Collectors Market, Eastbourne, Sussex East.
Seaquel Antique & Collectors Market, Eastbourne, Sussex East.
George Street Antiques Centre, Hastings, Sussex East.
Church-Hill Antiques Centre, Lewes, Sussex East.
Cliffe Antiques Centre, Lewes, Sussex East.
The Emporium Antique Centre, Lewes, Sussex East.
Lewes Antique Centre, Lewes, Sussex East.
Lewes Flea Market, Lewes, Sussex East.
The Hastings Antique Centre, St. Leonards-on-Sea, Sussex East.
Rocking Horse Antique Market, Ardingly, Sussex West.
The Old Cornstore Antiques, Arundel, Sussex West.
Almshouses Arcade, Chichester, Sussex West.
Chichester Antiques Centre, Chichester, Sussex West.
Petworth Antique Centre, Petworth, Sussex West.
Newcastle Antique Centre, Newcastle-upon-Tyne, Tyne and Wear.
Malthouse Antiques Centre, Alcester, Warks.
The Stables Antique Centre, Hatton, Warks.
Barn Antiques Centre, Long Marston, Warks.
Stratford Antique Centre, Stratford-upon-Avon, Warks.
The Stratford Antiques and Interiors Centre Ltd, Stratford-upon-Avon, Warks.
Vintage Antiques Centre, Warwick, Warks.
The Warwick Antique Centre, Warwick, Warks.
The Birmingham Antique Centre, Birmingham, West Mids.
Antiques Adventure, Coventry, West Mids.
Regency Antique Trading Ltd., Stourbridge, West Mids.
Wolverhampton Antiques and Collectors Market, Wolverhampton, West Mids.
Upstairs, Downstairs Collectors Centre, Devizes, Wilts.
The Marlborough Parade Antique Centre, Marlborough, Wilts.
King Street Curios, Melksham, Wilts.
Antique and Collectors Market, Salisbury, Wilts.
The Avonbridge Antiques and Collectors Market, Salisbury, Wilts.
Dairy House Antiques, Semley, Wilts.
Penny Farthing Antiques Arcade, Swindon, Wilts.
Warminster Antiques Centre, Warminster, Wilts.
Bewdley Antiques, Bewdley, Worcs.
The Hayloft Antique Centre, Fladbury, Worcs.
Worcester Antiques Centre, Worcester, Worcs.
St Crispin Antique Centre, Beverley, Yorks. East.
Vicar Lane Antique Centre, Beverley, Yorks. East.
The Georgian Rooms, Bridlington, Yorks. East.
Grannie's Treasures, Hull, Yorks. East.
Mount Pleasant Antiques Centre, Market Weighton, Yorks. East.
The Ginnel Antiques Centre, Harrogate, Yorks. North.
Montpellier Mews Antique Centre, Harrogate, Yorks. North.
Leyburn Antiques Centre, Leyburn Yorks. North.
Pickering Antique Centre, Pickering, Yorks. North.

Skipton Antiques Centre, Skipton, Yorks. North.
Antiques Centre York, York, Yorks. North.
Cavendish Antiques & Collectors Centre, York, Yorks. North.
The Red House Antiques Centre, York, Yorks. North.
York Antiques Centre, York, Yorks. North.
Foster's Antique Centre, Rotherham, Yorks. South.
Barmouth Court Antiques Centre, Sheffield, Yorks. South.
Chapel Antiques Centre, Sheffield, Yorks. South.
Court House Antique Centre, Sheffield, Yorks. South.
Langtons Antiques & Collectables, Sheffield, Yorks. South.
Nichols Antique Centre, Sheffield, Yorks. South.
Wentworth Arts, Crafts and Antiques Ltd, Wentworth, Yorks. South.
Halifax Antiques Centre, Halifax, Yorks. West.
Headrow Antiques Centre, Leeds, Yorks. West.
Victoria Antiques, Saltaire, Yorks. West.
Scottish Antique & Arts Centre, Abernyte, Scotland.
Clola Antiques Centre, Clola by Mintlaw, Scotland.
The Antiques Warehouse, Glasgow, Scotland.
The Victorian Village Antiques, Glasgow, Scotland.
Rait Village Antiques Centre, Rait, Scotland.
Cardiff Antiques Centre, Cardiff, Wales.
Jacobs Antique Centre, Cardiff, Wales.
Hay Antique Market, Hay-on-Wye, Wales.
Offa's Dyke Antique Centre, Knighton, Wales.
The Works Antiques Centre, Llandeilo, Wales.
Pembroke Antiques Centre, Pembroke, Wales.
Trecastle Antiques Centre, Trecastle, Wales.

Antiquarian Books

Barrie Marks Ltd, London N2.
Nicholas Goodyer, London N5.
Fisher and Sperr, London N6.
Keith Fawkes, London NW3.
Marcet Books, London SE10.
Rogers Turner Books, London SE10.
Classic Bindings Ltd, London SW1.
Thomas Heneage Art Books, London SW1.
Sims Reed Ltd, London SW1.
Hünersdorff Rare Books Ltd, London SW10.
John Thornton, London SW10.
Regent House Gallery, London SW11.
Paul Foster's Bookshop, London SW14.
Hanshan Tang Books, London SW15.
Ash Rare Books, London SW17.
Earlsfield Bookshop, London SW18.
Peter Harrington Antiquarian Bookseller, London SW3.
Russell Rare Books, London SW3.
Robin Greer, London SW6.
The Gloucester Road Bookshop, London SW7.
Paul Orssich, London SW8.
Altea Gallery, London W1.
G. Heywood Hill Ltd, London W1.
Holland & Holland, London W1.
Maggs Bros Ltd, London W1.
Marlborough Rare Books Ltd, London W1.
Pickering and Chatto, London W1.
Jonathan Potter Ltd, London W1.

SPECIALIST DEALERS

Bernard Quaritch Ltd (Booksellers), London W1.

Robert G. Sawers, London W1.

Shapero Gallery, London W1.

Henry Sotheran Ltd, London W1.

Crawley and Asquith Ltd, London W10.

Demetzy Books, London W11.

Peter Kennedy, London W11.

D. Parikian, London W14.

Hosains Books and Antiques, London W2.

Adrian Harrington, London W8.

Atlantis Bookshop, London WC1.

Cinema Bookshop, London WC1.

Fine Books Oriental, London WC1.

Michael Finney Antique Prints and Books, London WC1.

Robert Frew Ltd, London WC1.

Tim Bryars Ltd, London WC2.

David Drummond at Pleasures of Past Times, London WC2.

P. J. Hilton (Books), London WC2.

Marchpane, London WC2.

Henry Pordes Books Ltd, London WC2.

Bertram Rota Ltd, London WC2.

Storey's Ltd, London WC2.

Tindley and Chapman, London WC2.

Watkins Books Ltd, London WC2.

Nigel Williams Rare Books, London WC2.

Peter Shepherd Antiques, Hurst, Berks.

Eton Antique Bookshop, Windsor, Berks.

Penn Barn, Penn, Bucks.

The Bookshop, Cambridge, Cambs.

G. David, Cambridge, Cambs.

Sarah Key, Cambridge, Cambs.

Stothert Old Books, Chester, Cheshire.

Copnal Books, Crewe, Cheshire.

Lion Gallery and Bookshop, Knutsford, Cheshire.

Mereside Books, Macclesfield, Cheshire.

New Street Bookshop, Penzance, Cornwall.

Penzance Rare Books, Penzance, Cornwall.

Bonython Bookshop, Truro, Cornwall.

Norman Kerr - Gatehouse Bookshop, Cartmel, Cumbria.

Peter Bain Smith (Bookseller), Cartmel, Cumbria.

Archie Miles Bookshop, Gosforth, Cumbria.

Lakes Crafts & Antiques Gallery, Grasmere, Cumbria.

G.K. Hadfield, Great Salkeld, Cumbria.

Keswick Bookshop, Keswick, Cumbria.

The Book House, Ravenstonedale, Cumbria.

R. F. G. Hollett and Son, Sedbergh, Cumbria.

Michael Moon - Antiquarian Booksellers, Whitehaven, Cumbria.

Dartmoor Bookshop, Ashburton, Devon.

Exeter Rare Books, Exeter, Devon.

High Street Books, Honiton, Devon.

Graham York Rare Books, Honiton, Devon.

The Pocket Bookshop, Paignton, Devon.

P.M. Pollak, South Brent, Devon.

The Schuster Gallery, Torquay, Devon.

Collards Books, Totnes, Devon.

The Exchange, Totnes, Devon.

Pedlars Pack Books, Totnes, Devon.

Bridport Old Books, Bridport, Dorset.

Words Etcetera, Dorchester, Dorset.

Antique Map and Bookshop, Puddletown, Dorset.

Chapter House Books, Sherborne, Dorset.

Reference Works Ltd., Swanage, Dorset.

Books Afloat, Weymouth, Dorset.

Minster Books, Wimborne Minster, Dorset.

Castle Bookshop, Colchester, Essex.

Peter J. Hadley Bookseller, Harwich, Essex.

Bookworm, Holland-on-Sea, Essex.

Pastimes, Bristol, Glos.

David Bannister FRGS, Cheltenham, Glos.

Michael Rayner, Cheltenham, Glos.

Ian Hodgkins and Co. Ltd, Slad, Glos.

Wychwood Books, Stow-on-the-Wold, Glos.

Tetbury Old Books, Tetbury, Glos.

Laurence Oxley Ltd, Alresford, Hants.

Bookends, Emsworth, Hants.

Kingsclere Old Bookshop (Wyseby House Books), Kingsclere, Hants.

The Petersfield Bookshop, Petersfield, Hants.

Castle Hill Books, Kington, Herefs.

Keith Smith Books, Ledbury, Herefs.

Ross Old Book and Print Shop, Ross-on-Wye, Herefs.

Gillmark Gallery, Hertford, Herts.

Eric T. Moore, Hitchin, Herts.

Clive A. Burden Ltd, Rickmansworth, Herts.

Reg and Philip Remington, St. Albans, Herts.

Ventnor Rare Books, Ventnor, Isle of Wight.

The Canterbury Bookshop, Canterbury, Kent.

Chaucer Bookshop, Canterbury, Kent.

McConnell Fine Books, Deal, Kent.

Military History Bookshop, Folkestone, Kent.

Alan Lord Antiques, HytheKent.

Baggins Book Bazaar - The Largest Secondhand Bookshop in England, Rochester, Kent.

Hall's Bookshop, Tunbridge Wells, Kent.

Taylor-Smith Books, Westerham, Kent.

Siri Ellis Books, Bolton, Lancs.

Eric J. Morten, Manchester, Lancs.

Halewood and Sons, Preston, Lancs.

Preston Book Co, Preston, Lancs.

Clarendon Books, Leicester, Leics.

Elaine Lonsdale Bookseller and Bookbinder, Hemswell Cliff, Lincs.

P.J. Cassidy (Books), Holbeach, Lincs.

Golden Goose Books, Lincoln, Lincs.

Harlequin Gallery and Golden Goose Globe Restorers, Lincoln, Lincs.

Staniland (Booksellers), Stamford, Lincs.

C.K. Broadhurst and Co Ltd, Southport, Merseyside.

Ian Sheridan's Bookshop, Hampton, Middx.

Chris Hollingshead Horticultural Books, Teddington, Middx.

Anthony C. Hall, Twickenham, Middx.

John Ives Bookseller, Twickenham, Middx.

Rita Shenton, Twickenham, Middx.

The Brazen Head Bookshop & Gallery, Burnham Market, Norfolk.

Books Etc., Cromer, Norfolk.
Village Books, East Dereham, Norfolk.
David Ferrow, Great Yarmouth, Norfolk.
Baskerville Bindings, Holt, Norfolk.
Simon Finch Norfolk, Holt, Norfolk.
The Old Reading Room Gallery and Tea Room,
    Kelling, Norfolk.
The Angel Bookshop, North Walsham, Norfolk.
The Tombland Bookshop, Norwich, Norfolk.
Turret House, Wymondham, Norfolk.
The Old Hall Bookshop, Brackley, Northants.
Right Angle, Brackley, Northants.
Occultique, Northampton, Northants.
Park Gallery & Bookshop, Wellingborough, Northants.
Barter Books, Alnwick, Northumbs.
Priest Popple Books, Hexham, Northumbs.
Anthony W. Laywood, Balderton, Notts.
E.M. Lawson and Co, East Hagbourne, Oxon.
Jonkers Rare Books, Henley-on-Thames, Oxon.
Richard J. Kingston, Henley-on-Thames, Oxon.
Richard Way Bookseller, Henley-on-Thames, Oxon.
Blackwell's Rare Books, Oxford, Oxon.
Jericho Books, Oxford, Oxon.
Waterfield's, Oxford, Oxon.
Toby English, Wallingford, Oxon.
Tooley Adams & Co, Wallingford, Oxon.
Secondhand Bookshop, Uppingham, Rutland.
M. and M. Baldwin, Cleobury Mortimer, Shrops.
Candle Lane Books, Shrewsbury, Shrops.
George Bayntun, Bath, Somerset.
George Gregory, Bath, Somerset.
Patterson Liddle, Bath, Somerset.
Gresham Books, Crewkerne, Somerset.
Rothwell and Dunworth, Dulverton, Somerset.
Janet Clarke, Freshford, Somerset.
Rare Books and Berry, Porlock, Somerset.
Steven Ferdinando, Queen Camel, Somerset.
Sterling Books, Weston-Super-Mare, Somerset.
M.A.J. Morris, Burton-upon-Trent, Staffs.
Mike Abrahams Books, Lichfield, Staffs.
Besleys Books, Beccles, Suffolk.
Trinders' Fine Tools, Clare, Suffolk.
Abington Books, Finningham, Suffolk.
Claude Cox at College Gateway Bookshop, Ipswich,
    Suffolk.
R.E. and G.B. Way, Newmarket, Suffolk.
Honeypot Antiques Ltd, Elstead, Surrey.
Vandeleur Antiquarian Books, Epsom, Surrey.
J.W. McKenzie, Ewell, Surrey.
A. Burton-Garbett, Morden, Surrey.
Secondhand Bookshop, Oxted, Surrey.
Colin Page Antiquarian Books, Brighton, Sussex East.
Camilla's Bookshop, Eastbourne, Sussex East.
Roderick Dew, Eastbourne, Sussex East.
A. & T. Gibbard, Eastbourne, Sussex East.
Howes Bookshop, Hastings, Sussex East.
Bow Windows Book Shop, Lewes, Sussex East.
A. & Y. Cumming, Lewes, Sussex East.
The Fifteenth Century Bookshop, Lewes, Sussex East.

Chapter & Verse Booksellers, Rye, Sussex East.
The Book Jungle, St. Leonards-on-Sea, Sussex East.
Muttonchop Manuscripts, Petworth, Sussex West.
R.D. Steedman, Newcastle-upon-Tyne, Tyne and Wear.
Keel Row Books, North Shields, Tyne and Wear.
Olivers Bookshop, Whitley Bay, Tyne and Wear.
The Stratford Bookshop, Stratford-upon-Avon, Warks.
Duncan M. Allsop, Warwick, Warks.
David Temperley Fine and Antiquarian Books,
    Birmingham, West Mids.
Clive Farahar and Sophie Dupré - Rare Books,
    Autographs and Manuscripts, Calne, Wilts.
Hilmarton Manor Press, Calne, Wilts.
The Military Parade Bookshop, Marlborough, Wilts.
Heraldry Today, Ramsbury, Wilts.
Bookworms of Evesham, Evesham, Worcs.
Malvern Bookshop, Great Malvern, Worcs.
Antique Map and Print Gallery, Hallow, Worcs.
Grove Rare Books, Bolton Abbey, Yorks. North.
Potterton Books, Thirsk, Yorks. North.
Cobweb Books, Thornton-le-Dale, Yorks. North.
Barbican Bookshop, York, Yorks. North.
Fossgate Books, York, Yorks. North.
Minster Gate Bookshop, York, Yorks. North.
Janette Ray Rare and Out of Print Books, York, Yorks.
    North.
Ken Spelman, York, Yorks. North.
Alan Hill Books, Sheffield, Yorks. South.
The Toll House Bookshop, Holmfirth, Yorks. West.
Channel Islands Galleries Ltd, St. Peter Port, Guernsey,
    C.I.
John Blench & Son, St. Helier, Jersey, C.I.
The Selective Eye Gallery, St. Helier, Jersey, C.I.
Thesaurus (Jersey) Ltd, St. Helier, Jersey, C.I.
Stacks Bookshop, Dundonald, Co. Down, N. Ireland.
Foyle Books, Londonderry, Co. Londonderry, N.
    Ireland.
The McEwan Gallery, Ballater, Scotland.
Blairgowrie Books, Blairgowrie, Scotland.
Armchair Books, Edinburgh, Scotland.
Broughton Books, Edinburgh, Scotland.
McNaughtan's Bookshop, Edinburgh, Scotland.
The Old Town Bookshop, Edinburgh, Scotland.
Second Edition, Edinburgh, Scotland.
Marianne Simpson, Fochabers, Scotland.
Voltaire & Rousseau, Glasgow, Scotland.
Mair Wilkes Books, Newport-on-Tay, Scotland.
Penny Farthing, North Berwick, Scotland.
Ming Books, Wigtown, Scotland.
A.E. Morris (Books), Bethesda, Wales.
Books, Maps and Prints, Brecon, Wales.
Capel Mawr Collectors Centre, Criccieth, Wales.
Richard Booth's Bookshop Ltd, Hay-on-Wye, Wales.
Rose's Books, Hay-on-Wye, Wales.
Mark Westwood Antiquarian Books, Hay-on-Wye, Wales.
Dylan's Bookstore, Swansea, Wales.

Antiquities
C.J. Martin (Coins) Ltd, London N14.

SPECIALIST DEALERS

Aaron Gallery, London W1.
Charles Ede Ltd, London W1.
Hadji Baba Ancient Art Ltd, London W1.
Mansour Gallery, London W1.
Rabi Gallery Ltd, London W1.
Seaby Antiquities, London W1.
Rupert Wace Ancient Art Ltd, London W1.
Valued History, Ely, Cambs.
Potter's Antiques and Coins, Bristol, Glos.
Ancient & Oriental Ltd, Grimston, Leics.
Katharine House Gallery, Marlborough, Wilts.

Architectural Items

LASSCO, London EC2.
Westland London, London EC2.
Relic Antiques Trade Warehouse, London NW1.
Willesden Green Architectural Salvage, London NW10.
Davidson Antiques, London NW8.
Townsends, London NW8.
Lamont Antiques Ltd, London SE10.
CASA, London SE15.
Humphrey-Carrasco Ltd, London SW1.
Thornhill Galleries, London SW18.
Drummonds Architectural Antiques Ltd, London SW3.
Rodney Franklin Antiques, London SW9.
Architectural Antiques, London W6.
Architectural Antiques, Bedford, Beds.
The Studio Gallery, Datchet, Berks.
Dismantle and Deal Direct - Architectural Salvage
    Brokers, Aston Clinton, Bucks.
T. Smith, Chalfont St. Giles, Bucks.
Solopark Plc, Cambridge, Cambs.
Architectural Salvage Online, Chester Cheshire.
Willow Pool Garden Centre, Lymm, Cheshire.
Nostalgia Architectural Antiques, Stockport, Cheshire.
Cheshire Brick and Slate Co, Tarvin Sands, Cheshire.
The Great Northern Architectural Antique Company
    Ltd, Tattenhall, Cheshire.
Architectural Antiques, Kendal, Cumbria.
W.R.S. Architectural Antiques Ltd, Low Newton, Cumbria.
Cumbria Architectural Salvage, Raughton Head, Cumbria.
Havenplan's Architectural Emporium, Killamarsh,
    Derbys.
Adrian Ager Ltd, Ashburton, Devon.
Fagins Antiques, Exeter, Devon.
Yarrow, Honiton, Devon.
Dorset Reclamation, Bere Regis, Dorset.
Talisman, Gillingham, Dorset.
Minter Reclamation, Three Legged Cross Dorset.
Robert Mills Architectural Antiques Ltd, Bristol, Glos.
Cox's Architectural Reclamation Yard, Moreton-in-
    Marsh, Glos.
Minchinhampton Architectural, Stroud, Glos.
Architectural Heritage, Taddington, Glos.
Burgess Farm Antiques, Winchester, Hants.
The Pine Cellars, Winchester, Hants.
Baileys Home & Garden, Ross-on-Wye, Herefs.
Curios of Chale, Chale, Isle of Wight.
The Architectural Stores, Tunbridge Wells, Kent.

Old Smithy, Feniscowles, Lancs.
Antique Fireplace Warehouse, Manchester, Lancs.
In-Situ Manchester, Manchester, Lancs.
Old Bakery Antiques, Wymondham, Leics.
Lindsey Court Architectural, Horncastle, Lincs.
Architectural Salvage Online, Birkenhead, Merseyside.
Peco, Hampton, Middx.
Mongers, Hingham, Norfolk.
Stiffkey Antiques, Stiffkey, Norfolk.
Rococo Antiques, Architectural Goods and Furnishings,
    Weedon, Northants.
Woodside Reclamation (Architectural Antiques),
    Berwick-upon-Tweed, Northumbs.
Nottingham Architectural Antiques & Reclamation,
    Nottingham Notts.
Aston Pine Antiques, Faringdon, Oxon.
Oxford Architectural Antiques, Faringdon, Oxon.
The Country Seat, Huntercombe, Oxon.
North Shropshire Reclamation, Burlton, Shrops.
Priors Reclamation, Ditton Priors, Shrops.
Holloways of Ludlow, Ludlow, Shrops.
David Bridgwater, Bath, Somerset.
Walcot Reclamation, Bath, Somerset.
Chris's Crackers, Carhampton, Somerset.
Wells Reclamation Company, Coxley, Somerset.
Frome Reclamation, Frome, Somerset.
Castle Reclamation, Martock, Somerset.
J.C. Giddings, Wiveliscombe, Somerset.
Cawarden Brick Co Ltd, Rugeley Staffs.
Blackbrook Antiques Village, Weeford, Staffs.
E.T. Webster, Blythburgh, Suffolk.
Tower Reclaim, Mendlesham Suffolk.
Antique Buildings Ltd, Dunsfold, Surrey.
Drummonds Architectural Antiques, Hindhead, Surrey.
The Packhouse, Runfold, Surrey.
Antique Church Furnishings, Walton-on-Thames,
    Surrey.
Brighton Architectural Salvage, Brighton, Sussex East.
Shiners of Jesmond, Jesmond, Tyne and Wear.
Turnburrys, Jesmond, Tyne and Wear.
Tynemouth Architectural Salvage, Tynemouth, Tyne
    and Wear.
Thomas Crapper & Co, Stratford-upon-Avon, Warks.
Willow UK, Kington Langley, Wilts.
Harriet Fairfax Fireplaces and General Antiques,
    Langley Burrell, Wilts.
Kevin Marshall's Antiques Warehouse, Hull, Yorks.
    East.
Old Flames, Easingwold, Yorks. North.
The White House Antiques & Architectural
    Reclamation, Easingwold, Yorks. North.
Period Interiors, Guisborough, Yorks. North.
The Baildon Furniture Co. Ltd, Baildon, Yorks. West.
Andy Thornton Ltd, Halifax, Yorks. West.
Bingley Antiques, Haworth, Yorks. West.
EASY - Edinburgh Architectural Salvage Yard,
    Edinburgh, Scotland.
Holyrood Architectural Salvage, Edinburgh, Scotland.
Cardiff Reclamation, Cardiff, Wales.

Gallop and Rivers Architectural Antiques, Crickhowell, Wales.

Dyfed Antiques and Architectural Salvage, Haverfordwest, Wales.

Drew Pritchard Ltd, Llandudno Wales.

Arms & Armour

London Militaria Market, London N1.

Finchley Fine Art Galleries, London N12.

Laurence Corner, London NW1.

The Armoury of St. James's Military Antiquarians, London SW1.

Peter Dale Ltd, London SW1.

Blunderbuss Antiques, London W1.

Holland & Holland, London W1.

Michael German Antiques Ltd, London W8.

Amir Mohtashemi Ltd, London W8.

Raymond D Holdich International Medals & Militaria, London WC2.

MJM Antiques, Hungerford, Berks.

Anthony D. Goodlad, Chesterfield, Derbys.

Boscombe Militaria, Bournemouth, Dorset.

Sterling Coins and Medals, Bournemouth, Dorset.

Ickleton Antiques, Saffron Walden, Essex.

Chris Grimes Militaria, Bristol, Glos.

Pastimes, Bristol, Glos.

Q & C Militaria, Cheltenham, Glos.

J F F Fire Brigade & Military Collectables, Old Bedhampton, Hants.

New Forest Antiques, Ringwood, Hants.

H.S. Greenfield and Son, Gunmakers (Est. 1805), Canterbury, Kent.

Sporting Antiques, Tunbridge Wells, Kent.

Jean's Military Memories, Great Harwood, Lancs.

Anything Old & Military Collectables, Lancaster, Lancs.

Garth Vincent Antique Arms and Armour, Allington, Lincs.

The Old Brigade, Kingsthorpe, Northants.

Michael D. Long, Nottingham, Notts.

Quillon Antiques of Tetsworth, Tetsworth, Oxon.

English Heritage, Bridgnorth, Shrops.

West Street Antiques, Dorking, Surrey.

Casque and Gauntlet Militaria, Farnham, Surrey.

The Lanes Armoury, Brighton, Sussex East.

St. Pancras Antiques, Chichester, Sussex West.

Magpie Jewellers and Antiques and Magpie Arms & Armour, Evesham, Worcs.

Cairncross and Sons, Filey, Yorks. North.

Hanover Antiques & Collectables, Scarborough, Yorks. North.

J.K. Adamson - Adamson Armoury, Skipton, Yorks. North.

D.W. Dyson (Antique Weapons), Huddersfield, Yorks. West.

Angus Antiques, Dundee, Scotland.

Bow-well Antiques, Edinburgh, Scotland.

Huw Williams Antiques, Porthmadog, Wales.

Edred A.F. Gwilliam, Cricklade, Wilts.

Art Deco & Art Nouveau

Le Style 25, London E3.

After Noah, London N1.

The Antique Trader, London N1.

Charlton House Antiques, London N1.

Style Gallery, London N1.

Tadema Gallery, London N1.

Mike Weedon, London N1.

Crafts Nouveau, London N10.

Michael Slade Antiques, London N4.

Art Furniture, London NW1.

The Facade, London NW1.

Beverley, London NW8.

Bizarre, London NW8.

The Studio, London NW8.

Behind the Boxes - Art Deco, London SE26.

Ciancimino Ltd, London SW1.

Gallery '25, London SW1.

Keshishian, London SW1.

Bob Lawrence Gallery, London SW1.

Twentieth Century, London SW12.

After Noah, London SW3.

Butler and Wilson, London SW3.

David Gill, London SW3.

Gordon Watson Ltd, London SW3.

Rupert Cavendish Antiques, London SW6.

Victor Arwas Gallery - Editions Graphiques Gallery Ltd, London W1.

Liberty, London W1.

Mayfair Gallery Ltd, London W1.

Hickmet Fine Arts, London W11.

Themes and Variations, London W11.

Haslam and Whiteway, London W8.

John Jesse, London W8.

Pruskin Gallery, London W8.

Puritan Values, London W8.

Aldersey Hall Ltd, Chester, Cheshire.

Maggie Mays, Buxton, Derbys.

Altamiradeco, Bournemouth, Dorset.

Lionel Geneen Ltd, Bournemouth, Dorset.

Ruskin Decorative Arts, Stow-on-the-Wold, Glos.

Alexanders, Titchfield, Hants.

Brian West Antiques, Sandgate, Kent.

Peter Hoare Antiques, Southborough, Kent.

Joroen Markies, Tunbridge Wells, Kent.

The Design Gallery 1850-1950, Westerham, Kent.

A.S. Antique Galleries, Manchester, Lancs.

Circa 1900, Liverpool, Merseyside.

Osiris Antiques, Southport, Merseyside.

Arbiter, Wallasey, Merseyside.

Decorative Antiques, Bishop's Castle, Shrops.

Expressions, Shrewsbury, Shrops.

Puritan Values at the Dome, Southwold, Suffolk.

The Gooday Gallery, Richmond, Surrey.

Cockrell Antiques, Surbiton, Surrey.

Aspidistra Antiques, Woking, Surrey.

Peter Hancock Antiques, Chichester, Sussex West.

Tango Antiques, Warwick, Warks.

Willow UK, Kington Langley, Wilts.

SPECIALIST DEALERS

Muir Hewitt Art Deco Originals, Halifax, Yorks. West.
The Rendezvous Gallery, Aberdeen, Scotland.
The Meadows Lamp Gallery, Edinburgh, Scotland.
Jeremy Sniders Antiques, Glasgow, Scotland.
Strachan Antiques, Glasgow, Scotland.
Rhudle Mill, Kilmichael Glassary, Scotland.
Riverside Antiques (Wales) Ltd, Cardiff, Wales.
The House 1860-1925, Monmouth, Wales.

Barometers - see also Clock Dealers
Frosts of Clerkenwell Ltd, London EC1.
R.E. Rose FBHI, London SE9.
John Carlton-Smith, London SW1.
Trevor Philip and Sons Ltd, London SW1.
The Clock Clinic Ltd, London SW15.
Ronald Phillips Ltd, London W1.
Raffety & Walwyn Ltd, London W8.
The Clock Workshop, Caversham, Berks.
Alan Walker, Halfway, Berks.
The Old Malthouse, Hungerford, Berks.
Wyrardisbury Antiques, Wraysbury, Berks.
Carlton Clocks, Amersham, Bucks.
John Beazor and Sons Ltd, Cambridge, Cambs.
Antique Barometers, Ramsey, Cambs.
T. W. Pawson - Clocks, Somersham, Cambs.
Derek and Tina Rayment Antiques, Barton, Cheshire.
Andrew Foott Antiques, Cheadle Hulme, Cheshire.
Mike Read Antique Sciences, St. Ives, Cornwall.
Musgrave Bickford Antiques, Crediton, Devon.
Leigh Extence Antique Clocks, Honiton, Devon.
Honiton Clock Clinic, Honiton, Devon.
Barometer World Ltd, Merton, Devon.
M.C. Taylor, Bournemouth, Dorset.
Timecraft Clocks, Sherborne, Dorset.
Tom Tribe and Son Ltd, Sturminster Newton, Dorset.
Chris L. Papworth, Kelvedon, Essex.
Littlebury Antiques - Littlebury Restorations Ltd,
    Saffron Walden, Essex.
It's About Time, Westcliff-on-Sea, Essex.
Montpellier Clocks, Cheltenham, Glos.
Antony Preston Antiques Ltd, Stow-on-the-Wold, Glos.
Styles of Stow, Stow-on-the-Wold, Glos.
Vanbrugh House Antiques, Stow-on-the-Wold, Glos.
Wyndhams, Stow-on-the-Wold, Glos.
Bryan Clisby Antique Clocks, Hartley Wintney, Hants.
The Clock-Work-Shop (Winchester), Winchester, Hants.
G.E. Marsh Antique Clocks Ltd, Winchester, Hants.
The Barometer Shop Ltd, Leominster, Herefs.
Robert Horton Antiques, Hertford, Herts.
John Chawner, Birchington, Kent.
Patric Capon, Bromley, Kent.
Michael Sim, Chislehurst, Kent.
Neill Robinson Blaxill, Sevenoaks, Kent.
Drop Dial Antiques, Bolton, Lancs.
Harrop Fold Clocks (F. Robinson), Bolton-by-Bowland,
    Lancs.
Oaktree Antiques, Lubenham, Leics.
N. Bryan-Peach Antiques, Wymeswold, Leics.
Robin Fowler (Period Clocks), Aylesby, Lincs.

Time after Time, Hemswell Cliff, Lincs.
David J. Hansord & Son, Lincoln, Lincs.
Timepiece Repairs, Lincoln, Lincs.
Rita Shenton, Twickenham, Middx.
Keith Lawson Antique Clocks, Scratby, Norfolk.
Peter Wiggins, Chipping Norton, Oxon.
Rosemary and Time, Thame, Oxon.
R.G. Cave and Sons Ltd, Ludlow, Shrops.
Adrian Donnelly Antique Clocks, Shrewsbury, Shrops.
Dodington Antiques, Whitchurch, Shrops.
Kembery Antique Clocks Ltd, Bath, Somerset.
Bernard G. House, Wells, Somerset.
James A. Jordan, Lichfield, Staffs.
Patrick Marney, Long Melford, Suffolk.
Horological Workshops, Guildford, Surrey.
Surrey Clock Centre, Haslemere, Surrey.
B. M. and E. Newlove, Surbiton, Surrey.
Baskerville Antiques, Petworth, Sussex West.
Time in Hand, Shipston-on-Stour, Warks.
Summersons, Warwick, Warks.
P.A. Oxley Antique Clocks and Barometers, Cherhill,
    Wilts.
Time Restored Ltd, Pewsey, Wilts.
Inglenook Antiques, Ramsbury, Wilts.
Hansen Chard Antiques, Pershore, Worcs.
Time and Motion, Beverley, Yorks. East.
Lewis E. Hickson FBHI, Gilberdyke, Yorks. East.
Craiglea Clocks, Edinburgh, Scotland.

Beds
La Maison, London E1.
The Cobbled Yard, London N16.
Tobias and The Angel, London SW13.
And So To Bed Limited, London SW6.
The French House (Antiques) Ltd, London SW6.
Simon Horn Furniture Ltd, London SW6.
The French House (Antiques) Ltd, London SW8.
Hirst Antiques, London W11.
Town House Antiques, Marple Bridge, Cheshire.
The Country Bedroom and En-Suite, Keswick,
    Cumbria.
Staveley Antiques, Staveley, Cumbria.
The Antiques Warehouse, Buxton, Derbys.
R.C. Associates, Cullompton, Devon.
The Grove Antiques Centre Ltd, Honiton, Devon.
Pugh's Farm Antiques, Monkton, Devon.
Annterior Antiques, Plymouth, Devon.
Cartouche, Shaftesbury, Dorset.
Antique Bed Shop, Halstead, Essex.
Deja Vu Antiques, Leigh-on-Sea, Essex.
Antique Bed Company, Emsworth, Hants.
Victorian Dreams, Headley, Hants.
Serendipity, Ledbury, Herefs.
Peggottys, Teynham, Kent.
House Things Antiques, Hinckley, Leics.
A Barn Full of Brass Beds, Conisholme, Lincs.
Graham Pickett Antiques, Stamford, Lincs.
Antiques & Gifts, Downham Market, Norfolk.
Pearman Antiques & Interiors, Newark, Notts.

Manor Farm Antiques, Standlake, Oxon.
Swans, Oakham, Rutland.
Malthouse Antiques, Bridgnorth, Shrops.
Bedsteads, Bath, Somerset.
Wessex Antique Bedsteads, Stoke-sub-Hamdon, Somerset.
Yew Tree Antiques Warehouse, Wiveliscombe, Somerset.
Bed Bazaar, Framlingham, Suffolk.
Goodbreys, Framlingham, Suffolk.
Valentina Antique Beds, Brighton, Sussex East.
The Victorian Brass Bedstead Company, Cocking,
    Sussex West.
Le Grenier Antiques, Wootton Wawen, Warks.
Timeless Beds, Malvern Link, Worcs.
S.W. Antiques, Pershore, Worcs.
Penny Farthing Antiques, North Cave, Yorks. East.
Northern Antiques Company, Norton, Yorks. North.
The French House (Antiques) Ltd., York, Yorks. North.
Paraphernalia, Sheffield, Yorks. South.
Agar Antiques, Saintfield, Co. Down, N. Ireland.
P. J. Smith (Antiques), Stewartstown, Co. Tyrone, N.
    Ireland.
Seventh Heaven, Chirk, Wales.

Brass - see Metalware

Bronzes
Gladwell and Co., London EC4.
Style Gallery, N1.
Finchley Fine Art Galleries, N12.
Tara Antiques, London NW8.
Robert Bowman, London SW1.
Victor Franses Gallery, London SW1.
Brian Harkins Oriental Art, London SW1.
Hermitage Antiques Ltd, London SW1.
Jeremy Mason (Sainsbury & Mason), London SW1.
Peter Nahum At The Leicester Galleries, London SW1.
Tryon Gallery (incorporating Malcolm Innes), London
    SW1.
Christine Bridge, London SW13.
Anthony James and Son Ltd, London SW3.
Rogers de Rin, London SW3.
Victor Arwas Gallery - Editions Graphiques Gallery
    Ltd, London W1.
Eskenazi Ltd, London W1.
The Sladmore Gallery of Sculpture, London W1.
Elizabeth Bradwin, London W11.
Gavin Douglas Fine Antiques Ltd, London W11.
M. and D. Lewis, London W11.
Marshall Phillips, London W4.
David Brower Antiques, London W8.
Barry Davies Oriental Art, London W8.
H. and W. Deutsch Antiques, London W8.
John Jesse, London W8.
Pruskin Gallery, London W8.
Mary Wise & Grosvenor Antiques, London W8.
Griffin Fine Art & Antiques, Hungerford, Berks.
The John Davies Gallery, Stow-on-the-Wold, Glos.
Kenulf Fine Arts, Stow-on-the-Wold, Glos.
Michael Sim, Chislehurst, Kent.

Apollo Antique Galleries, Westerham, Kent.
London House Antiques, Westerham, Kent.
Edward Cross - Fine Paintings, Weybridge, Surrey.
Richard Hagen, Broadway, Worcs.
Falle Fine Art Limited, St Helier, Jersey, C.I.

Carpets & Rugs
Alexander Juran and Co, London N4.
Kennedy Carpets, London N4.
Joseph Lavian, London N4.
David J. Wilkins, London NW1.
Sabera Trading Co, London NW2.
Soviet Carpet & Art Galleries, London NW2.
Lida Lavender, London NW5.
Orientalist, London NW5.
Mayfair Carpet Gallery Ltd, London SE1.
Belgrave Carpet Gallery Ltd, London SW1.
S. Franses Ltd, London SW1.
Keshishian, London SW1.
Gideon Hatch Rugs, London SW11.
Shaikh and Son (Oriental Rugs) Ltd, London SW19.
Gallery Yacou, London SW3.
Orientalist, London SW3.
Robert Stephenson, London SW3.
Perez Antique Carpets Gallery, London SW6.
Polonaise Gallery, London SW7.
David Aaron Ancient Arts & Rare Carpets, London W1.
Sibyl Colefax & John Fowler, London W1.
John Eskenazi Ltd, London W1.
Essie Carpets, London W1.
C. John (Rare Rugs) Ltd, London W1.
Vigo Carpet Gallery, London W1.
A. Zadah, London W1.
Rezai Persian Carpets, London W11.
David Black Carpets, London W2.
Christopher Legge Oriental Carpets, Oxford, Oxon.
Oriental Rug Gallery Ltd, Oxford, Oxon.
Tattersall's, Uppingham, Rutland.
Haliden Oriental Rug Shop, Bath, Somerset.
Michael and Amanda Lewis Oriental Carpets and Rugs,
    Wellington, Somerset.
The Persian Carpet Studio Ltd, Long Melford, Suffolk.
Karel Weijand Fine Oriental Carpets, Farnham, Surrey.
Oriental Rug Gallery, Guildford, Surrey.
Clive Rogers Oriental Rugs, Staines, Surrey.
Lindfield Galleries - David Adam, Lindfield, Sussex West.
Persian Carpet Gallery, Petworth, Sussex West.
A.W. Hone and Son Oriental Carpets, Birmingham,
    West Mids.
D & J Lines Antiques, Wychbold, Worcs.
London House Oriental Rugs and Carpets, Harrogate,
    Yorks. North.
Omar (Harrogate) Ltd, Knaresborough, Yorks. North.
The Oriental Rug Shop, Sheffield, Yorks. South.
London House Oriental Rugs and Carpets, Boston Spa,
    Yorks. West.
R.L. Rose Oriental Carpets Ltd, Edinburgh, Scotland.
Samarkand Galleries, Edinburgh, Scotland.
R.L. Rose Oriental Carpets Ltd, Glasgow, Scotland.

C.S. Moreton (Antiques), Inchture, Scotland.
Gallery Persia, Inverness, Scotland.

Cars & Carriages

Fieldings Antiques, Haslingden, Lancs.
The Complete Automobilist, Greatford, Lincs.
Finesse Fine Art, Dorchester, Dorset.
C.A.R.S. (Classic Automobilia & Regalia Specialists),
Brighton, Sussex East.

Chinese Art - see Oriental

Church Furniture & Furnishings

LASSCO, London EC2.
Graham Kirkland, London SW6.
Tomkinson Stained Glass, Leagrave, Beds.
Cumbria Architectural Salvage, Raughton Head, Cumbria.
Havenplan's Architectural Emporium, Killamarsh, Derbys.
Robert Mills Architectural Antiques Ltd, Bristol, Glos.
Antique Church Furnishings, Walton-on-Thames, Surrey.
Cardiff Reclamation, Cardiff, Wales.

Clock & Watches

City Clocks, London EC1.
Frosts of Clerkenwell Ltd, London EC1.
Sugar Antiques, London N1.
Antiques 4 Ltd, London NW3.
North London Clock Shop Ltd, London SE25.
R.E. Rose FBHI, London SE9.
John Carlton-Smith, London SW1.
Charles Frodsham & Co Ltd, London SW1.
Harrods Ltd, London SW1.
Somlo Antiques, London SW1.
The Clock Clinic Ltd, London SW15.
Roger Lascelles, London SW17.
W. F. Turk Antique Clocks, London SW20.
Norman Adams Ltd, London SW3.
Gutlin Clocks and Antiques, London SW6.
A. & H. Page (Est. 1840), London SW7.
David Duggan Watches, London W1.
Mallett and Son (Antiques) Ltd, London W1.
Mallett at Bourdon House, London W1.
Pendulum of Mayfair Ltd, London W1.
Ronald Phillips Ltd, London W1.
Michael Rose - Source of the Unusual, London W1.
The Royal Arcade Watch Shop, London W1.
Central Gallery (Portobello), London W11.
Chelsea Clocks & Antiques, London W11.
Gavin Douglas Fine Antiques Ltd, London W11.
Raffety & Walwyn Ltd, London W8.
Roderick Antique Clocks, London W8.
The London Silver Vaults, London WC2.
The Old Malthouse, Hungerford, Berks.
Times Past Antiques, Windsor, Berks.
Wyrardisbury Antiques, Wraysbury, Berks.
Carlton Clocks, Amersham, Bucks.
Peter Wright Antiques, Great Missenden, Bucks.
Robin Unsworth Antiques, Olney, Bucks.
Peter Norman Antiques and Restorations, Burwell, Cambs.

John Beazor and Sons Ltd, Cambridge, Cambs.
T. W. Pawson - Clocks, Somersham, Cambs.
Antiques & Curios (Steve Carpenter), Wisbech, Cambs.
Chapel Antiques, Nantwich, Cheshire.
Coppelia Antiques, Plumley, Cheshire.
Little Jem's, Penzance, Cornwall.
Saint Nicholas Galleries Ltd. (Antiques and Jewellery),
   Carlisle, Cumbria.
G.K. Hadfield, Great Salkeld, Cumbria.
Westmorland Clocks, Kendal, Cumbria.
David Hill, Kirkby Stephen, Cumbria.
Hackney House Antiques & Clocks, Barlow, Derbys.
Heldreich Antiques & French Polishers, Brailsford,
   Derbys.
Derbyshire Clocks, Glossop, Derbys.
Antique, Electrical & Turret Clocks, Brixham, Devon.
Musgrave Bickford Antiques, Crediton, Devon.
Ivor Doble Ltd, Exeter, Devon.
Mortimers, Exeter, Devon.
Leigh Extence Antique Clocks, Honiton, Devon.
Honiton Clock Clinic, Honiton, Devon.
Carnegie Paintings & Clocks, Yealmpton, Devon.
M.C. Taylor, Bournemouth, Dorset.
Derek J. Burgess - Horologist, Branksome, Dorset.
Batten's Jewellers, Bridport, Dorset.
Timecraft Clocks, Sherborne, Dorset.
Tom Tribe and Son Ltd, Sturminster Newton, Dorset.
Eden House Antiques, West Auckland, Durham.
Chris L. Papworth, Kelvedon, Essex.
Harris Antiques, Thaxted, Essex.
It's About Time, Westcliff-on-Sea, Essex.
Antique Corner with A & C Antique Clocks, Bristol, Glos.
Montpellier Clocks, Cheltenham, Glos.
Woodward Antique Clocks, CheltenhamGlos.
School House Antiques, Chipping Campden, Glos.
Arthur S. Lewis, Gloucester, Glos.
Jeffrey Formby Antiques, Moreton-in-Marsh, Glos.
Jillings Antiques - Distinctive Antique Clocks, Newent,
   Glos.
Keith Harding's World of Mechanical Music,
   Northleach, Glos.
Styles of Stow, Stow-on-the-Wold, Glos.
Vanbrugh House Antiques, Stow-on-the-Wold, Glos.
Clockwise, Emsworth, Hants.
Bryan Clisby Antique Clocks, Hartley Wintney, Hants.
A.W. Porter and Son, Hartley Wintney, Hants.
Barry Papworth, Lymington, Hants.
Gaylords, Titchfield, Hants.
The Clock-Work-Shop (Winchester), Winchester, Hants.
G.E. Marsh Antique Clocks Ltd, Winchester, Hants.
Robin Lloyd Antiques, Ross-on-Wye, Herefs.
Howards, Baldock, Herts.
David Penney, Bishop's Stortford, Herts.
Robert Horton Antiques, Hertford, Herts.
Country Clocks, Tring, Herts.
Weston Antiques, Weston, Herts.
John Corrin Antiques, Douglas, Isle of Man.
Ye Olde Village Clock Shop, Freshwater, Isle of Wight.
John Chawner, Birchington, Kent.

Old Manor House Antiques, Brasted, Kent.
Patric Capon, Bromley, Kent.
Michael Sim, Chislehurst, Kent.
Neill Robinson Blaxill, Sevenoaks, Kent.
Gaby's Clocks and Things, Tenterden, Kent.
Derek Roberts Antiques, Tonbridge, Kent.
B.V.M. Somerset, Tonbridge, Kent.
Pantiles Spa Antiques, Tunbridge Wells, Kent.
Payne & Son (Silversmiths) Ltd, Tunbridge Wells, Kent.
The Vintage Watch Co., Tunbridge Wells, Kent.
The Old Clock Shop, West Malling, Kent.
Ancient and Modern, Blackburn, Lancs.
Drop Dial Antiques, Bolton, Lancs.
Harrop Fold Clocks (F. Robinson), Bolton-by-Bowland, Lancs.
Brittons - Watches and Antiques, Clitheroe, Lancs.
Fieldings Antiques, Haslingden, Lancs.
P.W. Norgrove - Antique Clocks, Haslingden, Lancs.
Charles Howell Jeweller, Oldham, Lancs.
H.C. Simpson and Sons Jewellers (Oldham)Ltd, Oldham, Lancs.
Hackler's Jewellers, Preston, Lancs.
Edmund Davies & Son Antiques, Whalley, Lancs.
Northern Clocks, Worsley, Lancs.
Lowe of Loughborough, Loughborough, Leics.
Oaktree Antiques, Lubenham, Leics.
Charles Antiques, Whitwick, Leics.
N. Bryan-Peach Antiques, Wymeswold, Leics.
Trade Antiques, Alford, Lincs.
Robin Fowler (Period Clocks), Aylesby, Lincs.
Grantham Clocks, Grantham, Lincs.
Marcus Wilkinson, Grantham, Lincs.
Time after Time, Hemswell Cliff, Lincs.
David J. Hansord & Son, Lincoln, Lincs.
Timepiece Repairs, Lincoln, Lincs.
Marcus Wilkinson, Sleaford, Lincs.
Penman Clockcare (UK) Ltd, Spalding, Lincs.
Weldons Jewellery and Antiques, Southport, Merseyside.
Rita Shenton, Twickenham, Middx.
Village Clocks, Coltishall, Norfolk.
R.C. Woodhouse (Antiquarian Horologist), Hunstanton, Norfolk.
Tim Clayton Jewellery Ltd, King's Lynn, Norfolk.
Jennifer and Raymond Norman Antiques, Needham, Norfolk.
Keith Lawson Antique Clocks, Scratby, Norfolk.
Parriss, Sheringham, Norfolk.
Norton Antiques, Twyford, Norfolk.
M.C. Chapman, Finedon, Northants.
Michael Jones Jeweller, Northampton, Northants.
Gordon Caris, Alnwick, Northumbs.
Gordon Caris, Hexham, Northumbs.
Goodacre Engraving, Sutton Bonington, Notts.
Horseshoe Antiques and Gallery, Burford, Oxon.
Hubert's Antiques, Burford, Oxon.
Jonathan Howard, Chipping Norton, Oxon.
Craig Barfoot, East Hagbourne, Oxon.
Rosemary and Time, Thame, Oxon.
W.R. Harvey & Co (Antiques) Ltd, Witney, Oxon.

Witney Antiques, Witney, Oxon.
C. Reynolds Antiques, Oakham, Rutland.
Harvey Art and Antiques, Uppingham, Rutland.
Mytton Antiques, Atcham, Shrops.
R.G. Cave and Sons Ltd, Ludlow, Shrops.
Adrian Donnelly Antique Clocks, Shrewsbury, Shrops.
Dodington Antiques, Whitchurch, Shrops.
Kembery Antique Clocks Ltd, Bath, Somerset.
Quiet Street Antiques, Bath, Somerset.
Bernard G. House, Wells, Somerset.
The Essence of Time, Lichfield, Staffs.
James A. Jordan, Lichfield, Staffs.
Winder's Fine Art and Antiques, Newcastle-under-Lyme, Staffs.
R.A. James - The Clock Shop, Tutbury, Staffs.
Mayflower Antiques, Long MelfordSuffolk.
Edward Manson (Clocks), Woodbridge, Suffolk.
Antique Clocks by Patrick Thomas, Dorking, Surrey.
The Howard Gallery, Dorking, Surrey.
The Coach House Antiques, Gomshall, Surrey.
Horological Workshops, Guildford, Surrey.
Surrey Clock Centre, Haslemere, Surrey.
West Street Antiques, Haslemere, Surrey.
B. M. and E. Newlove, Surbiton, Surrey.
S. Warrender and Co, Sutton, Surrey.
The Clock Shop Weybridge, Weybridge, Surrey.
Yellow Lantern Antiques Ltd, Brighton, Sussex East.
W. Bruford, Eastbourne, Sussex East.
John Cowderoy Antiques Ltd, Eastbourne, Sussex East.
Coach House Antiques, Hastings, Sussex East.
Lewes Clock Shop, Lewes, Sussex East.
The Old Mint House, Pevensey, Sussex East.
The Clock Shop, Hurstpierpoint, Sussex West.
Churchill Clocks, Midhurst, Sussex West.
Baskerville Antiques, Petworth, Sussex West.
Thakeham Furniture Ltd, Petworth, Sussex West.
Peter Smith Antiques, Sunderland, Tyne and Wear.
Time in Hand, Shipston-on-Stour, Warks.
George Pragnell Ltd, Stratford-upon-Avon, Warks.
Summersons, Warwick, Warks.
F. Meeks & Co, Birmingham, West Mids.
M. Allen Watch and Clockmaker, Four Oaks, West Mids.
Moxhams Antiques, Bradford-on-Avon, Wilts.
Trevor Waddington Antique Clocks, Bradford-on-Avon, Wilts.
P.A. Oxley Antique Clocks and Barometers, Cherhill, Wilts.
Time Restored Ltd, Pewsey, Wilts.
Inglenook Antiques, Ramsbury, Wilts.
Chris Wadge Clocks, Salisbury, Wilts.
Allan Smith Antique Clocks, Swindon, Wilts.
Hansen Chard Antiques, Pershore, Worcs.
The Barber's Clock, Worcester, Worcs.
Time and Motion, Beverley, Yorks. East.
Lewis E. Hickson FBHI, Gilberdyke, Yorks. East.
Milestone Antiques, Easingwold, Yorks. North.
Chris Wilde Antiques, Harrogate, Yorks. North.
Brian Loomes, Pateley Bridge, Yorks. North.
Tomlinsons, Tockwith, Yorks. North.

SPECIALIST DEALERS

Harpers Jewellers, York, Yorks. North.
Keith Stones Grandfather Clocks, Bessacarr, Yorks. South.
Fishlake Antiques, Fishlake, Yorks. South.
F S Antiques, Sheffield, Yorks. South.
Clock House Antiques, Haworth, Yorks. West.
A. and Y.M. Frost Antique Clocks, Honley, Yorks. West.
Robert Christie Antiques, Ballyclare, Co. Antrim, N. Ireland.
Fourwinds Antiques, Moira, Co. Armagh, N. Ireland.
Ian Burton Antique Clocks, Auchterarder, Scotland.
The Clock Showrooms, Canonbie, Scotland.
Bow-well Antiques, Edinburgh, Scotland.
Craiglea Clocks, Edinburgh, Scotland.
Donald Ellis incorporating Bruntsfield Clocks, Edinburgh, Scotland.
Harlequin Antiques, Edinburgh, Scotland.
John Whyte, Edinburgh, Scotland.
Bygones, Huntly, Scotland.
Ty-Llwyd Antiques, Cardiff, Wales.
Snowdonia Antiques, Llanrwst, Wales.
Rodney Adams Antiques, Pwllheli, Wales.

Coins & Medals

George Rankin Coin Co. Ltd, London E2.
C.J. Martin (Coins) Ltd, London N14.
Christopher Eimer, London NW11.
The Armoury of St. James's Military Antiquarians, London SW1.
Kenneth Davis (Works of Art) Ltd, London SW1.
Knightsbridge Coins, London SW1.
Beaver Coin Room, London SW5.
Michael Coins, London W8.
Spink and Son Ltd, London WC1.
A.H. Baldwin and Sons Ltd, London WC2.
M. Bord (Gold Coin Exchange), London WC2.
Philip Cohen Numismatics, London WC2.
Raymond D Holdich International Medals & Militaria, London WC2.
Valued History, Ely, Cambs.
B.R.M. Coins, Knutsford, Cheshire.
Souvenir Antiques, Carlisle, Cumbria.
Penrith Coin and Stamp Centre, Penrith, Cumbria.
Sterling Coins and Medals, Bournemouth, Dorset.
Dorset Coin Company, Parkstone, Dorset.
The Treasure Chest, Weymouth, Dorset.
Robin Finnegan (Jeweller), Darlington, Durham.
Potter's Antiques and Coins, Bristol, Glos.
Peter Morris, Bromley, Kent.
The Coin and Jewellery Shop, Accrington, Lancs.
Chard Coins, Blackpool, Lancs.
David M. Regan, Southport, Merseyside.
Gold and Silver Exchange, Great Yarmouth, Norfolk.
Clive Dennett Coins, Norwich, Norfolk.
Acanthus Antiques & Collectables incorporating Dutton & Smith Medals, Nottingham, Notts.
Collectors World, Nottingham, Notts.
D.D. and A. Ingle, Nottingham, Notts.
NSE Medal Dept., Nottingham, Notts.
Bath Stamp and Coin Shop, Bath, Somerset.
Neate Militaria & Antiques, Sudbury, Suffolk.

St. Pancras Antiques, Chichester, Sussex West.
Intercoin, Newcastle-upon-Tyne, Tyne and Wear.
Format of Birmingham Ltd, Birmingham, West Mids.
Castle Galleries, Salisbury, Wilts.
Whitmore, Great Malvern, Worcs.
B.B.M. Coins., Kidderminster, Worcs.
C.J. and A.J. Dixon Ltd, Bridlington, Yorks. East.
Cookstown Antiques, Cookstown, Co. Tyrone, N. Ireland.
The Collectors Shop, Edinburgh, Scotland.
Edinburgh Coin Shop, Edinburgh, Scotland.
A.D. Hamilton and Co, Glasgow, Scotland.
A. K. Campbell & Sons, Kirkcaldy, Scotland.
Abbey Antiques, Stirling, Scotland.

Dolls & Toys

Donay Games & Pastimes, London N1.
Dolly Land, London N21.
Engine 'n' Tender, London SE25.
Stephen Long, London SW10.
Mimi Fifi, London W11.
Victoriana Dolls, London W11.
London Antique Gallery, London W8.
Berkshire Antiques Co Ltd, Windsor, Berks.
Rosina's, Falmouth, Cornwall.
Spondon Antiques and Collectables, Spondon, Derbys.
Honiton Antique Toys, Honiton, Devon.
The Vintage Toy and Train Shop, Sidmouth, Devon.
Boscombe Models and Collectors Shop, Bournemouth, Dorset.
The Doll's House, Northleach, Glos.
Park House Antiques, Stow-on-the-Wold, Glos.
Peter Pan's of Gosport, Gosport, Hants.
The Attic, Baldock, Herts.
London House Antiques, Westerham, Kent.
C. and K.E. Dring, Lincoln, Lincs.
Norwich Collectors Toyshop, Norwich, Norfolk.
Trench Puzzles, Stowmarket, Suffolk.
C.A.R.S. (Classic Automobilia & Regalia Specialists), Brighton, Sussex East.
Paul Goble Jewellers, Brighton, Sussex East.
Sue Pearson, Brighton, Sussex East.
Coach House Antiques, Hastings, Sussex East.
The Old Cornstore Antiques, Arundel, Sussex West.
Recollect Dolls Hospital, Burgess Hill, Sussex West.
Antiquated, Petworth, Sussex West.
Dolly Mixtures, Birmingham, West Mids.
Grannie's Parlour, Hull, Yorks. East.
Classic Rocking Horses, Thirsk, Yorks. North.
Collectors Old Toy Shop and Antiques, Halifax, Yorks. West.
Memory Lane, Sowerby Bridge, Yorks. West.
Angus Antiques, Dundee, Scotland.
Bebes et Jouets, Edinburgh, Scotland.
Pastimes Vintage Toys, Glasgow, Scotland.
Museum of Childhood Memories, Beaumaris, Wales.

Etchings & Engravings

Gladwell and Company, London EC4.
Odyssey Fine Arts Ltd, London SW1.

Old Maps and Prints, London SW1.
The Map House, London SW3.
Old Church Galleries, London SW3.
Hilary Chapman Fine Prints, London SW6.
King's Court Galleries, London SW6.
The Wyllie Gallery, London SW7.
Agnew's, London W1.
Victor Arwas Gallery - Editions Graphiques Gallery
    Ltd, London W1.
William Weston Gallery, London W1.
Justin F. Skrebowski Prints, London W11.
Storey's Ltd, London WC2.
Antique Map and Bookshop, Puddletown, Dorset.
Black Ink, Stow-on-the-Wold, Glos.
Oldfield Gallery, Portsmouth, Hants.
The Shanklin Gallery, Shanklin, Isle of Wight.
Marrin's Bookshop, Folkestone, Kent.
London House Antiques, Westerham, Kent.
Graftons of Market Harborough, Market Harborough,
    Leics.
P.J. Cassidy (Books), Holbeach, Lincs.
TRADA, Chipping Norton, Oxon.
The Barry Keene Gallery, Henley-on-Thames, Oxon.
Elizabeth Harvey-Lee, North Aston, Oxon.
George Gregory, Bath, Somerset.
The Sadler Street Gallery, Wells, Somerset.
England's Gallery, Leek, Staffs.
King's Court Galleries, Dorking, Surrey.
Ronald Carr, Salisbury, Wilts.
Heatons, Tisbury, Wilts.
Heirloom & Howard Limited, West Yatton, Wilts.
The Drawing Room - Interiors & Antiques, Pershore,
    Worcs.
The Gallery (Nigel Stacy-Marks Ltd), Blair Atholl,
    Scotland.
Open Eye Gallery Ltd, Edinburgh, Scotland.
Royal Mile Gallery, Edinburgh, Scotland.
Ewan Mundy Fine Art Ltd, Glasgow, Scotland.
Mainhill Gallery, Jedburgh, Scotland.
Killin Gallery, Killin, Scotland.
David Windsor Gallery, Bangor, Wales.

Fire Related Items
Westland London, London EC2.
Chesney's Antique Fireplace Warehouse, London N19.
Amazing Grates - Fireplaces Ltd, London N2.
Acquisitions (Fireplaces) Ltd, London NW5.
Townsends, London NW8.
CASA, London SE15.
Ward Antique Fireplaces Ltd, London SE6.
Ward Antique Fireplaces Ltd, London SE7.
The Fireplace, London SE9.
Nigel A. Bartlett, London SW1.
Nicholas Gifford-Mead, London SW1.
H.W. Poulter and Son, London SW10.
Thornhill Galleries, London SW18.
Mr Wandle's Workshop Ltd, London SW18.
Drummonds Architectural Antiques Ltd, London SW3.
O.F. Wilson Ltd, London SW3.

Old World Trading Co, London SW6.
The Chiswick Fireplace Co., London W4.
Architectural Antiques, London W6.
Architectural Antiques, Bedford, Beds.
Sundial Antiques, Amersham, Bucks.
Dismantle and Deal Direct - Architectural Salvage
    Brokers, Aston Clinton, Bucks.
Grosvenor House Interiors, Beaconsfield, Bucks.
Architectural Salvage Online, Chester, Cheshire.
Nostalgia Architectural Antiques, Stockport, Cheshire.
Antique Fireplaces, Tarvin, Cheshire.
Architectural Antiques, Kendal, Cumbria.
W.R.S. Architectural Antiques Ltd, Low Newton,
    Cumbria.
Cumbria Architectural Salvage, Raughton Head,
    Cumbria.
Staveley Antiques, Staveley, Cumbria.
Finishing Touches, Derby, Derbys.
Havenplan's Architectural Emporium, Killamarsh,
    Derbys.
Adrian Ager Ltd, Ashburton, Devon.
Robson's Antiques, Barnard Castle, Durham.
Flame and Grate, Bristol, Glos.
Period Fireplaces, Bristol, Glos.
Cox's Architectural Reclamation Yard, Moreton-in-
    Marsh, Glos.
Minchinhampton Architectural, Stroud, Glos.
Ward Antique Fireplaces Ltd, Beckenham, Kent.
Bygones Reclamation, Canterbury, Kent.
Victorian Fireplace, Canterbury, Kent.
Elham Antiques, Elham, Kent.
Ward Antique Fireplaces Ltd, Sidcup, Kent.
The Architectural Stores, Tunbridge Wells, Kent.
Past & Present, Clitheroe, Lancs.
Old Smithy, Feniscowles, Lancs.
Antique Fireplace Warehouse, Manchester, Lancs.
In-Situ Manchester, Manchester, Lancs.
Colin Blakey Fireplaces, Nelson, Lancs.
House Things Antiques, Hinckley, Leics.
Britain's Heritage Ltd, Leicester, Leics.
Architectural Salvage Online, Birkenhead, Merseyside.
Antique Fireplaces, Liverpool, Merseyside.
Peco, Hampton, Middx.
Marble Hill Gallery, Twickenham, Middx.
Mongers, Hingham, Norfolk.
Woodside Reclamation (Architectural Antiques),
    Berwick-upon-Tweed, Northumbs.
Nottingham Architectural Antiques & Reclamation,
    Nottingham, Notts.
Hallidays (Fine Antiques) Ltd, Dorchester-on-Thames,
    Oxon.
Aston Pine Antiques, Faringdon, Oxon.
Oxford Architectural Antiques, Faringdon, Oxon.
Colin Greenway Antiques, Witney, Oxon.
Holloways of Ludlow, Ludlow, Shrops.
Walcot Reclamation, Bath, Somerset.
Cawarden Brick Co Ltd, Rugeley, Staffs.
Blackbrook Antiques Village, Weeford, Staffs.
Brighton Architectural Salvage, Brighton, Sussex East.

SPECIALIST DEALERS

Golden Cross Antiques, Hailsham, Sussex East.
Shiners of Jesmond, Jesmond, Tyne and Wear.
Turnburrys, Jesmond, Tyne and Wear.
Tynemouth Architectural Salvage, Tynemouth, Tyne and Wear.
Tudor House Antiques, Halesowen, West Mids.
Harriet Fairfax Fireplaces and General Antiques, Langley Burrell, Wilts.
The Antique Centre, Kidderminster, Worcs.
Old Flames, Easingwold, Yorks. North.
Period Interiors, Guisborough, Yorks. North.
Robert Aagaard & Co, Knaresborough, Yorks. North.
Andy Thornton Ltd, Halifax, Yorks. West.
Chapel House Fireplaces, Holmfirth, Yorks. West.
Kelly Antiques, Omagh, Co. Tyrone, N. Ireland.
P. J. Smith (Antiques), Stewartstown, Co. Tyrone, N. Ireland.
Burning Embers, Aberdeen, Scotland.
EASY - Edinburgh Architectural Salvage Yard, Edinburgh, Scotland.
Holyrood Architectural Salvage, Edinburgh, Scotland.
Neilsons Ltd, Edinburgh, Scotland.
Flame 'n' Grate, Barry, Wales.
Cardiff Reclamation, Cardiff, Wales.
Kings Fireplaces, Antiques and Interiors, Cardiff, Wales.

Frames
Paul Mason Gallery, London SW1.
Nigel Milne Ltd, London SW1.
Rollo Whately Ltd, London SW1.
Arnold Wiggins and Sons Ltd, London SW1.
Paul Mitchell Ltd, London W1.
Daggett Gallery, London W11.
Lacy Gallery, London W11.
Justin F. Skrebowski Prints, London W11.
The Fairhurst Gallery, Norwich, Norfolk.
Coulter Galleries, York, Yorks. North.
W. Greenwood (Fine Art), Burneston, Yorks. North.
Looking Glass of Bath, Bath, Somerset.
Huddersfield Picture Framing Co, Huddersfield, Yorks. West.

Furniture - Continental (mainly French)
La Maison, London E1.
Charlton House Antiques, London N1.
Frames Stop, London N12.
Relic Antiques Trade Warehouse, London NW1.
Davidson Antiques, London NW8.
The Galleries, London SE1.
Robert E. Hirschhorn, London SE5.
Didier Aaron (London)Ltd, London SW1.
ADEC, London SW1.
Appley Hoare Antiques, London SW1.
Blanchard Ltd, London SW1.
Andi Gisel, London SW1.
Ross Hamilton Ltd, London SW1.
Harris Lindsay, London SW1.
Hermitage Antiques Ltd, London SW1.

Carlton Hobbs, London SW1.
Christopher Howe, London SW1.
Jeremy Ltd, London SW1.
Odyssey Fine Arts Ltd, London SW1.
Mark Ransom Ltd, London SW1.
Rogier et Rogier, London SW1.
Kate Thurlow, London SW1.
LucyJohnson, London SW10.
Thomas Kerr Antiques Ltd, London SW10.
McVeigh & Charpentier, London SW10.
Orientation, London SW10.
Toynbee-Clarke Interiors Ltd, London SW10.
Garland Antiques, London SW11.
The Woodpigeon, London SW11.
Prides of London, London SW3.
Charles Saunders Antiques, London SW3.
O.F. Wilson Ltd, London SW3.
Antiques and Things, London SW4.
275 Antiques, London SW6.
I. and J.L. Brown Ltd, London SW6.
Rupert Cavendish Antiques, London SW6.
Decorative Antiques, London SW6.
Birdie Fortescue Antiques, London SW6.
The French House (Antiques) Ltd, London SW6.
Judy Greenwood, London SW6.
Christopher Jones Antiques, London SW6.
Mora & Upham Antiques, London SW6.
AnthonyOutred, London SW6.
M. Pauw Antiques, London SW6.
The French House (Antiques) Ltd, London SW8.
Adrian Alan Ltd, London W1.
H. Blairman and Sons Ltd., London W1.
Mallett at Bourdon House, London W1.
Partridge Fine Arts plc, London W1.
Pelham Galleries Ltd, London W1.
Jacob Stodel, London W1.
Windsor House Antiques Ltd, London W1.
Barham Antiques, London W11.
Curá Antiques, London W11.
M. and D. Lewis, London W11.
Robin Martin Antiques, London W11.
Myriad Antiques, London W11.
Marshall Gallery, London W14.
Reindeer Antiques Ltd, London W8.
Sinai Antiques Ltd, London W8.
Cox Interiors Ltd, London W9.
David Litt Antiques, Ampthill, Beds.
John A. Pearson Antiques, Horton, Berks.
Franklin Antiques, Hungerford, Berks.
Youll's Antiques, Hungerford, Berks.
La Maison, Bourne End, Bucks.
Phoenix Antiques, Fordham, Cambs.
Ivor and Patricia Lewis Antique and Fine Art Dealers, Peterborough, Cambs.
Sandra Harris Interiors and Antiques, Chester, Cheshire.
Manchester Antique Company, Stockport, Cheshire.
Old Town Hall Antiques, Falmouth, Cornwall.
Pine and Decorative Items, Ashbourne, Derbys.
R.C. Associates, Cullompton, Devon.

Hermitage Antiques, Honiton, Devon.
Merchant House Antiques, Honiton, Devon.
Pilgrim Antiques, Honiton, Devon.
Jane Strickland & Daughters, Honiton, Devon.
Pugh's Farm Antiques, Monkton, Devon.
Lionel Geneen Ltd, Bournemouth, Dorset.
Talisman, Gillingham, Dorset.
Cartouche, Shaftesbury, Dorset.
Piers Pisani Antiques Ltd, Sherborne, Dorset.
Deja Vu Antiques, Leigh-on-Sea, Essex.
West Essex Antiques (Stone Hall), Matching Green,
    Essex.
Mill Lane Antiques, Woodford Green, Essex.
The Roger Widdas Gallery, Moreton-in-Marsh, Glos.
Gary Wright Antiques, Moreton-in-Marsh, Glos.
Ashton Gower Antiques, Stow-on-the-Wold, Glos.
Annarella Clark Antiques, Stow-on-the-Wold, Glos.
Antony Preston Antiques Ltd, Stow-on-the-Wold, Glos.
The Decorator Source, Tetbury, Glos.
Sieff, Tetbury, Glos.
Townsend Bateson, Tetbury, Glos.
Westwood House Antiques, Tetbury, Glos.
Geoffrey Stead, Todenham, Glos.
Whittington Barn Antiques, Whittington, Glos.
Artemesia, Alresford, Hants.
Cedar Antiques Limited, Hartley Wintney, Hants.
David Lazarus Antiques, Hartley Wintney, Hants.
Wick Antiques, Lymington, Hants.
Gray's Antiques, Portsmouth, Hants.
Millers of Chelsea Antiques Ltd, Ringwood, Hants.
Antique Eyes, Stockbridge, Hants.
The Bakhtiyar Gallery, Stockbridge, Hants.
I. and J.L. Brown Ltd, Hereford, Herefs.
Great Brampton House Antiques Ltd, Hereford, Herefs.
Royal Standard Antiques, Cowes, Isle of Wight.
Gabrielle De Giles, Bilsington, Kent.
Lennox Cato, Edenbridge, Kent.
Chevertons of Edenbridge Ltd, Edenbridge, Kent.
Samovar Antiques, Hythe, Kent.
Gabrielle de Giles, Sandgate, Kent.
Henry Baines, Southborough, Kent.
Flower House Antiques, Tenterden, Kent.
Phoenix Antiques, Tunbridge Wells, Kent.
Up Country, Tunbridge Wells, Kent.
J. Green and Son, Queniborough,, Leics.
Graham Pickett Antiques, Stamford, Lincs.
Birkdale Antiques, Southport, Merseyside.
Twickenham Antiques Warehouse, Twickenham,
    Middx.
Anthony Fell, Holt, Norfolk.
Ron Green, Towcester, Northants.
Helios & Co (Antiques), Weedon, Northants.
Jonathan Fyson Antiques, Burford, Oxon.
Gateway Antiques, Burford, Oxon.
Hallidays (Fine Antiques) Ltd, Dorchester-on-Thames,
    Oxon.
Summers Davis Antiques Ltd, Wallingford, Oxon.
Swans, Oakham, Rutland.
Malthouse Antiques, Bridgnorth, Shrops.

Martin Quick Antiques, Cosford, Shrops.
Jadis Ltd, Bath, Somerset.
M.G.R. Exports, Bruton, Somerset.
Pennard House Antiques, East Pennard, Somerset.
Country Brocante, Godney, Somerset.
Gilbert & Dale, Ilchester, Somerset.
Edward Marnier Antiques, Shepton Mallet, Somerset.
The Walnut Tree, Wedmore, Somerset.
Yew Tree Antiques Warehouse, Wiveliscombe,
    Somerset.
Johnsons, Leek, Staffs.
Denzil Grant Antiques, Drinkstone, Suffolk.
Dix-Sept, Framlingham, Suffolk.
The Theatre Antiques Centre, Framlingham, Suffolk.
Adams Room Antiques, Dorking, Surrey.
Heytesbury Antiques, Farnham, Surrey.
Heath-Bullocks, Godalming, Surrey.
Marryat, Richmond, Surrey.
Dermot and Jill Palmer Antiques, Brighton, Sussex
    East.
Graham Lower, Flimwell, Sussex East.
Graham Price Antiques Ltd, Heathfield, Sussex East.
Claremont Antiques, Staplecross, Sussex East.
Julian Antiques, Hurstpierpoint, Sussex West.
Angel Antiques, Petworth, Sussex West.
Brownrigg @ Home, Petworth, Sussex West.
Heather Denham Antiques, Petworth, Sussex West.
Oliver Charles Antiques, Petworth, Sussex West.
Little Theatre Antiques Centre, Jesmond, Tyne and
    Wear.
Curio Corner, Tynemouth, Tyne and Wear.
Arcadia Antiques, Radford Semele, Warks.
Le Grenier Antiques, Wootton Wawen, Warks.
L.P. Furniture Ltd, Walsall, West Mids.
Avon Antiques, Bradford-on-Avon, Wilts.
Moxhams Antiques, Bradford-on-Avon, Wilts.
St Mary's Chapel Antiques, Devizes, Wilts.
Chloe, Warminster, Wilts.
Obelisk Antiques, Warminster, Wilts.
Coopers of Ilkley, Ilkley, Yorks. West.
Jacquart Antiques, Holywood, Co. Down, N. Ireland.
Neil Livingstone, Dundee, Scotland.
Gow Antiques, Forfar, Scotland.
Jeremy Sniders Antiques, Glasgow, Scotland.
Michael Vee Design - Birch House Antiques, Melrose,
    Scotland.

Furniture - Country
Relic Antiques Trade Warehouse, London NW1.
M. and D. Seligmann, London NW3.
Robert E. Hirschhorn, London SE5.
Rogier et Rogier, London SW1.
The Furniture Cave, London SW10.
Robert Young Antiques, London SW11.
Simon Coleman Antiques, London SW13.
I. and J.L. Brown Ltd, London SW6.
Alistair Sampson Antiques Ltd, London W1.
S. and S. Timms Antiques Ltd, Shefford, Beds.
Simon and Penny Rumble Antiques, Chittering, Cambs.

SPECIALIST DEALERS

A.P. and M.A. Haylett, Outwell, Cambs.
Adams Antiques, Nantwich, Cheshire.
Country Living Antiques, Callington, Cornwall.
Julie Strachey, Connor Downs, Cornwall.
Blackwater Pine Antiques, Truro, Cornwall.
Simon Starkie Antiques, Cartmel, Cumbria.
David Hill, Kirkby Stephen, Cumbria.
Pine and Decorative Items, Ashbourne, Derbys.
Peter Bunting Antiques, Bakewell, Derbys.
Byethorpe Furniture, Barlow, Derbys.
Godolphin, Chagford, Devon.
Rex Antiques, Chagford, Devon.
Cobweb Antiques, Cullompton, Devon.
Cullompton Old Tannery Antiques, Cullompton, Devon.
Miller Antiques, Cullompton, Devon.
The Grove Antiques Centre Ltd, Honiton, Devon.
Pilgrim Antiques, Honiton, Devon.
Pugh's Farm Antiques, Monkton, Devon.
Timepiece, Teignmouth, Devon.
Fine Pine Antiques, Totnes, Devon.
Ann Quested Antiques, Bridport, Dorset.
Macintosh Antiques, Sherborne, Dorset.
Piers Pisani Antiques Ltd, Sherborne, Dorset.
The Collector, Barnard Castle, Durham.
English Rose Antiques, Coggeshall, Essex.
The Stores, Great Waltham, Essex.
Lennard Antiques, Sible Hedingham, Essex.
J. and R. Bateman Antiques, Chalford, Glos.
John P. Townsend, Cheltenham, Glos.
Patrick Waldron Antiques, Cirencester, Glos.
Jon Fox Antiques, Moreton-in-Marsh, Glos.
Annarella Clark Antiques, Stow-on-the-Wold, Glos.
Keith Hockin Antiques, Stow-on-the-Wold, Glos.
Huntington Antiques Ltd, Stow-on-the-Wold, Glos.
The Chest of Drawers, Tetbury, Glos.
Peter Norden Antiques, Tetbury, Glos.
Westwood House Antiques, Tetbury, Glos.
Cedar Antiques Limited, Hartley Wintney, Hants.
Millers of Chelsea Antiques Ltd, Ringwood, Hants.
Burgess Farm Antiques, Winchester, Hants.
The Pine Cellars, Winchester, Hants.
I. and J.L. Brown Ltd, Hereford, Herefs.
Robin Lloyd Antiques, Ross-on-Wye, Herefs.
M. and J. Russell, Yazor, Herefs.
Tim Wharton Antiques, Redbourn, Herts.
Gabrielle De Giles, Bilsington, Kent.
Douglas Bryan, Cranbrook, Kent.
Elham Antiques, Elham, Kent.
Mill House Antiques, Goudhurst, Kent.
Gabrielle de Giles, Sandgate, Kent.
Henry Baines, Southborough, Kent.
Phoenix Antiques, Tunbridge Wells, Kent.
Up Country, Tunbridge Wells, Kent.
Edmund Davies & Son Antiques, Whalley, Lancs.
Oaktree Antiques, Lubenham, Leics.
Quorn Pine and Decoratives, Quorn, Leics.
Hunters Antiques & Interior Design, Stamford, Lincs.
Graham Pickett Antiques, Stamford, Lincs.
Sinclair's, Stamford, Lincs.

Andrew Thomas, Stamford, Lincs.
Paul Hopwell Antiques, West Haddon, Northants.
Tudor Rose Antiques, Carlton-on-Trent, Notts.
Horseshoe Antiques and Gallery, Burford, Oxon.
Swan Gallery, Burford, Oxon.
Key Antiques, Chipping Norton, Oxon.
Dorchester Antiques, Dorchester-on-Thames, Oxon.
Knights Antiques, Henley-on-Thames, Oxon.
Wychwood Antiques, Taynton, Oxon.
Quillon Antiques of Tetsworth, Tetsworth, Oxon.
Antiques of Woodstock, Woodstock, Oxon.
Chris Baylis Country Chairs, Woodstock, Oxon.
Oak and Country Furniture Partnership, Woodstock, Oxon.
Garrard Antiques, Ludlow, Shrops.
G. & D. Ginger Antiques, Ludlow, Shrops.
Richard Midwinter Antiques, Market Drayton, Shrops.
Marcus Moore Antiques, Stanton upon Hine Heath, Shrops.
Dodington Antiques, Whitchurch, Shrops.
Mary Cruz, Bath, Somerset.
Anthony Sampson Antiques, Dulverton, Somerset.
Pennard House Antiques, East Pennard, Somerset.
Gilbert & Dale, Ilchester, Somerset.
Johnsons, Leek, Staffs.
Michael Lewis, Leiston, Suffolk.
Noel Mercer Antiques, Long Melford, Suffolk.
Antiques Warehouse (inc. The Woodbridge Trading Co.), Marlesford, Suffolk.
Suffolk House Antiques, Yoxford, Suffolk.
Stoneycroft Farm, Betchworth, Surrey.
The Refectory, Dorking, Surrey.
Christopher's Antiques, Farnham, Surrey.
Anthony Welling Antiques, Ripley, Surrey.
E. and B. White, Brighton, Sussex East.
Hadlow Down Antiques, Hadlow Down, Sussex East.
Graham Price Antiques Ltd, Heathfield, Sussex East.
Pastorale Antiques, Lewes, Sussex East.
Claremont Antiques, Staplecross, Sussex East.
Ringles Cross Antiques, Uckfield, Sussex East.
Park View Antiques, Wadhurst, Sussex East.
Antiquities, Arundel, Sussex West.
Michael Wakelin and Helen Linfield, Billingshurst, Sussex West.
Angel Antiques, Petworth, Sussex West.
John Bird, Petworth, Sussex West.
Cosby Antiques, Petworth, Sussex West.
David Swanson Antiques, Petworth, Sussex West.
King's Cottage Antiques, Leamington Spa, Warks.
Arcadia Antiques, Radford Semele, Warks.
L.P. Furniture Ltd, Walsall, West Mids.
Calne Antiques, Calne, Wilts.
Matthew Eden, Corsham, Wilts.
Maxfield House Antiques, Warminster, Wilts.
D & J Lines Antiques, Wychbold, Worcs.
Smith & Smith Designs, Driffield, Yorks. East.
Elaine Phillips Antiques Ltd, Harrogate, Yorks. North.
Cellar Antiques, Hawes, Yorks. North.
Early Oak, Knaresborough, Yorks. North.

Northern Antiques Company, Norton, Yorks. North.
Country Oak Antiques, Pateley Bridge, Yorks. North.
John Gilbert Antiques, Robin Hood's Bay, Yorks. North.
E. Thistlethwaite, Settle, Yorks. North.
Coach House Antiques, Sleights, Yorks. North.
Ruth Ford Antiques, York, Yorks. North.
Fishlake Antiques, Fishlake, Yorks. South.
Cottage Antiques (1984) Ltd, Walsden, Yorks. West.
Audrey Bull, Carmarthen, Wales.
The Mount Antiques Centre, Carmarthen, Wales.
Havard and Havard, Cowbridge, Wales.
Gallop and Rivers Architectural Antiques, Crickhowell, Wales.
Tim Bowen Antiques, FerrysideWales.
Antiques in Wales, Kidwelly, Wales.
Country Antiques (Wales) Ltd, Kidwelly, Wales.
Islwyn Watkins, Knighton, Wales.
Jim and Pat Ash, Llandeilo, Wales.
Collinge Antiques, Llandudno Junction, Wales.
Malt House Antiques, Narberth, Wales.
Rodney Adams Antiques, Pwllheli, Wales.
Audrey Bull, Tenby, Wales.

Furniture - Georgian
John Jackson at Town House, London E1.
Peter Chapman Antiques and Restoration, London N1.
Furniture Vault, London N1.
Jonathan James, London N1.
Regent Antiques, London N1.
C. Tapsell, London N1.
Vane House Antiques, London N1.
Finchley Fine Art Galleries, London N12.
Martin Henham (Antiques), London N2.
Julian Alexander Antiques, London N20.
Michael Slade Antiques, London N4.
Betty Gould Antiques, London N6.
Dome Antiques (Exports) Ltd, London N7.
G. and F. Gillingham Ltd, London NW2.
Antiques 4 Ltd, London NW3.
Patricia Beckman Antiques, London NW3.
M. and D. Seligmann, London NW3.
Davidson Antiques, London NW8.
Patricia Harvey Antiques and Decoration, London NW8.
Young & Son, London NW8.
The Galleries, London SE1.
Tower Bridge Antiques, London SE1.
Walpoles, London SE10.
Robert E. Hirschhorn, London SE5.
Anno Domini Antiques, London SW1.
John Bly, London SW1.
Ross Hamilton Ltd, London SW1.
Harrods Ltd, London SW1.
Hotspur Ltd, London SW1.
Christopher Howe, London SW1.
Humphrey-Carrasco Ltd, London SW1.
Jeremy Ltd, London SW1.
Peter Jones, London SW1.
Westenholz Antiques Ltd, London SW1.

The Furniture Cave, London SW10.
Lucy Johnson, London SW10.
Stephen Long, London SW10.
Toynbee-Clarke Interiors Ltd, London SW10.
Pairs Antiques Ltd, London SW11.
The Dining Room Shop, London SW13.
H.C. Baxter and Sons, London SW16.
Chris Baron Interiors, London SW2.
Norman Adams Ltd, London SW3.
Apter Fredericks Ltd, London SW3.
Richard Courtney Ltd, London SW3.
Robert Dickson and Lesley Rendall Antiques, London SW3.
Michael Foster, London SW3.
General Trading Co Ltd, London SW3.
Godson and Coles, London SW3.
Michael Hughes, London SW3.
Anthony James and Son Ltd, London SW3.
John Keil Ltd, London SW3.
Peter Lipitch Ltd, London SW3.
Prides of London, London SW3.
Charles Saunders Antiques, London SW3.
313 Antiques, London SW6.
John Clay, London SW6.
Charles Edwards, London SW6.
HRW Antiques (London) Ltd, London SW6.
Christopher Jones Antiques, London SW6.
L. and E. Kreckovic, London SW6.
Nimmo & Spooner, London SW6.
Ossowski, London SW6.
AnthonyOutred, London SW6.
M. Pauw Antiques, London SW6.
Rogers & Co, London SW6.
H. Blairman and Sons Ltd., London W1.
Antoine Cheneviere Fine Arts, London W1.
Sibyl Colefax & John Fowler, London W1.
Mallett and Son (Antiques) Ltd, London W1.
Partridge Fine Arts plc, London W1.
Pendulum of Mayfair Ltd, London W1.
Ronald Phillips Ltd, London W1.
Jeremy Seale Antiques/Interiors, London W1.
M. Turpin Ltd, London W1.
Windsor House Antiques Ltd, London W1.
Judy Fox, London W11.
Robin Martin Antiques, London W11.
Trude Weaver, London W11.
Marshall Gallery, London W14.
J. Roger (Antiques) Ltd, London W14.
Eddy Bardawil, London W8.
Butchoff Antiques, London W8.
C. Fredericks and Son, London W8.
Raffety & Walwyn Ltd, London W8.
Reindeer Antiques Ltd, London W8.
Brian Rolleston Antiques Ltd, London W8.
Patrick Sandberg Antiques Ltd, London W8.
Neil Wibroe and Natasha MacIlwaine, London W8.
Fluss and Charlesworth Ltd, London W9.
Antiquarius of Ampthill, Ampthill, Beds.
Paris Antiques, Ampthill, Beds.

SPECIALIST DEALERS

Pilgrim Antiques, Ampthill, Beds.
S. and S. Timms Antiques Ltd, Shefford, Beds.
Town Hall Antiques, Woburn, Beds.
John A. Pearson Antiques, Horton, Berks.
Franklin Antiques, Hungerford, Berks.
Griffin Fine Art & Antiques, Hungerford, Berks.
Roger King Antiques, Hungerford, Berks.
The Old Malthouse, Hungerford, Berks.
Turpins Antiques, Hungerford, Berks.
Widmerpool House Antiques, Maidenhead, Berks.
Rupert Landen Antiques, Reading, Berks.
Cavendish Fine Arts, Sonning-on-Thames, Berks.
John Connell - Wargrave Antiques, Wargrave, Berks.
Eton Antiques Partnership, Windsor, Berks.
Marcelline Herald Antiques, Windsor, Berks.
Peter J. Martin, Windsor, Berks.
The Cupboard Antiques, Amersham, Bucks.
Grosvenor House Interiors, Beaconsfield, Bucks.
Period Furniture Showrooms, Beaconsfield, Bucks.
Leo Antiques & Collectables Ltd, Olney, Bucks.
Robin Unsworth Antiques, Olney, Bucks.
Peter Norman Antiques and Restorations, Burwell,
    Cambs.
Jess Applin Antiques, Cambridge, Cambs.
John Beazor and Sons Ltd, Cambridge, Cambs.
Tavistock Antiques Ltd, St. Neots, Cambs.
Antiques & Curios (Steve Carpenter), Wisbech, Cambs.
Trash 'n' Treasure, Alsager, Cheshire.
Church Street Antiques, Altrincham, Cheshire.
Andrew Foott Antiques, Cheadle Hulme, Cheshire.
Antique Exporters of Chester, Chester, Cheshire.
Sandra Harris Interiors and Antiques, Chester, Cheshire.
Melody's Antiques, Chester, Cheshire.
Moor Hall Antiques, Chester, Cheshire.
David Bedale, Mobberley, Cheshire.
Chapel Antiques, Nantwich, Cheshire.
Nantwich Antiques, Nantwich, Cheshire.
Coppelia Antiques, Plumley, Cheshire.
Romiley Antiques & Jewellery, Romiley, Cheshire.
Saxon Cross Antiques Emporium, Sandbach, Cheshire.
Manchester Antique Company, Stockport, Cheshire.
Antique Chairs and Museum, Launceston, Cornwall.
John Bragg Antiques, Lostwithiel, Cornwall.
Antiques & Fine Art, Penzance, Cornwall.
Victoria Antiques, Wadebridge, Cornwall.
Anthemion - The Antique Shop, Cartmel, Cumbria.
Johnson & Johnson, Kirkby Lonsdale, Cumbria.
Haughey Antiques, Kirkby Stephen, Cumbria.
Ashbourne Antiques Ltd, Ashbourne, Derbys.
Martin and Dorothy Harper Antiques, Bakewell,
    Derbys.
Michael Pembery Antiques, Bakewell, Derbys.
Hackney House Antiques & Clocks, Barlow, Derbys.
Heldreich Antiques & French Polishers, Brailsford,
    Derbys.
The Antiques Warehouse, Buxton, Derbys.
Ian Morris, Chesterfield, Derbys.
Wayside Antiques, Duffield, Derbys.
Shardlow Antiques Warehouse, Shardlow, Derbys.

Nimbus Antiques, Whaley Bridge, Derbys.
Kessler Ford, Ashburton, Devon.
Bampton Gallery, Bampton, Devon.
Robert Byles and Optimum Brasses, Bampton, Devon.
J. Collins and Son Fine Art, Bideford, Devon.
John Prestige Antiques, Brixham, Devon.
David J. Thorn, Budleigh Salterton, Devon.
Cullompton Old Tannery Antiques, Cullompton, Devon.
Miller Antiques, Cullompton, Devon.
Mills Antiques, Cullompton, Devon.
The Antiques Complex, Exeter, Devon.
Peter Wadham Antiques, Exeter, Devon.
Alison Gosling Antiques Studio, Exmouth, Devon.
Alexander Paul Antiques, Fenny Bridges, Devon.
Roderick Butler, Honiton, Devon.
The Grove Antiques Centre Ltd, Honiton, Devon.
Hermitage Antiques, Honiton, Devon.
Lombard Antiques, Honiton, Devon.
Merchant House Antiques, Honiton, Devon.
Pilgrim Antiques, Honiton, Devon.
Jane Strickland & Daughters, Honiton, Devon.
Upstairs, Downstairs, Honiton, Devon.
Guy Dennler Antiques & Interiors, Rackenford, Devon.
A. E. Wakeman & Sons Ltd, Tedburn St Mary, Devon.
Domani, Topsham, Devon.
Mere Antiques, Topsham, Devon.
Anthony James Antiques, Whimple, Devon.
Milton Antiques, Blandford Forum, Dorset.
Lionel Geneen Ltd, Bournemouth, Dorset.
Sainsburys of Bournemouth Ltd, Bournemouth, Dorset.
Benchmark Antiques, Bridport, Dorset.
Hamptons, Christchurch, Dorset.
Tower Antiques, Cranborne, Dorset.
Michael Legg Antiques, Dorchester, Dorset.
Legg of Dorchester, Dorchester, Dorset.
Hardy Country, Melbury Osmond, Dorset.
Laburnum Antiques, Poole, Dorset.
Stocks and Chairs, Poole, Dorset.
Shaston Antiques, Shaftesbury, Dorset.
Antiques of Sherborne, Sherborne, Dorset.
Phoenix Antiques, Sherborne, Dorset.
Renaissance, Sherborne, Dorset.
Wessex Antiques, Sherborne, Dorset.
James Hardy Antiques Ltd, Barnard Castle, Durham.
Joan, David and Richard White Antiques, Barnard
    Castle, Durham.
Margaret Bedi Antiques & Fine Art, Stockton-on-Tees,
    Durham.
Eden House Antiques, West Auckland, Durham.
Swan Antiques, Baythorne End, Essex.
Colton Antiques, Kelvedon, Essex.
Clive Beardall Restorations Ltd, Maldon, Essex.
West Essex Antiques (Stone Hall), Matching Green,
    Essex.
F.G. Bruschweiler (Antiques) Ltd, Rayleigh, Essex.
W.A. Pinn and Sons, Sible Hedingham, Essex.
Harris Antiques, Thaxted, Essex.
White Roding Antiques, White Roding, Essex.
Peter and Penny Proudfoot, Berkeley, Glos.

The Antiques Warehouse Ltd, Bristol, Glos.
Triton Gallery, Cheltenham, Glos.
Cottage Farm Antiques, Chipping Campden, Glos.
School House Antiques, Chipping Campden, Glos.
Forum Antiques, Cirencester, Glos.
Hares, Cirencester, Glos.
Patrick Waldron Antiques, Cirencester, Glos.
Bernard Weaver Antiques, Cirencester, Glos.
Blenheim Antiques, Fairford, Glos.
Benton Fine Art, Moreton-in-Marsh, Glos.
Berry Antiques Ltd, Moreton-in-Marsh, Glos.
Dale House Antiques, Moreton-in-Marsh, Glos.
Simply Antiques, Moreton-in-Marsh, Glos.
The Roger Widdas Gallery, Moreton-in-Marsh, Glos.
Gary Wright Antiques, Moreton-in-Marsh, Glos.
Robson Antiques, Northleach, Glos.
Ashton Gower Antiques, Stow-on-the-Wold, Glos.
Duncan J. Baggott, Stow-on-the-Wold, Glos.
Baggott Church Street Ltd, Stow-on-the-Wold, Glos.
Christopher Clarke Antiques Ltd, Stow-on-the-Wold,
    Glos.
Huntington Antiques Ltd, Stow-on-the-Wold, Glos.
Kenulf Fine Arts, Stow-on-the-Wold, Glos.
T.M. King-Smith & Simon W. Nutter, Stow-on-the-
    Wold, Glos.
La Chaise Antique, Stow-on-the-Wold, Glos.
Roger Lamb Antiques & Works of Art, Stow-on-the-
    Wold, Glos.
Malt House Antiques, Stow-on-the-Wold, Glos.
Antony Preston Antiques Ltd, Stow-on-the-Wold, Glos.
Queens Parade Antiques Ltd, Stow-on-the-Wold, Glos.
Michael Rowland Antiques, Stow-on-the-Wold, Glos.
Stow Antiques, Stow-on-the-Wold, Glos.
Styles of Stow, Stow-on-the-Wold, Glos.
Vanbrugh House Antiques, Stow-on-the-Wold, Glos.
Wyndhams, Stow-on-the-Wold, Glos.
Alderson, Tetbury, Glos.
Ball and Claw Antiques, Tetbury, Glos.
Breakspeare Antiques, Tetbury, Glos.
The Chest of Drawers, Tetbury, Glos.
Peter Norden Antiques, Tetbury, Glos.
Porch House Antiques, Tetbury, Glos.
Gainsborough House Antiques, Tewkesbury, Glos.
Whittington Barn Antiques, Whittington, Glos.
Berkeley Antiques, Winchcombe, Glos.
In Period Antiques, Winchcombe, Glos.
Prichard Antiques, Winchcombe, Glos.
Pineapple House Antiques, Alresford, Hants.
The Furniture Trading Co, Botley, Hants.
Brambridge Antiques, Brambridge, Hants.
F.E.A. Briggs Ltd, Brook, Hants.
Nicholas Abbott, Hartley Wintney, Hants.
Deva Antiques, Hartley Wintney, Hants.
David Lazarus Antiques, Hartley Wintney, Hants.
Lita Kaye of Lyndhurst, Lyndhurst, Hants.
Millers of Chelsea Antiques Ltd, Ringwood, Hants.
Antique Eyes, Stockbridge, Hants.
The Bakhtiyar Gallery, Stockbridge, Hants.
Gasson Antiques and Interiors, Tadley, Hants.

Gaylords, Titchfield, Hants.
Max Rollitt, Winchester, Hants.
Great Brampton House Antiques Ltd, Hereford, Herefs.
John Nash Antiques and Interiors, Ledbury, Herefs.
Serendipity, Ledbury, Herefs.
Farmers Gallery, Leominster, Herefs.
Jeffery Hammond Antiques, Leominster, Herefs.
Anthony Butt Antiques, Baldock, Herts.
Michael Lipitch Ltd, Barnet, Herts.
The Windhill Antiquary, Bishop's Stortford, Herts.
Tapestry Antiques, Hertford, Herts.
Michael Gander, Hitchin, Herts.
Phillips of Hitchin (Antiques) Ltd, Hitchin, Herts.
Tom Salusbury Antiques, Hitchin, Herts.
Bushwood Antiques, Redbourn, Herts.
J.N. Antiques, Redbourn, Herts.
Tim Wharton Antiques, Redbourn, Herts.
Charnwood Antiques and Arcane Antiques Centre,
    Sawbridgeworth, Herts.
John Bly, Tring, Herts.
New England House Antiques, Tring, Herts.
Weston Antiques, Weston, Herts.
Collins Antiques (F.G. and C. Collins Ltd.),
    Wheathampstead, Herts.
Michael Armson (Antiques) Ltd, Wilstone, Herts.
John Corrin Antiques, Douglas, Isle of Man.
Royal Standard Antiques, Cowes, Isle of Wight.
Stablegate Antiques, Barham, Kent.
David Barrington, Brasted, Kent.
Cooper Fine Arts Ltd, Brasted, Kent.
G. A. Hill Antiques, Brasted, Kent.
Keymer Son & Co. Ltd, Brasted, Kent.
Roy Massingham Antiques, Brasted, Kent.
Old Bakery Antiques, Brasted, Kent.
S. L. Walker, BrastedKent.
Conquest House Antiques, Canterbury, Kent.
Alan Lord Antiques, Chilham, Kent.
Chislehurst Antiques, Chislehurst, Kent.
Michael Sim, Chislehurst, Kent.
Lennox Cato, Edenbridge, Kent.
Chevertons of Edenbridge Ltd, Edenbridge, Kent.
Restall Brown & Clennell, Edenbridge, Kent.
Mill House Antiques, Goudhurst, Kent.
Alan Lord Antiques, Hythe, Kent.
Thanet Antiques, Ramsgate, Kent.
J.D. and R.M. Walters, Rolvenden, Kent.
Christopher Buck Antiques, Sandgate, Kent.
Finch Antiques, Sandgate, Kent.
Michael Fitch Antiques, Sandgate, Kent.
Freeman and Lloyd Antiques, Sandgate, Kent.
J. Luckhurst Antiques, Sandgate, Kent.
Steppes Hill Farm Antiques, Stockbury, Kent.
Sutton Valence Antiques, Sutton Valence, Kent.
Flower House Antiques, Tenterden, Kent.
Down Lane Hall Antiques, Tunbridge Wells, Kent.
The Pantiles Antiques, Tunbridge Wells, Kent.
Pantiles Spa Antiques, Tunbridge Wells, Kent.
Phoenix Antiques, Tunbridge Wells, Kent.
John Thompson, Tunbridge Wells, Kent.

Up Country, Tunbridge Wells, Kent.
Apollo Antique Galleries, Westerham, Kent.
London House Antiques, Westerham, Kent.
Taylor-Smith Antiques, Westerham, Kent.
Laurens Antiques, Whitstable, Kent.
Ascot Antiques, Blackpool, Lancs.
Brun Lea Antiques (J. Waite Ltd), Burnley, Lancs.
K.C. Antiques, Darwen, Lancs.
P.J. Brown Antiques, Haslingden, Lancs.
Luigino Vescovi, Morecambe, Lancs.
Alan Grice Antiques, Ormskirk, Lancs.
Sitting Pretty, Great Glen, Leics.
Magpie Antiques, Hinckley, Leics.
Withers of Leicester, Hoby, Leics.
Corry's Antiques, Leicester, Leics.
Treedale Antiques, Little Dalby, Leics.
Lowe of Loughborough, Loughborough, Leics.
Oaktree Antiques, Lubenham, Leics.
Walter Moores and Son, Market Harborough, Leics.
J. Stamp and Sons, Market Harborough, Leics.
J. Green and Son, Queniborough, Leics.
West Gate Antiques, GranthamLincs.
G. Baker Antiques, Horncastle, Lincs.
Alan Read - Period Furniture, Horncastle, Lincs.
Hansord at No 2 Antiques & Period Design, Lincoln, Lincs.
David J. Hansord & Son, Lincoln, Lincs.
Dawson of Stamford Ltd, Stamford, Lincs.
Hunters Antiques & Interior Design, Stamford, Lincs.
Graham Pickett Antiques, Stamford, Lincs.
St. George's Antiques, Stamford, Lincs.
Robin Shield Antiques, Swinstead, Lincs.
Underwoodhall Antiques, Woodhall Spa, Lincs.
V.O.C. Antiques, Woodhall Spa, Lincs.
Stefani Antiques, Liverpool, Merseyside.
Colin Stock, Rainford, Merseyside.
Tony and Anne Sutcliffe Antiques, Southport, Merseyside.
Helen Horswill Antiques and Decorative Arts, West Kirby, Merseyside.
Tobias Jellinek Antiques, Twickenham, Middx.
A.E. Bush and Partners, Attleborough, Norfolk.
Pearse Lukies, Aylsham, Norfolk.
M. and A. Cringle, Burnham Market, Norfolk.
Hamilton Antiques, Burnham Market, Norfolk.
Anthony Fell, Holt, Norfolk.
James K. Lee, King's Lynn, Norfolk.
James Brett, Norwich, Norfolk.
Nicholas Fowle Antiques, Norwich, Norfolk.
Priests Antiques Ltd, Ringstead, Norfolk.
Country House Antiques, Seething, Norfolk.
Stalham Antique Gallery, Stalham, Norfolk.
Jubilee Antiques, Tottenhill, Norfolk.
Norton Antiques, Twyford, Norfolk.
T.C.S. Brooke, Wroxham, Norfolk.
Simon Banks Antiques, Finedon, Northants.
M.C. Chapman, Finedon, Northants.
Robert Cheney Antiques, Finedon, Northants.
Blockheads and Granary Antiques, Flore, Northants.

Christopher Jones Antiques, Flore, Northants.
F. and C.H. Cave, Northampton, Northants.
Reindeer Antiques Ltd, Potterspury, Northants.
Granary Antiques, Woodford, Northants.
G.M. Athey, Alnwick, Northumbs.
James Miller Antiques, Wooler, Northumbs.
Dukeries Antiques Centre, Budby, Notts.
A.J. O'Sullivan Antiques, Darlton, Notts.
Ivory Gate, Hucknall, Notts.
No. 1 Castlegate Antiques, Newark, Notts.
Pearman Antiques & Interiors, Newark, Notts.
Ranby Hall, Retford, Notts.
William Antiques, Ascott-under-Wychwood, Oxon.
Burford Antique Centre, Burford, Oxon.
Gateway Antiques, Burford, Oxon.
Hubert's Antiques, Burford, Oxon.
David Pickup, Burford, Oxon.
Swan Gallery, Burford, Oxon.
Rupert Hitchcox Antiques, Chalgrove, Oxon.
Georgian House Antiques, Chipping Norton, Oxon.
Dorchester Antiques, Dorchester-on-Thames, Oxon.
Hallidays (Fine Antiques) Ltd, Dorchester-on-Thames, Oxon.
Brushwood Antiques, FaringdonOxon.
Richard J. Kingston, Henley-on-Thames, Oxon.
Stephen Orton Antiques, Henley-on-Thames, Oxon.
The Country Seat, Huntercombe, Oxon.
Winston Antiques, KinghamOxon.
de Albuquerque Antiques, Wallingford, Oxon.
Chris and Lin O'Donnell Antiques, Wallingford, Oxon.
Mike Ottrey Antiques, Wallingford, Oxon.
Summers Davis Antiques Ltd, Wallingford, Oxon.
Cross Antiques, Watlington, Oxon.
Colin Greenway Antiques, Witney, Oxon.
W.R. Harvey & Co (Antiques) Ltd, Witney, Oxon.
Joan Wilkins Antiques, Witney, Oxon.
Witney Antiques, Witney, Oxon.
Antiques of Woodstock, Woodstock, Oxon.
The Chair Set - Antiques, Woodstock, Oxon.
Swans, Oakham, Rutland.
Treedale Antiques, Oakham, Rutland.
John Garner, Uppingham, Rutland.
Harvey Art and Antiques, Uppingham, Rutland.
T.J. Roberts, Uppingham, Rutland.
Woodman's House Antiques, Uppingham, Rutland.
Robert Bingley Antiques, Wing, Rutland.
Mytton Antiques, Atcham, Shrops.
Martin Quick Antiques, Cosford, Shrops.
Bayliss Antiques, Ludlow, Shrops.
R.G. Cave and Sons Ltd, Ludlow, Shrops.
G. & D. Ginger Antiques, Ludlow, Shrops.
Richard Midwinter Antiques, Market Drayton, Shrops.
Raynalds Mansion, Much Wenlock, Shrops.
Brian James Antiques, Rodington, Shrops.
Corner Farm Antiques, Shifnal, Shrops.
Mansers Antiques, Shrewsbury, Shrops.
Marcus Moore Antiques, Stanton upon Hine Heath, Shrops.
Dodington Antiques, Whitchurch, Shrops.

Lawrence Brass, Bath, Somerset.
Mary Cruz, Bath, Somerset.
Jadis Ltd, Bath, Somerset.
Quiet Street Antiques, Bath, Somerset.
M.G.R. Exports, Bruton, Somerset.
Chris's Crackers, Carhampton, Somerset.
Anthony Sampson Antiques, Dulverton, Somerset.
The Crooked Window, Dunster, Somerset.
Freshfords, Freshford, Somerset.
Westville House Antiques, Littleton, Somerset.
Edward Marnier Antiques, Shepton Mallet, Somerset.
The Old Schoolrooms Antiques, Wincanton, Somerset.
Ottery Antique Restorers, Wincanton, Somerset.
Wincanton Antiques, Wincanton, Somerset.
J.C. Giddings, Wiveliscombe, Somerset.
John Hamblin, Yeovil, Somerset.
Page Antiques, Leek, Staffs.
Milestone Antiques, Lichfield, Staffs.
Winder's Fine Art and Antiques, Newcastle-under-Lyme, Staffs.
H.W. Heron and Son Ltd, Yoxall, Staffs.
Fauconberges, Beccles, Suffolk.
Bly Valley Antiques, Blyford, Suffolk.
Seabrook Antiques and Suffolk Antiques Centre, Cavendish, Suffolk.
Robin Butler, Clare, Suffolk.
F.D. Salter Antiques, Clare, Suffolk.
Debenham Antiques, Debenham, Suffolk.
Denzil Grant Antiques, Drinkstone, Suffolk.
English and Continental Antiques, Eye, Suffolk.
The Theatre Antiques Centre, Framlingham, Suffolk.
P & R Antiques Ltd, Halesworth, Suffolk.
Hubbard Antiques, Ipswich, Suffolk.
Richard A. Rush Antiques, Ipswich, Suffolk.
J. and J. Baker, Lavenham, Suffolk.
Warrens Antiques Warehouse, Leiston, Suffolk.
Sandy Cooke Antiques, Long Melford, Suffolk.
Alexander Lyall Antiques, Long Melford, Suffolk.
Matthew Tyler Antiques, Long Melford, Suffolk.
Martlesham Antiques, Martlesham, Suffolk.
Napier House Antiques, Sudbury, Suffolk.
Peppers Period Pieces, Wattisfield, Suffolk.
David Gibbins Antiques, Woodbridge, Suffolk.
Hamilton Antiques, Woodbridge, Suffolk.
Anthony Hurst Antiques, Woodbridge, Suffolk.
J.C. Heather, Woolpit, Suffolk.
Suffolk House Antiques, Yoxford, Suffolk.
John Anthony Antiques, Bletchingley, Surrey.
G. D. Blay Antiques, Charlwood, Surrey.
Adams Room Antiques, Dorking, Surrey.
Arkell Antiques Ltd, Dorking, Surrey.
Dolphin Square Antiques, Dorking, Surrey.
The Dorking Desk Shop, Dorking, Surrey.
Harman's, Dorking, Surrey.
Holmwood Antiques, Dorking, Surrey.
The Howard Gallery, Dorking, Surrey.
Malthouse Antiques, Dorking, Surrey.
Norfolk House Galleries, Dorking, Surrey.
Honeypot Antiques Ltd, Elstead, Surrey.

Christopher's Antiques, Farnham, Surrey.
Heytesbury Antiques, Farnham, Surrey.
Heath-Bullocks, Godalming, Surrey.
The Coach House Antiques, Gomshall, Surrey.
West Street Antiques, Haslemere, Surrey.
Glencorse Antiques, Kingston-upon-Thames, Surrey.
F.G. Lawrence and Sons, Redhill, Surrey.
M. & M. White Antique & Reproduction Centre, Reigate, Surrey.
Marryat, Richmond, Surrey.
J. Hartley Antiques Ltd, Ripley, Surrey.
Sage Antiques and Interiors, Ripley, Surrey.
Cockrell Antiques, Surbiton, Surrey.
B. M. and E. Newlove, Surbiton, Surrey.
Clifford and Roger Dade, Thames Ditton, Surrey.
Church House Antiques, Weybridge, Surrey.
Alexandria Antiques, Brighton, Sussex East.
Patrick Moorhead Antiques, Brighton, Sussex East.
Michael Norman Antiques Ltd, Brighton, Sussex East.
The North Laine Antiques Market, inc. Alan Fitchett Antiques, Brighton, Sussex East.
Yellow Lantern Antiques Ltd, Brighton, Sussex East.
Dycheling Antiques, Ditchling, Sussex East.
Hadlow Down Antiques, Hadlow Down, Sussex East.
The Old Mint House, Pevensey, Sussex East.
Bragge and Sons, Rye, Sussex East.
East Street Antiques, Rye, Sussex East.
Herbert Gordon Gasson, Rye, Sussex East.
The Old House, Seaford, Sussex East.
Bygones, Angmering, Sussex West.
Michael Wakelin and Helen Linfield, Billingshurst, Sussex West.
Frensham House Antiques, Chichester, Sussex West.
Gems Antiques, Chichester, Sussex West.
David Foord-Brown Antiques, Cuckfield, Sussex West.
Ashcombe Coach House, Henfield, Sussex West.
Stable Antiques, Lindfield, Sussex West.
Callingham Antiques, Northchapel, Sussex West.
Antiquated, Petworth, Sussex West.
Ronald G. Chambers Fine Antiques, Petworth, Sussex West.
Heather Denham Antiques, Petworth, Sussex West.
Elliott's, Petworth, Sussex West.
Richard Gardner Antiques, Petworth, Sussex West.
Granville Antiques, Petworth, Sussex West.
William Hockley Antiques, Petworth, Sussex West.
Oliver Charles Antiques, Petworth, Sussex West.
Thakeham Furniture Ltd, Petworth, Sussex West.
T.G. Wilkinson Antiques Ltd., Petworth, Sussex West.
Georgia Antiques, Pulborough, Sussex West.
Elaine Saunderson Antiques, Pulborough, Sussex West.
Wilsons Antiques, Worthing, Sussex West.
Graham Smith Antiques, Jesmond, Tyne and Wear.
Curio Corner, Tynemouth, Tyne and Wear.
Apollo Antiques, Warwick, Warks.
William J. Casey Antiques, Warwick, Warks.
Patrick and Gillian Morley Antiques, Warwick, Warks.
James Reeve, Warwick, Warks.
Peter Clark Antiques, Birmingham, West Mids.

Moseley Emporium, Birmingham, West Mids.
Yoxall Antiques, Solihull, West Mids.
Thomas Coulborn and Sons, Sutton Coldfield, West Mids.
Avon Antiques, Bradford-on-Avon, Wilts.
Mac Humble Antiques, Bradford-on-Avon, Wilts.
Moxhams Antiques, Bradford-on-Avon, Wilts.
Harley Antiques, Christian Malford, Wilts.
Edward Hurst, Coombe Bissett, Wilts.
William Cook (Marlborough), Marlborough, Wilts.
Katharine House Gallery, Marlborough, Wilts.
Dann Antiques Ltd, Melksham, Wilts.
Alan Jaffray, Melksham, Wilts.
21st Century Antics, Salisbury, Wilts.
Boston Antiques, Salisbury, Wilts.
Robert Bradley Antiques, Salisbury, Wilts.
Myriad, Salisbury, Wilts.
Salisbury Antiques Warehouse Ltd, Salisbury, Wilts.
Mike Scott Repair & Restoration, Salisbury, Wilts.
Cassidy's Antiques, Warminster, Wilts.
Maxfield House Antiques, Warminster, Wilts.
Obelisk Antiques, Warminster, Wilts.
Bay Tree Antiques, Wilton, Wilts.
A.J. Romain and Sons, Wilton, Wilts.
Barnt Green Antiques, Barnt Green, Worcs.
Stephen Cook Antiques, Broadway, Worcs.
Fenwick and Fenwick Antiques, Broadway, Worcs.
H.W. Keil Ltd, Broadway, Worcs.
Robert Belcher Antiques, Droitwich, Worcs.
Miscellany Antiques, Great Malvern, Worcs.
The Drawing Room - Interiors & Antiques, Pershore, Worcs.
Angel Antiques, Redditch, Worcs.
Lower House Fine Antiques, Redditch, Worcs.
Bygones by the Cathedral, Worcester, Worcs.
Bygones of Worcester, Worcester, Worcs.
M. Lees and Sons, Worcester, Worcs.
Priory Antiques, Bridlington, Yorks. East.
Houghton Hall Antiques, Market Weighton, Yorks. East.
Bennett's Antiques & Collectables, Bedale, Yorks. North.
John Wilson, Boroughbridge, Yorks. North.
R.S. Wilson and Sons, Boroughbridge, Yorks. North.
Milestone Antiques, Easingwold, Yorks. North.
Elm Tree Antiques, Flaxton, Yorks. North.
Dickinson's Antiques Ltd, Gargrave, Yorks. North.
R.N. Myers and Son, Gargrave, Yorks. North.
Nigel Adamson, Harrogate, Yorks. North.
Armstrong, Harrogate, Yorks. North.
Bryan Bowden, Harrogate, Yorks. North.
Garth Antiques, Harrogate, Yorks. North.
David Love, Harrogate, Yorks. North.
Charles Lumb and Sons Ltd, Harrogate, Yorks. North.
Thorntons of Harrogate, Harrogate, Yorks. North.
Walker Galleries Ltd, Harrogate, Yorks. North.
Paul Weatherell Antiques, Harrogate, Yorks. North.
Chris Wilde Antiques, Harrogate, Yorks. North.
Sturman's Antiques, Hawes, Yorks. North.
John Thompson Antiques, Knaresborough, Yorks. North.

Aura Antiques, Masham, Yorks. North.
Milton Holgate, Ripon, Yorks. North.
Sigma Antiques and Fine Art, Ripon, Yorks. North.
Anderson Slater Antiques, Settle, Yorks. North.
Antony, David & Ann Shackleton, Snainton, Yorks. North.
Alan Ramsey Antiques, Stokesley, Yorks. North.
Tomlinsons, Tockwith, Yorks. North.
Dovetail Antiques, Sheffield, Yorks. South.
Sarah Scott Antiques, Sheffield, Yorks. South.
The Baildon Furniture Co. Ltd, Baildon, Yorks. West.
Browgate Antiques, Baildon, Yorks. West.
Bingley Antiques, Haworth, Yorks. West.
Coopers of Ilkley, Ilkley, Yorks. West.
Geary Antiques, Leeds, Yorks. West.
Park Antiques, Menston, Yorks. West.
Victoria Antiques, Alderney, Alderney, C.I.
Robert Christie Antiques, Ballyclare, Co. Antrim, N. Ireland.
Oakland Antiques, Belfast, Co. Antrim, N. Ireland.
Dunluce Antiques, Bushmills, Co. Antrim, N. Ireland.
MacHenry Antiques, Newtownabbey, Co. Antrim, N. Ireland.
Millcourt Antiques, Seapatrick, Co. Down, N. Ireland.
Moy Antiques, Dungannon, Co. Tyrone, N. Ireland.
Kelly Antiques, Omagh, Co. Tyrone, N. Ireland.
Colin Wood (Antiques) Ltd, Aberdeen, Scotland.
Ian Whitelaw Antiques, Auchterarder, Scotland.
Coldstream Antiques, Coldstream, Scotland.
The Magic Lantern, Dunecht, Scotland.
Georgian Antiques, Edinburgh, Scotland.
Hawkins & Hawkins, Edinburgh, Scotland.
London Road Antiques, Edinburgh, Scotland.
Gow Antiques, Forfar, Scotland.
Cathedral Antiques, Fortrose, Scotland.
Butler's Furniture Galleries, Glasgow, Scotland.
Michael Young Antiques at Glencarse, Glencarse, Scotland.
C.S. Moreton (Antiques), Inchture, Scotland.
Kilmacolm Antiques Ltd, Kilmacolm, Scotland.
QS Antiques and Cabinetmakers, Kilmarnock, Scotland.
Rhudle Mill, Kilmichael Glassary, Scotland.
Osborne Antiques, Kirkcudbright, Scotland.
Michael Vee Design - Birch House Antiques, Melrose, Scotland.
Harper-James, Montrose, Scotland.
Newburgh Antiques, Newburgh, Scotland.
Crossroads Antiques, Prestwick, Scotland.
Coach House Antiques Ltd, Stanley, Scotland.
The Mount Antiques Centre, Carmarthen, Wales.
Havard and Havard, Cowbridge, Wales.
Renaissance Antiques - The Vale of Glamorgan Antiques Centre, Cowbridge, Wales.
Antiques in Wales, Kidwelly, Wales.
J. and R. Langford, Llangollen, Wales.
Snowdonia Antiques, Llanrwst, Wales.
Allam Antiques, Newbridge-on-Wye, Wales.
Rodney Adams Antiques, Pwllheli, Wales.
Barn Court Antiques, Crafts & Tearoom, Templeton, Wales.

F.E. Anderson and Son, Welshpool, Wales.

Furniture - Oak

Michael Slade Antiques, London N4.
Robert E. Hirschhorn, London SE5.
Christopher Howe, London SW1.
Kate Thurlow, London SW1.
The Furniture Cave, London SW10.
Robert Young Antiques, London SW11.
Apter Fredericks Ltd, London SW3.
Alistair Sampson Antiques Ltd, London W1.
Beedham Antiques Ltd, Hungerford, Berks.
Simon and Penny Rumble Antiques, Chittering, Cambs.
Melody's Antiques, Chester, Cheshire.
Adams Antiques, Nantwich, Cheshire.
Marhamchurch Antiques, Marhamchurch, Cornwall.
Simon Starkie Antiques, Cartmel, Cumbria.
Jennywell Hall Antiques, Crosby Ravensworth,
    Cumbria.
Sleddall Hall Antiques Centre inc. Kendal Studios
    Antiques, Kendal, Cumbria.
Johnson & Johnson, Kirkby Lonsdale, Cumbria.
Haughey Antiques, Kirkby Stephen, Cumbria.
J H S Antiques Ltd, Ashbourne, Derbys.
Peter Bunting Antiques, Bakewell, Derbys.
Byethorpe Furniture, Barlow, Derbys.
Richard Glass, Whaley Bridge, Derbys.
Kessler Ford, Ashburton, Devon.
Robert Byles and Optimum Brasses, Bampton, Devon.
Godolphin, Chagford, Devon.
Rex Antiques, Chagford, Devon.
Cobweb Antiques, Cullompton, Devon.
Cullompton Old Tannery Antiques, Cullompton, Devon.
Pilgrim Antiques, Honiton, Devon.
A. E. Wakeman & Sons Ltd, Tedburn St Mary, Devon.
The Collector, Barnard Castle, Durham.
Lennard Antiques, Sible Hedingham, Essex.
Peter and Penny Proudfoot, Berkeley, Glos.
J. and R. Bateman Antiques, Chalford, Glos.
William H. Stokes, Cirencester, Glos.
Duncan J. Baggott, Stow-on-the-Wold, Glos.
Baggott Church Street Ltd, Stow-on-the-Wold, Glos.
Keith Hockin Antiques, Stow-on-the-Wold, Glos.
T.M. King-Smith & Simon W. Nutter, Stow-on-the-
    Wold, Glos.
Malt House Antiques, Stow-on-the-Wold, Glos.
Michael Rowland Antiques, Stow-on-the-Wold, Glos.
Arthur Seager Antiques, Stow-on-the-Wold, Glos.
Day Antiques, Tetbury, Glos.
Peter Norden Antiques, Tetbury, Glos.
Westwood House Antiques, Tetbury, Glos.
In Period Antiques, Winchcombe, Glos.
Quatrefoil, Fordingbridge, Hants.
Cedar Antiques Limited, Hartley Wintney, Hants.
Robin Lloyd Antiques, Ross-on-Wye, Herefs.
M. and J. Russell, Yazor, Herefs.
Tim Wharton Antiques, Redbourn, Herts.
Collins Antiques (F.G. and C. Collins Ltd.),
    Wheathampstead, Herts.

R. Kirby Antiques, Acrise, Kent.
Douglas Bryan, Cranbrook, Kent.
Old English Oak, Sandgate, Kent.
Henry Baines, Southborough, Kent.
Edmund Davies & Son Antiques, Whalley, Lancs.
Treedale Antiques, Little Dalby, Leics.
Lowe of Loughborough, Loughborough, Leics.
West Gate Antiques, Grantham, Lincs.
Alan Read - Period Furniture, Horncastle, Lincs.
Sinclair's, Stamford, Lincs.
Tobias Jellinek Antiques, Twickenham, Middx.
Pearse Lukies, Aylsham, Norfolk.
Anthony Fell, Holt, Norfolk.
James Brett, Norwich, Norfolk.
Priests Antiques Ltd, Ringstead, Norfolk.
Country House Antiques, Seething, Norfolk.
Paul Hopwell Antiques, West Haddon, Northants.
No. 1 Castlegate Antiques, Newark, Notts.
Pearman Antiques & Interiors, Newark, Notts.
Horseshoe Antiques and Gallery, Burford, Oxon.
Swan Gallery, Burford, Oxon.
Key Antiques, Chipping Norton, Oxon.
Knights Antiques, Henley-on-Thames, Oxon.
Quillon Antiques of Tetsworth, Tetsworth, Oxon.
Witney Antiques, Witney, Oxon.
Antiques of Woodstock, Woodstock, Oxon.
Treedale Antiques, Oakham, Rutland.
John Garner, Uppingham, Rutland.
R.G. Cave and Sons Ltd, Ludlow, Shrops.
G. & D. Ginger Antiques, Ludlow, Shrops.
Richard Midwinter Antiques, Market Drayton, Shrops.
Marcus Moore Antiques, Stanton upon Hine Heath,
    Shrops.
Dodington Antiques, Whitchurch, Shrops.
Stuart Interiors Ltd, Barrington, Somerset.
Lawrence Brass, Bath, Somerset.
Anthony Sampson Antiques, Dulverton, Somerset.
The Crooked Window, Dunster, Somerset.
John Nicholls, Leigh, Staffs.
Winder's Fine Art and Antiques, Newcastle-under-
    Lyme, Staffs.
Seabrook Antiques and Suffolk Antiques Centre,
    Cavendish, Suffolk.
Quercus, Debenham, Suffolk.
Denzil Grant Antiques, Drinkstone, Suffolk.
J. and J. Baker, Lavenham,, Suffolk.
Noel Mercer Antiques, Long Melford, Suffolk.
Matthew Tyler Antiques, Long Melford, Suffolk.
Peppers Period Pieces, Wattisfield, Suffolk.
Hamilton Antiques, Woodbridge, Suffolk.
Anthony Hurst Antiques, Woodbridge, Suffolk.
Suffolk House Antiques, Yoxford, Suffolk.
Stoneycroft Farm, Betchworth, Surrey.
The Howard Gallery, Dorking, Surrey.
Malthouse Antiques, Dorking, Surrey.
The Refectory, Dorking, Surrey.
Sage Antiques and Interiors, Ripley, Surrey.
Anthony Welling Antiques, Ripley, Surrey.
B. M. and E. Newlove, Surbiton, Surrey.

SPECIALIST DEALERS

Graham Lower, Flimwell, Sussex East.
Herbert Gordon Gasson, Rye, Sussex East.
Ringles Cross Antiques, Uckfield, Sussex East.
Park View Antiques, Wadhurst, Sussex East.
Cosby Antiques, Petworth, Sussex West.
David Swanson Antiques, Petworth, Sussex West.
King's Cottage Antiques, Leamington Spa, Warks.
James Reeve, Warwick, Warks.
Mac Humble Antiques, Bradford-on-Avon, Wilts.
Louis Stanton, Mere, Wilts.
Boston Antiques, Salisbury, Wilts.
A.J. Romain and Sons, Wilton, Wilts.
Stephen Cook Antiques, Broadway, Worcs.
H.W. Keil Ltd, Broadway, Worcs.
R.N. Myers and Son, Gargrave, Yorks. North.
Derbyshire Antiques Ltd, Harrogate, Yorks. North.
Elaine Phillips Antiques Ltd, Harrogate, Yorks. North.
Thorntons of Harrogate, Harrogate, Yorks. North.
Cellar Antiques, Hawes, Yorks. North.
Early Oak, Knaresborough, Yorks. North.
Aura Antiques, Masham, Yorks. North.
Country Oak Antiques, Pateley Bridge, Yorks. North.
John Gilbert Antiques, Robin Hood's Bay, Yorks. North.
Coach House Antiques, Sleights, Yorks. North.
Tim Bowen Antiques, Ferryside, Wales.
Country Antiques (Wales) Ltd, Kidwelly, Wales.
Allam Antiques, Newbridge-on-Wye, Wales.

Furniture - Pine

Chest of Drawers, London N1.
The Cobbled Yard, London N16.
Squawk, London N19.
The Furniture Cave, London SW10.
The Pine Mine (Crewe-Read Antiques), London SW6.
The Pine Parlour, Ampthill, Beds.
Dee's Antique Pine, Windsor, Berks.
Bourne End Antiques Centre, Bourne End, Bucks.
T. Smith, Chalfont St. Giles, Bucks.
Pine Antiques, Olney, Bucks.
Ward Thomas Antiques Ltd, Balsham, Cambs.
Cambridge Pine, Bottisham, Cambs.
Abbey Antiques, Ramsey, Cambs.
Melody's Antiques, Chester, Cheshire.
Town House Antiques, Marple Bridge, Cheshire.
Chapel Antiques, Nantwich, Cheshire.
The Attic, Poynton, Cheshire.
The White House, Waverton, Cheshire.
Country Living Antiques, Callington, Cornwall.
Evergreen Antiques, Redruth, Cornwall.
Blackwater Pine Antiques, Truro, Cornwall.
Ben Eggleston Antiques Ltd, Long Marton, Cumbria.
Pine and Decorative Items, Ashbourne, Derbys.
Byethorpe Furniture, Barlow, Derbys.
Friargate Pine Company Ltd, Derby, Derbys.
Michael Allcroft Antiques, Hayfield, Derbys.
Pennsylvania Pine Co, Ashburton, Devon.
Robert Byles and Optimum Brasses, Bampton, Devon.
Cobweb Antiques, Cullompton, Devon.
Cullompton Old Tannery Antiques, Cullompton, Devon.

Mills Antiques, Cullompton, Devon.
Annterior Antiques, Plymouth, Devon.
Fine Pine Antiques, Totnes, Devon.
Chorley-Burdett Antiques, Bournemouth, Dorset.
Ann Quested Antiques, Bridport, Dorset.
Legg of Dorchester, Dorchester, Dorset.
English Rose Antiques, Coggeshall, Essex.
Partners in Pine, Coggeshall, Essex.
The Stores, Great Waltham, Essex.
Oldwoods, Bristol, Glos.
Relics - Pine Furniture, Bristol, Glos.
Berkeley Antiques, Winchcombe, Glos.
The Furniture Trading Co, Botley, Hants.
Brambridge Antiques, Brambridge, Hants.
Squirrels, Brockenhurst, Hants.
Burgess Farm Antiques, Winchester, Hants.
The Pine Cellars, Winchester, Hants.
Waterfall Antiques, Ross-on-Wye, Herefs.
Country Life Interiors, Bushey, Herts.
Back 2 Wood, Appledore, Kent.
Antique and Design, Canterbury, Kent.
Pinetum, Canterbury, Kent.
Old English Pine, Sandgate, Kent.
House Things Antiques, Hinckley, Leics.
Flagstones Pine & Interiors, Melton Mowbray, Leics.
Quorn Pine and Decoratives, Quorn, Leics.
R. A. James Antiques, Sileby, Leics.
Kate, Hemswell Cliff, Lincs.
Andrew Thomas, Stamford, Lincs.
Antiques & Gifts, Downham Market, Norfolk.
Earsham Hall Pine, Earsham, Norfolk.
Heathfield Antiques & Country Pine, Holt, Norfolk.
Laila Gray Antiques, Kingsthorpe, Northants.
The Country Pine Shop, West Haddon, Northants.
Granary Antiques, Woodford, Northants.
Bailiffgate Antique Pine, Alnwick, Northumbs.
Tudor Rose Antiques, Carlton-on-Trent, Notts.
Jack Spratt Antiques, Newark, Notts.
Harlequin Antiques, Nottingham, Notts.
Aston Pine Antiques, Faringdon, Oxon.
Cotswold Pine & Associates, Middle Aston, Oxon.
Times Past Antiques, Auchterarder, Scotland.
London Road Antiques, Edinburgh, Scotland.
QS Antiques and Cabinetmakers, Kilmarnock, Scotland.
Abbey Antiques, Stirling, Scotland.
Garrard Antiques, Ludlow, Shrops.
Chris's Crackers, Carhampton, Somerset.
Antiques and Country Pine, Crewkerne, Somerset.
Westville House Antiques, Littleton, Somerset.
Notts Pine, Radstock, Somerset.
Burton Antiques, Burton-upon-Trent, Staffs.
Antiques Within Ltd, Leek, Staffs.
Anvil Antiques Ltd, Leek, Staffs.
Gemini Trading, Leek, Staffs.
Roger Haynes - Antique Finder, Leek, Staffs.
Coblands Farm Antiques, Depden, Suffolk.
The Theatre Antiques Centre, Framlingham, Suffolk.
Hardy's, Hacheston, Suffolk.
Orwell Furniture For Life, Ipswich, Suffolk.

Michael Lewis, Leiston, Suffolk.
Mildenhall Antique Furniture, Mildenhall, Suffolk.
House of Christian, Ash Vale, Surrey.
Cherub Antiques, Carshalton, Surrey.
M. & M. White Antique & Reproduction Centre, Reigate, Surrey.
The Packhouse, Runfold, Surrey.
Antique Church Furnishings, Walton-on-Thames, Surrey.
Hadlow Down Antiques, Hadlow Down, Sussex East.
Graham Price Antiques Ltd, Heathfield, Sussex East.
Pastorale Antiques, Lewes, Sussex East.
Claremont Antiques, Staplecross, Sussex East.
Park View Antiques, Wadhurst, Sussex East.
Antiquities, Arundel, Sussex West.
Stable Antiques, Lindfield, Sussex West.
John Bird, Petworth, Sussex West.
Northumbria Pine, Whitley Bay, Tyne and Wear.
Arcadia Antiques, Radford Semele, Warks.
Pine and Things, Shipston-on-Stour, Warks.
Tudor House Antiques, Halesowen, West Mids.
The Red Shop, Wolverhampton, West Mids.
North Wilts Exporters, Brinkworth, Wilts.
Calne Antiques, Calne, Wilts.
Philip A. Ruttleigh Antiques incorporating Crudwell Furniture, Crudwell, Wilts.
Pillars Antiques, Lyneham, Wilts.
Sambourne House Antiques Ltd, Swindon, Wilts.
Smith & Smith Designs, Driffield, Yorks. East.
Imperial Antiques, Hull, Yorks. East.
L.L. Ward and Son, Brandsby, Yorks. North.
The Main Pine Co, Green Hammerton, Yorks. North.
Michael Green Pine & Country Antiques, Harrogate, Yorks. North.
Havelocks, Harrogate, Yorks. North.
Westway Pine, Helmsley, Yorks. North.
Northern Antiques Company, Norton, Yorks. North.
Manor Barn, Skipton, Yorks. North.
Eskdale Antiques, Sleights, Yorks. North.
Millgate Pine & Antiques, Thirsk, Yorks. North.
Ruth Ford Antiques, York, Yorks. North.
St. John Antiques, York, Yorks. North.
Fishlake Antiques, Fishlake, Yorks. South.
Penistone Pine and Antiques, Penistone, Yorks. South.
Beech House, Sheffield, Yorks. South.
Dovetail Antiques, Sheffield, Yorks. South.
Aberford Antiques Ltd t/a Aberford Country Furniture, Aberford, Yorks. West.
K.L.M. & Co. Antiques, Lepton, Yorks. West.
Memory Lane, Sowerby Bridge, Yorks. West.
Cottage Antiques (1984) Ltd, Walsden, Yorks. West.
The Pine Collection, St. Peter Port, Guernsey, C.I.
Attic Antiques & Pine, Saintfield, Co. Down, N. Ireland.
Homes, Pubs and Clubs, Coleraine, Co. Londonderry, N. Ireland.
The Furniture Cave, Aberystwyth, Wales.
Gallop and Rivers Architectural Antiques, Crickhowell, Wales.

Jim and Pat Ash, Llandeilo, Wales.
Carrington House, Llanrwst, Wales.
Frost Antiques & Pine, Monmouth, Wales.

Furniture - Victorian
John Jackson at Town House, London E1.
Peter Chapman Antiques and Restoration, London N1.
Furniture Vault, London N1.
Jonathan James, London N1.
Regent Antiques, London N1.
C. Tapsell, London N1.
The Waterloo Trading Co., London N1.
Finchley Fine Art Galleries, London N12.
Frames Stop, London N12.
Martin Henham (Antiques), London N2.
Julian Alexander Antiques, London N20.
Michael Slade Antiques, London N4.
Betty Gould Antiques, London N6.
Dome Antiques (Exports) Ltd, London N7.
Solomon, London N8.
G. and F. Gillingham Ltd, London NW2.
Antiques 4 Ltd, London NW3.
Patricia Beckman Antiques, London NW3.
Church Street Antiques, London NW8.
Davidson Antiques, London NW8.
Just Desks, London NW8.
Young & Son, London NW8.
The Galleries, London SE1.
Tower Bridge Antiques, London SE1.
Minerva Antiques, London SE10.
Walpoles, London SE10.
Robert Whitfield Antiques, London SE10.
CASA, London SE15.
Oola Boola Antiques London, London SE26.
Ward Antique Fireplaces Ltd, London SE7.
Hilary Batstone Antiques inc. Rose Uniacke Design, London SW1.
Blanchard Ltd, London SW1.
John Bly, London SW1.
Ross Hamilton Ltd, London SW1.
Harrods Ltd, London SW1.
Christopher Howe, London SW1.
Humphrey-Carrasco Ltd, London SW1.
Westenholz Antiques Ltd, London SW1.
Christopher Edwards, London SW11.
Garland Antiques, London SW11.
Overmantels, London SW11.
Pairs Antiques Ltd, London SW11.
A. and J. Fowle, London SW16.
Just a Second, London SW18.
Chris Baron Interiors, London SW2.
General Trading Co Ltd, London SW3.
Michael Hughes, London SW3.
Prides of London, London SW3.
Charles Saunders Antiques, London SW3.
275 Antiques, London SW6.
John Clay, London SW6.
Charles Edwards, London SW6.
HRW Antiques (London) Ltd, London SW6.

SPECIALIST DEALERS

Christopher Jones Antiques, London SW6.
L. and E. Kreckovic, London SW6.
Nimmo & Spooner, London SW6.
Rogers & Co, London SW6.
Adrian Alan Ltd, London W1.
H. Blairman and Sons Ltd., London W1.
Jeremy Seale Antiques/Interiors, London W1.
Windsor House Antiques Ltd, London W1.
Barham Antiques, London W11.
Judy Fox, London W11.
M. and D. Lewis, London W11.
Trude Weaver, London W11.
Marshall Gallery, London W14.
Craven Gallery, London W2.
Butchoff Antiques, London W8.
Haslam and Whiteway, London W8.
Antiquarius of Ampthill, Ampthill, Beds.
Paris Antiques, Ampthill, Beds.
Pilgrim Antiques, Ampthill, Beds.
Victoria House, Bedford, Beds.
W. J. West Antiques, Potton, Beds.
S. and S. Timms Antiques Ltd, Shefford, Beds.
Manor Antiques, Wilstead (Wilshamstead), Beds.
Town Hall Antiques, Woburn, Beds.
Franklin Antiques, Hungerford, Berks.
Griffin Fine Art & Antiques, Hungerford, Berks.
Roger King Antiques, Hungerford, Berks.
Hill Farm Antiques, Leckhampstead, Berks.
Widmerpool House Antiques, Maidenhead, Berks.
Rupert Landen Antiques, Reading, Berks.
John Connell - Wargrave Antiques, Wargrave, Berks.
Eton Antiques Partnership, Windsor, Berks.
Peter J. Martin, Windsor, Berks.
Studio 101, Windsor, Berks.
The Cupboard Antiques, Amersham, Bucks.
Grosvenor House Interiors, Beaconsfield, Bucks.
Period Furniture Showrooms, Beaconsfield, Bucks.
Bourne End Antiques Centre, Bourne End, Bucks.
Leo Antiques & Collectables Ltd, Olney, Bucks.
Robin Unsworth Antiques, Olney, Bucks.
Jess Applin Antiques, Cambridge, Cambs.
Ivor and Patricia Lewis Antique and Fine Art Dealers,
    Peterborough, Cambs.
Antiques & Curios (Steve Carpenter), Wisbech, Cambs.
Trash 'n' Treasure, Alsager, Cheshire.
Church Street Antiques, Altrincham, Cheshire.
Andrew Foott Antiques, Cheadle Hulme, Cheshire.
Antique Exporters of Chester, Chester, Cheshire.
Moor Hall Antiques, Chester, Cheshire.
The Old Warehouse Antiques, Chester, Cheshire.
W. Buckley Antiques Exports, Congleton, Cheshire.
Michael Allcroft Antiques, Disley, Cheshire.
David Bedale, Mobberley, Cheshire.
Limited Editions, Mobberley, Cheshire.
Chapel Antiques, Nantwich, Cheshire.
Nantwich Antiques, Nantwich, Cheshire.
Romiley Antiques & Jewellery, Romiley, Cheshire.
Saxon Cross Antiques Emporium, Sandbach, Cheshire.
Country Living Antiques, Callington, Cornwall.

Old Town Hall Antiques, Falmouth, Cornwall.
Antique Chairs and Museum, Launceston, Cornwall.
John Bragg Antiques, Lostwithiel, Cornwall.
Antiques & Fine Art, Penzance, Cornwall.
Evergreen Antiques, Redruth, Cornwall.
The Old Steam Bakery, Redruth, Cornwall.
Victoria Antiques, Wadebridge, Cornwall.
Haughey Antiques, Kirkby Stephen, Cumbria.
Ashbourne Antiques Ltd, Ashbourne, Derbys.
Martin and Dorothy Harper Antiques, Bakewell,
    Derbys.
Michael Pembery Antiques, Bakewell, Derbys.
Hackney House Antiques & Clocks, Barlow, Derbys.
The Antiques Warehouse, Buxton, Derbys.
Maggie Mays, Buxton, Derbys.
Ian Morris, Chesterfield, Derbys.
Wayside Antiques, Duffield, Derbys.
A.A. Ambergate Antiques, Ripley, Derbys.
Shardlow Antiques Warehouse, Shardlow, Derbys.
Nimbus Antiques, Whaley Bridge, Derbys.
Bampton Gallery, Bampton, Devon.
John Prestige Antiques, Brixham, Devon.
Miller Antiques, Cullompton, Devon.
Mills Antiques, Cullompton, Devon.
The Antiques Complex, Exeter, Devon.
Eclectique, Exeter, Devon.
Alison Gosling Antiques Studio, Exmouth, Devon.
Alexander Paul Antiques, Fenny Bridges, Devon.
Hermitage Antiques, Honiton, Devon.
Lombard Antiques, Honiton, Devon.
Merchant House Antiques, Honiton, Devon.
Jane Strickland & Daughters, Honiton, Devon.
Upstairs, Downstairs, Honiton, Devon.
Farthings, Lynton, Devon.
Pugh's Farm Antiques, Monkton, Devon.
Guy Dennler Antiques & Interiors, Rackenford, Devon.
A. E. Wakeman & Sons Ltd, Tedburn St Mary, Devon.
Domani, Topsham, Devon.
Mere Antiques, Topsham, Devon.
The Antique Dining Room, Totnes, Devon.
Anthony James Antiques, Whimple, Devon.
Milton Antiques, Blandford Forum, Dorset.
Chorley-Burdett Antiques, Bournemouth, Dorset.
Benchmark Antiques, Bridport, Dorset.
Hamptons, Christchurch, Dorset.
Tower Antiques, Cranborne, Dorset.
Michael Legg Antiques, Dorchester, Dorset.
Hardy Country, Melbury Osmond, Dorset.
Laburnum Antiques, Poole, Dorset.
Stocks and Chairs, Poole, Dorset.
Cartouche, ShaftesburyDorset.
Shaston Antiques, Shaftesbury, Dorset.
Antiques of Sherborne, Sherborne, Dorset.
Phoenix Antiques, SherborneDorset.
Renaissance, Sherborne, Dorset.
James Hardy Antiques Ltd, Barnard Castle, Durham.
Joan, David and Richard White Antiques, Barnard
    Castle, Durham.
Paraphernalia, Norton, Durham.

Margaret Bedi Antiques & Fine Art, Stockton-on-Tees, Durham.
Eden House Antiques, West Auckland, Durham.
Swan Antiques, Baythorne End, Essex.
Colton Antiques, Kelvedon, Essex.
Clive Beardall Restorations Ltd, Maldon, Essex.
West Essex Antiques (Stone Hall), Matching Green, Essex.
F.G. Bruschweiler (Antiques) Ltd, Rayleigh, Essex.
Bush Antiques, Saffron Walden, Essex.
Harris Antiques, Thaxted, Essex.
It's About Time, Westcliff-on-Sea, Essex.
White Roding Antiques, White Roding, Essex.
Peter and Penny Proudfoot, Berkeley, Glos.
The Antiques Warehouse Ltd, Bristol, Glos.
Oldwoods, Bristol, Glos.
Tower House Antiques, Bristol, Glos.
Cottage Farm Antiques, Chipping Campden, Glos.
School House Antiques, Chipping Campden, Glos.
Patrick Waldron Antiques, Cirencester, Glos.
Bernard Weaver Antiques, Cirencester, Glos.
Blenheim Antiques, Fairford, Glos.
Benton Fine Art, Moreton-in-Marsh, Glos.
Berry Antiques Ltd, Moreton-in-Marsh, Glos.
Dale House Antiques, Moreton-in-Marsh, Glos.
Simply Antiques, Moreton-in-Marsh, Glos.
Gary Wright Antiques, Moreton-in-Marsh, Glos.
Robson Antiques, Northleach, Glos.
Ashton Gower Antiques, Stow-on-the-Wold, Glos.
Duncan J. Baggott, Stow-on-the-Wold, Glos.
Christopher Clarke Antiques Ltd, Stow-on-the-Wold, Glos.
T.M. King-Smith & Simon W. Nutter, Stow-on-the-Wold, Glos.
La Chaise Antique, Stow-on-the-Wold, Glos.
Malt House Antiques, Stow-on-the-Wold, Glos.
Queens Parade Antiques Ltd, Stow-on-the-Wold, Glos.
Styles of Stow, Stow-on-the-Wold, Glos.
Alderson, Tetbury, Glos.
Ball and Claw Antiques, Tetbury, Glos.
Porch House Antiques, Tetbury, Glos.
Whittington Barn Antiques, Whittington, Glos.
Berkeley Antiques, Winchcombe, Glos.
Pineapple House Antiques, Alresford, Hants.
The Furniture Trading Co, Botley, Hants.
Brambridge Antiques, Brambridge, Hants.
F.E.A. Briggs Ltd, Brook, Hants.
Eversley Barn Antiques, Eversley, Hants.
Former Glory, Gosport, Hants.
Deva Antiques, Hartley Wintney, Hants.
Plestor Barn Antiques, Liss, Hants.
Wick Antiques, Lymington, Hants.
Gray's Antiques, Portsmouth, Hants.
Lorraine Tarrant Antiques, Ringwood, Hants.
Amber Antiques, Southampton, Hants.
Antique Eyes, Stockbridge, Hants.
Gasson Antiques and Interiors, Tadley, Hants.
Gaylords, Titchfield, Hants.
John Nash Antiques and Interiors, Ledbury, Herefs.

Serendipity, Ledbury, Herefs.
Farmers Gallery, Leominster, Herefs.
Jeffery Hammond Antiques, Leominster, Herefs.
Anthony Butt Antiques, Baldock, Herts.
Michael Lipitch Ltd, Barnet, Herts.
Wareside Antiques, Cottered, Herts.
Tapestry Antiques, Hertford, Herts.
Tom Salusbury Antiques, Hitchin, Herts.
Bushwood Antiques, Redbourn, Herts.
J.N. Antiques, Redbourn, Herts.
Charnwood Antiques and Arcane Antiques Centre, Sawbridgeworth, Herts.
New England House Antiques, Tring, Herts.
Collins Antiques (F.G. and C. Collins Ltd.), Wheathampstead, Herts.
Michael Armson (Antiques) Ltd, Wilstone, Herts.
John Corrin Antiques, Douglas, Isle of Man.
Royal Standard Antiques, Cowes, Isle of Wight.
Stablegate Antiques, Barham, Kent.
David Barrington, Brasted, Kent.
Bigwood Antiques, Brasted, Kent.
Cooper Fine Arts Ltd, Brasted, Kent.
Courtyard Antiques incorporating Southdown House, Brasted, Kent.
Keymer Son & Co. Ltd, Brasted, Kent.
Roy Massingham Antiques, Brasted, Kent.
Old Bakery Antiques, Brasted, Kent.
S. L. Walker, Brasted, Kent.
Conquest House Antiques, Canterbury, Kent.
Alan Lord Antiques, Chilham, Kent.
Chislehurst Antiques, Chislehurst, Kent.
Lennox Cato, Edenbridge, Kent.
Chevertons of Edenbridge Ltd, Edenbridge, Kent.
Restall Brown & Clennell, Edenbridge, Kent.
Mill House Antiques, Goudhurst, Kent.
Alan Lord Antiques, HytheKent.
Samovar Antiques, Hythe, Kent.
Northfleet Hill Antiques, Northfleet, Kent.
Thanet Antiques, Ramsgate, Kent.
J.D. and R.M. Walters, Rolvenden, Kent.
Finch Antiques, Sandgate, Kent.
Michael Fitch Antiques, Sandgate, Kent.
J. Luckhurst Antiques, Sandgate, Kent.
Brian West Antiques, Sandgate, Kent.
Ward Antique Fireplaces Ltd, Sidcup, Kent.
Steppes Hill Farm Antiques, Stockbury, Kent.
Sutton Valence Antiques, Sutton Valence, Kent.
Down Lane Hall Antiques, Tunbridge Wells, Kent.
The Pantiles Antiques, Tunbridge Wells, Kent.
Pantiles Spa Antiques, Tunbridge Wells, Kent.
Phoenix Antiques, Tunbridge Wells, Kent.
Up Country, Tunbridge Wells, Kent.
Apollo Antique Galleries, Westerham, Kent.
Taylor-Smith Antiques, Westerham, Kent.
Laurens Antiques, Whitstable, Kent.
Ascot Antiques, Blackpool, Lancs.
Brun Lea Antiques (J. Waite Ltd), Burnley, Lancs.
K.C. Antiques, Darwen, Lancs.
P.J. Brown Antiques, Haslingden, Lancs.

R.J. O'Brien and Son Antiques Ltd, Manchester, Lancs.
Luigino Vescovi, Morecambe, Lancs.
European Fine Arts and Antiques, Preston, Lancs.
Sitting Pretty, Great Glen, Leics.
House Things Antiques, Hinckley, Leics.
Magpie Antiques, Hinckley, Leics.
Withers of Leicester, Hoby, Leics.
Corry's Antiques, Leicester, Leics.
Lowe of Loughborough, Loughborough, Leics.
Oaktree Antiques, Lubenham, Leics.
J. Stamp and Sons, Market Harborough, Leics.
J. Green and Son, Queniborough,, Leics.
Charles Antiques, Whitwick, Leics.
Grantham Furniture Emporium, Grantham, Lincs.
G. Baker Antiques, Horncastle, Lincs.
Clare Boam, Horncastle, Lincs.
Alan Read - Period Furniture, Horncastle, Lincs.
Seaview Antiques, Horncastle, Lincs.
C. and K.E. Dring, Lincoln, Lincs.
Hansord at No 2 Antiques & Period Design, Lincoln, Lincs.
Antique & Secondhand Traders, Lound, Lincs.
Graham Pickett Antiques, Stamford, Lincs.
Sinclair's, Stamford, Lincs.
St. George's Antiques, Stamford, Lincs.
The Antique Shop, Sutton Bridge, Lincs.
Robin Shield Antiques, Swinstead, Lincs.
Underwoodhall Antiques, Woodhall Spa, Lincs.
V.O.C. Antiques, Woodhall Spa, Lincs.
Stefani Antiques, Liverpool, Merseyside.
Colin Stock, Rainford, Merseyside.
Tony and Anne Sutcliffe Antiques, Southport, Merseyside.
Gallerie Veronique, Enfield, Middx.
A.E. Bush and Partners, Attleborough, Norfolk.
Antiques & Gifts, Downham Market, Norfolk.
Eric Bates and Sons Ltd., Hoveton, Norfolk.
James K. Lee, King's Lynn, Norfolk.
Nicholas Fowle Antiques, Norwich, Norfolk.
Country House Antiques, Seething, Norfolk.
Stalham Antique Gallery, Stalham, Norfolk.
Jubilee Antiques, Tottenhill, Norfolk.
Norton Antiques, Twyford, Norfolk.
Simon Banks Antiques, Finedon, Northants.
Robert Cheney Antiques, Finedon, Northants.
Blockheads and Granary Antiques, Flore, Northants.
Christopher Jones Antiques, Flore, Northants.
Bryan Perkins Antiques, Great Cransley, Northants.
F. and C.H. Cave, Northampton, Northants.
Reindeer Antiques Ltd, Potterspury, Northants.
Granary Antiques, Woodford, Northants.
G.M. Athey, Alnwick, Northumbs.
James Miller Antiques, Wooler, Northumbs.
Dukeries Antiques Centre, Budby, Notts.
A.J. O'Sullivan Antiques, Darlton, Notts.
Ivory Gate, Hucknall, Notts.
No. 1 Castlegate Antiques, Newark, Notts.
Pearman Antiques & Interiors, Newark, Notts.
Ranby Hall, Retford, Notts.

William Antiques, Ascott-under-Wychwood, Oxon.
Burford Antique Centre, Burford, Oxon.
Gateway Antiques, Burford, Oxon.
Hubert's Antiques, Burford, Oxon.
David Pickup, Burford, Oxon.
Swan Gallery, Burford, Oxon.
Rupert Hitchcox Antiques, Chalgrove, Oxon.
Georgian House Antiques, Chipping Norton, Oxon.
Hallidays (Fine Antiques) Ltd, Dorchester-on-Thames, Oxon.
Brushwood Antiques, Faringdon, Oxon.
Richard J. Kingston, Henley-on-Thames, Oxon.
Stephen Orton Antiques, Henley-on-Thames, Oxon.
The Country Seat, Huntercombe, Oxon.
Winston Antiques, Kingham, Oxon.
de Albuquerque Antiques, Wallingford, Oxon.
Chris and Lin O'Donnell Antiques, Wallingford, Oxon.
Mike Ottrey Antiques, Wallingford, Oxon.
Cross Antiques, Watlington, Oxon.
Colin Greenway Antiques, Witney, Oxon.
Joan Wilkins Antiques, Witney, Oxon.
Bees Antiques, Woodstock, Oxon.
Swans, Oakham, Rutland.
John Garner, Uppingham, Rutland.
Harvey Art and Antiques, Uppingham, Rutland.
T.J. Roberts, Uppingham, Rutland.
Woodman's House Antiques, Uppingham, Rutland.
Robert Bingley Antiques, Wing, Rutland.
Mytton Antiques, Atcham, Shrops.
Malthouse Antiques, Bridgnorth, Shrops.
Martin Quick Antiques, Cosford, Shrops.
Bayliss Antiques, Ludlow, Shrops.
Brian James Antiques, Rodington, Shrops.
Corner Farm Antiques, Shifnal, Shrops.
A Little Furniture Shop, ShrewsburyShrops.
Mansers Antiques, Shrewsbury, Shrops.
Quayside Antiques, Shrewsbury, Shrops.
Lawrence Brass, Bath, Somerset.
Mary Cruz, Bath, Somerset.
Waterfall Antiques, Bath, Somerset.
M.G.R. Exports, Bruton, Somerset.
Chris's Crackers, Carhampton, Somerset.
Westville House Antiques, Littleton, Somerset.
Edward Marnier Antiques, Shepton Mallet, Somerset.
Selwoods, Taunton, Somerset.
Courtyard Antiques, Washford, Somerset.
The Old Schoolrooms Antiques, Wincanton, Somerset.
Wincanton Antiques, Wincanton, Somerset.
Yew Tree Antiques Warehouse, Wiveliscombe, Somerset.
John Hamblin, Yeovil, Somerset.
Gilligans Antiques, Leek, Staffs.
Page Antiques, Leek, Staffs.
Milestone Antiques, Lichfield, Staffs.
Winder's Fine Art and Antiques, Newcastle-under-Lyme, Staffs.
White House Antiques, Uttoxeter, Staffs.
H.W. Heron and Son Ltd, Yoxall, Staffs.
Fauconberges, Beccles, Suffolk.

Bly Valley Antiques, Blyford, Suffolk.
Robin Butler, Clare, Suffolk.
Debenham Antiques, Debenham, Suffolk.
English and Continental Antiques, Eye, Suffolk.
The Theatre Antiques Centre, Framlingham, Suffolk.
P & R Antiques Ltd, Halesworth, Suffolk.
A. Abbott Antiques Ltd, Ipswich, Suffolk.
The Edwardian Shop, Ipswich, Suffolk.
Hubbard Antiques, Ipswich, Suffolk.
Richard A. Rush Antiques, Ipswich, Suffolk.
Warrens Antiques Warehouse, Leiston, Suffolk.
Alexander Lyall Antiques, Long Melford, Suffolk.
Napier House Antiques, Sudbury, Suffolk.
Peppers Period Pieces, Wattisfield, Suffolk.
Ashe Antiques Warehouse, Wickham Market, Suffolk.
Hamilton Antiques, Woodbridge, Suffolk.
Anthony Hurst Antiques, Woodbridge, Suffolk.
R.A and S.M. Lambert and Son, Woodbridge, Suffolk.
J.C. Heather, Woolpit, Suffolk.
House of Christian, Ash Vale, Surrey.
Country & Town Antiques, Bagshot, Surrey.
Dolphin Square Antiques, Dorking, Surrey.
The Dorking Desk Shop, Dorking, Surrey.
Harman's, Dorking, Surrey.
Holmwood Antiques, Dorking, Surrey.
Malthouse Antiques, Dorking, Surrey.
Norfolk House Galleries, Dorking, Surrey.
Honeypot Antiques Ltd, Elstead, Surrey.
Christopher's Antiques, Farnham, Surrey.
The Coach House Antiques, Gomshall, Surrey.
West Street Antiques, Haslemere, Surrey.
Glencorse Antiques, Kingston-upon-Thames, Surrey.
F.G. Lawrence and Sons, Redhill, Surrey.
Marryat, Richmond, Surrey.
Sage Antiques and Interiors, Ripley, Surrey.
Cockrell Antiques, Surbiton, Surrey.
B. M. and E. Newlove, Surbiton, Surrey.
Brocante, Weybridge, Surrey.
Church House Antiques, Weybridge, Surrey.
Alexandria Antiques, Brighton, Sussex East.
Ashton's Antiques, Brighton, Sussex East.
Patrick Moorhead Antiques, Brighton, Sussex East.
The North Laine Antiques Market, inc. Alan Fitchett
    Antiques, Brighton, Sussex East.
Dycheling Antiques, Ditchling, Sussex East.
Timothy Partridge Antiques, Eastbourne, Sussex East.
Hadlow Down Antiques, Hadlow Down, Sussex East.
Coach House Antiques, Hastings, Sussex East.
Graham Price Antiques Ltd, Heathfield, Sussex East.
The Old Mint House, Pevensey, Sussex East.
East Street Antiques, Rye, Sussex East.
Wish Barn Antiques, Rye, Sussex East.
The Old House, Seaford, Sussex East.
Bygones, Angmering, Sussex West.
W.D. Priddy Antiques, Chichester, Sussex West.
Stable Antiques, Lindfield, Sussex West.
Callingham Antiques, Northchapel, Sussex West.
Antiquated, Petworth, Sussex West.
Heather Denham Antiques, Petworth, Sussex West.

Elliott's, Petworth, Sussex West.
Richard Gardner Antiques, Petworth, Sussex West.
Georgia Antiques, Pulborough, Sussex West.
Wilsons Antiques, Worthing, Sussex West.
Little Theatre Antiques Centre, Jesmond, Tyne and
    Wear.
Graham Smith Antiques, Jesmond, Tyne and Wear.
Ian Sharp Antiques Ltd., Tynemouth, Tyne and Wear.
Apollo Antiques, Warwick, Warks.
William J. Casey Antiques, Warwick, Warks.
Patrick and Gillian Morley Antiques, Warwick, Warks.
James Reeve, Warwick, Warks.
Peter Clark Antiques, Birmingham, West Mids.
Moseley Emporium, Birmingham, West Mids.
Martin Taylor Antiques, Wolverhampton, West Mids.
Mac Humble Antiques, Bradford-on-Avon, Wilts.
Cross Hayes Antiques, Chippenham, Wilts.
William Cook (Marlborough), Marlborough, Wilts.
Katharine House Gallery, Marlborough, Wilts.
Dann Antiques Ltd, Melksham, Wilts.
Alan Jaffray, Melksham, Wilts.
21st Century Antics, Salisbury, Wilts.
Myriad, Salisbury, Wilts.
Salisbury Antiques Warehouse Ltd, Salisbury, Wilts.
Mike Scott Repair & Restoration, Salisbury, Wilts.
Cassidy's Antiques, Warminster, Wilts.
Isabella Antiques, Warminster, Wilts.
Maxfield House Antiques, Warminster, Wilts.
Obelisk Antiques, Warminster, Wilts.
Hingstons of Wilton, Wilton, Wilts.
Barnt Green Antiques, Barnt Green, Worcs.
Gallimaufry, Broadway, Worcs.
Robert Belcher Antiques, Droitwich, Worcs.
Carlton Antiques, Great Malvern, Worcs.
Miscellany Antiques, Great Malvern, Worcs.
S.W. Antiques, Pershore, Worcs.
Angel Antiques, Redditch, Worcs.
Lower House Fine Antiques, Redditch, Worcs.
M. Lees and Sons, Worcester, Worcs.
Priory Antiques, Bridlington, Yorks. East.
Houghton Hall Antiques, Market Weighton, Yorks. East.
Penny Farthing Antiques, North Cave, Yorks. East.
Bennett's Antiques & Collectables, Bedale, Yorks. North.
John Wilson, Boroughbridge, Yorks. North.
R.S. Wilson and Sons, Boroughbridge, Yorks. North.
Milestone Antiques, Easingwold, Yorks. North.
Elm Tree Antiques, Flaxton, Yorks. North.
Garth Antiques, Harrogate, Yorks. North.
David Love, Harrogate, Yorks. North.
Chris Wilde Antiques, Harrogate, Yorks. North.
Sturman's Antiques, Hawes, Yorks. North.
John Thompson Antiques, Knaresborough, Yorks.
    North.
Milton Holgate, Ripon, Yorks. North.
Sigma Antiques and Fine Art, Ripon, Yorks. North.
John Gilbert Antiques, Robin Hood's Bay, Yorks. North.
Anderson Slater Antiques, Settle, Yorks. North.
Antony, David & Ann Shackleton, Snainton, Yorks.
    North.

Alan Ramsey Antiques, Stokesley, Yorks. North.
Acorn Antiques, Sheffield, Yorks. South.
Dovetail Antiques, Sheffield, Yorks. South.
N.P. and A. Salt Antiques, Sheffield, Yorks. South.
Paul Ward Antiques, Sheffield, Yorks. South.
Aberford Antiques Ltd t/a Aberford Country Furniture, Aberford, Yorks. West.
The Baildon Furniture Co. Ltd, Baildon, Yorks. West.
Browgate Antiques, Baildon, Yorks. West.
Bingley Antiques, Haworth, Yorks. West.
Geary Antiques, Leeds, Yorks. West.
Park Antiques, Menston, Yorks. West.
Victoria Antiques, Alderney, Alderney, C.I.
David Wolfenden Antiques, Antrim, Co. Antrim, N. Ireland.
Robert Christie Antiques, Ballyclare, Co. Antrim, N. Ireland.
Oakland Antiques, Belfast, Co. Antrim, N. Ireland.
Dunluce Antiques, Bushmills, Co. Antrim, N. Ireland.
MacHenry Antiques, Newtownabbey, Co. Antrim, N. Ireland.
Agar Antiques, Saintfield, Co. Down, N. Ireland.
Attic Antiques & Pine, Saintfield, Co. Down, N. Ireland.
Millcourt Antiques, Seapatrick, Co. Down, N. Ireland.
Foyle Antiques/Whitehouse Furniture, Londonderry, Co. Londonderry, N. Ireland.
Moy Antiques, Dungannon, Co. Tyrone, N. Ireland.
Kelly Antiques, Omagh, Co. Tyrone, N. Ireland.
Colin Wood (Antiques) Ltd, Aberdeen, Scotland.
Ian Whitelaw Antiques, Auchterarder, Scotland.
Treasures of Ballater & Rowan Antiques, Ballater, Scotland.
Coldstream Antiques, Coldstream, Scotland.
Cromarty Antiques, Cromarty, Scotland.
The Magic Lantern, Dunecht, Scotland.
Dunkeld Antiques, Dunkeld, Scotland.
Alan Day Antiques, Edinburgh, Scotland.
Georgian Antiques, Edinburgh, Scotland.
London Road Antiques, Edinburgh, Scotland.
Young Antiques, Edinburgh, Scotland.
Gow Antiques, Forfar, Scotland.
Cathedral Antiques, Fortrose, Scotland.
Butler's Furniture Galleries, Glasgow, Scotland.
Strachan Antiques, Glasgow, Scotland.
Michael Young Antiques at Glencarse, Glencarse, Scotland.
Kilmacolm Antiques Ltd, Kilmacolm, Scotland.
QS Antiques and Cabinetmakers, Kilmarnock, Scotland.
Rhudle Mill, Kilmichael Glassary, Scotland.
Osborne Antiques, Kirkcudbright, Scotland.
Cobwebs of Lockerbie Ltd, Lockerbie, Scotland.
Michael Vee Design - Birch House Antiques, Melrose, Scotland.
Newburgh Antiques, Newburgh, Scotland.
Design Interiors and Perth Antiques, Perth, Scotland.
Crossroads Antiques, Prestwick, Scotland.
Riverside Antiques (Wales) Ltd, Cardiff, Wales.
The Mount Antiques Centre, Carmarthen, Wales.

North Wales Antiques - Colwyn Bay, Colwyn Bay, Wales.
Havard and Havard, Cowbridge, Wales.
Renaissance Antiques - The Vale of Glamorgan Antiques Centre, Cowbridge, Wales.
Antiques in Wales, Kidwelly, Wales.
Collinge Antiques, Llandudno Junction, Wales.
J. and R. Langford, Llangollen, Wales.
Carrington House, Llanrwst, Wales.
Allam Antiques, Newbridge-on-Wye, Wales.
Barn Court Antiques, Crafts & Tearoom, Templeton, Wales.

Garden Furniture, Ornaments and Statuary
LASSCO, London EC2.
Westland London, London EC2.
Squawk, London N19.
Relic Antiques Trade Warehouse, London NW1.
Townsends, London NW8.
Appley Hoare Antiques, London SW1.
McVeigh & Charpentier, London SW10.
Drummonds Architectural Antiques Ltd, London SW3.
Chelminski Gallery, London SW6.
Mora & Upham Antiques, London SW6.
M. Pauw Antiques, London SW6.
Rodney Franklin Antiques, London SW9.
Mallett at Bourdon House, London W1.
Myriad Antiques, London W11.
Marshall Phillips, London W4.
Below Stairs of Hungerford, Hungerford, Berks.
Garden Art, Hungerford, Berks.
Dismantle and Deal Direct - Architectural Salvage Brokers, Aston Clinton, Bucks.
La Maison, Bourne End, Bucks.
The Antique Garden, Chester, Cheshire.
Cheshire Brick and Slate Co, Tarvin Sands, Cheshire.
The Great Northern Architectural Antique Company Ltd, Tattenhall, Cheshire.
Julie Strachey, Connor Downs, Cornwall.
Pine and Decorative Items, Ashbourne, Derbys.
Dorset Reclamation, Bere Regis, Dorset.
Talisman, Gillingham, Dorset.
I. Westrope, Birdbrook, Essex.
Jon Fox Antiques, Moreton-in-Marsh, Glos.
Robson Antiques, Northleach, Glos.
Duncan J. Baggott, Stow-on-the-Wold, Glos.
Minchinhampton Architectural, Stroud, Glos.
Architectural Heritage, Taddington, Glos.
Jardinique, Beech, Hants.
Baileys Home & Garden, Ross-on-Wye, Herefs.
Bygones Reclamation, Canterbury, Kent.
Jimmy Warren Antiques, Littlebourne, Kent.
The Architectural Stores, Tunbridge Wells, Kent.
Phoenix Antiques, Tunbridge Wells, Kent.
Architectural Miscellanea, Wingham, Kent.
Lindsey Court Architectural, Horncastle, Lincs.
Mongers, Hingham, Norfolk.
Renney Antiques, Corbridge, Northumbs.
Ranby Hall, Retford, Notts.

Colin Greenway Antiques, Witney, Oxon.
David Bridgwater, Bath, Somerset.
Walcot Reclamation, Bath, Somerset.
Cawarden Brick Co Ltd, Rugeley, Staffs.
Tower Reclaim, Mendlesham, Suffolk.
Drummonds Architectural Antiques, Hindhead, Surrey.
Sweerts de Landas, Ripley, Surrey.
The Packhouse, Runfold, Surrey.
Brighton Architectural Salvage, Brighton, Sussex East.
Dermot and Jill Palmer Antiques, Brighton, Sussex East.
Antiquated, Petworth, Sussex West.
John Bird, Petworth, Sussex West.
Matthew Eden, Corsham, Wilts.
Holloways, Suckley, Worcs.
Juro Antiques, Worcester, Worcs.
The White House Antiques & Architectural Reclamation, Easingwold, Yorks. North.
Flaxton Antique Gardens, Flaxton, Yorks. North.
Moy Antiques, Dungannon, Co. Tyrone, N. Ireland.
Coach House Antiques Ltd, Stanley, Scotland.

Glass - see also Glass Domes & Paperweights
Carol Ketley Antiques, London N1.
Mike Weedon, London N1.
Wilkinson plc, London SE6.
Antiquus, London SW1.
Pullman Gallery, London SW1.
Christine Bridge, London SW13.
The Dining Room Shop, London SW13.
Mark J. West - Cobb Antiques Ltd, London SW19.
W.G.T. Burne (Antique Glass) Ltd, London SW20.
Thomas Goode and Co (London) Ltd, London W1.
Ronald Phillips Ltd, London W1.
Pullman Gallery, London W1.
Wilkinson plc, London W1.
Mercury Antiques, London W11.
Craven Gallery, London W2.
H. and W. Deutsch Antiques, London W8.
Jeanette Hayhurst Fine Glass, London W8.
John Jesse, London W8.
Tomkinson Stained Glass, Leagrave, Beds.
Peter Shepherd Antiques, Hurst, Berks.
Cavendish Fine Arts, Sonning-on-Thames, Berks.
Berkshire Antiques Co Ltd, Windsor, Berks.
Gabor Cossa Antiques, Cambridge, Cambs.
Antiques, Marazion, Cornwall.
Just Glass, Alston, Cumbria.
Elizabeth and Son, Ulverston, Cumbria.
Martin and Dorothy Harper Antiques, Bakewell, Derbys.
Wessex Antiques, Sherborne, Dorset.
Robson's Antiques, Barnard Castle, Durham.
Jan Morrison, Bristol, Glos.
Potter's Antiques and Coins, Bristol, Glos.
Grimes House Antiques & Fine Art, Moreton-in-Marsh, Glos.
A.W. Porter and Son, Hartley Wintney, Hants.
Louisa Francis, Brasted, Kent.

Jack Moore Antiques and Stained Glass, Trawden, Lancs.
Keystone Antiques, Coalville, Leics.
Liz Allport-Lomax, Norwich, Norfolk.
Weedon Antiques, Weedon, Northants.
Acanthus Antiques & Collectables inc. Dutton & Smith Medals, Nottingham, Notts.
Laurie Leigh Antiques, Oxford, Oxon.
Joan Wilkins Antiques, Witney, Oxon.
Bees Antiques, Woodstock, Oxon.
Brian and Caroline Craik Ltd, Bath, Somerset.
Frank Dux Antiques, Bath, Somerset.
Robin Butler, Clare, Suffolk.
Marryat, Richmond, Surrey.
David R. Fileman, Steyning, Sussex West.
Drew Pritchard Ltd, Llandudno, Wales.
Delomosne and Son Ltd, North Wraxall, Wilts.
Dragon Antiques, Harrogate, Yorks. North.
Castle Gate Antiques, Helmsley, Yorks. North.
Dunluce Antiques, Bushmills, Co. Antrim, N. Ireland.
Brian R. Bolt Antiques, Portballintrae, Co. Antrim, N. Ireland.
Peter Francis Antiques, Saintfield, Co. Down, N. Ireland.

Glass Domes
Get Stuffed, London N1.
John Burton Natural Craft Taxidermy, Ebrington, Glos.
Heads 'n' Tails, Wiveliscombe, Somerset.

Icons - see Russian Art

Islamic Art
Polonaise Gallery, London SW7.
David Aaron Ancient Arts & Rare Carpets, London W1.
Aaron Gallery, London W1.
Emanouel Corporation (UK) Ltd, London W1.
Sam Fogg, London W1.
Hadji Baba Ancient Art Ltd, London W1.
Mansour Gallery, London W1.
Axia Art Consultants Ltd, London W11.
Hosains Books and Antiques, London W2.
Millner Manolatos, London W8.
Amir Mohtashemi Ltd, London W8.
Sinai Antiques Ltd, London W8.
Clive Rogers Oriental Rugs, Staines, Surrey.

Japanese Art - see Oriental

Jewellery - see Silver

Lighting
Rosemary Conquest, London N1.
Carlton Davidson Antiques, London N1.
Turn On Lighting, London N1.
David Malik and Son Ltd, London NW10.
Young & Son, London NW8.
B.C. Metalcrafts, London NW9.
Wilkinson plc, London SE6.

SPECIALIST DEALERS

Hilary Batstone Antiques inc. Rose Uniacke Design, London SW1.
Blanchard Ltd, London SW1.
Andi Gisel, London SW1.
Hermitage Antiques Ltd, London SW1.
Carlton Hobbs, London SW1.
Christopher Howe, London SW1.
Humphrey-Carrasco Ltd, London SW1.
Jeremy Ltd, London SW1.
Carlton Davidson Antiques, London SW10.
H.W. Poulter and Son, London SW10.
Joy McDonald Antiques, London SW13.
Chris Baron Interiors, London SW2.
W.G.T. Burne (Antique Glass) Ltd, London SW20.
Robert Dickson and Lesley Rendall Antiques, London SW3.
Antiques and Things, London SW4.
275 Antiques, London SW6.
The Antique Lamp Shop, London SW6.
Charles Edwards, London SW6.
Hector Finch Lighting, London SW6.
The French House (Antiques) Ltd, London SW6.
Mora & Upham Antiques, London SW6.
Old World Trading Co, London SW6.
M. Pauw Antiques, London SW6.
The French House (Antiques) Ltd, London SW8.
Partridge Fine Arts plc, London W1.
W. Sitch and Co. Ltd., London W1.
M. Turpin Ltd, London W1.
Wilkinson plc, London W1.
Jones Antique Lighting, London W11.
Marshall Gallery, London W14.
Marshall Phillips, London W4.
Mrs. M.E. Crick Chandeliers, London W8.
Denton Antiques, London W8.
Cox Interiors Ltd, London W9.
George and Peter Cohn, London WC1.
David Litt Antiques, Ampthill, Beds.
Manor Antiques, Wilstead (Wilshamstead), Beds.
Griffin Fine Art & Antiques, Hungerford, Berks.
Starlight Period Lighting, Wansford, Cambs.
Peter Johnson, Penzance, Cornwall.
Johnson & Johnson, Kirkby Lonsdale, Cumbria.
Staveley Antiques, Staveley, Cumbria.
Mill Lane Antiques, Woodford Green, Essex.
The Antiques Warehouse Ltd, Bristol, Glos.
Triton Gallery, Cheltenham, Glos.
Antony Preston Antiques Ltd, Stow-on-the-Wold, Glos.
Queens Parade Antiques Ltd, Stow-on-the-Wold, Glos.
Government House, Winchcombe, Glos.
Fritz Fryer Antique Lighting, Ross-on-Wye, Herefs.
Magic Lanterns, St. Albans, Herts.
Conquest House Antiques, Canterbury, Kent.
Chislehurst Antiques, Chislehurst, Kent.
The Architectural Stores, Tunbridge Wells, Kent.
Knicks Knacks Emporium, Sutton-on-Sea, Lincs.
Birkdale Antiques, Southport, Merseyside.
Period Style Lighting, Enfield, Middx.
The Stiffkey Lamp Shop, Stiffkey, Norfolk.

Renney Antiques, Corbridge, Northumbs.
Holloways of Ludlow, Ludlow, Shrops.
Antique Textiles & Lighting, Bath, Somerset.
Exning Antiques & Interiors, Exning, Suffolk.
Post House Antiques, Bletchingley, Surrey.
Woodall and Emery Ltd, Balcombe, Sussex West.
David R. Fileman, Steyning, Sussex West.
L.O.G.G. Lights, Tynemouth, Tyne and Wear.
Delomosne and Son Ltd, North Wraxall, Wilts.
Gray's Interiors, Worcester, Worcs.
Old Flames, Easingwold, Yorks. North.
The French House (Antiques) Ltd., York, Yorks. North.
Kelly Lighting, Sheffield, Yorks. South.
Sarah Scott Antiques, Sheffield, Yorks. South.
Jacquart Antiques, Holywood, Co. Down, N. Ireland.
Agar Antiques, Saintfield, Co. Down, N. Ireland.
Berland's of Edinburgh, Edinburgh, Scotland.
The Meadows Lamp Gallery, Edinburgh, Scotland.
Michael Vee Design - Birch House Antiques, Melrose, Scotland.

Maps & Prints
Frontispiece Ltd, London E14.
York Gallery Ltd, London N1.
Gallery Kaleidoscope incorporating Scope Antiques, London NW6.
The Warwick Leadlay Gallery, London SE10.
Adam Gallery Ltd, London SW1.
Isaac and Ede, London SW1.
The Mall Galleries, London SW1.
Paul Mason Gallery, London SW1.
Old Maps and Prints, London SW1.
The Parker Gallery, London SW1.
Michael Parkin Fine Art Ltd, London SW1.
Sims Reed Gallery, London SW1.
Ash Rare Books, London SW17.
The Map House, London SW3.
Old Church Galleries, London SW3.
20th Century Gallery, London SW6.
Hilary Chapman Fine Prints, London SW6.
King's Court Galleries, London SW6.
Trowbridge Gallery, London SW6.
York Gallery Ltd, London SW6.
Paul Orssich, London SW8.
Altea Gallery, London W1.
Andrew Edmunds, London W1.
Map World, London W1.
Jonathan Potter Ltd, London W1.
Shapero Gallery, London W1.
Henry Sotheran Ltd, London W1.
Crawley and Asquith Ltd, London W10.
Peter Kennedy, London W11.
Justin F. Skrebowski Prints, London W11.
Abbott and Holder Ltd, London WC1.
Austin/Desmond Fine Art, London WC1.
Michael Finney Antique Prints and Books, London WC1.
Robert Frew Ltd, London WC1.
Tim Bryars Ltd, London WC2.

Grosvenor Prints, London WC2.
Storey's Ltd, London WC2.
The Witch Ball, London WC2.
Graham Gallery, Burghfield Common, Berks.
The Studio Gallery, Datchet, Berks.
Eton Antique Bookshop, Windsor, Berks.
Penn Barn, Penn, Bucks.
The Lawson Gallery, Cambridge, Cambs.
J. Alan Hulme, Chester, Cheshire.
Moor Hall Antiques, Chester, Cheshire.
Cranford Galleries, Knutsford, Cheshire.
Lion Gallery and Bookshop, Knutsford, Cheshire.
John Maggs, Falmouth, Cornwall.
Souvenir Antiques, Carlisle, Cumbria.
Archie Miles Bookshop, Gosforth, Cumbria.
Sleddall Hall Antiques Centre inc. Kendal Studios
    Antiques, Kendal, Cumbria.
Keswick Bookshop, Keswick, Cumbria.
R.F.G. Hollett and Son, Sedbergh, Cumbria.
Medina Gallery, Barnstaple, Devon.
High Street Books, Honiton, Devon.
Graham York Rare Books, Honiton, Devon.
Devonshire Fine Art, Modbury, Devon.
The Schuster Gallery, Torquay, Devon.
Bridport Old Books, Bridport, Dorset.
Words Etcetera, Dorchester, Dorset.
F. Whillock, Litton Cheney, Dorset.
Antique Map and Bookshop, Puddletown, Dorset.
The Swan Gallery, Sherborne, Dorset.
The Treasure Chest, Weymouth, Dorset.
Castle Bookshop, Colchester, Essex.
Cleeve Picture Framing, Bishops Cleeve, Glos.
Alexander Gallery, Bristol, Glos.
David Bannister FRGS, Cheltenham, Glos.
Kenulf Fine Arts, Stow-on-the-Wold, Glos.
Talbot Court Galleries, Stow-on-the-Wold, Glos.
Vanbrugh House Antiques, Stow-on-the-Wold, Glos.
Laurence Oxley Ltd, Alresford, Hants.
Kingsclere Old Bookshop (Wyseby House Books),
    Kingsclere, Hants.
The Petersfield Bookshop, Petersfield, Hants.
Oldfield Gallery, Portsmouth, Hants.
The Olympic Gallery, Southampton, Hants.
Bell Fine Art, Winchester, Hants.
Ross Old Book and Print Shop, Ross-on-Wye, Herefs.
Gillmark Gallery, Hertford, Herts.
Eric T. Moore, Hitchin, Herts.
Antique Print Shop, Redbourn, Herts.
Clive A. Burden Ltd, Rickmansworth, Herts.
The Shanklin Gallery, Shanklin, Isle of Wight.
Ventnor Rare Books, Ventnor, Isle of Wight.
The Canterbury Bookshop, Canterbury, Kent.
Chaucer Bookshop, Canterbury, Kent.
Cranbrook Gallery, Cranbrook, Kent.
Marrin's Bookshop, Folkestone, Kent.
The China Locker, Lamberhurst, Kent.
Langley Galleries Ltd, Rochester, Kent.
London House Antiques, Westerham, Kent.
Halewood and Sons, Preston, Lancs.

P.J. Cassidy (Books), Holbeach, Lincs.
Golden Goose Books, Lincoln, Lincs.
Harlequin Gallery and Golden Goose Globe Restorers,
    Lincoln, Lincs.
Norman Blackburn, Stamford, Lincs.
David Ferrow, Great Yarmouth, Norfolk.
Baron Art, Holt, Norfolk.
The Old Reading Room Gallery and Tea Room,
    Kelling, Norfolk.
Crome Gallery and Frame Shop, Norwich, Norfolk.
Right Angle, Brackley, Northants.
Park Gallery & Bookshop, Wellingborough, Northants.
TRADA, Chipping Norton, Oxon.
The Barry Keene Gallery, Henley-on-Thames, Oxon.
Elizabeth Harvey-Lee, North Aston, Oxon.
Sanders of Oxford Ltd, Oxford, Oxon.
Toby English, Wallingford, Oxon.
Tooley Adams & Co, Wallingford, Oxon.
Marc Oxley Fine Art, Uppingham, Rutland.
The Antique Map Shop Ltd, Bath, Somerset.
Patterson Liddle, Bath, Somerset.
Sarah Russell Antiquarian Prints, Bath, Somerset.
Trimbridge Galleries, Bath, Somerset.
Michael Lewis Gallery - Antiquarian Maps & Prints,
    Bruton, Somerset.
Julian Armytage, Crewkerne, Somerset.
House of Antiquity, Nether Stowey, Somerset.
M.A.J. Morris, Burton-upon-Trent, Staffs.
Besleys Books, Beccles, Suffolk.
King's Court Galleries, Dorking, Surrey.
Vandeleur Antiquarian Books, Epsom, Surrey.
Leoframes, Brighton, Sussex East.
Murray Brown, Pevensey Bay, Sussex East.
Baynton-Williams, Arundel, Sussex West.
Julia Holmes Antique Maps and Prints, South Harting,
    Sussex West.
Andrew Dando, Bradford-on-Avon, Wilts.
Heatons, Tisbury, Wilts.
Antique Map and Print Gallery, Hallow, Worcs.
Grove Rare Books, Bolton Abbey, Yorks. North.
McTague of Harrogate, Harrogate, Yorks. North.
Minster Gate Bookshop, York, Yorks. North.
Alan Hill Books, Sheffield, Yorks. South.
Oakwood Gallery, Leeds, Yorks. West.
Channel Islands Galleries Ltd, St. Peter Port, Guernsey,
    C.I.
John Blench & Son, St. Helier, Jersey, C.I.
The Selective Eye Gallery, St. Helier, Jersey, C.I.
Thesaurus (Jersey) Ltd, St. Helier, Jersey, C.I.
Phyllis Arnold Gallery Antiques, Donaghadee, Co.
    Down, N. Ireland.
Colin Wood (Antiques) Ltd, Aberdeen, Scotland.
The McEwan Gallery, Ballater, Scotland.
Calton Gallery, Edinburgh, Scotland.
The Carson Clark Gallery - Scotland's Map Heritage
    Centre, Edinburgh, Scotland.
The Old Town Bookshop, Edinburgh, Scotland.
Royal Mile Gallery, Edinburgh, Scotland.
Second Edition, Edinburgh, Scotland.

SPECIALIST DEALERS

David Windsor Gallery, Bangor, Wales.
Books, Maps and Prints, Brecon, Wales.

Metalware/work
Robert Young Antiques, London SW11.
Christopher Bangs Ltd, London SW6.
Jack Casimir Ltd, London W11.
Johnny Von Pflugh Antiques, London W11.
Christopher Sykes Antiques, Woburn, Beds.
Turpins Antiques, Hungerford, Berks.
Peter J. Martin, Windsor, Berks.
Sundial Antiques, Amersham, Bucks.
Phoenix Antiques, Fordham, Cambs.
A.P. and M.A. Haylett, Outwell, Cambs.
Johnson & Johnson, Kirkby Lonsdale, Cumbria.
J H S Antiques Ltd, Ashbourne, Derbys.
Martin and Dorothy Harper Antiques, Bakewell,
  Derbys.
Michael Pembery Antiques, Bakewell, Derbys.
Roderick Butler, Honiton, Devon.
Ann Quested Antiques, Bridport, Dorset.
J.B. Antiques, Wimborne Minster, Dorset.
William H. Stokes, Cirencester, Glos.
Duncan J. Baggott, Stow-on-the-Wold, Glos.
Baggott Church Street Ltd, Stow-on-the-Wold, Glos.
Christopher Clarke Antiques Ltd, Stow-on-the-Wold,
  Glos.
Keith Hockin Antiques, Stow-on-the-Wold, Glos.
Huntington Antiques Ltd, Stow-on-the-Wold, Glos.
Prichard Antiques, Winchcombe, Glos.
Cedar Antiques Limited, Hartley Wintney, Hants.
Michael Gander, Hitchin, Herts.
V.O.C. Antiques, Woodhall Spa, Lincs.
James Brett, Norwich, Norfolk.
M.D. Cannell Antiques, Raveningham, Norfolk.
Blockheads and Granary Antiques, Flore, Northants.
Jonathan Fyson Antiques, Burford, Oxon.
Horseshoe Antiques and Gallery, Burford, Oxon.
Knights Antiques, Henley-on-Thames, Oxon.
Mike Ottrey Antiques, Wallingford, Oxon.
Colin Greenway Antiques, Witney, Oxon.
Joan Wilkins Antiques, Witney, Oxon.
R.G. Cave and Sons Ltd, Ludlow, Shrops.
Brian and Caroline Craik Ltd, Bath, Somerset.
Bernard G. House, Wells, Somerset.
Peppers Period Pieces, Wattisfield, Suffolk.
Anthony Welling Antiques, Ripley, Surrey.
Heritage Antiques, Brighton, Sussex East.
Golden Cross Antiques, Hailsham, Sussex East.
Park View Antiques, Wadhurst, Sussex East.
Michael Wakelin and Helen Linfield, Billingshurst,
  Sussex West.
Avon Antiques, Bradford-on-Avon, Wilts.
Harriet Fairfax Fireplaces and General Antiques,
  Langley Burrell, Wilts.
H.W. Keil Ltd, Broadway, Worcs.
D & J Lines Antiques, Wychbold, Worcs.
Derbyshire Antiques Ltd, Harrogate, Yorks. North.
Charles Lumb and Sons Ltd, Harrogate, Yorks. North.

Elaine Phillips Antiques Ltd, Harrogate, Yorks. North.
Aura Antiques, Masham, Yorks. North.
E. Thistlethwaite, Settle, Yorks. North.
Geary Antiques, Leeds, Yorks. West.
Unicorn Antiques, Edinburgh, Scotland.
Tim Wright Antiques, Glasgow, Scotland.

Miniatures
D.S. Lavender (Antiques) Ltd, London W1.
S.J. Phillips Ltd, London W1.
H. and W. Deutsch Antiques, London W8.
Ellison Fine Art, Beaconsfield, Bucks.
Michael Sim, Chislehurst, Kent.
Vintage Jewels, Westerham, Kent.
M B G Antiques, Fine Art & Jewellery, Newark, Notts.
Arden Gallery, Henley-in-Arden, Warks.
Phyllis Arnold Gallery Antiques, Donaghadee, Co.
  Down, N. Ireland.

Mirrors
Carlton Davidson Antiques, London N1.
Carol Ketley Antiques, London N1.
Relic Antiques Trade Warehouse, London NW1.
Young & Son, London NW8.
Minerva Antiques, London SE10.
Anno Domini Antiques, London SW1.
Hilary Batstone Antiques inc. Rose Uniacke Design,
  London SW1.
Chelsea Antique Mirrors, London SW1.
Ossowski, London SW1.
Thomas Kerr Antiques Ltd, London SW10.
McVeigh & Charpentier, London SW10.
Overmantels, London SW11.
Joy McDonald Antiques, London SW13.
Norman Adams Ltd, London SW3.
Robert Dickson and Lesley Rendall Antiques, London
  SW3.
Anthony James and Son Ltd, London SW3.
Peter Lipitch Ltd, London SW3.
275 Antiques, London SW6.
The French House (Antiques) Ltd, London SW6.
Judy Greenwood, London SW6.
House of Mirrors, London SW6.
Christopher Jones Antiques, London SW6.
Old World Trading Co, London SW6.
Ossowski, London SW6.
The French House (Antiques) Ltd, London SW8.
M. Turpin Ltd, London W1.
Through the Looking Glass Ltd, London W8.
Cox Interiors Ltd, London W9.
David Litt Antiques, Ampthill, Beds.
Manor Antiques, Wilstead (Wilshamstead), Beds.
Richmond Antiques, Bowdon, Cheshire.
Old Town Hall Antiques, Falmouth, Cornwall.
Peter Wadham Antiques, Exeter, Devon.
Alexander Paul Antiques, Fenny Bridges, Devon.
Jane Strickland & Daughters, Honiton, Devon.
Mill Lane Antiques, Woodford Green, Essex.
The Antiques Warehouse Ltd, Bristol, Glos.

Triton Gallery, Cheltenham, Glos.
Ashton Gower Antiques, Stow-on-the-Wold, Glos.
Stow Antiques, Stow-on-the-Wold, Glos.
Max Rollitt, Winchester, Hants.
The Windhill Antiquary, Bishop's Stortford, Herts.
David Barrington, Brasted, Kent.
G. A. Hill Antiques, Brasted, Kent.
Chislehurst Antiques, Chislehurst, Kent.
Phoenix Antiques, Tunbridge Wells, Kent.
Ranby Hall, Retford, Notts.
The Old French Mirror Co Ltd, Henley-on-Thames, Oxon.
W.R. Harvey & Co (Antiques) Ltd, Witney, Oxon.
Looking Glass of Bath, Bath, Somerset.
On-Reflection Mirrors Ltd, Charlton Horethorne, Somerset.
Country Brocante, Godney, Somerset.
Moorland Antique Mirrors, Leek, Staffs.
Malthouse Antiques, Dorking, Surrey.
Dermot and Jill Palmer Antiques, Brighton, Sussex East.
Julian Antiques, Hurstpierpoint, Sussex West.
T.G. Wilkinson Antiques Ltd., Petworth, Sussex West.
Annabelle Giltsoff, Warminster, Wilts.
The Drawing Room - Interiors & Antiques, Pershore, Worcs.
W. Greenwood (Fine Art), Burneston, Yorks. North.
The French House (Antiques) Ltd., York, Yorks. North.
Sarah Scott Antiques, Sheffield, Yorks. South.
Michael Vee Design - Birch House Antiques, Melrose, Scotland.

Musical Boxes, Instruments and Literature
Boxes and Musical Instruments, London E8.
Vincent Freeman, London N1.
Tony Bingham, London NW3.
Otto Haas, London NW3.
Talking Machine, London NW4.
Robert Morley and Co Ltd, London SE13.
J. & A. Beare Ltd, London W1.
Peter Biddulph, London W1.
Pelham Galleries Ltd, London W1.
Travis and Emery Music Bookshop, London WC2.
J.V. Pianos and Cambridge Pianola Company, Landbeach, Cambs.
Mill Farm Antiques, Disley, Cheshire.
Miss Elany, Long Eaton, Derbys.
M.C. Taylor, Bournemouth, Dorset.
Arthur S. Lewis, Gloucester, Glos.
Keith Harding's World of Mechanical Music, Northleach, Glos.
Vanbrugh House Antiques, Stow-on-the-Wold, Glos.
Thwaites Fine Stringed Instruments, Watford, Herts.
Old Smithy, Feniscowles, Lancs.
The Violin Shop, Hexham, Northumbs.
S. & E.M. Turner Violins, Beeston, Notts.
R.R. Limb Antiques, Newark, Notts.
Laurie Leigh Antiques, Oxford, Oxon.
Mayflower Antiques, Long Melford, Suffolk.

John Cowderoy Antiques Ltd, Eastbourne, Sussex East.
Pianos Galore, Little Horsted, Sussex East.
S. and E.M. Turner Violins, Birmingham, West Mids.
Time Restored Ltd, Pewsey, Wilts.
The Barber's Clock, Worcester, Worcs.
The Piano Shop, Leeds, Yorks. West.
K.L.M. & Co. Antiques, Lepton, Yorks. West.
Talking Point Antiques, Sowerby Bridge, Yorks. West.
San Domenico Stringed Instruments, Cardiff, Wales .
John Carpenter, Llanelli, Wales .
Keith Chugg Antiques, Swansea, Wales.

Nautical Items - see Scientific

Needlework - see Tapestries

Netsuke - see Oriental

Oil Paintings
Gladwell and Company, London EC4.
Peter Chapman Antiques and Restoration, London N1.
Swan Fine Art, London N1.
Finchley Fine Art Galleries, London N12.
Martin Henham (Antiques), London N2.
Lauri Stewart - Fine Art, London N2.
Chaucer Fine Arts Ltd, London N4.
Duncan R. Miller Fine Arts, London NW3.
Newhart (Pictures) Ltd, London NW3.
Gallery Kaleidoscope incorporating Scope Antiques, London NW6.
Nicholas Drummond/Wrawby Moor Art Gallery Ltd, London NW8.
Patricia Harvey Antiques and Decoration, London NW8.
Leask Ward, London NW8.
The Greenwich Gallery, London SE10.
Didier Aaron (London)Ltd, London SW1.
Ackermann & Johnson, London SW1.
Adam Gallery Ltd, London SW1.
John Adams Fine Art Ltd, London SW1.
Verner Åmell Ltd, London SW1.
Antiquus, London SW1.
Artemis Fine Arts Limited, London SW1.
Chris Beetles Ltd, London SW1.
John Bly, London SW1.
Brisigotti Antiques Ltd, London SW1.
Miles Wynn Cato, London SW1.
Cox and Company, London SW1.
Simon C. Dickinson Ltd, London SW1.
Douwes Fine Art Ltd, London SW1.
Eaton Gallery, London SW1.
Victor Franses Gallery, London SW1.
Frost and Reed Ltd (Est. 1808), London SW1.
Christopher Gibbs Ltd, London SW1.
Martyn Gregory, London SW1.
Ross Hamilton Ltd, London SW1.
Hazlitt, Gooden and Fox Ltd, London SW1.
Hermitage Antiques Ltd, London SW1.
Carlton Hobbs, London SW1.

SPECIALIST DEALERS

Derek Johns Ltd, London SW1.
MacConnal-Mason Gallery, London SW1.
The Mall Galleries, London SW1.
Paul Mason Gallery, London SW1.
Mathaf Gallery Ltd, London SW1.
Matthiesen Fine Art Ltd., London SW1.
Duncan R. Miller Fine Arts, London SW1.
Moreton Contemporary Art Ltd, London SW1.
Peter Nahum At The Leicester Galleries, London SW1.
Oakham Gallery, London SW1.
Paisnel Gallery, London SW1.
The Parker Gallery, London SW1.
Michael Parkin Fine Art Ltd, London SW1.
Portland Gallery, London SW1.
Steven Rich & Michael Rich, London SW1.
Royal Exchange Art Gallery, London SW1.
Julian Simon Fine Art Ltd, London SW1.
Bill Thomson - Albany Gallery, London SW1.
Trafalgar Galleries, London SW1.
Tryon Gallery (incorporating Malcolm Innes), London SW1.
Rafael Valls Ltd, London SW1.
Johnny Van Haeften Ltd, London SW1.
Waterman Fine Art Ltd, London SW1.
The Weiss Gallery, London SW1.
Whitford Fine Art, London SW1.
Wildenstein and Co Ltd, London SW1.
Jonathan Clark & Co, London SW10.
Hollywood Road Gallery, London SW10.
Thomas Kerr Antiques Ltd, London SW10.
Lane Fine Art Ltd, London SW10.
Offer Waterman and Co. Fine Art, London SW10.
Park Walk Gallery, London SW10.
Pairs Antiques Ltd, London SW11.
Regent House Gallery, London SW11.
New Grafton Gallery, London SW13.
John Spink, London SW13.
Ted Few, London SW17.
The David Curzon Gallery, London SW19.
The Andipa Gallery, London SW3.
20th Century Gallery, London SW6.
Robert Barley Antiques, London SW6.
Rupert Cavendish Antiques, London SW6.
The Taylor Gallery Ltd, London SW7.
The Wyllie Gallery, London SW7.
Agnew's, London W1.
Victor Arwas Gallery - Editions Graphiques Gallery Ltd, London W1.
Browse and Darby Ltd, London W1.
Burlington Paintings Ltd, London W1.
Andrew Clayton-Payne Ltd, London W1.
P. and D. Colnaghi & Co Ltd, London W1.
Connaught Brown plc, London W1.
The Fine Art Society plc, London W1.
Deborah Gage (Works of Art) Ltd, London W1.
Richard Green, London W1.
William Hanham Ltd, London W1.
Maas Gallery, London W1.
Mallett and Son (Antiques) Ltd, London W1.

Mallett Gallery, London W1.
Marlborough Fine Art (London) Ltd, London W1.
Messum's, London W1.
John Mitchell and Son, London W1.
Partridge Fine Arts plc, London W1.
W.H. Patterson Ltd, London W1.
Frank T. Sabin Ltd, London W1.
Stoppenbach & Delestre Ltd, London W1.
William Thuillier, London W1.
Waterhouse and Dodd, London W1.
Wilkins and Wilkins, London W1.
Williams and Son, London W1.
Crawley and Asquith Ltd, London W10.
Caelt Gallery, London W11.
Curá Antiques, London W11.
Charles Daggett Gallery, London W11.
Fleur de Lys Gallery, London W11.
Lacy Gallery, London W11.
Milne and Moller, London W11.
Piano Nobile Fine Paintings, London W11.
Justin F. Skrebowski Prints, London W11.
Stern Pissarro Gallery, London W11.
Johnny Von Pflugh Antiques, London W11.
Marshall Gallery, London W14.
Manya Igel Fine Arts Ltd, London W2.
Richard Nagy Fine Art Ltd, London W2.
Richard Philp, London W6.
Campbell's of London, London W7.
Baumkotter Gallery, London W8.
Butchoff Antiques, London W8.
The Lucy B. Campbell Gallery, London W8.
Pawsey and Payne, London W8.
Abbott and Holder Ltd, London WC1.
Austin/Desmond Fine Art, London WC1.
Woburn Fine Arts, Woburn, Beds.
Omell Galleries, Ascot, Berks.
Graham Gallery, Burghfield Common, Berks.
The Studio Gallery, Datchet, Berks.
John A. Pearson Antiques, Horton, Berks.
Grosvenor House Interiors, Beaconsfield, Bucks.
H.S. Wellby Ltd, Haddenham, Bucks.
Penn Barn, Penn, Bucks.
Cambridge Fine Art Ltd, Cambridge, Cambs.
Storm Fine Arts Ltd, Great Shelford, Cambs.
Baron Fine Art, Chester, Cheshire.
Sandra Harris Interiors and Antiques, Chester, Cheshire.
Lion Gallery and Bookshop, Knutsford, Cheshire.
Copperhouse Gallery - W. Dyer & Sons, Hayle, Cornwall.
Tony Sanders Penzance Gallery and Antiques, Penzance, Cornwall.
Peter Haworth, Sandside, Cumbria.
R. F. G. Hollett and Son, Sedbergh, Cumbria.
Medina Gallery, Barnstaple, Devon.
J. Collins and Son Fine Art, Bideford, Devon.
Godolphin, Chagford, Devon.
Mill Gallery, Ermington, Devon.
Honiton Fine Art, Honiton, Devon.
Skeaping Gallery, Lydford, Devon.

Farthings, Lynton, Devon.
Devonshire Fine Art, Modbury, Devon.
Gordon Hepworth Fine Art, Newton St. Cyres, Devon.
Michael Wood Fine Art, Plymouth, Devon.
Hampshire Gallery, Bournemouth, Dorset.
The Swan Gallery, Sherborne, Dorset.
Margaret Bedi Antiques & Fine Art, Stockton-on-Tees, Durham.
T.B. and R. Jordan (Fine Paintings), Stockton-on-Tees, Durham.
Brandler Galleries, Brentwood, Essex.
Neil Graham Gallery, Brentwood, Essex.
S. Bond and Son, Colchester, Essex.
Totteridge Gallery, Earls Colne, Essex.
Peter and Penny Proudfoot, Berkeley, Glos.
Cleeve Picture Framing, Bishops Cleeve, Glos.
Alexander Gallery, Bristol, Glos.
Manor House Gallery, Cheltenham, Glos.
Triton Gallery, Cheltenham, Glos.
Peter Ward Fine Paintings, Cheltenham, Glos.
School House Antiques, Chipping Campden, Glos.
Astley House - Contemporary, Moreton-in-Marsh, Glos.
Astley House - Fine Art, Moreton-in-Marsh, Glos.
Benton Fine Art, Moreton-in-Marsh, Glos.
Berry Antiques Ltd, Moreton-in-Marsh, Glos.
Grimes House Antiques & Fine Art, Moreton-in-Marsh, Glos.
The Roger Widdas Gallery, Moreton-in-Marsh, Glos.
Nina Zborowska, Painswick, Glos.
Baggott Church Street Ltd, Stow-on-the-Wold, Glos.
Cotswold Galleries, Stow-on-the-Wold, Glos.
The John Davies Gallery, Stow-on-the-Wold, Glos.
The Fosse Gallery, Stow-on-the-Wold, Glos.
Kenulf Fine Arts, Stow-on-the-Wold, Glos.
Roger Lamb Antiques & Works of Art, Stow-on-the-Wold, Glos.
Styles of Stow, Stow-on-the-Wold, Glos.
The Titian Gallery, Stow-on-the-Wold, Glos.
Century Fine Arts, Lymington, Hants.
Robert Perera Fine Art, Lymington, Hants.
The Petersfield Bookshop, Petersfield, Hants.
The Wykeham Gallery, Stockbridge, Hants.
Bell Fine Art, Winchester, Hants.
Lacewing Fine Art Gallery, Winchester, Hants.
Webb Fine Arts, Winchester, Hants.
The Shanklin Gallery, Shanklin, Isle of Wight.
Old Bakery Antiques, Brasted, Kent.
Michael Sim, Chislehurst, Kent.
Francis Iles, Rochester, Kent.
Langley Galleries Ltd, Rochester, Kent.
Sundridge Gallery, Sundridge, Kent.
Pantiles Spa Antiques, Tunbridge Wells, Kent.
Redleaf Gallery, Tunbridge Wells, Kent.
John Thompson, Tunbridge Wells, Kent.
Apollo Antique Galleries, Westerham, Kent.
London House Antiques, Westerham, Kent.
Vintage Jewels, Westerham, Kent.
Ascot Antiques, Blackpool, Lancs.
Fulda Gallery Ltd, Manchester, Lancs.

St. James Antiques, Manchester, Lancs.
European Fine Arts and Antiques, Preston, Lancs.
Henry Donn Gallery, Whitefield, Lancs.
Corry's Antiques, Leicester, Leics.
P. Stanworth (Fine Arts), Market Bosworth, Leics.
Coughton Galleries Ltd, Market Harborough, Leics.
Graftons of Market Harborough, Market Harborough, Leics.
Robin Shield Antiques, Swinstead, Lincs.
Baron Art, Holt, Norfolk.
Judy Hines of Holt - The Gallery, Holt, Norfolk.
The Old Reading Room Gallery and Tea Room, Kelling, Norfolk.
The Bank House Gallery, Norwich, Norfolk.
Crome Gallery and Frame Shop, Norwich, Norfolk.
The Fairhurst Gallery, Norwich, Norfolk.
Mandell's Gallery, Norwich, Norfolk.
The Westcliffe Gallery, Sheringham, Norfolk.
Staithe Lodge Gallery, Swafield, Norfolk.
Norton Antiques, Twyford, Norfolk.
Castle Ashby Gallery, Castle Ashby, Northants.
Bryan Perkins Antiques, Great Cransley, Northants.
Clark Galleries, Towcester, Northants.
Ron Green, Towcester, Northants.
Anthony Mitchell Fine Paintings, Nottingham, Notts.
Ranby Hall, Retford, Notts.
H.C. Dickins, Bloxham, Oxon.
Horseshoe Antiques and Gallery, Burford, Oxon.
Hubert's Antiques, Burford, Oxon.
Brian Sinfield Gallery Ltd, Burford, Oxon.
The Stone Gallery, Burford, Oxon.
Georgian House Antiques, Chipping Norton, Oxon.
The Barry Keene Gallery, Henley-on-Thames, Oxon.
Mike Ottrey Antiques, Wallingford, Oxon.
Marc Oxley Fine Art, Uppingham, Rutland.
Bebb Fine Art, Ludlow, Shrops.
Valentyne Dawes Gallery, Ludlow, Shrops.
Wenlock Fine Art, Much Wenlock, Shrops.
Adam Gallery Ltd, Bath, Somerset.
Chomé Fine Art, Bath, Somerset.
Mary Cruz, Bath, Somerset.
Anthony Hepworth Fine Art Dealers, Bath, Somerset.
Trimbridge Galleries, Bath, Somerset.
Freshfords, Freshford, Somerset.
Nick Cotton Fine Art, Watchet, Somerset.
The Sadler Street Gallery, Wells, Somerset.
Everett Fine Art Ltd, West Buckland, Somerset.
England's Gallery, Leek, Staffs.
Thompson's Gallery, Aldeburgh, Suffolk.
Debenham Antiques, Debenham, Suffolk.
J. and J. Baker, Lavenham,, Suffolk.
Peasenhall Art and Antiques Gallery, Peasenhall, Suffolk.
Suffolk House Antiques, Yoxford, Suffolk.
Cider House Galleries Ltd, Bletchingley, Surrey.
Glencorse Antiques, Kingston-upon-Thames, Surrey.
Bourne Gallery Ltd, Reigate, Surrey.
Roland Goslett Gallery, Richmond, Surrey.
Marryat, Richmond, Surrey.

SPECIALIST DEALERS

Sage Antiques and Interiors, Ripley, Surrey.
B. M. and E. Newlove, Surbiton, Surrey.
Edward Cross - Fine Paintings, Weybridge, Surrey.
Willow Gallery, Weybridge, Surrey.
Campbell Wilson, Brighton, Sussex East.
John Day of Eastbourne Fine Art, Eastbourne, Sussex East.
Murray Brown, Pevensey Bay, Sussex East.
E. Stacy-Marks Limited, Polegate, Sussex East.
Nicholas Bowlby, Poundgate, Sussex East.
Chichester Gallery, Chichester, Sussex West.
The Canon Gallery, Petworth, Sussex West.
Oliver Charles Antiques, Petworth, Sussex West.
Georgia Antiques, Pulborough, Sussex West.
Wilsons Antiques, Worthing, Sussex West.
MacDonald Fine Art, Gosforth, Tyne and Wear.
Ian Sharp Antiques Ltd., Tynemouth, Tyne and Wear.
Arden Gallery, Henley-in-Arden, Warks.
Fine-Lines (Fine Art), Shipston-on-Stour, Warks.
Astley House - Fine Art, Stretton-on-Fosse, Warks.
Oldswinford Gallery, Stourbridge, West Mids.
Driffold Gallery, Sutton Coldfield, West Mids.
Gallimaufry, Broadway, Worcs.
Richard Hagen, Broadway, Worcs.
Haynes Fine Art of Broadway, Broadway, Worcs.
John Noott Galleries, Broadway, Worcs.
The Highway Gallery, Upton-upon-Severn, Worcs.
James H. Starkey Galleries, Beverley, Yorks. East.
W. Greenwood (Fine Art), Burneston, Yorks. North.
Garth Antiques, Harrogate, Yorks. North.
Sutcliffe Galleries, Harrogate, Yorks. North.
Walker Galleries Ltd, Harrogate, Yorks. North.
E. Stacy-Marks Limited, Helmsley, Yorks. North.
Kirkgate Fine Art & Conservation, Thirsk, Yorks. North.
Coulter Galleries, York, Yorks. North.
Oakwood Gallery, Leeds, Yorks. West.
Monkman Antiques, Otley, Yorks. West.
Robin Taylor Fine Arts, Wakefield, Yorks. West.
Channel Islands Galleries Ltd, St. Peter Port, Guernsey, C.I.
Atelier Ltd, Grouville, Jersey, C.I.
Falle Fine Art Limited, St Helier, Jersey, C.I.
The Selective Eye Gallery, St. Helier, Jersey, C.I.
I.G.A. Old Masters Ltd, St. Lawrence, Jersey, C.I.
Grange Gallery - Fine Arts Ltd, St. Saviour, Jersey, C.I.
The Bell Gallery, Belfast, Co. Antrim, N. Ireland.
Dunluce Antiques, Bushmills, Co. Antrim, N. Ireland.
Atholl Antiques, Aberdeen, Scotland.
The Rendezvous Gallery, Aberdeen, Scotland.
Colin Wood (Antiques) Ltd, Aberdeen, Scotland.
The McEwan Gallery, Ballater, Scotland.
The Gallery (Nigel Stacy-Marks Ltd), Blair Atholl, Scotland.
Bourne Fine Art Ltd, Edinburgh, Scotland.
Calton Gallery, Edinburgh, Scotland.
Open Eye Gallery Ltd, Edinburgh, Scotland.
The Scottish Gallery, Edinburgh, Scotland.
Anthony Woodd Gallery Ltd, Edinburgh, Scotland.

Young Antiques, Edinburgh, Scotland.
The Roger Billcliffe Fine Art, Glasgow, Scotland.
Ewan Mundy Fine Art Ltd, Glasgow, Scotland.
Michael Young Antiques at Glencarse, Glencarse, Scotland.
Inchmartine Fine Art, Inchture, Scotland.
Mainhill Gallery, Jedburgh, Scotland.
Killin Gallery, Killin, Scotland.
Kilmacolm Antiques Ltd, Kilmacolm, Scotland.
Newburgh Antiques, Newburgh, Scotland.
Kirk Ports Gallery, North Berwick, Scotland.
St. Andrews Fine Art, St. Andrews, Scotland.
Abbey Antiques, Stirling, Scotland.
David Windsor Gallery, Bangor, Wales.
Michael Webb Fine Art, Bodorgan, Wales.
Welsh Art, Tywyn, Wales.
Rowles Fine Art, Welshpool, Wales.

Oriental Items
Japanese Gallery, London N1.
Kevin Page Oriental Art, London N1.
C. Tapsell, London N1.
Malcolm Rushton - Early Oriental Art, London NW3.
Leask Ward, London NW8.
B.C. Metalcrafts, London NW9.
Ciancimino Ltd, London SW1.
Brian Harkins Oriental Art, London SW1.
Jeremy Mason (Sainsbury & Mason), London SW1.
Opium, London SW10.
Orientation, London SW10.
Toynbee-Clarke Interiors Ltd, London SW10.
Sebastiano Barbagallo, London SW6.
Indigo, London SW6.
Daphne Rankin and Ian Conn, London SW6.
Soo San, London SW6.
Brandt Oriental Art, London W1.
Paul Champkins, London W1.
Eskenazi Ltd, London W1.
John Eskenazi Ltd, London W1.
Sam Fogg, London W1.
Robert Hall, London W1.
Gerard Hawthorn Ltd, London W1.
Roger Keverne, London W1.
Sydney L. Moss Ltd, London W1.
Gordon Reece Gallery, London W1.
Rossi & Rossi Ltd, London W1.
Robert G. Sawers, London W1.
A. & J. Speelman Ltd, London W1.
Jan van Beers Oriental Art, London W1.
Linda Wrigglesworth Ltd, London W1.
Sebastiano Barbagallo, London W11.
Graham and Green, London W11.
M.C.N. Antiques, London W11.
The Nanking Porcelain Co. Ltd, London W11.
Christina Truscott, London W11.
AntikWest AB, London W8.
Gregg Baker Asian Art, London W8.
David Brower Antiques, London W8.
Cohen & Cohen, London W8.

Barry Davies Oriental Art, London W8.
H. and W. Deutsch Antiques, London W8.
J.A.N. Fine Art, London W8.
Japanese Gallery, London W8.
Peter Kemp, London W8.
S. Marchant & Son, London W8.
R. and G. McPherson Antiques, London W8.
Millner Manolatos, London W8.
Santos, London W8.
Sinai Antiques Ltd, London W8.
Geoffrey Waters Ltd, London W8.
Jorge Welsh Oriental Porcelain & Works of Art, London
    W8.
Mary Wise & Grosvenor Antiques, London W8.
Glade Antiques, High Wycombe, Bucks.
Peter Johnson, Penzance, Cornwall.
Rex Antiques, Chagford, Devon.
Yarrow, Honiton, Devon.
The Dragon and the Phoenix, South Molton, Devon.
Lionel Geneen Ltd, Bournemouth, Dorset.
Artique, Tetbury, Glos.
Oriental Rug Gallery Ltd, St. Albans, Herts.
Michael Sim, Chislehurst, Kent.
Mandarin Gallery - Oriental Art, Otford, Kent.
Flower House Antiques, Tenterden, Kent.
The Rug Gallery, Leicester, Leics.
Roger Bradbury Antiques, Coltishall, Norfolk.
Country and Eastern Ltd., Norwich, Norfolk.
M.D. Cannell Antiques, Raveningham, Norfolk.
Cathay Antiques, Nottingham, Notts.
Haliden Oriental Rug Shop, Bath, Somerset.
Lopburi Art & Antiques, Bath, Somerset.
Antiquus, Castle Cary, Somerset.
The Crooked Window, Dunster, Somerset.
Oriental Rug Gallery, Guildford, Surrey.
Robin Kennedy, Richmond, Surrey.
Clive Rogers Oriental Rugs, Staines, Surrey.
Patrick Moorhead Antiques, Brighton, Sussex East.
Brian Page Antiques, Brighton, Sussex East.
Gensing Antiques, St. Leonards-on-Sea, Sussex East.
Fu Jen Ni Ltd, Petworth, Sussex West.
Paul Baxter, Birmingham, West Mids.
Indigo, Manningford Bruce, Wilts.
Heirloom & Howard Limited, West Yatton, Wilts.
Paul M. Peters Fine Art Ltd., Harrogate, Yorks. North.
Tansu Oriental Antiques, Batley, Yorks. West.
Two Dragons Oriental Antiques, Llanerchymedd,
    Wales.
Peter Wain, Menai Bridge, Wales.

Paperweights
Garrick D. Coleman, London W11.
Garrick D. Coleman, London W8.
Sweetbriar Gallery Ltd, Frodsham, Cheshire.
The Stone Gallery, Burford, Oxon.
David R. Fileman, Steyning, Sussex West.

Photographs & Equipment
Jubilee Photographica, London N1.

Shapero Gallery, London W1.
Jessop Classic Photographica, London WC1.
Medina Gallery, Barnstaple, Devon.
Peter Pan's Bazaar, Gosport, Hants.
Vintage Cameras Ltd, Deal, Kent.

Pottery & Porcelain
Finchley Fine Art Galleries, London N12.
Martin Henham (Antiques), London N2.
Sabera Trading Co, London NW2.
Klaber and Klaber, London NW3.
Albert Amor Ltd, London SW1.
Ross Hamilton Ltd, London SW1.
Stephen Long, London SW10.
Robert Young Antiques, London SW11.
The Dining Room Shop, London SW13.
Rogers de Rin, London SW3.
Davies Antiques, London SW8.
Thomas Goode and Co (London) Ltd, London W1.
Harcourt Antiques, London W1.
Brian Haughton Antiques, London W1.
Alistair Sampson Antiques Ltd, London W1.
Judy Fox, London W11.
M. and D. Lewis, London W11.
Mercury Antiques, London W11.
Schredds of Portobello, London W11.
David Brower Antiques, London W8.
H. and W. Deutsch Antiques, London W8.
Hope and Glory, London W8.
Jonathan Horne, London W8.
Peter Kemp, London W8.
Libra Antiques, London W8.
London Antique Gallery, London W8.
E. and H. Manners, London W8.
Simon Spero, London W8.
Stockspring Antiques, London W8.
Mary Wise & Grosvenor Antiques, London W8.
Anchor Antiques Ltd, London WC2.
Nick & Janet's Antiques, Leighton Buzzard, Beds.
Cavendish Fine Arts, Sonning-on-Thames, Berks.
Berkshire Antiques Co Ltd, Windsor, Berks.
Gabor Cossa Antiques, Cambridge, Cambs.
Abbey Antiques, Ramsey, Cambs.
Aldersey Hall Ltd, Chester, Cheshire.
Cameo Antiques, Chester, Cheshire.
K D Antiques, Chester, Cheshire.
Littles Collectables, Congleton, Cheshire.
Barn Antiques, Nantwich, Cheshire.
Romiley Antiques & Jewellery, Romiley, Cheshire.
Imperial Antiques, Stockport, Cheshire.
Antiques, Marazion, Cornwall.
Saint Nicholas Galleries Ltd. (Antiques and Jewellery),
    Carlisle, Cumbria.
Souvenir Antiques, Carlisle, Cumbria.
Dower House Antiques, Kendal, Cumbria.
Sleddall Hall Antiques Centre inc. Kendal Studios
    Antiques, Kendal, Cumbria.
The Good Olde Days, Ockbrook, Derbys.
Spondon Antiques and Collectables, Spondon, Derbys.

SPECIALIST DEALERS

Moor Antiques, Ashburton, Devon.
Bampton Gallery, Bampton, Devon.
David J. Thorn, Budleigh Salterton, Devon.
Honiton Pottery, Honiton, Devon.
Lombard Antiques, Honiton, Devon.
Mere Antiques, Topsham, Devon.
Box of Porcelain Ltd, Dorchester, Dorset.
Renaissance, Sherborne, Dorset.
Wessex Antiques, Sherborne, Dorset.
Reference Works Ltd., Swanage, Dorset.
Yesterdays, Wareham, Dorset.
James Hardy Antiques Ltd, Barnard Castle, Durham.
Robson's Antiques, Barnard Castle, Durham.
E. J. Markham & Son Ltd, Colchester, Essex.
Bush House, Corringham, Essex.
Bush Antiques, Saffron Walden, Essex.
Barling Fine Porcelain Ltd, Wickham Bishops, Essex.
Porchester Antiques, Bristol, Glos.
Stuart House Antiques, Chipping Campden, Glos.
Sodbury Antiques, Chipping Sodbury, Glos.
Berry Antiques Ltd, Moreton-in-Marsh, Glos.
Yvonne Adams Antiques, Stow-on-the-Wold, Glos.
Malt House Antiques, Stow-on-the-Wold, Glos.
Artemesia, Alresford, Hants.
Graylings Antiques, Andover, Hants.
Lita Kaye of Lyndhurst, Lyndhurst, Hants.
Lane Antiques, Stockbridge, Hants.
Goss and Crested China Centre and Goss Museum, Waterlooville, Hants.
The Collector Limited, Barnet, Herts.
Flagstaff Antiques, Cowes, Isle of Wight.
Louisa Francis, Brasted, Kent.
S. L. Walker, Brasted, Kent.
W.W. Warner (Antiques), Brasted, Kent.
Serendipity, Deal, Kent.
Toby Jug, Deal, Kent.
The China Locker, Lamberhurst, Kent.
Steppes Hill Farm Antiques, Stockbury, Kent.
Magpie Antiques, Hinckley, Leics.
Corry's Antiques, Leicester, Leics.
Underwoodhall Antiques, Woodhall Spa, Lincs.
Peter and Valerie Howkins Jewellers, Great Yarmouth, Norfolk.
Liz Allport-Lomax, Norwich, Norfolk.
Country House Antiques, Seething, Norfolk.
T.C.S. Brooke, Wroxham, Norfolk.
Weedon Antiques, Weedon, Northants.
Melville Kemp Ltd, Nottingham, Notts.
Swan Gallery, Burford, Oxon.
Winston Antiques, Kingham, Oxon.
Bees Antiques, Woodstock, Oxon.
John Howard, Woodstock, Oxon.
T.J. Roberts, Uppingham, Rutland.
Micawber Antiques, Bridgnorth, Shrops.
Bear Steps Antiques, Shrewsbury, Shrops.
Collectors' Place, Shrewsbury, Shrops.
David and Sally March Antiques, Abbots Leigh, Somerset.
Quiet Street Antiques, Bath, Somerset.

Antiquus, Castle Cary, Somerset.
T. J. Atkins, Taunton, Somerset.
Milestone Antiques, Lichfield, Staffs.
Eveline Winter, Rugeley, Staffs.
Burslem Antiques & Collectables, Stoke-on-Trent, Staffs.
The Potteries Antique Centre Ltd, Stoke-on-Trent, Staffs.
The Pottery Buying Centre, Stoke-on-Trent, Staffs.
White House Antiques, Uttoxeter, Staffs.
John Read Antiques, Martlesham, Suffolk.
David Gibbins Antiques, Woodbridge, Suffolk.
Decodream, Coulsdon, Surrey.
Dolphin Square Antiques, Dorking, Surrey.
Marryat, Richmond, Surrey.
Helena's Collectables, Shere, Surrey.
Brocante, Weybridge, Surrey.
Patrick Moorhead Antiques, Brighton, Sussex East.
Yellow Lantern Antiques Ltd, Brighton, Sussex East.
Southdown Antiques, Lewes, Sussex East.
Herbert Gordon Gasson, Rye, Sussex East.
Gems Antiques, Chichester, Sussex West.
Richard Gardner Antiques, Petworth, Sussex West.
Ian Sharp Antiques Ltd., Tynemouth, Tyne and Wear.
The Purple Antique Shop, Henley-in-Arden, Warks.
Andrew Dando, Bradford-on-Avon, Wilts.
Moxhams Antiques, Bradford-on-Avon, Wilts.
Antiques - Rene Nicholls, Malmesbury, Wilts.
Heirloom & Howard Limited, West Yatton, Wilts.
Gallimaufry, Broadway, Worcs.
Bygones by the Cathedral, Worcester, Worcs.
Bygones of Worcester, Worcester, Worcs.
M. Lees and Sons, Worcester, Worcs.
Worcester Antiques Centre, Worcester, Worcs.
The Crested China Co, Driffield, Yorks. East.
Antiques at Forge Cottage, Gargrave, Yorks. North.
Nigel Adamson, Harrogate, Yorks. North.
Bryan Bowden, Harrogate, Yorks. North.
David Love, Harrogate, Yorks. North.
Appleton Antiques, Middlesbrough, Yorks.North.
Country Collector, Pickering, Yorks. North.
Nanbooks, Settle, Yorks. North.
Anderson Slater Antiques, Settle, Yorks. North.
Eskdale Antiques Ltd, Whitby, Yorks. North.
Holly Farm Antiques, Rotherham, Yorks. South.
Muir Hewitt Art Deco Originals, Halifax, Yorks. West.
David Wolfenden Antiques, Antrim, Co. Antrim, N. Ireland.
Dunluce Antiques, Bushmills, Co. Antrim, N. Ireland.
Peter Francis Antiques, Saintfield, Co. Down, N. Ireland.
Duncan & Reid Books & Antiques, Edinburgh, Scotland.
Young Antiques, Edinburgh, Scotland.
Tim Wright Antiques, Glasgow, Scotland.
Grannie Used To Have One, Longhaven, Scotland.
Harper-James, Montrose, Scotland.
Newburgh Antiques, Newburgh, Scotland.
Nolton Antiques, Bridgend, Wales.

Islwyn Watkins, Knighton, Wales.
J. and R. Langford, Llangollen, Wales.
Passers Buy (Marie Evans), Llangollen, Wales.
Frost Antiques & Pine, Monmouth, Wales.
Magpie Antiques, Swansea, Wales.

Prints - see Maps

Rugs - see Carpets

Russian/Soviet Art
Chaucer Fine Arts Ltd, London N4.
Soviet Carpet & Art Galleries, London NW2.
Hermitage Antiques Ltd, London SW1.
Iconastas, London SW1.
Jeremy Ltd, London SW1.
Mark Ransom Ltd, London SW1.
The Andipa Gallery, London SW3.
Richardson and Kailas Icons, London SW6.
Antoine Cheneviere Fine Arts, London W1.
Wartski Ltd, London W1.
Caelt Gallery, London W11.
Temple Gallery, London W11.
The Mark Gallery, London W2.

Scientific Instruments
Finchley Fine Art Galleries, London N12.
Trevor Philip and Sons Ltd, London SW1.
Langford's Marine Antiques, London SW10.
Peter Delehar, London W11.
Humbleyard Fine Art, London W11.
Johnny Von Pflugh Antiques, London W11.
Gillian Gould at Ocean Leisure, London WC2.
Christopher Sykes Antiques, Woburn, Beds.
Principia Fine Art, Hungerford, Berks.
Mike Read Antique Sciences, St. Ives, Cornwall.
Branksome Antiques, Branksome, Dorset.
The Nautical Antiques Centre, Weymouth, Dorset.
The Chart House, Shenfield, Essex.
Chris Grimes Militaria, Bristol, Glos.
Malt House Antiques, Stow-on-the-Wold, Glos.
The Barometer Shop Ltd, Leominster, Herefs.
Michael Sim, Chislehurst, Kent.
Sporting Antiques, Tunbridge Wells, Kent.
Robin Fowler (Period Clocks), Aylesby, Lincs.
Rita Shenton, Twickenham, Middx.
Bernard G. House, Wells, Somerset.
Patrick Marney, Long Melford, Suffolk.
Mayflower Antiques, Long Melford, Suffolk.
Roy Arnold, Needham Market, Suffolk.
Odin Antiques, Brighton, Sussex East.

Sculpture
Mike Weedon, London N1.
Chaucer Fine Arts Ltd, London N4.
Duncan R. Miller Fine Arts, London NW3.
Gallery Kaleidoscope incorporating Scope Antiques,
     London NW6.
Tara Antiques, London NW8.

Robert E. Hirschhorn, London SE5.
Robert Bowman, London SW1.
Christopher Gibbs Ltd, London SW1.
Nicholas Gifford-Mead, London SW1.
Hazlitt, Gooden and Fox Ltd, London SW1.
MacConnal-Mason Gallery, London SW1.
The Mall Galleries, London SW1.
Duncan R. Miller Fine Arts, London SW1.
Whitford Fine Art, London SW1.
Jonathan Clark & Co, London SW10.
New Grafton Gallery, London SW13.
Ted Few, London SW17.
Joanna Booth, London SW3.
Robert Barley Antiques, London SW6.
Chelminski Gallery, London SW6.
Agnew's, London W1.
Adrian Alan Ltd, London W1.
Victor Arwas Gallery - Editions Graphiques Gallery
     Ltd, London W1.
Browse and Darby Ltd, London W1.
Eskenazi Ltd, London W1.
The Fine Art Society plc, London W1.
Daniel Katz Ltd, London W1.
Messum's, London W1.
Frank T. Sabin Ltd, London W1.
The Sladmore Gallery of Sculpture, London W1.
Stoppenbach & Delestre Ltd, London W1.
Curá Antiques, London W11.
Hickmet Fine Arts, London W11.
Hirst Antiques, London W11.
Milne and Moller, London W11.
Piano Nobile Fine Paintings, London W11.
Wolseley Fine Arts Ltd, London W11.
Richard Philp, London W6.
Arthur Seager Antiques, Stow-on-the-Wold, Glos.
Quatrefoil, Fordingbridge, Hants.
The Wykeham Gallery, Stockbridge, Hants.
Lacewing Fine Art Gallery, Winchester, Hants.
Francis Iles, Rochester, Kent.
Pearse Lukies, Aylsham, Norfolk.
James Brett, Norwich, Norfolk.
The Barry Keene Gallery, Henley-on-Thames, Oxon.
Mary Cruz, Bath, Somerset.
Anthony Hepworth Fine Art Dealers, Bath, Somerset.
Thompson's Gallery, Aldeburgh, Suffolk.
Nicholas Bowlby, Poundgate, Sussex East.
Patrick and Gillian Morley Antiques, Warwick, Warks.
Louis Stanton, Mere, Wilts.
Bruton Gallery, Holmfirth, Yorks. West.
Calton Gallery, Edinburgh, Scotland.
The Roger Billcliffe Fine Art, Glasgow, Scotland.
Intaglio, Chepstow, Wales.

Shipping Goods & Period Furniture for the Trade
Eccentricities, London N1.
Regent Antiques, London N1.
The Waterloo Trading Co., London N1.
Madeline Crispin Antiques, London NW1.
Tower Bridge Antiques, London SE1.

SPECIALIST DEALERS

Oola Boola Antiques London, London SE26.
Tavistock Antiques Ltd, St. Neots, Cambs.
Antique Exporters of Chester, Chester, Cheshire.
W. Buckley Antiques Exports, Congleton, Cheshire.
Michael Allcroft Antiques, Disley, Cheshire.
Mill Farm Antiques, Disley, Cheshire.
Manchester Antique Company, Stockport, Cheshire.
Shardlow Antiques Warehouse, Shardlow, Derbys.
John Prestige Antiques, Brixham, Devon.
The Antiques Complex, Exeter, Devon.
Fagins Antiques, Exeter, Devon.
Etcetera Antiques, Seaton, Devon.
Sandy's Antiques, Bournemouth, Dorset.
White Roding Antiques, White Roding, Essex.
Bristol Trade Antiques, Bristol, Glos.
The Barn, Petersfield, Hants.
Brun Lea Antiques, Burnley, Lancs.
Brun Lea Antiques (J. Waite Ltd), Burnley, Lancs.
West Lancs. Antique Exports, Burscough, Lancs.
P.J. Brown Antiques, Haslingden, Lancs.
Fernlea Antiques, Manchester, Lancs.
R.J. O'Brien and Son Antiques Ltd, Manchester, Lancs.
G G Antique Wholesalers Ltd, Middleton Village, Lancs.
Tyson's Antiques Ltd, Morecambe, Lancs.
John Robinson Antiques, Wigan, Lancs.
Trade Antiques, Alford, Lincs.
Grantham Furniture Emporium, Grantham, Lincs.
C. and K.E. Dring, Lincoln, Lincs.
Antique & Secondhand Traders, Lound, Lincs.
Swainbanks Ltd, Liverpool, Merseyside.
Molloy's Furnishers Ltd, Southport, Merseyside.
The Original British American Antiques, Southport, Merseyside.
Tony and Anne Sutcliffe Antiques, Southport, Merseyside.
Antiques Warehouse (Uxbridge), Uxbridge, Middx.
Pearse Lukies, Aylsham, Norfolk.
Bryan Perkins Antiques, Great Cransley, Northants.
T. Baker, Langford, Notts.
Red Lodge Antiques, Screveton, Notts.
Mitre House Antiques, Ludlow, Shrops.
M.G.R. Exports, Bruton, Somerset.
J.C. Giddings, Wiveliscombe, Somerset.
Brett Wilkins Ltd, Lichfield, Staffs.
Goodbreys, Framlingham, Suffolk.
A. Abbott Antiques Ltd, Ipswich, Suffolk.
The Edwardian Shop, Ipswich, Suffolk.
Laurence Tauber Antiques, Surbiton, Surrey.
The Old Mint House, Pevensey, Sussex East.
Monarch Antiques, St. Leonards-on-Sea, Sussex East.
Peter Smith Antiques, Sunderland, Tyne and Wear.
Martin Taylor Antiques, Wolverhampton, West Mids.
North Wilts Exporters, Brinkworth, Wilts.
Cross Hayes Antiques, Chippenham, Wilts.
Pillars Antiques, Lyneham, Wilts.
Alan Ramsey Antiques, Stokesley, Yorks. North.
Roger Appleyard Ltd, Mexborough, Yorks. South.
Philip Turnor Antiques, Rotherham, Yorks. South.

Dronfield Antiques, Sheffield, Yorks. South.
N.P. and A. Salt Antiques, Sheffield, Yorks. South.
Times Past Antiques, Auchterarder, Scotland.
Imrie Antiques, Bridge of Earn, Scotland.
Georgian Antiques, Edinburgh, Scotland.
Narducci Antiques, Largs, Scotland.
Narducci Antiques, Saltcoats, Scotland.

Silver & Jewellery
George Rankin Coin Co. Ltd, London E2.
Jonathan Harris (Jewellery) Ltd, London EC1.
Hirsh Ltd, London EC1.
Joseph and Pearce Ltd, London EC1.
A.R. Ullmann Ltd, London EC1.
Searle and Co Ltd, London EC3.
Eclectica, London N1.
John Laurie (Antiques) Ltd, London N1.
Piers Rankin, London N1.
Tadema Gallery, London N1.
J.H. Bourdon-Smith Ltd, London SW1.
Cobra and Bellamy, London SW1.
Cornucopia, London SW1.
Kenneth Davis (Works of Art) Ltd, London SW1.
Alastair Dickenson Ltd, London SW1.
N. and I. Franklin, London SW1.
Harvey and Gore, London SW1.
Longmire Ltd (Three Royal Warrants), London SW1.
Nigel Milne Ltd, London SW1.
thesilverfund.com, London SW1.
Mary Cooke Antiques Ltd, London SW14.
James Hardy and Co, London SW3.
McKenna and Co, London SW3.
Christine Schell, London SW3.
Gordon Watson Ltd, London SW3.
M.P. Levene Ltd, London SW7.
A. & H. Page (Est. 1840), London SW7.
Fay Lucas Artmetal, London SW8.
A.D.C. Heritage Ltd, London W1.
Armour-Winston Ltd, London W1.
Paul Bennett, London W1.
Bentley & Skinner, London W1.
Daniel Bexfield Antiques, London W1.
Bruford & Heming Ltd, London W1.
John Bull (Antiques) Ltd JB Silverware, London W1.
Carrington and Co. Ltd, London W1.
Sandra Cronan Ltd, London W1.
A. B. Davis Ltd, London W1.
Thomas Goode and Co (London) Ltd, London W1.
Simon Griffin Antiques Ltd, London W1.
Hancocks and Co, London W1.
Hirsh London, London W1.
Holmes Ltd, London W1.
Johnson Walker & Tolhurst Ltd, London W1.
D.S. Lavender (Antiques) Ltd, London W1.
Marks Antiques, London W1.
Moira, London W1.
Richard Ogden Ltd, London W1.
A. Pash & Sons, London W1.
S.J. Phillips Ltd, London W1.

David Richards and Sons, London W1.
Michael Rose - Source of the Unusual, London W1.
Tessiers Ltd, London W1.
Wartski Ltd, London W1.
Central Gallery (Portobello), London W11.
Portobello Antique Store, London W11.
Schredds of Portobello, London W11.
The Silver Fox Gallery (Portobello), London W11.
Craven Gallery, London W2.
H. and W. Deutsch Antiques, London W8.
Green's Antique Galleries, London W8.
Howard-Jones - The Silver Shop, London W8.
John Jesse, London W8.
Lev (Antiques) Ltd, London W8.
B. Silverman, London W8.
Koopman Ltd & Rare Art (London) Ltd, London WC2.
The London Silver Vaults, London WC2.
The Silver Mouse Trap, London WC2.
Styles Silver, Hungerford, Berks.
Berkshire Antiques Co Ltd, Windsor, Berks.
Turks Head Antiques, Windsor, Berks.
Buckies, Cambridge, Cambs.
Cameo Antiques, Chester, Cheshire.
Kayes of Chester, Chester, Cheshire.
Lowe and Sons, Chester, Cheshire.
D.J. Massey and Son, Macclesfield, Cheshire.
Romiley Antiques & Jewellery, Romiley, Cheshire.
Imperial Antiques, Stockport, Cheshire.
Little Jem's, Penzance, Cornwall.
Saint Nicholas Galleries Ltd. (Antiques and Jewellery),
  Carlisle, Cumbria.
Elizabeth and Son, Ulverston, Cumbria.
Moor Antiques, Ashburton, Devon.
Mark Parkhouse Antiques and Jewellery, Barnstaple,
  Devon.
David J. Thorn, Budleigh Salterton, Devon.
Ivor Doble Ltd, Exeter, Devon.
Mortimers, Exeter, Devon.
Otter Antiques, Honiton, Devon.
Extence Antiques, Teignmouth, Devon.
G.B. Mussenden and Son Antiques, Jewellery and
  Silver, Bournemouth, Dorset.
R.E. Porter, Bournemouth, Dorset.
Tregoning Antiques, Bournemouth, Dorset.
Batten's Jewellers, Bridport, Dorset.
Greystoke Antiques, Sherborne, Dorset.
Henry Willis (Antique Silver), Sherborne, Dorset.
Georgian Gems Antique Jewellers, Swanage, Dorset.
Heirlooms Antique Jewellers and Silversmiths,
  Wareham, Dorset.
James Hardy Antiques Ltd, Barnard Castle, Durham.
Robin Finnegan (Jeweller), Darlington, Durham.
E. J. Markham & Son Ltd, Colchester, Essex.
J. Streamer Antiques, Leigh-on-Sea, Essex.
Hedingham Antiques, Sible Hedingham, Essex.
Whichcraft Jewellery, Writtle, Essex.
Peter and Penny Proudfoot, Berkeley, Glos.
Caledonian Antiques, Bristol, Glos.
Grey-Harris and Co, Bristol, Glos.

Kemps, Bristol, Glos.
Jan Morrison, Bristol, Glos.
Greens of Cheltenham Ltd, Cheltenham, Glos.
Martin and Co. Ltd, Cheltenham, Glos.
Sodbury Antiques, Chipping Sodbury, Glos.
Walter Bull and Son (Cirencester) Ltd, Cirencester,
  Glos.
Howards of Moreton, Moreton-in-Marsh, Glos.
A.W. Porter and Son, Hartley Wintney, Hants.
Barry Papworth, Lymington, Hants.
Meg Campbell, Southampton, Hants.
Abbey Fine Jewellery & Silver, Hemel Hempstead,
  Herts.
Flagstaff Antiques, Cowes, Isle of Wight.
R. J. Baker, Canterbury, Kent.
Owlets, Hythe, Kent.
Gem Antiques, Maidstone, Kent.
Kaizen International Ltd, Rochester, Kent.
Gem Antiques, Sevenoaks, Kent.
Chapel Place Antiques, Tunbridge Wells, Kent.
Payne & Son (Silversmiths) Ltd, Tunbridge Wells,
  Kent.
Vintage Jewels, Westerham, Kent.
The Coin and Jewellery Shop, Accrington, Lancs.
Ancient and Modern, Blackburn, Lancs.
Brittons - Watches and Antiques, Clitheroe, Lancs.
Leigh Jewellery, Leigh, Lancs.
Cathedral Jewellers, Manchester, Lancs.
St. James Antiques, Manchester, Lancs.
Charles Howell Jeweller, Oldham, Lancs.
Marks Jewellers and Antique Dealers, Oldham, Lancs.
H.C. Simpson and Sons Jewellers (Oldham)Ltd,
  Oldham, Lancs.
Keystone Antiques, Coalville, Leics.
Corry's Antiques, Leicester, Leics.
Stanley Hunt Jewellers Ltd, Gainsborough, Lincs.
Marcus Wilkinson, Grantham, Lincs.
Rowletts of Lincoln, Lincoln, Lincs.
James Usher and Son Ltd, Lincoln, Lincs.
Marcus Wilkinson, Sleaford, Lincs.
Dawson of Stamford Ltd, Stamford, Lincs.
C. Rosenberg, Heswall, Merseyside.
Edward's Jewellers, Liverpool, Merseyside.
Weldons Jewellery and Antiques, Southport,
  Merseyside.
Bond Street Antiques, Cromer, Norfolk.
Folkes Antiques and Jewellers, Great Yarmouth,
  Norfolk.
Peter and Valerie Howkins Jewellers, Great Yarmouth,
  Norfolk.
Wheatleys, Great Yarmouth, Norfolk.
Tim Clayton Jewellery Ltd, King's Lynn, Norfolk.
Albrow and Sons Family Jewellers, Norwich, Norfolk.
Clive Dennett Coins, Norwich, Norfolk.
Leona Levine Silver Specialist, Norwich, Norfolk.
Maddermarket Antiques, Norwich, Norfolk.
Oswald Sebley, Norwich, Norfolk.
Timgems, Norwich, Norfolk.
Tombland Jewellers & Silversmiths, Norwich, Norfolk.

Parriss, Sheringham, Norfolk.
Michael Jones Jeweller, Northampton, Northants.
M B G Antiques, Fine Art & Jewellery, Newark, Notts.
D.D. and A. Ingle, Nottingham, Notts.
Melville Kemp Ltd, Nottingham, Notts.
Stanley Hunt Jewellers, Retford, Notts.
Reginald Davis Ltd, Oxford, Oxon.
Payne and Son (Goldsmiths) Ltd, Oxford, Oxon.
MGJ Jewellers Ltd., Wallingford, Oxon.
English Heritage, Bridgnorth, Shrops.
E.P. Mallory and Son Ltd, Bath, Somerset.
Castle Antiques, Burnham-on-Sea, Somerset.
M.G. Welch Jeweller, Taunton, Somerset.
Winston Mac (Silversmith), Bury St. Edmunds, Suffolk.
Robin Butler, Clare, Suffolk.
A. Abbott Antiques Ltd, Ipswich, Suffolk.
Temptations, Ashtead, Surrey.
Scotts of Dorking, Dorking, Surrey.
Temptations, Antique Jewellery & Silver, Dorking,
    Surrey.
Cry for the Moon, Guildford, Surrey.
Glydon and Guess Ltd, Kingston-upon-Thames, Surrey.
Horton, Richmond, Surrey.
S. Warrender and Co, Sutton, Surrey.
Church House Antiques, Weybridge, Surrey.
Not Just Silver, Weybridge, Surrey.
Harry Diamond and Son, Brighton, Sussex East.
Paul Goble Jewellers, Brighton, Sussex East.
Douglas Hall Ltd, Brighton, Sussex East.
Hallmark Jewellers, Brighton, Sussex East.
Harry Mason, Brighton, Sussex East.
W. Bruford, Eastbourne, Sussex East.
Trade Wind, Rottingdean, Sussex East.
Peter Hancock Antiques, Chichester, Sussex West.
Rathbone Law, Chichester, Sussex West.
Nicholas Shaw Antiques, Petworth, Sussex West.
A.C. Silver, Jesmond, Tyne and Wear.
Davidson's The Jewellers Ltd, Newcastle-upon-Tyne,
    Tyne and Wear.
Howards Jewellers, Stratford-upon-Avon, Warks.
George Pragnell Ltd, Stratford-upon-Avon, Warks.
Russell Lane Antiques, Warwick, Warks.
R. Collyer, Birmingham, West Mids.
Maurice Fellows, Birmingham, West Mids.
Rex Johnson and Sons, Birmingham, West Mids.
Piccadilly Jewellers, Birmingham, West Mids.
Cross Keys Jewellers, Devizes, Wilts.
Magpie Jewellers and Antiques and Magpie Arms &
    Armour, Evesham, Worcs.
B.B.M. Coins., Kidderminster, Worcs.
Lower House Fine Antiques, Redditch, Worcs.
Bygones by the Cathedral, Worcester, Worcs.
Guest & Philips, Beverley, Yorks. East.
Karen Guest Antiques, Driffield, Yorks. East.
Carlton Hollis Ltd, Harrogate, Yorks. North.
Ogden Harrogate Ltd, Harrogate, Yorks. North.
Castle Gate Antiques, Helmsley, Yorks. North.
Mary Milnthorpe and Daughters Antique Shop, Settle,
    Yorks. North.

Barbara Cattle, York, Yorks. North.
Golden Memories of York, York, Yorks. North.
Geoff Neary (incorporating Fillans Antiques Ltd),
    Huddersfield, Yorks. West.
Jack Shaw and Co, Ilkley, Yorks. West.
Aladdin's Cave, Leeds, Yorks. West.
N. St. J. Paint & Sons Ltd, St Peter Port, Guernsey, C.I.
Ray & Scott Ltd, St Sampson, Guernsey, C.I.
A. & R. Ritchie, St. Helier, Jersey, C.I.
Robert's Antiques, St Helier, Jersey, C.I.
Dunluce Antiques, Bushmills, Co. Antrim, N. Ireland.
Brian R. Bolt Antiques, Portballintrae, Co. Antrim, N.
    Ireland.
Cookstown Antiques, Cookstown, Co. Tyrone, N.
    Ireland.
McCalls (Aberdeen), Aberdeen, Scotland.
McCalls Limited, Aberdeen, Scotland.
Treasures of Ballater & Rowan Antiques, Ballater,
    Scotland.
Joseph Bonnar, Jewellers, Edinburgh, Scotland.
Bow-well Antiques, Edinburgh, Scotland.
Goodwin's Antiques Ltd, Edinburgh, Scotland.
Royal Mile Curios, Edinburgh, Scotland.
John Whyte, Edinburgh, Scotland.
Cathedral Antiques, Fortrose, Scotland.
A.D. Hamilton and Co, Glasgow, Scotland.
Jeremy Sniders Antiques, Glasgow, Scotland.
Kilmacolm Antiques Ltd, Kilmacolm, Scotland.
Harper-James, Montrose, Scotland.
Hardie Antiques, Perth, Scotland.
Henderson, Perth, Scotland.
Abbey Antiques, Stirling, Scotland.
Hazel of Brecon & Silvertime, Brecon, Wales.

Sporting Items & Associated Memorabilia
Holland & Holland, London W1.
Sean Arnold Sporting Antiques, London W2.
Below Stairs of Hungerford, Hungerford, Berks.
Sir William Bentley Billiards (Antique Billiard Table
    Specialist Company), Hungerford, Berks.
David Bedale, Mobberley, Cheshire.
Dolphin Antiques, Beer, Devon.
John Burton Natural Craft Taxidermy, Ebrington, Glos.
Hamilton Billiards & Games Co., Knebworth, Herts.
Halstead Antiques, Bromley, Kent.
Sporting Antiques, Tunbridge Wells, Kent.
Books Etc., Cromer, Norfolk.
Manfred Schotten Antiques, Burford, Oxon.
Quillon Antiques of Tetsworth, Tetsworth, Oxon.
Billiard Room Antiques, Chilcompton, Somerset.
Academy Billiard Company, West Byfleet, Surrey.
Burman Antiques, Stratford-upon-Avon, Warks.
Grant Books, Droitwich, Worcs.
Dunkeld Antiques, Dunkeld, Scotland.
The David Brown (St. Andrews) Gallery, St. Andrews,
    Scotland.
Old Troon Sporting Antiques, Troon, Scotland.

Sporting Paintings & Prints
Swan Fine Art, London N1.
Ackermann & Johnson, London SW1.
Frost and Reed Ltd (Est. 1808), London SW1.
Paul Mason Gallery, London SW1.
Tryon Gallery (incorporating Malcolm Innes), London SW1.
Old Church Galleries, London SW3.
Richard Green, London W1.
Holland & Holland, London W1.
Iona Antiques, London W8.
Grosvenor Prints, London WC2.
The Heritage Gallery, Tetbury, Glos.
Coltsfoot Gallery, Leominster, Herefs.
Marrin's Bookshop, Folkestone, Kent.
Sporting Antiques, Tunbridge Wells, Kent.
Paul Hopwell Antiques, West Haddon, Northants.
Sally Mitchell's Gallery, Tuxford, Notts.
H.C. Dickins, Bloxham, Oxon.
Quillon Antiques of Tetsworth, Tetsworth, Oxon.
Julian Armytage, Crewkerne, Somerset.
Julia Holmes Antique Maps and Prints, South Harting, Sussex West.
Anthony Woodd Gallery Ltd, Edinburgh, Scotland.

Stamps
Argyll Etkin Gallery, London W1.
Michael Coins, London W8.
Spink and Son Ltd, London WC1.
Stanley Gibbons, London WC2.
Penrith Coin and Stamp Centre, Penrith, Cumbria.
Jeremy's (Oxford Stamp Centre), Oxford, Oxon.
Bath Stamp and Coin Shop, Bath, Somerset.
Corbitt Stamps Ltd, Newcastle-upon-Tyne, Tyne and Wear.
J. Smith, York, Yorks. North.
Edinburgh Coin Shop, Edinburgh, Scotland.

Tapestries, Textiles & Needlework
Meg Andrews, London N1.
Annie's Vintage Costume & Textiles, London N1.
Alexander Juran and Co, London N4.
Joseph Lavian, London N4.
Gallery of Antique Costume and Textiles, London NW8.
Anno Domini Antiques, London SW1.
Antiquus, London SW1.
S. Franses Ltd, London SW1.
Joss Graham Oriental Textiles, London SW1.
Keshishian, London SW1.
Peta Smyth - Antique Textiles, London SW1.
The Dining Room Shop, London SW13.
Tobias and The Angel, London SW13.
Joanna Booth, London SW3.
Orientalist, London SW3.
Robert Stephenson, London SW3.
Antiques and Things, London SW4.
Christopher Bangs Ltd, London SW6.
Lunn Antiques Ltd, London SW6.
Perez Antique Carpets Gallery, London SW6.

Polonaise Gallery, London SW7.
John Eskenazi Ltd, London W1.
C. John (Rare Rugs) Ltd, London W1.
Partridge Fine Arts plc, London W1.
Pelham Galleries Ltd, London W1.
Linda Wrigglesworth Ltd, London W1.
A. Zadah, London W1.
Sheila Cook Textiles, London W11.
Rezai Persian Carpets, London W11.
Virginia, London W11.
Jonathan Horne, London W8.
Storm Fine Arts Ltd, Great Shelford, Cambs.
The House that Moved, Exeter, Devon.
The Honiton Lace Shop, Honiton, Devon.
Robson's Antiques, Barnard Castle, Durham.
Catherine Shinn Decorative Textiles, Cheltenham, Glos.
Anthony Hazledine, Fairford, Glos.
Huntington Antiques Ltd, Stow-on-the-Wold, Glos.
Queens Parade Antiques Ltd, Stow-on-the-Wold, Glos.
Teagowns & Textiles, Leominster, Herefs.
Farmhouse Antiques, Bolton-by-Bowland, Lancs.
Past Caring Vintage Clothing, Holt, Norfolk.
Country and Eastern Ltd., Norwich, Norfolk.
Witney Antiques, Witney, Oxon.
Antique Textiles & Lighting, Bath, Somerset.
Haliden Oriental Rug Shop, Bath, Somerset.
Ann King, Bath, Somerset.
Susannah, Bath, Somerset.
Avon Antiques, Bradford-on-Avon, Wilts.
Penny Farthing Antiques, North Cave, Yorks. East.
London House Oriental Rugs and Carpets, Boston Spa, Yorks. West.
Echoes, Todmorden, Yorks. West.
Hand in Hand, Coldstream, Scotland.

Taxidermy
Get Stuffed, London N1.
Below Stairs of Hungerford, Hungerford, Berks.
John Burton Natural Craft Taxidermy, Ebrington, Glos.
Quillon Antiques of Tetsworth, Tetsworth, Oxon.
Heads 'n' Tails, Wiveliscombe, Somerset.
The Enchanted Aviary, Bury St. Edmunds, Suffolk.
A.F.J. Turner Antiques, East Molesey, Surrey.
Hawkins & Hawkins, Edinburgh, Scotland.

Tools including Needlework & Sewing
Woodville Antiques, Hamstreet, Kent.
Norton Antiques, Twyford, Norfolk.
Trinders' Fine Tools, Clare, Suffolk.
Roy Arnold, Needham Market, Suffolk.
The Tool Shop, Needham Market, Suffolk.
Peppers Period Pieces, Wattisfield, Suffolk.

Toys - see Dolls

Trade Dealers - see Shipping Goods

Treen
Robert Young Antiques, London SW11.

Halcyon Days, London W1.
Phoenix Antiques, Fordham, Cambs.
A.P. and M.A. Haylett, Outwell, Cambs.
Baggott Church Street Ltd, Stow-on-the-Wold, Glos.
Peter Norden Antiques, Tetbury, Glos.
Prichard Antiques, Winchcombe, Glos.
Millers of Chelsea Antiques Ltd, Ringwood, Hants.
Brian and Caroline Craik Ltd, Bath, Somerset.
Peppers Period Pieces, Wattisfield, Suffolk.
Moxhams Antiques, Bradford-on-Avon, Wilts.
Stephen Cook Antiques, Broadway, Worcs.
Fenwick and Fenwick Antiques, Broadway, Worcs.
Michael Green Pine & Country Antiques, Harrogate, Yorks. North.
Brian R. Bolt Antiques, Portballintrae, Co. Antrim, N. Ireland.
Islwyn Watkins, Knighton, Wales.

Vintage Cars - see Cars and Carriages

Watercolours
Gladwell and Company, London EC4.
Finchley Fine Art Galleries, London N12.
Lauri Stewart - Fine Art, London N2.
Angela Hone Watercolours, London NW1.
Newhart (Pictures) Ltd, London NW3.
Gallery Kaleidoscope incorporating Scope Antiques, London NW6.
The Greenwich Gallery, London SE10.
Ackermann & Johnson, London SW1.
John Adams Fine Art Ltd, London SW1.
Chris Beetles Ltd, London SW1.
Miles Wynn Cato, London SW1.
Douwes Fine Art Ltd, London SW1.
Victor Franses Gallery, London SW1.
Frost and Reed Ltd (Est. 1808), London SW1.
Martyn Gregory, London SW1.
Moreton Contemporary Art Ltd, London SW1.
Oakham Gallery, London SW1.
Old Maps and Prints, London SW1.
Paisnel Gallery, London SW1.
Michael Parkin Fine Art Ltd, London SW1.
Royal Exchange Art Gallery, London SW1.
Bill Thomson - Albany Gallery, London SW1.
Waterman Fine Art Ltd, London SW1.
Hollywood Road Gallery, London SW10.
Offer Waterman and Co. Fine Art, London SW10.
Park Walk Gallery, London SW10.
Regent House Gallery, London SW11.
John Spink, London SW13.
The David Curzon Gallery, London SW19.
20th Century Gallery, London SW6.
Agnew's, London W1.
Victor Arwas Gallery - Editions Graphiques Gallery Ltd, London W1.
Andrew Clayton-Payne Ltd, London W1.
Connaught Brown plc, London W1.
The Fine Art Society plc, London W1.
Maas Gallery, London W1.

Mallett and Son (Antiques) Ltd, London W1.
Mallett Gallery, London W1.
John Mitchell and Son, London W1.
Piccadilly Gallery, London W1.
Waterhouse and Dodd, London W1.
Crawley and Asquith Ltd, London W10.
Charles Daggett Gallery, London W11.
Milne and Moller, London W11.
Justin F. Skrebowski Prints, London W11.
Richard Nagy Fine Art Ltd, London W2.
Campbell's of London, London W7.
Pawsey and Payne, London W8.
Abbott and Holder Ltd, London WC1.
Michael Finney Antique Prints and Books, London WC1.
Graham Gallery, Burghfield Common, Berks.
J. Manley, Windsor, Berks.
Windmill Fine Art, High Wycombe, Bucks.
Penn Barn, Penn, Bucks.
Cambridge Fine Art Ltd, Cambridge, Cambs.
Storm Fine Arts Ltd, Great Shelford, Cambs.
Baron Fine Art, Chester, Cheshire.
Lion Gallery and Bookshop, Knutsford, Cheshire.
Copperhouse Gallery - W. Dyer & Sons, Hayle, Cornwall.
Tony Sanders Penzance Gallery and Antiques, Penzance, Cornwall.
Peter Haworth, Sandside, Cumbria.
Medina Gallery, Barnstaple, Devon.
J. Collins and Son Fine Art, Bideford, Devon.
Cooper Gallery, Bideford, Devon.
Godolphin, Chagford, Devon.
Mill Gallery, Ermington, Devon.
Honiton Fine Art, Honiton, Devon.
Skeaping Gallery, Lydford, Devon.
Devonshire Fine Art, Modbury, Devon.
Michael Wood Fine Art, Plymouth, Devon.
Hampshire Gallery, Bournemouth, Dorset.
The Swan Gallery, Sherborne, Dorset.
Margaret Bedi Antiques & Fine Art, Stockton-on-Tees, Durham.
T.B. and R. Jordan (Fine Paintings), Stockton-on-Tees, Durham.
Brandler Galleries, Brentwood, Essex.
Neil Graham Gallery, Brentwood, Essex.
S. Bond and Son, Colchester, Essex.
Totteridge Gallery, Earls ColneEssex.
Barling Fine Porcelain Ltd, Wickham Bishops, Essex.
Cleeve Picture Framing, Bishops Cleeve, Glos.
Alexander Gallery, Bristol, Glos.
The Loquens Gallery, Cheltenham, Glos.
Manor House Gallery, Cheltenham, Glos.
School House Antiques, Chipping Campden, Glos.
The Roger Widdas Gallery, Moreton-in-Marsh, Glos.
Nina Zborowska, Painswick, Glos.
The Fosse Gallery, Stow-on-the-Wold, Glos.
Kenulf Fine Arts, Stow-on-the-Wold, Glos.
Roger Lamb Antiques & Works of Art, Stow-on-the-Wold, Glos.

Styles of Stow, Stow-on-the-Wold, Glos.
The Titian Gallery, Stow-on-the-Wold, Glos.
Laurence Oxley Ltd, Alresford, Hants.
J. Morton Lee, Hayling Island, Hants.
Century Fine Arts, Lymington, Hants.
The Petersfield Bookshop, Petersfield, Hants.
The Wykeham Gallery, Stockbridge, Hants.
Bell Fine Art, Winchester, Hants.
Lacewing Fine Art Gallery, Winchester, Hants.
Coltsfoot Gallery, Leominster, Herefs.
The Shanklin Gallery, Shanklin, Isle of Wight.
Cranbrook Gallery, Cranbrook, Kent.
Francis Iles, Rochester, Kent.
Langley Galleries Ltd, Rochester, Kent.
Sundridge Gallery, Sundridge, Kent.
Redleaf Gallery, Tunbridge Wells, Kent.
Apollo Antique Galleries, Westerham, Kent.
Fulda Gallery Ltd, Manchester, Lancs.
P. Stanworth (Fine Arts), Market Bosworth, Leics.
Coughton Galleries Ltd, Market Harborough, Leics.
Graftons of Market Harborough, Market Harborough, Leics.
The Boydell Galleries, Liverpool, Merseyside.
Crome Gallery and Frame Shop, Norwich, Norfolk.
The Fairhurst Gallery, Norwich, Norfolk.
Mandell's Gallery, Norwich, Norfolk.
The Westcliffe Gallery, Sheringham, Norfolk.
Staithe Lodge Gallery, Swafield, Norfolk.
Norton Antiques, Twyford, Norfolk.
Castle Ashby Gallery, Castle Ashby, Northants.
Anthony Mitchell Fine Paintings, Nottingham, Notts.
H.C. Dickins, Bloxham, Oxon.
Horseshoe Antiques and Gallery, Burford, Oxon.
Brian Sinfield Gallery Ltd, Burford, Oxon.
The Stone Gallery, Burford, Oxon.
Wren Gallery, Burford, Oxon.
The Barry Keene Gallery, Henley-on-Thames, Oxon.
Marc Oxley Fine Art, Uppingham, Rutland.
Adam Gallery Ltd, Bath, Somerset.
Chomé Fine Art, Bath, Somerset.
Trimbridge Galleries, Bath, Somerset.
The Sadler Street Gallery, Wells, Somerset.
England's Gallery, Leek, Staffs.
Thompson's Gallery, Aldeburgh, Suffolk.
J. and J. Baker, Lavenham, Suffolk.
Peasenhall Art and Antiques Gallery, Peasenhall, Suffolk.
Glencorse Antiques, Kingston-upon-Thames, Surrey.
Bourne Gallery Ltd, Reigate, Surrey.
Roland Goslett Gallery, Richmond, Surrey.
Marryat, Richmond, Surrey.
Sage Antiques and Interiors, Ripley, Surrey.
John Day of Eastbourne Fine Art, Eastbourne, Sussex East.
Nicholas Bowlby, Poundgate, Sussex East.
Chichester Gallery, Chichester, Sussex West.
The Canon Gallery, Petworth, Sussex West.
Wilsons Antiques, Worthing, Sussex West.
MacDonald Fine Art, Gosforth, Tyne and Wear.

Arden Gallery, Henley-in-Arden, Warks.
Fine-Lines (Fine Art), Shipston-on-Stour, Warks.
Oldswinford Gallery, Stourbridge, West Mids.
Driffold Gallery, Sutton Coldfield, West Mids.
Gallimaufry, Broadway, Worcs.
Richard Hagen, Broadway, Worcs.
Haynes Fine Art of Broadway, Broadway, Worcs.
John Noott Galleries, Broadway, Worcs.
The Highway Gallery, Upton-upon-Severn, Worcs.
James H. Starkey Galleries, Beverley, Yorks. East.
W. Greenwood (Fine Art), Burneston, Yorks. North.
Garth Antiques, Harrogate, Yorks. North.
McTague of Harrogate, Harrogate, Yorks. North.
Walker Galleries Ltd, Harrogate, Yorks. North.
E. Stacy-Marks Limited, Helmsley, Yorks. North.
Kirkgate Fine Art & Conservation, Thirsk, Yorks. North.
Coulter Galleries, York, Yorks. North.
Huddersfield Picture Framing Co, Huddersfield, Yorks. West.
Monkman Antiques, Otley, Yorks. West.
Robin Taylor Fine Arts, Wakefield, Yorks. West.
Beverley J. Pyke - Fine British Watercolours, Alderney, C.I.
Channel Islands Galleries Ltd, St. Peter Port, Guernsey, C.I.
Atelier Ltd, Grouville, Jersey, C.I.
Falle Fine Art Limited, St Helier, Jersey, C.I.
The Bell Gallery, Belfast, Co. Antrim, N. Ireland.
Phyllis Arnold Gallery Antiques, Donaghadee, Co. Down, N. Ireland.
The Rendezvous Gallery, Aberdeen, Scotland.
The McEwan Gallery, Ballater, Scotland.
The Gallery (Nigel Stacy-Marks Ltd), Blair Atholl, Scotland.
Calton Gallery, Edinburgh, Scotland.
Anthony Woodd Gallery Ltd, Edinburgh, Scotland.
Young Antiques, Edinburgh, Scotland.
The Roger Billcliffe Fine Art, Glasgow, Scotland.
Ewan Mundy Fine Art Ltd, Glasgow, Scotland.
Inchmartine Fine Art, Inchture, Scotland.
Mainhill Gallery, Jedburgh, Scotland.
Newburgh Antiques, Newburgh, Scotland.
Kirk Ports Gallery, North Berwick, Scotland.
St. Andrews Fine Art, St. Andrews, Scotland.
David Windsor Gallery, Bangor, Wales.
Michael Webb Fine Art, Bodorgan, Wales.
Rowles Fine Art, Welshpool, Wales.

Wholesale Dealers - see Shipping Goods

Wine Related Items
Christopher Sykes Antiques, Woburn, Beds.
Neil Willcox & Mark Nightingale, Penryn, Cornwall.
Malt House Antiques, Stow-on-the-Wold, Glos.
Robin Butler, Clare, Suffolk.
Andrew Jennings Antiques, Melksham, Wilts.

DEALERS' INDEX

In order to facilitate reference both the names of individuals and their business name are indexed separately. Thus A E Jones and C Smith of High Street Antiques will be indexed under:

Jones, A E, Town, County.
Smith, C, Town, County.
High Street Antiques, Town, County.

Bridges, Devon.
Alexander, Mrs M. and D., Portrush, Co. Antrim, N. Ireland.
Alexander, Peter, London W8.
Alexander, Tom, Castle Gate Antiques Centre, Newark, Notts.
Alexanders, Titchfield, Hants.
Alexandria Antiques, Brighton, Sussex East.
Alfandary, Alexandra, The Mall Antiques Arcade, London N1.
Alfies Antique Market, London NW8.
Alfred's "Old Curiosity Shop" and The Morris and Shirley Galleries, Mr., Southampton, Hants.
Alfreton Antiques Centre, Alfreton, Derbys.
Alice's, London W11.
Alicia Antiques, Lamb Arcade, Wallingford, Oxon
All Our Yesterdays & Chris Baker Gramophones, Sandwich, Kent.
All Our Yesterdays, Glasgow, Scotland.
Allam Antiques, Newbridge-on-Wye, Wales.
Allam, Paul, Newbridge-on-Wye, Wales.
Allan, Keith, Berwick-upon-Tweed, Northumbs.
Allcock, J. and P., Alcester, Warks.
Allcroft Antiques, Michael, Disley, Cheshire.
Allcroft Antiques, Michael, Hayfield, Derbys.
Allen Watch and Clockmaker, M., Four Oaks, West Mids.
Allen's (Branksome) Ltd, Branksome, Dorset.
Allen, Geoff, Lechlade, Glos.
Allen, M.A., Four Oaks, West Mids.
Allen, Mandy, Fakenham, Norfolk.
Allen, Martin, Brancaster Staithe, Norfolk.
Allen, N. and A., Moreton-in-Marsh, Glos.
Allenby, Mike, Sue and Ben, Uxbridge, Middx.
Allens, Chappells Antiques Centre, Bakewell, Derbys.
Allerston, Peter and Sonia, Chappells Antiques Centre, Bakewell, Derbys.
Allison, Paul, Preston, Lancs.
Allison, S.J., The Swan at Tetsworth, Oxon.
Allport-Lomax, Liz, Norwich, Norfolk.
Allsebrook, Robert, Ashbourne, Derbys.
Allsop, Duncan M., Warwick, Warks.
Allwright, C., Rochester, Kent.
Almshouses Arcade, Chichester, Sussex West.
Alpren, S.A., Solihull, West Mids.
Alston Antiques, Alston, Cumbria.
Altamiradeco, Bournemouth, Dorset.
Altea Gallery, London W1.
AM-PM, Antiquarius, London SW3.
Amadeus Antiques, Tunbridge Wells, Kent.
Amati, E., London SW1.
Amato, Alexia, Antiquarius, London SW3.
Amazing Grates - Fireplaces Ltd, London N2.
Amber Antiques, Southampton, Hants.

Ambergate Antiques, A.A., Ripley, Derbys.
Åmell Ltd, Verner, London SW1.
Amor Ltd, Albert, London SW1.
Amphora Galleries, Balfron, Scotland.
Ampthill Antiques Emporium, Ampthill, Beds.
Ampthill Antiques, Ampthill, Beds.
Amstad, R.J., Hastings Antique Centre, St. Leonards-on-Sea, E. Sussex
Amstad, R.J., St. Leonards-on-Sea, Sussex East.
Anchor Antiques Ltd, London WC2.
Ancient & Oriental Ltd, Grimston, Leics.
Ancient and Modern, Blackburn, Lancs.
Ancient and Oriental Ltd, Durham House Antiques Centre, Stow-on-the-Wold, Glos.
& Barrington, Castle Gate Antiques Centre, Newark, Notts.
And So To Bed Limited, London SW6.
Andersen, G. and V., London W8.
Anderson and Son, F.E., Welshpool, Wales.
Anderson, Gillian, Corbridge, Northumbs.
Anderson, I., Welshpool, Wales.
Anderson, Mark and June, Totnes, Devon.
Anderson, Mr and Mrs A., Bath, Somerset.
Anderton, K. and J., Darwen, Lancs.
Andipa Gallery, The, London SW3.
Andrew, Tony, Llanerchymedd, Wales.
Andrews Antiques, Paul, The Furniture Cave, London SW10
Andrews Gallery, Stephen, St Peter Port, Guernsey, C.I.
Andrews, D.A. and J.P., Bristol, Glos.
Andrews, Devonia, Bristol, Glos.
Andrews, Meg, London N1.
Angel Antiques, Petworth, Sussex West.
Angel Antiques, Redditch, Worcs.
Angel Arcade, The, London N1.
Angel Bookshop, The, North Walsham, Norfolk.
Angus Antiques, Dundee, Scotland.
Ann's Antiques, Stoke-on-Trent, Staffs.
Annette Antiques, Lincoln, Lincs.
Annie's Antiques, Farnham, Surrey.
Annie's Vintage Costume & Textiles, London N1.
Anno Domini Antiques, London SW1.
Annterior Antiques, Plymouth, Devon.
Anthea A.G. Antiques, Grays Antique Markets, London W1.
Anthemion - The Antique Shop, Cartmel, Cumbria.
Anthony James Antiques, Whimple, Devon.
Antichi, G. and M., London W11.
Antics, Almshouses Arcade, Chichester, Sussex West
Antik Dekor, Grays Antique Markets, London W1.
AntikWest AB, London W8.
Antiquarius of Ampthill, Ampthill, Beds.
Antiquarius, London SW3.
Antiquated, Petworth, Sussex West.
Antique & Secondhand Traders, Lound,

Lincs.
Antique and Collectors Market, Salisbury, Wilts.
Antique and Design, Canterbury, Kent.
Antique Barometer Co, The, The Mall Antiques Arcade, Lower Mall, London N1.
Antique Barometers, Ramsey, Cambs.
Antique Bed Company, Emsworth, Hants.
Antique Bed Shop, Halstead, Essex.
Antique Buildings Ltd, Dunsfold, Surrey.
Antique Centre on the Quay, The, Exeter, Devon.
Antique Centre, Cleobury Mortimer, Shrops.
Antique Centre, The, Kidderminster, Worcs.
Antique Centre, The, Preston, Lancs.
Antique Chairs and Museum, Launceston, Cornwall.
Antique Church Furnishings, Walton-on-Thames, Surrey.
Antique Clocks by Patrick Thomas, Dorking, Surrey.
Antique Corner with A & C Antique Clocks, Bristol, Glos.
Antique Dining Room, The, Totnes, Devon.
Antique Exporters of Chester, Chester, Cheshire.
Antique Eyes, Stockbridge, Hants.
Antique Fireplace Warehouse, Manchester, Lancs.
Antique Fireplaces, Liverpool, Merseyside.
Antique Fireplaces, Tarvin, Cheshire.
Antique Furniture Warehouse, Stockport, Cheshire.
Antique Garden, The, Chester, Cheshire.
Antique Lamp Shop, The, London SW6.
Antique Map and Bookshop, Puddletown, Dorset.
Antique Map and Print Gallery, Hallow, Worcs.
Antique Map Shop Ltd, The, Bath, Somerset.
Antique Print Shop, Redbourn, Herts.
Antique Rooms, The, Maldon, Essex.
Antique Shop, The, Blaenau Ffestiniog, Wales.
Antique Shop, The, Bruton, Somerset.
Antique Shop, The, Godalming, Surrey.
Antique Shop, The, Kirkcudbright, Scotland.
Antique Shop, The, Langholm, Scotland.
Antique Shop, The, Llandudno, Wales.
Antique Shop, The, Sutton Bridge, Lincs.
Antique Textiles & Lighting, Bath, Somerset.
Antique Trader, The, London N1.
Antique Warehouse, Worcester, Worcs.
Antique, Electrical & Turret Clocks, Brixham, Devon.
Antiques & Collectables & Gun Shop, Scunthorpe, Lincs.
Antiques & Collectors Centre (Diss), The, Diss, Norfolk.
Antiques & Collectors Centre,

DEALERS' INDEX

Ashby-Arnold, Sara, Norton, Yorks. North.

Ashcombe Coach House, Henfield, Sussex West.

Ashe Antiques Warehouse, Wickham Market, Suffolk.

Ashford, Paul, LeyburnYorks. North.

Ashley Antiques, Tudor House, Stow-on-the-Wold, Glos

Ashton Gower Antiques, Stow-on-the-Wold, Glos.

Ashton's Antiques, Brighton, Sussex East.

Ashton, B., Stow-on-the-Wold, Glos.

Ashton, Chris, Top Banana Antiques Mall 2, Tetbury, Glos.

Ashton, John and Rhian, Bristol, Glos.

Ashton, Mark and Nikki, Bath, Somerset.

Ashton, R. and P., Brighton, Sussex East.

Askew, J.S., Lostwithiel, Cornwall.

Aslangul, Veronica, Enfield, Middx.

Aslanian, Michael, Ross-on-Wye, Herefs.

Aspidistra Antiques, Woking, Surrey.

Aspidistra, Uppingham, Rutland.

Aspinall Antiques Ltd, Walter, Sabden, Lancs.

Aspinall, Jane, Talbot Walk Antique Centre, Ripley, Surrey.

Asplin, D.C., Cambridge, Cambs.

Assad, Elias, Grays Antique Markets, London W1.

Assembly Rooms Market, The, Lancaster, Lancs.

Astley House - Contemporary, Moreton-in-Marsh, Glos.

Astley House - Fine Art, Moreton-in-Marsh, Glos.

Astley House - Fine Art, Stretton-on-Fosse, Warks.

Aston Antiques, Durham House Antiques Centre, Stow-on-the-Wold, Glos.

Aston Pine Antiques, Faringdon, Oxon.

Aston, C.D. and Mrs I., Fordingbridge, Hants.

Aston, Fiona, Ginnel Antiques Centre, The, Harrogate, Yorks. North.

Aston, Fiona, Red House Antiques Centre, York, Yorks. North.

Aston, S., Alnwick, Northumbs.

Astra House Antiques Centre, Hemswell Cliff, Lincs.

Atelier Ltd, Grouville, Jersey, C.I.

Athey, G.M., Alnwick, Northumbs.

Athill, Philip, London WC1.

Atholl Antiques, Aberdeen, Scotland.

Atighi, Grays Antique Markets, London W1.

Atkin, Miss D.J., Nantwich, Cheshire.

Atkin, Miss S.E., Froncysyllte, Wales.

Atkins, Fiona, London E1.

Atkins, Jonathan, London SE10.

Atkins, T. J., Taunton, Somerset.

Atlantic Antique Centres Ltd, London W1.

Atlantic Antiques Centres Ltd, London N1.

Atlantic Antiques Centres Ltd, London SW3.

Atlantis Bookshop, London WC1.

Attfield, David, Holt, Norfolk.

Attic Antiques & Pine, Saintfield, Co. Down, N. Ireland.

Attic, The, Baldock, Herts.

Attic, The, Newton Abbot, Devon.

Attic, The, Poynton, Cheshire.

Auldearn Antiques, Auldearn, Scotland.

Aura Antiques, Masham, Yorks. North.

Aurum Antiques, Grays Antique Markets, London W1.

Austin, Barbara, Chappells Antiques Centre, Bakewell, Derbys.

Austin, G., Winchester, Hants.

Austin, J., London WC1.

Austin-Cooper, Matthew, Angel Arcade, London N1.

Austin-Fell, A.J. and C.R., Holt, Norfolk.

Austin-Kaye, A.M., Chester, Cheshire.

Austin/Desmond Fine Art, London WC1.

Austwick, Paul, Sowerby Bridge, Yorks. West.

Autodrome, Almshouses Arcade, Chichester, Sussex West

Automotive Art, Red House Antiques Centre, York, Yorks. North.

Avon Antiques, Bradford-on-Avon, Wilts.

Avon House Antiques/Hayward's Antiques, Kingsbridge, Devon.

Avonbridge Antiques and Collectors Market, The, Salisbury, Wilts.

Avrick Antiques, Top Banana Antiques Mall 1, Tetbury, Glos.

Axia Art Consultants Ltd, London W11.

Ayres, Lynne, Wansford, Cambs.

Aytac Antiques, Grays Antique Markets, London W1.

B

B & T Engraving, Grays Antique Markets, London W1.

B and B Antiques, Stickney, Lincs.

B. and T. Antiques, London W11.

B.B.M. Coins, Kidderminster, Worcs.

B.C. Metalcrafts, London NW9.

B.R.M. Coins, Knutsford, Cheshire.

Back 2 Wood, Appledore, Kent.

Bacon, Edward, Red House Antiques Centre, York, Yorks. North

Bacou, Guillaume and Louise, London E1.

Baddiel, Colin, Grays Antique Markets, London W1.

Baddow Antique Centre, Great Baddow, Essex.

Badland, Miss, Bradford, Yorks. West.

Baggins Book Bazaar - The Largest Secondhand Bookshop in England, Rochester, Kent.

Baggott Church Street Ltd, Stow-on-the-Wold, Glos.

Baggott, D.J. and C.M., Stow-on-the-Wold, Glos.

Baggott, Duncan J., Stow-on-the-Wold, Glos.

Baggott, Lucy and Henry, Stow-on-the-Wold, Glos.

Bagham Barn Antiques, Chilham, Kent.

Bail, A., Ash Vale, Surrey.

Baildon Furniture Co. Ltd, The, Baildon, Yorks. West.

Baile de Laperriere, H., Calne, Wilts.

Bailey, M. and S., Ross-on-Wye, Herefs.

Baileys Home & Garden, Ross-on-Wye, Herefs.

Bailiffgate Antique Pine, Alnwick, Northumbs.

Baillie, Anthea, Windsor, Berks.

Baines, Henry and Anne, Southborough, Kent.

Baines, Henry, Southborough, Kent.

Baird, R. and V., Langholm, Scotland.

Bairsto, Peter, Tetbury, Glos.

Baker Antiques, G., Horncastle, Lincs.

Baker Asian Art, Gregg, London W8.

Baker Fine Arts, Antiquarius, London SW3.

Baker, David, Grays Antique Markets, London W1.

Baker, J. and J., Lavenham, Suffolk.

Baker, K.R., Woking, Surrey.

Baker, Keith, Woking, Surrey.

Baker, Mrs B.A.J., Lavenham, Suffolk.

Baker, R. J., Canterbury, Kent.

Baker, Sandie and Chris, Sandwich, Kent.

Baker, T., Langford, Notts.

Baker, T.R., Stockbridge, Hants.

Bakhtiyar Gallery, The, Stockbridge, Hants.

Baldock, David, Birmingham, West Mids.

Baldry, Mrs J., Great Yarmouth, Norfolk.

Baldwin and Sons Ltd, A.H., London WC2.

Baldwin, L., Nottingham, Notts.

Baldwin, M. and M., Cleobury Mortimer, Shrops.

Baldwin, R.E. and P.J., Scarborough, Yorks. North.

Baldwin, R.J.S., London SW3.

Baldwin, V.F.S. and J.F., Alcester, Warks.

Bale, Craig, Bath, Somerset.

Bale, Errin, Alton, Hants.

Bale, Vicki, Ditton Priors, Shrops.

Ball and Claw Antiques, Tetbury, Glos.

Ball, Ann and John, Porthcawl, Wales.

Ball, G., Tattershall, Lincs.

Ball, John M., Marlesford, Suffolk.

Balloo Moon, Bangor, Co. Down, N. Ireland.

Bampton Gallery, Bampton, Devon.

Bananarama, Top Banana Antiques Mall 1, Tetbury, Glos.

Banbury Antique Centre, Banbury, Oxon.

Banbury Fayre, London N1.

Bangs Ltd, Christopher, London SW6.

Bangs, Christopher, London SW6.

Bank House Gallery, The, Norwich, Norfolk.

Banks Antiques, Simon, Finedon, Northants.

Bannister FRGS, David, Cheltenham, Glos.

Bannister, Kate, Angel Arcade, London N1.

Barbagallo, Sebastiano, London SW6.

Barbagallo, Sebastiano, London W11.

Bee, Linda, Grays Antique Markets, London W1.
Beech House, Sheffield, Yorks. South.
Beech, Garland, London SW11.
Beech, J.M. and A.J., Sheffield, Yorks. South.
Beedham Antiques Ltd, Hungerford, Berks.
Beedle, D.W., Sheffield, Yorks. South.
Beehive, Petts Wood, Kent.
Beeney, C., Ryde, Isle of Wight.
Beer, John, London NW8.
Beer, Reginald and Jennifer, London E14.
Bees Antiques, Woodstock, Oxon.
Beesley, Mike, Leckhampstead, Berks.
Beetles Ltd, Chris, London SW1.
Begley-Gray, Margaret, Newark, Notts.
Behari, Mrs G., Olney, Bucks.
Behind the Boxes - Art Deco, London SE26.
Belcher Antiques, Robert, Droitwich, Worcs.
Belcher, David, Chipping Norton, Oxon.
Belcher, Robert & Wendy, Droitwich, Worcs.
Belgrave Antique Centre, Darwen, Lancs.
Belgrave Carpet Gallery Ltd, London SW1.
Bell Antiques, Grimsby, Lincs.
Bell Antiques, J. and H., Castletown, Isle of Man.
Bell Antiques, Romsey, Hants.
Bell Antiques, Twyford, Berks.
Bell Fine Art, Winchester, Hants.
Bell Gallery, The, Belfast, Co. Antrim, N. Ireland.
Bell, Aline, Petworth, Sussex West.
Bell, E., Cockermouth, Cumbria.
Bell, J.N., Belfast, Co. Antrim, N. Ireland.
Bell, John, Jesmond, Tyne and Wear.
Bell, L.E., Winchester, Hants.
Bell, Mrs J., Alston, Cumbria.
Bell, R. and N., York, Yorks. North.
Bellinger Antiques, C., Barnet, Herts.
Bellis, Michael J., Holt, Norfolk.
Bellum Antiques, Antiquarius, London SW3
Belmonts, London Silver Vaults, London WC2.
Below Stairs of Hungerford, Hungerford, Berks.
Belsten, R., Stiffkey, Norfolk.
Benarroch, A., Bournemouth, Dorset.
Benchmark Antiques, Bridport, Dorset.
Bender, Marion, Manningford Bruce, Wilts.
Bennett Ltd, Alan, Truro, Cornwall.
Bennett's Antiques & Collectables, Bedale, Yorks. North.
Bennett, Alan, London SE1.
Bennett, Caroline, South Molton, Devon.
Bennett, F.R., Shipston-on-Stour, Warks.
Bennett, Louise, Jesmond, Tyne and Wear.
Bennett, Paul and Kim, Bedale, Yorks. North.
Bennett, Paul, London W1.
Bennett, Richard, Thirsk, Yorks. North.

Benson, Jane and Julian, Stockbridge, Hants.
Bentley & Skinner, London W1.
Bentley Billiards (Antique Billiard Table Specialist Company), Sir William, Hungerford, Berks.
Bentley, M.R., Knutsford, Cheshire.
Benton Fine Art, Moreton-in-Marsh, Glos.
Benton, J.G., Moreton-in-Marsh, Glos.
Benton, Mrs P. A., Church Stretton, Shrops.
Beresiner, Yasha, London N3.
Berg, Barbara, Grays Antique Markets, London W1.
Berkeley Antiques Market, Berkeley, Glos.
Berkeley Antiques, Winchcombe, Glos.
Berkshire Antiques Co Ltd, Windsor, Berks.
Berktay, Y., Somerton, Somerset.
Berland's of Edinburgh, Edinburgh, Scotland.
Berney, G. and M., Pickering, Yorks. North.
Berry Antiques & Interiors, LongridgeLancs.
Berry Antiques Ltd, Moreton-in-Marsh, Glos.
Berry Antiques, Lesley, Flamborough, Yorks. East.
Berry, Chris, Moreton-in-Marsh, Glos.
Berry, F.E., Disley, Cheshire.
Berry, Helen and Michael, Porlock, Somerset.
Berry, Mrs L., Flamborough, Yorks. East.
Berthoud, N., Bridgnorth, Shrops.
Beskin, Geraldine and Bali, London WC1.
Besley, P.A. and P.F., Beccles, Suffolk.
Besleys Books, Beccles, Suffolk.
Bett, H., London W1
Better Days, Menai Bridge, Wales.
Bettney, Julian, Datchet, Berks.
Bevan, D., Stourbridge, West Mids.
Beverley R, Grays Antique Markets, London W1.
Beverley, London NW8.
Bevins, J.R., Ulverston, Cumbria.
Bewdley Antiques, Bewdley, Worcs.
Bexfield Antiques, Daniel, London W1.
Beyer, Jane and Gerd, London N1.
Beyer, Jane and Gerd, London SW6.
Bhalla, Mrs A., Lincoln, Lincs.
Bianco, L., Cheltenham, Glos.
Bibby, R., Leigh, Lancs.
Biblion, Grays Antique Markets, London W1.
Bichard, R., J. and N., Bradford-on-Avon, Wilts.
Bickford, Mr and Mrs D.M., Crediton, Devon.
Bicknell, Willow, Kington Langley, Wilts.
Biddulph, Peter, London W1.
Bieganski, Z., Woburn, Beds.
Bigden Fine Art, Edward, Debenham, Suffolk.
Bigden, Chris, Debenham, Suffolk.
Biggs Antiques, Paula, Durham House Antiques Centre, Stow-on-the-Wold,

Glos.
Biggs, J. and P., Bideford, Devon.
Bigwood Antiques, Brasted, Kent.
Bigwood, C., Tunbridge Wells, Kent.
Bigwood, Hazel, Talbot Walk Antique Centre, Ripley, Surrey.
Bigwood, S., Brasted, Kent.
Billcliffe Fine Art, The Roger, Glasgow, Scotland.
Billiard Room Antiques, Chilcompton, Somerset.
Billing, David, Antiquarius, London SW3.
Billington, J.L., Sabden, Lancs.
Biltoft, Philip, Top Banana Antiques Mall 3, Tetbury, Glos.
Bingham, Tony, London NW3.
Bingley Antiques, Haworth, Yorks. West.
Bingley Antiques, Robert, Wing, Rutland.
Bingley, Robert and Elizabeth, Wing, Rutland.
Birch, C., Great Yarmouth, Norfolk.
Birch, T., Cheltenham, Glos.
Bird, John, Petworth, Sussex West.
Bird, M.J. and P.J., Cirencester, Glos.
Bird, R.J., Cambridge, Cambs.
Birkdale Antiques, Southport, Merseyside.
Birkett, Keith, The Mall Antiques Arcade, Lower Mall, London N1.
Birmingham Antique Centre, The, Birmingham, West Mids.
Bishop, Jeanette and Norman, Cleethorpes, Lincs.
Bishopsgate Antiques, York, Yorks. North.
Bizarre Antiques, Bristol, Glos.
Bizarre, London NW8.
Bjs.Online.com/Bijoux Signes, Grays Antique Markets, London W1.
Black Carpets, David, London W2.
Black Dog Antiques, Bungay, Suffolk.
Black Ink, Stow-on-the-Wold, Glos.
Black, David, London W2.
Black, Oonagh, The Swan at Tetsworth, Oxon.
Blackbrook Antiques Village, Weeford, Staffs.
Blackburn, Joan and David, Clola by Mintlaw, Scotland.
Blackburn, Mrs E.M., Tunbridge Wells, Kent.
Blackburn, Mrs G., Lancaster, Lancs.
Blackburn, Norman, Stamford, Lincs.
Blacker, Sue, Top Banana Antiques Mall 1, Tetbury, Glos.
Blackford, M., Calne, Wilts.
Blackwater Pine Antiques, Truro, Cornwall.
Blackwell's Rare Books, Oxford, Oxon.
Blair Antiques, Blair Atholl, Scotland.
Blair, J., Guildford, Surrey.
Blair, J., St. Albans, Herts.
Blair, Julian, Oxford, Oxon.
Blairgowrie Books, Blairgowrie, Scotland.
Blairman and Sons Ltd., H., London W1.
Blake, J., J. and S.T., Puckeridge, Herts.
Blake, Mark W.J., Taunton, Somerset.

Clubb, A., Twickenham, Middx.
Clure, Steve, Jubilee Hall Antiques Centre, Lechlade, Glos.
Cluzan, M., Framlingham, Suffolk .
Clyde Antiques, Patrington, Yorks. East.
Coach House Antiques Centre, Canterbury, Kent.
Coach House Antiques Ltd, Stanley, Scotland.
Coach House Antiques, Hastings, Sussex East.
Coach House Antiques, Sleights, Yorks. North.
Coach House Antiques, The, Gomshall, Surrey.
Cobbled Yard, The, London N16.
Coblands Farm Antiques, Depden, Suffolk.
Cobra and Bellamy, London SW1.
Cobweb Antiques, Cullompton, Devon.
Cobweb Books, Thornton-le-Dale, Yorks. North.
Cobwebs of Lockerbie Ltd, Lockerbie, Scotland.
Cobwebs, Southampton, Hants.
Cockburn, F.J., Northwich, Cheshire.
Cockermouth Antiques Market, Cockermouth, Cumbria.
Cockermouth Antiques, Cockermouth, Cumbria.
Cockram, Mrs A., Lincoln, Lincs.
Cockram, T.A.M., Cowes, Isle of Wight.
Cockrell Antiques, Surbiton, Surrey.
Cockrell, Sheila and Peter, Surbiton, Surrey.
Cockton, Mrs L., London SE26.
Cocoa, Cheltenham, Glos.
Cocoa, Top Banana Antiques Mall 1, Tetbury, Glos.
Cocoa, Top Banana Antiques Mall 2, Tetbury, Glos.
Coffey, Norman and Margaret, Louth, Lincs.
Cohen & Cohen, London W8.
Cohen Numismatics, Philip, London WC2.
Cohen, A., Antiquarius, London SW3.
Cohen, Ewa and Michael, London W8.
Cohn, George and Peter, London WC1.
Coin and Jewellery Shop, The, Accrington, Lancs.
Coinage Hall Antiques Centre, The, Truro, Cornwall.
Coldstream Antiques, Coldstream, Scotland.
Colefax & John Fowler, Sibyl, London W1.
Coleman Antiques, Robin, Piccadilly Antiques, Batheaston, Somerset.
Coleman Antiques, Simon, London SW13.
Coleman, Garrick D., London W11.
Coleman, Garrick D., London W8.
Coleman, M.L., Maidenhead, Berks.
Coles, Gail and Zachary, Blackburn, Lancs.
Coles, Gerard, Old Bank Antiques Centre, Bath, Somerset.
Coles, Graham, Newport, Wales.
Coles, Lorna, Tetbury, Glos.
Coleshill Antiques and Interiors Ltd, Coleshill, Warks.

Coll, Mrs P., Long Melford, Suffolk.
Collard, B., Totnes, Devon.
Collards Books, Totnes, Devon.
Collectables, Honiton, Devon.
Collectables, Kingston-on-Spey, Scotland.
Collection Antiques, Grays Antique Markets, London W1.
Collector Limited, The, Barnet, Herts.
Collector's Corner, Truro, Cornwall.
Collector, The, Barnard Castle, Durham.
Collector, The, Clevedon, Somerset.
Collectors Centre - Antique City, London E17.
Collectors Centre, The, St Peter Port, Guernsey, C.I.
Collectors Choice, Modbury, Devon.
Collectors Corner, Almshouses Arcade, Chichester, Sussex West.
Collectors Corner, Carshalton, Surrey.
Collectors Corner, Northallerton, Yorks. North.
Collectors Corner, Southport Antiques Centre, Southport, Merseyside
Collectors Old Toy Shop and Antiques, Halifax, Yorks. West.
Collectors Shop, The, Edinburgh, Scotland.
Collectors World, Cromer, Norfolk.
Collectors World, Nottingham, Notts.
Collectors' Paradise, Leigh-on-Sea, Essex.
Collectors' Place, Shrewsbury, Shrops.
Colledge, John and Margaret, Hatton, Warks.
Collett, J., Chipping Campden, Glos.
Collett, Sylvie, Castle Gate Antiques Centre, Newark, Notts.
Collie, Mr and Mrs James, Uppingham, Rutland.
Collinge Antiques, Llandudno Junction, Wales.
Collinge, Nicky, Llandudno Junction, Wales.
Collingridge Antiques Ltd, Peter, Angel Arcade, London N1.
Collingridge, Jeremy, Tudor House, Stow-on-the-Wold, Glos
Collingridge, Peter, Stow-on-the-Wold, Glos.
Collingridge, Peter, Tudor House, Stow-on-the-Wold, Glos
Collings, B.L., Cambridge, Cambs.
Collins and Son Fine Art, J., Bideford, Devon.
Collins Antiques (F.G. and C. Collins Ltd.), Wheathampstead, Herts.
Collins, Andy, Totnes, Devon.
Collins, B.L., London Silver Vaults, London WC2.
Collins, Barry, London Silver Vaults, London WC2.
Collins, Edwin, Leominster, Herefs.
Collins, J, London W1.
Collins, J., Llanrwst, Wales.
Collins, Len and Mary, Barkham, Berks.
Collins, M.C., Wheathampstead, Herts.
Collins, Olivia Howard, Grays Antique Markets, London W1.
Collins, Tracey, Horncastle, Lincs.
Colliton Antique Centre, Dorchester, Dorset.

Collyer, Bryan, Durham House Antiques Centre, Stow-on-the-Wold, Glos.
Collyer, R., Birmingham, West Mids.
Colnaghi & Co Ltd, P. and D., London W1.
Colquhoun, Wayne, Liverpool, Merseyside.
Colt, R., Farnham, Surrey.
Coltman, B.J., Ginnel Antiques Centre, The, Harrogate, Yorks North
Colton Antiques, Kelvedon, Essex.
Colton, Gary, Kelvedon, Essex.
Coltsfoot Gallery, Leominster, Herefs.
Colyer, J.M., Wallasey, Merseyside.
Colyton Antiques Centre, Colyton, Devon.
Comben, Chris, Rait Village Antiques Centre, Scotland
Comberton Antiques and Interiors, Comberton, Cambs.
Comer, Mrs S., Shaftesbury, Dorset.
Complete Automobilist, The, Greatford, Lincs.
Conder, R., Grantham, Lincs.
Connaught Brown plc, London W1.
Connell - Wargrave Antiques, John, Wargrave, Berks.
Conquest House Antiques, Canterbury, Kent.
Conquest, Rosemary, London N1.
Constable, John, London SW15.
Conway, M.J., Colyton, Devon.
Conway, Pauline, Red House Antiques Centre, York, Yorks. North
Cook (Marlborough), William, Marlborough, Wilts.
Cook Antiques, Stephen, Broadway, Worcs.
Cook Textiles, Sheila, London W11.
Cook's Cottage Antiques, Ginnel Antiques Centre, The, Harrogate, Yorks North
Cook, Bob and Brenda, North Shields, Tyne and Wear.
Cook, Diana, Henley-on-Thames, Oxon.
Cook, K.J., Rochester, Kent.
Cook, W.J., Marlborough, Wilts.
Cooke Antiques Ltd, Mary, London SW14.
Cooke Antiques, Sandy, Long Melford, Suffolk.
Cooksey, Elizabeth and Brian, Colchester, Essex.
Cooksey, G.L., West Haddon, Northants.
Cookstown Antiques, Cookstown, Co. Tyrone, N. Ireland.
Coom, J., Devizes, Wilts.
Coombe Antiques, New Malden Surrey.
Coomber, P.C. and E., Newcastle Emlyn, Wales.
Coombes, J. and M., Dorking, Surrey.
Cooney, Martin and Elaine, Darwen, Lancs.
Cooper Antiques, John, St. Helier, Jersey, C.I.
Cooper Antiques, Val, Angel Arcade, London N1.
Cooper Fine Arts Ltd, Brasted, Kent.
Cooper Gallery, Bideford, Devon.
Cooper, Ben, Top Banana Antiques Mall 3, Tetbury, Glos.
Cooper, Charles and Jane, Ilkley, Yorks.

SW6.

Crewkerne Antique Centre, Crewkerne, Somerset.

Cricieth Gallery, Criccieth, Wales.

Crick Chandeliers, Mrs. M.E., London W8.

Cridland and Vivienne King, David, Tudor House, Stow-on-the-Wold, Glos

Cringle, M. and A., Burnham Market, Norfolk.

Cripps, Lilian, Penrith, Cumbria.

Crispin Antiques, Madeline, London NW1.

Critchlow, Nigel, Shardlow, Derbys.

Crocket, Sue, Brockenhurst, Hants.

Crockwell Antiques, Durham House Antiques Centre, Stow-on-the-Wold, Glos.

Crofts, Mrs Pat L., Wisbech, Cambs.

Crofts, Peter A., Wisbech, Cambs.

Cromarty Antiques, Cromarty, Scotland.

Crome Gallery and Frame Shop, Norwich, Norfolk.

Cromwell House Antique Centre, Battlesbridge Antique Centre, Essex

Cronan Ltd, Sandra, London W1.

Crook, Sandra, Stockport, Cheshire.

Crook, W.V. and A., Kidderminster, Worcs.

Crooked Window, The, Dunster, Somerset.

Cross - Fine Paintings, Edward, Weybridge, Surrey.

Cross Antiques, Watlington, Oxon.

Cross Hayes Antiques, Chippenham, Wilts.

Cross Keys Jewellers, Devizes, Wilts.

Cross, B.J., Kendal, Cumbria.

Crossley, Peter and Mary, Haslingden, Lancs.

Crossroads Antiques, Prestwick, Scotland.

Crouchman, C.C., Shenfield, Essex.

Crowder, P., Talbot Walk Antique Centre, Ripley, Surrey.

Crown Arcade, London W11.

Crown Silver, London Silver Vaults, London WC2.

Crowson, Julie, Wainfleet, Lincs.

Crowther, D.J., Guisborough, Yorks. North.

Crowther, Mrs V., London SW4.

Crozier, G.R., Bishop's Stortford, Herts.

Crozier, Richard J., Beccles, Suffolk.

Cruz, Mary, Bath, Somerset.

Cry for the Moon, Guildford, Surrey.

Crystal Palace Antiques, London SE19.

Cufflink Shop, The, Antiquarius, London SW3.

Cull, Jonathan, Topsham, Devon.

Cullen, A. and R.S., Hemel Hempstead, Herts.

Cullen, James, Ripley, Derbys.

Cullimore, Hedley, Top Banana Antiques Mall 1, Tetbury, Glos.

Cullompton Antiques, Cullompton, Devon.

Cullompton Old Tannery Antiques, Cullompton, Devon.

Cumbria Architectural Salvage, Raughton Head, Cumbria.

Cumbrian Antiques Centre, The, Brampton, Cumbria.

Cumming, A. & Y., Lewes, Sussex East.

Cummins, Cornelius, Bristol, Glos.

Cunningham, David, Lamb Arcade, Wallingford, Oxon

Cunningham, J.R., Kilmarnock, Scotland.

Cupboard Antiques, The, Amersham, Bucks.

Curá Antiques, London W11.

Curio City., Southend-on-Sea, Essex.

Curio Corner, Tynemouth, Tyne and Wear.

Curios of Chale, Chale, Isle of Wight.

Curiosity Shop, The, South Shields, Tyne and Wear.

Curiosity Shop, The, St. Sampson, Guernsey, C.I.

Curiosity Shop, Uppingham, Rutland.

Curry, Peter, Finchingfield, Essex.

Curtis, P., London SW3.

Curzon Gallery, The David, London SW19.

Cusack, T., Barnstaple, Devon.

Cushion Corner, The, Grays Antique Markets, London W1.

Cyphus, Chloe, Warminster, Wilts.

Cyrlin & Co, Philip, Bond Street Antiques Centre, London W1.

Cyrus Antiques & Decorative Interiors, Petworth, Sussex West.

Czerek, John, Dundee, Scotland.

D

D & J Lines Antiques, Wychbold, Worcs.

D'Ardenne, P.J., Branksome, Dorset.

D'Eyncourt, Chertsey, Surrey.

D'Oyly, N.H., Saffron Walden, Essex.

D.M. Restorations, Weston-Super-Mare, Somerset.

Da Capo Antiques, Edinburgh, Scotland.

Dade, Clifford and Roger, Thames Ditton, Surrey.

Daggett Gallery, Charles, London W11.

Daggett Gallery, London W11.

Daggett, Caroline, London W11.

Daggett, Charles and Caroline, London W11.

Dahling Antiques, Oscar, Croydon, Surrey.

Daines, Christopher, Cheltenham, Glos.

Dairy House Antiques, Semley, Wilts.

Dale House Antiques, Moreton-in-Marsh, Glos.

Dale Ltd, Peter, London SW1.

Dale, Joan, Ilchester, Somerset.

Dale, John, London W11.

Daly, M. and S., Wadebridge, Cornwall.

Dams, Tim, Shifnal, Shrops.

Danbury Antiques, Danbury, Essex.

Dance, T.A.B., Martock, Somerset.

Dando, A.P. and J.M., Bradford-on-Avon, Wilts.

Dando, Andrew, Bradford-on-Avon, Wilts.

Daniel Charles Antiques, Ashbourne, Derbys.

Daniel, Anjula, Brighton, Sussex East.

Daniel, Francoise, Antiques at Heritage, Woodstock, Oxon.

Daniel, Francoise, Jubilee Hall Antiques Centre, Lechlade, Glos.

Daniell, J., Upton-upon-Severn, Worcs.

Daniels, P., London Silver Vaults, London WC2.

Dann Antiques Ltd, Melksham, Wilts.

Dann, M., Hatherleigh, Devon.

Daphne's Antiques, Penzance, Cornwall.

Darby, W., Framlingham, Suffolk.

Darley, Mike, Coltishall, Norfolk.

Dartmoor Bookshop, Ashburton, Devon.

David, G., Cambridge, Cambs.

David, P., Aberystwyth, Wales.

Davidge, Mrs Amanda, Lostwithiel, Cornwall.

Davidson Antiques, Carlton, London N1.

Davidson Antiques, Carlton, London SW10.

Davidson Antiques, London NW8.

Davidson's The Jewellers Ltd, Newcastle-upon-Tyne, Tyne and Wear.

Davidson, Anthony and Helen, Newcastle-upon-Tyne, Tyne and Wear.

Davidson, Edward, London NW8.

Davie, Janet, Pershore, Worcs.

Davies & Son Antiques, Edmund, Whalley, Lancs.

Davies Antiques, London SW8.

Davies Gallery, The John, Stow-on-the-Wold, Glos.

Davies Oriental Art, Barry, London W8.

Davies, Daphne, Penzance, Cornwall.

Davies, E. and P., Whalley, Lancs.

Davies, Elinor, Penzance, Cornwall.

Davies, G., Cockermouth, Cumbria.

Davies, G.D., South Shields, Tyne and Wear.

Davies, H., Coxley, Somerset.

Davies, H.Q.V., London SW8.

Davies, John, Piccadilly Antiques, Batheaston, Somerset.

Davies, L., Botley, Hants.

Davies, Mr and Mrs, Chertsey, Surrey.

Davies, P.A., Tunbridge Wells, Kent.

Davies, Rhys, Top Banana Antiques Mall 1, Tetbury, Glos.

Davies, S.E., Stamford, Lincs.

Davis (Works of Art) Ltd, Kenneth, London SW1.

Davis Antiques, Jesse, Antiquarius, London SW3.

Davis Ltd, A. B., London W1.

Davis Ltd, Reginald, Oxford, Oxon.

Davis, Andrew and Glynis, Kew Green, Surrey.

Davis, Andrew, Kew Green, Surrey.

Davis, Harry, Callington, Cornwall.

Davis, Mark, Exeter, Devon.

Davison Antiques, Stephanie, Chappells Antiques Centre, Bakewell, Derbys.

Davison, Chris and Barbara, Henley-in-Arden, Warks.

Davison, Diane, Bridlington, Yorks. East.

Davison, Gerald, Castle Cary, Somerset.

Dawson of Stamford Ltd, Stamford, Lincs.

Dawson, J., Stamford, Lincs.

Dawson, Sharon, Denby Dale, Yorks.

French-Greenslade, S., Tilston, Cheshire.
Frensham House Antiques, Chichester, Sussex West.
Freshfords, Freshford, Somerset.
Frew Ltd, Robert, London WC1.
Freya Antiques, Tacolneston, Norfolk.
Friargate Pine Company Ltd, Derby, Derbys.
Friday Street Antique Centre (The Ferret), Henley-on-Thames, Oxon.
Frings, S., Hoby, Leics.
Frith, I. and M., London W1.
Frith, Michael, Hemswell Cliff, Lincs.
Frodsham & Co Ltd, Charles, London SW1.
Frome Reclamation, Frome, Somerset.
Fronhouse Antiques, Barmouth, Wales.
Frontispiece Ltd, London E14.
Frost and Reed Ltd (Est. 1808), London SW1.
Frost Antique Clocks, A. and Y.M., Honley, Yorks. West.
Frost Antiques & Pine, Monmouth, Wales.
Frost, Alan and Yvonne, Honley, Yorks. West.
Frost, C.C., Bury St. Edmunds, Suffolk.
Frost, Nicholas, Monmouth, Wales.
Frost, P.J., Iver, Bucks.
Frost, R.F., Martlesham, Suffolk.
Frosts of Clerkenwell Ltd, London EC1.
Fryer Antique Lighting, Fritz, Ross-on-Wye, Herefs.
Fu Jen Ni Ltd, Petworth, Sussex West.
Fulda Gallery Ltd, Manchester, Lancs.
Fulda, M.J., Manchester, Lancs.
Fuller, Anthony, London EC4.
Fuller, Cory, Anthony and Glenn, London W1.
Fuller, Kenneth , London WC2.
Fuller, Nicholas, Potterspury, Northants.
Furniture Cave, The, Aberystwyth, Wales.
Furniture Cave, The, London SW10.
Furniture Mart, Margate, Kent.
Furniture Trading Co, The, Botley, Hants.
Furniture Vault, London N1.
Fyson Antiques, Jonathan, Burford, Oxon.
Fyson, J.R., Burford, Oxon.

G

G G Antique Wholesalers Ltd, Middleton Village, Lancs.
G.B. Antiques Ltd, Lancaster, Lancs.
G.D. and S.T. Antiques, Poole, Dorset.
Gaby's Clocks and Things, Tenterden, Kent.
Gadsden, P., Petersfield, Hants.
Gage (Works of Art) Ltd, Deborah, London W1.
Gainsborough House Antiques, Tewkesbury, Glos.
Gale, Mrs Joan, Norwich, Norfolk.
Galinsky, P., Edinburgh, Scotland.
Gallerie Antiques, Hainault, Essex.
Gallerie Veronique, Enfield, Middx.
Galleries, The, London SE1.
Gallery '25, London SW1.
Gallery (Nigel Stacy-Marks Ltd), The,

Blair Atholl, Scotland.
Gallery 23 Antiques, Chalfont St. Giles, Bucks.
Gallery Diem, Grays Antique Markets, London W1.
Gallery Kaleidoscope incorporating Scope Antiques, London NW6.
Gallery of Antique Costume and Textiles, London NW8.
Gallery Persia, Inverness, Scotland.
Gallery Yacou, London SW3.
Gallery, Aberdeen, Scotland.
Gallie, Jim and Fraser, Battlesbridge, Essex.
Gallie, Jim, Battlesbridge Antique Centre, Essex
Gallimaufry, Broadway, Worcs.
Gallison, Antiquarius, London SW3
Gallop and Rivers Architectural Antiques, Crickhowell, Wales.
Gallop, G. P., Crickhowell, Wales.
Galsworthy, A., Barry, Wales.
Gander, Michael, Hitchin, Herts.
Gander, Rachel, Brighton, Sussex East.
Gange, C.C., Marlborough, Wilts.
Garden Art, Hungerford, Berks.
Garden House Antiques, Red House Antiques Centre, York, Yorks. North
Garden House Antiques, Yoxford, Suffolk.
Garden House, Ginnel Antiques Centre, The, Harrogate, Yorks North
Gardiner Antiques, Charles, Lurgan, Co. Armagh, N. Ireland.
Gardiner Antiques, John, Somerton, Somerset.
Gardiner, G., Red House Antiques Centre, York, Yorks. North
Gardner Antiques, Richard, Petworth, Sussex West.
Gardner's The Antique Shop, Kilbarchan, Scotland.
Gardner, Allan and Deborah, Petworth, Sussex West.
Gardner, David, Bath, Somerset.
Gardner, G.D., R.K.F. and D.D., Kilbarchan, Scotland.
Gardner, J., Bishops Cleeve, Glos.
Gardner, Richard and Janice, Petworth, Sussex West.
Gargrave Gallery, Gargrave, Yorks. North.
Garland Antiques, London SW11.
Garner, G., Monkton, Devon.
Garner, John, Uppingham, Rutland.
Garrard Antiques, Ludlow, Shrops.
Garrard, Caroline, Ludlow, Shrops.
Garreta, C., Grays Antique Markets, London W1.
Garth Antiques, Harrogate, Yorks. North.
Gasson Antiques and Interiors, Tadley, Hants.
Gasson, Herbert Gordon, Rye, Sussex East.
Gasson, Patricia and Terry, Tadley, Hants.
Gatehouse Antiques, Macclesfield, Cheshire.
Gateway Antiques, Burford, Oxon.
Gatland, T. and Mrs D., Ashburton, Devon.

Gauld, J.A., Killin, Scotland.
Gauld, Maureen H., Killin, Scotland.
Gaunt, Peter, Grays Antique Markets, London W1.
Gavey, G.P. and Mrs C., St. Peter Port, Guernsey, C.I.
Gavin, J.M., Penryn, Cornwall.
Gay, M. and B.M., Romsey, Hants.
Gayler, A.P., Brighton, Sussex East.
Gaylords, Titchfield, Hants.
Gaze, John, London SW1.
Gazeley-Howitt, Michelle, Top Banana Antiques Mall 1, Tetbury, Glos.
GB Military Antiques, The Mall Antiques Arcade, London N1.
Gealer, Mrs R., Falmouth, Cornwall.
Geary Antiques, Leeds, Yorks. West.
Geary, J.A., Leeds, Yorks. West.
Geddes, J., St Peter Port, Guernsey, C.I.
Gee, Colin, Tetbury, Glos.
Geer, Deidre, Talbot Walk Antique Centre, Ripley, Surrey.
Geering, A.F., London W8.
Geering, A.F., Southwold, Suffolk.
Gelsthorpe, J. and E., Barlow, Derbys.
Gem Antiques, Maidstone, Kent.
Gem Antiques, Sevenoaks, Kent.
Gemini Trading, Leek, Staffs.
Gems Antiques, Chichester, Sussex West.
Geneen Ltd, Lionel, Bournemouth, Dorset.
General Trading Co Ltd, London SW3.
Gensing Antiques, St. Leonards-on-Sea, Sussex East.
Gent, Ann, Newport, Wales.
George Street Antiques Centre, Bath, Somerset.
George Street Antiques Centre, Hastings, Sussex East.
George, C., Hingham, Norfolk.
George, D., Felixstowe, Suffolk.
George, Dr J.D., London SW1.
George, Judy, Worcester, Worcs.
Georgia Antiques, Pulborough, Sussex West.
Georgian Antiques, Edinburgh, Scotland.
Georgian Gems Antique Jewellers, Swanage, Dorset.
Georgian House Antiques, Chipping Norton, Oxon.
Georgian Rooms, The, Bridlington, Yorks. East.
Georgiou, D., London N12.
Germain, T.C., Burnham-on-Sea, Somerset.
German Antiques Ltd, Michael, London W8.
German, P., Almshouses Arcade,Chichester, Sussex West
Gerrish, Olivia, Grays Antique Markets, London W1.
Geshua, Anthea, Grays Antique Markets, London W1.
Gestetner, Jonathan, London W1.
Get Stuffed, London N1.
Gewirtz, R., London N1.
Ghafoori, Ghazi, Grays Antique Markets, London W1.
Gibbard, A. & T., Eastbourne, Sussex East.

Kings Fireplaces, Antiques and Interiors, Cardiff, Wales.

Kingsclere Old Bookshop (Wyseby House Books), Kingsclere, Hants.

Kingston Antique Market, Kingston-upon-Thames, Surrey.

Kingston, Dennis, Antiquarius, London SW3.

Kingston, Richard J., Henley-on-Thames, Oxon.

Kingswood, T., London WC2.

Kinloch, Clare, Hastings Antique Centre, St. Leonards-on-Sea, E. Sussex

Kinnaird, Jane and John, Keswick, Cumbria.

Kinsey, Alan, London W1.

Kirby Antiques, R., Acrise, Kent.

Kirby, R.D. and M.W., Acrise, Kent.

Kirby, S.P.J., Stratford-upon-Avon, Warks.

Kirch, Richard, Grays Antique Markets, London W1.

Kirk Ports Gallery, North Berwick, Scotland.

Kirk, N.R., Honiton, Devon.

Kirkgate Fine Art & Conservation, Thirsk, Yorks. North.

Kirkland, Chris, Tetbury, Glos.

Kirkland, Graham, London SW6.

Kirsopp-Reed Antiques, Jane, Gosforth, Tyne and Wear.

Kirton Antiques, Kirton, Lincs.

Kismet, Ginnel Antiques Centre, The, Harrogate, Yorks. North.

Kitagawa, Ted, London N1.

Kitching, Tracy, London SW10.

Kitsch 22, Newport, Isle of Wight.

Klaber and Klaber, London NW3.

Klaber, Mrs B., London NW3.

Knapp, Mr and Mrs R., Bath, Somerset.

Knicks Knacks Emporium, Sutton-on-Sea, Lincs.

Knight and Sons, B.R., St. Ives, Cambs.

Knight, Caroline, Hadlow Down, Sussex East.

Knight, I.H. and G.M., Folkestone, Kent.

Knight, Michael, St. Ives, Cambs.

Knight, P., Christchurch, Dorset.

Knight, S.J. and M.L., Henley-on-Thames, Oxon.

Knight-Mudie, George, Aberdeen, Scotland.

Knights Antiques, Henley-on-Thames, Oxon.

Knights, P.H., Norwich, Norfolk.

Knightsbridge Coins, London SW1.

Knowles, Susan and Arnie, Hungerford, Berks.

Knowles, W.A. and M.A., Penkridge, Staffs.

Knutsford Antiques Centre, Knutsford, Cheshire.

Koll, A., London SW1.

Koopman Ltd & Rare Art (London) Ltd, London WC2.

Koopman, Timo, London WC2.

Korkis, Geoffrey Boyes, Walton-on-Thames, Surrey.

Korom-Vokis, Andrew, London SW1.

Kowalski, K. S., Macclesfield, Cheshire.

Kreckovic, L. and E., London SW6.

Krumrey, Caterina, Grays Antique Markets, London W1.

Kubacki, Edward, Finedon, Northants.

Kunz, Armin London SW1.

L

L.O.G.G. Lights, Tynemouth, Tyne and Wear.

L.P. Furniture Ltd, Walsall, West Mids.

La Chaise Antique, Stow-on-the-Wold, Glos.

La Maison, Bourne End, Bucks.

La Trobe, H., Brasted, Kent.

Laburnum Antiques, Poole, Dorset.

Laburnum Cottage Antiques, Eye, Suffolk.

Lacewing Fine Art Gallery, Winchester, Hants.

Lack, Stephen, Grays Antique Markets, London W1.

Lacquer Chest, The, London W8.

Lacy Gallery, London W11.

Laffling, Graham, Wickham Market, Suffolk.

Lagden, J., Penzance, Cornwall.

Laithwaite, Miss S., Macclesfield, Cheshire.

Lake Antiques, Lake, Isle of Wight.

Laker, I.A. and E.K., Somerton, Somerset.

Lakes Crafts & Antiques Gallery, Grasmere, Cumbria.

Lamb Antiques & Works of Art, Roger, Stow-on-the-Wold, Glos.

Lamb Arcade, The, Wallingford, Oxon.

Lamb, B. and J.E., Swanage, Dorset.

Lamb, S. and Mrs K., Sherborne, Dorset.

Lambert and Son, R.A and S.M., Woodbridge, Suffolk.

Lambert Antiques Centre, Dorrian, Lincoln, Lincs.

Lambert, R., Lincoln, Lincs.

Lamberty Ltd, London SW1.

Lamberty, Andrew, London SW1.

Lamond, David, Boscastle, Cornwall.

Lamont Antiques Ltd, London SE10.

Lamont, Ewan, Edinburgh, Scotland.

Lamont, N., London SE10.

Lamp Gallery, The, Talbot Walk Antique Centre, Ripley, Surrey.

Lampert, B., London Silver Vaults, London WC2.

Lancaster Leisure Park Antiques Centre, Lancaster, Lancs.

Lancaster, Peter A., Beverley, Yorks. East.

Lancaster, T.J., Leek, Staffs.

Lancastrian Antiques & Co, Lancaster, Lancs.

Landen Antiques, Rupert, Reading, Berks.

Lane Antiques, Russell, Warwick, Warks.

Lane Antiques, Stockbridge, Hants.

Lane Fine Art Ltd, London SW10.

Lane, Mrs E.K., Stockbridge, Hants.

Lane, R.G.H., Warwick, Warks.

Lane, Russell, The Swan at Tetsworth, Oxon.

Lanes Armoury, The, Brighton, Sussex East.

Lang, P., Leominster, Herefs.

Langer, M.T., Chipping Norton, Oxon.

Langford's Marine Antiques, London SW10.

Langford, Adam and Joel, London Silver Vaults, London WC2.

Langford, J. and R., Llangollen, Wales.

Langford, J., Shrewsbury, Shrops.

Langford, L.L., London SW10.

Langfords, London Silver Vaults, London WC2.

Langham, P.A., Haworth, Yorks. West.

Langley Galleries Ltd, Rochester, Kent.

Langton Family, Sheffield, Yorks. South.

Langton Green Antiques, Tunbridge Wells, Kent.

Langton, M., Hull, Yorks. East.

Langton, Mrs Teresa, Bath, Somerset.

Langtons Antiques & Collectables, Sheffield, Yorks. South.

Lankester Antiques and Books, Saffron Walden, Essex.

Lankester, P., Saffron Walden, Essex.

Lansdown Antiques, Top Banana Antiques Mall 1, Tetbury, Glos.

Lapham, Vivien and Robin, Kidderminster, Worcs.

Larner, P., Cirencester, Glos.

Lascelles, Roger, London SW17.

LASSCO, London EC2.

Latreville, Claude & Martine, Antiquarius, London SW3.

Laurence Corner, London NW1.

Laurens Antiques, Whitstable, Kent.

Laurens, G. A., Whitstable, Kent.

Laurie (Antiques) Ltd, John, London N1.

Lavender (Antiques) Ltd, D.S., London W1.

Lavender, Lida and Paul, London NW5.

Lavender, Lida, London NW5.

Lavian, Joseph, London N4.

Law, Mr and Mrs R., Chichester, Sussex West.

Law, Mrs P., Broadstairs, Kent.

Law, Rathbone, Chichester, Sussex West.

Lawrence and Sons, F.G., Redhill, Surrey.

Lawrence Antiques, J., Chappells Antiques Centre, Bakewell, Derbys.

Lawrence Gallery, Bob, London SW1.

Lawrence House Antiques, Redhill, Surrey.

Lawrence, C.V., Ripley, Derbys.

Lawrence, Chris, Redhill, Surrey.

Lawrence, F., Tunbridge Wells, Kent.

Lawrence, Mrs. Sheila, Redhill, Surrey.

Lawrence, T., Westerham, Kent.

Lawson and Co, E.M., East Hagbourne, Oxon.

Lawson Antique Clocks, Keith, Scratby, Norfolk.

Lawson Antiques, F. and T., Richmond, Surrey.

Lawson Gallery, The, Cambridge, Cambs.

Lawson MBE, W.J. and K.M., East Hagbourne, Oxon.

Lawson, Jennifer, Bridgend, Wales.

Magpie Arms & Armour, Evesham, Worcs.
Magpies, Rushden, Northants.
Magrath, P.W., Tetsworth, Oxon.
Mahboubian Gallery, London W1.
Mahboubian, H., London W1.
Main Pine Co, The, Green Hammerton, Yorks. North.
Main, C. and K.M., Green Hammerton, Yorks. North.
Mainhill Gallery, Jedburgh, Scotland.
Mair Wilkes Books, Newport-on-Tay, Scotland.
Mair, James, Newport-on-Tay, Scotland.
Mairs, Paul and Marisa, Kirkcudbright, Scotland.
Maison, La, London E1.
Malbon, C., Grays Antique Markets, London W1.
Malik and Son Ltd, David, London NW10.
Mall Antiques Arcade, The, London N1.
Mall Galleries, The, London SW1.
Mallett and Son (Antiques) Ltd, London W1.
Mallett at Bourdon House, London W1.
Mallett Gallery, London W1.
Mallory and Son Ltd, E.P., Bath, Somerset.
Maloney, E., Hunstanton, Norfolk.
Malt House Antiques, Narberth, Wales.
Malt House Antiques, Stow-on-the-Wold, Glos.
Malthouse Antiques Centre, Alcester, Warks.
Malthouse Antiques, Bridgnorth, Shrops.
Malthouse Antiques, Dorking, Surrey.
Malthouse Arcade, Hythe, Kent.
Malvern Bookshop, Great Malvern, Worcs.
Malvern Studios, Great Malvern, Worcs.
Mammon, C. and T., London Silver Vaults, London WC2.
Mammon, Claude, London Silver Vaults, London WC2.
Mancey, Michael, Hungerford, Berks.
Manchester Antique Company, Stockport, Cheshire.
Manchester House Antiques Centre, Chipping Norton, Oxon.
Mandarin Gallery - Oriental Art, Otford, Kent.
Mandegaran, Dr. Ali, Petworth, Sussex West.
Mandell's Gallery, Norwich, Norfolk.
Mandrake Stevenson Antiques, Ibstock, Leics.
Mangan, P., Glasgow, Scotland.
Manion Antiques, Ashbourne, Derbys.
Manion, Mrs V.J., Ashbourne, Derbys.
Manley, J., Windsor, Berks.
Manley, Stuart & Mary, Alnwick, Northumbs.
Mann, D., Hexham, Northumbs.
Mann, D., Stiffkey, Norfolk.
Mann, John R., Canonbie, Scotland.
Manners, Carol, Redditch, Worcs.
Manners, E. and H., London W8.
Manners, Errol and Henriette, London W8.
Manor Antiques, Wilstead

(Wilshamstead), Beds.
Manor Barn Furniture Ltd,, Skipton, Yorks. North.
Manor Barn, Skipton, Yorks. North.
Manor Farm Antiques, Standlake, Oxon.
Manor House Gallery, Cheltenham, Glos.
Manor House Old Pine, Old Bank Antiques Centre, Bath, Somerset.
Mansell Antiques and Collectables, Hoylake, Merseyside.
Mansell, Gary, Hoylake, Merseyside.
Mansers Antiques, Shrewsbury, Shrops.
Mansions, Lincoln, Lincs.
Manson (Clocks), Edward, Woodbridge, Suffolk.
Mansour Gallery, London W1.
Mantle, Susan and William, Bridgnorth, Shrops.
Manussis, V., London SW1.
Map House, The, London SW3.
Map World, London W1.
Mar Antiques, Stella, Red House Antiques Centre, York, Yorks. North
Marble Hill Gallery, Twickenham, Middx.
Marcet Books, London SE10.
March Antiques, David and Sally, Abbots Leigh, Somerset.
March Antiques, Ginnel Antiques Centre, The, Harrogate, Yorks. North.
March Antiques, Red House Antiques Centre, York, Yorks. North.
March, D. and S., Abbots Leigh, Somerset.
Marchant & Son, S., London W8.
Marchant, R.P. and S.J., London W8.
Marchpane, London WC2.
Marco Polo Antiques Ltd, Grays Antique Markets, London W1.
Marcovitch, Diana, Antiques at Heritage, Woodstock, Oxon.
Marhamchurch Antiques, Marhamchurch, Cornwall.
Mariad Antique Jewellery, Antiquarius, London SW3.
Marianski, N.J., Derby, Derbys.
Mark Gallery, The, London W2.
Mark, H., London W2.
Market Deeping Antiques & Craft Centre, Market Deeping, Lincs.
Markham & Son Ltd, E. J., Colchester, Essex.
Markies, Joroen, Tunbridge Wells, Kent.
Marks Antiques, London W1.
Marks Jewellers and Antique Dealers, Oldham, Lancs.
Marks Ltd, Barrie, London N2.
Marks Tinsley,, Newark, Notts.
Marks, Anthony, London W1.
Marks, B.J. and S., Oldham, Lancs.
Marks, Christopher R., Dorking, Surrey.
Marks, Michael, Grays Antique Markets, London W1.
Marlborough Fine Art (London) Ltd, London W1.
Marlborough Parade Antique Centre, The, Marlborough, Wilts.
Marlborough Rare Books Ltd, London W1.
Marles, O., Sutton Valence, Kent.
Marlow Antique Centre, Marlow, Bucks.

Marney, Patrick, Long Melford, Suffolk.
Marnier Antiques, Edward, Shepton Mallet, Somerset.
Marnier, E.F., Shepton Mallet, Somerset.
Marpole, A., Burwell, Cambs.
Marr Antiques, Iain, Beauly, Scotland.
Marr, I. and A., Beauly, Scotland.
Marrin's Bookshop, Folkestone, Kent.
Marrin, Patrick, Folkestone, Kent.
Marriott, Ann, Chipping Norton, Oxon.
Marriott, T.I., Beaconsfield, Bucks.
Marryat (Richmond) Ltd, Richmond, Surrey.
Marryat, Richmond, Surrey.
Marsden, Josie A., St. Albans, Herts.
Marsh Antique Clocks Ltd, G.E., Winchester, Hants.
Marshall Gallery, London W14.
Marshall Phillips, London W4.
Marshall's Antiques Warehouse, Kevin, Hull, Yorks. East.
Marshall, A.R. and Mrs S.B., Grantham, Lincs.
Marshall, A.R., Kirton, Lincs.
Marshall, D.A. and J., London W14.
Marshall, Mrs Phyllis M. and Simon, Burford, Oxon.
Marshall, P., Carhampton, Somerset.
Marshall, S., Norwich, Norfolk.
Marshall, Trevor, Wells, Somerset.
Marshalls of Wells, Wells, Somerset.
Martin & Son, Peter J., Windsor, Berks.
Martin (Coins) Ltd, C.J., London N14.
Martin and Co. Ltd, Cheltenham, Glos.
Martin and Parke, Farnborough, Hants.
Martin Antiques, Robin, London W11.
Martin, A., Sandgate, Kent.
Martin, C., Bagshot, Surrey.
Martin, Carol, Talbot Walk Antique Centre, Ripley, Surrey.
Martin, George Perez, Petworth, Sussex West.
Martin, J., Farnborough, Hants.
Martin, John R., Edinburgh, Scotland.
Martin, Paul, London W11.
Martin, Peter J., Windsor, Berks.
Martin, R. and S., Risby, Suffolk.
Martin, Tony, Looe, Cornwall.
Martinez Antiques, J., Edinburgh, Scotland.
Martinez-Negrillo, Antiquarius, London SW3.
Martlesham Antiques, Martlesham, Suffolk.
Martyn, Dee, Tunbridge Wells, Kent.
Mascaro, R., Plymouth, Devon.
Masham, Douglas, Rotherfield, Sussex East.
Maskill, Heather, ShrewsburyShrops.
Mason (Sainsbury & Mason), Jeremy, London SW1.
Mason Gallery, Paul, London SW1.
Mason, Bill and Sue, Great Shelford, Cambs.
Mason, Harry, Brighton, Sussex East.
Mason, M. and Mrs R., Peterborough, Cambs.
Mason, Nicola, Tunbridge Wells, Kent.
Mason, R.A., Bournemouth, Dorset.
Massada Antiques Ltd, Bond Street Antiques Centre, London W1

Massey and Son, D.J., Macclesfield, Cheshire.

Massey, Allison, Grays Antique Markets, London W1.

Massingham Antiques, Roy, Brasted, Kent.

Masters, John, Westerham, Kent.

Mathaf Gallery Ltd, London SW1.

Mathias, Gerald, Antiquarius, London SW3.

Mathias, R., Guildford, Surrey.

Mathias, R., St. Albans, Herts.

Mathias, Richard, Oxford, Oxon.

Matlock Antiques and Collectables Centre, Matlock, Derbys.

Matlock, Diane, Grays Antique Markets, London W1.

Matthiesen Fine Art Ltd., London SW1.

Maud's Attic, Ipswich, Suffolk.

Maxfield House Antiques, Warminster, Wilts.

Maxtone Graham, Mr and Mrs R.M., Hythe, Kent.

Maxwell, Margaret, Innerleithen, Scotland.

May Antiques & Collectables, Shirley, Chappells Antiques Centre, Bakewell, Derbys.

May Antiques, Greta, Tonbridge, Kent.

May, Desmond and Ann, Brambridge, Hants.

Mayes, R.K., Ginnel Antiques Centre, The, Harrogate, Yorks North

Mayfair Carpet Gallery Ltd, London SE1.

Mayfair Gallery Ltd, London W1.

Mayfield Antiques, Top Banana Antiques Mall 1, Tetbury, Glos.

Mayflower Antiques, Long Melford, Suffolk.

Mayhew, Paul, The Mall Antiques Arcade, London N1.

Maynard Antiques, Mark, London SW6.

Mays, Maggie, Buxton, Derbys.

Mazaheri-Asadi, Masoud, Stockbridge, Hants.

Mazar Antiques, Grays Antique Markets, London W1.

McAvoy, Mike, Ludlow, Shrops.

McBain Antiques, Ian, The Antiques Complex, Exeter, Devon.

McBain Exports, The Antiques Complex, Exeter, Devon.

McBain, Martin and Kathy, The Antiques Complex, Exeter, Devon

McCall, B., Aberdeen, Scotland.

McCalls (Aberdeen), Aberdeen, Scotland.

McCalls Limited, Aberdeen, Scotland.

McCann, Mrs A.D., Holyhead, Wales.

McCarthy, O., Ross-on-Wye, Herefs.

McCarthy, T.P. and C.A., Liss, Hants.

McCartney, Graham, The Swan at Tetsworth, Oxon.

McClaren, J., Gosport, Hants.

McCluskey, Alberta and Donald, Belfast, Co. Antrim, N. Ireland.

McConnell Fine Books, Deal, Kent.

McConnell, Audrey, Durham House Antiques Centre, Stow-on-the-Wold, Glos.

McConnell, Nick, Deal, Kent.

McCormick, P., Knaresborough, Yorks. North.

McCreddie, B.S., Ludlow, Shrops.

McCulloch Antiques, John, Felixstowe, Suffolk.

McDonald Antiques, Joy, London SW13.

McDonald-Hobley, Mrs N., Antiquarius, London SW3.

McEwan Gallery, The, Ballater, Scotland.

McEwan, D., P. and R., Ballater, Scotland.

McGonigle, Joseph, Glasgow, Scotland.

McGowan, P., Shenton, Leics.

McGregor, Veronica, Halstead, Essex.

McGregor, Veronica, Sudbury, Suffolk.

McHale, Tom and Mary, Chichester, Sussex West.

McHugo, M., Stourbridge, West Mids.

McKeivor, Mrs J., Chilcompton, Somerset.

McKenna and Co, London SW3.

McKenna, C. and M., London SW3.

McKenzie, J.W., Ewell, Surrey.

McKinley, D., Wiveliscombe, Somerset.

McKnight, E.W., Bury St. Edmunds, Suffolk.

McLaughlin, A.J. and Mrs B., Manchester, Lancs.

McLaughlin, Ronan, Ballymena, Co. Antrim, N. Ireland.

McLean, Mrs M., Antiquarius, London SW3.

McLeod, David and Patricia, Knutsford, Cheshire.

McLeod, Murdoch J., Edinburgh, Scotland.

McLeod-Brown, William, Antiquarius, London SW3.

McLoughlin, Alan, Truro, Cornwall.

McMonagle, David, Newcastle-upon-Tyne, Tyne and Wear.

McMullan & Son, D., Manchester, Lancs.

McNally, Trevor, Belfast, Co. Antrim, N. Ireland.

McNaughtan's Bookshop, Edinburgh, Scotland.

McNulty Wholesalers, Coleraine, Co. Londonderry, N. Ireland.

McPherson Antiques, R. and G., London W8.

McPherson, I. and H., Coalville, Leics.

McPherson, Robert and Georgina, London W8.

McQuade Antiques, Kilbarchan, Scotland.

McQuade, W. G. & W. J., Kilbarchan, Scotland.

McTague of Harrogate, Harrogate, Yorks. North.

McTague, P., Harrogate, Yorks. North.

McVeigh & Charpentier, London SW10.

McWhirter, James, London SW10.

McWhirter, London SW10.

Mead, M.C., Uffculme, Devon.

Meadows Lamp Gallery, The, Edinburgh, Scotland.

Meara, Richard, London N1.

Meddings, Gill, Sible Hedingham, Essex.

Medina Gallery, Barnstaple, Devon.

Mee, Roderick, London W8.

Meeks & Co, F., Birmingham, West Mids.

Megarry's and Forever Summer, Blackmore, Essex.

Melford Antique Warehouse, Long Melford, Suffolk.

Melody's Antiques, Chester, Cheshire.

Melody, M. and M., Chester, Cheshire.

Melton Antiques, Woodbridge, Suffolk.

Melton's, London W1.

Melvin, R., Edinburgh, Scotland.

Memories, Rochester, Kent.

Memory Lane Antiques Centre, Ripley, Derbys.

Memory Lane Antiques, Great Bookham, Surrey.

Memory Lane Antiques, Lower Stondon, Beds.

Memory Lane, Sowerby Bridge, Yorks. West.

Mennis, G., Hastings Antique Centre, St. Leonards-on-Sea, E. Sussex

Mercado, Mr and Mrs K., Baythorne End, Essex.

Mercer Antiques, Noel, Long Melford, Suffolk.

Merchant House Antiques & Interiors, Ipswich, Suffolk.

Merchant House Antiques, Honiton, Devon.

Mercury Antiques, London W11.

Mere Antiques, Topsham, Devon.

Meredith, John, Chagford, Devon.

Mereside Books, Macclesfield, Cheshire.

Merlin Antiques, Tetbury, Glos.

Merlins Antiques, Carmarthen, Wales.

Messum's, London W1.

Metcalfe, C.W., West Auckland, Durham.

Metcalfe, Mrs A., Frodsham, Cheshire.

Mews Antique Emporium, Holt, Norfolk.

Meyer, Atlanti, Tudor House, Stow-on-the-Wold, Glos

Meyler, Olivia, Red House Antiques Centre, York, Yorks. North.

Meysey-Thompson Antiques, Sarah, Woodbridge, Suffolk.

MGJ Jewellers Ltd., Wallingford, Oxon.

Mibus, Adrian, London SW1.

Micawber Antiques, Bridgnorth, Shrops.

Michael Coins, London W8.

Michael's Boxes, Grays Antique Markets, London W1.

Michael, Judith, Corbridge, Northumbs.

Michelson, E., Bond Street Antiques Centre, London W1.

Michieli, Robert, St Helier, Jersey, C.I.

Mick's Antiques, Red House Antiques Centre, York, Yorks. North.

Middleham Antiques, Middleham, Yorks. North.

Middlemiss, Janet, Sonning-on-Thames, Berks.

Middleton, Helen, Durham House Antiques Centre, Stow-on-the-Wold, Glos.

Midgley, J.L. and N.M., Settle, Yorks. North.

T

Tabbron, Geoffrey, Exning, Suffolk.
Tadema Gallery, London N1.
Tagg, Mr and Mrs H., Norwich, Norfolk.
Tags, Lamb Arcade, Wallingford, Oxon
Tait, S., North Berwick, Scotland.
Talbot Court Galleries, Stow-on-the-Wold, Glos.
Talbot Walk Antique Centre, Ripley, Surrey.
Talish Gallery, The, Edinburgh, Scotland.
Talisman, Gillingham, Dorset.
Talking Machine, London NW4.
Talking Point Antiques, Sowerby Bridge, Yorks. West.
Tamblyn, Alnwick, Northumbs.
Tango Antiques, Warwick, Warks.
Tankerton Antiques, Whitstable, Kent.
Tanner, J., Cavendish, Suffolk.
Tanner, J., Long Melford, Suffolk .
Tansu Oriental Antiques, Batley, Yorks. West.
Tanswell, P., Warminster, Wilts.
Tantalus Antiques, Troon, Scotland.
Tapestry Antiques, Hertford, Herts.
Tapestry, Cheltenham, Glos.
Tappin, Ruth, Leek, Staffs.
Tapsell, Andrew, Skipton, Yorks. North.
Tapsell, C., London N1.
Tara Antiques, London NW8.
Taramasco, A., London NW8.
Tarplett, Carrie and David, Durham House Antiques Centre, Stow-on-the-Wold, Glos.
Tarporley Antique Centre, Tarporley, Cheshire.
Tarrant Antiques, Lorraine, Ringwood, Hants.
Tartan Antiques, The Swan at Tetsworth, Oxon.
Tatham-Losh (Top Banana Antiques Mall), Julian, Cheltenham, Glos.
Tatham-Losh Ltd, Julian, Cheltenham, Glos.
Tatham-Losh, Julian, Tetbury, Glos.
Tatham-Losh, Julian, Top Banana Antiques Mall 1, Tetbury, Glos.
Tattersall's, Uppingham, Rutland.
Tattersall, J., Uppingham, Rutland.
Tauber Antiques, Laurence, Surbiton, Surrey.
Taunton Antiques Market - Silver Street, Taunton, Somerset.
Tavistock Antiques Ltd, St. Neots, Cambs.
Tawny Owl, Top Banana Antiques Mall 1, Tetbury, Glos.
Tayler, Ron and Sandra, Freshwater, Isle of Wight.
Taylor Antiques, Martin, Wolverhampton, West Mids.
Taylor Fine Arts, Robin, Wakefield, Yorks. West.
Taylor Gallery Ltd, The, London SW7.
Taylor, Allison, Dornoch, Scotland.
Taylor, B., Kingston-on-Spey, Scotland.
Taylor, B.R., Kelling, Norfolk.
Taylor, C.D., Hampton, Middx.
Taylor, D., Driffield, Yorks. East.
Taylor, D., Halesowen, West Mids.

Taylor, Jason, Manchester, Lancs.
Taylor, Jeremy, London SW7.
Taylor, L., London SE19.
Taylor, M., London SW12.
Taylor, M.C., Bournemouth, Dorset.
Taylor, Mark, Bournemouth, Dorset.
Taylor, Seth, London SW11.
Taylor, Stanley, Durham House Antiques Centre, Stow-on-the-Wold, Glos.
Taylor-Smith Antiques, Westerham, Kent.
Taylor-Smith Books, Westerham, Kent.
Taylor-Smith, Ashton, Westerham, Kent.
Tea & Antiques, Felixstowe, Suffolk.
Teagowns & Textiles, Leominster, Herefs.
Teapot World, Conwy, Wales.
Tebbs, J.J., Conisholme, Lincs.
Teger Trading, London N4.
Temperley Fine and Antiquarian Books, David, Birmingham, West Mids.
Temperley, D. and R.A., Birmingham, West Mids.
Temple Gallery, London W11.
Temple, K., Raughton Head, Cumbria.
Temple, R.C.C., London W11.
Templeman, Lynda, Rait Village Antiques Centre, Scotland
Templeman, Robert, Doune, Scotland.
Templemans,, Abernyte, Scotland.
Templeton, Paul, The Swan at Tetsworth, Oxon.
Temptations, Antique Jewellery & Silver, Dorking, Surrey.
Temptations, Ashtead, Surrey.
Tencati, Sergio, Bond Street Antiques Centre, London W1.
Tenterden Antiques and Silver Vaults, Tenterden, Kent.
Terrett, J.S., Truro, Cornwall.
Tessier, The Swan at Tetsworth, Oxon.
Tessiers Ltd, London W1.
Tetbury Old Books, Tetbury, Glos.
Tetlow, Robert, Debden, Essex.
Tew, T., London N2.
Tewkesbury Antiques & Collectables Centre, Tewkesbury, Glos.
Thakeham Furniture Ltd, Petworth, Sussex West.
Thames Oriental Rug Co, Henley-on-Thames, Oxon.
Thanet Antiques, Ramsgate, Kent.
Thatcher, K., Londonderry, Co. Londonderry, N. Ireland.
Theatre Antiques Centre, The, Framlingham, Suffolk.
Themes and Variations, London W11.
Theobald, D., Cambridge, Cambs.
Thesaurus (Jersey) Ltd, St. Helier, Jersey, C.I.
thesilverfund.com, London SW1.
Thirkill Antiques, Leyburn, Yorks. North.
Thistle & Rose, Rait Village Antiques Centre, Scotland
Thistle Antiques, Aberdeen, Scotland.
Thistlethwaite, E., Settle, Yorks. North.
Thomas H. Parker Ltd,, London SW1.
Thomas, Andrew, Stamford, Lincs.
Thomas, N., Talbot Walk Antique Centre, Ripley, Surrey.

Thomas, Rena, Norton, Durham.
Thomas, T., Bladon, Oxon.
Thompson Antiques, John, Knaresborough, Yorks. North.
Thompson's Gallery, Aldeburgh, Suffolk.
Thompson, B., London N1.
Thompson, Bruce, Norwich, Norfolk.
Thompson, C.A. and A.L., Lound, Lincs.
Thompson, J. and S., Aldeburgh, Suffolk.
Thompson, J.J., Easingwold, Yorks. North.
Thompson, John, Tunbridge Wells, Kent.
Thompson, N.D.A. and E.K., Honiton, Devon.
Thompson, N.F., Buxton, Derbys.
Thompson, S., Arundel, Sussex West.
Thomson - Albany Gallery, Bill, London SW1.
Thomson's, St Helier, Jersey, C.I.
Thomson, D., Ripon, Yorks. North.
Thomson, I.G.F., Chappells Antiques Centre, Bakewell, Derbys.
Thomson, R.N., St Helier, Jersey, C.I.
Thomson, W.B., London SW1.
Thorn, David J., Budleigh Salterton, Devon.
Thornbury, M., Brinkworth, Wilts.
Thornhill Galleries, London SW18.
Thornhill, J., Shrewsbury, Shrops.
Thornley, G. and E.M., Helmsley, Yorks. North.
Thornton Ltd, Andy, Halifax, Yorks. West.
Thornton, D., Oxford, Oxon.
Thornton, John, London SW10.
Thornton, R.H. and R.J., Harrogate, Yorks. North.
Thorntons of Harrogate, Harrogate, Yorks. North.
Thorp, John, Market Bosworth, Leics.
Thorpe, Bob and Sue, Canterbury, Kent.
Thorpe, Miwa, Antiquarius, London SW3.
Thorpe, P., Haverfordwest, Wales.
Thredder, Phil, Ross-on-Wye, Herefs.
Thrie Estaits, The, Edinburgh, Scotland.
Throckmorton, Lady Isabel, Market Harborough, Leics.
Through the Looking Glass Ltd, London W8.
Thrower, D. and V., Petworth, Sussex West.
Thuillier, William, London W1.
Thurlow, Kate, London SW1.
Thurstans, C.M. and D., Stillington, Yorks. North.
Thwaites Fine Stringed Instruments, Watford, Herts.
Tickety Boo Antiques, Rait Village Antiques Centre, Scotland
Tiffin, Sylvia, Penrith, Cumbria.
Tiffins Antiques, Emsworth, Hants.
Tildesley, B. and J., Thirsk, Yorks. North.
Till, Michael J., London N1.
Tilleke, David, Redbourn, Herts.
Tillett, P.J., Camelford, Cornwall.
Tilley's Vintage Magazine Shop,

PLEASE USE THIS FORM FOR A NEW OR SUBSTANTIALLY ALTERED ENTRY

Please complete and return this form; there is no charge

NAME OF SHOP ....

ADDRESS OF SHOP ....

....

full address including county and postal code

Name (or names) and initials of proprietor(s) ....

(Mr/Mrs/Miss/or title)

Previous trading address (if applicable) ....

State whether 'Trade Only' (Yes or No) ....

BADA (Yes or No) .... LAPADA (Yes or No) ....

Year Established .... Resident on premises (Yes or No) ....

OPENING (One entry, e.g. '9.30-5.30' if open all day or part day
HOURS: Two entries, e.g. '9.30-1.00, 2.00-5.30' if closed for lunch)

Please put 'CLOSED' and 'BY APPT.' where applicable

	Morning	Afternoon
Sunday	....	....
Monday	....	....
Tuesday	....	....
Wednesday	....	....
Thursday	....	....
Friday	....	....
Saturday	....	....

SIZE OF SHOWROOM: Small (up to 600 sq. ft.) ....

Medium (600 to 1,500 sq. ft.) ....

Large (over 1,500 sq. ft.) ....

HOW TO GET TO YOUR SHOP (BUSINESS)
Brief helpful details from the nearest well-known road:

....

....

....

....

OF WHAT DOES YOUR STOCK CHIEFLY CONSIST?

(A) Please list in order of importance	(B) Approximate period or date of stock	(C) Indication of price range of stock eg £50-£100 or £5-£25
1. (Principal stock)		
2.		
3.		

IS PARKING *OUTSIDE* YOUR SHOP (BUSINESS) Easy (Yes or No)

TELEPHONE NUMBER Business ....

Home ....

(only if customers can ring for appointments outside business hours)

V.A.T. scheme operated – Standard/Special/Both ....

SERVICES OFFERED:

Valuations (Yes or No) ....

Restorations (Yes or No) ....

Type of work ....

Buying specific items at auction for a commission (Yes or No) ....

Type of item ....

FAIRS:

At which fairs (if any) do you normally exhibit? ....

....

....

CERTIFICATION:

The information given above is accurate and you may publish it in the Guide.

I understand that this entry is entirely free.

Signed .... Date ....